# THE ENCYCLOPEDIA OF PARAPSYCHOLOGY AND PSYCHICAL RESEARCH

# THE ENCYCLOPEDIA OF PARAPSYCHOLOGY AND PSYCHICAL RESEARCH

Arthur S. Berger, J.D.
AND
Joyce Berger, M.A.

PARAGON HOUSE
NEW YORK

First edition, 1991

Published in the United States by

Paragon House
90 Fifth Avenue
New York, NY 10011



Library of Congress Cataloging-in-Publication Data
Berger, Arthur S., 1920–
The encyclopedia of parapsychology and psychical research / Arthur S. Berger and Joyce Berger.—1st ed.
p. cm.
Includes bibliographical references.
ISBN 1-55778-043-9, 1-55778-358-6 (pbk.)
1. Psychical research—Dictionaries. I. Berger, Joyce.
II. Title.
BF1025.B47 1991
133′.03—dc20 89-28857
CIP

Design: Stanley S. Drate/Folio Graphics Co. Inc.

10 9 8 7 6 5 4 3 2

Manufactured in the United States of America

The paper used in this publication meets the minimum requirements of American National Standard for Information Sciences—Permanence of Paper for Printed Library Materials, ANSI Z39.48-1984.

# CONTENTS

# PREFACE

Each year a sea of letters engulfs societies and laboratories dealing with the paranormal. Sometimes the writers want to know what some puzzling experiences in their daily lives mean or why they happened. But the one request common to all which, like a playful porpoise, keeps surfacing again and again is: "Please send me information about. . . ." People want to know about research and educational centers, publications, phenomena, individuals in the field, and technical language used in psychical research and parapsychology—terms often used interchangeably although the disciplines are different and occupy separate investigative areas.

This work—a special purpose, worldwide encyclopedia of parapsychology and psychical research—provides authoritative information about these things and more. This book will satisfy the general public's fascination with the subject matter in these areas. It is also a reference source for the growing number of science writers and journalists interested in the fields. It makes parapsychology and psychical research accessible to professionals in other fields (e.g. psychology, philosophy, psychiatry, archaeology, physics, and religion). A reference work of this sort also makes the subject matter accessible to educators. In addition, this encyclopedia makes it easier for those young scientists new to these fields to master the huge body of literature and to find the scattered sources that deal with pertinent concepts and methods. Seasoned professional parapsychologists and psychical researchers, too, will be able to gain access to a considerable range of subjects and concepts beyond the pale of their areas of specialization.

From time to time, reference works have appeared on the market that have tried to fill the need for similar information. Except for Nandor Fodor's *Encyclopedia of Psychic Science* (1933), however, no competent professionals have devoted the necessary time to the production of a *comprehensive* book. (Helene Pleasant's *Biographical Dictionary of Parapsychology with Directory* (1964), Robert H. Ashby's *The Guidebook for the Study of Psychical Research* (1972, rev. 1987) and Brian Inglis's *The Paranormal* (1985) are more specialized and cover much less material.)

Joyce Berger is an experienced investigator, researcher, and writer about paranormal phenomena who has done considerable editorial work in the field. Arthur S. Berger is president of the Survival Research Foundation, a full member of the Parapsychological Association (an affiliate of the American Association for the Advancement of Science), and author of many books and papers on the subject. Together they have supplied that missing, up-to-date book: the Encyclopedia of Parapsychology and Psychical Research.

This work is unique in many respects. It is an introductory reference source with over 1,400 succinct entries. They present a broad spectrum of the concepts, methods and phenomena of both disciplines, their research organizations and publications, and the biographies of past and present actors in the fields of both psychical research and parapsychology—from eminent scientists* to mediums to mind-reading animals. No other encyclopedia deals with *all* the specific terms previously or currently used in parapsychology. Many of these terms have appeared in the *Journal of Parapsychology,* are used with the kind permission of the editor, and are identified by the initials "JP."

This book has other key features that make it distinct from other books on the market or in reference libraries.

## SPECIAL PURPOSE

In this book, the authors have tried wherever possible to discuss and evaluate the significance of each entry from the perspective of parapsychology or psychical research and to show how it fits into one framework or the other.

## NOTED WITNESSES

There are few of us who are not curious about the lives and thoughts of the famous whose deeds or writings we have heard or read about. The strange tales of the paranormal told about or by prominent people may be more persuasive than stories appearing in the tabloids or those concerning complete strangers. Yet, this kind of collection has been made only once before and that over three decades ago. Dr. Walter F. Prince realized the importance of collecting what are called "spontaneous cases"—the stories of psychic experiences that just happen to people whose names are familiar to all. He called them "noted witnesses." We have followed in his footsteps and have collected and presented here the stories of extrasensory and other paranormal phenomena recognized, experienced, narrated by or credited to about ninety "noted witnesses."

## WEIRD, OCCULT, AND NEW AGE PHENOMENA

Parapsychologists complain when the discipline is rejected by orthodox science as *a priori* pseudoscientific. Yet, to try to protect its own hopes of being thought respectable and scientific parapsychology takes the same debunking attitude toward other areas. This concern with parapsychology's public image and credibility makes it overlook fringe areas that may be related directly or indirectly to its field of interest

*Except for one or two who have expressly asked to be excluded.

and which may contribute significant ideas. Our position is that both parapsychology and psychical research should take cognizance of *all* paranormal phenomena that lie outside the pale of orthodox science. We have tried to be open-minded and sympathetic toward all occult topics and have included them in this encyclopedia as long as they have some evidential basis and some connection to psychical research or parapsychology. We have also included New Age personalities and topics when they seemed relevant to either field. At the same time, we have tried to maintain throughout an objective forthright approach. If we suspect that some topics, persons, or events are not credible or that there is no evidence of the paranormal claimed for them, we have not hesitated to say so. Likewise, if there is too much evidence for us to dismiss a subject or individual, however bizarre or incredible, we have said so.

## ANTIQUITY AND NON-WESTERN CULTURE

Often the beginning of paranormal phenomena is traced to the Fox sisters in the United States or to the time of the organization of the English Society for Psychical Research in London. In this book, we have included entries to show that paranormal phenomena have always happened and can be found in the Old Testament, in ancient Greece, and in the experiences of people in the centuries long prior to the Fox sisters, including, for example, Martin Luther who, in the fifteenth century, heard strange raps, bangs and noises in his room. We also think that people want to know about psi–related practices and beliefs in both Western and non–Western, "civilized" and "primitive," cultures. So, we have presented here experiences or events down the centuries and across the world for which normal explanations do not account.

This book also includes an appendix of organizations and publications around the world, organized alphabetically by country.

## BIBLIOGRAPHY

Although there are bibliographical references at the end of most entires, at the end of the book there is a more complete bibliography. This bibliography contains English and foreign language books, journals, and articles relating to parapsychology and psychical research and is a rich mine of some of the best literature in these fields from their beginnings to the present time.

In carrying out the exacting task of compiling this work we have attempted to make this book as correct, authoritative, and up-to-date as possible.

We have used the following abbreviations: JASPR for the *Journal of the American Society for Psychical Research;* JSPR for the *Journal of the Society for Psychical Research;* JP for the *Journal of Parapsychology;* PASPR for the *Proceedings of the American Society for Psychical Research;* and PSPR for the *Proceedings of the Society for Psychical Research.*

*JB*
*ASB*

# ACKNOWLEDGMENTS

The authors gratefully acknowledge the cooperation of the following authorities who have given us information about parapsychology and psychical research in their countries: *Argentina*: Professor Enrique Novillo Pauli, Director of the Institute for Parapsychology, Universidad del Salvador. *Australia*: Dr. Harvey Irwin, Department of Psychology, the University of New England. *France*: Yves Lignon, President of the Organisation pour la Recherche en Psychotronique and Director of the Laboratoire Universitaire de Parapsychologie et d'Hygiène Mental de Toulouse; and Marc F. Michel, Secretary of the Organisation pour la Reserche en Psychotronique. *India*: Dr. Jamuna Prasad, Research Advisor for the Foundation for Reincarnation & Spiritual Research, Allahabad; and Dr. P. V. Krishna Rao, Professor and Head of the Department of Psychology and Parapsychology, Andhra University. *Italy*: Paola Giovetti, psychical researcher on the editorial board of *Luce e Ombra*; and Prof. Ugo Dettore, scholar, editor and author of works on parapsychology. *Japan*: Tosio Kasahara, Department of Psychology, Matui Hospital, Tokyo. *Mexico*: Marcela Gomezharper de Treviño, Secretary of the Mexican Parapsychological Society. *The Netherlands*: Jeff C. Jacobs, researcher in the Sychronicity Research Unit and co-editor of the *Sychronicity Research Unit Bulletin*. *Panama*: R. Manieri C., Director, Institute of Parapsychological Studies. *South Africa*: Dr. John C. Poynton, Department of Biology, University of Natal, Durban. *Spain*: Francisco Gavilán Fontanet, psychologist, parapsychologist, and member of the Spanish Parapsychological Society. *Switzerland*: Alex Schneider, professor of physics and President of the Swiss Parapsychological Society.

# THE ENCYCLOPEDIA OF PARAPSYCHOLOGY AND PSYCHICAL RESEARCH

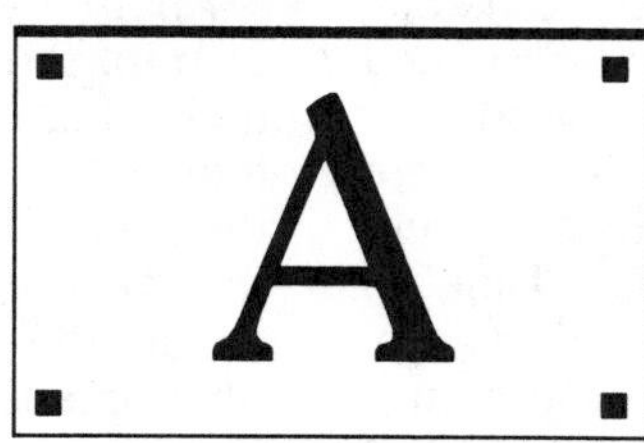

**Miss A.** The pseudonym used by **Frederic W. H. Myers** for **Kate Wingfield.**

**Mrs. A.** The pseudonym for Mrs. **Gladys Osborne Leonard** used by **Sir Oliver Lodge** in 1916 in his article on precognition and survival.

**Abdul Latif.** See **Garrett, Eileen J.**

**Aberfan Disaster.** Earthquakes, volcanic eruptions, tidal waves, airplane crashes, ship sinkings, and other catastrophes have produced deaths and property losses beyond estimate; they may have triggered, as well, puzzling cases of precognition in which details linked to the disasters have been foreseen.

One of the most closely studied from a parapsychological point of view is a disaster that struck Wales in the United Kingdom on October 6, 1966. On that date the mining town of Aberfan was buried under an enormous mass of waste coal that moved rapidly down a mountainside and tore up and covered everything in its path. Of the 144 people killed, 128 were schoolchildren in a junior high school in the direct path of the avalanche. J. C. Barker, a psychiatrist, confirmed twenty-four cases of precognition related to the disaster. In one case, one week before the disaster, a woman dreamed of screaming children buried by an avalanche of coal in a mining village; in a second, two weeks before, a woman dreamed of a school, children screaming, and a "creeping black shiny substance"; and in a third case, a woman received a **message** from a spirit about 100 children engulfed in black mud; and, most pathetically, one of the young victims dreamed the night before of the school's being buried in "something black."

Apart from its tragic aspect, the Aberfan incident is unusual because it generated a large number of reports of premonitions. The Barker study, however, is not accepted as hard evidence of precognition because the reports of people's experiences did not reach Barker until after the tragedy. The solution to this difficulty has been the setting up of central agencies (a "Disaster Early Warning System" in London and Central Premonitions Registries in New York and Toronto) to which premonitions of disasters can be reported before they take place in order to supply harder evidence of precognition than studies such as Barker's offer.

BIBLIOGRAPHY: Barker, J. C. 1967. "Premonitions of the Aberfan Disaster." JSPR 44:169; Barker, J. C. 1967. "Disaster Early Warning System." JSPR 44:107.

**Aborigines, Australian.** Inhabitants indigenous to Australia. About 250,000 years ago, either by raft and canoes or by land connections over the now submerged Sahul Shelf, the forerunners of the aborigines of Australia came from southeast Asia. With them came the dingo, a wild, wolf-faced dog. Some 500 tribes of these seminomadic people roamed the country to collect and hunt for food.

Although preliterate, the aborigines have a high intelligence and an interesting concept of "the Dreaming" or "Eternal Dream Time" in which supernatural, legendary beings created the land and human life. These beings continue in spirits, in totems, in natural features, or in human beings. In "the Dreaming" the aborigines connect their world with the invisible world. There is no line between the natural and supernatural. The two realms are interdependent.

It is in the "Eternal Dream Time" that the **Clever Men,** around whom paranormal phenomena are centered, consciously use their powers of extrasensory perception. According to **Ronald K. H. Rose** (1952), the distinction between the Clever Men and the ordinary members of a tribe is that the former are able to use their paranormal powers at will while ordinary aborigines occasionally have unexpected psychic experiences.

The aborigines place a high value on contemplation, in which state they transcend space and time and demonstrate telepathic abilities. Even during conversation, the aborigine may go into this trancelike condition and, after a few minutes, announce correctly the name of someone who will soon be making an appearance or who has just died or will know that an event has taken place far away and without any possibility of prior communication. The trance is important to the aborigines as a way of developing their Clever Men, and it is also a means of obtaining paranormal knowledge.

Smoke signals, whose use dates back to ancient Egypt, always have been thought of as a form of transmitting messages by code. Some anthropologists, however, believe that, for the aborigines, the smoke signal simply tells them to go into trance to try to use telepathy to obtain information. A similar effect is produced when totemic animals are seen. Rose reported the case of the aborigine who saw two sandpipers or plovers flying around his cottage. He knew that he was hallucinating, that the plovers were not really there, but, because plovers were his uncle's totem, he entered into a state of trance. He then announced that his uncle was dead. The next morning news came by telegram that the man's uncle had died the night before two hundred miles away.

Another method used by the aborigines to gain information paranormally is to send out their "familiars" or spirit-dogs or assistant totems to collect information even at a great distance. The aborigines, in a state of trance, receive the information as it is being collected. In such cases, if true, the paranormal phenomena involved would be either clairvoyance or telepathy.

Rose later conducted experiments in extrasensory perception and psychokinesis with semicivilized natives to determine the nature and degree of their paranormal gifts. While the tests in psychokinesis produced only chance results, the card-guessing tests for ESP were highly significant for a considerable number of subjects. These significant results suggest that the paranormal powers of the aborigines may be unusually strong. There may then be real psychic activity behind their beliefs and superstitions which, sadly, are fast dying out as the lore and culture of the aborigines fade in the advance of Western ideas.

BIBLIOGRAPHY: Rose, R. 1952. "Psi and Australian Aborigenes." JASPR 46:17–58.

**Absent Sitter.** The person for whom a reading is given but who is not present at a mediumistic session or experiment. The purpose of an absent sitting is to guard against sensory cues being given to the medium or to reduce the possibility of ESP from the mind of the sitter. In absent sittings, a substitute person or a material object may be used to assist the medium. See also **Linkage Experiment; Proxy Sitting.**

**Academy of Religion and Psychical Research.** Established in 1972 as an academic affiliate of Spiritual Frontiers Fellowship. Its purposes are, through conferences, symposia, and educational programs, to foment a dialogue among clergy, academics of religion and philosophy, and researchers in parapsychology as well as in all other scientific and humanistic disciplines. It is governed by a board of trustees and publishes the proceedings of its conferences and the *Journal of Religion and Psychical Research.* The address of the academy is P.O. Box 614, Bloomfield, Connecticut 06002.

**Accademia Tibernia.** Italian organization established in Rome in 1960 as the Facoltà di Scienze Psichiche e Psicologiche (Faculty of

Psychic and Psychological Sciences) of Accademia Tibernia. The "faculty," however, is not located within the walls of any university because of academic resistance in Italy to parapsychology and even to psychology which is only an optional subject in many universities. The primary function of the faculty is to offer a three-year course in parapsychology and another in psychology. Address: Via Dante 13/A, Padua, Italy.

**Acupuncture.** From the Latin *acus* or needle and *punctura* or puncture. Without surgery or drugs, can a gold, silver or brass-handled needle inserted into a point on the human body alleviate ulcers, arthritis, stomach upsets, improve hearing, or prevent or control disease? Unbelievable perhaps, yet this traditional Chinese medical art of sticking needles into specific points in the body in order to treat disorders seems to work. Some Western physicians seem slowly to be coming around to acceptance of the art. Their explanations for its empirical success range from the removal of interferons, the release of endorphins, or placebo effects. On the other hand, the theory of the ancient Chinese practitioners of acupuncture is that there is in the body a life energy current *(ch'i)* which flows along a system of twelve lines or meridians. Disorders occur when this flow is disturbed. There are 800–900 points on the meridians which, when punctured by needles, release or otherwise affect the flow of energy. Research in the Soviet Union has produced an instrument called the "tobiscope" that measures points on the body where there is low electrical resistance and which seem to correspond to the points of Chinese acupuncture. See also **Adamenko, Victor G.**

Acupuncture may be relevant to psychical research because the theorized energy force in the body may be the same energy hypothesized in psychic or spiritual **Healing** (Ostrander and Schroeder, 1974). Some (Tiller, 1976) feel that the "tobiscope" shows that such a nonphysical energy exists—although this claim seems extreme since all the device really does is measure skin resistance. In spite of the clinical successes of this ancient Chinese medical technique and the vital nonphysical energy force it supposes, its *modus operandi* as well as its relation to parapsychology remain the subject of pure speculation.

BIBLIOGRAPHY: Ostrander, S. and Schroeder, L. 1974. *Handbook of Psychic Discoveries*; Tiller, W. A. "Devices for Monitoring Nonphysical Energies." In E. G. Mitchell, *Psychic Exploration*, 1976, p. 488.

**Adamenko, Victor G.** Contemporary Soviet biophysicist. While in the Soviet Union, he studied laser medicine and electromagnetic biology. Deeply impressed with acupuncture and Kirlian photography, he invented the "tobiscope" to detect the electromagnetic properties of acupuncture points. His interest in parapsychology centered mainly on macro-PK. Adamenko published many scientific papers in the Soviet Union on his research in parapsychology and lectured widely there on the subject to scientists, cosmonauts, and students. However, when the climate in that country in the 1970s became hostile toward parapsychology and government authorities began to remove research from the hands of individual researchers, Adamenko was dismissed from his position. Eventually, he got out of the U.S.S.R and became a member of the faculty of Crete University in Greece and director of its psychobiophysics laboratory. In 1988, he came to the United States and worked for a while as a visiting scientist at the Foundation for Research on the Nature of Man, after which he returned to Greece.

**Adept.** While normally this term applies to one who is highly proficient in something, in **Theosophy** it designates a member of a brotherhood in Tibet which became interested in the Theosophical movement and whose members possess paranormal powers to produce marvels surpassing the powers of ordinary human beings. Adepts also are called Mahatmas. The question of the existence of the mysterious brotherhood is a vexed one. When **Richard Hodgson** investigated this as well as other phenomena connected with Theosophy, he concluded "that the strongest apparent evidence for the existence of the Mahatmas comes to nothing at all."

BIBLIOGRAPHY: Hodgson, R. 1885. " 'An Account of Personal Investigations in India, and Discussion of the 'Koot Hoomi' Letters.' " PSPR 3:207, 248.

**Ad Hoc.** An explanation or interpretation made up to try to account for an unanticipated experimental result.

**Adventure, An.** The title of a sensational book by "Miss Morison" and "Miss Lamont," pseudonyms respectively for C. A. E. Moberly and E. F. Jourdain. These English authors related their puzzling experiences in 1901 in Versailles, France, when they were on holiday and visited the gardens of the Petit Trianon where they saw and heard people whose dress and appearance seemed very strange. They spent years studying the history of the period of the French Revolution and became convinced that what they had witnessed were scenes out of the eighteenth century. Their book ran through four editions and continues to be mentioned whenever books or articles on the paranormal are written. But it is a controversial book that has divided readers into those who consider it the strongest case of retrocognition ever recorded and those who think it is the weakest. See also **Versailles, Apparitions at.**

BIBLIOGRAPHY: Moberly, C. A. E. ("Miss Morison") and Jourdain, E. F. ("Miss Lamont"). *An Adventure,* 1911.

**Agent.** A person in one location, whether in a building or in a room or behind an opaque screen, who stares at or focuses hard on an object, a number, a picture, or symbol while another person in a different location or on the other side of the screen tries to grasp, visualize or guess what the other is concentrating on. In spontaneous cases of telepathy, the agent generally is a person in a crisis situation. Yet, it is not clear what role an agent plays. Whether in experimental or spontaneous situations, the problem is whether any agent takes the initiative and actively transmits thoughts or whether the people who learn about those thoughts play the active role and take the initiative. In this state of our knowledge, it is better to define an "agent" as one who is either attempting to initiate or "send" an impression to another or who acts as a target individual whose mental states will be apprehended by the other. See also **percipient.**

**Akashic Records.** Scenic records or "memories" stored indelibly on Akasha, a fluid ether in the spiritual world, of all acts or thoughts that have taken place since time began. This mystical concept, which remains without empirical support, is invoked often as a counterhypothesis for cases of apparent retrocognition, reincarnation, and spirit communication. In such cases, a person claiming knowledge of past occurrences would be said to have read by some means, perhaps by an out-of-body experience, events stored in these mysterious archives. A person claiming a prior life would be said to "remember," through having gained access similarly to a deceased person's stored "memories," and a medium would be said to have used psychic abilities to read a deceased person's stored "memories."

**Akolkar, Vasant Vinayak. 1911—.** Indian academic. His voice is familiar to listeners to the All India Radio programs on parapsychology. Vinayak was a visiting research fellow at the Parapsychology Laboratory at Duke University. He is a retired professor of psychology at the University of Bombay and author of textbooks on general and social psychology and is currently an investigator of cases suggestive of reincarnation and poltergeist disturbances in India. He also has guided postgraduate dissertations on parapsychology at Nagpur University and has published several research reports in the *Journal of Parapsychology* and in Indian publications.

**Aksakoff, Alexander Nikolajewitsch, 1832–1903.** Russian investigator. He is one of the rare people in the history of psychical research who devoted his life and energies to obtaining proof of life after death. He first became acquainted with spiritualism in 1855 when he read the works of Emanuel Swedenborg and Andrew Jackson Davis which he translated into German and Russian. He was intelligent and critical and aware of the difficulties of the problem of proving survival of death. He was also fully cognizant of "the credulity, infatuation, fanaticism of Spiritists and Spiritualists, and, finally, the fraud which made its entrance into the inquiry." (Aksakoff, 1890). In 1874, he founded in Leipsig, Germany, the monthly parapsychological journal *Psychische Studien,* which he edited for twenty-five years.

Aksakoff had sittings with many famous mediums, among them William Eglinton, D. D. Home, Eusapia Palladino. In 1875, he brought other mediums to St. Petersburg (now Leningrad) to be examined by a scientific commission set up to look into physical phenomena and, over the years, provided the Society for Psychical Research with cases that he himself tried to verify. He conducted an investigation into an extraordinary and perplexing case of partial dematerialization.

On December 11, 1893, Aksakoff and a circle of fourteen other sitters gathered in Helsingfors, Finland, for a seance with the physical medium Madame Elizabeth D'Esperance. The chair in which she sat in front of a cabinet was large, upholstered, and the lower part of its back was open. After a hand and forearm, and then a luminous form, were seen reaching out of the cabinet, the medium began to pat her skirt which was spread almost to the floor. She began to sigh heavily and then asked a sitter to feel her chair. He and other sitters found it empty. The lower half of her body had disappeared. Before long, however, the sitters could see the medium's legs and feet reappearing under her skirt. Aksakoff presented this case to the world as, finally, the one which could not be explained on the ground of imposture.

Although the medium could not have simply spread her legs and pulled them back to the sides of the chair or curled them under her body because these maneuvers would have been noticed, Hereward Carrington suggested that the medium could have put her legs through the open back of the chair while her skirt was over the seat and kneeled in the cabinet just behind the chair while the upper part of her body was visible to the sitters.

The case shows nevertheless that Aksakoff tried to do all he could to bring light to the problem of materialization and dematerialization. He theorized that a materialization is the medium's double "so that if a materialized form . . . turns out to be the body of the medium [that] is not necessarily an indication of fraud: it may be fusion" (Inglis, 1985:282).

Aksakoff is remembered as one of the most dedicated of the early builders of facts as a basis for solving the riddle of human life.

Selected Writing: Aksakoff, A. N. *Animism and Spiritism: an Attempt at a Critical Investigation of Mediumistic Phenomena, with Special Reference to the Hypothesis of Hallucination and of the Unconscious; an Answer to Dr. E. von Hartmann's work, 'Der Spiritismus.' 1890. 2 Vols.*

BIBLIOGRAPHY: Carrington, H. 1907. "An Examination of Mons. Aksakoff's 'Case of Partial Dematerialization of a Medium's Body.'" PASPR 1:131; Inglis, B. *The Paranormal,* 1985, p. 282; Perovsky-Petrovo-Solovovo, M. 1903. "Obituary - Mr. A. N Aksakoff." JSPR 11:45

**Allison, Lydia Winterhalter, 1880–1959.** American psychical researcher. The death of her husband, Dr. Edward Wood Allison, in 1920 led Lydia Allison to psychical research. Her husband had believed in survival after death; she had not. But her hope of being able to communicate with him brought her to the American Society for Psychical Research and to sittings with the mediums Minnie Soule and Gladys Osborne Leonard. Her report of these sittings was Mrs. Allison's major contribution to experimental psychical research.

When in 1925 a rift developed in the ASPR over the Mina S. Crandon ("Margery") mediumship and the ASPR's policy of popularizing, Lydia Allison, along with Elwood Worcester, was instrumental in forming, in 1925, the Boston Society for Psychic Research. The achievements, mainly publications, of the Boston Society were largely due to Lydia Allison's work. At the same time she maintained good relations with the ASPR so that, when a change in administration there in 1941 made it possible, she was able to arrange for the amalgamation of the Boston Society into the ASPR. She then became chairperson of that body's Publication Committee and later its secretary.

Her obituary in JASPR (1959) described her as "[f]riendly, cooperative, shrewd, candid [and] discreet," shy and with a subtle sense of humor.

Selected Writings: 1934. "Proxy Sittings with Mrs. Leonard." PSPR 42:104; *Leonard and Soule Experiments in Psychical Research.* Boston, 1929.

BIBLIOGRAPHY: "Obituary and Tributes to Mrs. E. W. Allison." 1959. JASPR 53:81; "Obituaries. Mrs. Lydia Allison." 1959. JSPR 40:98.

**Alpha Rhythm Activity.** Electrical brain activity occurring eight to thirteen cycles per second whose presence can be recorded by an electroencephalogram. Alpha rhythm seems to be promoted by relaxation and meditation procedures and to be blocked by intellectual activity. In card-guessing tests with ten subjects, **Charles Honorton** found "a strong positive correlation . . . between the [subjects'] ESP calls and their alpha levels . . . ."

BIBLIOGRAPHY: Honorton, C. 1969. "Relationship between EEG Alpha Activity and ESP in Card-Guessing Performance." JASPR 63:365.

**Alpha Waves.** See **Alpha Rhythm Activity.**

**Altered State of Consciousness (ASC).** A state of consciousness dissociated from the normal waking state, sometimes induced deliberately by means of meditation, drugs or hypnosis or produced spontaneously through hypnagogic reverie. Investigations suggest that the ASC is conducive to ESP and creativity. See also **Ganzfeld Procedure; Relaxation; Trance.**

**Alternative Healing.** See **Healing, Unorthodox.**

**Alvarado, Carlos S., 1955–.** American parapsychologist. He was drawn to parapsychology in 1972 when, while in his native Puerto Rico, he began reading English-language parapsychological publications (the *Journal of the American Society for Psychical Research,* the *Journal of the Society for Psychical Research,* the *Journal of Parapsychology* and the *Parapsychology Review*). The University of Puerto Rico where he was an instructor of psychology sent him in 1978 to pursue graduate studies in parapsychology at John F. Kennedy University in California, after which he became Research Assistant at the Division of Parapsychology of the University of Virginia. He is now visiting scholar at the Institute for Parapsychology.

In recent years his interests, which include spontaneous cases and the survival of the human personality after death, have resulted in publications on the history of parapsychology (1982) and the out-of-body experience (1986). A doctoral student in the history department of Duke University, Mr. Alvarado has published widely in English language, Spanish and Italian parapsychological journals. He is also an abstractor for *Parapsychology Abstracts International.* He is a member of the American Society for Psychical Research, the International Association of Near-Death Studies and the Parapsychological Association.

Selected Writings: 1987. "Observations of Luminous Phenomena around the Human Body: A Review." JSPR 54:38; 1986. "ESP During Spontaneous Out-of-Body Experiences: A Research and Methodological Note." JASPR 53:393; 1986. "Ernesto Bozzano. Una Nota Bibliografica in Tre Reviste Straniere." *Luce e Ombra* 86:9; 1982. "Historical Perspective in Parapsychology: Some Practical Considerations." JSPR 51:265; 1980. "Joseph Banks Rhine (1895–1980): Pionero en la parapsicología experimental." *Psi Comunicación* 6:9.

**Amadou, Robert, 1924–.** French philosopher, theologian, and psychical researcher. Like a checkerboard, Amadou's life has been colored by alternating patterns. A student of Hebrew and the Kabbala, bound to the world of Islam, ordained in the Syrian church, a specialist in little known philosophies, a doctor of theology and in ethnology, Amadou is also one of the premier parapsychologists in France (he is a member of the Parapsychological Association). His contributions have made psychical research a respected field of inquiry there. He has been editor of *Le Journal Saint-Jacques-Bulletin de Parapsychologie* and of the *Revue Métapsychique.* He is the author of several books including one on physical mediums. Amadou selected for his book *Les Grands Médiums* those great physical mediums of the past—the Fox sisters, D. D. Home, Florence Cook, Mina Crandon, Eusapia Palladino among others—who did not resist rigid controls or investigations. After examining the phenomena produced by them, Amadou reached the conclusion distasteful to spiritualists that nothing ever supplied by these mediums stands as conclusive proof that paranormal physical phenomena exist. In another book, *La Parapsychologie,* rated by Jean Cocteau as fourth among "Books of the Year" in 1954, Amadou presented a valuable guide to the history, terms, and implications of parapsychology. Over the years he has maintained his interest in the field and is presently writing (with Léon-Jacques Delpech) another book on the subject entitled *La Parapsychologie, Dialogue Philosophique.*

Selected Writings: *Les Grands Médiums,* 1957; *La Parapsychologie,* 1954.

**American Association—Electronic Voice Phenomena.** American organization established in 1982 to encourage research into electronic voice phenomena, which it considers the best objective evidence of the survival of the human personality after bodily death. The association, which describes itself as "a metaphysical organization interested in spiritual evolvement", consists of 200 members, arranges conferences and publishes a quarterly newsletter. Address: 726 Dill Road, Severna Park, MD 21146.

**American Indians.** Among the Indians north of Mexico, not including the Eskimos, there are no separate domains of natural and spiritual. The forest is alive with spirits; there are living beings in every tree, every lake, every plant. Each male Indian seeks a guardian spirit or totem, an animal or bird god, or a spirit helper to accompany him on lonely journeys, guard and guide him, and to bring him success in life, especially in hunting. Dreams are used to find and communicate with spirit helpers.

For the Chippewas, the Ojibwa and the Algonkian-speaking Indians of Canada, the most terrible of the spirits is the **Windigo,** a monster who preys on flesh. Yet an individual may become a windigo, the basis of this belief being possession by the spirit of the monster.

Indians rarely report seeing apparitions, but other forms of paranormal phenomena, in addition to possession, are found among the Indians. **Hand-Trembling** is practiced among those Navajos who have psychic gifts to locate lost objects and perform other functions. Crystal gazing is an art among the Chippewas. The Sioux conduct a yuwipi ceremony with what is best called a physical medium in a darkened room in which mysterious lights and other physical phenomena are produced. Before the practice faded away as a result of contact with the white man, the Chippewas used in their conjuring lodges the **Shaking Tent** to call on the spirits. Shamans among the Indians use paranormal powers of clairvoyance to locate wild game or precognition to predict threats to the community from enemies. Poltergeist disturbances have been reported. V. Barnouw came across a case in which flying chips of wood in a forest frightened a man who found out subsequently that his brother-in-law had died at the same time. Andrew Lang described the case of a fourteen-year-old girl in whose presence heavy weights slid around the floor of her wigwam accompanied by intelligent scratches and knocks thought to be produced by the spirit of a dead medicine man.

Fire ceremonies for religious or healing purposes have been conducted by the tribes of American Indians for centuries. The **Fire Test,** generally associated with Hindus who walk without injury over glowing ashes in a fire, were part of the oldest but little recognized (by the white man) rituals of the Indians of America. As early as the seventeenth century, the Jesuit missionary, Father Le Jeune, witnessed a sick woman, with her feet and legs bare, marching through two or three hundred fires. In 1637, he saw healers place red-hot stones in their mouths and carry them without harm to patients. Patients were rubbed with glowing cinders without showing pain or effects on their skin. In all these fire ceremonies, there is manifested a fire magic that may involve a paranormal ability to be immune to flame and heat. Neither Le Jeune nor any other trader, missionary or explorer ever saw any preparation used to treat the skin to prevent injuries. Other natural explanations are possible, however. See **Fire Tests; Rolling Thunder; Shaman.**

BIBLIOGRAPHY: Barnouw, V. 1946. "Paranormal Phenomena and Culture." JASPR 40:2–21; Lang, A. 1903. "The Poltergeist, Historically Considered." PSPR 17: 305–326.

**American Institute for Scientific Research. James Hervey Hyslop**'s idea of forming an organization that would not compete with the **American Society for Psychical Research** but that would stir up interest in, and obtain funds for, psychical research was praised by William James, Charles Richet and others. By 1904, Hyslop was able to establish the American Institute for Scientific Research to investigate two fields. Its Section A was to inquire into psychopathology or abnormal psychology; its Section B was to investigate psychical research or what Hyslop called "supernormal psychology." When the American Society for Psychical Research was dissolved in 1906, the new ASPR became Section B.

**American Society for Psychical Research (ASPR).** In 1882, with the organization of the Society for Psychical Research in England, there was laid the true foundation of psychical research and parapsychology. Before then, physical phenomena, and other mysterious events in which people seemed to be in contact with a level of reality beyond time and space, were usually either believed naively or rejected without investigation. The Society for Psychical Research subjected these strange events to critical study. For the same purpose the American Society for Psychical Research was founded in 1885 largely as a result of the efforts of William Barrett and William James. In 1887, Richard Hodgson assumed the post of secretary. Two years later, for financial reasons, the ASPR became a branch of the Society for Psychical Research. It was dissolved in 1906 after Hodgson's death and became Section B of James Hervey Hyslop's **American Institute for Scientific Research.** It continued as an independent organization after the American Institute for Scientific Research was discontinued. In the 1920s a schism developed between those who thought scientific methods were being ignored (e.g. William McDougall, Walter Franklin Prince and Gardner Murphy) and those who wanted a more open society. This break led, in 1925, to the formation of the **Boston Society for Psychic Research** which was not reintegrated into the ASPR until 1941.

The purpose of the ASPR is to investigate all classes of paranormal phenomena including telepathy, clairvoyance, precognition, psychokinesis, psychometry and survival phenomena. It publishes a *Journal* and *Proceedings.* Archivists and researchers will be interested in its large and complete parapsychological library and in its invaluable collection of the records of the Boston Society for Psychic Research and the papers of the principal figures in parapsychology: Richard Hodgson, James H. Hyslop, Walter F. Prince, Gardner Murphy and Laura Dale. Its present address is 5 West 73rd Street, New York, New York 10023.

**Amityville Horror, The.** The best-selling book and blockbuster movie that bear this name are supposedly the true story of horrifying psychic phenomena that took place over the 28-day period in November and December, 1975, that George and Kathy Lutz lived in their home in Amityville, New York. A year earlier in that same house, Ronald De Feo, Jr. had murdered his mother, his father, his two sisters, and his two brothers. According to the book and movie strange noises were heard, doors and windows opened, a red-eyed pig and a horned creature were seen, a black substance lined the toilet bowl, a green substance oozed down from the ceiling, the personalities of the whole family began to change, etc. Indeed, the attorney for De Feo used this theory of "demonic possession" in his unsuccessful appeal of his client's conviction. The Psychical Research Foundation and other investigators looked into the alleged experiences, found nothing paranormal, and the suspicion has been that the Lutzes could not afford to keep the house and found a way at the same time of making a great deal of money. The present occupants of the house report no psychic phenomena of any kind. And so it seems that this "true story" is 99 percent fiction.

BIBLIOGRAPHY: Moran, R. and Peter, J. 1978. "The Amityville Horror Hoax." *Fate* 31(5): 43; Owen, I. and Mitchel, P. 1979. "The Alleged Haunting of Borley Rectory." JSPR 50: 149, 161.

**Anderson, Margaret L., 1920–1986.** American educator and parapsychologist. Her relatively short career in parapsychology began in the mid-1950s when, after many years of teaching, including a stint in Mexico, she joined J. B. Rhine's Parapsychology Laboratory. Working with Rhea White, she began testing ESP in children. They predicted that mutual teacher-pupil liking would produce ESP while disliking would obstruct it. The early series of tests (Anderson and White 1956, Anderson 1957, and Anderson and White 1957) were spectacularly successful and were picked up by other experimenters. Later experiments were not as successful. Anderson then turned from predicting ESP based on existing classroom conditions to creating conditions that would produce ESP. Working with students who were encouraged to play fantasy games and write "space music," she created feelings of excitement and enthusiasm that produced continuing excellent results (Anderson and Gregory 1959).

In 1961, Margaret Anderson returned to the University of Pittsburgh (she had taught there earlier) to obtain her doctorate in education and to work with Robert A. McConnell who was Research Professor in the Department of Biophysics. In 1961, working with McConnell, Anderson created a fantasy experiment in which one class launched an imaginary space rocket, a second class guided it and a third class reentered it. For this work she and McConnell in 1961 won the **McDougall Award for Distinguished Work in Parapsychology.**

She was president of the Parapsychology Association in 1962. Her last appearance in parapsychology seems to have been at a meeting of the American Society for Psychical Research where she presented a paper on the role of fantasies in liberating ESP (Anderson 1966).

Margaret Anderson received her Ph.D. in 1962 and began a career of teaching and educational research at the University of Pittsburgh from which she retired as professor of education in 1985. She died some nine months later of lung cancer.

Selected Writings: 1966. "The Use of Fantasy in Testing for Extrasensory Perception." JASPR 60:150; 1957. "Clairvoyance and Teacher-Pupil Attitudes in Fifth and Sixth Grades." JP 21:1; and E. Gregory. 1959. "A Two-year Program of Tests for Clairvoyance and Precognition with a Class of Public School Pupils." JP 23:149; and R. A. McConnell. 1961. "Fantasy Testing for ESP in a Fourth- and Fifth-Grade Class." *Journal of Psychology* 52:491; and R. White. 1956. "Teacher-Pupil Attitudes and Clairvoyance Test Results." JP 20:141; and R. White. 1957. "A Further Investigation of Teacher-Pupil Attitudes and Clairvoyance Test Results." JP 21:81.

BIBLIOGRAPHY: McConnell, R. A. *Parapsychology in Retrospect,* 1987, p. 67; Osis, K. 1987. "A Tribute to Margaret L. Anderson, 1920–1985" [*sic*]. JASPR 81:257.

**Anderson, Roger Ivan, 1943–.** American writer. A lifelong interest in the unknown, the supernatural, and the occult, and a fascination with ghost stories, all as fiction, eventually led Anderson to the classics of psychical research such as F. W. H. Myers's *Human Personality* and Edmund Gurney's *Phantasms of the Living.* Despite his own belief that telepathy, apparitions, and communications that seem to come from the dead actually do take place, he became actively involved in psychical research because he felt that writers on the subject were too uncritical. Yet, although he felt that certain cases, such as the Watseka Wonder, were not particularly impressive, he could not find any natural explanations for the proxy sittings with Gladys Osborne Leonard or the cross-correspondences such as Arthur Balfour's Palm Sunday case. Even the explanation of these latter cases as some form of super ESP would make the idea of survival plausible, he believes, because it would demonstrate that the human mind can function outside the limitations of space and time. His special interests in the field are survival after death, the history of spiritualism, and experimental research.

Holder of an M.S. in Philosophy received in 1974 from the University of Utah, Anderson has written articles on psychical research for the *Parapsychology Review,* the *Journal of the American Society for Psychical Research, Theta, The Journal of Religion and Psychical Research* and for popular magazines such as *Fate.*

Anderson, who won the Robert H. Ashby Memorial Award in 1983, is a Fellow of the American Society for Psychical Research, a member of the Psychical Research Foundation, a past academic member of the Academy of Religion and Psychical Research and is a contributing editor to Parapsychology Abstracts International.

Selected Writings: 1986. "Reincarnation: Can Christianity Accommodate It?" *Journal of Religion and Psychical Research* 9:189; 1985. "The Life and Works of James H. Hyslop." JASPR 79:167; 1984. "Psychometry or Survival, Parts I & II." *Parapsychology Review* 15(3,4):6, 10; 1984. "Cahagnet's Contribution to Psychical Research." *Theta* 12(4):74; 1983. "The Mediumship of Geraldine Cummins." *Theta* 11(3):50; 1981. "Contemporary Survival Research: A Critical Review." *Parapsychology Review* 12(5):8; with W. L. Anderson. 1982. "Veridical and Psychopathic Hallucinations: A Comparison of Types." *Parapsychology Review* 13(3):17.

**Andhra University.** The only university in India offering courses and research programs in parapsychology. The objectives of its Department of Psychology and Parapsychology, founded and chaired by **K. Ramakrishna Rao,** are instruction and research in psychology and parapsychology. The department offers two courses leading to an M.A. (psychology) in which parapsychology is an elective subject, a one-year research program in psychology and parapsychology leading to an M.Phil., and a three-year research program in psychology and parapsychology leading to a Ph.D. Six Ph.D. degrees in parapsychology have been granted so far. The research contributions of the department have considerably advanced the progress of parapsychology in India. The department also has a special arrangement with the **Institute for Parapsychology** by which students may enroll for the Ph.D. program at Andhra University but work at the Institute for Parapsychology for the preparation and completion of their dissertations for the Ph.D. degree. The Department of Psychology and Parapsychology publishes the *Journal of Indian Psychology*. The address of Andhra University is: Visakhapatnam 530 003, A.P., India.

**Angels of Mons.** In August 1914, the German army and British Expeditionary Force faced one another in southern Belgium. Superior German forces at Mons forced the B.E.F. to fall back as charging German cavalry pursued the retreating and helpless British. They turned to fight the Germans in the expectation of annihilation "when to their wonder they saw between them and the enemy a whole troop of angels. The German horses turned round terrified. . ." (Salter, 1915). One witness who had never believed in God said that, having seen the heavenly apparitions, he was forever after a changed man.

Many similar reports of angels who had taken up arms against the Germans circulated like the wind throughout England. But when serious efforts were made to trace them to authoritative sources, none of the reports, all second- or third-hand, could be corroborated. The probable source of the reports was an article published in *The All Saints' Clifton Parish Magazine* in May 1915, for all the reports repeated the text of the article almost verbatim. The article itself was based on stories narrated to the author by a woman who admitted later that she could not verify them and did not know where they came from. Another possible origin of the reports was a piece of fiction called *The Bowmen* written by Arthur Machen that appeared in the London *Evening News* in September 1914. It told of angelic intervention on the battlefield. A pamphlet by Harold Begbie entitled *On the Side of Angels*, however, claimed that British soldiers had seen angels in France prior to Machen's story and quoted some of the soldiers's experiences. But they were related long after the event when the factors of failing memory, suggestion, and imagination may have become operative.

The Angels of Mons case is relevant to psychical research because it illustrates that all reports of the paranormal are no more than fallible human testimony with which every lawyer, historian, and parapsychologist is familiar. All such reports must be investigated and appraised critically before any conclusions can be based on them. The case brings out the distinction between legend and fact and between unfounded rumor and testimony that can be corroborated by authoritative sources.

BIBLIOGRAPHY: Salter, H. de G. 1915. "An Enquiry Concerning 'The Angels of Mons.'" JSPR 17:106.

**Angoff, Allan, 1910–.** American librarian, book critic, and editor. He believes that a great deal of parapsychological literature is unknown to researchers and students of the subject and advocates the establishment of a central library of parapsychology. In his view, the greatest contribution to the field that could be made by owners of small libraries would be the donation of their books to the central library. Angoff had been editor in chief of New York University Press and Emerson Books, was managing editor and book review editor of *Tomorrow*, a publication of the Parapsychology Foundation, and editor of the *Proceedings* published by the foundation of its annual international conferences.

**Animal ESP.** See **ANPSI.**

**Animal Magnetism.** A psychic force or subtle fluid supposed to emanate from some human beings who are its conductors and to have healthful effects on other people who are its receptors. Franz Anton Mesmer, a Viennese doctor, invented the term. He had been a student of astrology and believed that the planets had a magnetic influence on human beings. He tried to effect cures by passing magnets over the bodies of patients. Later, he came to believe that the curative power did not lie in magnets, but in individuals who passed their hands over the bodies of others. Mesmer discontinued the use of magnets and, supposing that the curing power radiated from people, described his treatment as "animal magnetism" treatment. See also **Mesmerism.**

**ANPSI.** Paranormal abilities in animals and birds. Countless accounts have been received of the strange behavior of animals and birds that seems to have no sensory basis and so to lie in their ESP abilities. For example, a pet dog whines continuously at the time its master is killed or is in serious trouble many miles away; a cat abandoned by its owner travels fifty miles to the owner's new home in a strange town, a phenomenon called "psi-trailing." When some birds make their annual migrations from northern regions to the Southern Hemisphere, young birds on their first trip navigate directly toward the right areas and are there waiting to greet the flock and the older birds who have made the journey before, a phenomenon called "homing."

In addition to these and similar accounts, field investigations have been made of reports of spontaneous cases in which animals seem able to respond to questions by pawing or pointing their noses at letters or numbers or by barking. One hypothesis is that, if it is not the high intelligence of the animals that is responsible for their success, it must be their telepathic powers. There is little experimental evidence that ESP is responsible for homing. **Joseph G. Pratt** explored the subject of homing in pigeons and designed an ESP test for it that unfortunately was never carried out. W. Bechterev, the Soviet neurophysiologist who observed and conducted experiments with a circus trainer and his trained St. Bernard and fox terrier, concluded that the animals could be directly influenced by telepathy. Generally, however, other experimental results have produced evidence that is at best inconclusive. See also **Chris the Wonder Dog; Clever Hans; Lady Wonder; Missy; Rolf of Mannheim.**

**Anthony, Susan Brownwell,** 1820–1906. American reformer. She was active in abolition and temperance movements and, along with Elizabeth Cady Stanton, was a leader of the woman suffrage movement. Anthony's advocacy of woman suffrage led to the adoption of the 19th Amendment to the U.S. Constitution which forbids the states to deny the right to vote because of sex and extends suffrage to women.

Susan B. Anthony is a **Noted Witness** in support of the phenomenon of precognition and of the possibility of "intervention" to avoid a precognized event: Staying in a hotel in Atlantic City, Anthony had a vivid dream that she was burned alive in one of the Atlantic City hotels on the boardwalk. The following morning she packed up and left. The next day a raging fire destroyed her hotel and others along the boardwalk.

**Apparition.** The figure of a living or dead being (human or animal) seen at a time when in fact no human being or animal is physically present. The term sometimes is used interchangeably with "ghost." But an apparition is not a **Ghost** since there can be apparitions of living as well as of dead people.

Some distinctive characteristics of apparitions are: 1. They are not perceived as being within ourselves as in imagination or memory. They are external to us and occupy different kinds of settings in space. 2. They are not physical in character. For example, they may fade away or disappear from a locked room, yet they seem solid and no different from living people. 3. They seem as aware as living people of their surroundings and act as might be expected (i.e., they avoid furniture, usually enter through a door, turn their heads to watch movements). 4. The percipient of an apparition frequently feels a draft of cold air or a cold touch.

In Greek and Roman times, the appearance of apparitions seems to have been accepted by Cicero, Plutarch, and Pliny the Younger. In our day, John Palmer, who surveyed the psychic experiences of the residents of Charlottesville, Virginia, in 1974, found that 17 percent of the respondents had seen, touched or heard an apparition. In a later survey in Iceland, Erlendur Haraldsson found 31 percent of the 902 persons he surveyed reporting apparitional experiences.

While many reports of apparitions can be dismissed on the ground that they are subjective hallucinations of the individuals perceiving them, there are several classes of well-attested cases not accounted for by psychological explanations: 1. Collectively Seen Apparitions—when two or more people see the same apparition at the same time and in the identical location. In the **Census of Hallucinations,** this class of case constituted about 8 percent of the total of 1,087 cases of waking hallucinations; 2. Crisis Apparitions—in which a distant person is seen within twelve hours before or after undergoing a crisis, usually death, accident, or unexpected illness unknown to the see-er; 3. Postmortem Apparitions—where apparitions of long deceased people are seen and identified by individuals who had never seen or known them or where such apparitions provide information known only to the deceased person but not to anyone living; 4. Purposeful Apparitions—where apparitions display purpose and consciousness as in **Deathbed Visions,** usually the apparitions of deceased relatives whose ostensible purpose is to guide and take away dying people to another dimension.

There is still no generally accepted explanation for apparitional experiences, but different theories have been formulated to account for them. The first theory gained wide currency among parapsychologists: **F. W. H. Myers** and **Edmund Gurney** hypothesized that an apparition was a telepathic phenomenon, a mental hallucination created by a percipient as a result of telepathic information received from an appearer. Gurney further theorized, along with **Eleanor Sidgwick** and **H. H. Price,** that images might have been impressed by the appearer's physical organism on a region of physical space that was later perceived by sensitive people. **G. N. M. Tyrrell** thought that apparitions were idea-patterns projected by the cooperation between the subconscious of a percipient and that of an agent which together staged a creative apparitional drama. **Hornell Hart** offered the theory that the figure seen was the astral or etheric body of a person. **L. E. Rhine** put forward the theory that, as the result of information obtained through the clairvoyance of an appearer and the situation in which he or she had been placed, the mind of a percipient generated an apparition. Spiritualists maintain that apparitions are the spirits of dead people. At present, the data from apparitional cases not being strong enough to confirm any theory, the search for data continues. See also **Apparition, Experimental.**

**Apparition, Experimental.** In the classes of apparitions discussed under **Apparition,** the appearers were either already dead or in or near the dying state. But many experiments have been reported in which perfectly healthy people seem to have been successful in intentionally producing and projecting their own apparitions that have been visible to others at unexpected times and at distant places.

One such experiment was reported in *Phantasms of the Living*. About 9:30 P.M. on December 1, 1882, as B. sat by the fireside in a room in his home in the United Kingdom, he concentrated so strongly on the interior of a house where a Miss Verity and her two sisters lived that he believed that he was actually in their house. A half hour later, resolving that he would will his apparition to appear in the Verity house at twelve midnight, he went to bed. The following day, one of the sisters staying with Miss Verity said she was certain that she had seen B. at 9:30 P.M. as he was walking from one room to another in the house. Again at midnight, while she was still fully awake, she saw B. come into her bedroom, take her long hair into his hand and stare at it. The case is one of a conscious experiment made by an appearer. Apparitions of living people who have not made any deliberate effort at projection have also been seen.

**Apport.** The moving of living organisms or material objects into a permanently enclosed area in the absence of any known human agency, which implies the ability of one solid object to pass through another (the passage of matter through matter); generally a phenomenon of physical mediumship in which, after a seance in the darkness and in a closed room, the lights reveal a vase of flowers or a live animal on a table as if the spirits had transported them through the walls of the room. See also **Medium, Physical; Deport; Teleportation.**

**Aragón, Enrique O., 1879–1950.** Mexican doctor of medicine and dean of the Universidad Nacional Autónoma de México. In 1937, he followed the precedent set by Gustav Pagenstecher by using scientific methods to investigate paranormal phenomena. His first investigations were of poltergeist disturbances. In one of his cases involving a thirteen-year-old boy who appeared to be a poltergeist agent, Aragón used a device called a "stenometer" to measure the energy force that was the apparent cause of the disturbances. His other interests included haunts and the exposures of frauds in the field of the paranormal.

Selected Writing: *Historia del Alma,* Vol. 2, 1943.

**Archaeology.** Claims are sometimes made that psychics are capable of making contributions to the field of archaeology. David

Read Barker has pointed out that casual readers may be misled by exaggerated assertions that psychics have provided leads to archaeological excavations and finds. Yet, in spite of possible distortions, many archaeologists are taking the possibility seriously in the light of both old and new discoveries that have been made as a result of the work of psychics.

The Edgar Chapel in the twelfth century Glastonbury Abbey is a classic illustration of such a discovery. It was known that the Edgar Chapel had once existed but, among the ruins of the abbey, no one knew its site or character. In order to try to discover its location, **Frederick Bligh Bond,** who later became director of excavations at Glastonbury and who is considered the father of psychic archaeology, and a friend conducted experiments in automatic writing. A script was produced, sometimes in a language purporting to be Old English and sometimes in Latin, that spelled out the location, plan, and dimensions of the Edgar Chapel. Subsequent excavations verified the information.

**Stefan Ossowiecki** and **Stanislaw Poniatowski** for almost ten years, beginning in 1935, carried on experiments in psychic archaeology, the results of which were confirmed many years later. The Russians have used dowsing to locate archaeological sites. The most recent example of contributions by psychics to archaeology comes from **Stephan Schwartz's** attempt to establish the location of Alexander's tomb. He gave eleven psychics in the United States a map of forty square miles of a region around Alexandria, Egypt. With the information they supplied, three sites were excavated by archaeologists who made discoveries that seemingly could not have been made by using normal techniques. Other sites psychically located are still to be explored.

BIBLIOGRAPHY: Schwartz, S. A. *The Alexandria Project,* 1983; Schwartz, S. A. *The Secret Vaults of Time,* 1978.

**Archer, William, 1820–1874.** Australian architect and botanist. He was the first scientist in the history of psychical research in his country to conduct an experiment in the paranormal and to present his findings in a scientific paper (Archer, 1864) presented to the Royal Society of Tasmania. In his experiment with **Table-Tilting**, he organized a séance in which sitters seated themselves around a highly polished, slippery-surfaced table covered by a tablecloth. The sitters placed their hands on the table and exerted a downward pressure. The table tilted all right, but the tablecloth in front of one sitter was wrinkled. The sitter had consciously or unconsciously pushed toward the center of the table and so had produced the tipping movement of the table. The significance of this simple test is not merely that it was the first ever reported in Australia; it also had the distinction of dampening for a long time scientific and intellectual interest in paranormal phenomena.

Selected Writings: Archer, W. 1864. "Observations on Table-Moving." *Proceedings of the Royal Society of Tasmania* 4: 86.

BIBLIOGRAPHY: Irwin, H. J. 1988. "Parapsychology in Australia." JASPR 82:319.

**Archivo di Documentazione Storica Della Ricerca Psichica (Archives of Historical Documents on Psychical Research).** Italian organization founded in Bologna in 1985 that contains the most outstanding and important collection in all of Italy of books and materials pertaining to psychical research and parapsychology, their works and phenomena. The collection, based on the vast libraries assembled by **Gastone de Boni** and **Ernesto Bozzano,** makes the center a gold mine for researchers and archivists. The organization also publishes *Luce e Ombra.* Address: Via Orfeo 15, 40124 Bologna, Italy.

**A.R.E.** See **Association for Research and Enlightenment.**

**Arigo, José (José Pedro de Freitas), 1918–1971.** Brazil's most famous healer. He was an uneducated laborer who claimed that a deceased German doctor named "Dr. Fritz" was helping him. Arigo made medical diagnoses, used medical terms, prescribed medicines and, often on a discarded door made into an operating table, performed various medical procedures, such as inserting a pocket knife under the eyelid or into the body of a patient to remove a cataract or tumor, all without anesthesia or antisepsis. His patients, experiencing no pain, loss of blood, or infection, seemed cured of their disorders. While many "cures" can perhaps be put down to journalistic sensationalism, trickery, or patient motivation or expectation, trained physicians who studied Arigo were deeply impressed by his performances. Henry (Andrija) K. Puharich who watched him do surgery, for example, said: "every patient was helped and none had postoperative complications. It was truly a mind-shattering experience to see every principle of surgery violated with impunity" (Puharich, 1974). Arigo and his spirit guide continued his (or their) healing until Arigo lost his life in a car accident.

BIBLIOGRAPHY: Puharich, H. "Psychic Research and the Healing Process." In E. D. Mitchell (J. White, ed.), *Psychic Exploration*, 1976, p. 333.

**Aristotle, 384–322 B.C.** Greek thinker and one of the world's outstanding philosophers. His writings, which covered logic, physics, ethics, politics, metaphysics, and the philosophy of art, for centuries have greatly influenced thinkers everywhere.

Some of the phenomena of psychical research and parapsychology, namely, precognition and telepathy, played a role in his thought. He reacted to the evidence with the statement that one could neither believe nor ignore it. Generally, however, he accepted both, although in his *Eudemian Ethics* he expressed the opinion that these gifts were possessed only by people with a "melancholic" temperament, that is, he considered them emotionally or mentally disturbed. He deliberated over the problem of survival beyond physical death. In his philosophy, he pictured three kinds of souls: the rational, the animal, and the vegetable. Only the rational soul which was responsible for reflection, reasoning, and intellect and which was limited to human beings survived death. But Aristotle did not affirm personal survival. For while the rational element survived, memory did not. Without conscious memory of people, objects, events, or of information obtained before death, there cannot be any sense of continuity nor can evidence of personal identity be furnished to the living. Just what the future destiny of the rational element may be is not clear from Aristotle's philosophy, but it seems to be part of the divine essence and probably returns to God of which it is a part. See also **Identity, Personal.**

**Ashby, Robert Howe. 1930–1975.** American director of education and research of the Spiritual Frontiers Fellowship. His major interests were the question of survival and survival research. The one guiding principle of his life was "the desire and determination to investigate the mystery of life . . . of all the enigmas we face, none is more baffling or overarching in its significance than that of death and its impact. How we view death determines in large measure how we view life. . ." (Ebon, 1982).

His feelings about survival of death are revealed in his conception of what it means to be a person. "To be a person is to have the conviction that . . . death does *not* close all. . . . It is to see in the confidence that one's personality survives death, that one's life is a seamless garment unrent by the seeming edge of death still another shining answer to the question of what it is really to be a person? It is to be immortal" (Ashby, 1982). Ashby believed that the super ESP hypothesis was a fallacy unsupported by data. On the other hand, he saw support for the survival hypothesis in psychical research because "it tends to the view that man is more than merely physical; and if man is more, then physical dissolution of the body and brain would not necessarily mean the dissolution of the 'I' that is the individual" (Tribbe, 1982).

In order to prod other people's thinking about whether we survive death, Ashby prepared and distributed 1,000 questionnaires. From the responses, he arrived at the conclusion that, assuming survival after death, few of the respondents knew how to identify themselves after death to the living. This finding was important because it may explain why so many messages purporting to be from the dead are vague and cannot be clearly identified with a deceased person. This significant finding opened up new directions for other research, such as Gertrude R. Schmiedler's predictive research project (Schmeidler, 1977) and Arthur S. Berger's cipher test (Berger, 1987) which can be used to establish personal identity through the communication of secret information.

Prior to becoming associated with the Spiritual Frontiers Fellowship, Ashby was headmaster of the American School in London and before that had been headmaster of the American School in Tangier, Morocco. He was a Sherlock Holmes fan and was fascinated by the enigma of Sir Arthur Conan Doyle. While in England he became Rosalind Heywood's protégé. She was his link to nineteenth century psychical research. He also spent much time in the library and among the records of the Society for Psychical Research. The result was his principal work—a survey of the bibliography in parapsychology (Ashby, 1972).

Selected Writings: 1982. "Personhood." *Spiritual Frontiers* 14 (1): 7; *The Guidebook for the Study of Psychical Research,* 1972.

BIBLIOGRAPHY: Berger, A. S. *Aristocracy of the Dead,* 1987; Ebon, M. 1982. "In Memoriam - Ashby Remembered." *Spiritual Frontiers* 14 (1):3; Schmeidler, G. R. 1977. "Looking Ahead: A Method for Research on Survival." *Theta* 5 (1): 2; Tribbe, F. C. 1982. "Research Report: Robert Ashby and the Super ESP Hypothesis." *Spiritual Frontiers* 14 (1):33.

**Association for Research and Enlightenment.** A nonprofit educational organization founded in Virginia Beach, Virginia, in 1931 by **Edgar Cayce** for the purpose of storing and studying the material from his readings. During Cayce's life (he died in 1945) the organization had fewer than 150 members. In 1980, under Cayce's son Hugh Lynn (who died in 1982), the A.R.E. had a nationwide membership of about 20,000 and, in 1987, a staff of over 150 and a membership of over 70,000 (Vahle, 1987). The members of A.R.E. are interested in psychic experiences, dreams, meditation, unorthodox healing, and other similar topics and are predominantly white, female, married, fairly well educated, liberal politically, and rather religious (Kohr, 1980). All the activities of the A.R.E. are related to Cayce's readings.

The A.R.E. holds conferences at its headquarters in Virginia Beach from May to October and throughout the United States and Canada in the spring and fall. The organization puts out books and home study courses and publishes a bimonthly magazine, *Venture Inward.* A holistic health-care facility, the A.R.E. Clinic in Phoenix, Arizona, is not a part of the A.R.E. organization, but it treats patients and does research using the Cayce concepts of healing.

BIBLIOGRAPHY: Kohr, R. L. 1980. "A Survey of Psi Experiences among Members of a Special Population." JASPR 74:395; Vahle, N. 1987. "The Spiritual Legacy of Edgar Cayce." *New Realities.* 8(2):34.

**Association Theory of Telepathy.** Propounded by **Whately Carington** it holds that, if two ideas are paired in the mind of person A, and if later one of these ideas is presented again to that mind or to the mind of another person B, it is more probable that the second idea will accompany the first or follow it than if the two ideas had not been originally associated in the mind of A. Telepathy may take place more easily as agent and percipient share ideas in common. "K-idea" and "K-object" were terms Carington used to describe any idea or object with which another idea or object is associated and which may allow telepathy to take place more freely.

**Associazione Italiana Scientifica di Metapsichica** (Italian Scientific Association of Metaphysics). Founded in Milan in 1946, it supports rigorous investigation of paranormal phenomena by individuals, but primarily it carries out social and educational programs to disseminate information to parapsychological groups in Italy and abroad. The organization publishes *Metapsichica,* considered one of the best and most up-to-date parapsychological publications in Italy. Address: S. Vittore, 9, Milan, Italy.

**Astral Body.** A term used in the literature of Spiritualism and Theosophy which posits that the soul is never disembodied but is always dressed in a psychic covering or "perispirit" purported to be an exact counterpart of the physical body but composed of some kind of subtle matter. During waking hours, the astral body corresponds precisely to the physical body. But during sleep and at other times the astral body may separate from the physical body and travel to other places. According to some authorities, the astral body maintains its connection to the physical body by a silver cord that can be stretched without limit and is the vital mechanism. This cord is cut at death when it is said that the astral body enters an initial postmortem stage. The idea of an entity separable and independent of the body goes back thousands of years. The Egyptians believed in a *ka* which they conceived as a double of the body that came forth from it and moved wherever the *ka* wished. The oriental sages of long ago conceived of a "radiant body" that resembled the physical one and could move at will through solid objects. See also **Double; Out-of-Body Experience.**

**Astral Projection.** See **Out-of-Body Experience.**

**Astral Travel.** See **Out-of-Body Experience.**

**Astrology.** "According to the stars," says the astrologer, "if this is your birthday, you are surrounded by glamour and mystery and Pisces people will be important to you. If you're a Cancer, your mate is going to surprise you, if a Libra luck is with you." So do astrologers use their art to divine the personalities and fates of human beings and even earthly events from the positions of the stars and planets. The art is ancient having originated millennia before our era in Mesopotamia (now Iraq). It developed in Babylon, in classical antiquity, spread to India and China, and thrived in the Middle Ages when chairs of astrology were established at European universities. It continues today through horoscope columns in newspapers, astrological organizations, almanacs, journals and books. Great popular interest is stimulated by reports that investors hire astrologers to forecast the prices of stocks, bonds, and commodities and that celebrities use astrologers to make their decisions. The news in 1988, for instance, that the First Lady and President Reagan were interested in astrology and that astrologers shaped executive policies exploded like a bomb for some people.

The astrologer's craft consists of casting a horoscope by plotting twelve "houses of heaven," each governed by a heavenly body and each with its character type. The astrologer then determines what star or planet was in ascendency on the date of birth of an individual and places that person in one of the twelve character types. Astrology gave rise to astronomy, but that very science, beginning with the discovery of Nicolaus Copernicus, the sixteenth century Polish astronomer, exposed the error of astrology's key theory that the earth is the center of the universe. The vast majority of scientists and intellectuals deplore the absence of any scientific or intellectual merit in astrology. Thus in 1975, *The Humanist,* the journal of the American Humanist Association, published "Objections to Astrology" signed by eighteen Nobel laureates and 172 prominent scientists.

Most parapsychologists do not accept the art of the astrologer, either. Yet empirical evidence is not completely absent. Science might concede the fundamental premise of astrology—that the positions of heavenly bodies are important and may influence human beings. In medicine, correlations have been found between solar flares and coronary thrombosis. The sun affects our temperatures, and the lunar cycle and solar rhythms are related to the times of our births. While science still does not agree with the astrologer's claim that each individual is affected differently by the planets, the statistical procedures used by Michel Gauquelin, who concentrated on statistics and psychology at the Sorbonne in France, are provocative. He did not use the usual tools of the astrologer, the "houses," for instance, and he considers astrology just a superstition. Nevertheless, he determined the positions of the Sun, Moon, Mars, Venus, Jupiter, and Saturn and the dates of birth of 27,000 people. Making a quantitative study, he found that the positions of these bodies showed significant correlations with the professions of celebrities—sports champions, actors, soldiers—as opposed to ordinary people.

Gauquelin's findings are controversial but, if valid, make the basic premise of astrology more credible. But they do not mean that astrology is free from criticism or that its further premise that the moment of birth is the key factor is correct. Scientist Lyell Watson disagrees "that the moment of birth is the critical moment . . . cosmic forces are acting on everything all the time and . . . the moment of birth bears the same relation to the rest of life as the momentary position of Mars does to the rest of the cosmos." (Watson, 1973). Yet astrophysicist John Gribbin and physicist Stephen Plagemann write (1974) that "astrologers were not so wrong after all; it seems that the alignment of the planets can, for sound scientific reasons, affect the behavior of the earth."

Parapsychology should not overlook the important insight that cosmic forces always act on us. Astrology may pertain to at least two of parapsychology's concerns. We give the names extrasensory perception and psychokinesis to mental processes about which we know nothing. But whatever our minds are doing in these processes, cosmic forces may be influencing and interacting with them as well. A related point is that astrology's claim may also have a direct relation to the difficult problem of repeatability. Should cosmic forces always in flux be influencing our personalities, behavior, and performances, they may be affecting our psi abilities, too, and so be creating an enormous obstacle in the way of ever achieving the repeatable experiment. An experiment conducted in a parapsychological laboratory on one day when certain cosmic patterns prevail cannot be carried out with the same result on another day, whether in the same or another laboratory, when cosmic forces are different. If psi, like our lives, is correlated to heavenly bodies, it cannot manifest in the identical way twice because cosmic conditions are never identical or controllable.

BIBLIOGRAPHY: Gauquelin, M. *Cosmic Influence on Human Behavior,* 1974; Gribbin, J. and S. H. Plagemann. *The Jupiter Effect,* 1974; Watson, L. *Supernature,* 1973, p. 75.

**Atreya, Bhikhan Lal, 1897–1967.** Indian scholar who pioneered the development of parapsychology in his country. As the head of the Department of Philosophy and Psychology at Benares Hindu University, he paved the way for experimental research there and was instrumental in introducing parapsychology into the psychology and philosophy curricula of the universities in India. In 1957, a collection of Atreya's papers on parapsychology was published.

**Augustine, Saint, (Saint Augustine of Hippo), 354–430.** African Bishop of Hippo, great Christian theologian and one of the early fathers of the Catholic Church. Called the Christian "Aristotle," he was a philosopher who systematized religious truths and is acknowledged the greatest thinker of Christian antiquity. After his conversion to Christianity, he became a priest and later a bishop, teacher, and judge of civil cases. He wrote against heretics and was the author of *The Confessions* (397), in which he told the story of his life and conversion, and of the famous *City of God* (413) where he described the cities of heaven and earth and presented a philosophy of predestination.

Augustine, like others of his age, had no awareness of modern concepts of extrasensory perception or communicators. In keeping with the opinions of the early Christians, he attributed such phenomena to demonic possession or to a supernatural agency. But his presentation of such accounts as true make him a **Noted Witness** for the centuries-old existence of the phenomena. In his *De Genesi ad Litteram* (401–415), for example, he described a man on his sick bed who seemed to be in a delirium, yet who gave in minute and correct detail each phase of a priest's future trip from its start to the time of his arrival at the man's house. The account bears a strong family resemblance to hundreds of cases that are today classified as precognition. Augustine also related how a dead father advised his son where a missing receipt could be found—a case suggestive of a communicator and very similar to one of Emanuel Swedenborg's spirit communications in which a missing receipt also was found (*De cura pro mortuis* 11[13]).

BIBLIOGRAPHY: Thurston, H. *The Physical Phenomena of Mysticism,* 1952, pp. 332–33.

**Aura.** A luminous halo said to surround the head or a radiating mist or nimbus of many colors said to envelop the body. Against the possible contention that the aura is only an occult or religious idea or a phenomenon seen only by psychics, there is the testimony of Gerda Walther, a respected parapsychologist, that she saw the phenomenon and the work done by Walter J. Kilner which he claimed supported it. There are, as well, soundly based theories and observations in biology and physics which agree that every living organism creates an electromagnetic field and that a part of the field projects beyond the boundaries of the organism to produce an electromagnetic aura. See also **Kirlian Photography; Luminous Phenomena.**

BIBLIOGRAPHY: Kilner, W. J. *The Human Aura,* 1965; Bagnall, O. *The Origin and Properties of the Human Aura,* 1970; Ellison, A. J. 1962. "Some Recent Experiments in Psychic Perceptivity." *JSPR* 41:355; Sudre, R. *Treatise on Parapsychology,* 1960.

**Australian Society for Psychical Research.** Organized in the west of Australia in the early 1980s, this highly active group, through its meetings, seminars, and its newsletter "Psi," is attracting the attention of the public in Western Australia to research and issues in psychical research and parapsychology. The address of its founder and president is Prof. J. Frodsham, School of Communication, Murdoch University, Murdoch WA 6153, Australia.

**Australian Institute of Psychic Research.** Notwithstanding its name, this group conducts no active research. Rather, it is a membership organization whose aim is to function as a resource center, depository for books and investigative reports and, through its bulletin, to supply information about paranormal phenomena to its members as well as the general public and mass media. Address: P.O. Box 445, Lane Cove, NSW 2066, Australia.

**Australian Skeptics.** Founded in Australia as a branch of the Committee for the Scientific Investigation of the Claims of the Paranormal. With its meetings, conferences, and the publication of its journal *The Skeptic,* this organization subjects all claims of the paranormal to critical examination and has established effective relationships with the mass media. Address: P.O. Box 575, Manly, N.S.W. 2095, Australia.

**Automatic Writing.** See **Automatic Writing, Speaking or Spelling.**

**Automatic Writing, Speaking or Spelling.** Writing, speaking or spelling that is not done consciously or intentionally but nevertheless with purpose and intelligence. This type of activity in mediums is interpreted by some as communication of messages by spirits. The common notion that the activity began with the advent of Spiritualism must be taken with a grain of salt. Automatic writing descends to us from the Old Testament. For example, Jehoram, the king of Judah, received a writing from Elijah the Prophet, who had been dead for seven years, to the effect that Jehoram and all of Judah would be punished (II Chronicles 21:12–15). See also **Automatism; Ouija Board; Planchette.**

**Automatism.** An action carried out without the actor's conscious effort or control and generally in a dissociated state. **Dowsing, Automatic Writing, Speaking or Spelling,** sometimes using a ouija board, planchette, or a pendulum, are examples of motor automatisms. Visual or auditory images outside the conscious control of an individual in a dissociated or **Altered State of Consciousness** are examples of sensory automatisms. In mediumship, the issue is whether the action is merely a motor or sensory automatism or whether the content of the statement made or image experienced automatically by a medium can have been known normally by the medium. If it cannot have been, the activity may be classified as paranormal and perhaps interpreted as a communication from a deceased person.

**Automatist.** Generally applied to a medium; one who writes or spells automatically or uses a ouija board or makes automatic oral statements. See also **Automatism.**

**Autoscopy.** The hallucination of seeing, apparently from outside oneself, the image or **"Double"** of one's own body. See also **Out-of-Body Experience.**

**Azuma, Nagato, 1956–.** Japanese surgeon. He is the first physician in Japan to investigate unorthodox healing and, in particular, psychic surgery practiced in the Philippines. He made several field trips there where he witnessed and worked with practitioners as they wielded their knives and performed their "operations." See also **Healing, Unorthodox.**

Selected Writing: and Stevenson, I. 1987. "Difficulties Confronting Investigations of 'Psychic Surgery' in the Philippines." *Parapsychology Review* 18(2):6.

# B

**Ba.** Egyptian conception of the soul of the human being that would live forever with the gods in heaven and was pictured as a hawk with a human head. Of all the religious beliefs held by the Egyptians, the oldest and most prominent is their belief in human survival of physical death, the same subject that has absorbed psychical research since its inception. For parapsychologists, however, the human being was conceived dualistically with a mind that might continue to exist even when there was no longer a body. The Egyptians, on the other hand, conceived a tripartite division of the human being into the natural body that would remain in the tomb, the **Ka** that had all the attributes of a person and would be able to live with the gods, and finally the **Ba** or essence of the person that hovered about the tomb and also would enjoy eternal life. The *Ba* was thought to be an ethereal substance but, curiously enough, if it did not receive funerary offerings of food, some part of it might decay. The *Ba* also was believed capable of assuming any shape it pleased. Since apparitions are among the most ancient and best known of all paranormal phenomena, it is possible that this notion was produced gradually by mounting reports and experiences with apparitions.

BIBLIOGRAPHY: Budge, E. A. *The Book of the Dead,* 1950.

**Bach, Richard, 1935–.** American author. A direct descendant of the great composer, Johann Sebastian Bach, Richard Bach served from 1956 to 1959 as a U.S. Air Force officer and later worked as a letter carrier and editor of a magazine. In 1970, Bach published *Jonathan Livingston Seagull,* described by *Time* magazine as "perhaps . . . the decade's top publishing miracle." It was translated into many languages, was a Book of the Month selection and sold more copies than any other book in U.S. history; it surpassed even the record made by Margaret Mitchell's *Gone With the Wind*, published in 1936.

How Bach came to write his book is of interest to psychical research. He was in Belmont, California, in 1959 when: "One night I was out walking by the water wondering . . . how I was going to pay the rent. I was not in a strange state of mind at all, except I guess concern, when I heard this male voice say in a matter-of-fact way, 'Jonathan Livingston Seagull.' It stopped me cold and I felt the hair on the back of my neck rise up. It was a frightening thing because I knew I was alone. . . . I turned around to look for someone to attach the voice to, but there wasn't a soul."

This experience was followed by a vivid vision, again while he was awake, of a sunrise with a lone seagull in flight. The vision also contained images that he formed into the words and paragraphs that eventually became the first part of the book. Much of the remainder of the book came to Bach eight years later in a dream. Because the message of *Jonathan Livingston Seagull* has been interpreted in various ways, Bach has been asked what he meant to convey. His answer is: "If I had written the book myself I could say what it meant. But I didn't so I can't." Bach is a **Noted Witness** who testifies to the creative process and the inspirational nature of his achievement. His testimony also suggests clairaudience or the existence of a personal daemon such as those of Socrates or Camille Saint-Saens.

BIBLIOGRAPHY: Bolen, J. G. 1974. "Interview: Richard Bach." *Psychic* 5(6):6–10, 25–27.

**Backster, Cleve, 1924–.** Contemporary American polygraph expert. His remarkable claim that plants have "primary perception" (Backster, 1968) generated great interest among parapsychologists and the public alike. His polygraph recordings indicated to him that the electric potential of living vegetable tissue had been influenced by human emotion and thought and led him to the conclusion that plants have some sensory system or capacity that is similar to or identical with extrasensory perception. He also concluded that they use this capacity to perceive what human beings are feeling or thinking.

Backster formed this theory in 1966 when, engaged in polygraph research, he idly applied his testing equipment to a leaf of a philodendron potted plant. When he planned to strike a match to burn the leaf, there was a radical alteration in the sweep of the recording pen as the plant seemed to react to his intention to injure it. He conducted more experiments in which plants were exposed to another emotional situation (i.e., the deaths of brine shrimp in the vicinity of plants), and his conclusion that plants have some ability to perceive thoughts akin to human ability was reinforced.

The idea that plants have qualities usually attributed to human beings is not unique to Backster. The Malays and Dyaks believe that rice is animated by a soul (Frazer, 1951) and Aristotle taught that plants have souls although those of human beings possess higher powers. The Indian scientist Bose also found that the reactions of plants to electric currents are similar to those of human beings (Bose, 1929).

**Edgar Mitchell** is convinced that the phenomenon discovered (or rediscovered) by Backster "is now established beyond all doubt as genuine" (Mitchell, 1976). Nevertheless, independent researchers using Backster's procedures have not been able to confirm his results (Kmetz 1977; [Horowitz, Lewis, and Gasteiger 1975]) and Backster's claim remains inconclusive and without support from any empirical evidence. If plants do react to human thought, the cause of the response need not be some capacity within the plants but one within the human being. It may be a case of "mind over matter" with the human being influencing plant tissue by psychokinesis.

Selected Writing: Backster, C. 1968 "Evidence of Primary Perception in Plants." *International Journal of Parapsychology* 10:6.

BIBLIOGRAPHY: Bose, J. C. *Growth and Tropic Movements of Plants,* 1929; Frazer, J. G. *The Golden Bough,* 1951, p. 480; Horowitz, K. A., Lewis, D. C., Gasteiger, E. L. 1975. "Plant 'Primary Perception': Electrophysiological Unresponsiveness to Brine Shrimp Killing." *Science* 189:478; Kmetz, J. 1977. "A Study of Primary Perception in Plant and Animal Life." *JASPR* 71:157; Mitchell, E. "Introduction: From Outer Space to Inner Space." In E. D. Mitchell (J. White, ed.), *Psychic Exploration,* 1974.

**Baerwald, Richard, 1867–1929.** German psychologist and editor of an outstanding journal, *Zeitschrift für Kritischen Okkultismus.* He was a harsh critic of the research done by the Society for Psychical Research and a hard-line skeptic of physical phenomena, psychokinesis, and clairvoyance. He did not believe in survival after death because he considered the Christian notion of eternal life more frightening than annihilation at death. But he had no doubt whatever that telepathy is a fact, except that he did not conceive of the phenomenon as any paraphysical or paranormal event. He regarded it as a physical transmission of energy from brain to brain, comparable to a radio transmission, and believed that such unconscious emanations existed among all people. He explained all paranormal occurrences, including clairvoyance, on the basis of his conception of telepathy.

Others, such as Mark Twain and Upton Sinclair, also have thought of telepathy as "mental telegraphy" or "mental radio" and today the Soviets favor an electromagnetic hypothesis for it. Despite the fact that telepathy seems to work even when subjects are placed in a metal room or lead structure that shields radio waves and electromagnetic transmissions, the theory remains one of many theories to account for the still mysterious phenomenon of telepathy. No one can say with confidence which theory is right or wrong.

Selected Writing: "Die intellektuellen Phänomene." In M. Dessoir, ed., *Der Okkultismus in Orkunden,* 1925.

**Baggally, William Wortley, ?–1928.** British psychical researcher. Remembered best for his joint investigation with Everard Feilding and Hereward Carrington of the controversial physical medium Eusapia Palladino, he was a skilled, extremely skeptical, investigator and expert magician who knew the trick methods to look for. The report produced as a result of this investigation has been called "a classic of psychical research" (Nicol, 1972) that should be "mandatory reading" (Beloff, 1985) for all skeptics.

Baggally's hope of finding experimental proof of survival led him to join the Society for Psychical Research in 1896 and to his studying Spiritualism. He sat with William Eglinton, Florence Cook, and many others but felt that all their so-called phenomena had natural explanations. In 1900, he sat with Eusapia Palladino in his hotel room in Naples and was baffled by what he saw. And so, when, in 1909, he was asked to join in experiments with her, he happily complied. There were eleven sittings during which occurred 470 physical phenomena, including levitations of the séance table, movement of curtains, bulgings of Palladino's dress, psychokinesis, raps and sounds on musical instruments without contact, materialization of hands, unusual lights, and air currents. All the experimenters concurred that many of the phenomena were genuine. Baggally believed that during this investigation and for the only time in his life he had seen paranormal phenomena. He discounted the theory that he and the others experienced collective hallucinations. He responded sharply (1910) to Frank Podmore's criticisms of the investigation aimed chiefly at Baggally—Podmore claimed that Baggally could not have been controlling Eusapia's hands and feet—as "an admirable example of special pleading" limited "to three seances" (p. 227). Baggally did not think, however, that Eusapia's phenomena had any bearing on his search for evidence for survival. For that he turned to the cross-correspondences that he felt did afford such evidence.

From 1902 on, Baggally was a member of the SPR Council whose duties he carried out faithfully despite failing health. He died on March 14, 1928, on his way home from a council meeting.

Selected Writing: 1910. "The Naples Report on Eusapia Palladino." JSPR 14:213; and Feilding, E. and Carrington, H. 1909. "Report on a Series of Sittings with Eusapia Palladino." PSPR 23:309.

BIBLIOGRAPHY: Beloff, J. "What Is Your Counter-Explanation? A Plea to Skeptics to Think Again." In P. Kurtz, ed. *A Skeptic's Handbook of Parapsychology,* 1985; Nicol, F. 1972. "The Founders of the S.P.R." PSPR 55:341.

**Bailey, Charles (Charles Beasmore), 1870–1947.** Australian physical medium. He has the distinction of being one of the most praised and one of the most condemned mediums of all time. When Charles Beasmore was eighteen, he attended a séance at which he was told that he, too, was a medium. He joined a circle, went into trances and soon received spirit communications that told him he could produce apports, and, indeed, at one séance, a stone appeared out of nowhere still wet from the sea. He then decided to make mediumship a profession and adopted "Charles Bailey" as a stage name.

He was supported by the wealthy Spiritualist, Thomas Welton Stanford, who held sittings with Bailey over the next twelve years. More striking even than his spirit messages were Bailey's apports which included live fish, plants, old coins, birds, eggs, and even a human skull. The greatest of all the apports were clay cylinders and tablets, supposedly Babylonian, whose cuneiform texts were translated at no cost by friendly spirit scholars. Authorities of the British Museum who examined the cylinders and tablets, however, declared them bogus.

Bogus or not, how did the cylinders and tablets get into the séance room at Stanford's office in the center of busy Melbourne where all séances were held? In order to prevent fraud, in 1903 and 1904 Bailey was tested in a lengthy series of séances by Charles MacCarthy, a distinguished doctor from Sydney. MacCarthy searched Bailey before each test, enveloped him in a bag leaving only his head and hands free or placed him in a wooden frame screwed to the floor with top and sides covered with mosquito netting. Still the apports continued. Among the fifty-four items apported were more clay tablets with inscriptions, an Arabic newspaper, a rug, and a living shark. MacCarthy's report on Bailey as the genuine article sent Spiritualist stock in Australia to a new high. Australian Spiritualism and Bailey were synonymous.

Bailey was next tested in Melbourne by A. W. Dobbie, an Australian parapsychologist, who asked Bailey's Hindu control to translate a sentence into Hindustani. The translation turned out to be "meaningless scribble" (Mediumship of Mr. C. Bailey, 1905). Now famous abroad, Bailey was invited to Italy in 1904 to be investigated by the Milan Society for Psychical Studies. In spite of being put in a bag or mosquito netting, Bailey continued to produce apports—birds, coins, seeds. The Italians believed that some fraud must have been committed, such as regurgitation of the objects at appropriate times in the dark séance room. In 1910, in an investigation in Grenoble, France, by a French team of parapsychologists, Bailey, although again in a bag, produced a pair of birds, but the investigators found that Bailey had bought the birds in town. In a series of tests in 1911 in England, Bailey was investigated by a group of researchers, among them Everard Feilding and W. W. Baggally. The latter found that Bailey's production of a pair of tiny birds was fraudulent—he had apparently had the birds with him in the bag in which he was enclosed. In Sydney, in 1914, he was exposed again during a materialization séance.

While Bailey has been extolled as "the greatest apport medium the world has ever seen" (Morrison, 1948) and the medium who "influenced the minds of the leading citizens of the capital and European Universities towards Spiritualism" (Wallis, 1946), he also has been censured as "a mediumistic trickster" (Marriott, 1911) and, by Eric J. Dingwall, as "one of the most objectionable of all apport mediums" (Irwin, 1987). But in any case he had a tremendous buoying effect on Spiritualism in Australia and possibly elsewhere in the world. At the same time, Bailey completely stopped psychical research and parapsychology in Australia for decades as few serious researchers were willing to jeopardize their careers and reputations by getting involved with and perhaps being deceived by tricksters.

BIBLIOGRAPHY: Irwin H. J. 1987. "Charles Bailey: A Biographical Study of the Australian Apport Medium." JSPR 54:97; MacCarthy, C. W. *Rigid Tests of the Occult: Being a Record of Some Remarkable Experiences Through the Mediumship of Mr. C. Bailey with a Critical Examination of the Origin of the Phenomena,* 1904; Marriott, W. A. "A Mediumistic Trickster." *Mainly About People,* June 24, 1911: 777; Morrison, J. S. 1948. "Greetings from Australia." *Harbinger of Light* 79 (3):8; "Mediumship of Mr. C. Bailey." 1905. JSPR 12: 77, 109; Wallis, W. K. 1946. "Spiritualism in Australia." *Harbinger of Light* 77(5):36.

**Balfour, Arthur James, 1848–1930.** Eminent British statesman. Best known to the world at large for the Balfour Declaration (1917), this prime minister of England (1902–1905) and first earl of Balfour (1922) was one of the most brilliant of **Henry Sidgwick**'s pupils. Like him and Edmund Gurney and F. W. H. Myers, and others from Trinity College, Cambridge, Balfour was also interested in psychical research. He was an early member of the Society for Psychical Research and its president in 1893.

Balfour had several experiences that qualify him as a **Noted Witness.** Two of them support the phenomena of clairvoyance and crystal gazing. One Sunday at about 5 P.M. he was looking into a crystal ball and saw a woman he knew seated under a lamp making tea in the company of a man with a moustache who was wearing a blue serge suit. The following Tuesday he met the lady who confirmed what he had seen. On another occasion he and **Andrew Lang** spoke of **Ada Goodrich-Freer.** Later that day, in Lang's study, Balfour was gazing into a glass bowl of water and saw in it the picture of a house with its flooring, doors, windows, and a white Persian cat on the stairs. Miss Goodrich-Freer, whom Balfour had never met in his life, verified that he had truly seen her house and cat.

It is, however, the "Palm Sunday Case" with which Balfour's name is usually linked and that makes him a *Noted Witness* for survival and for communication with the dead. In 1870, Balfour fell in love with Mary Catherine Lyttleton. She died suddenly on Palm Sunday 1975. Balfour was grief stricken, never married and, for 55 years until his death, spent Palm Sunday, the anniversary of Mary's death, with her sister and her family. On Palm Sunday 1912, thirty-seven years after Mary Lyttleton's death, **Mrs. Willett** (Mrs. Coombe-Tennant) produced the first script in the Palm Sunday cross-correspondence case that seemed to deal with the love of Arthur Balfour and Mary Catherine Lyttleton. Over a period of eighteen years as the scripts continued to be received, until his death, Balfour gradually came to accept the continuing communications as genuine and the communicator as his dead love, Mary Catherine Lyttleton. He believed he would be reunited with her after death and looked forward to that reunion. The Palm Sunday Case is considered one of the strongest cases in favor of the survival hypothesis.

BIBLIOGRAPHY: Balfour, J. 1960. "The 'Palm Sunday' Case." PSPR 52:79; Prince, W. F. *Noted Witnesses for Psychical Research,* 1963.

**Balfour, Gerald William, 1853–1945.** British statesman and psychical researcher. A younger brother of Arthur Balfour and Eleanor Sidgwick, Gerald Balfour attended Trinity College, Cambridge, as had so many of the young men who were the mainspring of the early Society for Psychical Research. He was elected president of the SPR in 1906, the year he left public life. He then took up the study of the **Cross-Correspondences** and, in particular, the mediumship of **"Mrs. Willett"** of whose supernormal powers he was convinced. He, his sister Eleanor Sidgwick, and J. G. Piddington lived in one household for many years. At the expense of all other areas of psychical research, they devoted their time to analyzing the cross-correspondences that allegedly were communications from their dead colleagues and relatives, received by various automatists.

Selected Writings: 1935. "A Study of the Psychological Aspects of Mrs. Willett's Mediumship, and of the Statements of the Communicators Concerning Process." PSPR 43: 43; 1905–7. "Presidential Address." PSPR 19: 373.

**Bangs, May and Lizzie, late nineteenth–early twentieth century American mediums.** Sisters who gained fame in Chicago near the turn of the century; their methods were detected and reported as fraudulent (Krebs, 1901). In the light of this exposé, history generally condemns them as cheap tricksters. It should be noted, however, that while their spirit paintings can easily be duplicated by conjurors, **Isaac Funk,** who conducted experiments with mediums, had a sitting with them that cannot be ignored. He had an old photograph of his mother that he never showed to the pair. Yet the picture they produced was a good likeness of her, and his son also thought it resembled his grandmother. Because the sisters could not have been familiar with the photograph, Funk could not account for the phenomenon (Hyslop 1919).

BIBLIOGRAPHY: Hyslop, J. H. *Contact with the Other World,* 1919, p. 290; Krebs, S. L. 1901. "On the Trick Methods of The Misses L. and H. Bangs." JSPR 10:7.

**Banshee.** In Gaelic thought, a female entity who, by wails, groans, or blood-curdling screams, heralds the approaching death of a member of the family. Generally, the banshee is dismissed as a myth invented or accepted by uncritical minds. Yet there have been first-hand accounts: "On the night preceding my father's death, my mother was reading in the dining-room. . . . Suddenly, from apparently just under the window, there rang out the most harrowing screams. Immeasurably startled. . . , my mother summoned the servants, and they all listened. The sounds went on, every moment increasing in vehemence, and there was an intensity and eeriness about them that speedily convinced the hearers that they could be due to no earthly agency" (Fodor, 1938). Several days later, the news came that the father had died the day following the screaming. In a second account, a series of heartrending screams about midnight woke up a man and his wife. The screams went on and then stopped with one long drawn out wail. The husband waited and when the sound was not repeated "got up and not, I confess, without considerable apprehensions, and went out on to the landing, where I found several of the other inmates of the house collected together discussing with scared faces the screams which they, too, had heard. An examination of the house and grounds was at once made, but nothing was discerned that could in any way acount for the sounds" (Fodor, 1938). Some days afterward, the husband learned that his aunt in County Kerry had died within twenty-four hours of the time the screams were heard.

Is the banshee a myth? It is not easy to ignore the phenomenon when there are firsthand accounts of the sounds heard collectively by several people. A classification in psychical research into which the screaming banshee could fall is the **Haunt,** one of whose manifestations is auditory. Because the death of a family member is foretold the phenomenon also becomes prophetic or precognitive.

BIBLIOGRAPHY: Fodor, N. 1938. "A Letter from England—The Man Who Heard the Banshee." JASPR 32:286.

**Baraduc, Hyppolite, 1850–1902.** French investigator who used photography to try to detect radiations issuing from or near the human body. When he reported some successful detections in 1897, he did not know that ten years later personal tragedy would lead him to take the most dramatic pictures he had ever taken. In 1907, nine hours after his son André died, Baraduc photographed the coffin in which André's body lay. The resulting photograph showed radiations of a formless mist from the coffin. Six months later Baraduc's wife lay dying. Baraduc set up a camera at his wife's deathbed and photographed her as she died. He found on the developed plates three luminous spheres emitting thin fingers of light just above her body. Another photograph taken fifteen minutes later showed the three globes united and concealing the corpse's head. Luminous cords could be seen around them. Three and a half hours later, the globes, which Baraduc could see with the naked eye, hovered over the body, then, emitting cold breezes, separated from the body and eventually floated away from it and finally disappeared. Over the next few days by means of automatic writing an amateur psychic received a communication that the globe was the encasement of his wife's still living soul (Carrington, 1921).

Results and reports such as Baraduc's suggest that the age-old beliefs in a soul or astral body may be valid but that these entities are not ethereal as is supposed but sufficiently material to reflect light and be photographed. However, such reports and results must be repeated and confirmed under controlled conditions. The problem is that 90 percent of us die in hospitals where cooperation in a Baraduc-like experiment cannot be expected. It is therefore improbable that replication of his work will ever be attempted.

Selected Writing: *L'Ame Humaine: Ses Mouvements, ses Lumières et l'Iconographie de l'Invisible Fluidique,* 1897.

BIBLIOGRAPHY: Carrington, H. *The Problem of Psychical Research,* 1921, pp. 182–185.

**Barbanell, Maurice, 1902–1981.** British editor, author, and co-founder of the **Survival Joint Research Committee Trust.** He founded, in 1932, the spiritualist newspaper *Psychic News,* which he edited until his death. He wrote numerous books to educate tyros in Spiritualism. He instructed them on how and where to locate mediums, establish a circle and to receive what he considered evidence of life after death. His prolonged experience with mediumistic practices and communications and his interesting popular style of writing made his literary output effective.

As a dyed-in-the-wool Spiritualist, Barbanell was convinced beyond doubt of human survival of bodily death and of the genuineness of messages from "across the gulf"—the title of one of his books. For him the evidence of postmortem survival and communication could both comfort mourners and sometimes prevent disastrous or fatal events. In this latter connection, he would remind his readers of the R-101 whose doom had been foretold in spirit messages received by Emilie Hinchcliffe from her dead husband, Captain Walter Raymond Hinchcliffe. "Over fifty lives could have been saved, and the terrible tragedy averted if only these warnings had been attended to," wrote Barbanell. "Mrs. Hinchcliffe, widow of the famous airman, twice went to Cardiff and pleaded with Squadron Leader S. L. Johnston, who was the navigator of R-101 to listen to the repeated warnings she had received in messages from her husband: but he was sceptical and her pleading was in vain" (Barbanell, 1940).

Barbanell may not have succeeded in persuading skeptics, such as the R-101 squadron leader and the scientific community in general, to pay more serious attention to what to him were facts of spirit survival, but his life was one long effort to do so.

Selected Writing: *Across the Gulf,* 1940.

**Bardo Thodol.** See Book of the Dead, Tibetan.

**Barham, Allan.** Contemporary British Clergyman. His study of religion led him to the field of psychical research where his main interests are survival and psychokinesis. He formed the "Daventry Group" which held successful sittings over a period of months between January 1971 and July 1972 with Colin Brookes-Smith. "The intention [of the sittings] was to explore the technical possibilities of data-tape recording for measuring mechanical forces and some other variables associated with psychokinetic table levitation phenomena" (Brookes-Smith, 1973:69). Kenneth Batcheldor's method for producing the proper psychological conditions was used. Mr. Barham for the last few years has been attempting to repeat some of Brooke-Smith's experiments.

Mr. Barham was chairman of the committee of the Churches' Fellowship for Psychical and Spiritual Studies (CFPSS), which first produced and privately published *The Christian Parapsychologist,* and was research officer of the CFPSS and chairman of its Speakers Panel for Schools and Colleges. He has written two popular books (1980/1984, 1982), both of which were selections of the Psychic Book Society, and was a contributor to *Life, Death and Psychical Research*, published in 1973. He has recently written an article on William J. Crawford and his PK work (1988) and another on Colin Brookes-Smith, both published in the *Journal of the Society for Psychical Research.*

Mr. Barham is a member of the Society for Psychical Research, the Survival Joint Research Committee, the CFPSS, and the College of Psychic Studies.

Selected Writings: 1988. "The Crawford Legacy: Part II." JSPR 55:196; 1988. "Dr. W. J. Crawford, His Work and his Legacy in Psychokinesis." JSPR 55:113; *Strange to Relate,* 1980/1984; *Life Unlimited,* 1982.

BIBLIOGRAPHY: Brookes-Smith, C. 1973. "Data-Tape Recorded Experimental PK Phenomena." JSPR 47:69.

**Barlow, Fred, ?–1964.** British photographic expert and longtime member of the Society for Psychical Research. Barlow was the photographic expert to whom the SPR turned to investigate any instances of **Spirit Photography.** At one time secretary of the Society for the Study of Supernormal Pictures, and on the basis of numerous experiments and much time and thought, he was at first a believer in and staunch defender of spirit photography. Further investigations, however, particularly into the work of spirit photographers George Moss and William Hope, forced him to the unwelcome conclusion that in every case he ever investigated the "extra" (or "spirit") that appeared on the photograph was an exact copy of some existing photograph or painting. His judgment was that he had never had a successful sitting in which there was not some possibility of fraud. None of the "spirit photographs" he examined ever proved to be genuine, yet he did not go so far as to claim that genuine "extras" or "spirits" on film had never been produced.

On his death his collection on spirit photography went to **Eric J. Dingwall** who cataloged and arranged it and contributed it to the occult section of the Department of Printed Books in the British Museum.

Selected Writing: Rampling-Rose, W. 1933. "Report of an Investigation into Spirit-Photography," PSPR 41:121.

BIBLIOGRAPHY: Dingwall, E. J. "The Need for Responsibility in Parapsychology." In P. Kurtz, ed. *A Skeptic's Handbook of Parapsychology,* 1985, p. 168.

**Barrett, Sir William Fletcher, 1844–1925.** British physicist. Imbued with an eagerness to stir up an interest in paranormal phenomena, Barrett had all the attributes of an erudite and daring huckster. In 1876, he tried to sell telepathy to the staid British Association by reading a paper on experiments he had conducted with a hypnotized girl who seemed to know what ideas and images were in his mind. His paper asked that a scientific commission be set up to examine the phenomenon. The *London Times* and many distinguished scientists ridiculed him, but others, including Sir William Crookes and Lord Rayleigh, came to his support. The controversy created by the paper both in the press and in the local and spiritualist journals promoted just the kind of interest in the subject Barrett wanted.

Barrett now beat the drum even more vigorously to stimulate interest on the part of key scholars, such as Henry Sidgwick, F. W. H. Myers and Edmund Gurney, in the formation of a group to press for a collective inquiry into paranormal phenomena of which Barrett already had collected a large number of cases. Barrett became the moving force behind the formation, in 1882, of the **Society for Psychical Research,** a vice president of the SPR and, in 1884, proposed that it publish a *Journal* of which he became the editor during its first year. In 1884, also, Barrett toured the United States where he interested scientists and scholars, among them William James, in psychical research and persuaded them to form the **American Society for Psychical Research.** Barrett was president of the SPR in 1904.

Barrett was a recognized authority on **Dowsing,** conducted experiments in **mesmerism,** and, after receiving a letter from William Crookes reporting that he had seen D. D. Home handle red-hot coals as if they were oranges, undertook a long series of experiments with physical phenomena. The only case of materialization he ever witnessed occurred during a séance with the medium Cecil Husk (who was caught cheating many years later [1890]), in which a clothed human figure whose bearded face was illuminated by a bluish light appeared and identified itself in a guttural voice as **"John King."** Such experiments convinced Barrett that he had witnessed "striking evidence of amazing supernormal power." It has been suggested that Barrett's devotion to the study of physical phenomena, as well as being out of favor with the powers of the SPR, caused his reputation to be less than it deserved to be.

His scientific work outside of psychical research was noteworthy. He was assistant to the British physicist John Tyndall at the Royal Institution from 1862 to 1867, conducted investigations into entropic vision, and made discoveries of alloys of iron. In 1899, Barrett was elected a Fellow of the Royal Society.

Selected Writings: 1924. "Some Reminiscences of Fifty Years of Psychical Research." PSPR 34:275; 1897. "On the So-Called Divining Rod, Or Virgula Divina: A Scientific and Historical Research as to the Existence and Practical Value of a Peculiar Human Faculty Unrecognized by Science, Locally Known as Dowsing." PSPR 13:2; 1900. "On the So-Called Divining Rod: A Psycho-Physical Research on a Peculiar Faculty Alleged to Exist in Certain Persons Locally Known as Dowsers." PSPR 15: 130.

BIBLIOGRAPHY: Inglis, B. 1988. "Sir William Barrett (1844–1925)." JSPR 55:16; Sidwick E. M. 1925 "In memory of Sir William Fletcher Barrett, F.R.S." PSPR 35:413.

**Barrington, Mary Rose, 1926–.** British lawyer and psychical researcher. Her interest in psychical research began with reading works by Sir Oliver Lodge and increased at Oxford when she was involved with the Oxford Society for Psychical Research. She now gives lectures in psychical research and plays an active role in the conduct of experiments and investigations for the Society for Psychical Research. One of her investigations involved the poltergeist case of a bath thermometer that seemed to lift itself off a hook in a bathroom and fly diagonally through the room at about a thirty degree angle before it fell to the floor (Barrington, 1976, 1965). Miss Barrington theorized that the phenomenon might have centered on either the mother or child who occupied the residence. She also conducted an ingenious experiment in extrasensory perception in which agents by ESP were to influence percipients to recall false memories of themes and pictures on target cards. The results, however, were only marginally significant (Barrington, 1973). Miss Barrington is a member of the SPR Council.

Selected Writings: 1976. "A Poltergeist Revived: The Flying Thermometer Case Again." JSPR 48:293; 1973. "A Free Response Sheep/Goat Experiment Using an Irrelevant Task." JSPR 47:222; 1965. "The Case of the Flying Thermometer." JSPR 43:11.

**Basic Limiting Principles.** C. D. Broad's term for "certain very general principles . . . which practically everyone who has been brought up within or under the influence of Western industrial societies assumes without question. . ." (Broad, 1962). We cannot know another person's experiences except by hearing that person describe them, or by reading about them, or by interpreting gestures, or by making inferences from material objects that that person made or used. We cannot foresee an event that has not yet happened. Except for being able to move parts of our own bodies, our minds cannot influence matter. And we take for granted that, at death, consciousness either ceases altogether or certainly cannot in any way interact with the living. "An event that seems *prima facie* to conflict with one or more of the *basic limiting principles,* and not merely with some well-established uniformity of nature, may be called an 'ostensibly paranormal phenomenon'" (Broad, op. cit.).

BIBLIOGRAPHY: Broad, C. D. *Lectures on Psychical Research,* 1962; Broad, C. D. *Religion, Philosophy and Psychical Research,* 1953;

Price, H. H. 1954. "Professor C. D. Broad's *Religion, Philosophy and Psychical Research.*" JASPR 48:56.

**Basic Technique (BT).** The term used to describe the method in **clairvoyance** tests of having the experimenter, after the top card of a facedown deck of cards is called by a subject, place that card to one side to be checked after a run. See also **Call; Check.**

**Batcheldor, Kenneth, 1921–1988.** English psychologist. He revived the Victorian after dinner séance in the hope of inducing psychokinesis and paranormal events and thereby overcame one of the great problems in the investigation of physical phenomena. These phenomena are generally thought of as belonging only to the heyday of Spiritualism and to the famous (or infamous according to one's point of view) purportedly gifted mediums of the past, such as Mina S. Crandon, Eusapia Palladino and Daniel D. Home.

Batcheldor, inspired by a social evening in 1964 where a group of friends tried Table-tilting for fun, worked with ordinary people, such as himself and friends, who made no claim to mediumistic gifts. The group met over a period of weeks in séances resembling those of the Victorian era and, before long, apports, levitations, table-tilting, raps, breezes, and intense cold were produced. Unlike the Spiritualist séances, there was a complete absence of spiritualistic assumptions of a spirit world and spirit communicators. There were no prayers and no one went into trance. On the contrary, the group was relaxed, engaged in animated conversation, joked and sometimes sang songs. Batcheldor realized that the mood and belief of people are important factors in the induction of paranormal occurrences. He showed successfully that, if the right conditions to affect mood and belief are set up, psychokinesis and physical phenomena can occur in a small and informal group meeting regularly under conditions resembling a séance and without the help of a medium (although he did find in the 1980s that a specific sitter produced remarkable results). The four elements essential to the production of phenomena, according to Batcheldor, are: 1. Complete belief that something paranormal is going to take place. 2. Artifacts that create or contribute to belief. (Artifacts are normal events that are mistaken for, or thought to be, paranormal, i.e., a draft which is interpreted as a psychic breeze, a spark thought to be a psychic light). 3. Suggestion based either on an artifactual or real paranormal event that heightens expectancy of a genuine paranormal occurrence. 4. Overcoming the resistance that arises out of fear of the unknown and uncontrolled. Batcheldor identified two types of resistance: "ownership resistance"—resistance to the feeling that one possesses paranormal powers; and "witness inhibition"—resistance to witnessing a display of the paranormal; both to be overcome by the encouragement of a lighthearted atmosphere. In Batcheldor's view, it is the state of mind of the sitter-group that brings about paranormal phenomena, not deceased people who manage to come from the "other side" to set up a rapport with the living.

Of course, there are difficulties with Batcheldor's approach. Since many meetings must be held over a period of weeks or months before any phenomena take place, a group may slowly fall apart. The loss of even one regular member can radically alter the group. Nevertheless, other investigators are trying what is now known as "Batcheldor's technique" in their work with psychokinesis and in other areas of psi research.

In his later years, Batcheldor devoted himself to practicing and testing his technique for inducing PK out of unconscious muscular activity. And, in the years just before his death, he was paying special attention to materialization and to the effect of an intention to verify on the reality of one's experience. He made infrared videotapes of psychic phenomena, including what looks like ectoplasm, and had a collection of apports that had materialized over twenty years of research but did not publicize them. Batcheldor left an enormous quantity of material that one hopes will someday be published. Writing of the varieties of PK phenomena Batcheldor produced, his obituarist (Shields, 1988) says in William Crookes's words: "I am not saying all this is possible. I am saying it is true" and calls Batcheldor "the greatest contemporary practitioner of macro-PK in England" (p. 110).

Selected Writings: 1984. "Contributions to the Theory of PK Induction from Sitter-Group Work." JASPR 78:105; 1966. "Report in a Case of Table Levitation and Associated Phenomena." JSPR 43:339.

BIBLIOGRAPHY: Giesler, P. V. 1988. "Kenneth J. Batcheldor: Friend, Colleague and Teacher." *ASPR Newsletter* 14(4):32; Shields, J. 1988. "Obituary Kenneth J. Batcheldor." JSPR 55:110.

**Bauer, Eberhard, 1944–.** German historian of parapsychology and managing editor of *Zeitschrift für Parapsychologie und Grenzgebiete der Psychologie,* the only high quality journal of parapsychology in Germany. Besides being the leading authority in Europe on the history of parapsychology and the circumstances of its contemporary situation, he is involved in the theoretical and experimental aspects of the field and in studies of psychokinesis. Bauer is one of the cofounders of the **Wissenschaftliche Gesellschaft zur Förderung der Parapsychologie** (Scientific Society for the Advancement of Parapsychology). In public recognition of his work the Society for Psychical Research has made him a Corresponding Member.

Selected Writing: 1984. "Criticism and Controversies in Parapsychology." *European Journal of Parapsychology* 5:141.

**Bayless, Raymond, 1920–.** American author and psychical researcher, he seems to have been the first to discover the existence of **Electronic Voice Phenomena.** In 1959, he reported that he had recorded more than 100 strange voices on tape. He later worked with inaudible raps, rather than voices, on tape because he considers the rap phenomenon more readily repeatable than the voice phenomenon. With a special interest in survival research, Bayless claims to have observed numerous kinds of physical phenomena, an out-of-body experience and apparitions. He is the author of several books and articles on survival-related phenomena.

Selected writings: 1959. "Correspondence." JASPR 53:35; and E. E. McAdams. *The Case of Life After Death: Parapsychologists Look at the Evidence,* 1981; and D. S. Rogo. *Phone Calls from the Dead,* 1980.

**Beard, Paul, 1906–.** British authority on the psychic. His major interest for thirty years has been the study of the qualitative evidence for the survival of the human personality after bodily death and the conduct of experimental research with mediums. He has ignored physical phenomena because of the fallibility of human observation and because he believes that the future lies "in the mental field . . . because here the evidence . . . [has] been recorded verbatim . . . [and] its *existence* . . . is unchallengeable" (Beard, 1966:8).

President of the College of Psychic Studies for sixteen years, Mr. Beard has been a frequent contributor to *Light* and is the author of books on assessing the value of personal evidence of survival (1966) and the analysis of the teachings of important communicators regarding the nature of postmortem existence (1981).

Selected Writings: *Living On,* 1981; *Survival of Death,* 1966.

**Belasco, David, 1853–1931.** Renowned American theatrical producer and dramatic author. His plays, famous for their marvelous effects and settings, included *Madame Butterfly, Girl of the Golden West, Zaza, The Heart of Maryland,* and *The Return of Peter Grimm.* The inspiration for this last-named play in which the spirit of the dead returns occurred in Belasco's home in Newport, Rhode Island, when he was awakened from a deep sleep "to see my dear mother (whom I knew to be in San Francisco) standing close by me. As I strove to speak and to sit up she smiled at me a loving-reassuring smile, spoke my name—the name she called me in my boyhood—'Davy, Davy, Davy,' then, leaning down, seemed to kiss me; then drew away a little and said, 'Do not grieve. All is well and I am happy'; then moved toward the door and vanished."

The following day, a telegram arrived with the news that Belasco's mother had died at about the hour she had appeared to him. He was told that just before she died, she smiled and said three times, "Davy, Davy, Davy." Belasco's experience makes him a **Noted Witness** to the phenomenon of an apparition that was veridical.

BIBLIOGRAPHY: Prince, W. F. *Noted Witnesses for Psychic Occurrences,* 1963.

**Belly-Talkers.** In the ancient Roman-Greco world, the official oracles were not the sole means of obtaining answers to anxious questions. Also sought out were private individuals who spoke automatically while in a trance and were called "belly-talkers." These mediums were considered to have a **Daemon** in their bellies that used the mediums' vocal organs to foretell the future in an apparent demonstration of precognition. See also **Automatic Writing, Speaking, or Spelling.**

**Beloff, John, 1920–.** British psychologist. Long interested in parapsychology because of its implications for the philosophy of mind, he considers one of his major achievements in the field his involvement, as trustee of **Arthur Koestler**'s bequest, in the establishment in 1984 of the Koestler Chair of Parapsychology at Edinburgh University.

His open-mindedness on the subject of psi has made him respected by parapsychologists and skeptics alike even though he has written that he "side[s] with the believers rather than the skeptics . . . less [because of] this or that particular case than the global impression [he] derive[s] from [his] survey of the literature that something real is going on that defies conventional explanation" (Beloff, 1985). Dr. Beloff believes that the report of Everard Feilding, Hereward Carrington, and W. W. Baggally on the physical medium Eusapia Palladino "should be made mandatory reading" for skeptics. He believes that "the more fantastic phenomena are not necessarily any less real than those of lesser magnitude" and that "we can no longer justify dismissing materializations as too preposterous to warrant serious consideration." He also feels that one must look with a fresh eye on the physical mediumship of Florence Cook, Eva C., Margery, and, especially, Carlos Mirabelli whose feats purportedly surpassed even D. D. Home's.

Dr. Beloff, a dualist, believes that psychical research is important because an affirmative answer to the question of whether "human beings [can] ever interact with their environment otherwise than through the recognized sensory and motor channels . . . would cast doubt on the prevailing 'physicalist' view of man and of his place in nature . . . [O]n the practical side, it would mean having to reckon with a range of human potentialities that go beyond anything now acknowledged by official scientific psychology. . ." (Beloff, 1988:1).

Dr. Beloff has written also on all aspects of parapsychology, his articles having appeared mainly in the parapsychological journals, and is the author of the "Historical Overview" for *The Handbook of Parapsychology* (1977). Of his books, *Psychological Sciences* (1974) has been published in Dutch, Spanish, and German. He edited *New Directions in Parapsychology* (1975) which has been translated into Dutch, German, and Japanese, and is coeditor of *The Case for Dualism* (1988).

Dr. Beloff received his B.A. with honors in psychology from the University of London in 1952 and, in 1956, his Ph.D. from the University of Belfast where he was a lecturer in the Department of Psychology from 1953 to 1962. From 1963 until his retirement in 1985 he was senior lecturer in the Department of Psychology at the University of Edinburgh except for a year as visiting professor at Cornell University in 1966. He is a Fellow of the British Psychological Society and has been a council member of the Society for Psychical Research since 1964. Since 1981 he has been editor of the *Journal of the Society for Psychical Research.* He is a member of the Parapsychological Association, has served on its council and was its president in 1972 and again in 1982.

Selected Writings: *The Importance of Psychical Research,* 1988; "What Is Your Counter-Explanation? A Plea to Skeptics to Think Again." In P. Kurtz, ed. *A Skeptic's Handbook of Parapsychology,* 1985; "Historical Overview." In B. B. Wolman, ed. *The Handbook of Parapsychology,* 1977; *Psychological Sciences,* 1974; *The Existence of Mind,* 1964; Editor, *New Directions in Parapsychology,* 1975; with J. Smythies, eds., *The Case for Dualism,* 1988.

**Bender, Hans, 1907–.** German psychologist. He has been the doyen of Continental parapsychologists since World War II and was the holder of the first chair of parapsychology in German academic history at the Albert-Ludwig University in Freiburg. A former president of the Parapsychological Association, founder of the *Zeitschrift für Parapsychologie und Grensgebiete der Psychologie*—one of the outstanding journals in the field of parapsychology—and founder and director of the *Institut für Grenzgebiete der Psychologie und Psychohygiene* (The Institute for Border Areas of Psychology and Mental Hygiene), he became interested in the paranormal because he had a "spiritual constitution" (Bender, 1987) and because at the age of seventeen he was deeply affected by messages received on a ouija board.

While studying under Pierre Janet at the College of France in Paris in the 1930s,

Bender experimented with automatic writing, which led him to consider the possibility of extrasensory perception. On the basis of this work in 1936 he was awarded his Ph.D. from the Psychological Institute of Bonn University despite opposition to the subject matter from many of the professors there and despite a general Nazi hostility to psychical research and parapsychology.

Following World War II, he taught psychology at Freiburg University and introduced parapsychology into his courses. When a chair of psychology and border areas was established there in 1954, he became its occupant. This marked the initial entrance of parapsychology into the German academic framework. He considers his integrating parapsychology into the university curriculum at Freiburg his most important contribution to the subject. He has done research both in the laboratory and in the field. He and Wilhelm H. C. Tenhaeff conducted "chair tests" with Gerard Croiset, and he has also investigated metal-bending, mediums, unorthodox healing, astrology, and precognitive dreams. He is best known, however, for his investigations of poltergeists, his most famous cases being the Nickelheim Poltergeist and the Rosenheim Poltergeist. During his investigations of these cases, he used videotapes of moving objects to convince people of the reality of the phenomena.

Dr. Bender has said that "I don't feel I have made essential mistakes. Neither do I feel that the beliefs that I had when I entered the field have been fundamentally changed because of my experiences. From the very beginning I expected that nearly all is possible in the 'magic reality'"(Bender, 1987:116). This last belief has caused Bender to be harshly criticized by German rationalists who call him "der Spukprofessor." The German Society for Protection Against Superstition once charged him with generating the spread of superstition. His book, *Unser sechster Sinn (Our Sixth Sense)* (1982) has also been criticized for stating Bender's beliefs as if they were scientific facts, for not including fraudulent or erroneous cases, for taking as proved the metal-bending feats of Uri Geller and the supposed clairvoyance and precognition of Gerard Croiset, but, most of all, for regaling us "with the success story of a triumphant new science [parapsychology] with revolutionary implications for our views of God, Man, and the Universe" (Hoebens, 1986:33) instead of sticking to pure scientific inquiry.

In any case, Hans Bender is appreciated by all as a man of high integrity, and he is certainly considered throughout the world to be the representative of parapsychology in continental Europe.

Selected Writings: "A Positive Critic of Superstition." In R. Pilkington, ed. *Men and Women of Parapsychology,* 1987; "Poltergeists." In I. Grattan-Guiness, ed. *Psychical Research,* 1982; *Unser sechster Sinn,* 1982 (originally published 1972); with R. Vandrey and S. Wendlandt. "The 'Geller Effect' in Western Germany and Switzerland." In J. D. Morris, W. G. Roll, and R. L. Morris, eds. *Research in Parapsychology 1975,* 1976; "Modern Poltergeist Research." In J. Beloff, ed. *New Directions in Parapsychology,* 1974.

BIBLIOGRAPHY: Hoebens, P. H. "Sense and Nonsense in Parapsychology." In K. Frazier, ed. *Science Confronts the Paranormal,* 1986.

**Benedict XIV (Prospero Lambertini), 1678–1758.** Italian pope who reigned from 1740 to 1758. Of noble birth, with a doctorate in law and theology, he was ordained to the priesthood, made a cardinal in 1728 and archbishop of Bologna three years later. In 1740, he succeeded Pope Clement XII and assumed the name of Benedict XIV. A friend of Voltaire, whose dramatic work *Mahomet* was dedicated to him, Lambertini was known for his wit, enlightenment, and scholarship. To him can be credited the first objective study of the paranormal in Italy.

Beginning in 1702 and for twenty years, he acted in canonization procedures as *Promotor Fidei,* Promoter of the Faith,—otherwise known as "Devil's Advocate." His task was to make a case *against* the holiness of anyone being considered for canonization. As a theologian, he was concerned with miracles and accepted the possibility of their occurrence. But, just as any parapsychologist would be, he was extremely cautious and refused to admit the miraculous powers of candidates for canonization, regardless of how impressively paranormal their feats seemed to be, if they could be explained naturalistically. Lambertini studied luminous phenomena and many cases of what today would be called unorthodox healing and extrasensory perception. He considered the gift of extrasensory perception simply a natural fact that did not constitute evidence either of sanctity or of diabolical possession. In this recognition, Lambertini went against the tide of religious thought of the time.

His four-volume work *De Canonizatione Sanctorum,* published between 1734 and 1738, is a study of canonization procedures and of the alleged miracles he examined with the eye of a psychical researcher and parapsychologist.

BIBLIOGRAPHY: Haynes, R. *Philosopher King: The Humanist Pope Benedict XIV,* 1970.

**Béraud, Marthe** See **Eva C.**

**Berendt, Heinz C., 1911–.** German-born Israeli dentist and parapsychologist interested in metal-bending. In controlled experiments conducted in Jerusalem, he was able to capture on film the paranormal bending by a young male Israeli of spoon, forks, keys, and metal rods of different strengths, lengths, and materials, all supplied by the experimenter or observers. Berendt is convinced that paranormal metal-bending is a fact that can be accomplished without physical force and requires us to reorient our thinking in relation to the question of mind and matter.

Selected Writing: "A New Israeli Metal-Bender (with Film)." In W. G. Roll, J. Beloff, and R. W. White, eds. *Research in Parapsychology 1982,* 1983, p. 43.

**Bergen, Edgar John, 1903–1978.** American ventriloquist. For over half a century in vaudeville, on radio, and in motion pictures he entertained audiences everywhere, principally with his dummy "Charlie McCarthy" and with other characters such as "Mortimer Snerd." Bergen is also a **Noted Witness** for the paranormal. As Jean Houston writes: "One time my father [who was writing the Edgar Bergen show] and I came into Edgar's room. . . . Edgar was talking to Charlie and we thought he was rehearsing, but he was not rehearsing. He was asking Charlie questions: 'Charlie, what is the nature of life? Charlie, what is the nature of love?' And this wooden dummy was answering quite unlike the being I knew on the radio. A regular wooden Socrates, he was. It was the same voice but it was a very different content altogether. And Bergen would get fascinated and say, 'Well, Charlie, what is the nature of true virtue?' and the dummy would just pour out this stuff; beauty, elegance, brilliant. . . . [T]hen . . . Bergen looked around and turned beet red and said, 'Oh, hello, you caught us. . . . I was talking with Charlie. He's the wisest person I know.' And my father said, 'But that's your mind; that's *your* voice coming through that wooden creature.' And Ed said, 'Well, I guess ultimately it is, but I ask Charlie these questions and he answers, and I haven't the faintest idea of what he's going to say and I'm astounded by his brilliance—so much more than I know.' "

"Charlie McCarthy" could have been the instrument for several kinds of phenomena: a personal daemon, monition, guide, communicator or channeling.

BIBLIOGRAPHY: Klimo, J. *Channeling,* 1987, p. 229.

**Berger, Arthur Seymour, 1920–.** American attorney, author, thanatologist, and historian and encyclopedist of parapsychology and psychical research. His inability to answer such questions as "Why am I here?" and "What is my ultimate destiny?" turned him to psychical research. Berger ultimately became president of the Survival Research Foundation. He has received grants to pursue original research into the question of the possible postmortem continuation of human consciousness, has published theoretical and experimental papers on this subject, has designed a posthumous experiment called the **Dictionary Test** to test the hypothesis of survival after death, and has both contributed to and authored several books, one of which Prof. Anthony Flew has called a significant step forward in the investigation of the question of human survival after death (Flew, 1987). Objective and skeptical regarding postmortem survival, he has written over thirty articles on the subject, for one of which he received the Robert H. Ashby Memorial Award in 1985, and a casebook (Berger, 1988a) to help people make critical evaluations and informed judgments about the so-called evidence for life after death. As a historian of parapsychology, Berger has written a "superb" (Rogo, 1989) and "unusually interesting history of the field . . . an excellent introduction to scientific study of the paranormal" (Child, 1989) that also contains biographies of its dominant figures (Berger, 1988b).

As director of the International Institute for the Study of Death and vice president for Cross-Cultural Affairs of Columbia University's Foundation of Thanatology, he has explored bioethical issues and has convened conferences for universities and the Florida Endowment for the Humanities. He has edited books on these issues and on death and dying (Berger, A., Badham, Kutscher, Berger, J., Perry, and Beloff, 1989). Berger is a member of the Society for Psychical Research, the American Society for Psychical Research and the Parapsychological Association.

Selected Writings: *Evidence of Life after Death: A Casebook for the Tough-Minded,* 1988a; *Lives and Letters in American Parapsychology: A Biographical History 1850–1987,* 1988b; *Aristocracy of the Dead,* 1987; "Bridging the Gap: A Critical Survey of the Latest Types of Prima Facia Survival Evidence." In P. and L. Badham, eds., *Death and Immortality in the Religions of the World,* 1987; 1984. "Experiments with False Keys." JASPR 78:41; and Badham, P., Kutscher, A. H., Berger, J., Perry M., Beloff, J., *Perspectives on Death and Dying: Cross-Cultural and Multi-Disciplinary Views,* 1989.

BIBLIOGRAPHY: Child, I. L. "Berger, A. S. Lives and Letters in American Parapsychology: A Biographical History, 1850–1987". *Choice,* March 1989; Flew, A. Foreword. In A. S. Berger, *Aristocracy of the Dead,* 1987; Rogo, D. S. 1989. "Book Review. Lives and Letters in American Parapsychology—A Biographical History, 1859–1987 by Arthur S. Berger." *Parapsychology Review* 20 (3):12.

**Berger, Rick E., 1952–.** American parapsychologist. He designs, develops, and uses microcomputers, such as the Apple II, to conduct research in parapsychology. He also carries on psi experiments with "psi games" or tests in which subjects interact with computers and random number generators. His work has included the design and construction of an automated **Ganzfeld Procedure.** Besides research, Berger devotes much time to shaping programs for conventions of the Parapsychological Association.

Selected Writings: "Psi Effects without Real-Time Feedback". In D. H. Weiner and R. L. Morris, eds., *Research in Parapsychology 1987,* 1988, p. 14; and Honorton, C. "Psi Lab//:A Standardized Psi-Testing System". In R. A. White and J. Solfvin, eds., *Research in Parapsychology 1984,* 1985, p. 68.

**Bergson, Henri-Louis, 1859–1941.** Eminent French philosopher. He was the first process philosopher and greatly influenced the great philosopher Alfred North Whitehead. Bergson's most famous metaphysical work is his *Creative Evolution.*

He early differentiated between lived time as opposed to spatialized or clock time measured by science and felt that scientific determinism was baseless. In one of his most important works, *Matière et Mémoire (Matter and Memory)* (1896), he concluded that memory—mind or soul—is independent of the body that it uses to carry out its purposes, a conclusion clearly of interest to psychical research.

In his presidential address to the Society for Psychical Research, in 1913, Bergson stated that perception is a practical function but that the range of unconscious function is far wider. When "the barrier imposed by the brain is weakened, some of those . . . perceptions may be able to pass the threshold of consciousness, and telepathy or clairvoyance may occur" (Price, 1941). "[C]onsciousness is not a function of the brain, [but the brain] is the organ of attention to life" (Bergson, 1913). This fact makes the brain as well an organ of limitation, a filter. Bergson believed that survival is more likely than not because "the mental life of the embodied human personality is far wider than its cerebral life" (Price, 1941: 276).

Bergson was Jewish by birth. In his will, dated 1937, he said that over the years he had come closer and closer to Catholicism which he felt fulfilled Judaism, but he did not convert because of the wave of anti-Semitism which he foresaw was about to break upon the world. Just two years later, sick, he stood in line on a bitterly cold December day to register as a Jew in occupied France, even though he had been offered exemption. A pulmonary disorder resulted, and a few weeks later he was dead.

Selected Writing: 1913. "Presidential Address." PSPR 26:462.

BIBLIOGRAPHY: Dale, L. A. 1941. "Henri Bergson, Realist." JASPR 35:57; Price, H. H. 1941. "Henri Bergson." PSPR 46:271; Thibaudet, A. and Bird, O. A. "Bergson, Henri-Louis." In the *New Encyclopaedia Britannica,* Vol. 2, 1986, pp. 129–131.

**Bernadette, Saint (Marie-Bernarde Soubirous), 1844–1879.** French shepherdess; canonized in 1933. When she was fourteen years of age, Bernadette claimed to see at Lourdes, not once but eighteen times, an apparition she took to be the Virgin Mary. Saying to the girl, "I am the Immaculate Conception," the vision told her to return to the place for a fortnight and she would be happy in the next world. Many people also were to come, and the girl was to tell the priests to build a chapel near the fountain in which she was to wash and from which she was to drink.

Such is the account. From the point of view of psychical research, the apparition the girl said she saw was seen by no one else and can be considered a subjective hallucination. Nor did the vision say anything whatever about the healing properties of the waters at Lourdes. Nevertheless, Lourdes has become one of the world's great shrines for pilgrimages and the scene of reports of miraculous cures.

Bernadette's story does not end there, however. Thirty years after her death at the age of thirty-four, her body was exhumed. An eyewitness reported: "Not the least trace of corruption nor any bad odour could be perceived in the corpse of our beloved sister. Even the habit in which she was buried was intact. The face was somewhat brown, the eye slightly sunken, and she seemed to be sleeping." See also **Incorruptibility; Lourdes, Miracles of.**

BIBLIOGRAPHY: Thurston, H. *The Physical Phenomena of Mysticism,* 1952, p. 235.

**Bersani, Ferdinando, 1942–.** Italian lecturer in physics. On the Faculty of Medicine and Surgery at the University of Bologna he has broad interests ranging from biophysics to telepathy, psychometry, physical phenomena and electronic voice phenomena. He stoutly opposes the belief that this last category has shown that electronic communication with the dead has been established. He explains the phenomena away by a theory of "psycholinguistic PK," which holds that motivated people can convert random sounds into meaningful ones through the action of psychokinesis. He has developed methods for discovering this kind of action on fragments of sounds.

**Besant, Annie, 1847–1933.** English social reformer, leader of Indian independence, and ardent Theosophist. After carrying the flag for the emancipation of women and birth control and marching in the ranks of the Fabian Socialists, in 1889 she fell under the spell of Mme **H. P. Blavatsky.** Besant became a loyal follower of Theosophy and one of its most effective exponents whose lectures, articles, and books are rated with the most influential in all of Theosophical literature. When Richard Hodgson published his report damning Madame Blavatsky and the Theosophical Society as fraudulent, Besant sprang to the Madame's defense in March 1891 in an article in *Time* magazine. Hodgson, she charged, was prejudiced, dishonest, and suffering from typical English ignorance of Indian thought. Madame Blavatsky could not have asked for a better or more determined advocate. Although Hodgson answered every criticism (1893), the battle over his report in which Besant fired the first shot still goes on (Berger, 1988).

In 1907, Besant became president of the Theosophical Society, a position she held until her death. In 1911, she proclaimed Jiddu Krishnamurti the New Messiah, a role with which he was never comfortable, but in 1927 she withdrew her claims. Gifted in oratory and organization, she founded a college in Banares, India, where she became active in the Indian nationalist movement. She established the Indian Home Rule League and was president of the Indian National Congress in 1917. For her role in the movement for Indian independence she was jailed in 1917. Annie Besant spent her remaining days in India whose cause she espoused and where she could be close to the headquarters of the Theosophical Society in Madras.

BIBLIOGRAPHY: "Annie Besant." *Encyclopaedia Britannica,* 1958, pp. 470–471; Hodgson, R. 1893. "The Defence of the Theosophists." PSPR 9:129; Berger, A. S. *Lives and Letters in American Parapsychology,* 1988.

**Bessent, Malcolm, 1945–.** British psychic and high-scoring subject. His psychic experiences dated back to an early age, but he "developed" his gifts under the tutelage of **Douglas Johnson.** In 1969, he left England for the United States and parapsychological tests.

In precognition tests with a random event generator, Bessent scored significantly above chance in forecasting which of two colored targets would light (Honorton, 1971). He went on to a series of tests at the Maimonides Medical Center Dream Laboratory. In experiments with precognitive dreams over a period of eight nights, experimenters found that Bessent had the ability to dream the elements of randomly determined events that would occur the next day and highly significant results were recorded (Krippner, Ullman, and Honorton, 1971).

There was another interesting six-night dream study. A group of 2,000 young people attending a rock concert was asked to transmit target pictures to Bessent over a distance of forty-five miles, while he was dreaming at the Maimonides Laboratory. His dreams again were statistically significant (Krippner, Honorton, and Ullman, 1973). Bessent, who meditates to prepare for experiments, is one of the rare professional psychics who has cooperated fully and been successful in laboratory testing.

BIBLIOGRAPHY: Krippner, S. Honorton, C., and Ullman, M. 1973. "A Long-Distance ESP Dream Study with the 'Grateful Dead.'" *Journal of the American Society of Psychosomatic Dentistry and Medicine* 20:9; Krippner, S., Ullman, M. and Honorton, C. 1971. "A Precognitive Dream Study with a Single Subject." JASPR 65:192; Honorton, C. 1971. "Automated Forced-Choice Precognition Tests with a 'Sensitive.'" JASPR 65:476.

**Besterman, Theodore Deodatus Nathaniel, 1904–1976.** British psychical researcher. How gladly he was welcomed into this world by his parents is evidenced by his given names, all of which mean "gift of God" (in Greek, Latin, and Hebrew). (Quite different from "that young swine Besterman," as **Harry Price** called him [quoted in Inglis, 1984]).

Besterman came to psychical research by way of Theosophy. In 1930, he wrote a defense of Mme H. P. Blavatsky and asked for better understanding between Theosophists and the Society for Psychical Research. Yet, he was known as an arch critic of psychical research, particularly of the physical phenomena of Spiritualism. His attack on Ernesto Bozzano's report of sittings at Millesimo Castle in Italy was the final straw that caused Sir Arthur Conan Doyle to resign from the SPR. Besterman had written that "Signor Bozzano's reports . . . show an almost complete lack of understanding of what constitutes good evidence and adequate recording of mediumistic sittings. . . . [T]o put forward such a book as this as a serious contribution to psychical research, and to put it forward with such dogmatic claims of infallibility as Signor Bozzano's, is to bring our subject into contempt and disrepute" (JSPR 26:10, 11, 14). A year earlier he had written a critical review of certain aspects of Margery's mediumship (JSPR 38:399). And his book *Some Modern Mediums,* which questioned the investigations of Charles Richet, Albert von Schrenck-Notzing, and Gustave Geley, caused a furor.

In 1931, Besterman conducted an interesting experiment which, like Richard Hodgson's and S. J. Davey's, again showed how fallible eyewitness testimony is: The testimony of the sitters at a simulated séance was correct only 33.9 percent of the time on average. Indeed, he was so certain of the unreliability of everyone's observations, including his own, that he never reported the most remarkable paranormal phenomena he ever saw (for example, with Rudi Schneider) because they depended solely on his own testimony.

His reports in psychical research all date from the late 1920s and early 1930s. Yet thirty-odd years later, in the Preface to his *Collected Papers* (1968), he wrote that he continued to be amused by the virulence of the attacks against him and still could not understand why he had been thought hypercritical: "I am struck . . . not merely by the tone of sweet reasonableness, but by the extent to which I leaned over backwards to present my conclusions in the most favorable light" (p. viii).

Besterman became SPR librarian in 1927 and editor of the *Journal* and *Proceedings* in 1929 and was also the society's Investigations Officer. He resigned from all his positions in 1935. Besterman co-authored with **Sir William Barrett** a book on dowsing, *The Divining Rod,* published in 1926. In later years he became a world-famous bibliographer.

Selected Writings: 1930. "Review of Modern Psychic Mysteries, Millesimo Castle, Italy." JSPR 26:10; 1932. "The Psychology of Testimony in Relation to Paraphysical Phenomena." PSPR 40:365; *Collected Papers on the Paranormal,* 1968.

BIBLIOGRAPHY: Inglis, B. *Science and Parascience,* 1984; Manning, W. E. 1968. "Collected Papers on the Paranormal." JSPR 44:407.

**Betz, Hans D., 1940–.** German professor of

physics at the University of Munich. He has conducted ingenious experiments in psychokinesis which suggest that a subject can influence electrical circuits by unknown means. Currently the German federal government is supporting his research in dowsing.

Selected Writing: 1975. "Experimentelle Untersuchung ungewohnlicher Metall-Beigeeffekte." *Zeitschrift für Parapsychologie und Grenzgebiete der Psychologie* 17:241.

**Bierman, Dick, 1943–.** Dutch lecturer in parapsychology at the University of Amsterdam. He is openly critical of people who naively worship before the god of scientific technology and believe that, with modern instrumentation, a "fraud-proof" parapsychological experiment can be produced that will overcome the objections of skeptics and convince nonbelievers. The whole idea, Bierman says, "is a fiction" (Bierman, 1981) because the same modern technology that can be used for controls in experiments can be employed as well for fraud. This does not mean that psi phenomena do not exist; it signifies only that a "fraud-proof" experiment can never be achieved. He pointed out that it is therefore wrong to report any of **William Edward Cox**'s "mini-lab" experiments as fraud-proof and even bet $200 that he could reproduce any events taking place in the mini-lab by instrumentation alone and without paranormal means.

With a Ph.D. in physics, Bierman also is interested in the relation between psi phenomena and physics and in fitting the results of parapsychological experiments into observational theories.

Bierman cofounded the **Research Institute for Psi and Physics.**

Selected Writing: 1981. "An Open Letter to Julian Isaacs." JSPR 51:183.

**Billet Reading.** A question is written on a piece of paper, the paper is folded, perhaps placed in a sealed envelope, and given to a person purporting to possess psychic powers. The alleged psychic then tells the writer what is written on the paper and answers the question. Many performers who specialized in billet reading, such as Bert Reese, impressed people with what appeared to be a demonstration of paranormal powers but, in reality, they were tricksters who managed to switch billets so that they were able to read the questions in advance.

**Bilocation.** The experience of being in two different places simultaneously or of observing an individual in one location while that person is physically in another. See also **Out-of-Body Experience.**

**Biocommunication.** A Soviet term for **Telepathy.**

**Bioenergetics.** What the Soviets call **Psychokinesis.**

**Biofeedback.** A method that uses instruments to monitor unconscious bodily functions, such as the heartbeat rate and that may allow individuals to control such functions consciously by learning from data received from the instruments.

**Bird, James Malcolm, 1886–.** American psychical researcher. No more voluble and vigorous advocate of the controversial medium, Mina S. Crandon, ever existed than Bird. A teacher of mathematics at Cooper Union and Columbia University, Bird became associate editor of *Scientific American* which, in 1925, offered $2,500 to anyone who could produce physical phenomena to the satisfaction of its committee. Bird organized and served as secretary of that committee, which included William McDougall, Walter F. Prince, Hereward Carrington and Harry Houdini. The committee conducted sittings with Mina Crandon whose pseudonym "Margery" was invented by Bird in an article published in the *Scientific American.* A divided committee decided against Margery's mediumship. Bird, as secretary of the committee had no vote, but he was seemingly convinced of Margery's paranormal powers. His book *Margery the Medium* (1925) has been called "one of the most unreliable and often duplicitous works ever published in the field" (Tietze, 1976).

In that same year Bird was appointed with Prince as co-research officer of the American Society for Psychical Research, an appointment that so infuriated Prince who had nothing but contempt for Bird's methods and abilities that he resigned from the ASPR. Equally disaffected were McDougall, Elwood Worcester and Gardner Murphy who also resigned from the ASPR and, in 1925, formed an independent organization, the Boston Society for Psychic Research, that Prince joined as director.

Despite his steady defense of Margery's mediumship, in 1930 Bird submitted a confidential report to the ASPR Board of Trustees in which he revealed that some, at least, of Margery's phenomena has been "normally" (i.e., fraudulently), produced and that she had even, during Houdini's investigation, asked Bird to ring a bell or do anything else he could think of that would pass for paranormal activity. Accusations and counteraccusations of sexual impropriety seem to have passed between the Crandons and Bird, and his second volume of the ASPR *Proceedings* dealing with the Margery mediumship was never published, another being printed in its place. Bird's manuscript, which was thereafter offered to both the Boston Society for Psychic Research and the SPR, has disappeared.

Prince saw Bird on December 8, 1932. What happened to him after that remains a mystery (Tietze, 1973:136–143).

Selected Writings: Ed. 1928. "The Margery Mediumship." PASPR 20–21, Vol. 1; *Margery the Medium,* 1925.

BIBLIOGRAPHY: Berger, A. S. *Lives and Letters in American Parapsychology: A Biographical History, 1850–1987,* 1988; Tietze, T. R. 1976. "Ursa Major: An Impressionistic Appreciation of Walter Franklin Prince." JASPR 70:1, 14–15; Tietze, T. R. *Margery,* 1973.

**Bishop, Washington (possibly Wellington) Irving, 1856–1889.** American stage entertainer and self-styled "World's First Mind Reader." He was really **Muscle-Reading,** a trick he learned by watching J. Randall Brown, the originator of the modern thought reading act. In the 1870s Bishop, whose mother was a medium and whose father was a Spiritualist, joined the stage troupe of Annie Eva Fay, the foremost American physical medium of her day. Bishop became her manager, and in 1876 made his stage debut by performing her effects and showing how she could untie herself in her cabinet and then retie herself so that it looked as if she had never moved.

Bishop was an enormous success in the United States, and on the Continent where he appeared before the crowned heads of Romania, Greece, Norway, Sweden, Russia, and in Mexico. His usual method of "mind-reading" was to grab someone's hand and rush around frenetically until he had found the answer or person he was looking for; sometimes, however, he merely stayed close to someone. To avoid comparison with Brown, Bishop had gone to England in 1877 where he came to the attention of Society for Psychical Research. Their conclusion was that there was nothing paranormal about his performances. They could all be explained "by the perception by a trained operator of involuntary and unconscious muscular movements." Nonetheless his successful career continued.

Unfortunately, Bishop was subject to sudden fits of catalepsy. On May 12, 1889, while performing before show business notables at the Lambs Club in New York City, he fell unconscious. Neither a heartbeat nor breath could be detected. Although Bishop always carried a note that explained his condition and forbade autopsy (he had once purportedly been in trance for three weeks), an overzealous doctor—strangely a friend who knew of Bishop's cataleptic trances—performed an autopsy in the course of which he removed Bishop's brain. Thus ended a short and colorful career.

BIBLIOGRAPHY: Barrett, W. F., Gurney, E., and Myers, F. W. H. 1882. "First Report on Thought Reading." PSPR 1:13; Jay, R. *Learned Pigs and Fireproof Women,* 1986.

**Black Box.** A device invented in the 1950s by **George De La Warr** who claimed to have used it successfully in the paranormal diagnosis and treatment of ailments. The box consisted of a diagnostic apparatus, a camera, and a device for treatment. A spot of blood supplied by a patient who might be hundreds of miles away was placed in the diagnostic device. The blood spot was then "tuned" by the device to certain frequencies. Dials and reference tables provided the diagnosis. The camera then confirmed the diagnosis. The blood spot was next placed on the treatment device and "tuned," whereupon the device sent healing rays out to the patient. De La Warr seemed convinced that his box would perform as advertised although, in at least one case, the inventor and his device were charged with being fraudulent.

**Black Magic.** Spells, incantations, rituals, practiced from the earliest times in order to kill or injure. It is one of the darker areas in the regions occupied by occultism. While parapsychology and psychical research have no wish to enter it and few parapsychologists have done so to date, nevertheless, sometimes essays in black magic are connected to paranormal phenomena. Possession by spirits or gods is found in voodooism, for instance, and, in that cult as well as in bone-pointing, extrasensory perception may be making its appearance. In witchcraft also, many parallels with parapsychology can be found.

**Black Mass.** A Satanic ceremony conducted as a burlesque of the Christian mass. White vestments become black, prayers are gibberish, chastity becomes sexuality, the sacrifice of Christ becomes human sacrifice, and not God but the devil is worshipped. But, with a single exception, widespread stories of such rites have no historical authentication. The exception occurred in the 1670s in France when Mme de Montespan, one of King Louis XIV's mistresses, lay naked on a slab draped in black and surrounded by seven burning candles. Her body served as an "altar" over which a baby was sacrificed to Astarte (or Ashtoreth), an ancient Syrian deity whose attributes were fertility, reproduction, and immorality. The frustrated lady's aim was to bring the straying monarch back to her bed. The Black Mass is one area of occultism from which parapsychology and psychical research can learn nothing except that being a royal mistress was not always a happy lot and that its practice did not keep Mme de Montespan from becoming Mother Superior of the convent of St. Joseph in Paris.

**Blackmore, Susan Jane, 1951–.** British psychologist and parapsychologist. During her undergraduate years (1970–1973) at the University of Oxford from which she received her B.A. with honors in Physiology and Psychology, Susan Blackmore as president and secretary of the Oxford University Society for Psychical Research developed her interest in parapsychology.

Proceeding on the hypothesis that memory is not stored in individual brains but is common to everyone, she pursued a Ph.D. in parapsychology (awarded in 1980) at Surrey University by assuming the existence of psi and looking for the processes involved. Her Ph.D. thesis entitled "Extrasensory Perception as a Cognitive Process" reported completely negative results. Dr. Blackmore was unable to find any evidence for ESP (or psi) then, and she has never found any since.

Starting as a believer in ESP, Dr. Blackmore thought at first that she had just had bad luck, then, as negative results continued, that her experimental designs were wrong, then that null results might be due to experimenter effect, or that she might find psi, not in the laboratory, but in a study of spontaneous cases. As, over a period of ten years, she never got anything but negative results—in studies with children, with Tarot cards, with Ganzfeld experiments, with out-of-body experiences (she has had many)—she came to think at first that psi might not exist and, finally, that it does not exist. She believes now that we need a "New Parapsychology." In other words, there are "spontaneous experiences interpreted as ESP or PK, out-of-body experiences, apparitions and hauntings, near-death and deathbed visions, poltergeists, and so on. . . . Let us define parapsychology as the study of these phenomena rather than as the study of psi. . . . [T]he schism between the proponents and the skeptics might [then] be healed, the repeatability problem could be shelved, and we might find ourselves studying all the same phenomena we have always studied but also able to tackle those human experiences and occult and mystical teachings that we could never approach through the study of psi" (Blackmore, 1985:441, 445–46).

Dr. Blackmore is presently visiting research fellow at the Brain and Perception Laboratory of the University of Bristol and is one of the very few parapsychologists who were considered for the newly created Koestler Chair of Parapsychology at the University of Edinburgh. She has written three books (1978, 1982, 1986), has contributed to several others, and has published numerous papers in the parapsychological and other professional journals as well as in popular magazines such as *The Unexplained, Science Now,* and *Fate.* She has appeared many times on radio and television and since December 1986 has been presenting a monthly magazine program on the BBC. She has taught courses in psychology and parapsychology and has lectured at many universities both in England and abroad. Among other associations, she is a member of Mensa, the Bristol Theosophical Society, the Society for Psychical Research, the Association for the Study of Anomalous Phenomena, the British UFO Research Association, and the Parapsychological Association.

Selected Writings: "A Theory of Lucid Dreams and OBEs." In J. Gackenbach and S. LaBarge, eds., *Lucid Dreaming*, 1988; 1987. "A Report of a Visit to Carl Sargent's Laboratory." JSPR 54:186; *The Adventures of a Parapsychologist*, 1986; "The Adventures of a Psi-Inhibitory Experimenter." In P. Kurtz, *A Skeptic's Handbook of Parapsychology*, 1985; 1984. "ESP in Young Children." JSPR 52:311; 1983. "Divination with Tarot Cards: An Empirical Study." JSPR 51:97; *Beyond the Body*, 1982-1983; *Parapsychology and Out-of-the-Body Experiences*, 1978.

**Blake, William, 1757–1827.** English poet, engraver, and painter. He was endowed with emotion and mystical imagination, which he expressed in art and extraordinary poetry whose influence continues to grow. His poetry and engraving skills are found in *Songs of Innocence* (1789) and the so-called "Prophetic Books," *The Marriage of Heaven and Hell* (1790), *The Gates of Paradise* (1793), *The Vision of the Daughters of Albion* (1793), *Milton* (1804), and *Jerusalem* (1820). He also wrote *Songs of Experience* (1794) and contributed beautiful illustrations to Robert Blair's poem *The Grave* (1804–1805). Blake lived uneventfully and one step ahead of poverty. When he died, he was buried in an unmarked grave, evidence of the lack of recognition accorded his genius during his lifetime.

Blake sits in the box as a **Noted Witness.** He seems to have been a psychic. When he was four, he had a vision of God and when ten a vision of angels. His work was the product of his paranormal experiences. His brother, Robert, who died in 1787, was his communicator. In a letter to his patron William Hayley, Blake said, "Thirteen years ago I lost a brother, and now with his spirit I converse hourly and daily. . . . I hear his advice, and even now write from his dictate." Blake said that he learned from the deceased Robert the technique of engraving text on copper plate. Blake had visions of spirits and wrote automatically as they communicated with him. He spoke of writing daily and nightly "under the direction of Messengers from Heaven." When he wrote to his friend Thomas Butts about his poem *Jerusalem* he confessed, "I have written this poem from immediate dictation. . . . I can praise it, since I do not pretend to be any other than the secretary; the authors are in eternity." The poem, he said, "was written . . . twelve or sometimes twenty or thirty lines at a time, without premeditation and against my will." This statement makes him a witness for the creative process, also. Inspiration was the key to Blake's concept of survival beyond death. Through the creative process and the imaginative art it produces, the artist achieves not personal survival but a permanent reality and in this way survives the death of the mortal body. See also **Automatic Writing, Speaking, or Spelling.**

BIBLIOGRAPHY: Gibbes, E. H. 1939. "Influenced or Inspirational Writing." JASPR 33:270.

**Blavatsky, Helena Petrovna (Hahn), 1831–1891.** the Russian-born founder of **Theosophy.** Helena Hahn was born to the daughter of a princess and a Russian captain. As a child she believed she could control goblins and spirits, even to the extent of causing the death of a young serf. At seventeen she married Nikifor V. Blavatsky, vice-governor of a province on the Armenian border; three months later she ran away to Constantinople. During the next ten or fifteen years, she seems, among other adventures, to have been an equestrienne in a circus, to have toured Europe with an operatic bass (at the same time searching for the Ancient Wisdom), to have had an illegitimate son, to have functioned as a medium and to have become a Spiritualist. She later claimed that during this period she had been in India and Tibet where she learned the secrets of the Masters.

In Vermont in 1874, she met Colonel **Henry Steel Olcott** who, abandoning his wife and family, became her close associate, first, in the promotion of Spiritualism, then in the development of a secret society known as the Brotherhood of Luxor and, finally, in 1875, in the foundation of the Theosophical Society as an answer to the conflict between science and religion.

In 1877 Mme Blavatsky's first book, *Isis Unveiled*, was published. According to Olcott, much of it was dictated by "Tibetan masters." With the help of "Neoplatonism, the Cabala and certain texts from India [the book] reveals the making up of the universe and the individual human being by the conjoining of . . . matter, an invisible energizing spirit, and immortal consciousness" (Ellwood, 1983).

In 1879, HPB (as she liked to be called) and Olcott went to India, for Mme Blavatsky believed that India and Tibet were the sources of spiritual wisdom. In 1882, HPB and Olcott established their Theosophical Society headquarters at Adyar, near Madras, and began publication of *The Theosophist*, which Mme Blavatsky edited from 1879 to 1888.

In 1884, the Society for Psychical Research sent **Richard Hodgson** to India to study the alleged paranormal phenomena taking place at the Theosophical Society headquarters in India. Hodgson concluded that all the phenomena were fraudulently produced with the help of accomplices, that the allegedly paranormally delivered letters supposedly written by the Mahatmas (enlightened Masters living in Tibet) were instead written by Mme Blavatsky herself (or by an accomplice) and that incriminating letters to her accomplices, which Mme Blavatsky claimed were forgeries, had indeed been written by her. (Hodgson also accused her of being a spy for the Russian government, but that charge seems to have been definitely untrue.) The SPR on the basis of Hodgson's report condemned Mme Blavatsky as "One of the most accomplished, ingenious, and interesting imposters in history."

The controversy, over whether or not the Blavatsky phenomena were genuine, continues because accusing HPB of fraud is, for her thousands of followers worldwide, the same as it would be for Christians if someone accused Jesus of using conjuring tricks to produce fake miracles (Thouless, 1968). Thouless thinks that Hodgson was probably right but does not think he proved it. Indeed, Harrison (1986) has shown that, by using Hodgson's methods of handwriting analysis, "One could prove that HPB wrote *Huckleberry Finn.*"

In 1885, in ill health, HPB left India forever. She spent her last years writing *The Secret Doctrine*, her most important work which presents an overview of Theosophical doctrine, *The Voice of the Silence*, and *The Key to Theosophy*. White Lotus Day—the day of her death, May 8—is commemorated every year by her followers.

Selected Writings: *The Voice of the Silence*, 1889; *The Key to Theosophy*, 1889; *Secret Doctrine*, 1888; *Isis Unveiled*, 1877.

BIBLIOGRAPHY: Carrithers, W. A., Jr. 1962. "Madame Blavatsky: 'One of the World's Great Jokers'." JASPR 56:131; Ellwood, Jr., R. S. "The American Theosophical Synthesis." In H. Kerr and C. L. Crow, eds., *The Occult in America*, 1983; Harrison, V. 1986. "J'Accuse. An Examination of the Hodgson Report of 1885." JSPR 53:286; Hodgson, R. 1885. "Account of Personal Investigations in India, and Discussion of the Authorship of the 'Koot Hoomi' Letters." PSPR 3:207; Meade, M. *Madame Blavatsky*, 1980; "Report of the Committee Appointed to Investigate Phenomena Connected with the Theosophical Society." 1885. PSPR 3:201; Symonds, J. *The Lady with the Magic Eyes*, 1960; Thouless, R. H. 1968. "Review of *Obituary - The 'Hodgson Report' on Madame Blavatsky.*" JSPR 44:341; Williams, G. M. *Madame Blavatsky: Priestess of the Occult*, 1946.

**Bleeding Pictures and Statues.** Sometimes things as seemingly bloodless as pictures and statues do bleed. Just before the first World War, such a phenomenon occurred in Mirabeau en Poitou, near Poitiers, France, where the retired Abbé Cesaire de Grateloup lived. The case was so remarkable that Everard Feilding, an extremely skeptical investigator of the paranormal, called it "the strangest in the whole course of my experience." (Feilding, 1963).

The picture involved was an oleograph (color lithograph) of Jesus Christ on canvas or cloth pinned to an ordinary wooden frame hanging above the altar in the Abbé's private chapel. One morning in 1911, as he began to say the Mass as usual, he noticed red marks on Christ's forehead in the picture. Two mornings later, he saw a blood-like substance starting to ooze from the wounds. In the days succeeding, there were more wounds, more bleeding. The next month the Host began to bleed also. Great crowds clamored for a view of the bleeding picture. After the picture was examined by the bishop of Poitiers, the Abbé was ordered to let no one see it. Some skeptical workmen, however, got hold of a key and stole into the house. They saw that the picture continued to bleed as did the Host. When Feilding arrived in 1914, the blood flowed from the Host so freely that it ran down the altar. In 1916, a Frenchwoman Feilding knew well observed blood flowing from the picture with such force that it covered and was soaked up by the white linen that had been placed under the picture. In 1919, Feilding returned and took specimens of the substance. Analysis by the Lister Institute confirmed that the liquid was real human blood. Yet, the Abbé, persecuted by the bishop of Poitiers, had been excommunicated in 1915 without an examination of the case. Feilding's efforts to have the case reviewed by clerical authorities failed.

In an Italian home in 1971, genuine human blood fell in drops from the eyes, hands and feet of a picture of the Virgin Mary. A small statue of Jesus Christ above an altar in a house in Pennsylvania started bleeding in 1975. After inspection by a priest and a doctor, the statue was placed in the local church where it continued to bleed and was revered as a miracle.

But can there be a natural or, failing that, a paranormal explanation, for bleeding pictures or statues? In none of the French, Italian, or American cases did careful inspection show fraud, such as concealed tubes, holes or gadgets that might have produced blood. Psychokinesis seems to have shown that, at times, human beings possess the mental ability to influence objects. Perhaps owners of the pictures or statue were poltergeist agents whose especially strong religious emotions enabled them to produce, not necessarily consciously, a poltergeist manifestation that gave every appearance of divine action. But such a theory seems altogether unsatisfactory in the cases of both the Abbé's picture and the Christ statue in Pennsylvania, both of which continued to bleed when the owners, the supposed poltergeist agents, were not present. The only other parapsychological theory that might account for the phenomenon is the rather farfetched explanation that there had been an apport of human blood to the picture or statue.

Such cases seem to be enigmas as to which we can only admit, along with Feilding, that we are "unable . . . to come to any kind of conclusion, or to decide which of all the possible hypotheses about its character seemed the most probable, or the least improbable." (Feilding, 1963). See also **Crying Pictures and Statues.**

BIBLIOGRAPHY: Feilding, E. *Sittings with Eusapia Palladino & Other Studies,* 1963, pp. 299–314; Rogo, D. S. *Miracles: A Parascientific Inquiry into Wondrous Phenomena,* 1982, pp. 159–162.

**Bleeding, Posthumous.** The flowing of blood from a corpse for a considerable time after death. Saint Francis of Geronimo died in 1716 at 10 o'clock in the morning. His fellow monks decided to cut out the corns from his feet in order to keep them as relics. When they cut the first corn a half hour later, the blood flowed so profusely that they had to find material to absorb it all. The body continued to bleed unchecked until seven in the evening. Most medical authorities maintain that generally corpses do not bleed. A corpse has no blood pressure to create blood circulation, and lacking circulation little, if any, blood will flow. Yet medical people have noticed that incisions made on dead people a few hours after death may still cause them to bleed. But when a corpse continues to bleed months and years subsequent to death, the atmosphere of the ordinary changes to the rarefied air of the outer reaches of the extraordinary. Such extraordinary cases have been observed, usually when bodies have been exhumed as part of the process of beatification or canonization carried out by the Roman Catholic church. For example, nine months after his death in 1591 blood flowed from the fingers of Saint John of the Cross when they were cut off; liquid blood was found in the body of Saint Andrew Avellino the year following his death in 1608; blood flowed from the body of Saint Francis Carraciolo twenty years after his death in 1608; and blood was discharged from the severed fingers of Saint Peter Regalatus thirty-six years after death in 1456.

Was each of these cases a miracle resulting from divine intervention? Although the cases just given were all of saints, there are other instances of people bleeding long after death who were never thought of as saints. Not every extraordinary occurrence can be classified as miraculous, and it is possible that someday medical science will be able to explain posthumous bleeding as an event that is within nature, not beyond it and therefore supernatural. Meanwhile, the subject continues to be a puzzle of interest to medical scientists, theologians, and parapsychologists alike. See also **Catherine of Bologna.**

BIBLIOGRAPHY: Thurston, H. *The Physical Phenomena of Mysticism,* 1952, pp. 247–251, 287, 288–289.

**Bleksley, Arthur Edward Herbert, 1908–1984.** South African scientist, astrophysicist, and mathematician. He was a distinguished leader of parapsychology who gave it prestige in the eyes of the general public and universities in his country. His interest in the field focused on research on extrasensory perception during sleep and brought him the McDougall Award for Distinguished Work in Parapsychology.

This research started with a letter sent to him by one W. van Vuurde who lived 600 miles away and of whom Bleksley had never heard. Van Vuurde said that, by using his psi ability, he could wake up at any randomly selected hour, even though he did not know what it was. Did van Vuurde have some remarkable paranormal ability or, as he was sleeping, did his body have some motor process that enabled him to know when to wake up? Bleksley found out that van Vuurde normally slept between midnight and 7:59 A.M. The experimenter used a randomizing procedure to set a broken alarm clock to a target time. Hundreds of miles away van Vuurde was to wake up at the preset time. On each of 161 nights the subject sent to the experimenter the hour he (van Vuurde) awakened. The results of the experiment were statistically remarkable: On ten nights the subject awakened within one minute of the target time. These highly statistically significant results suggested that the ability of the man to awaken at a preset time indicated an ESP mechanism that was directing the subject toward the randomly set hands of the distant clock. What is also interesting about the experiment is that, although Bleksley let the subject stay in his own home where he felt comfortable and where he thought the conditions were conducive to ESP, Bleksley was still able to control the test and obtain significant results.

Bleksley was president of the South African Society for Psychical Research and was later appointed research director for the South African Institute for Parapsychological Research. As a creative mathematician who invented axioms, methods, techniques, and mathematical entities, he was interested in the creative process. While he had no personal experience of his own to narrate, he carefully studied the history of other creative mathematicians, such as Henri Poincaré, and concluded that mathematical creation "is not a conscious phenomenon . . . [it] may have at least one foot in the extrasensory universe. . . . That this may indeed be the case is borne out by some well-recorded cases in the history of mathematics, in which mathematicians have done better than they should have done." (Bleksley, 1970).

Selected Writings: "Creativity in the Mathematical Field." In A. Angoff and B. Shapin, eds., *Psi Factors in Creativity,* 1970, p. 85; 1963. "An Experiment of Long-Distance ESP During Sleep." JP 27:1.

**Blind.** When a subject is prevented from knowing about the procedures or conditions of an experiment. See also **Double-Blind.**

**Blind Matching Test.** A test of **Clairvoyance.** It requires subjects who never look at or have any way of knowing the symbols on the ESP cards they are holding to match them against the five groups of key cards that have been placed in black envelopes and that are also concealed from and unknown to the subjects. See also **Open Matching Test.**

**Boehme, Jakob, 1575–1624.** German mystic and philosopher. His writings are widely studied today. Originally a shoemaker, he wrote philosophical treatises and in 1621 aroused such antagonism on the part of the clergy and municipal authorities that his works were confiscated and he was ordered to write no more. But he did resume writing to expound his speculations on the unity of the many in the One and the manifestations of God in the world and the human being.

Boehme is another of the creative individuals who received, from a source beyond their conscious minds, information and inspiration for their writings. From the following testimony given in one of his books, he becomes a **Noted Witness** for the creative process and for automatic writing, speaking or spelling: "Art has not wrote this, neither was there any time to consider how to set it punctually down, according to the right understanding of letters, but all was ordered according to the direction of the Spirit, which often went in haste. . . . The Penman's hand, by reason he was not accustomed to it, did often shake; and though I could have wrote in a more accurate, fair and plain manner, yet the reason I did not was this, that the burning fire often forced forward with speed, and the hand and pen must hasten directly after it; for that fire comes and goes, as a sudden shower. I can write nothing of myself, but as a child which neither knows or understands anything, which neither has ever been learnt; and I write only that which the Lord vouchsafes to know in me according to the measure as he himself manifests in me. . . ."

BIBLIOGRAPHY: Gibbes, E. H. 1939. "Influenced or Inspirational Writing." JASPR 33:270

**Boirac, Emile, 1851–1917.** French parapsychologist. He resurrected Franz Anton Mesmer's theory of animal magnetism. He postulated that this invisible, effluence supposed to radiate from some people and affect others was not only the causative agent in hypnosis as Mesmer believed, but also in telepathy and psychokinesis and the physical phenomena of Spiritualism.

Selected Writing: *La Psychologie Inconnu: Introduction et Contribution a l'Etude Experimentale des Sciences Psychiques,* 1908.

**Bolton, Frances Payne, 1885–1977.** American member of the U.S. Congress for almost 30 years. She was a leader in philanthropic and governmental causes, including nursing education, and was vitally interested in parapsychology. The Frances Payne Bolton School of Nursing at Western Reserve University was created because of her influence and support, and it was her bill in Congress that established the U.S. Cadet Nurse Corps during World War II.

Her meeting with the medium **Eileen Garrett** and the close friendship that ensued became "the basis for one of the significant partnerships in scientific psychic research. . ." (Loth, 1957). The congresswoman crossed the threshold of the mundane world and entered the bizarre one of the paranormal. She gave financial support to **Joseph B. Rhine's** research at the Parapsychology Laboratory at Duke University. She cofounded with Eileen Garrett and was vice president of the **Parapsychology Foundation** through which she provided funds to subsidize researchers. Mrs. Bolton's financial support also made it possible to hold the First International Congress of Parapsychological Studies in Utrecht in 1953. She once said: "To me the whole area of parapsychology . . . is something the future must understand" (*Parapsychology Review*, 1977).

Until her last illness, she remained actively interested in the affairs of the foundation and in the cause of parapsychology to which she had given herself. She is remembered in Congress as the ranking Republican member of the Foreign Affairs Committee. In parapsychology, she is remembered as a devoted and generous supporter.

BIBLIOGRAPHY: "Frances P. Bolton Dies." 1977 *Parapsychology Review* 8 (2): 1; Loth, D. *A Long Way Forward: The Biography of Congresswoman Frances P. Bolton,* 1957.

**Bond, Frederick Bligh, 1864–1945.** British architect and archaeologist. Early interested in Spiritualism and the occult, Bond had little formal education but learned architecture as an apprentice. In 1897 he became a Fellow of the Royal Institute of British Architects. In 1903 he was accepted as a member of the Somerset Archaeological and Natural History Society as a result of which he was named director of excavations (a nonpaying job) at Glastonbury Abbey.

In connection with these excavations, Bond and his friend James Allen Bartlett turned, no one seems to know why, to psychic sources of information, specifically to automatic writing. "The response was a contact with a flow of information that would eventually overpower all else in his life. He had begun his conversations with the Company of Avalon, the 'Watchers' from the other side" (Schwartz, 1978: 13). As a result of these conversations Bond became the father of psychic **Archaeology.** At first he thought he had reached some "well of memory" but later came to believe that he was indeed in touch with the spirits of former monks who had lived and worked at Glastonbury. They told him where to dig to find the remains of various parts of the almost completely destroyed abbey, what their lives had been like, and why they built where and when they did. G. W. Lambert (1968), however, feels that "no detail in the script[s] . . . compel[s] . . . us to look beyond the memories and subconscious inventive powers of the two friends" (p. 278), and that, although the experiments with automatic writing gave an impetus to the work, "Bond greatly exaggerated the value of the script as a contribution to his discoveries by excavation" (1966:306). Bond's book *The Gate of Remembrance* sets forth the story as he saw it.

In any case, his involvement with the psychic (he was also at this time editing *Psychic Science,* the journal of the College of Psychic Science), together with the machinations of his extremely vindictive wife from whom he had been long separated, resulted in his loss, first, of his archaeological work, second, of his architectural practice and, at last, of the small amounts of money he was able to make from lecturing and from running a guest house in Glastonbury.

During the 1920s Bond sat with an automatist with whom he produced the "Gospel of Philip." He was then asked by the person who was paying for the sittings to sit instead with Geraldine Cummins who later, as a result of these sittings, produced the Cleophas scripts. Bond felt that his presence was necessary for the production of the scripts and that he should receive compensation when they were published. After a great deal of acrimony, a court held otherwise.

A short time later a patron brought Bond to the United States where he became educational director of the American Society for Psychical Research and from 1930 to May 1935 the editor of its *Journal*. During the period of his editorship Bond became involved in the controversial Margery (Mina Crandon) mediumship and was at first convinced of its genuineness. But in May 1935, evidence presented to him forced him to publish in JASPR that one of Margery's famous phenomena ("Walter's" thumbprints) was a fraud. The Board of Trustees of the ASPR reacted violently, published their own disclaimer of Bond's publication and fired him forthwith.

By January 1936 Bond had returned to England. He died in 1945.

Selected Writings: 1935. "Editorial Notes: 'Walter' Thumbprints: Dr. Cummins's Report." JASPR 29:130; *The Gospel of Philip the Deacon*, 1932; *The Gate of Remembrance*, 1918, 1921.

BIBLIOGRAPHY: Kenawell, W. W. *The Quest at Glastonbury: A Biographical Study of Frederick Bligh Bond*, 1965; Lambert, G. W. 1966. "The Quest at Glastonbury." JSPR 43:301; Lambert, G. W. 1968. "Johannes, the Monk: A Study in the Script of J. A. in 'The Gate of Remembrance'." JSPR 44:271; Schwartz, S. A. *The Secret Vaults of Time*, 1978; Supplemental Number. 1935. JASPR 29 (5, sup.): 153.

**Bone-Pointing.** A "perfect murder" technique among the aborigines of Australia and used by their **Clever Men.** It consists of taking a bone, perhaps a kangaroo bone, pointed at one end with a hole at the other end through which a tuft of human hair has been passed, and pointing it at a person who, in effect, becomes a victim. Once victims become aware that they have been its target, they become persuaded that they will die. Frequently death comes to them regardless of good health or of the efforts or orthodox medicine to save them. Awareness is not always necessary, however. In one case, a victim who was ignorant that he had been pointed at died when the absent "clever man" pronounced that he had "got him." Such a case might be an example of the bone having become a deadly spear of thought and a killing by telepathy. Ronald K. H. Rose (1952) associates the loss of the will to live with a belief in reincarnation and believes that the only way the fatal effect of the technique can be counterbalanced is by the superior powers of another "clever man."

To kill by bone-pointing is not a homicide punishable by law. Autopsies of victims reveal death from natural causes. To kill by pointing a bone, then, is to commit the perfect crime. See also **Aborigines, Australian; Curse; Voodooism.**

BIBLIOGRAPHY: Rose, R. 1952. "Psi and Australian Aborigines." *JASPR* 46: 17.

**Book of the Dead, Egyptian.** A collection of funerary hymns and prayers, formulae, and magical words of power written by scribes between 1100 B.C. and 900 B.C. It was a guide book for pious Egyptians, rich or poor, on how to travel the road beyond death. It is a monument to their firmly held belief in human survival after physical death and in the eternal light and happiness they would enjoy. The texts are of significance to psychical research and parapsychology because they postulate a *ka*, an exact double of the physical body, which has an existence entirely independent of the physical body and can travel at will from place to place. It is clear that the astral body and out-of-body experience were phenomena well-known in ancient Egypt. Closely linked to the *ka* was the *ba* or soul that was to enjoy eternal life.

**Book of the Dead, Tibetan.** Also known as the *Bardo Thodol*, meaning "Liberation by Hearing on the After-Death Plane." A book of instructions for the dying and dead that describes right thinking for the dying, what occurs at the moment of death, the stage immediately following death, and that preceding reincarnation. The message of the book is that dying is an art as important as the art of living. In the belief of the East, the final thought at death, the last moment of life, shapes the character of the incarnation to come. The book is a manual for the technique of dying calmly and in right understanding that permits death not only to be an ecstatic experience, but also an initiation into good reincarnations until Nirvana is attained. In effect, a person will be what that person thinks. A guru or lama attends the dying process, directs the thoughts of the dying, and keeps them placid as they enter the next or Bardo stage. The book is read also to the corpse by the lama or guru.

Of interest to psychical research is that, according to the book's teachings, several paranormal phenomena are recognized. Survival after physical death and reincarnation are plainly accepted in the teaching that there is at the moment of death a separation from the physical body of the "knower" or principle of consciousness. This principle of consciousness enters the Bardo stage between death and rebirth and afterward enters a womb to be reborn in a flesh and blood body. According to a further teaching, the counterpart to the astral body is recognized, since about three and a half days after death the knower will rise up in a "radiant body resembling the former body" and will spring forth. It "is not a body of gross matter, so that thou hast the power to go right through any rock-masses, hills, boulders, earth, houses. . . . Even the King of Mountains, Mt. Meru itself, can be passed through by thee, straight forwards and backwards unimpededly."

BIBLIOGRAPHY: Evans-Wentz, W. Y. *The Tibetan Book of the Dead,* 1960.

**Book Test.** An effort, supposedly initiated by a deceased communicator, to supply evidence of his or her survival of physical death. In the test, the communicator instructs a sitter to look in a specified place for a specified book not normally known to the sitter or medium. The sitter is further instructed to open the book to a specified page where, on a certain place on the page, is a passage that can be considered an appropriate message from the communicator. The test is designed to eliminate telepathy from the sitter as an explanation of the purported communication. It does not, however, exclude clairvoyance by the medium, or cryptomnesia, or the possibility that on any page of any book some phrase can be interpreted as a message. See also **Newspaper Test; Picture Test.**

**Borley Rectory.** Called by Harry Price "the most haunted house in England," Borley Rector was the center of his books, the focus of many sensational articles in the press and the most famous ghost story in the history of psychical research. Before it was destroyed by fire in 1939, Borley Rectory stood atop a hill in Essex, a great red-brick house with bay windows, a glass veranda and twenty-three rooms connected by three staircases, all made dark and gloomy by the tall trees that ringed it. A lawn stretched from the house down to a stream.

The house was also surrounded by several legends, one of which set the stage for the stories of ghostly coaches, headless men, and nuns supposed to frequent the place. It was rumored that the rectory had been constructed on the site of a monastery built in the thirteenth century and that a monk from the monastery had a clandestine love affair with a nun from a nearby convent. But when the ill-fated pair ran away together, they were pursued and captured. The monk was executed by beheading or hanging, the nun was taken back to the nunnery to be bricked alive into it. This tale was generally accepted until 1938, when the Essex Archaeological Society announced that, except for a twelfth-century church, no religious building had even been constructed on the site at Borley, nor was there any record of a convent in the vicinity.

But whatever legends about Borley Rectory may have been circulated and disproved, there are some historical facts that cannot be contradicted. The house was built in 1863 by the Rev. Henry D. E. Bull who, with his family, occupied it up to his death in 1892. His place was taken by his son, the Rev. Harry F. Bull, and the rectory remained in the possession of the Bull family until 1927 when Harry Bull died. The rectory remained unoccupied for over a year because, although offered in succession to twelve clergymen, each refused to live in it because of its local reputation as a haunt.

In 1928, however, the Rev. G. E. Smith, who did not know of the rumors, became rector. Upset by them after he moved in and more so by the unwillingness of people to attend meetings at the rectory, he contrived the idea of getting psychical researchers to make an investigation that would clear the rectory's name. In 1929, he sent a letter asking for help to the *Daily Mirror,* and a reporter was dispatched. After the newspaper editor received the reporter's account of footsteps in empty rooms and other phenomena, Harry Price, well-known as a psychic investigator and author, was asked to take charge of the case. Price went to the rectory in June 1929, to begin what would be almost twenty years of inquiry. A couple of days later, the bad condition of the house plus the publicity generated by the *Daily Mirror* that brought hundreds of curiosity seekers to Borley, forced the Rev. Smith and his wife to flee the rectory permanently. From 1930 to 1935, the Rev. L. A. Foyster and his family lived in the house and in May 1937, Price himself rented it for a year. It was then purchased by Captain W. H. Gregson. In February 1939, the rectory was gutted by fire. Price's extensive investigations led to two major books.

It is not possible to deal with all the aspects of the case or all the manifestations alleged to have taken place, but some of the chief reports of apparitions and physical phenomena can be mentioned. Shaw Jeffrey, an undergraduate staying at the rectory, said he saw the phantom of a nun and a coach and witnessed poltergeist phenomena; four members of the Bull family saw on the lawn the apparition of a woman in a flowing black robe such as nuns wear; Ethel Bull, one of the sisters, saw a tall man dressed in black clothes standing by her bed and once or twice felt someone sitting at the side of her bed; the Rev. Harry Bull claimed to have observed a nun's apparition, possibly a man without a head in the garden, and a ghostly coach pulled by two horses controlled by a headless coachman. On the occasion of Price's visit to the rectory in 1929, poltergeist phenomena made their appearance in the rectory with a shower of pebbles and keys. Among the objects were two medallions, one related to Roman Catholicism, the other issued in Paris was related to France. At this time as well, Mary Pearson, a servant, told Price that she had not only seen the strange nun but also a headless man behind a tree. Two days later, the *Daily Mirror* reporter caught sight of an apparition near the lawn. In addition, candlesticks flew and bells rang without explanation.

During the period of the Foyster occupancy, Price said that almost 2,000 manifestations occurred including apparitions, poltergeist phenomena, footsteps, and the ringing of bells. When Price was a tenant in 1937, he advertised for and organized a group of observers whom he instructed on how to watch for strange phenomena. Many were noted such as thuds and pencil marks on walls. There took place in the rectory in 1937 also table-tipping and messages received through a planchette from a deceased personality with the name of Marie Lairre. She claimed to have been a French Catholic nun at a convent near Borley and that she had been murdered and interred in the rectory grounds. The claim seemed supported by the French and Catholic medallions which had appeared earlier and in turn bolstered the sightings of a nun's apparition. While Gregson was the owner of the rectory, he said the whole atmosphere of it made his flesh crawl and that a spaniel he owned had gone wild in the rectory's courtyard and had run yelping from the place to disappear for good. In 1943, Price made excavations under the cellar of the rectory and discovered a part of a human jawbone and a human skull, which were thought to be what was left of the nun sighted so often.

Following Price's death, Eric J. Dingwall, K. M. Goldney and Trevor Hall were invited by the Society for Psychical Research to interview all witnesses who were living and make a critical survey of the evidence. Their work, finished in 1956, concluded that the accounts given in Price's books were uncorroborated, that he himself had exaggerated and distorted the testimony of witnesses and that, worse, he had manufactured the evidence and cheated in many ways. This exposé stood until Hastings, on a re-examination of the case published in 1969, showed that the study was a one-sided case for the prosecution. In his defense of Price, he argued that the interviews of the witnesses cross-examined by Price's critics had not demonstrated Price's dishonesty and that Price's books were not intended to be pieces of scientific research but simple narratives corroborated by records that could be examined by researchers at the University of London. It was on Price's documents not his books that the genuineness of the phenomena rested and on which all criticisms should be based. It is a justifiable inference that Price had nothing to hide or he would not have deposited the documents with the University of London and so opened them up to examination by researchers.

So, after a century and a quarter of reports of strange happenings at Borley Rectory, there is still no real agreement on whether the case of the old house on the hill in Essex is a first-class ghost story or the story of a first-class rogue.

BIBLIOGRAPHY: Dingwall, E. J., Goldney, K. M. and Hall, T. H. 1956. "The Haunting of Borley Rectory: A Critical Survey of the Evidence." PSPR 51:1; Hastings, R. J. 1969. "An Examination of the 'Borley Report'." PSPR 55:65; Price, H. *The End of Borley Rectory,* 1946; Price, H. *The Most Haunted House in England,* 1940.

**Bosco, Saint John (Don), 1815–1888.** Italian founder of the Society of St. Francis de Sales or the Salesians of Don Bosco, a Roman Catholic religious order for men. Their purpose is to provide a Christian education to the poor. He was also a co-founder of a similar order for women known as the Daughters of Our Lady Help of Christians or the Salesian Sisters. He was canonized in 1934. When the Roman Catholic church was considering his beatification, an eyewitness substantiated a remarkable feat of food multiplication that makes him a **Noted Witness** to the phenomenon.

In 1860, when John Bosco was at one of the Salesian establishments in Turin where 300 young boys were being given religious instruction, there was not enough bread to feed them at breakfast. John Bosco gave instructions that whatever bread could be found should be collected and said that he would see that the boys were fed. The witness said, "I fixed my eyes upon the basket . . . and I saw that it contained fifteen or twenty rolls at the most. Meanwhile, Don Bosco carried out the distribution, and to my great surprise, I saw the same quantity remain which had been there from the first, though no other rolls had been brought and the basket had not been changed."

Parapsychologists like lawyers know from their study of cases that human testimony is fallible. Yet this witness's story was given under oath. Would his being a Salesian with a greater sense of obligation to God than the ordinary witness make him less apt to have been mistaken? See also **Food, Multiplication of.**

BIBLIOGRAPHY: Thurston, H. *Physical Phenomena of Mysticism,* 1952, p. 389.

**Boston Society for Psychic Research.** Founded in 1925 in Boston by **Elwood Worcester** with the help of **William McDougall** after their break from the American Society for Psychical Research because they believed it was disregarding scientific standards, particularly in its support of Mina S. Crandon. With Worcester as its first president and **Walter F. Prince** its research officer and editor, the organization tried to regain and perpetuate those standards. Gardner Murphy was also a member of the Boston Society and Lydia W. Allison was its secretary. It is mainly noted for some brilliant publications (for example, works by Prince, J. B. Rhine and Allison). After Prince's death in 1934 the society began to flounder and, after a change in the administration of the ASPR in 1941 made it possible, the BSPR was amalgamated with that latter society.

**Bowditch, Henry Pickering, 1840–1911.** American physiologist. He was co-founder of the American Physiological Society. In 1884, Bowditch, then of the Harvard Medical School, became a member of a committee to consider whether a society for psychical research should be formed in the United States. Upon the formation in 1885 of the **American Society for Psychical Research,** Bowditch was on its council and was one of its vice presidents. He joined with William James in issuing a call for the formation of committees in the new ASPR to report on special subjects.

**Bozzano, Ernesto, 1862–1943.** Italian psychical researcher. Self-taught, he read widely in literature, philosophy, and science and demonstrated the defects, lacunae, and enthusiasms of this kind of education. Until 1891 a positive materialist (he idolized Herbert Spencer who was also self-taught), he became convinced of survival after death and the validity of Spiritualism as a result of a careful reading of the *Annales des Science Psychique,* a response by Charles Richet in defense of psychical research and a communication in 1893 through a medium from his adored dead mother of two lines of an inscription on her tomb.

Between 1899 and 1904, he sat with a group studying mediumship, including that of Eusapia Palladino who produced apparently genuine materializations. But he himself was not an experimenter. He lacked the scientific base and rigorous discipline necessary. Bozzano developed a systematic classification in an attempt to present "metapsychic facts in a theoretical system forming the basis of a new 'science of the soul'" (Alvarado, 1987:39). Between 1920 and 1930 he published many articles outside Italy in *Light, Psychic News, Revue Spirite, Revue Métapsychique,* and the *Journal of the American Society for Psychical Research.* In order to advance his Spiritualist beliefs and his "science of the soul," he collected hundreds of cases of haunts to show that apparitions are not limited to places where they once lived and that movements of objects suggest a physical presence (1920). He made a collection of cases of xenoglossy in which mediums seemed to speak and respond in real languages unknown to them (1932). He published as well an important study of deathbed visions (1923) and ethnographic accounts of paranormal manifestations among primitive people (1974).

The scathing criticism by **Theodore Besterman** (1930) of Bozzano's report on sittings held at Millesimo Castle in Savona was the direct cause of **Sir Arthur Conan Doyle**'s resignation from the Society for Psychical Research.

Bozzano included in his studies any published case, whether or not investigated and without regard for documentation and evidential value. "Bozzano basically considered psychic phenomena as objects to be classified . . ." and thought that he obtained "'legitimate and conclusive' proofs . . . for the phenomena through 'comparative analysis and convergence of proofs'" (Alvarado, 1987:42) based on a formula enunciated by Robert Dale Owen in 1861.

Bibliographically, Bozzano is considered of the highest importance and is looked on as one of the major figures to have emerged from Italian psychical research. His historical influence and importance are just beginning to be studied.

Selected Writings: *Popoli Primitivi e Manifestazioni Supernormali,* 1974; *Polyglot Mediumship,* 1932; *Phénomènes Psychiques au Moment de la Mort,* 1923; *Les Phénomènes de Hantise,* 1920.

BIBLIOGRAPHY: Alvarado, C. S. 1987. "The Life and Work of an Italian Psychical Researcher: A Review of *Ernesto Bozzano: La Vita e l'Opera* by Giovanni Iannuzzo." JASPR 81:37; Besterman, T. 1930. "Review of *Modern Psychic Mysteries, Millesimo Castle, Italy.*" JSPR 26:10; Dettore, U., ed., *L'uomo e L'ignoto,* 1979.

**Braud, William G., 1942–.** American psychologist and parapsychologist. Recipient in 1967 of a Ph.D. in experimental psychology from the University of Iowa, Dr. Braud's first professional involvement with parapsychology seems to have occurred during the years 1972 to 1974 when, as an associate professor of Psychology at the University of Houston, he served as a consultant to Edgar D. Mitchell and Associates. According to Dr. Braud, his major interests in parapsychology are the psychokinetic influences of living systems, psychic healing, and the laboratory study of psi-conducive states. In his profile he writes that he considers his major contributions to the field "psi facilitation through . . . relaxation and Ganzfeld studies. . . , studies of psychokinetic influences upon living systems, inertia and lability studies and models, role of autonomic arousal in psi, studies of psychological and psychic blocking and shielding of psi."

Since 1975, Dr. Braud has been senior research associate at the **Mind Science Foundation** in San Antonio, Texas, and during this same period has served as adjunct professor at several local colleges and was visiting professor of parapsychology at the Graduate School of Consciousness Studies at John F. Kennedy University in Orinda, California.

Dr. Braud has published articles on parapsychology in both parapsychological and other scientific journals, his most recent writing being a monograph entitled *Biological Psychokinesis: A Systematic Research Program* to be published by the Parapsychology Foundation.

Among other affiliations, Dr. Braud is a member of the American Association for the Advancement of Science, the New York Academy of Sciences, the Society of Neuroscience, the American Society for Psychical Research, the Parapsychological Association, the Biofeedback Society of Texas, and the Society for Scientific Exploration.

Selected Writings: 1987. "Dealing with Displacement." JASPR 81:209; "The Two Faces of Psi: Psi Revealed and Psi Obscured." In B. Shapin and L. Coly, eds., *The Repeatability Problem in Parapsychology,* 1985, pp. 150–182.; 1983. "Psychokinetic Influence on Electrodermal Activity." JP 47:95; "Lability and Inertia in Psychic Functioning." In B. Shapin and L. Coly, eds., *Concepts and Theories of Parapsychology,* 1981, pp. 1–36; "Psi Conducive Conditions: Explorations and Interpretations." In B. Shapin and L. Coly, eds., *Psi and States of Awareness,* 1978, pp. 1–41.

**Braude, Stephen, 1945–.** American philosopher. In the tradition of philosophers C. D. Broad, C. J. Ducasse and H. H. Price, Dr. Braude has recognized the relevance of psychical research and parapsychology to philosophy. His interest dates from his graduate student days at the University of Massachusetts from which he received his Ph.D. in 1972. There he wrote a dissertation on temporal logic, and "just for fun, . . . [he and some friends] held a seance during which [his] own table rose and nodded in response to questions." He put the whole question aside, however, for fear of jeopardizing his career and waited to pick it up again after he became tenured at the University of Maryland where he is an associate professor, and after he had made his reputation as a philosopher.

In numerous articles in scholarly and parapsychological journals and in his book *ESP and Psychokinesis* (1979), Braude has analyzed the complex philosophical and theoretical issues raised by parapsychology, the conceptual foundations of parapsychology, and what makes something paranormal. In his recent book *The Limits of Influence* (1986), Dr. Braude makes it clear that he regards most quantitative experimental work in the field of parapsychology as worthless because he believes that we have no idea why a given experimental result occurs or who the agent really is. For this reason he has turned to the physical mediums of the past who seem to have produced large-scale physical effects. The book on which he is presently working deals with multiple personality and will include the evidence for mental mediumship and survival.

Dr. Braude has also been a professional musician since 1961 and continues to perform and compose.

Selected Writings: *The Limits of Influence: Psychokinesis and the Philosophy of Science,* 1986; 1982. "Precognitive Attrition and Theoretical Parsimony." JASPR 76:143; 1981. "The Holographic Analysis of Near-Death Experiences: The Perpetuation of Some Deep Mistakes." *Essence* 5:53; *ESP and Psychokinesis,* 1979; 1979. "The Observational Theories in Parapsychology: A Critique." JASPR 73:349; 1979. "Objections to an Information-Theoretic Approach to Synchronicity." JASPR 73:179.

**"Bridey Murphy".** The name of a personality supposedly born in Cork, Ireland, in 1798 and who Ruth Simmons (pseudonym for Virginia Tighe) born in 1923 in Iowa remembered having been in a former life. The best-selling book *The Search for Bridey Murphy* (Bernstein, 1956) describes the author's use of **Past Life Regression** with Ruth Simmons. During the experiments, the hypnotized subject assumed the personality of the Irish girl, described scenes and details in her life which the subject, who had never been in Ireland, probably could not have known normally. The "search" was the search for the details that could be verified.

That many details were verified seemed to support the hypothesis of reincarnation, an idea distasteful to many Western religious and scientific people. The book therefore became the center of controversy. Critics debunked the book and offered many theories (as distinguished from evidence) to explain the possible sources of information about Ireland that the American woman might have tapped. One of the claims urged most strongly by psychologists and psychiatrists (Kline, 1956) was based on cryptomnesia: that the subject's memories of an earlier life were the submerged memories of the woman's childhood or of matters relating to Ireland that she had once read or heard about from people who were Irish or knew about that country.

The method used to regress the subject was to regress her first to her early childhood and then to her first year of age. The hypnotist then said: "Oddly enough, you can go even farther back. I want you to keep on going back and back and back in your mind. And, surprising as it may seem, strange as it may seem, you will find that there are other scenes in your memory. There are other scenes from faraway lands and distant places in your memory . . . and when I talk to you again you will tell me about it" (Bernstein, 1956:111). To this kind of coaxing and suggestion, it is said, the subject responded by dramatizing out of her memories the personality of Bridey Murphy. This theory, however, does not account for several obscure facts, such as the reference by the Irish girl to a tuppence, a coin used in Ireland only between 1797 and 1850, and the subject's correct mention of the names of a rope company and two grocers in Belfast not known even to experts. They were verified subsequently by an independent investigator. These facts do not necessarily establish either that "Bridey Murphy" had been reincarnated or that this was a case of possession by the spirit of the dead "Bridey Murphy." But they do suggest that, in all likelihood the subject did not come by her knowledge in any normal manner and that its acquisition was paranormal.

BIBLIOGRAPHY: Bernstein, M. *The Search for Bridey Murphy,* 1956; Kline, M. V., ed., *A Scientific Report on "The Search for Bridey Murphy",* 1956.

**Brier, Robert, 1943–.** American philosopher, Egyptologist, and parapsychologist. He became interested in parapsychology after reading Joseph B. Rhine's *Reach of the Mind.* He co-edited with Rhine a cross section view of research activities in parapsychology (Rhine and Brier, 1968) and in 1969 became a research fellow at the Institute for Parapsychology where he conducted investigations into extrasensory perception and psychokinesis. He also carried out interesting research on gambling to see if psi could be applied to practical purposes (i.e., winning at a roulette wheel), at craps, and at baccarat in a gambling casino (Brier and Tyminski, 1971).

He received his Ph.D. from the University of North Carolina and is currently the chairman of the Philosophy Department at the C. W. Post Campus of Long Island University. His interest in parapsychology continues, specifically in experiments with psychic Ingo Swann. Dr. Brier is a member of the Parapsychological Association and of the American Society for Psychical Research.

Selected Writings: *Precognition and Philosophy,* 1974; and Tyminski, W. V. "Psi Application." In J. B. Rhine, ed., *Progress in Parapsychology,* 1971, p. 36; and Rhine, J. B. *Parapsychology Today,* 1968.

**Bristol, John I. D., 1845–1932.** American insurance agent. Under his administration as president of the **American Society for Psychical Research** the prestige of the organization suffered. During the six years of his presidency which began in 1926, the ASPR was controlled by enthusiasts who had little regard for the scientific standards of investigation established by **James H. Hyslop,** who had personally managed it for over a decade.

BIBLIOGRAPHY: Berger, A. S. *Lives and Letters in American Parapsychology,* 1988.

**Brittain, Annie.** Early twentieth century British medium whose control was "Belle." Many impressive sittings were held with her. Among her numerous sitters were Sir Arthur Conan Doyle and Samuel G. Soal who reported that his interest in Spiritualism would have languished had it not been for her. In 1919, when he was a complete stranger to her, she asked him if he knew "Canuter" or "Canuder" because someone there wished to speak with him. In fact, "Canewdon" was a little village he knew well. It was near the home where he still lived and where his deceased brother Frank had lived. The medium also gave a good description of Frank together with his name. Soal recorded his "high opinion of her honesty and sincerity" (Soal, 1953).

BIBLIOGRAPHY: Soal, S. G. 1953. "My Thirty Years of Psychical Research." PSPR 50:67.

**Broad, Charlie Dunbar, 1887–1971.** Eminent British philosopher. Because of his international reputation, his lifelong interest in psychical research gave it a certain respectability. As early as 1920 he was a member of the Society for Psychical Research; he was its president in 1935–1936 and again in 1958–1960.

Although according to one of his students at Trinity College, Cambridge, Broad was "mild and cherubic and [played] with a yo-yo" and although he retained a boyish interest in model trains, he had a keen analytical mind and dealt brilliantly with the theoretical problems of psychical research. His early writings on paranormal phenomena dealt with their philosophical implications for an understanding of the nature of man. One of his most important contributions was his *Religion, Philosophy and Psychical Research* (1953) in which he set forth his **Basic Limit-**

**ing Principles** that he believed form the framework of belief in our Western technological society. Any event that conflicts with any of these principles is ostensibly paranormal.

He gradually became interested in the psychical research as such. He was also interested in the people involved in early research, especially Henry Sidgwick whom he admired, and he wrote long, unfortunately unpublished, essays on Edmund Gurney and F. W. H. Myers. He published a report on Gladys Osborne Leonard's mediumship in the *Journal of the American Society for Psychical Research* and on her mediumship and Mrs. Willett's in his *Lectures on Psychical Research.* This work also dealt with other aspects of psychical research, including what he called the **"Psi-Component,"** which he pictured "as a kind of highly complex and persistent vortex in the old-fashioned ether; associated (as a kind of 'field') with a living brain and nervous system and with events and processes in the latter . . . and capable of persisting . . . after the destruction of the brain and nervous system, as a vortex on the surface of a pond may persist after the dropping of a stone into the water." This psi-component, together with the physical component, he hypothesized, made up the human being. He was convinced of the existence of telepathy and felt survival of the psi-component was possible. He was uneasy, however, about what an afterlife might bring and hoped not to survive death. He died peacefully, in full possession of his faculties, in his rooms at Cambridge.

Selected Writings: *Lectures on Psychical Research,* 1962; *Personal Identity and Survival.* (The Thirteenth Frederick W. H. Myers Memorial Lecture), 1958; 1955. "The Phenomenology of Mrs. Leonard's Mediumship." JASPR 49:47; *Religion, Philosophy and Psychical Research,* 1953; *The Mind and its Place in Nature,* 1925.

BIBLIOGRAPHY: "In Memoriam: Professor C. D. Broad 1887–1971." 1971. JSPR 46:103; Price, H. H. 1954. "Professor C. D. Broad's *Religion, Philosophy and Psychical Research.* JASPR 48:56.

**Brookes-Smith, Colin H. W., 1899–1982.** British instrumentation engineer. Upon his retirement in 1960, he became a member of the Society for Psychical Research and devoted the remainder of his life to parapsychology. This work he considered his most important achievement. In 1966 he visited Kenneth J. Batcheldor's table-tilting group and thereafter devoted most of his research to table-tipping and levitation. Using Batcheldor's psychological methods, he conducted successful experiments whose aim was to make measurements during table levitations in the hope of interesting others in the application of instrumentation in that area. He created and built devices for this purpose that are described in articles in the *Journal of the Society for Psychical Research,* the most important one having been published in 1973. He also wrote handbooks of *Operating Instructions* and privately published a series of monographs on the subject.

Like William J. Crawford, Brookes-Smith thought in mechanical terms. He believed that table levitation might be caused by "a kind of 'hovercraft effect' . . . [or] that psychokinesis, even ESP, worked through the medium of some usually invisible, quasi-material substance (like 'ectoplasm')" (Batcheldor, 1982:404). He also conducted several long-range ESP experiments and felt that his results showed "a finite velocity of propagation and a fall-off in success with distance" (Batcheldor, 1982:404).

Brookes-Smith had studied engineering at University College, London, but did not receive a degree. After serving in the army at the end of WWI, he built what were then called wireless sets for the early days of broadcasting. His later work involving measuring rapidly varying mechanical phenomena was applied to his study of psychokinesis.

Selected Writing: 1973: "Data-Tape Recorded Experimental PK Phenomena." JSPR 47:69.

BIBLIOGRAPHY: Batcheldor, K. J. 1982. "Obituary C. H. W. Brookes-Smith." JSPR 51:403.

**Brougham, Henry Peter, 1778–1868.** English lawyer and Lord High Chancellor of England. One of the leading figures of his time, he contributed to politics, science, education, law reform, and literature.

In his autobiography, *Life and Times of Lord Brougham* (1871), he wrote that he and a friend had "actually committed the folly of drawing up an agreement, written with our blood, to the effect that whichever of us died the first should appear to the other, and thus solve any doubts we had entertained of the 'life after death.'" A few years later, at about 1 A.M., on December 19, 1799, Brougham stopped at an inn in Sweden. At about 2 A.M. while he was taking a hot bath, he saw his friend sitting in a chair calmly looking at him. How he got out of the bath, Lord Brougham did not know but suddenly he found himself sprawling on the floor. The apparition disappeared. On his return to Edinburgh, Lord Brougham received a letter from India announcing his friend's death there on December 19. Lord Brougham attributed this experience to a dream.

That he remembered the experience all his life is indicative that, if it was a dream, it was not an ordinary one. The case suggests that Lord Brougham, however unwilling, may be a **Noted Witness** to an apparition and compact which his friend tried to fulfill. The case also brings out the importance of distinguishing between a possible paranormal experience and ordinary sleep and underlines the mind-set of many people, such as Lord Brougham, to explain away such an experience as an ordinary dream. See also **Life After Death Pact.**

BIBLIOGRAPHY: Gurney, E. and F. W. H. Myers and F. Podmore, *Phantasms of the Living,* 1918, pp. 255–256.

**Broughton, Richard S., 1946–.** American parapsychologist. While serving as secondary school instructor at the Schutz American School in Alexandria, Egypt, from 1969 to 1971, he read widely. In the course of his reading he came across an article by Lawrence LeShan which aroused his interest in parapsychology. On his return to the United States in 1971 he took graduate courses at Seton Hall University from which he had received his B.A. degree in 1969 and continued his reading in parapsychology. In 1973 he applied for and became the Society for Psychical Research's Cutten Student in Parapsychology and, for the years 1974–1977, held the Perrott Studentship in Psychical Research (Trinity College, Cambridge) for Ph.D. work at the University of Edinburgh. In 1978 he was awarded his Ph.D. from that university for his thesis "Brain Hemisphere Differences in Paranormal Abilities with Special Reference to Experimenter Expectancies."

Dr. Broughton's main interests in parapsychology are computerized psi research, the investigation of psi ability in real life, and the study of the relationship between brain hemisphere specialization and ESP. At the University of Edinburgh with **Dr. John Beloff** he worked to develop the first computer "game" to test psychokinesis. In 1978–1979 as a visiting lecturer at the Parapsychology Laboratory at the University of Utrecht he developed widely acclaimed computer methodology for parapsychology experiments. In 1981, Dr. Broughton joined the Institute for Parapsychology as senior research associate and, in the absence of K. Ramakrishna Rao, acted as its director of research. In addition to his responsibilities for the research and educational activities of the institute, Dr. Broughton has developed two major lines of investigation. One project investigates factors leading to success in Ganzfeld studies; the other uses computer "game" tests to probe the unconscious use of PK and may lead to practical applications.

Dr. Broughton was president of the Parapsychological Association in 1986, is responsible for the management of the *Journal of Parapsychology,* and is an editorial consultant for the *Journal of the Society for Psychical Research.*

Selected Writings: "Brain Hemisphere Specialization and ESP: What Have We Learned?" In R. A. White and R. S. Broughton, eds., *Research in Parapsychology 1983,* 1984; "The Use of Computers in Psychical Research." In I. Grattan-Guinness, ed., *Psychical Research: A Guide to Its History, Principles and Practices,* 1982, Chapter 19; 1975. "Psi and the Two Halves of the Brain." JSPR 47:133; and Perlstrom, J. R. "A Competitive Computer Game in PK Research: Some Preliminary Findings." In R. White and J. Solfvin, eds., *Research in Parapsychology 1984,* 1985.

**Brown, Rosemary Eleanor, 1938–.** British automatist. The piano sonatas she claims come from the beyond seem authentic compositions to some and sour notes to others. With some piano lessons in her background as mother and office worker, Brown says that she is the agency through whom famous deceased composers, including Beethoven, Schubert, Chopin, Brahms, and Liszt, have dictated musical pieces. In a normal conscious state, she takes down these compositions note by note (Brown, 1974). The true origin of her music, which now can be heard in her piano album, vexes musical authorities. Some who have heard it believe that it is too technically flawed, banal, and lacking the touch of genius to be the work of its purported composers. Other musical experts think that the music is genuine and remarkable. If they and we accept the claim that the compositions come from musical communicators, we must also accept Brown's assertion that Chopin suspends his musical dictation long enough to tell her when her bathtub is overflowing and that Liszt stops playing his heavenly piano in order to advise her how to shop for bananas in the supermarket. We may also ask why German, Austrian, Polish, and Hungarian composers should have chosen a London widow to take down their music.

Possible counterhypotheses to the spiritistic one are that the music is a product of Mrs. Brown's subconscious mind or that we have here a case of cryptomnesia in which she recalls great music once heard but forgotten. Some might argue that Mrs. Brown has gained access to Akashic Records or cosmic memory where all events, including music, are supposed to be stored imperishably. Then again parapsychology might apply the field theory and suggest that Mrs. Brown uses her extrasensory perception to pick up musical traces from a psi field. The figures of Beethoven and the rest may be mediating vehicles that allow the information acquired by ESP to surface.

Whatever the real explanation and true source of Brown's musical compositions, the case is challenging and ripe for parapsychological study.

Selected Writing: *In Her Own Write: A Note on Rosemary Brown. The Rosemary Brown Piano Album,* 1974.

**Browning, Elizabeth Barrett, 1806–1861.** English poetess of the Victorian era. Her genius is reflected in her *Sonnets from the Portuguese* (1850), love poems written by an adoring poet-wife to an equally adoring poet-husband, **Robert Browning**. (He called her his "Portuguese" because she was dark.) He had first loved her verses and, although she was a semi-invalid, then had fallen in love with her as a woman and as an intellectual equal. Even before her famous love poems, she had been ranked with Tennyson, had translated the *Prometheus Unbound* of Aeschylus (1833), and had written *The Seraphim and Other Poems* (1838) and *Poems* (1844).

After her marriage she developed an interest in Italian politics (*Casa Guidi Windows* [1851]) and in slavery in the United States against which she protested in *Poems Before Congress* (1860). These interests were accompanied by a growing attraction to Spiritualism.

In 1855, the Brownings, then living in Florence, visited London. While there they attended a séance with Daniel D. Home during which raps were heard, table-tilting occurred, there were materializations of spirit-hands, and even the levitation from the table of a wreath of clematis that settled on the astonished poetess's brow. Although Browning was sure that it was all a delusion and that the medium had cheated, Mrs. Browning was convinced that the phenomena were real. Yet, to keep peace in the family, she could never again see or speak of Home in her husband's presence.

Her testimony as a **Noted Witness** to the séance and its manifestations deserves to be considered, however:

"I went with my husband to witness the so-called spiritual manifestations at Ealing. . . . The class of phenomena in question appears to me too numerous not to be recognized as facts. I believe them to occur often under circumstances which exclude the possibility of imposture. . . . [I]f you ask me (as you do) whether I would rank the phenomena witnessed at Ealing among the counterfeits, I sincerely answer that I may be much mistaken, of course, but for my own part, and in my own conscience, I find no reason for considering the medium in question responsible for anything seen or heard on that occasion. . . . You may be unaware that many persons . . . believe simply in the physical facts, attribute them to physical causes, and dismiss the spiritual theory as neither necessary nor tenable.

"This is not my view, however" (1903).

BIBLIOGRAPHY: "Mr. Browning on D. D. Home." 1903. JSPR 11:12.

**Browning, Robert, 1812–1889.** Great English poet. His works, including *The Ring and the Book, Paracelsus, Men and Women* and *Sordello* demonstrate learning, spiritual insight, dramatic monologue, and psychological analysis of characters. He was the husband of **Elizabeth Barrett Browning,**

the celebrated English poetess. She was a Spiritualist; he found Spiritualism repugnant. He believed that the spirits the adherents of this queer doctrine produced were frauds. He savagely attacked the famous medium D. D. Home who became the model for the deceitful Sludge in Browning's *Mr. Sludge the Medium.*

Yet in some areas of parapsychology his skepticism was shaken. In Florence, Italy, an Italian count who claimed to have paranormal powers asked him for a few personal articles. Browning gave him the gold studs he was wearing. The count held them in his hands and then spoke: "There is something here which cries out in my ear, 'Murder, murder.'" Browning said: "And truly those very studs were taken from the dead body of a great-uncle of mine, who was violently killed on his estate in St. Kitts, nearly eighty years ago." The skeptical Browning may be considered a **Noted Witness** to the phenomenon of psychometry or telepathy.

BIBLIOGRAPHY: Prince, W. F. *Noted Witnesses for Psychic Occurrences,* 1963.

**Brugmans, Henri J. F. W., 1885–1961.** Dutch experimental psychologist. He pioneered experimental research in parapsychology at the University of Gröningen where he was a professor of psychology. Gertrude Schmeidler thought his experiments there in 1919 with Gerardus Heymans to test for telepathy (1922) were well-planned and obtained an "astonishing result . . . 60 successes in 187 tries" (1958:7). But Sybo Schouten and Edward F. Kelly in 1978 reanalyzed these experiments and thought they could be explained by normal means or sensory cues.

In other imaginative experiments, Brugmans recorded physiological changes, such as skin resistance during some psi tests (1921), and found when he administered small doses of alcohol to a subject in other tests that the subject's scores were the highest ever recorded (1923). Brugmans's work is considered among the best in parapsychology prior to the advent of the experiments done by Joseph B. Rhine.

Selected Writings: 1923. "De 'Passieve Toestand' van een Telepaath door het Psychogalvanisch Phenomeen Gecontroleerd." *Overdruk vit Mededeelingen Der Studievereeniging voor Psychical Research* 7; 1922. and Heymans, G. and Weinberg, A. "Une communication sur des expériences télépathiques au laboratoire de psychologie à Groningue." *Compte Rendu Officiel du Premier Congrès International de Recherches Psychiques,* p. 396; 1921. "Some Experiments in Telepathy Performed in the Psychological Institute of the University of Groningen." *Compte-Rendu du Premier Congrès International de Recherches Psychiques.*

BIBLIOGRAPHY: Schmeidler, G. R. and McConnell, R. A. *ESP and Personality Patterns,* 1958; Schouten, S. A. and Kelly, E. F. 1978. "On the Experiments of Brugmans, Heymans and Weinberg." *European Journal of Parapsychology* 2:247.

**Bucke, Richard Maurice, 1837–1902.** Canadian psychiatrist. He is best known outside of psychical research and parapsychology as the author of the first major biography of his admired and close friend, the American poet Walt Whitman.

At the age of thirty-five, Bucke had a deeply moving, life-transforming experience during which he momentarily left his everyday world of sight, sound, and smell and entered a new dimension of consciousness far above his normal one. This experience made him see the universe in a fresh light. To this mystical experience, he gave the name **"Cosmic Consciousness,"** which became the title of his book lauded by William James. Bucke, who was president of the Psychological Section of the British Medical Association and professor of mental and nervous Diseases at Western University in Ontario, was so convinced of the significance of his experience that it became his preoccupation and led him over the next thirty years to seek out and study people who had had similar experiences. Bucke's prestige and work gave the mystical experience a value and seriousness it had never before had. Raynor C. Johnson saw Bucke's work as a "challenge . . . to those who are disposed to class the phenomena of mysticism with psychopathic manifestations of the human mind" (Johnson, 1953).

Selected Writing: *Cosmic Consciousness,* 1923.

BIBLIOGRAPHY: Johnson, R. C. *The Imprisoned Splendour,* 1953.

**Bull, Titus, 1871–1946.** American medical doctor and neurologist. As early as 1908, he worked with James H. Hyslop in the latter's experiments with Frederic L. Thompson. Later, Bull joined Hyslop in applying spiritistic methods of treatment to patients who were mentally dissociated and suffering from spirit "obsession" or possession. Bull believed that mentally dissociated minds provided an opportunity for telepathy from the minds of living people and from beings in the spirit world. In the latter case, although telepathy from "an adjusted member of the spirit realm" was relatively harmless, "a suggestion from a maladjusted disembodied spirit" (Bull, 1938) could be coercive and destructive. If a patient under the influence of an evil spirit could not be cured by orthodox medical techniques, Bull used a medium to make contact with the troublemaking spirit and try to persuade it to abandon its possession of the patient.

Bull was convinced that psychical research should be accepted as a legitimate branch of science. It must have support, he said, "in the same manner as other branches of investigation . . . before psychic phenomena can reveal their usefulness and purpose in the universe" (Bull, 1927).

Selected Writings: 1938. "Mental Obsession and the Latent Faculty." JASPR 32:260; 1927. "Resistance to Metaphysical Science." JASPR 17:645.

**Burbank, Luther, 1849–1926.** American originator of new flowers, trees, grasses, fruits, and vegetables. His experimental farms stimulated the growth of plant breeding. His personal experiences make him a **Noted Witness** to telepathy. He wrote: "I inherited my mother's ability to send and receive communications. So did one of my sisters. In tests before representatives of the University of California she was able, seven times out of ten, to recognize messages sent to her telepathically. My mother, who lived to be more than ninety-six years of age, was in poor health the last years of her life. On such occasions I never had to write, telephone or telegraph to [my sister]. Instead, I sent her messages telepathically, and each time she arrived in Santa Rosa, California, where I live, on the next train."

BIBLIOGRAPHY: Prince, W. F. *Noted Witnesses for Psychic Occurrences,* 1963.

**Burt, Sir Cyril, 1883–1971.** English psychologist knighted in 1946. He was famous for his work on the importance of heredity in the development of intelligence and the application of psychology to education. Like psychologists William McDougall and William James, he was strongly drawn to psychical research and parapsychology. He observed and assisted in **Samuel G. Soal's** experiments when Soal was a student in Burt's laboratory at University college where Burt was a professor. Burt also conducted research with mediums, collaborated with McDougall in some investigations, and, with James, felt that, insofar as personal survival after death was concerned, the Creator must have intended this department of nature to baffle us eternally. Although Burt was much impressed by the cross-correspondences, he did not regard this or any other evidence as establishing personal survival. Yet he thought that one result of parapsychological investigation was to demonstrate "in the face of confident denials of the materialists and the behaviourists, *at least the possibility* of survival in some form or other, though not necessarily in the form depicted by traditional piety or fourth-century metaphysics" (Burt 1967).

Much stronger was Burt's belief in the importance of extrasensory perception in relation to perception. He felt that "we ought . . . to interpret ordinary perception in the light of what we have learned about ESP" (1972). In an extremely significant paper delivered as the Seventeenth Myers Memorial Lecture (1968), Burt discussed the importance of psychology to psychical research.

Since his death, Burt has been revealed as a fraud who doctored data to support his work on the effect of heredity on intelligence and who appropriated the work of other people as his own. The strong case against Burt shows that fraud is a problem for psychology (and for other sciences as well) and is not limited to the field of parapsychology as some critics like to think. Whatever Burt may have done in psychology, however, does not eliminate or diminish his contributions to parapsychology.

Selected Writings: "The Implications of Parapsychology for General Psychology." In R. Van Over, ed., *Psychology and Extrasensory Perception,* 1972, p. 344; "Psychology and Psychical Research," 1968; "Psychology and Parapsychology." In J. R. Smythies, ed., *Science and ESP,* 1967, p. 61.

BIBLIOGRAPHY: Hearnshaw, L. S. *Cyril Burt-Psychologist,* 1979.

**Bury, Dennis, 1943–.** British accredited counsellor in higher education and Anglican parish priest. He has spent many years in the study of the paranormal and is co-founder of the Association for the Scientific Study of Anomalous Phenomena. As secretary to the Survival Joint Research Committee Trust, he arranges public conferences and develops experimental programs for its inquiries into the question of the survival of the human personality after bodily death.

**Bushmen, African.** The African world is a world of the paranormal. Mediums and possession by spirits are not uncommon. Apparitions of gods are frequent. But so are those of *bibendi,* dead human beings, who will seize people, principally women and children, as they walk along the roads, to take and keep them in towns occupied by *bibendi.* Apparitions of dead people are seen at night in cemeteries and are to be avoided, also.

Reincarnation is another belief held by the natives of Africa. An interesting notion is that a pregnant woman's deceased husband may be reborn as his own child so that the child would be the husband of his mother and his own father!

Folk healers practice their skills in Africa as elsewhere. The !Kung bushmen display their curative powers in group dances. Nonbushman groups in Rhodesia (Zimbabwe and Zambia), such as the Shona, also believe that diseases are inflicted on them by spirits, their doctors, or *nganga,* derive their curative powers from the spirits of dead relatives. Sometimes the *nganga* are possessed by a spirit or sometimes the patients are possessed by evil entities who cause them to suffer. In the latter case, the patients are exorcised to force the evil ones into a fowl or animal that is released later in the woods.

The out-of-body experience is suggested by numerous accounts of individuals having traveled during the night or the day before to a place impossible to reach by ordinary means. Other stories told by the African bushmen may be evidence of the acquisition of knowledge over great distances by telepathy or clairvoyance. One such story is of Cogaz who was sent by his father, Kaang, to a region occupied by baboons to find sticks in order to make bows. As Kaang slept, the son was killed by the baboons. On awakening, Kaang by "magic" knew his son's fate and set out after the baboons for revenge.

An illustration of telepathy comes from a report made by the director of Kenya National Parks. Several Africans in Tanganyika were living and hunting with lions. The local villagers believed that the lion-men controlled the animals with their thoughts. When the lions began to threaten and cause panic among the villages, one of the lion-men was put in jail. The accused man warned the chief that, if he was not set free the very next day, he would command the lions to attack the chief's cattle. His demand was refused. The following day, fourteen of the cattle belonging to the chief were found killed by the lions.

**Button, William Henry, 1871–1944.** American lawyer. Under his administration as president of the American Society for Psychical Research the organization was involved in a scandal that nearly wrecked it. The ASPR had been the staunch champion of Mina S. Crandon, the medium known as "Margery," in one of whose seánces fingerprints were allegedly left by her dead brother. Button was advised by a fingerprint expert that the fingerprints actually were those of a living person but refused to publish these findings. In 1935, when Frederick Bligh Bond was editor of the ASPR's *Journal*, he too came into possession of information that strongly suggested that the fingerprints were a fraud and felt it his moral duty to publish the facts. When Button denied his request to do so, Bond went ahead anyway with the publication to save the face of the organization. Button repudiated what Bond had done and fired him. In the furor that followed, many key members of the organization resigned. Although the ASPR was not totally wrecked, its reputation was severely injured.

Button served as the president of the organization from 1932 to 1941. During this time he supported Gardner Murphy's ESP experiments and helped bring Murphy recognition as an important figure in psychical research and parapsychology. But the seeds of revolt already had been planted and, in 1941, Button and those associated with him were ousted from office.

BIBLIOGRAPHY: Berger, A. S. *Lives and Letters in American Parapsychology,* 1988.

**Bux, Kuda, 1905–1981.** Pakistani (originally Indian) stage performer. Again and again, seemingly in trance, he paced up and down trenches of glowing beds of embers and coals. The heat was so intense that people near the trenches could not bear it yet Kuda Bux never burned his feet. Those observers who attempted to duplicate his achievement were badly burned in the blistering heat before they could go halfway. Bux repeated his exploit by walking through a bed of fire that Harry Price, the famous investigator, constructed to test him. Price had no explanation (Price, 1936). Kuda Bux maintained that without the technique of yoga he would not have been able to pass the fire tests, and it may be that an altered state of consciousness produces immunity to injury in these tests. Yet many people nowadays, including Larissa Vilenskaya, have walked over beds of coals without seeming to be in an altered state of consciousness.

Bux was famous also for his "eyeless vision." Experts would blindfold him or investigators would cover his eyes with sticky dough, plaster, and bandages, yet he could read any material presented to his uncovered nose. As long as his nose was not covered, he could "see." Perhaps he could see down the side of his nose although the precautions taken were meant to prevent this possibility. This additional skill contributed much to his success as an entertainer, but it did not make him a psychic. Today we are familiar with the phenomenon of dermo-optic perception. If he indeed read with his nose (instead of seeing through some crack in the blindfold or dough), the feat may be similar to reading with fingertips and need not be paranormal.

BIBLIOGRAPHY: Price, H. 1936. "A Report on Two Experimental Fire Walks." *Bulletin II, University of London Council for Psychical Investigation.*

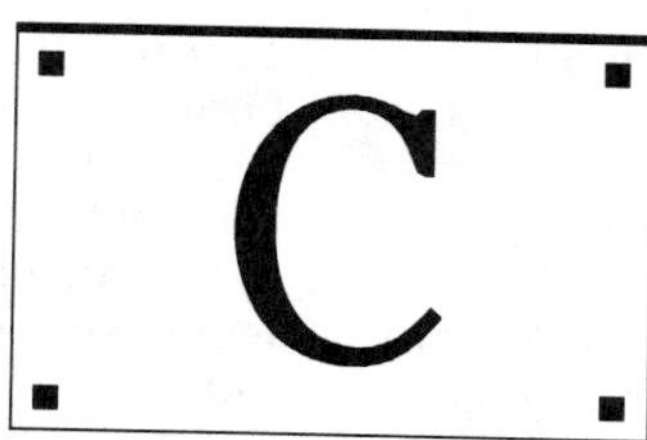

**Cabinet.** An enclosure in which a physical medium is seated and often fastened during a séance and from which, in due course, breezes, strange lights, or materializations may issue. The enclosure may be curtained, barricaded, or made of glass as it was in the case of Mina S. Crandon.

**Cadoret, Remi Jere, 1928–.** Canadian physiologist. He is important to parapsychology for having conducted some noteworthy experiments in extrasensory perception. In some he used the physiological approach to the subject. For example, he made electroencephalographic (EEG) recordings during tests of clairvoyance to see if there might be any correlation between the alpha rhythm activity of the brain of a subject and ESP performance (Cadoret, 1964). Cadoret was also one of the earliest experimenters to attempt to determine whether psi could be applied for practical purposes. He had a subject perform one ESP task and then used it to predict ESP performance in another task (Cadoret, 1955).

Selected Writings: 1964. "An Exploratory Experiment: Continuous EEG Recording During Clairvoyant Card-Guessing." JP 28:226; 1955. "The Reliable Application of ESP." JP 19:203.

**Cagliostro, Alessandro Conte di (Giuseppe Balsamo), 1743–1795.** Italian conjurer and con man. He lit up the sky of eighteenth century Europe with astonishing apparently paranormal powers that enabled him to predict the future by communicating with the dead and to diagnose and heal sickness. He also maintained that he possessed the alchemist's ability to transmute base metal into silver and gold.

After his marriage to the beautiful Lorenza Feluciani, they held themselves out as Count and Countess Cagliostro. Now in France he asserted that he had learned the secrets of Egyptian Freemasonry which promised all who joined the movement moral and physical benefits of which they had never dreamed. Handsome initiation fees charged their disciples seemed to assure the count and countess of luxurious lives among the cream of society until Cagliostro was suddenly imprisoned in the Bastille along with Cardinal de Rohan, bishop of Strasbourg, for his part in an intrigue in the court of Louis XVI and Marie Antoinette over a diamond necklace. Driven from France after his imprisonment, he went to Rome where he attempted to establish Freemasonry, an act for which, in 1789, his wife reported him to the Inquisition. Arrested by the Holy Office and tried for this offense, he was placed in the prison in the castle of San Leo where he spent his final days. He died lonely and forgotten and was buried in unconsecrated ground.

**Cahagnet, Louis Alphonse, 1809–1885.** Pioneering French Spiritualist. Using hypnosis ("animal magnetism") he was researching psychical phenomena before the formation of the Society for Psychical Research. The arch-skeptic Frank Podmore considered his methods of investigation beyond reproach.

He was a materialist and an atheist whose reading of **Emanuel Swedenborg** converted him to the latter's philosophy. In order to replicate Swedenborg's assertions Cahagnet "magnetized" a number of subjects and was amazed that sometimes they knew things they could not have learned normally. His best subject was Adèle Maginot Théodule whom Eric J. Dingwall, another arch-skeptic, considered an especially remarkable medium.

Cahagnet's purposes in his research were to explore the world of spirits and to obtain evidence that purported communications came from spirits of the dead and not from the mind of the medium. Several sensitives, including Adèle Maginot Théodule, described this spirit world in pretty much the same way, but this similarity could have been caused by suggestion of the magnetist, by an underlying likeness of all subconscious selves, or by the fact that all spirit teachings are based on Swedenborg. The communications that Adèle Maginot Théodule received, however, were amazingly accurate, even in what are now called proxy sittings, but are open to the same questions that mediumship must still answer: Are they communications from the dead or are they the result of the medium's ESP? Nevertheless, Cahagnet is said to have laid a secure foundation for demonstrating the survival of the "soul" after bodily death.

Selected Writings: *The Celestial Telegraph,* 1850; *The Sanctuary of Spiritualism,* 1851; *Arcanes de la Vie Future Dévoilés,* 1860.

BIBLIOGRAPHY: Anderson, R. I. 1984. "Cahagnet's Contributions to Psychical Research." *Theta* 12:74.

**Caldwell, Taylor, 1900–1985.** British writer of best-selling novels. She was psychic, believed in extrasensory perception and thought she had seen ghosts but was horrified by the prospect of reincarnation. "What person of intelligence," she asked, "could endure other 'rounds' in this dreadful existence in this most dreadful world?" (Caldwell, 1973: 316).

Yet the possibility that she had lived previous lives taunted her because she could find no explanation for material in her books she was certain did not come from episodes in her present life. There were, for example, correct historical descriptions in her books—such as *The Earth Is the Lord's* in which she wrote about Genghis Khan with such authority that scholars were astounded by the accuracy of detail; there was her correct description of Paris in *The Arm and the Darkness* though she had never been there; and there were her two medical novels "at which eminent physicians marveled for their accuracy" (Caldwell, 1973:319) although she had no medical education. Because she was anxious to see if reincarnation might be true, she consented to being regressed and was "astounded at what I had said" (Caldwell, 1973: 318). Under hypnosis, she had "remembered" having been a scullery maid to George Eliot and she spoke with an Irish brogue; she demonstrated knowledge of medicine and described a brain operation.

Taylor Caldwell said flatly, "I do not believe in reincarnation" (Caldwell, 1973:320). But her belief is unimportant. Her case has to be judged on its facts. All of her statements while regressed could have been unconscious fantasies. None of the details she gave were ever verified. And some of her statements under hypnosis and all of the material for her books might have had one of two paranormal explanations other than reincarnation: 1. The novelist gained her knowledge through extrasensory perception; or 2. cryptomnesia—although it is hard to pinpoint the exact books or individuals from which or from whom the information was derived. Mentioning these difficulties does not positively exclude the possibility that Caldwell's memories really came from prior lives. But they need to be weighed carefully before concluding that reincarnation accounts for her case.

Selected Writing: "Epilogue by Taylor Caldwell." In J. Stearn, *The Search for a Soul: Taylor Caldwell's Psychic Lives,* 1973.

**Call.** The guess made by a subject who speaks, writes, or points to indicate the target in an ESP experiment. See also **Extrasensory Perception.**

**Calvin, John (adapted from the French name Jean Cauvin), 1509–1564.** French Protestant reformer. His theological and ecclesiastical doctrines were major factors in the formulation of the doctrines of the Puritan religion in England and the United States and of the Reformed Church. His radical views forced him to leave France and to settle in Geneva where he wrote and enforced his dogmatic theological doctrines. On December 19, 1562, while confined to his bed with gout, Calvin told his followers that he heard the sound of drums (used in the wars of that time) and warned them that some vitally important event was then taking place. It turned out that on that very day the first great battle of the Wars of Religion was fought in France; the Huguenots in whom Calvin was intensely interested being badly defeated in a bloody struggle at Dreux more than 300 miles from Geneva where Calvin lived.

The event was of great importance to Calvin because it signified to him the defeat of Protestantism in France. Calvin's experience entitles him to be summoned as a **Noted Witness** in favor of telepathy from someone at the battle or of clairvoyance of the actual battle.

BIBLIOGRAPHY: Prince, W. F. 1920. "Peculiar Experiences Connected with Noted Persons." JASPR 14:362.

**Canavesio, Orlando, 1915–1957.** Argentinian physician. Deeply impressed by parapsychology, he used the electroencephalograph (EEG) to explore for relations between extrasensory perception and brain physiology. In 1946, he founded the Asociación Médica de Metapsíquica Argentina (Argentine Metapsychic Medical Association), the first organization formed anywhere that encouraged physicians to investigate ESP. He was also editor of the *Revista Médica de Metapsíquica* (Medical Journal of Metapsychics). Canavesio, chief of psychiatry on the Faculty of Medicine at the University of Córdoba, was made the head of the Instituto de Psicopatología de la Secretaria de Salud Pública (Institute of Applied Psychopathology of the Department of Public Health), an agency created by the government of Argentina with a parapsychological section. Its purpose was to determine whether Spiritualist activities in Argentina were injurious to the health of the population and to take steps to control Spiritualistic practices. Canavesio, the author of several important papers, was the only Spanish-speaking parapsychologist invited in 1953 to the University of Utrecht to make a presentation at the International Conference on Parapsychological Studies that was being held there. His work and his role in Argentinian parapsychology came to an end in 1957 when he was killed in an automobile accident.

**Carancini, Francesco, c.1863–1940.** Italian physical medium. His impressive phenomena were the subjects of glowing articles in Italian newspapers and commentaries in parapsychological publications such as *Annales des Sciences Psychiques.* These phenomena included apports, levitation, materializations, and writing in Latin and ancient Greek. Photographs were taken of floating musical instruments and of Carancini himself apparently levitated. But since all phenomena always were produced in absolute darkness, the medium was suspected of trickery. Yet, although Carancini was studied extensively by parapsychologists and scientists including Theodore Flournoy in Geneva and Everard Feilding who went to Rome, no trickery could be established. Then in 1909, after Carancini gave a series of séances in England at which Sir William Crookes and William W. Baggally were present, the medium finally was detected using his hands to produce the phenomena, all of which, it was concluded, had been fraudulently produced.

BIBLIOGRAPHY: Baggally, W. W. 1910. "Some Sittings with Carancini." JSPR 14:193.

**Card-Guessing.** This method of testing for ESP was used by **J. B. Rhine** and for decades was the principal investigating technique. It merely consisted of shuffling a deck of ESP cards and, using the **Basic Technique** or one of the other matching methods, required subjects to make calls. Since calls were either right or wrong and it was relatively uncomplicated to determine the mathematical odds against chance and to evaluate result statistically, this form of ESP experiment was simple and easy to conduct. In view of the objections to early experiments that sensory clues from experimenter to subject were invalidating experiments, techniques, such as **Screened Touch Matching,** were designed to eliminate such clues. But more difficult to overcome was the boredom most subjects felt after several runs with the unexciting cards. Nevertheless, card-calling tests represented a means of obtaining mathematical evidence and an objective demonstration of ESP. See also **Blind Matching Test; Down Through; Open Matching Test.**

**Carey, Ken.** Contemporary American channeler whose books are considered among the most beautiful and moving of channeled literature. The books, whose source is "Raphael" (or even Christ) tell us "that we are spiritual beings who are awakening . . . into the organic unity of a planetary species operating in harmony with the larger Creation. . . .[;] that we are the bridge between spirit and matter, Creator and Creation, between the spirit and the forms through which spirit flows. . . ." (Klimo, 1987:58).

BIBLIOGRAPHY: Klimo, J. *Channeling,* 1987.

**Cargo Cult.** A politico-religious phenomenon of New Guinea and Melanesia. Its leaders prophesy that material goods and gifts brought by the spirits of ancestors or tribal deities will be transported in ships or planes of the white race to make the natives rich without working for it. Such prophesies were made as early as the nineteenth century but were kindled and spread like wildfire in the twentieth because of the "Vailala Madness." It started in 1919 in Papuan New Guinea when a villager, while affected by convulsions, claimed the power to foresee that wealth would be brought to the people by an airplane, that all white men would be expelled and that a period of great happiness and plenty would dawn. Three years later, an airplane landed with gifts for the Papuans. The prophesy confirmed, other Papuans began to convulse and make predictions of cargos coming by ships and planes and the movement grew in intensity and swept through the southeast Pacific islands and beyond. Docks and airstrips were built to receive the expected cargos. The result was the mass neglect of regular sources of food (i.e., animals and gardening), and repressive measures taken by colonial authorities against the natives.

From the angle of psychical research, the prophesies are of no value as examples of precognition. Native jealousies of the white race with its civilization and riches and native hopes that whites would bring the islanders help and share great material wealth with them are at least a century old.

**Carington, Walter Whately, 1884–1947.** British psychical researcher. Born Walter Whately Smith, in 1933 he resumed the family name of Carington (from Carentan in Brittany). His interest was divided equally between science and psychical research. Even though he was very poor, he eventually refused a well-paying distinguished academic post in science to live in incredible poverty and hardship because he considered psychical research, to which he devoted all his time, the most important work in the world and the basis of a new metaphysic.

In December 1916 he had his first sitting with the mental medium Gladys Osborne Leonard who produced what he considered striking evidence. Later, he investigated the physical medium Kathleen Goligher and believed, and continued to believe, that at that time her phenomena were genuine. He also investigated the materializing medium Eva C. but was not convinced by her materializations.

Carington came to think that the continuing work with spontaneous cases and qualitative studies was a dead end and that researchers had to turn to quantitative methods. To that end he devoted four years (1935–1939) of daily work to a series of papers entitled "The Quantitative Study of Trance Personalities" whose ideas have been praised although his statistical methods have been criticized (Thouless, 1937). As a result of this study Carington concluded that controls are secondary personalities of the medium, but he also felt there was a case for the independent existence of the communicators.

He was anxious for telepathy to be demonstrated to scientists by a method they would consider cogent because he hypothesized that "a telepathic endowment . . . is a common property of the human race" (Murphy, 1947:127). He published many papers on the subject and demonstrated the **Displacement** effect. His book entitled *Telepathy,* most of which was written in just three weeks, gained immediate recognition. He had a lively way of writing: Fraser Nicol has said that his "words jump and dance on the page." His "conception is that all human minds are one mind, arbitrarily viewed by a sort of prism which artificially separates them. . . . This is, of course, a version of the theory of 'one big mind,' the doctrine developed by the sages of ancient India, by Plotinus, and by many Western mystics" (Murphy, 1947: 130–131).

Carington believed in a form of survival and wrote "that Conscious Existence does not terminate with the death of the body," but he did not believe in Spiritualism. He had developed a view of survival and of postmortem existence, the **Psychon Hypothesis,** which stated that "a cluster of associations belonging to a single mind . . . is only loosely hung together. . . . Post-mortem . . . psychon systems may well continue—and indeed under certain circumstances may in death make progressive consolidation. . . . The concept of a psychon system was in fact for Carington much more than a theory of mind; it was a theory of the cosmos." (Murphy, 1947: 130–131). At his death Carington was working on a definitive study of the subject, *Matter, Mind and Meaning,* his most ambitious creative work. **H. H. Price** subsequently edited and prepared it for publication.

His two most important papers were "Steps in the Development of a Repeatable Technique" and a paper on the Association Theory of Psychical Phenomena.

In 1940 Carington was awarded a Perrott Studentship in Psychical Research and a little later a Leverhulme Research Grant. He had been a pilot in World War I and was left in poor health for the rest of his life. In the late 1930s he carried out the daring rescue from Nazi Germany of the woman (Hedda Enders) who became his wife and helper in his research.

Selected Writings: *Telepathy: An Outline of Its Fact, Theory and Implications,* 1972; *Matter, Mind and Meaning,* 1949; 1934, 1935, 1937. "The Quantitative Study of Trance Personalities. Part I." PSPR 42:173; 43:319; 44:189; 1944. "Experiments on the Paranormal Cognition of Drawings: III. Steps in the Development of a Repeatable Technique." PASPR 24:3; 1944. "Experiments on the Paranormal Cognition of Drawings. IV." PSPR 47:155.

BIBLIOGRAPHY: Murphy, G. 1947. "W. Whately Carington: In Memoriam." JASPR 41:123; "Obituary: Mr. W. Whately Carington, M.Sc." 1947. PSPR 48:197; Thouless, R. H. 1937. "A Review of Mr. Whately Carington's Work on Trance Personalities." PSPR 44:223.

**Carlson, Chester F., 1906–1968.** American physicist. He invented the process of reproducing called xerography ("dry writing") developed by the Xerox Corporation which has come to be used universally and which made him a multimillionaire. His wealth went to support various causes, political, social, humanitarian. Surprisingly, because he always had been a materialist, parapsychology also benefited greatly from his philanthropy.

His conversion from materialism and his interest in parapsychology can be attributed to his wife, Dorris Carlson, who began to have psychic experiences in about 1948. One evening Carlson tried to have a psychic experience of his own. He sat in his chair by the fire, closed his eyes and for about twenty minutes concentrated on hearing a sound. All at once a sound like an explosion came from the center of the room so loud and real that it made his wife start and made a cocker spaniel who had been asleep on the floor leap up. (Carlson, 1969).

Now he began to read the literature of parapsychology and became convinced that extrasensory perception and other data related to spiritual dimensions in the human being. But he wanted more empirical data and he began to contribute large sums, especially to the American Society for Psychical Research, to support parapsychological research. His generous support broadened its areas of investigation, opened up new ones, and made possible the appointment to the ASPR of Karlis Osis as director of research with whom Carlson worked closely. He also served as a member of the ASPR Board of Trustees from 1964 until his death. After Carlson's death, the ASPR received his bequest of one million dollars and honored its benefactor by establishing the Chester F. Carlson Research Laboratory.

BIBLIOGRAPHY: Carlson, D. 1969. "The Beginnings of Chester Carlson's Interest in Parapsychology." PASPR 28:5.

**Carr, Bernard John, 1949–.** British researcher on cosmology and astrophysics. He is a lecturer at Queen Mary College, University of London, whose main interests in parapsychology are its relationship to physics and experiments in extrasensory perception and psychokinesis. He serves as vice president of the Cambridge University Society for Psychical Research and chairman of the Education Section of the Society for Psychical Research.

**Carrel, Alexis, 1873–1944.** French biologist and surgeon in the front rank of the intellectual and scientific world of his time. In 1904 he was a member of the Rockefeller Institute for Medical Research; in 1912 he was awarded the Nobel Prize in physiology and medicine; and in 1930, the Nordhoff-Jung prize for cancer research. He added to his achievements with his work on suturing blood vessels. Collaborating in experiments with the American airman Charles A. Lindbergh, he opened the way for future organ transplantation by keeping heart tissue alive in a test tube.

His best-selling book *Man the Unknown* pointed to the disparity between the sciences of inert matter and those of life, especially the biological sciences that are still ignorant about the nature of the human being. He argued that many important facts elicited by parapsychology should not be ignored. "At the present time, scientists who are concerned solely in the physical, chemical and physiochemical aspects of physiological processes still look upon telepathy and other metaphysical phenomena as illusions" (Carrel, 1935:40). Thus, Carrel became one of the few scientists of his era to recognize the existence and importance of extrasensory perception. "Clairvoyance and telepathy are a primary datum of scientific observation," he wrote. "Those endowed with this power grasp the secret thoughts of other individuals without using their sense organs. They also perceive events more or less remote in space and time. . . . Thus, knowledge of the external world may come to man through other channels than sense organs. It is certain that thought may be transmitted from one individual to another, even if they are separated by long distance. These facts . . . must be accepted just as they are. They constitute a part of the reality. They express a rare and almost unknown aspect of ourselves." (Carrel, 1935:124–126). Carrel became convinced of the phenomena, not because of the opinions of researchers or others, but because he "began their study when he was a young medical student . . . [and] made his own observations and experiments" (Carrel, 1935:124n).

Carrell's book not only stimulated interest in and study of parapsychology. It makes him one more **Noted Witness** whose testimony favors the acceptance of paranormal phenomena as new information to help us understand the nature of the human being.

Selected Writing: *Man the Unknown*, 1935.

**Carrington, Hereward, 1880–1958.** Anglo-American author and psychical researcher. Born in St. Helier, Jersey, UK, Carrington came to the United States in 1899. In 1900 he joined the American branch of the Society for Psychical Research. After Richard Hodgson's death in 1905, he became for three years James Hervey Hyslop's assistant. His *Physical Phenomena of Spiritualism*, which explained the fraudulent practices of physical mediums, appeared in 1907.

In 1908, he, Everard Feilding and, later, W. W. Baggally, all skeptics, were sent to Naples by the SPR to investigate Eusapia Palladino, the famous and controversial physical medium. Their report has been called "a classic of psychical research (Nicol, 1972)" and required reading for all skeptics (Beloff, 1985). A series of eleven sittings was held, of which Carrington attended ten. He came away convinced of the reality of some of the phenomena, particularly the touches by seemingly human hands while the medium's hands were controlled. He was also very impressed by the sound of a guitar string being plucked when it was out of the medium's reach and by a cool breeze that issued from the medium's forehead. After the sittings in Naples, Carrington organized an American tour for Eusapia, which proved to be a disaster.

In 1921 Carrington founded the American Psychical Institute and Laboratory. In 1923, in connection with a prize offered by the magazine *Scientific American* for a "visible physical manifestation," a committee composed of William McDougall, Daniel Frost Comstock, Walter Franklin Prince, Harry Houdini, and Hereward Carrington investigated the sensational medium known as "Margery" **(Mina S. Crandon)** who literally tore the ASPR asunder. Carrington was the only one of the committee who voted for the genuineness of her phenomena.

Carrington investigated many areas of parapsychology, including the poltergeist and other manifestations of psychokinesis. His interest in **astral projection** led him to publish several books with **Sylvan J. Muldoon** who reported on his Out-of-Body Experiences. He also carried on experiments (later criticized as showing an inadequate understanding of psychology) with **Eileen J. Garrett** that he thought indicated that her controls were separate, independent entities.

Selected Writings: *The Case for Psychic Survival*, 1957; *The Physical Phenomena of Spiritualism*, 1907; with Muldoon, S. J., *The Phenomena of Astral Projection*, 1951; with

Muldoon, S. J., *The Projection of the Astral Body,* 1929; with Feilding, E., Baggally, W. W., 1909. "Report on a Series of Sittings with Eusapia Palladino." PSPR 23:309.

BIBLIOGRAPHY: Beloff, J. "What is Your Counter-Explanation? A Plea to Skeptics to Think Again." In P. Kurtz, ed., *A Skeptic's Handbook of Parapsychology,* 1985; Nicol, F. 1972. "The Founders of the SPR." PSPR 55:341.

**Cassadaga.** A town located southwest of Daytona Beach, Florida, it is the site of one of the most famous Spiritualist camps in the United States. Mediums approved by the camp association, most with the protective title of "Reverend," give readings, what is called spiritual counseling, or perform unorthodox healing for a fee. A bronze plaque at the First Spiritualist Church there announces that the camp was founded in 1875 by one George P. Colby. Colby was supposed to have been led through the wilderness to the area where the camp is now located by three guides from the spirit world named "Seneca," "the Philosopher," and "the Unknown." They told Colby to establish a psychic center in the area. Colby did so especially since, the story goes, a prophesy had been made when he was a child that he would found such a center in the South and he aimed to fulfill it. Colby's three spirit guides may not travel to the site any more but today other spirits make the trip from their unearthly abodes as long as clients with money are willing to pay expenses.

**Cassirer, Manfred, 1920–.** German-born British parapsychologist. Former chairman of the Physical Phenomena committee of the Society for Psychical Research, his main interests are in unidentified flying objects, mediums, and spontaneous cases. Among his frequent contributions to the *Journal of the Society for Psychical Research* are articles on Eusapia Palladino (Cassirer, 1983) and Helen Duncan (Cassirer, 1985). Cassirer, who has a master's degree from Oxford University, is listed in *Who is Who in Western Europe.*

Selected Writings: 1985. "Helen Duncan: A Reassessment." JSPR 53:138; 1983. "The Fluid Hands of Eusapia Palladino." JSPR 52:105.

**Cassoli, Piero, 1918–.** Italian physician and parapsychologist. He was one of the founders of **Centro Studi Parapsicologia** (Center for Parapsychological Studies) in Bologna. Convinced that the scientific-experimental method of investigation should be followed in parapsychology, he organized and directs within the center a study and expermentation group to carry out careful examinations of paranormal phenomena and subjects who ask to be investigated.

He has been attracted to many branches of parapsychology including fire tests and precognition with which he experimented with financial support provided by the Parapsychology Foundation. His rigorous studies of mediums "uncovered many tricks, some trivial, others complex and shrewd" (Cassoli, 1971). As a physician, he undertook surgical operations under hypnosis (an appendectomy and tonsillectomy) with controls that excluded the possibility of fraudulent pharmacological intervention and achieved "positive and exceptional results." The road of his long career in parapsychology has not always been smooth, but, says Cassoli, "I continued working amid the difficulties, the disbelief, the distrust and continuous professional injury, for what in my opinion is, today more clear than ever, this wonderful but grievous ordeal, the study of parapsychology in Italy" (Cassoli, 1971).

Selected Writing: "Parapsychology in Italy Today." *Proceedings of an International Conference. Parapsychology Today: A Geographical View,* 1971, p. 187.

**Casteñeda, Carlos, 1925 (or 1935)–.** Pseudonym of the best-selling Brazilian (or perhaps Peruvian) author of reported teachings relating to the out-of-body experience and altered states of consciousness. Casteñeda claims to have been the pupil in Mexico of one Don Juan Matus, a Yaqui Indian sorcerer, who trained Casteñeda to become a "man of knowledge." Since the publication of Casteñeda's first (his master's thesis) and other books, doubt has been expressed concerning their factuality and whether Don Juan really exists. Few parapsychologists today are willing any longer to use Don Juan as an authority to buttress their discussions of out-of-body experiences and altered states of consciousness. However, if the mysterious Mexican mentor is fictitious, we should not be confused into thinking that these phenomena are also.

Selected Writing: *The Teachings of Don Juan,* 1968.

**Catherine of Bologna, Saint, 1413–1463.** Italian Abbess of the Franciscan convent of Poor Clares. Her writings have given spiritual inspiration for four centuries. She was canonized in 1712.

Catherine's is a startling case. On her death, she was not placed in a coffin, but simply laid in a grave in the ground. Soon a wonderful sweet smell was noticed at the burial site, and before long marvelous cures were reported there. The nuns of her convent asked for and, about three weeks later, received permission to disinter her remains. The new abbess recorded the following: "One of the Sisters seeing a little bit of skin, which hung from one of the feet, pulled it off, and instantly red blood flowed from out of the place, as if the body were alive. . . . Three months after death, she twice bled at the nose so copiously as to fill a cup with the blood."

The bleeding of a corpse after so much time had elapsed since death is a subject beyond medical explanation, but within the pale of parapsychological study. Assuming the trustworthiness of the accounts, Catherine belongs in the box as a **Noted Witness** for posthumous bleeding and **Incorruptibility.** See also **Bleeding, Posthumous.**

BIBLIOGRAPHY: Thurston, H., *The Physical Phenomena of Mysticism,* 1952, p. 285.

**Catherine of Genoa, Saint, 1447–1510.** Italian mystic of noble birth. Her spiritual writings are considered inspired and sensitive, and she was utterly devoted to helping the poor and sick. She was honored as a saint in 1737. Following the practice of other mystics, such as Therese Neumann, she went without eating for seventy days each year over a period of twenty years. In spite of these fasts, her mind and body were always vigorous.

Before her death, an eyewitness described how, when Catherine was experiencing great pain in her arm, "the arm grew more than one half a palm longer than it was by nature." The growth of an arm is less spectacular than the feats of D. D. Home by which he stretched his body by a few inches, but Catherine qualifies as **Noted Witness** for the phenomenon of elongation.

After she died her body manifested the puzzling state of **Incorruptibility.** Her body was buried next to a wall of the hospital church and left there. An old account tells how, after eighteen months, it was discovered that the burial site was always damp because of water running under the wall. Catherine was disinterred "and the holy body was found entire from head to foot without any kind of lesion."

BIBLIOGRAPHY: Thurston, H. *The Physical Phenomena of Mysticism,* 1952, p. 202, 344.

**Cayce, Edgar, 1877–1945.** American psychic known as "the sleeping prophet." His reputation is based mainly on his success as a healer. Given the name and address of the person (usually unknown to him and at some distant location) who wanted a reading, the entranced Cayce, speaking in a difficult and convoluted language that sometimes required "translation," would then diagnose the person's condition and prescribe treatment. The treatment was often a combination of salt packs and baths, massage, diet (an almond a day to prevent cancer, for example), herbs, and occasionally drugs. Jess Stearn (1967) writes that "Healthwise, Cayce had a virtually infallible record, when his recommendations were followed." Although this statement is an exaggeration, many people do seem to have been helped by Cayce. And today, through the work of the **Association for Research and Enlightenment (ARE)** at Virginia Beach, founded by Cayce in 1931 and carried on by his sons, people continue to follow the recommendations set out in his 30,000 or so medical readings.

Cayce also gave "life readings" in which he told people about their previous lives in, perhaps, Ireland, Rome, Syria, Peru, Atlantis (which he expected to resurface), and in our own early West. He prophesied cataclysms for the earth beginning in 1958. He also made predictions of political and economic events. These predictions were often wrong. "No one is served, certainly not Cayce's memory, by overstating the case for his prophetic abilities. However, Cayce's healing 'readings' . . . contained much seemingly precognitive detail . . . proved correct by subsequent events. . . . His astonishing health and life readings . . . demand further study. . ." (Ebon, 1968) writes an admirer.

Cayce's readings contained "literally volumes of archaeological and cultural-anthropological data" (Schwartz, 1978), but the first evidence of their validity was the discovery in 1947 of the Dead Sea Scrolls that verified what Cayce had been saying since 1934 about an Essene community at Qumran in what is today Israel. Other statements about Egypt and Persia that disagree with orthodox archaeology have yet to be tested.

A central idea running through Cayce's readings is that mind shapes our reality. Other ideas that were often repeated were that we all have a purpose to accomplish; that we can all heal ourselves; that our dreams offer us wisdom and guidance; that the body is the temple of the soul; that an understanding of our past lives will explain problems in this life.

Not everyone is an admirer, however. Critics say that Cayce's medical readings are often wrong (his misdiagnosis of J. B. Rhine's daughter is an often quoted example), that his treatments reflect his association with osteopaths and homeopaths, that his remedies include inventions of his own subconscious without any medical value, and that his metaphysics is "a confusing hodge-podge of Christianity, astrology, Pyramidology, Theosophy and other occult traditions" (Gardner, 1957).

BIBLIOGRAPHY: Ebon, M. *Prophecy in Our Time,* 1968, pp. 30–43; Gardner, M. *Fads and Fallacies in the Name of Science,* 1957, pp. 216–219; Schwartz, S. A. *The Secret Vaults of Time,* 1978, pp. 165–197; Stearn, J. *Edgar Cayce - The Sleeping Prophet,* 1967; Vahle, N. 1987. "The Spiritual Legacy of Edgar Cayce." *New Realities* 8(2):34.

**Census of Hallucinations.** The title of a landmark inquiry into waking telepathic experiences of the hallucinatory type among sane people. The Society for Psychical Research in Great Britain in the late nineteenth century asked: "Have you ever, when believing yourself completely awake, had a vivid impression of seeing or being touched by a living being or an inanimate object or of hearing a voice; which impression, so far as you could discover, was not due to any external physical cause?" From the 17,000 responses, it was ascertained that about ten percent of the population had such an experience. The inquiry represented the first attempt at statistical evaluation of spontaneous cases.

BIBLIOGRAPHY: "Report on the Census of Hallucinations." 1894. PSPR 10:25.

**Center for Scientific Anomalies Research.** Critics, such as the Committee for the Scientific Investigation of the Claims of the Paranormal, claim that parapsychology is a "pseudoscience." Sociologist Marcello Truzzi decided that parapsychology was included with occult beliefs because it was isolated from other areas of scientific research. He formed the Center for Scientific Anomalies Research in Ann Arbor, Michigan, in 1981 in order to promote better communication between critics and proponents of this research as well as to promote responsible and open scientific and skeptical inquiry into the claims of the paranormal and other anomalies. The organization publishes the *Zetetic Scholar.* Address: Prof. Marcello Truzzi, Center for Scientific Anomalies Research, P.O. Box 1052, Ann Arbor, MI 48106.

**Centro di Ricerca Psichica del Convivio (Psychical Research Center of the Convivium).** Italian organization in Rome that conducts investigations of mediums and, by various experiments, seeks to determine the identity and autonomous existence of discarnate communicators. The center also teaches a course on the research it and others have conducted and its theoretical implications for the survival and ultimate destiny of the human being. Address: Via dei Serpenti, 100, 00184 Rome, Italy.

**Centro Italiano di Parapsicologia (Italian Center of Parapsychology).** Italian membership and research organization established in 1960 by **Giorgio Di Simone** to carry out investigations of mediums and the hypothesis of human survival after death. Communications allegedly from "Dimension X" have been received in hundreds of medimistic sittings. The organization also distributes questionnaires on paranormal phenomena and holds monthly meetings and lectures to implement its educational program. It publishes *Informazioni di Parapsicologia.* Address: Via Poggio De'Mari, 16–80129, Naples, Italy.

**Centro Studi Parapsicologici (Center of Parapsychological Studies).** Italian organization founded in Bologna in 1954. Its organizers had broken away from a group known as "Centro Emiliano di Metapsychica" because it was too spiritistic for them and because they wanted to pursue statistical and experimental avenues of research. Since 1954 the center has arranged parapsychological congresses at the University of Rome, has persuaded the Italian medical journal *Minerva Medica* to publish articles on parapsychology, and, with its investigations of fire tests, palmistry, telepathy, and the use of drugs in parapsychological experiments, has become the most active organization of its kind in Italy. In addition to such investigations, since 1968 a "Gruppo di Ricerce e Sperimentazione" (Study and Experimentation Group) under the direction of **Piero Cassoli** that consists of graduate students in physics, biology and medicine has conducted experiments in unorthodox healing, mediumistic art, and the so-called "Geller Effect." The group also offers courses on parapsychology at the university level. Besides all these activities, the center offers lectures, holds public meetings and organizes major scientific meetings called "Giornata Parapsicologiche Bolognesi." It publishes *Bolletini,* a semiannual review for members, and *Quaderni di Parapsicologia,* the *Proceedings* of its annual congresses. Address: Via Valeriani, 39, 40134 Bologna, Italy.

**Chaffin Will Case.** A well-known and well-authenticated case in which a deceased person apparently took the initiative in order to convey information not known to any living person and to rectify a mistake. In 1905 James L. Chaffin wrote his own will in which he left everything to one of his four sons. He made no provision for his wife or other three sons. Fourteen years later, he apparently wrote out a second will to put things right but, instead of telling anyone about it, he placed the will in an old Bible and sewed a note in the inside pocket of his overcoat telling where the will was. After Chaffin died in 1921, the first will was filed in a North Carolina court by the son named in that will and duly probated. The other sons and the widow did not contest the will for the obvious reason that they did not know about the later will. Four years after the probate, one of the sons who was cut out of the 1905 will began to have vivid dreams about his father. In one of them, the father appeared to give him information about the location of the second will. The note was found in the overcoat as was the will in the Bible. The second will was probated in North Carolina and the old will annulled (Case, 1927).

The family insisted over and over again that they had never heard of the second will until the visitation from the spirit of old Chaffin. They believed the dead father had come back to right a wrong. A critical assessment of this case, however, may lead to other conclusions, among them, the possibilities of clairvoyance or forgery. (Berger, 1988).

BIBLIOGRAPHY: 1927. "Case of the Will of James L. Chaffin." PSPR 36:517; Berger, A. S. *Evidence of Life After Death: A Casebook for the Tough-Minded,* 1988.

**Chance.** The complex of undefined causal factors irrelevant to the purpose at hand (JP).

**Channeling.** The receipt of information purportedly from discarnate entities. Channeling is a direct descendant of mediumship and is related as well to shamanism and to religious prophecy. Mediumship as it has been studied in psychical research has noteworthy differences from channeling. The medium in trance is taken over by a **Control,** such as Gladys Osborne Leonard's Feda, Leonora Piper's Phinuit and "G. P." and Eileen Garrett's Uvani and Abdul Latif. The controls always claimed to be the spirits of deceased human beings, while the entities being channeled today often claim never to have been incarnate (Jane Roberts's **Seth**—the first modern channeled entity—and Jach Pursel's **Lazaris,** for example) but to be beings from another dimension. Some of them, such as J. Z. Knight's **Ramtha** and Alan Vaughan's Li Sung, do claim to have lived on earth, Ramtha some 35,000 years ago and Li Sung 1,200 years ago. The purpose of mediumship is to have the control bring the departed spirit of a sitter's loved one and to provide both solace to the bereaved and proof of the continuance of consciousness after bodily death.

Although some channeled entities give advice to individuals, their main purpose seems to be to deliver metaphysical messages and to provide inspiration. The "channeled material is clearly tuned to the culture and themes of the time" (Hastings, 1987: 153). Sometimes they make predictions, often about cataclysmic events: earthquakes, floods, pestilence, etc. These prophecies have usually been wrong. Different entities bring different messages. But all agree that "All human beings: Are fragments of the one source, the universal I Am. Reincarnate in order to choose each life situation. . . . Experience many different life sitations based on their needs . . . to [understand] . . . being in a physical body. May achieve inner peace and celebrative lifestyles. . . . Who are currently on the Earth plane have chosen to participate in the evolution of the Earth as it moves into the vibration of the Aquarian or New Age" (Nickell quoted by Vaughan, 1987:46).

In any event, channeling seems to be a phenomenon whose time has come. Channeled books outsell all others. Channeled entities, such as Lazaris, evidently fill a need and people are willing to spend large sums of money to hear "him," buy "his" audio and video tapes, etc. "He" is advertised as "a nonphysical entity whose immense wisdom, powerful techniques, and unparalleled concern for and understanding of people have transformed the lives of tens of thousands. Lazaris is there to love you when you are ready to be loved and to guide you on your Spiritual Journey Home" (Advertisement in *New Realities* 1987:7(6), 33). And groups have grown up around Lazaris, **"Seth,"** a **"Course in Miracles," "Michael,"** and "Ramtha," among others.

So who or what are these entities? Are they what they claim to be? Although mediumship was studied very seriously over many years, with the exception of a roundtable discussion of the subject at the 1986 Parapsychological Association convention, parapsychologists have been conspicuously absent from the channeling scene. Is it because researchers feel that the kindest thing that can be said about the channeled entities is that they are dissociated states, creations of the channelers' own subconscious or unconscious (much as the medium's controls are thought to be) and that in any event, even if they are not fraudulent, they are products of the "lunatic fringe" of the paranormal? **Charles Tart** thinks that the real reason is fear of possession (which which he equates channeling) and of psi in general (1987:159). But **Arthur Hastings** urges that "Studies of channeling phenomena are relevant to the nature of personality, depth psychology, models of nonphysical realities, and transpersonal processes [and that the] content is relevant to social themes and movements, spiritual teachings, and human potential" (1987:153).

BIBLIOGRAPHY: Hastings, A. "The Study of Channeling." In D. H. Weiner and R. D. Nelson, eds., *Research in Parapsychology 1986,* 1987; Klimo, J. *Channeling,* 1987; *New Realities.* 1987. 7(6): 25–44; Tart, C. "Psychological Resistance in Research on Channeling: A Discussion of the Channeling Panel." In D. H. Weiner and R. D. Nelson, eds., *Research in Parapsychology 1986,* 1987; Vaughan, A. 1987. "Channeling." *New Realities* 7(3):43.

**Charcot, Jean-Martin, 1825–1893.** distinguished French physician, medical clinician, and member of the French Academy of Sciences. Since Franz Anton Mesmer's day, hypnosis had been regarded with hostility by the scientific conventions of the time. In spite of the hypnotic cures he effected, Mesmer had been attacked and discredited by those conventions. Some years later, with the same spirit of intolerance, authorities at London University in England forbade John Elliotson, a professor of medicine, to use hypnosis in his experiments and forced him to resign. But then Charcot established a neurological clinic at the Salpêtrière Hospital in Paris for hysterics, a form of neurosis in which patients experience different bodily disorders. Charcot introduced and dared to conduct hypnotic experiments at the hospital. Through hypnosis and suggestion that their symptoms would disappear, he found that the symptoms of hysteria could be alleviated. It even became possible to hypnotize and then suggest to healthy people that they would suffer symptoms of hysteria and they did. The hypnotic experiments showed that bodily disorders can have psychological rather than organic causes.

**Sigmund Freud** studied under Charcot as did **Pierre Janet**. As a result of Charcot's work, hypnosis no longer lay beyond the pale. The French Academy of Sciences was compelled to accept it as a valid therapeutic tool. Hypnosis was established as a fact by Charcot who also helped stimulate and advance psychology and medical science. See also **Mesmerism.**

**Chari, Cadambur Tiruvenkatachari Krishnama, 1909—.** Indian scholar. He is one of the leading philosophers of parapsychology both in his country and in the world. His interest in parapsychology began when he was sixteen and read the works of William Stainton Moses. Over the years, parapsychology developed into "a passionate and absorbing hobby for me" (Chari, 1988). Because of this passion, he has written extensively on yoga, reincarnation, precognition, extrasensory perception, psychometry, cryptomnesia, poltergeists, psychokinesis, spontaneous cases, and Gladys Osborne Leonard—in short, about virtually everything parapsychology covers. Because of his perceptive papers contributed to the philosophical and parapsychological journals of the United Kingdom, France, Switzerland, Italy, Germany, and the United States, he has achieved his reputation as a foremost philosopher in the field of parapsychology.

He was chairman of the Department of Philosophy and Psychology at Madras Christian College, president of the Logics and Metaphysics Sections of the India Philosophical Congress in 1950, president of the Madras Psychology Conference in 1959, and consulting editor to the *Journal of Indian Psychology*.

Selected Writings: (January 4, 1988) Letter to authors; "Some Generalized Theories and Models of PSi: A Critical Evaluation." In B. Wolman, ed., *Handbook of Parapsychology*, 1977, p. 803; 1973. "Regurgitation, Mediumship and Yoga." JSPR 47:156.

**Chauvin, Remy, 1913—.** French ethologist (expert on animal behavior) and parapsychologist. His major interests in parapsychology are anpsi (animal psi), telepathy, clairvoyance, and psychokinesis. In 1960 he was a member of the French National Bee Laboratory, in 1961 became a visiting research consultant to the Parapsychology Laboratory at Duke University, and in 1964 was director of the Experimental Ethology Laboratory.

In 1959 he published the results of an exploratory investigation into the effect on subjects's ESP of their differing positions in relation to the target cards and, in 1961, a study that seemed to suggest that subjects scored better on large targets than on small. In 1968, under the pseudonym Pierre Duval, he published with Jean Mayer, who used the pseudonym E. Montredon ("Why," asked John Beloff [1969], "are our French Colleagues so bashful?") two "astonishing" papers on ESP in mice. His interest in anpsi continued and resulted in 1986 in a PK experiment with mice using the **Tychoscope.** His most recent paper (1988) deals with attempts to accelerate water cooling by psychokinesis.

Selected writings: 1988. "'Built upon Water' Psychokinesis and Water Cooling: An Exploratory Study." JSPR 55:10; 1986. "A PK Experiment with Mice." JSPR 53:348; and Montredon, E. (J. Mayer) 1968a. "ESP Experiments with Mice." JP 32:153; and Montredon, E. (J. Mayer) 1968b. "Further Psi Experiments with Mice." JP 32:260.

BIBLIOGRAPHY: Beloff, J. 1969. "Review of Periodical Literature 1968," JSPR 45:60, 72.

**Check.** Following the end of an ESP test, the determination of a score by matching the calls made by a subject with the targets. See also **Extrasensory Perception; Run Score Variance.**

**Chenoweth, Mrs. (Minnie Meserve Soule), 1867–1936.** American trance medium. Extensively studied by James Hervey Hyslop, who gave her the psuedonym Mrs. "Chenoweth," in early adolescence she began having precognitive dreams and after her marriage in 1897 began to hear names clairaudiently and to receive descriptions, later verified, of people unknown to her. She then began automatic writing during which she received messages from people long dead. Although she and her husband were Unitarians, they were introduced to Spiritualism during an experience with table-tilting. At that time Mrs. Soule began speaking automatically and turned out to be a gifted medium. She had several American Indian guides, one of whom, "White Cloud," was a healer who would prescribe herbs for Mrs. Soule's sitters. Her guide "Sunbeam" (called "Starlight" by Hyslop) spoke Choctaw (a language that, presumably, Mrs. Soule could not have known). Later she received communications from the Imperator Group who had supposedly also communicated through Stainton Moses and Leonora Piper.

From 1907 to Hyslop's death in 1920, Mrs. Chenoweth worked with him and eventually gave up her lecturing career to devote full time to research with him for the American Society for Psychical Research. Many of the studies of her trance communications, mainly produced by automatic writing, were published in enormous volumes of the *Proceedings of the American Society for Psychical Research*. One of Hyslop's purposes in working with Mrs. Chenoweth was to try to prove the identity of those purportedly communicating through her, and he did come to believe in the reality of her controls. Hyslop used Mrs. Chenoweth in the apparent case of possession of Frederic L. Thompson by the spirit of the artist Robert Swaine Gifford and in an attempt to learn whether it was the deceased Mark Twain who had dictated the books *Jap Herron* and *Brent Roberts* to mediums Mrs. Hays and Emily Grant Hutchings. She was the medium who produced evidential material from the "spirit" of "Emma Fischer" in the famous Doris Fischer case of multiple personality.

In 1920 Walter Franklin Prince found her good enough to be compared to the most famous mediums of the time, Gladys Osborne Leonard and Leonora Piper, and received through Mrs. Chenoweth evidential communications from his deceased wife. These experiments were reported by Lydia Allison and published by the Boston Society for Psychic Research.

Mrs. Soule had been a school teacher and had organized the Young People's Psychical Inquiry Club. Gertrude Tubby (1941) described her as "[s]imple but dignified, kind but firm, gentle but strong, a loyal friend and an uncompromising foe, a daring pioneer in the psychic science field, undergoing all required tests willingly . . ." (p. 39).

BIBLIOGRAPHY: PASPR Vols. 3, 4, 5, 6, 7, 9, 14 (1909–1920); Tubby, G.O. 1941. "Mrs. Chenoweth (In Memoriam)." JASPR 35:31.

**Chiaia, Ercole, ?–1905.** Italian Spiritualist. He rediscovered **Eusapia Palladino** after she had virtually vanished following the death of Enrico Damiani, her original discoverer. Chiaia resumed studies with her. In 1888 he published an open letter to **Cesare Lombroso** in which Chiaia stated that he was persuaded that the phenomena occurring in the presence of the medium could not be explained by natural laws and in which he invited Lombroso to a sitting with Eusapia. Lombroso finally agreed. Chiaia must be credited with having brought this medium to the attention of Lombroso and the scientific world beyond the confines of Neapolitan Spiritualism. Nicolas Camille Flammarion called Chiaia "the apostle of a good cause."

**Child, Irvin L., 1915—.** American humanistic psychologist, professor emeritus, Department of Psychology, Yale University. Possibly telepathic and precognitive experiences of his maternal grandfather stimulated an early interest in parapsychology that was reinforced when, in his teens, Dr. Child read Upton Sinclair's *Mental Radio.* He has found Gertrude Schmeidler's "sheep-goat" research and the attempts by Thelma Moss and Joseph Gengerelli to use emotional stimuli in ESP experiments extremely impressive. He considers worthy of careful consideration by parapsychologists and psychologists alike the work in the relationship of dreams to extrasensory perception (including precognition) carried on at the Maimonides Medical Center Dream Laboratory.

His own research has dealt with the relationship between a subject's errors in standard ESP tasks and in visual tasks and the effect of unbalanced target decks on ESP performance. In 1972 he made his first personal observations of what he took to be genuine ESP by a second-year law student who performed possibly precognitive tasks and PK tests successfully both at Yale and at J.B. Rhine's Institute of Parapsychology under fraud-proof conditions. Dr. Child considered these tests dependable repeatable evidence. He has therefore become less interested in testing for the occurrence of ESP than in attempts "to identify . . . the conditions that influence ESP. . . . To both kinds of research, I believe," he wrote (1973:201), "a humanistic approach contributes a great deal."

Dr. Child was president of the Parapsychological Association in 1981, has written analyses and reviews of parapsychological experimentation and of its critics, and has published approximately twenty-five articles dealing with parapsychology.

Selected Writings: "Criticism in Parapsychology." In S. Krippner, ed., *Advances in Parapsychological Research 5,* 1987; 1985. "The Question of ESP in Dreams." *American Psychologist* 40 (11):1219; "Implications of Parapsychology for Psychology." In S. Krippner, ed., *Advances in Parapsychological Research 4,* 1984; *Humanistic Psychology and the Research Tradition.* 1973.

BIBLIOGRAPHY: Berger, A. S. *Lives and Letters in American Parapsychology,* 1988; Sinclair, U. *Mental Radio,* 1930.

**Chi Square.** A sum of quantities, each of which is a **Deviation** squared by an expected value. Also a sum of the squares of CR's [**Critical Ratios**]. (JP).

**Chris the Wonder Dog.** A pet dog supposed

to be able to answer questions by pawing at the arm of its master to indicate its responses. When no sensory cues could be observed to guide the pawing of the dog and the premise of ESP was suggested to account for the dog's success, the Parapsychology Laboratory undertook an investigation of Chris in the 1950s. The highly intelligent animal learned a code for making calls of ESP cards (i.e., the dog would paw once for a circle, twice for a plus sign, etc). The dog's scores were significantly beyond mean chance expectation for one series of tests and then well below chance for another. This inconsistency plus the possibility that the human experimenters or the dog's owner might have used their own ESP and then unconsciously given sensory cues to Chris rendered the evidence in Chris's case, as it has been in the investigations of other animals, weak and insufficient for conclusions to be drawn. See also **Anpsi; Clever Hans; Lady Wonder; Missy.**

**Christ.** See **Jesus Christ.**

**Christian Parapsychologist.** A quarterly journal published in England by the **Churches' Fellowship for Psychical and Spiritual Studies.** It presents current developments in parapsychology and psychical research that may be of interest to Christians. The journal also provides comments on these developments from a theological viewpoint, book reviews, and letters from readers. The editor is The Venerable Michael Perry whose address is 7 The College, Durham DH1 3EQ, England.

**Christian Science.** A term probably invented by Phineas P. Quimby but, in its present form, begun in 1866 by **Mary Baker Eddy** who had been his pupil. In 1879, she founded the Church of Christ, Scientist, which is based on biblical teachings, a belief in an omniscient God as a universal Divine Mind, on fundamental Christian beliefs in the Resurrection, and in the deity (not the divinity) of Christ.

It is also a curative system outside of conventional medicine to heal disease by spiritual means. It regards medical intervention as erroneous and unnecessary. Basically, it holds that the antidote to all sickness lies in the immortal, Divine Mind, that we are not material beings but pure spirits who need not be attacked by pain or disease. There is in us a power to control our own health. Church publications contain over 50,000 testimonials to its healing of various disorders, including conditions diagnosed as terminal or degenerative. Some of these are astonishing, but it is not known how many, if any, of these have ever been evaluated by competent investigators.

People who believe in Spiritualism, Theosophy, or hypnosis are denied admission to the Church and those who intend or are determined to receive conventional medical treatment would not seek admission anyway. Nevertheless, membership in the Church has increased and branches of the movement have spread regularly since its founding throughout the United States, United Kingdom, Europe, and the Third World countries. Among the reasons for its appeal may be, as Bronislaw Malinowski said of Spiritualism and Theosophy, that its ministry of spiritual healing offers "a genuine response to a real need." It is also the only Christian Church where equality of the sexes is respected and women are active as practitioners and officers. The Mother Church, the First Church of Christ Scientist, is in Boston. The respected *Christian Science Monitor* is published by the Church.

The movement has been and continues to be the target of many criticisms from Christian and scientific quarters because of its fundamentalist doctrines and departure from traditional Christian teachings about creation. Christian Science practices, however—by which diseases of the body appear to be cured by the mind of a patient, or by which a healing practitioner distant from a patient may effect a cure—fall into the sphere of parapsychological interest. To dismiss apparently successful cases of healing with the explanation that they are only the therapeutic effects of "suggestion" does not entirely explain the matter. The healing process seems to be started by some unknown mental power or by some interaction between thought and body by which the mind controls the body. What is "suggested" is that there may reside in us some resource or ability that, under some circumstances, has the power to heal, but, as things now stand, an ability that still remains unknown and is a subject for investigation. A term such as "mind-cure" seems to express best the movements' basic curative principle of the power of mind over body.

**Christopher, Milbourne, 1914–1984.** American magician. He was at one time president of the Society of American Magicians and later chairman of its Occult Investigation Committee, a post once held by **Harry Houdini**. Christopher's interest in the paranormal started when he witnessed trickery practiced by mediums. Thus, he followed in Houdini's footsteps in searching for those who produce psychic phenomena by deception and in discrediting fraudulent claims of such phenomena. He included Uri Geller in this group. Christopher thought that Geller uses tricks and illusions to give the impression that his metal-bending is a paranormal feat. He was convinced that there are no genuine paranormal phenomena, that what passed for them can be produced by sleight of hand and various other methods used by magicians. He urged parapsychologists to consult with magicians who are familiar with parapsychological research and with the techniques that may be used by charlatans for producing spurious phenomena. It is generally agreed among parapsychologists that his advice is sound. There is a definite need for cooperation with magicians. But there are two qualifications: Cooperating magicians should have no vested interest in the results of any investigation, and they should receive no publicity as a result of it.

Selected Writing: *Mediums, Mystics and the Occult,* 1975.

**Churches' Fellowship for Psychical and Spiritual Studies.** British organization founded in 1953 "for the study of the wide reaches of the paranormal and extra-sensory perception in their relation to Christian faith." While some branches of the Christian Church from time to time have appointed committees to make inquiries into the relationship between parapsychology and the Christian faith, this is the first Christian body, albeit private, to recognize parapsychology and its phenomena. The CFPSS is a membership organization and anyone who is a practicing member of a church and believes in Jesus Christ may became a member. The organization publishes **The Christian Parapsychologist.** Address: St. Mary Abchurch, Abchurch Lane, London EC4 7BA, England

**Cipher Test.** Information that comes through a medium is sometimes considered evidence that the surviving spirit of a deceased person has communicated. A counterexplanation always is, however, that the medium, by telephathy, has read the mind of a sitter or other living person who knows the facts or, by clairvoyance, has "seen" a written document in which the information has been recorded.

The cipher test has been designed to avoid this objection. It consists of a message enciphered before death by an individual who intends after death to try to communicate the key word or words that will allow the enciphered message to be read. The key must not be known to any person alive (except the individual) and must not be recorded in any document. **Robert H. Thouless** is called the "father" of this test because he was the first to design such a test, which he based on the Vigenère method (Thouless, 1948). **Frank C. Tribbe** in association with Clarissa Mulders of the Survival Research Foundation devised another based on key quotations from standard reference works (Tribbe, 1980). **Arthur S. Berger** devised a third based on a key word selected from entries in a dictionary (Berger, 1987).

The basic premise of such tests is that, without the unrecorded key known to the communicator alone, enciphered test messages cannot be read. A posthumous communication of the correct key could not be explained away easily by telepathy or clairvoyance and would stand as strong evidence of postmortem survival. Berger (1980), however, conducted experiments to examine the basic premise of the tests. He demonstrated that some tests can be deciphered by false keys unless safeguards are adopted. See also **Dictionary Test; Life After Death Pact.**

BIBLIOGRAPHY: Berger, A. S. *Aristocracy of the Dead,* 1987; Berger, A. S. 1984. "Experiments with False Keys." JASPR 78:41; Tribbe, F. C. 1980. "The Tribbe/Mulders Code." *Journal of the Academy of Religion and Psychical Research* 3:44; Thouless, R. H. 1948. "A Test of Survival." PSPR 48:257.

**Circle.** A group of people who hold séances with a medium. In the séances, individuals sit in a circle around the medium, their hands or knees in physical contact in order to set up a claimed and undefined psychic energy to aid the medium or communicators to produce paranormal phenomena.

**Clairaudience.** The paranormal hearing of sounds or of voices, generally internal ones, through which information is sometimes obtained.

**Clairsentience.** A paranormal faculty or means of obtaining information other than through **Clairaudience** or **Clairvoyance.**

**Clairvoyance.** Night after night from June to September, 1888, a determined Nobel laureate conducted tedious experiments with a hypnotized woman. Charles Richet of France placed playing cards in opaque envelopes and carefully closed them. Then, without knowing which cards were in which envelopes, he handed them to the subject who named the card. Richet had worked out the mathematics of probability and knew that her successes in this experiment could not be explained by chance. He was sure that he had discovered a capacity to obtain knowledge that was entirely different from telepathy and which was absolutely unknown. He called it "lucidity" or "second sight." It has also been called "telesthesia" and "cryptesthesia" but today it is commonly called "clairvoyance." Although the term is often applied to all forms of ESP and is confused with seeing apparitions, with obtaining information about the thoughts of another, or with obtaining information via the out-of-body experience, its proper meaning, in keeping with its etymological derivation from the French—"clear-seeing"—is the faculty of getting information about physical objects or distant events of which no one else is aware.

The phenomenon of clairvoyance was known in antiquity. The Bible contains experiences that look very much like clairvoyance, for example, Samuel's knowing that Saul's father's asses, lost three days before, had been found (1 Samuel 9:20). And in the fifth century A.D., the Emperior Trajan tested the oracle at Baalbek who claimed to be able to read sealed letters without opening them by forwarding to the oracle a blank set of sealed tablets. He asked the god Jupiter to whom the oracle was dedicated to read them without opening them. The god's response was to return to Trajan, along with the sealed tablets that remained undisturbed, a blank sheet of papyrus. The experiment is not fundamentally different from the experiment Richet conducted in which his subject named cards hidden in an opaque envelope.

Richet's work was followed in 1920 by Gerardus Heymans of Holland and by Joseph B. Rhine in the United States. In more recent clairvoyance experiments Joseph Gaither Pratt, adopting Richet's technique of asking subjects to identity cards concealed in opaque envelopes, used concealed white and green cards to obtain highly significant results with Pavel Stepanek.

**Clairvoyance, Traveling.** The experience of observing while at a point in space outside the physical body. See also **ESP Projection.**

**Clairvoyant.** See **Psychic.**

**Clairvoyant Reality.** A term invented by **Lawrence Le Shan** to describe a level of reality, different from the normal everyday one, which is glimpsed during moments when extrasensory perception is occurring. In this reality, all and everyone are interrelated, time is different since the past, present and future exist equally and simultaneously, judgments of "good" and "evil" cannot be made, and information is passed, not through the senses, but by accepting the oneness of the reality in which all information circulates.

BIBLIOGRAPHY: Le Shan, L. *The Medium, the Mystic and the Physicist,* 1966.

**Clark, Walter Houston, 1902—.** American, professor emeritus of Psychology of Religion, Andover Newton Theological Seminary, and former president of the Academy of Religion and Psychical Research. He has pioneered in the investigation of psychedelic drugs, which he believes release spiritual development and experiences of a religious nature. In experiments with psilocybin, an active principle of a Mexican mushroom, he found his subjects having deep mystical experiences (Clark, 1969). His studies have convinced him also that religion and the paranormal are linked in many ways, as evidenced by the accounts of paranormal events in the Bible and the similarity between the attitudes of mystics and psychics toward reality (Clark, 1977). See also **Drugs, Studies of.**

Selected Writings: "Parapsychology and Religion." In B. J. Wolman, ed., *Handbook of Parapsychology,* 1977, p. 769; *Chemical Ecstacy: Psychedelic Drugs and Religion,* 1969.

**Clemens, Samuel Langhorne** See **Mark Twain.**

**Clever Hans.** One of the renowned Elberfeld horses in Germany, famous for his ability to spell, write, make mathematical calculations, tell time, and even indicate when the wrong musical chord was played on a piano. Hans's responses were made by shaking his head to indicate "yes" or "no," by tapping a foreleg on the ground, or by pressing his nose against alphabet blocks. To the horse was attributed either an intellectual capacity equal to any human being's or a power to use ESP to obtain the correct information from human minds. The more probable explanation for Hans's success, however, was that, while tapping, the horse would watch very closely the head and body movements of the person questioning him (Pfungst, 1965). When the horse's tapping reached the right answer, the questioner's head or body would change position unconsciously, and, even though slight, enough to signal the watchful Hans that it was time to stop tapping. When the questioner did not know the answer, the horse tapped on and on without stopping. See also **ANPSI.**

BIBLIOGRAPHY: Pfungst, O. *Clever Hans,* 1965.

**Clever Men.** In the aboriginal tribes of Australia, clever men are witch doctors who appear to possess both extrasensory perception and powers of psychokinesis and to use these abilities at will in order to practice black magic, obtain paranormal knowledge, or communicate with the spirits of the dead. Although the majority are males, some females are "clever" as well. In order to become initiated as a clever man, **Ronald K.H. Rose** reports that novices must endure sometimes painful physical rituals, including the pulling out of fingernails. They must enter into a trance, sometimes called "death," to seek help from the spirits of the dead. During the rituals, clever men may produce ectoplasm that they use to climb toward the sky. In spite of their apparent paranormal gifts and the respect in which tribal members hold them, clever men have no special privileges and apart from their powers are not distinguishable from the rest of the tribe. See also **Aborigines, Australian; Bone-Pointing.**

**Closed Deck.** A deck of ESP cards that contains twenty-five cards, five of each of the five symbols; star, circle, cross, square, and wavy lines. See also **Open Deck.**

**Cloud Busting.** The alleged distintegration of a cloud by the exercise of will power or psychokinesis. In 1955 in England, for example, several people including one Rolf Alexander claimed to have this ability. Alexander said that, in hundreds of demonstrations, he was able on any clear day to make a target cumulus cloud dissipate merely by staring at it and willing its disintegration while leaving unaffected control clouds next to it.

An ability such as this which others, including Wilhelm Reich, had claimed as well would have great implications for parapsychology, which is searching for the repeatable experiment, and for meteorology. Meteorologists, however, know that cumulus clouds in good weather generally disappear within fifteen or twenty minutes whether or not weather-psychics are staring at them so that, with the help of nature, anyone can be a cloud-buster.

In most parapsychological investigations, the claims made are generally difficult to test. This investigation of cloud busting was unusual because here a clear claim was made that could be easily verified or disproved. Unfortunately for the claimant, for parapsychology and for meteorology, it was disproved.

BIBLIOGRAPHY: Parsons, D. 1956. "Cloud Busting: A Claim Investigated." JSPR 38:352.

**Cock Lane Ghost.** A famous case dating back to 1762. It focused on the child Elizabeth Parsons who lived with her family in a house on Cock Lane in London. Raps heard near her bed or person attracted crowds and investigators. In answer to questions, the source of the noises, rapping once for "yes" and twice for "no," declared that its messages came from a young woman who had been poisoned by her lover who had been a lodger in the house. The belief prevailed that little Elizabeth was producing the raps by trickery, but there were those who replied that the raps were heard even when the child was asleep or tied up. The case is over two centuries old and still there is no agreement on the true origin of the mysterious sounds.

BIBLIOGRAPHY: Lang, A. *Cock Lane and Common Sense,* 1894.

**Cocteau, Jean, 1889–1963.** French poet, novelist, painter, surrealist, and director of motion pictures. He is considered the greatest many-sided artist of his time. In 1955, he was invited to become a member of the Academie Française.

Cocteau joins the ranks of famous artists who attribute their achievement to sources outside their control; he is a **Noted Witness** to the creative process. In the "Process of Inspiration" he wrote: "I do not believe that inspiration falls from heaven. I think it rather the result of a profound indolence and of our incapacity to put to work certain forces in ourselves. These unknown forces work deep within us, with the aid of the elements of daily life. . . . When the work that makes itself in us and in spite of us demands to be born, we can believe that this work comes to us from beyond and is offered us by the gods. . . . The poet is at the disposal of his night. His role is humble, he must clean house and await its due visitation.

"The play that I am producing at the Théâtre de l'Oeuvre, *The Knights of the Round Table,* is a visitation of this sort. I was sick and tired of writing, when one morning, after having slept poorly, I woke with a start and witnessed, as from a seat in a theatre, three acts which brought to life an epoch and characters about which I had no documentary information and which I regarded moreover as forbidding."

BIBLIOGRAPHY: Ghiselin, B. *The Creative Process,* 1952, pp. 81–82.

**Coffins, Disturbed.** Among the most bizarre cases in the records of psychical research are unexplained occurrences in cemeteries. The most noteworthy of these took place in Arensburg, a town on the large Baltic Sea island of Saarema (formerly called Oesel) now a part of the Soviet Union. Coffins had been placed side by side in a burial vault under a private chapel. When the vault was entered in 1844 on the occasion of a funeral, the coffins were found heaped one on the other. The coffins were restored to their original positions and the doors to the vault secured. Nevertheless the coffins were again discovered lying atop one another. The bishop of the province and the municipal authorities then made an official inquiry in the course of which the coffins were put once more in their original positions, the vault inspected for secret entrances and the floor of the vault and the stairs covered with a fine wood ash. The doors were locked again, sealed with official seals, and soldiers were posted to guard and watch the building. However, in spite of these precautions, the official investigators found on their return that the coffins had been scattered with some set up on end and one with its lid forced open. The seals on the door had not been broken and there were no footsteps in the ash covering the floor and stairs of the vault.

A possible paranormal explanation is the poltergeist which is famous for disturbances in buildings. A normal explanation could be underground waters that might have flooded the vault and caused the coffins to float. After the waters subsided, the coffins would have been in odd positions and the wood ash would have been left smooth and apparently undisturbed. Yet this explanation does not account for the forcing open of one of the coffins.

It is also interesting to recall that other cases of disturbed coffins have occurred for which neither floods, earthquakes, nor any human agency could have been the cause. Such a case took place a century later, in August 1943, in a cemetery in Barbados. A vault containing two coffins had been hermetically sealed by a brick wall. When it was opened for repairs a large lead coffin was found propped up against a wall. The other coffin had vanished altogether. All that remained of its former occupant was a skull and some bones on a ledge on the vault. The case remains a total mystery.

BIBLIOGRAPHY: "A New Case of Disturbed Coffins in the Barbados." 1947. JSPR 34:11; Wallace, A. R. 1899. "Mr. Podmore on Clairvoyance and Poltergeists." JSPR 9:22.

**Coleman, Michael Herder, 1927—.** British research scientist. He is chairman of the Survival Joint Research Committee Trust and has been a frequent contributor to the pages of the *Journal of the Society for Psychical Research* on a variety of topics ranging from the experimental aspects of extrasensory perception and psychokinesis to discussions of witchcraft, poltergeists, and mediums. His principal contributions have dealt with Sir William Crookes (1974) and Borley Rectory (1956).

Selected Writings: 1974. "William Crookes to Charles Blackburn." JSPR 47:306; 1956. "Borley Rectory: Some Criticisms." JSPR 38:249.

**Coleridge, Samuel Taylor 1772–1834.** English poet, essayist and dramatist. He wrote with a pen of such beauty, imagination, and mystery as to make him one of the most prominent figures in English literature. He was known also as a prose critic. Because of his *Biographia Literaria* (1817), he was acknowledged a critic of poetry superior to any. He was a brilliant conversationalist and lecturer and spoke and wrote on politics and religion. He thought of becoming a Unitarian minister. Had he not been diverted by his other interests, a terrible procrastinator and addicted to opium, he might have taken his place in the first rank of literature. As it was, however, he met and collaborated with William Wordsworth to publish *Lyrical Ballads* (1798) to which Coleridge contributed one of the greatest of English ballads, *The Rime of the Ancient Mariner,* as well as the *Nightingale,* and two scenes from his play *Osorio.* A year earlier, Coleridge had written his fragmentary masterpiece, *Kubla Khan.*

In *The Rime of the Ancient Mariner,* Coleridge displayed his leaning toward the paranormal. The ancient mariner and his shipmates see an apparition in the form of a female specter. Her skeleton ship is also a specter.

Again in his *Biographia Literaria,* he shows an interest in the paranormal. Coleridge described a case in Göttingen, Germany, of an uneducated girl who spoke Latin, Greek, and Hebrew. It seemed a remarkable case of xenoglossy until investigation showed that she had been employed by a Protestant clergyman who, while she was working in his kitchen, was in the habit of intoning aloud from Latin, Greek, and Hebrew books. Many of her utterances were from passages in the books.

But the real strength of Coleridge's testimony as a **Noted Witness** lies in his acknowledging a force or source beyond his will or control that led him to write his *Kubla Khan.* The creative process that produced fifty-four lines of the poem Coleridge described in "Prefatory Notes to Kubla Khan": "In the summer of 1797, the Author, then in ill health, had retired to a lonely farmhouse. . . . [F]rom the effects of [an anodyne] he fell asleep in his chair at the moment he was reading the following sentence . . . in 'Purchas's Pilgrimage': 'Here the Khan Kubla commanded a palace to be built, and a stately garden thereunto. And thus ten miles of fertile ground were inclosed with a wall.' The Author continued for about three hours in a profound sleep, at least of the external senses, during which time he . . . composed from two to three hundred lines . . . without any sensation or consciousness of effort. On awaking he appeared to have a distinct recollection of the whole, and taking his pen, ink and paper, instantly and eagerly wrote down the lines. . . ."

In another writing Coleridge admits that he had actually taken two grains of opium and fallen into a reverie. In any case, on waking from the sleep or reverie, he was writing down the 200 or more lines when someone on business called him away from his writing for more than an hour. When the visitor left, the remainder of the poem "had passed away like the images on the surface of a stream into which a stone has been cast, but alas! without the after restoration of the latter!"

**Collective Apparition.** See also **Apparition.**

**College of Psychic Studies.** Founded in 1884 in London by **William Stainton Moses,** and formerly known as the London Spiritualist Alliance, the aims of the college are to inquire into Psychic phenomena, provide a platform for lectures, hold workshops, give courses, and provide sessions with mediums. It publishes the magazine *Light.* Of value to researchers and archivists are Moses's papers and the records of the British National Association of Spiritualists and London Spiritualist Alliance stored here. The office of the college is at 16 Queensbury Place, London SW7 2EB, England.

**Coly, Eileen, 1916—.** American president of the Parapsychology Foundation. Her mother, **Eileen Garrett,** was the most famous medium of her time. As a child she had always trailed in her mother's shadow. She remembers "being subjected to dear old ducks asking, 'Do you have your mother's gifts, dear?' " (Pilkington, 1987). She reacted negatively to such questions and the patronizing attitudes of her mother's admirers. If she did inherit any of Eileen Garrett's psychic abilities, she deliberately repressed them. In fact, she said to herself, "No, no, no, I have no psychic gift, and I wouldn't want it anyway." (Pilkington, 1987).

But extinguishing any psychic abilities she might have possessed did not extinguish her interest in parapsychology. Although during her mother's lifetime she was not active in the field or in the Parapsychology Foundation her mother helped to establish, she was intimately familiar with its meetings and conferences and with the people in parapsychology. Telepathy and parapsychological research especially interested her. With her mother's death, Eileen Coly was precipitated into parapsychology and into the presidency of the Parapsychology Foundation. As its chief executive, her position is: "The research must go on . . . We can't stop because we haven't solved the mystery of psychic phenomena yet. It's got to be out there somewhere" (Pilkington, 1987).

BIBLIOGRAPHY: Pilkington, R. "Eileen Coly: Interview, January 20, 1986." In R. Pilkington, ed., *Men and Women of Parapsychology: Personal Reflections,* 1987.

**Coly, Lisette, 1950—.** American vice president of the Parapsychology Foundation. She oversees all of its activities and organizes its international conferences. She was drawn irresistibly into the field of parapsychology and into the Parapsychology Foundation because her grandmother was Eileen Garrett, the celebrated medium and co-founder of the foundation, and her mother is **Eileen Coly,** current president of the foundation. Although the foundation was not designed as a family affair, with Lisette Coly's entrance into it, it seems to have become one. The opportunity to brush shoulders with the leaders in the field whenever they came to the offices of the foundation where she had worked since 1972 also contributed to her entrapment by parapsychology. Lisette Coly also is associate editor of the foundation's *Parapsychology Review* and co-editor of the *Proceedings* it publishes of its annual international conferences.

**Combination Lock Test.** A test developed on the same principles as the cipher test in order to provide strong evidence of postmortem survival. In the lock test, a combination padlock of special design is left by an individual whose intention is to try to communicate, after death, its six-digit combination or a verbal key that will allow the lock to be opened. This correct communication will signal the individual's postmortem survival and identity. Neither the combination nor the verbal key have been told to anyone or written down. The secret verbal key can be a six-letter word or a six-word sentence selected by the individual. The letters of the word or sentence are translated into the numbers of the combination according to a formula provided by the designer of the test. Thus, the six-letter verbal key "living" can be converted into 29 29 47, to which a lock can be set and by which it can be opened again. See also **Life After Death Pact.**

BIBLIOGRAPHY: Stevenson, I. 1968. "The Combination Lock Test for Survival." JASPR 62:246.

**Combustion, Paranormal.** The sudden eruption of fire in a living human being in the absence of flame or heat from any source. In contrast to fire tests in which individuals demonstrate a total physical immunity to fire, in spontaneous paranormal combustion the bodies of people are completely consumed by flames even when other combustible matter remains unscathed. Thus, in 1904 in the United Kingdom, a woman was burned to ashes in a chair whose cushions were not even burned, and in India in 1907, the clothes worn by a woman destroyed by fire were not scorched and the room in which she died was unaffected. The phenomenon remains one of the most mysterious.

The nearest psychical research can come to an explanation is through its studies of the **Poltergeist.** This phenomenon generally is limited to damages and disturbances in houses. But vicious assaults have been noted from time to time against people who have been slapped, pinched, pulled, pushed, scratched, hit with bottles and clubs, even covered with excrement. Among the poltergeist phenomena are also outbreaks of fire. The poltergeist has made some objects burn and not others and ignited fires in one part of a house and not in another. Perhaps a **Poltergeist Agent,** consciously or unconsciously intending to harm a victim, might cause the victim to burst into flames while leaving other combustibles untouched.

BIBLIOGRAPHY: Mitchell, J. and Rickard, R. J. M. *Phenomena: A Book of Wonders,* 1977, pp. 34–35.

**Committee for the Scientific Investigation of the Claims of the Paranormal.** Headed by Paul Kurtz, a professor of philosophy at the State University of New York, scientists and philosophers organized this committee because they were driven by a concern that a mounting wave of public gullibility over pseudoscientific beliefs, such as astrology and other (to them) implausible subjects, was threatening rational thought and the scientific outlook in the United States.

Parapsychology, included in the list of occult beliefs and practices condemned by the group, was singled out as trying to introduce into modern science metaphysics, and particularly, the "soul" and Cartesian dualism that science has rudely rejected. The object of the committee is to question critically many of the claims of the paranormal, to suggest normal alternative explanations, and to urge the mass media to scrutinize more critically the claims of the paranormal before presenting them to the public. When NBC-TV offered as "documentaries" programs on the "Bermuda Triangle" and "The UFO Incident," the committee filed a complaint with the Federal Communications Commission. The committee also objected to articles on parapsychology carried by the *Reader's Digest* on the ground that they were misleading.

The committee does not disguise its hardline scepticism and has been charged frequently, both by people inside the committee as well as outside, with being unfair and with carrying on a debunking "crusade" against parapsychology and the individuals who work in the field. The organization's journal is the *Skeptical Inquirer.* Address of the committee: P.O. Box 229, Buffalo, New York, 14215-0229. See also **Skeptics.**

**Communicator.** Purportedly the discarnate personality of a deceased human being that manifests itself or communicates directly with the living through a mental medium, or communicates indirectly with the living through the mental medium's control.

**Conley Case.** Classic case, frequently cited to support the survival hypothesis. In this case the apparition of a dead man revealed the location of money that no living person knew about. In 1891, Michael Conley, a farmer in Iowa, died in a place distant from his home. His filthy clothes were removed at a morgue in this distant place before the body was brought home. On its arrival, one of his daughters fainted. When she recovered, she asked: "Where are father's old clothes? He has just appeared to me and told me that after leaving home he sewed a large roll of bills inside his grey shirt with a piece of my red dress and the money is still there." A search for the clothes found them still in the morgue, and when the gray shirt was examined, the roll of bills was discovered sewed inside it with a piece of red cloth (Myers, 1892).

BIBLIOGRAPHY: Myers, F.W.H. 1892. "On the Indications of Continued Terrene Knowledge." PSPR 8:200.

**Control.** A purported deceased personality apparently and habitually in control of the speech or actions of a mental or physical medium. This personality, as general communicator, purports to describe other discarnate personalities or to transmit messages from them through the medium.

One of the most famous controls was Mrs. Gladys Osborne Leonard's "Feda." The control spoke with her own peculiarities and preserved her individuality throughout every sitting. When the medium entered into a trance, her own individuality seemed to fade into Feda's. When a communicator was supposed to be giving her a message, Feda (i.e., the medium) would lean forward as if listening carefully and then would tell a sitter how the communictor looked and what was being said. A typical example was one of Helen de G. Salter's sittings where Feda described a communicator as "a bit thin, a bit of a cough. His nose comes out, it's bent down a little. He's been good-looking. The eyebrows are brown, a little arched, the hair brown, the temples bare, have a bony look. 'Arthur' [is his name]." Mrs. Salter allowed that this was a good description of her dead father. Another sitting with Mrs. Salter illustrate how Feda transmitted messages: "He says he's met an old friend lately . . . he means a man, not a lady." In C. Drayton Thomas's sitting with Mrs. Leonard, Feda described how the messages came to her from communicators: "They try any way, feeling, seeing or hearing, but Feda finds feeling the easiest."

On those occasions when ostensible communicators other than the control are communicating directly through a medium, a control seems to function as a master of ceremonies to assist them in their attempts at communication.

In 1900, the able Eleanor Sidgwick carefully investigated the mediumship of Leonora

Piper and concluded that the medium's control Phinuit and other *soi-disant* personalities appearing in her trances, were Mrs. Piper's own trance personality or dream personality, conveying information she had fished from sitters or learned from them by ESP. The great majority of psychical researchers today, following Mrs. Sidgwick's hypothesis, tend to believe that a control is not the independent intelligence of a surviving spirit of some deceased person, but the medium herself. Much as in cases of split personalities studied by psychiatrists such as Morton Prince, the control is thought to be a secondary personality of the medium formed around a center of repressed material. See also **Trance-Control.**)

**Control Experiment.** In order to determine whether results in quantitative ESP experiments can be explained by chance, one method is to calculate the deviation from mean chance expectation. Another, which has the advantage of avoiding such mathematical calculations, is to set up a "control" experiment that resembles the ESP experiment in every way with the one difference that the scoring results must be attributable to chance and not to any ESP process. J. B. Rhine pioneered one of the earliest control experiments by merely shuffling a pack of ESP cards and seeing if there was any correspondence between the pack and calls made through ESP.

BIBLIOGRAPHY: Thouless, R. H. *Experimental Psychical Research,* 1963.

**Cook, Florence Eliza (later Mrs. E. E. Corner), 1856–1904.** British physical medium. W. H. Salter believed that there was no single episode in psychical research more important than the sittings held between December 1873 and May 21, 1874 by William Crookes with Florence Cook. And there is little doubt that, without the endorsement of the famous scientist Crookes, Florence Cook would have been merely a footnote in the history of psychical research as is her sister **Kate Cook** who allegedly produced the same sorts of phenomena.

Young and pretty, Florence (called Florrie) originally gave private sittings for wealthy Spiritualist Charles Blackburn who supported her and her family and later sponsored her sister Kate. Her principal phenomenon, vouched for by Crookes, and the *ne plus ultra* of physical mediumship, was the production of the full-form **Materialization** "Katie King," the daughter of **"John King"** (allegedly the spirit of the pirate Sir Henry Morgan). Florrie's Katie King was seen together with Florence Cook herself and was therefore claimed to be something or someone other than the medium—the interpretation, according to Spiritualism, being that Katie King was the materialized spirit of a once-living human being. On the other hand, Dutch parapsychologist George Zorab, while accepting the reality of the materialized Katie King, does not believe "she" was a spirit; he thinks she was a double of the medium. (A rival Spiritualist medium, Mrs. Agnes Guppy, was supposed to have plotted to have acid thrown in Katie King's face in the hope of exposing Florence Cook as the "spirit" and at the same time destroying her beauty.) Prior to Crookes's beginning his investigations, there is conflicting evidence about whether or not Florence Cook had been detected impersonating Katie. The crucial incident in the Crookes-Cook sittings was the report by Crookes himself of having seen "Katie" and another materialization, "Florence," (the control of Rosina Showers), walking arm in arm in his laboratory. Although Crookes later concluded that Rosina Showers was a fraud, he never seems to have thought that if Rosina Showers was a fraud so was Florence Cook.

"Katie King" was reported to have departed on May 21, 1874 and was succeeded by "Leila" and then by "Marie." On January 9, 1880, Sir George Sitwell took hold of "Marie" and found himself holding Florence Cook clad in her underwear. Florence Cook was also caught cheating in June 1899, in Warsaw. Nevertheless, Charles Richet was convinced that Katie King was a genuine materialization.

Forty-five years after Florence Cook's death, one F.G.H. Anderson told the Society for Psychical Research that he had at one time been her lover and that she had confessed to him that her phenomena had been fraudulent, the sittings with Crookes having been held to conceal their illicit affair. The French author, Jules Bois, told much the same story to Eileen Garrett. The Anderson statements in the SPR files were the basis of Trevor Hall's allegations in *The Spiritualists* (1963) put out by Eileen Garrett's publishing house that the Crookes-Cook séances were fraudulent and a coverup for their affair.

Since some of the investigations were conducted under very stringent conditions (the best of them not being mentioned by Hall who relies on "innuendo, irrelevant detail, avoidance of relevant detail, and transparently fallacious arguments" [Braude, 1986]), the question remains whether Florence Cook's phenomena were fraudulent, and, if they were, if Crookes knew it. (The *Journal of the American Society for Psychical Research* in its issues of October 1963 (57:215), January 1964 (58:57), and April 1964 (58:128) contain a running argument on this question.) See also **Cox, Edward William.**

BIBLIOGRAPHY: Beloff, J. "George Zorab and 'Katie King.'" In F. W. J. J. Snel, ed., *In Honour of G. A. M. Zorab,* 1986; Braude, S. E. *The Limits of Influence,* 1986; Hall, T. H. *The Spiritualists: The Story of Florence Cook and William Crookes,* 1963 (reissued as *The Medium and the Scientist,* 1984); Medhurst, R. G. and Goldney, K. M. 1964. "William Crookes and the Physical Phenomena of Mediumship." PSPR 54:25; Salter, W. H. 1962. "Review of The Spiritualist." JSPR 41:372; Thouless, R. H. 1963. "Correspondence. Crookes & Cook." JSPR 42:203.

**Cook, Kate Selina (The second Mrs. E. E. Corner), 1859–1923.** British physical medium. The younger sister of **Florence Cook,** Kate Cook—who was described as "decidedly *spirituelle* in appearance"—from 1875 to 1891 produced manifestations similar to those of her older sister, including a full-form **Materialization** ("Lily" or "Lillie Gordon") who, just as with Florence, was seen at times together with the medium. It is said that Kate's manifestations were fraudulent, her sole purpose being to bilk the wealthy Spiritualist Charles Blackburn. He did, in fact, support her and her family and, at his death, left them, with the exception of Florence, the bulk of his fortune. W. Stainton Moses sat with Kate on October 27, 1878, and was convinced that she and the alleged spirit were one and the same. Yet F. W. H. Myers sat with her on numerous occasions from 1878 to early 1882, and she supposedly produced phenomena similar to D. D. Home's and Stainton Moses's.

In 1907, three years after Florence's death (and as soon as it was legally possible in England to do so because of a new law), her widower married Kate and upon Kate's death inherited what was left of Charles Blackburn's fortune.

BIBLIOGRAPHY: Medhurst, R. G. and Goldney, K. M. 1964. "William Crookes and the Physical Phenomena of Mediumship." PSPR 54:25.

**Coombe-Tenant, Winifred.** See "**Willett, Mrs.**"

**Cooper, Blanche,** See **Soal, S. G.**

**Cooperator.** In psychometry, the individual associated with the physical object from which information is sought by ESP and who may verify the correctness of any information obtained.

**Coover, John Edgar, 1872–1938.** American experimental psychologist. His apparently valid but mistaken scientific report in 1917 on extrasensory perception undermined scientific interest in parapsychology. Coover, the first Fellow in psychical research appointed by Stanford University under a gift from **Thomas W. Stanford,** was also the first representative of a large American university to conduct a serious experimental investigation of telepathy and clairvoyance. With an agent in one room and a percipient in another, he carried out well-designed experiments with decks of forty playing cards. Ten thousand trials with 100 students from his psychology classes were reported by Coover in a 600-page volume in 1917. In the report, Coover presented the results as negative and only at chance.

Since the report was so large and detailed and filled with impressive statistics, and, in addition, since it came out of a prestigious university department of psychology, it was regarded with great respect by the scientific community. It had the natural effect of discouraging further investigation into extrasensory perception and of strengthening already existing hostile attitudes toward parapsychology on the part of academic psychologists and others. It turned out, however, that Coover's conclusion was completely erroneous. Several independent evaluators, including Robert H. Thouless (1935), found hidden under a cover of statistics that Coover's results from his experiments actually were significantly above chance.

It is difficult to say now how really fair-minded Coover had been when he reached his conclusion. Perhaps he simply would not report evidence favorable to extrasensory perception. He is known to have written to the president of Stanford University that his research dealt with material "offensive in the nostrils of my fellow psychologists" (Mauskopf and McVaugh, 1980:50). Joseph B. Rhine suggested that Coover reached a conclusion opposite to the true one because he "was under a great deal of stress because of the critical attitude of psychology in his day" and so he "concealed the significance of his findings" (Rhine, 1977). Whatever the truth, Coover's work was one of major influence for a long time. It is also of interest for another reason. Undoubtedly Coover was extremely skeptical. His having obtained positive results gives the lie to a hypothesis commonly accepted by skeptics that only those who believe in the paranormal obtain favorable evidence while skeptics always obtain chance or negative results.

Selected Writing: *Experiments in Psychical Research,* 1917.

BIBLIOGRAPHY: Mauskopf, S. H. and McVaugh, M. R. *The Elusive Science,* 1980; Rhine, J. B. "History of Experimental Studies." In B. Wolman, ed., *Handbook of Parapsychology,* 1977, p. 25; Thouless, R. H. 1935. "Dr Rhine's Recent Experiments in Telepathy and Clairvoyance and a Reconsideration of J. E. Coover's Conclusions on Telepathy." PSPR 43:24.

**Cornell, Anthony Donald, 1923—.** British councilor in Cambridgeshire County and president of the Cambridge University Society for Psychical Research. During the last quarter century, he has established himself as an investigator of haunts, apparitions, and poltergeists and has conducted experiments to see how many people claim to have observed a ghost or apparition (Cornell, 1959). He has made, as well, investigations of strange bangs, crashes, and creaks in a farmhouse for which he could find no normal explanation (Cornell and Gauld, 1960). With **Alan Gauld,** he is co-author of an important critical analysis and assessment of the poltergeist phenomenon (Gauld and Cornell, 1979).

Selected Writings: 1959. "An Experiment in Apparitional Observation and Findings." JSPR 40:120; and Gauld, A. *Poltergeists,* 1979; 1960, and Gauld, A. "A Fenland Poltergeist." JSPR 40:343.

**Corroboration.** Since reports of spontaneous cases depend primarily upon the statements of people who may be: 1. emotionally involved in their experiences or those they claim to have witnessed; 2. may be mistaken or merely credulous; or 3. may be exaggerating a story for purposes of publicity or money, psychical researchers must always try to obtain independent evidence of the trustworthiness of these reports. Witnesses and relevant documents must be examined. Occasionally, such careful investigations show that a case, apparently valuable on its face, is a deliberate hoax, as was the claimed communication from a soldier supposedly killed in action who, after inquiries were made, turned out to be nonexistent.

BIBLIOGRAPHY: "A Fictitious Communicator." 1924. JSPR 21:306.

**Cosmic Consciousness.** A consciousness of the life and order of the cosmos; a higher level of consciousness "not simply an expansion or extension of the self-conscious mind with which we are all familiar, but the superaddition of a function as distinct from any possessed by the average man as *self*-consciousness is distinct from any function possessed by one of the higher animals" (Bucke, 1923). The term also is the title of a book by **Richard M. Bucke** in which he described an experience he had had while riding in a hansom. With his mind calm and peaceful yet flowing with ideas and images, he experienced what he labelled a "cosmic consciousness: a subjective flash, a great joyousness accompanied by an intellectual illumination" that made him aware of the life and order of the universe and of the immortality of the soul. It lighted up the rest of his life. Gardner Murphy believed that what really happens in individuals to give rise to such creative or mystical experiences has something in common with paranormal experiences and that efforts should be made to investigate that possibility. In view of the numerous reports of creative people and of mystics having had paranormal abilities or experiences, there may be a close connection between the creative, the mystical and the paranormal.

BIBLIOGRAPHY: Bucke, R. M. *Cosmic Consciousness,* 1923.

**Cosmic Memory.** A concept that can be described as the mind of a deity or, in this age of computers, as a super-mundane computer memory bank that constitutes an imperishable storehouse of information about every act and thought that has occurred since the beginning of time and which can be retrieved. Like the notion of Akashic Records, cosmic memory serves as a convenient counterhypothesis for cases of retrocognition, reincarnation, and communications from the dead. All evidential material otherwise supporting such cases can be attributed to the cosmic source of information to which some people whose psi or consciousness have reached high enough levels have gained access and from which they have been able to retrieve "memories."

**Counseling, Parapsychological.** Therapeutic support for people who, having had psychic experiences, have difficulty in understanding or integrating these experiences into their lives. The result can be fear or emotional or mental disorder. Generally, the essential steps in the counselling procedure are: to listen carefully to the individual's description of the experience, assure the individual that other people have had the same type of experience and that it is not a sign of insanity, identify the kind of experience and inform the person what is known about it, and finally to confront the emotional reactions resulting from the experience. The aim is to support the troubled person and to encourage him or her to see what happened with emotional balance.

BIBLIOGRAPHY: Hastings, A. 1987. "Therapeutic Support for Initial Psychic Experiences." *ASPR Newsletter* 13(2):11.

**Course in Miracles, A.** A 1,200 page book in three volumes (Volume 1: Text; Volume 2: Workbook for Students; Volume 3: Manual for Teachers) channeled through Helen Cohn Schucman, a professor of medical psychology in the Psychiatric Department of Columbia University College of Physicians and Surgeons in New York City. She was an atheist who did not believe in paranormal phenomena.

Beginning in 1965 she heard an inner voice that kept repeating. "This is a course in miracles. Please take notes." She did take notes, which she says were not automatic writing; she was taking dictation from this inner voice. The "material provide[s] an extraordinarily clear attempt to explain the maya, or illusionlike nature, associated with our day-to-day ego, which we are told we mistakenly take to be our true and only self. At the same time, the material pictures the larger spiritual reality within which our true identity resides . . ." (Klimo, 1987:38). Volume 2, the workbook, provides an exercise for every day of the year. The three volumes, published in 1975, merely by word of mouth have sold hundreds of thousands of copies in the United States, and in 1985 were introduced into Britain.

Many readers, but not James McHarg (1986) or Renée Haynes (1982), are deeply impressed. Dr. McHarg, a psychiatrist, was unable to plow through the entire work and questions the soundness of its teachings. Ms. Haynes dismisses it as "a sort of Do-It-Yourself Psi" having nothing to do with God or prayer.

The source of the material remains a question. Some contend that the author is Christ. Others feel that Helen Schucman was tapping into her own higher Self, some universal source, or her own subliminal mind. She herself came to believe that the Christ Spirit was the source of the material and that its message was love. She died in 1981.

BIBLIOGRAPHY: Anon. *A Course in Miracles,* 1975; Klimo, J. *Channeling.* 1987, pp. 37–42; Haynes, R. 1982. "Are Unusual Phenomena Signs of Holiness?" *The Christian Parapsychologist* 4(6): 179; McHarg, J. 1986. "A Course in Miracles." *The Christian Parapsychologst* 6:109.

**Coven.** A group or meeting of **Witches** and wizards, usually thirteen: six males, six females, and a high priestess.

**Cox, Edward William, 1809–1879.** British Spiritualist and investigator of the physical phenomena of Spiritualism. A barrister of the highest rank comparable to a doctor of civil law (serjeant-at-law),—he was always referred to as Serjeant Cox—he founded a Psychological Society that studied the physical phenomena associated with Spiritualism.

He worked closely with William Crookes in the investigation of the medium D. D. Home, but parted company with Crookes when it came to the latter's endorsement of Florence Cook. Cox believed her to be a fraud because he had been present (as Crookes had been) at a joint materialization by her and Rosina Showers of their controls Katie and Florence. In a lengthy letter Cox said: "I have seen the forms of Katie and Florence together in full light, coming out from the room in which Miss Cook and Miss Showers were placed. . . . They were solid flesh and blood and bone. They breathed, and perspired, and ate. . . . On that occasion there was nothing . . . but the bare assertion of the forms in white that they were not what they appeared to be . . . and that the real ladies were at that moment asleep on the sofa behind the curtain . . ." (Hall, 1962). Cox repeatedly urged that the only way to be sure that the materializations were not the mediums in costume was to open the curtains and see and touch the entranced mediums, but this was never done.

Serjeant Cox also tried "to give articulate expression to the current metaphysics of the Spiritualists . . . without having recourse to disembodied spirits. . . . Serjeant Cox . . . attributed the phenomena in which he believed . . . to the extra-corporeal action of the human soul" (Podmore, 1897). Several of Cox's cases from *The Mechanism of Man* (1876) were incorporated in *Phantasms of the Living* written by Edmund Gurney with F. W. H. Myers and Frank Podmore.

Selected Writings: *The Mechanism of Man, an Answer to the Question "What Am I?"* 1876.

BIBLIOGRAPHY: Hall. T. *The Spiritualists,* 1962; Podmore, F. *Studies in Psychical Research,* 1897.

**Cox, William Edward, 1915—.** Mechanical engineer, semi-professional magician, and parapsychologist. An interest in magic led him, in 1932, to parapsychology and J. B. Rhine's works. From 1957 on, Cox began to devote most of his time to experiments in psychokinesis. At about the same time he became a research associate at the Parapsychology Laboratory at Duke University and later of the Institute for Parapsychology. Although it has been said (Brian, 1982:253) that "much of Cox's work has a certain wild, almost Alice-in-Wonderland quality . . . [for example] his investigation to see if Nature is benevolent . . . [o]r his construction of a bubble-producing machine to test the power of mind over matter. . . ," Charles Honorton in his Presidential Address to the Parapsychological Association in 1975 remarked that PK research would probably have died in the 1940s had Ed Cox not "nurtured" it for almost twenty years.

As the "bubble-producing machine" shows, Cox has invented numerous PK testing devices. In 1951 he introduced the widely used **"PK-Placement"** method and adapted the **Majority-Vote Technique** for use in PK tests. The *European Journal of Parapsychology* (1978) referred to Cox's creative and ambitious work in PK research, and in 1957 he won the Society for Psychical Research's prize for the best and most original essay on parapsychology. He is nowadays, however, known for his work with the **SORRAT** experiments, principally with a wide range of physical effects—direct writing, inflation of balloons, apports, metal-bending, etc.—inside a "mini-lab", a sealed aquarium tank. These experiments have been severely criticized. Cox, however, writes (1985:28): "[L]et my reputation as a specialist in quantitative and qualitative PK perish if clear and unrestricted evidences are ever found in favor of outright fraud at Rolla", Missouri, where the mini-lab was located.

Author of over fifty articles on parapsychological subjects, Cox was a founding member of the Parapsychological Association and served on the Board of Trustees of the Foundation for Research on the Nature of Man. See also **Bierman, Dick.**

Selected Writings: 1985. "An Invited Rebuttal to George Hansen's 'Critique' of Mr. Cox's Mini-Lab Experiments." *Archaeus* 3:25; 1979. "A Comparison of Two Machines Using Water Bubbles as PK Target." JP 43:44; 1957. "The Influence of 'Applied Psi' upon the Sex of Offspring." JSPR 39:65.

BIBLIOGRAPHY: Berger, A.S. *Lives and Letters in American Parapsychology,* 1988; Brian, D. *The Enchanted Voyager,* 1982; Honorton, C. "Science Confronts the Paranormal." In *Research in Parapsychology 1975,* 1976, p. 213.

**Crandon, Le Roi Goddard, 1873-1939.** American physician. A medical doctor (he was graduated from Harvard College in 1894 and obtained his medical degree in 1898), he was intensely interested in psychical research. At a séance held five years after his marriage to **Mina (Stinson) Crandon** and attended by his wife, himself, and four other people, table-tilting took place. After that Mina Crandon developed rapidly as a physical medium over the next years during which she seemed to produce an assortment of paranormal phenomena that made her into a sensation. Crandon was stage manager at all her seances and was the most persevering and eloquent of all who defended her against critics. See also **Bird, J. M.; McDougall, William; Prince, Walter F.**

**Crandon, Mina Stinson, 1889–1941.** Canadian-born American physical medium. Married (after an unsuccessful earlier marriage) to **Le Roi G. Crandon,** a Boston surgeon, Mina Crandon, under the pseudonym "Margery," became the brightest and most controversial star ever seen in the sky of American physical mediumship. In a dark séance room, phosphorescent lights appeared, objects moved, electric bell boxes rang, linkages of wooden rings and levitations occurred, ectoplasmic arms and legs emerged from her body, and spirit fingerprints were left by "Walter," allegedly the spirit of her deceased brother. The newspapers of the time covered her extensively and her name was spoken from coast to coast. People from all over the world came to have sittings with her and hundreds were astonished by the marvels of her séances.

Then came intensive observations and investigations of her and a troubled period of acrimonious charges and countercharges. She was investigated by a committee formed by the *Scientific American.* Hereward Carrington, one of is members, was convinced of the genuineness of her phenomena, but the other three members—Harry Houdini, William McDougall and Walter Frankin Prince—thought otherwise. The committee secretary, J. Malcolm Bird, "Margery's" most active defender next to her husband, thought that the phenomena were of first quality. But the verdict of four instructors from Harvard University who observed her later, although their methods were somewhat questionable, was that trickery accounted for the phenomena. Eric J. Dingwall who had come from England and the Society for Psychical Research to investigate her wrote enthusiastically to Albert von Schrenck-Notzing of his remarkable sittings with her, yet his final written report (probably influenced by William McDougall) stated that he was not convinced that any of the phenomena were authentic. J. B. Rhine sat with her and was horrified at what he believed to be evidence of fraud.

The American Society for Psychical Research, however, would have none of the insinuations and diatribes against her. With Bird its research officer, the pages of its *Journal* contained material written by him, Crandon, Mark W. Richardson and others favorable to "Margery's" cause and, in effect, became platforms for her defense and powers. Indeed, the ASPR's advocacy in the case was one of the reasons for the alienation in 1925 of some of its key members—McDougall, Prince, Elwood Worcester, Gardner Murphy—and the formation of the Boston Society for Psychic Research. In sum, Mina Crandon's demonstrations inspired some who believed that they were signs from another world and disillusioned and angered others who were convinced that the phenomena were no more than trickery in this world.

The controversy over whether her phenomena were genuine or spurious goes on. Whether genuine or not, however, "Margery" must be credited with altering the course of parapsychology in the United States. Unlike Charles Bailey, another physical medium, who effectively stopped parapsychology in Australia, she helped transformed parapsychology in her country for she made Rhine believe that investigations of mediums could not be carried out in a dark séance room and led him to set up experiments in the laboratory and to convert parapsychology into a science instead of a study of psychical research.

BIBLIOGRAPHY: Berger, A. S. *Lives and Letters in American Parapsychology,* 1988; Bird, J. M., ed., 1928. "The Margery Mediumship." PASPR 20–21:1; Rhine, J. B. and L. E. Rhine. 1927. "One Evening's Observation on the Margery Mediumship." *Journal of Abnormal and Social Psychology* 21:401; Tietze, T. *Margery,* 1973.

**Crawford, William Jackson, 1881–1920.** New Zealand-born British mechanical engineer. "[R]esponsible for the most intriguing series of experiments which have been performed in the field of parapsychology" (Barham 1988:116), Crawford, the holder of a D.Sc. from the University of Glasgow, investigated the physical phenomena of **Kathleen Goligher** from about 1914 when the medium was in her mid-teens until his death in 1920. The phenomena consisted of raps and knocks, often on request, and of table levitations. Sometimes the table turned upside down in the air and moved up and down. On one occasion a stool was levitated to the height of a man's head. Since Crawford was convinced that there was no fraud either on the part of the medium or of the sitters—an opinion shared by Sir William Barrett (1919) and Whateley Carington (then Smith) (1919), both of whom had observed the phenomena—he developed what he called "the rod theory," that is, he theorized that a paranormal cantilever of some kind was used in some of the levitations. This "rod," extruded from the medium's body, was, he thought, made up of very fine, transparent and invisible threads that were projected under the table and attached to its surface at which time the threads stiffened and became a rigid "girder" able to levitate the table. This exteriorized "plasma" or ectoplasm, was, however, sometimes visible and in Crawford's book *Psychic Structures* there are twenty-six photographs showing the material, which looks suspiciously man-made, coming from the medium. Eric J. Dingwall was favorably impressed and thought the photographs might "be the ultimate means of understanding the mechanics of these phenomena" (Dingwall, 1921).

Although Crawford became a convert to Spiritualism and came to believe in "operator" spirits, he theorized that the energy necessary to cause the levitations came, not from spirits and not from the medium, who supplied the ectoplasm, but from the sitters. His developing mechanical means for measuring the force involved was a major contribution to parapsychology.

Crawford finished his book *Psychic Structures* early in 1920 and seemed satisfied both with the experiments and with the photographs of the phenomena. On July 26, 1920, he wrote to the editor of the magazine *Light* that he had had a mental breakdown that had nothing to do with the work with Kathleen Goligher, that he was getting worse daily and that he was afraid of becoming a danger to those he loved. On July 30, 1920, he committed suicide.

After Crawford's death, Fournier d'Albe conducted twenty experiments with Kathleen Goligher in an attempt to confirm Crawford's work. He failed and in his book *The Goligher Circle,* published in 1921, implies that the phenonena were fraudulently produced. Partly because Crawford had refused to work with the Society for Psychical Research in his experiments, this assessment has stood and has damned Crawford's work despite Dingwall's belief in their extreme importance to the study of psychokinesis. Recently, however, there has been a rebirth of interest in Crawford's experiments and a reassessment of their value. Colin Brookes-Smith thought the phenomena were genuine and John Beloff and Mary Rose Barrington have given them serious attention.

Selected Writings: *The Psychic Structures of the Goligher Circle,* 1921; *The Reality of Psychic Phenomena,* 1916.

BIBLIOGRAPHY: Barham, A. 1988. "Dr. W. J. Crawford, His Work and His Legacy in Psychokinesis." JSPR 55:113; Barrett, W. 1919. "Report on Dr. Crawford's Medium." PSPR 30:334; Carington, W. (W. Whately Smith). 1919. "'The Reality of Psychic Phenomena.'" PSPR 30:306; Dingwall, E. J. 1921. "The Psychic Structures of the Goligher Circle." PSPR 32:147.

**Creative Process.** To try to define this process is to attempt to define the undefinable. Many creative people oppose any too close scrutiny of creativity because, as Yeats put it, it would be "muddying the spring." Yet two things seem clear. The process interlocks and interplays at several points with the paranormal and is the production of something new or imaginative. For this reason the tendency to use intuition as a synonym for the creative process is erroneous since "just knowing" something does not necessarily involve the novel production of anything.

The experience of Henri Poincaré, the mathematician, gives us one insight into creative activity. He had set himself to analyzing the problem of the solution of algebraic equations. He had tried unsuccessfully for days to arrive at some theory. Then on a sleepless night, he observed the working of his own creative activity: "Ideas rose in clouds; I felt them collide until pairs interlocked, so to speak, making a stable combination. By the next morning I had established [the solution] . . . I had only to write out the results which took a few hours." Although some creative people believe that they produce by consciously calculating every step, B. Ghiselin, a poet who studied the process, states that this claim "does not fit the facts reported almost universally in every field of creative work." Poincaré, for example, took no conscious control of the creative process. It went on automatically, involuntarily, and outside his conscious control until the process produced a concept.

Poincaré is only one example of many outside mathematics who do not know in advance the content of their art, fiction, or poetry. It seems suddenly to unroll in their minds like a picture scroll as they compose. The whole process is on all fours with the process used by mediums who do automatic writing, speaking, or spelling. The impressions or images received by them and purporting to come from communicators are also beyond their conscious direction. Creative people and mediums are, as Friedrich Nietzsche said, "mouthpieces of an outside force" and as William Blake expressed it, secretaries taking dictation involuntarily from authors within or outside them. There is little difference between the Poincaré creation and the creation of Pearl Lenore Curran, except that in her case there is the assumption of a spirit communicating.

The creative process has a similarity with spontaneous cases where the life experience is sudden. The created product also comes without warning. After the original concept came to Poincaré, he was struck by an additional idea when he was on a trip and had just mounted the step of a bus.

The creative process is indistinguishable from extrasensory perception in that it does not depend on the normal channels of sense for the acquisition of material for the production of something. The process seems also to be one that is penetrated by psychic elements that work below or beyond the threshold of consciousness. For in this submerged strata of our beings, along with memories and thoughts, ESP takes place. While the basic ESP process still is little understood, there is general agreement that, like creativity, it cannot be consciously controlled. Telepathy surfaces from the unconscious to the conscious along with other elements, such as dreams and memories, which we do not think of as paranormal. ESP makes its appearance in a number of familiar forms of mental activity such as dreams, and it probably appears also in the creative process, which may contain information obtained by ESP from outside sources, such as the information that came from within Jean Cocteau of a long ago age he knew nothing about. The uprushes from the hidden strata below consciousness all very likely containing impressions gained by ESP are like the "spring bubbling up," in A. E. Housman's words and are fully in line with F. W. H. Myers' concept of a "subliminal self." He believed that these uprushes produced inspiration, genius and originality.

BIBLIOGRAPHY: Ghiselin, B., ed., *The Creative Process*, 1952.

**Creery Sisters (Alice, Emily, Mary, Maud, Kathleen).** Nineteenth-century British subjects in the earliest experiments in telepathy. **Sir William Barrett, F. W. H. Myers and Edmund Gurney** who tested them in 1881 considered that they had proved that telepathy is a genuine phenomenon (Barrett, Gurney, and Myers 1882). But in later experiments with the sisters in Cambridge, two were caught using a crude code of signals. As a result, Henry Sidgwick, Gurney and others said that the "detection must throw discredit on the results of all previous trials" (Gurney, 1888:268). This decision was not well received by Barrett who considered the Creery girls his protégés. He defended the early experiments on the ground that subsequent cheating should not be allowed to invalidate the early trials. Barrett may have had a point. If no signals had been used, it is difficult to see why the earlier successes should not retain their evidential value when there was no evidence of cheating. Nevertheless, following the principle of the dirty test tube, the entire case is tainted, provides skeptics with more ammunition and few parapsychologists today cite the experiments with the Creery sisters as part of the evidential base for psi.

BIBLIOGRAPHY: Barrett, W. F., Gurney, E., and Myers, F. W. H. 1882. "First Report on Thought-Reading," PSPR 1:13; Gurney, E. 1888. "Note Relating to Some of the Published Experiments in Thought-Transference." PSPR 5:269.

**Crewe Circle.** A group of mediums who gathered at Crewe, England, and who specialized in **Spirit Photography.** The most famous of them was **William Hope.**

**Crime Detection.** When cases remain unsolved by normal police methods, law enforcement officials sometimes reach the point where they will try anything, even psychics. Because of sensational reporting and public relations propaganda put out by psychics it is difficult to know if or how many cases really have been solved by extrasensory perception. Peter Hurkos, for example, claimed to have solved the theft of the Stone of Scone from Westminster Abbey in 1950; Scotland Yard has denied that he played a significant part in solving the case.

Debunkers disclaim the ability of psychics to solve crimes and support their opinions with experiments. In 1979, for example, M. Reiser et al. reported experiments in which twelve psychics were given samples of physical evidence from four major crimes. The lack of agreement among the subjects led to the conclusion that there was little basis for believing that psychics are useful in criminal investigation.

A famous case involves **W. H. C. Tenhaeff's** report of an apparent hit in the case of the disappearance of ten-year-old Dirk Zwenne of The Netherlands for whom police searched unsuccessfully for three days. When the psychic **Gerard Croiset** was consulted, according to Tenhaeff he "saw" a raft and a sail boat in a harbor, the boy playing on the raft, falling into the water, and drowning when the left side of his head struck the boat. A few days later, the child was discovered drowned with a wound in the left side of his head. The raft and boat also were found (Pollack, 1964). But the actual report of the incident reveals that the boy's body *was* found but not where Croiset said it would be, that it was found four or five days earlier than he had predicted, and that it has never been established where or how the boy fell into the water (Hoebens, 1986).

On the other hand, some data suggest that psychics have actually been useful in locating missing persons or corpses in homicide cases and in supplying the details of crimes. To investigate this possibility the **Center for Scientific Anomalies Research (CSAR)** has initiated a long-term project researching psychic detectives. Irene Hughes, the Chicago psychic, has affidavits from police officials stating that she has helped in solving murder cases. In Germany, Frau Gunther-Geffers (1928), a professional psychic, was acquitted of fraud after much evidence was produced confirming her paranormal powers in finding dead bodies and uncovering thefts. In Holland, based on official reports of the police in Amsterdam, Tenhaeff and van Woudenberg have described valuable services by psychics that included tracing missing people and successfully discovering a theft. In the United States, although police usually report that information received from psychics has rarely helped in the solution of police cases, a New Jersey police chief has confirmed that Peter Hurkos furnished leads and gave the complete name of the person who was eventually arrested in a homicide case (Hoebens with Truzzi, 1985).

But are the few successes by psychic sleuths due to psychic causes? It has been suggested (Hoebens with Truzzi, 1985) that psychics may use the same natural methods employed by normal detectives or that they may have especially acute normal abilities or that they "trigger" information already in a police officer's mind.

BIBLIOGRAPHY: Guarino, R. 1975. "The Police and Psychics." *Psychic* 6(2):9; Gunther-Geffers Case. 1928. JSPR 24:306; Hoebens, P. H. "Investigation of the Mozart of 'Psychic Sleuths.'" and "Gerard Croiset and Professor Tenhaeff." in K. Frazier, ed., *Science Confronts the Paranormal,* 1986, pp. 122–132, 133–141; Hoebens, P. H. with Truzzi, M. "Reflections on Psychic Sleuths." In P. Kurtz, ed., *A Skeptic's Handbook of Parapsychology,* 1985; Pollack, J. H. *Croiset the Clairvoyant,* 1964; Reiser, M., Ludwig, L., Saxe, S., and Wagner, C. 1979. "An Evaluation of the Use of Psychics in the Investigation of Major Crimes". *Journal of Police Science and Administration* 7:18; Tenhaeff, W. H. C. and van Woudenberg, G. D. H. 1964. "Practical Achievements of Sensitives." *Zeitschrift für Parapsychologie und Grenzgebiete der Psycholoqie* 7:159; Trubo, R. 1975. "Psychics and the Police." *Psychic* 6(2):8.

**Crisis-Apparition.** See **Apparition.**

**Critical Ratio (CR).** A measure to determine whether or not the observed deviation is significantly greater than the expected random fluctuation above the average. The CR is obtained by dividing the observed deviation by the **Standard Deviation.** (The probability of a given CR may be obtained by consulting tables of the probability integral, such as Pearson's.) (JP)

**Critics.** See **Skeptics.**

**Croesus, ?–546 B.C.** Mighty king of Lydia, conquerer of the ancient Greeks, whose name is a synonym for fabulous wealth. He was the first parapsychologist in history. Concerned about the increasing strength of the Persians, he decided to consult the best of the oracles to advise him. To determine which oracle had the greatest ability, Croesus devised a test. The king sent out seven messengers on the same day to seven of the foremost oracles. On the hundredth day after their departure each messenger was to ask the oracle, to whom he had been sent, what the king was doing on that particular day. He was careful not to disclose the answer to any of his messengers. When they returned, Croesus found that six of the seven were wrong. Only the **Delphic Oracle** (Pythia) gave a reply that described a most unusual activity of the king, so unusual that it would have been impossible to guess. He was cutting up a tortoise and a lamb and boiling them in a brazen cauldron.

Like others of his time who consulted oracles to ask questions of the gods, he had no conception of the paranormal, parapsychology, or extrasensory perception. Yet in his test, Croesus demonstrated that he was a highly successful experimeter in ESP whose result could not be explained by chance coincidence or sensory leakage. In addition to being the first parapsychologist, he qualifies as the first **Noted Witness** to the paranormal.

In a footnote to this experiment, it should be added that, as a result of Pythia's success, Croesus asked her about the war he intended to make against Persia. The answer he received was: "When Croesus passes over the river Halys, he will overthrow the strength of an empire." As usual, it was another of Pythia's ambiguous answers. The king interpreted it as signifying that he would overthrow the Persian Empire. He was wrong. The war destroyed his own.

**Croiset, Gerard, 1909–1980.** Dutch "paragnost" (psychic). Made famous by **W. H. C. Tenhaeff,** Croiset is known internationally as a "super sleuth" and an outstanding precognitive clairvoyant. According to Tenhaeff, the many hits Croiset made while helping the Dutch police solve cases are shining examples of extrasensory perception.

His precognition was demonstrated most clearly in the so-called "chair tests" in which he predicted who would sit in a particular chair in a particular concert hall or auditorium on a particular day at a particular time. Recent close scrutiny of these claims has revealed the Croiset never actually solved any police cases and was wrong thousands of times and that the accuracy of his predictions with regard to the chair tests has also been overstated. If someone resembing the person he described sat anywhere near the target seat ("hits-by-displacement"), he was credited with a direct hit. On at least one occasion the person he described and who did indeed sit in the correct chair at the correct time was the only person not invited to the function and Croiset had had time to arrange for her cooperation. Another carefully controlled test was downright wrong (Zorab, 1965).

On the other hand, both Lawrence LeShan (1969) and Jule Eisenbud (1973) report very interesting chair tests in which some of Croiset's predictions were very striking and in which the possibility of fraud seems to have been ruled out. Many people, including George Zorab, believe that Croiset was a talented psychic and some have witnessed what they considered "miracles." See also **Crime Detection.**

BIBLIOGRAPHY: Eisenbud, J. 1973. "A Transatlantic Experiment in Precognition with Gerard Croiset." JASPR 67:1; Hoebens, P. H. "Gerard Croiset: Investigation of the Mozart of 'Psychic Sleuths'" and "Gerard Croiset and Professor Tenhaeff: Discrepancies in Claims of Clairvoyance." In K. Frazier, ed., *Science Confronts the Paranormal,* 1986; LeShan, L. and Esser, A. H. 1969. "A Transatlantic 'Chair Test'." JSPR 45:167; Zorab G. "Croiset the Clairvoyant." JSPR 43:209.

**Crookall, Robert 1890–1981.** British geologist. He is best-known in psychical research as the foremost collector of events and experiences relating to the out-of-body experience (astral projection).

Some religions or philosophies assert the existence of an entity supposed to separate from the physical body. Crookall made a survey of hundreds of personal accounts that not only testified to the existence of this separable entity; they related what happened after the separation. Among these occurrences were a loss of consciousness ("blackout" as Crookall called it), the rising of the entity or "double" above the physical body, the horizontal position of the double, the appearance of a silver cord attaching the double to the physical body, and more. Among the experiences reported were seeing the abandoned physical body, a review of one's past life, the disappearance of pain, the awareness that the entity or double was the real body, the sight of apparitions of dead family members or friends, the knowledge that there is survival of death, and the loss of any fear of death. In addition, Crookall's books indicate that out-of-body experiences can occur in almost every circumstance: gradually and slowly under "natural" conditions (when people are well, exhausted, ill, near death); or abruptly under "enforced" conditions (when people are under anesthesia, are falling, or being suffocated) (Crookall, 1964, 1966).

Although the objectivity of the out-of-body experience remains a hotly debated issue, Crookall was firmly convinced of it based on the data he collected that showed significant percentages of people having the experience. Crookall also had no doubt that the human soul, spirit, or mind continued after death.

In another work (1961), he collected and analyzed communications through mediums to show the process of death and used statements made by communicators to describe the nature of life after death.

Crookall was a determined and careful worker, but his conclusions may be marred because of his Spiritualist bias, his willingness to use popular books as his sources, and his acceptance of material at face value without any attempt at critical evaluation.

Selected Writings: *The Study and Practice of Astral Projection,* 1966; *More Astral Projections,* 1964; *The Supreme Adventure,* 1961.

**Crookes, Sir William, 1832–1919.** Eminent British scientist and psychical researcher. President of the Society for Psychical Research from 1896 to 1899, he is best known in parapsychology for his investigations of the physical mediums **D. D. Home** and **Florence Cook.**

Although he did not have a university education, he became a famous and widely respected experimental chemist and physicist. In 1861 he made his first great discovery: the element thallium. In 1876 he discovered cathode rays; he was the first to discover that helium could be obtained from the disintegration of radium; he did research on the rare earths and their spectra.

He was also an author of many scientific works and the editor both of scientific (e.g., the *Chemical News* and the *Quarterly Journal of Science*) and Spiritualist journals. He was fascinated by the area of uncertainty between the known and the unknown both in physical and psychical research. From 1870 to 1874 he investigated the phenomena of Spiritualism. His writings on these investigations, while they horrified most of the scientific community, greatly interested Lord Rayleigh, himself a famous scientist.

Crookes was convinced that D. D. Home produced remarkable genuine physical phenomena, such as levitation, handling red-hot coals, and materialization of spirit hands and forms. To explain away the apparent paranormality of these phenomena critics have invoked trickery, hallucination, hypnotism, and even, in the case of Florence Cook's phenomena—which Crookes also said were genuine—sexual involvement. (Hall, 1963/1984; Medhurst and Goldney, 1964).

In his crucial statement concerning the Crookes-Cook sittings Crookes wrote that he had seen Florence Cook's full-form materialization "Katie King" and Rosina Showers's materialized "Florence" walking arm in arm in his laboratory. Yet his later conclusion that Rosina Showers was a fraud puts Florence Cook's honesty—and his own—and the genuineness of Katie King in doubt. In fact were Crookes not a famous scientist, had honors not been heaped upon him by universities throughout the world, had he not been knighted in 1897, and had he not received the highest order the English king can confer, the Order of Merit, it is unlikely that much attention would still be paid to Florence Cook. It has been suggested, however, (Brandon, 1983) that Crookes, in his work in psychical research, was not the objective, noninvolved scientist, but that, because of grief over the death in 1867 of his brother Philip he wanted very much to prove Spiritualism by scientific means.

So the questions remain: Did Crookes believe that "Katie King" was a full-form materialization? If he did, why did he think so? Because she *was* or because he wanted to believe? And if he didn't believe in "Katie King," why did he not reveal her to be a hoax?

Selected Writings: 1896. "Address by the President." PSPR 12:338; 1889. "Notes of Seances with D. D. Home." PSPR 6:98; *Researches in Spiritualism,* 1875.

BIBLIOGRAPHY: Barrett, W. 1920. "In Memory

of Sir William Crookes, O.M., F.R.S." PSPR 31:1; Beloff, J. "George Zorab and 'Katie King,'" In F. W. J. J. Snel, ed., *In Honour of G. A. M. Zorab,* 1986; Brandon, R. *The Spiritualists,* 1983; Hall, T. *The Spiritualists,* 1963 (reissued as *The Medium and the Scientist,* 1984); Medhurst, R. G. and Goldney, K. M. 1964. "William Crookes and the Physical Phenomena of Mediumship." PSPR 54:25; Thouless, R. H. "Correspondence. Crookes & Cook." JSPR 42:203.

**Cross-Correspondences.** A description applied to fragments of sentences often of a classical nature in the famous cases of the Society for Psychical Research that occur in the writings or speech of two or more mediums working independently of one another. The fragments by themselves are without significance, but when fitted together like a jigsaw puzzle result in an understandable message. One illustration comes from **Alice Johnson's** report of medium **Mrs. Verrall**'s automatic writing and that of another automatist containing references to Attila's appearance at the gates of Rome and to the pope's pleading with Attila not to sack the city. The separate fragments together created an integrated and meaningful picture. Again, on January 6, 1909, Mrs. Verrall's script contained verses relating to St. Paul on the road to Damascus and a note signed with F. W. H. Myers's initials with an allusion to Renan's *Chemin de Damas.* On January 8, **Mrs. Willett** received a message to write to Mrs. Verrall the words "Eikon Renam. Eikon Renam." (Renam is apparently a misspelling of Renan.) It was found that in the *Chemin de Damas,* Renan had described St. Paul seeing Jesus, the Eikon, on the road to Damascus. And so again the pieces of the two messages fitted together to make one whole.

The cross-correspondences started soon after the deaths of Henry Sidgwick, F. W. H. Myers and Edmund Gurney and involved, among others, automatists **Helen de G. Verrall,** Mrs. A. W. Verrall, Mrs. Willett, and **Mrs. Holland.** Many students of the cross-correspondences believe that they give evidence of survival after death because they seem to have been thought of and designed by dead individuals. It is hard to explain the purposeful communicator behind the messages as one of the automatists or a sitter. Others, however, believe that the cross-correspondence can be explained by ESP among the automatists. This objection might be answered if pieces of evidence characteristic of two or more deceased people and of something they had in common were given. This evidence, at the same time, should be mysterious and beyond the understanding of living people until the final piece of the jigsaw puzzle is provided.

A scheme of this kind was the classic "Ear of Dionysius" case reported by **Gerald Balfour.** The "Ear of Dionysius" referred to stone quarries with acoustical properties where Athenian slaves were imprisoned. The case suggested that two deceased men, both classical scholars, had thought up a scheme containing a literary association of ideas characteristic of their interests in and knowledge of the classical literature. The ideas were given through the automatist Mrs. Willett who was not a classical scholar. They even baffled people who were classicists until all the literary topics given—the ear of Dionysius, Syracuse, the heel of Italy, and others—were finally understood as parts of a united plan.

**Eric J. Dingwall,** however, was contemptuous of the "renowned cross-correspondences" because they "have proved impossible to investigate since we are not yet permitted to examine the original documents" (Dingwall, 1985:167). He thought they were the result of selection of material by his pet hate **J. G. Piddington.**

BIBLIOGRAPHY: Balfour, G. W. 1917. "The Ear of Dionysius: Further Evidence Affording Evidence of Personal Survival." PSPR 29:197; Dingwall, E. J. "The Need for Responsibility in Parapsychology." In P. Kurtz, ed., *A Skeptic's Handbook of Parapsychology,* 1985; Johnson, A. 1908–1909. "On the Automatic Writing of Mrs. Holland." PSPR 21:297.

**Cross References.** Where two or more mediums independently provide the same information. The technique was first used by **James H. Hyslop** in his investigation of the case of **Frederic L. Thompson** who was having strange experiences. Hyslop wanted to see if the same phenomena taking place in Thompson would be repeated through the mediums who had no knowledge of Thompson's situation. If he could, he believed the repetition would establish the paranormal character of the phenomenon.

BIBLIOGRAPHY: Hyslop, J. H. 1909. "A Case of Veridical Hallucinations." PASPR 3:1.

**Crowley, Aleister (Edward Alexander), 1875–1947.** British occultist. "The Great Beast," "a monster of wickedness," "the wickedest man in the world," these epithets coined by James Douglas, editor of the *Sunday Express* and Horatio Bottomley of the English periodical *John Bull* have caused us to remember Crowley as we do.

His father was a wealthy brewer; his mother was a religious fanatic who is supposed to have believed that her son was the Beast 666 of the Apocalypse, the Antichrist. Yet there is much evidence that Crowley was actually a spoiled and pampered child who had very little capacity for affection.

Shortly after he entered Trinity College, Cambridge, in 1893, he heard of the secret Masonic order called the White Brotherhood that guides the evolution of humankind. Crowley yearned to join and in 1898 was at last initiated into the Hermetic Order of the Golden Dawn, the most powerful secret society in England, whose members included William Butler Yeats. The order used ceremonial magic to facilitate reaching higher levels of consciousness and attempted to teach astral projection, telepathy, and psychokinesis.

On his honeymoon in Cario in 1904 he had dictated to him the three chapters of the *Book of the Law (Liber Al ver Legis)* under the guidance of a communicator that identified itself as Aiwass. All of humanity was to follow a new law, the law of Thelema: "Do what thou wilt shall be the whole of the Law," which seems to mean "Do as you please" but actually meant something like the Taoist principle of letting things take their course without interference from the rational mind. (One wonders how much of Crowley's law of Thelema—interpreted as "do as you please"—influenced the "do your own thing" of the hippies and youth rebels of the 1960s and 1970s.)

In 1908 in China a fall from a cliff produced a vision which indicated to him that he was the prophet of a new age. He returned to England and founded the Order of the Silver Star (Argenteum Astrum). Between 1908 and 1914 he wrote hundreds of books on his new philosophy. He advocated the use of drugs (legal in England at that time) and sexual freedom. In 1914 his support of Irish nationalism and Imperial Germany led to his villification by the British press and to his spending 1915–1919 in the United States where he underwent a series of magical ordeals. In both the United Kingdom and the United States, he preached Satanism and magical sexual techniques adapted from the sexual practices of Tantric yoga. In 1920 he moved to Sicily where he established the Abbey of Thelema from which he began to propound the mystery of the eon of Thelema, which is the eon of Horus, the conquering child. Crowley identified himself both with the child and with Beast 666, and, with the Scarlet Woman (actually many women), practised sexual magic (the passionate union of opposites, cosmic union, which he interpreted as sexual union), and explored unseen worlds.

The hatred of the English press followed him to Sicily. He was falsely accused of blackmail, murder, and the ritual sacrifice of his daughter (she actually died of influenza). In 1922 Mussolini expelled Crowley from Italy. Although he had inherited money from his mother who died in 1903, by 1929 he was impoverished. A heroin addict, he then revealed that he was the incarnation of the hawk-headed god Horus. Although he produced some of his major works on magic after this time, he was no longer the public figure that he had been. Only thirteen people attended his funeral in England in 1947.

Who and what he was remains a mystery: "Was he a fraud; was he deranged; was he a legitimate psychic; was he a prophet, saint, and god? . . . [O]ne peels away layer after layer only to reveal another. . . . [T]he Great Beast elude[s] us . . ." (Briggs, 1976).

BIBLIOGRAPHY: Briggs, K. C. 1976. "The Great Beast: the Legend of Aleister Crowley." *Psychic* 7(5):39; Grant, K. "Aleister Crowley (1875–1947)." In R. Cavendish, ed., *Encyclopedia of the Unexplained,* 1974.

**Crying Pictures and Statues.** Historians have recorded for centuries the tears that statutes shed. From the books of Livy, the Roman historian, we learn that a statue of Apollo cried for three days. In 1527, just before the terrible sack of Rome by the German and Spanish mercenaries of Charles I in which even the pope was taken prisoner, a statue of Jesus Christ is supposed to have wept. As Syracuse in Sicily was being besieged in 1719, a statue of St. Lucy, who had lived in Syracuse, shed tears. Such cases are analogous to **Bleeding Pictures and Statues** of religious figures.

The ancient pattern has not changed to this day. Statues continue to cry. For example, on August 29, 1953, a plaster statue of the Virgin Mary on a wall in the house of Antonietta and Angelo Janusso in Syracuse, Italy, began to cry and went on crying for four days. It cried on the wall or when laid in a drawer. The tears shed were identified as the same saline fluid secreted by human eyes. In March 1960, tears flowed from a picture of the Virgin Mary kept in a home of a Greek family in Island Park, New York. A pastor from the St. Paul Greek Orthodox Church who examined it reported: "When I arrived, a tear was drying beneath the left eye. Then just before the devotions ended, I saw another tear well in the left eye. It started as a small, round globule of moisture in the corner of her left eye, and it slowly trickled down her face." As the news spread about the plaster statuette in Italy and the lithograph in New York thousands of people filed through each residence to see for themselves the running tears and to pray. Even skeptics were convinced by the startling and apparently inexplicable phenomena. Indeed, on December 18, 1953, even the generally inflexible Holy Office of the Catholic Church, after a series of inquiries, sanctioned the weeping statue in the Janusso home as a genuine miracle.

Nevertheless, there may be a paranormal explanation. **Poltergeist** phenomena that have been reported over the years by careful observers have taken a variety of forms—from houses being bombarded with stones and fires being set to houses flooding with water from unknown sources. This last form comes close to cases of weeping objects, especially if the **Poltergeist Agent** in whose home a religious statue or picture is kept is in an intense emotional state (i.e., a highly charged religious fervor), which may produce the phenomenon. If crying religious figures or images are a poltergeist phenomenon they would be unique in the history of parapsychology and would force parapsychologists to look anew at the old problem of the poltergeist. For generally the poltergeist is hostile, frightening, and destructive. Since crying religious statutes and pictures usually inspire great religious faith and joy, even bring about remarkable cures, it would seem that, when the religious element enters the picture, the wild poltergeist becomes tamed and changed for the better.

BIBLIOGRAPHY: Fodor, N. *Between Two Worlds,* 1964, pp. 282–286; Michell, J. and Rickard, R. J. M. *Phenomena: A Book of Wonders,* 1977, pp. 20–21.

**Cryptesthesia.** See **Clairvoyance.**

**Cryptomnesia.** A term invented by **Theodore Flournoy** and which **F. W. H. Myers** defined as "submerged memory." It denotes memories of events, experiences, or information, none recognized as memories, whose original acquisition is completely forgotten and which surface as new experiences. It is encountered sometimes in cases of plagiarism in which authors, such as Friedrich Nietzsche, without deliberately intending to commit literary theft, use words and phrases they have read in some other author's work but which they do not remember having read. In parapsychology, phenomena such as messages given by mediums, extrasensory perception, xenoglossy, or reincarnation cannot be considered paranormal unless there is a satisfactory demonstration that information given has not been obtained previously in some normal way, such as by having read or heard it somewhere at sometime.

A contemporary case reported by James F. McHarg shows how "memories of a past life" were probably due to cryptomnesia rather than reincarnation. A twenty-nine year-old man, regaining consciousness after a serious head injury, remembered having been a major in the Confederate Army. It was a puzzling case of post-traumatic personation until a magazine article about Civil War buffs who identified themselves with the Confederate Army and wore its uniforms was brought to the man's attention. He was surprised but remembered having read it prior to his injury. See also **Déjà Vu**.

**Crystal Gazing.** Also called "crystal vision" or "scrying." The steady staring at a reflecting surface of liquid, metal, crystals, stones, or glass, such as the well-known crystal ball, in order to divine the future, ease troubles, or solve problems. These and similar methods were in use in the earliest cultures and were almost universal. Among the Arabs, the custom was to write on the edge of a mirror words from the Koran about the power of God and the names Gabriel, Azrael, Raphael, and Assafel. The person then fasted for seven days, and, as prayers were recited, saw in the mirror what was to be done or decided. In ancient Greece, oracles were delivered before the temple of Demeter by tying a cord to a mirror and lowering it into a fountain until the lower edge of the mirror touched the surface of the water. The figures or images seen in the mirror were the basis for predictions. And in the royal court of the queen of France, Catherine de Medici asked her magician to look into a mirror to tell her how long her sons would rule as kings of France.

The individual who uses this technique is a "seer" or "scryer." The technique is employed to induce images in the reflecting surface. The pictures, however, exist in the mind of the individual and not on the surface.

Crystal gazing looms large in the history of the occult but belongs in the domain of psychical research as a means of facilitating mental and physical concentration and the acquisition of impressions through telepathy or clairvoyance. It is another possible sensory **Automatism,** like the motor automatism of automatic writing, which may facilitate the appearance and use of psi abilities and the obtaining of paranormal knowledge.

The experience of Ada Goodrich-Freer is a possible example of telepathy. She had concentrated her gaze on a magnifying glass placed on a dark background and saw in it a picture of a small bunch of daffodils although she wanted to see a figure she was thinking about. But the bunch of flowers kept presenting itself. Three days later, there arrived unexpectedly for her a painting of a bunch of daffodils that corresponded exactly with the bouquet she had seen in the glass. She found out that, on the very day she had seen the flowers in the glass, the artist had worked on the painting. See also **Balfour, Arthur J.; Shelley, Percy B**

**Crystals.** Thought to contain a cosmic energy that, through reflections and radiations of pure light, acts upon the people who see, touch, wear, or meditate with them. Crystals are believed to transmit energy to guide, stimulate awareness, raise consciousness, promote spiritual growth, and produce healing and other marvels. Crystals have different powers and product different effects. Smoky quartz, for example, promotes serenity while milky quartz helps establish contact with the mysterious. There is a clear connection between the claims made for crystals and those made for pyramids in that both are believed somehow to collect a universal life force and to channel it.

Such a life force would be of interest to parapsychology because its existence would change the way psychokinesis is understood. Instead of conceiving of psychokinesis as a "mind over matter" effect and a power unique to the human mind, it would need to be viewed as a cosmic, not a human, power, one channeled through us as it is supposed to be channeled through crystals and pyramids. But, as with pyramids, there is as yet no scientific documentation for crystals and the cosmic energy assumed. Until there is, there is little likelihood of any alteration in the present conception of psychokinesis as the influence of a human mind over matter.

**Cummings, Geraldine Dorothy, 1890–1968.** Outstanding Irish sensitive and automatist. Although she felt that at least some of her trance scripts gave strong evidence of survival after bodily death, she herself did not wish to survive, longed for eternal sleep, and felt that life was meaningless and worthless. As early as 1917 she took part in the "Pearl Tie-Pin Case" in which Sir. W. F. Barrett was the experimenter. She ("Miss D. C.") and Hester Travers Smith, the sitters, played with a kind of ouija board. Although Barrett wrote that the resulting communication "points unmistakably to a telepathic message" from the dead, Geraldine Cummins herself at the time thought that it could better be explained by a forgotten telepathic communication from the alleged communicator (her cousin) to herself. In 1923 Miss Cummins met Miss E. B. Gibbes, a member of the Society for Psychical Research, who for the next twenty-five years worked with her as investigator and protector.

Between 1928 and 1950 Geraldine Cummins wrote automatically six books known collectively by the title of the first book, *The Scripts of Cleophas,* which deal with the rise of Christianity during the first century A.D. Fascinating as they are, it has been pointed out (Anderson, 1983) that they contain nothing that "might reasonably be attributed to a discarnate source." The same is true of other similar works written by her and that Anderson feels must simply be considered historical romances.

Along with her brother, Dr. R. Cummins (called R. Connell in the reports) Geraldine Cummins did intersting work in psychometry with patients whose phobias or neuroses did not respond to conventional treatment. The method employed was to have Miss Cummins psychometrize an object owned by the patient and to have her in this way determine the source of the problem. In every case the patient's difficulty was traced to some sort of genetic memory and not to any fault of the patient. Although there is no way of determining the veridicality of the readings, the important point is that the therapy worked and the patients were cured.

There were many scripts that purported to be communications from the dead. The most impressive is her last series of scripts, ostensibly communicated by Winifred Coombe-Tenant (Mrs. Willett) published as *Swan on a Black Sea* with a forward by **C. D. Broad.** Broad thought that the survival hypothesis was the simplest and most plausible for explaining the scripts, and a reviewer (Thouless 1966) thought the book added to the "weight of evidence for post mortem communication from a surviving personality . . .". But the question has been raised of how much Geraldine Cummins knew or had at one time known and forgotten about Mrs. Coombe-Tenant. See also **Bond Frederick Bligh**.

Selected Writings: *The Scripts of Cleophas,* n.d. [1928]; *Swan on a Black Sea,* 1965/1970.

BIBLIOGRAPHY: Anderson, R. I. 1983. "The Mediumship of Geraldine Cummins." *Theta* 11:50; Barrett, W. F. 1918. "Evidence of Super-Normal Communications through Motor Automatism." PSPR 30:230,235; Barrington, M. R. 1966. "Swan on a Black Sea: How Much Could Miss Cummins Have Known?" JSPR 43:289; Heywood, R. 1970. "Notes on the Mediumship of Geraldine Cummins." JSPR 45:396; Thouless, R. H. 1966. "Swan on a Black Sea: A Study in Automatic Writing." JSPR 43:267.

**Cuna Indians.** A people indigenous to Panama who live principally on its Atlantic Coast and on the San Blas Islands off the east coast of the country. Among the Cunas are the *Avisua* who sing songs of magic which can cure the sick, influence a person to act, or change atmospheric conditions; the *Ina-Duledi* who use plants to prepare curative medicines; and the witch doctors or *Neles* who claim to possess powers of extrasensory perception that are used to heal or to acquire paranormal information about the past, present, or future.

The main source of the powers of the *Neles* comes in dreams in which *nuchus* (magical wooden dolls) come to life in some unexplained way and provide the *Neles* with their training, paranormal information and even trigger out-of-body-experiences. Unlike the clever men of the Australian Aborigines, the *Neles* are granted special privileges and given special training to permit them to perform their roles in Cuna society. *Neles* are identified at once at birth because they are born with amniotic membranes veiling their faces and covering parts of their bodies.

A well-known parapsychologist, drawn to the San Blas Islands by the provocative stories told about the Cunas, tried to test their psi abilities. From 1968 to 1972, **Robert L. Van De Castle** carried out a program of ESP tests among Cuna boys and girls. The tests involved colored drawings of canoes, sharks, jaguars, conch shells, and airplanes—all objects with which the Cuna adolescents were familiar. The overall results were at the chance level although the girls outscored the boys. It was not clear, however, that any of the young subjects tested were the fascinating *Neles* who continue to be untested from a parapsychological point of view.

BIBLIOGRAPHY: Van de Castle, R. "An Investigation of Psi Abilities Among the Cuna Indians of Panama." In A. Angoff and D. Barth, eds., *Parapsychology and Anthropology,* 1974, pp. 80–97.

**Curé of Ars (Saint Jean-Baptiste-Marie Vianney), 1786–1859.** French patron saint of priests. His devoutness made Ars, France, a pilgrimage center for thousands. Over a period of eighteen years until his death, they made their way to his small village church to receive from him spiritual guidance and to have him hear their confessions. He was honored as a saint by Pope Pius XI.

The curé, around whom an aura was a often seen, once described in a catechism a discussion he had had with two Protestant ministers who doubted the presence of Christ in the Holy Eucharist: "I said to them. 'Do you believe that a piece of bread could detach itself and, of its own accord, place itself upon the tongue of a person who was approaching to receive it?' 'No.' . . . Now listen well to what I am going to tell you. I do not say that it happened *somewhere or other,* but I say that it happened to me. When that man presented himself to receive Holy Communion, the Sacred Host detached Itself from my fingers while I was yet a good distance from him, and went and placed Itself upon the tongue of that man."

Both for communicant and priest, the phenomenon was a divine gift. But in the eyes of parapsychology, it is so similar to the action of objects influenced by the mind that has been observed from parapsychology laboratories to Spiritualist séances that the good priest's testimony may make him a **Noted Witness** for psychokinesis or "mind over matter."

BIBLIOGRAPHY: Thurston, H. *The Physical Phenomena of Mysticism,* 1952, p. 143.

**Curran, Pearl Lenore (Pollard), 1883–1937.** American housewife through whom the Patience Worth material came. On July 8, 1913, the words "Many moons ago I lived. Again I come—Patience Worth my name" were spelled out on a ouija board with which Mrs. Curran, a St. Louis housewife, and her friend Emily Grant Hutchings were playing. Thus began one of the most intriguing parapsychological mysteries of all time. Over the next twenty-four years Mrs. Curran received, at first through the ouija board but eventually without it, millions of words, comprising poetry, aphorisms, prayers, and several full-length books. The poetry and books (especially *The Sorry Tale* dealing with the time of Christ) were praised for their literary quality and for the authenticity of setting and characters. The *New York Times* book reviewer called *The Sorry Tale* "a wonderful, a beautiful, and a noble book . . .". William Marion Reedy, a noted literary critic, said that *The Sorry Tale* was "the most remarkable piece of literature [he had] ever read. . . . The story is a fifth gospel." The material was produced rapidly and spontaneously. If, for example, someone asked for a poem on whatever subject, it was given instantaneously. Sometimes "Patience" would work on three or four things at a time, alternating line by line among the different compositions; yet, when they were separated they each read perfectly. The language of the material, especially for the first six or seven years, was in a form of seemingly archaic English (Patience Worth claimed to have lived in the seventeenth century). It proved to be a language never actually spoken, however but, remarkably, it was made up almost entirely of Anglo-Saxon root-words with no modernisms.

Praise for Patience Worth was not unanimous. Some saw no merit in the literature. **James H. Hyslop,** secretary of the American Society for Psychical Research and editor of its *Journal,* claimed that the case was a fraud, that Mrs. Curran's knowledge of the dialect of the Ozarks explained Patience Worth's language and that the desire for notoriety and money were behind the entire matter. Hyslop was wrong about the language, and the Currans never made any money from Patience Worth. Mrs. Curran did not charge people who came to marvel at the miracle of Patience Worth; the books which were written in a very difficult language for modern readers did not sell well; and the costs of maintaining records, entertaining people, etc. came out of the Currans' pocket.

If we accept the entire good faith of Mrs. Curran, that she really believed that Patience Worth was a separate individual, the wise spirit of a young woman who had lived in the seventeenth century—and it certainly seems so since the Currans adopted a child at Patience's direction—the question of who or what Patience was has not been settled. Many have concluded that she was a secondary personality of Mrs. Curran's. The problems with this theory, however, are that Mrs. Curran was not in a dissociated state during the time that the material came through and, especially, that the subject matter and language of the material were completely beyond Mrs. Curran's knowledge and abilities. After ten months of exhaustive study, noted psychical researcher Walter Franklin Prince concluded: *"Either our concept of what we call the subconscious must be radically altered, so as to include potencies of which we hitherto have had no knowledge, or else some cause operating through but not originating in the subconsciousness of Mrs. Curran must be acknowledged."*

BIBLIOGRAPHY: Litvag, I. *Singer in the Shadows: the Strange Story of Patience Worth,* 1972; Prince, W. F. *The Case of Patience Worth,* 1964.

**Curse.** Words spoken or written out of revenge or hate with the intention of bringing misfortune, harm or death to others. We may ask what power to hurt or kill could possibly lie in words. We remember from our childhood the little saying: "Sticks and stones may break my bones, but words will never hurt me." But to some people even today and certainly to the people of antiquity words had great potency.

In some instances, particularly those in which Egyptian tombs have been opened and desecrated or mummies carried away, an argument can be made for the power of the curse extending over thousands of years and operating against those who violated the tombs or disturbed the bodies. It was the custom of Egyptian priests to utter these incantations. There is the famous case of the Egyptian king Tut-Ankh-Amen whose tomb was found and entered in 1927 by the archaeologist Howard Carter and Egyptologist Lord Carnarvon in the most exciting and impressive discovery ever made in Egyptian archaeology. It is an astonishing fact that many who were connected directly or indirectly with the tomb or the excavations met with disaster. Lord Carnarvon died as the result of mosquito sting in the tomb. Richard Bethell, co-investigator of the tomb, died suddenly and his father, Lord Westbury, committed suicide. Sir Archibald Douglas Reid who X-rayed the mummy died unexpectedly as did Colonel Herbat and Jonathan Carver both of whom were at the tomb when it was opened. Only Howard Carter remained unaffected—except that on the same day that he entered the tomb, his pet canary was swallowed by a python, the emblem of the royal house of Tut-Ankh-Amen.

Curses normally do not fall into that class of subject studied by psychical research, but they should for the same reason that unorthodox healing, **Bone-Pointing** or voodoo-death do. They will involve the power of the mind over the body. It can cure in some circumstances or, if the victims of a curse worry over it, it can kill. Perhaps Lord Carnarvon *et al.* did die because they knew of the curse, but what about Carter's canary? The case raises the difficult yet key question in the investigation of all paranormal phenomena and one which psychical research always must face: the question of chance-coincidence. Were the deaths in the Tut-Ankh-Amen case just coincidences as many prudent people would argue, or did they exceed what we generally think of as chance? If we can say that there was some causal connection between the excavation (some would say "desecration") of the tomb and the deaths of those who had something to do with it, then the coincidences are evidence of something paranormal—perhaps a deadly telepathic message across time or a thought-form that had impressed itself in the space of the tomb for centuries until called up by people with the sensitivity to receive it. Edmund Gurney suggested a similar theory for apparitions. He thought they were images impressed on a house by people long since dead. See also **Voodooism**.

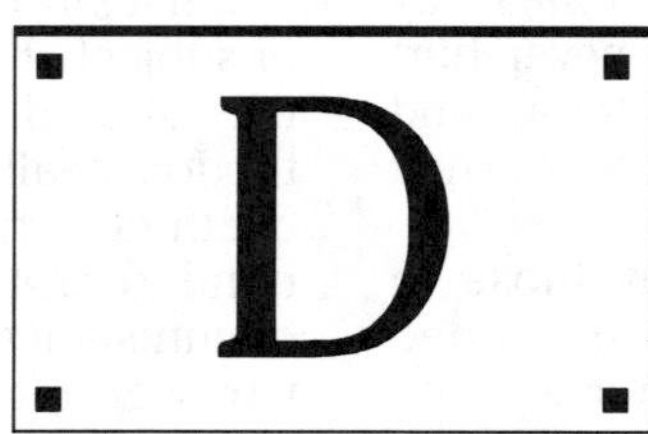

**Daemon (or Daimon).** To be distinguished from "demon." An inward monitory voice, guardian spirit, or guide that inspires or counsels. Although hearing voices is often regarded as a symptom of madness, in some cases there is no other indication of insanity except for the voices. Sometimes, too, the messages conveyed by the voices are greater in insight than the normal level of thought and consciousness can attain. Examples are the voices heard by **Socrates** that he believed to be a divine power and by **Joan of Arc** that she thought came from God or saints. See also **Fox, George; Goethe, Johann Wolfgang von; Gregory, Saint.**

**Dale, Laura Abbott, 1919–1983.** American editor of the *Journal of the American Society for Psychical Research.* Over a period of almost three decades of devotion to this publication, she made it into a valuable scientific journal. She was stubborn as a mule in her refusal to publish any material that fell below her standards of high scientific excellence, accuracy, and English usage.

Apart from her editorial skills, she was a vigorous researcher whose name has come to be associated with the myth of Midas who wanted to turn everything he touched into gold. Dale came to realize that she had the "Midas touch in reverse" (Dale, 1943), the decline effect, her experience and that of many other experimenters as well. If extrasensory perception can be compared to gold, all Dale and some other experimenters touched turned from initial positive (golden) scores into dross—a decline from successful scores to scoring at chance.

She also cast a net out for spontaneous experiences and her investigations of them were outstanding. She was, said Gardner Murphy with whom she worked closely, "the primary research worker of the [ASPR], to whose imagination, energy, and skill most of its effective contribution . . . has been due" (Murphy, 1957). Laura Dale also collaborated with Rhea A. White in preparing a valuable survey of the many books in parapsychology.

Selected Writings: and White, R. A. *Parapsychology: Sources of Information,* 1973; and Murphy, G. *Challenge of Psychical Research,* 1966; and Taves, E. 1943. "The Midas Touch in Reverse." JASPR 37:57.

BIBLIOGRAPHY: Berger, A. S. *Lives and Letters in American Parapsychology,* 1988; Murphy, G. 1957. "Notes for a Parapsychological Autobiography." JP 21:173.

**Damiani, Enrico, ?–1886.** Italian Spiritualist. He is famous for having discovered the physical medium **Eusapia Palladino.** After he found that this ignorant daughter of a peasant in Bari, Italy seemed to be able to produce surprising manifestations at séances, he helped develop her powers and methodically investigated them with a rigor new to the Spiritualist thought and practice of the time. His death led to her temporary disappearance from Spiritualist circles.

**Dangers of the Paranormal.** The paranormal has its bright side. Extrasensory perception and psychokinesis seem to suggest that human beings possess powers that go beyond their sensory organs, and survival research has provided data that may suggest that death is not the end of the individual. But fascination with this field should not blind us from seeing that it has its dark side, also. Dangers lurk in many areas whose phenomena can be conveniently divided into "after death" and "before death" types.

*After Death.* Messages, whether received through the ouija board or through automatic writing, if taken seriously, can disturb or disrupt lives. Whether the messages are from some discarnate agency or are the externalizing of the subconscious of the people doing the writing or operating the ouija board, following the messages can lead to unwise decisions: for example, to sell or to buy property, to make or to terminate intimate personal relationships, or even to take one's life on the lure of a promised glorious meeting in the Great Beyond. The danger is also that automatic writing or the ouija board can be used to escape work or family or in place of normal conversations. In the séance room, messages coming through mediums can be dangerous for the same reasons. In addition, however, the séance can be used as the base of operations for the unscrupulous and fraudulent ready to take advantage of the innocent and bereaved. People should realize that there is no reason to believe that the dead are made wiser by reason of death or that the "other side" is a Heavenly Information Bureau. The sole object of communication from the perspective of parapsychology should be to try to get evidence that deceased people have survived death.

*Before Death.* Telepathy is believed to be strong enough to produce or aggravate illness. Psychiatrist **Berthold E. Schwarz** maintains that "telepathy offers an attractive hypothesis for the understanding of psychosomatic disease" (Schwarz, 1980:114). One of the effects of the out-of-body experience may be the nightmarish experience of meeting an "astral fiend" (Muldoon and Carrington, 1973:292). Poltergeists may create turmoil in home or office and even cause personal harm. Precognition can make one fearful of being hurt by an event precognized or of being responsible either for the event or for averting it. Psychokinesis can bring on the fear that one has lost control because an unknown force seems to be taking over. Psi abilities may create a terrible concern that one is tapping into other dimensions and worlds. Psychics who try to cope with the problems of clients complain of becoming ill or confused as a result or, on the other hand, either of feeling mentally unbalanced or powerful and unique because of their psychic gifts.

The paranormal holds no dangers for those who deny the existence of paranormal phenomena. But if one does not deny their reality, one should acknowledge the dangers and heed warning signs posted at every entrance to the paranormal.

BIBLIOGRAPHY: Muldoon, S. and Carrington, H. *The Projection of the Astral Body,* 1973; Schwarz, B. E. *Psychic Nexus: Psychic Phenomena in Psychiatry and Everyday Life,* 1980.

**Davenport Brothers: William Henry, 1841–1911; Ira Erastus, 1839–1877.** American physical mediums. They received widespread publicity because they were the first to focus public attention on rope-tying. The brothers followed an interesting procedure for their performances. First they would insist on being searched and that the ropes to be used to tie them be examined as a precaution against trickery. Then they would go into a cabinet and be bound to their seats by someone from the audience who was highly skilled in making knots, perhaps an old sea captain. Their arms would be lashed to their sides and legs lashed together. The audience by this time would be convinced that now the brothers would never be able to escape. The cabinet doors would be shut—only to be opened by the brothers a moment or two later as they emerged completely free of the rope now dangling from their hands. The audience would applaud wildly not suspecting that "the performance of the brothers Davenport was trickery, and nothing but trickery" (Carrington, 1907). As they were being tied, the Davenports had expanded parts of their bodies, raised their shoulders, held their hands away from their bodies, or used other methods, to ensure that there would be slack in the rope. The rope could then be worked and pulled until one hand was freed, then the other, while the teeth were used to untie knots. After their performance the brothers would go back into the cabinet, close its doors and really start their show of marvellous physical phenomena, including the blowing of horns and ringing of bells, to astonish the spectators even more.

BIBLIOGRAPHY: Carrington, H. *The Physical Phenomena of Spiritualism,* 1907.

**Davey, S. John, 1864–1891.** British psychical researcher. Although cut short by death from typhoid fever at the age of twenty-seven, Davey's work was extremely important, revealing as it did the fallibility of eyewitness accounts of events. He began to look into psychical research in 1883, his interest having been stimulated by the apparent apparition of a deceased friend.

In 1884 he met William Eglinton, the famous physical medium, and was enormously impressed by and convinced of the paranormality of the latter's slate-writing. Once given some idea of how slate-writing might be produced by natural means, however, Davey experimented and found that, by sleight of hand, he could produce many (but not all) of the same effects that Eglinton produced, including writing on the inside of slates that were screwed together. With **Richard Hodgson** as his accomplice, Davey pretended to be a medium and convinced his sitters, specially selected for their intelligence and supposed investigative ability, that his slate-writing was paranormal. Even conjurors, if not aware of the specific methods by which fraudulent results could be obtained, were persuaded of the genuineness of his "phenomena."

Selected Writings: 1887. "The Possibilities of Malobservation &c. from a Practical Point of View." JSPR 3:8; and Hodgson, R. 1887. "The Possibilities of Malobservation and Lapse of Memory from a Practical Point of View." PSPR 4:381.

BIBLIOGRAPHY: Hodgson, R. 1892. "Mr. Davey's Imitations by Conjuring of Phenomena Sometimes Attributed to Spirit Agency." PSPR 8:252.

**Davis, Andrew Jackson, 1826–1910.** "The Poughkeepsie seer." He provided the philosphical basis for **Spiritualism**—a philosophy largely ignored by run-of-the-mill Spiritualists who were interested only in communicating with the spirits of the dead.

Born into a poor family, uneducated, with an alcoholic father, Davis as a boy, after hearing a lecture on animal magnetism, began to go into trance. In 1844 while he was mesmerized he had a vision of **Emanuel Swedenborg** and the Greek physician Galen who gave him a magic staff. His early lectures beginning in 1845, published as *The Principles of Nature,* were a mixture of Swedenborg's cosmology (he claimed Swedenborg dictated the work to him) and the socialism of Charles Fourier. In that same year Davis became a spiritual healer. In *The Great Harmonia* (1850–1855) Davis wrote that to rid society of all its evils it was necessary to understand that there is no such thing as sin and that good and evil play a necessary role in God's plan for the world. Human beings, by following the "harmonious principles of nature [would reach] the successively higher stages of development . . . inherent in each individual" (Isaacs, 1983:81). Alan Gauld (1968:24) considers Davis's writings tedious but remarkable for an uneducated young man. Davis also wrote and lectured on women's rights and insisted on the absolute equality of the sexes. His work was said to have influenced the metaphysics of Christian Science.

Although Davis had early endorsed the physical phenomena of the Fox Sisters, he minimized the importance of mediumship which he felt was unreliable and emphasized instead the importance of social reform. Nevertheless, his reports of spirits living in "Summerland" have influenced mediums from his day to this.

In 1880 when the New York State legislature outlawed the practice of spiritual healing, Davis enrolled in medical school, obtained degrees in medicine and anthropology, and moved to Watertown, Massachusetts where he treated people regardless of their ability to pay.

Selected Writings: *The Principles of Nature, Her Divine Revelations, and a Voice to Mankind,* 1847; *The Great Harmonia: Being a Philosophical Revelation of the Natural Spiritual, and Celestial Universe,* 5 vols., 1850–1855.

BIBLIOGRAPHY: Cavendish, R., ed., *Encyclopedia of the Unexplained,* 1974, p. 173; Gauld, A. *The Founders of Psychical Research,* 1968; Isaacs, E. "The Fox Sisters and American Spiritualism." In H. Kerr and C. L. Crow, eds., *The Occult in America: New Historical Perspectives,* 1983; Moore, R. L. "The Occult Connection? Mormonism, Christian Science, and Spiritualism." In H. Kerr and C. L. Crow, eds., *op. cit.*

**Davis, Gordon.** The most celebrated and cited case in the history of psychical research of a communicator ostensibly from the "other side" who turned out not to be dead. In a sitting in 1922 with the medium Blanche Cooper, **Samuel G. Soal** apparently received a communication from his dead brother Frank. "Frank" said, "Sam, I've brought someone who knows you." The next speaker identified himself as Gordon Davis from "Roch," which Soal took to be Rocheford. The accent and the tone of the voice were very familiar to Soal. In fact, he exclaimed, "By Jove, and it's like Gordon Davis, too." Soal had known Davis when, as boys, from 1898 to 1901 they attended the same school.

Two years before the sitting, Soal had heard that Davis had been killed in World War I. And now Davis was speaking to him and giving all sorts of correct information about the names of the people and the places they had known together. "Davis" also spoke of his "poor wife" and "kiddie." In a later sitting, through one of Mrs. Cooper's controls, "Davis" accurately described parts of a house and its contents. It all looked decidedly like a genuine and impressive spirit communication until 1925 when Soal found out that Davis was not dead. Gordon Davis was very much alive and working as a real estate agent.

When Soal visited Davis three years after the first sitting, he found from Davis's diary that the latter had been conducting an interview with a client at the time of the supposed spirit communication. In addition, Davis did not move into the house described until some time after the sitting. This strange and interesting case seems to presents the paradox of a "spirit communication" from a living person. Since Soal knew much of the information given, the medium could have acquired it through telepathy. Yet some of the information seems to have been precognitive so that "the material could have been obtained neither by telepathy from the sitter nor wholly by telepathy with the Gordon Davis of 1922. Precognitive telepathy or clairvoyance must seemingly have been involved and 'super-ESP' does not seem too strong a term to apply to it" (Gauld, 1977:614).

BIBLIOGRAPHY: Gauld, A. "Discarnate Survival." In B. Wolman, ed., *Handbook of Parapsychology,* 1977, pp. 613–615; Soal, S. G. 1925. "A Report on Some Communications Received Through Mrs. Blanche Cooper." PSPR 35:471.

**Dayal, Parmeshwar, 1931–.** Indian psychologist. Since 1961 he has been involved with psychical research. He has been associated with **Karlis Osis** in the study of deathbed visions in India and has also investigated there cases suggestive of reincarnation. Dayal works in the Bureau of Psychology in Allahabad and is senior research fellow of the Foundation for Reincarnation and Spiritual Research where he assists Dr. Jamuna Prasad.

**Dean, E(ric) Douglas, 1916–.** British parapsychologist living in the United States. His active work in parapsychology began in 1959 when he was assistant director of research at the Parapsychology Foundation, a post he held until 1962, during which time he worked on developing electroencephalographic and plethysmographic methods of measuring telepathy. His main interests in parapsychology have been the use of scientific instruments to measure ESP, PK, and healing; the study of precognition in business executives and the attempt to formulate a theory to account for it. Dr. Dean describes himself in his *curriculum vitae* as having an "intense interest in the Shift of Physics via Quantum Theory to include Consciousness and the Jahn-Dunne method of measuring Consciousness variables in a similar manner to measuring physical variables . . .".

From 1962 to 1976, Dr. Dean was research director of the Psi Communications Project at the New Jersey Institute of Technology and has held many positions in industry, research, and College Board testing. He is presently head of the Parapsychology/Paraphysics Department of the International College of Montreal, Canada. As president of the Parapsychological Association in 1967 he initiated and in 1969 completed affiliation of that body with the American Association for the Advancement of Science. In the years 1970–1973, as president of the New Jersey Society of Parapsychology, he introduced high-voltage testing of psychic healing by means of Kirlian photography. From 1975 to 1978 he was president of the International Kirlian Research Association and since 1976 has been president of the American Healers Association. In 1977 he was elected vice president of the World Federation of Healing. He is on the

Board of the Academy of Religion and Psychical Research.

Dr. Dean has written many articles (1966), two chapters in books (1974a; 1974b), has published one book (1987), is working on another, and has co-authored (1974) a third.

After receiving a bachelor's degree, a second bachelor's degree with honors and a master's degree in electrochemistry from Liverpool University in England, Dr. Dean received his Ph.D. in 1983 from the Humanistic Psychology Institute, now Saybrook Institute, for his dissertation, "An Examination of Infra-Red and Ultra-Violet Techniques to Test for Changes in Water Following the Laying-on-of-Hands."

Selected Writings: *The Mystery of Healing: Still a Mystery after 60,000 Years,* 1987; "Precognition and Retrocognition." In E. D. Mitchell (J. White, ed.) *Psychic Exploration,* 1974a, pp. 173–178; "The Kirlian Aura." In S. Krippner and D. Rubin, eds., *The Energies of Consciousness,* 1974b, Chapter 5; 1966. "Plethysmographic Recordings as ESP Responses." *International Journal of Neuropsychiatry* 2:439; with Mihalasky, J., Schroeder, L. and Ostrander, S. *Executive ESP,* 1974.

**Death.** "Death," wrote **Nicolas Camille Flammarion,** "is the profoundest subject that has ever occupied the thoughts of men, the supreme problem of all times and all peoples" (Flammarion, 1921). The problem is whether death is extinction or a transition.

Those who see consciousness and mind as only epiphenomena or by-products of the brain and body believe that consciousness cannot exist after the death of the brain and body and that death is extinction. But those who, on the ground of religion or personal experience, believe that the human being has a spiritual part (the soul) distinct from the physical part or a non-physical mind that will persist after the death of the body think that death is a transition. One of the aims and tasks of psychical research is carefully and systematically to collect evidence that may throw light on which of these conflicting beliefs is correct. It conducts survival research to inquire into what, if anything, survives death and, if something does, how it survives. Many areas have been and are being studied as part of this task: **Reincarnation, Deathbed Visions, Near-Death Experiences, Out-of-Body Experiences, Apparitions, Haunts, Poltergeists, Mediums,** and **Communicators.**

A recent survey of authorities in parapsychology who have examined all these lines of evidence (Berger, 1987) shows that there is no agreement on whether survival after death has been established. The "supreme problem" is not yet solved. As Robert H. Thouless said: "It is a future task of parapsychology to reduce to a minimum this uncertainty and to find out all we can about the nature [of death]. Its task is very far from being yet completed" (Thouless, 1984).

BIBLIOGRAPHY: Berger, A. S. *Aristocracy of the Dead,* 1987; Flammarion, C. *Death and its Mystery,* 1921; Thouless, R. H. 1984. "Do We Survive Bodily Death?" PSPR 57:1.

**Deathbed Visions.** A phenomenon sometimes reported by a dying person who claims to see or otherwise be aware of dead relatives or friends, or religious figures, or of otherworldly scenes marked by beautiful color and intense light. Psychological, cultural, and medical explanations are advanced for such claims so that no special weight is given the phenomenon as evidence of postmortem survival.

Yet, there are some striking cases in which dying people "see" dead individuals they thought were still alive. William Barrett, for example, reports the case of a young girl who was dying and, who for many days, seemed totally oblivious of her surroundings. Suddenly she opened her eyes and seemed to be aware of the presence of her three dead sisters. She called out their names—Susan, Jane, Ellen—and then, as though completely taken aback at seeing him with them, she called out the name of her brother—Edward—whom she supposed to be alive in India. Later, from letters from India that came after the girl died, it was learned that Edward had died accidentally a week or two prior to his sister's death.

**Karlis Osis** and **Erlendur Haraldsson** made a cross-cultural survey of dying people. They interviewed physicians and nurses in the United States and northern India, the focus of the interviews being on the visions apparently experienced by dying patients. They found that 90 percent of the apparitions perceived were of close relatives and that neither mind-altering medications nor brain pathology produced the apparitional experiences. They concluded that these experiences constitute true glimpses of what lies beyond the present world. See also **Near-Death Experience; Peak in Darien; R. Warcollier.**

**Deathwatch.** The belief that a mysterious ticking sound such as the ticking of a watch signifies that someone is going to die or has died. Several cases in the annals of parapsychology report this strange phenomenon. In one such case, a man narrated that, after he and his wife had gone to bed and to sleep, "I awoke suddenly, with all my senses alive . . . and heard what is commonly called the death-watch ticking. . . . I was well aware that such ticking was caused by some insects in the woodwork, and was not alarmed in the very least degree. The noise continuing, however, for a long time, curiosity got the better of me, and I . . . got softly out of bed, and tried to find out in what part of the room the ticking was. But . . . when I went to one part of the room, it went to another . . . I must have disturbed my wife, for she said to me . . . 'Alfy, your watch is going!' . . . At breakfast my wife said, 'Alfy, I had such a funny dream. I saw your mother with a handkerchief tied under the chin, making such faces at me, and moving her jaws in a most extraordinary manner.' We both laughed. . . . [Then came] a knock at the door. It is the servant, handing me a telegram. It was from my father and ran: 'Mother died last night. Letter to follow.' In the evening I received the letter, which stated among others:—'Mother was paralysed . . . for 6 hours before death. . . . All this time she struggled fearfully to articulate, and the doctor tied, at last, her jaw with a cloth, to prevent her opening it. She died at 4 o'clock this morning." (Cases, 1885).

Was the elusive ticking sound connected with the mother's death? This case resembles those in which the fall of a picture or the stoppage of a clock are reported as presaging death. If these events do not have a normal explanation, psychokinesis, by which human will may produce physical effects, may then be the responsible factor, but whose—mother's, husband's or wife's? The wife in her dream by extrasensory perception seems to have received veridical information about her mother-in-law's death. Yet to attempt to explain physical effects, such as ticking sounds, falling pictures or stopping clocks on the basis of psychokinesis is to try to explain these events with an as yet unexplained phenomenon. Until more research clears up the question, however, the explanation is a possible hypothesis for a baffling mystery.

BIBLIOGRAPHY: "Cases Received by the Literary Committee." 1885. JSPR 1:487.

**De Boni, Gastone, 1908–1986.** Italian physician. He was introduced to psychical research by reading the works of Nicolas Camille Flammarion. His long friendship with Ernesto Bozzano served to deepen his interest in the field. He collected over the years an enormous library of over 10,000 volumes dealing with the paranormal. In 1941, he published the first book on psychical research ever to appear in Italy and six years later became director of the Italian publication *Luce e Ombra.* Under his direction the publication took on a Spiritualist flavor.

De Boni was sometimes criticized by Italian parapsychologists, including Piero Cassoli, for his leanings toward Spiritualism and for his treatment of paranormal phenomena. "In no way can we agree to his standards of control," they said (Cassoli, 1971). Nevertheless, De Boni became president of the Società Italiana di Parapsicología in 1955 and continued firmly in charge of *Luce e Ombra* until his death.

BIBLIOGRAPHY: Cassoli, P. "Parapsychology in Italy Today." *Proceedings of an International Conference Parapsychology Today: A Geographical View,* 1971, p. 187.

**Deck, ESP Card.** A pack containing twenty-five cards consisting of five duplicates of five symbols: a star, a circle, a square, a cross, and wavy lines.

**Decline Effect.** Also called "decline curve." In many extrasensory perception and psychokinesis tests, the deterioration of a scoring rate from the start of a run or experimental series to the end.

**Déjà Vu.** French words meaning "already seen." The feeling or belief that a place or event is familiar and has been experienced before. Nathaniel Hawthorne and **Charles Dickens,** among other authors, have written about it and General George S. Patton was one of many notables who have experienced it. This feelings or belief is not in itself a parapsychological phenomenon. Nevertheless, the déjà vu experience is of interest in psychical research because sometimes it is adduced as evidence of **Reincarnation.**

Many cases of déjà vu that seem to suggest a previous lifetime can, however, be accounted for on other grounds. There was, for instance, an instructive case (Lewis, 1936) of a British army officer who, with his wife, was on a tour of a section of Great Britain that neither had visited before. Adjacent to the road they came across a pool that, along with other objects in the area, seemed so entirely familiar to them that they thought they must have lived in the area during a prior incarnation. Following the trip, they went back to London and revisited an art gallery. There they found a painting—which they had seen before they left on their trip—of a pool beside a road. Neither had remembered the picture until their return visit to the gallery. **Cryptomnesia** rather than reincarnation was the more probable explanation for their déjà vu experience. See also **Paramnesia.**

BIBLIOGRAPHY: Lewis, L. S. May 11, 1936. Correspondence. *Morning Post.* London.

**Delanne, Gabriel, 1857–1926.** Eminent French psychical researcher. He was one of the pioneers in the use of paraffin casts, such as were used later by Gustave Geley, to obtain evidence of materialization. Reincarnation interested him and he gathered many documented and impressive cases of the reincarnation-type from letters and other sources (Delanne, 1924). Editor of *Revue Scientifique et Moderne de Spiritisme,* Delanne was an ardent advocate of Spiritism and convinced beyond doubt of life after death: "We are now able to assure ourselves that the individual human soul is not, as materialists claim, a function of the nervous system; it is a being which can exist independently of the physical organism, and which gives evidence of its existence and of the possession of all its faculties. . . . We consider that we possess abundant proof of all descriptions to attest the fact of the survival of the intelligent principle, with all its mental and moral attributes, through the crisis of physical disintegration called death. The evidence which supports this assertion is extensive and weighty" (Delanne, 1904:25, 260). Although Delanne's books were written with this foregone conclusion, they are all interesting and instructive in their manner of presenting experiments and facts.

Selected Writings: Delanne, G. *Documents pour Servir à l'Étude de la Reincarnation,* 1924; *Evidence for a Future Life (L'Âme est Immortelle)* (E. T. H. A. Dallas), 1904.

**De La Warr, George, 1904–1969.** British engineer. Of him it was said: "Either de la Warr should be placed in the scientific stocks and have things thrown at him or else he should be awarded a fellowship in the Royal Society and a knighthood without delay" (Parsons, 1961). De la Warr developed a **Black Box** that he claimed would provide diagnoses and treatments for disorders, human or animal. Among other things, he claimed four hundred successful diagnoses with the apparatus, in one case diagnosing the pregnancies of a woman and a cat just by using the box's camera to photograph blood spots belonging to them; in another case diagnosing fetal sex from blood spots (Day with De La Warr, 1956). These and other claims challenging conventional medicine were of great interest to psychical research as possible instances of diagnostic tools for paranormal healing. But after inquiry and examination, investigators decided the evidence was not strong enough to support the claims (Parsons, 1961). As if to buttress this conclusion, it is worth noting the 1960 "Black Box Case" in which De La Warr was sued for damages on the ground of fraud. The plaintiff who purchased a black box claimed that it was a fake. For example, according to the box, her patients changed sex every day. The court thought that the equipment was all fake, too, but, because De La Warr seemed honestly to believe that his boxes were really diagnostic tools, found for the defendant.

Selected Writing: Day, L. with De La Warr, G. *New Worlds Beyond the Atom,* 1956.

BIBLIOGRAPHY: Parsons, D. 1961. "The Black Boxes of Mr De La Warr." JSPR 41:12.

**Delphic Oracle.** One hundred miles from Athens, Greece, the oracle of Delphi lived on the slopes of Mt. Parnassus where the temple of Apollo was located. The greatest oracle in Greece, the Delphic oracle was the most famous of **Oracles** anywhere and represented the most respected wisdom in the ancient world. The medium was always female, over fifty years of age, separated from her husband and was known as the Pythia. While in trance, she would become possessed and a voice different from her own would speak in the first person as a god to counsel, usually on political matters, or, as in the case of **Croesus,** on military questions. Advice was given generally in obscure language that required interpretation although sometimes the Pythia gave clear and specific information.

One explanation for the trance is that it was caused by sulfurous fumes at Delphi breathed in by the medium. But geologists have discovered no signs of vapors there. The trance was induced either by chewing potent laurel leaves or by going through ritualistic acts such as occupying the holy seat of Apollo or touching his sacred laurel. The trance seemed geniune because once, according to Plutarch, a Pythia, seemingly possessed by an evil spirit, ran screaming in a hoarse voice from the temple. Within a few days she was dead.

**Dematerialization.** Following a period of time after the **materialization** of figures or objects, their gradual dematerializing or fading away completely as sitters watch with no trace left behind; also the paranormal vanishing of a portion of a living human being. See also **Aksakoff, Alexander.**

**De Morgan, Augustus, 1806–1871.** English logician. He was a professor of mathematics at the University College of London whose studies in logic and whose treatise, *Formal Logic, or the Calculus of Inference, Necessary and Probable* (1847), helped to develop mathematical logic.

He is a **Noted Witness** to support clairoyance for he said: "I had frequently heard of the thing called clairvoyance . . . but always considered it as a thing of which I had no evidence direct or personal, and which I could not admit till such evidence came. . . . One evening I dined at a house about a mile from my own in which my wife had never been at that time." While he was visiting at the house, a young girl who was with his wife outside the house said that she "saw" De Morgan talking to an old gentleman and that there were ladies there. "This was a true description of the party, except that the other gentleman was not old . . .". (Of course, to a young person someone over forty years of age seems old.) The girl then described the room as having white and red curtains made up into a loop and said there were wine, water, and biscuits on the table. Of the curtains, De Morgan said the girl's description was "true to the letter" and the reference to wine, water, and biscuits "was literally true. . . . All this is no secret. You may tell whom you like, and give my name."

BIBLIOGRAPHY: Prince, W. F. *Noted Witnesses for Psychic Occurrences,* 1963.

**Deport.** The movement of living organisms or material objects out of a permanently enclosed area without any known human or animal agency and implying the passage of one solid body through another. See also **Teleportation.**

**Dermal Perception.** Also called "skin sight". See **Dermo-Optic Perception.**

**Dermo-Optic Perception.** Also called "eyeless vision" and "dermal perception." Feats such as that of the blindfolded **Kuda Bux** who could "read" print with his nose, or of the Soviet woman **Rosa Kuleshova** who had the ability while blindfolded to identify colors with her fingertips, suggested to many people a paranormal phenomenon. It was thought that extrasensory perception might be providing individuals such as Bux and Kuleshova with the power to perceive external objects without the use of the organ of sight. But this theory seems to have been overthrown by experiments **Carroll B. Nash** and others conducted in the United States. In his experiment, Nash tested thirty-six subjects to determine if, with the tips of their fingers, they could distinguish between concealed black or red target paper. In some runs, the target paper, either black or red, was not covered, in some it was covered with cellophane and in some with glass. The subjects were able to distinguish the colors when they touched the paper directly or the cellophane covering but could not identify the colors through the glass covering. If ESP were working, it should have operated under all conditions. The result of the experiment therefore suggests not ESP but a "cutaneous color sensitivity." Indeed, Barbara Ivanova of the Soviet Union ruled out any possibility of ESP by Rosa Kuleshova and called her faculty "dermo-optic perception," the same term that had been used years before by her countryman Professor A. S. Novomeysky of the Sverdlovsk Pedagogical Institute in the Soviet Union.

Since 1960, investigations carried out in the United States, in the Soviet Union, and in

France by **Yvonne Duplessis** have strongly suggested that the human skin is sensitive to radiations of the electromagnetic spectrum in the infrared range. Dermo-optic perception, therefore, has to do with the ability of the human being to respond to colored surfaces whether they are at a distance, hidden in darkness, or under opaque screens. See also **Exceptional Human Body Function.**

**Despard, Rosina Clara ("Rose Morton"), 1863–?.** The principal witness on whose paper (Morton, 1892) and testimony the famous "Morton Ghost" case depends. When, in 1882, the family of Captain F. W. Despard occupied the house in Cheltenham, England, where the strange phenomena occurred, Rosina Clara Despard was unmarried, the eldest of the captain's daughters, and was described as "a lady of scientific training, now preparing to be a physician" (Myers, 1892). In fact, she went on to study at the London School of Medicine that had just begun its operations in 1874. She passed her final examination with honors. London medical degrees were granted to women for the first time in 1878, and when she became a medical doctor in 1895, no more than 200 women were shown in the medical register (Huby, 1970). For a woman to have achieved so much in the nineteenth century was a noteworthy accomplishment and evidence of Despard's high intellectual and other qualities. The observations she made in the Morton Ghost case, therefore, must be given considerable weight. See also **Ghost.**

Selected Writing: Morton, R. C. 1892. "Record of a Haunted House." PSPR 8:311.

BIBLIOGRAPHY: Huby, P. M. 1970. "New Evidence About 'Rose Morton'." JSPR 45:391; Myers, F. W. H. 1892. "Prefatory Note. Record of a Haunted House." PSPR 8:311.

**D'Esperance, Elizabeth, 1855–1919.** pseudonym of Elizabeth Hope Reed, British physical medium. In 1893 she was investigated by Alexander N. Aksakoff and, during a séance with him and other sitters, was the star of one of the most spectacular shows of partial dematerialization ever put on. The lower half of her body seemed to disappear completely while the upper half was visible, talked, and drank water.

**Dessoir, Max, 1867–1947.** German "uomo universale." Like the great Leonardo da Vinci, he was versatile and knowledgeable about everything. As a child, he played the violin with such perfection that Kaiser Wilhelm presented the young virtuoso with one. As he grew into adulthood, he was the multifaceted Renaissance man, an expert in psychology, physiology, a professor of philosophy, a medical doctor, a radio broadcaster on culture and history, and one of the foremost aestheticians who worked out a system of the general theory of art. He believed that the term "aesthetics" should be applied to the philosophical approach and "art" to the scientific approach. Finally, he was a psychical researcher with a lifelong interest in the field.

By the time he was nineteen, he had already conducted successful experiments in telepathy. In 1888, he co-founded in Germany the Gesselschaft für Experimental-Psychologie (Society for Experimental Psychology) to study hypnosis and paranormal phenomena. In 1889, he coined the term "parapsychology," which many erroneously attribute to Joseph Banks Rhine who adopted it and made it a word of general use. Dessoir went on to investigate mediums, among them Eusapia Palladino, to found the parapsychological publication *Zeitschrift für kritischen Okkultismus,* and to write extensively on psychical research. Although extremely critical, he thought that "the Piper case . . . contains a residuum of which there is not, so far, any normal explanation" (Schiller, 1921:146). He saw himself as an educator in psychical research for the German public. Dessoir is one of the little-known but extraordinary figures in the history of the field.

Selected Writings: 1889. "Die Parapsychologie. Eine Entgegnung auf den Artikel 'Der Prophet'." *Sphinx* 7:341; 1886. "Experiments in Muscle-Reading and Thought-Transference." PSPR 4:111.

BIBLIOGRAPHY: Hövelmann, G. H. "Neglected Figures in the History of Parapsychology. I. Some General Reflections." In F. W. J. J. Snel, ed., *Liber Amicorum in Honour of G. A. M. Zorab,* 1986, p. 94; Schiller, F. C. S. 1921. "Vom Jenseits der Seele." PSPR 32:146.

**Dettore, Ugo, 1905–.** Italian novelist and scholar. He taught history and philosophy and has been interested in parapsychology for more than thirty years. He used his scholarship and literary skills to prepare and edit encyclopedias of parapsychology and a work on the history of the field to which Italian parapsychologists responded enthusiastically. In several of his works will be found a philosophy and theory of the paranormal.

Selected Writings: Dettore, U., ed., *L'Uomo e l'Ignoto,* 1978. 5 vols.; *L'Altro Regno,* 1973.

**Deviation.** The amount an observed number of hits or an average score varies (either above or below) from mean chance expectation of a run or series or other unit of trials (JP).

**Dice-Throwing Tests.** Dice-throwing by hand, by cup, or by a mechanical device to determine whether a subject can will certain die faces to come up in a proportion significantly greater than mean chance expectation has been one of the traditional methods used in tests of **Psychokinesis.** There are three forms of dice-throwing tests: 1. the "high dice" test—in which two dice are thrown and the subject wills die faces of eight or more to come up; 2. the "seven" or gambler's test—in which two dice are thrown and the subject wills die faces totalling seven to be uppermost; 3. the "low dice" test—in which two dice are thrown and the subject wills them to fall with die faces adding up to six or less uppermost.

**Dickens, Charles, 1812–1870.** English novelist. He achieved unparalleled success as the writer of stories that, because of their unforgettable characters, sentimentality, humor, and melodramatic plots, were and continue to be enjoyed by the mass of readers. Among his best-known works are *Pickwick Papers* (1836), *A Christmas Carol* (1843), *David Copperfield,* (1850), *Oliver Twist* (1837–1839), and *A Tale of Two Cities* (1859).

In the 1830s Dickens became friendly with Prof. John Elliotson of the University Hospital in London. Elliotson demonstrated mesmerism to Dickens who, despite initial strong preconceptions against it, became a believer. He even used it to treat himself and his family and cured the wife of a Swiss banker of a nervous tic.

With his unhappy marriage broken, Dickens set up a liaison with a young actress. At about the same time he recorded an experience that makes him a **Noted Witness** for the paranormal. On May 20, 1863, Dickens wrote: "On Thursday night in last week, . . . I dreamed that I saw a lady in a red shawl with her back to me (whom I supposed to be E). On her turning round I found that I did not know her, and she said. 'I am Miss Napier'. All the time I was dressing the next morning I thought—What a preposterous thing to have so very distinct a dream about nothing! for I never heard of any Miss Napier. That same Friday night, I read. After the reading, came into my retiring-room, Mary Boyle and her brother, and *the* Lady in red, whom they present as 'Miss Napier'. These are all the circumstances exactly told."

Besides this dream suggestive of precognition, Dickens had another experience that suggests déjà vu or reincarnation. He went to Ferrara in Italy for the first time and when he saw it, he recorded: "In the foreground was a group of silent peasant girls leaning over the parapet of a little bridge, looking now up at the sky, now down into the water. In the distance a deep dell; the shadow of approaching night on everything. If I had been murdered there in some former life I could not have seemed to remember the place more thoroughly or with more emphatic chilling of the blood . . .".

BIBLIOGRAPHY: Inglis. B. *Natural and Supernatural,* 1977, p. 175; Shirley, R. *The Problem of Rebirth,* n.d.; Forster, J. *The Life of Charles Dickens,* 1874. 3 Vols. III, pp. 484–485.

**Dictionary Test.** To try to obtain stronger evidence to support the hypothesis of human survival of bodily death, **Arthur S. Berger** devised this test based on the same principles as the **Cipher Test.** Under his method, the letters of a key word chosen at random from a dictionary, and its definition, are translated into numbers following a formula provided by Berger. A test message is then enciphered. Here "enciphered" means that numbers are substituted for the real letters of a message so that the message cannot be read by anyone who does not have the verbal key to decipher it. The individuals enciphering messages keep their keys to themselves and do not reveal them to anyone. They do not even write them down. Their intentions are, if they survive death, to communicate their secret verbal keys in order to decipher their messages. It is the furnishing of their keys, which no one else could have known and without which their messages cannot be deciphered, that will stand as *prima facie* evidence of their postmortem survival and identity. Antony Flew has called Berger's test, expecially when used by people fitting the profile of the "ideal" communicator Berger's research has identified, a "significant step forward" (Flew, 1987) in survival research.

BIBLIOGRAPHY: Berger, A. S. *Aristocracy of the Dead,* 1987; Flew, A. Foreword. In A. S. Berger, *Aristocracy of the Dead,* 1987.

**Didier, Alexis, c. 1847–c. 1888.** French clairvoyant. After being hypnotized and having his eyes bandaged by his manager, Didier was said to be able to name cards lying face down on a table, describe the contents of a closed tin box, and read passages ten or twenty pages ahead of the page to which a book brought by a stranger was open. The psychical researchers of the time, especially Frank Podmore, thought Didier an imposter and that the bandages over his eyes were put on so unsatisfactorily that he could see. But it is difficult to find any normal explanation for the testimony of Robert Houdin who was a trained observer and famous conjuror. He asked Didier what was written on a piece of paper Houdin had folded in fours. Didier replied that the test was not difficult and said: "Receipt of MM. Saquier and Bray, booksellers, 64, Rue des Saint-Pères, for 15 francs, 20 cents." The astonished Houdin verified the correctness of Didier's description (Extract 1899).

BIBLIOGRAPHY: "Extract from J. E. De Mirville's 'Des Esprits et de Leurs manifestations Fluidiques.'" 1899. PSPR 14:373.

**Dieppe Raid.** One of the most impressive paranormal auditory experiences ever recorded, the Dieppe Raid case sounds like an audio tape recording of a battle during World War II played back almost a decade later. On August 19, 1942, the British commenced what was to be for them a costly operation against the Germans. The strategy was to have commandos land in two surprise thrusts on the French coast, one to the east of Dieppe, one to the west. Then after an air attack and bombardment by destroyers, the main assault by Canadian forces was to begin. Just before 4 A.M., assault craft accidentally encountered a German convoy and firing began that probably alerted the Germans at Puys, two miles east of Dieppe and started them shouting as they got ready to defend the beaches. At 5:07 A.M., the assault craft began their landings at Puys in the face of heavy defensive fire. At 5:15 A.M., allied aircraft attacked. At 5:20 A.M., the main assault was launched against Dieppe as firing by the Germans became intense. At 5:40 A.M., destroyers ceased bombarding Dieppe. At 5:50 A.M., Royal Air Force planes attacked. But the results for the invaders were horrendous. Within a few hours, half their force was lost along with many planes and landing craft.

Nine years later, Dieppe was quiet and peaceful again. Two sisters-in-law from England decided to take their holiday at Puys. One of them brought along her two children and a nurse. Like most people who had lived through World War II, they knew about the raid on Dieppe but were not any more knowledgeable about that operation than other important operations, such as the invasion of Normandy.

The Englishwomen shared one bedroom in a house where German troops had been quartered at the time of the Dieppe operation. The nurse and children occupied another bedroom a couple of doors away on the same floor. At about 4 A.M., both sisters-in-law were disturbed in their sleep by noises that resembled a storm at sea and by the sounds of men coming from the direction of the beach. At 5:05 A.M., one of the women heard the noise of gunfire, shell-fire, men's cries, and landing craft. Two minutes later the other woman heard the same noises. Shortly thereafter sounds like dive-bombers were heard. At 5:40 A.M., the sounds stopped but at 5:50 A.M. began again with airplane noises predominating.

The two women stood on the balcony of their room, listened and took notes but saw nothing. It was as if the battle were being fought over again by unseen soldiers. As noted by the parapsychologists who investigated the case: "The remarkable feature of this case is the close correspondence between the times of the 'battle sounds' heard by the percipients on the 4th of August, 1951, and the times of the actual battle sounds resulting from the operations on the 19th August 1942." The investigators concluded: "Both as regards form and content we think the experience must be rated as a genuine psi phenomenon, of which little or nothing was derived from previously normally acquired knowledge" (Lambert and Gay, 1952).

Subsequent to this conclusion, however, it came to light that a dredge had been operating in the Dieppe Harbor from about midnight to 8:15 A.M. when the women were on their holiday. The sound it made coming from a distance and distorted by the cliffs near Dieppe could have been interpreted by the women as battle-sounds. Yet, later in the day, after the women had taken their notes, they asked other people whether they also had been disturbed by noises during the night and all replied that they had not been. Neither the nurse nor the children heard any sounds, either. The failure of other people to hear any sounds suggests that the noises noted did not come from the dredge, from water in the pipes, or from a radio. No theory or fact has been put forward satisfactory enough to change the investigators' conclusion of paranormality.

The Dieppe Raid case bears an interesting resemblance to the case reported in *An Adventure* which took place in the gardens of the Trianon in Versailles, France. In both cases, two English ladies on a holiday had unusual experiences in France. The Dieppe case, however, seems the more evidential of the two. See also **Adventure, An; Versailles, Apparitions At.**

BIBLIOGRAPHY: Lambert, G. W. and Gay, K. 1952. "The Dieppe Raid Case." JSPR 36:607.

**Differential Effect.** Significant difference between scoring rates when subjects are participating in an experiment in which two procedural conditions (such as two types of targets or two modes of response) are compared. See also **Score.**

**Dingwall, Eric John, 1890–1986.** British investigator of the paranormal. Known as the *enfant terrible* of parapsychology, Dingwall was for six decades a prominent and respected (if feared) worker in the field. In 1969, he abruptly abandoned parapsychology, however, because he said he did not want to waste any more time on parapsychologists' "hoaxes and fictional reports."

Early in his career, Dingwall had been the director of the Department of Physical Phenomena at the American Society for Psychical Research and from 1922 to 1927 the paid research officer of the Society for Psychical Research. Although he was discharged from that post in 1927, he continued to be an active force in the SPR for the next forty-odd years. Dingwall devoted considerable study to mental mediums. But, above all, he was the cautious and keen observer and critic of experiments conducted by others in physical mediumship, which was his particular interest. As research officer of the SPR, he conducted his own experiments with Mina S. Crandon ("Margery"). Although he considered her one of the most remarkable of physical mediums and wrote enthusiastically to Albert von Schrenck-Notzing of sittings with her in 1924, he could not bring himself to state that the phenomena (ectoplasm) produced from a "bodily opening" at the sittings were authentic. (Some have said that the so-called "ectoplasm" was really animal lung tissue.)

He was extremely critical of the work of most parapsychologists and wrote a scathing study of Harry Price's investigations of Borley Rectory. He was contemptuous of Gilbert Murray's informal experiments in telepathy and of the cross-correspondences that he thought were based on material carefully selected from a mass of unrevealed writings. His "pet aversion" was J. G. Piddington. He did, however, respect **Helen Salter,** thought the best psychical researcher of the past had been Charles Richet and, as both a researcher and a person, admired Everard Feilding most of all.

At the end of his long career, Dingwall concluded that most of the leading parapsychologists he had known during his sixty years in the field were not objectively in search of truth and were only out to prove their preconceived theories. "During the past 60 years," he wrote (1985:171), "I have noted . . . incidents in which leading parapsychologists and their propagandists have been shown to be barefaced liars." Alan Gauld (1987) has described him as "an historical rationalist of anti-clerical tendencies. . . . [H]e looked upon what he saw as a rapidly growing tendency toward 'occultism'. . . . (ESP and PK being, of course, the modern jargon terms for such powers)." Yet Dingwall had had some experiences that he could not explain: a pseudopod that he had seen creep across the floor in a sitting with Stella C., a cold wind that blew through Eva C.'s cabinet and some haunting-like phenomena that occurred in his own home.

He was an expert archivist who helped catalogue the SPR's library. He thought that psychical researchers and subjects alike had been interested in (and practiced) sexual deviation (West, 1987). And he was, in fact, widely known outside of parapsychology in academic circles as an expert on "obscure sexual practices, and as the honorary curator of the 'locked case' in the British Museum Library" (Gauld, 1987). The British Museum was his second home and it was to the British Museum that he left the bulk of his estate.

Selected Writings: "The Need for Responsibility in Parapsychology." In P. Kurtz, ed., *A Skeptic's Handbook of Parapsychology,* 1985; *Some Human Oddities,* 1962; *Very Peculiar People,* 1962; 1970. "Responsibility in Parapsychology." *Parapsychology Review.* 1:13; *Ghosts and Spirits of the Ancient World,* 1930; 1926. "A Report on a Series of Sittings with the Medium Margery." PSPR 36:79; 1924. "Telekinetic and Teleplastic Mediumship." PSPR 34:324; 1922. "The Hypothesis of Fraud." PSPR 32:309.

BIBLIOGRAPHY: Gauld, A. 1987. "Recollections of E. J. Dingwall." JSPR 54:230; West, D. J. 1987. "Obituary." JSPR 54:92.

**Direct Voice.** A voice ostensibly of and from a deceased person and not of or from the physical medium in whose presence it is heard. Occasionally, words seemingly spoken directly by communicators themselves are heard in whispers. Since the direct voice usually seems to come from inside a luminous trumpet whirling or floating in the dark above the heads of sitters, sittings with direct voice mediums are often called trumpet sittings. See also **Mark W. Richardson.**

**Direct Writing.** Writing by unseen hands on paper or slate of spirit messages or answers to sitters' questions. Some remarkable instances of such writing were reported during the mediumships of **William Stainton Moses** and **Daniel D. Home.** In Moses's case, "Direct writing was often given, sometimes on a sheet of paper placed in the centre of the table and equidistant from all the sitters; at other times one of us would place our hands on a piece of paper previously dated and initialled, and usually a message was found written upon it at the conclusion of the seance. We always placed a pencil upon the paper, but sometimes we only provided a small piece of lead, the results being the same in both cases" (Myers, 1893).

When **Sir William Crookes** had a sitting with Home and asked for a written message, the following took place: "A pencil and some pieces of paper were lying on the centre of the table; presently the pencil rose on its point, and after advancing by hesitating jerks to the paper, fell down. It then rose and again fell. A third time it tried, but with no better result. After this a small wooden lath, which was lying upon the table, slid towards the pencil, and rose a few inches from the table; the pencil rose again, and propping itself against the lath, the two together made an effort to mark the paper. It fell again and then a joint effort was again made. After a third trial, the lath gave it up and moved back to its place, the pencil lay as it fell across the paper, and an alphabetic message told us, 'We have tried to do as you asked, but our power is exhausted'" (Crookes, 1875).

Fraud is always a possible explanation for reports such as these, yet the Crookes sitting took place in Crookes's own home and in full light. The experiments conducted by Richard Hodgson and S. J. Davey, however, show that there can be much lapse of memory and malobservation on the part of sitters (1887). Even if no fraud is detected, these experiments suggest that reports of direct writing be looked on with great caution.

BIBLIOGRAPHY: Crookes, W. *Researches in Spiritualism,* 1875, p. 93; Hodgson, R. and Davey, S. J. 1897. "The Possibility of Malobservation and Lapse of Memory." PSPR 4:381; Myers, F. W. H. 1893. "The Experience of W. Stainton Moses—I." PSPR 9:245.

**Dirty Test Tube.** This metaphor is used when the conditions of an experiment have been found below the standards generally accepted by scientists so that the results of the experiment are in question and must be rejected. A test tube must be clean when doing research; the presence of any dirt in the tube implies that the entire experiment is faulty. This kind of approach, of course, allows skeptics to use any kind of weakness in an experiment, for example, overcomplicated design or poor control or documentation, as a reason for throwing out all the evidence. Most parapsychologists feel that the results of an experiment should not be dismissed unless critics can show a connection between the results and the suspect conditions and that only those results clearly linked to the dirt in the test tube should be rejected.

A similar problem has always existed in psychical research and parapsychology. Mediums in séances, notably Eusapia Palladino, cheated when they could and subjects in experiments, among them the "Jones Boys" and the Creery Sisters, used signals. Under the strict rule laid down by the English and American psychical researchers, namely, once a cheat always a cheat, all results produced by cheating mediums or subjects were questioned. But is this policy correct? Should any cheating by mediums or subjects invalidate the results of other rigorously controlled séances or experiments in which genuine paranormal gifts may have been demonstrated? See also **Jones, Glyn** and **Ieuan.**

**Discarnate.** An incorporeal entity or spirit. Although the term is usually applied to the personality of a deceased individual believed to have survived physical death and to continue without a physical body, there are discarnate entities that claim never to have been incarnate. See also **Channeling; Communicator; Survival; Survival Research.**

**Di Simone, Giorgio, 1925–.** French psychotherapist now residing in Italy and teaching at the University of Naples. He has been preoccupied with psychical research since 1947. His primary interest has been in paranormal dreams, in studying the survival hypothesis, and in the critical and scientific investigations of mediums. In the course of these last investigations he uses voice prints to compare the voice of the medium with that of a purported discarnate communicator. From 1973 to 1986, he issued reports of his experiments with mediumistic communications from "Dimension X."

Di Simone, who received a prize from the Schweizerische Vereinigung für Parapsychologie (Swiss Association for Parapsychology) in 1980, founded and is director of the **Centro Italiano di Parapsicología** and also established and is president of **Instituto "Gnosis" per la Ricérca Sulla Ipòtesi Soppravvivenza.**

Selected Writings: Di Simone, G. *Rapporto dalla Dimensione X,* 1973–1986; *Dialoghi con la Dimensione X. (Beyond Death),* 1981.

**Displacement.** ESP responses to targets other than those for which the calls were intended. Backward displacement: ESP responses to targets preceding the intended targets. Displacement to the targets one, two three, etc. places preceding the intended target are designated as (−1), (−2), (−3), etc. Forward displacement: ESP responses to targets coming later than the intended targets. Displacement to the targets one, two, three, etc., places after the intended target are designated as (+1), (+2), (+3), etc. (JP).

**Dissociation.** A term for an **Altered State of Consciousness.** See also **Trance.**

**Divination.** It can mean water divining or dowsing. A forked "divining rod" or *virgula divina,* as the philosopher John Locke called it in 1691, is held by those claiming the power to find underground water or objects. Divination also refers to methods famliar to classical antiquity that were employed to obtain knowledge of things to come. Plato and Cicero distinguished between two types of divination—*ominal,* which included divining by augury, astrology, lots or entrails; and *intuitive,* which included dreams and trances.

Psychical research finds divination interesting in both these senses. Dowsing may possibly be a form of clairvoyance. Since some of the strongest data in support of extrasensory perception come from veridical dreams and the trance state, diviners using the intuitive type of divination may have acquired information by extrasensory perception, also. Even Democritus in the fifth centry B.C. believed that a kind of telepathy was responsible for the content of diviners' dreams. He believed that the images and thoughts projected by living people entered into dreams through the pores of the body of the dreaming diviner (Dodds, 1971). It is probable that those individuals the ancients and cultures outside our own call "diviners" we would call psychics.

BIBLIOGRAPHY: Barrett, W. F. 1900. "On the So-Called Divining Rod." PSPR 15:130; Dodds, E. R. 1971. "Supernormal Phenomena in Classical Antiquity." PSPR 55:189.

**Diviner.** An individual who forecasts the future either by using innate abilities to converse with spirits, as in the **Shaking Tent** phenomenon, or through techniques such as reading **Tarot Cards, Crystal-Gazing,** or **Astrology.** It is unfortunate that diviners in non-Western societies tend to resist scientific investigation. In South Africa, for example, attempts by parapsychologists to conduct scientific studies of African black diviners in that country have failed. The reason may be the difficult race relations there but, more fundamentally, it seems that scientific study is the tool of Western culture and does not operate well in a very different one.

**Dixon, Jeane Pinckert, 1918–.** American prophetess. One of the most famous of America's psychics, whose predictions have made headlines in the tabloids since 1952, her greatest prestige and fame stem from her reported (some say they never happened) predictions of the assassination of President **John F. Kennedy.** As a result, her biography *A Gift of Prophecy: The Phenomenal Jeane Dixon* (1965), written by **Ruth Montgomery,** was a pre-publication best-seller. Although many of her prophecies have been completely wrong—that the Vietnam War would be over in the summer of 1966; that Red China would plunge the world into war in 1958; that Walter Reuther would win a bid for the presidency in 1964, etc.—she has made others that have been inexplicably correct, including her prediction that Dag Hammerskjold would die in an airplane crash in mid-September, 1961 (he was killed on September 18 of that year).

Mrs. Dixon, who never charges for her services, believes that her visions come from God and that inaccuracies are due to her misinterpretation of what she sees. In any event, she does seem to have psychic ability, and it has been suggested that "a qualified parapsychologist [should] study Mrs. Dixon and make his findings known" (White, 1966). See also **Precognition.**

BIBLIOGRAPHY: Ebon, M. *Prophecy in Our Time,* 1968; Montgomery, R. *A Gift of Prophecy,* 1965; White, R. 1966. "A Gift of Prophecy: The Phenomenal Jeane Dixon." JASPR 60:297.

**Doctrinal Compliance.** Term used by **Jan Ehrenwald** to describe thoughts, wishes, and expectations in a therapist's mind that are conveyed via telepathy to a patient under analysis. Ehrenwald also observed the tendency of patients to use symbols in their dreams in line with the different schools of psychoanalysis to which their analysts belong.

**Dodds, Eric Robertson, 1893–1979.** English classical scholar. Dodds combined two interests "which have been with me through most of my working life—curiosity about the religious ideas of classical antiquity and curiosity about those oddities of human experience which form the subject-matter of psychical research or, to use a more pretentious word, 'parapsychology'" (Dodds, 1971:189).

His latter curiosity began as a result of reading another classical scholar, Frederic W. H. Myers. He was drawn to many aspects of psychical research and parapsychology. He made a survey of paranormal phenomena in the ancient world (Dodds, 1971). He was impressed by telepathy but insisted that the direction and method of experiments be changed to "shift from the question 'Whether' to the question 'How' . . . [T]o show *that* telepathy works, the mass quantitative experiment was the ideal instrument because of its logical simplicity and controllability; but for discovering *how* telepathy works it is a blunt tool—partly because it yields no insight into the mind of either agent or percipient, and partly because it is inadequate to the concrete richness of the phenomena as it occurs in nature." (Dodds, 1962:256). He surveyed Gilbert Murray's experiments in telepathy (Dodds, 1972) and even conducted his own. He had sittings with mediums, both mental and physical, including Rudi Schneider and his brother, Willi.

A regius professor of Greek at Oxford University, Dodds also focused his interest on the question of human survival after death. In what has become a classic paper (Dodds, 1934), he cited his reasons for not believing in survival and for thinking that the hypothesis of super ESP covers all the evidence from mediumship. The sheer triviality of mediumistic communications from spirits and the unintellectual afterlife they were supposed to be leading disgusted him: "How is it that these countless Columbuses, returning to us (if but for an hour) from the supreme voyage of discovery, describe the life beyond the tomb in terms that are equally applicable to life in Putney, or alternatively, are borrowed from cheap theosophical literature? Can the vivid literary talent of a Verrall or the philosophic insights of a Myers do no more than this? And why, in general, do the 'spirits' of intellectually gifted persons produce no evidence that they retain their gifts in the other world?" (Dodds, 1934:171).

President of the Society for Psychical Research from 1961 to 1963, Dodds is described as "a deep thinker and a stimulating teacher . . . [who gave] wise, witty and gentle—but far from weak—guidance" (Heywood, 1979). When Dodds talked, people listened and when he wrote, they read.

Selected Writings: 1972. "Gilbert Murray's Last Experiments." PSPR 55:371; 1971. "Supernormal Phenomena in Classical Antiquity." PSPR 55:189; 1962. "Experimental Research at the Universities and in the Society." PSPR 53:247; 1934. "Why I Do Not Believe in Survival." PSPR 42:147.

BIBLIOGRAPHY: Heywood, R. 1979. "Professor E. R. Dodds, D. Litt., F.B.A." JSPR 50:171.

**Doppelganger.** The subject of much European folklore, the doppelganger has been studied by European scientists. It is usually the mirror image of the subject and appears without warning. Sometimes this **Double** has warned the experiencer of danger; sometimes it has appeared to foretell a future event, that is, it is older than the person is at the time of the experience and is either dressed in clothes the person does not yet own or has a disability the person later acquires. See also **Autoscopy; Goethe, Johann Wolfgang von.**

**Double.** Sometimes believed to be the **Astral Body,** or psychical or spiritual one, which has been exteriorized from the physical body and which is supposed to function independently from the physical body as a conscious and perceiving entity. See also **ESP Projection; Out-of-Body Experience.**

**Double-Blind.** Any experiment where subject and experimenter are given no information about the conditions involved in the test. An example in parapsychology is an experiment in remote viewing in which neither the subject nor the experimenter knows anything about the distant target area that the subject is to describe or draw. See also **Blind.**

**Down Through (DT).** The clairvoyance technique in which ESP cards or other cards are called down through the pack before any are removed or checked (JP).

**Dowsing.** The detection of oil, coal, water, precious metals, minerals, lost jewelry or treasure, or other objects concealed beneath the ground, and even the location of corpses, by the use of a variety of instruments including a pendulum, a so-called divining rod or forked twig, or even a wire coat hanger. Individuals who employ this method are "dowsers."

The practice appeared in Germany in the fifteenth century and from there made its entry into France and England. But it is more ancient than that. Eight-thousand-year-old rock paintings in Algeria depict what seems to be dowsing; Confucius mentions it; the ancient Egyptians practised it as did the Hebrew Kabbalists. Albert Einstein is supposed to have dowsed the location of a leak, and dowsing is said to have been used in Vietnam to locate Viet Cong tunnels. The Swiss pharmaceutical company Hoffman-La Roche is said routinely to dowse for water before building a new plant, and General George Patton in World War II used a dowser to find water in the desert. The Russians are said to use dowsing to solve geological problems.

Dowsing of underground water or minerals may be no more than a sensory process. The physical properties of underground objects may produce electromagnetic changes to which dowsers are sensitive, and this sensitivity may result in neuromuscular reactions that cause the instruments they hold to move in the direction of locating a hidden object.

But the subject may have a legitimate place in psychical research on the theory that the process may be paranormal, especially where the successful dowsing is of a map or a sketch or is used to locate missing people and animals. Although the actual movement of the instrument may be caused by motor automatism and the neuromuscular actions of the dowser, the correct location of an object or person of which or of whom neither the dowser nor anyone else had any knowledge may be a form of clairvoyance. Critics, however, will tell you that successful on-the-spot dowsing is due to knowledge by the dowser of the kinds of areas where water (or whatever) is likely to be found and that successful map-dowsing is due to chance. See also **Pendulum.**

BIBLIOGRAPHY: Barrett, L. *Psi Trek,* 1981, pp. 164–167; Bird, C. 1982. "Fruitful Searches." *New Realities* (5):45; Gardner, M. *Fads and Fallacies in the Name of Science,* 1957, pp. 101–115.

**Doyle, Sir Arthur Conan, 1859–1930.** Eminent British author and Spiritualist. A medical doctor who was knighted for his service as historian during the Boer War he is, of course, best known as the author of the Sherlock Holmes stories. Doyle, a big man who participated in many sports—boxing, cricket, football, and skiing among others—was a materialist in 1886 when he was persuaded to look into psychic phenomena for the purpose of extending scientific knowledge. But it was Spiritualism as a religion to which he was gradually converted. A message, never revealed, from his wife's brother who was killed in World War I in September 1914 changed Doyle's life.

He was an inspired orator. During the war when he found that his lectures on Spiritualism comforted the bereaved he decided to devote all his time to testing mediums, studying the literature, and keeping in touch with psychical research. Thus he effectively ended the career of Sherlock Holmes (of whom it has been suggested [Yellen, 1965] he was jealous because Holmes had become more famous than his creator).

From 1916 on, he used his "superb reasoning faculties . . . in building elaborate, well-wrought cases for the psychic upon the most unreliable foundations of physical mediumship . . .". He was convinced, no matter how often or how vociferously **Harry Houdini** denied it, that the latter was a physical medium and insisted that Houdini had intimated as much. Doyle endorsed all the physical phenomena of the Fox Sisters, the Davenport Brothers, Eva C., Kate Goligher, Florence Cook, Mina S. Crandon, and many others who had at least sometimes, and often many times, been caught cheating. In *The Case for Spirit Photography,* and to the end of his days, Doyle defended the questionable mediumship of **William Hope.**

*The Coming of the Fairies* (1921) perhaps strained credulity most. In 1917 Elsie Wright, sixteen years of age, had taken a series of photographs of fairies. The Kodak Company suggested that the pictures could have been produced by natural means. To the disinterested observer the "fairies" look exactly like paper cutouts and, in fact, have been identified as having been taken from a drawing illustrating Alfred Noyes's poem, "A Spell for a Fairy" (Brandon, 1983:224). Doyle, however, accepted them at face value and found them "epoch making." Since then, computer enhancement technology has confirmed that the fairies in the pictures are two-dimensional, flat figures, just as paper cutouts would be (Randi, 1980). And, to make the whole matter moot, the principals, now elderly ladies, have admitted that the pictures were faked (Inglis, 1985).

Doyle had joined the Society for Psychical Research in 1894 and was early active on its committees. He became more and more estranged from the society, however, because of what he considered its "tradition of obtuse negation" of Spiritualist phenomena. In April 1930, ill and incensed at **Theodore Besterman's** attack on Prof. **Ernesto Bozzano,** he resigned from the society.

At about the same time he began to wonder if he and his wife had been "victims of some extraordinary prank . . . from the other side." Lady Doyle, who had developed mediumistic powers, had received communications from an Arabian spirit (Pheneas) who told Doyle that he was to prepare people for the calamities—tidal waves, earthquakes, etc.—that would signal the end of the world. Doyle, however, was to "survive till the end, then pass over with [his] whole family" (Brandon:227). It never seems to have occurred to Doyle that the messages might not have come from "the other side," yet none of Pheneas's predictions came true. Still in this state of perplexity, Doyle died on July 7, 1930. See also **Spirit Photography.**

Selected Writings: *The Edge of the Unknown,* 1968/1930; *The Complete Sherlock Holmes,* 1938; "The Psychic Question as I See It." In C. Murchison, ed., *The Case for and Against Psychical Belief,* 1927; *The Case for Spirit Photography,* 1923; *The Coming of the Fairies,* 1921.

BIBLIOGRAPHY: Brandon, R. *The Spiritualists,* 1983; Carr, J. D. *The Life of Sir Arthur Conan Doyle,* 1949; Ebon, M. *They Knew the Unknown,* 1971; Inglis, B. *The Paranormal,* 1985, p. 183; Randi, J. *Flim-Flam!* 1980; Yellen, S. 1965, "Sir Arthur Conan Doyle: Sherlock Holmes in Spiritland." *International Journal of Parapsychology* 7(1):33.

**Dream, Announcing.** Among some cultures with the belief in **Reincarnation,** a dream signalling the rebirth of an individual. Generally a pregnant woman has a dream of some deceased person, such as a relative or friend, that persuades her that this person has come back in her body and will be returned by her to life on earth. Sometimes a female friend or relative of the pregnant woman may have the dream. A child born may then be given the name of the deceased and may exhibit some knowledge of that person's life. Such dreams seem to occur frequently among the Tlinglit Indians of Alaska, the Burmese and, but not as often, in India.

**Dream Laboratory.** See **Maimonides Medical Center, Dream Laboratory of.**

**Dreams, Lucid.** Dreams in the course of which dreamers know they are dreaming. The term was invented by Frederick van Eeden (1913).

BIBLIOGRAPHY: van Eeden, F. 1913. "A Study of Dreams." PSPR 26:431.

**Dreams, Paranormal.** In which the dream imagery corresponds in all material respects to the details of some situation or event that took place prior to, simultaneous with, or subsequent to the dream and of which the dreamer did not know or could not have inferred through any normal means. Such dreams tend to be more vivid than ordinary dreams.

In ancient Greece, where omniscient gods were worshipped and believed to make their will known to believers, people consulted belly-talkers and oracles. But dreams were also accepted as divine messages. Plutarch, the Greek author, called the dream "the oldest oracle." In it the dreamer was told what to do or not to do, what would or would not take place, or where to find lost objects. For example, after a boy from Haliesis had fallen or dived from a cliff there, his father went to the temple of Asclepius in the city of Epidaurus to ask the oracle about the fate of his son. It was the practice to sleep in the temple to see if the responses to questions would be given in dreams. The father slept in the temple and dreamed that Asclepius led him to where the boy was. After going back to Haliesis, he found the place, opened up a passage in the rock and found his son there (whether dead or alive the temple record does not say).

Telepathy may account for the following dream of a simultaneous event taken from Louisa E. Rhine's collection. Unable to sleep one night, a woman started to read a book in which a girl was attacked by a gang and forced into a garage and raped. The story was so upsetting that the woman closed the book and decided to try to get some sleep. Just then, her adolescent daughter, who had been asleep in her own bedroom, burst into her mother's room in an emotional state. She had just had a nightmare in which a gang had pulled her into a garage to rape her.

**Mark Twain's** dream of his brother Henry (who was then alive) as a corpse is an example of a precognitive dream of a subsequent event as was Michael Gabriele's dream in July 1988 of his recently deceased daughter who told him to "Play the numbers." Using the numbers on his daughter's New Jersey lottery ticket, he bought a Florida lottery ticket and won $10,500,000.

Besides such reports of spontaneous cases, experiments in dream telepathy done at the **Maimonides Medical Center** (Dream Laboratory) suggest that there is a close association between ESP and dreams. See also **American Indians: Lincoln, Abraham)**

BIBLIOGRAPHY: Dodds, E. R. 1971. "Supernormal Phenomena in Classical Antiquity." PSPR 55:189,200; Hyslop, J. H. *Contact with the Other World,* 1919; "Lotto Winner: Play, Dead Daughter Told Me." *Miami Herald,* July 7, 1988; Rhine, L. E. *Psi What Is It?* 1975.

**Driesch, Hans Adolf Eduard, 1867–1941.** German philosopher, scientist, and last distinguished biological advocate of the doctrine of vitalism. He was active and deeply interested in psychical research and was president of the Society for Psychical Research, the first German to be awarded that honor. Although "I have never made a successful psychical experiment, though I have tried to do so," said Driesch (1926), his interest in psychical research arose partly because he felt that its work and results "show a relation to a great number of different problems of general philosophy" (Driesch, 1927).

But primarily Driesch was interested in psychical research because of his vitalistic conception of biology. His famous experiments in 1891 led him to it. When he separated the first two or four cleavage cells of a sea urchin's egg, he found that he had two or four whole organisms. Even though he removed the cells or changed their position, normal embryos developed. Complete organisms developed though the cells were cut into pieces. Driesch was now persuaded that the mechanistic theory of life was not tenable. There was something else at work in life, some nonmaterial, mind-like, soul-like, agent that did not create matter or material processes but guided and controlled them. He used for this something the Aristotelian term "entelechy."

He saw in the physical mediums, such as Eusapia Palladino and Eva C., who produced ectoplasm and materializations in direct continuity with their bodies, a similar controlling and ordering of existing matter. Driesch perceived vitalistic biology to be "a bridge leading into physical parapsychological phenomena" (Driesch, 1926) and he looked on these phenomena as coinciding with his vitalistic theory. "Think of the little material body, called an egg, and think of the enormous and very complex material body, say, an elephant, that may come out of it: here you have a permanent stream of materializations before your eyes . . . a spreading of entelechial control" (Driesch, 1926). Materialization and ectoplasmic substances emerging from the bodies of physical mediums were phenomena produced by the same biological processes that developed whole embryos, were a continuation of his vitalist theory, and were made intelligible by it. Today such an argument falls on deaf ears. Although he made vitalism a growing and established doctrine among scientists and philosophers in his time, it has been attacked since and has become a dead issue in ours.

But he remains an interesting figure for another reason. He was a scientist and not an easy man to convince. In his séance with Carlos Mirabelli in Brazil in 1928, he was extremely skeptical about some of the phenomena such as xenoglossy, apports, and some messages supposedly received when the medium was in trance (Driesch, 1930). But when a vase on a table moved and then fell down, he was convinced that psychokinesis had been demonstrated and was "rather impressive." On another occasion, he had been asked by Albert von Schrenck-Notzing to be a spectator at a séance given by the physical medium Willi Schneider. He came back from it absolutely persuaded (Sudre, 1926). Thus Driesch becomes another **Noted Witness** for some of the physical phenomena that harmonized with his vitalist theory.

Driesch was a professor of philosophy at many German universities as well as an active psychical researcher and supporter of the field. Because of his convictions, he was deprived of his professorships when the Nazis came to power.

Selected Writings: "Die wissenschaftliche Parapsychologie der Gegenwart". In H. de Geymuller, ed., *Swedenborg und die übersinnliche Welt,* 1936, p. 351; 1930. "The Mediumship of Mirabelli." *Psychic Research* 24:486; "Psychical Research and Philosophy." In C. Murchison, ed., *The Case for and Against Psychical Belief,* 1927, p. 163; 1926. "Presidential Address: Psychical Research and Established Science." PSPR 36:171.

BIBLIOGRAPHY: Sudre, R. 1926. "The Ideas of Hans Driesch." JASPR 20:193.

**Drop-in Communicator.** A communicator who, prior to manifesting or communicating through a mental medium, is unknown both to the medium and the sitters. The identity of the "drop-in" or the information communicated is unknown but is verified later.

For example, at a sitting held in Zurich, Switzerland, in 1962 with a trance medium, a child unexpectedly "dropped-in." He said, "You have never known me" and added that his name was now Hans-Peter and that he had a second name, an Indian name—Pasona. The boy said also that he had died of appendicitis in a children's hospital but had also had an unusual illness accompanied by much fever. He had lived in the seventh district of the city. His father had some connection with tea and drank a lot of it. The sitters attempted to verify this communication after the sitting by searching the telephone directory for the name "Pasona." There was no such name. Instead they found the name "Passanah." John Passanah, who had been four years old at the time of his brother's death, verified that the family were importers of tea, drank a great deal of it, lived in the seventh district of Zurich and also verified, mistakenly, that the child had died of appendicitis in Kinderspital (Children's Hospital). From an examination of various records, it was established that the family were Indians and that their son Robert had died in Kinderspital when about twenty months old not of appendicitis but of severe pneumonia with continuous high fever. All items provided by the communicator were accurate except for his first name and the nature of the disease that killed him.

BIBLIOGRAPHY: Stevenson, I. 1970. "A Communicator Unknown to Medium and Sitter." JASPR 64.53.

**Drugs, Magical.** To bring forth visions, mystical and transcendental experiences, union with the divine, and to foretell the future, it has been the practice among ancient and primitive people to use magical beverages, herbs, mushrooms, flowers, and drinks such as *yaje* in South America and the kava drink made from pepper in the South Pacific. The initiates into the Eleusinian Mysteries of ancient Greece drank *kykeon* to commune with the gods, the Delphic oracle chewed laurel leaves to go into trance, and the Mexican Indians ate *peyotl* (in Nahuatl meaning "divine messenger") to produce euphoria and paranormal powers. Prophets, mystics, sorcerers, religious worshippers—all have used similar agents to give them new insights and powers.

The use of magical drugs has a significance for psychical research and parapsychology. Spontaneous cases occurring everywhere and psi experiments done in laboratories suggest that psi ability is not confined to certain kinds of people and that everyone seems to have the dormant ability which given the right setting or procedure can be brought out. If people who use magical drugs demonstrate psi powers they have not manifested before, then psi capacity is not limited to exceptional people. The only thing necessary is a way to make it manifest itself. See also **Drugs, Studies of.**

**Drugs, Studies of.** Investigators always have had to face two problems. Subjects who show psi ability in parapsychological experiments are not reliable and cannot maintain a high scoring rate. And in psychical research, one can never tell where or when spontaneous cases will occur so that, by the time investigators arrive at the place of occurrence, it is usually to late to find anything to investigate.

Psychopharmacology may offer parapsychology and psychical research a new research tool to overcome these difficulties. In the history of religion, there is much to indicate that psi capacity can be brought out and developed by procedures or circumstances. Magical drugs have been used to stimulate psychic experiences. Some studies suggest that in the psychedelic drug state great imagery is produced but not necessarily any paranormal effects. The conclusion from these studies is that psi occurs as often in situations where psychedelic drugs are used as in those in which none are used (Masters and Houston, 1973).

In other early studies parapsychologists used alcohol, sodium amytal, caffeine, and dexedrine on subjects. It was found that scoring was reduced in laboratory experiments with alcohol (Averill and Rhine, 1945) and increased with caffeine (Coca-Cola) (Rhine, Humphrey and Averill, 1945). In later experiments, marijuana and the more powerful psychedelic (meaning "mind-manifesting") drugs such as LSD 25, mescaline, and psilocybine also were used by investigators, including Jan Kappers (1966) to see if psi could be induced. While there have been some positive results, the general run of evidence thus far indicates that these drugs produce a great variety of individual responses in experiments. Drugs affecting one person may not affect another. Studies do not point clearly to a correlation between paranormal mental states and psychedelic substances. And little has been done by parapsychologists since 1966 to clarify the murky psychedelic situation. The discharge of Harvard professor Timothy Leary who allowed students to use psychedelic drugs and his advocacy of their use as less dangerous than alcohol or nicotine contributed to legislation against LSD and other restrictions on using psychedelic drugs for research. There is no telling when or if these drugs will be used again in parapsychological research. In the meantime, parapsychologists are concentrating on other mind-altering procedures, such as sensory bombardment, meditation, and hypnosis. See also **Drugs, Magical.**

BIBLIOGRAPHY: Averill, R. L. and Rhine, J. B. 1954. "The Effect of Alcohol Upon Performance in PK Tests." JP 9:32; Kappers, J. with van Asperen de Boer and Barkema, P. R. 1966. "Is It Possible to Induce ESP with Psilocybine? An Exploratory Investigation." *International Journal of Neuropsychiatry* 2 (5): 447; Masters, R. L. and Houston, J. *The Varieties of Psychedelic Experience,* 1973; Rhine, J. B., Humphrey, B. M., and Averill, R. L. 1945. "An Exploratory Experiment on the Effects of Caffeine Upon Performance in PK Tests." JP 9:80.

**Ducasse, Curt John, 1881–1969.** Eminent French-born American philosopher. He came to the United States as a teenager, became an American citizen, and eventually chairman of the Department of Philosophy at Brown University. He was one of the few philosophers with the intellectual courage to brave academic displeasure and disdain by daring to study and write about the paranormal. He wrote and lectured extensively on psychical research and parapsychology, held sittings with mediums, travelled to centers of parapsychological research, and attended international conferences on parapsychology because he believed that the facts of parapsychology were sufficiently established to pose important philosophical problems. Ducasse realized the absurdity of trying to philosophize about human nature and mind without taking these facts into account. Yet he knew that his colleagues and others ignored, derided, or denied them as radical phenomena that seemed to clash with accepted assumptions. Perhaps while smelling a flower in his buttonhole as he liked to do, he told a story to illustrate this attitude: "There is an old story, that one day a student brought to his professor a sea shell which did not fit into the accepted scientific classification, and that the professor, after puzzling over it a few moments, dropped the shell on the floor, ground it under heel, and declared: 'There is no such shell!'" (Ducasse, 1954).

Apart from the philosophical importance of psychical research and parapsychology that he tried to spell out for his fellow philosophers and the problem of precognition which intrigued him, he devoted his ability and scholarship mainly to the question of human survival beyond death, which is what led him into parapsychology in the first place. His last book, *A Critical Examination of the Belief in a Life After Death,* remains a masterful examination of the question. As he perceived it, we must first ask if survival is impossible on theoretical grounds. If it is not theoretically impossible, we ask next if it is empirically possible. If it is both theoretically and empirically possible, we should ask finally what *prima facie* positive evidence there is which makes survival a fact. In the end, Ducasse felt that it was a fact and that the evidence for reincarnation was particularly impressive.

Although actively concerned with psychical research and parapsychology, Ducasse was a leading and original philosopher with several important philosophical works to his credit. He was a member of the Board of Trustees of the American Society for Psychical Research from 1951 to the day he died. If reincarnation is the fact Ducasse thought it was, his wisdom and wit may reappear among us one of these days.

Selected Writings: *A Critical Examination of the Belief in a Life After Death,* 1961; 1954. "Some Questions Concerning Psychical Phenomena." JASPR 48:3; *Nature, Mind and Death,* 1951.

**Duke University.** In 1930, Duke became the first university in the United States to grapple in the laboratory with extrasensory perception. Under the guidance of **William McDougall,** head of its Department of Psychology, and with the help of others in the department, including Karl Zener, **Joseph B. Rhine** began the **Parapsychology Laboratory** there. ESP tests in the laboratory and in buildings on campus were conducted with many of the gifted subjects who emerged from the enthusiastically cooperative undergraduate student body.

With an administration less sympathetic to parapsychology than in the past and with Rhine's retirement from the institution, parapsychological links with the university were broken. Rhine established off campus the **Foundation for Research on the Nature of Man** and the **Institute for Parapsychology** as a successor to the Parapsychology Laboratory. The Perkins Library at Duke which contains collections of the papers of Rhine, Louisa E. Rhine, McDougall, Joseph G. Pratt and Gertrude R. Schmeidler is important to archivists and researchers. Also collected there are the records of the Parapsychological Association and Parapsychology Laboratory and the editorial records of the *Journal of Parapsychology.*

**Dumas, Alexandre, Père, 1802–1870.** Popular French novelist and dramatist. Besides his plays such as *Napoleon Bonaparte* (1831), his best-known historical romances are *The Three Musketeers* (1844) and *The Count of Monte Cristo* (1844).

He is a **Noted Witness** for the paranormal. He held séances at his villa Monte Cristo and had a personal experience suggestive of telepathy or clairvoyance, which he narrated in his *Memoirs.* His father, a general in Napoleon's army, died unexpectedly in a faraway place. At the hour of his father's death, Dumas, only four years of age, was awakened by a knock at the door and, as he went to answer it, he cried out, "Good-by, papa!" This experience remained a vivid memory for him throughout his life.

BIBLIOGRAPHY: Prince, W. F. *Noted Witnesses for Psychic Occurrences,* 1963.

**Duncan, Helen Victoria, 1898–1956.** Scottish physical medium. In the 1930s, she gave impressive demonstrations of her powers during fifty sittings at the London Spiritualist Alliance and elsewhere. Her performances generally consisted of entering a cabinet, being taken over by a **control**, "Albert Smith," then producing ectoplasm from which were formed materializations which gasping sitters recognized as dead relatives or friends.

The medium's greatest performance came, however, when she was forced to defend herself in 1944 in London's Central Criminal Court known as the Old Bailey. The Crown had charged her with claiming falsely to be in contact with the spirits of the dead. The prosecution showed that the defendant's "ectoplasm" was no more than cheesecloth and the materializations impersonations by the medium or perhaps confederates wearing white sheets in which anxious or hoping sitters saw likenesses of people they wanted to see. But Duncan called a stream of witnesses in her behalf to give testimony that her phenomena were genuine. Commenting on this aspect of the case, Donald J. West, a criminologist as well as parapsychologist, said, "most of the testimony was valueless from the psychical researchers' point of view, the narrators being obviously credulous and gullible" (West, 1946). Apparently the testimony of the defendant's witnesses was considered valueless at the trial also because the medium was convicted as charged and imprisoned for nine months.

The conviction could have come as no surprise to Harry Price who had investigated Duncan thirteen years earlier in his **National Laboratory of Psychical Research.** Flashlight photographs he took during her séances showed that her "ectoplasm" was cheesecloth complete with holes and creases and that a "materialization" was a rubber glove (Price, 1931). But neither this early exposure nor the later conviction at Old Bailey seem to have prevented Duncan's devotees from claiming her innocence to this day (Cassirer, 1985).

BIBLIOGRAPHY: Cassirer, M. 1985. "Helen Victoria Duncan: A Reassessment." JSPR 53:138; Price, H. "Regurgitation and the Duncan Mediumship." *Bulletin of the National Laboratory of Psychical Research,* 1931; West, D. J. 1946. "Trial of Helen Duncan." PSPR 48:32.

**Dunne, John W., 1866–1949.** English aeronautical engineer, designer of England's first military plane. His book *An Experiment with Time* (1927) described his precognitive dream experiences and those of others and promoted much scientific interest in and controversy about his new concept of multidimensional time.

One of his dreams makes him a **Noted Witness** in support of **Precognition.** In the spring of 1902, while Dunne was in a place where mail and newspapers arrived only rarely, he had a vivid and very unpleasant dream of "an island which was in imminent peril from a volcano. And, when I saw the vapor spouting from the ground, I gasped: 'It's the island! Good Lord, the whole thing is going to *blow up!*'. . . Forthwith I was seized with a frantic desire to save the four thousand (I knew the number) unsuspecting inhabitants." In the dream, he tried to get French authorities on a neighboring island to send ships to evacuate the inhabitants from the threatened island. Some time later when newspapers finally did arrive, the article that caught his eye at once was "Volcano Disaster in Martinique—Town Swept Away—An Avalanche of Flame—Probable Loss of Over 40,000 Lives." The volcano of Mt. Pelee had erupted on May 8, 1902, some weeks after Dunne's dream.

Dunne's testimony is strong because of the many correspondences between his dream and the event: the volcano; on an island; French authorities and inhabitants on the island of St. Lucia which was nearest to Martinique; in the dream the island was going to "blow up," and on Martinique the mountain split open down the side; in the dream ships were sent, and, in reality, in the harbor of Martinique there were many ships; 4,000 people were going to be killed in the dream and in the report the same figures were given for lost lives with one cipher added.

Selected Writing: *An Experiment with Time,* 1927.

BIBLIOGRAPHY: Prince, W. F. *Noted Witnesses for Psychic Occurrences,* 1963.

**Duplessis, Yvonne, 1912-.** French specialist

in dermo-optic perception. Since receiving her degrees from Paris and Montpellier universities, she has conducted research on dermo-optic perception at the Institut Métapsychique International in Paris, has carried on her work with grants from the Parapsychology Foundation and has written many books and articles on her specialty.

Thirty years before, author Jules Romains, her countryman, had written about experiments that convinced him that colors could be perceived without using normal vision. But his writings convinced no one else because he was a novelist, not a scientist. But work in the Soviet Union, in the United Kingdom, and the United States since then, and particularly the research of Duplessis in France have shown that Romains's claims should not have been dismissed. Dr. Duplessis's conduct of numerous experiments with both blind and sighted subjects led her to theorize that the skin contains receptors of information that are responsive to infrared radiation and that dermo-optical sensitivity is separate and distinct from normal vision. This suggests, as have experiments by others, that ESP is ruled out. The interesting conclusion she also draws from her work is that some colors act not only on the eyes; their invisible radiations act also on the entire body—and, at times, without our knowing it, some may actually harm us.

Selected Writings: 1985. "Dermo-Optical Sensitivity and Perception." *International Journal of Biosocial Research* 7 (2):76; *La Vision Parapsychologique des Couleurs*, 1974.

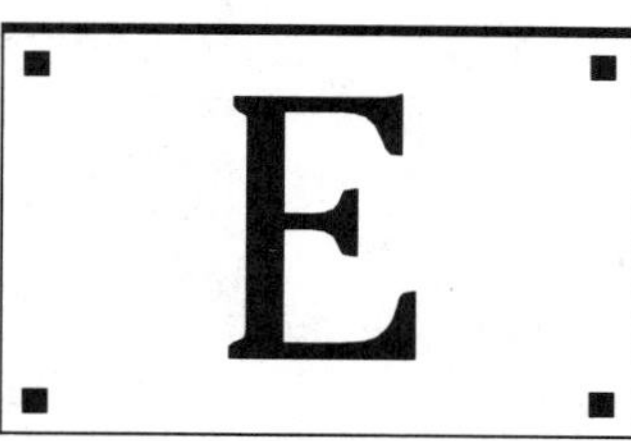

**Ebon, Martin, 1917–.** German-born lecturer and author living in New York and Greece. He has written and edited more than thirty books, most of which deal with some aspect of psychical research, for example, prophecy (1968), people of letters who have had psi experiences (1971), exorcism (1974), the dangers of the paranormal (1976), and the data relating to survival after death (1977). For twelve years until 1965, he was the administrative assistant of the Parapsychology Foundation. The post gave him the opportunity to work with Eileen Garrett, meet the outstanding figures in psychical research and parapsychology, travel extensively, and read and learn much about research. His lectures, books, book reviews, and articles in magazines all reflect serious treatment of the field of parapsychology and are a far cry from other popular writings that are less concerned with its scientific aspect than with titillating the public and selling books. Ebon's expertise also extends to the Soviet Union and the state of parapsychological research there (1983).

Selected Writings: *Psychic Warfare: Threat or Illusion,* 1983; *The Evidence for Life After Death,* 1977; *The Satan Trap,* 1976; *The Devil's Bride,* 1974; *The Knew the Unknown,* 1971; *Prophecy in Our Time,* 1968.

**Ecsomatic.** See **Out-of-Body Experience.**

**Ecstacy.** An intensely pleasurable mental and emotional state that may be produced by sexual stimulation, drugs, rhythmic dance, or, in the religious sphere, an immense tranquility and illumination such as mystics experience when they believe they are one with God. In the sphere of psychical research, ecstacy is an **Altered State of Consciousness** in which one's vision or spirit is transferred to a spiritual world; in the words of **F. W. H. Myers** "a spontaneous transfer of the center of perception into that region from whence discarnate spirits" communicate. If a spirit of the dead can come to enter into a living being from the outside, a spirit from the inside can go out and alter its center of perception. Ecstacy is the complementary or correlative aspect of spirit-control as **W. Stainton Moses** and **Emanuel Swedenborg** reported of their journeys into the spirit world.

**Ectoplasm.** Also known as "teleplasm." From the Greek *ektos.* Ectoplasm denotes a strange cold and clammy substance said to be produced by and then to exist outside the body of a physical medium. See also **Ectoplasy.**

**Ectoplasy.** A term used by **F. W. H. Myers** to describe the alleged power of forming, outside the body of a physical medium, a concentration of what is said to be a vital energy, or vitalized matter, called **Ectoplasm.** The substance is said to be produced by the medium and can emerge from any of the openings of the body. This collection of vital energy operates in the same way as the physical body from which it emerges and can form into visible, tangible phenomena known as **Materializations.**

**Eddy, Mary Baker, 1821–1910.** American healer and founder of Christian Science. Mary Baker Eddy became the founder of a new religion when she established the Church of Christ, Scientist, and the religious and healing system known as Christian Science.

She was born on a New England farm and was a beautiful girl. But she was subject to epileptic seizures, had a violent temper, and like Joan of Arc, heard voices. Her reading was limited to one book in the family library—the Bible—and her education was extremely limited. In 1843, she married George Washington Glover, a bricklayer, who died of yellow fever a year later. At this time, she began to go into trance, saw visions, heard raps, and became attracted to Spiritualism.

In 1843, she married a dentist named Daniel Patterson. Her health having deteriorated, her husband was forced to carry his bedridden wife up and down the stairs. After sixteen years Patterson abandoned her.

Her life reached a turning point when she came under the influence of Phineas Parkhurst Quimby, an uneducated but intelligent clockmaker who believed that sickness was a delusion, a misconception of the mind. Cure could be affected by stimulating the faith and expectations of patients. Quimby achieved a reputation for amazing cures. His ideas about "mind-cure" were embodied in a manuscript he called "The Science of Christ." After the then Mrs. Patterson went to him for help, her ailments virtually vanished. She learned from Quimby all she could about his theories and system. In 1864 in Spiritualistic-type experiments Eddy (Patterson) acted as medium, went into trance and communicated with her dead brother Albert.

Quimby died in 1866 of a cancer which not even his system could cure. In 1866 Eddy was badly crippled as the result of a fall and seemed again doomed to invalidism. Suddenly and astonishingly she was healed following her reading of the Bible and her application of "The Science of Christ." The year 1866 therefore marks the start of Christian Science: Eddy now went from place to place to talk about the system to anyone who would listen. She even attended Spiritualist séances and occasionally, in order to teach the system, went into trance to bring messages from Christ and the Apostles. Before long she had filled the waiting rooms of practitioners of the system with paying patients. In 1875, she published *Science and Health* in which, without any acknowledgment to Quimby, she presented "my discovery" of Christian Science and stated that "no human pen or tongue taught me the Science contained in this book." She also said in the book: "I could never believe in Spiritualism."

Her marriage to Patterson having been dissolved in 1873, in the same year she married Asa Gilbert Eddy, a sewing machine salesman. Two years later, she established the Church of Christ, Scientist, in Boston.

Eddy has been criticized for denying to Quimby the credit he deserved for teaching her Christian Science and for her denial of Spiritualism after she had practised it. Sometimes she has also been accused of having been motivated by money in the establishing of her system. But she seems to have shared Quimby's sincere desire to alleviate human suffering and to present a real truth (i.e., that within us there may be a mental or psychical curative agency).

**Edge, Hoyt L., 1944–.** American philosopher. He was introduced to things psychic during his college days when he had several readings from mediums at Cassadaga, Florida, a Spiritualist community, but he was not impressed. Indeed, in his doctoral dissertation—he received his Ph.D. from Vanderbilt University in 1970—he denied the possibility of ESP's being mental and suggested that it might be fraudulent. But after an impressive reading from another psychic, Dr. Edge offered a course at Rollins College, where he is professor of philosophy, on the philosophical implications of parapsychology and became, as he says "hooked."

Dr. Edge's interest in parapsychology relates to his main philosophical interests: what it means to be a person and the matter of human potentials. "Insofar as the data of parapsychology points [*sic*] to aspects of the person which are not fully explainable at this time by our traditional worldview," he wrote in a letter to Arthur S. Berger, "it tells us something about what can be a new vision of what it means to be human."

Dr. Edge has met and worked with experimental parapsychologists both here and abroad, notably at the University of Utrecht and at the University of Freiburg with Eberhard Bauer. He has published widely in parapsychological journals and, in 1976, he co-edited with philosopher James M. O. Wheatley *Philosophical Dimensions of Parapsychology.* In 1986 he wrote, with Robert L. Morris, Joseph Rush and John Palmer, *Foundations of Parapsychology.*

Dr. Edge is a member of the American Philosophical Association, the Society for Psychical Research, and is on the Board of Trustees of the American Society for Psychical Research. In 1989, he served as president of the Parapsychological Association.

Selected Writings: with Morris, R. L., Rush, J. and Palmer, J. *Foundations of Parapsychology,* 1986; 1985. "The Dualist Tradition in Parapsychology." *European Journal of Parapsychology* 53; 1985. "Parapsychology and Atomism." JSPR 53:78; 1978. "A Philosophical Justification for the Conformance Behavior Model." JASPR 72:215; "The Place of Paradigms in Parapsychology." In B. Shapin and E. Coly, eds., *The Philosophy of Parapsychology,* 1977; and J. M. O. Wheatley, eds., *Philosophical Dimensions of Parapsychology,* 1976.

BIBLIOGRAPHY: Berger, A. S. *Lives and Letters in American Parapsychology,* 1988.

**Edison, Thomas Alva, 1847–1931.** American inventor. Included among over a thousand patents were the incandescent electric lamp, the phonograph (his most original invention), the carbon telephone transmitter, the motion picture projector, the mimeograph, the fluoroscope, and the alkaline storage battery. Uneducated, deaf from a childhood attack of scarlet fever, he applied himself to technology rather than to pure science. From his electric light system he earned $4,000,000 (at a time when money was worth many times what it is today) but lost it all in an attempt to develop a magnetic ore-separating process for low-grade iron deposits. He made a great deal of money, however, from the mass entertainment industry.

Edison is of interest to psychical research because of his belief in telepathy and because of his attempt to build a machine for communicating with the dead. Edison felt that he himself had telepathic abilities—he would concentrate on someone who would then come to see him or he would pass mental messages to someone. He sometimes felt that his ideas came to him from some outside source, which he considered telepathic, and had conducted what he considered to be successful experiments with a professional clairvoyant.

Edison had been a friend of Sir William Crookes and shared with the latter his interest in the survival of human personality after death. Edison was quoted in the October 30, 1920 issue of the *Scientific American* as saying that "If our personality survives, then it is strictly logical and scientific to assume that it retains memory, intellect, and other faculties and knowledge that we acquire on this earth. . . . I am inclined to believe that our personality hereafter will be able to affect matter . . ." (Ebon, 1971). He therefore thought it should be possible to build a machine that would permit communication with the dead without the aid of mediums. The device was never built in Edison's lifetime. Ten years after Edison's death, a medium transmitted a purported message from Edison that gave the names and addresses of three people who might have the blueprint for his machine. One of them had a drawing that was supposedly Edison's. Perhaps it was, but the device built from it didn't work.

On Sunday, October 18, 1931, at 3:24 A.M. the clocks of three of Edison's associates stopped: It was the moment of Edison's death.

BIBLIOGRAPHY: Ebon, M. *They Knew the Unknown,* 1971, pp. 125–133; Josephson, M. "Edison." In *Encyclopedia Britannica,* 15th ed., 1986, pp. 1049–51.

**Edmonds, John, 1816–1874.** American judge. He became the "first martyr" (Moore, 1977) in the cause of **Spiritualism.** Convinced of the validity of the movement and persuaded of the geniuneness of its mental and physical phenomena based on his own abilities as a medium and those of his daughter, Laura, Edmonds became an ardent and evangelical Spiritualist. Although he was respected as a jurist, his political enemies soon accused him of basing his legal decisions not only on the law books but also on messages he was receiving from the spirits. As a result of the controversy that followed these charges, he gave up his place on the bench of the Supreme Court of the State of New York and devoted himself to lectures and the writing of books, letters, and articles both to defend and advance Spiritualism.

BIBLIOGRAPHY: Moore, R. L. *In Search of White Crows,* 1977.

**Edwards, Harry (Henry James Edwards) 1893–1976.** British healer and founder of the National Federation of Spiritual Healers. Over a period of forty years, he gained a worldwide reputation for his unorthodox healing ministry. Over one million letters were received by him from sufferers asking to come to his treatment center in Surrey, England, or to his public demonstrations. In the United Kingdom, where medical treatment is provided without charge, this is noteworthy. Edwards claimed to have the power to do absent healing as well as direct healing when he would run his hands over a patient's body. He attributed his power to spirit doctors and maintained that, because of it, he had benefitted 85 percent of the thousands of cases that had come to him (Edwards, 1952; 1971).

Some question may be raised about his phenomenal success rate. When surveys have been made of claims such as his, a large percentage of successes could not be confirmed and, in other instances, there was a great variance between the actual records and the claims (Rose, 1955). See also **Healing, Unorthodox**).

Selected Writings: *The Healing Intelligence,* 1971; *Evidence for Spirit Healing,* 1952.

BIBLIOGRAPHY: Rose, L. 1955. "Some Aspects of Paranormal Healing." JSPR 38:105.

**Eglinton, William, 1857–1933.** British physical medium. From his youth, Eglinton traveled worldwide and was renowned for his alleged complete materializations in good light when he himself was in full view. Many people converted to Spiritualism after seeing him perform. Yet on one occasion he was caught in fraud by Archdeacon Colley, and he was exposed by **Richard Hodgson** when he cooperated in 1882 with **Mme H. P. Blavatsky** in producing a fraudulent letter from the "Masters."

By 1884 Eglinton had turned to slate-writing. Again, in good light, he was supposed to have produced messages, many evidential, on a slate pressed against the underside of a table, or on the hidden surface of a slate held firmly above the table, or on the inside of a closed and locked folding slate, or on the portion of a slate underneath a drinking glass placed face downward on the slate. At that time Eleanor Sidgwick and Richard Hodgson of the Society for Psychical Research were investigating physical phenomena. Eleanor Sidgwick felt that conjuring was the explanation for the phenomena and Hodgson noted how Eglinton distracted his sitters. The greatest damage to Eglinton's claims, however, were sittings by S. J. Davey who produced his results by conjuring, and yet whose sitters were as convinced of the paranormality of his effects as Eglinton's sitters were of his. Davey, however, never produced all of Eglinton's phenomena. (For example, he was never able to write an intelligible message underneath a drinking glass.)

Many Spiritualist members of the SPR, including W. Stainton Moses, resigned from the society as a result of what they considered a too harsh and unfair judgment of Eglinton. Most psychical researchers, however, then believed, as do parapsychologists now, that Eglinton's phenomena were produced by conjuring.

BIBLIOGRAPHY: Aksakoff A. *Animisme et Spiritisme,* 1895; Farmer, J. S. *'Twixt Two Worlds: A Narrative of the Life and Work of William Eglinton,* 1886; Gauld, A. *The Founders of Psychical Research,* 1968; Hodgson, R. 1892. "Mr. Davey's Imitations by Conjuring of Phenomena Sometimes Attributed to Spirit Agency." PSPR 8:253; Hodgson R. and Davey, S. J. 1886–1887. "The Possibilities of Mal-Observation and Lapse of Memory from a Practical Point of View." PSPR 4:381.

**Egypt, Marian Apparitions In.** Claims of appearances of the Virgin Mary have been recorded in several countries. But "probably the greatest of all Marian visitations" (Rogo, 1982) began in Cairo, Egypt, on April 2, 1968 when two Moslem workers noticed what they thought to be a nun in white standing near the dome of St. Mary's Church of Zeitoun, a shabby district of Cairo. The church was part of the Coptic church a Christian church in the midst of Moslem Egypt, had been converted to Roman Catholicism. During the months of April and May, the radiant figure materialized out of light over the dome of the church and again and again and again was visible in front of the dome, over it, walking on the roof of the church, inclining its body to salute the onlookers, and even making blessing signs with its hands. Frequently, the **Apparition**

would remain in view for hours at a time and then would dematerialize. An **Aura** surrounded it and glittering lights resembling flying birds appeared near the church dome before the figure materialized or while it was in view. The crowds who came to see what was now believed to be the Virgin Mary filled the streets around the church. One estimate placed the number on April 6 alone at 100,000. Photographs of professional quality of the figure were taken. Numerous manifestations went on through 1968. In 1969 the figure appeared only a dozen times. There were a few appearances in 1970, and by 1971 they had stopped altogether.

There were hundreds of thousands of witnesses, both Christian and Moslem, to the event. The duration of the phenomenon was extraordinary: It lasted almost three years. The figure was seen near or on the church for hours at a time. It was accompanied by birdlike flashes of light. There is overwhelming photographic and testimonial evidence in support of the phenomenon. And whereas in other countries where Mary's apparitions have been claimed the majority of the population is Roman Catholic, the visions in Cairo took place in a predominantly Moslem country and the first witnesses were Moslems. Religious influence, therefore, cannot have accounted for what transpired.

This spectacular event is of enormous interest to parapsychology as an evidential case. There is ample reason to think that the apparition was seen by people numbering in the hundreds of thousands. The impressive photographs taken of the figure suggest an authentic phenomenon.

St. Mary's Church was erected in 1925 as a result of a dream in which the Virgin Mary requested its construction. She was supposed to have appeared in a later dream in which she promised to return to the church. One theory (Rogo, 1982) is that the appearances were thought-forms physically objectified by crowds who knew of her promise and of the fact that, after Herod commanded all male infants to be killed, Mary fled with Joseph and Jesus to Egypt and, specifically, to Zeitoun. Whatever the merits of the theory, what happened at Cairo is such a startling paranormal phenomenon that it warrants the closest study. See also **Mary, Saint.**

BIBLIOGRAPHY: Rogo, D. S. *Miracles: A Parascientific Inquiry into Wondrous Phenomena,* 1982, pp. 250–257.

**Egyptian Book of the Dead.** See **Book of the Dead, Egyptian.**

**Ehrenwald, Jan, 1900–1988.** American psychiatrist born in Hungary. Dr. Ehrenwald's interest in parapsychology began in the 1920s when he was studying neuropsychiatry at the University Hospital in Vienna and came across a mentally defective girl who might have been receiving telepathic impressions from her mother. He later noted the telepathic aspects of schizophrenia. His insistence on publishing his material (*Telepathy and Medical Psychology* [1948]) caused his forced resignation from the British mental hospital where he was working at the time.

In a later book, *New Dimensions of Deep Analysis: A Study of Telepathy in Interpersonal Relationships* (1954), Dr. Ehrenwald "argued that psi impressions emerge from the unconscious, from the Freudian Id or from Myers' subliminal domain" (Berger, 1988). Along with most modern neuroscientists, Dr. Ehrenwald believed "that the brain's hemispheres allow an individual to operate in two different cognitive styles" (1987) and that psi is probably a right hemispheric function "e.g. in the child-parent symbiosis and in the doctor-patient relationships" (Berger, 1988).

Along with Jule Eisenbud, Montague Ullman and others, Dr. Ehrenwald was a member of the Medical Section of the American Society for Psychical Research. He never considered himself "a dyed-in-the-wool parapsychologist" but felt that psychical research was one of the important elements in his development.

Selected Writings: "An Autobiographic Fragment." In R. Pilkington, ed., *Men and Women of Parapsychology,* 1987; *Anatomy of Genius: Split Brains and Global Minds,* 1984; *The ESP Experience: A Psychiatric Validation,* 1978; *New Dimensions of Deep Analysis,* 1954; *Telepathy and Medical Psychology,* 1948.

BIBLIOGRAPHY: Berger, A. S. *Lives and Letters in American Parapsychology,* 1988.

**Eisenbud, Jule, 1908–.** American psychiatrist and parapsychologist. Best known in parapsychology field for *The World of Ted Serios* (1967), his book on **Thoughtography,** Dr. Eisenbud has been familiar with telepathy all his life: His mother often knew what his father was thinking and his "wife is a telepathist of no mean ability" (Eisenbud, 1987). Precognition in the form of precognitive dreams has also figured in his life, and he witnessed what he considered genuine psychokinesis during some table-turning sessions he attended with a friend.

Dr. Eisenbud's real interest in parapsychology began, however, with his psychiatric and psychoanalytic practice in which his patients provided examples of telepathic dreams. In 1942, along with Montague Ullman, Laura Dale and others, he began attending sessions held by Gardner Murphy at the American Society for Psychical Research. In these sessions Dr. Eisenbud found confirmation for his observation of the key role of the analyst in these telepathic situations. Jan Ehrenwald and others eventually joined this group which became the Medical Section of the ASPR.

In 1945, Dr. Eisenbud's first paper in the field of parapsychology, "Telepathy and Problems of Psychoanalysis," presented to the New York Psychoanalytic Society inspired a movement for his expulsion from that society. There followed snubbings and a loss of a certain number of patient referrals, and the general attitude, even among his friendly colleagues, was that he was crazy.

"The research that more than any other has affected my views about just about everything under the sun," writes Dr. Eisenbud (1987), "was my work with Ted Serios. . . . There is no escape for me either from the data and their far reaching implications or from the furor these have evoked on all sides." Dr. Eisenbud is convinced that Serios was able paranormally to imprint pictures on Polaroid film. Skeptics, of course, think otherwise.

In *Paranormal Foreknowledge* (1982), Dr. Eisenbud suggests that precognition is the sometimes conscious, sometimes unconscious, psychokinetic production of a future event.

Dr. Eisenbud feels that real progress in parapsychology can be made only by turning away from scientists and scientific institutions because he believes that science and the psychic side of the human being are irreconcilable. See also **Serios, Ted.**

**Selected Writings:** 1946. "Telepathy and Problems of Psychoanalysis." *Psychoanalytic Quarterly* 15:32; *The World of Ted Serios,* 1967; *Paranormal Foreknowledge,* 1982; "My Life with the Paranormal." In R. Pilkington, ed., *Men and Women of Parapsychology,* 1987.

BIBLIOGRAPHY: Berger, A. S. *Lives and Letters in American Parapsychology,* 1988.

**Electronic Voice Phenomena (EVP).** Also called "Raudive voices," they are physical effects somehow and unaccountably recorded on electromagnetic recording tape. These sounds are not heard until the tapes are played back. The phenomenon is a very recent one made possible by technological advances in recording devices. During the last three decades, a growing number of individuals throughout the world have conducted experiments with tape recorders in an attempt to obtain these effects. They report that they have established electronic communication with people who are deceased and that their recordings are the voices of dead communicators.

The first indication that such "voices" were being tape-recorded seems to have come in a 1959 report by parapsychologist **Raymond Bayless.** But the work of **Friedrich Jürgenson** and **Konstantin Raudive** brought the subject worldwide attention.

While the great majority of enthusiasts believe that the voices recorded have their origins in the spirit world, the dominant view taken by parapsychology is that these are not messages from the surviving spirits of the dead. There may be no "voices" at all. What is "heard" may be wishful thinking or some arbitrary misinterpretations of random noises, involuntary whispers from those present during experiments or of stray fragments of radio broadcasts. If there are indeed paranormal voices on the tape, still they need not be evidence of spirit messages. They may be caused by psychokinesis from the living experimenters that has converted stray sounds into meaningful ones.

BIBLIOGRAPHY: Bayless, R. 1959. "Correspondence." JASPR 53:36; Ellis, D. T. *The Mediumship of the Tape Recorder,* 1978; Raudive, K. *Breakthrough,* 1971.

**Eliade, Mircea, 1907–1986.** Romanian historian of religion distinguished for his researches into religious traditions and his study of shamans and their ecstatic states. This study is well-known in psychical research and is of particular value because it shows that, outside the Western traditions, out-of-body experiences and paranormal healing and other occurrences take place. Eliade wrote: "We now touch upon a problem of the greatest importance . . . that is, the question of the *reality* of the extrasensory capacities and paranormal powers ascribed to the shamans and medicine-men. Although research into this question is still at its beginning, a fairly large number of ethnographic documents has already put the authenticity of such phenomena beyond doubt" (Eliade, 1966).

Selected Writing: *Shamanism: Archaic Techniques of Ecstacy,* 1966.

**Eliot, George (Mary Ann Evans), 1819–1880.** English novelist. Her prose fiction was of the first rank in the literature of the nineteenth century. She is often considered the equal of such contemporary authors as Charles Dickens and William Makepeace Thackeray. While her historical novels such as *Romola* (1863) stressed the strict morality of the Victorian era, it was her psychological novels in which her characters were subjected to powerful psychological analyses that earned her her reputation. Among her best known works are *Adam Bede* (1859), *The Mill on the Floss* (1860), *Silas Marner* (1861), and *Middlemarch* (1871–1872). Eliot defied Victorian morality by living openly for twenty-four years with George Henry Lewes until his death in 1878.

Her scholarly and intellectual achievements surely contributed to making her one of the foremost writers of her time but so did the creative process which her testimony as a **Noted Witness** supports. "[I]n all that she considered her best writing, there was a 'not herself' which took possession of her, and . . . she felt her own personality to be merely the instrument through which this spirit, as it were, was acting. . . . Then, abandoning herself to the inspiration of the moment, she wrote the whole scene exactly as it stands, without alteration or erasure."

BIBLIOGRAPHY: Cross, J. W. *George Eliot's Life As Related in Her Letters and Journals,* 1885. 3 Vols.

**Ellison, Arthur James, 1920–.** British engineer. Now professor emeritus, Professor Ellison's career, as his numerous publications, honors, and patents show, has been devoted to research and teaching in the field of engineering. His interest in psychical research and parapsychology, however, was sparked by his own experiences that, over the years, have included "a haunting type apparition, materialization, apports, and, later, altered states of consciousness including out-of-body experiences" (Ellison, 1977:237). He is sympathetic to the Hindu idea of our physical world as illusion or as Sir James Jeans put it as "more like a great thought than like a great machine." Professor Ellison urges the importance to parapsychologists of training themselves at other "levels" of consciousness and of the value of meditation in reaching these levels. He urges also continuation of the physical work begun by Kenneth Batcheldor and carried on successfully by A. R. G. and Iris Owen.

Theosophy, Huna, yoga and unorthodox healing may all be important and useful to parapsychologists, he believes. Professor Ellison is convinced that telepathy, clairvoyance and psychokinesis do occur and that precognition has been shown to exist. He believes that there is excellent evidence of reincarnation and that survival of death therefore follows. As do so many psychical researchers, Professor Ellison considers the cross-correspondences the best evidence we have so far had of survival. He has himself done some research with hypnosis, random number generators, and metal-bending in children.

Professor Ellison's parapsychological writings include his two presidential addresses (1978, 1982a) to the Society for Psychical Research, papers in the *Journal of the Society for Psychical Research,* articles in the weekly *The Unexplained,* a chapter on Kirlian photography (1982b) and a book (1988). He also teaches occasional courses in parapsychology at universities and other institutions of learning.

The recipient in 1945 of a B.S. in engineering with first class honors, Professor Ellison worked for some years in industry before serving as lecturer and senior lecturer at Queen Mary College. In 1959 he was visiting professor at M.I.T. After receiving his D.Sc. in engineering from the University of London in 1970, he became head of the Department of Electrical and Electronic Engineering there from 1972 until his retirement. He is a Fellow of the Institute of Mechanical Engineers, a Fellow of the Institute of Electrical Engineers, senior member of the Institute of Electrical and Electronic Engineers, and chairman of the Theosophical Research Centre.

Selected Writings: *The Reality of the Paranormal,* 1988; 1982a. "Psychical Research: After 100 Years What Do We Really Know?" PSPR 56:384; "Kirlian Photography." In I. Grattan Guinness, ed., *Psychical Research,* 1982b; 1978. "Mind, Belief and Psychical Research." PSPR 56:236.

**Elongation.** A paranormal increase in the normal length of the human body or its limbs. Well-attested instances of the phenomenon have been noted in the case of mystics and devout people. During one of her ecstasies, the Blessed Stefana Quinzana, a Dominica nun, extended her arms and the left one stretched beyond its natural length. Veronica Laparelli, a nun who died in 1620, did something even more spectacular. A witness said: "[W]hen [the nun] being in the trance state was reciting her Office alternately with some invisible being, she was observed gradually to stretch out until the length of her throat seemed to be out of all proportion in such a way that she was altogether much taller then usual. . . . So, to make sure, we took a yard-measure and measured her height, and afterwards when she had come to herself we measured her again, and she was at least [ten inches] shorter. This we have seen with our own eyes, all of us nuns who were in the chapel."

Lest it be thought that the phenomenon is confined to mysticism and religion, it should be noted that some physical mediums have seemed able to grow beyond their normal measure. During a séance with D. D. Home, for example, the earl of Dunraven, with Home standing beside him, saw the medium stretch his body so that, said Dunraven, "Home grew, I should say, at least, six inches. Mr. Jencken, who is a taller man than Home, stood beside him, so that there could be no mistake about it. Home's natural height is, I believe, 5 feet 10 inches. I should say he grew to 6 feet 4 inches or 6 feet 6 inches. I placed my hands on his feet, and felt that they were fairly level on the ground. He . . . unbuttoned his coat. He was elongated from his waist upwards, there was a space of, I suppose, 4 inches between his waistcoat and the waistband of his trowsers [*sic*]."

BIBLIOGRAPHY: Dunraven, earl of. 1924, "Experiences in Spritualism with D. D. Home." PSPR 35:1, p. 63; Thurston, H. *The Physical Phenomena of Mysticism,* 1952, p. 198.

**Epworth Rectory.** One of the "best authenticated ghost stories" (Price, 1945) in the literature of psychical research. It is based on a contemporary journal record kept by the Reverend Samuel Wesley, father of the famous Anglican clergyman, John Wesley, and on letters from John's mother and sisters. John himself was away from home but, based on letters and conversations with the family, published the account in the *Arminian Magazine.*

Samuel Wesley was the rector of the Epworth Parsonage in Lincolnshire, England, where he lived with his wife and seven daughters. They were prevented from sleeping in December 1716 and January 1717 because of frightening and inexplicable disturbances that included knocks, footsteps, groans, and creaks in various parts of the house. They heard bangs as if large lumps of coal were being rolled down the stairs and cups and china were smashed in the cupboard. On several occasions, they saw a creature that looked like a badger or rabbit but gobbled like a turkey. When pursued, it vanished. Samuel Wesley noted, "I have been thrice pushed by an invisible power, once against the corner of my desk in the study, a second time against the door of the matted chamber, a third time against the frame of my study door as I was going in" (Sitwell, 1940). When he heard knocking, he rapped with his cane, and the knocks answered him rap for rap. The family referred to the cause of the disturbances as "Old Jeffery" possibly because it seemed to be an intelligent entity.

But who or what was the real author of the outbreaks? For the religious Samuel Wesley and his family who shared the convictions of the eighteenth century, it was the devil himself. Modern day parapsychologists theorize differently. One theory is that subterranean flood waters underneath the parsonage may have tilted the house to such an extent that its timbers groaned, windows rattled and a desk, door, and door frame moved toward Samuel Wesley instead of his being pushed toward them as he thought (Lambert, 1955).

Opposed to the physical theory of earth movements and noises that would not seem to cover all of the phenomena are paranormal theories. The case might be a **Poltergeist** outbreak centering around a **Poltergeist Agent,** a daughter of the Wesleys who, because she trembled exceedingly in her sleep, may have had medical or emotional problems. Frank Podmore believed that the agent was the nineteen-year-old Mehetabel (called Hetty). The noises that seemed to emanate from her bed started and went on as she trembled in her sleep. They followed her and she seemed to attract more of "Jeffery's" attention than anyone else. Particularly significant was the fact that, although Samuel Wesley's other daughters wrote letters describing the occurrences, she alone wrote none and remained silent (Podmore, 1899). At the same time, the Epworth disturbances that extended through two months and were observed by nine or ten witnesses manifest many of the visual and auditory phenomena generally associated with a haunt. The old case remains a fascinating one.

BIBLIOGRAPHY: Lambert, G. 1955 "Poltergeists: A Physical Theory." JSPR 38:49; Podmore, F. 1899. "Correspondence" JSPR 9:37; Price, H. *Poltergeist Over England,* 1945, p. 81; Sitwell, S. *Poltergeists,* 1940.

**Ermacora, Giovanni, 1850–1898.** Italian physicist and one of Italy's first investigators of the paranormal. After Cesare Lombroso's conversion by Eusapia Palladino and his statement that the phenomena he witnessed during a sitting with her were genuine, Ermacora was one of the innumerable scientists who rushed to conduct experiments with her. In 1895, together with another physicist, Giorgio Finzi, he founded the *Revista di Studi Psichica* (Journal of Psychic Studies), which proposed a program of rigorous scientific investigation with methods similar to those used by the Society for Psychical Research. Ermacora was interested in all branches of the paranormal, especially telepathy, and, between 1892 and 1895, was the first person anywhere to carry on experiments to study the possible influence of telepathy on dreams.

**Esalen Institute.** Founded in California in 1962 to explore human potentials, to encourage mental training in sports, to give courses and workshops, and to hold encounter groups in consciousness expansion and biofeedback. It has also established a Soviet-American Exchange Program to sponsor seminars and to promote dialogue and the dissemination of information among scientists in the two countries who are working for the development of human potential. This is an area that includes holistic health, sports psychology, and parapsychology.

**ESP.** See **Extrasensory Perception.**

**ESP Cards.** Cards on each of which one of the following symbols appears: three wavy lines, a circle, a star, a square, a plus sign. A deck contains five of each symbol for a total of twenty-five cards. Also called Zener cards. See **Rhine, Joseph B.; Zener, Karl.**

**ESP Projection.** The apparent separation from the physical body of a center of consciousness that, after its return to the physical body, remembers places, events, or people observed while out-of-body. In a survey of college students conducted by **Hornell Hart,** 20 percent claimed that they had experienced an ESP Projection. See **Out-of-Body Experience.**

**Estebany, Oskar.** Twentieth century Hungarian healer with a wide reputation for successfully healing the sick by **Laying-on-of-Hands.** Estebany maintained that he could feel a "healing energy," "sensations of 'something' moving in his hands as well as vibrations of heat particularly on those places where the patient claimed to feel ill" (Grad, 1987:149). After this former cavalry officer in the Hungarian army moved to Canada, Bernard Grad tested his "healing energy" with positive results. Similar results were produced when Estebany was studied by M. Justa Smith and again by Dolores Krieger. Whatever the "something" is, the studies of Estebany suggest that he has it. See also **Healing, Unorthodox.**

BIBLIOGRAPHY: Grad, B. "Experiences and Opinions of an Unconventional Scientist." In R. Pilkington, ed., *Men and Women of Parapsychology,* 1987.

**Estabrooks, George Hoben, 1895–1980s.** Canadian-born psychologist. He pioneered in experimental parapsychology when, in 1926, he conducted experiments in telepathy under William McDougall at Harvard University. He used a large number of subjects who were students at Harvard. In one room he placed an agent concentrating on a card chosen at random from a shuffled pack and in a different room a percipient who wrote down the name of a card that came to him after the click of a telegraph key. After a large number of tests, Estabrooks got positive results suggestive of telepathy. Since the experiments excluded sensory cues, they were a significant although little noticed advance in 1926.

Estabrooks also was the first to observe another matter of significance. He noted that the hits of his subjects in the second half of their runs dropped well below chance in contrast to high scores posted in the first half. He did not attach much importance to this discovery, but he put his finger on what is by now a phenomenon familiar in parapsychology and in psi experiments—the falling off of success and the declination of scores in the course of an experiment.

Selected Writings: 1927. "A Contribution to Experimental Telepathy." *Bulletin of the Boston Society for Psychic Research* 5:1.

**European Journal of Parapsychology.** Semiannual publication in the English language of the Parapsychology Laboratory of the University of Utrecht. Although it contained theoretical articles on parapsychology, its primary emphasis was on experimental papers. The aim of the *Journal,* whose publication began in 1975, was to stimulate parapsychological activity in Europe. Its editorial staff consisted of English and European workers, including **John Beloff** and **Hans Bender.** Submissions from non-European authors, however, were accepted. With the closing of the Parapsychology Laboratory, the status of the *Journal* is in doubt.

**Eva C(arriere) (Marthe Béraud), 1886–?.** French materializing medium. Her career began in 1903 in Algiers at the home of her fiancé's parents when she materialized the spirit "Bien Boa" and his sister "Bergolia." In 1905, **Charles Richet** went to Algiers to investigate Marthe's phenomena and concluded that they were almost certainly geniune even though the materialized figure breathed and produced carbon dioxide, just like a human being. Richet wrote that Bien Boa was either a phantom who had human attributes or a person playing the part of a phantom. He opted for the former explanation. Shortly after Richet's report, one Dr. Z and a lawyer named Marsault living in Algiers alleged that all the phenomena were fraudulently produced with the aid of accomplices and that Marthe had admitted that she had entered into the whole affair for fun. Richet nevertheless never accepted the fraudulent explanation of the phenomena and Stephen E. Braude (1986) considers the charges irrelevant "in view of the excellent eyewitness accounts of materializations in the process of formation" (p.149).

In 1908, now known as "Eva C.," Marthe, then twenty-two years of age, went to Paris where she was introduced to sculptress Juliette Bisson. In 1909, Eva C. began giving private sittings to a small circle and for nearly twenty years thereafter was investigated under the most rigorous conditions that included rectal and vaginal examinations and the ingestion of emetics. In 1910 she moved into Mme Bisson's studio and in 1912, on the death of Mme Bisson's husband, Eva "moved in to live with her, sharing her life in every detail" (Brandon, 1983)—a clear suggestion of lesbianism. (Some fourteen years later, however, Eva C. did marry.) In 1909, **Albert von Schrenck-Notzing** began attending Eva's séances. He, too, became convinced of the genuineness of her phenomena, which consisted of materializations from various parts of her body of either vague masses or arms (with hands and fingers) and heads.

Helen Verrall **(Helen de G. Salter)** and many later investigators as well suggest that most of the material could have been regurgitated. Yet Schrenck-Notzing (1927) could find no substantiation for this charge and Richet ( 1923/1975) wrote that prior to a sitting Eva C. ingested a syrup that would have colored any regurgitated matter. That many of the materializations looked like cutouts from newspapers neither Richet nor Braude consider evidence against their being genuine because materializations need not be three-dimensional and because they were formed from "ectoplasm [which] emerged in a thin stream, from different parts of the body, and then developed into forms. . . . What appeared in photographs as 'still life' was to onlookers very much alive, but rarely still, and never the same for long" (Inglis, 1983:71).

**Gustave Geley** also studied Eva C. and reported that her phenomena were genuine. Much later Rudolf Lambert (1954) reported that, after Gustave Geley's death, his papers revealed that Mme Bisson had been an accomplice in Eva C.'s fraud and that Geley's stereoscopic pictures of the medium that showed that the materializations had been attached by wires to her hair had been suppressed. But the problem with the photographs has been partially countered by the witnesses' observations mentioned above and by the further suggestion that the photographs could have been altered psychokinetically.

BIBLIOGRAPHY: Brandon, R. *The Spiritualists,* 1983; Braude, S. E. *The Limits of Influence,* 1986; Geley, G. *L'Ectoplasmie et la Clairvoyance,* 1924; Inglis, B. "Retrocognitive Dissonance," In *Research in Parapsychology, 1982,* 1983; Lambert, R. 1954. "Dr. Geley's Report on the Medium Eva C." JSPR 37:682; Richet, C. *Thirty Years of Psychical Research,* 1923/1975; Richet, C. 1905. "De Quelques Phénomènes dits de Materialisation." *Annales des Sciences Psychiques,* 129ff.; von Schrenck-Notzing, A. *The Phenomena of Materialization,* 1927 (originally published as *Materialisationsphänomene,* 1914); Verrall, Helen de G. 1914. "The History of Marthe Beraud." PSPR 27:333.

**Evil Eye.** The power ascribed to some people who, merely with a glance, can cause injury or death. The belief is found everywhere and can be traced to antiquity. Democritus, a philosopher of ancient Greece, thought that living people could emit images from their eyes. If the images were filled with hostile intent, they could cling to a victim and cause injury. Plato held similarly in his *Timaeus* that a fiery current could be emitted by an eye. Defenses—charms, for example, or gestures, such as crooking a finger—vary with the culture. In Africa, where it is believed that people are more exposed to harm when their mouths are open while eating or drinking, food and drink are taken when alone or inside a house whose doors are locked. The source of the evil eye is thought to be the devil or witchcraft. If indeed it is a real power and not just an old and ubiquitous superstition, however, perhaps some basic concepts and phenomena in psychical research can explain it. A noted psychiatrist believes that telepathy can cause illness (Schwarz, 1980:114). Victims of the "evil eye," therefore, may receive telepathically the hostile thoughts of a person looking at them and subconsciously become persuaded that they will be injured or die. Or, victims may be influenced by psychokinesis as a hostile mind concentrates its power on them. Charms and signs have not been shown to be effective against telepathy or psychokinesis; there are no known measures that can be taken to ward them off.

BIBLIOGRAPHY: Schwarz, B. E. *Psychic Nexus: Phenomena in Psychiatry and Everyday Life,* 1980.

**Evola, Natuzza, 1922–.** Italian stigmatic and psychic. Over the last forty years, hundreds have come to her for inspiration or help in the belief that she is a modern saint. This illiterate peasant of Calabria in the south of Italy and devout mother of five children by her carpenter husband is purported to possess psi abilities, such as clairvoyance in the diagnosis of disease or in the location of missing objects or people, and the power of bilocation of which some fifty-five cases have been documented. In addition, she perspires blood, and stigmata similar to Christ's wounds appear on her body. She produces haemography—the arrangement of the blood from her wounds in the form of crosses, faces, figures, or rosaries on materials that have come into contact with her body, such as shirts or handkerchiefs. Natuzza will not submit to any scientific testing of her powers, but neither does she accept money from those who come to her for consultations. Nor has she ever been detected in trickery. In many ways, she resembles the Catholic mystics, such as **Padre Pio,** and seems to carry on the tradition associated with them.

BIBLIOGRAPHY: Nanko, M. 1985. "A Report on the Case of Natuzza Evolo." *Journal of the Southern California Society for Psychical Research* 3:5.

**Exceptional Human Body Function. (EHBF).** In 1979, the ability of a twelve-year-old boy in China to read printed ideograms when they were applied to his ears excited the minds of scientific people. The hypothesis of ESP to explain the acquisition of knowledge without the use of the organ of sight was rejected by the Chinese scientists, however. They theorized that some physical explanation existed for the phenomenon analogous to **Dermo-Optic Perception.** They called the phenomenon Extraordinary Human Body Function and began and have continued successful experiments with other children. But foreign scientists who have witnessed the children's "performances" have not been impressed.

**Exorcism.** Brought to public attention by the best-selling book and sensational movie *The Exorcist,* the rite of exorcism is used in various religions to expel possessing demons, devils, and evil spirits. What constitutes possession is a basic problem and is defined differently by shamans, witch hunters, parapsychologists, psychiatrists, or priests. The subjects of "possession and exorcism . . . have from time immemorial been a hodgepodge of superstition, primitive lore, musty theological dogma, esoteric doctrine, and largely preconceived psychiatric opinion" (Ehrenwald, 1975). "Madness, epilepsy, religious ecstasy, prophecy, poetic and artistic inspiration, drunken or sexual frenzy, states of trance . . . have been explained . . . as [possession] by a . . . god or spirit or demon . . ." (*Encyclopedia of the Unexplained,* 1974). Modern findings in psychology, psychical research, and medicine make it questionable that there is really such a thing as demonic possession. "Diabolical possession is caused by belief in diabolical possession; possession without the devil remains simply an autosuggestive trance or a hysterical fit" (Kelly, 1970).

Nevertheless, belief in demonic possession and in the efficacy of exorcism continues. Exorcistic rites have ranged from a parapsychologist's closeting himself in a room where poltergeist phenomena had taken place and then asserting that "it" would not come back (it didn't) (Gauld and Cornell, 1979); to the religious rites of *The Exorcist* (the commands to the demon to leave; the demon's abusive replies and disgusting and horrible behavior; the final triumph of the exorcist); to the beating to death (beating and ill-treatment are often part of the exorcism) in 1966 of a young Swiss girl who claimed to be possessed by the devil.

BIBLIOGRAPHY: Blatty, W. P. *The Exorcist,* 1971; Cavendish, R., ed., *Encyclopedia of the Unexplained,* 1974; Ebon, M. *The Devil's Bride: Exorcism, Past and Present,* 1974a; Ebon, M. 1974b. "Exorcism beyond the Chaos." *Psychic* 5(6):50; Ehrenwald, J. 1975. "The Devil's Bride." JASPR 69:292; Gauld, A. and Cornell, A. D. *Poltergeists,* 1979; Kelly, H. A. 1970. (quoted in Ebon, "Exorcism beyond the Chaos," p.52).

**Expectation.** The number of trials times the probability of success on each trial.

**Experiment, Control.** See **Control Experiment.**

**Experimenter.** The designer of an experiment or the conductor of one, or both.

**Experimenter Effect.** The hypothesis that experimenters may be key factors in the success or failure of experiments. Subjects may respond to the needs, wishes, unintentional sensory cues, personalities, or psi abilities of experimenters. Experimenter effect is an explanation often given for the success or lack of it in many psi experiments.

**Extended Telepathy.** See **Super ESP.**

**Extra.** See **Spirit Photography.**

**Extrachance.** Not due to chance alone (JP).

**Extrasenser.** Russian term for psychic or sensitive.

**Extrasensory Perception (ESP).** A general term covering Clairvoyance, Telepathy and Precognition, that is, modes of obtaining information about an event, object, or situation outside oneself without the use of any of the known sensory processes. ESP continues to be reported, as it has been throughout the ages, in daily life experiences or spontaneous cases. A woman drops a cup she had been drying and exclaims: "My God, he's hurt!" At that very moment, her husband is struck by a car as he is crossing a road miles away from his home. Another woman has a dream heralding the death of a friend. A man wakes in the middle of the night and sees an apparition by his bedside. A medium displays knowledge during a séance she could never have gotten through the use of her eyes, ears, and wits.

If the reports of such phenomena are totally false, if the events reported never took place, the fact that they have been reported by, and have been accepted by, individuals of sound mind and good moral character is intriguing from the viewpoint of the psychology of human testimony, hallucination, and credibility. On the other hand, if these reports have been confirmed, they would have diverse and far-reaching implications. That so many highly intelligent and well-educated people continue to deny such occurrences is then equally intriguing from the viewpoint of the psychology of human bias and incredulity.

If the reports of such events are true, they are exceedingly interesting from a philosophical perspective, for they raise the ancient question of the relationship between mind and brain. Dualism long ago was toppled in favor of a materialist view that mind is a function of processes of the brain and totally dependent on it. But the occurrence of paranormal events that seem to resist and baffle physical explanations may point to the existence of a nonphysical mental component interacting with, yet autonomous of, the brain and which, at certain times, has the ability to influence physical objects or become aware of other minds whose physical bodies may be either living or dead. Such events, if they in fact occur, collide with materialism and the impact could restore mind-body dualism to the attention of thinkers. From the standpoint of religion, the ability of one mind to be conscious of or to affect another despite the distance between them and without the use of the senses, would also be of great interest because it suggests an unseen order beyond the visible world of space and time.

The term "extrasensory perception" was not introduced by J. B. Rhine as is popularly supposed. Others, including Oskar Fischer, a German professor who wrote about the nomenclature of parapsychology in 1926, used it before Rhine. They, like Rhine, intended the term to mean perception without the function of any recognized sense. Robert H. Thouless has criticized the term and its concept as committing us to the perhaps incorrect theory that what is occurring in the ESP process is a form of "perception." So he urged a more neutral term that commits us to no theory. But whether the term is good or bad, the interpretation of the phenomenon as non-sensory and the question of what really is taking place in the process are all secondary to the primary question of whether the phenomenon does in fact exist.

There are two major fields, one in psychical research, the other in parapsychology in which attempts are made to answer that question. One is the examination of spontaneous cases in which all the abilities of a lawyer, detective, and historian are required in order to assess the value of the evidence. The other is experimental research with statistical evaluations such as card-guessing. Among the experiments considered strong evidence for the existence of ESP are the Pearce-Pratt and Pratt-Woodruff experiments conducted at Duke University in the United States. Some psychologists, however, have strongly criticized the evidence for ESP. Although Joseph G. Pratt, J. B. Rhine and other parapsychologists believed that they had silenced these criticisms in 1940, the question remains controversial even today. Psychologists such as Ray Hyman and Charles E. M. Hansel believe that the results of even the best experiments must have been produced by fraud or experimenter incompetence.

BIBLIOGRAPHY: Hansel, C. E. M. *ESP: A Scientific Evaluation,* 1966; Pratt, J. G. and Rhine, J. B. 1954. "A Review of the Pearce-Pratt Distance Series of ESP Tests." JP 18:165; Pratt, J. G., Rhine, J. B., Smith, B. M., Stuart, C. E. *Extrasensory Perception after Sixty Years,* 1940; Pratt, J. G. and Woodruff J. L. 1939. "Size of Stimulus Symbols in Extra-Sensory Perception." JP 3:121; Rhine, J. B. *Extra-Sensory Perception,* 1934.

**Eyeless Vision.** See **Dermo-Optic Perception.**

**Eysenck, Hans Jurgen, 1916–.** German psychologist. Professor emeritus of the University of London, he studied under Sir Cyril Burt and is the author or editor of over 800 articles and forty books on personality and individual differences, social attitudes, and intelligence and cognitive abilities. He developed one of the psychological tests known as the Eysenck Personality Scale which is in wide use in parapsychology and applied in extrasensory perception experiments. His theory that extraverts will produce high ESP scores (Eysenck, 1967) is one that parapsychologists also use in their predictions. Eysenck considers the evidence for the paranormal favorable (Eysenck and Sargent, 1982) and even has designed instructions for anyone interested in the conduct of ESP exercises and tests (Eysenck and Sargent, 1983).

Selected Writings: and Sargent, C. *Know Your Own PSI-IQ,* 1983; and Sargent, C. *Explaining the Unexplained,* 1982; 1967. "Personality and Extrasensory Perception." JSPR 44:55.

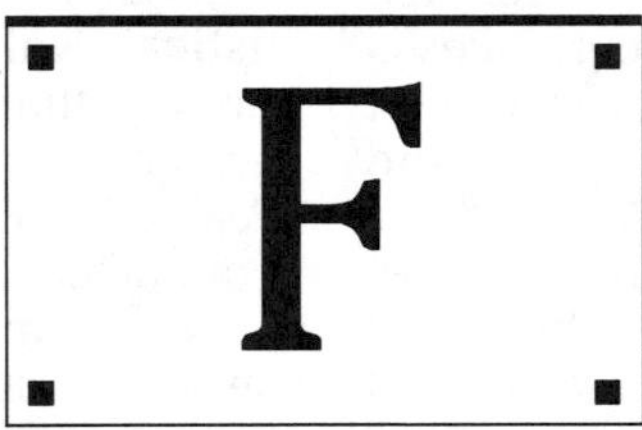

**Fairies.** A race of beings who live on earth in human form, are generally handsome or beautiful, but sometimes are only a few inches in height. They can be kind or cruel and possess the power to cause mysterious occurrences in human affairs. The belief in fairies can be found in the traditions of virtually all people and in the earliest literature. If claims of having seen them accord with objective reality and are not imagination, the existence of these creatures totally unknown to science would be of great importance. The evidence for their existence is weak. Photographs are unsatisfactory because there are many techniques for faking pictures and, like photographs of unidentified flying objects, they may be clever fakes.

A case in point are the photographs that **Sir Arthur Conan Doyle** in 1920 accepted as proof for his belief in fairies and which, a quarter century later, were still being presented as absolutely genuine (Gardner, 1945). They have now been shown by computer enhancement technology (Randi, 1980) and the recent confessions of the women who took them, then sixteen and ten years of age, (Inglis, 1985) to have been faked.

If fairies are real, it is possible that those few who see them have some psychic faculty for doing so. Psychical researchers may agree that there is a psychic ability to perceive apparitions or even to obtain information from communicators. But apparitions and communicators, if they in fact exist, are nonphysical inhabitants of another level of reality and not physical beings whose home is this planet. Neither parapsychology in its laboratories nor psychical research in **Spontaneous Cases** has discovered the paranormal ability to see fairies.

BIBLIOGRAPHY: Gardner, F. L. *Fairies,* 1945; Inglis, B. *The Paranormal,* 1985; Randi, J. *Flim-flam!,* 1980.

**Faith Healing.** See **Healing, Unorthodox.**

**Faraday, Michael, 1791–1867.** Eminent British physicist and chemist. In 1853, his interest shifted from physics and chemistry to table-tilting, which Spiritualists considered a manifestation of spirits. He invented a device that would record the muscular movements of anyone whose hands were on it. Using the device in table-tilting experiments, he demonstrated that the movements of a table were not attributable to spirits but rather to the unconscious push-pull force exerted by people seated around the table with their hands resting on it. Faraday's experiments, which he published as a letter in the *Times,* seemed effectively to tilt the table against table-tilting. But it really fell short of explaining the phenomenon completely—for example, when no human hands are on or near a moving or rapping table or when raps supply information unknown to sitters and which may have a faraway telepathic source.

The great scientist, however, seems to have lost his scientific attitude in the case of **Daniel Dunglas Home.** When he received an invitation to investigate Home, Faraday insisted as a condition of the investigation that Home first agree that his phenomena were fraudulent. When Home would not agree, Faraday refused to investigate. "The position taken was quite indefensible. . . . [T]o enter upon a judicial inquiry by treating the subject matter as a *chose jugée* was surely a parody of scientific methods" (Podmore, 1902).

Selected Writing: Letter to the *Times*, June 30, 1853.

BIBLIOGRAPHY: Podmore, F. *Modern Spiritualism: A History and a Criticism*, 1902, Vol. II, pp. 145–146.

**Fate.** A popular monthly magazine. Although many of its articles dealing with strange subjects and experiences must be taken with a grain of salt, often it carries significant and interesting reports, critiques, and book reviews dealing with topics and issues in psychical research and parapsychology. D. Scott Rogo is on its editorial board.

**Fatima, Marian Apparitions at.** Fatima, once a sleepy village in central Portugal, is one of the largest pilgrimage centers in the world because of what happened there between May 13 and October 13, 1917.

On May 13, three young children, two girls and a boy, were taking care of sheep just outside the village when there was a flash of lightning and they saw a beautiful young woman standing atop a small tree. She said she came from heaven and that they would go there one day. She asked them to come back to the same place on the thirteenth day of each month for six months. One of the children, without any basis for saying so, told her parents that she had seen the Blessed Virgin. The children claimed more appearances at the tree in the months that followed. All were scolded by their parents and were repeatedly cross-examined by church and municipal authorities, but their accounts did not vary. In August, when another apparition was expected, the political authorities, concerned about religious demonstrations, kidnapped the children and threatened them with being boiled in oil unless they either admitted they were lying or revealed what secrets the Mother of God had entrusted to them. Each child was warned on the way to the non-existent kettle that the others had been cooked and that the boiling would be repeated if the child did not speak. But the children remained tight-lipped. That month the apparition was late for its appointment.

The vision had promised that she would disclose her identity and, to persuade skeptics, would perform a miracle on October 13. On the designated day, 70,000 people, both hostile and friendly to religion, assembled to see the miracle. Troops were on hand to keep order. When nothing but heavy rains had taken place by noon, there were murmurs, complaints, and jokes from the drenched crowd. The editor of *O Seculo*, an anti-religious publication, was already making sarcastic notes for the next edition. Suddenly, through an opening in the thick clouds, the mass of witnesses reported that the sun, looking like a great silver disc, rose and fell and gyrated. It produced colors of the rainbow whose hues appeared on the faces of the astonished crowd and on the surrounding countryside. Then it fell on a trajectory that took it toward earth. The heat it gave off was intense. People in the crowd cried and prayed in the face of the approach of the end of the world. Then the disc climbed back toward the sky. A shout of relief and happiness went up from the watchers.

National pilgrimages to Fatima began ten years later and a basilica was built at the Shrine of Our Lady of Fatima. The normal population of Fatima is about 600. In 1967, when Pope Paul VI said mass on the fiftieth anniversary of the first vision, one million pilgrims inundated the village.

The apparition never seems to have revealed that she was Mary, but it is generally assumed that it was she. If it was Mary, it was, with Egypt, her most dramatic appearance. Religion aside, it was a genuine paranormal occurrence. Yet, it defies any parapsychological explanation. Apparitions can be explained as subjective experiences when seen by a single person or as a collective and infectious hallucination when seen by several. But here the phenomenon was observed in towns eight and forty kilometers away. Children poured out of schools to witness what scholars have called "the dance of the sun." The phenomenon was not a collective hallucination, for it was seen both by 70,000 people in one place and by others far away who should not have been caught by the contagion.

It seems on its face a genuine wonder for which no natural causes can account and before which science and psychical research stand mute. Yet, those standing on this planet have always seen objects in the sky. Perhaps what was seen on October 13 was misidentified as the sun. The mysterious disc with its curious pattern of movements has all the earmarks of an unidentified flying object. But then, we must ask, why should a UFO have appeared on the very day designated by the vision? If it was a UFO, its appearance would be an astonishing coincidence, which leads us back to evaluating the "dance of the sun" as an inexplicable chapter in the book of the paranormal. See also **Egypt, Marian Apparitons at; Mary, Saint.**

BIBLIOGRAPHY: Walsh, W. T. *Our Lady of Fatima,* 1949.

**Fay, Annie Eva, 1855—1927.** American physical medium. Slender, small, with grey eyes and blonde hair, she became the most famous psychic performer in America. Her specialty was the alleged paranormal movement of objects while she was firmly tied to a wooden post. During most of 1874 she gave stage performances in London. William Crookes investigated her at this time and apparently got successful results, but Frederic W. H. Myers and Count Perovsky-Petrovo-Solovovo believed she was a cheat. The most important test Crookes made involved the use of an electrical circuit designed by **Cromwell Varley.** The test seems to have shown that Mrs. Fay produced physical phenomena without breaking an electrical circuit of which she was part which should have meant that the phenomena were paranormal. The possibility of the aid of an accomplice in such tests, however, has been suggested (Broad, 1964). In April 1876 the *New York Daily Graphic* exposed her and in May of that year **Washington Irving Bishop,** her onetime manager, duplicated her feats and showed how she freed herself (and then retied herself) by means of extraordinary physical contortions. Despite these exposures, however, she continued to be a successful performer into the 1920s.

BIBLIOGRAPHY: Broad, C. D. 1964. "Cromwell Varley's Electrical Tests with Florence Cook." PSPR 54:158; Jay, R. *Learned Pigs and Fireproof Women,* 1986; Medhurst, R. G. and Goldney, K. M. 1964. "William Crookes and the Physical Phenomena of Mediumship." PSPR 54:25.

**Fear of Psi.** Although many of us have positive attitudes toward psi and see it as a potential means of learning more about the nature of the human personality, of spiritual growth, personal development or healing, others have negative attitudes toward it. As a president of the Society for Psychical Research said, "We are working in a region densely populated with the hopes and fears of men, and not only with hopes and fears but with superstitions, obsessions, preconceptions and fixed ideas innumerable. These things swarm round the inquirer like the evil spirits which beset the path of Bunyan's Pilgrim when he passed through the Valley of Humiliation" (Jacks, 1917).

Largely as the result of "horror" movies and books in which psychokinesis is portrayed as demolishing buildings or producing fiery infernos, or, as in the case of **The Amityville Horror,** where evil psychic phenomena are everywhere, a number of people think of psi as harmful, violent, destructive. Some people are afraid that they are being exposed to the psi abilities of others who have access to their thoughts and feelings. Often, too, there are deep ethical concerns; people are alarmed by the possible use of psi for sinister and antisocial purposes, such as altering or manipulating minds or causing disease, even death. Such fears are voiced often in connection with reported research in parapsychology by the military-scientific complexes of the great powers who realize that the cost of using psychics to destroy an enemy is far less than that of missiles. Other groups are frightened by psi because they see psychic phenomena as a threat to the picture of the world orthodox science has built up.

Psychics, too, who deal with psi on a daily basis, have their own fears, which fall into these categories: 1) loss of control and the feeling that the unseen source contacted may use the psychic; 2) distortions of self resulting from a need to please clients; 3) the confusion resulting when clients do not accept a reading; 4) becoming ill from dealing with the problems of clients; 5) personal problems arising from the knowledge that they have and can use new and extraordinary powers (Tart, 1985).

Fear of psi is a matter of great concern to parapsychologists because it creates resistance to parapsychology and impedes both real life psi experiences and psi performance in laboratory experiments. In one experiment with psychokinesis, for example, a subject was afraid that if she demonstrated her psychokinetic powers too well, she would be kidnapped by government agents and sent to a secret military research installation.

BIBLIOGRAPHY: Jacks, L. P. 1917. "Presidential Address." PSPR 29:287; Tart, C. T. 1985. "Psychics' Fears of Psychic Powers." In D. H. Weiner and D. I. Radin, eds., *Research in Parapsychology 1985,* 1986, p. 151.

**Feda.** See **Garrett, Eileen J.**

**Feedback.** In tests of extrasensory perception and psychokinesis, the practice of supplying a subject with immediate information of successes or failures in order to improve the subject's performance.

Some parapsychologists are attempting to devise methods of feedback in order to induce an incline effect in ESP tests. An interesting illustration of one of these methods is an unusual experiment conducted at the Mind Science Foundation where thirty subjects volunteered to participate in feedback tests involving telepathy and the Ganzfeld procedure. One group of subjects would one by one lie in a curtained waterbed in one room with their eyes covered with translucent hemispheres and wearing headphones which gave off a pleasant "white noise" with the lower frequencies a little increased. Through the headphones recorded timing signals were cues for the subjects to start describing impressions as an agent in another room concentrated on randomly selected target slides. The subject's impressions were heard by the agent through an intercom. If there was a correspondence between the content of the slide and the description given by the subject, immediate feedback would be supplied by a special tone a little more intense than the volume of noise normally heard through the headphones (Braud and Wood, 1977). Another unusual method of feedback was designed by **Richard Broughton** and others who developed a random event generator that gives the subjects a painful electric shock if their scores are low.

There are some indications that feedback may have improved the performances of subjects in ESP tests. In the experiment at the Mind Science Foundation, for example, the subjects who received feedback scored more significantly than the control group who were not given feedback. In the majority of tests of psychokinesis, however, in which feedback was used in an attempt to train subjects or improve their performance, no significant relation between feedback and performance has yet been noted.

BIBLIOGRAPHY: Braud, W. G. and Wood, R. 1977. "The Influence of Immediate Feedback on Free-response GESP Performance During Ganzfeld Stimulation." JASPR 71:409.

**Feilding, (Francis Henry) Everard (Joseph), 1867–1936.** British barrister and psychical researcher. Educated at Oxford, he was the second son of the earl of Denbigh. A visit to Lourdes in 1892 made a profound impression on Feilding and sparked his interest in strange occurrences. The shock of his sister Clare's death in 1895 from influenza led him to look for evidence of survival after death more solid than that offered by the Catholic church of which he was a member.

He joined the Society for Psychical Research in 1890 and little by little became involved in its investigations. His principal contribution to psychical research was his study, along with his friend William W. Baggally and Hereward Carrington, of Eusapia Palladino who, they all concluded, produced some genuine phenomena under very strict experimental conditions. Fraser Nicol (1972) has called their report of this investigation "a classic of psychical research" and John Beloff (1985) believes it should be "mandatory reading" for all skeptics. Feilding wrote that during the eleven séances with Eusapia he experienced an emotional thrill on only two occasions: once, when he was touched by a hand and distinctly felt the fingers and nails, and, secondly, when a guitar string was plucked at a distance from the medium during the second séance. Sadly, his sittings with Eusapia in Naples in 1910 (with co-experimenter and conjurer W. Marriott) were a failure.

He was secretary of the Society for Psychical Research from 1903 to 1920. He had sittings with **Florence Cook** and many other physical mediums and investigated haunted houses. In 1919 he married **Stanislawa Tomczyk,** a physical medium whom he had studied and who he thought had paranormal powers. After 1920 he withdrew gradually from active participation in the SPR although he continued to be interested in events outside England, such as the mediumship of

Rudi Schneider and his brother Willy and the Margery (Mina S. Crandon) mediumship.

He was an extreme skeptic but "was always ready to disregard the waste of time and money, to laugh at the exposure of trickery, and to suggest by way of consolation that after all we had gained some further knowledge of mediumistic psychology" (Bennett, 1936). Eric J. Dingwall (1963) wrote that Feilding was "beloved . . . among all who knew him" and his obituarist added: "He died amid the love and esteem of all who knew him, without an enemy in the world. . ." (Bennett, 1936).

Selected Writings: *Sittings with Eusapia Palladino and Other Studies,* 1963; and W. W. Baggally and H. Carrington. 1909. "Report on a Series of Sittings with Eusapia Palladino." PSPR 23:309.

BIBLIOGRAPHY: Beloff, J. "What Is Your Counter-Explanation? A Plea to Skeptics to Think Again." In P. Kurtz, ed., *A Skeptics' Handbook of Parapsychology,* 1985; Bennett, E. W. 1936. "In Memory of Everard Feilding." PSPR 44:5; Dingwall, E. J. "Introduction." In Feilding, E. *Sittings with Eusapia Palladino and Other Studies,* 1963; Nicol, F. 1972. "The Founders of the SPR." PSPR 55:341.

**Feola, Jose Maria, 1926–.** Argentinian mathematician, physicist and radiobiologist. His interest in parapsychology began when he read about the physical phenomena produced by such mediums as Daniel D. Home and Rudi Schneider. While a professor of physics and mathematics at the University of La Plata in Argentina, he began to conduct his own table-tilting experiments. When he came to the United States in 1959 to study at the University of Rochester, his interest in psychic phenomena drew him inevitably to the Institute for Parapsychology where he talked with Joseph B. Rhine and Louisa E. Rhine. The relation of extrasensory perception to brain changes interested him as it did other parapsychologists and he carried out experimental investigations to see if ESP was related to alpha rhythm activity. He found a positive relationship after a subject making calls on hidden pictures scored higher when high alpha activity was present than when it was low (Rao and Feola, 1973). Dr. Feola is also intensely interested in electronic voice phenomena.

Selected Writing: and Rao, K. R. "Alpha Rhythm and ESP in a Free Response Situation." In W. G. Roll et al., eds., *Research in Parapsychology 1972,* 1973.

**Fernandez, Jose S., 1893–1967.** Argentinian university professor and engineer who adopted the quantitative methodology of **Joseph B. Rhine** and conducted the first serious investigations of parapsychology in his country. He was one of the founders of the Sociedad Argentina de Parapsicología (Argentine Society of Parapsychology) and its first president. Fernandez also helped found the **Instituto Argentino de Parapsicología** (Argentine Parapsychology Institute) and was the author of several publications both on physics and parapsychology.

**Field Theory.** Attempts have been made to apply field theory in parapsychology as it has been applied in physics and psychology. The Soviets have put forward the concept of a physical field to explain telepathy. A **PSI Field Theory** has been proposed by **William G. Roll** who suggests that all living organisms and inanimate objects have some force field or "psi field" around them. These fields interact. If an event takes place in one field when another field is in its neighborhood, the event in the first field will be registered as a trace in the second field. This trace will remain in the second field after the first is gone and, later, can stimulate the ESP of a psychic or percipient and will allow that person to pick up the trace. Field theory has been applied by **Gardner Murphy** to the question of survival after death to suggest that what might survive death are the psychical activities of an individual in time and space which that individual leaves in an interpersonal field and which become aspects of the field.

**Fire Tests.** For centuries, stories of saints and yogis walking on beds of red-hot coals have been told. The dervishes of Egypt are known to have placed glowing coals in their mouths. On the island of Bali in Indonesia, A. Passeron describes how, after a bonfire of coconut shells has been allowed to subside into a mass of hot coals, entranced dancers mounted on broomsticks simulating horses dance barefooted on the coals and gradually extinguish them with their feet without being burned.

Among the phenomena produced by physical mediums, notably **Daniel D. Home,** was also the apparent ability to withstand extreme heat, that is, they not only walked on hot coals with impunity but buried their faces among burning coals as though bathing in water. In one of Home's feats, he stirred the coals of a fire with his hand, removed a burning coal as large as an orange, placed it in one hand, covered it completely with another and, as he blew on the coal to make it white-hot, demonstrated to observers how the flames flickered around the coal and his hand. Throughout he seemed to suffer no pain or burns.

A natural explanation for resistance to fire could be that the skin has been treated with fire resisting substance. In Home's case, however, **William Crookes,** one of the great chemists of the time, said that there was no chemical preparation known that could protect Home's hand against the heat.

It has been demonstrated, however, that nothing paranormal is involved in firewalking: No burning will occur if exposure to the fire is under one second per step. Even more fantastic effects—such as entering a blazing oven with raw steaks and emerging unharmed with the steaks cooked—have been performed by entertainers for hundreds of years.

There may also be other and rather simple explanations for the ability to withstand fire. Home and others who handle fire (e.g., American Indians), may have achieved a self-induced trance or hypnosis and, in this altered state of consciousness, have become immune to injury. Coe and other chemists theorize that the ability to resist burns from incandescent objects is caused by the vapor created by the sweating of the skin. This vapor, they think, enters into a spheroidal state and protects the skin. For glowing coals, a combination of the spheroidal condition, the brief duration of contact mentioned above, skin thickness, and the insulation of wood ash may account for what seems a mysterious phenomenon.

BIBLIOGRAPHY: Coe, M. R. C. 1958. "Fire-Walking and Related Behaviors." JASPR 52:85; Jay, R. *Learned Pigs and Fireproof Women,* 1986; Passeron, A. 1983. "Trances and Dances." *Revue Métapsychique* 17:9; Rogo, D. S. 1973. "Fakers and Fakirs." *Psychic* 5(2):50.

**Fire Walking.** See **Fire Tests.**

**Fisher, Sir Ronald Alymer, 1890–1962.** British statistician who developed classical statistical analysis and was knighted in 1952. His statistical formulae and methods provided valuable guides to quantitative research workers in parapsychology in every part of the world. They agree with Fisher's observation that "in the investigation of living beings by biological methods statistical tests of significance are essential. Their function is to prevent us from being deceived by accidental circumstances, due not to the causes we wish to study, or are trying to detect, but to a combination of the many other circumstances we cannot control" (Fisher, 1929).

Selected Writing: 1929. "The Statistical Method in Psychical Research." PSPR 39:189.

**Fisk, George William, 1882–1972.** British experimental parapsychologist. All Fisk's efforts were concerned with the experimental quantitative side of parapsychology. His published experiments date mainly from the 1950s after his retirement, yet he did contribute importantly in 1935 and 1936 to G. N. M. Tyrrell's pioneering ESP experiments by pointing out how a subject could by normal means produce above chance scores.

It was from China, where he spent most of his working life, that Fisk joined the Society for Psychical Research in 1910. He saw many striking examples of ESP in China and noted the ability of many Chinese to orient themselves even in complete darkness. He was the editor of the *Journal* and the *Proceedings* of the SPR for nine years beginning 1957. In 1958, together with D. J. West, he received the McDougall Award for Distinguished Work in Parapsychology.

According to Rosalind Heywood (1973), Fisk was the ideal psychical researcher: "sceptically scientific, yet open-minded and humorous, humble and kind." D. J. West said that, unlike himself, Fisk had the "'magic' necessary to elicit successful psi results" which pointed to the importance of the role of the experimenter in obtaining positive results. Fisk was convinced by the evidence of ESP and told Rosalind Heywood that he would communicate with her after death if he could. The impressions she received, however, do not point clearly to such a communication.

Selected Writings: And D. J. West. 1956. "ESP and Mood: Report of a 'Mass' Experiment." JSPR 38:320; and D. J. West. 1953. "A

Dual ESP Experiment with Clock Cards." JSPR 37:185.

BIBLIOGRAPHY: Heywood, R. 1973. "G. W. Fisk and ESP." JSPR 47:24; West, D. J. 1973. "Obituary: G. W. Fisk." JSPR 47:21.

**Flammarion, Nicolas Camille, 1842–1925.** French astronomer. He founded the French Astronomical Society and, in 1882, the monthly review, *L'Astronomie,* which he edited. He was distinguished for his work on the motion of the stars, on double and triple stars, on the physical characteristics of Mars, and was one of the pioneers in the use of the balloon to study the stars. Recipient in 1922 of the award of the Commander of the Legion of Honor, he was known as the "Poet of the Heavens" for his books on astronomy. Running into several editions and published in many languages, they presented the subject in lucid terms understandable to the layman. His works on the topography of the red planet combined with the impression of what seemed constructed canals on it not only produced the popular idea of intelligent life on Mars but also contributed heavily to one of the classics in psychical research: **Theordore Flournoy's** study of the medium **Hélène Smith** who claimed to be in communication with a Martian speaking in the dialect of the planet.

Flammarion's contributions to psychical research were more direct than that, however. It became his object of study for fifty years after his interest was stimulated when he saw a book by Alan Kardec on a Paris book stand. He put down the apathy of others to ignorance. "It is particularly in psychic matters that this ignorance is remarkable and regrettable, for we are all concerned here. The psychical world is vaster and more immense than the physical world" (Flammarion, 1935). His concern with the psychical world led him to investigate haunts, participate in experiments in materialization with Franek Kluski and hold a series of experiments with Eusapia Palladino. He also wove the phenomenon of retrocognition into a story in *Lumen,* published in 1873, about a man who in 1864 said he was able to see the Place de la Concorde at the time of the French Revolution.

But he was especially fascinated by these great questions: "What is our true nature? What is our future destiny? Are we merely ephemeral flames shining in an instant to be forever extinguished? Do there exist proofs, evidences of the survival of the human being after the destruction of the living organism?" (Flammarion, 1921:4). He addressed these questions in his masterpiece, *Death and its Mystery,* which he divided into three books: *Before Death, At the Moment of Death,* and *After Death.* These works had one aim: "to establish the positive proofs of survival" (Flammarion, 1921:26). To accomplish this aim from 1900 to 1923 he collected letters written to him and all the facts he could find dealing with paranormal phenomena, including apparitions, in order to present them to convince others—as he was convinced—that the human soul lives on after death.

Flammarion was president of the Society for Psychical Research in 1923.

Selected Writing: 1935. "The Unknown of Yesterday is the Truth of Tomorrow." JASPR 29:339; *Death and its Mystery: Before Death,* 1921.

**Fleming, Alice MacDonald (Kipling), 1868–1948.** British mental medium. The sister of author **Rudyard Kipling,** Mrs. Fleming (who used the pseudonym "Mrs. Holland" because of her family's opposition to her involvement in psychic matters) was one of the seven principal mediums involved in the famous **Cross-Correspondences** cases, the others being Margaret Verrall, Helen Verrall, Leonora Piper, "Mrs. Willett," Dame Edith Lyttleton and Mrs. Stuart Wilson.

Mrs. Fleming was married to an army officer and lived in India. In 1893 she began writing automatically, usually poetry but sometimes letters to (always) new acquaintances that purported to come from their deceased loved ones. In 1903 after reading **F. W. H. Myer's** *Human Personality and Its Survival of Bodily Death* her writings changed. She began to receive messages purportedly from the deceased Myers, among others, that were part of the cross-correspondences. She continued to receive these messages until 1910 when she had a mental breakdown. She and her work were studied extensively by the Society for Psychical Research.

BIBLIOGRAPHY: Johnson, A. 1908. "On the Automatic Writing of Mrs. Holland." PSPR 21:166; Johnson A. 1910. "Second Report on Mrs. Holland's Script." PSPR 24:201; Johnson, A. 1911. "Third Report on Mrs. Holland's Script." PSPR 25:218; Podmore, F. *The Newer Spiritualism,* 1910, pp. 237–238.

**Flew, Anthony Garrard Newton, 1923–.** British philosopher. He is an internationally know sceptic who has written at length in the field of psychical research and parapsychology in order to present their theoretical difficulties.

He considers spontaneous cases of dubious validity and has put forward logical arguments against the backward causation implied by precognition. He believes that the survival beyond death of a discarnate personality is a logical impossibility. He maintains that we cannot even describe what it means to be a "spirit" or "soul" or discarnate being. He goes further and argues that bodily continuity is a necessary condition of personal identity and that it is impossible to understand how a separate discarnate being can be identified or reidentified as the same person who once lived after much time has gone by. Flew was of the opinion that the question of survival and personal identity was one that never could be tested empirically. It appears, however, that his stand has been modified in this respect since he now considers "a significant step forward" (Flew, 1987a) **Arthur S. Berger's** research and Dictionary Test according to which select communicators will be able to identify themselves as the encipherers who left messages before death (Berger, 1987).

Flew, the author of important books and articles relative to parapsychology, is distinguished research fellow at the Social and Policy Center at Bowling Green University in Ohio and professor emeritus of the University of Reading in England.

Selected Writings: *Foreword.* In A. S. Berger, *Aristocracy of the Dead,* 1987a; *The Logic of Mortality,* 1987b; 1972. "Is There A Case for Disembodied Survival?" JASPR 66:129; *A New Approach to Psychical Research,* 1953.

BIBLIOGRAPHY: Berger, A. S. *Aristocracy of the Dead,* 1987.

**Flint, Leslie, 1911–1980s.** British physical medium. He gained a worldwide reputation as a **Direct Voice** medium. In all his public demonstrations and private séances, his cockney control "Mickey" would introduce communicators whose voices and messages were so convincing that audiences and sitters were satisfied that strong evidence of the spirit world had been produced.

A few incidents in Flint's career, however, suggest that on occasions audiences or sitters may have been guilty of malobservation or that normal or paranormal explanations other than survival after death may account for some or all of his phenomena. There was, for example, Flint's refusal in 1947 to submit to an investigation by the Society for Psychical Research that wanted a demonstration of his gifts (Result of Prize Offer 1948). In 1948, during one of Flint's public demonstrations, microphones outside the cabinet in which he was enclosed produced impressive voices, but SPR investigators found that the microphones could pick up clearly the voice of anyone inside the cabinet (Annual Report of SPR, 1949).

In 1972, Flint was the medium in a direct voice séance held in Reading, England. A communicator appeared to identify herself as "Sheargold" and to refer to "Badminton" (Sheargold, 1980). "Sheargold" was the name of **Richard Sheargold** and "Badminton" was not a reference to the game but to his address at 32 Badminton Road in Maidenhead. The communication seemed a "bull's eye" hit and evidence of the survival of Sheargold's dead mother. Sheargold, however, a prominent psychical researcher interested in the survival question, was chairman of the Survival Joint Research Committee Trust, and his address had appeared since 1932 in a widely distributed publication, in the lists of members of the SPR, and on his stationery. This information, therefore, might have been available to the medium before the séance or, without any conscious fraud, might have been obtained by cryptomnesia or the medium's clairvoyance.

All in all there would appear to be some blemishes on Flint's record and legitimate questions about the authenticity of Flint's phenomena.

BIBLIOGRAPHY: Annual Report. JSPR 35:2; Sheargold, R. K. 1980. "A Drop-In Communicator." JSPR 50:420; "The Result of the Prize Offer to Physical Mediums." 1948. JSPR 34:153.

**Flournoy, Theodore, 1854–1920.** Swiss psychologist. He received an M.D. degree in 1878, studied under Wilhelm Max Wundt, the noted German physiologist and psychologist, and held the Chair of Experimental Psychology at the University of Geneva. Besides psychology, psychical research was Flournoy's absorbing interest.

In his *From India to the Planet Mars* (1901), he made a study of the psychological aspects of mediumship so remarkable that William James wrote to the author: "Upon my word, dear Flournoy, you have done a bigger thing here than you know; and I think that your volume has probably made the decisive step in converting psychical research into a respectable science" (LeClair, 1966:90). The book, still cited today, provided parapsychology with an instructive study of Héléne Smith, a medium whose automatic writing and utterances in a hypnotic state Flournoy observed and analyzed over a period of six years. She relived prior lives, spoke in strange languages, wrote in Sanskrit, was in communication with the spirits of the dead. One personality claimed to be from Mars and spoke in a language described as a Martian dialect. Flournoy spent five years analyzing it and concluded that the language was a complex transposition from the French (which the medium spoke) and was based on French syntax and grammar. The words in Sanskrit by a personality who claimed to be a Hindu princess he found had been acquired by the medium through reading a grammar to which she had access. In her belief that she remembered an earlier existence, the medium said she had been Sivrouka, the wife of an Indian potentate. Flournoy discovered two copies in Geneva of an old history of India in which the name "Sivrouka" was given. He concluded that Hélène Smith's mediumship was made up of a chain of impersonations and complicated languages originating in the medium's subconscious and "refuse[d] to admit that it would have been through occult means. I believe it was only by some natural process" (Flournoy, 1901:307).

Flournoy considered himself a Spiritualist, yet he was not persuaded of the reality of communicators from the "other side." In his *Esprits et Médiums,* he presented many cases of apparent messages from the spirit world that others thought adequate evidence but that did not convince him, other counterhypotheses, such as cryptomnesia and super ESP not having been ruled out. But when it came to discussing the mediumship of Leonora Piper and the cross-correspondences, his rejection of the evidence was less forceful; he was aware of the great difficulty of the super ESP theory requiring as it does the assumption of astonishing powers by a medium to select from out of millions of minds the single person with the information needed. Originally he was sceptical about physical phenomena but Eusapia Palladino produced phenomena he could not explain: "Ten years ago I expressed my invincible scepticism regarding the apparitions of Katie King which Mr Crookes observed . . . I now hasten myself to admit that I have changed my opinion since that time. . ." (Flournoy, 1911:422).

Flournoy carried on a correspondence with William James from 1890 to 1910, Flournoy writing in French, James in English. They were friends, two remarkable men with close intellectual and spiritual affinities. "[T]here is hardly a human being," wrote James, "with whom I feel as much sympathy of aims and character, or feel as much 'at home', as I do with you" (LeClair, 1966).

Selected Writings: *Esprits et Médiums,* 1911; *From India to the Planet Mars,* 1901.

BIBLIOGRAPHY: Le Clair, R. C. *The Letters of William James and Theodore Flournoy,* 1966.

**Fly-in Experiment.** Conducted by Karlis Osis in connection with his research at the American Society for Psychical Research into the Out-of-Body Experience. He made a nationwide appeal to individuals who thought they had the ability to induce such an experience at will and asked them to "fly-in" from their homes to his office at the ASPR at a certain hour. Osis had arranged targets on a table there at which the "fly-inners" were to look. Later, they were to report their observations. Those whose observations seemed correct would then be invited as subjects for later testing in the ASPR laboratory. Osis tested over one hundred people who thought they were talented OBERs but the results were not significant (Osis, 1978).

BIBLIOGRAPHY: Osis, K. "Out-of-Body Research at the American Society for Psychical Research." In D. Scott Rogo, ed., *Mind Beyond the Body: The Mystery of ESP Projection,* 1978, p. 162.

**Flying Saucers.** See **Unidentified Flying Objects.**

**Focussing Effect.** A response pattern demonstrated in tests of extrasensory perception (ESP) in which the subject tends to concentrate more on certain targets presented under concealed conditions than on other targets presented under the same conditions. See also **Liking Effect**.

**Fodor, Nandor, 1895–1964.** Hungarian-born psychoanalyst and well-known psychical researcher. He was the author of a leading reference work and of books and articles on psychical research and parapsychology. In 1936, while research officer for the International Institute for Psychical Research that he helped found in England, he became the English correspondent for the American Society for Psychical Research. As such, he contributed a series of notes called "A Letter from London," which appeared regularly in the *Journal of the American Society for Psychical Research* and which discussed events and developments in psychical research and parapsychology in the United Kingdom.

During this time, Fodor published one book (Fodor, 1935) and devoted an enormous amount of industry to the preparation of a parapsychological reference work (Fodor, 1934) that included theoretical and historical articles, biographies of mediums and researchers, descriptions of publications and organizations, and even the tables of contents of the *Journal* and *Proceedings of the American Society for Psychical Research.* For years his encyclopedia remained a valuable source of information for workers in the fields of psychical research and parapsychology.

His taking up the practice of psychoanalysis in New York in 1939 did not stop his investigations of psychic phenomena and his continuing stream of books (Fodor, 1953, 1958, 1959, 1964). These works generally contained some noteworthy theoretical contributions and were effective and clearly written popular presentations on various aspects of the paranormal. From his experience as an analyst, he was able to throw different light on the subjects of his books and was one of the first to analyze the poltergeist phenomenon from a psychological point of view. Fodor also turned his attention to shared dreams in which telepathy appeared in the dreams of two or more dreamers (Fodor, 1951).

Selected Writings: *Between Two Worlds,* 1964; *The Haunted Mind: A Psychoanalyst Looks at the Supernormal,* 1959; *On the Trail of the Poltergeist,* 1958; *New Approaches to Dream Interpretation,* 1951; *The Mysterious People,* 1935; *Encyclopedia of Psychic Science,* 1934; and Carrington, H. *The Story of the Poltergeist Down the Centuries,* 1953.

**Food, Multiplication of.** The unexplained duplication or extension of items of food. This phenomenon often is reported in a religious context as a supernatural manifestation.

An instructive instance of food multiplication was reported in the last century in the Good Shepherd Convent of Bourges, France. Because the supply of flour and bread was running short in the dead of a terrible winter and starvation was facing 116 people, the Mother Superior, goes the account, prayed to Ste. Germaine Cousin: " 'Make the quantity of flour suffice for twenty loaves. . .'. The miracle took place. The first batch . . . produced twenty large loaves. . . . The second batch was even more marvellous . . . yet only four bushels of flour had been used. Five days later the same multiplication took place with two batches. . . . In the convent granary was a supply which at most would last, with care, for two months. . . .'Wishing', as they said, 'to surprise the little Saint red-handed in a miracle,' at the beginning of February [the Sisters] began to measure the flour. Again at the end of a fortnight they did the same. The flour weighed exactly what it had done a fortnight before, in spite of two bakings, so without knowing it the Community had been drawing direct from the granaries of Divine Providence" (Thurston, 1952:390–91).

While the multiplication of food is considered by many, as it was in this case and in the case of Jesus's multiplying the loaves and the fishes, to be a true miracle, the phenomenon may not be limited to the religious sphere. There is at least one report of a person replicating food who thought of himself merely as a psychic. Philip Haley, a dentist in the San Francisco area, who regarded himself as having psychic abilities apparently was successful in experiments he conducted in psychokinesis. After saying the Lord's prayer and reading from the Bhagavad Gita, he supposedly increased slices of bread and slices of apple over the number when the experiments began (Rogo, 1982). If the incident really happened, the phenomenon of the multiplication of food may be as much of psychic as of supernatural origin. See **Bosco, John.**

BIBLIOGRAPHY: Rogo, D. S. *Miracles: A Parascientific Inquiry into Wondrous Phenomena,*

1982, pp. 303–305; Thurston, H. *The Physical Phenomena of Mysticism,* 1952, pp. 390–391.

**Forced Choice Experiments.** An experiment in extrasensory perception or in **Psychokinesis** in which the number of targets as to which a subject is to make calls is limited and sharply defined. This method of research began with **Joseph B. Rhine** and is illustrated by the pack of twenty-five ESP cards with which he conducted card-guessing experiments.

**Ford, Arthur, 1897–1971.** American medium. He gained fame as perhaps the greatest medium of the century because of two startling achievements. Called "the most puzzling human being . . . an incredible mixture of heaven and earth; a man who lived in two worlds but was at home in neither" (Spraggett with Rauscher, 1973), Ford was a drug addict and alcoholic and may have been a total fraud. At the same time, as pastor of the First Spiritual Church in New York, a founder of Spiritual Frontiers Fellowship and president of the National Association of Spiritualists, he was worshipped as a saint.

Ford claimed that "[a]s a boy [he] always seemed to know what other people were thinking" (Ford with Ellison, 1971:16) and that during World War I at Camp Grant he dreamed of a sheet of paper on which were written the names of the soldiers in camp who were going to die that night of influenza during the epidemic. The camp bulletin the following day supposedly confirmed the list he saw (Ford with Ellison, 1971:16–17). Soon he developed as a medium and gave impressive public performances. Because of the "crowds of discarnates who pressed about me" (Ford and Ellison, 1971), he felt that he needed a control to act as a policeman and regulate the crowd. Then he found "Fletcher," supposedly a French Canadian killed in World War I, who acted as his spirit in charge while Ford was in trance. The pair gave sittings, even to royalty, public demonstrations, and lectures. In London in 1927, Ford was lauded by Sir Arthur Conan Doyle. The next year an event took place that made Ford a household name as the foremost medium of all time.

**Harry Houdini** was said to have told his wife, Beatrice, that he would identify himself from the beyond by sending her a message in a code they had used in their vaudeville act. Over several séances, Ford gave a ten word message to Houdini's widow who, according to Ford, "exclaimed: It's right!" (Spraggett with Rauscher, 1973:148). She signed a statement to that effect. The event made the headlines and made Ford. Charges of fraud and collusion between Mrs. Houdini and Ford were made but denied. Later, however, Beatrice Houdini denied that her husband had sent a message.

The second event that precipitated Ford into the front pages and fame again took place forty years later in 1967. A television séance with Ford for Bishop James A. Pike was arranged on Canadian television by Allen Spraggett. During the séance Ford conveyed information that seemed to Pike highly evidential.

Then Ford made the greatest mistake of his career: he died. The result was that his files came into the possession of William V. Rauscher, his literary executor. The papers revealed that Ford had been a cheat whose custom it was to clip obituaries, consult school directories or records or *Who's Who,* and keep a notebook with entries on people that he used as references for "messages." He called his notes "poems" (Spraggett with Rauscher, 1973) and, after peeking at the lists of people who had appointments with him, used his "poems" to be ready for them. Ford also had a photographic memory that enabled him to remember all sorts of significant (and—maybe even more convincing—insignificant) details. Obituaries had, in fact, supplied the material that so impressed Pike.

Psychical researchers long had had reason to be suspicious of Ford. In June 1928, at a public demonstration in London, he called out the name of a person in the audience and said that her brother had died and that he gave the name "Arthur" as belonging to a dead father or brother. The audience was impressed but, in fact, the named individual had furnished the information to Ford before the public meeting and during a conversation with him after a private sitting ("The Rev. Arthur Ford," 1928). In 1953, Ford was carefully tested by the American Society for Psychical Research in five proxy sittings. The results were null. His performance did not show any psi powers in operation (MacRobert, 1954). And the keen Laura A. Dale, who had an infallible instinct for people, said: "I have no hard-core evidence that Ford cheats, but my strong impression is that he has certainly done so in the past" (Berger, 1988:248).

In fairness to Ford, since he seems to have supplied correct information to some people in his public audiences and sittings, it is possible that he did have psychic powers and cheated when he had to in order to be able to perform on command. But fraud or not, he undoubtedly brought comfort to the grieving and left his mark on history as "a fascinating, fantastic character" (Spraggett with Rauscher, 1973:14).

Selected Writings: *Nothing So Strange*, 1958; with Ellison, J. *The Life Beyond Death*, 1971.

BIBLIOGRAPHY: Berger, A. S. *Lives and Letters in American Parapsychology*, 1988; MacRobert, A. F. 1954. "Proxy Sittings: A Report of the Study Group Series with Arthur Ford." JASPR 58:71; Spraggett, A. with Rauscher, W. F. *Arthur Ford: The Man Who Talked with the Dead*, 1973; 1928. "The Rev. Arthur Ford." JSPR 24:357.

**Forecasts.** See **Precognition.**

**Fort, Charles Hoy, 1874–1932.** American journalist, collector of the fantastic and rebel against scientific dogma. After receiving a modest inheritance at the age of forty-two, he abandoned journalism and spent the rest of his life collecting clippings, which he stored in cardboxes in his Bronx apartment, and doing research in the New York City Public Library and the British Museum. His purpose was to discover what he called the "damned facts," his description for all sorts of anomalies science found embarrassing, for which it could not or would not account and preferred to ignore.

Fort was therefore at heart a psychical researcher since psychical research also studies and collects phenomena that are ignored and not accepted as part of the current scientific outlook. But Fort's mind soared into regions where psychical researchers and parapsychologists trying to maintain a facade of scientific respectability would never dare go, and his interests went far beyond the conventional forms of phenomena that concern them. Fort collected data on such things as showers of blood, stones, frogs, or fish; red rain or rains of mud, dead birds, or metal objects. His files bulged with accounts of a city in the sky over Ohio, a horse running in the sky above West Virginia, divisions of infantry marching through the skies over Hungary.

Fort had a particular grievance against the "scientific priestcraft" (Fort, n.d.) and all forms of scientific dogma that made science and others blind to "data upon data of new lands that are not far away" (Fort, n.d.), which he had come upon. These new lands were in the sky. One of his theories was that above the earth was a Super-Sargasso Sea into which all sorts of phenomena had blown from earth a long time ago. From an island located on the great sea there came back to earth showers of the strange things that had left it. But although Fort is not your ordinary psychical researcher, in one respect he contributed to the field. His collection of mysterious disappearances led him to believe that objects as well as people were being transported across space, from earth to space, from space to earth. His term for this phenomenon was **"Teleportation,"** a word that has since passed into the vocabulary of psychical research.

Few people, including Fort's distraught wife, understood what Fort was doing, or why, or understood him. But the intellectuals of the day did—Theodore Dreiser, Booth Tarkington, Ben Hecht, Alexander Woolcott, Tiffany Thayer. To continue in his honor the attack he started against the "scientific priestcraft," they founded the Fortean Society, an organization still going strong.

Selected Writing: *Lo!*, 1931; *New Lands*, n.d.; *The Book of the Damned*, 1919.

**Forthuny, Pascal (Georges Cochet), 1872–1962.** French art critic of *Le Matin*, musician, novelist. He was numbered among the Parisian literati until his son's death in a plane crash precipitated Forthuny into mediumship. In 1920, he was in the midst of writing a novel when "his hand suddenly ceased to obey his conscious thought and began, as if moved by some impulsive extraneous force, to make a whole series of strokes just like a little child at its first writing lesson." On a separate piece of white paper the strokes went on, followed by curves, then letters, finally words. He turned to his wife and said, "Here's a funny thing. I'm a medium" (Osty, 1926:26).

Still another paranormal experience persuaded him that he had psychic gifts. He was away from Paris when he had a vision of a coffin. Forthuny returned immediately to the city in time to see his mother before she died unexpectedly. As his mediumship developed along with his automatic writing, his dead son and a guide began to give him messages.

In 1921, however, these gifts took a new turn in the direction of clairvoyance and psychometry. He found that he could "read" the contents of folded letters. On one occasion, as he held a fan, he had the sense of suffocation and heard the name "Elisa." In fact, the fan had belonged to a woman of that name who had died from a lung ailment.

Forthuny was investigated by Eugene Osty who asked him to display his gifts at the Institut Métapsychique International in Paris. There Forthuny would sit facing a large audience and tell people of the impressions he received about them and their lives. In the course of these public demonstrations, Osty found that about 34 percent of the medium's statements were true and about 31 percent were partly true.

In England, Forthuny was investigated by the Society for Psychical Research. He was handed two objects in psychometric tests. One was a sealed matchbox in which there was a small piece of aluminum. A tiny hole in the top of the matchbox allowed the aluminum to be seen and touched. He identified the object correctly as a piece of a Zeppelin that had been shot down near London and associated it with a crew member who had been killed. Another object was a piece of canvas sealed in an envelope one side of which was open to permit a part of the canvas to be seen and touched. Forthuny gave the names "Michael" and "Hardy" which were closely connected with the woman who brought the canvas (Woolley, 1931).

Forthuny's reputation was marred by an accusation that, in one of his public demonstrations, an accomplice gave him signals. (Notes on Periodicals, 1930). But outside of this charge angrily denied by Forthuny, the bulk of the evidence redounds to his credit.

BIBLIOGRAPHY: "Notes on Periodicals." 1930. JSPR 26:87; Osty, E. *Une Faculté de Connaissance Supra-Normal. Pascal Forthuny,* 1926; Woolley, V. J. 1931. "The Visit of M. Pascal Forthuny to the Society in 1929." PSPR 39:347.

**Fortune-Telling.** The art of reading the future practiced in ancient Babylonia, Egypt, Greece, and Rome and still widely practiced today although the United Kingdom and some American communities have laws against it. Several techniques and objects are used in the art, including **Astrology**, tea leaves, **Tarot Cards, Palmistry** and **Crystal Gazing.** The difference between fortune-tellers and psychics who, like fortune-tellers, sometimes deal with the concerns and fortunes of people who consult them, is very small, if not nonexistent.

Fortune-telling may be another form of psi, and the techniques and objects used to tell fortunes may merely be means to facilitate impressions gained through telepathy, clairvoyance, or precognition. Not all these impressions are pleasant and, for one's own safety, some should be taken lightly. A case in point is that of a young woman in good physical condition who died after having had minor surgery. An autopsy showed no reason for her death. But it seemed that she was afraid of operations and, just prior to being admitted to the hospital, had gone to a fortune-teller who forecast that she would die from the surgery. The woman took the prediction seriously and was literally "scared to death" by autosuggestion (Barker, 1968). See also **Reader.**

BIBLIOGRAPHY: Barker, J. C. *Scared to Death: An Examination of Fear, its Causes and Effects,* 1968.

**Forwald, Haakon Gabriel, 1897–1978.** Norwegian-born Swedish electrical engineer. He held over 500 invention patents and was design engineer for Sweden's largest electric company. A part-time parapsychologist, he became interested in the field after experimenting with table-tilting with some friends. Joseph B. Rhine to whom Forwald wrote about his experiences advised him to devote his time to PK placements tests which he did for some twenty-odd years and for which, together with Joseph G. Pratt, in 1956 he received the McDougall Award for Distinguished Work in Parapsychology.

"Haakon Forwald's work is unique in the annals of parapsychology. . . . His experimental procedure has varied only in details. He releases several cubes (i.e., unmarked dice) from an elevated slide onto a level tabletop, and tries mentally to influence them to deviate toward the right or the left of their statistically normal forward path" (Rush, 1971:223). As an engineer, Forwald was interested in the physical operation of psychokinesis rather than its psychological aspects and tried to find a physical basis of PK.

Over the years, beginning in about 1952, he carried out an enormous number of experiments with cubes made of different materials or covered with foil. Since he found that the positive results he obtained were not caused by electrostatic, magnetic, or nuclear effects, he theorized that his mental efforts, actually mental imaging of the results he wanted to obtain, "somehow cause[d] a local gravitational field to be applied to the moving cube so as to deflect it in the desired direction" (Rush, 1971:225). The chief objection to Forwald's work (other than his unusual hypothesis) is that he was both experimenter and subject, that he designed the experiments, produced the phenomena and evaluated the results without any blind or double-blind controls. He did, however, produce positive results before witnesses during an eight week visit to the Parapsychology Laboratory at Duke University. Robert A. McConnell who evaluated this series of experiments and worked with Forwald in setting up and analyzing a further series carried out in Sweden between March and November 1960 considers Forwald to have been the foremost PK experimenter of the 1950s, the other major experimenter of the period being William E. Cox.

Forwald wrote a great number of papers, most of which were published in the *Journal of Parapsychology,* and a monograph (1970) in which he set forth his experiments and theories.

Selected Writings: *Mind, Matter and Gravitation,* 1970; 1955. "A Study of Psychokinesis and Physical Conditions." JP 19:133; 1952. "A Continuation of the Experiments in Placement PK." JP 16:273; and R. A. McConnell. 1967. "Psychokinetic Placement: I. A Re-examination of the Forwald-Durham Experiment." JP 31:51; and R. A. McConnell. 1968. "Psychokinetic Placement: III. Cube-Releasing Devices." JP 32:9; and J. G. Pratt. 1958. "Confirmation of the PK Placement Effect." JP 22:1.

BIBLIOGRAPHY: McConnell, R. A. *An Introduction to Parapsychology in the Context of Science,* 1983; Rush, J. H. 1971. "Mind, Matter, and Gravitation: A Theoretical and Experimental Study." JASPR 65:223.

**Foundation for Reincarnation and Spiritual Research.** Established in 1985 in India to undertake an in-depth study of **Reincarnation** and, by using empirical methods, to collect evidence through the investigation of cases suggestive of the phenomenon. The further aim is to coordinate the evidence with ancient Vedic and Yogic literature and thus bring science and spirituality together, an attempt unique in India and the world. The foundation is a membership organization and collaborates with researchers from other countries. The research advisor for the organization is **Dr. Jamuna Prasad** who leads investigative teams. The office of the foundation is at 109 Rami Mandi, Allahabad, 211003, U.P., India.

**Foundation for Research on the Nature of Man. (FRNM).** Created by **Joseph B. Rhine** at Durham, North Carolina, as an independent organization and an outgrowth of the **Parapsychology Laboratory** after Duke University was no longer willing to continue supporting it, FRNM conducts inquiries into puzzling human experiences that suggest still unrecognized capacities or principles and which seem to distinguish the peculiar nature of the human being. It publishes the *Journal of Parapsychology.* The present director of FRNM is **Dr. K. Ramakrishna Rao** and its current address is Box 6847, College Station, Durham, North Carolina 27708. See also **Institute for Parapsychology.**

**Fox, George, 1624–1690.** British religious leader and founder of the Society of Friends (or Quakers). He was imprisoned eight times for his missionary zeal and opposition to government interference with religion.

From his writings, he stands out as a **Noted Witness** for paranormal phenomena. His *Journal,* which recorded many of his personal experiences, reported monitions, or his personal daemon during times of severe stress: "When all my troubles and torments were great, when all my hopes in all men were gone so that I had nothing outwardly to help me, nor could I tell what to do, then, O then, I *heard a voice* which said, 'There is One, even Jesus Christ, that can speak to thy condition.'" Fox also wrote a *Book of Miracles* in which he narrated his powers of unorthodox healing and his remarkable curing of the disorders of many people. Although he and other Quakers believed that the curative force was supernatural in origin and miraculous, we might think it a natural power that resides within us. In any case, Fox shows that the phenomenon of healing was recognized and practiced in seventeenth century England.

BIBLIOGRAPHY: Cadbury, H. J. *George Fox's 'Book of Miracles,'* 1948.

**Fox Sisters, Leah, c.1811–1890, Margaretta (or Margaret), c.1834–1893, Kate, c.1836–1892.** American Spiritualist mediums. Although Margaret and Kate, who became the first professional mediums, are considered the founders of **Spiritualism** and Leah made it into the worldwide religious movement that it became, Spiritualism actually got its start in 1844 with **Andrew Jackson Davis's** vision of Emanuel Swedenborg. Spiritualism began in earnest, however, on March 31, 1848 in Hydesville, New York. On that day the young Kate and Margaret Fox received an intelligible reply by way of the raps the Fox household had been hearing. The knocking continued all night, the final message being that a murdered peddler was buried under the house. Upon excavation, some hair, two human teeth and a piece of jawbone were found. (In 1904 more bones were dug up at the house but proved upon examination to have been placed there as a trick [Hyslop, 1909]).

As a result of public meetings and private séances arranged by Leah, Spiritualism spread rapidly throughout the United States and by 1853 had spread to Europe, its adherents at that time being estimated between two and four million, and mediums multiplied almost as rapidly. Supporters of the Fox Sisters, including Horace Greeley, the editor of *The New York Tribune* who gave them publicity, came from all walks of life, but there were skeptics, of course, also. Three medical professors from the University of Buffalo reported in 1851 that the raps were made by the dislocation of the bones of the girls' knees, toes, or ankles, and Louis Agassiz of Harvard University said, in 1857, that the raps were produced by the bones of their feet. (Count Perosky-Petrovo-Solovovo [1893] was apparently able to imitate rappings by cracking his feet.)

Of the three, Kate was the most notable medium. In her presence almost all known physical phenomena—automatic writing, levitation, materialization—occurred. She sat jointly with Daniel D. Home and was investigated by Eleanor Sidgwick, Sir William Crookes and Lord Rayleigh. Although all reported some phenomena, only Crookes was convinced of their genuineness. Lord Rayleigh said only that they could not be readily explained. In 1888 Margaretta confessed that the raps were made by "joint-cracking" but Kate repudiated the confession as did Leah. Leah's life was the most stable of the three, the other two sinking into alcoholism.

Whether or not the raps were fraudulent, the other aspects of their mediumship seem truly to have puzzled and confused Kate and Margaret. Nor did they ever understand the philosophical side of Spiritualism. Because of the emotional claims and counterclaims surrounding the Fox Sisters and the paucity of research, a certain decision as to the genuineness of their phenomena has not been possible.

BIBLIOGRAPHY: Berger, A. S. 1985. "The Early History of the ASPR." JSPR 79:39; Crookes, W. *Researches in the Phenomena of Spiritualism,* 1874; Hyslop, J. H. 1909. "Editorial." JASPR 3:19; Isaacs, E. "The Fox Sisters and American Spiritualism." In Kerr, H. and C. L. Crow, eds., *The Occult in America,* 1983; Nicol, F. 1948. "The Fox Sisters and the Development of Spiritualism." JSPR 34:271; Perosky-Petrovo-Solovo, Count. 1893. "On the Production of Spurious 'Spirit Raps.'" JSPR 6:120; Pond, M. B. *The Unwilling Martyrs,* 1947; Rayleigh, Lord. 1919. "Presidential Address." PSPR 30:275; Sidgwick, E. M. 1886. "Results of a Personal Investigation into the Physical Phenomena of Spiritualism." PSPR 4:45.

**Francis of Assisi, Saint, 1182–1226.** Italian founder of the Franciscan order, the Patron Saint of Italy. He was baptised Giovanni by his mother. His father, Pietro di Bernardone, on his return from a trip to France, changed the infant's name to Francis. As a youth, he was as wild as any young man, learned Latin at school and French from travelling minstrels. Then, after visions and invisible voices bade him to surrender himself to prayer, he renounced his family and wealth to live in poverty among the poor, the sick, and the lepers. Although not ordained within the Church, he became an itinerant preacher of poverty, devotion, repentance, human brotherhood, and nature. The people in the towns of Italy through which he passed loved him. Their warm support and his rule of life—to live as Christ had lived—soon drew disciples. In 1209, with the backing of Pope Innocent III, the Franciscan order began. The Vatican finally ratified it in 1223, and eventually it spread to the rest of Europe.

Francis loved nature and called all living beings his "brothers" or "sisters." Thus Francis expressed the unusual idea that in all living beings are the same elements as in his human "brothers" and "sisters," and that, if human beings survive death, so will they. Such an insight, if shared more generally in psychical research, might open up new avenues of survival research.

There is some evidence that Francis was able to take aerial flights and so becomes a **Noted Witness** for levitation. When Brother Leo, for instance, beheld "how many a time and oft St. Francis was rapt in God and uplifted from the ground. . . ; and sometimes he beheld him raised so high in the air and surrounded with such radiance, that scarcely could he see him."

Better attested is another phenomenon he produced. In 1224, while deep in meditation and prayer in a cave near Assisi, a seraph with six glowing wings, a beautiful face and its body affixed to a cross descended toward him from heaven. When the winged figure disappeared, Francis was left with five lesions on his feet, hands and side like those left on the body of Christ by the crucifixion. Among the eyewitnesses who observed and actually touched them was Pope Alexander IV. Francis's biographer, Thomas of Celano, described the wounds: "[M]arks of nails began to appear in his hands and feet. . . . His hands and feet seemed pierced in the midst by nails, the heads of the nails appearing in the inner part of the hands and in the upper part of the feet and their points over against them. . . . Moreover his right side, as [if] it had been pierced by a lance, was overlaid with a scar, and often shed blood so that his tunic and drawers were many times sprinkled with the sacred blood." Even after his death, the **Stigmata** continued on Francis's body with the nails formed out of his flesh as black as iron and his right side red with blood.

Most of Francis's biographers assert that instances of stigmata had never been recorded previously, yet the phenomenon seems to have been familiar to Christians such as St. Paul. Be that as it may, Francis, if not the first, is at any rate the most famous noted witness for the reproduction on a human body of Christ's wounds. After his stigmata had received worldwide attention, they became a Roman Catholic phenomenon. Claims and observations of Christ-like markings among Catholics started and have persisted until modern times. See also **Evola, Natuzza: Neumann, Thérèse; Pio, Padre.**

BIBLIOGRAPHY: H. Thurston, *The Physical Phenomena of Mysticism,* 1952, pp. 5, 45–46.

**Fraud.** The constant charges and exposures of fraud in the past in the kinds of phenomena studied by psychical research and parapsychology have given rise to the skeptical supposition that fraud is still likely today in parapsychology. The psychologist **Charles E. M. Hansel,** for example, who assumes that psi is *a priori* impossible maintains that fraud committed by the experimenter or subject or both is the only possible explanation of any successful experiment in parapsychology that seems to show the existence of psi. "If the result could have arisen through a trick, the experiment must be considered unsatisfactory evidence of ESP, whether or not it is finally decided that such a trick was in fact used" (Hansel, 1966:18). If this principle were to be applied generally in science, no new discovery could ever be accepted. "Every research worker who has ever published his own findings, in whatever field of science, knows that he could not completely disprove irresponsible accusations of fraud leveled against his own results. Why, therefore, should parapsychologists be required to do so?" (Pratt, 1973, 167).

Yet, responsible scepticism is healthy and can help prevent fraud or potential fraud, and it is interesting that the main exposures of fraud in parapsychology have not come from sceptics outside the field but rather from parapsychologists themselves. **Joseph B. Rhine** and his associates at the Institute for Parapsychology exposed a fraudulent experimenter there (Rhine, 1947) and **Betty Markwick** showed that **Samuel G. Soal** mainpulated data in his research in telepathy (Markwick, 1978).

Spiritualism and fraud are entwined. Its history "is saturated with fraud . . . the vast majority of the phenomena obtained through mediums are fraudulent in character" (Carrington, 1907:9). The numbers of purported mediums, for example, who have been found impersonating spirits (or having accomplices do so) or who have done research on their sitters (or are simply good at giving "cold readings") are legion.

But what of the medium Eusapia Palladino and others like her? She was often caught cheating and yet, under the strictest conditions of control, also produced remarkable paranormal phenomena. And what about experimenters such as S. G. Soal? He did excellent experimental work for years and yet he doctored the scores in his most famous series of experiments. Many have said, "Once a cheat, always a cheat" and have concluded that all the results of anyone ever caught cheating must be swept away. On the other hand, it has been pointed out that psychic ability and mental dissociation frequently go hand in hand—often in subjects (such as Palladino) and occasionally in experimenters (such as Soal who was subject to trance states and "afflicted with the mental distemper of automatism" [Soal, 40:176]).

**Robert A. McConnell** (1983) has pointed out that those who dissociate readily are untrustworthy because they "can smile the sweet smile of innocence while they deceive us with another consciousness" (p. 60). And Betty Markwick writes that "even ostensibly genuine mediums may . . . resort to deception. . . , *especially in a dissociated state*" (Markwick, 1978:274). She hypothesized that Soal was guilty of either "dissociated manipulation" or "data massage" (1978:272, 274). The latter suggests conscious deception, not necessarily initially intended, as a result of persistent negative results and would apply to other scientists, in and out of parapsychology, who have been caught cheating. **Anita Gregory** (1979) has written that parapsychology belongs to "the realm of the magical" in which there is "the possibility . . . of the extension of the supremacy of the imagination over the realm of the physical" (p. 257) and that this realm of imagination is shared with the liar and the confidence man, among others.

The question of fraud, then, is not simple. At times, it need not even involve the conscious, deliberate intention of either subject or experimenter to cheat.

BIBLIOGRAPHY: Carrington, H. *The Physcial Phenomena of Spiritualism,* 1920; Gregory, A. 1979. "Cyril Burt—Psychologist. By L. S. Hearnshaw." JSPR 50:249, 257; Hansel, C. E. M. *ESP: A Scientific Evaluation,* 1966; Markwick, B. 1978. "The Soal-Goldney Experiments with Basil Shackleton: New Evidence of Data Manipulation." PSPR 56:250; McConnell, R. A. *An Introduction to Parapsychology in the Context of Science,* 1983; Pratt, J. G. *ESP Research Today,* 1973; Rhine, J. B. 1974. "A New Case of Experimenter Unreliability." JP 38:215; Soal, S. G. 1932. "Experiments in Supernormal Perception at a Distance." PSPR 40:165.

**Free Response Test.** An experiment in which a subject, through drawing or oral description, responds to a set of concealed targets on the basis of feelings or impressions. A typical test is the **Picture Drawing Experiment.** Other situations illustrative of free responses include **Séances** in which mental mediums give descriptions of or messages from deceased people or tests of psychometry where information derived from physical objects is given. **Joseph G. Pratt** and others developed procedures to try to measure the verbal material quantitatively to see if correct information was beyond what might be attributed to chance.

**Frei, Gebhard, 1905–1967.** Swiss psychologist and Catholic priest. Among the Catholic clergy, he was the foremost parapsychologist and the Vatican's specialist in the field. He founded the Jung Institute in Zurich, was president of **Imago Mundi,** was a contributor to *Neue Wissenschaft,* a parapsychological journal, and to *Breakthrough,* Konstantin Raudive's book on electronic voice phenomena.

**Freitas, Jose Pedro de.** See **Arigo, Jose.**

**Freud, Sigmund, 1856–1939.** Viennese physician and father of psychoanalysis. In 1882 Freud began working with Josef Breuer using the latter's pioneering treatment of hysteria by hypnosis. Between 1892 and 1895, however, Freud developed the technique of free association and gradually abandoned the use of hypnosis. Freud's and Breuer's joint book, *Studies in Hysteria* published in 1895, marked the beginning of psychoanalysis but was denounced by the German medical world (so much so that Breuer lost faith in his own theory). Freud received no recognition from orthodox science at this time, but Frederic W. H. Myers in 1893 wrote appreciatively in the *Proceedings* (9:12–15) of the Society for Psychical Research of Freud's and

Breuer's article "The Psychical Mechanism of Hysterical Phenomena."

Between 1895 and 1899 Freud researched and wrote *The Interpretation of Dreams,* considered his most original and brilliant work. Although in the popular mind Freud and the unconscious are synonymous, his first systematic statement about the subject did not appear until 1912 when it was published in PSPR (26:312). (He had become a member of the SPR in 1911. He was also a member of the American Society for Psychical Research.) At about the same time came his break with **Carl Gustav Jung**—who had been his heir apparent—over Freud's insistence that sexuality was the basis of human behavior and his unhappiness over Jung's "occult" tendencies.

Yet Freud himself was extremely interested in psychical research. He allowed himself, however, to be persuaded not to make public statements of that interest. In 1921 he wrote an essay entitled *Psychoanalysis and Telepathy* but it was not published until after his death. In that same year he wrote to Hereward Carrington, "If I had my life to live over again I should devote myself to psychical research rather than to psychoanalysis." In 1922 he published "Dreams and Telepathy" in which he said that, despite distortions that occur in dreams, the telepathic interpretation is plausible. In 1925 he published "The Occult Significance of Dreams" (against precognition, for telepathy) and, in 1933, in Lecture 30 of his *New Introductory Lectures on Psychoanalysis* he dealt directly with telepathic phenomena during analysis. He thought that telepathy might have been humankind's archaic way of communicating.

In his last work, *Moses and Monotheism* (1939), he asserted that "the archaic heritage" of mankind includes not only dispositions, but also ideational contents, memory-traces of the experiences of former generations" which sounds very much like Jung's collective unconscious or what is sometimes called "genetic memory."

For many years Freud had smoked twenty or more cigars a day, as a result of which he developed cancer of the jaw and palate. Beginning in 1923 he underwent thirty-three operations and was in constant pain, but he continued to work and publish important books. In 1938 when the Nazis entered Vienna he was persuaded to leave for London where, in 1939, the pain from his disease having become unbearable, his physician administered a dose of "adequate sedation," and Freud died.

Of Freud T. W. Mitchell wrote (1939a): "His undeviating search for truth in spite of all opposition and opprobrium has never been surpassed in the history of science. His equanimity under neglect and misrepresentation, his serenity under trial and affliction, his bearing under cruelty and injustice, are the marks of a truly great man."

Selected Writings: 1912. "A Note on the Unconscious in Psycho-Analysis." PSPR 26:312; "Dreams and Telepathy," "The Occult Significance of Dreams" and "New Introductory Lectures on Psycho-Analysis." In G. Devereux, ed., *Psychoanalysis and the Occult,* 1953.

BIBLIOGRAPHY: Jephson, I. 1954. "Psychoanalysis and the Occult." JSPR 37:235; Mitchell, T. W. 1939a. "Obituary Professor Sigmund Freud." PSPR 45:344; Mitchell, T. W. 1939b. "Sigmund Freud. *Moses and Monotheism.*" PSPR 45:347; Servadio, E. "Psychoanalysis and Parapsychology." In J. R. Smythies, ed., *Science and ESP,* 1967, pp. 255–261; West, D. J. 1956. "Centenary of Sigmund Freud." JSPR 38:265; West D. J. 1958. "Sigmund Freud: Life and Work. Vol. III. The Last Phase." JSPR 39:242.

**FRNM Bulletin.** Published quarterly by a publishing subsidiary of the **Foundation for Research on the Nature of Man,** it contains descriptions of the Summer Study Program there and of the work done by FRNM's staff as well as news of topics and events of interest to parapsychologists.

**Fujiwara, Sakuhei, 1884–1950.** Japanese critic. In a devastating report, he lashed out against the experiments on thoughtography and clairvoyance carried out by **Tomokichi Fukurai.** In Japan as in the Western world criticisms serve the important function of alerting parapsychologists to possible flaws in their experiments. Whether or not Fukiwara's criticisms were justified, they were responsible for Fukurai's resignation of his professorial post, the abandonment of his research, then the most important in Japan, and the eventual suicide of **Chizuko Mifune.**

Selected Writing: Fukiwara, S. *Senrigan Jikkenroku* (Record on Experiments of Clairvoyance), 1911.

**Fukurai, Tomokichi, 1869–1952.** Japanese pioneer in psychical research. His main interest was in the conduct of experiments in **Thoughtography,** a term he invented. He was at the same time professor of psychology at the Tokyo Imperial University (now University of Tokyo), from whose Department of Psychology he was graduated in 1899.

In his experiments he sandwiched together three photographic plates and asked his subjects to place on the middle one a language character he had chosen. He selected the middle plate because he believed that such a hit was "pregnant with meaning in the study of the psychic problem." He also carried on experiments in clairvoyance. Because of a tragic incident involving **Chizuko Mifune,** one of his star subjects, criticisms of his work by **Sakuhei Fukiwara** and **Taranosuke Oguma** and heated controversy among leading scientists and scholars over his work, he was compelled to resign his university post in 1913 and his inventive tests ceased. As a result, in addition to Fukurai's resignation, the majority of scholars and scientists who had entered psychical research felt obliged to leave the field and all such research not only at the university but also in Japan was terminated for decades.

Selected Writings: Fukurai, T. *Toshi to Nensha,* 1913, republished as *Clairvoyance and Telepathy,* 1930.

**Fukurai Institute of Psychology.** Japanese organization that surveys and investigates paranormal phenomena with a special emphasis on experiments in thoughtography. It publishes a *Bulletin.* Its office is located at 10-3 Niizaka-machi, Sendai-shi, Miyagi-ken, 980 Japan.

**Fundacíon Internacional Subdud (International Subdud Foundation).** A branch of Subdud Brotherhood International Foundation. Mexican charitable organization established in 1982 which works with the University of Zacatecas and the Instituto Politécnico Nacional to help in the rehabilitation of handicapped adults and children in the rural areas of Mexico.

Two of its techniques may possibly be relevant to psychical research. While some of its methods are bizarre, such as the use of energized gems which, in some way, are supposed to help the handicapped; it also uses acupuncture to treat patients. Although over the years the use of Kirlian photography as a diagnostic tool has been questioned, the foundation is using it as a method of diagnosing and evaluating the psychophysiological conditions of handicapped children while they are receiving various types of therapy. The address of the organization is Plutarcho Elias Calles No. 702, Col. Club de Golf, Cuernavaca, Morelos, 62030 Mexico.

**Funk, Isaac Kauffman, 1839–1912.** American editor, publisher, clergyman, investigator of mediums such as May and Lillie Bangs and of psychic phenomena. Educated for the Lutheran ministry, he was ordained in 1861 and held pastorates in Indiana, Ohio, and Brooklyn, New York, from 1861 to 1872 when he resigned to take trips through Europe, Egypt, and Palestine. When Funk returned in 1873, he became editor of *The Christian Radical* and soon founded a publication to help the clergy prepare its sermons. By 1891, he had become editor-in-chief and president of the publishing house of Funk and Wagnalls which published high quality books including the *Standard Dictionary of the English Language.* He was active in his attempts to simplify spelling and make it phonetic.

Funk was also an ardent believer in the temperance movement and in psychic phenomena. He was James H. Hyslop's friend and tried to help promote Hyslop's American Institute for Scientific Research. Funk also earned a reputation as an investigator of psychic phenomena through his two books, *The Widow's Mite* and *The Psychic Riddle.* But although his reputation as a publisher and temperance leader was high, his reputation as a psychic investigator was low. People thought him a credulous Spiritualist and extremely naive. But this was far from true. Hyslop, who knew him well, believed that Funk "was quite willing for the public to think that he was deceived, if only he could get to the bottom of a case." Funk, he thought, was "a keenly critical man and sceptical about the phenomena in psychical research" (Berger, 1987).

Following his death, Funk was an excellent communicator. Hyslop reported receiving from him evidential messages consisting of a secret sign and references to a cemetery in Brooklyn where Funk was buried (Berger, 1987).

BIBLIOGRAPHY: Berger, A. S. *Aristocracy of the Dead,* 1987.

# G

**Galloway, Donald D. G., 1929–.** British medium. For forty years, he has been associated with international organizations oriented toward psychical research and has been active in mediumship, unorthodox healing and, recently, channeling. He has been general secretary of the College of Psychic Studies. Galloway was one of the mediums who participated in a controlled, cross-correspondences type, experiment conducted in 1983 to test the hypothesis of survival after death. None of the mediums knew or was in communication with the others. They were to know nothing of the test and the fragmentary pieces of information they received would mean nothing to them. But when all fragments were put together, the experimenters would know if they were supplemental to one another and corresponded to one plan. Through Galloway's mediumship, the experimental results were highly suggestive of the survival of and communication by a young man who died in 1978 and who seemed to fit the description of the "ideal" communicator identified by rigorous research into two population samples and 100 of the best cases reported in the parapsychological literature (Berger, 1987).

BIBLIOGRAPHY: Berger, A. S. *Aristocracy of the Dead,* 1987.

**Galsworthy, John, 1867–1933.** British author who won the Nobel Prize in literature in 1932 and was as eminent a novelist as a dramatist. Although a member of the English bar, he left the law for literature. The presentation of *The Forsyte Saga* (written between 1906 and 1920) on television resurrected Galsworthy's fame. He addressed social and political problems in plays such as *The Silver Box* (1906), *Strife* (1909), and *Justice* (1910).

Two years before he died, Galsworthy discussed how inspiration helped him create the characters of his novels: "I sink into my morning chair, a blotter on my knees, the last words or deed of some character in ink before my eyes; a pen in my hand, a pipe in my mouth, and nothing in my head. I sit. I don't intend; I don't expect; I don't even hope. . . . Suddenly, my pen jots down a movement or remark, another, and goes on doing this, haltingly perhaps for an hour or two. When the result is read through it surprises one by seeming to come out of what went before, and by ministering to some sort of possible future. Those pages, adding tissue to character, have been supplied from the cupboard of the subconscious, in response to the appeal of one's conscious directive sense. . . ."

Poet and author Brewster Ghiselin (1952) felt that these last words meant that Galsworthy believed he consciously directed the creative process, which "does not fit the facts" of the involuntary nature of the process that is outside conscious control. In fact, Galsworthy was not saying that his conscious mind operated the process, but simply that he appealed to his unconscious to do something. Witness his statements that "there is nothing in my head," "I don't intend," and that what he finally jots down "surprises one." When these are considered, his case "fits the facts" and really looks like another one in which writers, poets, or artists are only mouthpieces of an outside force. It makes Galsworthy an important **Noted Witness** to the creative process.

BIBLIOGRAPHY: Ghiselin, B. *The Creative Process,* 1952; Gibbes, E. B. 1939, "Influenced or Inspirational Writing." JASPR 33:271, pp. 274–275.

**Ganzfeld Procedure.** From the German meaning "entire field." This procedure is used to reduce sensory alertness, which is believed to impede ESP functions. The Ganzfeld sensory deprivation technique is used in ESP tests to create a homogeneous, unpatterned, sensory stimulation, that is, an effect of featureless light (for example, by placing translucent screens such as halved ping pong balls over a subject's eyes) or by placing earphones on a subject's ears to produce random or "white" noise. From the number of Ganzfeld experiments reported (Honorton, 1985) in which significant ESP scoring has been found, this technique appears to be an effective means for eliciting psi and achieving replication of psi experiments.

Work in this field has encountered increasing criticisms, however, that sensory leakages and faulty methods of analyzing data have greatly exaggerated their significance (Hyman, 1985). And Rex Stanford "laments the fact that research on the supposedly psi conducive effects of these techniques for modifying consciousness have not been more systematic and more theoretically oriented" (Beloff, 1988:159).

BIBLIOGRAPHY: Beloff, J. 1988. "Advances in Parapsychological Research, Vol. 5." JSPR 55:157; Honorton, C. 1985. "Meta-Analysis of Psi Ganzfeld Research: A Response to Hyman." JASPR 49:59; Hyman, R. 1985. "The Ganzfeld Psi Experiment: A Critical Appraisal." JP 49:3.

**Gardner Murphy Research Institute.** American organization founded in 1971 by a small group of parapsychologists to promote **Gardner Murphy's** dream: interdisciplinary research which would point up the relevance of psi to human affairs and the importance of parapsychology to other disciplines. With **Montague Ullman** as its first president, the organization held annual meetings with Murphy and generally strove to attain its goal. But, although the group succeeded in fostering some conjoint studies and deepening some professional ties, "it never got much beyond that and was finally dissolved" (Ullman, 1988).

BIBLIOGRAPHY: Ullman, M. "Autobiographical Notes." In A. S. Berger, *Lives and Letters in American Parapsychology,* 1988, p. 288.

**Garibaldi, Giuseppe, 1807–1882.** Italian revolutionary and patriot. He helped to overthrow the Kingdom of Naples and to unite Italy under King Victor Emmanuel by conquering Naples and Sicily and driving out the royal forces. At the age of forty-six he was on a vessel at sea when, on the very day that his mother died in Nice, France, he dreamed that she was being carried to her grave. He is a **Noted Witness** to the existence of telepathy or clairvoyance.

BIBLIOGRAPHY: W. F. Prince, *Noted Witnesses for Psychic Occurrences,* 1963.

**Garrett, Eileen, J., 1892–1970.** Famous Irish-American trance medium. Born Emily Jane Savage on March 14, 1892—it was until recently thought that she was born Eileen Jeannette Vancho on March 17, 1893 (Healy, 1987)—she was known variously as Jane Savage, Jean Lyttle (under which pseudonym she wrote four novels), and Eileen J. Garrett. She was "good company, amusing, generous, impulsive, imaginative, creative . . . and a stern disciplinarian."

Eileen Garrett became famous as a result of apparent communications of technical information, which she supposedly could not have known and claimed not to understand, from the dead captain of the airship R-101 that had crashed and burned on October 5, 1930, on its maiden voyage. (Sceptics, however, have suggested that the R-101 had a long and troubled history before its maiden voyage and that Eileen Garrett could easily have known a good deal about it [Booth, 1984].)

Training as a Spiritualist medium under J. Hewat McKenzie at the British College of Psychic Science in London (although she herself never espoused Spiritualism) "channel[ed] her propensity for mental dissociation—if not psychotic disorganization—into a means of creative self-expression" (Ehrenwald,

1984). She did not like the occult but was fascinated by philosophy, politics, and the new physics. She rubbed elbows with, among others, H. G. Wells, George Bernard Shaw, D. H. Lawrence, and Aldous Huxley.

Unlike the lengthy investigations made of Leonora Piper and Gladys Osborne Leonard, her mediumship was never studied extensively for the paranormal content of the material she received although "the combined record of Mrs. Garrett's life as a trance medium and experimental ESP subject has gone far to suggest the reality of her paranormal abilities" (Ehrenwald, 1984). Indeed, J. B. Rhine's and Joseph Gaither Pratt's research with her changed the course of parapsychology. Showing as it did that information is readily accessible to a medium's ESP—she did well in tests both of clairvoyance and telepathy—it threw into doubt the interpretation that "messages" received by a medium come from the dead.

Other investigations—by Hereward Carrington, Whately Carington, Ira Progoff, Jan Ehrenwald and others—tried to explain who or what Eileen Garrett's controls, Abdul Latif, Uvani, Tahoteh (Giver of Words), and Ramah (Giver of Life) might be. Uvani, her first control, manifested toward the end of 1926 when she was training in mediumship with McKenzie. Uvani insisted that he was the surviving spirit of one Yusuf ben Hafik ben Ali from a noble merchant family of Basrah who had lived in the early 1800s and died at age forty-eight fighting against the Turks. Abdul Latif claimed to have been the historical Abdul Latif, a Persian physician and astronomer connected with the court of Saladin at the time of the Crusades at the end of the twelfth and the beginning of the thirteenth centuries. Eileen Garrett, however, never believed that her controls were independent intelligences but thought instead, as do most parapsychologists, that they were in fact symbols, creations or projections of some level of her own being.

She was also an author and publisher. In 1951 she founded the **Parapsychology Foundation.**

Selected Writings: *My Life as a Search for the Meaning of Mediumship,* 1939; *Awareness,* 1943; *Many Voices: The Autobiography of a Medium,* 1968.

BIBLIOGRAPHY: Angoff, A. *Eileen Garrett and the World Beyond the Senses,* 1974; Booth, J. *Psychic Paradoxes,* 1984; Ehrenwald, J. *Anatomy of Genius,* 1984, pp. 161–173; Fuller, J. G. *The Airmen Who Would Not Die,* 1979; Healy, J. 1987. "Correspondence." JSPR 54:90; Price, H. 1931. "The R-101 Disaster." JASPR 25:268; Progoff, I. *The Image of an Oracle: A Report on Research into the Mediumship of Eileen J. Garrett,* 1964; Rhine, J. B. 1971. "Eileen J. Garrett as I Knew Her." JSPR 46:59; Stevenson, I. 1971. "Eileen J. Garrett—An Appreciation." JASPR 65:336.

**Gauld, Alan, 1932–.** British psychologist. Presently senior lecturer in psychology at the University of Nottingham in England, Dr. Gauld's interest in psychical research dates back to at least 1955 when, as an undergraduate, he was secretary of the Cambridge University Society for Psychical Research. His main interest in the field has been the study of spontaneous cases and his main contribution, in addition to numerous articles in the parapsychological literature, has been the publication of three very important books. The first (1968) is the authoritative history of the early Society for Psychical Research. In the second, *Poltergeists,* written with **A. D. Cornell,** Dr. Gauld demonstrates how complex poltergeists really are, that not all can be attributed to a single cause, such as the RSPK (recurrent spontaneous psychokinesis) of a focal agent, and that some cases seem to indicate the agency of an external, possibly discarnate, entity.

His most recent book (1982), *Mediumship and Survival,* has been called "the best review of its topic" (Stevenson, 1983) since W. H. Salter's *Zoar.* Dr. Gauld concluded that mediums' controls are creations of some level of their own minds and that the super-ESP theory cannot explain all mediumistic phenomena. While he feels that survival after death does not explain all cases of mediumistic communications, he does think that the hypothesis can explain many of them.

Dr. Gauld has been editor of both the *Journal* and the *Proceedings* of the Society for Psychical Research and has been a member of the SPR Council since 1962. He is also a member of the Parapsychological Association.

Selected Writings: *The Founders of Psychical Research,* 1968; *Mediumship and Survival,* 1982; and A. D. Cornell, *Poltergeists,* 1979.

BIBLIOGRAPHY: Stevenson, I. 1983. "Mediumship and Survival." JSPR 52:203.

**Gavilan Fontanet, Francisco, 1936–.** Spanish psychologist. Specializing in extrasensory perception and the investigation of spontaneous cases, he is the author of approximately 100 articles in *Psi-Comunicación* and other periodicals on parapsychology. One of his special interests is the motives that prompt parapsychologists to give time to their field, the chief ones being the desires to obtain knowledge, to help humanity, and to gain personal experiences.

Selected Writings: 1978. "Los Factores Motivacionales del Investigador en Parapsicología". *Psi Comunicación* 7–8:9.

**Gay, Kathleen Robson, 1890–1968.** British psychical researcher. She met G. N. M. Tyrrell in the 1930s and through him became interested in psychical research. She was said to be an ideal researcher with "a cool head, a warm heart, an eye for the unexpected, and the patience to record all data with methodical accuracy. . . . [S]ympathetic as she was with honest mediums, she was not easily fooled by frauds" (Heywood, 1969). Her forte seems to have been long-term investigations, her most important for the Society for Psychical Research being the **Edgar Vandy Case.** She carried out proxy sittings for J. B. Rhine and with G. W. Lambert reported on the Dieppe Raid Case. She was working on a survey of spontaneous cases when her final crippling illness made it impossible for her to continue.

Selected Writing: 1957. "The Case of Edgar Vandy." JSPR 39:1; with G. W. Lambert. 1952. "The Dieppe Raid Case." JSPR 36:607.

BIBLIOGRAPHY: Heywood, R. 1969. "Obituary. The Hon. Mrs Cyril Gay." JSPR 45:92.

**Geley, Gustave, 1868–1924.** French psychical researcher. A medical doctor, he gave up his profession in 1918 to accept the post of first director of the **Institut Métapsychique International** in Paris. In France at that time hostility to psychical research was virulent, and Geley was accused, not of credulity or malobservation, but of fraud. To combat these accusations Geley permitted his premises to be searched and agreed to be chained and controlled during experiments.

His work with Eva C. whose materializations he pronounced genuine came into question thirty years after his death when Rudolf Lambert reported that Geley's papers revealed Eva to have been a fraud and that stereoscopic pictures indicating it had been suppressed. Lambert added that he did not believe Geley cheated intentionally but that he was "incapable of any accurate observations at all when he attempted to realize his loftiest strivings and hopes for mankind by the help of our field of enquiry" (1954:386).

Geley's strongest evidence consists of the paraffin casts, mainly of hands, which he, sometimes with co-experimenter Charles Richet, obtained in carefully controlled experiments through the mediumship of Franek Kluski. Sir Oliver Lodge (1924) called the casts "a standing demonstration of something inexplicable by normal science; . . . a permanent material record, which can be examined at leisure, and which . . . are, as it were, a standing miracle."

Geley wrote (1919) that "robbed of its illusions individual existence seems a real misfortune if it endures only from birth to death." For this reason he accepted survival and reincarnation (which he called "palingenesis") and communications with the dead although he did not believe that banal trance communications came from discarnate beings. He believed reincarnation was true because it was just.

Geley was killed in an airplane crash on his way back to Paris from Warsaw after some sittings with Franek Kluski.

Selected Writings: *From the Conscious to the Unconscious,* 1919; 1923. "Experiments in Materialization." JASPR 17:233; 17:423; 17:555; 17:630; 17:677.

BIBLIOGRAPHY: Lambert, R. 1954. "Dr. Geley's Report on the Medium Eva C." JSPR 37:682; Lodge, O. 1924. "In Memoriam—Gustave Geley. 1868–1924." PSPR 34:201; Sudre, R. 1925. "The Philosophy of Geley." JASPR 19:30.

**Geller, Uri, 1946–.** Israeli physical medium. He traces his psychic abilities back to an early age. "I've had telepathy since I was very small," he said in an interview. When he was seven years old, "I noticed that my watch would show a different hour than what it really was. . . . I began to notice that the hands would change their positions almost instantaneously—very fast—like dematerializing from one hour to another . . . Not very long after that, the wristband bent and broke. That was the first time I became aware of something bending and breaking near me." After his release from military service at the end of the Arab-Israeli War in 1967, Geller began to perform publicly and before long excited audiences all over Israel and the world with his apparent gifts of extrasensory perception and psychokinesis.

According to **Henry K. (Andrija) Puharich** (1974), Geller's biographer, under hypnosis Geller revealed that his ESP abilities and powers of psychokinesis emanate from a computer-like mechanical extraterrestrial entity designed and code named "Spectra" by beings from the planet Hoova (which is outside our universe). Geller's (and Puharich's) mission is to bring to humankind the truth about the existence of superior beings from outer space. Geller, now a millionaire living in England—Puharich calls him an "unabashed egomaniac" interested only in fame and fortune—seems a strange choice for such a mission.

Whether or not we find this claim believable, however, there is no doubt that Geller's feats of metal-bending performed on television have sparked an extraordinary public reaction and seem to have caused apparently authentic spontaneous cases of psychokinetic phenomena. Following the television programs on which he has appeared, Hans Bender and other German parapsychologists interviewed and sent questionnaires to viewers in West Germany and Switzerland who had called in. 402 of them described 599 cases of watches and clocks starting and 151 people reported 243 instances of twisted or bent cutlery and 36 instances of fractured cutlery.

Because of the "Geller Effect," as it is called, and of reports of his other ostensible gifts of ESP and psychokinesis Russell Targ and Harold Puthoff, two physicists then at the Stanford Research Institute in California, conducted laboratory tests with Geller after he said he was given permission by the extraterrestrial entity who supplies his powers to go ahead with experiments. The tests began in 1972. Under strictly controlled experimental conditions, Geller did not demonstrate psychokinetic abilities to Targ and Puthoff's satisfaction, a result that supplies ammunition both for those who question Geller's abilities and those who doubt the genuineness of metal-bending. (John Booth, [1984], for example, reveals how many of Geller's "phenomena" have been produced and states categorically that Geller is a fraud.)

Targ and Puthoff, however, looking for another avenue of exploration, conducted experiments in telepathy. Geller, in a shielded isolation chamber, was to duplicate target pictures hung by the experimenters on the wall of another room. Geller saw purple circles and made a drawing which very closely resembled the target, a picture of a bunch of grapes. But a demonstration of this kind is not unusual in the history of parapsychology. Picture drawing experiments have been carried out successfully many times and with many subjects. And a series of 100 similar tests run at SRI with Geller by Dr. Charles Rebert and Leon Otis were a complete failure (Randi, 1980:140).

On the other hand, Ila Ziebell, a young researcher, writes (1976) that Geller, without touching her, dematerialized a ring she was holding in her closed hand and that in his presence all kinds of fantastic UFO phenomena took place. And she is just one of many seemingly disinterested and honorable people who have witnessed equally remarkable happenings in Geller's presence.

And so the question remains: Is Geller just an entertainer or are his abilities real? (And what about Hoova?)

BIBLIOGRAPHY: Booth, J. *Psychic Paradoxes,* 1984; Puharich, A. *Uri: A Journal of the Mystery of Uri Geller,* 1974; Randi, J. *Flim-Flam!,* 1980; Targ, R. and Puthoff, H. E. *Mind-Reach: Scientists Look at Psychic Ability,* 1977; White, J. 1975. "Uri." *Psychic* 6(2):40; Ziebell, I. 1976. "Through the Looking Glass with Uri Geller." *Psychic* 6(6):17.

BIBLIOGRAPHY: "Interview: Uri Geller." 1973. *Psychic* 4(5):6.

**General Extrasensory Perception (GESP).** Undifferentiated ESP in which either or both telepathy or clairvoyance may be in operation—or even precognition or retrocognition.

**GESP.** See **General Extrasensory Perception.**

**G. P.** See Piper, Leonora E.

**Ghost.** A term popularly used to describe the spirit of a dead person. A ghost is often thought of as clanking down dark hallways or making a misty spectral appearance in houses, gardens, or special places, usually, but not necessarily, over a prolonged period of time. The "Morton Ghost," for example, is one of the most famous ever recorded.

In June 1882, Rose Morton (pseudonym of Rosina C. Despard), then a medical student saw in the light of her candle the figure of a tall lady dressed in black at the head of the stairs. From 1882 to 1884, Rose Morton saw the figure half a dozen times and a servant, Miss Morton's sister and brother, and his friend, saw it three times. It was so solid and lifelike that it seemed like a real person. From 1885 to 1889, other witnesses saw the figure, too, in the house or the garden. During the final two years, the figure was observed less and less frequently but its footsteps were heard by approximately twenty people, including visitors and servants. The eyewitnesses agreed generally in their description of the woman: a tall lady dressed in a soft, woollen, black garment resembling widow's weeds. She wore a dark hood or veil. Rose Morton tried to photograph the ghost but with no results. She fastened strings across the stairs; the ghost passed through without disturbing them. Miss Morton spoke to the ghost without results. She tried to touch it but the ghost eluded her. The identity of the "ghost" has never been established.

Many English manor houses and castles are said to be haunted. Raynham Hall in Norfolk, England, is haunted by a frightful, eyeless lady in brown who has the distinction of having been photographed in 1936 by a photographer from *Country Life* magazine! Abraham Lincoln's ghost is said to haunt the White House, particularly the Lincoln Room where he has often been seen.

There are also many ghost stories in folklore—often of a young woman hitchiking along the road who vanishes somewhere along the way and turns out to be the ghost of someone killed years before at the spot where the ghost was picked up. (The Mexican La Llorona, the weeping woman, belongs to this category as do the Lost Seminole Indians.) Ghosts ships (e.g., the Flying Dutchman) are legion.

The difference between a ghost and an **Apparition** is that a ghost is usually less purposeful and more somnambulistic than an apparition, and an apparition may be of a living person.

BIBLIOGRAPHY: Cohen, D. *The Encyclopedia of Ghosts,* 1984; Morton, R. C. 1892. "Record of a Haunted House." PSPR 8:311; Schaffer W. 1988. "Miss Seminole Blends Cultures Old and New." *The Miami Herald* (Neighbors, 8/14/88), p. 14.

**Ghost Society.** British group formed in 1851. It was the earliest organization established anywhere to investigate paranormal phenomena. Apart from this noteworthy feature, it could also boast that one of its members, and the most prominent, was **Henry Sidgwick** who later became a key figure in the formation and work of the Society for Psychical Research.

**Giesler, Patric V., 1950–.** American parapsychologist and anthropologist. He early came to see, as had Andrew Lang almost 100 years ago, the significance of psychical research for anthropology. His main interests in the field include altered states of consciousness (shamanism, trance mediumship and hypnosis), research on spontaneous cases, poltergeists, sitter group psychokinesis à la Kenneth Batcheldor and synchronicity. He believes the development of unobtrusive experimental methodologies for field work is of extreme importance and is interested in psi-related belief systems in general. A major field study in parapsychological anthropology (1984a, 1985a) was funded by the Parapsychology Foundation.

Presently the holder of an M.S. degree in parapsychology from John F. Kennedy University, Mr. Giesler is a Ph.D. student in anthropology at Brandeis University. He has been a visiting research associate at the Foundation for Research on the Nature of Man and at the Division of Parapsychology, University of Virginia. He has written many papers for the parapsychological literature (for example, 1984a, 1985a, 1985b, 1986) and is a member of the Parapsychological Association, the American Anthropological Association, the Society for Psychological Anthropology, the Society for Psychical Research and the American Society for Psychical Research.

Selected Writings: 1986. "GESP Testing of Shamanic Cultists: Three Studies and Evaluation of Dramatic Upsets during Testing." JP 50:123; 1984a. "Parapsychological Anthropology: I. Multi-Method Approaches to the Study of Psi in the Field Setting." JASPR 78:289; 1984b and 1985b. "Batcheldorian Psychodynamics in the Ubanda Ritual Trance Consultation: Part I and II." *Parapsychology Review* 15(6):5 and 16(1):11; 1985a. "Parapsychological Anthropology: II. A Multi-Method Study of Psi and Psi-Related Processes in the Umbanda Ritual Trance Consultation." JASPR 79:114.

**Gift of Tongues.** Also called "speaking in tongues" or "glossolalia." It is unidentifiable and unintelligible speech in a language not known to the speaker who seems to speak without conscious effort or control. It is often observed during religious fervor or hypnotic regression. The phenomenon is of interest to the linguist who sees it as a reduction of one's native tongue to phonological components. It is equally interesting to clergy and theologians because the gift of tongues has a long history, especially in Christianity, and is known as baptism in the Holy Spirit. In some religious views of "speaking in tongues," the one speaking is controlled by a holy spirit and is using an unknown language to communicate with the realm of the supernatural. Cases of tongue-speaking sometimes are referred to parapsychologists as instances of **Xenoglossy.** But when, on investigation, it is found that the so-called language is not a real language, this discovery usually spells *finis* to a case from the parapsychological viewpoint.

**Giovetti, Paola, 1938–.** Italian author and journalist. Her interest in psychical research, particularly in regard to the possibility of human survival of death, began when she was near death as the result of an accident. She has had sittings with the medium Gustavo Adolfo Rol (Giovetti, 1984), has conducted research into the near-death experience and the out-of-body experience and has written books on various aspects of the paranormal, including mediumistic art (Giovetti, 1982). Dr. Giovetti is on the editorial staff of *Luce e Ombra* and writes regularly for newspapers on parapsychological topics.

Selected Writings: 1984. "An Extraordinary Medium: Gustavo Adolfo Rol." *Theta* 12:29; *Arte Medianica,* 1982.

**Gladstone, William Ewart, 1809–1898.** British statesman and prime minister of England. His four ministries opened the way for outstanding legislative achievements, liberal reforms and the establishment of modern services and institutions. Gladstone, "The Grand Old Man," is a **Noted Witness** for the significance of psychical research. In 1885 he called it "the most important work being done in the world. By far the most important" (Myers, 1898). Gladstone became an Honorary Member of the Society for Psychical Research and never tried to conceal his sympathy and support for its aims or his belief in the possibility of communication with the dead. If a political figure today of Gladstone's stature were to declare as openly as he did endorsement of the objects and work of psychical research, one wonders if he would remain in office for very long.

BIBLIOGRAPHY: Myers. F. W. H. 1898. "The Right Hon. W. E. Gladstone." JSPR 8:260.

**Glanvil (or Glanvill), Joseph, 1636–1680.** British philosopher. The author of works on religious themes, a Fellow of the Royal Society, rector of the Abbey Church in Bath, and chaplain to Charles II, Glanvil can be considered one of the earliest psychical researchers. He believed that, in contrast to religious dogmatism, the scientific approach was the best one for the acquisition of knowledge. In an era dominated by the belief in witchcraft, he advocated the calm and careful investigation of paranormal phenomena. He advised people investigating haunts or ghosts to write down carefully what was observed and to get the confirmation of witnesses.

He himself conducted investigations in which he observed phenomena and interviewed witnesses in an attempt to make a critical evaluation of the data, and he compiled accounts of cases involving apparitions, ghosts and poltergeists (Glanvil, 1700). His personal experiences also make him a **Noted Witness** for poltergeist phenomena. In one case, which became known as the Drummer of Tedworth, he visited a house in 1662 where he heard scratching and panting and saw movements in a bed occupied by two little girls, saw movements in a bag that hung near the bed, and was awakened the following morning by a strange knocking (Glanvill, 1700). In another case, he observed: "As soon as Prayers were done, and then in sight of the Company, the Chairs walkt about the Room of themselves, the Children's shoes were hurled over their Heads and every loose thing moved about the Chamber" (Glanvil, 1700).

Selected Writing: *Saducismus Triumphatus,* 1700.

**Goat.** See **Sheep-Goat Experiments.**

**Goethe, Johann Wolfgang von, 1749–1832.** German poet, playwright, philosopher, and novelist. He is one of the leading figures in literature. His poems include *Hermann* *and Dorothea* (1797); his dramas *Iphegenia* (1787), *Egmont* (1788), *The Sorrows of Werther* (1774), and *Faust* (1790–1833); his novels *Wilhelm Meister* (1821–1829). His scientific studies and philosophical thought are reflected in his work.

His grandfather had significant dreams that seemed to foretell events to come. Goethe himself seems to have been similarly psychic. When he had to leave Fredericka Brion, the woman he loved, as he wrote in *Wahrheit und Dichtung:* "I now rode on horseback over the footpath to Drusenheim, when one of the strangest experiences befell me. Not with the eyes of the body, but with those of the spirit, I saw myself on horseback coming toward me on the same path dressed in a suit as I had never worn, pale-gray with some gold. As soon as I had shaken myself out of this reverie the form vanished. It is strange, however, that I found myself returning on the same path eight years afterward to visit Fredericka once more and that I then wore the suit I had dreamt of, and this not by design but by chance. Be this as it may, the strange phantasm had a calming influence on my feelings in those moments following the parting." This part of Goethe's testimony qualifies him as a **Noted Witness** to support the phenomena of the doppelganger and of precognition and possibly also that of trance (Goethe was forced to "shake himself out" of his state of mind).

Goethe is also a noted witness for the creative process and to the inspiration many creative individuals have received from a source outside themselves. He told a friend: "No productivity of the highest order, no invention, no lofty thought that bore fruit and led to results was ever due to a human agency, but sprang from a source above the earthly. . . . In these cases I look upon man as merely an instrument of a Higher Power, as a vessel found worthy to receive a divine influx." He also said: "In poetry, especially in that which is unconscious, before which reason and understanding fall short and which therefore produces effects so far surpassing all conceptions, there is always something daemonic." Goethe here was probably referring to a daemon, guide or control.

He also believed in reincarnation. In *Selig Sehn Sucht,* he wrote: "As long as you are not aware of the continual law of Die and be Again, you are merely a vague guest on a dark earth." And in a letter to Christoph Wieland, he said: "I cannot explain the significance to me of this woman or her influence over me, except by the theory of metempsychosis. Yes, we were once man and wife." And when he attended Wieland's funeral in 1813, Goethe said that "I am certain that I have been here as I am now a thousand times before, and I hope to return a thousand times. . .". He believed that thousands of years hence he would meet Wieland again.

BIBLIOGRAPHY: Gibbes, E. B. 1939, "Influenced or Inspirational Writing." JASPR 33: 270; Head, J. and Cranston, S. L., eds., *Reincarnation,* 1967, pp. 268–169; Prince, W. F. *Noted Witnesses for Psychic Occurrences,* 1963.

**Goldney, Kathleen Mary, 1894–.** British investigator of psychic phenomena. In terms of age and length of time dedicated to the work of the Society for Psychical Research, she is one of the oldest members of that organization. Her investigations began in the 1930s when she trained under and worked with Samuel G. Soal in experiments with Basil Shackleton. She co-authored with Soal the Shackleton report (Soal and Goldney, 1943) considered for decades one of the most important series of experiments ever conducted in parapsychology.

Mrs. Goldney conducted other experiments in extrasensory perception, analyzed the material in the famous R-101 case and carried out investigations of Helen Duncan. The more outstanding of her studies are tests conducted of the physiological conditions during the trance state of the medium Eileen Garrett (Goldney and Soal, 1938), her critical survey of the evidence relating to the Borley Rectory and her charge of misconduct on the part of Harry Price in that case (Dingwall, Goldney and Hall, 1956) and her analysis of the sittings held by Sir William Crookes with Florence Cook (Medhurst and Goldney, 1964).

When the Soal-Goldney experiments with Shackleton were attacked in 1974, she defended Soal on the basis of the facts then available. But when Betty Markwick investigated the data and found damaging evidence of Soal's manipulation, Mrs. Goldney cooperated fully by giving Ms. Markwick access to all records and by discussing experimental procedures with her. For Mrs. Goldney, "the object of all our studies is to find and establish the truth" (Goldney, 1978).

Selected Writings: 1978. "Statement by Mrs

K. M. Goldney." In B. Markwick, "The Soal-Goldney Experiments." PSPR 56:278; and Medhurst, R. G. 1964. "Sir William Crookes and the Physical Phenomena of Mediumship." PSPR 54:25; and Dingwall, E. J. and Hall, T. H. 1956. "The Haunting of Borley Rectory." PSPR 51:1; and Soal S. G. 1943. "Experiments in Precognitive Telepathy." PSPR 47:21; and Soal, S. G. 1938. "Report on a Series of Experiments with Mrs Eileen Garrett." PSPR 45:43.

**Goligher, Kathleen, 1898–.** Irish physical medium. The outstanding medium in a family of mediums, Kathleen Goligher was brought to world attention by **Dr. William Crawford** of the University of Belfast who began to study her in 1914 when she was sixteen years of age. He continued to study her until 1920 when he committed suicide. The phenomena consisted mainly of raps (often thunderous, which rocked the room) and levitation of a table which weighed ten and one-half pounds, sometimes for as long as five minutes at a time. Crawford was sure that there was no fraud involved and that the phenomena were genuine, the levitations being caused by a cantilever of **Ectoplasm** excreted from the lower portions of the medium's body. He succeeded in photographing these structures which, in the photographs, look like physical rods. (When Crawford showed these pictures to Harry Houdini and said he was going to use them in his book, Houdini concluded that Crawford was insane.)

Sir William Barrett attended a sitting in 1915 and was favorably impressed. In 1916 W. Whately Carington (then Smith) sat with the Goligher family. In good light he witnessed the levitation and turning of the table, looked underneath it and could see all four legs off the floor with nothing supporting them and found that, using all his strength, he could not force the table down and toward the medium. He was at that time convinced of the genuineness of the phenomena although four years later he found that the mediumship had deteriorated and concluded that, although it had originally been honest, it had become fraudulent.

Three months after Crawford's death plasma issuing from the medium's body was photographed and considered genuine. In 1922, Dr. E. E. Fournier d'Albe had twenty sittings with the Golighers and decided that he had seen nothing but fraud. Although in 1933, after more than ten years of retirement, Kathleen (Now Mrs. Donaldson) once more produced cloth-like ectoplasm, researchers did not study her again.

The principal importance of her mediumship to parapsychology seems to be the introduction of technological equipment and methods by Dr. Crawford in his study of her.

BIBLIOGRAPHY: Barrett, W. 1919. "Report on Dr. Crawford's Medium." PSPR 30:334; Brandon, R. *The Spiritualists,* 1983, pp. 150–151, 160–161; Dingwall, E. J. 1921. "The Psychic Structures at the Goligher Circle." PSPR 32:147; Nicol, J. F. "Historical Background." In B. Wolman, ed., *Handbook of Parapsychology,* 1977, pp. 317–318; Smith, W. W. 1919. "The Reality of Psychic Phenomena." PSPR 30:306; Tietze, T. R. 1974. "The Great Physical Mediums, Part II." *Psychic* 5(3):30–33.

**Goligher Circle.** See **Crawford, William J.; Goligher, Kathleen.**

**Goodrich-Freer, Ada, 1857–1931.** British psychic and psychical researcher. She was a practicing medium whose "safe field [was] clairvoyance, visions, telepathy, shell-hearing, [crystal-gazing] and the like" (Lambert, 1969:53). Physical phenomena, such as the movement of a table, also occurred in her presence, but she considered them due to her own unconscious muscular movements and not in any way paranormal.

Ada Goodrich-Freer was apparently of humble origins (about which she lied) and somehow managed to learn the speech and mannerisms of a "lady." In the 1890s she was assistant editor of William T. Stead's *Borderland,* a Spiritualist magazine, and in that capacity published a six-page article praising **Leonora Piper.** Later, however, when the Society for Psychical Research published voluminous material on Mrs. Piper's mediumship while ignoring Miss Goodrich-Freer, she became highly critical of the Piper mediumship.

During this same time the SPR was inquiring into "second sight" (i.e., clairvoyance and precognition, in the Scottish Highlands). Miss Goodrich-Freer was entrusted with the job of following up the affirmative responses to the original inquiry. In the course of her investigation in the Highlands and the Hebrides she met Rev. Peter Dewar and through him Fr. Allan McDonald who had a large collection of stories. Miss Goodrich-

Freer borrowed heavily from Fr. McDonald's work but failed to acknowledge her debt to him. No report of the inquiry was ever published in the *Proceedings*—whether because the material was not worthy of publication or because of a break between Miss Goodrich-Freer and **Frederic W. H. Myers** is not clear.

Miss Goodrich-Freer had also become involved in 1897 in an abortive investigation of an alleged haunted house, Ballechin House, in connection with which there have been suggestions of a sexual involvement between her and Myers and a subsequent quarrel. (Campbell and Hall, 1968). But it has also been suggested that the break came, not over a love affair, but because of the SPR's decision not to print anything about the "ghost hunt" at Ballechin House (Campbell, 1969). In that same year of 1897 her employment by W. T. Stead came to an end and in 1900 her patron (Lord Bute) died.

Trevor Hall (1968) has accused her of thereafter using fraud in her sittings—after all she "practised life-long deception in her personal and social life. . . ; in addition, she was guilty of grievous plagiarism in her folklore lectures and literary publications: can anyone reasonably believe that her career as a clairvoyant is likely to have been spotless?" (Campbell, 1969).

Miss Goodrich-Freer went to Palestine in 1901 and from then on had nothing more to do with psychical research. She died in 1931 in America.

BIBLIOGRAPHY: Campbell, J. L. 1969. "Correspondence. Strange Things and Ada Goodrich-Freer." JSPR 45:183; Campbell, J. L. and Hall, T. H. *Strange Things,* 1968; Lambert, G. W. 1969. "Stranger Things: Some Reflections on Reading 'Strange Things' by John L. Campbell and Trevor H. Hall." JSPR 45:43.

**Grad, Bernard, 1920–.** Canadian biochemist. Dr. Grad's main interest has been in healing by touch.

Always aware of a surrounding energy connected with the body's well-being, he "came to experience energy as a tide, flowing in during one time of the day and flowing out later in the day" (Grad, 1987:147) while he was lying ill with tuberculosis in 1942. He felt the need to understand this experience after August 6, 1945, the day the first atomic bomb was dropped and he felt a "sensation . . . as intense as if I had put my finger in an electrical outlet. . ." (Grad, 1987: 148).

In 1948 he began the regular use of **Wilhelm Reich's** orgone accumulator (a device that supposedly accumulates atmospheric bioenergy) during which he felt bioenergetic "streamings" on his back, heard oceanic sounds and felt "charged up after a half-hour of its use." From 1949 to 1953 Grad experimented with the effect of the orgone accumulator on lymphatic leukemia in mice and found that the lowered incidence of the disease in the treated mice was highly significant.

In 1957 Grad met the healer Oskar Estebany who claimed to heal by the **Laying-on of Hands** by which he believed he transmitted energy from the atmosphere (like a human orgone accumulator). Estebany also felt heat in his hands at the place of a patient's illness. In order to circumvent the criticism that any healing from laying-on of hands was due to suggestion or hypnosis, Grad's experiments dealt with nonhumans (animals and plants) and nonliving things, such as cloth. He was astonished that laying-on of hands regularly affected biological processes in mice. A later successful series of experiments with plants dealt with the "mummification" of bananas. He was the first to report studies with laying-on-of-hands in the scientific literature, after which other parapsychologists began to experiment in the field.

"I became involved in the LH [laying-on of hands] phenomenon because I was interested in bioenergy . . . I am convinced now more than ever that there is energy at work. . . . [and that] healers can make a significant impact on disease. . . . [T]he patient [should] have an open mind about the possibility of being healed. . . . [T]here is a rational, scientifically investigatable, objective core to the LH phenomenon" (Grad, 1987: 154–155).

Because his studies have been met with silence from the scientific community and because of his accompanying isolation Grad feels that to work successfully in this field one should have, among other things, "lots of money, preferably [one's] own. . . ; a group of close friends. . . ; [and] no great hankering for honors or promotions to positions of influence or power" (Grad, 1987:159).

Dr. Grad has been lecturer and then associate professor at the Gerontologic Unit of the Allan Memorial Institute of Psychiatry, McGill University, became associate director of biological studies in 1969, and in 1972 associate scientist at the Royal Victoria Hospital in Montreal. Since 1985 he has been associate professor at the University of Quebec, Montreal.

Selected Writings: "Experiences and Opinions of an Unconventional Scientist." In R. Pilkington, ed., *Men and Women of Parapsychology,* 1987; 1965. "Some Biological Effects of the 'Laying-on of Hands': A Review of Experiments with Animals and Plants." JASPR 59:95; "The Biological Effects of the 'Laying-on of Hands" in Animals and Plants: Implications for Biology." In G. Schmeidler, ed., *Parapsychology: Its Relation to Physics, Biology, Psychology and Psychiatry,* 1976; 1981. "Paranormal Healing and Life Energy." ASPR *Newsletter* 7:21; 1961. with R. J. Cadoret and G. I. Paul. "An Unorthodox Method of Treatment of Wound Healing in Mice." *International Journal of Parapsychology* 3:5.

**Grattan-Guiness, Ivor, 1941–.** British editor of the science journal *Annals of Science* and founder-editor of the journal *History and Philosophy of Logic.* He is deeply involved in parapsychology. His interests in this field are coincidences which he believes may be forms of psi phenomena and the history and philosophy of psi research that were discussed in a recent book he edited (Grattan-Guinness, 1982). He is managing editor of the *Journal of the Society for Psychical Research* as well as president of the British Society for the History of Mathematics.

Selected Writing: *Psychical Research. A Guide to its History, Principles and Practice,* 1982.

**Greeley, Horace, 1811–1872.** American journalist and editor. The **Fox Sisters** and Spiritualism owe him much. He was the editor of *The New Yorker* magazine in 1834 and seven years later established the *New York Tribune.* He edited the paper until he died and made it into one of the most influential newspapers in the United States. Greeley supported Abraham Lincoln, opposed slavery and helped found the Republican party.

While he is famous for his advice to the young men of America—"turn your face to the great West, and there build up a home and fortune"—it is not so well known that he is one of the distinguished Americans who attended séances, was drawn to Spiritualism (Berger, 1988), and used the powerful *Tribune* to publicize the feats of Leah, Kate, and Margaretta Fox. Indeed, it was only because Greeley's paper "had given favorable notice to the seances the girls conducted . . . [that] they emerge[d] to any degree as leading figures of a new profession" (Moore, 1977). Thus did Greeley play an important role in promoting the spread of the movement and marvels of Spiritualism. The spirits did not help him win the presidency in 1872 when he made an unsuccessful bid for it against Grant, but it is to be hoped that they brought him some comfort for the grief he felt at the death of a son.

BIBLIOGRAPHY: Moore, R. L. *In Search of White Crows,* 1977.

**Green, Celia, 1935–.** British director of the Institute of Psychophysical Research. Her valuable surveys of interest to psychical research include lucid dreams (Green, 1968a) and the **Out-of-Body Experience** (Green, 1968b, 1967). She also completed a lengthy and creative tabulation and extended discussion of the data relating to spontaneous cases (Green, 1960).

Former research secretary of the Society for Psychical Research, she was elected in 1958 to the Perrott Studentship in Psychical Research.

Selected Writings: *Lucid Dreams,* 1968a; *Out-of-Body Experiences. Proceedings of the Institute of Psychophysical Research,* 1968b; 1967. "Ecsomatic Experiences and Related Phenomena." JSPR 44:111; 1960. "Analysis of Spontaneous Cases." PSPR 53:97.

**Greenwood, Joseph Albert, 1906–1988.** American mathematician and statistician. As a young geometer at Duke University, he was recruited by Joseph B. Rhine in 1937 to improve the statistical evaluations of the experimental work at the Parapsychology Laboratory and to counter criticisms. Greenwood "gradually made himself over into a statistician at Rhine's instigation." He, along with Charles Stuart, "assume[d] the responsibilities of studying the criticisms being made of the Duke work and of deciding what changes or developments in theory and technique ought to be undertaken" (Mauskopf and McVaugh, 1980:187)

It was largely Joseph Greenwood's work that brought mathematical respectability to the field of parapsychology. It also made it clear that experimental parapsychologists would either have to have a sound training in statistics or to employ competent statisticians and that "they would have to understand the mathematical consequences of experimental design" (Mauskopf and McVaugh, 1980:201).

From 1937 to 1979 Dr. Greenwood (he had received his Ph.D. in 1931) published authoritative articles on the use of statistics in parapsychology. He was a co-author of *Extra-sensory Perception after Sixty Years* (1940) and from 1942 to 1982 was statistical editor of the *Journal of Parapsychology.*

Dr. Greenwood was an assistant professor of mathematics at Duke University from 1930 to 1942. From 1942 to 1957 he was a statistician for the U.S. Navy's Bureau of Aeronautics where he developed sampling and quality control methods for which he is widely known. He was a Fellow of the American Society for Quality Control and received an Outstanding Performance Award from the Air Force Intelligence Center and the Drug Enforcement Agency's Exceptional Service Award.

Selected Writings: 1940. "A Reply to Dr. Feller's Critique." JP 4; 1939. "Some Mathematical Problems for Future Consideration Suggested by ESP Research." JP 3; 1937. "Mathematical Techniques Used in ESP Research." JP 1; with J. G. Pratt, J. B. Rhine, B. M. Smith, and C. E. Stuart. *Extra-sensory Perception after Sixty Years, 1940–1966.*

BIBLIOGRAPHY: "Joseph A. Greenwood 1906\1988." *FRNM Bulletin* 37:2, Spring 1988; Mauskopf, S. H. and McVaugh, M. R. *The Elusive Science,* 1980, pp. 197–201.

**Gregory, Anita (Kohsen), 1925–1984.** German-born British parapsychologist. Anita Gregory was an author and teacher of psychology and parapsychology in the School of Education in the Polytechnic of North London and earned her Ph.D. in parapsychology shortly before her death. She was also an investigator of paranormal phenomena.

Her interest in psychical research and parapsychology centered mainly on work in the field done in the Soviet Union, on the British psychic Matthew Manning and on the mediumship of Rudi Schneider about which she became a leading authority. She also served devotedly on the Council of the Society for Psychical Research and as its Honorary secretary and vice president. Her search to find truth in life and parapsychology ended with her death in 1984 and seems to have been epitomized by her last words before she slipped into unconsciousness and death. Arthur Ellison, who was at her bedside, heard her say in German: "ich weiss nicht!" ("I don't know!")

Selected Writings: *The Strange Case of Rudi Schneider,* 1985; Gregory, A., ed., 1982. "London Experiments with Matthew Manning." PSPR 56:283.

**Gregory, Clive C. L., ?–1964.** British astronomer and director of the University of London Observatory. He became interested in psychical research and had sittings with mediums Rudi Schneider and Stella C. After his marriage to Anita Kohsen, he co-authored with her a book on research in parapsychology (Gregory and Kohsen, 1954). Gregory, realizing that there still existed no adequate theory to accommodate the findings of parapsychology and fit them into a scientific framework, with his wife formulated a theoretical model for parapsychology (Gregory and Kohsen, 1958). A car accident in 1964 terminated his life and work.

Selected Writings: and Kohsen, A. 1958. "A Cosmological Approach to a Theory of Mental Images." PSPR 52:33; and Kohsen, A. *Physical and Psychical Research,* 1954.

**Gregory Thaumaturgus, Saint, c. 213–270.** Greek bishop of Neocaesarea. He came to Christianity under the tutelage of the great theologian, Origen. He earned his Greek name Thaumaturgus, meaning "wonder worker," as a result of **Miracles** he was supposed to have performed. He was said to have written his major work, *Exposition of Faith,* because of a vision of St. John the Evangelist. His other works included the *Panegyric to Origen* which analyzed the difference between pagan and Christian philosophy.

In the *Panegyric,* he described "that holy angel of God who led me from my youth . . . that angel who still at this present time sustains, and instructs, and conducts me; and who, in addition to all these other benefits has brought me into connection with [Origen] which, in truth, is the most important of all the services done me." Later on in the *Panegyric,* Gregory spoke again of that "certain divine companion and beneficent conductor and guardian, ever leading us in safety through the whole of this present life. . .".

It is not likely that by the term "holy angel" Gregory meant one of God's winged messengers. It is possible that, like Socrates, Gregory had a personal daemon, or, even likelier, a guide if Gregory's reference to the entity as a "beneficent conductor and guardian" means anything. His testimony as a **Noted Witness** is supportive of any of these phenomena.

BIBLIOGRAPHY: Prince, W. F. *Noted Witnesses for Psychic Occurrences,* 1963.

**Greville, Thomas Nall Eden, 1910–.** American mathematician. He has been concerned with developing statistical methods for the evaluation of data in quantitative experimental parapsychology (Greville, 1941, 1944) and for the evaluation of verbal material produced by mediums (Greville, 1949). The wide and long use of his methods by parapsychologists everywhere suggests that the relationship between statisticians and parapsychologists that began in the Joseph B. Rhine era is a close and continuing one.

Dr. Greville's interests spread beyond statistics, however. He inclines strongly toward a belief in reincarnation and rejects the doctrine of materialism. "It is one of the strangest developments in the annals of human thought that most establishment scientists have come to accept this bizarre hypothesis, for which there is no hard evidence, and which is contradicted by the daily experience of every human being" (Greville, 1983).

A past president of the Psychical Research Foundation, Greville now is associated with the Department of Personality Studies (formerly the Division of Parapsychology) at the University of Virginia.

Selected Writings: "Some Views of Survival." In W. G. Roll, J. Beloff, R. A. White, eds., *Research in Parapsychology 1982,* 1983, p. 120; 1949. "On the Number of Sets Required for Testing the Significance of Verbal Material." JP 13:137; 1944. "On Multiple Matching with One Variable Deck." *Annals of Mathematical Statistics* 15:432; 1941. "The Frequency Distribution of a General Matching Problem." *Annals of Mathematical Statistics* 12:350.

**Grof, Stanislav, 1932–.** Czechoslovakia-born physician and psychiatrist. He has conducted pioneering research at the Psychiatric Research Institute in Prague and at the Maryland Psychiatric Research Center in Baltimore into the psychedelic experience. Appointed chief of psychiatric research at the Maryland Psychiatric Research Center after he chose to remain in the United States, he carried out a program of psychedelic therapy there with people dying of cancer, psychiatric patients, and others.

Their experiences embraced a broad spectrum—from prenatal and childhood memories to an awareness of having gone beyond the limits of time and space to find cosmic unity. They also had symbolic encounters with death and rebirth (Grof and Halifax, 1978). The effects of these experiences contributed to improved emotional and physical functioning and self-actualizing and led to a harmonious adjustment to life (Grof and Halifax, 1978:220). The experience also overcame negative concepts of death and suggested that death was not final: "Individuals who have suffered through the death-rebirth phenomenon in their psychedelic sessions usually become open to the possibility that consciousness might be independent of the physical body and continue beyond the moment of clinical death. . . . Those who were previously convinced that death was the ultimate defeat and meant the end of any form of existence discovered various alternatives to this materialistic and pragmatic point of view. They came to realize how little conclusive evidence there is for any authoritative opinion in this matter and often began seeing death and dying as a cosmic voyage into the unknown" (Grof and Halifax, 1978:52).

The experiences resembled the accounts given in the ancient manuals developed in Egypt and Tibet to guide people approaching physical death or attempting to experience it symbolically. Indeed this resemblance may force sceptics "to reevaluate their position, to raise questions rather than to reject the new area of research in existence after physical death. They should ask themselves . . . why there is this recurrence of certain motifs and themes in remote countries, and different time periods, and cultures, and religions" (Kübler-Ross, 1978:vii–viii).

Dr. Grof in now a scholar in residence at the Esalen Institute and consulting editor for the *Journal of Near-Death Studies.*

Selected Writing: and Halifax, J. *The Human Encounter with Death,* 1978.

BIBLIOGRAPHY: Kübler-Ross, E. Foreword. In

Grof, S. and Halifax, J. *The Human Encounter with Death,* 1978.

**Grosso, Michael, 1937–.** American philosopher and classical scholar. He has deep and broad ranging interests in psychical research and parapsychology. A frequent contributor to the *Journal of the American Society for Psychical Research* and *Theta,* he is the author of numerous book reviews and papers on the near-death experience, out-of-body experience, the evolutionary implications of psi and the parapsychology of religion.

The question of survival after death, particularly the difficult problem of continuing personal identity (Grosso, 1979), occupies him. His most recent writings draw on the near-death and out-of-body experiences to deal with the psycho-spiritual transformation of St. Paul (Grosso 1989a) and use psychical research, channeling and apparitions of the Virgin Mary as data to support what he sees as a new image of humankind and a new "postmodern mythology of death" (Grosso, 1989b).

Of great concern to him is the survival of the human race as it lives under the shadow of the Bomb (Grosso, 1985). In this latter connection, he finds in psi abilities and near-death and out-of-body experiences many resources and elements for the emergence of a powerful archetype for human transformation. This psychic mechanism, which he dubs the Archetype of Death and Enlightenment, will help us lose the fear of death, transform consciousness, and help humankind find its way out of the shadow and into the light. Dr. Grosso, who received a Ph.D. in philosophy from Columbia University, is on the editorial staff of the *Journal of Religion and Psychical Research.*

Selected Writings: "St. Paul's *Metanoia:* An Essay in Psycho History." In A. S. Berger and H.Thompson, eds., *Religion and Parapsychology,* 1989a; "A Post-Modern Mythology of Death." In A. S. Berger, J. Berger, A. H. Kutscher, eds., *Cross-Cultural Perspectives on Death and Dying,* 1989b; *The Final Choice: Playing the Survival Game,* 1985; 1979. "The Survival of Personality in a Mind-Dependent World." JASPR 73:367.

**Grunewald, Fritz, 1885–1925.** German engineer and inventor who furthered serious laboratory experiments in psychical research. He was the first in Germany to construct a private workshop so that he could experiment with physical mediums and the phenomena they are said to produce. He devised ingenious apparatus to measure, record, and photograph phenomena. Among his apparatus were platforms for weighing mediums and materializations, a special table to test for table-tilting and levitations and a box containing microphones to register raps. In all of Europe and the United Kingdom only in France at the Institut Métapsychique International was there a laboratory comparable to Grunewald's. In the United States only at Stanford University did a similar facility exist. So that others could also do laboratory investigations of physical phenomena, Grunewald described his laboratory and devices in detail (Grunewald, 1920). His descriptions continue to be valuable even for modern day researchers with their electronically controlled laboratories.

Selected Writings: *Physikalisch-mediumistische Untersuchungen,* 1920.

BIBLIOGRAPHY: Hövelmann, G. H. "Neglected Figures in the History of Parapsychology." In F. W. J. J. Snel, ed., *Liber Amicorum in Honour of G. A. M. Zorab,* 1986, p. 94.

**Guererro, Bárbara (Pachita), c. 1900–1979.** Mexican psychic surgeon known throughout the world for her powers of unorthodox healing. She claimed that the spirit of Cuauhtemoc, emperor of the Aztecs hanged by the Spaniards in the sixteenth century, used her as an instrument. She called him "little brother" and, with his guidance, performed her surgery with a kitchen knife. She worked in darkness relieved only by a few candles as she opened her patients, removed a diseased organ or other problem and then closed, all without anesthesia. If her patients cried out in pain and suffering, she had only to touch their foreheads gently and they became calm and peaceful. After the operations, she wrapped her patients in sheets and sent them home to remain in bed for three days. At the end of that time, they would usually just remove their bandages, bathe, take the herbal medicines, tea or syrup she had given to them and resume their normal lives.

Her patients of course included Mexicans, but many also came from the United States and the rest of Latin America to her simple home on the outskirts of sprawling Mexico City. She would do her work with them all day long and into the nights. But when midnight came, she refused to work any more because she was fearful of the dark spirits then abroad.

Besides patients, parapsychologists came to her door, among them Stanley Krippner and investigators from the Sociedad Méxicana de Parapsicología. Representatives of orthodox medicine do not admit or confirm that "Pachita" effected any cures—despite her many satisfied patients.

Sometime around midyear 1978, she announced to her friends and assistants that her mission was completed and that she would die soon. Her "little brother" did not want her to die and, through her assistants, directed the removal of two of her organs. But even he could not save her and she died in 1979. Today, the *hombres* and *mujeres* of her *pueblo* claim that they still see her walking its streets.

BIBLIOGRAPHY: Krippner, S. and Villoldo, A. *The Realms of Healing,* 1976.

**Guess.** See **Call.**

**Guide.** Said to be a wise and kindly spirit always vigilant and ready to help a chosen individual to find the path to spiritual wisdom and growth.

**Guppy, Agnes (Nichol), ?–1917.** British physical medium. Her marvels included materializations, levitation of herself while she was seated in a chair, Apports of fresh fruits and flowers and teleportation of her body from her home to the center of London three miles away. Since she was of considerable size and weight, her ability to achieve levitation and teleportation must have been marvellous indeed. When still Agnes Nichol (prior to her marriage to Samuel Guppy), she so impressed Alfred R. Wallace with her feats that he asked his scientific colleagues to come to see her demonstrations and to become persuaded of Spiritualism as he was.

Mrs. Guppy was an exceedingly popular figure with many patrons and supporters and contributed to the development of Spiritualism in England. She was determined to protect against any rival medium and at all costs her popularity and high position. She did not hesitate, for example, to send hirelings to break up their séances and tear down their cabinets. She had a particular fear and jealousy of **Florence Cook** and did what she could to undermine that medium's reputation. Apparently she succeeded to a degree because Miss Cook was reported in 1873 to have "been greatly vexed by some reports spread about her by Mrs. Guppy" (Medhurst and Goldney, 1964:56). In the same year, Mrs. Guppy tried to enlist the help of others "in a plot whereby [some people] were to be hired to attend a seance at Miss Cook's, and watching their opportunity, at a favourable moment, while the manifestations were in progress *to throw vitrol* [sic] *in the face of the spirit,* hoping thereby to destroy forever the handsome features of Miss Florrie Cook, and thus at one fell stroke to effectually remove from further use a medium who, Mrs. Guppy claimed, had and was taking all her, Mrs. Guppy's, friends away from her and upon whose patronage Mrs. G. had long depended" (Medhurst and Goldney, 1964:58).

After the death of her husband, Mrs. Guppy married William Volckman, one of those she planned to hire in the plot to throw acid in her rival's face, and instigated him later in 1873 to attend a Cook séance and to attack her in a fight that cost him part of his beard. The accounts of the time make Mrs. Guppy rather a repulsive character even to people who were not her competitors. John W. Strutt (Lord Rayleigh) said, "Mrs. Guppy I don't think I could stand, even in the cause of science and philosophy!" (Medhurst and Goldney, 1964:57).

BIBLIOGRAPHY: Medhurst, R. G. and Goldney, K. M. 1964. "William Crookes and the Physical Phenomena of Mediumship." PSPR 54:25.

**Gurney, Edmund, 1847–1888.** British psychical researcher. Perhaps the most important figure in the early days of the **Society for Psychical Research** to which he devoted nearly all his time. He did extensive work in hypnosis and developed a theory of apparitions (hallucinations). *Phantasms of the Living,* published in 1886, was principally his work (with help from **Frederic W. H. Myers** who wrote the Introduction and **Frank Podmore** who investigated many of the cases). It still remains the beginning point for any study of crisis-apparitions and has been called "the greatest work on the subject that had ever been launched on the world in two thousand years of Western culture" (Nicol, 1966).

Gurney could be gay and witty; he was a delightful and sympathetic companion. Yet there was a strain of melancholy in his nature that worried his friends. In 1875 three of his sisters drowned, and he was thereafter obsessed with the "indefensibility of human suffering."

His early interests had been, in turn, music (a career considered most unsuitable at that time), medicine, and law, but he found at last that he had no talent for any of them—although his interest in music resulted in the important book *The Power of Sound* (1880). He also published a series of valuable philosophical essays in his several volumes of *Tertium Quid.*

After his early failures, he turned to psychical research mainly because of his sensitivity to the grief and suffering of others. He felt that he had at last found an absorbing profession that might give him an opportunity to help others. He had become interested in the phenomena of Spiritualism when, in 1874, and still a Fellow of Trinity College, Cambridge, he attended a séance of the famous medium Stainton Moses. He was a charter member of the Society for Psychical Research upon its formation in 1882 and became its honorary secretary in 1883 and the editor of its *Proceedings.*

During the three years (1883–1886) of work on *Phantasms of the Living,* Gurney was also doing extensive studies in hypnosis as well as carrying on all his other duties. American philosopher C. S. Peirce raised serious objections to *Phantasms of the Living,* however: that the cases reported were the result of chance coincidence only; that people are more likely to remember hallucinations that coincide with deaths and to forget others that have no meaning; and that the percentage of people reporting these experiences was considerably smaller than Gurney had estimated. Gurney answered these objections as well as he could; the *Census of Hallucinations* published after his death vindicated him.

Gurney died in a hotel in Brighton from an apparently self-administered dose of chloroform. Whether his death was accidental, the chloroform being administered to control pain (the position of the SPR), or suicide because he realized that his work in psychical research, like his earlier work, was also a failure (Hall, 1964) remains a mystery. Yet chloroform was routinely used in those days to control pain, and "Gurney's accident was not unique, except in its finality. For Cromwell Varley almost died in similar circumstances" (Nicol, 1972). It has been said that Gurney's death was the single greatest blow psychical research has ever suffered. After his death Gurney was allegedly one of the principal communicators in the **Cross-Correspondences** cases.

Selected Writings: 1889: "Remarks on Mr. Peirce's Rejoinder." PASPR 1:285; 1884. "The Problems of Hypnotism." PSPR 2:265; 1888. "Hypnotism and Telepathy." PSPR 5:215; with Myers, F. W. H. and Podmore, F. *Phantasms of the Living,* 1886.

BIBLIOGRAPHY: Gauld, A. *The Founders of Psychical Research,* 1968; Hall, T. H. *The Strange Case of Edmund Gurney,* 1964; Myers, F. W. H. 1889. "Postcript on Mr. Gurney's Reply to Professor Peirce." PASPR 1:300; Nicol, F. 1972. "The Founders of the S.P.R." PSPR 55:341, 349; Nicol, F. 1966. "The Silences of Mr. Trevor Hall." *International Journal of Parapsychology* 8(1):5.

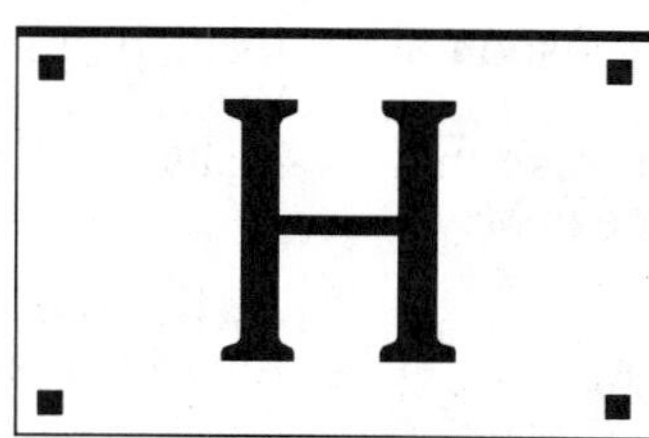

**Haggard, Sir Henry Rider, 1856–1925.** British novelist. His chief works included *Allan Quartermain* (1887), *She* (1887), and *Ayesha* (1905). His *King Solomon's Mines,* published in 1885, has been made into a motion picture several times; the most recent version stars Richard Chamberlain.

Haggard's own real-life story, first published in *The Times* for July 21, 1904 marks him as a **Noted Witness** for Telepathy between him and a dog. On Sunday morning, July 10, 1904, Haggard went to bed at about 12:30 A.M. At about 2 A.M. he was awakened by his wife who said he had been making moaning animal-like sounds. As Haggard awakened, he knew that he had had a nightmare that seemed associated with a terrible struggle for life such as when one is drowning. Between the time he heard his wife's voice and became conscious enough to respond to her, he had another dream, this time of Bob, his daughter's black retriever. In the dream, Bob seemed to be lying in rough undergrowth next to water and to be trying to speak to him or to transmit to him in some way that the dog was dying.

The following day, Haggard dismissed the dream as a very disagreeable experience, even laughed at it, until he discovered that Bob was missing. A few days later, Haggard and a servant found the broken body of the dog floating in a river. It had been on a bridge when struck by a train a little after 10:25 P.M. on July 9 and fallen from the bridge into the reeds of the river. Apparently, the accident occurred about two hours before Haggard went to bed and prior to his dream of the dog's attempt to tell him that it was dying. Eleanor Sidgwick described the case as unusual and well-authenticated.

BIBLIOGRAPHY: Sidgwick, E. 1922, "Phantasms of the Living." PSPR 33:23.

**Hailstones, Miraculous.** Situated in eastern France on the Moselle River, the town of Remiremont gained power and fame in the Middle Ages. The nuns of its convent were chosen from the nobility and its abbess, consecrated by the pope, was a princess of the Holy Roman Empire. In the sixteenth century, however, a victory for the duke of Lorraine ended the power of Remiremont and, two centuries later, the French Revolution crushed the nunnery altogether. Fame came to Remiremont once more in 1907 when it was the focus of a case called by the French "grêlons-medailles" (hailstorm-medallions)—a case so startling that the Society for Psychical Research delegated a representative to collect information and evidence on the spot.

"Notre-Dame du Trésor" (Our Lady of the Treasure) had been given to the convent of Remiremont by Charlemagne in the eighth century and was believed by the people of Remiremont to have the power to bring rain or to avert calamities. On May 12, 1682, for example, a strong earthquake demolished a great number of houses and its aftershocks forced the terrified population to sleep in the fields surrounding the town. But as soon as "Notre Dame du Trésor" was carried through Remiremont, the calamity ceased. After that, there was a procession of the statue in May of each year so that the town would not be devastated by another earthquake. The local clergy, with the approval of Pope Pius X, planned a procession on May 20, 1907, in honor of the coronation of the holy image. But Remiremont was divided into clerical and anti-clerical parties, and, on May 13, the Town Council forbade the procession. The procession was not held.

On the following Sunday, May 26, a storm struck toward evening. Heavy rain was followed by a violent hailstorm. Some of the hailstones were extraordinarily large and heavy, yet they fell slowly, like snow. The hailstones destroyed porches, tiles and bricks but, amazingly, spared the vegetable and flower gardens. Soon the cry echoed throughout the town—"Notre Dame du Trésor is on the hailstones!" Father Vuillemin, the parish priest, conducted an inquiry into the facts and collected the depositions of 107 witnesses who said they saw the images on the hailstones. The clergy were convinced that Rome would declare the event a miracle and that Remiremont would become a pilgrimage center.

If this were a real miracle, it would stand outside the pale of psychical research. But the representative of the Society for Psychical Research did not find any basis for a miracle—or for a paranormal occurrence, either, for that matter. He concluded that the slowly falling hailstones had been merely an optical illusion and that the witnesses had seen the Blessed Virgin's image on the hailstones only after the suggestion had been made to them that the image was there. Anyway, the witnesses were ignorant peasants influenced by religious fervor. Although a Parisian, the representative applied the double standard of the snobbish English society that, unlike ladies and gentlemen, peasants cheat or can be deceived.

But perhaps it was a paranormal event after all. Perhaps, as a result of the pent-up frustration in the town psychokinesis combined with a poltergeist effect that sometimes takes the form of stones or rocks being thrown or falling could have caused the phenomenon (Rogo, 1982).

BIBLIOGRAPHY: Rogo, D.S. *Miracles: A Parascientific Inquiry into Wondrous Phenomena,* 1982, p. 156; Sage, M. 1909. "The Alleged Miraculous Hailstones of Remiremont." PSPR 21:405.

**Hall, Granville Stanley, 1844–1924.** American psychologist. He founded the disciplines of education psychology and child psychology, and the *American Journal of Psychology,* the first journal of its kind in the United States. He held a professorship at Johns Hopkins University and went on to help found Clark University of which he became president.

While lecturing at Harvard University, Hall met **William James,** a leading force in the formation of the American Society for Psychical Research and became one of the ASPR's vice presidents upon its founding in 1885. One wonders why Hall ever accepted the post. Like most academic psychologists, he was hostile toward psychical research. He "tabooed" and tried to discourage **James H. Hyslop** from entering the field (Berger, 1988) and when one of his assistants wrote a book to demolish Hyslop and his experiments with mediums, Hall contributed a lengthy preface that said in part. "It is significant . . . that the chief works of the English Psychic Research Society [*sic*] have never before had such a searching, impartial, critical estimate, often as they have been worked over by believers. Those with skepticism enough to have been impartial have never been able to arouse interest enough to treat these studies thoroughly. Thus, I cannot but hope that this book will make a turn of the tide" (Hall, 1910).

Hall seems to have assumed that in order to be impartial one had to be sceptical. Yet the book which was to "turn the tide" has been forgotten now for almost eighty years.

Selected Writing: Preface. In A. E. Tanner, *Studies in Spiritism,* 1910.

BIBLIOGRAPHY: Berger, A.S. *Lives and Letters in American Parapsychology,* 1988.

**Hall, Prescott F., 1868–1921.** American lawyer Besides his practice in Boston, he worked with Richard Hodgson, James H. Hyslop and the American Society for Psychical Research on the vexing question of proving human survival after death. In the experiments with mediums that he analyzed, he remained skeptical, lawyerlike, and insistent that it was not possible to draw conclusions from incomplete records of sittings or of psychic phenomena.

"A record of an incident is much like the abstract of title to a piece of land. It is not enough that the instruments reported are sufficient on their face to pass title; it must also appear that nothing was omitted, and that everything was examined that should have been. Nothing can be left to the private information or memory of the searcher, if the record is to be of any value to others. It is true that in law we might be willing to rely upon the summary of an abstract made by an examiner of high repute; but we cannot do so with psychic records. In law the canons of investigation have long been established; there is no doubt as to what constitutes a thorough examination of title. But, in psychical research, we have no such precision of method. What appears of no importance today may turn out to be of the greatest importance tomorrow; and therefore we are obliged to insist on the fullest measure of detail in the matters reported" (Hall, 1914:150–151).

The salutary rule he urged unfortunately has not been recognized or applied. Inadequate reporting continues to impede important survival research (Berger, 1988).

Selected Writing: 1914. "Experiments with Mrs. Caton." JASPR 8:1.

BIBLIOGRAPHY: Berger, A.S. 1988. "Two Unrecognized Problems in Survival Research." In D.H. Weiner and R.L. Morris, eds., *Research in Parapsychology 1987,* 1988, p. 140.

**Hall, Trevor Henry, 1910–.** British author. A surveyor by profession, Mr. Hall was awarded the Perrott Studentship in Psychical Research at Trinity College, Cambridge, in 1954. His principal contributions to psychical research have been his writings on the subject.

His first work, undertaken with **Eric J. Dingwall** and **Kathleen M. Goldney** (1956), was published in the *Proceedings of the Society for Psychical Research* and was a critical survey of the evidence for the hauntings at Borley Rectory. The authors concluded that Harry Price invented or distorted the evidence and that the enormous publicity given the alleged phenomena persuaded "otherwise sensible people" that what was going on was paranormal.

In 1958, again with Eric J. Dingwall, Hall wrote a book on ghosts which was favorably reviewed in the *Journal* of the SPR (Stratton, 1958). Thereafter, as he began to write for the general public and therefore to look for more sensational subject matter, parapsychologists came more and more to feel that he could no longer be considered "a serious worker in a research field" (Medhurst, 1967:100).

His book (1963) on the William Crookes-Florence Cook sittings in which he branded Florrie Cook's materializations fraudulent and claimed that she had been sexually involved with Crookes caused, and continues to cause, a furor among psychical researchers. The furor still continues as well over his next book (1964) in which he theorizes that Edmund Gurney committed suicide (and that the powers that were at the SPR lied to conceal that fact) and, in passing, that Frank Podmore was a homosexual whose sexual preference somehow was involved with his mysterious death. His 1984 book that seeks to debunk the *ne plus ultra* of physical mediumship, D.D. Home, has also met with disapproval from the parapsychological community (Braude, 1985).

On the other side of the coin, however, many readers of his books, among them members of the SPR and including his co-author John L. Campbell (1968), have been persuaded by his arguments. Campbell wrote that before meeting with Mr. Hall he "had read his book on Edmund Gurney and considered that he had made his case, and now hold[s] the same views regarding his other writings on psychical research, particularly his book on Florence Cook and William Crookes" (Campbell, 1969:183–184).

Hall's and his co-authors' words referring to Harry Price in the Borley Rectory case perhaps now sum up best parapsychologists's attitude toward Hall: "With all that can be said against him, it must be admitted that it was he who . . . put psychical research on the map for the man-in-the-English-street. But was it the right map?" (Dingwall, Goldney and Hall, 1956:175). See also **Goodrich-Freer, Ada.**

Selected Writings: *The Enigma of Daniel Home,* 1984; *The Strange Case of Edmund Gurney,* 1964; *The Spiritualists* 1963 (reissued as *The Medium and the Scientist,* 1984); with J.L. Campbell. *Strange Things,* 1968; with E. J. Dingwall. *Four Modern Ghosts,* 1958; with E. J. Dingwall and K.M. Goldney, "The Haunting of Borley Rectory." PSPR 51.1.

BIBLIOGRAPHY: Braude, S.E. 1985. "The

Enigma of Daniel Home." JSPR 53:40; Campbell, J.L. "Correspondence. Strange Things and Ada Goodrich Freer." JSPR 45:183; Medhurst, R.G. 1967. "New Light on Old Ghosts." JSPR 44:94; Stratton, F.J.M. 1958. "Four Modern Ghosts." JSPR 39:288.

**Hallucination.** The experience of sense-imagery that in no way corresponds with a physical fact in any manner consistent with normal perception; the experience of touching, seeing, hearing, or in any other way perceiving a person, object, or event although no physical person or object or event actually is stimulating the sensory organs. A dream is an example of an hallucination. Sometimes hallucinations may be the result of physical or mental disturbance (i.e., alcoholic delirium). In psychical research, some possible examples of hallucinations are **Apparitions** and **Out-of-Body-Experiences.** The question in every case is whether the hallucinatory experience is veridical.

**Hand-Trembling.** On the Indian reservations in the states of Arizona and New Mexico, a technique for **Divination** used by Navajo psychic detectives. As their hands tremble and shake and they enter into an **Altered State of Consciousness,** these gifted Navajos may sing or scatter corn pollen on their hands. In a trance state, they appear to use paranormal powers to diagnose illness or locate lost or stolen objects. In one case, for instance, two traders employed a hand-trembler to find jewelry valued at $3,000 that had been stolen from their trading post. The Navajo located the jewelry in a cave where it had been secreted. In another case, lost horses were found through the services of a hand-trembler and, in a third example, the technique traced a would-be murderer to his hideout.

In the culture of the Navajos, the hand-trembler is used for the benefit of society and occupies a respected place.

**Hankey, Muriel, 1895–1978.** British psychical researcher. In 1915, as secretary to **J. Hewat McKenzie** she was introduced to Spiritualism and in that same year to **Gladys Osborne Leonard,** the famous medium. Over the next 45 years as sitter, proxy sitter, or recorder she had hundreds of sittings with Mrs. Leonard of whose integrity and sincerity she was convinced. Mrs. Hankey also accepted Mrs. Leonard's control, Feda, at face value as a separate entity.

In 1924, Mrs. Hankey met **Eileen Garrett** whom she considered the most "versatile, dedicated and accomplished" sensitive "in the field of psychical research" (Hankey, 1970:407). Mrs. Hankey's interest in mediumship was so great that at one time she "gave up a fixed job and spent two whole years devoted to note-taking at séances, mostly with Mrs. Leonard, and many with Mrs. Garrett" (Hankey, 1969:106).

Author of a biography of J. Hewat McKenzie (1963), Mrs. Hankey was a member of the council of the Society for Psychical Research from 1965 to 1970 and was principal of the College for Psychic Studies for seven years.

Selected Writings: 1970. "Mrs. Eileen Garrett." JSPR 45:406; 1969. "Mrs. Gladys Osborne Leonard: Some Reminiscences." JSPR 45:105; *James Hewat McKenzie. A Personal Memoir,* 1963.

BIBLIOGRAPHY: Heywood, R. 1978. "Mrs. Muriel Hankey." JSPR 49:824.

**Hansel, Charles Edward, 1917–.** British psychologist. Head of the Department of Psychology at the University of Wales at Swansea, he is one of the most formidable opponents of parapsychology to appear in the last two decades. His full-scale criticisms in 1966 and 1980 attacked the field and left it a smoking ruin.

Parapsychology "is even more beleaguered now than at any time in the past" (Berger, 1988:237) because recent scathing criticisms have come from well-informed sceptics such as Ray Hyman and Hansel. Hansel, a Fellow of the Committee for the Scientific Investigation of the Claims of the Paranormal, which looks on parapsychology as a "pseudoscience" anyway, launched the first of his attacks against certain key experiments that parapsychologists regard as providing them with a solid base supporting the existence of extrasensory perception (1966).

In his second attack (1980), he covered more of the same ground but enlarged his critique to include remote viewing and experiments conducted by Helmut H.W. Schmidt. Hansel began his critique with the assumption that extrasensory perception is impossible. He doggedly pursued his aim which was "to isolate the conclusive experiments and then to indicate that other explanations than ESP can account for their results" (Hansel, 1966:240). While he found no evidence of actual cheating, he concluded that "in the case of each of these experiments, the result could have arisen through a trick on the part of one or more of those taking part" (Hansel, 1966:240). Samuel G. Soal was one of the experimenters Hansel attacked, and, in Soal's case, Hansel's attack turned out to be justified.

The assumption of the impossibility of ESP and the mere suspicion of the possibility of fraud, however slight and even if not proved, makes it easy for sceptics to reason that no experiment can be genuine and that ESP does not exist. But few of those who read and accepted Hansel's work realized that he had not always been accurate factually and that he had often described experiments incorrectly in order to be able to question their results (Stevenson, 1967).

From a narrow parapsychological perspective, the work of this psychologist has greatly influenced many people to reject out of hand all psi research as fraudulent. From a wider perspective, however, Hansel's work is valuable because it is the first serious attempt since George R. Price to warn us to be alert against fraud and to examine all claims in parapsychology with a vigilant eye.

Selected Writings: *Esp and Parapsychology: A Critical Re-Evaluation,* 1980; *ESP: A Scientific Evaluation,* 1966.

BIBLIOGRAPHY: Berger, A.S. *Lives and Letters in American Parapsychology,* 1988; Stevenson, I. 1967. "An Antagonist's View of Parapsychology." JASPR 61:254.

**Hansen, George P., 1951–.** American parapsychologist. One of his main interests in parapsychology is **Dowsing,** a subject whose history and experimental investigation he examined (Hansen, 1982). He also has focussed much of his attention on **SORRAT** and reported, as have other parapsychologists (Berger, 1988:80–82), highly suspicious circumstances in connection with the "mini-lab" and with other claims made by the group (Hansen and Broughton, 1983).

Mr. Hansen has been a research fellow at the Institute for Parapsychology and technical associate for the Psychophysical Research Laboratories.

Selected Writings: 1982. "Dowsing: A Review of Experimental Research." JSPR 51:343; and Broughton, R.S. "An Investigation of Macro-PK: The Sorrat." In W.G. Roll, J. Beloff, and R.A. White, eds., *Research in Parapsychology 1982,* 1983, p. 115.

BIBLIOGRAPHY: Berger, A.S. *Evidence of Life After Death: A Casebook for the Tough-Minded,* 1988.

**Hanussen, Erik Jan (Hermann Steinschneider). 1889–1933.** Austrian self-styled "Prophet of the Third Reich." Flamboyant, self-aggrandizing, a consummate showman, he was a "mixture of real talent, fakery, misanthropism, and political compromise" (Raeder, 1988). Born in Vienna, he went into show business at the age of twelve. He learned conjuring and in 1917 wrote a book on the origins and practice of stage telepathy. Over the years he perfected the techniques of billet-reading and muscle-reading and demonstrated his abilities so well in a court of law that charges of fraudulent clairvoyance against him were dropped.

Although reputedly a Jew, Hanussen believed that Germany's future lay with Hitler and, before the latter's rise to power, prophesied, both in his stage performances throughout the country and in a tabloid he published, the historic inevitable destiny of a Nazi-dominated Europe. He committed himself completely to the Nazi cause. To ingratiate himself with the powers-to-be he lent large sums of money to Nazi officials and wangled an introduction to Hitler in 1931 who spoke to him about the importance of the occult. Goebbels, however, did not like him. On January 30, 1933, Hitler was named chancellor of Germany. On February 26 Hanussen opened his flamboyant "Palace of the Occult" with a prophetic vision of the burning of a large public building and the people's call for Hitler. On February 27, the Reichstag was burned; on February 28, Hitler declared himself dictator.

In the early weeks of Hitler's regime, Hanussen was "riding high," had his own Storm Trooper bodyguard, lived lavishly and expensively, secured favors for his friends and gloated over the discomfiture of his enemies. But when Hanussen asked Storm Trooper commander von Ohst to repay a debt, he had gone too far. On the evening of March 24, 1933, before his scheduled performance, Hanussen was arrested on the grounds of having used forged papers. On April 7 his partially decomposed body was found south of Berlin. He had been shot—either because he knew too much or was getting too greedy.

The prophet of the " 'Thousand Year Reich' whose birth he had prophesied . . . survived less than two months" after its inception (Ebon, 1968).

BIBLIOGRAPHY: Ebon, M. *Prophecy in Our Time,* 1968; Raeder, K. 1988. "Klaus Maria Brandauer." *European Travel and Life* 4(4):57.

**Haraldsson, Erlendur, 1931–.** Icelandic psychologist and parapsychologist. Originally a student of languages and philosophy at the University of Edinburgh in Scotland and at the University of Freiburg in Germany, he was a journalist in Reykjavik, Iceland, and a freelance writer in Berlin, the Middle East and Asia from 1958 to 1964.

His interest in psychical research and parapsychology led him to study psychology at the University of Freiburg and at the University of Munich from which he obtained his degree in 1969. He then (1969–1970) became a research fellow at Joseph B. Rhine's Institute for Parapsychology and did an internship in clinical psychology (1970–1971) at the Department of Psychiatry of the University of Virginia Medical School. Working under Hans Bender, in 1972 he received his Ph.D. from the University of Freiburg with a dissertation entitled "Vasomotoric Reactions as Indicators of Extrasensory Perception."

Dr. Haraldsson's interest and work in psychical research and parapsychology are equally divided among the study of spontaneous cases in Iceland, the evidence for survival after death, in connection with which he has studied mediums and the experiences of dying patients, and experimental research into "the relationships between physiological variables and ESP, the effects of feedback, dream recall, and personality and attitudinal variables in ESP performance" (1977:209). He is now undertaking research in Sri Lanka and India in cases of the reincarnation type.

The author of numerous papers in the parapsychological and psychological journals, he has also written four books, two of which—*Modern Miracles* (1988), on the Indian religious leader and "miracle worker" Sathya Sai Baba, and *At the Hour of Death* (1977) with Karlis Osis—have been published in English. *Modern Miracles* took ten years of research in India and was first published in German (1986). *At the Hour of Death,* a cross-cultural study (in the U.S. and India) of the experiences of dying patients, has been published in fourteen countries. The authors reported that "the dying do experience much that has some bearing on the question of postmortem survival—for example, having extrasensory glimpses of a possible afterlife" (p. 27).

Dr. Haraldsson was a research associate at the American Society for Psychical Research from 1972 to 1974, became assistant professor of psychology at the University of Iceland in 1974, an associate professor in 1978, and a full professor in 1988. He was visiting professor at the Department of Psychiatry of the University of Virginia Medical School for the scholastic year 1985–1986. In addition to membership in professional psychological associations, he is a member of the Parapsychological Association and of the Society for Psychical Research.

Selected Writings: *Modern Miracles,* 1988; 1985. "Representative National Surveys of Psychic Phenomena: Iceland, Great Britain, Sweden, USA and Gallup Multinational Survey." JSPR 53:145; 1981. "Some Determinants of Belief in Psychical Phenomena." JASPR 75:297; 1980. "Confirmation of the Percipient-Order Effect in a Plethysmographic Study of ESP." JP 44:105; and L.R. Gissurarson. 1988. "The Icelandic Medium Indridi Indridason." PSPR 58:1; and K. Osis, *At the Hour of Death,* 1977; and I. Stevenson. 1975. "A Communicator of the 'Drop In' Type in Iceland: The Case of Runolfur Runolfsson." JASPR 69:33.

**Harary, Keith (Stuart Blue), 1953–.** American psychologist, author, and parapsychological subject. Presently president and research director of the Institute for Advanced Psychology in San Francisco, Dr. Harary, who received his Ph.D. from Union Graduate School in 1986, is best known in parapsychology for his work as a subject in experiments dealing with the out-of-body experience and, particularly, for experiments in the early 1970s at the Psychical Research Foundation (as Stuart Blue Harary) in which he seemed while out of body to interact with a kitten. Another widely publicized feat was the successful predicting of silver futures for a commercial client while he was a partner with **Russell Targ** in Delphi Associates (1982–1986) whose purpose was the practical applications of psi.

Known as Keith Harary since 1982, he would like to bring the study of both human and animal **(Anpsi)** psi into scientific research. He has theorized (1982a) that psi is "a lawful process which permeates nature," that there is no distinction between subjectively experienced psi and the study of psi in the laboratory. He has tried, in addition, to educate the public about psi research and to make expansive psychological experiences available to the public. To this end, he has co-authored a psychological approach to inducing and exploring the out-of-body experience (Harary and Weintraub, 1989a) and another similar approach to inducing and exploring lucid dreams (Harary and Weintraub, 1989b). Harary is also concerned with ethical guidelines for psychical and parapsychological researchers. He urges that terms such as "parapsychology," "extrasensory perception," and "paranormal," for example, be avoided and that expressions such as "mental noise," "extended perception," and "associative targeting" be introduced. He has also investigated clinical issues relating to psi and has used psychological counseling to eliminate the sighting of an apparition (1982b).

Dr. Harary has written for both parapsychological and popular publications and is the co-author with Russell Targ of *Mind Race* whose conclusions, he now says, are outdated. He is currently writing a book on his new material as well as editing an anthology dealing with the clinical side of psi. He has lectured before the USSR Academy of Sciences and is a member, among other organizations, of the American Psychological Association, the American Association for the Advancement of Science, the American Society for Psychical Research, the Society for Psychical Research and the Parapsychological Association.

Selected Writings: and Weintraub, P. *The Free Flight Program,* 1989a; and Weintraub, P. *The Creative Sleep Program,* 1989b; "Psi as Nature." In W.G. Roll, R.L.Morris and R.A. White, eds., *Research in Parapsychology, 1981,* 1982a, pp. 75–78; "The Marshmallow Ghost." In W.G. Roll, R.L. Morris and R. A. White, eds., *Research in Parapsychology, 1981,* 1982b, pp. 187–189; "A Personal Perspective on Out-of-Body Experiences." In D. Scott Rogo, ed., *Mind Beyond the Body,* 1978; and R. Targ, *Mind Race,* 1985.

**Hardy, Sir Alister, 1896-1985.** Eminent British marine biologist. Populating the restless seas and oceans that cover almost three-quarters of the surface of the earth are life forms more fantastic than even Jules Verne could have imagined. But it was for something more than these that Hardy searched on his extensive voyages as a marine biologist. He was searching for a certain prestige that would allow him to act as the advocate of religion against orthodox scientists who viewed the world as a blindly moving machine.

He found what he needed by becoming professor of zoology at Hull and Oxford Universities, by writing the two-volume *The Open Sea* (1956 and 1958), and by founding the Religious Experience Research Unit, now called the Alister Hardy Research Centre, at Manchester College in Oxford. The object of the centre is to study and record human religious experiences and their importance. Hardy was drawn to psychical research because he thought that it was "one of the most important branches of investigation that the human mind has ever undertaken" (Hardy, 1965). He believed that its findings might revolutionize the outlook of biologists and that telepathy might be a factor in the molding of behavior patterns. He also wanted to uncover the relationship between extrasensory perception and religious experience. He believed that the discovery that people might be in telepathic connection across space might be one of the most revolutionary ever made.

If only 1 percent of the money now expended on the biological and physical sciences were to be applied instead to religious experience and to investigations in psychical research he maintained, we would not have long to wait for the dawning of a new age of faith.

He served as president of the Society for Psychical Research from 1965 to 1969.

Selected Writings: *The Divine Flame,* 1966; *The Living Stream,* 1965; 1953. "Biology and Psychical Research." PSPR 50:96; 1950. "Telepathy and Evolutionary Theory." JSPR 35:225.

**Hare, Robert, 1781–1858.** American chemist. He set out "to bring whatever influence he possessed to the attempt to stem the tide of popular madness which, in defiance of reason and science, was fast setting in in favour of the gross delusion called Spiritualism" (quoted in Doyle, 1968:172). He used spring balances and other equipment in experiments to trap fraudulent mediums. But soon he found himself going along with the tide "of popular madness" and accepting the revelations made by the spirits. One of them, for example, described the spirit world as made up of six spheres not counting the earth, the last sphere being exactly 120 miles above the surface of the earth.

Hare became one of the strong supporters of the movement he planned to destroy. His published experiments and conclusions (Hare, 1855) are used by Spiritualists as impressive authority favorable to their cause. Although Hare was emeritus professor of chemistry at the University of Pennsylvania and a noted inventor, he was "boycotted and bullied by the American Scientific Association" (Doyle, 1968:172) because, Sir Arthur Conan Doyle thought, Hare had become convinced that Spiritualism was absolutely justified. The real reason may have been, however, that Hare took too much at face value and "seems not to have thought of such a things as careful sifting and criticism of the evidence for spirit existence, much less to have established any criteria for determining the validity of statements about the spiritual world" (Hyslop, 1919:339)

Selected Writing: *Experimental Investigation of the Spirit Manifestations,* 1855.

BIBLIOGRAPHY: Doyle, A.C. *The Edge of the Unknown, 1968*\1930; Hyslop, J. H. *Contact with the Other World,* 1919.

**Harribance, Lalsingh (Sean), 1940–.** West Indian psychic. After he gained fame in Trinidad for his readings, Harribance came to the United States to be tested for his psychic gifts by the Institute for Parapsychology and the Psychical Research Foundation. At the PRF, he was given concealed photographs. His task was to guess the sexes of the people in the pictures. The results showed statistically significant evidence of extransensory perception. Harribance is one of the rare breed of psychics who are eager to have their abilities verified scientifically—and it proved profitable for him since he now frequents horse races and uses his confirmed psychic gifts to pick winners (Cantwell, 1977).

BIBLIOGRAPHY: Cantwell, R. 1977. "Win, Place and Glow." *Sports Illustrated* 7:32.

**Hart, Hornell Norris, 1888–1967.** American sociologist. Hornell Hart's principal interest in psychical research was the study of spontaneous cases of apparitions, particularly as they relate to the question of survival after death. His eventual belief in the survival of consciousness after bodily death was based on his studies of out-of-body experiences. His wife, Ella Brockhauser, shared his interests. Together they published (in 1933) a long paper entitled "Visions and Apparitions Collectively and Reciprocally Perceived" in which they concluded that the reality of such apparitions had been demonstrated and that apparitions of the dead are evidence for survival.

Hart developed an interesting five-dimensional explanation of the universe that he expounded both in JASPR (1953) and in a monograph (whose philosophical speculations John Beloff [1966] criticized sharply) published by the Parapsychology Foundation. He wrote that "in the five-dimensional psychic continuum there is room for all dreams, all memories, all imaginative fictions, all visualized plans, all heavens, hells and purgatories, the astral world of the Theosophists, and the 'branching time-lines' of the science-fictioneers."

In 1959 his book entitled *The Enigma of Survival* was published. At the time of his death he had just completed a book entitled *Survival After Death* that he considered his most important contribution to parapsychology and which superseded his earlier book. Sadly, with his death, this manuscript seems to have disappeared.

Hornell Hart was a professor of sociology at Duke University from 1938 until his forced retirement in 1957 because of the university's compulsory retirement rule. During his twenty years at Duke he took a keen interest in the work going on at the Parapsychology Laboratory there and became friends with the staff, notably J.B. Rhine and J.G. Pratt.

He was an outspoken person who, despite threats, dared to challenge McCarthyism. To its credit, the university administration backed him in his position. After his retirement from Duke he was, in turn, John Hay Whitney Professor of Sociology at Centre College of Kentucky and chairman of the Sociology Department of Florida Southern College. He contributed many papers and reviews to the *Journal of the American Society for Psychical Research* and to the *Journal* and *Proceedings* of the Society for Psychical Research.

He was a charter member of the Parapsychological Association and member of both the British and American Societies for Psychical Research See also **Persona Hypothesis** and **Super ESP**.

Selected Writings: *Toward a New Philosophical Basis for Parapsychological Phenomena,* 1965; *The Enigma of Survival,* 1959; 1956. "Six Theories about Apparitions." PSPR 50:153; 1953. "The Psychic Fifth Dimension." JASPR 47:3 and 47:47; and Hart, E.B. 1933. "Visions and Apparitions Collectively and Reciprocally Perceived." PSPR 41:205.

BIBLIOGRAPHY: Beloff, J. 1966. "Review." JSPR 43:317; Nicol, F. 1967. "Obituary: Professor Hornell Hart." JSPR 44:165; Pratt, J.G. 1968. "In Memory of Hornell Hart: A Personal Appreciation." JASPR 62:80.

**Hastings, Arthur, 1935–.** American professor at the Institute for Transpersonal Psychology. He provides parapsychological counseling and therapy to people who are troubled by their psychic experiences. Although his work and articles are concentrated on this form of therarpy (Hastings, 1983), his interests extend to channeling whose phenomena he believes are relevant to the nature of personality, depth psychology, models of nonphysical realities, and transpersonal processes (Hastings, 1987). Hastings also has studied remote viewing and the poltergeist. He could find no normal explanation for one poltergeist case in which electric typewriters in the office of a court reporter repeatedly malfunctioned despite numerous repairs and eight telephones kept falling off the desks on which they had been placed.

Selected Writing: "The Study of Channeling." In D.H. Weiner and R.D. Nelson, eds., *Research in Parapsychology 1986,* 1987, p. 151; 1983. "A Counselng Approach to Parapsychological Experience." *Journal of Transpersonal Psychology* 15:145.

**Haunt.** No one who has tried has been able to sleep peacefully through the night in the corner bedroom next to the study on the first floor of Hannath Hall near Wisbech, England. For, so the rumor goes, it was in this large brick farmhouse built in the nineteenth century by Jonathan Hannath, that his wife lay for six weeks after her death while, at Hannath's stern command, obedient but trembling servants brought meals to the corpse. In the summer and fall of 1957, tenants in the house heard early morning crashes on the bedroom door, taps in the rooms on the second floor, footsteps, groans, and raps. So terrible were her dreams that one member of the family could not bear to remain in the house. **Anthony Cornell** and **Alan Gauld,** two parapsychologists sent by the Society for Psychical Research to investigate the reported haunt, spent the night in the bedroom described by legend as the corpse's dining room. About 1:30 A.M., they heard gentle taps followed by raps that gradually became louder. The raps were responsive to the investigator's questions. Rapping once for "yes" and twice for "no," "it" identified itself as a woman who had met foul play in the house near the turn of the century. The investigators could assign no visible, normal cause to these phenomena or to any of the other equally mysterious occurrences they and others observed over a period of several visits to the place from 1957 to 1960.

Hannath Hall is fairly representative of a haunt. But a haunt need not be confined to a house or to the auditory phenomena noted in this case. For a haunt may be defined more generally as any place, whether house, palace, rectory, garden, or other location, where apparently any or all of the following paranormal phenomena have been experienced over a long period of time by one or more living people: visual—such as apparitions; auditory—such as footsteps, blows on walls, moving furniture, groans, cries; and tactile—including cool touches, winds, or shudders.

The phenomena occurring at haunts are different from poltergeist phenomena. The latter seem usually to be connected to an individual and are sudden, unexpected, comparatively short-lived. Haunting phenomena, on the other hand, seem to be connected to a place rather than to a person, may be witnessed by many individuals as in Hannath Hall, and may extend over years as they were purported to have done at Borley rectory and in the case of the "Morton Ghost".

It is commonly supposed that such phenomena are produced by deceased persons. A theory favored by many parapsychologists, however, is that the location may contain impressions of prior occupants which the ESP of living people pick up later and project as apparitions, noises, or sensations.

**Haynes, Renée, (Mrs. Jerrard Tickell), 1906–.** British author and editor. A witty and charming writer and conversationalist, this great-granddaughter of T. H. Huxley coined the now generally used phrase "the boggle threshold" ("There's glory for you," she wrote in a letter to Arthur S. Berger in 1988). A "recognition of significant form in art and nature, in sensory and in extrasensory perception, together with Croce's argument that beauty cannot be proved or disproved by the scientific method, helped me to yield," she writes (1985) "to an increasing conviction that . . . scientific materialism . . . could not explain the universe at large, that living was not a meaningless process, and that reality inhered in God."

Her principal interests in psychical research are spontaneous experiences—telepathy, retro- and precognition, mind-body and parent-child interactions—and historical instances of psi. She says that she is less interested in mass experiments and statistical evaluations and feels that there is "undue reverance for that sacred object the computer" (1987). Indeed, alleged proof by computer of Samuel G. Soal's fraud has left her unconvinced.

Ms. Haynes believes that "psi is interwoven with the general nature of things" and has herself had many trivial experiences as well as some vivid precognitive dreams—of apes, of Greek gods, of black and white cattle, and of a procession of mentally handicapped boys, for example.

As editor (1970–1981) of the *Journal of the Society for Psychical Research*—she joined the society in 1946—she emphasized the importance of writing in a language all educated people, not just mathematicians or physicists, can understand. She has contributed chapters to many books and has written numerous articles in a variety of publications, including *The Christian Parapsychologist, Theta, Parapsychology Review, The International Journal of Parapsychology, Fate,* JSPR and others. Her books include a history of human beliefs and attitudes about psi from ancient times to the present day (1961); a work whose subtitle reflects its subject matter; *Perception, Sensory and Extrasensory* (1976); a history of the Society for Psychical Research (1982); and, perhaps her favorite, *Philosopher King: The Humanist Pope Benedict XIV* (1970) who wrote a long treatise on psychical phenomena in which he "distinguished very clearly between occurrences that could . . . be explained by science, occurrences due to paranormal causes, and occurrences that could be ascribed to the direct action of God. . ." (1987:107).

Renée Haynes received her B.A. and M.A. degrees from Oxford. She is a vice president of the SPR and is on its council, is a member of the Alistair Hardy Research Centre and the Churches' Fellowship for Psychical and Spiritual Studies. She is also interested in the work of the Scientific and Medical Network.

Selected Writings: "Aspects of Psychical Research." In R. Pilkington, ed., *Men and Women of Parapsychology,* 1987; 1985–6 "A Life-Long Look at Psi." *Theta* 13/14:14; *The Society for Psychical Research 1882–1982: A History,* 1982; *The Seeing Eye, the Seeing I,* 1976; *Philosopher King,* 1970; *The Hidden Springs,* 1961.

**Healing.** See **Healing, Unorthodox.**

**Healing, Unorthodox.** Sometimes called "alternative," "psychic," or "spiritual" healing. The act or process of curing that is not compatible with principles accepted by conventional or orthodox medicine in a particular society. Such healing can be divided into three basic types: "faith-healing," such as the healings reported at Lourdes; "mind-cure," such as are said to take place in **Christian Science;** "Spirit-cures," where the healings are attributed to the spirits of deceased doctors or other spiritual helpers. Those who purport to have the power of unorthodox healing are known as "healers."

Reports of miraculous healings have echoed through the ages. The Greco-Roman god of medicine, Aesculepius, who learned the healing arts from a centaur, effected countless cures by prescribing medications for the sick. Apollonius of Tyana, who lived in the first century A.D., performed healing wonders similar to **Jesus Christ's.**

For a long time, psychical research and parapsychology failed to pay attention to healing because many claims could be dismissed as trickery or lacked authentication and evidential value. Healings were discounted as being caused by suggestion (without explaining how or why suggestion works). Reasons advanced for the healing process, such as God, immortal Mind, spirit, or some species of energy, have been thought too nebulous to be taken seriously.

But in recent years the light of parapsychological inquiry has been turned on the area of health and healing. The evidence from Lourdes and Christian Science strongly suggests that medically inexplicable healings occur at least some of the time. Sometimes, suddenly, "the blind see and the lame walk" so that some unknown element of mysterious origin and character seems to be in operation. In addition, experiments have been conducted that seem to suggest the existence of the healing phenomenon (i.e., when "healers" perform certain acts), either physical or mental, there is a positive alteration in the "healee's" physical condition that, in the normal course of events, could not have been predicted. Western observers also have testified to **Qigong** healing in the People's Republic of China. Qigong practitioners are said to channel "qi" or vital energy into their palms and then apply it to pressure points on the bodies of their patients.

**Lawrence Le Shan** has separated unorthodox healers into two types: Type 1 in which healers in altered states of consciousness attain the **"Clairvoyant Reality"** where they feel a "oneness" with healees and healing takes place; and Type 2 in which a healer's hands appear to be the means of restoring health. Le Shan's healing theories and techniques have attracted many followers.

Included under the heading of unorthodox healing are apparently skillful and successful acts of surgery by healers, for example, removal of tumors previously diagnosed as inoperable, performed without anesthesia, gloves, hemostatic procedure, and with dirty knives or unsterilized razors. Generally, such successful healing procedures are without postoperative infections. Although sleight-of-hand, rather than actual surgery, may be involved (Randi, [1980] assures us that that is all that is ever involved), some people are cured, perhaps because of a combination of motivation, expectation, and commitment. Many healing practioners, as in the cases of **Harry Edwards** and **Jose Arigo,** claim to be directed in their diagnoses and procedures by spirit doctors or guides.

The success rate claimed by healers is fantastic—Edwards, for instance, claimed that 85 percent of the many thousands who had been treated by him had been benefitted. A British psychiatrist, however, investigated ninety cases in which a healer or patient claimed that, after orthodox medicine had failed, the healer had improved or cured the patient's condition. The investigator found that the claims for fifty-eight cases could not be confirmed, that in twenty-two cases there was a considerable variance between the records and the claims, in three cases improvement was followed by relapse, in four, improvement occurred when healing and orthodox treatment were given concurrently, and in one case there was no benefit. In just a single case had an organic disability been helped or cured (Rose, 1955).

Such findings seem contradicted by Lourdes, Christian Science, healing experiments, and qigong. But even if there were little empirical data to substantiate the claims of healers, thousands of people who have received no benefit from or have been cast out by orthodox medicine are persuaded that they are helped or believe that there is a prospect of help. This in itself is a good that should not be dismissed.

The phenomenon of unorthodox healing is an outstanding candidate for study by psychical researchers because of its genuine importance to human welfare and because it may point to our possession of powers that transcend our physical beings. After all, most proponents of unorthodox healing believe that "ultimately, all healing is self-healing." Such a study may determine how to clear away the blockage between our minds and bodies, perhaps between our world and other worlds.

BIBLIOGRAPHY: Eisenberg, D. with Wright, L.T. *Encounters with Qi,* 1985; Grad, B. 1965. "Some Biological Effects of the 'Laying on of Hands.'" JASPR 59:95. Le Shan, L. *The Medium, the Mystic and the Physicist,* 1966; Puharich, H.K. "Psychic Research and the Healing Process." In Mitchell, E. (J. White, ed.). *Psychic Explorations,* 1976; Quing Nan, Z. 1985. "Qigong- Ancient Way to Good Health." *China Reconsructs* 34(7):56; Randi, J. *Flim-Flam!* 1980; Rose, L. 1955. "Some Aspects of Paranormal Healing." JSPR 38 105; Watkins, G.K. and Watkins, A.M. 1971. "Resuscitation of Anesthetized Mice." JP 35:251.

**Heard, Gerald, 1889–1971.** British mystic, author, philosopher, and UFOlogist. Long interested in psychical research, Gerald Heard was a member of the council of the Society for Psychical Research in the 1930s and, in 1933, with Theodore Besterman investigated the claim that at times direct voice phenomena occurred during sittings with Gladys Osborne Leonard. (Their results were negative).

In 1934 Heard participated in a series of radio broadcasts on psychical research, the other participants being Lord Charles Hope, Dame Edith Lyttleton, Sir Oliver Lodge and C.D. Broad. He has been described as "an adventurer upon the frontiers of knowledge, and . . . an adventurer unusually well equipped, by wide reading in many fields . . . Mr. Heard takes the findings of parapsychology fully into account . . . not only the assured facts but also the margin where those facts shade off into hypotheses, and where the work of Rhine and Soal has to be given its place beside that of the most recent physicists and astronomers" (Grensted, 1950: 347–8). Heard himself, speaking of psychical research, said: "No other inquiry and research is more promising or more pressing. . ." (1953a:122).

In 1950, after six years of study, Heard came to the conclusion that UFOs are really out there, that they come from Mars, that the Martians are probably "super-bees" approximately two inches long and that they are hovering over us as "companions—yes, and possibly guides—minds that have gone ahead of ours. . . . There seems . . . no . . . right and adequate reason . . . why we should refuse . . . the present possibility that hangs over us" (1953b:181–2).

Selected Writings: 1953a. "A Philosophical Scrutiny of Religion. By C. J. Ducasse." JASPR 47:119; *Is Another World Watching?* 1953b; and T. Besterman. 1933. "Note on an Attempt to Locate in Space the Alleged Direct Voice Observed in Sittings with Mrs Leonard." JSPR 28:84.

BIBLIOGRAPHY: Grensted, L.W. "Is God Evident? An Essay towards a Natural Theology. By Gerald Heard." JSPR 35:346; Haynes, R. *The Society for Psychical Research 1882–1982,* 1982.

**Helmholtz, Herman von, 1821–1894.** German scientist. A professor of physics at the University of Berlin and director of the Physico-Technical Institute of Berlin, he studied the function and structure of the eye, invented the opthalmoscope and contributed to the knowledge of optics. He also increased understanding of the electron, physiology, mathematics, electrodynamics, and established the principle of conservation of energy. Helmholtz rightfully is accorded recognition as a great scientist.

Yet he refused absolutely to look at evidence he did not wish to accept or at facts that might compel him to reevaluate his preconceptions. Thus did Helmholtz tell Sir William Barrett in a conversation about telepathy: "I cannot believe it. Neither the testimony of all the Fellows of the Royal Society, nor even the evidence of my own senses would lead me to believe in the transmission of thought from one person to another independently of the recognized channels of sensations. It is clearly impossible" (Barrett, 1904). Helmholz is an extreme example of the conceptual sceptic.

BIBLIOGRAPHY: Barrett, W.F. 1904. "Address by the President." PSPR 18:323.

**Herne, Frank, c.1850–?.** British professional physical medium of the 1870s. He is remembered because of his relationships with the famous scientist William Crookes and the medium Florence Cook. In 1871 and through at least 1873 he was in partnership with Charles Williams. On April 11, 1871, Crookes attended a joint sitting of Herne, D.D. Home and Charles Williams at which Crookes reported all sorts of remarkable phenomena (which, however, he attributed to Home's presence). In 1872 Herne gave joint sittings with Florence Cook, but in these sittings phenomena, including materializations, were produced when neither he nor she was under any restraint.

Herne and Williams were supposed to have been the subjects in successful spirit photographs taken by a Mr. Russell, but neither prints nor negatives were ever produced to corroborate their claims and Herne was accused on other occasions with the photographer Frederick A. Hudson of having "sat for the ghost" which appeared on other "spirit" photographs. In December of 1875, Herne was caught impersonating the spirit "John King."

BIBLIOGRAPHY: Medhurst, R.G. and Goldney, K. M. 1964. "William Crookes and the Physical Phenomena of Mediumship." PSPR 54:25; Sidgwick, E.M. "On Spirit Photographs; A Reply to Mr. A.R. Wallace." PSPR 7:268, 271–272.

**Hettinger, John, 1880–?.** British electrical engineer. In the 1930s, he pioneered and conducted experimental investigations in

**Psychometry** in which he used highly inventive methods to discover and evaluate the phenomenon. One was to get from their owners various objects, such as keys, combs, letters, or pencils, and place them in sealed envelopes. An envelope would be given to a psychic who, without opening it, would make statements about the absent owner of the article. The statements were recorded and then sent on to the owner for comment. Hettinger found that about 40 percent of the statements were correct and this suggested to him what he called "the ultraperceptive faculty" (Hettinger, 1940).

Another method used by Hettinger was to test for both psychometry and **Telepathy.** He would ask a subject to look at an illustrated magazine at a prearranged time for the experiment. Subjects were to mark each page with the time when they perused the pictures or articles on the page. Simultaneously, a psychic miles away would be handed a sealed envelope in which there was an object belonging to the subject and Hettinger recorded the impressions the psychic described. The psychic's impressions were then compared with the picture or article on the page perused by the subject. Hettinger found many resemblances between the psychic's description and the material looked at by the subject (Hettinger, 1941).

His reports were widely read and generally accepted by the public. But parapsychological reactions were antipodal. On the one side, Hettinger's work was said to have "established the phenomenon with a very high degree of probability" (Johnson, 1953: 175) but, on the other, his experimental techniques were sharply criticized and the conclusion reached "that very little weight can be attached to any of the evidence put forward in these reports" (Scott, 1949:49). In spite of the division of parapsychological opinion concerning Hettinger's investigations, there seems an ample body of evidence supporting the existence of psychometry.

Selected Writings: *Exploring the Ultra-Perceptive Faculty,* 1941; *The Ultra Perceptive Faculty,* 1940.

BIBLIOGRAPHY: Scott, C. 1949. "Experimental Object-Reading: A Critical Review of the Work of Dr. J. Hettinger." PSPR 49:16; Johnson, R.C. *Imprisoned Splendour,* 1953.

**Heymans, Gerardus, 1857–1930.** Dutch psychologist and philosopher. He was a pioneer in experimental parapsychology in The Netherlands. In 1919, with Henri J.F.W. Brugmans, he conducted tests in telepathy at the Psychology Department of the University of Groningen with a gifted subject. The blindfolded student sat before a board resembling a checkerboard whose rows were identified by numbers and whose columns by the letters A to H. His task was to hit the target square that had been predetermined before a trial by one expermenter's picking a slip from each of two bags, one containing slips with numbers, one with slips with the letters A to H.

Although parapsychologists long cited the experiment as evidence of extrasensory perception because it was so well designed, its precautions were rigorous, and the results astonishing (60 hits out of 187 trials), Sybo Schouten and Edward F. Kelly (1978) reanalyzed the experiments and concluded that the results could have been produced by the motor automatism of the subject.

Heymans later founded the **Studievereniging Voor Psychical Research.**

Selected Writing: and Brugmans, H.J.F.W., and Weinberg, A. "Une communication sur des expériences télépathiques au laboratoire de psychologie à Groningue." *Compte Rendu Officiel du Premier Congrès International des Recherches Psychiques,* 1922, p. 396.

BIBLIOGRAPHY: Schouten, S.A. and Kelly, E.F. 1978. "On the Experiments of Brugmans, Heymans and Weinberg." *European Journal of Parapsychology* 2:247.

**Heywood, Rosalind (Hedley), 1895–1980.** British psychic and psychical researcher. Her first experiences with ESP came during World War I when, as a nurses' aide, she would get what she called "Orders—for want of a better word . . . they were confident and not initiated by my conscious self" (Heywood, 1982:66). These "orders"—"Do this, do that"—were always right. Often they told her of unorthodox ways to treat dying patients who then recovered. During her wartime service, she also had her first experiences with telepathy and deathbed visions.

After her marriage in 1921 to Frank Heywood, whom she had met in Macedonia during the war and who became a member of the British diplomatic corps, her interest in psychic matters increased because of the frequent telepathic exchanges between her and her husband. She was sure that if she and her husband were in telepathic contact, then others are as well. In the early 1920s she had an out-of-body experience whose result was a sort of split personality. "When I have been aware of duality in myself," she wrote (1982:76), "the split seemed to be because a hidden part of me wanted to act on information which the conscious part did not possess." She felt it was a mistake to make a sharp distinction between sensory perception and extrasensory perception and that people are more likely to have psychic experiences if they accept them as possible. She wrote that "conscious attention and effort inhibit the emergence of ESP impressions" and that one "must really *want* to communicate at moments when sensory methods of doing so are not available" (1982:80). She also felt that in psychical research "'we keep asking the wrong questions.' . . . [I]nstead of asking [for example] 'What is an apparition?' [we] should be asking 'What is man?'" (MacKenzie, 1980)

In 1938 she joined the Society for Psychical Research and from that time forward until her death was an active member, cooperating in experiments and writing many articles for the society's *Journal.* In 1959 she wrote an excellent book on psychical research in which she discussed both quantitative and qualititative methods, and in 1964 she published her psychic autobiography.

Selected Writings: "Autobiography." In R.A. McConnell, ed., *Encounters with Parapsychology,* 1982; *The Sixth Sense: An Enquiry into Extra-sensory Perception,* (American edition entitled *Beyond the Reach of Sense*) 1959\1971; *The Infinite Hive* (American edition entitled *ESP: A Personal Memoir*), 1964\1972.

BIBLIOGRAPHY: Haynes, R. 1980. "Rosalind Heywood 1895–1980." JSPR 50:521; MacKenzie, A. 1980. "Talks with Rosalind Heywood." JSPR 50:523; Vaughan, A. 1973. "Interview; Rosalind Heywood." *Psychic* 5(2):6.

**High Variance.** See **Variance, High.**

**Hit.** An accurate **Call.**

**Hitler, Adolph (Adolf Schicklegruber), 1889–1945.** Der Fuehrer of the Third Reich. An Austrian painter of posters and an obscure orderly in a Bavarian infantry regiment in the first World War, he became founder and leader of the National Socialist party and absolute dictator of Germany. By the time he had committed suicide in a bunker in Berlin on April 3, 1945, the face of the world had been covered with blood and changed permanently.

Anyone who has seen or heard Hitler's angry and passionate harangues gets the feeling that he was a master hypnotist who had the power to influence a nation to become his fanatic followers. Hitler believed that Providence had sent him and that he was the divine presence in the form of a man. His followers proclaimed his divinity.

On July 24, 1944, an attempt was made on his life: A time bomb went off at a staff meeting attended by Hitler and his officers. Many were killed. Hitler, only slightly wounded, said: "Who says I am not under the special protection of God?"

Hitler was supposed to have his personal astrologer and to make decisions and predictions based on horoscopes. The British even employed their own astrologers in an attempt to find out what Hitler was being told.

The Nazis used prophesy as a propaganda tool. The prophesies of **Nostradamus** on the basis of which they predicted that they were going to win World War II were circulated throughout Germany and France. The prophet who had the greatest influence in Hitlerite Germany was Hans Horbiger with his doctrine of the eternal ice or Cosmic Ice, which explained the origins of the solar system and the Earth, and the beginning and destiny of the Aryan race. Although contrary to astronomy and mathematics, Horbiger's doctrine received Hitler's support as a Nordic and Nazi science as opposed to Jewish-liberal science. Hitler's adherence to the doctrine influenced the war in the Soviet Union. Horbiger predicted that the winter of 1941 would be mild. In addition, Hitler's own mystical belief was that the ice and cold could not resist him or his armies. But in December 1941, the weather went against prophesy and mysticism and Hitler's soldiers, with only a pair of gloves and a scarf to protect them, retreated or froze.

Hitler's *Mein Kampf* discloses his belief that he came by information and knowledge he had no ordinary way of knowing through visions, hunches, and intuition, all likely instances of extrasensory perception. When he was soldiering in the trenches of World War I, for example, a voice told him to get out before an explosion buried him under the earth. He obeyed it; as soon as he did so a grenade exploded and buried his comrades who were at the position he had just vacated. Another instance occurred on November 8, 1939, when Hitler gave a speech at the Buergerbrau Keller in Munich. His life was saved again because he left ahead of schedule just before a bomb which killed and injured many exploded next to the podium where he had been standing. **Jan Ehrenwald,** who heard the speech, described it as "heavily laden with premonitions of impending death for some of those present" (Ehrenwald, 1984). Again, in February 1945, when Hitler had moved his Chancery to a bunker in Berlin, Albert Speer, Hitler's minister for war production and armaments, planned to introduce poison gas into the bunker to kill Hitler and negotiate a peace. But immediately prior to the plan's being put into execution, Hitler issues unexpected orders to build a chimney which connected to an air vent. These examples hint strongly that Hitler might have had psychic gifts and make him a **Noted Witness** for precognition or telepathy.

The account of H. Rauschning, one of Hitler's followers and governor of Danzig (now Gdansk), Poland, describes some of Hitler's strange experiences which suggest that Hitler was a noted witness for possession and apparitions. Rauschning said that Hitler "wakes up in the night screaming and in convulsions. He calls for help, and appears to be half paralyzed. He is seized with a panic that makes him tremble until the bed shakes." And again: "Hitler was standing up in his room, swaying and looking all around him as if he were lost. . . . His lips were white; he was sweating profusely. . . . It was terrifying. He used strange expressions strung together in bizarre order. . . . Then suddenly he screamed: 'There! there! Over in the corner! He is there!'—all the time stamping with his feet and shouting." (Pauwels and Bergier, 1960).

Besides his testimony as a noted witness, Hitler's case is of interest and concern to psychical research because it involves mysticism, intuition, hunches, and paranormal gifts and experiences gone wrong. Their use by such a man gives powerful ammunition to all who want to keep the occult, mystical, and psychic at arm's length for fear of their use for evil. Hitler is a prime example of the horrors that can be produced when the psychic and the mystical are combined in a demagogue who imagines himself on a divine mission.

Strangely, although the Fuehrer gave every indication of being psychic and was interested in astrology and the occult, his regime brought German parapsychology to an end. The parapsychological journal founded by **Alexander N. Aksakoff** as *Psychische Studien* but at that time called *Zeitschrift für Parapsychologie* was forbidden and punitive action was taken against many of the leaders of parapsychology such as Hans Driesch. See also **Hanussen, E.J.**

BIBLIOGRAPHY: Ehrenwald, J. *Anatomy of Genius,* 1984, p. 193; Heiden, K. *Der Fuehrer,* 1944, p. 758; Pauwels, L. and Bergier, J. *The Morning of the Magicians,* 1968, pp. 219–220.

## Hodgson, Richard, 1855–1905.

Australian-born psychical researcher. He had three loves, but, although he had an LL.D. from the University of Melborune, none of them included the law, which he thought "horrid." Neither did they include women. In fact, Hodgson seemed to keep himself away from all fleshly pursuits (Berger, 1988). He was a terrible prude who once said that the only virtuous women in Cambridge were the stone monuments on its courthouse. His true loves were poetry, philosophy, and psychical research. Reading about Spiritualism had sparked his interest in the field, and, once in England, he was active in an undergraduate society at the University of Cambridge that investigated paranormal phenomena.

In 1884, Hodgson was sent to India by the Society for Psychical Research to investigate Madame H.P. Blavatsky and the Theosophical Society of which she was the founder and leader. Hodgson's conclusion was that all the marvellous phenomena connected with the Theosophical Society were part of a huge scheme concocted by Madame Blavatsky and that she was a fraud. True or false, the report effectively finished her as far as parapsychology was concerned. Her followers screamed at the time at the dishonor cast upon their movement and the name of their founder, and they do still. Today, Hodgson's report continues to stir the flame of heated controversy even among those who are not Theosophists. Vernon Harrison (1986) has claimed, for example, that Hodgson acted in bad faith and "bamboozled" the SPR. Conversely others (Coleman 1987 and Berger 1988) have maintained that he was justified in his report.

In a non-controversial highly praised investigation of slate-writing (1887) Hodgson showed that witnesses can be guilty of poor memory and malobservation.

Impressed by Hodgson's report on the phenomena associated with **Theosophy,** the American Society for Psychical Research offered him its secretaryship. He accepted the post in 1887. Under his management, the ASPR began to make tangible progress. Hodgson became obsessed with the medium Leonora Piper and devoted almost all his time and energy to observations of her mediumship. At first he considered the evidence supplied through her insufficient to establish the reality of survival after death. Gradually, however, skepticism was overcome by messages which convinced him that the personalities purporting to communicate through her were truly personalities who had survived death.

Hodgson also examined the report of researchers who had investigated the physicial medium Eusapia Palladino and himself sat with her. Finding at this sitting that she maneuvered one of her hands, he declared that all her phenomena—wherever and whenever—produced fraudulent results.

In 1905, while playing handball Hodgson dropped dead. One of the most critical and hard-headed of the early workers in psychical research, Hodgson received William James's tribute as a "man among men."

Selected Writings: 1898. "A Further Record of Observations of Certain Phenomena of Trance." PSPR 13:284; 1895. "The Value of the Evidence for Supernormal Phenomena in the Case of Eusapia Paladino [*sic*]." JSPR 7:36; 1887. "The Possibilities of Malobservation and Lapse of Memory from a Practical Point of View." PSPR 4:381; 1885. "An Account of Personal Investigations in India, and Discussion of the Authorship of the 'Koot Hoomi' Letters." PSPR 3:207.

BIBLIOGRAPHY: Berger, A.S. *Lives and Letters in American Parapsychology,* 1988; Coleman, M.H. 1987. "Correspondence." JSPR 54:158; Harrison, V. 1986. "J'Accuse. An Examination of the Hodgson Report." JSPR 53:286.

**Hodgson Memorial Fund.** Created in 1912 at Harvard University, it was the first stride made in the United States toward the recognition of psychical research by an American university. It was set up by individuals who wanted to commemorate the life and achievements of **Richard Hodgson** and to provide money for the investigation of those "mental or physical phenomena the origin or expression of which appears to be independent of the ordinary sensory channels." Henry James, Jr., son of William James, acted as attorney for the contributors and transmitted to Harvard on their behalf what was big money when Woodrow Wilson was president—the sum of $10,000 as a gift which Harvard accepted for the support of psychical research. Money from the fund has been used to encourage the work of a few investigators, such as Gardner Murphy, but mainly the fund has been administered sparingly and with extreme conservatism.

**Mrs. Holland** See **Fleming, Alice Macdonald (Kipling).**

**Holmes, Nelson, Mr. and Mrs.** Nineteenth century American physical mediums. They produced materializations and other physical phenomena both in the United States and in England, to which they went in 1873. In England, they were subjected to a series of tests by Sir William Crookes. Like most professional mediums, the Holmeses laid claim to a control named **"John King"** said to have been the pirate Sir Henry Morgan. He seems to have influenced the pair to commit a few crimes themselves during their séances. A letter from Ellen Crookes to Daniel D. Home in 1876 reports, for instance, that "when the Holmes were in England they were denounced several times, but with the usual result. Finding how loth spiritualists are to believe that they have been deceived, they got more and more daring, and even now there are people who support them and attend their seances" (quoted in Medhurst and Goldney, 1964:110).

If the Holmeses deserve a place in parapsychological history, it is because of the "Guppy Warfare on the Holmeses." The jealous and vicious medium **Agnes Guppy** was suppposed to have tried to enlist their cooperation in a plot to throw acid in the face of Florence Cook. The Holmeses refused. But the affair was far from over. Nelson Holmes wrote: "From Miss Cook, Mrs. Guppy now turned her rage against us, and soon after sent a party . . . to tear down our cabinet and otherwise break up our seances in London" (quoted in Medhurst and Goldney, 1964:59), but Mrs. Guppy's attempt to destroy them was foiled.

BIBLIOGRAPHY: Medhurst, R.G. and Goldney, K.M. 1964. "William Crookes and the Physical Phenomena of Mediumship." PSPR 54:25.

**Holmes, Oliver Wendell, 1809–1904.** American man of letters, author, and poet. He was famous for the satirical and humorous character of his works as well as for the poems *Old Ironsides* (1830) and *The Chamber'd Nautilus* (1858). His *Breakfast Table* essays first appeared in 1857 in the *Atlantic Monthly.*

In one of his essays,*Over the Teacups* (1891), he wrote: "Remarkable coincidence. On Monday, April 18, being at table from 6:30 P.M. to 7:30 with [two ladies] I told them of 'trial of battel' offered by Abraham Thornton in 1817. I mentioned his throwing down his glove, which was not taken up by the brother of his victim, and so he had to be let off, for the old law was still in force. I rose from the table and found an English letter waiting for me . . . [the letter read:] 'Dear Sir: In traveling the other day I met with a reprint of the very interesting case of Thornton for murder, 1817. the prisoner succesfully pleaded the old Wager of Battel. I thought you would like to read the account, and sent it with this. . . .- Yours faithfully, Fred. Rathbone.'"

Holmes had not referred to the Thornton case for years, knew of no reason why he should have spoken of it on that day, and had never spoken of it to Rathbone whom he knew in England. That he received a letter from England about the case just as he was thinking and talking about it at his table makes Holmes another **Noted Witness** for the phenomenon of telepathy between Rathbone and himself or of clairvoyance of the letter or of synchronicity.

BIBLIOGRAPHY: Prince, W.F. *Noted Witnesses for Psychic Occurrences,* 1963.

**Holzer, Hans, 1920–.** Austrian-born American writer. He likes to be called "the ghost hunter." Author of numerous popular books on psychical research, he has not, with one notable exception, been reviewed in the parapsychological literature. That exception is a discussion of a portion of one of his books, dealing with the use of ESP to investigate the past (1970), in the *Journal of the Society for Psychical Research* in December 1970. The chapter in question deals with the alleged haunting of a house by the ghost of Nell Gwyn.

As is his wont, Mr. Holzer took two mediums to the supposedly haunted house. They identified the ghost as Nell Gwyn and gave the cause of the haunting as the murder of one of her lovers on orders from Charles II who had given the house to her. She was supposed to have acted at the adjacent Royalty Theatre. It was also stated that the house had formerly housed the Royal Stables.

The JSPR article reveals that just about everything the mediums said was incorrect, the house not having been built until after Nell Gwyn's death, the theatre not having been built until about 150 years later, and the Royal Stables never having been located anywhere near the site. "Whatever may be the truth about the ESP investigations carried out by Mr Holzer, his treatment of his historical sources is so unsatisfactory, on the evidence of this case, as to cast considerable doubt on the objectivity and reliability of his work as a whole" (Green, 1970:431).

Selected Writing: *Window to the Past, Exploring History through Extra Sensory Perception,* 1970.

BIBLIOGRAPHY: Green, H.J.M. "Correspondence." JSPR 45:428.

**Home, Daniel Dunglas, 1833–1886.** Scottish-American physical medium. Reputedly the greatest of all physical mediums and upon whom the case for physical mediumship was said to stand or fall. He was the focus around which occurred all known physical phenomena (except apports): shaking of the room (earthquake effects), table-tilting, movement of heavy objects (PK), levitation (of himself and of furniture), materialization, elongation, playing of musical instruments without contact. Although there has been much speculation (Hall, 1984; Booth, 1984) that he must have been guilty of fraud, there is no compelling evidence that he was. The so-called "mystery of iniquity" that was said to have led to his leaving France was first suggested (Dingwall, 1962) to have related to homosexuality but apparently was only a misunderstanding about a greatcoat (Dingwall, 1970)!

His phenomena apparently first appeared during the heyday of American Spiritualism when he was a young boy living with his aunt in Connecticut who was so frightened by them that she turned him out of the house. He spent the rest of his youth with neighbors. In 1855, a Spiritualist committee raised money and sent him to Europe. The poets Elizabeth Barrett Browning and Robert Browning attended one of Home's séances in July 1855 in England. Elizabeth Barrett Browning was sure the phenomena were genuine (she, of course, was a Spiritualist); Robert Browning, no Spiritualist, was just as sure that Home was "a cheat" and an "imposture." (Home was the model for Browning's *Mr. Sludge the Medium*).

It has been suggested that Home's (false) claim to a relationship with the earls of Home (to which end he changed the spelling of his name from Hume) was the reason for his being the darling of European society and for his being accepted by the aristocracy into which he twice married. (Both his wives were Russian noblewomen.) Count Perovsky-Petrovo-Solovovo, himself a member of the Russian nobility, was not, however, impressed by the aristocracy's powers of observation and writes very critically of Home and of the possibilities (indeed, probabilities) of fraud in his manifestations.

Home never charged money for his séances but did accept lodging and gifts. That his séances were usually held in the homes of his hosts has been an argument for the genuineness of his phenomena since he could not have arranged trap doors and other artifices. The counterargument is that parlor entertainment is less criticially examined than is professional mediumship. Then, too, Home was involved in a sensational court case (Lyon *v.* Home) in which the plaintiff won a judgment against him for a considerable sum of money she had given him, supposedly on the basis of messages Home allegedly received from her dead husband who told her to do so. The evidence in the case, however, has been criticized, the judge having ruled against Home solely for the reason that he was a medium.

In 1871, William Crookes, an eminent scientist of his day, in connection with a study he was making of the phenomena of Spiritualism, conducted a series of sittings with Home. Crookes confirmed the geniuneness of Home's phenomena, which Crookes felt demonstrated the existence of a psychic force. (G.W. Lambert [1976], onetime President of the Society for Psychical Research, believes that the so-called "psychic force" can be explained by underground water, high winds, or engineering work going on at the time.) Home's séances usually took place in good light .and usually without his being in trance.

Perhaps his most sensational, most often discussed and criticized demonstration took place on December 16, 1868, when in the presence of the earl of Dunraven, Lord Adare, and the Master of Lindsay he went into trance and was supposed to have floated out one window, to have remained in the air outside the window for a few seconds and then to have floated back into another window, the space between the two windows being a distance of about seven and a half feet. In order to explain away the apparent phenomena, it has been suggested that Home was a superhypnotist or a supermagician or that those present were all gullible and remembered imperfectly what had actually happened.

"If incredible phenomena were being built up around [him] by a process of suggestion and hallucination on the grand scale, then that was not [his] fault, but [his] good fortune" (Dingwall, 1962:128). One modern critic (John Booth) believes that Home could have levitated by using a double rope sling. Sir William Crookes, however, writing of Home's levitations in the *Quarterly Journal of Science* for January 1874, said that either they were genuine or there was no alternative but "to reject all human testimony whatever." To this day much that Home was reported to have done remains an unexplained mystery.

BIBLIOGRAPHY: Beloff, J. "Historical Overview." In B. Wolman, ed., *Handbook of Parapsychology,* 1977, pp. 3–24; Booth, J. *Psychic Paradoxes,* 1984; Crookes, W. 1889. "Notes of Seances with D.D. Home." PSPR 6:98; Dingwall, E.J. 1970. "D.D. Home and the Mystery of Iniquity." JSPR 45:316; Dingwall, E.J., *Some Human Oddities,* 1962, pp. 91–128; Douglas, A. *Extra-Sentory Powers: Century of Psychical Research,* 1977; Gauld, A. *The Founders of Psychical Research,* 1968; Hall, T.H. *The Enigma of Daniel Home,* 1984; Jenkins, E. *The Shadow and the Light: A Defence of Daniel Dunglas Home, the Medium,* 1982; Lambert, G. W. 1976. "D.D. Home and the Physical World." JSPR 48:298; "Mr. Browning on D.D. Home." 1903. JSPR 11:11; Perovsky-Petrovo-Solovovo, M. 1911. "Les Phénomènes Physiques du Spiritisme." PSPR 24:413, 442–443; Podmore, F. *Modern Spiritualism: a His-*

*tory and Criticism,* 1902; Zorab, G. 1970. "Test Sittings with D.D. Home at Amsterdam." JP 34:47.

**Homing.** See **Anpsi.**

**Honorton, Charles, 1946–.** American parapsychologist. After joining the **Maimonides Medical Center Dream Laboratory** as senior research associate in 1967 and later being appointed director of research, he became the recipient, along with Montague Ullman and Stanley Krippner, of a grant from the U.S. Public Health Service, National Institute of Mental Health, the first federal grant ever made for research in parapsychology. In 1979, he became the director of the **Psychophysical Research Laboratories.**

Honorton has designed techniques and experiments to explore, through the Ganzfeld procedure, the relationship between psi and altered states of consciousness. The procedure is said to be effective in facilitating psi. For example, in an experiment with thirty subjects with halved ping-pong balls over their eyes to produce a homogeneous visual field and headphones over their ears to provide a repetition of seashore sounds, agents in other rooms viewing images were able to affect the subjects' images and ideation to a statistically significant degree (Honorton and Harper, 1974).

The validity of evidence based on the Ganzfeld procedure, however, has been seriously challenged (Hyman, 1985). Honorton, nevertheless, in a meta-analysis of twenty-eight Ganzfeld studies by investigators in ten different laboratories found an overall significance in the outcomes (Honorton, 1985). For this work in 1988 he was awarded the Exceptional Contribution Award by the Parapsychological Association.

Some parapsychologists have proposed that the search for a repeatable experiment is futile and should be given up. But Honorton is absolutely convinced that, in order for parapsychology to advance, this kind of experiment is a must. He believes that "Parapsychology will stand or fall on its ability to demonstrate replicable and conceptually meaningful findings. Future critics who are interested in the resolution rather than the perpetuation of the psi controversy are advised to focus their attention on systematic lines of research which are capable of producing such findings" (Honorton, 1981). In his opinion the Ganzfeld procedure is the line of research that has the best potential for producing the repeatable experiment.

Mr. Honorton has also developed computer games for the study of psychokinesis.

He has been a member of the Board of Trustees of the American Society for Psychical Research and is on the Board of Directors of the Parapsychological Association.

Selected Writings: 1985. "Meta-Analysis of Psi Ganzfeld Research: A Response to Hyman." JP 49:59; 1981. "Beyond the Reach of Sense: Some Comments on C.E.M. Hansel's *ESP and Parapsychology: A Critical Re-Evaluation.*" JASPR 75:155; and Harper, S. 1974. "Psi-Mediated Imagery and Ideation in an Experimental Procedure for Regulating Perceptual Input." JASPR 68:156.

BIBLIOGRAPHY: Hyman, R. 1985. "The Ganzfeld Psi Experiment: A Critical Appraisal." JP 49:3.

**Houston, Jean.** Contemporary American psychologist. Together with her husband, R.E.L. Masters, Dr. Houston has been engaged in the study of altered states of consciousness (ASCs) because "ASCs = expanded possibilities of mind. ASCs = deconditioned, deautomatized mind-brain system. ASCs disinhibit, give access to new experiences, ordinarily unused and largely unusable capacities" (Masters and Houston, 1972:7). Their pioneering study of the effects of LSD on altering consciousness (1966) made them famous. When LSD could no longer be used in research, Masters and Houston turned to mental exercises to induce altered states of consciousness without the use of drugs. Their Foundation for Mind Research has also conducted dream telepathy experiments with the Maimonides Medical Center Dream Laboratory with interesting results.

Dr. Houston has taught at Columbia University, Hunter College, the New School for Social Research and Marymount College. See also Bergen, Edgar.

Selected Writings: and R.E.L. Masters. *Mind Games,* 1972; and R.E.L. Masters. *The Varieties of Psychedelic Experience,* 1966.

BIBLIOGRAPHY: Douglas, A. *Extra-Sensory Powers,* 1977.

**Hope, Lord Charles, ?–1962.** British investigator of the paranormal, especially of physical mediums. His long series of sittings with Rudi Schneider convinced him "that impressive phenomena were observed at all these sittings" (Hope,1958). Hope was sharply critical of Harry Price's charges that Schneider cheated. "What does emerge damaged from Mr. Price's report," wrote Hope, "is his own reputation as controller, conductor of investigations and critic" (Hope, 1933). As far as Hope's own reputation was concerned, he "was seeking quite simply for the truth, whatever it might be" (Heywood, 1962).

Selected Writings: 1958. "Rudi Schneider: Recollections and Comments." JSPR 39:214; 1933. "Report of a Series of Sittings with Rudi Schneider." PSPR 41:255.

BIBLIOGRAPHY: Heywood, R. 1962. "Lord Charles Hope." JSPR 41:395.

**Hope, William, 1863–1933.** British "spirit photographer." He worked both in Crewe, England, and out of the offices of the British College of Psychic Science in London. His "spirit photograph" of someone Sir William Crookes took to be his late wife convinced him of her survival after death. The plate from which the photograph was made, however, supposedly shows that it had been produced by a double exposure. Harry Price reported that he had caught Hope in fraud, but Oliver Lodge (who nonetheless believed that Hope was a fraud) showed that the x-ray method Price had used was not foolproof, and Brian Inglis (1985) felt Price had framed Hope. Frank Barlow, however, stated that all Hope's **Spirit Photography,** that is, all his photographs with "extras," were fraudulently made as were his **Psychographs.**

BIBLIOGRAPHY: Barlow, F. and Rampling-Rose, W. 1933. "Report of an Investigation into Spirit-Photography." PSPR 41:121; Inglis, B. *The Paranormal,* 1985; Lodge, O. 1922. "On the Making of Test Plates by Previous Exposure." JSPR 20:370; Price, H. 1922. "A Case of Fraud with the Crewe Circle." JSPR 20:271.

**Horse Races.** Along with deaths, tragedies, wars and disasters, they are among the most common subjects of **Precognition.** People such as Brian Inglis frequently report precognitive dreams of winners that paid off. But it is impossible to be sure that any paranormal elements are present even in these dreams. Since thousands of people may be dreaming about a big race, some dreams must come true occasionally just by chance. Nevertheless, it is hard to dismiss the successful forecast of racing, reported in the *Journal of the Society for Psychical Research* (Case, 1947), in which a man had four dreams of actual winners in 1946 that resulted in substantial winnings for the dreamer's family and supporters.

Were these dreams then paranormal? Or had the dreamer studied racing so that he was familiar with horses, had picked up information that the winners were good horses, the information then emerging in his dreams?

BIBLIOGRAPHY: 1947. "Case: Forecasts of Horse Races." JSPR 34:63.

**Houdini, Harry (Erik Weisz or Weiss), 1874–1926.** Pre-eminent Hungarian-born American escape artist and magician. Although Houdini claimed to have been born on April 6, 1874, in Appleton, Wisconsin, he had in fact been born in Pest, Hungary, on March 24 of that year (Gresham, 1959:9).

Chained, Houdini was able to escape from a locked, weighted box tied with rope and submerged in water. He frequently freed himself from a straitjacket while suspended upside down seventy-five feet above the ground. With hands tied behind his back, in a sack in a locked box which in turn was tied with rope, Houdini was free in three seconds and out of the locked and tied box. But his wife, inside the sack with her hands tied behind her back, was now in it! He freed himself while hanging shackled, upside down in a locked tank filled with water. No manacles or locks could hold him. His exploits seemed so impossible that Sir Arthur Conan Doyle, a convinced Spiritualist, was sure that Houdini was a physical medium who dematerialized and then rematerialized.

Now it so happens that Houdini wanted to believe in Spiritualism; he longed to communicate with his beloved mother who had died in 1913. To try to demonstrate survival after death he made pre-mortem compacts with friends—even to the extent of creating codes and handgrips. But none of these people ever communicated. And as a conjurer he knew all the tricks of physical mediumship: how to untie and then retie oneself, use misdirection, etc. He claimed that he never found anything but conjuring tricks among the mediums he sat with, including Mina S. Crandon (he was on the *Scientific American* committee that investigated her).

Houdini and Conan Doyle became friends. Doyle admired Houdini's warmth and extreme generosity (if not his conceit and brashness "like a side show barker," as Fulton Oursler said). But their friendship was destroyed as the result of a séance held especially by Doyle for Houdini in 1922 on June 17, his mother's birthday, in which Lady Doyle was the reluctant amateur medium. The automatic writing, supposedly from Houdini's mother, began with a cross at the top of the page and was written in English. According to Doyle, Houdini accepted the message and was "walking on air." Houdini himself violently repudiated the suggestion that the message was from his mother because she had been Jewish, the wife of a rabbi, and because she could neither speak, read, nor write English. Doyle tried to point out that mediums normally translate their impressions into their own languages and that the cross was for the medium's protection. But the relationship between Doyle and Houdini was irremediably damaged.

Houdini was said to have told his wife Beatrice that, if he could, he would communicate with her from beyond the grave by means of the code they had used in their magic act. As a result of a ruptured appendix caused by severe blows to the body, Houdini died on Halloween 1926. Every year after that on that date attempts were made to reach him. Arthur Ford, the American medium, claimed to have recieved the message, a claim at first endorsed by Beatrice Houdini. But she eventually withdrew her endorsement and said later that there had never been a message and that Houdini was not coming back. Beatrice has been dead since 1943; still, every Halloween, attempts to reach Houdini continue.

Selected Writing: "A Magician among the Spirits." In C. Murchison, ed., *The Case for and against Psychical Belief,* 1927.

BIBLIOGRAPHY: Cohen, D. *The Encyclopedia of Ghosts,* 1984; Doyle, A.C. *The Edge of the Unknown,* 1930; FitzSimons, R. *Death and the Magician: The Mystery of Houdini,* 1980; Gresham W.L. *Houdini: The Man Who Walked through Walls,* 1959; Jay, R. *Learned Pigs and Fireproof Women,* 1986.

**Housman, Alfred Edward, 1859–1936.** English poet and Latin scholar. In spite of having written fewer than 100 poems, he is considered among the great poets of England. It took twenty-three years for him to write the poem that finally became *A Shropshire Lad* (1896). His *Last Poem* did not appear until 1922. Although his first volume was not immediately appreciated, his second volume was the most popular book of verses of the time. His poetry is easy, direct, and economical and shows Housman's great learning and strength of intellect.

In *The Name and Nature of Poetry* (1933), Houseman added his testimony as a **Noted Witness** to the creative process: "Meaning is of the intellect, poetry is not. If it were, the eighteenth century would have been able to write it better. . . . I think that the production of poetry, in its first stage, is less an active than a passive and involuntary process. . . . Having drunk a pint of beer at luncheon—beer is a sedative to the brain, and my afternoons are the least intellectual portions of my life—I would go out for a walk of two or three hours. As I went along, thinking of nothing in particular, . . . there would flow into my mind, with sudden and unaccountable emotion, sometimes a line or two of verse, sometimes a whole stanza at once, accompanied, not preceded, by a vague notion of the poem which they were destined to form part of. Then there would usually be a lull of an hour or so, then perhaps the spring would bubble up again."

BIBLIOGRAPHY: Ghiselin, G. *The Creative Process,* 1952.

**Hövelmann, Gerd, 1956–.** German linguist and philosopher. He is on the staff of the Institut für Philosophie at Phillips-Universität and is a soft-line sceptic who has published extensively on philosophical, sociological, methodological, and terminological aspects of parapsychology.

Also concerned with the ongoing debate between sceptics and parapsychologists, he has contributed an overview of articles in parapsychological and non-parapsychological journals written by hard-line sceptics, the first such survey ever made by a self-confessed sceptic. In it, Hövelmann provides an annotated bibliography in which he points out the pluses and minuses of the sceptical writings. With the controversy over parapsychology always heated and sometimes hysterical, it is Hövelmann's hope that his systematic analysis "will be used in [the] spirit and serve [the] end" (Hövelmann, 1985) of producing some spirit of cooperation between sceptics and parapsychologists.

Another of his hopes is that parapsychology will be recognized as a science, but he believes that such recognition requires throwing on the scrap heap many of parapsychology's outworn and even harmful conceptions, theories, and practices. Among his recommendations are that parapsychologists stop describing their field as "revolutionary." The application of orthodox scientific methods does not fit in well with revolutionary slogans. Another problem he sees is with the vague terminology in the field that explains nothing. He believes that a standardized and methodically constructed terminology should be developed. If we understand the etymology of words and their conceptual background, we will think, talk, and write better. A further recommendation is the abandonment of Thomas Kuhn's conception that scientific theories and branches develop irrespective of efforts to justify them. Hövelmann urges that there should be a valid and critical foundation for any scientific theory. One advantage of this kind of justification for parapsychology would be to enable it to meet criticisms better. Hövelmann also questions the importance of survival research. He asks: "Would we profit in one way or another by finding out whether we will survive? Would this knowledge be useful to meet our vital interests. . . ?" (Hövelmann, 1983).

While many parapsychologists would accept his other proposals, some would balk at abandoning investigative efforts to find out if survival after death is a reality. Many still feel that "experimental resolution one way or another of the [survival] hypothesis . . . would have sweeping implications" (Berger, 1987) for religion, medicine, psychology, and philosophy and would "color our lives, affect our thoughts and impinge upon some of the problems confronting us" (Berger, in press).

As might be expected of a sceptic, Hövelmann is a consultant to the Committee for the Scientific Investigation of Claims of the Paranormal. He abstracts articles in German language periodicals for *Parapsychology Abstracts International* and is a member of the Parapsychological Association.

Selected Writings: 1984. "Are Psi Experiments Repeatable?" *European Journal of Parapsychology* 5:285; 1983. "Cooperation Versus Competition: In Defense of Rational Argument in Parapsychology." *European* Journal of Parapsychology 4:483. "Some Recommendations for the Future Practice of Parapsychology." In W.G. Roll, J. Beloff, R.A. White, eds., *Research in Parapsychology 1982,* 1983, p.137; with Truzzi, M. and Hoebens, P.H. "Skeptical Literature on Parapsychology—An Annotated Bibliography." In P. Kurtz, ed., *A Skeptic's Handbook of Parapsychology,* 1985, p. 449.

BIBLIOGRAPHY: Berger, A.S. *Aristocracy of the Dead,* 1987, p. 176; Berger, A.S. "Three Views of Death and Their Implications for Life." In P. Badham, ed., *The Value of Human Life,* in press.

**Huby, Pamela Margaret, 1922–.** British philosopher. Although she has come up with interesting evidence about the life of "Rose Morton," the main witness in the famous "Morton Ghost" case (Huby, 1970), her main interests in psychical research are spontaneous cases, reincarnation and the perennial question of whether the human being survives death. She has applied philosophical reasoning (Huby, 1976) to try to answer this important parapsychological question. Dr. Huby has also studied what the effect of psychedelic drugs might be on extrasensory perception. She conducted two experiments with drugs but did not obtain any statistically significant results (Huby and Wilson, 1961). Dr.Huby taught philosophy at the University of Liverpool and has contributed many book reviews to the *Journal of the Society for Psychical Research.*

Selected Writings: "Some Aspects of the Problem of Survival." In S.C. Thakur, ed., *Philosophy and Psychical Research,* 1976; 1970. "New Evidence About 'Rose Morton.'" JSPR 45:391; and Wilson, C.W.M. 1961. "The Effects of Centrally Acting Drugs on ESP Ability in Normal Subjects." JSPR 41:60.

**Hudson, Frederick A.** Late nineteenth century famous British spirit photographer. Beginning his work about 1872, Hudson soon became one of the best-known practitioners of **Spirit Photography**—and soon was accused of cheating. The *Spiritualist* magazine for September 1872 revealed that some of Hudson's photographs were obvious double exposures and that others had been altered by hand. In still others medium Frank Herne had clearly "sat for the ghost." Nevertheless, even his most outspoken enemies believed that Hudson at times produced genuine spirit photographs, and his supporters maintained that Hudson had never cheated, that the double exposures and changes on the plates were the work of spirits. Several people, whose honesty seems unquestionable, were certain that the "extras" Hudson obtained on photographs made in their presence were undoubtedly genuine. "In the particular case of spirit photography [however] . . . the great complication of the process of photography and the number of ways in which sham ghost pictures may be done . . . make it especially hard to detect trickery" (Sidgwick, 1891:276–7).

Recognition of "spirits" in photographs does not mean that they are genuine, either. "Some people would recognize anything. A broom and a sheet are quite enough to make up a grandmother for some wild enthusiasts . . ." (W. Stainton Moses as quoted in Sidgwick 1891:277). Yet Alfred Russel Wallace, among others, was completely convinced of the genuineness of Hudson's photographs, and Hudson was never actually caught in fraud.

BIBLIOGRAPHY: Sidgwick, E. (Mrs. Henry) 1891. "On Spirit Photographs; A Reply to Mr. A.R. Wallace." PSPR 7:268.

**Hudson, Thomas Jay, 1834–1903.** American author. His popular books were intended to bring psychical research to the attention of the general reader. He seems to have been one of the first to conceive of the **Cosmic Memory.** Since this notion has been used to explain away various psychic phenomena, James H. Hyslop was cranky with Hudson and called him an "irresponsible thinker" (Hyslop, 1918:121).

Hyslop said nothing, however, about Hudson's claim to have formulated an original hypothesis that would embrace and permit the study of psychic occurrences (Hudson, 1893). His theory was that the human being was a divided personality with two minds, one objective, one subjective. The latter, lying below ordinary consciousness, has great powers demonstrated by psychic phenomena. This dual personality theory tied psychology in with the paranormal and was introduced before Freudian psychology came on the scene but is only a restatement of Frederic W.H. Myers's conception of the **Subliminal Self.**

Hudson's second book which set out to "demonstrate" a future life (1895) went wide of its mark. It merely reported some of the phenomena of Spiritualism. It was valuable, however, in provoking interest in the subject and in the field of psychical research in general.

Selected Writings: *A Scientific Demonstration of a Future Life,* 1895; *The Law of Psychic Phenomena,* 1893.

BIBLIOGRAPHY: Hyslop, J.H. *Life After Death: Problems of the Future Life and Its Nature,* 1918.

**Hugo, Victor Marie, 1802–1885.** French writer and poet. A founder of the French Romantic school, he was a leading figure in French nineteenth century literature. His famous historical novels include *Les Misérables* (1862) and *The Hunchback of Notre Dame* (1831). In addition, poems and plays poured from his creative talents.

His political activity led to his being exiled by Emperor Napoleon III in 1852. As a result, he took up residence on the English island of Jersey. The island turned out to be the home of people who were curious and enthusiastic about Spiritualism and table-tilting. Hugo's daughter, Leopoldine, had drowned in an accident in 1843. Hugo gave vent to some of his grief in a book of poems, *Les Contemplations,* published in 1856. At first he was sceptical about seeking and finding an additional means of solace in table-tilting and séances. He went so far as to be present at them, but would not participate.

At length, however, a spirit identifying itself as that of his dead daughter seemed to communicate through the table. Hugo's wife cried. His son, Charles, asked questions of the spirit and, in the end, Hugo was deeply impressed and moved. Thereafter, for a period of two years, a frenzy of séances, which lasted from noon until the following morning, took place. Hugo attended daily. But he would never place his hand on the table. He would suggest questions or ask them of a spirit while his son managed the séance. Dante, Aesop, Shakespeare, Moliere, Racine, Jesus, Muhammad, Galileo, Plato, Isaiah, doves from Noah's ark, the lion of Androcles[!], Lord Byron, Walter Scott—even Napoleon III who was very much alive (but perhaps asleep?)—all communicated.

Hugo seems to have felt that the spirits had a close telepathic rapport with him for he said: "These grand mysterious beings that listen to me look into my mind whenever they wish to do so, quite as one looks into a cave with a torch." They changed Hugo's life and "enhanced the prophetic-messianic view which Victor Hugo had of himself" (Ebon, 1971).

In addition to being a **Noted Witness** who was satisfied that he had received communications from beyond the grave, Hugo seemed also to lean toward reincarnation for he wrote in his journal: "Man suffers because he has to expiate in this world a fault committed in an anterior world."

When Hugo died at the age of eight-four, all France mourned and a million people lined the route of his funeral cortège.

BIBLIOGRAPHY: Ebon, M. *They Knew the Unknown,* 1971; Sudre, R. 1929. "The Case of Victor Hugo and the Collective Psychism." *Psychic Research:* 23:337.

**Humphrey, Betty.** See **Nicol, Betty H.**

**Huna ("secret" in the Hawaiian language).** A Polynesian (specifically, Hawaiian) psycho-religious system. The Kahuna, the practitioners of Huna, used **Precognition** and **Clairvoyance,** and their folklore tells of their miracles and magic. According to Huna, each person has three selves: the high *(aumakua),* the middle *(uhane),* and the low *(unihipili),* which seem very like modern concepts of the superconscious, the conscious, and the subconscious. Each self has a subtle or etheric body *(kino-aka).* Each self uses a form of energy or vitality, the highest *(Mana Loa),* the life force used by the high self, being able to heal and perform other miracles. "There is only one sin in the Huna concept. That is the sin of hurting another self. The Huna way of life is a harmless, hurtless way" (Hoffman, 1976:16).

Knowledge of Huna was brought to the West by Max Freedom Long who went to Hawaii in 1917 to work with Dr. William Tufts Brigham, the first westerner to investigate Huna. Brigham had seen the Kahuna walk on hot coals, had seen healings, had witnessed weather control, had seen Kahuna call sharks to the beach. But he never learned how they did these things, and by the time Long came to Hawaii the last of the expert Kahuna had died, the ancient religion having been suppressed by the missionaries. Long, however, by studying the root vocabulary of the Hawaiian language and its symbolism rediscovered the secret of the Kahuna. He has written several books on the subject. His second book *The Secret Science behind Miracles* (1948) explains the Huna system. He also founded Huna Research Associates to study and develop Huna techniques.

**Arthur Ellison** has pointed out the similarity of the ideas in Huna to those of the ancient Hindus and their resemblance as well to the hypotheses of Freud and Jung. He also comments on their relevance to parapsychology and suggests that they should be studied and tested.

BIBLIOGRAPHY: Ellison, A. 1977. "Mind, Belief and Psychical Research." PSPR 56:236, 245; Hoffman, E. *Huna: A Beginner's Guide,* 1976; Long, M.F., *The Secret Science behind Miracles,* 1948.

**Hunch.** See **Intuition.**

**Hurkos, Peter (Pieter Van der Hurk), 1911–1988.** Dutch psychic. He was known for his appearances on television and in the theater. His autobiography states that "scientific authorites have come to agree" (Hurkos, 1962:6) that he was the greatest psychic in the world.

According to Hurkos, his remarkable talents started in 1941 when, while painting a house, he fell thirty-six feet from a ladder and landed on his head. After the injury, he had the paranormal ability to obtain information about people and objects. At the end of World War II, he went on the stage. In his performances, he would be blindfolded and then, using psychometry, would use photographs put into his hands to provide correct information about the people in the pictures. In 1947, Hurkos related how he became a psychic Sherlock Holmes who helped the police of several countries solve many cases of murder, theft, and missing people. Hurkos went on to state that later he was brought to the United States by **Henry K. (Andrija) Puharich** and was studied in experiments at a laboratory in Maine.

After Hurkos gave his impressive stage performances with photographs, he refused to agree to conditions proposed by a Belgian committee set up to look into parapsychological claims. The conditions were simply that the eye-bandaging procedure be omitted and that Hurkos just hold a photograph behind his back (Zorab, 1962). His ability as a psychic sleuth also has been called into question by George Zorab. Hurkos had related in his book the case of a four-year-old girl named Joelle Ringot. But Zorab remembered that the "villagers collected a large sum of money as a fee for Hurkos to come over and find the girl. Days passed and though Hurkos, with a whole gang of journalists at his heels, searched for the girl by means of 'paranormal' clues, he failed utterly. Sometime later the police discovered the girl had been strangled by an insane woman and thrown into a cesspool" (Zorab, 1962:430).

Surprisingly also, we find no mention in Hurkos's book that he was ever tested by parapsychologists in the Studievereniging voor Psychical Research (Dutch Society for Psychical Research) which had been in existence since 1920. It is a significant fact, too, that, after he came to the U.S., he refused Joseph B. Rhine's request to come to Duke University for tests and was never scientifically investigated by any other respected parapsychologist except Charles C. Tart whose findings concerning him were negative. The Maine tests have only a doubtful value because they were never submitted for publication to any established parapsychological journal and Hurkos's "account of these loosely knit experiments leaves much to be desired" (Cox, 1963:46).

Yet Hurkos is reported to have helped new Jersey police in solving a murder case (Hoebens with Truzzi, 1985) so that it is possible that Hurkos possessed at least some of the paranormal gifts he claimed. See also **Crime Detection.**

Selected Writing: *Psychic: The Story of Peter Hurkos,* 1962.

BIBLIOGRAPHY: Cox, W.E. 1963. "Reviews. Psychic: The Story of Peter Hurkos." JSPR 57:44; Hoebens, P.H. with Truzzi, M. "Reflections on Psychic Sleuths." In P. Kurtz, ed., *A Skeptic's Handbook of Parapsychology,* 1985; Zorab, G. 1962. "Reviews. Psychic: The Story of Peter Hurkos." JASPR 41:429.

**Huxley, Aldous, 1894–1963.** British novelist and essayist. Born of a famous family (great-nephew of Matthew Arnold, grandson of Thomas Huxley, brother of Julian Huxley), his reputation as a man of letters seemed assured from birth and was reinforced by his witty and satirical writings on the decadence of English high society. After he came to live in Hollywood, California, in 1937, he became interested in Hindu philosphy, in the mystical experience and became one of the many men of letters drawn to parapsychology. He acted as agent in experiments in telepathy conducted by Gilbert Murray. In an article in *Life* in 1954, he discussed extrasensory perception and parapsychology. He described the experience of his mother who dreamed correctly of the death of her absent son Jack. Huxley also wrote for *Life*'s readers that the work of Joseph B. Rhine had established a base for psi too solid to be ignored.

Most observers believe that psi is an unconscious function and that, whether in spontaneous cases or laboratory tests, subjects are never aware of whether their feelings or calls are right or wrong. Huxley's own experiences or impressions are exactly in line with this belief: "In . . . those who undergo tests for ESP, or prevision, there is no perceptible distinction between success and failure. The process of guessing *feels* exactly the same, whether the result be a score attributable to mere chance, or markedly above or below that figure" (Huxley 1952:72). He also shared the belief of many parapsychologists that academic philosophers feel menaced by psi phenomena: "The great majority of philosophers have not treated hypnotism and the allied phenomena of healing and extrasensory perception as the serious study of a year or even a semester. And yet if they had looked into the matter, if they had examined the masses of carefully sifted evidence accumulated by such scientific organizations as the Society for Psychical Research, they would have found themselves confronted with strange data very hard to explain in terms of the philosophic systems recently current in the West" (Huxley, 130).

One of the most convincing reasons for the belief that the survival of the human consciousness beyond death is not possible is the contention that consciousness is produced by the brain—in William James's simile, as steam is produced by the tea-pot. If this is the case, when the brain dies so must consciousness. But based on his experience with psychedelic drugs, Huxley came to see the brain as a "cerebral reducing valve" which, instead of producing consciousness, eliminates much of reality and perception if it is not relevant to our biological needs. Under the influence of mescaline, he experienced brightly lit and beautiful landscapes like the fairylands of religion and folklore with brilliant colors and from which objects shone like gems. Under the influence of the drug, finally the "Mind at Large" which we all possess managed to get through the "cerebral reducing valve." His mescaline experience also convinced him that beautiful visions come if one begins the drug experience with positive feelings, such as love. But if the feelings are negative, such as fear or malice, the visions may be hellish. He believed that in the postmortem state something similar happens. Some people may find themselves in a blissful heaven, some in an appalling hell, and some in a spirit plane resembling earthly existence (Huxley, 1956).

As he was dying of cancer, Huxley asked for—and got from his wife—LSD to reduce his pain. His death on November 22, 1963 came on the very day that a sniper's bullet killed John F. Kennedy.

Selected Writings: *Heaven and Hell,* 1956; *The Doors of Perception,* 1954; *The Devils of Loudon,* 1952; *Themes and Variations,* 1950.

**Hyman, Ray.** Contemporary American psychologist. He is one of the principal evaluators of parapsychology on the National Research Council of the National Academy of Sciences. In 1987 the National Research Council found no scientific justification for the existence of parapsychological phenomena. Hyman is one of the leading sceptics and one of "a new generation of psychologists who are more rational, systematic, and deadly in their criticisms" (Berger, 1988:232) than earlier psychologists such as Joseph Jastrow, Granville S. Hall and Hugo Münsterberg whose attacks were frequently marred by the neglect or falsification of facts. Hyman is a responsible critic who has attempted to examine the evidence for the reality of extrasensory perception. In one paper, he concentrated on the Ganzfeld procedure which many parapsychologists feel increases scores in ESP tests and represents the promise of providing the elusive repeatable experiment. Hyman found the Ganzfeld studies to be filled with statistical and methodological flaws (Hyman, 1985). In another writing, Hyman discredited as defective some of the best cases and experiments that seemed to point to psi (Hyman, 1986).

Dr. Hyman is a member of the Department of Psychology at the University of Oregon, is active in the **Committee for the Scientific Investigation of the Claims of the Paranormal** and is on the its executive council.

Selected Writing: 1986. "Parapsychological Research: A Tutorial Review and Critical Appraisal." *Proceedings of the IEEE* 74:823; 1985. "The Ganzfeld Psi Experiment: A Critical Appraisal." JP 49:3.

BIBLIOGRAPHY: Berger, A.S. *Lives and Letters in American Parapsychology,* 1988).

**Hynek, Josef Allen, 1910–1986.** American astrophysicist. He was widely respected as a leading investigator of unidentified flying objects and for his scientific attitude which neither debunked nor sensationalized the subject but approached it impartially. In 1948, he became a United States Air Force scientific consultant on the subject.

During his career, Hynek examined over 10,000 reports of sightings and concluded that, while more than 90 percent could be discounted as aircraft, planets, meteors, weather balloons, birds, hallucinations or frauds, about 500 reports could not be accounted for and suggested extra terrestrial beings. Hynek classified UFO sightings into close encounters of the first kind (a sighting within 200 yards of a witness), close encounters of the second kind (besides the sighting, physical marks on the ground or physical influences on a witness), and close encounters of the third kind (in which alien beings interact with human beings). The last classification was used by Steven Spielberg as the title of a movie on UFOs.

To try to resolve some of the difficulties and the ongoing controversey between UFO buffs and debunkers, Hynek established and became the director in 1973 of a Center for UFO Studies to collect data and get positive or negative evidence of UFOs. He died before this goal could be realized.

Selected Writing: *The UFO Experience,* 1972.

**Hyperaesthesia.** A form of unconscious sense-perception developed to a high degree (e.g., a superior hearing faculty). Hyperaesthesia of the recognized senses sometimes has been used as an explanation for cases claimed to be instances of telepathy.

BIBLIOGRAPHY: Murray, G. 1916. "Presidential Address." PSPR 39:46.

**Hypermnesia.** See **Cryptomnesia.**

**Hypnagogic.** The state between sleep and waking when, as sleep is coming on or is leaving, visual or auditory impressions, some of which may be paranormal, may occur.

**Hypnosis.** An altered state of consciousness bearing a superifical resemblance to sleep. It is induced in a subject by a hypnotist or operator. In this state, subjects are highly suggestible and may permit the operator to control their thoughts and actions. The technique has been used in the performance of surgical operations and as a therapeutic tool in the treatment of mental disorders, the control of pain, in the relief of symptoms of disease and in the healing process.

The phenomenon, earlier called **Mesmerism,** had fallen into disrepute but the work of **Jean-Martin Charcot** and others in the mid-nineteenth century brought it scientific respectability and marked one of the beginnings of parapsychology. For, in their investigations of the phenomenon, medical people noticed that patients in "mesmeric" trance seemed to demonstrate psychic faculties with powers of **Clairvoyance** or **Telepathy.** When the Society for Psychical Research was organized, hypnosis was a priority subject, one of its committees being charged with collecting evidence on the mesmeric trance and the paranormal phenomena allied to it.

In recent times, hypnosis has been used by L.L. Vasiliev, the Soviet experimenter, and by the American researcher Stanley Krippner to induce telepathy. The Czech parapsychologist Milan Ryzl found hypnosis a tool to train people, notably Pavel Stepanek, to exhibit ESP ability. Hypnosis also is now being used with increasing frequency as a way to induce subjects to describe experiences and events in prior lives. As evidence of reincarnation, however, most cases suffer from the defect that statements about past lives have not been verified against historical facts and "interest and enthusiasm on the part of the general public has far outrun respectable data" (Stevenson, 1977).

BIBLIOGRAPHY: Stevenson, I. "Reincarnation: Field Studies and Theoretical Issues." In B. Wolman., ed., *Handbook of Parapsychology,* 1977, p. 631.

**Hypnotism.** See **Hypnosis; Mesmerism.**

**Hyslop, George, H., 1892–1965.** American physician. It was inevitable that, as the son of **James H. Hyslop** who had maintained the American Society for Psychical Research for two decades, he would dedicate forty active years to the work and financial affairs of that organization.

George Hyslop was exposed to psychical research from an early age. He was a young doctor in 1921 when he was elected to the ASPR Board of Trustees and in the 1930s was highly critical of the ASPR's slippage away from the high standards his father had established. He also demanded along with Frederic Bligh Bond that the facts revealing the fraudulent character of Mina S. Crandon's most impressive phenomena—the spirit fingerprints of her dead brother—be published by the ASPR. Hyslop became the ASPR's president in 1941 after a revolt by its members drove its officers out of office and he proceeded to reinstitute his father's standards, protect the public image of the organization and direct its financial program.

BIBLIOGRAPHY: Berger, A.S. *Lives and Letters in American Parapsychology,* 1988.

**Hyslop, James Hervey, 1854–1920.** Noted American psychical researcher. With his death, Hyslop finally may have confirmed a proposition that he defended strenuously all his life: that the so-called dead live on and are able to communicate with the living. But although, because of this belief, he seemed to the orthodox to be only a credulous spook-chaser, in reality Hyslop was an investigator who, like Richard Hodgson, began his career in psychical research as a skeptic and only after serious scientific study became a believer.

A farm boy who took care of cows and horses, he became leader of the **American Society for Psychical Research.** The intensity with which he pursued the path of psychical research is underscored by the almost twenty years he devoted to it, by his voluminous writings on the subject, by his refusal to accept any salary for his labors as founder and secretary of the ASPR and by not merely braving but lashing out against critics who heaped ridicule on him for chasing spooks.

His policy in the *Journal* of the ASPR was to show no mercy to people who did not adhere to the strict truth in their treatment of psychical research. He was so merciless that even some of Hyslop's friends were taken aback by his fiery responses and lack of diplomacy. William James once said that Hyslop had no more idea of policy than a street terrier. But Hyslop was persuaded that psychical research was a subject of great importance which, if understood and presented fairly, might bring about a radical change in thought. And so when ill health forced him to resign his post as professor of logic and ethics at Columbia University, he concentrated on psychical research and tried to gain financial support for its work by organizing the **American Institute for Scientific Research.**

With the death of Hodgson and the dissolution of the ASPR, then a branch of the English Society for Psychical Research, Hyslop took over organized psychical research in America. The ASPR became a section of the American Institute for Scientific Research. Hyslop managed the ASPR single-handedly for over a decade and assured its stability and growth. He contributed many important books to psychical research as well as experimental reports of investigations into cases of possession and sittings with mediums that are unique because of their detail and volume.

Selected Writings: *Contact with the Other World,* 1919; *Life After Death: Problems of the Future Life and its Nature,* 1918; 1909. "Observations on the Mediumistic Records in the Thompson Case." PASPR 3:1; *Psychical Research and the Resurrection,* 1908; 1901. "A Further Record of Observations of Certain Phenomena of Trance." PSPR 16:1.

BIBLIOGRAPHY: Berger, A.S. *Lives and Letters in American Parapsychology,* 1988.

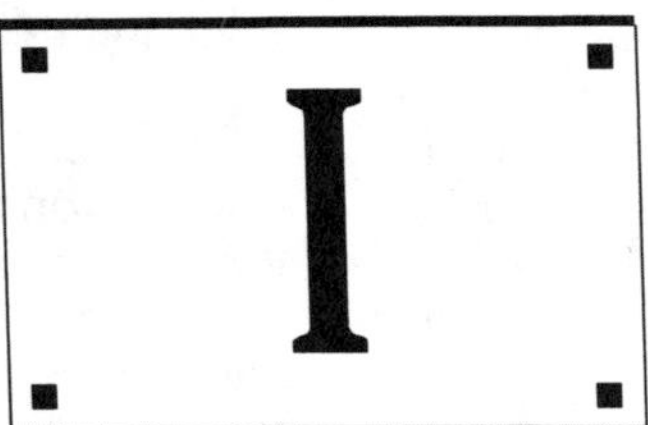

**I Ching.** Also called Book of Changes and one of the Five Classics of Confucianism. An ancient Chinese text containing sixty-five symbolic hexagrams with solid lines representing the yang and broken lines representing the yin principle, it is used to guide people in their daily lives and toward more profound knowledge of themselves. It is also a very elaborate method for predicting the future. People with questions they want answered cast yarrow stalks or toss coins until they have constructed a hexagram that indicates which paragraph to read in the book. The I Ching may be relevant to the psi abilities of people who use it. The unconscious and psychokinesis may play a role in directing the casting of the stalks or coins and extrasensory perception may be used to locate an appropriate passage.

Controlled experiments to test the efficiency of the ancient system and for the presence of psi are rare. In one such experiment involving the I Ching and hidden targets, forty subjects were told to seek an answer to questions important to them. As they thought of their questions, they kept tossing three pennies until their hexagrams were completed. Each subject was provided with two paragraphs to read from the book, one of which fit the completed hexagram, although the subjects did not know it; the other, a control hexagram completed by a randomizing procedure, did not. The tasks of the subjects were to rate the passages relevant to their questions. The scores of the subjects who were **Sheep** were statistically significant and showed psi-hitting but the scores of **Goats** were not significant and showed psi-missing (Rubin and Honorton, 1971). The results of the experiment strongly suggest that there is a connection between psi and the I Ching and that psychokinesis may operate with targets hidden in the I Ching.

BIBLIOGRAPHY: Rubin, L. and Honorton, C., 1971. "Separating the Yins from the Yangs: An Experiment with the I Ching." *Proceedings of the Parapsychological Association 8:6.*

**Identity, Personal.** The greatest problem facing so-called evidence supporting the hypothesis of personal survival after physical death is identifying the alleged spirits of deceased individuals as one and the same people who once lived and who they claim to be. In normal life, people are identified by voice, physical appearance, fingerprints. But these forms of evidence are not possible when the personal identities of spirits of the dead must be established.

The **Dictionary Test, Cipher Test** or **Combination Lock Test** which require the communication of information known to no one but the deceased individual may be one form of evidence of identity. Another form is the transmission of messages characteristic of communicators—for example, the **Cross-Correspondences** in which automatists's scripts contained just the kind of material that might have been produced by the deceased (often classical scholars).

A third form of evidence that might identify a surviving personality would be the mention or description of objects or events associated with the personality. James H. Hyslop maintained that a conspicuous event in a life would not be particularly good evidence because a medium or other person might easily be familiar with it. The best evidence of personal identity, therefore, would be a very private and trivial event, for example, a message Hyslop received supposedly from a dead uncle about the shaft of a wagon in which they had been riding having had to be repaired with rope.

**Illusion.** The drawing of an erroneous conclusion from data presented to the senses, for example, a bush mistaken in the dark for an apparition or a figure draped in muslin mistaken for the spirit of a dear departed one. In experiments conducted by **Theodore Besterman** (1932) to test the testimony of witnesses regarding physical phenomena supposedly occurring in séances, sitters suffered from various kinds of illusions. They misinterpreted physical objects and movements and were unable to report correctly the actual episodes or scenes that took place.

BIBLIOGRAPHY: Besterman, T. 1932. "The Psychology of Testimony in Relation to Paraphysical Phenomena." PSPR 40:365.

**Image, Religious.** The image of some divine personage which does not fade with time and which is produced in a manner and by a medium that cannot be explained by present day science. The most famous such image is that on the **Shroud of Turin.** It appears to be of a crucified man and, until 1988 when carbon-dating seems to have ruled out the idea, was thought by Christians to be the burial cloth and image of Jesus Christ. A similar religious relic is the **Lady of Guadalupe,** a Mexican *tilma* or cotton blanket used as a cloak on which, supposedly supernaturally produced, is a high quality lifelike picture in color of the Virgin Mary.

**Imago Mundi.** An international organization of Roman Catholic parapsychologists and philosophers that studies, gives lectures on and holds conferences in Rome and elsewhere in Europe on parapsychology. "Imago Mundi" also is the name of a journal published by the Pontifical University of Lateran and edited by **Andreas Resch.**

**Immortality.** There are at least six different conceptions of immortality ranging from continuing after death through one's descendants, through the persisting influence of one's spirit or thought to being absorbed in Nature or the One (Berger, 1987a). But if we are thinking of personal immortality then these are pale substitutes. Every religion holds that, in one form or another, there will be personal continuance beyond the death of the physical body. While not all teach that the immortal soul survives death forever, Judaism is one that does and the Christian faith also teaches the soul's eternal life as well as the resurrection of the body.

The **Survival Research** carried out by psychical research throws light on these teachings to a limited extent. Evidence that an individual consciousness may have persisted after death for some period of time although not forever is not proof of the immortality of the soul. But if it were possible to obtain "convincing findings that a human consciousness had survived the blow of death . . . such findings would support the fundamental precondition of the eternal life promised by Western religions" (Berger, 1987b) and also would verify and support religious beliefs in a future life.

BIBLIOGRAPHY: Berger, A. S. *Aristocracy of the Dead,* 1987a; Berger, A. S. "Bridging the Gap: A Critical Outline of the Prima Facie Evidence for Survival." In P. Badham and L. Badham, eds., *Death and Immortality in the Religions of the World,* 1987b, p. 188.

**Imperator Band.** A group of forty-nine spirits with highly impressive credentials who specialized in providing religious and moral teachings. They were supposed to include Elijah, St. John the Baptist, Plato, and Aristotle with the Old Testament prophet, Malachi, their leader. The first appearance of a spirit who signed himself "Imperator" occurred in 1872 during the automatic writing of the medium **W. Stainton Moses.** Imperator became the control or leading guide for the phenomena produced by Moses. Later, Imperator and his group purported to communicate through the medium **Leonora E. Piper** and to become her controls.

**Incline Effect.** The improvement of a scoring rate toward the end of a run or experimental series.

**Incorporeal Personal Agency. (IPA).** A term used to designate a deceased human personality or consciousness that presumably has survived death. Since the postulated surviving personality or consciousness need not be bodiless and may have an **Astral Body** or other quasi-physical one, the term may be misleading.

**Incorruptibility.** Weeks, months, or years after death, the freedom from natural decay of a corpse that has not been embalmed, frozen, dessicated, or placed in a sealed metal coffin. Bodies found entire have been reported in the cases of many famous Christian religious figures: St. Francis de Sales died in 1622, but his body remained uncorrupted ten years after death; the body of St. John of God was not affected twenty years after death except for the tip of the nose; St. Francis of Paula's body was not decayed although fifty-five years had elapsed since death; even more striking, the body of St. Antoninus of Florence who died in 1459 showed no sign of corruption by 1589; and though the body of St. Paschal Baylon had been covered with lime in 1592, it was still absolutely preserved in 1611.

It does not necessarily mean, however, that incorruptibility is a miracle brought about by God. The number of such cases is too great to assume that supernatural intervention has taken place. Moreover, some of the most venerated of saints, such as Catherine of Siena, St. Ignatius of Loyola and St. Francis of Assisi, who might have been expected to have been granted the divine favor of incorruptibility, were not. Why some bodies remain free of decay and others do not remains an enigma for which medical science has no explanation but which, as an unexplained phenomenon, is of potentially great interest for psychical research. See **Bernadette, Saint; Catherine of Bologna, Saint; Teresa of Avila, Saint; Vincent de Paul, Saint.**

BIBLIOGRAPHY: Thurston, H. *The Physical Phenomena of Mysticism,* 1952, pp. 247–248.

**Indians, American.** See **American Indians.**

**Indridason, Indridi, 1883–1912.** Icelandic physical medium. The first outstanding physical medium in the history of Iceland, he became aware of his psychic talents in 1905 upon attending a circle. As his powers developed and his reputation in his country increased, he was investigated extensively by representatives of the Experimental Society in Reykjavik, among them the most illustrious scientist of the day, Gudmundur Hannesson, a professor of medicine at the University of Iceland.

During the tests and while in trance, Indridason produced, often in well-illuminated séance rooms, a full array of impressive and varied physical phenomena ranging from apports, direct voice, levitation and luminous phenomena to raps and materializations. For example, in the full light of a séance room in 1906, a deceased being purporting to be one "Jensen," wrote an investigator, "showed himself . . . where we sat, with the medium among us—do not forget that! The medium was in a very deep trance. The new visitor was dressed in a very fine white drapery . . . and the light was radiating from him. We saw him at different places in the room. Once he stood on a sofa, and behind him was a red light, which was similar to a little sun, with whitish light steaming out from it. . . . Frequently he managed to appear 7–8 times the same evening in different places in the room. Many times we saw the medium and this materialised being simultaneously. But this extraordinary visitor could not be visible for more than a few seconds each time. . . . and he always allowed us to touch his materialised body before he dematerialised it again" (Gissurarson and Haraldsson, 1989:83). This startling event and many others took place in the presence of the medium despite rigorous controls and steps to avoid trickery.

All the investigators involved were absolutely sure that what they had observed could not be explained. Even the great Hannesson stated that it was "my firm conviction, that the phenomena are unquestionable realities" (Gissurarson and Haraldsson, 1989:125). And the authors of a treatise on the medium "feel confident in saying that all those who are intent on disbelieving and, if possible, discrediting all claims of paranormality are likely to find this case a tough nut to crack" (Gissurarson and Haraldsson, 1989:56).

Indridason died of tuberculosis at the age of 29. Had he not died prematurely and unknown outside of Iceland, historians of psychical research might have ranked him the equal of D. D. Home and Eusapia Palladino, the greatest physical mediums of the time.

BIBLIOGRAPHY: Gissurarson, L. R. and Haraldsson, E. 1989. "The Icelandic Physical Medium Indridi Indridason." PSPR 57:53.

**Inglis, Brian, 1916–.** Irish columnist, feature writer for the *Irish Times* and *Spectator*, television commentator, historian and author. He dreamed the winner of the Grand National (wrong name, right number) and won some money. As a result of his precognitive dream, he reviewed a book on precognition, came to realize that the unexplained ought to be investigated, and wrote articles on the paranormal for the *Times* and *Guardian*. He also began writing books for the general reader on unorthodox healing or "natural medicine" (Inglis, 1979) and on the history of parapsychology, physical phenomena, and the paranormal (Inglis, 1985; 1977).

Inglis does, however, "have a curious penchant for white-washing the careers of psychics and researchers he favors" (Rogo, 1985) and fails on occasion to bring out evidence of fraud that has been uncovered. So convinced is he of the reality of extrasensory perception, psychokinesis, and other paranormal phenomena that he charges to attack skeptics who would debunk and undermine parapsychology (Inglis, 1986). Inglis cofounded the KIB Foundation to encourage research into areas outside orthodox science. He has a Ph.D. from Dublin University and is a Fellow of the Royal Society of Literature.

Selected Writings: *The Hidden Power*, 1986; *The Paranormal: An Encyclopedia of Psychic Phenomena*, 1985; "Power Corrupts: Skepticism Corrodes." In W. G. Roll and J. Beloff, eds., *Research in Parapsychology 1980*, 1981; *Natural Medicine*, 1979; *Natural and Supernatural: A History of the Paranormal from the Earliest Times*, 1977.

BIBLIOGRAPHY: Rogo, D. S. 1985. "Book Review. The *Paranormal* by Brian Inglis." JSPR 53:180.

**Inoue, Enryo, 1859–1919.** Japenese philosopher. He founded Toyo University, organized Fushigi Kenkyukai (Society for Anomalous Phenomena) at the Imperial University of Tokyo in 1888 and pioneered critical investigations of spontaneous cases with particular reference to ghost lore.

Selected Writing: Inoue, E. *Shinkai* (Real Mystery), 1919.

**Inspiration.** See **Creative Process.**

**Institute for Parapsychology.** Founded by J. B. Rhine's Foundation for Research on the Nature of Man. It is the successor to the methods and standards of the Parapsychology Laboratory at Duke University. As FRNM's research unit it explores all unusual types of experiences that seem to transcend the known forces of our physical environment and may make the individual unique. The Institute for Parapsychology also offers summer study programs for advanced undergraduate and graduate-level students and contains a library with a complete collection of parapsychological journals. Stored here is the huge collection of spontaneous cases that had been gathered over the years by the Parapsychology Laboratory. The address of the institute is Box 6847, College Station, Durham, North Carolina 27708.

**Institute for Yoga and Consciousness.** Established at Andhra University, the Institute for Yoga and Consciousness is an interdisciplinary center in India supported by the government of Andhra Pradesh. It conducts research on mind-matter interaction and is the only center in India studying consciousness and paranormal powers in the context of Indian philosophy. It also conducts programs to assist people to discover their inner selves and their potentials. Programs on yoga, meditation, psychotherapy, and counseling also are carried on. See also **Rao, K. R.**

**Institute of Noetic Sciences.** American organization established in California in 1972 by **Edgar D. Mitchell** to conduct a general study of and encourage research in human consciousness. The institute is a vehicle for carrying out Mitchell's dream of making "psychenauts" of us all, travellers in inner space who will transform our consciousness and those of humankind so that we can become aware of our spiritual aspects and of our unity with one another and the universe. Parapsychology is linked to the project because parapsychology seems to undermine the physicalist view of the human being. Address: 2658 Ridgeway, Sausalito, CA 94965.

**Institute of Transpersonal Psychology.** American organization that provides a Spiritual Emergency Network with therapists and counsellors to help people troubled by psychic or spiritual experiences, practices, or development. It also offers an M.A. and Ph.D. in transpersonal psychology. Address: 250 Oak Grove Ave., Menlo Park, CA 94025.

**Institut für Grenzgebiete der Psychologie und Psychohygiene. (Institute for Border Areas of Psychology and Mental Hygiene).** Founded in 1950 by **Hans Bender,** this German organization once was described by Joseph B. Rhine as a "splendid" plant any parapsychologist would be happy to use. It investigates paranormal phenomena with instrumentation as the best means of effective documentation. The institute has carried on, for example, several poltergeist studies, Bender's speciality, with video recorders that can easily be brought to the scenes of ongoing investigations. The presentation of videotapes showing objects in movement can be very convincing to sceptics. The dual name of the organization comes from Bender's belief that coping with the paranormal entails more than scientific investigation. It also requires changing the thinking of the public which, on one hand, is irrational and superstitious, and, on the other, is negative and sceptical. The institute attempts to attack the psychology of superstitution and scepticism by using scientific methodology to establish the reality of the paranormal. The institut also offers courses on the methods and history of parapsychology and awards diplomas to psychologists completing such courses. It publishes *Zeitschrift für Parapsychologie* and, for interested archivists and researchers, maintains a collection of the papers of Albert von Schrenck-Notzing. The office of the organization is located at Eichhalde 12, 7800 Freiburg i. Br., West Germany.

**Institut Métapsychique International.** The founding in 1919 of this French organization by Jean Meyer, an ardent Spiritualist, marked a high point in the history of French psychical research. Meyer provided a large endowment in the belief that only through the scientific method could the paranormal phenomena in which he believed be generally accepted. He organized a committee consisting of scientific men, among them Charles Richet, Nicolas Camille Flammarion, Gustave Geley, Sir Oliver Lodge and Ernesto Bozzano. The high scientific standing of these people conveys the kind of dream and expectation Meyer had for the organization. Richet became its president and Geley its director. In subsequent years Rene Warcollier took over the presidency and Eugene Osty the directorship.

Among the outstanding studies made by the institut were those of Geley who had sittings with Franek Kluski and Osty who, just before and after World War I, devoted years to the investigations of mediums. Since its founding, the goal of the organization remains that of Meyer and it continues the scientific and rational study of paranormal phenomena. Anxious to integrate its research with other disciplines, the institut is now made up of ten committees that welcome qualified collaborators from other disciplines. The results of all research done by the institut along with other parapsychological topics are published in its organ, *Revue Métapsychique.* A Society of Friends of the Institut has been organized to arrange conferences, courses, work groups and the promulgation of a newsletter. The present address of the institut is Place de Wagram, 1. 75017, Paris, France.

**Instituto Argentino de Parapsicología.** Established in 1949 as the Argentine Parapsychology Society, this organization was reorganized as the Argentine Parapsychology Institute (Instituto Argentino de Parapsicología) to provide lectures and courses in parapsychology to an increasing membership and to publish the quarterly *Review of Parapsychology,* the first parapsychological journal published in Spanish anywhere. The importance of the organization during its early years lay in its close association with universities since many of its directors and lecturers on parapsychology were academics and since the organization provided much informational material to academics teaching parapsychology.

**Instituto de Estudios Parapsicologicos (Institute of Parapsychological Studies).** The first and only parapsychological organization in Panama and, in fact, in all of Central America, it was established in 1982 to study the nature of the human being as revealed by telepathy, clairvoyance, precognition, and psychokinesis. The founders intended to study spontaneous cases as well as to make laboratory investigations and to conduct survival research. Research programs are underway to study the native groups in Panama, including the Chocoes and Guaymies. Experiments are carried out at the School of Psychology at the University of Panama. The organization is the strongest link in Panama, and in all of Central America, between parapsychology and university support. It is also working toward offering a regular course in parapsychology at the University of Panama.

Educational programs were offered as were public lectures on parapsychology from 1982 to 1985. They have been suspended for the present. However, the plan is to resume them in 1990. The organization initially was open to membership but, since 1985, has limited itself to research activities. It publishes a bulletin, *Boletín Informativo.* Address: Apartado 8000, Panama 7, Panama.

**Instituto de Parapsicología (Parapsychology Institute).** Argentinian parapsychological organization founded in 1972 in order to conduct experimental investigations, particularly to replicate experiments conducted in the United States and reported in the *Journal of Parapsychology.* The institute offers courses in parapsychology as well as public lectures and, four times a year, publishes *Cuadernos de Parapsicología.* Address: Calle Ramón Lista 868, 1706 Domingo F., Sarmiento Haedo, Prov. Buenos Aires, Argentina.

**Instituto "Gnosis" per la Ricérca Sulla Ipòtesi della Sopravvivenza. (Institute "Gnosis" for Research on the Survival Hypothesis).** Italian organization created in 1981 in Naples by **Giorgio Di Simone.** In order to study the question of survival after death, it collects and evaluates data on paranormal phenomena, such as out-of-body experiences, deathbed visions, and mediums, in the belief that these data may increase our understanding of the destiny of the human being. The institute also believes that the importance of its research lies in its method of combining statistics with a critical examination of material. The organization is open to members, tries to cooperate with other organizations and individual researchers and publishes *Quadèrni Gnosis.* Address: Via Belvedere, 87/80127, Naples, Italy.

**Instituto Mexicano de Investigaciones Síquicas. (Mexican Institute of Psychical Investigations).** Formerly called the Circulo de Investigaciones Metasíquicas de México, this organization was established in 1939 as the first parapsychological group in Mexico with a membership of some 200 people. Since its first president was the dean of the National University of Mexico, it enjoyed great prestige. It was created primarily to investigate the physical medium **Luis Martínez,** and the séances it held with him were always crowded with the elite of Mexican society and politics. Soon the bloom faded from the rose, however, and the organization disappeared and no longer exists.

**International Association for Near-Death Studies.** American association established in 1981 as an organization of scholars, scientists, near-death experiencers, and the general public to encourage and support research into the nature and significance of the **Near-death Experience.** It also created a network of regional coordinators in the United States as well as an affiliated organization in the United Kingdom. Besides encouraging research, IANDS aims to sponsor symposia and conferences on the NDE, educate the public, hospitals, hospices, and nursing homes about the NDE and its implications and provide a supportive environment for near-death experiencers and their families. The association's publications include the *Journal of Near-Death Studies* and *Revitalized Signs.* Address: IANDS, Department of Psychiatry, University of Connecticut Health Center, Farmington CT 06032.

**International Institute for Religion and Parapsychology.** A Japanese organization called Kokusai Shukyo Cho-Shinri Gakkai. Consisting of about 1,000 members, it gives courses in yoga, studies religious experiences and psi and investigates psi processes by using psychophysiological and parapsychological methods. It publishes the periodical *Shukyo to Cho-Shinri* (Religion and Parapsychology). The founder of the organization is **Hiroshi Motoyama.** The office of the institute is located at 11-7, Inokashira 4-chome, Mitaka-shi, 180 Tokyo, Japan.

**International Institute for the Study of Death.** Organized in 1985 as the scholarly and scientific affiliate of the **Survival Re-**

**search Foundation,** the International Institute for the Study of Death was the first multidisciplinary and multicultural organization established to stimulate and organize scientific, philosophical, religious, and parapsychological inquiries into and cross-cultural dialogue on the many aspects of death and dying, including the question of the survival of the human personality or consciousness beyond death. Its aim is to provide an international forum in which, without advocating a particular doctrine, all cultures and disciplines can relate to, learn from, and cross-fertilize one another with respect to the many aspects of death. It has a branch in the United Kingdom. Its director is **Arthur S. Berger** and its main headquarters is in the United States. Address: P.O. Box 8565, Pembroke Pines, FL 33084, USA.

**International Journal of Parapsychology.** A quarterly journal which, beginning in 1959, was published by the **Parapsychology Foundation.** Before it became defunct, it provided a forum for authorities in all fields to discuss parapsychology. Research papers and major articles were published in English and summarized in French, German, Italian, and Spanish.

**Intervention.** Applied to any action taken to prevent or avoid a precognized event. See also **Precognition.**

**Intuition.** Derived from the Latin *intueri* meaning to look at or contemplate. "Hunch," "feeling," or "just knowing" are other terms used. One has an intuitive experience when, while awake and without any rational or sensory process, one has a thought that brings a true insight, information, or belief about some person or something outside oneself.

Twenty-nine percent of Louisa E. Rhine's spontaneous cases were intuitive. A typical case is that of a young woman in Chicago who was in her kitchen while her baby was asleep in the bedroom and her three year-old child was in the living room. All at once the mother felt that the baby was choking on something her older sister had put in the baby's mouth. The baby had not cried out, there was no reason to suspect that such a thing had happened, yet the woman "just knew." She ran into the bedroom, took the baby up, held her with her head down, pushed a finger into the baby's throat and extracted a piece of candy lodged in it. The older girl had wanted to be kind to her little sister.

The case shows how information can be received without use of the sense organs and, in this respect, makes intuition virtually the same as **Extrasensory Perception.** ESP does not appear in any particular form. It appears in many familiar forms including dreams and the creative process. Intuition may be another way that information received by ESP comes into consciousness.

BIBLIOGRAPHY: L. E. Rhine. *Psi: What Is It?,* 1975.

**Iredell, Denise, 1926–.** British industrial lecturer and psychical researcher. Daughter of **Muriel Hankey,** her involvement in psychical research began early and has continued for a lifetime. She was president of the **College of Psychic Studies,** editor of *Light,* investigated physical phenomena, worked with Kathleen R. Gay, had sittings with medium Geraldine D. Cummins and was also a sitter in the famous Sir Oliver Lodge posthumous test for survival at the time that his sealed packets were opened. Mrs. Iredell is a member of the Royal Institution of Great Britain, an old scientific learned society, and has served as secretary to the Survival Joint Research Committee trust.

**Irwin, Harvey Jon, 1943–.** Australian lecturer in psychology. Although Australia is a great distance from the centers of parapsychological research and theory across the seas, Dr. Irwin has helped put his country on the parapsychological map with a new approach to understanding the out-of-body experience as a psychological rather than a paranormal phenomenon. Considerable respect also is accorded Irwin's work relating to the psychological dimension known as "absorption"—the total imperviousness to normally distracting events and total attention paid to an object of thought. Paranormal experiences and out-of-body experiences may occur in people who have the capacity and need to enter into a state of absorption.

Besides teaching parapsychology at the University of New England and being on the editorial boards of two parapsychological journals, Dr. Irwin's other interests include the impact of the out-of-body experience and the near death experience on experiments, the belief in and the fear of psi and the history of Australian parapsychology. He is a Fellow of the American Society for Psychical Research from which he received the Mid S. Weiss award in 1979.

Selected Writings: 1988. "Parapsychology in Australia." JASPR 82:319; *Flight of Mind: A Psychological Study of the Out-of-Body Experience,* 1985; 1985. "Parapsychological Phenomena and the Absorption Domain." JASPR 79:1.

**Ivanova, Barbara Mikhailovna, 1917–.** Soviet healer, psychic and parapsychologist. In 1971 she developed powers of unorthodox healing and, from the testimony of her patients, cured cases of pneumonia, sciatica, infection, and toothaches (Mir and Vilenskaya, 1986).

Before she begins her healing, she stands quietly beside a patient with her head bowed because she is "asking the higher forces to assist me. I am asking to be a clear and pure channel for the highest energies." Then she says, "I vibrate my fingers until I begin to feel a prickling sensation at the end of them, which tells me that I am connected to the higher forces. Then, I imagine a *golden chalice* full of light and love . . . It is this energy which will heal . . . , not me." (Mir and Vilenskaya, 1986:25).

Ivanova became the first teacher of this subject in the Soviet Union. The students she trained in the process of healing reported a variety of results, including the decrease or disappearance of tumors and the anesthetizing of pain. In addition, according to Ivanova, "the normalizing of blood pressure . . . can be achieved by each of my students after two days of learning" (Ivanova, 1986:43). She also conducted experiments in telepathy and clairvoyance. In the belief that all people possess psi abilities and that these capacities can be developed, she trained her students to use their psi capacities to create psychographs and to obtain information about disorders in the human body and to make medical diagnoses.

She herself was the subject in an experiment in 1977 in a Moscow research laboratory. While in one room in the laboratory, she was given the task of describing objects in another of the rooms in which she had never been. She successfully described the shapes and colors of the targets in minute detail and with 90 percent accuracy (Vilenskaya, 1984).

In 1973, because of opposition to parapsychology, Dr. Ivanova "was fired from her job at the Moscow State Institute for International Relations. She was dismissed by blackmail and threats, with infringing Soviet labor laws. She has, since that time, remained without employ . . ." (Vilenskaya, 1980:208).

Selected Writing: "A Letter from Barbara Ivanova." In Mir, M. and Vilenskaya, L., eds., *The Golden Chalice,* 1986, p. 43.

BIBLIOGRAPHY: Mir, M. and Vilenskaya, L., eds., *The Golden Chalice,* 1986; Vilenskaya, L. 1984. "Investigation and Application of Telepathy, Clairvoyance and Psychokinesis in the USSR and in the West." Paper presented at the Second International Congress on Interdisciplinary Discussions of Border Area Problems of Science, Basel, Switzerland, November 1984; Vilenskaya, L. "On PK and Related Subjects' Research in the U.S.S.R." In W. and M. Uphoff, eds., *Mind Over Matter,* 1980, p. 205.

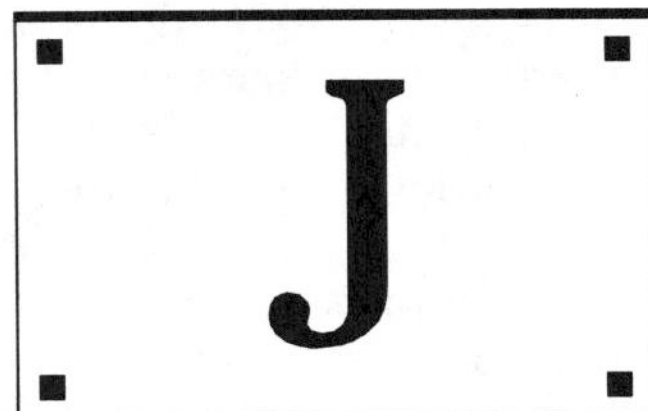

**Jacks, Lawrence Pearsall, 1860–1955.** British professor of philosophy and Unitarian minister. L. P. Jacks, who had a large following in the United States, was best known as the editor of the *Hibbert Journal,* which was open to all schools of thought, even psychical research. He sat with Gladys Osborne Leonard (who gave him a message from his "dead" son who was then very much alive) and tried to investigate (unsuccessfully) a ghost.

His main interests in psychical research, however, were dreams and survival of death, the latter being the subject of his presidential address to the Society for Psychical Research of which he was president for the years 1917 and 1918. He felt that the principal problem in both areas (dreams and survival) was that of the identity (of the character in the dream or of the communicator) and that we need more data. He suggested that those we call dead are now where they have always been and "that we have simply found them in one of their many houses. . . . [N]o man knows how many lives he lives, and how many worlds he inhabits here and now." He wrote many books and published in the *Journal* and the *Proceedings* of the SPR.

Selected Writings: 1917. "Presidential Address: The Theory of Survival in the Light of its Context." PSPR 29:287; 1915. "Dramatic Dreams, an Unexplored Field for Psychical Research." JSPR 17:178.

BIBLIOGRAPHY: Haynes, R. *The Society for Psychical Research 1882–1892: A History,* 1982; Stratton, F.J.M. 1955. "Obituary: Dr. L. P. Jacks." JSPR 38:100.

**Jack the Ripper.** Unknown murderer of seven harlots who walked the streets of London in 1888. He killed them by cutting their throats, butchering their bodies (hence the name "Ripper") and removing their organs with a skill that showed great anatomical knowledge. In spite of determined efforts by the police to find the killer, the gruesome crimes were never solved. Public indignation resulted in the resignations of the honorable secretary and the police commissioner.

Yet a psychic Sherlock Holmes claimed to have discovered the killer's identity. According to newspaper interviews and accounts beginning in 1895, a medium named **Robert Lees** maintained that he had foretold when a murder by Jack the Ripper was going to be committed. On one occasion, Lees reported to Scotland Yard that he "saw" a man and woman enter a small court, he saw its name and a clock that showed the time as 12:40 A.M. The man in the vision cut the woman's throat and slashed her body. The police paid no attention to him. He following night, however, according to the medium, a woman was killed at the hour and location revealed by the vision.

The next time he went to the police he told them that there would be another murder and that the woman's ears would be cut off. Scotland yard now listened to him because the police had received a postcard from Jack the Ripper in which he said that he was going to cut off the ears of his next prey. Lees again went to Scotland Yard when he had still another psychic impression of another murder. After the police were notified that in fact the Ripper had slain another victim, the medium said that a police inspector took him to the scene of the crime. Lee's gifts supposedly enabled him to identify a well-known London doctor who, of course, had the requisite knowledge of human anatomy and who, in addition, the police found to be a split personality capable of terrible cruelty. The physician, whose identity was never revealed, was allegedly determined to be insane and put in an asylum.

Thus, from the newspaper accounts, Lees tracked down Jack the Ripper in one of the earliest example of psychic crime detection. Scotland Yard, however, denied that any medium had been used in the case or that they knew who the murderer was. Also, the police kept arresting men suspected of the murders, which they would not have done if the real murderer had been identified. The unsolved case goes on as the perennial motivator of articles, books, and television plays as journalists, authors, detectives and others speculate on the true identity of Jack the Ripper.

BIBLIOGRAPHY: West, D. J. 1949. "The Identity of 'Jack the Ripper.'" JSPR 35:76.

**Jacobs, Jeff C., 1950–.** Dutch engineer and statistician. He founded the **Synchronicity Research Unit,** conducts research in psychokinesis, and is interested in synchronicity and in that special form of estrasensory perception that seems to waken us from sleep.

This latter interest led him to seek out W. van Vuurde after the latter had returned from South Africa to his native Holland. Jacobs's aim was to review and reconstruct the records van Vuurde had kept of home experiments he had conducted between 1951 and 1954. (They had so impressed Arthur E. H. Bleksley that he used van Vuurde in a series of award-winning tests.) Yet these valuable records had never been organized and examined before Jacobs undertook to analyze and evaluate them. His evaluation confirmed that extrasensory perception had been involved in van Vuurde's awakening from sleep at a predetermined time. The records showed hits of the target time so far in excess of chance and over such an extended period of years that Jacobs was led to describe van Vuurde as one of the outstanding subjects in parapsychological history.

Selected Writing: 1985. "PSI-Guided Awakening From Sleep 1: The Original Experiments of W. Van Vuurde." JSPR 53:159.

**Jacobson, Nils O., 1937–.** Swedish psychiatrist and author interested in psychical research. His book (Jacobson, 1971) brought to the attention of general readers how the findings of psychical research, in particular, the out-of-body experience, apparitions, possession, electronic voice phenomena, reincarnation, and xenoglossy bear on the question of the survival of the human personality after death. But all that Jacobson can say is that the material he presents cannot prove survival. It can only "motivate a *rationally based belief* in survival" (Jacobson, 1971:289). His conclusion is no more or less than that which psychical researchers have reached and been expressing since the late nineteenth century and is a sad reminder of how little they have been able to accomplish in survival research over the last 100 years.

Selected Writing: *Life without Death? On Parapsychology, Mysticism, and the Question of Survival,* 1971.

**Jaffé, Aniela, 1903–.** German-born psychologist. Secretary of the C. J. Jung Institute in Zurich, Switzerland, from 1947 to 1955, Miss Jaffé worked closely with **Carl Gustav Jung.** It was she who took down his reminiscences (1963) in the course of which she reported that she "often asked for specific data, but asked in vain" (Burt 1963:175). Miss Jaffé made an important contribution to psychical research in her book *Apparitions and Precognition* (1963), in which she dealt with spontaneous cases from three points of view: first, from their significance for the experiencer; second, from the Jungian view of the unconscious mind; and third, according to Jung's theory of synchronicity. She also wrote a study of Jung and parapsychology (1967).

Selected Writings: "C. J. Jung and Parapsychology." In J. R. Smythies, ed., *Science and ESP,* 1967; *Apparitions and Precognition,* 1963; ed., Jung, C. J. *Memories, Dreams, Reflections,* 1963.

BIBLIOGRAPHY: Burt, C. 1963. "Jung's Account of his Paranormal Experiences." JSPR 42:163; Eastman, M. 1964. "Apparitions and Precognition." JSPR 42:303.

**Jahn, Robert G., 1930–.** American engineer, dean of the School of Engineering/Applied Sciences at Princeton University. Dean Jahn, whose background is in engineering and applied physics, came to parapsychology in about 1978 when he supervised a student's independent project in psychical research and concluded that it was a valid subject for study. Accordingly, in mid-1979, he organized the Princeton Engineering Anomalies Project (PEAR) at Princeton whose work has been supported by grants from, among others, the James S. McDonnell Foundation, the John E. Fetzer Foundation, and the Ohrstrom Foundation.

PEAR has turned its attention mainly to investigations in remote viewing, low level psychokinesis, and theory. As a non-parapsychologist, Dean Jahn has recommended that "this community concentrate on clean, conservative experiments that are firmly rooted in ground familiar to established science . . . [and] that are characterized by . . . (a) *A well-defined purpose and protocol* . . . (b) *Theoretical exploration of one parameter at a time* . . . (c) . . . *elegant and sophisticated instrumentation and data processing* . . . (d) *Attention to baseline stability against artifact* . . . (e) *The use of bi-directional protocols whenever possible* . . . (f) *Very large data bases* . . . (g) *Theoretical models* . . . (h) *More attention to results generated by . . . people who make no claims of special gifts* . . ." (1983:134–136). He also believes that topics that will have practical applications should be selected to study and that the various psychical research and parapsychological organizations should merge to give the field greater "clout." Dr. Jahn's methods of accumulating large quantities of data has been praised (Beloff, 1985).

Dean Jahn has published papers on parapsychological subjects both in the parapsychological literature and in reports put out by PEAR.

Selected Writings: "On the Representation of Psychic Research to the Community of Established Science." In R. A. White and R. S. Broughton, eds., *Research in Parapsychology 1983,* 1984, pp. 127–138; and Dunne, B. J. and Nelson, R. D. 1985. *Princeton Engineering Anomalies Research.* Technical Note PEAR 85003; and Dunne, B. J. and Jahn, E. G. "Analytical Judging Procedure for Remote Perception Experiments." In W. G. Roll and J. Beloff, eds., (J. McAllister, ass't ed.) *Research in Parapsychology, 1980,* 1981.

BIBLIOGRAPHY: Beloff, J. "Parapsychology and the Expectation of Progress." In D. H. Weiner and D. I. Radin, eds., *Research in Parapsychology 1985,* 1986, pp. 106–107.

**James, William, 1842–1910.** One of America's foremost psychologists. He wrote widely in psychology (1890), philosophy (1897, 1902, 1907, 1909) and religion (1902), and when some Intellectual Hall of Fame is established, the millions who have savored and have been inspired by the eloquence, lucidity, and quotability of James's writings will see that he is honored as one of America's foremost intellects. His interests were wide-ranging and took in any phenomenon that involved some aspect of the human mind or personality. In this category was, first of all, "mental healing." To test it and try to cure his persistent insomnia he paid several visits to "a mind-cure doctress" who was none other than Lydia E. Pinkham of female home remedy fame. Since she seemed to help him, he became the foe of all bills in the Massachussetts Legislature that required the licensing of mental healers.

After mental healing, James's interest turned to psychical research. It has been said that "[m]odern insight into psychic phenomena begins and ends with William James . . ." (Ebon, 1971). James was attracted by the paranormal both as a psychologist hoping to find some depth of the human mind still to be discovered and as a philosopher concerned with the place of the human being in the cosmos. One of his essays contained a powerful criticism of orthodox science for ignoring as popular delusions paranormal phenomena, such as "spooks," telepathy, and raps. He thought these phenomena might be part of a genuine realm of natural phenomena. His interest in the subject led him to cooperate in the formation of the Society for Psychical Research in 1882. James also played a leading part in the formation in 1885 of the **American Society for Psychical Research.** He participated actively in the investigations of apparitions, haunts, and mediums.

In the autumn of 1885, after members of his family told him that a certain medium in Boston had given them facts and names that defied normal explanation, James could not resist paying her a visit himself. This first visit was followed by twelve more visits and these in turn by a "lightning-stroke" belief that the medium's many hits when she was in trance suggested that she possessed supernormal powers he could not explain. And so he discovered **Leonora E. Piper,** one of the great mediums in the history of parapsychology. She was James's "white crow," all that he needed to upset the law that all crows are black.

James was elected president of the SPR in 1894. He was a friend and admirer of F.W.H. Myers and wrote an enthusiastic review of the latter's posthumous treatise *Human Personality and its Survival of Bodily Death.* When Myers was dying in a hotel room in Rome, James, stricken with grief, sat just outside the dying man's bedroom, pen in hand, notebook on his lap, ready to record any message Myers would give after crossing the threshhold of death. But, to James's despair, there was no message.

Later, after the death of Richard Hodgson, James made a detailed study of Mrs. Piper's mediumship and Hodgson's purported communications through her.

Whether or not an Intellectual Hall of Fame is ever established, James already occupies a niche in psychical research as one of its early leaders who called for serious study of the paranormal and helped to organize its collective investigation in the United States.

Selected Writings: "What Psychical Research Has Accomplished." In his *The Will to Believe and other Essays in Popular Philosophy,* 1956. First published 1897; 1909. "Report of Mrs. Piper's Hodgson-Control." PSPR 23:2; *The Meaning of Truth,* 1909; *Pragmatism,* 1907; 1903. "Reviews: Human Personality and its Survival of Bodily Death." PSPR 18:22; *Varieties of Religious Experience,* 1902; *Principles of Psychology,* 1890.

BIBLIOGRAPHY: Berger, A. S. *Lives and letters in American Parapsychology: A Biographical History, 1850–1987.* 1988; Ebon, M. *They Knew the Unknown,* 1971; Murphy, G. and Ballou, R. O. *William James on Psychical Research,* 1960.

**Janet, Pierre (Marie-Felix), 1859–1947.** French psychologist and physician. A student and colleague of Jean-Martin Charcot, he attempted to link psychology and medicine and emphasized hypnosis as a treatment for mental disorders. He also was one of the earliest investigators of the paranormal and among the first to observe that psi was closely connected to altered states of consciousness.

Janet found that patients deep in a hypnotic sleep and isolated from the sensory world had the power of extrasensory perception. This finding shows how difficult it is to distinguish between trance and hypnosis since all the great mediums also were able to exercise paranormal abilities while in a dissociated state. In his experiments, Janet discovered "hypnosis at a distance": he could induce or end a person's hypnotic sleep by a mental command sent by telepathy from a distance and at random times (Janet, 1886).

Selected Writing: 1886. "Deuxième Note sur la Sommeil Provoqué à Distance et la Suggestion Mentale Pendant l'État Somnambulique." *Revue Philosophique de la France et de l'Étranger.* August 21: 212.

**Januarius, Saint (San Gennaro in Italian), ?–c.305 A.D..** Bishop of Benevento and patron saint of Naples. During the reign of Diocletian, the final massive persecution of the Christians by Rome took place. Diocletian set out to compel all Christians to give up their faith and pay homage to pagan gods. Januarius preferred martyrdom to abandoning his faith. Although the account of his martyrdom may be a fabrication, it is related that when the Romans threw him to the lions the animals refused to harm him. So he and others were removed from the arena and beheaded on September 19, 305. A cathedral was erected in Naples between 1294 and 1323 dedicated to Januarius and festivals are held in May and another in September to commemorate his martyrdom.

Januarius was not known for any paranormal gifts or feats during his lifetime. But he has achieved lasting fame as a noted witness to the paranormal because during May, September, and December of each year, the solid substance in two sealed glass ampules reputed to be the dried blood of the martyr liquifies during public ceremonies in honor of the saint. The weight and volume of the substance also change. The liquefaction phenomenon, which was first recorded in 1389, is of great interest and importance to the residents of Naples who believe, with good reason, that if the blood does not liquify they will have bad luck. When the phenomenon failed to occur in 1527, Naples was struck by a plague. In 1569 when it did not take place, there was a famine in the city and in 1941 when the blood again did not liquify, there was an eruption of Vesuvius and a bombing by planes from the Allied forces.

Since all attempts to provide any physical explanation for the liquefaction of Januarius's blood, when it does occur, have failed, it continues to be a subject that holds fascination for psychical research.

**Japanese Society for Parapsychology.** Founded in 1968 by Soji Otani, Akira Onda and others, it is a membership organization that promotes research in parapsychology, holds annual conventions and publishes the results of its work in a *Newsletter* and a *Proceedings*. Its office is located at 26-14 Chuo 4-chome, Nakano-ku, 164 Tokyo, Japan.

**Jastrow, Joseph, 1863–?.** Polish-born psychologist. He attended the University of Pennsylvania, became professor of psychology at the Universities of Wisconsin and Minnesota and emerged as "a spokesman for academic psychologists hostile to parapsychology" (Berger, 1988:110). Although it seemed to contradict his role as a member of the Advisory Council of the American Society for Psychical Research to which he was appointed in 1921, at every opportunity he lectured or wrote articles attacking the phenomena of psychical research and parapsychology from mediums to experiments in extrasensory perception carried out by Joseph B. Rhine at Duke University.

Jastrow opposed them all to the "last ditch" (Jastrow, 1927)—but not because he had any personal or experimental knowledge of the phenomena. Indeed, Jastrow believed "there is no real obligation to consider minutely all of the circumstances" (Jastrow, 1923). He thought that those who are "drawn to such experiments and observations are under the influence of a strong will to believe" (Jastrow, 1923:10). Yet it is interesting that the great majority of parapsychologists have recorded no psychic experiences as they should have if they were under the influence of a "will to believe" (Berger, 1988:104). Instead we find such experiences reported by Noted Witnesses who were not dominated by a "will to believe."

Selected Writings: "The Animus of Psychical Research." In C. Murchison, ed., *The Case for and against Psychical Belief*, 1927, p. 281; 1923. "A Reply to Mr. Prince." JASPR 17:15.

**Jephson, Ina (Selina), 1890s–1961.** British psychologist and psychical researcher. Her experiments in the late 1920s in clairvoyance (as opposed to telepathy) in card-guessing experiments were considered by the council of the Society for Psychical Research "as among the most important pieces of experimental work which have been undertaken on the Society's behalf." Gardner Murphy in America was equally enthusiastic. But a confirmatory series of experiments under stricter conditions conducted by Miss Jephson in 1929 with Theodore Besterman and Samuel G. Soal yielded negative results.

Miss Jephson was the first experimenter to notice the **Decline Effect** which she called "the fatigue curve." She also carried out an innovative series of experiments (sadly also with nul results) in which she was looking for what she called "Intuitive Perception" (Jephson, 1933).

A shy, reserved woman, Miss Jephson studied psychology in Munich and worked with disturbed children at a psychology clinic in London and, during the war years 1939–1945, in Oxford. She became a member of the Society for Psychical Research in 1920 and was on its council from 1928 until her death.

Selected Writings: 1933. "A Behaviourist Experiment in Clairvoyance." PSPR 41:99; 1928. "Evidence for Clairvoyance in Card-Guessing: A Report on Some Recent Experiments." PSPR 38:223; with Soal, S. G. and Besterman, T. 1931. "Report of a Series of Experiments in Clairvoyance Conducted at a Distance under Approximately Fraud-proof Conditions." PSPR 39:375.

BIBLIOGRAPHY: Berger, A. S. *Lives and Letters in American Parapsychology*, 1988; Goldney, K. M. 1962. "Obituary." JSPR 41:271.

**Jesus Christ (Jesus of Nazareth), c.6 B.C.—30 A.D.** Founder of the Christian faith. His name "Jeshua" in Aramaic became Jesus in Greek. When Jesus was thirty years old, he was baptized by John the Baptist and, according to one Gospel, the Spirit of God descended on him like a dove (Luke 3:22). The gospel of Jesus then began (Mark 1:1) preceded by forty days of fasting, prayer and meditation. At the end of that time, Jesus went on his mission, which lasted about three years before his trial and execution, to preach that all repent their sins because the Kingdom of God was at hand. He not only preached the highest moral teachings and visions of God and human destiny but also performed "mighty works" in the form of miracles reported in the New Testament that may have been paranormal phenomena. These can be pigeon-holed in several categories.

Early in his ministry, he demonstrated miraculous healing. One of his works was the healing of a woman who had been bleeding for twelve years. She just touched the hem of his cloak and, when he turned and declared her cured by her faith, she was cured (Matt. 9:20–22). Another instance was Jesus's healing of a nobleman's son dying of a fever (John 4:50–53). Such examples fall into the category of medically unexplained and unorthodox healing.

Another kind of feat psychical research and parapsychology would class today as telepathy. In one case, Jesus was able to tell a woman he had never known all the things she had ever done (John 4:29) and that, after having had five husbands, she was living with a man who was not her husband (John 4:18).

Other of Jesus's works could have been psychokinesis in operation. An instance is the biblical account of multiplication of food when Jesus fed the hungry with five loaves of bread and two fishes (Mark 6:36–44). (There is one report of a psychokinetic experiment having achieved a similar result [Rogo, 1982], and research in this area indicates that matter may be influenced by mental ability alone.) Jesus's psychokinetic ability would have been very great because of his great spirituality.

Jesus also excelled as a prophet and in his forecasts of future events gave evidence of precognitive ability.

In the case of some religious figures, there were wondrous manifestations after death. In the case of Jesus, too, death marked the start of new wonders. The Gospel reports that he rose after death and made postmortem appearances on several occasions (John 20:15, 19; John 21:4). Perhaps what was seen, however, was not his physical body returned. The appearances may have been apparitions, a paranormal event commonly reported in psychical research.

The miracles of Jesus tax the credence of many people today. But the miracles reported in the Gospels cannot be ignored. Psychical research and parapsychology suggest that at least some of Jesus's works of wonder could have been genuine paranormal phenomena and that Jesus had advanced and powerful psychic gifts. He is an extraordinary **Noted Witness** whose testimony in support of the paranormal should be considered. See also **Food, Multiplication of.**

**Joan of Arc, Saint (the Maid of Orleans), 1412–1431.** National heroine of France canonized in 1920. As a sixteen-year old girl on a divine mission to save France, she assumed leadership of its forces, lifted the siege of Orleans by the English in 1429, and had the Dauphin Charles VII crowned king of France. Captured by the English, she was burned at the stake as a sorceress in 1431.

Joan's place in psychical research, in contrast to her place in history, rarely has been explored. When she was about twelve years of age, a child she was playing with cried, "Joan, I see you flying near the ground!"—a possible instance of levitation. What drove the Maid on her great mission on behalf of France and finally on to her death were the visions she saw and the monitions or voices she said she heard. At first the voice simply told her to go home or to behave and to go to church. But subsequently the voice instructed her to go on her mission to save France and lift the siege of Orleans. Soon the voice she heard was accompanied by waking visions of saints and angels, invisible to anyone else. They sometimes spoke to her and she could even touch them.

Joan was illiterate, but she had a keen intellect as her organization of military campaigns and her successful parrying of the hostile questions of her accusers and judges demonstrate. Perhaps the Maid's visions and voices were the delusions or hallucinations of a disturbed girl, but she believed as did Socrates of his daemon that they were objective facts. And she did receive knowledge from her voices that she could not have obtained in any normal way or through her channels of sense.

Precognition is suggested by some examples in her brief life. Joan was able to tell the dauphin in April 1429, that, at Orleans, she would be wounded under the right shoulder by an arrow or crossbow bolt but that the would would not be mortal. On May 6 of that year, she was wounded by an arrow and recovered. Orleans had been under siege by the English since October 12, 1428, and it seemed a military impossibility to lift it. Yet on May 4, 1429, the voices predicted correctly that Joan would attack the English strongholds and raise the siege. The voices also prophesied that Charles VII would be crowned at Rheims and the prediction was fulfilled. On another occasion, Joan was advancing toward a castle when a man on horseback insulted and swore at her. She said to him, "In God's name, do you swear, and you so near your death?" An hour later, the man fell into a moat and was drowned. Finally, in Easter week of 1430, the voices told her that she would be captured before Midsummer Day and would suffer long captivity. She was in fact captured by the Burgundians in May 1430, a month before Midsummer Day, delivered by them to the English, imprisoned, tried, and burned a year later.

When Joan took over the military leadership of France, she needed a sword. In the church at Sainte-Catherine-de-Fierbois, the voices told her in a possible example of clairvoyance, there was hidden beneath the altar under the earth a rusty sword with five crosses on it. A man she had never seen and did not know was sent from Tours. He found the sword and presented it to Joan.

Another psychic phenomenon—telepathy—is suggested by incidents with the dauphin. When Joan was granted her first audience with him, he concealed himself among his court attendants. Yet she found him at once because, she said, she knew him through her voices. She then gave him information on a subject known only to him obtained from her voices and which she might have learned through telepathy. It had to do with his legitimacy and what she told him delighted him.

On the question of whether the voices were genuine or she was plain mad, Andrew Lang, who studied the Maid, concluded his study with the story of the scientist who said, "Come to the Salpêtrière [a hospital in Paris for hysterical women] and I will show you twenty Jeannes d'Arc." "Has one of them given us back Alsace and Lorraine?" he was asked. That is the crux of the problem of Joan of Arc and warrants numbering her among the **Noted Witnesses** for the paranormal.

BIBLIOGRAPHY: Lang, A. 1895. "The Voices of Jeanne d'Arc." PSPR 11:198.

**Johnson, Alice, 1860–1940.** British psychical researcher. Demonstrator in animal morphology in charge of the Balfour Laboratory at Newnham College, Cambridge, and **Eleanor Sidgwick's** private secretary until 1899, she became editor of the *Proceedings of the Society for Psychical Research* and ultimately research officer of the SPR, a post she held until 1916. She sat with Mrs. Leonora Piper during the latter's visit to England in 1889 and was one of the principal workers on the *Census of Hallucinations* (1894). In 1895 she sat for the first (and only) time with a physical medium during Eusapia Palladino's "disastrous" sittings in Cambridge. Fraser Nicol (1972) is extremely critical of her lack of knowledge and experience. Yet she felt strongly, along with Richard Hodgson and Frank Podmore, that even the best witnesses (including herself) were unreliable so that no physical phenomena could be considered genuine. Her work therefore mainly dealt with mental mediums. She noted the similarity between multiple personalities and mediumistic controls.

Alice Johnson (with some help from Richard Hodgson) did most of the work to complete (and, it seems, expurgate) **F. W. H. Myers's** posthumous great work, *Human Personality and its Survival of Bodily Death.* For thirty years she worked with Eleanor Sidgwick, Gerald Balfour and J. G. Piddington in analyzing alleged communications from their dead co-workers. Her most important papers dealt with the **Cross-Correspondences** and discussed mainly the automatic writing of Mrs. Holland (Mrs. Fleming) and Mrs. Verrall. She was one of the investigators in the Palm Sunday case involving Arthur Balfour. She argued that the cross-correspondences showed the active participation of intelligence and were evidence for human survival of bodily death.

Selected Writings: 1908. "On the Automatic Writing of Mrs. Holland." PSPR 21:166; (see also PSPR 24:201 and 25:218); 1914. "A Reconstruction of Some 'Concordant Automatisms.'" PSPR 27:1; with Sidgwick, H. and Committee. 1894. "Report on the Census of Hallucinations." PSPR 10:25.

BIBLIOGRAPHY: Gauld, A. *The Founders of Psychical Research,* 1968; Nicol, F. 1972. "The Founders of the S.P.R." PSPR 55:341, 361.

**Johnson, Douglas.** Contemporary British trance medium. He traces his psychic history to an aunt who was a medium and to an experience with levitation and table-tilting when he was eleven years old. As he lay on a heavy table as a group sat around it without touching it, it rose slowly upward. When he was sixteen he entered into a trance state for the first time and encountered a control named "Chiang." But "this frightened me very much, and I determined not to have anything to do with psychic things for a long time." After he was discharged from the Royal Air Force after World War II, however, apparently he overcame his fear and began his mediumship.

Johnson has been the subject of experiments conducted by parapsychologists both in the United Kingdom and the United States to try to confirm his psychic gifts in scientific tests. At the Psychical Research Foundation, for example, his task was to try to get images or impressions about strangers who were physically present or deceased people connected with them. In this experiment he received immediate feedback. In another set of tests, he was given objects and asked to use psychometry to get information about the absent people to whom the objects belonged. Johnson scored hits in both experiments, but there were many more when there was sensory contact and feedback. Johnson also was used in the investigation of a haunt in Florida. His impressions of a man, a girl, and a gray-haired lady all corresponded to apparitions the occupants of the house had seen (Joines and Artley, 1969).

Johnson, who conducts "development classes" in London to discover people, such as Malcolm Bessent, with psychic abilities, was featured in 1966 on an American Broadcasting Company television broadcast called "the Baffling World of ESP." While in trance during the broadcast, he gave information to a sitter about her dead father which so impressed her that she wept openly.

BIBLIOGRAPHY: "Interview: Douglas Johnson." 1971. *Psychic* 2:5; Joines, W. T. and Artley J. L. 1969. "Study of a Haunted House." *Theta* 27:2.

**Johnson, Gertrude M. (Nancy Sinclair), c. 1905–?.** British amateur sensitive. The adopted daughter of G. N. M. Tyrrell, she was the principal subject in his ESP experiments that seemed to give evidence of clairvoyance and precognition. In 1935 and 1936, using an electrical apparatus of his own design, Tyrrell carried out a long series of experiments with her and with G. W. Fisk, who acted sometimes as experimenter and sometimes as subject. Even after the introduction of randomizing procedures and other adaptations, Miss Johnson continued to score enormously above chance expectation.

BIBLIOGRAPHY: "Mr. T." (Tyrrell, G. N. M.) 1922. "The Case of Miss Nancy Sinclair." JSPR 20:294; Tyrrell, G. N. M. 1936. "Further Reserach in Extra-Sensory Perception." PSPR 44:99.

**Johnson, Martin.** Contemporary Swedish parapsychologist. A former professor of psychology at Lund University, Sweden, he has, since 1973, been "professor ordinarius" and director of the Parapsychological Division of the Psychological Laboratory at the University of Utrecht in The Netherlands. Respected by parapsychologists and sceptics alike (although his predecessor at Utrecht, **Wilhelm Tenhaeff,** called him a "Nordic woodchopper" who would destroy Tenhaeff's life work), Johnson feels that the evidence for psi is weak and ambiguous but that there is enough evidence to warrant further research in the field. He believes that there is evidence for something like extrasensonsory perception and psychokinesis but that theories propounded to explain psi raise questions rather than answer them.

Dr. Johnson is convinced that Sai Baba (and other Babas), Uri Geller and the other metal-benders are obviously frauds. In his 1982 book *Parapsychologie* Johnson wrote: "I think that parapsychology is presently in a critical stage. More unambiguous and robust findings will have to be presented if we want to justify its continued presence at the universities." Apparently, these findings have not been forthcoming since the Parapsychology Laboratory at Utrecht is being shut down. See also **University of Utrecht.**

Selected Writings: *Parapsychologie, Onderzoek in de Grensgebieden van ervaring en wetenschap,* 1982; "ESP and Subliminality." In W. G. Roll, R. L. Morris and J. D. Morris, eds., *Research in Parapsychology 1973,* 1974, pp. 22–24; 1971. "An Attempt to Manipulate the Scoring Direction of Subjects by Means of Control of Motivation of the Subjects." *Research Letter,* Parapsychological Division of the Psychological Laboratory of the University of Utrecht (Mar.):1; 1968. "Relationship between Dream Recall and Scoring Direction." JP 32:56; and Kanthamani, B. K. 1967. "The Defense Mechanism Test as a Predictor of ESP Scoring Direction." JP 31:99; and Nordbeck, B. 1972. "Variation in the Scoring of a 'Psychic' Subject." JP 36:311.

BIBLIOGRAPHY: Hoebens, P. H. "Sense and Nonsense in Parapsychology." In K. Frazier, ed., *Science Confronts the Paranormal,* 1986; Wolman, B., ed., *Handbook of Parapsychology,* 1977.

**Johnson, Raynor C., 1901–1987.** Australian physicist. He set out to explore questions that are or should be central to everyone's thinking and living: Why do we exist, what kind of a world do we live in, and why is there a world at all? For him to have satisfactory answers to such questions would have been more precious than all the wealth of the Indies. He was one of those rare scientists who recognized that science is not the only means through which answers can be gotten; psychical research and mystical experience also can bring us closer to an understanding of our world and our destiny. Johnson believed, too, that all facts—not only those acknowledged by orthodox science—must be considered. He perceived in the findings of psychical research much significant data to be used in the search for answers. At the end of his own search, he concluded that we probably can never get satisfying answers to all of our questions, perhaps to none of them. "But," he wrote, "even to look fearlessly is to be strangely comforted. We live in a universe more wonderful than all our dreams: this at least seems clear. The faint and far-off voices that come to us seem wholly friendly" (Johnson, 1953).

Johnson was master of Queens College, University of Melbourne, and "his considerable academic status may have been conducive to the emergence of university parapsychologists" (Irwin, 1988) in Australia. After his retirement in 1964 from Queens College, he became less and less interested in parapsychology and more and more absorbed in spirituality and the path of the mystic. But still he remained "amply satisfied that the evidence of [psychical research] is good . . . of our survival of death I am completely satisfied" (Johnson, 1953).

Selected Writings: *The Imprisoned Splendour,* 1953, pp. ix, 18, 410.

BIBLIOGRAPHY: Irwin, H. 1988. "Parapsychology in Australia." JASPR 82:319.

**Johnson, Samuel, 1709–1784.** British poet, critic, journalist, lexicographer, and the outstanding literary figure of his time. His *Dictionary of the English Language* appeared in 1755. It was the most extensive English dictionary ever undertaken and laid the basis for Noah Webster's *American Dictionary of the English Language* published in 1828 and for all subsequent English dictionaries. Adding to Johnson's fame was his gift for brilliant conversation, his essays, his editing of parliamentary reports, his poems, and his six-volume critical work *Lives of the Most Eminent English Poets* (1779–1781). But even more than by his own writings, Johnson was made immortal by his biographer James Boswell in *Life of Samuel Johnson, LL.D.* (1791).

From Boswell we learn that Johnson was deeply interested in the paranormal. On the subject of ghosts, Johnson said: "[T]his is a question which, after five thousand years, is yet undecided; a question, whether in theology or philosophy, one of the most important that can come before the human understanding" (Boswell, 1901, vol. IV:299–300). Johnson applied critical parapsychological standards of evidence to any situation. Again with respect to ghosts, he told Boswell: "Sir, I make a distinction between what a man can experience by the mere strength of his imagination, and what imagination cannot possibly produce. Thus, suppose I should think that I saw a form, and heard a voice cry, 'Johnson, you are a very wicked fellow, and unless you repent you will certainly be punished,' my own unworthiness is so deeply impressed upon my mind that I might imagine I thus saw and heard, and therefore I should not believe that an external communication had been made to me. But if a form should appear, and a voice should tell me that a particular man had died at a particular place and a particular hour, a fact which I had no apprehension of, nor any means of knowing, and the fact, with all its circumstances, should afterwards be unquestionably proved, I should in that case be persuaded that I had a supernatural intelligence imparted to me" (Boswell, 1901, vol. II: 72).

Johnson was extremely cranky with John Wesley because he thought the preacher accepted ghost stories and possibly the disturbances at Epworth Rectory "not on sufficient authority" (Boswell, 1901, vol. IV:299–300). In 1769, Johnson was drawn with so many others to Cock Lane in London to see for himself the **Cock Lane Ghost.** Contrary to the British historian Thomas Macauley's statement that Johnson was credulous about the Cock Lane Ghost, "Johnson was one of those by whom the imposture was detected. . . . [A]fter the gentlemen who went and examined into the evidence were satisfied of its falsity, Johnson wrote in their presence an account of it which was published in the newspapers and *Gentlemen's Magazine,* and undeceived the world" (Boswell, 1901, vol. II:72–73).

Boswell wrote that Johnson "will be regarded by the present age, and by posterity, with admiration and reverence." From the perspective of psychical research and parapsychology, he is remembered as the forerunner of modern inquiry in these fields.

BIBLIOGRAPHY: Boswell, J. *Life of Samuel Johnson, LL.D,* 1901.

**Jones, Cecil B. ("Scott") 1928–.** American research scientist. As special assistant to United States senator Claiborne Pell (from Rhode Island), Jones tries to promote government support of parapsychology and to facilitate applications by parapsychologists for funding by government agencies. As founder and president of the Center for Applied Anomalous Phenomena, he is also interested in programs for the development of psi and for the application of psychic phenomena to the law enforcement and intelligence communities. With a Ph.D. from American University, Jones was a carrier pilot and intelligence officer for the United States Navy and is on the Board of Trustees of the American Society for Psychical Research.

**Jones, Glyn (1942–) and Ieuan (1942–).** Welsh subjects, known as the "Jones Boys" in the literature of parapsychology. They were described as "invincible high scorers" (Soal and Bowden, 1959:235).

On the theory that uneducated and ingenuous children might have more psychic abilities than other people, **Samuel G. Soal** tested these adolescent cousins in rural Wales for telepathy in card-guessing experiments. But since the boys were not at all interested in extrasensory perception or tiresome experiments that made them give up their holidays and weekends, Soal had to encourage them by offering them monetary rewards for their scores. The resultant unprecedented high scores forced Soal to pay the boys large sums of money. He wrote: "Glyn and Ieuan have taught us nothing about the nature of telepathy. . . . What this investigation does demonstrate is the all-powerful influence of an intense motivation (in this case the love of money) in maintaining scores at a high level" (Soal and Bowden, 1959:235). (Their parents were equally greedy, demanding money, free holidays, etc.)

Sadly, the love of money was so strong that the "ingenuous" boys began to cheat. Ieuan moved his knee or foot to send signals to Glynn in the course of the experiments, coughed at regular intervals although he had no cold, or creaked his chair to guide Glyn's calls. The cheating was crude and they were caught and scolded. The experimenters did what they could to make the conditions of later experiments more rigorous. But the boys might have been too clever for them. Some critics think that the boys could have signalled with a supersonic whistle which adult ears cannot hear but which dogs, children, and adolescents can. The two cousins, after all, lived in a section of Wales where sheep dogs were controlled by "silent" dog whistles. Alternatively, they could have made a whistling sound through the teeth.

The noted sceptic, Charles E. M. Hansel said: "Such a technique could quite easily have been employed without fear of detection" (Hansel, 1966:149), especially since the experimenters were adults over fifty years of age who would not have heard a supersonic whistle. Yet Soal had the boys wear bathing suits and searched them to eliminate the possibility of their using a whistle or miniature radio. And, if the boys had a perfect system for cheating with the whistle, why would they have resorted to crude cheating such as with a knee, cough, or creaking chair? Still it has been pointed out, as James Randi said in another connection, that the mice were running the experiment (Nicol, 1960) and it is surely suspicious that the boys could score only when they were in a direct line with no closed doors between them.

The Jones Boys seem to "have succeeded in hoodwinking so many of the experts [that] their place in the history of [parapsychology] will be almost as important as if they are proved innocent" (Thouless, 1959:96).

BIBLIOGRAPHY: Hansel, C. E. M. *ESP: A Scientific Evaluation,* 1966; Nicol, B. H. 1960.

"The Jones Boys: A Case for Telepathy Not Proven." JASPR 54:118; Soal, S. G. and Bowden, H. T. *The Mind Readers,* 1959; Thouless, R. H. 1959. "The Mind Readers. By S. G. Soal and H. T. Bowden." JSPR 40:84.

**Jones, Sir Lawrence J., c. 1870–1955.** British member of the Society for Psychical Research from 1888 and its president in 1928 and 1929. His principal interest in psychical research was the mediumship of Kate Wingfield whom he described as "a very remarkable crystal-gazer and automatist."

Jones and his wife, who had never before sat with any medium, turned to Mrs. Wingfield after the death of their fourteen year old son in 1898. She convinced him of the reality of survival and of communication and was the subject of his *Presidential Address* to the SPR in 1928. He advised against resorting to mediums once "assurance of Survival has been obtained. . . . Still, [this] assurance . . . and the hopeful interpretation of the Universe which goes with it . . . has upheld me through many bereavements, and enlarged my sympathy with struggling humanity" (Jones, 1928: 47, 48).

At a time when the SPR was torn by dissension between Spiritualists (e.g., Sir Arthur Conan Doyle) and the more scientifically minded, his "geniality and courtesy . . . together with his dignified presence proved him to be exactly the President the Society needed during one of its most agitated periods" (Salter, 1955.)

Selected Writings: 1928. "Presidential Address." PSPR 38:17.

BIBLIOGRAPHY: Salter, W. H. 1955. "Obituary: Sir Lawrence J. Jones." JSPR 38:48.

**Jonson, Ben (Benjamin Johnson), 1572–1637.** English actor, man of letters, and playwright. He was a contemporary of William Shakespeare after whom he enjoys the reputation of being England's foremost dramatist. After working as a bricklayer and soldiering in Flanders, he became the "King's poet" under James I and Charles I. His plays included *"Every Man in His Humour* (1598), *Cynthia's Revels* (1600), and *Volpone, or the Fox* (1606).

During a visit, Jonson told the Scottish poet William Drummond of the following incident: "At that tyme the pest was in London; he being in the country with old Cambden, he saw in a vision his eldest son, then a child and at London, appear unto him with the mark of a bloodie cross in his forehead, as it had been cutted with a sword, at which amazed he prayed unto God, and in the morning he came to Mr. Cambden's chamber to tell him; who persuaded him it was but an apprehension of his fantasie; at which he should not be disjected; in the mean tyme comes then letters from his wife of the death of that boy in the plague . . . ." Ben Jonson becomes a **Noted Witness** to a veridical paranormal experience either of telepathy from his son or of his son's apparition.

BIBLIOGRAPHY: Prince, W. F. 1918. "Peculiar Experiences Connected with Noted Persons." JASPR 12:678.

**Jonsson, Olof, 1918–.** Swedish psychic residing in Chicago. While in Sweden in 1952, he claimed to have solved thirteen murders by using his psi abilities to identify as the murderer a mad police officer who killed his victims to steal their money and then burned their homes to conceal any clues. The officer committed suicide after leaving a note confessing the crimes and expressing his fear that Jonsson had found him out (Steiger, 1971).

However accurate this claim is, Jonson's abilities have been investigated by various parapsychologists including Joseph B. Rhine, Joseph G. Pratt and William E. Cox. But his reputation was established when *Life* magazine revealed that he was one of the percipients on earth with whom astronaut Edgar Mitchell, acting as agent, conducted a test of telepathy from outer space during the Apollo 14 lunar expedition in 1971. The results of the test were statistically significant, not for the number of hits but, rather, for the number of misses that was so large that the results could not be attributed to chance.

BIBLIOGRAPHY: Steiger, B. *The Psychic Feats of Olof Jonsson,* 1971.

**Jordan Peña, José Luis, 1932–.** Spanish psychologist. He is one of his country's most illustrious investigators of the paranormal and creator of advanced methodology for unmasking fraud in the field. He is a member of the Sociedad Española de Parapsicología and has directed about 250 conferences on parapsychology. He has also published several books and monographs on the subject. Jordan Peña has in addition conducted investigations into poltergeist phenomena and altered states of consciousness.

**Joseph of Copertino, Saint, 1603–1663.** Levitating Franciscan monk. Joseph, 300 years before the invention of the airplane, is reported to have had the astounding bird-like ability to take aerial flights that might attain sixty feet in height and were so spectacular that he earned the reputation of the "flying friar".

Born Guiseppe Desa in southeastern Italy, he was called "Open Mouth" because he used to sit staring skyward with his mouth open. He was also called simpleminded and ignorant but liked to be known as "The Ass." When he was seventeen years old, he decided to make religion his life's work. Rejected as unfit by the Capuchin Order, he was later accepted into the Order of Conventuals, whose monastery was not far from Copertino, and charged with taking care of a mule in the stable. In 1625, he was admitted to the Order of St. Francis and, as the result of a mistake, received the sacrament of ordination as a priest in the Catholic church.

Then began experiences that make Joseph a **Noted Witness** for the paranormal. He seems to have had the gift of telepathy because he was able to know what his confessants were thinking. Joseph is also said to have had the power of clairvoyance as he was able to find lost objects. But he is most famous for his well-substantiated flights that make him a noted witness for the phenomenon of levitation. Catholic hagiography presents a number of cases of saints who have levitated. But the case of Joseph of Copertino is so extraordinary that the bull of canonization of this saint proclaims that no other saint can be compared to him in this respect.

Joseph's levitations took place in the daylight and were in full view of people from all walks of life, including bishops and cardinals, who watched them closely. When he was in Rome and about to kiss the feet of Pope Urban VIII, Joseph floated up into the air and remained there while the Supreme Pontiff sat in his chair agape. Joseph did not confine his flights to the interiors of buildings. Once he was walking in a garden with the priest Antonio Chiarelli when Joseph, observed by eyewitnesses, "uttered a shriek, sprang from the ground and flew into the air, only coming to rest on the top of an olive tree where he remained in a kneeling position for half an hour . . ." until rescued.

Another account tells of a time in 1645 when Joseph went to a church to see the spanish ambassador to the Papal Court, the high admiral of Castile, and the admiral's wife. "[N]o sooner had he entered the church," runs the account, "than his eyes rested on a statue of Mary Immaculate which stood over the altar, and he at once flew about a dozen paces over the heads of those present to the foot of the statue. Then after paying homage there for some short space and uttering his customary shrill cry he flew back again and straightway returned to his cell, leaving the Admiral and his wife and the large retinue which attended them speechless with astonishment."

John Frederick, duke of Braunschweig-Luneberg, known principally as the patron of the great philosopher Gottfried W. Leibniz, in 1649 traveled to Assisi to attend masses conducted by Joseph. There, like the Spanish admiral and his wife, he was astounded by two of the saint's levitations. The effect on the duke was so great that he was converted from Lutheranism to Catholicism as was one of the officers in his entourage.

Joseph also transported others on his flights. During a service at the Church of Santa Chiara in Copertino, he gave out his usual shriek, ran towards the convent's father confessor who was at the service, took his hand and "both rose into the air in an ecstacy, the one being borne aloft by Joseph and the other by God himself . . . the one beside himself with fear but the other with sanctity."

There were over 100 different levitations by Joseph and they continued over a period of forty years. Even on his deathbed, while he lay dying of a fever, he thought he heard a bell calling him to God. He soared from his bed to his chapel where he said, "the little Ass is beginning to ascend the mountain." Then on September 18, 1663, Joseph's soul took its final flight toward heaven, this time without his body. Joseph was canonized in 1752.

BIBLIOGRAPHY: Dingwall, E. J. *Some Human Oddities,* 1947; Thurston, H. *The Physical Phenomena of Mysticism,* 1952, p. 16.

**Journal of Indian Psychology.** Published twice a year by Andhra University, this Indian periodical publishes reviews of books, theoretical papers and empirical reports dealing with psychology. Equal emphasis, however, is placed on papers and reports on issues in parapsychology in order to try to integrate normal, abnormal, and paranormal experiences and to stimulate alternative models for the study of the nature of the human personality. The editor is **K. Ramakrishna Rao.**

**Journal of Near-Death Studies.** Published quarterly in the United States and sponsored by the International Association for Near-Death Studies, it publishes empirical and theoretical papers and book reviews on the near-death experience and other phenomena, including deathbed visions and the out-of-body experience, which may have implications for understanding the processes of life and death and their relation to human consciousness. The editor is Bruce Greyson, M.D.

**Journal of Paraphysics.** Published quarterly in Downton, Wilts, England, by the Paraphysical Laboratory, the publication aims at being a link between East and West. It contains information on the paranormal from behind the iron curtain with contributions from Soviet and East European authors. The *Journal* also publishes investigations of paranormal phenomena but especially effects that do not appear to be attributable to human beings. Book reviews and articles on haunts, poltergeists, and psychokinesis are carried as well. The editor is **Manfred Cassirer.**

**Journal of Parapsychology.** Publication of this organ by the Parapsychology Laboratory at Duke University in Durham, North Carolina began in 1937. It is now published quarterly by the Foundation for Research on the Nature of Man and consists principally of experimental research and theoretical papers on ESP and psychokinesis. It also contains book reviews, announcements, correspondence and glossaries. Its editor is **K. Ramakrishna Rao.**

**Journal of Religion and Psychical Research.** An organ to encourage the exchange of ideas among members of the Academy of Religion and Psychical Research and others relating to the area where religion and parapsychology interact, this quarterly *Journal* published in the United States by the academy consists of general articles, reports of conferences, research papers, book reviews, and correspondence. The present editor is Mary Carman Rose.

**Journal of Scientific Exploration.** Published semi-annually in the United States by the Society for Scientific Exploration and addressed primarily to those in the mainstream of science. By presenting scientific papers on anomalous phenomena which exist beyond the normal paradigms of the physical, psychological, biological, and earth sciences, or within such paradigms but at variance with them, it presents a forum for removing the isolation of orthodox scientists from these anomalies. Editor is Ronald A. Howard.

**Journal of the American Society for Psychical Research.** The quarterly publication of the American Society for Psychical Research in New York. It consists of research reports, papers on investigations of spontaneous cases, general articles, reviews of books, and correspondence. It was published first in 1907 by **James H. Hyslop** after the establishment of the American Institute for Scientific Research. The present editor is **Rhea A. White.**

**Journal of the Society for Psychical Research.** The Society for Psychical Research started its publication in England in 1884 for the purpose of advising its members of the business and work of the organization. Because it was originally privately circulated among members only, people were willing to send in accounts of their paranormal experiences without fear of embarrassment by undue publicity. As spontaneous cases meeting high standards of evidence were collected, they were published in the *Journal.* Even cases that did not meet these standards were published, with their faults noted, for their educational value.

The *Journal* also contains reports on experimental research, reviews of periodicals and books, and correspondence. Throughout its years of existence, the *Journal,* published four times a year, has served as a means of promoting an active interest on the part of members and of encouraging sometimes deadly exchanges of criticism among members who feel they are protected against publicity by the privacy of the publication. The editors originally were members who were interested in the general work of the SPR. Today, however, the editors will be academics. The first in this new line is **Dr. John Beloff,** retired in 1985 from the Department of Psychology, University of Edinburgh.

**Judaism.** See **Kabbalah.**

**Judge, William Q., 1851–1896.** Irish-born lawyer who kept the Theosophical Society in New York from dying after Madame **Helena P. Blavatsky,** its founder, left for India to set up Theosophical Headquarters there. In anticipation of Richard Hodgson's investigation of her and the Theosophical Society, she had Judge come to India from New York to "save the situation." The "situation" included letters allegedly written by Mme Blavatsky which involved her in a conspiracy to commit fraud (Berger, 1988:17). It also involved phenomena taking place in a shrine in the so-called "Occult Room" in Theosophical Headquarters in Adyar. The "Shrine," although only a cupboard adjoining madame's bedroom, was an object of awe. It was revered as the means by which the brotherhood of adepts communicated through letters and other objects that appeared in it by apparently paranormal means. Hodgson during his investigation found that the shrine had disappeared and that in fact Judge had tried to "save the situation" by removing it and then chopping it up and burning it, piece by piece, perhaps to remove all signs of any trick apparatus. Hodgson did learn that there had been a sliding panel at the back of the shrine through which the shrine's miracles could have been produced from the bedroom (Hodgson, 1893:140–142).

Judge then returned to New York and, after Mme Blavatsky's death, had the American wing of the Theosophical movement break away from and become independent of the Indian branch.

BIBLIOGRAPHY: Berger, A. S. *Lives and Letters in American Parapsychology,* 1988; Hodgson, R. 1893. "The Defence of the Theosophists." PSPR 9:129.

**Jung, Carl Gustav, 1875–1961.** Eminent Swiss psychiatrist. Early a disciple of **Sigmund Freud** whose heir apparent Jung was, he broke with Freud in 1913 partly over Freud's insistence on the sexual basis of neurosis, partly because Freud did not understand Jung's "aspirations for a higher spiritual purpose" (Ehrenwald, 1984).

From childhood Jung (who, on his mother's side, came from a family which had frequent psychic experiences) had had paranormal experiences: visions, precognitive dreams, out-of-body experiences, poltergeist-like phenomena, awareness of ghosts, automatic writing, and a striking near-death experience. He often knew things he could not have known except by telepathy—as when he had a pain in his forehead and skull at the moment that a patient shot himself in the head (Jung, 1962).

He was fascinated by Goethe (Jung's grandfather was reputedly Goethe's natural son) and fancied himself living simultaneously in the eighteenth and nineteenth centuries. He had an early interest in Spiritualism and its literature, his experiments with a sixteen-year old medium (his cousin Helene [Helly] Preiswerk) being published in his doctoral dissertation. It has been suggested (Fodor, 1964) that her death was a blow from which Jung never recovered. He came to believe that the dead live but can only experience through the consciousness of the living. His *VII Sermons ad Mortuos,* published anonymously and written semi-automatically are instructions to the dead. The book shows Jung's indebtedness to Gnostic and Eastern thought. Jung read a great deal of **Emanuel Swedenborg** and, part of the Germanic mystical movement of the time, he used occult ideas, Eastern philosophies, astrology, I ching, and alchemy in the development of his thought on "the Heilsweg, the journey of the soul" (Webb, 1974a). Yet "the ultimte synthesis of knowledge and intuition eluded him" (Ehrenwald, 1984).

The Jungian concepts of most interest to psychical research are the collective unconscious (whose contents "appertain [not] to one individual only, but . . . to a whole nation and . . . to the whole of mankind . . . [;] congenital instincts and primordial forms of apprehension, the so-called archetypes or ideas" [Jung, 1920]) and synchronicity, an "a-causal connecting principle" (Jung, 1955).

The collective unconscious, the transpsychic reality carried by archetypes, has been used to explain, among other psychic phenomena, mediumship and retrocognition. It has also connected Jung and nazism because of his association with the founder of the Nordic Faith movement and its use of the idea of a racial unconscious (together with "some unfortunate statements [by Jung] about the difference between German and Jewish psychology" [Webb, 1974a]).

Synchronicity could explain many paranormal phenomena. Jung found that "objective events often significantly paralleled inner psychic events, without the presence of any causation . . . ," a famous case being the appearance of a scarab beetle just when a patient was describing a dream about a scarab. "[T]he appearance of these synchronicities usually hinged on the action of some one or another of the archetypes" (Adams, 1957), most frequently death or the imminent danger of death (Jaffé, 1967).

In later life Jung was professor of psychology at the Federal Polytechnical University in Zurich and professor of medical psychology at the University of Basel. Of himself, he wrote, "I have no judgment about myself and my life. There is nothing I am quite sure about."

Selected Writings: 1920. "The Psychological Foundations of Belief in Spirits." PSPR 31:75; *Synchronicity: an Acausal Principle,* 1955; *Archetypes and the Collective Unconscious,* 1959; *Memories, Dreams, Reflections,* 1962; *Synchronicity,* 1972.

BIBLIOGRAPHY: Adams, F. C. 1957. "The Possible Bearings of the Psychology of C. G. Jung on Psychical Research." JASPR 50:25; Beloff, J. 1963. "Explaining the Paranormal." JSPR 42:101; Burt, C. 1963. "Jung's Account of his Paranormal Experiences." JSPR 42:163; Ehrenwald, J. *Anatomy of Genius,* 1984, pp. 88–101; Fodor, N. *Between Two Worlds,* 1964; Jaffé, A. "C. J. Jung and Parapsychology." In Smythies, J. R., ed., *Science and Esp,* 1967; Webb, J. "Carl Gustav Jung." In Cavendish R., ed., *Encyclopedia of the Unexplained,* 1974a; Webb, J. "Synchronicity." In Cavendish, R., ed., *Encyclopedia of the Unexplained,* 1974b.

**Jürgenson, Friedrich, 1903–1987.** Swedish producer of films and television documentaries. Although not the discoverer of the **Electronic Voice Phenomena**—Raymond Bayless seems to have been the first to report them—Jurgenson brought them to the attention of the world.

In 1959, while trying to record bird songs, he heard a male voice speaking in Norwegian about "nocturnal bird songs." Subsequently, he recognized on electro-magnetic recording tape the voice of his dead mother saying, "Friedel, my little Friedel, can you hear me?" Over the next twenty-five years he continued to make recordings and concluded that the strange voices he taped belonged to deceased people he had once known. In 1963 and 1964, Jürgenson reported on his work to conferences in Sweden and, in 1967, published a book in Swedish describing his experiments and findings. He also worked in close collaboration with Hans Bender and with Konstantin Raudive.

He had considered Raudive his friend and pupil. Then suddenly their relationship changed: "It was after one of my lectures in Freiburg, in October 1969," Jürgenson wrote, "when I noticed signs of rivalry, a fact which was commented on by many friends who were present" (Bander, 1973). But Jürgenson, although disappointed and disillusioned, felt that "the bridge to another dimension of life is far more important, not only for scientific but for humanitarian reasons; I shall never allow personal ambitions and egocentric tendencies in researchers to cast a shadow over the project as a whole." (Bander, 1973:127).

In 1969, Pope Paul VI awarded Jürgenson the Commander's Cross of the Order of St. Gregory whether for his work with the voice phenomena or as the producer of films and documentaries is not clear.

Selected Writings: Jürgenson, F. *Sprechfunk mit Verstorbenen,* 1967.

BIBLIOGRAPHY: Bander, P. *Voices from the Tapes,* 1973.

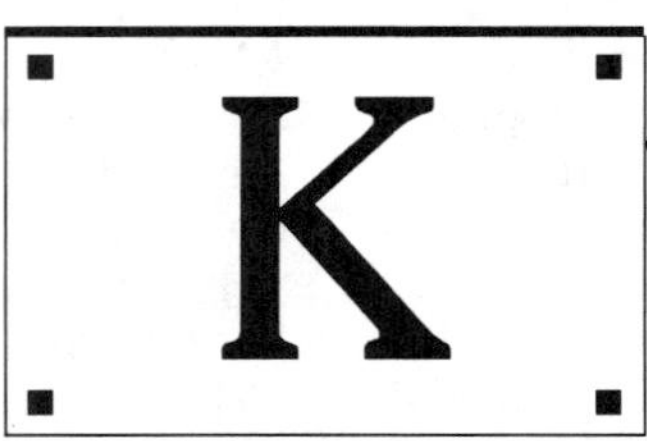

**KA.** Tied in closely with the Egyptian belief in human survival of physical death is the concept of the *ka* or **Double** of a human being. It resembles closely the notion of an **Astral Body.** It is similar also to the center of consciousness that is supposed to leave the physical body in an out-of-body experience, for the *ka* can separate itself from or rejoin the body when it wishes, can move about at will and can enjoy an existence apart from the body. The *ka* also is able to dwell with the gods in heaven. The *ka* is different from the astral body and center of consciousness, however, since it requires food and, in fact, was given funerary gifts of bread, cake, and wine and, failing these, fed on gifts painted on the walls of the tomb it inhabited. The *ka* also needs to be distinguished from the **Ba,** another division of the human being conceived by the Egyptians.

BIBLIOGRAPHY: Budge, E. A. *The Book of the Dead,* 1950.

**Kabbalah. (Also Kabala, Kabbala, Cabala, Cabbalah).** A stream of mystical thought and practice in Judaism, a religion that cannot be fully understood without taking the Kabbalah into account. It made its appearance in southern France in the thirteenth century. The word is derived from the Hebrew word "to receive" although its more probable meaning is "tradition" because it denotes secrets and teachings dealing with the mysteries of God and the world handed down over the centuries. Kabbalah has been defined as "a massive, detailed, and coherent view of our relation to the universe" (Hoffman, 1981:7).

Its speculations about God and the world touch psychical research at many points. The Kabbalah, for example, relates how dying people encounter the souls of the dead who accompany their souls to their future abode—a clear reference to deathbed visions. Survival after death and reincarnation are phenomena recognized by the Kabbalah in its teachings about the existence of a spiritual world beyond the physical one and the return of souls to earth in another form. The Jewish mystical tradition "has also embraced such intriguing phenomena as clairvoyance, telepathy, trance mediumship, spiritual healing, and prophecy" (Hoffman, 1981:167). These paranormal powers seem to arise when one is able to transcend the world of time and space.

It is interesting to note that Abraham, Ezekial, Daniel, and others who underwent spiritual practices were considered psychics. Writes one Hebrew scholar: "the Kabbalah regards their inspiring messages to our still conflicted world as genuine paranormal visions and not simply as poetic commentaries on the human condition. When individually they evolved to a certain state of awareness, the Kabbalah indicates, the biblical Prophets achieved their powers—even if they were not conscious of the process as it was occurring before the full-blown psychic state was manifested" (Hoffman, 1981:167).

BIBLIOGRAPHY: Hoffman, E. *The Way of Splendor: Jewish Mysticism and Modern Psychology,* 1981.

**Kaempffert, Waldemar Bernhard, 1877–1956.** American science writer. For over twenty-five years he was science editor of the influential *New York Times.* Kaempffert was interested in parapsychology because it asks the "fundamental question. . . . Is the spiritual or the materialistic interpretation of the universe the true one? Philosophers and theologians have debated that question for centuries without result. We need a new approach. It may be that that new approach will come through parapsychology?" (Kaempffert, 1956:136).

In 1934 he praised Joseph B. Rhine's *Extra Sensory Perception* in his column in the most powerful newspaper in the United States as "the most important study ever made" of telepathy and clairvoyance. Singlehandedly with this enthusiastic review of a book that otherwise would surely have escaped public notice, Rhine's book published by the obscure Boston Society for Psychic Research put Rhine, parapsychology, and Duke University into the public consciousness (Berger, 1988:212).

Holder of a degree in law (he never practiced), Kaempffert had majored in science in college. He counted among his friends Walter Franklin Prince, Alexis Carrel, and James H. Hyslop. He admired the latter as "a man of great intellectual power, great courage at a time when courage was needed" (Kaempfert, 1956:134). In 1921, Kaempfert was appointed to the Advisory Council of the American Society for Psychical Research and was elected to its Board of Trustees in 1941. He was on the Research Committee of the ASPR when the Hyslop-Prince Fellowship was established. He was for many years a trustee of the ASPR and just eight months before his death, on the occasion of the fiftieth anniversary of the society (as reestablished under Hyslop), made the opening address.

Dr. Kaempffert was also the author of many popular books on science that explained in language understandable to the layman the discoveries of scientists.

Selected Writing: 1956. "Dr. James H. Hyslop and Psychical Research." JASPR 50:134.

BIBLIOGRAPHY: Allison, L. W. 1957. "In Memory of Waldemar B. Kaempffert." JASPR 51:84; Berger, A. S. *Lives and Letters in American Parapsychology,* 1988.

**Kahn, S. David, 1929–.** American psychiatrist. His interest in psychic matters dates from his childhood, Edgar Cayce having been a long-standing friend of his family's. His mother's report of Gardner Murphy's lectures in 1947 at the New School of Social Research in New York introduced him to experimental and scientific psychical research. He was then attending Harvard University where his courses in science, philosophy, and psychology were in direct conflict with his interest in parapsychology, especially since psychologist B. F. Skinner assured him that sensory cuing explained all apparently successful ESP experiments and that Kahn's interest in psychical research indicated his lack of balanced judgment.

Nevertheless, Kahn and a few like-minded students in 1949 formed the Harvard Society for Parapsychology, and Gardner Murphy, who at that time was Richard Hodgson Fellow at Harvard and Chairman of the Department of Psychology at the City College of New York, accepted their invitation to speak. Later the Department of Psychology did finance (to the tune of forty dollars) Kahn's group's experiments in extrasensory perception using an electric scoring device. Kahn's thesis based on these experiments and arguing as well for the goal of repeatability was accepted by the Department of Social Relations (not by the Department of Psychology) at Harvard in partial fulfillment of the requirements of the B.A. degree. Gardner Murphy then edited the report and had it published in the proceedings of the American Society for Psychical Research (1952).

In 1951 Eileen Garrett through the Parapsychology Foundation gave some financial support to Kahn's research. Kahn's group also persuaded Mrs. Garrett to subsidize researchers under Gardner Murphy's guidance and suggested the establishment of an experimental laboratory at the foundation of which, in 1957, **Karlis Osis** became director.

In 1962, the now medical Dr. Kahn published a paper in which he theorized that psi might be something different from perception and that "not until we look to other possible manifestations of psi shall we find its essential character" (p. 124). A later paper (1976) suggested that we live in a "sea of psi" and that enhancement techniques might solve the problem of repeatability. Dr. Kahn, in his tribute to Gardner Murphy (1980), called him William James's equal and a man who was "faultless to a fault."

Until 1988 Dr. Kahn was a member of the Board of Trustees of the ASPR.

Selected Writings: 1980. "*Ave Atque Vale*: Gardner Murphy." JASPR 74:37; "Myers' Problem Revisited." In G. R. Schmeidler, ed., *Parapsychology: Its Relation to Physics, Biology, Psychology, and Psychiatry,* 1976; 1962. "The Enigma of Psi: A Challenge for Scientific Method." JASPR 56:114; 1952. "Studies in Extrasensory Perception." PASPR 25:i.

**Kant, Immanuel, 1724–1804.** German philosopher. He is considered one of the greatest philosophers of modern times. He was a lecturer *(privat dozent)* at the University of Königsberg and, in 1770, became a professor of logic and metaphysics there. His was a quiet, bachelor's life in Königsberg. His existence was so mechanical that his neighbors knew without looking at their clocks when it was precisely 9:30 A.M. or 4:00 P.M.

Kant never journeyed more than 100 miles outside of Königsberg, yet his mind soared. His system of critical philosophy or Kantian scepticism embodied in his three major works, *Critique of Pure Reason* (1781), *Critique of Practical Reason* (1788), and *Critique of Judgment* (1790) established a powerful tradition in philosophy. His "transcendental philosophy," concerned as it was with *a priori* concepts, also influenced subsequent philosophy. Kant presented as well strong moral arguments for the freedom of the will, the existence of God, and the belief in immortality. God, having given the human being moral duties that cannot be completed in one lifetime, will provide immortality to permit us to accomplish our tasks.

Kant's relation to psychical research began when he was about forty. He was attracted and impressed by the experiences and doctrines of another Immaneul—Emanuel Swedenborg. Kant's letter to Charlotte von Knobloch written in 1763 described Swedenborg's apparently successful attempt to communicate with the dead brother of the wife of King Alfred Fridrik of Sweden. Kant confessed to his correspondent that he was a pronounced sceptic with regard to such stories, but that Swedenborg's accomplishments had made him reconsider. He related also that he tried to investigate many of the Swedish seer's feats and was regretful that he could not question Swedenborg himself.

In Kant's *Dreams of a Spirit Seer (Träume eines Geistersehers erläutert durch die Trä ume der Metaphysik)* which he wrote in 1766, he discussed the philosophical problems related to the concepts of a disembodied soul and spirit world, Swedenborg's doctrines, and described Swedenborg's feats that had originally drawn his close and admiring attention. But now they left him "serious and undecided." He felt that it is quite pointless to speculate about a spirit world or listen to what any medium says. Since on moral grounds we are assured by God of an eternal life, it is unnecessary to rely on mediumistic evidence or metaphysics. The book shows Kant's flirtation with psychical research to have been short-lived and that Swedenborg did not succeed in converting him from a sceptic into a believer.

Why then did Kant bother to write *Dreams of a Spirit Seer,* especially since he published it anonymously in Königsberg—perhaps to protect his post at the university? We can but speculate that out of fear that his authorship would be discovered he pooh-poohed Swedenborg's phenomena to placate academic circles.

BIBLIOGRAPHY: Broad, C. D. 1950. "Immanuel Kant and Psychical Research." PSPR 49:79.

**Kapchan, Jack, 1922–.** American psychologist. His first introduction to parapsychology seems to have come in the early 1940s when, a student at the City College of New York, he studied under Gardner Murphy. After serving in the army during World War II, he continued this interest by working as a laboratory research assistant at Joseph B. Rhine's Parapsychology Laboratory at Duke University while he was pursuing his Ph.D. in psychology there. During this period both Robert H. Thouless and Donald J. West met him at the Parapsychology Laboratory. Dr. West spoke of his "somewhat formidably extravert personality" (West, 1950: 169) while Dr. Thouless remarked on his "ingenious method of [ESP] experimenting which may prove to be more fruitful than those now generally used" (Thouless, 1949:15).

Since 1952, Dr. Kapchan has been on the faculty of the University of Miami where he is now professor of psychology. One of his major areas of interest continues to be parapsychology.

BIBLIOGRAPHY: Thouless, R. H. 1949. "Report of a Visit to the United States." JSPR 35:14, 15; West, D. J. 1950. "The Parapsychology Laboratory at Duke University, and the American Society for Psychical Research: Some Impressions." JSPR 35:165, 169.

**Kappers, Jan, 1914–.** Dutch medical doctor. He has a practice in Amsterdam but is also a "half time parapsychologist" (Kappers, 1988). With a considerable grant from his government, he led a team of investigators in an attempt to induce paranormal events instead of waiting for them to occur either in the laboratory or in spontaneous cases. He also wanted to resolve the question of whether psi ability is a dormant human gift common to all that can be induced with drugs. And, if people have demonstrated some psychic ability, will a drug improve and make the ability stronger?

The drug he used was psilocybine extracted from the mushroom *Psilocybe Mexicana.* Although powerful, it is not as productive as LSD of vivid hallucinations that distract and disturb subjects. In experiments of his design he tested thirty subjects. There were tests with ESP cards, tests of psychometry, telepathy, and clairvoyance—eighty in all, forty-four under normal conditions without the drug and thirty-six after oral ingestion of the drug. After all tests were completed, he found that, while some subjects seemed to show a slight improvement in their scores when in a state of psilocybine intoxication, on the whole drugs did not improve or induce psi (Van Asperen de Boer, Barkema, Kappers, 1966). Rightfully, he considers this investigation one of his "major contributions" to parapsychology.

Another contribution was the work he did in Prague with Pavel Stepanek in which he noticed this star subject producing a focussing effect (Kappers, Ryzl, Barendregt, 1965).

Besides having been editor of *Spiegel der Parapsychology* (Mirror of Parapsychology), Dr. Kappers was the first president of the **Nederlandse Vereniging Voor Parapsychologie** and founded many "Parapsychological Circles" in towns in The Netherlands. As he looks back on his parapsychological career, he admits that "I have been very lucky to have had and witnessed several rare phenomena, like haunting, very significant clairvoyant dreams and ectoplasma [*sic*] and not to forget some very remarkable paranormal healings" (Kappers, 1988).

Selected Writings: (December 1, 1988) Letter to authors; with van Asperen de Boer and Barkema, P. R. 1966. "Is It Possible to Induce ESP with Psilocybine? An Exploratory Investigation." *International Journal of Neuropsychiatry* 2 (5): 447; with Ryzl, M., Barendregt, J. T. and Barkema, P. R. 1965. "An Experiment in Prague." JP 29:176.

**Karagulla, Shafica, 1914-late 1980s.** Turkish-born American neuropsychiatrist. Her studies of the "creative frontiers of the human mind" (1963: dust jacket) make her of interest to parapsychology. Educated at the American University in Beirut, Lebanon, she took her residency at the Royal Edinburgh Hospital for Mental and Nervous Disorders in Scotland. In 1948 she received her diploma in psychological medicine from the Royal College of Physicians and Surgeons in England, and in 1952 her research into hallucinations in abnormal mental states brought her to Dr. Wilder Penfield at McGill University in Montreal, Canada.

In 1957, by this time an American citizen on the faculty of the State University of New York's Department of Psychiatry, Dr. Karagulla read a book about Edgar Cayce and concluded that he "did not fit into any of my categories of the insane or the neurotic or even the sane. . . . Edgar Cayce shattered my theories about the nature of man's mind" (1967:24–5). Dr. Karagulla thereupon left her position, turned down an assistant professorship at a new medical school and set out to investigate what she calls "higher sense perception" (HSP) which is not extrasensory but physical. "HSP abilities are those special abilities which the individual is able to use and direct, or experience consciously, using his own initiative and free will" (1967:231). She found that people with HSP could heal, could make medical diagnoses, could "tune in" on things and people and often exhibited telepathy, clairvoyance and clairsentience.

Dr. Karagulla published a widely read book (1967) on her investigations and continued her research into energy fields, healing and higher sense perception. She was convinced of the reality of possession and of reincarnation and thought that children chose their parents. She also warned against "dabbling with kundalini" because it can be dangerous.

Dr. Karagulla was president and director of research of the Higher Sense Perception Research Foundation in Beverly Hills, California.

Selected Writing: *Breakthrough to Creativity,* 1967.

BIBLIOGRAPHY: Bolen, J. G. 1973. "Interview: Shafica Karagulla, M.D." *Psychic* 4(6):6.

**Kardec, Allan (Hippolyte Léon Denizard Rivail), 1804–1869.** French medical doctor. Kardec, who was greatly influenced by the Swiss reformer Johann Heinrich Pestalozzi, founded **Spiritism.** Kardec based his doctrine in part on messages in the form of automatic writings that he collected principally from two mediums. He felt he "had discovered . . . a perfectly coherent picture of the universe through the mediumship of two young girls" (Webb, 1974:33) and was therefore less concerned with proofs of the identity of the spirits than with what they said. He considered it rude to demand such proofs of spirits "who under [such] provocation" would refuse to reply or would withdraw.

In consequence of his unwillingness to offend the spirits, the messages on which Kardec depended for his doctrine are not evidential from the point of view of psychical research, yet millions have accepted Spiritism—perhaps because "[t]he religion is much more than Spiritualism. . . . It is a syncretism of the French 'magnetism' (Mesmerism), nineteenth century folk beliefs in spirits and spirit intervention, . . . [Emanuel] Swedenborg's ideas about the concentration of God's peace in human hands (i.e. healing), Hinduism (reincarnation and karma), Catholicism (morality), and some of Kardec's own metaphysics" (Giesler, 1985:116). This form of Spiritism, or Kardecismo, took firm root in Brazil where it still has many followers who continue to combine their founder's religious beliefs with his social conscience.

In addition, "Kardecismo philosophy teaches that three psychological disorders can sometimes be caused by spirits of the dead: . . . epilepsy, schizophrenia, and . . . multiple personality . . . and that sometimes we can be possessed by elements . . . inherited from our past experiences" (Rogo, 1988:221).

Selected Writing: *Le Livre des Médiums,* 1861.

BIBLIOGRAPHY: Giesler, P. V. 1985. "Parapsychological Anthropology: II." JASPR 79:113, 116; Rogo, D. S. *The Infinite Boundary,* 1988, p. 221; Webb, J. *The Occult Underground,* 1974, pp. 33–34.

**Karma.** A moral law of causation under which what is done in one life will bear fruit in a later one, a reaping in the future of what has been sown in the past. The scientific proposition that every cause will have its effects has been made by karma into a moral proposition that the causes operating in an earlier life will produce effects in the present or later one. Under karmic law, the merits or demerits of physical or mental action will produce appropriate effects such as physical state, mental capacity, sorrow or joy, ability or opportunity (i.e., an evil act will produce undesirable personal fortunes or economic conditions of one kind or another). But these effects need not show up in the same life in which a physical or mental act is done. They may be postponed until the next life or many lives later. Karma, in operation with reincarnation, brings to the world moral justice which redresses wrongs and provides a reasonable explanation for the baffling problem of great human inequalities that begin at birth.

Because in Hinduism and Buddhism the doctrines of reincarnation and karma are intimately related, it is sometimes thought that the one depends on the other. Yet some cultures, such as the Druses of Lebanon and Syria, embrace a belief in reincarnation but do not tie it into the doctrine of karma. Investigations by psychical researchers of cases of the reincarnation-type have thus far not provided evidence that there is any karmic law in operation although the lack of evidential support cannot rule it out. Since effects may be postponed for a number of lives following the one in which good or bad deeds are committed, the difficulty of getting evidence is very great. Karma may be a poetic doctrine that can never be verified or falsified.

**Kasahara, Tosio, 1947–.** Japanese clinical psychologist and parapsychologist. He is interested in psi and its elusiveness. He has translated many books on parapsychology into Japanese and, through controlled experiments, brought the Japanese psychic **Masuaki Kiyota** to the attention of Western parapsychologists. With colleagues at the Japanese Society for Parapsychology, he conducted formal tests of Kiyota's ability to produce thoughtography and metal-bending and, finding results suggestive of these abilities, made the results known to the Parapsychological Association. Kasahara also is one of the abstractors for *Parapsychology Abstracts International* and prepares for it abstracts from articles and papers in Japanese language periodicals.

Selected Writings: *Sai no Senjo (The Battlefield of Psi),* 1987; and Kohri, N., Ro, Y., Imai, S., Otani, S. 1981. "A Study on PK Ability of a Gifted Subject in Japan." In J. Beloff and W. G. Roll, eds., *Research in Parapsychology 1980,* 1981, p. 39.

**Keil, Jürgen, 1930–.** Australian psychologist. Having migrated from Germany to Australia, Keil received his education at the University of Tasmania where he became senior lecturer in the Department of Psychology and one of the individuals whose teaching and scientific integrity have helped parapsychology become a legitimate field of study in Australia. His principal interests are ESP, poltergeist phenomena and psychokinesis.

With J. G. Pratt, Keil investigated Nina Kulagina in Moscow and spent a six-month sabbatical from the University of Tasmania at the Division of Parapsychology, University of Virginia where he collaborated with Pratt on ESP tests with Pavel Stepanek related to the Focussing Effect. After Pratt's death, Keil described the former's life, career, and contributions to parapsychology in a book written from the vantage point of a close friend and colleague.

Selected Writings: *Gaither Pratt: A Life for Parapsychology,* 1987; and Pratt, J. G. 1973. "First Hand Observations of Nina S. Kulagina Suggestive of PK on Static Objects." JASPR 67:381; 1971. "A Wider Conceptual Framework for the Stepanek Focusing Effect." JASPR 65:75; and J. G. Pratt. 1969. "Further ESP Tests with Stepanek in Charlottesville Dealing with the Focusing Effect." JASPR 63:253.

**Kellog, Chester Elijah, 1888–1948.** Canadian psychologist on the faculty of the Department of Psychology of McGill University in Montreal. One of the most vigorous opponents of extrasensory perception, he published a series of criticisms following the publication in 1934 of Joseph B. Rhine's *Extra Sensory Perception.* Kellog condemned the "craze" for guessing ESP cards that might distract young men and women from more important problems (Berger, 1988:218) and he was sharply critical of the mathematical methods used by Rhine to show that the results of his ESP experiments could not be attributed to chance. When, however, in 1937 the Institute of Mathematical Statistics gave Rhine's methods a clean bill of health (Berger, 1988:218), his criticisms were largely silenced. Kellog also objected that "Rhine takes it for granted that the special capacity [extrasensory perception] exists, but only in isolated individuals, and also that it may appear and disappear. This belief . . . begs the whole question at issue, and removes the problem from the realm of scientific research" (Kellog, 1937).

Selected Writing: 1937. "The Problems of Matching and Sampling in the Study of Extra-Sensory Perception." *Journal of Abnormal and Social Psychology* 32:462.

BIBLIOGRAPHY: Berger, A. S. *Lives and Letters in American Parapsychology,* 1988.

**Kelly, Edward F., 1940–.** American cognitive psychologist and parapsychologist. Founder in 1983 and president of Spring Creek Institute, he became interested in parapsychology (or "psi" research as he prefers to call it) as a graduate student at Harvard because of his sister's sudden development of mediumistic abilities. After receiving his Ph.D. in psycholinguistics from Harvard in 1970, his interest eventually led him, in 1972, to J. B. Rhine's Institute of Parapsychology in Durham, North Carolina. For a year and a half he held the position there of postdoctoral research fellow. From 1973 to 1983 he worked at the Electrical Engineering Department of the School of Engineering at Duke University where the psychophysiological approach to psi research that he follows was being developed.

Dr. Kelly believes that the existence of psi has been established but that "not everyone has it to the same degree." He therefore tries "to study exceptional individuals in great detail using noninvasive psychophysiological methods, especially emphasizing the measurement of brain activity in conjunction with unusual psi performance" (Kelly, 1983). One of the "star" subjects with whom he worked in the early seventies was the same person who convinced Irvin L. Child of the existence of psi. Kelly believes that the kind of work he and his associates are doing is important because, by correlating "psi with other kinds of measurable phenomena[,]" statistical control and experimental control, possibly through training procedures, may be achieved that in turn may lead to detection of weak ESP, to the identification of the source of psi effects (the experimenter or the subject, for example), and ultimately to "discriminating among contending theories of psi" (Kelly, 1983). He also feels very strongly that the study of psi should be tied to the investigation of altered states of consciousness (for example, hypnosis, mediumistic trance and meditation) (Kelly and Locke, 1981).

Dr. Kelly also acts as a critic inside the field of parapsychology. With Sybo A. Schouten, he reanalyzed an important experiment carried out by Gerardus Heymans and other investigators that previously had been considered rigorous and extraordinary and found unsuspected flaws (Schouten and Kelly, 1978).

In the course of their studies Dr. Kelly and his associates have come up with technical inventions, such as a pasteless electrode, which they hope to exploit commercially in order to obtain funds for their research. Dr. Kelly has written a chapter for *The Handbook of Parapsychology* (1977), has published approximately thirty scientific articles and has presented numerous research papers.

Selected Writings: 1983. "A Psychobiological Framework for Psi Research." *Proceedings: Symposium on Applications of Anomalous Phenomena, November 30-December 1, 1983,* pp. 365–405; 1982. "On Grouping of Hits in Some Exceptional Psi Performers." JASPR 76:101; "Converging Lines of Evidence on Mind/Brain Relations." In B. Shapin and L. Coly, eds., *Brain/Mind and Parapsychology,* 1979, pp. 1–34; and Locke, R. G. "Altered States of Consciousness and Psi: An Historical Survey and Research Prospectus." *Parapsychology Foundation Monograph,* 1981; and Lenz, J. E. and Artley, J. L. 1980. "A Computer-Based Laboratory Facility for the Psychophysiological Study of Psi." JASPR 74:149; and Schouten, S. A. 1978. "On the Experiment of Brugmans, Heymans, and Weinberg." *European Journal of Parapsychology* 2:247; and Burdick, D. S. "Statistical Methods in Parapsychology Research." In B. Wolman, ed., *The Handbook of Parapsychology,* 1977.

BIBLIOGRAPHY: Berger, A. S. *Lives and Letters in American Parapsychology,* 1987.

**Kennedy, John Fitzgerald, 1917–1963.** Thirty-fifth president of the United States. On November 22, 1963, riding in an open limousine through the streets of Dallas, Texas, he was shot and killed. His assassination, in addition to being one of the most traumatic, was "one of the most extensively predicted personal disasters of our time. . . . **Mrs. Jeane Dixon** spoke of [it] as early as 1956 . . . [and] up to the day of Kennedy's violent death . . ." (Ebon, 1968:202).

In addition to many anecdotal reports, there are recorded predictions of many astrologers in various astrological publications around the world and the exceptional prediction of David Williams, an astrologer and economics specialist, who wrote and had witnessed by six people on August 4, 1960, that Kennedy would be elected president, would die in office, and be succeeded by Johnson. There is in addition the relation of "'the twenty years periodicity of Jupiter and Saturn with deaths of presidents in office'" (Ebon, 1968:206): 1840 Harrison; 1860 Lincoln; 1880 Garfield; 1900 McKinley; 1920 Harding; 1940 Roosevelt; 1960 Kennedy (but Reagan [1980] broke the cycle).

Kennedy himself was aware of his danger, was supposed that very morning to have pointed his finger at his head, and playfully to have pretended to be shot. Yet he insisted on riding in an open limousine. Was his assassination a self-fulfilling prophecy? See also **Precognition.**

BIBLIOGRAPHY: Ebon, M. *Prophecy in Our Time,* 1968.

**Kennedy, John L.** Twentieth century American psychologist. He was appointed fellow in psychical research by Stanford University under a gift from Thomas W. Stanford. After the publication in 1934 of Joseph B. Rhine's *Extra Sensory Perception,* Kennedy became one of the foremost critics of Rhine's work. In maintaining that no extra-chance results had been obtained by Rhine, Kennedy pointed out that the symbols on the ESP cards used in Rhine's experiments could be identified from their backs (Kennedy, 1938). Rhine, however, replied that, while this may have been true of the cards printed commercially, those used in experiments were not faulty.

Kennedy's other critiques were based on assertions of errors in recording results (Kennedy, 1939) and at a symposium on ESP held in 1938 by the American Psychological Association, he told the press that he had the nails ready for ESP's coffin. But when **Gardner Murphy** debated with Kennedy at the symposium over the issues and showed that all experimental methodology had been corrected, Kennedy was silenced (Berger, 1988:162).

Selected Writings: 1939. "A Methodological Review of Extra-Sensory Perception." *Psychological Bulletin* 36:59; 1938. "The Visual Clues from the Backs of ESP Cards." *Journal of Psychology* 6:149.

BIBLIOGRAPHY: Berger, A. S. *Lives and Letters in American Parapsychology,* 1988.

**Key Card.** In ESP card-guessing tests, a card believed by a subject to match a target card in the target pack. See also **ESP Cards.**

**K.I.B. Foundation.** British organization founded by Arthur Koestler, Instone Bloomfield and Brian Inglis "to support research in areas where funds have ordinarily been hard to come by, because they are regarded as just outside the boundaries of conventional science." These areas include the paranormal. In the past, the foundation has funded tests of Matthew Manning conducted by members of the Society for Psychical Research, such as Anita Gregory, and research into unorthodox healing, metal-bending, and psychokinesis with children. Address: 23 Harley House, Marylebone Road, London NW1 5HE, England.

**Kidd, James, c. 1879–1949.** American miner. After he disappeared in the Superstition Mountains of Arizona, his will became the focal point of a sensational and prolonged court battle known as the "Great Soul Trial."

Kidd was the picture of extreme frugality. He lived in the least expensive rooms, smoked the cheapest cigars, and read cast-off newspapers. Yet when he died somewhere in the Arizona hills, he left $270,000 in securities. The uneducated miner who had written his own will with a pencil left all his money "for research or some scientific proof of a soul of the human body which leaves it at death." Almost immediately 130 litigants flew into an Arizona court and descended on Kidd's estate like scavenging vultures. The trial court's decision awarded the Kidd estate to an Arizona-based institute that admitted that it never had and never would conduct research into the human soul and would use the money instead for brain research with cats and dogs. After appeal by the other disgruntled claimants, the lower court's decision was reversed. Two-thirds of the Kidd money was awarded to the American Society for Psychical Research and one-third to the Psychical Research Foundation. Among all the soul-searching decisions that are made by people in the course of a lifetime, this may be the only one that made the law reports and the pages of *Life* and *Reader's Digest.*

BIBLIOGRAPHY: Berger, A. S. *Lives and Letters in American Parapsychology,* 1988.

**K–Idea.** See **Association Theory of Telepathy.**

**Kilner, Walter John, 1847–1920.** British medical doctor. Fascinated by the human **Aura,** he was the first to conduct experiments with it, describe its colors, and develop special goggles stained with dye that would allow everyone to see what he believed to be a physical phenomenon with an objective existence. Kilner's work and conclusions, however, are controversial. While one colleague confirmed them (Bagnall, 1970), other notable investigators, such as René Sudre (1960) and Arthur J. Ellison (1962), have questioned his research, goggles, and the very existence of the aura, itself. There remains, however, a body of evidence, both anecdotal and scientific, that seems to support the phenomenon.

Selected Writing: *The Human Aura,* 1965.

BIBLIOGRAPHY: Bagnall, O. *The Origin and Properties of the Human Aura,* 1970; Ellison, A. J. 1962. "Some Recent Experiments in Psychic Perceptivity." *JSPR* 41:355; Sudre, R. *Treatise on Parapsychology,* 1960.

**"King, John."** Often claiming to be the spirit of the pirate Sir Henry Morgan, "John King," his wife, "Katie," and his daughter (also "Katie") have appeared frequently as the controls of many different mediums. Almost every nineteenth century medium seems to have had a John King Control: Madame H. P.

Blavatsky, the Davenport Brothers, Agnes Guppy, Nelson Holmes, Frank Herne, Charles Williams, Rosina Showers, Eusapia Palladino and others. In the 1920s and 30s, John King was still around helping Gladys Osborne Leonard and Etta Wriedt. Sir Oliver Lodge believed that he had spoken to John King, and as late as 1963 John and Katie King appeared in sittings with the Danish medium Einer Nielsen. Spiritualists theorized that "John King" was either a pseudonym for a group of controls or was a "symbol of power."

BIBLIOGRAPHY: Medhurst, R. G. and Goldney, K. M. 1964. "William Crookes and the Physical Phenomena of Mediumship." PSPR 54:25.

**King, Mrs.** See **Lyttleton Dame Edith.**

**King, William Lyon Mackenzie, 1874–1950.** Canadian economist, statesman, and prime minister of Canada. King is known for having concluded a trade treaty with the United States in 1935 and for having dominated the Canadian scene during World War II and the postwar years. But, behind the public facade, King was a **Noted Witness** for the paranormal who concealed his private life and deepest beliefs from the public.

One event in his life suggested precognition. A lonely man who never married, his one close companion was Pat, an Irish terrier. On the night prior to Pat's death, King's watch, which had been resting on a table next to his bed, dropped suddenly and unexpectedly face down to the floor. It stopped at 4:20. For King, it was a sign: "I am not psychic," he said, "but I knew then, as if a voice were speaking to me, that Pat would die before another 24 hours went by." (Quoted Fodor, 1964:14). Twenty-four hours after the watch had stopped, the dog left its basket, jumped on King's bed for the last time and died.

Behind the scenes also, King was a believer in Spiritualism. He consulted mediums, such as Geraldine Cummins, and was convinced that he had conversed with his dead mother, brother, and sister. After Nandor Fodor gave him a book dealing with evidence of human survival of death, he wrote that its words "appealed very strongly to me, and were in the nature of confirmation of experiences of my own concern, of which there can be no doubt whatever" (Quoted Fodor, 1964:13).

King was careful to keep his convictions from the public. "[I]t has seemed to me," he wrote, "inadvisable to become too actively identified with Psychical Research work, pending the time that I may continue to hold my present position" (Quoted Fodor, 1964:12). King died eight months after he left office. Following his death, the Canadian publication, *MacLean's Magazine,* revealed his secret life.

BIBLIOGRAPHY: Fodor, N. *Between Two Worlds,* 1964.

**Kipling, Rudyard, 1865–1936.** English author and poet. He was awarded the Nobel Prize for literature in 1907. Famous for bringing India and Burma to readers as the colorful and exciting places where brave British Tommies fought, for his defense of British imperialism, and for children's stories, Kipling began as a journalist and as sub-editor of the *Civil and Military Gazette.* His reputation was made when he published a volume of short stories among which were *Soldiers Three, The Phantom Rickshaw, and Wee Willie Winkie.* In 1887, he travelled to India and wrote the popular *Barrack-Room Ballads* (1892). After marrying an American, and living for some years in the United States, he wrote the children's stories the *Jungle Books* (1894 and 1895). Other famous works are *Captains Courageous* (1897), *The Light that Failed* (1890), and *Kim* (1901). His Cockney-dialect poetry includes *Fuzzy-Wuzzy, Tommy Atkins, Mandalay,* and *Gunga Din.*

Although his sister was **Alice Fleming,** the celebrated medium ("Mrs. Holland"), he did not write about mediums. He wrote instead about ghosts. In Kipling's stories, such as *The Phantom Rickshaw,* ghosts are taken for granted as realities like stones or sunsets and might qualify Kipling as **Noted Witness** for this phenomenon.

Much clearer, however, is his testimony for a personal daemon and the creative process. He is one more creative individual who claimed that his inspiration and information came to him from an external source beyond his conscious control. Thus he wrote in his autobiography: "Let us now consider the Personal Daemon of Aristotle . . . Mine came to me early when I sat bewildered among other notions, and said: 'Take this and no other.' . . . . [Under the influence of his daemon, he wrote *The Eye of Allah* and *The Captive.* Also] My Daemon was with me in the *Jungle*

*Books, Kim,* and both Puck books, and good care I took to walk delicately, lest he should withdraw. . . . [W]hen those books were finished they said so themselves with, almost, the water-hammer click of a tap turned off. . . . *Note here.* When your Daemon is in charge, do not try to think consciously. Drift, wait, and obey . . .".

BIBLIOGRAPHY: Ghiselin, B. *The Creative Process,* 1952, pp. 157–158.

**Kirlian Photography.** A method of high voltage, high frequency photography discovered in the Soviet Union by Semyon Davidovitch Kirlian and Valentina Kirlian and introduced to the West by Sheila Ostrander and Lynn Schroeder (1974). It aroused much interest because it seemed to be a technique that could be used for diagnosing and evaluating medical and psychophysiological states. Kirlian photographs of the fingers of human subjects (generally, it is the fingers that are photographed) show emotional and physical changes and reportedly show structures in pregnant women different from non-pregnant women (Treviño and Flores, 1985). But, because of many physical factors that are not easily controlled, such as skin hydration, temperature, and the pressure of the finger on a photographic plate, the technique has not proved reliable.

The significance of Kirlian photography for psychical research appears in photographs revealing a multicolored glow surrounding the contour of a leaf from a tree or human fingers or hands. It seems to provide evidence of the astral body or the aura a psychic may claim to see. Studies by **Carroll B. Nash** (1978) and others, however, do not seem to support such conclusions. The glow seems no more than an electrical corona discharge made up of ionized air molecules and ultraviolet radiation that may be affected by sweating or skin hydration. When an animate object, such as a human finger is photographed, the mental or physical state of a person may also affect the corona. But it does not appear to be the result of any paranormal factor.

Similarly, **Brian Millar's** research with Kirlian photographs convinced him that the effect bore no relationship to the human aura or astral body. In the case of the "phantom leaf" effect—in which the entire leaf appears on a photograph although a part of it has been torn away—Millar suggested that artifactual explanations for it exist, such as tearing or cutting the leaf with a blade and adjusting the voltage frequency to produce a corona from the sharp cut ends. In short, from present indications, it is difficult to perceive any relationship between Kirlian photography and psychical research. But the case is not closed and future discoveries may restore faded psychical research interest in the subject.

BIBLIOGRAPHY: Millar, B. 1974. "Correspondence." JSPR 47:461; Nash, C. B. 1978. "Correspondence. Aura. Kirlian Photography and Acupuncture." JSPR 49:764; Ostrander, S. and Schroeder, L. *Handbook of Psychic Discoveries,* 1974; Treviño, M. G. de and Flores, A. C. 1985. "Kirlian Photography and Pregnancy." *Psi Research* 4 (3,4): 232.

**Kiyota, Masuaki, 1962–.** Japanese psychic. He has been called "probably the most powerful in the world" (Kasahara, 1987) with the ability to produce thoughtography and metal bending. On October 30, 1977, an NBC-TV program called "Exploring the Unknown" showed a fourteen year old Japanese boy. A Polaroid camera with its lens capped and film provided by American visitors were handed to him. The boy stared at the camera, gathered up all his energy and uttered a shout as he let it go. Thirty seconds later the developed photograph showed the Tokyo Tower. The boy had apparently succeeded in imprinting on film the image that had been in his mind. He was Kiyota and had just demonstrated thoughtography for the video audience.

The year before, in his home and in the presence of other American visitors who gave him a heavy tablespoon made of stainless steel to hold, he simply twisted his wrist and threw the spoon into the air. When it fell to the floor, it had a twist in the handle of 180 degrees, a demonstration of metal-bending. These abilities first developed when Kiyota was ten but he did not realize that they were unusual until he saw Uri Geller on Japanese television.

In psychical research and parapsychology, however, demonstrations on television or at informal parties have little or no scientific value. Japanese parapsychologists, therefore, including Toshio Kasahara, made him the subject of metal-bending and thoughtography experiments in 1979 and 1980 in which he produced some paranormal spoon-bending and phenomena on Polaroid film. In 1982, he came to the United States to be tested at several parapsychological laboratories. Tests conducted by Jule Eisenbud in Denver for example, resulted in more paranormal effects on film and metal. Then in 1984, the proverbial roof fell in when, during a television program in Japan to show his metal-bending powers, Kiyota admitted that he had used normal force from his hands to supplement his psychic power to twist or break metal. His confession applied not only to the program he was on but also to previous demonstrations he had given. It produced the kind of hostility and controversy among Japanese scientists and scholars that had not been seen since the heated debates over the work of Tomokichi Fukurai and it had a harmful impact on other metal-benders and on parapsychologists.

The episode was a repeat of the old story well-known in psychical research of psychics and mediums who, required to perform on demand and produce results, resort to trickery, especially when loose conditions provide them with the opportunity. But, as in the case of Eusapia Palladino, the question is whether any of Kiyota's phenomena are genuine. After all, the successful experiments by Kasahara and Eidenbud took place under controlled conditions where fraud seems to have been impossible.

BIBLIOGRAPHY: Eisenbud, J. 1982. "Some Investigations of Claims of PK Effects on Metal: The Denver Experiments." JASPR 76:218; Kasahara, T. (November 26, 1987) Letter to authors; Kasahara, T., Kohri, N., Ro, Y., Imai, S., Otani, S. 1981. "A Study on PK Ability of a Gifted Subject in Japan." In J. Beloff and W. G. Roll, eds., *Research in Parapsychology, 1980,* 1981, p. 39.

**Klinckowstroem von, Carl (Count), 1884–1969.** German scientist and amateur conjuror. He was an authority on and supporter of dowsing. His interesting theory was that the dowser's response to stimuli from the ground was an allergic reaction produced by a "geopathic" constitution. He was on firmer ground when, as a member of the German Society for the Prevention of Superstition, he fought belief in witchcraft and astrology and cast a faultfinding eye on psychical research. He made a critical survey of physical mediums and the physical phenomena they allegedly produced. Count v. Klinckowstroem presented confessions by mediums of the frauds they had committed and published a letter that implicated Eva C. He was especially carping of the flaws in mediumistic investigations conducted by researchers such as Albert von Schrenk-Notzing.

The count was important to German psychical research as the severe critic who exposed weaknesses in investigations and forced psychical researchers to toe the line of higher scientific standards. What he did not do, however, was to add to his destructive criticisms constructive suggestions for improving investigations and evidence, a common failing among critics of psychical research and parapsychology, old and new.

Selected Writings: 1958. "Ist Die Wünschhelrute ein Aberglaube?" *Erfahrungsheilkunde* 3:211; with Rosenbusch H. and von Gulat-Wellenberg, W. "1: Der physikalische Mediumismus." In M. Dessoir, ed., *Der Okkultismus in Urkunden,* 1925.

**Kluski, Franek, 1874–?.** Polish physical medium. According to Gustave Geley, Kluski "follow[ed] a broad profession," was a poet and writer, was extremely intelligent and well educated and spoke several languages. He never accepted payment for his sittings but, simply because of his interest in science, agreed, first, to be investigated by the Warsaw Society for Psychical Research (beginning in the summer of 1919) and then by the Institut Métapsychique International in Paris.

Although a variety of physical phenomena took place in his presence, the most impressive were the production of paraffin molds which Sir Oliver Lodge (1924) called "a standing demonstration of something inexplicable by normal science; . . . a standing miracle." The method used was to place near the medium a receptacle containing melted paraffin floating on warm water. "The materialised entity is requested to plunge a hand, foot, or even part of his face, several times in the paraffine [*sic*]. . . . Then the materialised part . . . dematerialises and leaves the mould to the experimenters" (Geley, 1923). To ensure against prepared molds being smuggled into the séance room, the experimenters (Gustave Geley and Charles Richet) added cholesterin to the paraffin which could be tested for after the experiments.

Beautiful molds were obtained: a child's foot, the mold of the lower part of an adult male's face, four right and three left hands, and a left foot. The molds were extremely thin. In one the last three fingers were folded with the index finger outstretched. The lines of the hands were visible and did not match the medium's. How these molds could have been produced by normal means has not been demonstrated.

BIBLIOGRAPHY: Geley, G. 1923. "Experiments in Materialization." JASPR 17:233, 27:423, 27:555, 27:630, 27:677; Lodge, O. 1924. "In Memoriam—Gustave Geley." PSPR 34:201.

**Knight, J. Z.** Contemporary American trance channeller. Born Judy Hampton about forty years ago in Roswell, New Mexico, and now living in Yelm, Washington, where she moved on the advice of her control (Ramtha) to avoid the catastrophes that are about to beset the world, she has become—thanks to Shirley MacLaine's *Dancing in the Light*—America's most famous trance channeller and one of its richest. She earns millions yearly from her trance lectures and tapes.

**Knox, John, 1514–1572.** Scottish religious reformer. He was the fanatical leader of the Reformation in Scotland. When Mary Tudor (Henry VIII's daughter) became queen of England on the death of her brother, Edward VI, Knox preached resistance against the reign of a Catholic ruler over Protestant subjects. He spent three years with John Calvin in Geneva but returned to Scotland to become the fiery spokesman again. "Bloody Queen Mary" had him tried for treason but he was exonerated by the Privy Council. He wrote many treatises on religion including *Blasts of the Trumpet Against the Monstrous Regiment of Women* (1558).

One of his writings seems to make him a **Noted Witness** for either clairvoyance of distant objects or events or of precognition: "I dare not deny, lest I be injurious to the giver, that God has revealed unto me secrets unknown to the world; yea, certain grave revelations of mutations and changes where no such things were feared, nor yet were appearing. Notwithstanding these revelations I did abstain to commit anything to writing, contented only to have obeyed the charge of Him who commanded me to cry."

BIBLIOGRAPHY: Prince, W. F. *Noted Witnesses for Psychic Occurrences,* 1963.

**K-Object.** See Association Theory of Telepathy.

**Koestler, Arthur, 1905–1983.** Hungarian-born British writer. Known for his novels and essays touching on political, scientific, moral, and philosophic themes, Koestler had also been deeply interested in the paranormal from childhood when he took part in table-tilting séances. At about this same time he had the experience of feeling himself "peacefully dissolving in nature as a grain of salt dissolves in the ocean" (Koestler, 1952:37). As a young man, in 1931, he advertised in the newspapers for which he was science correspondent for verifiable accounts of telepathy, clairvoyance, and levitation—with no results. Sentenced to death and confined to one of Franco's prisons during the Spanish Civil War, he had a profound mystical experience that persuaded him that death was not final.

In *Roots of Coincidence* (1972), he argued "that the unthinkable phenomena of ESP appear somewhat less preposterous in the light of the unthinkable propositions of physics" and, as he surveyed the "ascent of parapsychology towards respectability," he was impressed by the rigorous scientific methods used in the investigation of paranormal phenomena and by the sheer weight of the number of spontaneous cases that had been collected. The book was especially important because it reached a general audience for whom it "destroy[ed] any remaining skepticism about telepathy" (Inglis, 1984:266). And in a tribute to Joseph B. Rhine (1982), Koestler wrote that "J. B. Rhine will be recognized by future historians as one of the pioneers of the new age." He was also fascinated by meaningful coincidences (synchronicity) which he wrote about in 1974.

His study of yoga in the 1950s led him into an investigation of levitation. It seemed to him that a loss of weight, even for a few seconds, might indicate the possibility of levitation. His early experiments using an old railway scale yielded one positive result with a child. In 1981, a new series of experiments was started with a new scale that could register very small and short variations of weight. Early results were promising, but Koestler's failing health precluded him from continuing with the experiments.

With "some trepidation" Koestler agreed to become one of the trustees, along with Brian Inglis and Instone Bloomfield, of the KIB Foundation whose purpose is to promote research in fields beyond the pale of orthodox science, such as psychical research and parapsychology. A member of the Society for Psychical Research and of the Parapsychological Association, he bequeathed his estate for the establishment in the United Kingdom of a Chair of Parapsychology.

"In 1934, plunged into self-pity by his failure as a writer and his growing disillusionment with the [Communist] party, Arthur [Koestler] tried to commit suicide" (Inglis, 1984:264). In 1983, suffering from the final stages of Parkinson's disease and with the help of his wife who died with him, he succeeded. See also **Koestler Chair of Parapsychology.**

Selected Writings: "J. B. Rhine's Impact." In K. R. Rao, ed., *J. B. Rhine: On the Frontiers of Science,* 1982, p. 144; *The Roots of Coincidence,* 1972; *Arrow in the Blue.* 1952; *The Challenge of Chance,* 1973.

BIBLIOGRAPHY: Inglis, B. 1984. "Arthur Koestler and Parapsychology." JASPR 78:263.

**Koestler Chair of Parapsychology.** This chair was made possible by the wills of Arthur Koestler and his wife, Cynthia, both of whom died in 1983 as the result of a suicide pact. It was founded at the University of Edinburgh within its Department of Psychology. Principally a Research Chair, it is the first such chair in the United Kingdom. See also **Beloff, John; Morris, Robert L.**

**Koot Hoomi Lal Singh.** According to Theosophy, he is one of its sages whom Theosophists call "Mahatmas" (meaning "great soul"). Mahatmas were said to possess marvellous paranormal powers and to be interested in the Theosophical movement. Koot Hoomi was supposed to have come from the Punjab region of India, to have travelled widely, and to have studied at the University of Leipzig. As a Mahatma, he projected his apparition to distant places and, with the initials "K. H.", signed the letters that were received so mysteriously in the shrine in Theosophical Headquarters in Adyar, India, that people prostrated themselves before it in awe and reverence. After Richard Hodgson of the Society for Psychical Research investigated **Madame Helena P. Blavatsky** and the Theosophical Society, he concluded that the remarkable stories circulated about the Mahatmas's powers were the result of deception carried on by Madame Blavatsky, that Koot Hoomi was a fictitious personality she had invented, that she was the real author of the Koot Hoomi letters, and that the letters had been inserted secretly into the shrine by means of a sliding panel at the back.

BIBLIOGRAPHY: Berger, A. S. *Lives and Letters in American Parapsychology,* 1988.

**Kornwachs, Klaus, 1947–.** German physicist. Lecturer in philosophy at the University of Stuttgart, he conducts laboratory studies of psychokinesis, is interested in the philosophical and social aspects of parapsychology, and is involved in the development of systems theory and observational theories to be used in experimental approaches to parapsychology.

In collaboration with Walter von Lucadou, he formulated a new concept in an effort to settle some issues related to the employment of observational theory in parapsychological experiments.

Selected Writings: and von Lucadou, W. 1983. "On the Limitations of Psi—A System-Theoretical Approach." In W. G. Roll, J. Beloff, R. A. White, eds., *Research in Parapsychology 1982,* 1983, p. 85; and von Lucadou, W. 1980. "Development of the Systemtheoretic Approach to Psychokinesis." *European Journal of Parapsychology* 3 (3):297.

**Kreiman, Naum, 1919–.** Argentinian statistician and professor at the Universidad del Museo Social. Since 1963, he has been an experimental parapsychologist and has conducted more than fifty systematic experiments in extrasensory perception and has tested mediums. In 1972, he founded the **Instituto de Parapsicología** (Parapsychology Institute) whose president and scientific advisor he became. Kreiman also has given courses in parapsychology and statistics at the institute.

**Kreskin (George Kresge), 1935–.** American entertainer. Although he has a degree in psychology, it was the comic book character Mandrake the Magician that inspired him at the age of five to begin to learn about "thought reading" and magic. He says he is neither a psychic, a medium, nor a magician—even though he uses magic in his act, or "concert" as he prefers to call it. He also claims that he uses telepathy to read people's social security numbers from their minds and to guess their thoughts. He insists that he does not use hypnosis (in fact that hypnosis does not exist) but suggestion instead to make people see flying saucers, topple from non-existent tightropes, forget their names, obey unspoken commands, converse in "moon" language, and lead him to the place where his paycheck is hidden (the last undoubtedly through muscle reading). He does slate-writing and, without admitting that he uses sleight-of-hand, calls it a "physical effect" and not psychokinesis. He was a failure at laboratory tests. And cynics cannot help believing that many of "amazing" Kreskin's feats must involve the use of confederates.

At any rate this extremely successful entertainer has worked with psychologists, doctors, and dentists and with police departments as a consultant in the use of suggestion—and has been awarded an honorary doctorate in humanities by Seton Hall University.

Selected Writing: *The Amazing World of Kreskin*, 1973.

BIBLIOGRAPHY: Bolen, J. 1978. "Kreskin: Mind Star in a Universe of Realities." *New Realities* 1(6):8.

**Krieger, Dolores.** Contemporary American nurse researcher. As professor of nursing in the Division of Nursing Education at New York University she was intrigued by the laying-on-of-hands technique used by the healer **Oskar Estebany** and by **Bernard Grad's** laboratory studies of him that showed the technique affecting non-human organisms. But she wanted to see if the technique could be used outside the laboratory and in the clinic in everyday life situations. "The challenge . . . to the nurse researcher," she said, "lies in the living individual, rather than specimens in vitro, or in plants and animals" (Krieger, 1976a:122).

In 1971, she went ahead with her own studies of Estebany and discovered that in vivo human hemoglobin, a protein pigment in the red blood cells, was increased when the healer's laying-on-of-hands method was used on patients. The hemoglobin in people not treated by Estebany was not affected (Krieger, 1976a). These results were confirmed by a second experiment (Krieger, 1976b). This provocative outcome led Krieger to teach what she calls the "therapeutic touch" to practicing nurses throughout the United States to help them help their patients. Krieger also established an organization of nurse healers.

Selected Writings: 1976a. "Healing by the 'Laying-On' of Hands as a Facilitator of Bioenergetic Change: The Response of In-Vivo Human Hemoglobin." *Psychoenergetic Systems* 1:121; 1976b. "A Second Experiment in 'Laying-on-of-Hands.'" *Psychoenergetic Systems* 7.

**Krippner, Stanley, 1932–.** American psychologist and parapsychologist. His principal interests in psychical research have been in altered states of consciousness (including dreams), in healing, and in international interaction in consciousness research in Europe, Asia, the Soviet Union, and Latin America.

He was introduced to things psychic at the age of fourteen when he was suddenly sure that an uncle was dead—and his uncle had, in fact, just died. His continued interest in psi led him, when a student at the University of Wisconsin in 1953 and despite opposition from the university's Psychology Department, to arrange to have Joseph B. Rhine invited to speak there. After graduation, he visited Rhine's laboratory at Duke University several times. There he met Louisa Rhine, Karlis Osis, William Edward Cox and J. Gaither Pratt (and there he learned that "parapsychology was one of the most financially hazardous of professions" [Krippner, 1975:11]). As director of the Kent State University Child Study Center, a position he assumed in 1961 after receiving his doctorate from Northwestern University, he ran parapsychological experiments with students in addition to his regular work involving children with reading problems and learning disabilities.

In 1964 Gardner Murphy and Montague Ullman invited Dr. Krippner to become director of the newly organized Maimonides Medical Center Dream Laboratory in Brooklyn dedicated to the investigation of the relationship between telepathy and dreams. There he worked out the research methodology for the experiments. Striking results with a variety of subjects and techniques were often obtained and a rigorous scoring technique was ultimately implemented to meet criticisms that the experimenters were finding what they expected to find. This research produced a monograph written with **Montague Ullman** (1970) and a popular book written with Ullman and one of their subjects, the psychic **Alan Vaughan** (1973).

Dr. Krippner's interest in consciousness led him to take psilocybin (in 1962 when it was still legal) and to look into yoga, zen meditation, t'ai chi, aikido, sensory awareness, and Rolfing. In 1971 he gave a lecture on parapsychology at the USSR Academy of Pedagogical Sciences in Moscow and in 1981 presented a paper on parapsychology at the Chinese Academy of Sciences in Beijing. His notable contributions to parapsychology were acknowledged by his being presented with the Marius Volkoff Award in 1980. He was president of the Parapsychological Association in 1982.

Dr. Krippner is the author of numerous articles and of ten books, has edited or co-edited nine others and is editor-in-chief of *Advances in Parapsychological Research: A Bienneal Review.* He is currently the director of the Center for Consciousness Studies at Saybrook Institute, San Francisco, California.

Selected Writings: *Song of the Siren: A Parapsychological Odyssey,* 1975; and Villoldo, A. *The Realms of Healing,* 1976; and M. Ullman, with A. Vaughan, *Dream Telepathy,* 1973; and M. Ullman, *Dream Studies and Telepathy,* 1970.

BIBLIOGRAPHY: Berger, A. S. *Lives and Letters in American Parapsychology,* 1988.

**Kübler-Ross, Elisabeth, 1926–.** Swiss born medical doctor. An identical twin and a triplet to boot, the "death and dying lady," as she has been called, is known throughout the world for her compassionate work to help both the dying and their families deal with death as part of life. Her life has been as adventurous as any romance novel. In addition, without any help and without the requisite academic background, she managed to earn her medical degree in 1957 from the University of Zurich. She feels that her early loneliness and isolation (she was odd-man-out in her family) and the incredible and tragic experiences she lived through, taught her "that it is our choice . . . whether we want to [live] as victims . . . or view such tragedies as the windstorms of life which . . . strengthen us and help us grow." *Life* magazine in 1969 first brought her work with the dying to the attention of the world, and in that same year her book *On Death and Dying* was published and soon became a best-seller. Her anecdotal reports of the experiences of dying patients brought the near-death experience to public attention. She endorsed Raymond Moody's work on the subject (1975) and stimulated Kenneth Ring's.

In the course of her numerous interactions with dying patients, Elisabeth, as she prefers to be called, has become firmly convinced of survival after death. She accepts at face value the reports of NDErs that they were making a "transition to another plane of existence [where they were] greeted by loved ones who had died before them" (1975:xii). And later she wrote that a dying child was making "the transition to yet another form of existence. There she would wait for her mother . . ." (1978:67). "I have had many wonderful mystical experiences," she writes, "from cosmic consciousness to the awareness and ability to be in touch with my own guides . . ." (Kübler-Ross, 1980:328). Elisabeth also became convinced that spirit guides can materialize. "Materialized guides" were active in her workshops at her center (Shanti Nilaya in California).

In the mid 1980s Elisabeth moved her operations to the Elisabeth Kübler-Ross Center/Shanti Nilaya in Head Waters, Virginia. Although she continues her worldwide lecturing, she hopes to make the center a place for the development of "physical, intellectual, emotional and spiritual help" and, specifically, for workshops with children and a hospice for babies with AIDS.

Selected Writings: "Epilogue." In D. Gill's *Quest: The Life of Elisabeth Kübler-Ross,* 1980; *To Live until We Say Goodbye,* 1978; "Foreword." In R. Moody's *Life after Life,* 1975; *On Death and Dying,* 1969.

BIBLIOGRAPHY: Gill, D. *Quest: The Life of Elisabeth Kübler-Ross,* 1980; Hardy, J. M. and Searls, D. 1978. "Impressions of Elisabeth." *Theta* 6(2/3):1.

**Kuhlman, Kathryn, 1907 (or 1910)–1976.** American healer. Convinced that God worked through her, she was the most famous faith healer of her time. She healed at emotion laden services that began with music and prayer and ended with those who had been healed coming forward and falling prostrate when she touched them. Her diagnoses of illnesses were often accurate but were more likely the result of clairvoyance rather than, as she believed, a direct communication from God. As always in cases of faith healing, documentation is rare and follow-ups rarer, but her biographer investigated as well as he could and was satisfied that there were a number of genuine, lasting cures. He believed that she was a saint who felt universal love for all mankind and that she was the most remarkable person he had ever met.

BIBLIOGRAPHY: Spraggett, A. *Kathryn Kuhlman The Woman Who Believes in Miracles,* 1970.

**Kuhn, Thomas, 1922–.** American historian and philosopher of science at Massachussetts Institute of Technology. His theory of science has been embraced by parapsychologists as squarely applicable to parapsychology, its true position and the problems it faces vis-à-vis scientific circles. Kuhn distinguishes between "normal" science that functions within accepted boundaries and familiar explanatory models or "paradigms" and "extraordinary" or revolutionary science that bursts out of the old boundaries because it has taken account of fresh insights that revise the old explanatory models (Kuhn, 1962).

Under the Kuhn theory, there are seven steps in any field of science (McConnell, 1983:198–199). The first step is always a preparadigmatic period of confusion. This step is followed by others—the emergence of a prevailing paradigm from crude theories and the start of a mature science, a period of normal science in which the paradigm is explored, a crisis in which unexplainable anomalies become apparent, the emergence of a new paradigm, revolutionary struggle between new and old and, finally, a return to normal science when one side is victorious. Parapsychologists see themselves as in the first preparadigmatic phase. Kuhn has shown them how many more revolutionary changes or paradigm switches need to be made, one at a time, before parapsychology can be considered a part of normal science.

Selected Writing: *The Structure of Scientific Revolutions,* 1962.

BIBLIOGRAPHY: McConnell, R. A.. *An Introduction to Parapsychology in the Context of Science,* 1983.

**Kulagina, Nina Sergeyevna (pseudonym Nelya Mikhailova), c. 1925–.** Soviet housewife and grandmother. She lives in Leningrad but has attracted the attention of the world by her apparent power to will the movements of small objects of all shapes and materials. She had no awareness of any unusual abilities until she realized that she had a faculty for **Dermo-Optic Perception.** When **Prof. Leonid L. Vasiliev** carried out some experiments with her in this area in the 1960s, he discovered to his surprise (and to hers as well) that she was able to move a compass needle by psychokinesis.

Foreign scientists learned about Kulagina when they attended an international conference on parapsychology in Moscow in 1968. In what Joseph G. Pratt described as "the high point of the conference" (Pratt, 1973:72), a film was shown in which, just by staring at them, she made a compass needle swing and a plastic pen cap and wooden matches move along a table. From then on, she was studied by Dr. Genady A. Sergeiev, a neurophysiologist at the Utomskii Physiological Institute in Leningrad, at the University of Leningrad and at the U.S.S.R. Academy of Sciences. In 1978 at the latter, for example, she so convinced the scientists who conducted various experiments with her that an official document stating that her psychokinetic abilities were real was drawn up (Vilenskaya 1980:205).

Dr. Sergeiev's research "registered heightened biological luminescence radiating from Kulagina's eyes during the apparent movement of objects by PK . . . [A]t the moment an object begins to move, all her body processes speed up drastically—heart, breathing, brain activity—and the electromagnetic force fields around her body, all begin to pulse in rhythm" (Ostrander and Schroeder, 1971:11–12). After testing Kulagina is exhausted, her pulse becoming faint and her coordination poor.

Western scientists have studied her also. Dr. Pratt and Dr. Montague Ullman went to the Soviet Union to observe her. Dr. Ullman declared that he "witnessed several striking psychokinetic effects performed by her in my hotel room" (Ullman 1988:301). Among the effects produced by this woman are moving tennis balls and standing cigarettes on end, moving one selected object among others, altering the heartbeat rate of a frog's heart, and reviving apparently dead fish. While there are many others who have demonstrated the process of psychokinesis, "there is little doubt that Kulagina has been and probably still is the most successful subject with respect to directly observable PK" (Keil, Herbert, Ullman, Pratt, 1976:219).

BIBLIOGRAPHY: Keil, H. H., Herbert, B., Ullman, M., Pratt, J. G. 1976. "Directly Observable Voluntary PK Effects: A Survey and Tentative Interpretation of Available Findings from Nina Kulagina and Other Known Related Cases of Recent Date." PSPR: 56:197; Ostrander, S. and Schroeder, L. 1971. "Psychic Enigmas & Energies in the U.S.S.R." *Psychic* 2(6):8,11–12; Pratt, J. G. *ESP Research Today,* 1973; Rejdak, Z. 1971. "Phenomena: Nina Kulagina's Mind over Matter." *Psychic* 2(6):24; Rejdak, Z. 1969. "The Kulagina Cine Films: Introductory Notes." *Journal of Paraphysics* 3:64; Ullman, M. "Autobiographical Notes." In A. S. Berger, *Lives and Letters in American Parapsychology,* 1988, p. 288; Vilenskaya, L. "On PK and Related Subjects' Research in the U.S.S.R." In W. and M. Uphoff, eds., *Mind over Matter,* 1980, p. 205.

**Kuleshova, Rosa A., 1955–1978.** Soviet subject. Her exploits with dermo-optic perception beginning when she was a child in 1960 aroused both scientific and popular interest, articles about her appearing in Soviet newspapers and in popular science magazines. While blindfolded, she was able to "see" print and identify colors with her fingertips. Investigated by scientists at the Nizhne-Tagil Pedagogical Institute and the U.S.S.R. Academy of Sciences Institute of Radio Engineering and Electronics in 1978, scientists found that the phenomena she produced "are by no means tricks but rather the existence of a manifestation of unusual capabilities in man" (Vilenskaya, 1980:205). These capabilities, however, are not paranormal because investigations in the Soviet Union and elsewhere indicate a normal explanation for them.

BIBLIOGRAPHY: Ivanov, A. 1964. "Soviet Experiments in 'Eyeless Vision.'" *International Journal of Parapsychology* 6:5; Vilenskaya, L. "On PK and Related Subjects' Research in the U.S.S.R." In W. and M. Uphoff, eds., *Mind over Matter,* 1980. p. 205.

**Kundalini.** So intimate is the connection between yoga and Kundalini that it is claimed that there can be no yoga without the activation of Kundalini (Krishna 1972:181). The doctrine posits a fabulous source of strength and nerve energy located near the base of the spine. It is conceived as a serpent coiled within the bowl or basin *(kunda)* created by the pelvis. When stimulated by meditation and breathing techniques, this serpent or kundalini giving off energy and sensations of heat rises up a narrow duct in the spinal cord until it reaches the brain. The nerve energy is extolled as "so marvellous, so potent, and so precious for the peace and happiness of mankind that no price paid for it and no sacrifice made to acquire the secret would be too great" (Krishna, 1972:66). Kundalini is supposed to be "the spiritual as well as biological base of all the phenomena connected with religion, the occult, and the supernatural" (Krishna, 1972:180) and when it reaches *sahasara,* the crown of the head, the individual has mystical experiences, and experiences altered states of consciousness and psychic powers. It is here that kundalini yoga makes its connection with psychical research.

BIBLIOGRAPHY: Krishna, G. *The Secret of Yoga,* 1972.

**!Kung.** A group among the bushmen indigenous to South Africa who hunt with spears, bows, and poisoned arrows and live in bands of twenty to thirty people. The !Kung believe in the spirits of the dead and practice unorthodox healing as an important part of their social system. Whereas in the West healers are wont to pray, meditate, or rely on spirit doctors for help, the !Kung prepare for their healing practice by engaging in a ritual dance, known as the Giraffe dance, in which males and females dance around a fire from dusk to dawn. The dance releases their strong healing power.

How this release is achieved is interesting. "You dance, dance, dance, dance," say the !Kung. "Then n/um lifts you in your belly and lifts you in your back, and then you start to shiver. N/um makes you tremble; it's hot. Your eyes are open but you don't look around; you hold your eyes still and look straight ahead. But when you get into !kia, you're looking around because you see everthing, because you see what's troubling everybody. . . . Rapid shallow breathing, that's what draws n/um up . . . then n/um enters part of your body, right to the tip of your feet and even your hair. . . . In your backbone you feel a pointed something, and it works its way up . . ." (Katz, 1973:140).

In this concept of n/um, we see a close connection with the doctrine of **kundalini,** the very essence of **yoga,** which is drawn up the spine by breathing techniques to produce great psychic and spiritual awareness. This similarity between two disconnected cultures is striking.

BIBLIOGRAPHY: Katz, R. 1973. "Education for Transcendence: Lessons from the !Kung Zhu/Twasi." *Journal of Transpersonal Psychology* 5:136.

**Kurtz, Paul, 1925–.** American educator, philosopher, editor, and chairman of the Committee for the Scientific Investigation of the Claims of the Paranormal. He says that his "interest in parapsychology has been life long in teaching courses in philosophy and the philosophy of science." But his interest is that of a hard-line skeptic. To him parapsychology is a pseudoscience. In his view, it cannot be a legitimate science unless the reality of the psi it hypothesizes is established (Kurtz, 1978a).

Kurtz also is largely motivated by the belief that there is an antiscientific trend in society today, a growth in the forces of unreason and that all the claims of psychic phenomena "go far beyond the range of hard evidence and can only leave the scientifically-minded flabbergasted" (Kurtz, 1978b:356). As head of CSICOP, he has made it the strongest and most well-known organization in the world of skeptics who deny the claims of parapsychology. Although headquartered in the United States, his leadership has stimulated the formation in other countries of clone organizations with the same objects as CSICOP's. Under Kurtz's editorship, the *Skeptical Inquirer,* whose articles debunk parapsychology, reaches thousands of readers in fifty-two countries. As editor-in-chief of a large publishing house, he sees to it that titles critical of parapsychology are published (Kurtz, 1985).

While Kurtz considers his to be a rationalist and scientific position, many supporters of parapsychology look on his attacks against the field as no more than a "crusade" based on his assumption that parapsychology and its phenomena contravene the basic tenets of orthodox science. Kurtz's opinion that parapsychology is a pseudoscience because its fundamental hypothesis of psi has not been verified is also subject to criticism, they say. They maintain that what ought to determine whether parapsychology is a legitimate science is not the validity of its hypotheses but its methods of investigation.

Selected Writings: (Ed.) *Skeptic's Handbook of Parapsychology,* 1985; 1978a. "Is Parapsychology a Science?" *The Skeptical Inquirer* 3:14; 1978b. "The Humanists' Crusade Against Parapsychology: A Discussion. Part One. On the Art of Quoting Out of Context: A Response to the Rockwells' Critique." JASPR 72:349.

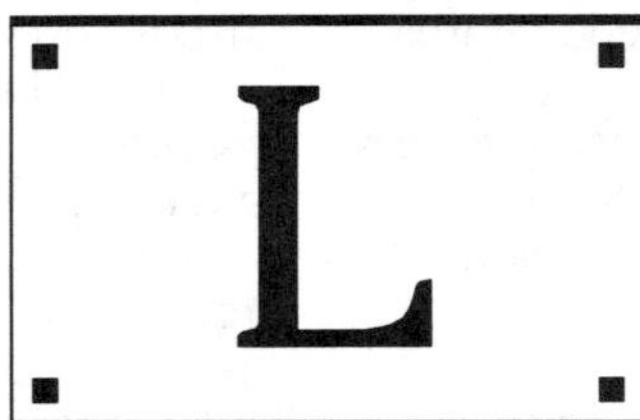

**Laboratoire Universitaire de Parapsychologie et d'Hygiène Mental.** An active center of research in parapsychology in France, this organization was established in May, 1974, at the University of Toulouse and is made up of university people. Taking no religious or philosophical position, they conduct scientific studies of paranormal phenomena and make field investigations of apparitions, dowsing, haunts, healing, and spontaneous cases. In laboratory studies, experiments are designed to study both previous experimental work done on established phenomena and the possible reality of yet unestablished phenomena.

In its studies of extrasensory perception, the laboratory uses three kinds of card-guessing experiments with conventional ESP cards. Ordinary playing cards are used also with statistical methods devised by the mathematician, Sir R. A. Fisher. Experiments are conducted, too, to determine whether there are differences between the extrasensory perception of colors and the extrasensory perception of geometric figures. In tests of psychokinesis, the center uses random event generators and random number generators and conducts trials of retro-PK proposed by the physicist Costa de Beauregard.

The laboratory also publishes experimental results, holds annual conferences, and conducts information meetings in public schools and workshops for the general public in the hope of controverting irrational opinions about occult subjects. The director of the laboratory is Yves Lignon. Address: Laboratoire de Parapsychologie, UER Mathématiques, Université Toulouse-Le-Mirail 31058, Toulouse CEDEX, France.

**Lady of Guadalupe.** A cloak made of cactus-fiber on exhibition in the Basilica of Guadalupe in Mexico City. On the cloak is a beautiful image in color of the Virgin Mary still plainly visible after four and one half centuries, and, assuming the truthfulness of the account of its manufacture, the first and only physical evidence of Mary's appearance.

According to historical facts investigated and authenticated by the Catholic church, the owner of the cloak was Juan Diego, a poor Indian, who had become a pious Christian. Walking toward a monastery on December 9, 1531, he reached a hill known as Tepeyac. There the Blessed Virgin surprised him and, speaking to him in Nahuatl, his native dialect, identified herself and asked that a church dedicated to her be erected on the very hill where he had seen her apparition. After a fruitless attempt to persuade the incredulous bishop in Mexico City of his meeting with Mary, Juan went back to the hill and saw her again. The next day, he returned to the bishop who, this time, demanded that Mary provide some sign. Juan went back to Tepeyac and once more Mary appeared and agreed to supply evidence of her identity. She told Juan to carry to the bishop as a sign flowers she had placed in Juan's cloak. He did as she asked and, when he opened his cloak in the presence of the bishop, in addition to the flowers, there was on the cloak an image of Mary in vivid color and so perfect that the bishop was awed and now completely convinced. A church was erected according to Mary's wishes.

The facts demand that the story be taken seriously. Although any ordinary cactus-fiber cloak can last no more than twenty years before falling apart, Juan Diego's has not disintegrated. Neither art experts nor scientists who have studied the image from 1666 to 1953 have been able to account for how the image was produced on the cloak or why the image, like the cloak, should have survived so long without deterioration or why its remarkable and sensitive quality should have continued after more than 400 years. Some people believe that the image of the "Lady of Guadalupe," was impressed supernaturally and is a miracle. But it is not easy to put up a fence with the miraculous on one side and the paranormal on the other. The "Lady of Guadalupe" presents mysteries that seem legitimate for psychical research to examine.

BIBLIOGRAPHY: Demarest, D. C. Taylor, eds., *The Dark Virgin,* (n.d.).

**Lady Wonder.** Known as the "mind-reading horse," Lady Wonder used her muzzle to multiply, subtract, tell time, and respond to questions by pointing to numbers and alphabet blocks. When Joseph B. Rhine tested her in 1927, he was fully familiar with the "Clever Hans" effect (i.e., unconscious guidance of an animal by minute, involuntary changes in the posture of the head or body of human questioners.) So Rhine, by excluding the horse's owner from the tests, took precautions in his experiments with the horse to eliminate all bodily cues. In spite of this handicap, Lady Wonder showed good form and came through the test a winner. As far as Rhine was concerned, the only tenable hypothesis for the results produced by the horse was telepathy.

After a second investigation in 1928, however, Lady Wonder did not seem to have been able to get out of the starting gate. This time Rhine found that the horse had lost whatever ESP ability she might once have had and merely reacted to her owner's whip, body movements or inflections of voice. Interestingly, Rhine did not retract his earlier finding that, whatever may have happened to her later, in the initial test Lady Wonder had brought strong evidence of telepathy across the finish line. See also **Anpsi.**

**Lambert, Guy William, 1889–1983.** British under secretary of state in the War Office between 1938 and 1951. His "life-long interest in psychical research" (Lambert, 1956:276) began with his reading the work of Frederic W. H. Myers who, like Lambert, had been a student at Cheltenham College. Lambert's interest led him to make detailed examinations of many of the phenomena of psychical research including some of its most famous cases: Frederick Bligh Bond's Glastonbury scripts (Lambert, 1966), the Dieppe Raid (Lambert and Gay, 1952), the Versailles ghosts (Lambert, 1962) and the Morton ghost (Lambert, 1958).

He was particularly drawn to the study of poltergeist phenomena and plotted them on a map to try to find a pattern for them. Lambert discovered that in countries bordering on the sea the phenomena were more likely to occur along the coast, including the tidal reaches of rivers and estuaries. If they occurred inland, the phenomena seemed to occur on the sides of valleys with rivers at the bottom (Lambert, 1956). From this observation, Lambert went on to develop a geophysical theory of poltergeists, that the majority of poltergeist phenomena are produced by tides, earth tremors or underground streams. Although the theory has been sharply criticized (Cornell and Gauld, 1961) and is not plausible in many poltergeist cases, it does suggest that physical, not paranormal, causes at times may account for mysterious noises and movements of objects.

Lambert was a member of the Society for Psychical Research for the record number of seventy years and had served as its president from 1955 to 1958.

Selected Writings: 1966. "The Quest at Glastonbury." JSPR 43:301; 1962. "Richard's Garden Revisited." JSPR 41:279; 1958. "The Cheltenham Ghost: A Reinterpretation." JSPR 39:267; 1956. "The Use of Evidence in Psychical Research." PSPR 50 275; and Gay, K. 1952. "The Dieppe Raid Case." JSPR 36:607.

BIBLIOGRAPHY: Cornell, A. D. and Gauld, A. 1961. "The Geophysical Theory of Poltergeists." JSPR 41:148.

**Lang, Andrew, 1844–1912.** Scottish man of letters. Called "the greatest bookman of his age," he wrote numerous books on topics ranging from anthropology to mythology to French and Scottish history to fairy tales and ghost stories and verse. Lang's chief contribution to psychical research, according to Alan Gauld, was that he made it a subject worthy of exploration by serious students. In addition, as a professional writer he was able to bring psychical research to the attention of the general public.

He had a lifelong interest in the subject (it seemed to him inseparable from folklore and anthropology), but he did not join the Society for Psychical Research until 1904. He was its president in 1911. In that same year and in the year before, he wrote articles on apparitions, crystal-gazing, hauntings, poltergeists, and psychical research in general for the 11th edition of the *Encyclopaedia Britannica* and defended Edmund Gurney against the charge of having been credulous and easily imposed upon. He saw Mrs. Leonora Piper at her worst, was convinced that her controls Phinuit and G. P. were secondary personalities and that all Mrs. Piper's successes were the result of either telepathy or muscle reading of her sitters. He did not believe that she ever communicated anything known only to a dead person but unknown to anyone living. He had "a deep-seated feeling that no educated or honourable person could, after death, conceivably wish to speak in American slang through the mouth of an uneducated lower-middle class lady hired at so many dollars a sitting" (Gauld, 1983). "In the matter of experiments," Lang (1911b) said, "I prefer to deal with highly-educated British subjects . . ." (p. 374).

He carried on a running argument with Frank Podmore about poltergeists whose phenomena Podmore considered in every case to be fraudently produced, usually by children. (Lang, [1901–1903] wrote, "If the things can be done so easily, will no young person do them?") Unlike William James (and many others) he was not particularly impressed by F. W. H. Myers's *Human Personality and its Survival of Bodily Death.* Lang's only experiments were in crystal gazing with Miss "Angus," actually a Miss Fyfe. Gauld (1983) considers Lang's *Cock Lane and Common-Sense* "the most enjoyable . . . book in the whole literature of psychical research."

Lang was deeply influenced by his Scottish boyhood and by Scottish literature. He began his career as a free-lance writer on every conceivable subject and was soon "a household word." In 1886 he wrote about an experience that makes him a **Noted Witness** in support of the phenomenon of the apparition: "It was when I was living in St. Giles that I saw the real or sham J. C. [Professor J. Conington]. I was under the lamp in Oriel Lane, about 9 at night, in winter and I certainly had a *very good view of him.* I believe this to have been a Thursday, but it may have been a Friday. I think it was on a Saturday that Scott Holland did not come to a breakfast party, and sent a note that Conington was dangerously ill. I said, 'He can't have been ill on Thursday (or yesterday, I can't remember which), for I met him near Corpus.' I am constantly failing to recognize people. Conington, however, was not easily mistaken, and I know of no one in Oxford who was at all like him." It was determined later that Conington knew he was dying on Thursday and did die on Saturday.

After 1893 and until his death in 1912 he produced forty-nine works, most of them involving original thought and research, two of them on psychical research. He liked "cricket, angling, book-collecting, spooks, mysteries, Scotland, Jacobitism, . . . children and animals" (Gauld, 1983). He had a melancholy strain, was very shy and so seemed aloof. He seemed to have psychic ability. He once found a missing object by table-tilting, wrote automatically and "saw his family death omen, a hideous cat," shortly before his death.

Selected Writings: "Edmund Gurney." In *Encyclopaedia Britannica,* 11th ed. Cambridge, 1911a; 1911b. "Presidential Address." PSPR 25:364; 1903–1904. "The Poltergeist at Cideville." PSPR 18:454; 1903–1904. "'The Nineteenth Century' and Mr. Frederic Myers." PSPR 18:62; 1901–1903. "The Poltergeist, Historically Considered." PSPR 17:305; 1900. "Discussion of the Trance Phenomena of Mrs. Piper." PSPR 15:39; *Cock Lane and Common-Sense,* 1896.

BIBLIOGRAPHY: Bayfield, M. A. 1913. "Andrew Lang and Psychical Research." PSPR 27:419; Gauld, A. 1983. "Andrew Lang as Psychical Researcher." JSPR 52:161 (contains a complete bibliography of Lang's works); Podmore, F. *Modern Spiritualism,* 1902; Prince, W. F. *Noted Witnesses for Psychic Occurrences,* 1963.

**Lawrence, Thomas Edward (Lawrence of Arabia, T. E. Shaw), 1888–1935.** British soldier, archaelogist, and author. No hero of fiction could have achieved more or been more admired by the world for his exploits than Lawrence who, almost single-handedly during World War I, successfully organized an Arab rebellion in Syria and coordinated the Arab forces against the Turks, then Germany's ally. His military strategy, personal courage, and charisma resulted in the capture of Aqaba and later Damascus. Lawrence's *Seven Pillars of Wisdom* (1926), which documented the uprising and his role in it, was much sought after. Following the war, he became the advisor on Arab affairs to Winston Churchill and worked with the Royal Air Force in the designing and testing of seaplanes. In 1925 he changed his name legally to T. E. Shaw—perhaps because of his friendship and admiration for George Bernard Shaw. Lawrence (Shaw) died in a motorcycle accident in Moreton, Dorset.

For years after he died, rumors circulated that Lawrence was not dead but had been seen in foreign countries. In 1938, the villagers of Dorset reported a ghostly motorcyclist racing along the streets at night. They believed that it was not Lawrence's ghost but his double's. The double, according to them, had been substituted for Lawrence by the secret service, lived in his cottage in Dorset, had been murdered in his place and buried under Lawrence's name. A medium from London was summoned to find out what she could about the ghostly motorcyclist. She headed directly for a garden shed near Lawrence's cottage, reached into a rubbish heap and withdrew Lawrence's dispatch box which had been forced open. Whatever papers had been in it were gone.

Nandor Fodor wrote: "It is certainly odd, whether the information can be verified or not, that [the medium] should so unhesitatingly walk to a spot unknown to her and unearth some of Lawrence's personal property with evidence pointing to a burglary. If it were indeed true that burglars had entered his cottage sometime before or after his death and stole important papers, the haunting of the village street by a phantom cyclist at least has an emotional motive" (Fodor, 1938).

BIBLIOGRAPHY: Fodor, N. 1938. "Letter from England—The Ghost of Lawrence of Arabia." JASPR 32:311.

**Laying-on-of-hands.** Also called by **Dolores Krieger** "therapeutic touch." One of the acts performed by "healers" who wish to help or heal an afflicted individual. It consists of a healer placing his or her hands near or on the body of a "healee" for about ten or fifteen minutes. Some healers pray aloud or silently during the procedure, some always touch the skin, others do not. Investigations such as those conducted by Dr. Krieger and Bernard Grad suggest that some curative force may be at work because plants, animals, and human beings seem affected by the technique. See also **Healing, Unorthodox.**

**Lazaris,** the entity channelled by **Jach Pursel** when he is in trance. Lazaris is, in his own words, "a non-physical entity, who is aware of themselves [*sic*] and the multiplicity of personality and identity, but has never put that into a bodily form. We are boundaryless consciousness. . . . We are not here in total, but a piece of us is here." "He" says that he does not possess Pursel's body but "rather project[s] thought patterns. . . . About one percent of our energy is involved in these transmissions. We are very active and involved with many consciousnesses who are not in body, who are in other systems of reality, in different levels of evolution. For them also, we are a friend on the way Home" [presumably to God?]. Lazaris says that he observed Pursel through many lifetimes during which the latter was influenced so as to make communication possible in this life. Lazaris further says that he has come at this time because of the "unfolding of the New Age . . . a new time of consciousness and evolution, a new way of reaching and returning Home." Lazaris says we grow through "love and joy and laughter," that we "do create [our] own reality" and that there is a "God/Goddess/All That Is, and that Force is real and loves" us. He also stresses that not all channelled information is true (presumably his is).

Whatever Lazaris is (what he says he is or a creation of Jach Pursel's subconscious), he draws people of all ages, incomes, backgrounds; he draws New Agers, business executives and show biz personalities (Shirley MacLaine, Michael York, Sharon Gless, etc.) We are told that his video tapes have been studied by traditional doctors and psychiatrists and that he has addressed all sorts of groups, including an international peace conference, and that people have come from Australia, Argentina, Switzerland, and Hong

Kong to hear him. They come presumably to learn. See also **Channeling.**

BIBLIOGRAPHY: Martin, K. 1987. "The Voice of Lazaris." *New Realities* 7(6):26.

**Leadbeater, Charles Webster, 1854–1934.** British Theosophist and psychic. A controversial figure, he was extolled as a saint and as the possessor of great powers of clairvoyance taught him by Eastern sages. He was leader of the Theosophical Society along with Annie Besant. At the same time, he was despised as an evil sex pervert who, in ritual masturbation, taught his young disciples that the orgasm was an ecstatic mystical experience and the key to psychic powers. Among his pupils was the young Jiddu Krishnamurti, later an eminent Indian philosopher, to whom he tried to teach the means of bringing a new Christ to the world. In the end, however, Krishnamurti abandoned Leadbeater's great scheme.

Leadbeater believed in the human aura and, with Besant, claimed to have discovered the "ajna chakram," an etheric organ between the eyes, with remarkable powers (Besant and Leadbeater, 1919).

Whether saintly or evil, Leadbeater is "a fascinating and remarkable human being whose character contained that mixture of diverse and contradictory elements that makes for eccentricity and unique individuality" (Tillett, 1982).

Selected Writings: and Besant, A. B. *Occult Chemistry*, 1919.

BIBLIOGRAPHY: Tillett, G. *The Elder Brother: A Biography of Charles Webster Leadbeater*, 1982.

**Leaf, Walter, 1852–1927.** British psychical researcher. Son of an extremely wealthy merchant banker, he was one of the Trinity College, Cambridge, group who were so important in the early years of the Society for Psychical Research. He joined the SPR in 1884, two years after its founding. Long before the organization of the SPR, he, with F. W. H. Myers, Edmund Gurney and Henry Sidgwick, had sittings over a period of time with some Spiritualist mediums, an experience they all remembered chiefly for its boredom. He was also a classical scholar and, during this period, in 1883, together with Andrew Lang and Ernest Myers (F. W. H. Myers's brother), translated the *Iliad*.

In 1889–1890 he was one of a committee, the others being Sir Oliver Lodge and F. W. H. Myers, who invited Leonora Piper to England. He both helped organize sittings with her and sat with her himself. He wrote a major portion of the lengthy report of that investigation in which he said "success and failure alternated in a puzzling manner."

In addition to his other papers and reviews which appeared in the *Proceedings* of the SPR, he wrote an insightful review of Myers's *Human Personality and Its Survival of Bodily Death.* He said (1903) that Myers "nowhere conceals his overwhelming desire that . . . human personality should be proved to survive death. . . . [yet] Myers's work . . . greatly weakens my sense of personality, to such an extent that I am rather less than more willing to believe that my personality will survive death. . . . This result is clearly not what Myers would have wished . . . yet . . . [his] hypothesis . . . to my mind reduces the notion of personality almost to vanishing point . . . because [personality] loses its limitations, and, with its limitations, its unity."

In his later years Leaf was not active in the work of the SPR.

Selected Writings: 1903. "Review of *Human Personality and Its Survival of Bodily Death.*" PSPR 18:53; 1890. "A Record of Observations of Certain Phenomena of Trance. Part II." PSPR 6:558.

BIBLIOGRAPHY: Gauld, A. *The Founders of Psychical Research,* 1968; "Obituary: Dr. Walter Leaf," 1927. JSPR 24:52.

**Leek, Sybil, 1923–1982.** British witch. Her best-selling *Diary of a Witch* made her the most famous witch in the United States (she came to the US in 1964). High priestess of a coven, she believed that witchcraft is an "Old Religion because it seems to go back to the time when man was first on earth, when he had those religious, spiritual feelings. I think it is a great mistake to think that man did not have religion until Christ and Buddha appeared." While this description of witchcraft gives it a gentle and pious public image, it is not clear that everyone would agree to it. What does seem clear, however, is that many of the phenomena associated with witchcraft are paranormal. Leek, for example, who worked with Hans Holzer, believed that she was a medium and that her psychic abilities were "as much a part of me [as] sitting here smoking or as walking."

BIBLIOGRAPHY: "Interview: Sybil Leek". 1969. *Psychic* 1:6.

**Lees, Robert, 1849–1931.** British medium purportedly used by Queen Victoria. Lees's fame, however, rests on his claim that his psychic powers detected the identity of the horrible murderer known as **Jack the Ripper.** Lees maintained that he had been sworn to secrecy and could not disclose who the murderer was but that he had led the police to the Ripper. But Scotland Yard denied that there were any records in its office to support the medium's claim.

**Leibniz, Gottfried Wilhelm, 1646–1716.** German philosopher, mathematician, scientist, and advisor to the royal House of Brunswick. One of the great intellects of history, he was the inventor of the differential and integral calculus and of a calculating machine. As a philosopher, he formulated a concept of "monadology" that has influenced philosophical thought down the centuries and has been of considerable use to parapsychology and psychical research.

In monadology, the world consists of an infinite number of substances or "monads," each reflecting the universe in microcosm and from its point of view. Philosophers of parapsychology and psychical research see this idea casting light on clairvoyance: A psychic might be a mirror of the universe. Leibniz followed the Cartesian proposition that substances cannot interact. He believed, however, that each had the power of "perception" that was reciprocally related to the perceptions of all other monads. This power has been interpreted as the power of telepathy, an intrinsic ability in monads. Leibniz's philosophy also helped **William McDougall** develop his monadic view of the human personality (Berger 1988:127).

BIBLIOGRAPHY: Berger, A. S. *Lives and Letters in American Parapsychology,* 1988.

**Leonard, Gladys Osborne, 1882–1968.** British trance medium. One of the two (the other being Leonora Piper) most famous trance mediums of her time. In 1914, at the insistence of her control Feda, she gave up her not very successful acting career for mediumship. Feda said that something terrible was going to happen soon (presumably World War I) and that Mrs. Leonard would be needed (presumably to bring messages from those killed in the war). Feda usually spoke through Mrs. Leonard when she was in trance, but sometimes messages came through table-tilting or automatic writing. Feda, who spoke a kind of pidgin English baby talk, claimed to be the spirit of the historical young Hindu wife (whose story Mrs. Leonard knew) of Mrs. Leonard's maternal great-great grandfather. Feda said she communicated with Mrs. Leonard by manipulating the latter's brain, but the communicators themselves said that the communication was effected by telepathy.

According to C. D. Broad, Feda was either, as she claimed to be, the surviving spirit of the dead Hindu girl or a secondary personality of Mrs. Leonard's. Self-consistent secondary personalities which, with the primary personality, alternately control the same body have long been studied by psychiatrists. Mrs. Leonard was also occasionally possessed directly by a communicator. And at times a direct voice would be produced (C. D. Broad witnessed this phenomenon), often at the same time that her control was speaking.

Mrs. Leonard became famous as a result of communications allegedly from Sir Oliver Lodge's son Raymond who was killed in World War I. She also produced evidential material through book tests (in which the communicator refers to a certain page in a certain book that yields a meaningful message for the sitter) and was equally successful in proxy sittings that eliminated the possibility of telepathy from the sitter.

There are more than thirty articles about Mrs. Leonard in the publications of the Society for Psychical Research and seven in the *Journal of the American Society for Psychical Research.* Their consensus is that neither fraud, natural explanations, telepathy, nor coincidence can explain all the positive results Mrs. Leonard obtained. Of course, like all mediums, she had her good days and her bad days, and, although she often produced strikingly evidential material, she was also sometimes completely wrong. There was also a noticeable sameness about most of the supposed communications from those killed in battle.

Selected Writing: Leonard, G. O. *My Life in Two Worlds,* 1931.

BIBLIOGRAPHY: Broad, C. D. 1955. "The Phenomenology of Mrs. Leonard's Mediumship." JASPR 49:47; Heywood, R. 1969. "Mrs. Gladys Osborne Leonard: A Biographical

Tribute." JSPR 45:95; Lodge, O. *Raymond,* 1916; Sidgwick, Mrs. H. 1921. "An Examination of Book-Tests Obtained in Sittings with Mrs. Leonard." PSPR 31:241; Smith, S. *The Mediumship of Mrs. Leonard,* 1964; Thomas, C. D. 1939. "A Proxy Experiment of Significant Success." PSPR 45: 257; Thomas, C. D. 1928. "The Modus Operandi of Trance Communication According to Descriptions Received Through Mrs. Osborne Leonard." PSPR 38:49.

**LeShan, Lawrence, 1920–.** American psychologist, parapsychologist, and psychic healer. He writes that his major interests in parapsychology are the "theoretical and scientific models of psi" for the development of which in the late 60s and early 70s he worked closely with the famous medium Eileen Garrett, collaborated with Dr. Gertrude R. Schmeidler in studying data from ESP tests and investigated how consciousness, reality, and paranormal perception interrelate.

The paranormal moment of perception Dr. LeShan calls the "Clairvoyant Reality," in which everything is and where everything is one. It is in this clairvoyant reality that one kind of healing is possible (God is within). In a second type of healing the cure seems to be effected by the healer's hands (God is without). Dr. LeShan has developed techniques for psychic healing and has held many training seminars in which people have learned to heal. His views on psychic healing were set out in the widely read *The Medium, the Mystic and the Physicist* (1974). Dr. LeShan's research into psychic healing was funded by a grant from Life Energies Research, Inc.

The recipient of a Ph.D. in human development from the University of Chicago in 1954, Dr. LeShan did intensive work to see if there is a carcinogenic personality and found that there are indeed factors that differentiate cancer patients from others. Dr. LeShan has written numerous professional papers and several books. He has since 1964 been Director of the Ayer Foundation's Research Project on the Development of a Scientific Model for Paranormal Phenomena.

Selected Writings: *From Newton to ESP,* 1984; *The Mechanic and the Gardener: Understanding the Wholistic Revolution in Medicine,* 1982; *You Can Fight for Your Life: Emotional Factors in the Development of Cancer,* 1980; *The Medium, the Mystic and the Physicist,* 1974.

**Levitation.** From the Latin term levis or "light," it is the paranormal elevation from the earth or floor and the suspension in space of a human body or inanimate physical object. In effect, it is a phenomenon that repeals the fundamental law of gravity.

Those sceptical of the phenomenon may think of it as a delusion, illusion, fraud, or dream. Yet reports of it are very old. Chrysanthius, the theurgist, and Iamblichus, the founder of Syrian Neoplatonism who thrived in the fourth century, both experienced it. Both the new and old evidence for levitation is striking. Beds have levitated in the presence of the British psychic **Matthew Manning,** and the Soviet subject **Nina S. Kulagina** has been observed levitating a ball between her hands. Much evidence exists as well in the cases of the mediums **Daniel Dunglas Home, Eusapia Palladino** and **W. Stainton Moses.** In one of Moses's séances, reported by **F. W. H. Myers,** a "table, untouched by us, rose and gently touched my throat and chest three times. . . . I was three times raised on to the table, and twice levitated in the corner of the room."

Levitation is not confined to sinners. It is recorded that about seventy saints, including **Francis of Assisi, Joseph of Copertino** and **Teresa of Avila,** have experienced it. But even among the lesser servants of God, we find a series of levitations. The Carmelite nun Sister Mary of Jesus Crucified, for example, was reported to have risen to the top of a tree and Suor Maria del Passione seemed to fly up a flight of stairs. If heaven and God are in or beyond the sky, it is reasonable that pious souls should try to proceed upward dragging their reluctant bodies along with them. Catholic hagiography makes levitation out to be a long and well-attested tradition in the Church.

It is also known among the fakirs and yogis of India. They bring on levitations by breathing exercises that are supposed to prevent gravity from pulling the body down.

The physical character of the levitating force has not been discovered. There seems to be a disappearance of the weight of a human body or inanimate object. Neither age nor sex seem factors. Levitation has been reported at age ninety and at age forty and about as many women as men levitate. It is noteworthy that no cases of levitations among animals have been recorded.

Levitation remains an exceptional phenomenon that seems to speak of a mysterious power within us that cries out for investigation.

BIBLIOGRAPHY: Myers, F. W. H. 1893. "The Experiences of W. Stainton Moses." PSPR 9:243, pp. 260–261; Thurston, H. *The Physical Phenomena of Mysticism,* 1952, pp. 29–30.

**Life After Death Pact.** An agreement between two people that the one dying first will communicate with or appear to the survivor. Among the best-known of the life after death pacts are those of Henry P. Brougham, Harry Houdini and Arthur G. Rubinstein in which the parties said they would "come back" in various ways. In some of these compacts the parties agree to try to demonstrate life after death through the Cipher Test, Combination Lock Test, Dictionary Test, or Sealed Envelope Test. In these tests, a person agrees to try, after death, to communicate a piece of information the other party to the contract can verify as having come from the one now dead.

**Life Review.** A reliving of memories. One of the elements associated with the **Near-Death Experience** and reported by 55 per cent of accident victims who have had a close call with death (Ring, 1980:115). It consists of vivid visual images in chronological order generally but not necessarily of highlights in one's life that pass before the mind with such rapidity that the review seems instantaneous. These flashbacks may be presented by a being of light (another element of the typical NDE). The process seems to be a kind of stocktaking as the individual is trying to decide whether to die or return to life (Ring, 1980).

BIBLIOGRAPHY: Ring, K. *Life At Death: A Scientific Investigation of the Near-Death Experience,* 1980.

**Light.** A quarterly publication of the College of Psychic Science. Of all the journals still extant that publish on paranormal subjects, *Light* is the oldest, having been established in 1881 even before the Society for Psychical Research was organized. It publishes materials relating to the psychic and spiritual aspects of life and, as stated on its title page, "Light exists for the reasoned and courteous examination" of these aspects. Since anything to do with the paranormal generally excites emotions and acrimony, it is nothing short of remarkable to find them discussed "courteously."

**Liking Effect.** A term describing the preference of subjects for certain targets. It has been found by some researchers that where subjects like a target, their ESP performances are significantly better than when the target is not to their liking. See also **Focusing Effect.**

**Lily Dale.** One of the best-known of the Spiritualist communities. It is located south of Buffalo, New York. There professional mediums who charge fees for their services hold séances or sittings for anyone who has the requisite desire and money.

**Lincoln, Abraham, 1809–1865.** The sixteenth president of the United States. After an early life spent on a farm in Kentucky and in the backwoods of Indiana where his schooling lasted no more than one year, Lincoln became a lawyer, was elected to Congress in 1846 and then to the presidency of the United States in 1861. His rich command of language has made his prose a classic in American literature.

The issue splitting the country in 1860 was slavery. Lincoln's election triggered the secession of the southern states and the ensuing Civil War. In September 1862, as a military measure, Lincoln made a preliminary proclamation emancipating the slaves, and, on January 1, 1863, he issued a final proclamation. In 1864, "the Great Emancipator" was re-elected to another presidential term. On April 26, 1865, the war ended largely because of his efforts, but Lincoln was already dead, shot twelve days before by an assassin.

It has been claimed that Lincoln is a noted witness for the phenomena of psychical research including mediums, communicators and séances. According to Colonel S. P. Kase, the president showed great interest in Spiritualism and attended séances in December 1962 at which a young medium, Nettie Colburn, in trance lectured him on the importance of emancipating the slaves and on abolishing slavery. Kase, a Spiritualist, was sure that these spirit messages convinced Lincoln to issue his Emancipation Proclamation a few weeks later, and this story has been reported in the Spiritualist literature for over a hundred years now. But the preliminary proclamation Kase said had been produced by the medium's spirit-messages and had been issued in September, 1862, before the séances, and took effect on January 1, 1863.

Lincoln is, however a **Noted Witness** for precognition. In 1860, in his home in Springfield, he saw a double image of himself in a looking glass. One face shone with life and breath, the other was ghostly white. The image glowing with life meant to him that he would live through his first presidential term, the death-like one meant that he would die before his second term was ended. During the second week in April 1865, he had his famous dream. "There seemed to be a death-like stillness about me. Then I heard subdued sobs, as if a number of people were weeping. . . . I went from room to room; no living person was in sight, but the same mournful sounds of distress met me as I passed along. . . . I was puzzled and alarmed. . . . I kept on until I arrived at the East Room, which I entered. . . . Before me was a catafalque, on which rested a corpse wrapped in funeral vestments. Around it were stationed soldiers who were acting as guards; and there was a throng of people, some gazing mournfully upon the corpse, whose face was covered, others weeping pitifully. 'Who is dead in the White House?' I demanded of one of the soldiers. 'The President,' was his answer; 'he was killed by an assassin!' Then came a loud burst of grief from the crowd, which awoke me from my dream."

The dream preceded by a few days Lincoln's assassination by John Wilkes Booth who put a lead ball in the back of Lincoln's head. The president died on April 15. He was embalmed and lay in a coffin in the East Room of the White House on a platform beneath a canopy of black silk. Thousands of weeping people thronged into the White House to pass by his coffin. The close correspondence between the dream and the event is extraordinary and makes the dream seem veridical.

BIBLIOGRAPHY: "President Lincoln's Manifesto for the Abolition of Slavery: The Narrative of Colonel Kase." 1930. *Psychic Research* 24:115; Sandburg, C. *The War Years, 1864–1865. Vol. III,* 1959, pp. 823–826.

**Linkage Experiment.** An attempt to reduce the possibility that a medium could have obtained information about a deceased person by telepathy from a living person. Such a mediumistic experiment is an extension of the proxy sitting method and places a series of minds between the medium and the knowledgeable living person. In an experiment conducted by Karlis Osis, for example, between the living wife of a deceased person and the mediums were the experimenter and several assistants who submitted questions to the mediums.

**Linnaeus, Carolus (Carl von Linne), 1707–1778.** Swedish naturalist. He developed principles for the definition of species of organisms. His principal work, *Systema Naturae,* published in 1735, described plants according to what became known as the Linnaean classification and helped advance the natural sciences. His *Species Planetarium* (1735) supplied a basis for botanical nomenclature.

He is a **Noted Witness** to the paranormal on the basis of this statement: "On the night of July 12–13, 1765, toward midnight, my wife heard for a long time someone walking, with a heavy step, in my museum. . . . I also heard it, although I was quite certain that no one could be there, for the doors were fastened and the key in my pocket. Some days later, I learned that my very faithful friend, the commissary Karl Clerk, *died precisely at that hour.* It was certainly his step. I used to recognize Clerk, in Stockholm, merely by the sound of his footstep."

BIBLIOGRAPHY: Prince, W. F. *Noted Witnesses for Psychic Occurrences,* 1963, pp. 32–33.

**Liverziani, Filippo, 1926–.** Italian professor on the Pontifical Theological Faculty and director of the Centro di Recerca Psichica del Convivio. His principal interest lies in experimental research and theory concerning the hypothesis of human survival beyond physical death. He has been active in the investigations of mediums, near-death experiences, and out-of-body experiences. Dr. Liverziani is a contributor to *Luce e Ombra* and the author of several books on the survival question.

Selected Writings: *La reincarnazione e i*

*suoi fenomeni—"chi" o "cosa" si reincarna,* 1985. English edition: *Reincarnation and Its Phenomena—"Who" or "What" Become Reincarnated,* 1988; *La esperienze di confine e la vita dopo la morte,* 1986.

**Locher, Theo, 1921–.** Swiss president of Schweizerische Vereinigung für Parapsychologie (Swiss Association for Parapsychology). The association was founded as a result of courses in parapsychology Dr. Locher gave at high schools in Switzerland. He is also editor of a *Swiss Bulletin for Parapsychology* and author of important works that describe the history and important figures in Swiss parapsychology (Locher, 1986; 1971).

Selected Writings: *Parapsychologie in der Schweiz,* 1986; "History of Psychical Research in Switzerland." *Proceedings of an International Conference Parapsychology Today: A Geographic View,* 1971, p. 131.

**Lodge, Sir Oliver Joseph, 1851–1940.** Eminent British scientist. From sittings with Leonora Piper and Rosalie Thompson, Lodge became convinced of the survival of the human personality after death. He was introduced to psychical research by Edmund Gurney. He met Frederic W. H. Myers in 1884 and in that year became a member of the Society for Psychical Research. That same year he wrote on telepathy and the importance of statistics in evaluating telepathic experiments.

He and Charles Richet became close friends but differed over the significance of the findings of psychical research. Lodge, unlike Richet, felt that "[s]ubjective metapsychics is [easy] to associate with human survival" and that "the personality having lost its own instrument may be able . . . to work . . . on the brain of some hospitable person," (i.e., a medium). As a physicist Lodge saw physics taking on the characteristics of metaphysics. Through Richet, Lodge took part in sittings with Eusapia Palladino and, despite Richard Hodgson's criticisms of the control used over the medium, continued to be favorably impressed by her phenomena.

Lodge had twenty-three sittings with Mrs. Piper when she visited England in 1889 and concluded (1890) that "the information she possesses in the trance state is not acquired by ordinary commonplace methods, but that she has some unusual means of acquiring information . . . by none of the ordinary methods known to physical science." Yet, he noted that in "the midst of this lucidity mistaken and confused statements are frequently made . . .".

When the SPR came close to foundering in 1901 after the deaths of Henry Sidgwick and Myers, Lodge's acceptance of the presidency saved it. He served in that capacity in 1902 and 1903 as well and again in 1932 as joint president of honour with Eleanor Sidgwick.

Lodge was involved in the cross-correspondences and brought **Gladys Osborne Leonard** to the attention of the SPR. Through her he received the alleged communications from his dead son which in 1916 he published in his famous book *Raymond.*

In his professional life, Lodge was in 1879 assistant professor of applied mathematics at University College, London. In 1881 he was appointed to the chair of physics at University College, Liverpool. He perfected a radio wave detector and in 1894 developed a type of radio receiver that continued to be used into the 1900s. He was the first, some years before its verification, to suggest that the sun is a source of radio waves. In 1900 he became the first principal of Birmingham University. He was knighted in 1902.

Lodge left a series of sealed packets as a posthumous test of survival. He assumed that "the experimenter would be in free communication with him through some medium or automatist" (Tyrrell, 1948). "No such clear and unambiguous conditions" were reached by the committee set up jointly by the SPR and the London Spiritualist Alliance (later the College of Psychic Science). Partly because Lodge left a series of "hints" that were supposed to jog his memory after his death, the results were at best ambiguous. Robert H. Thouless, one of the committee appointed to evaluate the test, concluded that a better posthumous test of survival, one on which an indefinite number of "checks" could be made, was needed.

Selected Writings: *Raymond,* 1916; 1890. "A Record of Observations of Certain Phenomena of Trance—Part I." PSPR 6:443; and Richet, C. 1924. "For and Against Survival." PSPR 34:107.

BIBLIOGRAPHY: "Lodge, Sir Oliver Joseph." 1986. *The New Encyclopaedia Britannica* 7:440; "Report on the Oliver Lodge Posthumous Test." 1955. JSPR 38:121; Thouless, R. H. 1955. "The Oliver Lodge

Posthumous Test of Survival: Some Comments." JSPR 38:172; Tyrell, G. N. M. 1948. "The O. J. L. Posthumous Packet." JSPR 34:269.

**Lombroso, Cesare, 1835–1909.** Italian anthropologist and criminologist. He founded a school of criminal anthropology whose influence resulted in a trend to study criminals scientifically. Lombroso held professorial posts in psychiatry at the Universities of Pavia and Turin and in 1876 published *L'uomo delinquente (The Criminal Man)* which brought him fame as a criminologist. He also studied cretinism, pellagra, and the relation between crime and serious disease.

Physical phenomena and séances interested him but little. In 1891, however, he decided to accept a three-year old invitation from Ercole Chiaia to attend a sitting with Eusapia Palladino. After the sitting Lombroso's apologetic testimony makes him another **Noted Witness** to the authenicity of physical phenomena. He said: "I am embarrased and sorry for having fought with such obstinacy the possibility of the so-called spiritistic facts" (our translation). Lombroso, who often boasted that he was the slave of facts, was certain that no fraud had produced the phenomena and he could no longer doubt their genuineness. He did not, however, accept a spiritistic explanation for them.

Lombroso was the first respected scientist to be converted by Palladino. An acknowledgement from one of the world's great criminologists that the phenomena were authentic immediately lighted fires of interest under scientists everywhere and made Eusapia Palladino the center of numerous investigations.

Lombroso's conversion did not end with Eusapia. He began investigations of poltergeist cases and said of them: "My researches, incomplete as they were, had been sufficient to persuade me that the phenomena . . . must be genuine as a whole" (1906:367). This observation is enough to place him among other noted witnesses to the authenticity of poltergeists.

Selected Writings: Lombroso, C. *After Death—What?*, 1909; 1906. "The 'Haunted Houses' Which I Have Studied." *Annals of Psychical Research* 3:361.

**London, Jack (John Griffith Chaney), 1876–1916.** Popular American novelist. His natural father (a well-known astrologer) abandoned his common-law wife (a Spiritualist medium). Upon her subsequent marriage her baby was given his stepfather's surname.

London is best known for his Alaskan novels *Call of the Wild* (1903) and *White Fang* (1906) and his adventure *The Sea Wolf* (1904). Although he is not remembered as a prophetic writer, prophesy plays a part in many of his stories, in particular in *The Iron Heel* (1907), a terrifying anticipation of "Nazism and Soviet-style communism, confrontation between student radicals and the conservative 'establishment' in various cities (starting in none other than Berkeley, Calif.), the burnings of great cities in ghetto uprisings, civil rights demonstrations and even government scandal—such as Watergate" (Wingfield, 1975:75). In his *The Star Rover* (1915\1963—there is an afterword in the 1963 edition by Gardner Murphy dealing with reincarnation—the narrator tells how he survived the brutality of his jailers by astral projection into his past lives.

At fourteen, London left home to find adventure and seek his fortune. He explored San Francisco Bay, went to Japan as a sailor and rode the rails in the United States. He was largely self-educated although he spent one year at the University of California at Berkeley, which he left in 1897 to look for gold in the Klondike. His first book, *The Son of the Wolf* (1900), was well-received. Although he became the highest paid writer in the United States, he always spent lavishly, built a grandiose house (Wolf House), and was always in need of money. He was and still is popular throughout the world, especially in the Soviet Union, perhaps because in 1894 he had become a militant Socialist and is still thought of as such there even though in later years he lost all interest in the class struggle.

The hero of London's autobiographical novel *Martin Eden* (1909) commits suicide after achieving fame. London's death in 1916 from a drug overdose is usually considered suicide.

Selected Writing: *The Star Rover,* 1963 (orginally published 1915).

BIBLIOGRAPHY: Backus, J. M. "Parapsychology and Literature." In B. Wolman, ed., *Handbook of Parapsychology,* 1977; Wingfield, W. 1975. "Jack London and the Occult." *Fate* 28(7):70.

**London Dialectical Society.** British organization established "for the purpose of affording a hearing to subjects which are estranged elsewhere." With Alfred R. Wallace its most distinguished member, it was formed in the nineteenth century prior to the formation of the Society For Psychical Research and was one of the first organizations anywhere to investigate paranormal phenomena (e.g., it appointed committees to investigate the phenomena of Spiritualism and mediums such as Daniel Dunglas Home.)

**Lorimer, David, 1952–.** British author and director of the UK branch of the International Institute for the Study of Death. Lorimer "first became interested in parapsychology through reading the works of Emanuel Swedenborg. . . . Swedenborg was particularly concerned with the nature of human beings in relation to death, maintaining that the only real change at death was the abandonment of the physical body" (Lorimer, 1989). This interest, in turn, led him to study psychic experiences, including apparitions, out-of-body experiences, and near-death experiences. He concluded that: "If reports of apparitions, OBEs, NDEs and death experiences are accepted as valid evidence, then . . . [t]he materialistic analysis of the phenomenon of death is highly misleading: apparent loss of consciousness is interpreted from the outside as extinction, while from the inside conscious experience may well be continuing in an enhanced state, released from the cramping confines of space-time, the physical body, and perhaps even the separate ego . . ." (Lorimer, 1984:304).

Lorimer, who taught modern languages at Winchester College, is also chairman of the UK branch of the International Association for Near-Death Studies and director of the Scientific and Medical Network.

Selected Writing: Letter to authors, 1989; *Survival? Body, Mind and Death in the Light of Psychic Experience,* 1984.

**Loudun, Demons of.** A classic seventeenth century case of apparent possession in which the Ursuline Roman Catholic nuns in the convent at Loudun, France, believed that they were controlled by demons. The case centered on priest Urbain Grandier whose appeal to, and conquests of, women produced such intrigues, animosities, envies, and motives of revenge among the nuns that the only means of explaining and expressing their natural desires and emotions seemed to them to be diabolical possession. The tormented women were exorcised again and again, and the priest, first admired and loved, became the object of fear and hate. He was accused of having bewitched them and was burned alive in 1634.

Soeur Jeanne, the superior of the Ursulines, at the beginning one of Grandier's ardent admirers became his implacable enemy. She believed that, because of him, a variety of demons possessed her—Asmodeus, Leviathan, Behemoth, Isacaaron, Balaam, Gresil, and Aman. But two centuries later, after the autobiography she left was examined along with the letters allegedly written by the demons, the letters were found to have been written by the sister, the utterances being the products of her own twisted mind. All in all Loudun is a story of ignorance, hatred, imagination—and, for Urbain Grandier, torture and death at the stake.

BIBLIOGRAPHY: Huxley, A. *The Devils of Loudun,* 1952.

**Lourdes, Miracles of.** Three million pilgrims go to Lourdes each year to bathe in or drink the waters. One of the cases that has contributed to Lourdes's fame as a faith-healing shrine is that of a stonecutter whose eyesight, lost when a stone pierced his eye, was restored instantly after he washed in the waters at Lourdes. In another case, the bones of a man's leg, broken into pieces, were healed as soon as he bathed in the waters at Lourdes.

The main operative factor in the healings at Lourdes is religious faith. To be considered miraculous the cures must be instantaneous and no remedies can have been used. Even so, questions arise whether the medical conditions have been properly diagnosed and whether an explanation other than the miraculous can be offered. The Medical Bureau of the Catholic church attempts to determine if the sick and suffering who come to Lourdes for a cure have the ailments they claim. If they do, the bureau further decides if a cure has taken place. Ninety percent of the cases are rejected. Should a cure be found by the Medical Bureau, however, an International Medical Commission composed of 100 doctors from various countries examines the case a year or two later to reconfirm the cure. If the commission decides that the cure is genuine, a Canonical Commission must certify that the case has been the result of God's special intervention. So far, out of the many thousands of cases certified by the International Medical Commission as genuine, only sixty-four have been certified as **miracles** by the Sacred Congregation of Rites.

An example of a miraculous cure was that of Louis-Justin Bouhohurts, an infant of eighteen months of age who was dying of consumption and osteomalacia. The child was unable to leave his cradle, to sit up, stand, or walk. He was immersed in the pool at Lourdes for fifteen and one-half minutes. Immediately, he left his cradle, walked without ever having learned to do so and eventually grew into adulthood.

Lourdes presents an intriguing religious phenomenon for psychical research. It is no wonder that, at its very start one hundred years ago, F. W. H. Myers and his brother A. T. Myers should have undertaken an examination of reports from Lourdes of "the blind seeing, the lame walking." The most recent examination was conducted by the physician-parapsychologist D. J. West who went through the dossiers of eleven cases which, between 1937 and 1950, were called miraculous cures by the Canonical Commission. He also looked at the testimony of the examining physicians. West's conclusion was that the evidence for "miracles" in the cases examined was "extremely meagre," that the diagnoses of the cases were either inadequate or incorrect and that negative, critical opinion had been suppressed. In effect, the facts were distorted to measure up to and to fit the criteria necessary to a judgment that a case was "miraculous." Miracles not being a subject for scientific inquiry, however, West's analysis was limited to seeing by what criteria judgments of miracles were made and if those criteria were met by the eleven cases.

There are thus only two questions for psychical research. The first is whether there is good evidence of medically inexplicable healings. Fifty-three cases certified as miraculous cures by the Church have not been evaluated by outside sources and therefore still stand. Other cases of the blind seeing and the lame walking cannot be dismissed out of hand as fairy tales. They force the conclusion that cases have occurred at Lourdes that are beyond medical explanation. The second question is, if medically inexplicable cures have occurred at Lourdes, what else can explain them. It is not enough to say "suggestion." How or why it operates is unknown. It would be of extreme importance to human life if the method could be discovered that sets into motion, wholly or in part, the curative process of suggestion that causes the mind to heal the body. Apart from its religious significance, Lourdes presents this challenge to parapsychology. See also **Bernadette, Saint; Healing, Unorthodox.**

BIBLIOGRAPHY: Myers, A. T. and Myers, F. W. H. 1893. "Mind-Cure, Faith-Cure and the Miracles of Lourdes." PSPR 9:160; West, D. J. *Eleven Lourdes Miracles,* 1957.

**Low Variance.** See **Variance, Low.**

**Lowell, Amy, 1874–1925.** American poet. She was the leader of the Imagist movement of poetry in the United States and the United Kingdom. This movement avoided mystical themes and used concrete ideas and images. She contributed to the technique of free verse and, like Robert Browning, used the monologue in narrative poetry. Her *John Keats* (1925) was a critical biography of the poet. Probably the most intellectually gifted and surely the most liberated woman of her day, she defied convention by smoking big black cigars and by using language not even sailors knew.

Amy Lowell's *The Process of Making Poetry* began with the question: How are poems made? She answered frankly and flatly, "I don't know." But then, in testimony that makes her a **Noted Witness** for the **Creative Process,** she went on: "All that I can confidently assert from my own experience is that it is not a daydream, but an entirely different psychic state and one peculiar to itself. . . . It would seem that a scientific definition of a poet might put it something like this: a man of an extraordinarily sensitive and active subconscious personality, fed by, and feeding, a non-resistant consciousness. A common phrase among poets is, 'It came to me.' So hackneyed has this become that one learns to suppress the expression with care, but really it is the best description I know of the conscious arrival of a poem. . . . How carefully and precisely the subconscious functions, I have often been a witness to in my own work. An idea will come into my head for no apparent reason; 'The Bronze Horses,' for instance. I registered the horses as a good subject for a poem; and, having so registered them, I consciously thought no more about the subject. But what I had really done was to drop my subject into the subconscious, much as one drops a letter into the mail-box. Six months later, the words of the poem began to come into my head, the poem—to use my own private vocabulary—was 'there.' "

BIBLIOGRAPHY: Ghiselin, B. *The Creative Process,* 1952, p. 110.

**Lucadou von, Walter, 1945–** German psychologist and physicist. He has studied parapsychology and helped found the Wissenschaftliche Gesellschaft zur Förderung der Parapsychologie (Scientific Society for the Advancement of Parapsychology). The holder of both D.Sc. and Ph.D. degrees, he is active in experimental and theoretical research in the field with a particular emphasis on psychokinesis, systems theory and observation theories. With **Klaus Kornwachs,** he proposed a new concept to simplify some of the problems with observation theory as it is being used in experimental approaches in parapsychology. Another central area of his work is the education in parapsychology of both undergraduate and graduate students.

Dr. von Lucadou is co-editor of *Zeitschrift für Parapsychologie* and was an assistant professor at the Institut für Grenzgebiete der Psychologie und Psychohygiene where he built a parapsychological laboratory. He was also a visiting research associate at the Parapsychological Laboratory at the University of Utrecht.

Selected Writings: and Kornwachs, K. "On the Limitations of Psi—A System-Theoretical Approach." In W. G. Roll, J. Beloff, R. A. White, eds., *Research in Parapsychology 1982,* 1983, p. 85; and Kornwachs, K. 1980. "Development of the Systemtheoretic Approach to Psychokinesis." *European Journal of Parapsychology* 3 (3):297.

**Luce E Ombra (Light and Shadow).** Italian parapsychological periodical published quarterly by the Archívio di Documentazione Stòrica Della Ricérca Psichica. Founded in 1900 by Angelo Marzorati and for almost forty years directed by Gastone de Boni, it is the oldest publication in Italy dedicated to all types of paranormal phenomena and to book reviews and general news in Italy and abroad in the field of parapsychology. The present editor is Silvio Ravaldini.

**Lucidity.** See **Clairvoyance.**

**Luminous Phenomena.** Strange lights glowing around or emanating from objects have always captivated the human mind. Baron Karl von Reichenbach claimed that, in a dark room, psychics could detect flames around the poles of magnets. His researches were among the initial problems tackled by the Society for Psychical Research when it was first organized. Even more fascinating and mysterious were the luminous phenomena visible around the human body. Prospero Lambertini, who became Pope Benedict XIV, considered and defined these phenomena in the eighteenth century in his *De Beatificatione et Canonizatione*: "It seems to be a fact that there are natural flames which at times visibly encircle the human head, and also that from a man's whole person fire may on occasion radiate naturally . . . ; further, that some people become resplendent in a blaze of light . . . which attaches . . . to their clothes, or to the staff or to the spear which they are carrying."

There have been many instances of a glowing aura around the bodies of holy personages or of a radiance lighting up their faces. When Moses came down from Mt. Sinai with the commandments, his face shone so brightly that the people of Israel were afraid to go near him (Exodus 34:29–30). Sometimes the radiance illuminates a room. In the case of Saint Lidwina of Schiedam, it was said by Thomas à Kempis: "[V]ery often by day and night . . . She was discovered by her companions to be surrounded by so great a divine brightness that, seeing the splendour and struck with exceeding fear, they dared not approach nigh to her. And although she always lay in darkness . . . the divine light . . . whereby her cell was often so wondrously flooded by night [made] the cell itself appear . . . full of material lamps or fires."

Luminous phenomena have been observed as well in the field of psychical research. In Lord Dunraven's experiments with D. D. Home, Home's "hand became quite luminous," witnesses "saw tongues or jets of flame proceeding from Home's head" and, also, Home's "head became quite luminous at the top, giving him the appearance of having a halo around it. When he was raised in the air, he waved his arms about, and in each hand, there came a little globe of fire (to my eyes, blue); the effect was very pretty" (Dunraven, 1924). In experiments conducted with Home and Florence Cook by Sir William Crookes, the latter saw luminous clouds appear and on one occasion "under strict test conditions," he said "I have seen a solid self-luminous body, the size and nearly the shape of a turkey's egg, float noiselessly about the room . . . and then gently descend to the floor" (Barrett, 1918).

Such phenomena frequently have been interpreted as the products of a paranormal force at work in the form of a vital energy within the medium often associaed with ectoplasm and materialization. Some cases are especially puzzling, particularly when a dying or dead person seems to emit light. A 1981 case in a hospice in Southern California was investigated by parapsychologist Elizabeth McAdams (1984). A chaplain, nurses, the hospice supervisor, and members of a dying patient's family all reported that they had observed a glowing light extending from the man's head. In the 1930s, the physician Protti looked into a strange case in a hospital in Pirano, Italy, where nurses, nuns and doctors were startled to see a usually blue-green, but sometimes pink, light emanating for about three to four seconds from the chest of a female patient who seemed totally unaware of it.

The most famous experiments dealing with the emission of light from a corpse are those of Dr. Hyppolite Baraduc who, on photographing his dead son and dying wife, discovered striking emanations from their bodies. If such luminous phenomena are an objective reality, they give some support to the notion of an astral body, to the religious idea of a soul, and to that of a conscious self-moving to another existence. See also **Reichenbach's Experiments.**

BIBLIOGRAPHY: Barrett, W. *On the Threshold of the Unseen,* 1918, pp. 86–87; Carrington, H. *The Problems of Psychical Research,* 1921, pp. 182–184; Dunraven, E. 1924. "Experiences in Spiritualism with D. D. Home." PSPR 35:1; McAdams, E. 1984. "Reported Near-Death Observations in a Hospice in California." In *1983 Annual Conference Proceedings of the Academy of Religion and Psychical Research: "The Synergy of Religion and Psychical Research: Past, Present and Future",* 57; Thurston, H. *The Physical Phenomena of Mysticism,* 1952, p. 167.

**Luther, Martin, 1483–1546.** German founder of the Reformation and of Protestantism. A member of the mendicant order of St. Augustine, he was ordained a priest in 1507. He took his doctor of theology degree in 1512 and succeeded to the chair of biblical theology at the University of Wittenberg. On October 31, 1517, he nailed to the door of All Saints Church there ninety-five propositions attacking the ecclesiastical practice of indulgences. The act led to his excommunication and eventually shook Christianity. He became the tireless advocate of views that soon produced the Reformation. In 1521, when he was declared an outlaw, he was hidden at the castle of Wartburg where he remained for a year, wrote *On Monastic Vows,* and translated the New Testament into German.

The experiences he related in *Table Talk* occurred in his rooms at the castle: "I dwelt far apart from the world in my chamber, and no one could come to me but two youths, sons of noblemen, who waited on me with my meals twice a day. Among other things, they brought me a bag of nuts, which I had put in a chest in my sitting-room. One evening, after I had retired to my chamber . . . and gone to bed, it seemed to me all at once that the nuts had put themselves in motion; and jumping about in the sack, and knocking violently against each other, came to the side of the bed to make noises at me. . . . By and by I was awakened by a great noise on the stairs, which sounded as though somebody was tumbling down them a hundred barrels, one after the other. Yet I knew very well that the door at the bottom of the stairs was fastened with chains, and that the door itself was of iron, so that no one could enter. I rose immediately to see what it was, exclaiming, 'Is it thou? Well, be it so!' (meaning the devil) and I recommended myself to our Lord Jesus Christ and returned to bed . . .".

There were other and similar incidents in his life: "Once in our monastery at Wittenberg," Luther wrote, "I distinctly heard the devil making a noise. I was beginning to read the Psalms . . . when . . . the devil came into my cell, and there made a noise behind the stove, just as though he was dragging some wooden measure along the floor. As I found that he was going to begin again, I gathered together my books and got into bed. . . . Another time in the night, I heard him above my cell, walking in the cloister, but as I knew it was the devil, I paid no attention to him, and went to sleep."

Luther's opinion that Satan was the cause of mysterious raps, footsteps, scrapings, knockings, and bangings was shared by all Christians of his day. In our time the parapsychological opinion would be that the phenomena described are of the poltergeist variety. Luther's testimony makes him a **Noted Witness** to its existence and perhaps to his having been a poltergeist agent.

BIBLIOGRAPHY: Prince, W. F. *Noted Witnesses to Psychic Occurrences,* 1963.

**Lyttelton, Dame Edith, c. 1865–1948.** British public figure and psychic. Active in politics, she became a delegate to the League of Nations. She was also a playwright. Dame Edith Lyttelton is best known in psychical research, under the pseudonym "Mrs. King," as one of the automatists in the **Cross-Correspondences** cases and for her apparent prediction through automatic writing in February and May 1914 of the sinking of the *Lusitania* which took place in May 1915. She felt that precognition was a demonstration of the psychic power of what she called the "superconscious" mind.

Edith Lyttelton had joined the Society for Psychical Research in 1902, her interest having been aroused by the death of her infant son. She began writing automatically in 1913 after the death of her husband. In January and May of 1915 her scripts spoke of the Munich Pact and of Berchtesgaden, references which made no sense until some twenty years later. She was president of the SPR in 1933 and 1934.

She wrote several books and, at the time of her death, was working on a book "on the soul as a link between time and eternity" (Salter and Richmond, 1949:335)

Selected Writings: *Some Cases of Prediction: A Study,* 1938; *Our Superconscious Mind,* 1931.

BIBLIOGRAPHY: Piddington, J. G. 1923. "Forecasts in Scripts Concerning the War." PSPR 33:438; Piddington, J. G. 1916. "Cross-Correspondences of a Gallic Type." PSPR 29:1; Salter, W. H. and Richmond, Mrs. 1949. "Obituary. The Hon. Mrs. Alfred Lyttelton, G.B.E." PSPR 48:333.

**MacKenzie, Andrew, 1911–.** New Zealand-born journalist, author, and investigator of spontaneous cases. After coming to London in 1939, he joined the Society for Psychical Research and worked with Guy W. Lambert in the study of cases of the paranormal. MacKenzie, basing his articles and books on publications of the SPR and on his own personal inquiries and information obtained from witnesses, narrates in clear and readable British prose well-authenticated and well-selected cases of apparitions and haunts (MacKenzie 1982, 1971, 1966) as well as poltergeists and precognition (MacKenzie, 1968).

Although some scientifically minded people believe that the only evidence for psi can come from experimental parapsychology carried out in laboratories, MacKenzie has shown that natural spontaneous events such as he writes about can be extremely valuable in providing clues to the mystery of psi. He serves on the council of the SPR and also lectures at colleges on parapsychology.

Selected Writings: *Hauntings and Apparitions,* 1982; *Apparitions and Ghosts,* 1971; *Frontiers of the Unknown,* 1968; *The Unexplained: Some Strange Cases of Psychical Research,* 1966.

**MacLaine, Shirley, 1934–.** American dancer, actress, and vocal proponent of the New Age. Born Shirley Beatty (she is actor Warren Beatty's sister; her mother's maiden name was MacLean), she was a political activist, feminist, an outstanding performer and world traveller until her late 40s when an affair with an English politician started her on a quest for self-understanding.

Unwilling to believe that the problems she was experiencing in this relationship could be caused by anything as obvious as the guilt her partner was feeling (he was married and had two children), she turned to mediumship, her first experience being with Thure Johanssen of Sweden and the entity, Ambres, which he channeled. Thereafter in the United States she had sittings with **Kevin Ryerson** and his entity Tom McPherson (and later with Jach Pursel's **Lazaris** and J. Z. Knight and her entity **Ramtha**—who told Ms. MacLaine that she had been his brother in Atlantis 35,000 years ago). Her quest took her from belief in spirit entities to reincarnation to unidentified flying objects and extraterrestrials. Eventually, through past-life recall of some of her previous incarnations she came to believe that her experiences, both good and bad, in this lifetime were the result of her own actions in past lifetimes and that we are all connected in love and light and purpose. At last she came to understand that she is God because we are all God (as the word God is used by the process philosophers).

Her autobiographical writings describing—often in tedious detail—her spiritual (and sexual) journey seem to be just what the American public had been waiting for, because the books have been enormous best-sellers. Surprisingly, though, the tabloids have mainly ignored her.

Ms. MacLaine travels extensively giving seminars and is planning to build Ariel Village in Colorado where people can come for meditation, past-life regressions and other alternative healings. She points out that, although she charges rather considerable fees, she makes more money simply performing, which she also continues to do. Many people have found in Shirley MacLaine a way to spiritual awakening; others think she is completely crazy.

Selected Writings: *Out on a Limb,* 1983; *Dancing in the Light,* 1985; *It's All in the Playing,* 1987.

BIBLIOGRAPHY: Friedrich, O. 1987. "New Age Harmonies." *Time* 130 (23): 62; Zuromski, P. 1987. "A Conversation with Shirley MacLaine." *Body, Mind and Spirit* 6(5):19.

**Macro-PK.** To be distinguished from "micro-PK". A class of effects produced by psychokinesis that are directly observable physical effects as distinguished from effects that can be inferred only from statistics. Examples of macro-PK effects are metal-bending, table-tilting, influencing the fall of dice, or a phenomenon claimed by the Society for Research on Rapport and Telekinesis group, rings interlocking.

**Maeterlinck, Maurice (Polydore-Marie-Bernard), 1862–1949.** Belgian poet, playwright, and dramatist. Best known for the opera *Pelléas and Mélisande* set to music by Debussy and for his play *The Blue Bird,* this 1911 Nobel laureate in literature was always deeply concerned about the meaning of death and the possibility of life after death. This concern led him to psychical research and a study of apparitions, hallucinations, haunts, psychometry, precognition and extrasensory perception in animals **(Anpsi).** In connection with the latter he studied the "Elberfeld horses" owned by Karl Kroll of Munich and was convinced that, in the absence of their owner, three of them could rap out correct numbers that at the time were unknown to any living person. Maeterlinck considered this evidence proof of the existence of "subliminal faculties." Despite his belief, however, that the subconscious self is free of limitations of time, he found no evidence for clairvoyants, fortune-tellers, or mediums being able to foresee the future.

Maeterlinck believed in life after death but was unconvinced that reincarnation had been demonstrated even though he thought it a pure and consoling creed. And despite his belief in life after death, he did not think that psychic phenomena need be the products of spirit actions. In his philosophical works, such as *The Life of the Bee* and *The Intelligence of Flowers,* Maeterlinck sought to come to terms with the human condition. To the end he was concerned with death—and with what may come after.

BIBLIOGRAPHY: Ebon, M. *They Knew the Unknown,* 1971, pp. 187–193; Inglis, B. *The Paranormal,* 1985, pp. 23–24; "Maeterlinck, Maurice." In *The New Encyclopaedia Britannica,* Vol. 7, 1986, pp. 664–665; Piddington, J. G. 1903.; "Le Temple Enseveli, by Maurice Maeterlinck." PSPR 17:411.

**Mafu.** See **Torres, Penny.**

**Magic.** The art or practice of affecting human beings or influencing events either beneficially ("white" magic) or inimically ("black" magic) by calling on and using external powers that are beyond or contrary to nature. To be distinguished from **Witchcraft** which for similar ends uses powers innate in a **Witch.** A belief in magic has existed from the time of the earliest human societies.

**Magic, Black.** See **Black Magic.**

**Magic, White.** See **White Magic.**

**Magician.** In non-Western societies, one who uses spells, objects, or rituals to practice and carry out the aims of magic. Sometimes known as a **Medicine Man** or **Sorcerer** as distinguished from a **Diviner, Shaman** or **Witch.**

In modern Western society, the magician is a professional performer who uses illusion and legerdemain to entertain and amaze audiences. Some Western magicians believe that psi is a reality; others are persuaded that authentic paranormal phenomena do not exist and that anything that seems paranormal can be produced by conjuring tricks. **Harry Houdini,** for example, was convinced that all mediums used such tricks and devoted his time to exposing them. Some magicians, however, are willing to cooperate and consult with parapsychologists by pointing out the techniques that can be used to simulate paranormal phenomena and so improve parapsychological research. The Parapsychological Association has gone on record as endorsing such consultations.

**Mahatma Letters.** See **Koot Hoomi Lal Singh.**

**Maimonides Medical Center, Dream Laboratory.** The relationship between dreams and the paranormal has been noted repeatedly. It had not been possible, however, to investigate that relationship until the mid-1950s when monitoring of dreams by electroencephalogram (EEG) and by the measurement of rapid-eye-movements (REM) enabled experimenters to know when a sleeping subject was dreaming.

As the result of a grant obtained by **Gardner Murphy, Montague Ullman** in 1961 established the Dream Laboratory at Maimonides Medical Center in Brooklyn, New York, to study ESP in dreams and other altered states of consciousness. Experiments were conducted to see if the content of dreams could be influenced by target material, such as art prints, on which agents were concentrating.

**Stanley Krippner** joined the staff of the Dream Laboratory in 1962 and developed its research methodology. In nine of the twelve studies, positive results supported the conclusion that ESP takes place during dreaming. At the University of Wyoming, two attempts at replication gave results approximately at chance; an attempted replication at Boston University School of Medicine, however, gave encouragement for further experimentation as did other small-scale studies.

**Charles E. M. Hansel** (1980) argued (incorrectly [Akers 1984]) that the Maimonides results were due to sensory cuing. But although Hansel's and some other "books by . . . psychologists . . . engage in nearly incredible falsification of the facts about the experiments, . . . [the] experiments at the Maimonides Medical Center on the possibility of ESP in dreams clearly merit careful attention . . ." (Child, 1985:1228). Yet, "when the big experimental push was made to prove dream telepathy under the impetus of a National Institute of Mental Health grant the result was a dismal failure . . . as the goal became proof rather than understanding . . ." (Ullman, 1987:28).

The Dream Laboratory was succeeded by the Division of Parapsychology and Psychophysics of the Department of Psychiatry at Maimonides Medical Center. This division enlarged the work of the laboratory to include research into feedback methods, and tests of psychokinesis.

BIBLIOGRAPHY: Akers, C. "Methodological Criticisms of Parapsychology," In S. Krippner, ed., *Advances in Parapsychology. Vol 4,* 1984, pp. 112–164; Child, I. L. 1985. "The Question of ESP in Dreams." *American Psychologist* 40 (11):1219, 1228; Hansel, C. E. M. *ESP and Parapsychology: A Critical Re-evaluation,* 1980; Krippner, S. and Ullman, M., *Dream Studies and Telepathy,* 1970; Ullman, M. "The World of Psychic Phenomena as I Came to Know It." In *Men and Women of Parapsychology,* 1987; Ullman, M., Krippner, S., and Vaughan, A. *Dream Telepathy,* 1973.

**Mainieri, Roberto C., 1949–.** Panamanian parapsychologist. He is the only parapsychologist in Panama and in all of Central America. He became interested in parapsychology while studying Rosicrucianism and, in 1979, founded a parapsychology study group of the Rosicrucian Lodge of Panama. Three years later he established and became director of the **Instituto de Estudios Parapsicológicos** (Institute for Parapsychological Studies) whose work and activities he manages in an effort to attract serious attention in Panama and Central America to the field of parapsychology. He sees his task as introducing parapsychology to these areas of the world through television and radio programs, conferences, courses, and assistance to high school and university students interested in parapsychology. He is also trying to set up links with the University of Panama. Mainieri, who studied at the Foundation for Research on the Nature of Man, is interested in altered states of consciousness, personality and psi, poltergeist phenomena and, especially, in investigating the native populations of Panama whose culture and practices are still neglected but should be prime targets for parapsychological study.

**Majority-Vote Technique.** In ESP (extrasensory perception) tests, a scoring method whereby the most frequent call, from a number of calls made for the same target, is defined as a single response to that target. In PK (psychokinesis) tests, an analogous technique, whereby the most frequently occurring target event, from a number of attempts on the same target, is defined as the single outcome for that target (JP).

**Mann, Thomas, 1875–1955.** German scholar, essayist, and novelist. Recipient of the Nobel Prize in literature in 1929, he is ranked with Marcel Proust and James Joyce as one of the foremost novelists of the twentieth century. His literary fame began with his first novel, *Buddenbrooks* (1901). Other novels from his pen are: *The Magic Mountain* (1924); *Joseph and His Brothers* (1933, 1934, 1936, 1943), a group of four novels; and *Doctor Faustus* (1948). In addition, he was the master of the short story, his masterpiece being *Death in Venice* (1912), in which art, eros, and death are interwoven themes. Although during and after the First World War, Mann expressed anti-democratic and pro-authoritarian sentiments, in 1930 he gave a lecture in Berlin against the policies of the National Socialist party. When Hitler and the Nazis came to power, Mann took up residence in Switzerland and the United States and never returned to Germany.

In Germany, as everywhere after the First World War, Spiritualism attracted millions who hoped to establish communication with soldiers slain in the conflict. Mann, too, was interested and was as much the critical observer as any parapsychologist. After attending a séance with the medium **Willi Schneider,** Mann wrote a letter about it dated December 21, 1922, to Baron **Albert von Schrenck-Notzing** at whose home in Munich the séance had been held and also described this sitting in an essay (1929). Before the séance began, Mann wrote, he had taken the "opportunity to look around the seance room and to examine the cabinet. . . . Then, along with others, I watched the medium dress and convinced myself that the black tights . . . and the black silk-quilted dressing gown with luminous stripes . . . contained no device that might have served to delude the onlookers. Willi's oral cavity was also examined. . . . A ceiling light with a red and black shade and a red table lamp diffused a dim reddish light. . . . At about 11.30 . . . a handkerchief that had been lying on the floor beside the little table was lifted. . . . by a support inside it . . . and was violently manipulated from within. . . .[T]he surface of the handkerchief clearly disclosed the working of an apparently claw-like organ considerably smaller than a human hand. . . . [Then] an indefinable something . . . arose from the same place as the handkerchief. . . . [and] glowed greenish-white. In falling, it disappeared. . . . [A] table bell, which had been standing on the floor, began to ring violently and was flung under the chair of one of the participants. . . . [A] luminous ring with a luminous cord attached rose up to the table top. . . . Several times, bright round spots or nebulae, tinged red by the lamp light, appeared on or near the wall in the vicinity of the medium, then vanished. . . . [A]ny thought of a swindle in the sense of a conjuring trick is absurd. There was simply no one there who could have rung and thrown the bell. Willi could not have done so because his extremities were being held, and besides, he was five feet away, sunk in . . . sleep. . . . [Yet] I saw it with my unprejudiced eyes which were quite prepared to see nothing if there was nothing to be seen." (Willi Schneider became the inspiration for a character with mediumistic experiences in Mann's major novel *the Magic Mountain* [1924]).

This extraordinarily detailed and objective description of his observations makes Mann a **Noted Witness** in support of physical mediumship and physical phenomena.

Selected Writings: "Thomas Mann and the Occult: An Unpublished Letter." *Encounter,* April, 1976, pp. 21–24; "An Experiment in the Occult." In his *Three Essays,* 1929.

**Manning, Matthew, 1955–.** British psychic. When he was a teenager poltergeist activity, investigated by Dr. A. R. G. Owen, erupted in his home. Gradually, he developed the apparent ability to do automatic drawing (which ceased in 1975) and, in a handwriting different from his own style and allegedly that of a deceased person **Automatic Writing** by means of which, among others, he produced five scripts in Arabic. He also found that he could bend metal paranormally, affect electrical equipment, move compass needles, and make medical diagnoses. He found himself experiencing telepathy, which he described as seeing "scenes flash across quickly," and once or twice got voices on tape. He also began having out-of-body experiences and participated in two OBE experiments.

Until 1979 Manning willingly cooperated with parapsychologists, among them Anita

Gregory, in scientific experiments most of which tested his ability to disrupt electronic equipment or bend metal. He became disillusioned with this experimental work when he became convinced that many scientists were interested only in the possible application of his talents to psychic warfare.

Stimulated by Cleve Backster's work in Plantpsi, by an experience which made him feel that when we abuse our bodies and minds we damage others psychically as well and by a mystical experience in the foothills of the Himalayas, Manning has turned to healing in an attempt to prove that we are all interconnected.

Selected Writings: *The Strangers,* 1978; *The Minds of Millions,* 1977; *The Link,* 1975.

BIBLIOGRAPHY: Gregory, A., ed., 1982. "London Experiments with Matthew Manning." PSPR 58:283; *New Realities,* eds., 1979. "Matthew Manning beyond Spoon Bending." *New Realities* 2(6):28; *Psychic,* eds., 1975. "Interview: Matthew Manning." *Psychic* 6(5):58.

**Margery** See **Crandon, Mina S.**

**Marian Apparitions.** See **Bernadette, Saint; Egypt, Marian Apparitions in; Fatima, Marian Apparitions at; Mary, Saint.**

**Markwick, Betty, 1933–.** British mathematician, computer programmer, and statistical consultant. Just a few years after receiving her B.Sc. in mathematics with highest honors and while she was working as a computer programmer and specialist in data correlation, Betty Markwick chanced upon a book entitled *Modern Experiments in Telepathy* (1954) by S. G. Soal and F. Bateman. This book piqued Ms. Markwick's interest in parapsychology and led to her eventual membership in the Society for Psychical Research—she joined in 1969 and has been a council member since 1983—and in the Para psychological Association. And so it is ironic that Betty Markwick's principal contribution to parapsychology has been the discrediting of Soal's research described in that book.

Ms. Markwick is also very interested in dreams and lucid dreams, and it was an intense dream in 1971 of Dr. R. G. Medhurst, who had recently died, followed five days later by the receipt of the *Journal of the Society for Psychical Research* with a posthumous article by Dr. Medhurst (1971) that started her on the investigation suggested by the dream. The Soal-Shackleton experiments in telepathy (1941–1943) had been considered the strongest evidence to date for ESP. But in 1960 a Mrs. Gretl Albert accused Soal of having altered the score sheets. There followed heated discussions pro and con. Dr. Medhurst's posthumous article (Medhurst had until then been a strong supporter of Soal's honesty) described the failure of his computer search to find the source of the prepared random numbers in the Shackleton target sequences, this failure casting doubt on Soal's explanation of how he had obtained his random digits. Eventually after examining the record sheets in the Shackleton file—all 262 of them—Betty Markwick discovered long duplicated sequences and what she called interrupted duplicated sequences with extra digits that indicate manipulation of the data. Ms. Markwick sadly concluded that "all the experimental series in card-guessing carried out by Dr. Soal must, as the evidence stands, be discredited" (1978:276) and urged (1985) the need for involving skeptics and magicians in independent replication of research.

Selected Writings: "The Establishment of Data Manipulation in the Soal-Shackleton Experiments." In P. Kurtz, ed., *A Skeptic's Handbook of Parapsychology,* 1985; 1978. "The Soal-Goldney Experiments with Basil Schakleton: New Evidence of Data Manipulation." PSPR 56:250; and Beloff, J. "Dream States and ESP." In D. H. Weiner and R. L. Morris, eds., *Research in Parapsychology, 1987, 1988;* and Beloff, J. "Dream States and ESP." In W. G. Roll, J.Beloff and R. A. White, eds., *Research in Parapsychology,* 1982, 1983.

BIBLIOGRAPHY: Medhurst, R. G. 1971. "The Origin of the 'Prepared Random Numbers' Used in the Shackleton Experiments." JSPR 46:39; Soal, S. G. and Bateman, F. *Modern Experiments in Telepathy,* 1954; Soal, S. G. and Goldney, K. M. 1943. "Experiments in Precognitive Telepathy." PSPR 47:21.

**Martínez, Luis, 1898–1973.** also called "Don Luisito," the most famous Mexican physical medium. His séances were attended by leaders of high society and the intellectual world of Mexico, by high government officials, army generals, and all the presidents of Mexico from Elias Calles in 1928 to López

Mateos in 1964. During these seances, the medium was hypnotized and went into trance. While in that state, he produced all the well-known physical phenomema of Spiritualism, including apports and materializations. He even managed his own leviation, although he weighed 200 pounds. He was best known for his materialization of "Maestro Amajur," a deceased oriental doctor.

Martínez was closely investigated by the Instituto Mexicano de Investigaciones Síquicas. On one occasion, after "Don Luisito" had been hypnotized and was in trance, the investigators tied and placed him in a cage suspended from the ceiling. It did not matter. The materialized form of "Maestro Amajur" made its appearance anyway. Since Martínez could not have been impersonating the form and assuming that the investigators exercised care to see that no confederate posed as the "Maestro," the medium seems to have furnished significant evidence. But the whole record of materializations is replete with one case of fraud after another so that one must be caution in accepting evidence for it.

**Mary, Saint.** Mother of Jesus. She occupies first place among all the saints and produced a special cult devoted to her that is mirrored in the organizations of nuns and priests who revere her and in the shrines dedicated to her.

She is also first among **Noted Witnesses** for her stupendous record of postmortem apparitions. There have been Marian appearances in all times and places. In Mexico, in 1531, Mary was said to have been seen by an Indian and in Lourdes in 1854 by a peasant girl; 1889 witnessed the appearance of the Blessed Virgin to a young girl in Pontinet, Dordogne, France, then to other children and finally to a large number of adults. They saw her sometimes in black, sometimes in white, sometimes large, sometimes as small as a statuette, sometimes as a vague form, sometimes illuminated in a golden light. In 1907, images of Mary were seen in hailstones in Remiremont, France; in 1917, three children encountered her in Fatima, Portugal; and in 1968 a horde of witnesses said they watched Mary in Egypt. The latest visions of Mary began on June 24, 1981, in Medugorje, Yugoslavia, when six children said they saw the Mother of God—or the "Gospa" in Croatian—and that her message was peace.

These events stir up great religious emotion and excitement. In Yugoslavia, for example, since 1981, almost eight million people have climbed the hill where the children claimed to have seen the apparition. The Marian apparitions in Pontinet and Medugorje have not been recognized by the Church although they have been corroborated by many witnesses; yet the vision at Lourdes seen by a single girl was recognized.

None of these appearances would be considered evidential enough for psychical research to accept them. In respect to Pontinet, it is arguable that the visions became contagious as suggestions and anticipation spread from one to the other to produce a collective hallucination. A similar phenomenon could have occurred among the six children at Medugorje. The vision at Lourdes, which rests on the uncorroborated word of one girl, could be a purely subjective experience.

There is a case, however, in which visions of Mary resulted in the fulfillment of a prophesy—the "dance of the sun" that took place in Fatima after Marian apparitions promised a miracle. The solar phenomenon was witnessed by people at three different locations at considerable distances from one another. The phenomenon remains one that neither natural causes, science, nor parapsychology can explain. Nor can anything but speculation account for the Marian apparitions in 1968 in a suburb of Cairo, Egypt, where hundreds of thousands of witnesses and many photographs attested to a spectacular series of appearances. It is such appearances as these that give weight to Mary's testimony as a noted witness. See also **Bernadette, Saint; Egypt, Marian Apparitions in; Fatima, Marian apparitions at; Hailstones, Miraculous; Lourdes, Miracles of.**

**Massey, Charles Carleton, 1838–1905.** British lawyer, Spiritualist, and Theosophist. Massey who never married and lived alone was so intensely interested in philosophy, psychology, and paranormal phenomena that he abandoned the law to study these subjects and make them his companions. He returned to the practice of law only once: to defend the medium Henry Slade who was prosecuted for swindling a sitter.

Massey was one of the first and among the most zealous supporters of the Society for Psychical Research and one of the Spiritualists on its council when the organization was formed. As a convinced Spiritualist, he was persuaded that he had evidence from sittings with mediums of the genuineness of the physical phenomena of Spiritualism (Massey, 1886). But he was not altogether credulous. Although a believer in Theosophy, he wanted evidence for the existence of the adepts and asked Madame H. P. Blavatsky for proof. Soon after he found a letter addressed to him that purported to come from one of the adepts. But it was a fraud as Massey learned from a letter from Mme Blavatsky to the person who "planted" the letter to him (Report, 1885:207, 397–400).

Massey translated into English the writings of Johann K. F. Zöllner and wrote articles for *Light.* **Sir William Barrett,** with whom he had formed an intimate friendship characterized Massey as "one of the most unselfish and lovable of men, ever modest and retiring, yet with a rare and resolute moral courage" (Barrett, 1905:96).

Selected Writing: 1886. "The Possibilities of Mal-Observation in Relation to Evidence for the Phenomena of Spiritualism." PSPR 4:75.

BIBLIOGRAPHY: Barrett, W.F. 1905. "Obituary. C. C. Massey." JSPR 12:95; 1885. "Report of the Committee Appointed to Investigate Phenomena Connected with the Theosophical Society." PSPR 3:201.

**Matching.** In ESP **Card-Guessing** experiments, the laying next to a key card of a **Target Card** as it is called or "guessed" by a subject.

**Matching, Blind.** See **Blind Matching Test.**

**Matching, Open.** See **Open Matching Test.**

**Materialization.** The purported appearance during a séance or sitting with a physical medium of visible, tangible objects or human faces, hands, or life-sized forms supposed to be materialized out of **Ectoplasm** emitted by the medium. Generally, the medium is seated and secured in a Cabinet while observers remain outside in a dark or dimly lighted séance room. Faces, objects or forms may issue from the cabinet or appear in the room.

That they need not be hallucinations and that forms appear to be real living beings is suggested by the fact that they may walk next to sitters, touch them, even drink water. Often the objects or figures are said to dematerialize and fade away completely with no trace left behind. It is commonly supposed that any interference with a materialized form may bring harm or even death to a medium. But in the records of parapsychology many such forms have been rudely grabbed by aggressive skeptical investigators and no injury to a medium has ever been reported. The result of a seizure often has been the exposure of a fraudulent medium caught in some disguise while impersonating a "spirit."

Should materialization be a reality, "it would mean that a solid body had been fashioned out of nothing—an incredible accomplishment" (Berger, 1988). Yet many researchers, including William Crookes, Charles Richet and Gustave Geley in the past and George Zorab today, have accepted materializations as real. Nevertheless, since the history of materialization is replete with exposures of physical mediums who have been detected in one kind of trickery or another, extreme wariness in accepting materialization as a fact and in insisting on decisive evidence are advisable. D. D. Home and Florence Cook were the most famous materializing mediums of the late nineteenth century. Carlos Mirabelli and George Spriggs were sensational materializing mediums of this century. See also **Dematerialization; Ectoplasy; Mellon, Annie.**

BIBLIOGRAPHY: Berger, A. S. *Evidence of Life After Death: A Casebook for the Tough-Minded,* 1988.

**Mattiesen, Emil, 1875–1939.** German composer of ballads and prolific writer. He had a strong belief in survival after death which he thought was based on ample evidence. Many consider his three-volume work written in the 1930s a complete and authoritative presentation of the question. In 1927 and 1928, he published a series of articles in the Spiritualist periodical *Zeitschrift für Psychische Forschung* in which he analyzed mediums and their trances and concluded that communicators are real and independent entities.

**Count Perovsky-Petrovo-Solovovo** (1928) scoffed at Mattiesen as a "convinced spiritist" and attacked his treatment of the whole subject and his uncritical acceptance of the survival hypothesis. But Mattiesen retorted that the attack was "ill-considered" and that the count was a "negativist" engaged in "endless fastidious cavilling at details" (Mattiesen, 1929).

Sixty years after Mattiesen's death the emotional issue of survival after death still divides people into two camps from each of which come the same charges and countercharges hurled by Perovsky-Petrovo-Solovovo and Mattiesen.

Selected Writings: *Das persönliche Überleben des Todes. Eine Darstellung der Erfahrungsbeweise,* 1936–1939; 1929. "A Reply to Count Perovsky-Petrovo-Solovovo." JSPR 25:27.

BIBLIOGRAPHY: Petrovsky-Petrovo-Solovovo, M. 1928. "On Some 'Critical' Methods." JSPR 24:361.

**Mayne, Alan James, 1927–.** British mathematician and computer expert. As a parapsychologist, he has developed models of psi to try to detect it and see how it operates. He has also designed and conducted experiments in extrasensory perception, in particular, "indirect experiments," in which the conscious inhibition of psychic talents is reduced because the subjects are not aware that their psi abilities are being tested. Mayne's major interest has been the stimulation of research in parapsychology by qualified research teams using essential scientific equipment (Mayne, 1963).

Selected Writing: 1963. "The Promotion of Research." JSPR 42:202.

**McClenon, James, 1947–.** American sociologist. His main interests in parapsychology include the sociology of science, the sociology of the paranormal, poltergeist phenomena, shamanism, and healing. Dr. McClenon's principal contribution to parapsychology has been to place the field under a sociologist's magnifying glass to see why it is considered a deviant science by orthodox scientists. He found that conventional science is compelled to condemn some disciplines as deviant just as society is compelled to brand some acts as crimes (i.e., to set limits on what is permissible and what is not). Parapsychology, therefore, is important to orthodox science because it helps that science to continue its activity (McClenon, 1984).

Dr. McClenon also believes that scientists, particularly the elite among them, are sceptics in regard to parapsychology because they are more committed to a mechanistic view of the world. Since in their eyes and those of orthodox science in general parapsychology is an aberration, what allows parapsychology to survive at all? It would appear to be only the support given to it by the general public and a few philanthropists such as James S. McDonnell and Chester F. Carlson.

Dr. McClenon who received his Ph.D. in sociology from the University of Maryland in 1981 is now assistant professor at Elizabeth City State University in North Carolina.

Selected Writing: *Deviant Science: The Case of Parapsychology,* 1984.

**M'Connel Case.** See **Pilot Case.**

**McConnell, Robert A., 1914–.** American biophysicist and parapsychologist. "Why," asks Dr. McConnell (1987:2), "would a physicist, already well-launched on a successful career, suddenly, at age 33, . . . set sail on the uncharted sea of parapsychology?" Because, in 1943 while working at the Radiation Laboratory at the Massachusetts Institute of Technology, he read in *Time* magazine about Joseph B. Rhine's experiments in psychokinesis. His interest aroused, he read the cases reported in the *Proceedings of the Society for Psychical Research* and came to the conclusion then, which he still believes, that "any competent scientist . . . who can lay aside his cultural preconceptions . . . and who is skilled at inductive thinking . . . cannot fail to be convinced of the reality of an extrasensory perception of some kind or other" (1987:6).

At the end of World War II Robert McConnell decided to get his Ph.D. as quickly as possible—he received it from the University of Pittsburgh in 1947—and then go to work in parapsychology. He is one of the fortunate few who have been able to work full time in the field. He has mainly studied psychokinesis at the University of Pittsburgh, from 1947 to 1952 in the Physics Department and thereafter as research professor in the newly formed Department of Biophysics. In 1984 he was named research professor emeritus.

Dr. McConnell believes that mental dissociation is important for the production of

ESP and PK and that hypnosis is the psychokinetic control of one brain by another.

He was the first president of the Parapsychological Association, founded in 1957. He co-authored (1958) with **Gertrude R. Schmeidler** a widely acclaimed book for which he provided the statistical analyses. In the hope of increasing interest in teaching parapsychology in the schools he wrote *ESP Curriculum Guide* (1970). He has published widely in scientific and parapsychological journals and has distributed worldwide to scientists and teaching libraries 4,800 copies of three books he has written (1982, 1983a, and 1983b) to try to combat the indifference or hostility of conventional scientists to parapsychology. His most recent book (1987) is a summary of his forty years in the field.

Selected Writings: *Parapsychology in Retrospect: My Search for the Unicorn,* 1987; *Parapsychology and Self-Deception in Science,* 1983a; *An Introduction to Parapsychology in the Context of Science,* 1983b; *Encounters with Parapsycholoyg,* 1982; *ESP Curriculum Guide,* 1970; and G. R. Schmeidler, *ESP and Personality Patterns,* 1958.

**McDonnell, James S., 1899–1980.** American aircraft manufacturer and philanthropist. He founded the McDonnell Aircraft Company that produced carrier-based jet fighters during World War II and merged his company with the Douglas Company to make jet fighters, cruise missiles, and commercial airliners.

As a student at Princeton, he had read the writings of Frederic W. H. Myers, was intrigued by the question of human survival after death, and developed a deep interest in psychical research. His father, however, advised him to go into some pursuit with a better future. Although he followed his father's counsel, he never lost his interest in the field. He established the James S. McDonnell Foundation whose increasing grants to the psychical research and parapsychological community provided it with money to support almost half the researchers in the United States. Among those who received the largest grants were the Psychophysical Research Laboratories and the Division of Parapsychology of the University of Virginia. The Parapsychological Association benefitted as well from McDonnell's generosity. In 1979, his foundation made a grant of $600,000 for the creation of the McDonnell Laboratory for Psychical Research in St. Louis. With McDonnell's death, parapsychology lost one of its few major philanthropists.

**McDougall, William, 1871–1931.** Anglo-American psychologist. Wilde Reader in Mental Philosophy at Oxford University and later holder of the chair of psychology at Harvard University, McDougall rebelled against the mechanistic school of thought that he felt denied that in every living thing there is a vital non-mechanistic element that strives toward goals. His contemporaries tried to ignore him, but his articulate and determined writings, such as *Body and Mind,* attacked mechanism and argued effectively that the soul should be accepted as a scientific hypothesis. The book also contained a chapter on psychical research and a discussion of the **Cross-Correspondences.** However the latter were to be explained, McDougall said, the explanation was fatal to the mechanistic order of things.

It is interesting that McDougall should have been drawn to psychical research at all in view of what happened at one of the first séances he attended with an obscure physical medium. In the dark room, the medium's spirit control, with its face glowing dimly, emerged from the cabinet and made its rounds slowly past the circle of sitters. When it reached McDougall, he grabbed the spirit's head and found the struggling body of the medium attached to it. McDougall nevertheless continued to believe that psychical research consisted of a body of phenomena supported by strong testimony that upset the creed of mechanism and suggested that mind transcends matter. It was orthodox science's denial of these phenomena that gave McDougall another reason to rebel—and to become active in psychical research.

In 1920, he was elected president of the Society for Psychical Research and, in 1921, also became President of the American Society for Psychical Research. He took part in the investigation of Mina Crandon ("Margery") (he thought she was a fraud) and helped Elwood Worcester found the Boston Society for Psychic Research when the ASPR became too unscientific for him to continue to support it. He also strongly influenced the trend toward making psychical research a subject of study by universities. In 1927, McDougall became head of the Department of Psychology at Duke University and paved the way for Joseph B. Rhine's work and the creation of the Parapsychology Laboratory there. McDougall became editor with Rhine of the *Journal of Parapsychology.*

Selected Writings: "Psychical Research as a University Study." In C. Murchison, ed., *The Case for and Against Psychical Belief,* 1927; *Body and Mind: A History and Defense of Animism,* 1911.

BIBLIOGRAPHY: Berger, A. S. *Lives and Letters in American Parapsychology: A Biographical History, 1850–1987,* 1988; Over, R. van and Oteri, L., eds., *William McDougall: Explorere of the Mind,* 1967.

**McDougall Award for Distinguished Work in Parapsychology.** Established in 1957 by the Parapsychology Laboratory at Duke University. An award of $1,000 has been made each year to a worker in parapsychology, whether in the United States or elsewhere in the world, who, in the previous year, contributed the most conspicuous research to the field. Awards have not been made to members of the Parapsychology Laboratory staff. Recipients of the award have included Arthur E. H. Bleksley, Haakon G. Forwarld, Milan Ryzl, Gertrude R. Schmeidler and Donald J. West.

**McHarg, James F., 1917–.** British psychiatrist. Like Jan Ehrenwald and Jule Eisenbud, Dr. McHarg's practice of psychiatry led him to his interest in psychical research, especially veridical visions in clinical practice, apparitions with veridical content in cases of temporal lobe epilepsy, and synchronistic phenomena as a basis of some psychotic illness. He is also interested in poltergeist outbreaks and is currently preparing a paper on a case from Argyll. He considers his main contributions to parapsychology to be his papers on these topics and, from his clinical experience in general psychiatry, his recognition of what he calls "pseudo-psi" and "of subjective distress based on actual psi-experiences."

Dr. McHarg is a graduate in medicine of Edinburgh University, having received his M.B. and Ch.B. in 1940 and his M.D. in 1959. Since 1958 he has been a Fellow of the Royal College of Physicians of Edinburgh and, in 1970, was a Founder Fellow of the Royal College of Psychiatrists, London. He is consultant psychiatrist at the Royal Dundee Liff Hospital. In 1982 he retired from the University of Dundee where he held the post of honorary senior lecturer in psychiatry. Dr. McHarg is a member of the Parapsychological Association and of the council of the Society for Psychical Research.

Selected Writings: "Psychose und Synchronizität." In *Grenzgebiete der Wissenschaft, I,* 1985, pp. 23–31; "Psychical Research and Psychiatry." In I. Grattan-Guiness, ed., *Psychical Research,* 1982; 1978. "A Vision of the Aftermath of the Battle of Nechtanesmere, AD 685." JSPR 49:938; "A Poltergeist Case from Glasgow." In J. D. Morris, W. G. Roll and R. L. Morris, eds., *Research in Parapsychology, 1976,* 1977, pp. 13–15; "Poltergeist and Apparitional Haunting Phenomena Affecting the Family and Associates of an Adolescent Girl with Well-controlled Epilepsy." In J.D. Morris, W. G. Roll and R. L. Morris, eds., *Research in Parapsychology, 1972,* 1973, pp. 17–19.

**McKenzie, James Hewat, 1870–1929.** British Spiritualist. Born in poverty, he was "a hard-headed practical man" (Hankey, 1963), a successful businessman who made a fortune. This fortune he devoted to the British College of Psychic Science which he founded after World War I in order to train mediums and to prove survival after death according to the tenets of Spiritualism.

Perhaps the most famous of the mediums he trained was Eileen Garrett who wrote that "Whatever integrity and seriousness I have been able to achieve in my attitude towards using my supernormal supersensitivity I feel I owe to the untiring patience and faith of this unflinching and courageous man" (quoted in Hankey 1970:407). He worked with Hereward Carrington in 1922 in the study of spirit photography and endorsed William Hope although Carrington was unwilling to give an opinion one way or the other (1925).

Eric J. Dingwall said of McKenzie that he "had not the slightest idea of the real meaning of scientific work. . . . His treatment of the spirit photographer, William Hope, was typical. Although it was strongly suspected that Hope never produced any genuine psychic effects, Mr. McKenzie defended him vehemently, . . . found apparatus for producing these frauds, published nothing about it, and the facts only emerged long afterwards" (Hankey, 1963:139). McKenzie's secretary Muriel Hankey, on the other hand, admired him enormously and it has been pointed out (Heywood, 1964) that the development of Spiritualism in England owes him much.

BIBLIOGRAPHY: Carrington, H. 1925. "Experiences in Psychic Photography. JASPR 19:258,263; Hankey, M. 1970. "Mrs. Eileen Garrett." JSPR 45:406,407; Hankey, M. *James Hewat McKenzie: A Personal Memoir,* 1963.

**McMahan, Elizabeth Anne, 1924–.** American zoologist and parapsychologist. When she was a sophomore in college, she found out about the work in parapsychology being done by Joseph B. Rhine, wrote to him and in 1943 was invited to become a research assistant at the Parapsychology Laboratory. A problem facing Rhine at the time was whether there was any evidence for telepathy that could not be accounted for on the grounds of clairvoyance. One of Elizabeth McMahan's important experiments at the laboratory gave significant results to show that pure telepathy exists as distinguished from clairvoyance (McMahan, 1946). During her eleven years at the Parapsychology Laboratory which she described as "some of the most exciting years of my life" (McMahan, 1982:14), she conducted numerous other experiments in extrasensory perception and psychokinesis and met outstanding personalities who had come there to talk about psi phenomena.

Selected Writings: "Joseph Banks Rhine: Teacher and Friend." In K. R. Rao, ed., *J. B. Rhine: On the Frontiers of Science,* 1982, p. 13; 1946. "An Experiment in Pure Telepathy." JP 10:224.

**Mead, George Robert Stowe, 1863–1933.** British scholar and Theosophist. As secretary of the Theosophical Society, he worked with his close friend Madame H. P. Blavatsky and, after Annie Besant took over the responsibilities for the society, Mead helped in attempts to plan its future program. Mead also founded and edited *Quest,* a publication dealing with Mysticism, philosophy and religion.

**Mead, Margaret, 1901–1978.** American anthropologist. A close friend of psychologist Gardner Murphy, in 1942 (along with Joseph B. Rhine and William James's son Henry) she became a member of the Board of Trustees of the American Society for Psychical Research as part of Murphy's efforts to restore the prestige of the ASPR after its long decline from academic respectability.

As a member of the Research Committee she criticized the experimental methods then in use: "Our approach is in error—our approach must be a study of the nature of what occurs in its whole setting, not just a search for the paranormal *element* in an unspecified context. . . . A study of times and circumstances of telepthic experience is necessary. . . . Our testing procedures are dull. Our methods are a cultural punishment of psychic ability" (quoted in Osis, 1985:505).

It was also because of her friendship for Murphy that, in 1969, she pushed vigorously for, and gained, acceptance for the Parapsychological Association as an affiliate of the American Association for the Advancement of Science. (She argued that "the PA used scientific methods and . . . it is methodology, not hypotheses, that determine what is a science" [Berger, 1988:157].)

Margaret Mead did not write on parapsychological subjects *per se* but naturally was involved with them in her anthropological studies. She did discuss hypnotic trance in her preface to a book by Jane Belo (1960). "As an anthropologist, she was best known for her studies of the nonliterate peoples of Oceania, especially with regard to various aspects of psychology and culture. . . . As a celebrity, she was most notable for her forays into such far-ranging topics as women's rights, childrearing, sexual morality, nuclear proliferation, race relations, drug abuse, population control, environmental pollution, and world hunger (*The New Encyclopaedia Britannica* 1986: Vol. 7, 987).

Dr. Mead studied under anthropologist Franz Boas at Columbia University and received her Ph.D. there in 1929. She wrote twenty-three books. Her first (1928\1961) is a continuing best-seller. She was for many years with the American Museum of Natural History in New York, where she served successively as assistant curator, associate curator, and curator emeritus of ethnology. In 1973 she was elected president of the American Association for the Advancement of Science and, in 1979, she was awarded posthumously the highest civilian honor, the Presidential Medal of Freedom.

Selected Writings: "Preface." In J. Belo, *Trance in Bali,* 1960; *Coming of Age in Samoa,* 1928\1961).

BIBLIOGRAPHY: Berger, A. S. *Lives and Let-*

*ters in American Parapsychology,* 1988, p. 157; "Margaret Mead." *The New Encyclopaedia Britannica,* 1986, Vol. 7, p. 987; Osis, K. 1985. "The American Society for Psychical Research 1941–1985: A Personal View." JASPR 79:501, 505.

**Mean Chance Expectation.** The most likely score if only chance is involved (JP).

**Mean Variance.** See **Variance, Mean (Theoretical).**

**Medhurst, Richard George, 1920–1971.** British mathematician. Introduced to parapsychology by Samuel G. Soal whose lectures he attended in the early 1940s, he took part in the famous experiments with Basil Shackleton which at the time he thought were "virtually conclusive evidence in favour of ESP" (Barrington, 1971:125). He very much admired Sir William Crookes and, with Kathleen M.Goldney, wrote a noteworthy paper (1964) dealing with him and his sittings with Florence Cook.

Because of his involvement in the Soal-Shackleton experiments he defended Soal against the charges of fraud leveled at these experiments and, to vindicate Soal, made a study (1971) of the random number sequences used in these experiments. Unfortunately, the results of his investigation, published posthumously, cast further doubt on Soal's work and led directly to Betty Markwick's proof of data manipulation.

Dr. Medhurst—he received his D.Sc. from London University shortly before his death—after his office hours at the General Electric Company would devote three or four hours a day to psychical research (ESP and hypnosis tests, for example) and to his work as chairman of the Library Committee of the Society for Psychical Research.

At the time of his death from a malignant brain tumor he was collecting material on Sir William Crookes for publication.

Selected Writings: 1971. "The Origin of the 'Prepared Random Numbers' Used in the Shackleton Experiments." JSPR 46:39; and K. M. Goldney. 1964. "William Crookes and the Physical Phenomena of Mediumship." PSPR 54:25.

BIBLIOGRAPHY: Barrington, M. R. 1971. "Obituary. Dr. R. G. Medhurst 1920–1971." JSPR 46:124.

**Mediating Vehicles.** A term coined by **G. N. M. Tyrrell** to describe a subconscious and psychological creation of a percipient that conveys to consciousness knowledge of information obtained by ESP. Dreams are an example.

**Medicine Man/Woman.** Also called witch doctor. Among the American Indians and some people of the Pacific, a male or female in whom rest all their hopes, fears, and beliefs. Believed to possess great powers of healing, the medicine man or woman performs rituals and uses material objects such as stones, feathers, and plants to cure the sick. Some authorites, such as Mircea Eliade, recognize that these individuals may also possess other paranormal powers.

BIBLIOGRAPHY: Eliade, M. *Shamanism: Archaic Techniques of Ecstasy,* 1966.

**Meditation.** A technique for keeping the conscious mind as tranquil and free from the agitation of thought as a motionless pool is from currents of wind. Usually, but not always, by following Eastern methods, such as Zen or **Yoga,** it is a means of achieving deep relaxation and inducing an altered state of consciousness. In this state, parapsychologists believe that transpersonal or spiritual elements may be released to facilitate the emergence of psi abilities and experiences.

To explore the influence of meditation on extrasensory perception and to test the hypothesis that meditation is another mental state favorable for the manifestation of psi, Gertrude R. Schmeidler asked six graduate students in psychology at City College of New York to act as subjects and make calls on ESP targets. After they had done so, she had a swami give the subjects meditation training and breathing exercises during which the subjects closed their eyes. After a few minutes, Dr. Schmeidler conducted a second experiment with ESP targets. The finding was that ESP performance by the subjects before meditation had been at chance while performance after meditation was significantly beyond chance.

BIBLIOGRAPHY: Schmeidler. G. R. 1970. "High ESP Scores After a Swami's Brief Instruction in Meditation and Breathing." JASPR 64:100.

**Medium.** A person said to be an intermediary or link between the living and the dead. Mediums fall into two classes: physical and mental. In the presence of physical mediums, there take place physical effects, such as psychokinesis (the movement of objects without physical contact); levitation; materialization of figures or portions of figures; the paranormal transportation of physical objects from one place to another (apports), usually including the passage of matter through matter; and the production of raps and direct voices. **D. D. Home** and **Eusapia Palladino** were two of the most famous physical mediums. Because of the amount of fraud discovered in the investigations of physical mediums, psychical researchers for the past fifty years have been loath to take them seriously and, when they do, discover that such mediums are reluctant to submit to controls.

Mental mediums (the two most famous being **Leonora Piper** and **Gladys Osborne Leonard**) are thought either: 1) presumably by telepathy, to receive communication from the dead directly or by means of "controls" who receive the communication and relay it to the medium or 2) to have their organisms controlled or possessed directly by the spirits of the dead. In either case, the medium sometimes goes into trance. In the first case, often called "clairvoyant" mediumship, mediums frequently claim to hear or to see the spirits of the dead, and they may present the "communication" in dramatic and convincing form. Clairvoyant mediumship is practiced in Spiritualism. In the second case, the medium may speak with the voice of the dead or may write or even paint or play the piano, all automatically. Automatic writing, speaking or spelling usually involves short messages but has produced entire books (e.g., **Pearl Lenore Curran's** production of the Patience Worth books).

Sometimes a medium will receive a fragmentary message that will make no sense until it is combined with other fragmentary messages received by other mediums. These messages, known as **"Cross-Correspondences,"** are considered the best evidence that there is a disembodied consciousness communicating. Yet it has often been held that the entire process of "communication" is a product of some subconscious level of the medium's mind (that is, that the intelligence communicating with the medium is the medium him/herself) and that all information given is the result of some form of extrasensory perception.

Mediumship has been studied extensively by psychical researchers throughout the world.

BIBLIOGRAPHY: Aksakoff, A. *Animismus and Spiritismus,* 1898; Amadou, R. *Les grands médiums,* 1957; Gauld, A. J. "Discarnate Survival." In B. Wolman, ed., *Handbook of Parapsychology,* 1977; Murphy, G. 1957. "Triumphs and Defeats in the Study of Mediumship." JASPR 52:125.

**Mediumistic Record.** Verbatim and accurate handwritten notes, or a tape recording, of all material presented during a mediumistic sitting. It is advisable to make such a record so that the material can be analyzed and evaluated because the memory of what is said or done at a sitting becomes dim or distorted with time. See also **Script.**

**Mediumistic Trance.** See **Trance.**

**Meek, George, 1910–.** American engineer. In 1982, he made the startling announcement to the world that his invention which he called **Spiricom** had achieved electronic communication with people who had died. He told the National Press Club in Washington, D.C.: "For the first time we have electronic proof that the mind, memory banks, and personality survive death of the physical body" (Swain, 1982).

After his retirement in 1970 from engineering and the invention of air and heat transfer devices, Meek founded the **Metascience Foundation** to do research into the nature of the human personality. He became interested in electronic voice phenomena and saw the work of Friedrich Jürgenson and Konstantin Raudive as a step toward setting up communication with another world. He set to work to develop a sophisticated apparatus for doing so. By 1982, he thought he had achieved his goal with the development and apparent success of Spiricom in communicating with a deceased American physicist. This success prompted Meek to assert that "it has been proven incontestably that death is merely a door to continuing life" (Meek, 1982). The problem is that the one and only success with Spiricom took place when the operator who has since disappeared from the scene was alone with the equipment. It is possible, then, that the operator was a medium so that Spiricom's electronic system worked only in combination with human psychic abilities. Nevertheless, since the dead physicist supplied details that subsequently were verified, the claim of success cannot be dismissed lightly.

Now at work on the development of systems for obtaining pictures of the dead on a television screen, Meek is the author of several books, including one (1980) that answers questions about life after death. It has been published in English, Japanese, Portuguese, and some of the languages of India.

Selected Writings: 1982. "The Significance of the Spiricom Breakthrough." *New Realities* 4(6):14; *After We Die, What Then?*, 1980.

BIBLIOGRAPHY: Swain, B. 1982. "Metascience News." *New Realities* 4(6):8.

**Meier, Carl Alfred, 1905–.** Swiss physician and psychiatrist who held the post of director of the Jung Institute. His interest in parapsychology was sparked by **Carl Gustav Jung** himself who told Dr. Meier of his (Jung's) many paranormal experiences. Dr. Meier was also Jung's assistant, succeeded him as professor of psychology at the Eidgenossische Technische Hochschule in Zurich and admired him as "not only a great doctor of individuals and collectivity, but also one of the most distinguished scientists" (Meier, 1961).

Meier's interest was stimulated as well by his own experiences in his private practice where he saw many cases of parapsychological phenomena. His deepening interest in parapsychology led him to study all the relevant literature, to organize colleagues for the purpose of conducting experimental research, to lecture on parapsychology in Zurich in conjunction with psychology courses he gave, and to write about the subject in his books. Dr. Meier participated in many international conferences, including the First International Conference for Parapsychological Studies held in 1953 at the University of Utrecht and the Cambridge Conference on spontaneous cases held in 1955.

Selected Writings: 1961. "Obituaries. C. G. Jung." JSPR 41:216.

**Mellon, Annie Fairlamb, c.1850–c.1935.** British physical medium. Of all the mediums claiming the power of materialization, she was acclaimed by Spiritualists, including William T. Stead, as the only one who had never been detected in a fraud. She seems to have started the development of her powers in 1874. The following year, she was investigated in Newcastle, England, by Henry Sidgwick, Eleanor Sidgwick, Frederic W. H. Myers and Edmund Gurney who were later to organize the Society for Psychical Research. As she sat tied in a cabinet, the investigators sitting outside in subdued light, forms issued from the cabinet. The skeptical investigators, unsatisfied, realized that the medium might have freed herself from a strap they had fastened loosely around her waist so as not to cause her discomfort. They therefore asked to search her after the séance but she refused. The investigators were suspicious but had not detected any outright trickery. That remained for another séance thousands of miles away.

The medium had immigrated to Australia in 1891. There she married J. B. Mellon, and there, as a professional medium, she gave séances in her home. Several sitters during these séances suspected that the forms they saw might have been impersonations by Mrs. Mellon. On October 12, 1894, as a form came out of Mrs. Mellon's cabinet, a sitter seized it "and found that I held the form of Mrs. Mellon, and that she was on her knees, and had a white material like muslin round her head and sholders. . . . I looked inside the cabinet, and saw, lying upon the floor (inside the cabinet) a false beard . . . a small black shawl, some old muslin, Mrs. Mellon's shoes and stockings . . ." (Henry, 1894). For his pains and aggressiveness, the sitter was attacked by the medium's husband and other men, but he succeeded in catching Mrs. Mellon red-handed and in showing her *modus operandi* of using various disguises to impersonate "spirits."

Mrs. Mellon's is another fraudulent case in the story of materialization.

BIBLIOGRAPHY: Henry, T. S. *"Spookland!": A Record of Research and Experiment in the Much Talked of Realm of Mystery,* 1894; Sidgwick, Mrs. H. 1886. "Results of a Personal Investigation into the Physical Phenomena of Spiritualism." PSPR 4:45.

**Mental Medium.** See **Medium.**

**Mental Phenomena.** Distinguished from **Physical Phenomena,** these phenomena include: 1) communications purportedly from deceased communicators through the organism of a mental medium; 2) apparitions; 3) out-of-body experiences; 4) the acquisiton of information by means other than the recognized senses (i.e, extrasensory perception), with or without a physical instrument such as a crystal ball, a dowsing implement, a psychometric object, or any device for writing or spelling, including a pen, ouija board or planchette. See also **Crystal-Gazing; Psychometry.**

**Mental Telegraphy.** See **Telepathy.**

**Mesmerism.** So called after Franz Anton Mesmer, an Austrian physician. He believed that the **Animal Magnetism,** a mysterious force, passed from him to his patients and produced an artificial trance by means of which he treated his patients' disorders. For his concept and techniques, Mesmer was opposed as a charlatan by his colleagues and fled from Vienna in 1778 to Paris where he practiced his technique and generated a mesmeric movement that attracted many followers. Mesmerism was induced by a mesmeriser who, after having established a rapport with a subject, made passes or wavings of the hand to induce a state of receptivity to suggestions.

Mesmerism, the forerunner of hypnosis, is important as a precursor of parapsychology. When medical people finally got around in the mid-nineteenth century to using the "mesmeric" trance for surgical or healing purposes, they noticed that entranced patients often displayed paranormal abilities for perceiving objects or events through clairvoyance or for obtaining knowledge through telepathy. The French psychologist Pierre Janet is reported to have used telepathy to place his patients in a mesmeric trance. Indeed, the newly organized Society for Psychical Research made the mesmeric trance one of its first objects of study.

**Message.** Applied to a communication in the form of speech, writing, percussive sounds, or any other form purporting to originate with a deceased person and to be intended for the living. In mediumship such a communication may be from an intelligence external to the medium through whom it comes or it may originate in an alternate personality of the medium. See also **Communicator.**

**Messing, Wolf, 1899–1974.** Polish-born Russian psychic. Forced to flee the Nazis, Messing found that he was already famous in Russia and that the story of his escape had made him something of a folk hero. (He was supposed, by suggestion or some form of hypnosis, simply to have walked out of a jail cell unnoticed by the guards.) Once in Russia his feats of telepathy and prophesy brought him to Stalin's attention.

The story goes that he persuaded Stalin of his abilities by making a teller in the state bank give him a large sum of money in exchange for a blank piece of paper. He was an enormously popular stage performer who, from his earnings, presented two fighter planes to the Russian Air Force during World War II and who apparently made huge sums of money for the Russian government.

Although he was reputed to possess supernormal (if not supernatural) powers, in fact he did exactly what Kreskin and all stage mentalists have always done, most of it by muscle-reading. He, like Washington Irving Bishop, was subject to cataleptic trances. Unlike the unfortunate Bishop, however, he learned to control them and they, too, became part of his stage performances.

Stories of his influencing events from afar and of his prophetic powers abound, but most of them are just that—unsubstantiated stories. His biographer (Lungin, in press) did, however, have many first hand experiences with Messing. Assuming the truthfulness of her accounts, we then have some basis for thinking that Messing was an unusual PSYCHIC. For example, she relates how, from a distance, he influenced a malevolent professor who intended to fail her son to be unaware of her son's presence so that he could be examined, and passed, by another. She also says that Messing predicted correctly that her son and his then fiancée would marry, have great trouble at the beginning of their marriage, would have two sons and a daughter, and that the son would eventually become a prosperous physician. At least for his biographer, Messing was never wrong.

BIBLIOGRAPHY: Lungin, T. *Wolf Messing: The True Story of Russia's Most Famous Psychic,* in press.

**Metagnone.** A French word for a **Psychic.**

**Metagnomy.** Awareness beyond normal knowledge.

**Metal-Bending.** Metal can be bent by physical force or, if internal stresses can be relaxed, the metal can bend spontaneously. Paranormal metal-bending through psychokinesis supposedly occurs when a piece of metal is bent, broken, or deformed without natural explanations: 1. by just being touched or stroked lightly with the fingers of one hand; or 2. by the simple influence of someone who does not touch it—sometimes even at a distance. The leading pretender to metal-bending is **Uri Geller** whose public performances have focussed attention on this phenomenon. But its genuineness has been seriously questioned by conjurers such as James Randi who contend that it is only another one of the many illusions in the magician's bag of tricks. Other skeptics claim the feat is the result of cleverly substituting an already bent metal specimen for the original.

The evidence for the phenomenon in the scientific journals is mixed. In Japan, Sasaki and others have reported tests in which four subjects broke stainless steel spoons or platinum wires by stroking the metal with their thumbs and forefingers. But in the West, there is little supportive date published by responsible scientists. The one exception in the parapsychological or other journals is an article by J. B. Hasted, a British professor of physics at the University of London and a parapsychologist, who reported a "scrunch" experiment in which bending or "scrunching" of paper clips placed in a glass sphere 131 millimeters in diameter with an eight millimeter hole in it was declared "impossible" unless it were done paranormally. Nevertheless, a subject did accomplish the "scrunch." This single experiment, unwitnessed by any other scientist, has not convinced the rest of the scientific community, however, it being claimed that the "scrunching" could take place normally through the hole in the sphere. John Taylor, another physicist, also reported "scrunches" and accepted the reality of the so-called "Geller effect" (Taylor, 1975) but later changed his mind (Taylor, 1980).

In contrast to the absence of scientific evidence for metal-bending are two other kinds of evidence. One are the spontaneous cases of metal-bending that seem to have been generated by Uri Geller's television appearances. The "Geller Effect" also has been responsible for widespread "PK Parties"—social occasions in which people meet and, in an atmosphere of fun and excitement, finger cutlery and shout at forks and spoons to bend. Many of the parties have reported a high success rate and the resultant belief of many attendees that they have demonstrated their own PK abilities and the genuineness of metal-bending.

BIBLIOGRAPHY: Hasted, J. B. *The Metal Benders,* 1981; Hasted, J. B. 1976. "An Experimental Study of the Validity of Metal-Bending." JSPR 48:365; Taylor, J. *Superminds,* 1975; Taylor, J. *Science and the Supernatural,* 1980.

**Metapsychics.** Meaning after or beyond psychic phenomena. From the French *métapsychique* invented by **Charles Richet** and H. A. Jules-Bois to include extrasensory perception, apparitions, haunts, mediums and unorthodox healing. Sometimes used as a synonym for psychical research.

**Metascience Foundation.** Established in the United States in 1970 by **George Meek** to conduct instrumental research into the question of human survival beyond death. The emphasis is upon designing, constructing, and developing highly sophisticated "hardware" in an attempt to produce instrumental communication with the spirits of the dead. Address: P.O. Box 73, Franklin, North Carolina 28734.

**Metempsychosis.** See **Reincarnation.**

**"Michael."** An entity channeled first in 1970 in the San Francisco Bay area by Jessica Lansing (a pseudonym). Her **Channeling** is described in two best-selling books. "Michael" had come through to Jessica and her husband while they were playing with the Ouija board. " 'Michael' indicated that it was a 'recombined entity' made up of more than a thousand 'old soul' fragments. . . . According to 'Michael,' 'all that is' is contained within the 'Tao'. . . . The essence of this Tao separates into entities and fragments, which then go through a complex evolutionary path. . . . In the vast journey out of and back to the Tao, souls must ascend through seven planes of existence" (Klimo, 1987:50). Interestingly, the same "Michael" is supposedly being channeled by others in the San Francisco area.

BIBLIOGRAPHY: Klimo, J. *Channeling,* 1987;

Yarbro, C. Q. *Messages from Michael*, 1979; Yarbro, C. Q. *More Messages from Michael*, 1986.

**Micro-PK.** To be distinguished from "Macro-PK". Effects based on microscopic-scale random event generators that use radioactive decay or electronic noise sources to indicate whether a subject's consciousness has been able to use psychokinesis to influence the action of microscopic random systems. The evidence for any such influence is purely statistical, not physical.

**Mifune, Chizuko, 1886–1911.** Japanese psychic. Tomokichi Fukurai considered her one of the most powerful of his subjects. She worked with Fukurai in his tests of clairvoyance and thoughtography. Because of criticisms from both Sakuhei Fujiwara and the press she committed suicide. The tragedy not only effectively terminated her life but Fukurai's career also and affected the course of parapsychology in Japan.

**Millar, Brian, 1947–.** Scottish editor of *Theoretical Parapsychology* now living in The Netherlands. One of his interests is "tasting wine" (Millar, 1987), perhaps for pleasure, perhaps as a connoisseur, or perhaps as a libation to the gods. But his profession is parapsychology. He has conducted parapsychological research under John Beloff, has been a visiting member of the staff at the Parapsychology Laboratory at the University of Utrecht, and is at present a Council Member of the Studievereniging voor Psychical Research and an active force in the Synchronicity Research Unit. Millar's work has covered Kirlian photography, electronic testers for extrasensory perception, experiments with rodents, precognition, psi and its distribution, and experimenter effect. But **Observational Theories** constitute his major interest in the field. Indeed, his publication in this area has become a standard work (Millar, 1978). As an observational theorist he has challenged the "cybernetic view" of psychokinesis which parapsychologists have taken for a long time. A living organism, by some means, perhaps by extrasensory perception, receives information to guide its mental force to a physical object or system. But in Millar's "non-cybernetic" view the PK guiding "genius" (if it can be called that) behind the PK function is not ESP-obtained information but sensory feedback that comes with actually observing the results of psi trials and results. His theory offers researchers a new avenue to explore that concentrates on the effects of observation and observer.

Selected Writings: (September 22, 1987) Letter to authors; 1978. "The Observational Theories: A Primer." *European Journal of Parapsychology* 2(3):304.

**Mind-Cure.** See **Healing, Unorthodox.**

**Mind-Kin.** Term invented by **C. D. Broad.** He theorized that the human mind consisted of a psychic factor and a bodily factor. After death, the psychic factor might continue and at times merge temporarily with the mind of a living medium. The merger would produce a "mind-kin," a composite of the characteristics of the living person and of the characteristics and memories of the deceased person.

**Mind-Reading.** See **Telepathy.**

**Mind-Reading Performance.** Although "mind-reading" sometimes is used as a synonym for telepathy, the mind-reading act performed for the entertainment of an audience is quite different from the phenomenon. Some of the methods used to transfer information normally between performers and their audiences or assistants include **Muscle-Reading,** codes of various kinds, and even secret electric devices by which signals are communicated by assistants to performers.

**Mind Science Foundation.** Established in 1958 to conduct scientific studies of the human mind. While other avenues of research are followed—into creativity, psychoneuronimmunology, and Alzheimer's disease—two aspects of parapsychology are investigated also: **Remote Viewing** (the clairvoyant or telepathic ability to perceive objects and events at a distance) and **Psychokinesis** with respect to living systems and to random-number generators. The address of the organization is 8301 Broadway, Suite 100, San Antonio, Texas 78209

**Minus Function.** Jan Ehrenwald's term for an altered state of consciousness (i.e., sleep, absent-mindedness, or hypnotic trance on the part of one person that may facilitate communication by telepathy between that person and another). An illustration of the cooperation of neurophysiological and psychodynamic factors in the production of the phenomenon is the case Ehrenwald studied of a mentally retarded nine-year old girl who could read only some letters of the alphabet. She was diagnosed as a case of dyslexia or alexia. She demonstrated an extrasensory perception awareness of passages her mother was then reading in another room by a robot-like repeating of the words then being read.

**Mirabelli, Carlos, 1889–1951.** Brazilian mental and physical medium. Theodore Besterman (1935) called him "[g]enial, temperamental, dynamic [and] unreliable . . ." (p. 141). The phenomena which Mirabelli purportedly produced were so remarkable and so varied—full materializations and dematerializations, transportation of the medium from one location to another, levitation, psychokinesis, automatic writing, and xenoglossy (in twenty-six languages, including Latin, Persian, English, French, Spanish, African, Chinese, Japanese, and other Oriental languages and even hieroglyphics), apports, paranormal odors, and trance addresses on theological, philosophical, medical, political and economic subjects—that Helen Salter was moved to wonder "to what modest dimensions all these preposterous claims would dwindle supposing Mirabelli were to appear" at the offices of either the English or one of the European societies for psychical research (H. Salter, 1927). Her skepticism seemed vindicated by Hans Driesch's report of a séance with Mirabelli held at a private home. Driesch reported some very minor and suspect phenomena and supposed xenoglossy (Italian—but Mirabelli's parents were Italian—and Estonian—but he had with him a young Estonian girl) that Driesch felt was all too natural (Driesch, 1930).

Mirabelli had been extensively studied in Brazil, first, by a commission of medical and other prominent men, and then by the Cesare Lombroso Academy of Psychical Studies. The latter's report was published in 1926. The objectivity of this report, however, was called into question by Besterman, (1935) who claimed that the "Academia and Mirabelli are . . . to all intents and purposes, one and indivisible" (p. 142). According to the report, Mirabelli's phenomena, including materializations, psychokinesis, and levitations were produced either in broad daylight or under strong electric light and often, it was claimed, with the medium tightly bound. There were 392 sittings reported, of which 337 were positive: 189 instances of xenoglossy, 85 of automatic writing, and 63 of physical phenomena. 349 of the sittings were held in the rooms of the academy in the presence of a total of 555 witnesses. Often the phenomena were photographed.

"What," Eric J. Dingwall (1930) asked, "are we to make of these amazing reports? . . . I will . . . grant the possibility of wholesale confederacy and assume . . . that the materializations are confederates. . . . But confederates are human beings and human beings do not usually rise into the air, dissolve into pieces and float about in clouds of vapor. Confederates do not lose half their bodies, feel like flaccid sponges and give violent shocks to people who try to seize them" (pp. 301–302).

In 1933, Mary S. Walker of the American Society for Psychical Research attended three séances with Mirabelli and witnessed movements of objects at a distance (including her own camera and her hat) and apports. In 1934, Besterman, sent by the Society for Psychical Research to South America to investigate Mirabelli, attended a few séances in which the medium was under no control. Besterman reported that all the phenomena, save one, were fraudulently produced. There were no materializations, and the claim of xenoglossy was ludicrous. Cromwell, for example, speaking of the "loved English tongue that I spook . . ." and Crookes (misspelled Crooks by the "spirit") exhorting the "purest ghosts to "learn you to partake of their elsarness [*sic*]." Besterman concluded that Mirabelli had some paranormal abilities "round which he . . . erected, for commercial purposes, an elaborate structure of fraud" (p. 153).

Dingwall, however, was sharply critical of Besterman's report because the investigator had failed to interview any of the important witnesses who had seen the impressive phenomena (Dingwall, 1936). In Dingwall's eyes, Mirabelli vied with D. D. Home as one of the great mediums of all time. He described Mirabelli's case as one "in which the most extraordinary occurrences are recorded, so extraordinary that there is nothing like them in the whole range of psychical literature" (Dingwall, 1930:296).

It is too late now for further investigation and so Mirabelli's case becomes another of psychical research's enigmas.

BIBLIOGRAPHY: Besterman, T. 1935. "The Mediumship of Carlos Mirabelli." JSPR 29:141; Dingwall, E. J. 1936. "Correspondence. The Mediumship of Mirabelli." JSPR 29:169; Dingwall, E. J. 1930. "An Amazing Case: The Mediumship of Carlos Mirabelli." *Psychic Research* 24(7):296; Driesch, H. 1930. "The Mediumship of Mirabelli." *Psychic Research* 24(11):486; Inglis, B. *Science and Parascience,* 1984, pp. 221–227, 297–298; Salter, H. 1927. "Notes on Periodicals." JSPR 24:125, 127.

**Miracle.** An event or experience in the physical world caused by a supernatural agency often as the result of prayer. Common sense bids us not to accept an event or experience as miraculous unless we have rejected the possibilities of a natural or paranormal explanation for it. When events or experiences have their analogues in psychical research, it is difficult to assume that they are miraculous.

Many strange phenomena occur in our world. One group belongs in the realm of the paranormal: apparitions, communicators, out-of-body experiences, levitation, extrasensory perception with all its subdivisions and psychokinesis. Many so-called "miracles" can be explained in these terms and so are not miracles. For the paranormal is not outside of nature but part of it. Many highly religious people have demonstrated extraordinary paranormal talents or produced paranormal physical phenomena which are not proof of sainthood or the miraculous.

In the second group are things that occur because of the action of God. The line between the two groups is often difficult to draw for both theologians and parapsychologists. **Renée Haynes,** a Catholic psychical researcher, has wrestled with the problem and has tried to draw a distinction. If new matter comes into existence, she says, the paranormal cannot account for the event, and it is a true miracle. Jesus Christ's multiplication of five loaves of bread and two fishes (Mark 6:36–44) would be an example. But what of materialization, which, if genuine, involves the formation of new matter but is a paranormal not a miraculous event? Another criterion suggested is the raising of the dead as Jesus raised Lazarus from the dead. Such an event would be a true miracle since nothing like it has ever occurred in the history of parapsychology. Other events that might possibly be considered miracles are the "dance of the sun" in Portugal, the blood phenomenon of Januarius, religious images, such as the "Lady of Guadalupe," and some cures medicine cannot explain. See also **Bosco, Saint John; Fatima, Marian Apparitions at; Food, Multiplication of; Images, Religious; Lourdes, Miracles of; Saints.**

BIBLIOGRAPHY: Haynes, R. *The Hidden Springs: Enquiry into Extra-Sensory Perception,* 1961.

**Miss.** An incorrect **Call.**

**Missie.** "The Psychic Dog of Denver." Unlike other cases of **Anpsi** in which animals respond to conscious or unconscious cuing by their masters, Missie (by barking to indicate yes, no, the letters of the alphabet, and numbers) gave information no one knew and accurately forecast future events. On October 15, 1964 she predicted that Lyndon Johnson would be elected president. She predicted other elections, the outcome of court cases, and on a radio show on New Year's Day 1966 she accurately predicted that the Dodgers would win the World Series that coming fall and that the score of the final game would be 6–0. On New Year's Eve 1966, again on the radio, she accurately forecast scores for events occurring each month for the next year—and she was 100 percent accurate.

Her owner, Mildred Probert, has notarized affidavits from a variety of people in many professions attesting to the accuracy of Missie's forecasts. She predicted that a woman who was due to be delivered by Cesarean section on October 6, 1965, of what the doctor assured her was a girl would in fact be delivered on September 28 and the child would be a boy. Missie was right! In February 1965 she correctly forecast the death of one C. Kincaid on January 9, 1967. But she apparently could not foresee her own end, for she choked to death on May 21, 1966 just three days before her eleventh birthday.

BIBLIOGRAPHY: Cerminara, G. 1973. "Missie The Psychic Dog of Denver." *Psychic* 5(1):37.

**Mitchell, Edgar D., 1930–.** American astronaut and the sixth man to walk on the moon. After being graduated from the Carnegie Institute of Technology in 1952, he became an aircraft pilot in the United States Navy and was assigned to the National Aeronautics and Space Administration's astronaut program at the Manned Spacecraft Center in Houston, Texas. He was pilot of the lunar module on the Apollo 14 flight in 1971.

Six years before the flight his interest in parapsychology had begun. "At that time," he said, "I was feeling a deep dissatisfaction with the ability of philosophy and theology . . . to give answers to my questions about the meaning of life and man's place in the universe" (Mitchell, 1974:32). He came to parapsychology for those answers.

For Mitchell the 1971 lunar expedition was a chance to conduct a test in telepathy in the far reaches of space for the first time. During rest periods in the flight to and from the moon, Mitchell attempted to act as agent and "send" symbols on ESP cards to four people on earth, including Olof Jonsson. The data, evaluated by Joseph B. Rhine, Karlis Osis and Mitchell himself after the conclusion of the test, showed that the number of misses was amazingly high and the number of hits amazingly low—a significant **Psi-Missing** effect (Mitchell, 1971).

After Mitchell saw the earth floating like a jewel in black space and perceived what few of us will ever perceive, "My sense of wonderment gradually turned into something close to anguish" (Mitchell, 1974:29). He realized how small our planet is and how we are destroying it and ourselves. It became his grand mission to promote "metanoia"—a new awakening in humanity, a transformation of consciousness that would bring about the unity of people with themselves and their environment. Awareness could be increased by religious experience, mystical experience, and psychic experience. Parapsychology fitted into this project because it "can be the key to unlock the missing experiential component with which to expand consciousness. . . . It can be the means of supporting the further evolution of the race and of developing the universal man of cosmic consciousness" (Mitchell, 1974:36). In short, Mitchell sees parapsychology as a weapon to be used in his fight to transform world consciousness. Many supporters of parapsychology, however, are afraid that Mitchell's use of their discipline "will confirm the widespread belief that parapsychology is some kind of religious cult rather than a scientific discipline" (Beloff, 1975:363).

In his desire to make the most of parapsychological experiences and phenomena, it seems that Mitchell has not been sufficiently critical. He concludes, for example, that "primary perception" in plants is "genuine" (Mitchell, 1974:40) even though there does not seem to be any empirical evidence to support this claim made by Cleve Backster.

After his retirement from the navy, Mitchell established the Institute for Noetic Sciences of which he is president.

Selected Writings: "Introduction: From Outer Space to Inner Space . . ." In E. D. Mitchell, ed., *Psychic Exploration: A Challenge for Science,* 1974, p.25; 1971. "An ESP Test from Apollo 14." JP 35.

BIBLIOGRAPHY: Beloff, J. 1975. "Reviews. Psychic Exploration: A Challenge for Science. By Edgar D. Mitchell and Others." JSPR 69:361.

**Mitchell, Thomas Walker, 1869–1944.** British physician. He was the first practicing medical doctor to be elected president of the Society for Psychical Research (in 1921). Mitchell was a psychologist and psychotherapist who often served as an interpreter of the work of each to psychical researchers on the one hand and psychoanalysts on the other.

He joined the SPR in 1906 and was made Honorary Secretary of the newly formed Medical Section in 1911. In 1912 he produced a Special Medical Part of the *Proceedings of the Society for Psychical Research* (26:257) that included a paper by Sigmund Freud and, in 1914, a Special Medical Supplement (PSPR 27:370). The SPR's medical section was dissolved at the end of World War I when the British Psychological Society created its own medical section.

Mitchell was impressed with Edmund Gurney's work on hypnosis but thought the most important problem in psychical research was the question of the mind from which a medium occasionally acquired information in some paranormal way. He was himself, however, most interested in the secondary personality or "control" which seemed to possess the medium's body during trance and in dissociated states and in multiple personality in general. He contributed numerous papers on these subjects to the *Journal* and *Proceedings* of the SPR.

Despite his considerable expertise and reputation, Mitchell preferred to remain a country doctor. He hated cities and "his capacity for getting lost in London unless placed firmly in a taxi" was a standing joke at the SPR.

Selected Writings: 1931. "Beneath the Threshold." Myers Memorial Lecture; 1922. "Presidential Address." PSPR 33:1; 1920. "The Doris Fischer Case of Multiple Personality." PSPR 31:30; 1912. "Some Types of Multiple Personality." PSPR 26:257; 1912. "A Study in Hysteria and Multiple Personality, with Report of a Case." PSPR 26:286.

BIBLIOGRAPHY: Salter, W. H. 1944. "Obituary. II T. W. Mitchell, M.D." PSPR 47:258; Wright, M. 1944. "Obituary. II T. W. Mitchell, M.D." PSPR 47:259.

**Miyauchi, Tsutomu, 1910–.** Japanese parapsychologist. He was the first experimenter in Japan, after the death of Tomokichi Fukurai, to investigate thoughtography. He carried on controlled experiments with Masuaki Kiyota and other psychics. He is also president of Nikon Nensha Kyokai (Japanese Association for Thoughtography).

**Mobius Society.** Founded in the United States in 1977 by S. A. Schwartz in order to conduct experiments in applied parapsychology. Beyond theoretical and experimental problems in the field is the additional problem of how to make practical and best use of psi abilities. One example of the work done by this organization to address this problem is the use of psi to obtain data for explorations in archaeology. Address: 7801 Wilshire Boulevard, Los Angeles, CA 90010.

**Monition.** The receipt of information not normally known from a voice within the individual. This voice seems wiser than the person in the ordinary conscious state and brings a message to warn, advise, restrain, or to take action. The message seems to originate in a deep strata within the individual and to rise up to consciousness. Examples are the well-known "voice of conscience," the monitory voices of Joan of Arc and the daemon of Socrates.

**Monroe, Robert A., 1915–.** American businessman. Famous in parapsychology for his books (1985, 1971) on his out-of-body experiences, Monroe's first paranormal experiences were apparent examples of precognition: a vision at the age of eight of himself seated before what he years later recognized as a color television set and, at the age of fifteen, his knowing, when there was no way that he could have known, that he would find $2 under an old plank lying near his home.

His OBE experiences began in 1958. They began with a cramp or constriction, followed by what he called a "ray" from the north and catalepsy. He next felt a vibratory sensation accompanied by the seeing of electrical sparks and the hearing of a soft high-pitched hiss. Three months from his first "symptoms," he had his first involuntary OBE during which his "fingers seemed to penetrate the rug. . . . [His] fingers went through the floor and there was the rough upper surface of the ceiling of the room below. . . . [His hand] went through the first floor ceiling . . . and touched water" (Monroe, 1971:26). Monroe then began to go out of body in his immediate local area.

During his OBEs he became aware of having a second body which has weight, is subject to gravity, can be visible, can feel and touch, is very plastic, and seems to be connected to the physical body by a cord. He thinks many, if not all people go out of body during sleep and that the familiar falling dreams we all have take place when the second body falls back into the physical body. Monroe found that sexual desire was very strong in the OBE state. He was also able to leave our physical plane and go into other dimensions, including the postmortem where he saw his doctor and his father and what seemed to be a parallel universe, similar to but different from ours. He also had very frightening experiences when he was attacked by entities and when he had difficulty in returning to his body. His later experiences include many levels of consciousness and experiences with various astral levels.

Mr. Monroe, who believes that anyone can consciously learn to have OBEs, has founded the Monroe Institute (RT. 1, Box 175, Faber, VA 22938) to do research into OBEs and related phenomena, including altered states of consciousness.

Selected Writings: *Far Journeys,* 1985; *Journeys out of the Body,* 1971.

**Montgomery, Ruth.** Contemporary American author and psychic. Originally a syndicated Washington columnist dealing with politics and world affairs, she was told in the early 1960s by medium Arthur Ford that she was able to do automatic writing (in her case automatic typing). Although skeptical, she tried and met her spirit guides, or as she calls them "mysterious penpals," "souls like ourselves who have had many previous lifetimes but are currently in the spirit plane . . . [and who] are always on tap for the daily sessions" (Montgomery, 1988:9). After his death in 1971 Ford joined her group of guides.

Eight books have resulted from her joint enterprise with her guides who choose the subjects—life after death, reincarnation, walk-ins, "who rejuvenate dying or unwanted bodies in order to help humankind," and New Age concepts. She modestly credits her first book (1967) with initiating the interest in New Age subjects, her second (1968) for the flood of books on reincarnation, and her book on what happens after death (dictated by the spirit of Arthur Ford) (1971) for "doctors and psychiatrists rush[ing] into print with books about the experiences of their patients who came back after clinical death . . ." Montogomery, 1988:9).

Two of her books (1979, 1982) deal with walk-ins who take over a physical body of someone "who desperately wishes to depart, or who . . . is unable to keep his/her body alive. . . . They are required to pledge that they will work for the common good . . ." (Montgomery, 1988:112). She names Moses, Christ, Abraham Lincoln, Mahatma Gandhi, Anwar Sadat, Dick Sutphen, and Jason Winters (the latters two exponents of the New Age) as walk-ins but no longer identifies walk-ins, perhaps because a few whom she has named "apparently retrogressed."

Her most recent book (1986) is an autobiography whose purpose is "to inspire others to set forth on their own voyage of discovery, to awaken the slumbering awareness within, and to realize that we are . . . individual sparks of the Creator."

Selected Writings: In *The New Age Catalogue,* 1988; *Threshold to Tomorrow,* 1982; *Strangers among Us,* 1979; *A World Beyond,* 1971; *Here and Hereafter,* 1968; *A Search for the Truth,* 1967; with Joanne Garland. *Ruth Montgomery: Herald of the New Age,* 1986.

**Moody, Raymond A., Jr., 1944–.** American physician, philosopher, and forensic psychiatrist. His book on the near-death experience, a best-seller in the United States and throughout the world (Moody, 1975), catapulted the NDE into the public consciousness. The impetus for the book was the discussion of the subject of survival of death in his courses on philosophy that prompted students to come to him with their near-death experiences.

For his book, he gathered case histories of and interviewed about fifty people who had been resuscitated after having been believed or declared dead by medical personnel. Their descriptions of their experiences made death seem a kind of voyage and were reminiscent of the accounts given in the *Tibetan Book of the Dead.* He found a striking similarity among the accounts and was able to pick out many recurring elements, including, for example, experiencers's becoming aware, after they thought they had separated from their physical bodies, "of other spiritual beings in their vicinity, beings who apparently were there to ease them through their transition into death" (Moody, 1975:55).

This research and finding of deceased people who came to help is similar to findings of other researchers, such as Kenneth Ring and Karlis Osis, and suggests to some people evidence of life after death. The title of his book *Life after Life* also implies this idea. Dr. Moody states, however, that he was "not trying to prove there is life after death" (Moody, 1975:5) and that "the reports of persons who have come close to death do not constitute proof or even evidence of that issue" (Moody, 1977:133). This cautious approach is justified since, as in the cases of deathbed visions and out-of-body-experiences, the question of whether to interpret the NDE naturalistically remains wide open.

Dr. Moody's work was purely anecdotal, was highly selective, and was not based on any statistical analyses. It failed to settle many issues, for example, whether the NDE is shaped by the reasons or physical conditions that brought a person to the brink of death or whether religious belief brings a religious quality to the experience. Nevertheless, Dr. Moody stimulated scientific studies by others and because of his work the NDE has emerged as a subject of clinical, psychological, and parapsychological significance.

Dr. Moody is now professor of psychology at West Georgia College.

Selected Writings: *Life after Life,* 1975; *Reflections on Life after Life,* 1977.

**Morphic Resonance.** A concept in plant physiologist Rupert Sheldrake's theory of formative causation. Morphic resonance is the means by which a morphogenetic field interacts with a crystallized structure that develops from a substance. Although Sheldrake did not set out to apply his theory to paranormal phenomena, it may account for some of them. A morphogenetic field, for example, might be a vehicle for the conveyance of information whether normally acquired or acquired by extrasensory perception.

**Morris, Robert Lyle, 1942–.** American parapsychologist. He is the first occupant of the Koestler Chair of Parapsychology at the University of Edinburgh, Scotland.

Fascinated by the unexplored aspects of both human and animal experience, Morris wrote his doctoral dissertation on avian social behavior. After receiving his Ph.D. from Duke University in 1969, he began his formal study of parapsychology at Joseph B. Rhine's Institute for Parapsychology by working with animals (Anpsi) and with people in PK experiments.

After two years of postdoctoral work at Duke University, Dr. Morris joined the staff of the Psychical Research Foundation where he explored internal states associated with extrasensory perception and out-of-body experiences. He then taught parapsychology and psychology courses at the University of California at Santa Barbara and at Irvine, at the same time looking into techniques that can mislead us into believing that something psychic is happening and into imagery techniques for improving psychokinesis. At the School of Computer and Information Science at Syracuse University he continued these investigations and developed computer programs for use in parapsychological research until he was named to the Chair of Parapsychology established under the will of Arthur Koestler.

Dr. Morris was president of the Parapsychological Association in 1974 and again in 1985, in which year he was also vice president of the Society for Scientific Exploration. He has been on the council of the American Association for the Advancement of Science and on the Board of Trustees of the American Society for Psychical Research for which he served as secretary from 1980–1982. In 1973 he received the Mid S. Weiss Award for the most distinguished contribution to the ASPR.

He is the author, with Hoyt Edge, John Palmer and Joseph Rush of *Foundations of Parapsychology,* has contributed to books, and has published widely in parapsychological and non-parapsychological journals. He was associate editor of *Research in Parapsychology* from 1970 through 1977 and again in 1981 and since 1983 has been associate editor of the *Journal of the Society for Scientific Exploration.*

Selected Writings: with Edge, H., Palmer, J. and Rush, J. *Foundations of Parapsychology,* 1986; 1982. "Assessing Experimental Support for True Precognition." JP 46:321; "A Survey of Methods and Issues in ESP Research." In S. Krippner, ed., *Advances in Parapsychological Research 2: Extrasensory Perception,* 1978; 1970. "Psi and Animal Behavior: A Survey." JASPR 64:242.

**Morselli, Enrico, 1852–1929.** Italian neurologist and eminent professor at the University of Genoa. In 1908, he brought out a two-volume work on twenty-eight sittings he had had with the medium **Eusapia Palladino** in Turin between 1901 and 1902 and in Genoa in 1906 and 1907. He was a convinced materialist and opponent of the reality of physical phenomena; nevertheless the conclusion he was forced to draw from his series of sittings was that the phenomena were not produced by trickery and could not be explained by any known physical laws.

Anticipating by many decades what became known as psychokinesis, he was also convinced, however, that the phenomena could be explained by forces connected with the human organism and were not necessarily related to spirit agencies as Spiritualists believed. Morselli also concluded that **"John King,"** Eusapia's spirit guide or control, was not a real entity.

His work created great interest at the time and made an important contribution to the Palladino case as an outstanding critique of the medium's séances and the manifestations at them.

Selected Writing: Morselli, E. *Psicología e 'Spiritismo'; Impressióni e nòte crítiche sui fenòmeni medianici di Eusapia Paladino,* 1908. 2 vols.

**Morton Ghost.** See **Ghost.**

**Moser, Fanny Hoppe, 1872–1953.** Swiss biologist. As the result of having been profoundly impressed by dramatic levitation phenomena in Berlin in 1914, she was drawn into psychical research. In her classic work on the subject (1935), she was one of the first to express the belief that there is an intimate connection between psi and altered states of consciousness. In addition, she was interested in haunts and in 1950 published twenty-seven of the most striking of the cases she had collected.

Selected Writings: *Okkultismus, Täuschungen und Tatsachen,* 1935; *Spuk–Irrglaube oder Wahrglaube?* 1950.

BIBLIOGRAPHY: Locher, T. "History of Psychical Reserach in Switzerland." *Proceedings of an International Conference Parapsychology Today: A Geographic View,* 1971, p. 131.

**Moses, c.1571–1451,B.C.** Hebrew leader, prophet, and lawgiver. After Egypt's pharoah commanded that all male Hebrew infants be killed, his mother placed him in a basket which she hid in the reeds on the banks of the Nile. He was found there by the pharoah's daughter and educated as a prince. But when he killed an Egyptian taskmaster for whipping a Hebrew slave unmercifully, Moses was forced to flee into exile. He became a shepherd and eventually guided the Israelites out of Egyptian captivity through the wilderness of Sinai into the Land of Canaan. While in Sinai, he was given the Ten Commanments, and a covenant was made between Israel and God.

According to the tradition of the **Kabbalah,** Moses was greater than all the prophets. Apparently he had the gift of prophesy or precognition to such an extent that, whereas the visions of other prophets were clouded, his were clear. He, unlike other prophets, was able to remain conscious and aware during his paranormal experiences. Moses was said to have believed in reincarnation and to have died in remorse because he had not fulfilled all the commandments and thus would have to reincarnate. In the Scriptures, the possibility is raised that he did reincarnate as John the Baptist.

Some interesting psychic phenomena are associated with Moses. There is the account in the Gospels to the effect that Moses and Elijah appeared on the Mount with Jesus Christ. In parapsychological terms, the dead Moses may have been perceived as an apparition. And while he appeared, Moses is supposed to have foretold correctly the death of Jesus and where it would occur, an instance of precognition. Strangely, some of the very people who believe that Moses returned from the dead and spoke deny that spirits of the dead can manifest and communicate with the living.

BIBLIOGRAPHY: Hoffman, E. *The Way of Splendor,* 1981, pp. 170, 201.

**Moses, William Stainton, 1839–1892.** Leading British spiritualist. An ordained Anglican clergyman, he became one of the leading Spiritualist mediums and teachers of his time. Physical phenomena in his presence began in 1872 shortly after he had sittings with several mediums, Daniel Dunglas Home among them. These physical phenomena over a period of time included raps, table-tilting, movement of large objects (or psychokinesis), direct voice, production of music without instruments, movement of matter through matter (apports), the production of psychic lights, scents (the so-called "odor of sanctity") and levitation. In 1873 mental mediumship began with the production of automatic writing in the tradition of Spiritualism. Moses advocated mediumship as the way to understanding God's will. His controls and communicators included the **Imperator Band,** purportedly made up of forty-nine spirits.

Moses was a founding member in 1882 of the Society for Psychical Research, but he resigned in 1886 because he disagreed with the attempt to use the scientific method in investigations of mediums, and of William Eglinton, in particular. Moses's physical phenomena came to an end about 1881 but he continued automatic writing for the rest of his life.

Perhaps relying too heavily on their belief that someone of Moses's integrity could not be guilty of fraud, those who tried to explain the physical phenomena purportedly produced by Moses agreed (with the exception of Frank Podmore) that, whatever their explanation, they were not fraudulently produced. As F. W. H. Myers wrote (1893), "That they were not produced fraudulently by Dr. Speer or other sitters I regard as proved . . . by moral considerations. . . . That Mr. Moses should have himself fraudulently produced them I regard as both morally and physically incredible."

Selected Writing: ("M. A. Oxon.") *Spirit Teachings,* 1949‹883.

BIBLIOGRAPHY: Gauld, A. *The Founders of Psychical Research,* 1968; Myers, F. W. H. 1893. "The Experiences of W. Stainton

Moses.—I." PSPR 9:245; Myers, F. W. H. 1892. "Supplement." PSPR 8:597.

**Moss, George.** Early twentieth century British spirit photographer. Originally a chauffeur, in May 1924, he showed his then employer some "extras," presumably spirits that he had obtained on photographic plates. His reputation as a medium became so widespread that in April 1925, he quit his job and became a member of the staff of the British College of Psychic Studies. Their magazine *Light* recommended him and endorsed him as genuine. In June 1925, Fred Barlow, a photographic expert, member of the Society for Psychical Research and former Honorary Secretary of the Society for the Study of Paranormal Pictures, examined the photographic plates on which "extras" appeared and found that in every case one edge of the plates had been roughened. Moss always insisted that photographic plates, prior to use, be left with him to be "magnetized." Plates not magnetized produced no results. When confronted with proof that during "magnetization" he was photographing the so-called "extra" that appeared when the plate was exposed again and then developed, he at first denied everything but later confessed and said that he had never produced genuine phenomena. He then resigned from the College of Psychic Studies.

J. Malcolm Bird, in the *Journal of the American Society for Psychical Research,* wrote a scathing attack on J. Hewat McKenzie, the president of the College of Psychic Studies, for his support of Moss and for his handling of the entire matter. See also **Spirit Photography.**

BIBLIOGRAPHY: Barlow, F. and Rampling-Rose, W. 1933. "Report of an Investigation into Spirit Photography." PSPR 41:121; Bird, J. M. 1926. "Observations on the Moss Case." JASPR 20:41; "The Cases of Mr. Moss and Mr. Munnings." 1926. JSPR 23:71.

**Moss, Thelma S.** Contemporary American medical psychologist (at the Neuropsychiatric Institute of the University of California) and parapsychologist.

Her acting career on the Broadway stage and in motion pictures and television having come to an end with the sudden death of her husband, Thelma Moss, after therapy with LSD, entered the field of psychology. The LSD experiences provided her with "glimpses of psychic phenomena. And they were shattering." She became active in many areas of parapsychology. She studied the relationship between creativity and psi and found that, in ESP experiments with targets consisting of slides, the scores of artists were significantly higher than nonartists (Moss, 1969).

Dr. Moss also found that emotional stimuli play an important role in eliciting psi. In one experiment a sender was looking at slides showing John F. Kennedy's assassination while listening to a funeral dirge; the percipient reported feelings of sadness over something tragic such as the funeral of a well-known figure (Moss and Gengerelli, 1967).

Together with Gertrude R. Schmeidler, she made a controlled investigation of a haunt in Los Angeles. Their methodology was to use psychics who toured the house independently and recorded their impression of the resident ghosts. When these descriptions were compared to those given by witnesses, the reports of three of the psychics showed a significant correspondence to the witnesses's statements and suggested something paranormal: either that there was a genuine haunting or that the psychics had gotten their information by ESP from the witnesses (Moss and Schmeidler, 1968).

Through her work, Thelma Moss has contributed to research advances in parapsychology.

Selected Writings: 1969. "ESP Effects in 'Artists' Contrasted with Non-Artists." JP 33:57; and Schmeidler, G. R. 1968. "Quantitative Investigation of a 'Haunted House' with Sensitives and a Control Group." JASPR 62:399; and Gengerelli, J. 1967. "Telepathy and Emotional Stimuli: A Controlled Experiment." *Journal of Abnormal Psychology* 72:341.

BIBLIOGRAPHY: "Interview: Thelma S. Moss." 1970. *Psychic* 2(1):4.

**Mother Ann (Ann Lee), 1736–1784.** English Shaking Quaker, the leader of the **Shakers** and founder of their basic doctrine of celibacy. She was an illiterate and uneducated blacksmith's daughter. She was deeply religious and seems, from an early age, to have formed an obsessive hatred of sexual intercourse whether within or outside wedlock. But she was forced by her father to marry another blacksmith who saw to it that the marriage was consummated again and again with his unwilling wife. Four children were born to Ann Lee. When each child died within a year of its birth, the mother saw their deaths as evidence of the divine retribution meted out for lust and the iniquity between the sexes.

At the age of 23 she became a member of the United Society of True Believers in Christ's Second Appearing and called the first day that she received the Gospel "my birthday." She began to hold meetings of the Believers. They worshipped by a sort of dancing during which their heads would move from side to side, their arms would be extended in front of and behind their bodies, and they would twitch and jerk in odd and apparently uncontrolled ways. In this state, the worshippers, including Ann Lee, went into trance during which they had visions, made prophecies, and may have had psychic experiences.

Following one especially noisy and excited session of worship, Ann Lee was arrested on a charge of disturbing the peace and of breaking the Sabbath. She was placed in a tiny cell and given no food. When her cell door was opened by the jailers after two weeks, instead of a corpse, they found a strong, healthy woman which convinced everyone that she was indeed the miraculous instrument of God. In reality, a young boy had been secretly providing the prisoner with milk and wine. While Ann Lee was in her cell Jesus appeared to her and made her understand clearly that sexual lust was the root of all human depravity and that the only way to the resurrection of the soul and spiritual life was celibacy. Perhaps this vision was a delusion or hallucination, but she did demonstrate a considerable amount of psychic ability all her life, being able, for instance, to know by telepathy the sins of people before they confessed. So it is possible that the revelation in the cell was genuinely paranormal. The experience with its divine message produced the basic tenet of the Shakers, brought Ann Lee the reputation as the mother of everything spiritual, and earned her the title of "Mother Ann."

Her persecution still continued. She was accused of blasphemy, the punishment for which would have been a hot poker run through her tongue. Summoned before four Anglican clergymen, "Mother Ann amazed and disarmed them by "speaking in tongues." Although this **Gift of Tongues** is well-known in Christianity, "These clergymen were great linguists, and they testified that she had spoken in seventy-two different tongues" (Evans, 1859). The case—allowing for the exaggeration in the number of languages—may therefore be an actual case of **Xenoglossy.**

"Mother Ann" had a vision of America: "I saw a large tree, every leaf of which shone with such brightness as made it appear like a burning torch." The tree symbolized the Shaker movement to be planted in America. She led the small band of Shakers out of England and, in 1774, brought it to the colonies in America. The Shakers believe that God is both male and female. "Mother Ann" died recognized by them as the female part of God's dual nature just as Jesus represented God's masculine part.

BIBLIOGRAPHY: Evans, F. W. *Ann Lee, Shakers and Shakerism, a Compendium of the Origin, History, Rules and Regulations, Government and Doctrines of the United Society of Believers in Christ's Second Appearing,* 1859; Pierson, J. 1938. "Psychic Manifestations Among the Shakers—Part 1." JASPR 32: 301.

**Motor Automatism.** See **Automatism.**

**Motoyama, Hiroshi, 1925–.** Japanese director of Kokusai Shukyo Cho-Shinri Gakkai (International Institute for Religion and Parapsychology). He has devoted himself to the study of the relationship between mind and body and has conducted tests in his laboratory with psychics, including Masuaki Kiyota, whom he studied for physiological changes during tests of psychokinesis.

Motoyama carried on successful experiments to show that psychokinesis can be used by one person to influence the galvanic skin responses and respiration of another person although the two are separated by a lead-shielded room. He also has examined unorthodox healers from the point of view of *ki* energy or oriental medicine and thinks that his instrumentation has picked up "energy from an awakened chakra [a center of the subtle or astral body] which [he] believe[s] to be the origin of paranormal phenomena" (quoted in Bartlett, 1981:202).

Selected Writings: Motoyama, H. *Psi to Ki no Kankei* (The Correlation Between Psi Energy and Ki), 1987; 1977. "Physiological Measurements and New Instrumentation." In G. W. Meek, ed., *Healers and the Healing Process,* 1977.

BIBLIOGRAPHY: Bartlett, L. *Psi Trek, 1981.*

**Mozart, Wolfgang Amadeus, 1756–1791.** Austrian composer. Joseph Haydn called him "the greatest composer I know." He is usually considered the greatest composer who ever lived. Mozart produced over 600 incomparable compositions. He is venerated as a genius by generations of music lovers. His works include masses, dances, symphonies, concerti for piano and orchestra, for violin and orchestra, and operas. He enjoyed great triumphs and material success for a time, but he died impoverished and ingloriously with no one to mourn him or attend his burial except the man who dug his unmarked grave.

A few months before Mozart's death, a mysterious man requested and paid in advance for the composition of a requiem. Mozart, whose health was failing, saw in the stranger a supernatural messenger and composed the requiem with all his genius to mark his own death. He died before he could complete it. The episode was not a paranormal foretelling of death, however, because the mysterious visitor was merely an agent of a nobleman who paid for musical pieces and performed them as his own.

Mozart is, however, a **Noted Witness** for the **Creative Process,** another creative individual who attributed his achievements to a source beyond his understanding and conscious control. In a letter to a friend, Mozart wrote: "When I am, as it were, completely myself, entirely alone, and of good cheer—say, travelling in a carriage, or walking after a good meal, or during the night when I cannot sleep; it is on such occasions that my ideas flow best and most abundantly. *Whence* and *how* they come, I know not; nor can I force them. Those ideas that please me I retain in memory, and am accustomed, as I have been told, to hum them to myself. . . . All this fires my soul, and provided I am not disturbed, my subject enlarges itself, becomes methodized and defined, and the whole, though it be long, stands almost complete and finished in my mind, so that I can survey it, like a fine picture or a beautiful statue, at a glance."

Mozart was a child prodigy. At four years of age, he was playing the clavier (a predecessor of the piano), at five composing minuets and other pieces and, at seven, performing on the harpsichord and playing violin concerti while he read music at sight. Many think he is a noted witness for reincarnation because they believe his musical genius must have carried over from a previous life. But it must be noted that his father, Leopold Mozart, was a composer and violinist who probably contributed heavily to his son's extraordinary talents.

BIBLIOGRAPHY: Ghiselin, B. *The Creative Process,* 1952, pp. 44–45.

**Muir, John, 1838–1914.** Scottish-born American naturalist and geologist. He was the discoverer of the Muir glacier in Alaska and his work for the cause of forest conservation contributed to the creation of Yosemite and Sequoia national parks in 1890.

Muir is a **Noted Witness** for monition or telepathy. In 1869, he had been camping in the mountains in the Yosemite Valley when, as he wrote in a letter dated in August of that year, "suddenly I was seized with the idea of going down into the valley to find Professor Butler. . . . I felt that I should be resisting the spirit if I did not go. . . . I lay in wait for the Prof. at a place near the Nevada rapids, on a trail I knew he must take. Towards evening he came to light among the rocks. . . . Then I sprang in front of him and asked if he did not know me." Butler had been on the faculty of the University of Wisconsin where Muir was educated and had been one of Muir's teachers.

In a note added to Muir's letter, Butler said, "When the feeling above described arose in Muir that he might reach me, his old teacher . . . the word telepathy—*far feeling*—had not been coined . . . but for this appearing 'as an angel dropped down from the clouds,' I must have been lost in the darkness then coming on. . .".

BIBLIOGRAPHY: Prince, W. F. *Noted Witnesses for Psychic Occurrences,* 1963, p. 37–38.

**Muldoon, Sylvan Joseph, 1903–1971.** American pioneer investigator of astral projection. His first astral projection (out-of-body experience) occurred when he was twelve years old after a visit to a Spiritualist camp. As a sickly boy who spent much of his time in bed, he had hundreds of out-of-body experiences that he learned to control and to induce at will. In 1927 he read some books by Hereward Carrington. Their ensuing correspondence resulted in his writing three now classic books on astral projection, two of them in collaboration with Carrington.

Carrington and Muldoon claimed that all psychical experiences, including telepathy, clairvoyance, psychokinesis, hauntings, psychic healing, and survival, can be explained on the hypothesis that we all have two bodies: the physical body and the astral body. They also stressed the importance of strong sexual feelings in astral projection.

Muldoon's experiences led him to conclude (1935) that "had a book on immortality never been written, had a lecture on 'survival' never been uttered, had I never witnessed a seance or visited a medium; in fact, had no one else in the world ever suspected 'life after death,' I should still believe implicity that I am immortal—for I have experienced the projection of the astral body."

Selected Writings: *The Case for Astral Projection,* 1935; and Carrington, H. *The Projection of the Astral Body,* 1970; and Carrington, H. *The Phenomena of Astral Projection,* 1970.

BIBLIOGRAPHY: Schwartz, E. K. 1952. "The Phenomena of Astral Projection." JASPR 46:161.

**Muller, Karl E., 1893–1969.** American-born linguist and parapsychologist. His interest in psychical research started when, as a child, he lived with his great-grandmother in Switzerland and took part in her Spiritualist séances. He remained in Switzerland and, in adulthood, conducted experiments with mediums whom he developed, observed various kinds of physical phenomena, took infrared photos of materializations and manifestations of psychokinesis. Reincarnation was his principal interest. He supplied investigators with data and himself wrote a book on the subject.

Selected Writing: *Reincarnation Based on Facts,* 1970.

BIBLIOGRAPHY: Locher, T. "History of Psychical Research in Switzerland". *Proceedings of an International Conference Parapsychology Today: A Geographical View,* 1971, p. 131.

**Mumler, Wiliam, ?–1884.** American jewelry engraver who became the first "spirit photographer" in the history of Spiritualism. Beginning operations in Boston in 1862, he produced the first photographs showing the pictures of deceased people together with the images of the living people who had been posing before the camera. These "extras" were acclaimed by Spiritualists as proof of life after death.

A year later, however, Mumler was charged with fraud when an "extra" turned out to be very much alive. Mumler fled Boston and into temporary obscurity. He resurfaced in another photographic studio in New York City in 1869, where more marvellous spirit photographs were taken and again delighted Spiritualists. Within a few months, however, Mumler was in criminal court charged with having swindled people with his spirit photographs. But the case against him was not strong enough and he was acquitted, the judge saying: "That, however he might believe that trick and deception had been practised by the prisoner, yet . . . he was compelled to decide that . . . the prosecution had failed to prove the case" (Sidgwick, 1891:270). Of course, the acquittal did not absolve Mumler of the previous fraud in Boston.

Whether or not he was an outright fraud, Mumler was a trail-blazer. Although the first spirit photographer, he was not the last.

BIBLIOGRAPHY: Sidgwick, E. 1891. "On Spirit Photography: A Reply to Mr. A. R. Wallace." PSPR 7:268.

**Mundle, Clement Williams Kennedy, 1916–1989.** British philosopher. His interest in parapsychology having been aroused by C. D. Broad's *Mind and its Place in Nature* and Joseph B. Rhine's *Extra-Sensory Perception,* Prof. Mundle joined the Society for Psychical Research in 1949. His first published article on the subject appeared in the *Journal* of that society in 1950 and dealt with the problem of distinguishing experimentally between cases of psychokinesis and cases of precognition.

In the 1960s he wrote a lengthy article entitled "ESP Phenomena, Their Philosophical Implications" for *The Encyclopedia of Philosophy* and, in 1965, a paper in which he examined the evidence for telepathy and clairvoyance. He concluded that "if all ESP were reducible to telepathy . . . we already have several alternative theories . . . which render the facts more or less intelligible. If clairvoyance is an irreducible phenomenon, as it seems to be, the theoretical problems are *very* much more formidable" (p. 229). In his Presidential Address (Prof. Mundle was president of the SPR from 1971–1974) he said that "psychical research originated as a theory in search of facts" and concludes that "we should not talk as if 'ESP' is the name of a positive and explanatory hypothesis. . . . [A]ll that psychical research has established is the occurrence of various phenomena which cannot yet be understood" (1973:1, 20). His last written contribution dealt with ESP in animals (Anpsi) (1976).

Prof. Mundle was educated at the University of St. Andrews and at Oxford University, from both of which he was graduated with highest honors. He served six years in the RAF during World War II. From 1947 to 1955 he was head of the Department of Philosophy at the University of Dundee and from 1955 to 1976 was professor and head of the Department of Philosophy at the University of Bangor, North Wales.

Selected Writings: "On the 'Psychic' Powers of Non-Human Animals." In S. C. Thakur, ed., *Philosophy and Psychical Research,* 1976; 1973. "Strange Facts in Search of a Theory." PSPR 56:1; 1965. "The Explanation of ESP." *International Journal of Parapsychology* 7(3):221; 1950. "The Experimental Evidence for PK and Precognition." PSPR 49:61.

**Munnings, Frederick Tansley, "Mr. Gaulton", ? c.1928.** British trumpet medium. Brought first to the notice of the public by the Spiritualist publication *Light,* Munnings at one of his sittings produced a full-form materialization that reportedly shook hands with some of the sitters. Although opinions were violently divided about the genuineness of his phenomena, many Spiritualists, including Sir Arthur Conan Doyle, maintained that he was "a very strong physical medium." In March 1926, when a light went on during a séance, Munnings was caught cheating. Conan Doyle then joined others in writing a letter published in the March 13, 1926, issue of *Light,* in which they warned the public about Munnings but still stated that at times his "psychic result has been beyond suspicion."

BIBLIOGRAPHY: "The Cases of Mr. Moss and Mr. Munnings." 1926. JSPR 23:71.

**Münsterberg, Hugo, 1863–1916.** German-born psychologist concerned with the practical application of psychology to business, law, sociology, teaching, and other areas. William James admired him and invited him from Germany to teach at Harvard University in 1892. In 1897, Münsterberg held the chair of psychology there.

His application of psychology to psychical research took the form of critical attacks published in newspapers and magazines (Münsterberg, 1899). His critiques, however, were described by the philosopher Ferdinand C. Schiller as a mass "of misrepresentations and misconceptions" emerging from a "shelter of ancient prejudices" (Schiller, 1899).

Perhaps such a prejudice was behind Münsterberg's refusal to accept James's invitation to sit with medium Leonora E. Piper. Nevertheless, Münsterberg was interested enough in psychical research to attack it, particularly messages through Mrs. Piper purportedly from the dead Richard Hodgson. He declared that the communications were characteristic, not of Hodgson, but of the medium—a strange criticism since he knew very little about Hodgson and nothing at all about Mrs. Piper with whom he had never sat. James H. Hyslop, who knew them both, rejected Münsterberg's opinion. Indeed, Hyslop went further and described the psychologist's attack as "the kind of evasion, prevarication and misrepresentation which this subject has to meet at the hands of persons who cannot keep company with the best men in Europe and America" (Hyslop, 1908).

Nevertheless, Schiller rather than Hyslop was most likely right about Münsterberg's prejudices. The fear of having his fundamental views and beliefs shaken could easily have made it impossible for him to imagine the possibility of a spirit of a dead person communicating and could have led to his avoidance of séances and his critiques of spirit messages. If this is the case, Münsterberg throws much light on the psychology of some psychologists.

Selected Writing: 1899. 1908. "Professor Muensterberg and Dr. Hodgson." JASPR 2:23. "Psychology and Mysticism." *Atlantic Monthly.*

BIBLIOGRAPHY: Berger, A. S. *Lives and Letters in American Parapsychology,* 1988; Schiller, F. C. S. 1899. "Psychology and Psychical Research. A Reply to Professor Munsterberg." PSPR 14:348.

**Murphy, Gardner, 1895–1979.** American psychologist. From the start, everything converged to force Murphy to lead, by his own admission, a "double life." One life began when he was sixteen and read William Barrett's book on psychical research. (Interestingly, his grandfather had been the attorney for the famous medium Leonora

Piper.) In addition, his father and mother were deeply interested in psychical research and were admirers of William James who himself had been drawn to the field. He even lectured at Concord where Murphy lived. In 1916, at Graduate School at Harvard, Murphy was introduced to much research material by Leonard Troland and, when he was overseas with the American Expeditionary Forces in 1917, joined the Society for Psychical Research.

Murphy began to read long and hard about spontaneous cases, the cross-correspondences and mediums. The material was so stimulating that he asked **William McDougall** about employment by the Society for Psychical Research. But the British psychologist offered him instead the **Hodgson Memorial Fund** at Harvard to conduct psychical research. A failure of health forced him to abandon the fund for some years. But Murphy returned to psychical research and parapsychology. He cooperated with Joseph B. Rhine, defended parapsychology with all his vigor when it was attacked in 1938 at an American Psychological Association Symposium on ESP, and became a co-editor of the *Journal of Parapsychology* which he opened up as a channel of communication with psychologists.

When the Boston Society for Psychic Research was formed as a result of disenchantment with the policies of the American Society for Psychical Research, Murphy was on its council and when the ASPR was reorganized in 1941, he played a leading role.

Murphy was ASPR president for twenty years during which time he recruited talented and productive people, stimulated research ideas and helped others such as Gertrude Schmeidler in their work. For many people, Murphey *was* the American Society for Psychical Research. In addition, he published over 100 papers in the *Journal* of the ASPR, in the *Journal of Parapsychology* and in other periodicals and books. He also authored and co-authored books dealing with parapsychology.

It is especially interesting that, although Murphy himself never had any paranormal experiences and was a failure as an experimenter (anything that was accomplished experimentally having been the result of his research ideas and support of other experimenters), he was still willing to dedicate his zeal and energies to parapsychology. The flame that had been ignited when he was sixteen simply could not be extinguished.

While Murphy kept a firm toehold in parapsychology, he carried on another life, his distinguished career in psychology. He had decided to major in this field at Yale because parapsychology and his religious convictions at the time motivated him to try to prove that mind or personality transcend mechanistic concepts and are not dependent on the brain. He became an instructor in psychology at Columbia, authored or co-authored books which gave psychology a "new look," and received many honors including the Butler Medal from Columbia. He served as consultant to UNESCO and was a member of the Ministry of Education of the Indian government. He became chairman of the Psychology Department at City College of New York where anonymous balloting of class after class of graduating seniors elected him "best-liked teacher." Later, Murphy was director of the Menninger Foundation.

The seminal papers and books Murphy generated both in parapsychology and psychology continue to be read.

Selected Writings: and R. O. Ballou, eds., *William James on Psychical Research,* 1961; with L. A. Dale. *The Challenge of Psychical Research,* 1961; 1953. "The Importance of Spontaneous Cases." JASPR 47:89; *Personality: A Biosocial Approach to Origins and Structure,* 1947; 1945. "An Outline of Survival Evidence." JASPR 39:2; 1945. "Difficulties Confronting the Survival Hypothesis." JASPR 39:67; 1945. "Field Theory and Survival." JASPR 39:181; 1943. "Psychical Phenomena and Human Needs." JASPR 37:163; *Historical Introduction to Modern Psychology,* 1929.

BIBLIOGRAPHY: Berger, A. S. *Lives and Letters in American Parapsychology,* 1988.

**Murphy, Michael, 1930–.** American cofounder of the Esalen Institute in California. His interest in mysticism and Eastern philosophy began at Stanford University and led to his taking up the study of yoga and meditation and to his eventually spending a year and a half at the Sri Aurobindo Ashram in Pondicherry, India. He thinks that psychic phenomena are "Lanterns along the way of our evolutionary development, harbingers of our emerging self mastery. . . . [I]f we undertake a sustained yoga or contemplative discipline there is a natural progression in the ways these powers unfold . . ." (Interview, 1976:18). He finds "analogies between yoga, sport and physical training . . . [and that the] phenomena of bodily luminosity, levitation and psychokinesis, the changing of body shape and size . . . all the varieties of stigmata, demonstrate the latency of spirit within matter" (Interview, 1976:20,21).

His interest in parapsychology led him in 1971 to visit the Soviet Union and to conduct an experiment in telepathy between the US and a Soviet telepathist in Moscow. His first novel (1972) contributed to his interest in the altered states of consciousness and peak experiences of athletes and culminated in his collaboration with **Rhea A. White** (1978) in their book dealing with psychic events in sports, including extrasensory perception and out-of-body experiences.

In 1975 *Time* magazine named Murphy one of the "200 Leaders of the Future."

Selected Writings: *Golf in the Kingdom,* 1972; and R. A. White. *The Psychic Side of Sports,* 1978.

BIBLIOGRAPHY: Bolen, J., ed., 1976. "Interview: Michael Murphy." *Psychic* 7(3):16.

**Murray, (George) Gilbert (Aime), 1866–1957.** Eminent Anglo-Australian classical scholar. A world-renowned Greek scholar (he was named to the Chair of Greek at Glasgow University at the age of twenty-three and in 1908 was appointed regius professor of Greek at Oxford University) and noted internationalist, he was caricatured by his friend George Bernard Shaw in the latter's play *Major Barbara.*

**Margaret de G. Verrall** was a close friend with whom he shared an interest in psychical research. He was reputed to have remarkable telepathic gifts, yet, as Fraser Nicol (1972) and Eric J. Dingwall point out, he was never under any kind of control during the experiments that were reported in the *Journal* and the *Proceedings of the Society for Psychical Research.* Because of the SPR's double standard (ladies and gentlemen did not cheat—"peasants" did) it was assumed that Murray could not or would not cheat.

He was president of the SPR in 1915 and 1916 and again in 1952. In his second Presidential Address he stated that, although he was uneasy at the idea of precognition and telekinesis and believed that most wonders—"spirit photographs, haunted houses, extensions of the human body and the great majority of poltergeists"—were either misreported, misobserved, or fraudulent, he knew from his own experience that telepathy did take place and operates best where language fails. He thought that telepathy was a prelinguistic or supralinguistic skill and was linked to genius.

Outside of psychical research he wrote many brilliant books on Greek literature and religion, translated Greek dramas, and wrote two original plays. "To hear Murray read aloud and interpret a passage of Greek poetry brought to successive generations of his students the intoxicating illusion of direct contact with the past . . ." (Salter, 1957). He worked indefatigably for the League of Nations and later for the United Nations. He was a dedicated humanitarian, yet he had "an irrepressible sense of the ridiculous." Upon his death his ashes were placed in Westminster Abbey.

Selected Writings: 1952. "Presidential Address." PSPR 49:155; 1916. "Presidental Address." PSPR 29:46.

BIBLIOGRAPHY: Dodds, E. R. and Salter, H. de G. 1957. "Obituary. Gilbert Murray, O. M." JSPR 39:150; Nicol, F. 1972. "The Founders of the S.P.R." PSPR 55:341,352; Sidgwick, E. M. 1924. "Report on Further Experiments in Thought-Transference Carried Out by Professor Gilbert Murray, LL.D., Litt.D." PSPR 34:212; Verrall, M. de G. 1916. "Report on a Series of Experiments in 'Guessing.'" PSPR 29:64.

**Muscle-Reading.** Sometimes mistaken for telepathy or mind-reading. In typical muscle-reading performances blindfolded performers name numbers or find or tell where to find objects whose location is unknown to them but is known to the members of the audience. It is the unconscious movements of a member of the audience whose hands they hold that guide the performers in giving dates of coins, denominations of bills, combinations of safes, location of hidden objects, etc. See also **Bishop, Washington Irving.**

**Mushroom, Sacred.** A mushroom grown in Oaxaca, Mexico, (botanical designation *Psilocybe Mexicana*) from which the psychedelic drug psilocybine is extracted. These mushrooms are eaten by the natives as an aid to divination and psychic powers and in sacred rituals by *curanderos* (shamans and healers) to effect cures. This use of the drug does not differ markedly from the use of Mexican Indians of peyote and ololiuqui, the ingestion by the Assyrians of poppy, mandrake and hemlock, the chewing of laurel leaves by the Delphic oracle, and the ingestion by the Vedas of soma (a kind of milkweed) for the same purposes. See also **Drugs, Magical; Sabina, Maria Magdelena.**

**Mushroom Cult.** Among the Mexican Indians, the people of eastern Siberia, and some tribes in northeastern New Guinea, the use of hallucinogenic mushrooms to produce paranormal abilities and experiences. See also **Drugs, Magical; Mushroom, Sacred.**

**Music.** Has been used in the classroom with apparent success in increasing the ability to learn. In parapsychology, it has been used to try to release psi abilities. The effect of music on the emergence of these abilities, however, seems negligible since in tests of extrasensory perception in which music was played for subjects no significant scores have been produced (Eilbert and Schmeidler, 1950).

BIBLIOGRAPHY: Eilbert, L. and Schmeidler, G. 1950. "A Study of Certain Psychological Factors in Relation to ESP Performance." JP 14:53.

**Myers, Arthur Thomas, 1851–1894.** British medical doctor. The youngest brother of F. W. H. Myers, he too was a classical scholar from Trinity College, Cambridge, and a founding member of the Society for Psychical Research. He was particularly interested in that work of the SPR that had relevance to his profession (i.e., the action of the mind on the body, popularly called "faith healing," and hypnosis). After Edmund Gurney's death he directed the SPR's study and research on hypnotism and built up the best library on that subject in the country. His medical practice, and later his incurable illness, prevented his being very active in the work of the SPR, but he was involved in many of its projects, including the **Census of Hallucinations** which was published in the year of his death.

Trevor Hall in *The Strange Case of Edmund Gurney* (1964) has accused Myers of giving false testimony at the inquest after Gurney's death in order to make the latter's death appear to have been an accident rather than suicide.

Selected Writings: and Crookes, W., Horsley, V., Bull, W. C. 1885. "Report on an Alleged Physical Phenomenon." PSPR 3:460; and Myers. F. W. H. 1893. "Mind-Cure, Faith-Cure, and the Miracles of Lourdes." PSPR 9:160; and Sidgwick, H., Sidgwick, E. M., Johnson, A., Myers, F. W. H., and Podmore, F. 1894. "Report on the Census of Hallucinations." PSPR Research 10:25.

**Myers, Frederic William Henry, 1843–1901.** Prominent British psychical researcher. One of the founders of the **Society for Psychical Research** and so truly its architect that his death almost sounded its death knell. Like so many of the early researchers, he was a classical scholar who had studied at Trinity College, Cambridge. As a young child he was extremely religious and, having experienced "the first horror of a death without resurrection . . . ," was preoccupied with death and the afterlife. By 1869 he had lost his faith as had most of the outstanding Cambridge intellectuals of his period. In the 1870s he became interested in the physical phenomena of Spiritualism and was impressed with Stainton Moses.

Despite his later quite happy marriage, he loved for his entire life his cousin's wife, Annie Marshall, who committed suicide in 1876. Messages from her which he considered genuine came through Rosalie Thompson (and also through Leonora Piper) and convinced him of survival after death. Unfortunately, he died before he could write his report on Mrs. Thompson. His wife destroyed his notes and Alice Johnson removed the chapter he had written about Mrs. Thompson from his posthumous *Human Personality and Its Survival of Bodily Death.*

He sat with all the mediums, both physical and mental, of his time and was involved in every facet of psychical research. He coined the word **"Telepathy"** which he discussed both in his Foreword to *Phantasms of the Living,* co-authored with **Edmund Gurney** and **Frank Podmore,** and in other writings.

In 1889 Myers, his brother (A. T. Myers), Henry Sidgwick, Eleanor Sidgwick, Frank Podmore and Alice Johnson began work on the **Census of Hallucinations** which was published in 1894. Myers published often in the *Proceedings* of the SPR and on a great variety of subjects, including **Telekinesis** (a word he coined) and in one of his writings theorized that telepathy was a function of the right hemisphere of the brain.

Myers was a seminal thinker who greatly influenced William James and was one of the first to take Freud seriously. Myers was a pioneer in psychology as well as in parapsychology. His concept of the "subliminal self" preceded and presaged that of the "unconscious." He perceived that, below the threshold of consciousness, exists another hidden strata of our being in which is found material more precious than that repressed from consciousness. In that deeper region where the individual has no conscious control much of the creative process goes on. Dreams and visions mingle with information, ideas and images obtained by extrasensory perception which also operates beyond consciousness. Long before modern physics he conceived of the structure of the atom as a miniature solar system. In his great work, *Human Personality and its Survival of Bodily Death,* he linked psychic functioning with psychiatry and outlined the evidence for survival.

Myers left a message in a sealed envelope and hoped to prove his survival by communicating its contents after death. The test, unfortunately, has usually been considered a failure, and at the best the results were ambiguous. So sure was Myers of survival that he welcomed death. He was supposedly one of the chief communicators in the **Cross-Correspondences** cases. See also **Sealed Envelope Test.**

Selected Writings: *Human Personality and its Survival of Bodily Death,* 1903; 1891–1892. "On Alleged Movement of Objects, Without Contact, Occurring Not in the Presence of a Paid Medium." PSPR 7:383; 1885. "Automatic Writing." PSPR 3:1; and Sidgwick, H., Sidgwick, E. M., Johnson, A., Myers, A. T., and Podmore, F. 1894. "Report on the Census of Hallucinations." PSPR 10:25; and Lodge, O., Leaf, W., and James, W. 1890. "A Record of Observations of Certain Phenomena of Trance." PSPR 6:436; and Gurney, E., and Podmore, F. *Phantasms of the Living,* 1886.

BIBLIOGRAPHY: Gauld, A. *The Founders of Psychical Research,* 1968; Salter, W. H. 1958. "F. W. H. Myers's Posthumous Message." PSPR 52:1.

**Mystic.** Sometimes used disapprovingly or disdainfully of someone hopelessly romantic, illogical, or unscientific, it also means one who enters into that experience in which William James believed all personal religious experience has its root and center. Mystics may be Christians, Moslems, Buddhists, or Hindus. They may be Jews in search of the wisdom of the Kabbalah. Or they may be independent of any organized religion or philosophy. The mystical experience of the Roman Catholic saint is the same as that of any other seeker of the contemplative and divine.

Mysticism is not easy to define in a few words. Love, humility, and purity of heart no doubt are elements in it. The term probably derives from the Greek word *myein* meaning to initiate into secret rites. Mystics of both East and West try to connect with and obtain another vision of the things unseen behind the external world. In effect, they deny the world in order to find reality. They strive for loss of separateness, a dissolution of individuality in the timeless cosmos, and a oneness with the All or reality.

The poet Alfred Tennyson expressed this sense of loss of individuality in the eternal. James also found the mystical state of consciousness to have additional qualities that mark it off from other states: *ineffability*—the state defies expression; *insight*—it provides knowledge, illumination, revelation; *transiency*—the state lasts only a short time and then fades; *passivity*—while the state may be brought on by certain deliberate techniques or disciplines, the mystic feels taken over by a greater power.

Mystical states often have been criticized as neurotic or pathological disorders. Visions, revelations, and other experiences are downgraded as paranoid delusions, childlike dependence on parent-figures or perhaps just what happens when the internal plumbing is out of order. But the origin of the state is less important than its value and its fruits and is of great interest to psychical research. The very states of mystical consciousness that modify or transform mystics's lives and make many of them saints or founders of religions or religious societies have also produced a variety of striking physical phenomena and remarkable psychic gifts. Mystics are therefore also suitable subjects for research on the paranormal who should provide a direct and effective approach to its study.

Mystical experience and mediumistic experience are fundamentally different in one way. In the former, the ecstatic state is a means of communing with the All or God. In the latter, the trance is a means of conversing with the spirits of the dead. Yet in a very important respect mystical experiences and states of mind appear to bear a strong resemblance to psychic experiences and altered states of consciousness. The transcendental experiences reported by mystics seem to possess four characteristics: 1) there is a better way of gaining information than via the senses; 2) there is a basic connectedness among all things; 3) time is illusory; 4) evil is illusory. When **Lawrence LeShan** compared mystics' and psychics's attitudes regarding reality, he found them in complete accord concerning all these elements. This agreement and the recording of similar mystical and psychical experiences in every place and time is prima facie evidence that may suggest "an aspect of reality with which these persons came in contact" (Broad, 1953) and that cannot be ignored.

BIBLIOGRAPHY: Broad, C. D. *Religion, Philosophy and Psychical Research,* 1953, p.242; James, W. *The Varieties of Religious Experience,* 1958, pp.292–293; LeShan, L. *The Medium, the Mystic and the Physicist,* 1975.

**Mystical Experience.** See **Mystic.**

**Mysticism.** See **Mystic.**

**Naegli-Osjord, Hans, 1909–.** Swiss psychiatrist. President of the Schweizer Parapsychologische Gesellschaft (Swiss Parapsychology Society) from 1958, he remained in that post for twenty-two years. His interest in psychical research began in his youth with stories of paranormal phenomena and with a personal experience. He encountered a ghost in an old castle. His interests today include haunts, possession, and lecturing on parapsychological topics both at home and abroad. But of all, he considers his primary interest and most important work to be in the area of psychic healing in the Philippines to which he has travelled frequently to observe the medical and psychiatric aspects of the practices of healers there. Dr. Naegli-Osjord received first prize from the Schweizerische Vereinigung für Parapsychologie (Swiss Association for Parapsychology) which he helped found.

Selected Writing: *Possession and Exorcism,* 1988.

**Nash, Carroll Blue, 1914–.** American zoologist and parapsychologist. Now emeritus professor of biology at St. Joseph's University in Philadelphia, he became professor of biology there in 1948 and founded a Parapsychology Laboratory at the University in 1956. In 1940, a year after receiving his Ph.D. from the University of Maryland and now a member of the Biology Department at the University of Arizona, he developed, independently of J. B. and Louisa Rhine, the use of dice to test for psychokinesis. At American University in 1945 and at Washington College in 1947 he continued his PK work. At St. Joseph's College, now university, he taught the first parapsychology course for credit ever given in the United States and the first laboratory parapsychology course.

Dr. Nash was the first American recipient of the William McDougall Award for Distinguished Work in Parapsychology and was the first to conduct ESP tests on television and to provide experimental evidence that subjects may use ESP unconsciously to fulfill a need or desire.

In addition to research, Dr. Nash has developed theoretical concepts dealing with ESP and PK. His 122 articles on psi, 23 coauthored with **Catherine S. Nash,** his wife, published in the *Journal of the Society for Psychical Research,* the *Journal of the American Society for Psychical Research* and the *Journal of Parapsychology* deal with a variety of parapsychological subjects including PK and precognition. Dr. Nash is also the author of two books.

Dr. Nash has been president of the Parapsychological Association. As holder of that office he initiated steps leading to affiliation with the American Association for the Advancement of Science.

Selected Writings: *Parapsychology The Science of Psiology,* 1986; 1986. "Comparison of Subliminal and Extrasensory Perception." JSPR 52:435; 1984. "Test of Psychokinetic Control of Bacterial Mutation." JASPR 78:145;

1983. "An Extrasensory Observational Theory." JSPR 52:113; *Science of Psi: ESP and PK*, 1978.

BIBLIOGRAPHY: Berger, A. S. *Lives and Letters in American Parapsychology*, 1988.

**Nash, Catherine Stifler, 1919–.** American biologist and parapsychologist. She and her husband, **Carroll B. Nash,** both worked in the Biology Department at St. Joseph's College (now university) in Philadephia for forty-five years and shared identical interests in laboratory research, extrasensory perception and psychokinesis.

Dr. Nash says that her husband "initiated experimentation in parapsychology and I followed along. Early contact with J. B. Rhine during summers when we visited Carroll's family in Henderson, N. Car., kindled my interest but housework, teaching, advising, etc. limited the time I was able to devote to research" (letter to authors). She did find time, however, to co-author, with Carroll Nash, twenty-three papers on their joint experiments. These papers have been published in the *Journal of the American Society for Psychical Research,* the *Journal of Parapsychology* and the *International Journal of Parapsychology.* In addition, she has made presentations at conventions of the Parapsychological Association.

Catherine Nash is now professor emeritus of biology at St. Joseph's University and is listed in *American Men and Women of Science.*

Selected Writing: and Nash, C. B. 1962. "Negative Correlations Between the Scores of Subjects in Two Contemporaneous ESP Experiments." JASPR 56:80.

**National Laboratory of Psychical Research.** British organization conceived and founded in 1923 by **Harry Price.** Renting space from the London Spiritualist Alliance (of which Sir Arthur Conan Doyle, Price's friendly enemy, was president), he set up a workshop, laboratory, and séance room to provide the first sophisticated facility in the world where famous mediums and investigators could come together to conduct experiments. With its cameras, Bunsen and gas burners, special lighting, including ultraviolet light, dark room for photographic processes, glass-blowing apparatus, chemical balances, barographs and thermographs, dictaphones, note-taker's table, musical vibrations, microscopes, lathes and tools of all kinds, it was in reality a veritable trap for fraudulent mediums. The laboratory published a bulletin and had one of the great libraries of some 20,000 volumes on psychical research and related subjects. When the laboratory was discontinued in 1937, its equipment and library went to the University of London.

BIBLIOGRAPHY: Price, H. 1926. "Science in the Seance Room." JASPR 20:202.

**NDE.** See **Near Death Experience.**

**Near-Death Experience (NDE).** Also called "pseudo-death" experience. A phenomenon resembling the **Deathbed Visions** associated with dying people except that, in the case of near-death experiences, patients, although often declared clinically "dead," are revived. The elements that seem to recur generally but not universally in the NDE are: 1. hearing a buzzing or ringing noise; 2. moving through a dark void or tunnel; 3. having an **Out-of-Body Experience** during which the physical body is viewed from another point in space; 4. being, while at that point, the detached observer of events, people and objects in the vicinity of the body and seeing and hearing, sometimes in great detail, what is said and done; 5. encountering deceased relatives or friends apparently come to lead patients to a different dimension; 6. seeing a loving being of light; 7. going through a **Life Review** and evaluation of their lives; 8. coming to a border; 9. returning to the physical body and life. A striking effect in the common pattern is the vastly increased appreciation of life and of others and the radically decreased fear of death felt after the return.

Although the NDE lately has become tremendously popular with the general public and the focus of interest on the part of professionals throughout the world, psychical research has been studying its major paranormal elements for a century. For example, investigations have been conducted of many claimed out-of-body experiences and claims that during the out-of-body state others have seen the OBErs's apparitions. The pioneers of psychical research, such as **Sir William Barrett** and **James H. Hyslop,** also studied the deathbed visions that constitute the fifth element of the NDE.

Psychical researchers also have long investigated the question of survival after death which many people believe the NDE has proved. After **Kenneth Ring** concluded his study of the phenomenon, he found "a huge effect here—one of the strongest of the entire investigation" (Ring, 1980:169), namely, the experiencers's belief beyond doubt in a life after death.

If the NDE amounts to evidence of survival after death, it seems reasonable to expect that close relatives or friends who are deceased wil be there to greet us and to act as our guides. Nevertheless, it is not reasonable to regard the NDE as survival evidence unless other naturalistic causes for these experiences can be excluded. It is possible that all the NDEs can be explained on naturalistic grounds, that is, there may be good psychological, physiological, or pharmacological reasons for them. Religious beliefs, wishful thinking, or medications such as morphine may facilitate the experience. Disturbance of brain function and cerebral anoxia are known causes of hallucinations and may occur in nearly dying or dying patients before they sink into unconsciousness.

Nevertheless, the fact is that we still don't know what the NDE really means or how to explain it. "Those who argue that the near-death experience tells us what death is like have taken a jump into the unknown, for they have assumed that near-death experience is continued into death experience, and in this they may or may not be justified. But those who say that the near-death experience is an experience of this life are also taking a leap from known facts. They are claiming that the NDE . . . can be accounted for in terms of psychological or physiological processes, but they have not yet proven their case" (Blackmore, 1982/1983:152).

BIBLIOGRAPHY: Blackmore, S. J. *Beyond the Body,* 1982\1983; Ring, K. *Life At Death: A Scientific Investigation of the Near-Death Experience,* 1980; Moody, R. A., Jr. *Life After Life,* 1975.

**Nederlandse vereniging Voor Parapsychologie.** This Dutch Society for Parapsychology was created in 1960 as the result of a rift in the Studievereniging voor Psychical Research that caused dissatisfied parapsychologists to leave that organization and to form another. The aim of the Dutch Society for Parapsychology is the popularization of parapsychology and its primary activity consists of lectures to carry out a program of public education in parapsychology. Some limited research in the field is conducted. Its journal is *Spiegel der Parapsychologie* (Mirror of Parapsychology). Address: Laan van Meerdervoort 554,2563 BL's-Cravenhage, The Netherlands.

**Neihardt, John Gneisenau, 1881–1973.** American poet, authority on the history and customs of the Plains Indians, and psychical researcher. A professor (poet in residence) at the University of Missouri from 1947 to 1967, a Socialist, and Indian Rights activist—among his last public acts were his broadcasts in favor of the Indian Rights movement during the confrontation at Wounded Knee in 1973—he considered himself a "pragmatic mystic." By pragmatic mysticism Neihardt seems to have meant the attainment of truths about the nature of the universe through heightened awareness and then the application of these insights to the world in order to make it a better place.

Neihardt was a psychic. Indeed, it was for this reason that the Oglala Sioux tribe made him a member and a recipient of their sacred knowledge. He is best known in psychical research because of **Sorrat** (Society for Research on Rapport and Telekinesis). The purpose of the group was to investigate PK phenomena. Neihardt believed that everyone had ESP abilities and thought that group rapport would provide the proper conditions for "the conscious manipulation of matter by means of controlled mental effort alone . . ." (Richards, 1982:107). (This same idea was later used by Kenneth Batcheldor and by Iris Owen and her group in the Philip experiments.) Neihardt's experimenters began in 1961 at Neihardt's home, Skyrim Farm near Columbia, Missouri. Eventually, the technique was successful and an enormous variety of apparently paranormal physical effects—raps, levitation of objects, apports—occurred.

Neihardt's interest in psychical research stemmed from a vivid out-of-body experience at the age of eleven and continued all his life. His wife, Mona, whom he married in 1908, was an amateur mental medium. Neihardt studied other mediums as well, including Pearl Lenore Curran. He concluded that there was no way she could have known the things "Patience Worth" knew.

A small man (5′ 2″ tall) of powerful build, Neihardt's attractive personality won him friends and disciples (Sorrats) in all walks of life—politics, the arts, and entertainment. He appeared often on radio and television, his classes at the University of Missouri were always full and visitors came from far and near to speak to him.

BIBLIOGRAPHY: Richards, J. T. *SORRAT: A History of the Neihardt Psychokinesis Experiments, 1961–1981,* 1982.

**Nester, Marian L., 1910–.** Daughter of Mark W. Richardson, Marian Nester has been associated with the Parapsychology Foundation where she worked with Karlis Osis and with the American Society for Psychical Research where she was editor of its *Newsletter* and director of education.

**Neumann, Therese, 1898–1962.** German stigmatic *extraordinaire.* She also claimed to live without eating or drinking.

One of ten children of a devoutly Catholic tailor, Therese was born in the Bavarian village of Konnersreuth. In 1918, when she was twenty, after two hours of demanding work helping fight a fire, she felt pain in her back and was compelled to rest. A few days later she fell, hit her head, and over a period of months underwent a terrible series of ailments. By 1920, she was totally blind and paralyzed. In 1923, she believed she saw Saint Thérèse of Lisieux, the "Little Flower," and her blindness disappeared, but not her paralysis and other problems. From that time until her death, Therese supposedly took no food at all except some gruel and drank nothing except some drops of water at Holy Communion.

Therese's own personality kept disappearing in favor of another that spoke differently and addressed the parish priest and her confessor as "du," the familiar second person singular. Her case might have been one of alternating personality, like the "Doris Fischer" case investigated by Walter Franklin Prince, or of possession by an alien entity or deceased human being or, as the parish priest believed, of Jesus Christ using Therese as an earthly instrument for his voice.

During Lent in 1926, Therese went into what the priest called an "exalted repose" or trance during which she claimed to have had a vision of the agony of Christ in the Garden of Gethsemane. She experiences these trances and visions over a period of years from every Thursday at midnght to early Friday morning. When each weekly series of trances and visions began, Therese seemed to be experiencing them for the first time and had no recollection of the identical prior trances and visions. During these states Therese gave evidence, as have other mystics in states of ecstacy of the strongest paranormal powers. By telepathy Therese seemed to know the thoughts of people present. There were manifestations of xenoglossy as she spoke words in a strange and ancient tongue she did not know, had never learned and which was identified later as Aramaic. She spoke just as if she were possessed by someone who had lived during the time of the Passion.

But outside of psychical research, the stigmata made her a world-wide celebrity. Black scabs looking like nail heads appeared on the palms of her hands which showed raw, red wounds. A wound in her side flowed blood and stained her white robe. Her forehead bled from wounds resembling Christ's crown of thorns, her blood staining a headcloth she wore. Her eyes oozed with blood-colored fluid that streamed down her cheeks.

Another central feature of Therese's case was her fast. Her total abstinence from food and drink, exceeding even that of Catherine of Genoa, is a feat which, if true, would involve nothing short of a biological miracle. In 1932, the Catholic Church requested Therese to submit to a scientific investigation at a university clinic of her claim that she had neither eaten nor drunk for twenty-nine years. Her father opposed any investigation and insisted on conditions to which the Church could not agree. No investigation was ever conducted.

Why should a thirty-four year old woman have permitted her father's opposition to prevent an important investigation? And, after he died and all excuse for her not being investigated was removed, Therese still refused. As a result, the Church declined to sponsor her claim of fasting or even to acknowledge any of the other phenomena she produced.

From the perspective of psychical research, it is curious that a person like Therese Neumann who appeared to demonstrate impressive paranormal powers should never have been investigated by any psychical researcher. The case of Therese Neumann must therefore remain as much an enigma for psychical research as it is for religion and medicine.

BIBLIOGRAPHY: Thurston, H. *The Physical Phenomena of Mysticism,* 1952, p. 114.

**Newbold, William Romaine, 1865–1926.** American philosopher. Greatly interested in psychical research, he reviewed cases of apparent possession with a critical eye (Newbold, 1897). He also recorded cases in which the creative process seemed at work during sleep when dreamers were able to reason out solutions to problems (Newbold, 1896). He had twenty-six sittings with the medium Leonora E. Piper that suggested to him the actual presence of communicators from the beyond (Newbold, 1898).

Newbold told his close friend James H. Hyslop about Mrs. Piper. As a result, Hyslop became interested in psychical research (Newbold, 1920:497). Later, Hyslop told Newbold that his (Hyslop's) belief in spirit communications had made him an "outcast" among his fellow philosophers (Berger, 1988:45).

Newbold was a professor of philosophy at the University of Pennsylvania when he was appointed to the Advisory Council of the American Society for Psychical Research. Later he became advisor to Elwood Worcester upon the latter's forming the Boston Society for Psychic Research (Berger, 1988:65,93).

Selected Writings: 1920. "An Estimate." JASPR 14:493; 1898. "A Further Record of Observations of Certain Phenomena of Trance. Part II." PSPR 14:6; 1897. "Demon Possession and Allied Themes. By John L. Nevius, D.D." PSPR 13:602; 1896. "Subconscious Reasoning." PSPR 12:11.

BIBLIOGRAPHY: Berger, A.S. *Lives and Letters in American Parapsychology,* 1988.

**Newcomb, Simon, 1835–1909.** Canadian-born mathematician, astronomer, and founder of the American Astronomical Society. He calculated the movement of celestial bodies and formulated important astronomical tables. Newcomb was appointed head of the American Nautical Almanac Office in Washington and was in charge of the Astronomy Department at Johns Hopkins University.

In 1885, upon becoming president of the American Society for Psychical Research, Newcomb did all he could to discourage the investigation of telepathy which he thought was not a paranormal phenomenon. In his view, it was merely a bodily function incapable of transfer over any distance (Berger, 1988:9). In his Presidential Address to the ASPR, he compared efforts to investigate telepathy to efforts to find a new kind of gold. Both investigations would be foolish and futile (Newcomb, 1886). **James H. Hyslop** charged Newcomb with "being entirely ignorant of the evidence" (Hyslop, 1909:285). But ignorant or not, Newcomb was merely expressing a viewpoint that was and is the opinion of the scientific community.

The real question is why Newcomb was appointed to, and why he accepted, the post of head of a psychical research organization one of whose primary objects was the investigation of a phenomenon he made no secret of repudiating.

Selected Writing: 1886. "Address of the President." PASPR 1:84.

BIBLIOGRAPHY: Berger, A. S. *Lives and Letters in American Parapsychology,* 1988; Hyslop, J.H. 1909. "Professor Newcomb and Occultism." JASPR 5:255.

**New Frontiers Center.** American organization established in 1970 by **Walter Uphoff** to explore and disseminate data related to psychic phenomena, survival after death and unorthodox healing. It holds major seminars and publishes a newsletter. Address: Fellowship Farm, Rt. 1, Oregon, Wisconsin 53575.

**Newlove, Bobbie, 1922–1932.** British youth who was the purported communicator in a famous case in the annals of psychical research. After Bobbie's death from diphtheria, **C. Drayton Thomas** held eleven proxy sittings with the medium **Gladys Osborne Leonard.** In apparent communication with the deceased boy, she related facts about his possessions, friends, games, and places he knew. She also relayed information about pipes that discharged water into a pool where he had bathed, the polluted water leading to the condition that killed him.

Neither Thomas nor the medium knew anything about Bobbie's possessions, friends, games, and places familiar to him. No one knew that the pipes even existed or that there was any connection between them and Bobbie's fatal illness. That was established later, after the investigation. The case, recently subjected to critical analysis (Berger, 1988), has long been considered by Thomas and others as extremely strong evidence for survival after death.

BIBLIOGRAPHY: Berger, A. S. *Evidence of Life After Death: A Casebook for the Tough-Minded,* 1988; Thomas, C.D. 1935. "A Proxy Case Extending over Eleven Sittings with Mrs. Gladys Osborne Leonard." PSPR 43:435.

**Newman, Seraine Deene, 1942–.** American medium. The product of three generations of psychics in her family, she had her first out-of-body experience when she was six years of age. In 1973, she received an apparent communication from a deceased relative who said Mrs. Newman's brother had lost valuable securities the relative wanted her to have. When confronted with this information, her brother confessed that he had lost the stocks but that no one alive knew that he had done so. In 1983, Mrs. Newman was one of several mediums who participated in an experiment to investigate whether a young man who died in a traffic accident in 1978 had survived death and could communicate. The young man was chosen as a target of the experiment because he corresponded to the "ideal" communicator **Arthur S. Berger** (1987) had identified through previous research. In this cross-correspondences type of experiment, the communicator attempts to communicate fragmentary pieces of information to several mediums that is meaningless to them. When the fragments are assembled, however, the experimenters can tell whether they make up an integrated picture that corresponds to a plan. Mrs. Newman's mediumship together with that of **Donald D. G. Galloway** helped produce results suggestive of the survival of and communication by the young man (Berger, 1987).

BIBLIOGRAPHY: Berger, A. S. *Aristocracy of the Dead,* 1987.

**Newspaper Test.** An apparent effort by a deceased communicator to supply evidence of survival after death by forecasting an item that will appear the next day on a specified page and column of a specified newspaper. A typical test consists of referring to names in the item that can be linked with the communicator's name or to names known to the sitter. For example, C. Drayton Thomas in a sitting with Gladys Osborne Leonard on October 10, 1919, was told by a communicator claiming to be her father that in *The Times* of the next day in the second column on the front page would be his name and his father's, his name coming first. On the next day in the place indicated appeared the name of Charles John Workman—Thomas's name was Charles; his father's name was John. The test eliminates the explanation of telepathy from the sitter but does not exclude the possibility of precognition by the medium or sitter. See also **Book Test.**

BIBLIOGRAPHY: Thomas, C. D. 1921. "Newspaper Tests." JSPR 20:89.

**Newton, Isabel, ?–1950.** British secretary to the Society for Psychical Research. She served as its mainspring from 1908, the time she was appointed to the post. She was devoted to the interests of the organization and was of enormous assistance as a sympathetic and patient counsellor to all who knew her. As director of studies, Isabel Newton was particularly helpful to American visitors. For example, she told Gardner Murphy just what to read and in what order to read it in order to increase his understanding in the field of the paranormal (Berger, 1988:159). She was fully familiar with the work that had been done by the brilliant figures associated with the SPR and particularly admired Alice Johnson and Eleanor Sidgwick. She was fond of saying that no one could come up with a brilliant idea that had not already been thought of and expressed better by Mrs. Sidgwick.

**Nickelheim Poltergeist.** Hans Bender who investigated the case said it "presented an extraordinary accumulation of 'oddities' or events which can by no means be understood in the framework of known physical laws." (Bender, 1969). The "oddities" began in the small Bavarian village of Nickelheim in 1968. Strange knockings typical of poltergeist disturbances first were heard on the windows and doors of a house occupied by a couple and their teenage daughter. Further poltergeist activity followed as stones were thrown against the house succeeded by toilet articles and dolls flying through the rooms, at times around corners. Water was poured into shoes and eggs were sometimes broken into the hats of visitors.

There were even odder "oddities" and the most bizarre poltergeist happenings of all: the advent of teleportation phenomena. As a priest gave the house a very badly needed blessing, suddenly a stone fell from the ceiling in the kitchen although all its doors and windows were shut. A lawyer also came to the house. He placed a perfume bottle and a bottle filled with tablets on a table in the kitchen. Before long, the bottle containing the perfume was seen in the air outside the house and, a little later, the other bottle was seen high in the air moments before it zigzagged to the ground. On still another occasion, Bender was sure that his coat, which had been hung in the wardrobe next to the kitchen, had been teleported outside and laid in the snow. Teleportation, or the penetration of matter through matter, is among the most inexplicable of all the weird things that take place in the world of the paranormal. It seems to have occurred in Nickelheim.

BIBLIOGRAPHY: Bender, H. 1969. "New Developments in Poltergeist Research." *Proceedings of the Parapsychological Association* 6:81.

**Nicol, Betty Humphrey, 1917–.** American parapsychologist. Her interest in parapsychology began when, in the 1930s, she was attending Earlham College in Indiana as a philosophy major. She did research there in extrasensory perception, went to Duke University for graduate work in parapsychology, and so impressed Joseph B. Rhine that he invited her to continue her research at the **Parapsychology Laboratory.** Dr. Nicol was in the forefront of parapsychologists seeking to find out if the personalities of individuals affect their psi abilities. Her research with her husband, **J. Fraser Nicol,** suggested that the people who make the highest scores in tests of extrasensory perception are extroverted, confident, calm, and emotionally stable (Nicol and Humphrey, 1953). People's moods have always been thought to affect their psi performances. Using drawings in tests for clairvoyance, Dr. Nicol found that people she called "expansives"—because they made drawings covering a large area of the paper—made significantly higher scores than "compressives"—who limited their drawings to a small part of the paper (Humphrey, 1949). Psychokinesis was another special area on which Dr. Nicol focussed her inquiries.

Although psi seems to be a gift of which we are not conscious, yet it is not totally beyond our control. Apparently, for example, psi can be directed to a particular card in a deck of cards so that a correct call can be made. Dr. Nicol addressed this point by having her subjects try to influence red and white dice simultaneously so that the "one" face would turn up on the red but not on the white. This task was successfully performed (Humphrey, 1947). Among Dr. Nicol's other accomplishments is her book describing in lucid detail the procedures to be followed for the conduct of ESP tests (Humphrey, 1948).

Selected Writings: 1949. "ESP Subjects Rated by Two Measures of Personality." JP 4:274; *Handbook of Tests in Parapsychology,* 1948; 1947. "Simultaneous High and Low Aim in PK Tests." JP 11:160; and J. Fraser Nicol. 1953. "The Exploration of ESP and Human Personality." JASPR 47:133.

**Nicol, J. Fraser., ?–1989.** Scottish-born parapsychologist. As early as 1934, Mr. Nicol was working in psychical research with the Society for Psychical Research. By 1951, he was at Joseph B. Rhine's Parapsychology Laboratory at Duke University where he met his future wife and collaborator, Betty Humphrey.

While at the Parapsychology Laboratory they began a study (1955), funded in part by the Rockefeller Foundation, of paranormal cases in which percipients' responses indicated their beliefs that their experiences were real. The remainder of the project was supported by grants from the Parapsychology Foundation and the American Society for Psychical Research. The ASPR continued to support Mr. Nicol's research until 1964; the Parapsychology Foundation funded his work until 1968.

Mr. Nicol was in addition a distinguished historian of psychical research, having written, among others, an historical background of the physical phenomena of parapsychology (1977), a history of the founding of the SPR (1972) and, earlier, a history of the Fox Sisters and their relationship to Spiritualism (1948).

Mr. Nicol was educated in Scotland and held a degree from the University of Edinburgh. He was at one time a member of the council of the SPR and was chairman of its Research Committee. He was a member of the American Statistical Association.

Selected Writings: "Historical Background." In B. Wolman, ed., *Handbook of Parapsychology,* 1977; 1972. "The Founders of the S.P.R." PSPR 55:341; 1961. "The Silences of Trevor Hall." *International Journal of Parapsychology* 8(1):5; 1948. "The Fox Sisters and the Development of Spiritualism." JSPR 34:271; and Nicol, B. M. (then

Humphrey). 1955. "The Feeling of Success in ESP." JASPR 49:3.

**Nielsen, Einer, ?–1965.** Danish physical medium. One of the leading mediums of his time. "John King" at times was his control. The physical phenomena he purportedly produced were as impressive as any associated with the mediumship of Mina S. Crandon ("Margery"). Among these phenomena were materializations of what seemed to be real human beings who walked, talked, and could be photographed.

The medium's own story of his life supplied further evidence of his paranormal powers (Nielsen, 1950). But in spite of this evidence and although Albert von Schrenck-Notzing thought that Nielsen's phenomena were genuine, for several reasons grave doubts exist. The medium held his sittings in dim light and the controls were not strict. Materializations could have been confederates or dummies. In addition, in 1922, during séances arranged by the Norwegian Society for Psychical Research in Oslo, the investigating committee detected Nielsen using trickery. Eric J. Dingwall was not satisfied with the committee's verdict of fraud (Dingwall, 1922), but it seems rather significant that thereafter Nielsen would not submit to further scientific investigations and limited his performances to the "faithful."

Selected Writing: *Solid Proofs of Survival,* 1950.

BIBLIOGRAPHY: Dingwall, E. J. 1922. "Einer Nielsen." JSPR 20:327.

**Nietzsche, Friedrich Wilhelm, 1844–1900.** German philosopher and poet. His writings bitterly critical of Christianity, democracy, and the basic values of civilization have influenced generations of philosophers, poets and writers. His superman replaces God. His Zarathustra is anti-Christ. His "will to power" is the main value of life and the driving force to what is good for the individual. After poor health forced him to resign his post as professor of philosophy in Basel, Switzerland, Nietzsche published his masterpiece, *Thus Spake Zarathustra* (1883–1885) in which Zarathustra, in the style of an Old Testament prophet, narrates Nietzsche's philosophy of the superman and the doctrine of eternal recurrence. Besides being one of the most influential and controversial philosophers of all time Nietzsche is a **Noted Witness** whose testimony has a direct bearing on several aspects of parapsychology.

A fundamental doctrine of *Thus Spake Zarathustra* is that of eternal recurrence under which all the states of the world and all the forms its elements take have been many times before and will recur and recur again and again in the future. All is endless coming and going. Under the doctrine, human consciousness is annihilated at death. Nietzsche's novel concept of personal immortality, however, is of interest to survival research even if it can never be tested: The "I" who lives and dies in this instant and who lived and died repeatedly before, will be reproduced throughout eternity exactly as "I" am now and have been previously. The doctrine also provides a key to precognition which really becomes retrocognition. If all the details of future events have already occurred in the past, not once but repeatedly, one need only read the past to forecast exactly what will recur in the future.

Carl Gustav Jung has pointed out that some of the ideas and images in Nietzsche's work were derived from a work by Justinus Kerner published fifty years earlier and which Nietzsche, when young, had read. In Nietzsche therefore we may have an unwilling but noted witness for cryptomnesia.

Nietzsche's testimony also relates to the creative process. In "Composition of Thus Spake Zarathustra" from his posthumously published autobiography *Ecce Homo* (1908), he dealt with the question of inspiration: ". . . Zarathustra himself as a type, came to me—perhaps I should rather say—*invaded* me. . . . one can hardly reject the idea that one is the mere incarnation, or mouthpiece, or medium of some almighty power. The notion of revelation describes the condition quite simply; by which I mean that something profoundly convulsive and disturbing suddenly becomes visible and audible with indescribable definiteness and exactness. One hears—one does not seek; one takes—one does not ask who gives: a thought flashes out like lightning, inevitably without hesitation—I have never had any choice about it."

BIBLIOGRAPHY: Jung, C. L. *Kryptomnesie,* 1966.

**Noetics.** From the Greek *noûs* meaning "mind." A term proposed by **Edgar D. Mitchell** to signify the general study of consciousness. See also **Institute of Noetic Sciences.**

**Nostradamus, 1503–1566.** French doctor of medicine who became the most famous of all prophets since the Delphic oracle. Born Michel de Notredame or Nostredame, he took the pen name Nostradamus in 1555 when he published a book called *Centuries.* It contained 1,000 four-line verses that were supposed to announce events to come. With the apparent fulfillment of his prophecies came a considerable reputation and a place in the court of Charles IX as physician-in-ordinary.

From his day to ours, his fame as a seer has grown. His significance for psychical research lies in his apparent powers of precognition that a good many people believe his quatrains show. There is, for example, the famous quatrain (Century 9, quatrain 20) that goes:

> "By night will come through the forest of Reines
> Two married people by a circuitous route—
> Herne, the white stone,
> The monk in grey—into Varennes,
> Elected Cap; result, tempest, fire, blood, slice."

This quatrain has been taken to foretell the attempt by Louis XVI and Marie Antionette to escape from Paris in 1791 during the French Revolution. But they were captured at Varennes, returned to Paris and guillotined ("sliced") in Paris in 1793.

Nostradamus's precognitive gifts were not typical. The usual types of precognitive experiences relate to events that occur very soon, usually within days, and deal with personal events. Nostradamus's predictions had to do with events distant in time and beyond his lifetime. Also, they dealt with epic, historical events. There are, in addition, certain general objections to accepting Nostradamus's prophesies as evidence of precognition. We have to remember that his quatrains were written in archaic French. For anyone who cannot read sixteenth century French, a translation is necessary and translations are often inaccurate. The quatrains are written in a difficult and obscure style. Since they must be interpreted, there can be many interpretations and all different. Any interpretation must be arbitrary and depend on the ingenuity of the interpreter to force the prophesy to fit into events. The quatrain that is supposed to prophesy the journey and "slicing" of the king of France at the time of the French Revolution does refer to the Capets. But all the kings who ruled France for nine hundred years came from the Capetian family. To make the quatrain apply only to Louis XVI is arbitrary.

It is also the case that many of Nostradamus's predictions have not turned out as advertised. One example is his supposed prediction that Adolf Hitler and the Nazis would be victorious in World War II. Another example is the alleged prediction that Los Angeles would be destroyed by an earthquake in May, 1988, and would fall into the sea. Frightened people made plans to evacuate Los Angeles while others besieged the U.S. Geological Institute and the California Institute of Technology with calls and letters.

These predictions were wide of the mark yet others seemed to come true. Nostradamus wrote 1,000 quatrains. A prediction of his that apparently fits one of the myriad events that occurred anywhere from the sixteenth century onward would not be surprising. The number of events is so great that it would not be hard to find resemblances to one or more quatrains. If we were to shoot 1,000 missiles at anything that moved over a period of 400 years, we might expect to strike a target or two. But it would not be evidence of any paranormal ability to fire missiles.

**Noted Witnesses.** From the book *Noted Witnesses for Psychic Occurrences* by **W. F. Prince.** From the beginning of psychical research, and with the **Census of Hallucinations,** the actual psychic experiences of people in daily life—spontaneous cases—have been collected. These experiences, however, do not prove the case for the paranormal. After all, reports of such experiences are the same fundamentally fallible human testimony every lawyer and historian encounters over and over again. It is always a question of how reliable and honest the reporter is.

The people designated "noted witnesses" in this work, some of whom were selected by Prince and some by the authors from the ranks of outstanding figures from saints to sinners, were chosen to meet this problem. When people are known to us, it may be easier to judge if they are reliable. We tend to give weight to the declarations of people whose careers have been in public view, whose deeds and writings are known to us, who have no professional fees or reputations as mediums to earn, and no wish to draw attention or seek publicity. What happened to them happened without warning or effort and was not deliberate. The testimony of noted witnesses may serve to introduce and shed light on many entries here, help readers make sense of them, and even supply clues to help guide further reading and research. See **Augustine, Saint; Bach, Richard; Balfour, Arthur J.; Belasco, David; Bergen, Edgar J.; Blake, William; Bleksley, Arthur E. H.; Boehme, Jakob; Brougham, Henry P.; Browning, Elizabeth B.; Browning, Robert; Burbank, Luther; Calvin, John; Carrel, Alexis; Cocteau, Jean; Catherine of Bologna, Saint; Coleridge, Samuel T.; Croesus; Cure of Ars; De Morgan, Augustus; Dickens, Charles; Driesch, Hans; Dumas, Alexandre; Dunne, John W.; Eliot, George; Fox, George; Francis of Assisi, Saint; Galsworthy, John; Garibaldi, Giuseppe; Gladstone, William E.; Glanvill, Joseph; Goethe, Johan W. V.; Gregory Thaumaturgus, Saint; Haggard, Sir Henry R.; Hitler, Adolf; Holmes, Oliver W.; Housman, Alfred E.; Hugo, Victor M.; Januarius, Saint; Jesus Christ; Joan of Arc, Saint; Jonson, Ben; Joseph of Copertino, Saint; King, William L. M.; Kipling, Rudyard; Lang, Andrew; Lincoln, Abraham; Linnaeus, Carolus; Lombroso, Cesare; Luther, Martin; Mann, Thomas; Mary, Saint; Mozart, Wolfgang A.; Muir, John; Nietzsche, Frederich W.; Obregon, Alvaro; Otis, James; Paine, Albert B.; Pickett, George E.; Pio, Padre; Poincare, Henri; Prince, Walter F.; Roberts, Kenneth; Robertson, Morgan; Romains, Jules; Rubinstein, Anton G.; Ruskin, John; Saint-Saens, Charles C.; Samuel, Hebrew Prophet; Schumann, Robert A.; Schurz, Carl; Scott, Sir Walter; Sellers, Peter R. H.; Shelley, Percy B.; Socrates; Somerville, Edith O.; Stanley, Sir Henry M.; Stead, William T.; Stevenson, Robert L.; Stowe, Harriet B.; Swedenborg, Emanuel; Tennyson, Alfred Lord; Teresa of Avila, Saint; Thackeray, William M.; Twain, Mark; Victoria; Warcollier, Rene.**

BIBLIOGRAPHY: Prince, W. F. *Noted Witnesses for Psychic Occurrences,* 1963.

**Novillo, Paulí Enrique, 1919–.** Argentinian parapsychologist. He is the author of the only complete textbook on parapsychology in Argentina and since 1971 has been that country's leading lecturer and researcher in the field. Novillo Paulí studied at the Foundation for Research on the Nature of Man, was a professor of parapsychology at the Catholic University of Córdoba until 1979 when he became professor of parapsychology at the Universidad del Salvador. As the present director of the Institute for Parapsychology there, his special interests include the study of psychokinesis, the relation between philosophy and parapsychology, unorthodox healing, and the blood phenomenon of Saint Januarius. He is also author of over a dozen papers.

Selected Writings: Novillo, Paulí, E. *Los Fenómenos Parapsicológicos—Psi en el Laboratorio,* 1984.

**Object Association.** See **Psychometry.**

**Object Reading.** See **Psychometry.**

**Obregón, Álvaro, 1880–1928.** Mexican politician and soldier. During the presidency of Francisco Madero, he led forces against the rebel Pascal Orozco and allied himself with Venustiano Carranza against Pancho Villa, Victoriano Huerta, and Emiliano Zapata. Obregón became president of Mexico in 1920, was reelected in 1928, and assassinated shortly afterward.

In his youth Obregón and his brother worked at an isolated hacienda many miles distant from the place where their mother lived. There was no telephone or telegraph connections with their mother's town. One night, Obregon's brother twice roused him from sleep, each time reporting the apparition of the mother. Two days later, a horseman brought news of the mother's death at the same time the first apparition had been seen. Obregón is one of the **Noted Witnesses** to a paranormal phenomenon: either of an apparition or the paranormal acquisition of knowledge through telepathy or clairvoyance.

BIBLIOGRAPHY: Prince, W. F. *Noted Witnesses for Psychic Occurrences,* 1963.

**Observational Theories.** These assume that observers influence psi events (i.e., that paranormal effects are the result of the later observation of an outcome or data by a conscious human observer who has received sensory feedback).

**Obsession.** See **Possession.**

**Occam's Razor (Ockham's Razor).** Also known as the Law of Parsimony. Attributed to William of Ockham, a fourteenth century British theologian in the Franciscan order, it may, however, have been the name given in 1852 by Sir William Hamilton, the Irish mathematician, to a law formulated by John Ponce in 1639. The law states that it is vain to do with more complicated explanations of facts when the simplest will suffice. The **Super ESP** hypothesis is an example of how Occam's Razor has been used to shave the explanation of spirit entities from cases that otherwise might be construed as suggesting the survival after death of a deceased person.

**Occultism.** A term to describe ideas, techniques, or rituals based on secret teachings or ancient writings related to divination, witchcraft, astrology, alchemy, and various forms of magic. "Occult" means "hidden" and occultism is the search for the hidden in the realm of the mysterious forces and spiritual entities that are supposed to fill the universe. Although occultism started in the United States with the witchcraft trials of the seventeenth century, it has existed for centuries almost everywhere in the form of beliefs ranging from the notion that gods or devils cause storms or disease to the idea of stabbing the shadow of a man in order to kill him.

One of the most striking phenomena of the 1960s was the revival of occultism everywhere. Although the occult revival has been criticized as a threat to reason and as fomenting dangerous doctrines and sects among the uneducated segments of society, in prior periods the teaching and rituals of occultism appealed to many of the best and most respected minds of the times: Giordano Bruno, Johannes Kepler, Francis Bacon, Isaac Newton. In spite, therefore, of the dogmatic, strange, seemingly irrational and unscientific theories and practices occultism embraces, it may contain important elements of wisdom and knowledge worth finding out about. Indeed psychical researchers and parapsychologists should search out those who work in the occult world because all seem to believe that extrasensory perception is possible and the overwhelming majority have had psychic experiences (Roney-Dougal, 1984).

Nevertheless, the relationship between occultism and parapsycology is curious. Some parapsychologists, such as **Serena Roney-Dougal** and **W. G. Roll,** maintain the occult "deserves the serious attention of parapsychologists. . . . [W]e need to stop and ask ourselves if they may not be expressions . . . of the very subject matter of parapsychology. For one way of looking at ESP and PK is to regard them as evidence that the human self extends into the environment in ways that have not so far been brought out by science" (Roll, 1976). It is important to bear in mind, however, that occultism and parapsychology are not alike in their methodology. Occultism is an esoteric art while parapsychology, because of its methods of investigation, is a science.

BIBLIOGRAPHY: Roll, W. G. *The Poltergeist,* 1976; Roney-Dougal, S. 1984. "'Occult' Conference Questionnaire." JSPR 52:379.

**Ochi, Yasou, 1944–.** Japanese engineer and professor at the Tokyo Institute of Technology. He has a major interest in psychokinesis and metal-bending and has conducted a series of experiments with Masuaki Kiyota to elicit evidence of these phenomena.

Selected Writing: 1982. "Some Observations on Metal Bending of Pure Aluminum Plate by Psychokinesis." *Journal of the Psi Institute of Japan* 17:7; and Tokaoka and A. Sasaki. 1978. "Some Observations with Scanning Electronic Microscope (SEM) of Fracture Surface of Metals Fractured by Psychokinesis." *Journal of the PSI Institute of Japan* 2:15.

**Odic Force.** Baron Karl von Reichenbach believed it was what he called the odic force that made crystals, magnets, and human bodies self-luminous in the dark and that produced various odd sensory effects on people. See also **Reichenbach's Experiments.**

**Odors, Paranormal.** Mysterious sweet smells rivalling the fragrance of perfume, flowers, or sweet spices. The Christian tradition associates a delicious fragrance known as the "odor of sanctity" with many devout people. The tradition stretches back to St. Paul: "For we are unto God a sweet savour of Christ" (II Corinthians 2:15).

The fragrance has been described in Christian accounts as emanating from the bodies of dead religious personages. When Saint Polycarp, the bishop of Smyrna, was burned at the stake in 155 A.D., witnesses who smelled the burning flesh "perceived such a fragrant smell, as if it were the wafted odour of frankincense or some other precious spice" (Thurston, 1952). The body of Saint John of the Cross was fragrant nine months after he died in 1591; Saint Lawrence Justinian's body, left above ground for sixty-seven days following his death in 1455, was still fragrant; and the body of Saint Thomas of Villanova, who died in 1555, gave off a delicious smell twenty-seven years later.

Perhaps the bodies of these and other pious people whose bodies gave off an "odor of sanctity" had been anointed with spices or herbs or perhaps incense had been placed in their coffins or burial places. The odors when natural, however, are not confined to the pious. The same phenomenon also has its secular analogues. It appears in Sir Thomas Malory's *Le Mort d'Arthur*: "[W]hen Sir Bors and his fellows came to [Sir Lancelot's] bed they found him dead, and as he lay he smiled, and the sweetest savour about him they ever felt."

Lovely fragrances have also been noticed by Spiritualists and mediums. Mina S. Crandon produced a variety of pleasing scents in her séances. So did William Stainton Moses: ". . . the room is pervaded by odours of subtle and delicate, or strong, perfume. . . . If a new intelligence is to communicate . . . the room is pervaded by perfumes which grow stronger as the spirit enters. . . . Indeed, when we have been in the country, far from the polluted atmosphere of smoke and dirt, . . . the air of the seance-room is always laden with perfumes. . . . Sometimes the odour is like nothing of this earth's production, ethereal, delicate, and infinitely delightful" (Myers, 1893).

One distinction between the "odor of sanctity" and smells emanating from Spiritualist séances may be that, in the former, the fragrances are not intentional while in the case of mediums they may be produced naturally and deliberately in order to impress.

But there is no difference between the "odor of sanctity" and fragrances occurring spontaneously in paranormal situations in which ordinary individuals have found themselves. For example, in 1963, the secretary to a dean of Nebraska Wesleyan University in Lincoln, Nebraska, saw an apparition of a tall, black-haired lady in a shirtwaist and ankle-length skirt and felt the presence of a man in the room. When she looked out a window, there was not one modern building and not even the familiar street. She said, "I realized that these people were not in my time, but I was back in their time." Simultaneously, "the strong odor hit me. When I say strong odor, I mean the kind that simply stops you in your tracks . . .". This was a case of retrocognition accompanied by a paranormal odor that "hit" a very "down-to-earth" woman who was no psychic. There is as yet no normal explanation for such odors. They remain as much a parapsychological phenomenon and puzzle as they are a religious one.

BIBLIOGRAPHY: Murphy, G. and Klemme H. L. 1966. "Unfinished Business." JASPR 60:306; Myers, F. W. H. 1893. "The Experiences of W. Stainton Moses.—I." PSPR 9:245, pp. 269–270; Thurston, H. *The Physical Phenomena of Mysticism,* 1952, p.222.

**Odour of Sanctity.** See **Odors, Paranormal.**

**Oguma, Taranosuke, 1888–1978.** Japanese researcher of paranormal phenomena famous for his sceptical investigations and exposures of fraudulent psychics. He was one of those whose violent criticisms of the work of Tomokichi Fukurai forced him to resign his university post and to stop his parapsychological experiments. Oguma, a psychologist at Meiji University, was the first president of the **Japanese Society for Parapsychology** and author of several books on parapsychology.

Selected Writing: Oguma, T. *Shinrei-Gensho no Mondai* (Problems of Psychical Research), 1918.

**Olcott, Henry Steel, 1832–1907.** American editor, newspaper reporter and attorney. He was the co-founder of theosophy. At twenty-six he was the agricultural editor of the *New York Tribune.* After becoming a colonel in the Civil War and a commissioner in the United States War and Navy Departments, Olcott was admitted to the New York bar.

He also wrote articles for the *New York Graphic.* Among them were reports of séances: Olcott like so many others was intrigued by Spiritualism. One of the interested readers of his exciting accounts of spirit manifestations was **Madame H. P. Blavatsky** who sought him out in October 1874. A year later he had left his wife and family and become her partner in the founding in New York City of the Theosophical Society. Olcott accompanied Mme Blavatsky to India where they took up residence in 1879 and set up the main headquarters of the society. In 1884, he went with her to England where they were examined by a committee of the Society for Psychical Research on the doctrines of Theosophy.

Although the SPR later condemned Mme Blavatsky and the phenomena as fraudulent, Olcott was specifically exempted from the condemnation because of his "extraordinary credulity, and inaccuracy in observation and inference" (Report, 1885:205). He was, in effect, a perfect partner for Mme Blavatsky in her promotion of Theosophy: honest, respected, influential, and with the will to believe. Olcott later helped Annie Besant found a college in Benares, India, and contributed to the renascence of Buddhism in India, Ceylon, and Burma.

BIBLIOGRAPHY: "Report of the Committee Appointed to Investigate Phenomena Connected with the Theosophical Society." 1885. PSPR 3:201; Williams, G. M. *Madame Blavatsky: Priestess of the Occult,* 1946.

**Onda, Akira, 1925–.** Japanese professor of psychology at Tokyo University. He helped found the Japanese Society for Parapsychology. His major interests are in survival after death, especially near-death experiences, psychokinesis, and the relation of the creative process to psi.

Selected Writing: 1964. "A Study of the Relationship between Creativity and ESP." *Bulletin* of Tokyo University 18:1.

**One-Tailed Test.** A measure of psi experimental results in which the movement of the deviation below or above mean chance expectation has been determined prior to the experiment. See also **Two-Tailed Test.**

**Open Deck.** A deck of ESP cards in which the symbols are selected randomly so that there can be more or fewer than five of a particular symbol. See also **Closed Deck.**

**Open Matching Test.** A test of clairvoyance that requires subjects, while holding **ESP Cards** face up, to distribute them into five groups and to match them against **Key Cards** that have been placed in black envelopes and so are concealed from the subjects. See also **Blind Matching.**

**Oracles.** In the ancient world, a response to questions thought to come from the gods. Also, a shrine where such responses were given. Many shrines thrived. There were oracles at Thebes, Dodona, Didyma, Olympia, Siwa, Sibyl, Clarus, Tegyra, Colchis, Athens, Thrace, Boetia, Paphos, Patrae, Baalbek, Delphi, and elsewhere. Each was dedicated to a god or goddess. Delphi was dedicated to Apollo, Dodona to Zeus, Colchis to Diana, Athens to Hercules, Thrace to Mars, Petrae to Demeter, Baalbek to Jupiter. The most famous of all was the **Delphic Oracle.**

In the ancient Greek religion dieties were worshipped. By means of signs or by responses at oracles, the gods spoke to believers to let their wills be known on all issues ranging from matters of great importance to the state, such as political or military decisions, to very personal concerns, such as "Did someone steal my ring?" or "Shall I marry?" and "Is this a good investment?" (Besides the oracles, people might also consult **Belly-Talkers.**)

At the oracles, questioners put their questions directly to a priestess, such as the Pythia at Delphi. The priestesses, seated on tripods, were in effect mediums and were unable to obtain answers unless they first entered into a state of trance which might be induced by drinking from a sacred spring as did the priestess at Didyma or by chewing laurel leaves as did the one at Delphi. In their normal waking state, the priestesses were ordinary women, but in trance and apparently possessed, a priestess spoke in a voice alien to her own and was transformed in facial expression and bearing. A god spoke through her to respond to questions on the basis of divine foreknowledge of the future. The priestesses's oral utterances, generally in the form of riddles or cryptic, ambiguous or symbolic verses, were recorded and later interpreted. The ambiguity and difficulty of interpreting the messages is illustrated by the unfortunate case of **Croesus** whose misinterpretation cost him his empire.

In the oracles, there is a marked similarity to modern sittings and séances, trance mediumship, possession and precognition. But whereas Spiritualists see sittings, séances, and trance mediums as connected with the spirits of dead human beings, the Greeks and Romans perceived their oracles as connected to the gods or nonhuman entities. Communication with the spirits of dead people was not denied but neither was it attempted. See also **Prophesy.**

**Organisation pour la Recherche en Psychotronique.** Created in January 1987, as an independent agency by the Laboratoire Universitaire de Parapsychologie et de Hygiène Mental de Toulouse. The purpose of the Organisation pour la Recherche en Psychotronique is to promote research in parapsychology, first in France and French-speaking countries and then in Europe. A data bank has been established as a tool both for research and for communication so that interested people can know what scientists are working on and in what fields of research they are working. A library, called l'Oeil (the Eye), mails members articles they request from French and foreign publications, analyzes protocols, and generally tries to avoid the pursuit of useless work (i.e., the repetition of experiments caused by the fact that heretofore there has been no way of keeping track of what other workers in the field have been doing). Support is given for work in the field and facilities provided to publish the results of the work. Beginning in 1988, the organization started to publish the *Revue*

*Française de Parapsychologie,* which is intended to be the equal of the *Journals* of the English and American societies for psychical research. A Bulletin also is published. Address: Yves Lignon-OEIL, Laboratoire de Parapsychologie, UER Mathématiques, Université Toulouse-Le-Mirail 31058, Toulouse CEDEX, France.

**Orgone Energy.** Theorized by Wilhelm Reich, its discoverer, to be a life force that is bluish in color and the source of all sexual energy in the human being. He based his theory on experiments with the sexual functioning of human beings and animals. "Orgone" comes from "orgasm" and "organism."

Reich invented a structure called the Orgone Energy Accumulator that was supposed to attract the life force and both charge with orgone energy and heal the body of anyone sitting inside. Reich's theory is controversial. If it is not a crack-pot theory, the discovery of a universal life force would be relevant to psychical research and parapsychology because it would force a modification of views of some paranormal phenomena. It might explain the process of unorthodox healing and might present psychokinesis in a new light. This phenomenon is now understood as "mind over matter"—a power by the human mind to influence matter. Orgone energy would make us think instead of a cosmic power that influences matter and that is channeled through us. See also **Reich, Wilhelm.**

**Osborn, Arthur W., 1891–.** British author who moved to Australia. He has surveyed and then based philosophical speculations on the meaning of life (Osborn, 1966) and the significance of reincarnation (Osborn, 1962) on the empirical data uncovered by parapsychology. The difficulty with efforts such as his to interpret the as yet inconclusive data is that interpretations are bound to be as varied as the backgrounds and disciplines of the people doing the interpreting. Spiritualists, psychologists, philosophers, psychical researchers, and parapsychologists speculating on the same data will see the data in radically different ways. For the present psychical researchers and parapsychologists are or should be mainly limiting themselves to the systematic collection and enlargement of the data base before attempting speculations.

Selected Writings: *The Meaning of Personal Existence,* 1966; *The Future is Now: The Significance of Reincarnation,* 1962.

**Osis, Karlis, 1917–.** Latvian-born American parapsychologist. When he was in his early teens and suffering from tuberculosis, he felt, just at the moment that his aunt died, a "tremendous wave of joy" and he and the room were filled with a "living light." This "call of the mysteriously sublime" led into psychical research and parapsychology because, he writes, "Belief was not enough; I had to *know.*" He feels that these spontaneous paranormal experiences can be life-transforming in a way that laboratory research cannot be.

In 1950 after receiving his Ph.D. in psychology from the University of Munich with a doctoral thesis on a very unusual subject for the time—interpretations of ESP—he came to the United States under the displaced persons program. On writing to J. B. Rhine about some crude experiments he was doing in anpsi (animal psi—in Osis's case with hens), he was amazed at being invited to Duke University to work on animal ESP.

Thus began a long and illustrious career in psychical research and parapsychology. From 1957 to 1962 he was director of research for the Parapychology Foundation. In 1962, he became director of research at the American Society for Psychical Research and was later Chester F. Carlson Research Fellow there, now emeritus.

Among Osis's many parapsychological experiments was the most elaborate ever conducted to find if ESP is independent of space and time (1970). Contrary to expectations, he found that there is a decline in ESP over distance. He is one of the very few psychical researchers researching the question of whether there is some aspect of the human being that survives death. In this connection he has investigated apparitions, designed a series of experiments to study the out-of-body experience (this research continues), made a pioneer survey of physicians and nurses in India and, with **Erlendur Haraldsson,** studied the experiences of dying people. The published results of this study (1977) indicate to Osis's satisfaction that survival fits the data better than does death as destruction. He also managed a technical, carefully conducted experiment on the effect of meditation on ESP but found that many colleagues were offended by the subject matter of the study. Along with Haraldsson, he began to investigate Sathya Sai Baba who, in Osis's presence, apparently materialized an unusual object and dematerialized a stone in his ring. Lack of funding, however, forced him to abandon this study which Haraldsson continued.

Karlis Osis is the author of seventy-odd scientific articles, was president of the Parapsychological Association and is a member of the American Psychological Association, the Eastern Psychological Association, the Society for Psychical Research and the American Association for the Advancement of Science, is a Fellow of the Society for the Scientific Study of Religion, and is on the board of the Academy of Religion and Psychical Research.

Selected Writings: "The Paranormal: My Window to Something More." In R. Pilkington, ed., *Men and Women of Parapsychology,* 1987; 1970. "ESP over Long Distances: In Search of Transmitting Energy." Paper presented at the 137th Meeting of the American Association for the Advancement of Science; *Deathbed Observations by Physicians and Nurses,* 1961; and E. Haraldsson. *At the Hour of Death,* 1977; with D. McCormick. 1980. "Kinetic Effects at the Ostensible Location of an Out-of-Body Projection during Perceptual Testing." JASPR 74:319.

BIBLIOGRAPHY: Berger, A. S. *Lives and Letters in American Parapsychology,* 1988.

**Ossowiecki, Stefan, 1877–1944.** Polish engineer and psychic. Born into an aristocratic Polish family living in Russia, he saw auras as a child and as a young man, stripped and wrapped in a straitjacket, was supposed to have demonstrated psychokinesis by moving objects at a distance (in one instance a large marble statue). In 1898 he met his guru, a dying Jewish yogi named Wrobel (Schwartz, 1978) or Vorobej (Borzymowski, 1965) who taught him visualization and concentration as a bridge from the conscious to the superconscious state. From Wrobel-Vorobej, Ossowiecki also learned psychometry. His time with Wrobel-Vorobej was the major spiritual experience of Ossowiecki's life. During the Russian Revolution, in prison and expecting to be executed, Ossowiecki came to believe that there is a higher, immortal life and that with his psychic gifts he could help others.

Upon his release from prison in 1919 he and his family returned to Poland. He made his living as an engineer and never accepted payment for his psychic services—not even from Eugene Rothschild whose blank check sent in payment for clairvoyant services rendered was returned. From 1920 on Ossowiecki was tested by psychical researchers, including, among others, Charles Richet, Gustave Geley, Theodore Besterman, Eric J. Dingwall, and Albert von Schrenck-Notzing. The experiments involved either astral projection (Ossowiecki claimed to be able to free his "etheric double" and to make himself appear to people at a distance) or the reading of messages in sealed envelopes (probably by clairvoyance). It was found that he never cheated and that he could perform at will. Richet said that Ossowiecki's results were "the most positive in the whole history of mental metapsychics" (Inglis, 1984:123) and Dingwall and Besterman, both extreme skeptics, were also favorably impressed. Ossowiecki always insisted that his psychic gifts which enabled him to "see and hear outside time and space" were merely a by-product of his search for enlightenment.

In 1935 several experiments showed that Ossowiecki when presented with an object was able to see into the past. This led directly to his long series of experiments in psychic archaeology with Stanislaw Poniatowski, experiments that were continued at great risk to the participants during the Nazi occupation of Warsaw. In the course of these experiments Ossowiecki gave information often unknown at the time but verified by later archaeological discoveries.

During World War II he refused to leave Poland. He felt he was needed to help the hundreds of people who came to him for information (which he received through psychometric readings of photographs or personal belongings) about the fates of their loved ones being held by the Nazis or fighting at the front.

Just before the German surrender on May 8, 1945, Stanislaw Poniatowski died in a Nazi concentration camp. He had survived Ossowiecki by nine months, however, the latter having been killed by the Nazis in August 1944 in the Warsaw uprising in a massacre of 9500 civilians. Miraculously, the records of the archaeological experiments survived and in 1952 were retrieved by Ossowiecki's widow.

BIBLIOGRAPHY: Besterman, T. 1933. "An Experiment in 'Clairvoyance' with M. Stefan Ossowiecki." PSPR 41:345; Borzymowski, A. 1965. "Experiments with Ossowiecki." *International Journal of Parapsychology.* 7(3):259;

Dingwall, E. J. 1924. "An Experiment with Polish Medium Stefan Ossowiecki." JSPR 21:259; Inglis, B. *Science and Parascience,* 1984; Richet, C. 1925. "Des Conditions de la Certitude." PSPR 35:422, 433–438; Schwartz, S. A. *The Secret Vaults of Time,* 1978, pp. 57–107.

**Osterreich, Traugott Konstantin, 1880–1949.** German professor of philosophy. His reputation in psychical research was established by his book (Osterreich, 1921) showing that the phenomena of possession and trance are common occurrences among all peoples in all ages. He also undertook investigations of the physical mediums Kathleen Goligher and Stanislawa Tomczyk (Osterreich, 1926), was among the first academics to try to integrate psychical research into the German academic framework, and argued for the improvement of terminology in psychical research. When the Nazis rose to power, Osterreich, along with others also active in psychical research, such as Hans Driesch, was compelled to resign his professorship. His academic position was not regained until after World War II.

Selected Writings: "Kathleen Goligher" and "Stanislawa Tomczyk." In A. Schrenck-Notzing, ed., *Die physikalischen Phänomene der grossen Medien. Eine Abwehr,* 1926, pp.105, 171; *Die Besessenheit,* 1921. (English edition *Possession: Demoniacal and Other, Among Primitive Races, in Antiquity, the Middle Ages, and Modern Times,* 1966).

**Osty, Eugene, 1874–1938.** French physician and psychical researcher. His open-mindedness in dealing with his medical practice ("I use any treatment that will effect a cure") was carried over into his researches in psychical research. He is often credited, along with Charles Richet, with being the founder of psychical research in France.

Originally a scientific materialist, he became interested in what he called clairvoyance (but which seems to have been psi in general, including telepathy and psychometry) when in 1909 a palmist gave accurate character analyses of subjects unknown to her but known to Osty (including an accurate description of his own character). In 1910 he began a long-term study of clairvoyance. He was soon publishing articles in the journals dealing with psychical research in France: *Les Annales des Sciences Psychiques, Psychica,* and the official organ of the Institut Métapsychique International, *La Revue Métapsychique.* He published several books beginning in 1913, the most important of which was *La Connaissance Supranormale* in 1923. G. N. M. Tyrrell thought the research work described was extremely important and that it was a great mistake that investigators never followed up Osty's promising leads.

In 1924, upon Gustave Geley's death in an airplane crash, Osty became director of the Institut Métapsychique International and from then on devoted all his time to it and to the publication of the *Revue.* Experimental research was unfortunately limited for want of funds.

A chair test, à la Gerard Croiset, (a psychic gave a very accurate description of the life and problems of an unknown person who would sit in a particular unreserved seat at a public function) with its apparent precognition, published in the *Revue* in 1936, very much impressed Tyrrell. Osty also did research on premonitions which caused him to hypothesize that, unconsciously, on some psychic plane, we all know our own futures.

Osty worked with Charles Richet, Henri Bergson, and Emile Boirac. He was present at experiments with Franek Kluski and was absolutely convinced of the latter's ability to produce paraffin gloves by paranormal means. He held many séances, both public and private, with mediums, the principal one being **Pascal Forthuny** on whom he wrote a monograph (Osty, 1926). He also worked extensively in research on physical phenomena with his son who was an engineer, his goal being to substitute instrumentation for fallible human observation. A successful use of this methodology employing a circuit of infrared lights was carried out in experiments with the medium **Rudi Schneider.** They seemed to suggest the conscious use of some invisible force by the entranced medium. The results of this work were published in *Les Pouvoirs Inconnus de l'Esprit sur la Matière* written with his son Marcel.

Osty was also interested in hypnotism, the creative process, paranormal crime detection, unorthodox healing, haunts, and the question of survival. He had collected material on all these matters and on all his work over a period of thirty years and was writing a definitive work at the time of his death. That book, sadly, was never published.

Selected Writing: *Une Faculté de Con-*

*naissance Supra-Normale. Pascale Forthuny,* 1926; (trans. by S. de Barth) *Supernormal Faculties in Man,* 1923.

BIBLIOGRAPHY: Johannet, R. 1938."Dr. Eugene Osty." JASPR 32:363; Osty, M. 1959. "Eugene Osty: Pioneer Researcher." *Tomorrow* 7(1):96; Pleasants, H., ed., *Biographical Dictionary of Parapsychology,* 1964; Tyrrell, G. N. M. 1947. "The Modus Operandi' of Paranormal Cognition." PSPR 48:65, pp. 100–108, 119.

**Otani, Soji, 1924–.** Japanese professor of psychology at the National Defense Academy and founder of the Japanese Society for Parapsychology. He surveyed the attitude of Japanese psychologists toward parapsychology. He read the works of Joseph B. Rhine, conducted psi experiments with Rhine's quantitative methods and introduced them to Japanese parapsychologists. Dr. Otani studied at the Parapsychology Laboratory and in 1964, at a meeting of the Japan Psychological Association, presented the first paper on parapsychology ever presented to Japanese psychologists.

Dr. Otani has contributed many papers to the *Journal of Parapsychology,* has co-authored reports of experiments conducted by Japanese parapsychologists with psychic Masuaki Kiyota and has carried out experiments to show that scores in extrasensory perception are affected by a sound stimulus. His major contribution has been his attempt to establish parapsychology as a branch of science in Japan.

Selected Writing: "Effect of Short-Term Stimulus upon ESP Functions." In J. Beloff and W. G. Roll, eds., *Research in Parapsychology 1980,* 1981, p.89; and Kohri, N., Ro, Y., Imai, S., 1981. "A Study on PK Ability of a Gifted Subject in Japan." In J. Beloff and W. G. Roll, eds., *Research in Parapsychology, 1980,* 1981, p. 39.

**Otis, James, 1725–1783.** American lawyer and orator from Massachusetts. In the days just prior to the American revolutionary war, he mobilized the opinions of the thirteen colonies against the Stamp Act and the interference of the British in the lives and businesses of Americans. He was a delegate to the first intercolonial Congress in New York in October 1765 to deliberate over the Stamp Act threat.

Otis is a **Noted Witness** to the phenomenon of precognition. Once, after putting a picture up on a wall, he said: "Don't take this down, for the next news you hear of me will be that I am killed by lightning." He also told his sister: "My dear sister, I hope when God Almighty, in his righteous providence, shall take me out of time into eternity, that it will be by a flash of lightning." He expressed this wish often. On May 23, 1783, while standing at the front door of a house with a group of people, a heavy cloud passed, a shower fell and a flash of lightning struck and killed him instantly. The correct prediction of death by lightning, hardly one of the major causes of death, is extraordinary and is suggestive of precognition.

BIBLIOGRAPHY: Prince, W. F. *Noted Witnesses for Psychic Occurrences,* 1963, pp. 67–69.

**Ouija Board.** The word "ouija" is a combination of the French and German words for "yes," ("oui" and "ja"). A ouija board has printed on it the letters of the alphabet, the numbers 0 through 9 and the words "Yes" and "No." A **planchette** glides over the board when touched by an operator or operators. Some think the words or sentences spelled out or numbers indicated in this way are messages from a deceased communicator. Others think the movement of the planchette is produced by the operators's unconscious muscular push-pull exertions and that it is a form of automatism, that is, that it is their own extrasensory perception that obtains information they could not have been known in any normal way.

A device strongly resembling a ouija board is described by Marcellinus Ammianus, the Roman historian of the fourth century A.D. He recorded that, in 371 A.D., at a trial for treason, a circular metal disk that one of the accused men confessed he and his co-defendants had used was brought into court. It stood on a tripod and had the twenty-four letters of the Greek alphabet engraved around its outside border. Someone stood over the disk holding above it a pendulum, a thread at the end of which was a ring. The defendants had prayed to the gods to tell them who would be emperor after Valens who ruled the eastern part of the Roman Empire. As the ring swayed, it began to spell first the Greek letter "theta" (TH in English), then "E", then "O." At this point the defendants decided that the ring was going to spell "Theodorus," stopped the operation and left.

Unfortunately for them, information about their activities leaked out to Valens and all, including Theodorus, were executed. In fact, it was Theodosius, not the unfortunate Theodorus, who assumed the throne after Valens was killed by the Huns in 378.

**Oursler, Charles Fulton, 1893–1952.** American author, music and drama critic, and editor of *Liberty* magazine. He was Harry Houdini's friend and shared with him extreme skepticism about anything smacking of the paranormal. Oursler even openly criticized **Walter F. Prince** for accepting phenomena Oursler could not. At Prince's urging, however, he began to record his dreams.

One dream impressed him as of "very considerable scientific importance. . . . On Saturday night, June 16 [1923], I dreamed that I saw in my apartment, Mrs. Oursler, my wife, running toward me in an almost nude condition, with her hands uplifted covered with blood. The floors were wet with it, and the walls were stained with it. I said, 'Look at all this blood.' She replied, 'Isn't the smell terrible?' I saw then immediately on my right a strip of blue serge cloth and two hands reach down and sweep away some of the wet blood from the serge." Mrs. Oursler certified that her husband had told her about the dream on Sunday morning. At 8 P.M. that Sunday, Oursler looked up from his desk and saw his wife in the doorway almost nude. Her hands were raised. She was so excited, she could not talk. She pointed outside. He ran out and into the street and found that a car had run over his Airedale terrier. The dog was bleeding profusely. After Oursler carried him into the house, the dog's blood covered the walls and floor of the hall and bathroom. Mrs.Oursler, crying, said to her husband, "Doesn't the blood smell terrible?" The family doctor came to attend the dog. His blue serge suit became spattered with blood and his hands wiped the blood away.

In many respects, the dream tallied with the actual event: Mrs.Oursler almost nude in both; her hands were raised in both; in both blood stained the walls and floors of the apartment; in both Oursler's wife remarked on the terrible smell of blood; there was in the dream blue serge cloth and in the event the blue serge suit worn by the doctor; in both the cloth was stained with blood; in both hands swept the blood from the suit. All these correspondences suggest that the skeptical Oursler is a good **Noted Witness** for the phenomenon of precognition.

BIBLIOGRAPHY: Prince, W. F. *Noted Witness for Psychic Occurrences,* 1963, pp. 216–217.

**Ouspensky, Peter Demianovitch, 1878–1947.** Russian philosopher and mystic. A disciple of Georges I. Gurdjieff, he collaborated with the Russo-Greco-Armenian mystic and perpetuated his teachings in writings studied by philosophers, psychologists, and physicists.

His works attract psychical researchers as well. He has recorded a number of his own veridical psychic experiences and has theorized the existence of a higher spiritual dimension (Ouspensky, 1950). His novel (1966) which deals with the nature of time has interesting relationships to Friedrich Nietzsche's eternal recurrence and to reincarnation. Ouspensky suggests that the only way out of a cycle of endless lives is by living, not selfishly for oneself, but for others.

Selected Writing: *Strange Life of Ivan Osokiń,* 1966; *In Search of the Miraculous,* 1950.

**Out-of-Body Experience (OBE).** The sensation that one's center of consciousness literally has withdrawn from one's physical body and has functioned, often in full consciousness and with unimpaired faculties, at other points in space not coincident with one's physical body. From these points people have sometimes perceived and obtained knowledge of events they could not have known normally. This type of phenomenon has also been called "ESP projection" by **Hornell Hart,** "ecsomatic experiences" by **Celia Green** "travelling clairvoyance," "bilocation" and "astral projection" or "astral travel."

The experience has been described since ancient times. St. Paul, referring to himself in the third person, said: "I knew a man . . . whether in the body, I cannot tell; or whether out of the body, I cannot tell: God knoweth . . . How that he was caught up into paradise, and heard unspeakable words . . ." (II Corinthians 12:2,4). In the second century A.D., Lucius Apuleius, the philosopher who wrote many treatises including *Metamorphoses,* spoke of the art of traveling from the body to a plane beyond this world: "I drew nigh to the confines of death. I trod the threshold of

Prosperine [the world of the dead]. I was borne through all the elements, and I returned to Earth again." Long before him, the Egyptians conceived of the **KA,** an entity which left the body and corresponds to whatever supposedly withdraws from the physical body in the out-of-body experience.

In modern times **Robert Crookall** collected and analyzed many recent case histories of people who had out-of-body experiences naturally or whose experiences were forced by anesthesia, suffocation, or falling. Oliver Fox, **Sylvan J. Muldoon, Yram** and **Robert Monroe** have written first-hand accounts of their out-of-body experiences. A typical experience was described to Dr. Raymond Moody: A woman's heart stopped beating. She then had the sensation of moving out of her physical body, on to the floor, and of beginning to ascend slowly toward the ceiling like a piece of paper blown in the wind. As she floated near the ceiling, she could see her physical body plainly and the medical personnel attempting feverishly to resuscitate her. She wondered why all the fuss since she was fine now (Moody, 1975).

Several curious effects seem to accompany an apparent separation of consciousness from the physical body. Subjects may report a sense of paralysis or catalepsy in their physical bodies, sometimes sexual arousal or the hearing of noises such as ringing bells or the rushing of air. Most dramatic is the feeling of many that, during separation, they have discovered finally what it really means to live. Joseph H. M. Whiteman is in this class as is Sylvan Muldoon who, over a period of a dozen years, claimed hundreds of experiences. Muldoon said: "We call ourselves physically alive, but in reality the material part of us is as dead as a door-nail. It is the energy behind the physical mechanism that is the real 'live' thing" (Muldoon and Carrington, 1973:48).

While there may be some agreement on the effects of the experience, the question of how to interpret it continues to be disputed. In theosophical and Spiritualist writings, every individual has a soul for which the astral body is the non-physical vehicle. Apparitions of the living and the accounts of people who have had near-death experiences or out-of-body experiences have been cited in support of this hypothesis. If it is valid, the monist conception that individuals are one-to-one with their bodies and their bodies to them would be contradicted. This interpretation of the out-of-body experience is challenged, however, by Susan J. Blackmore and others who explain the out-of-body experience as a psychological rather than a paranormal phenomenon. It is, they say, an hallucinatory experience, a lucid dream, an altered state of consciousness, or, as Harvey J. Irwin argues, a loss of bodily sensation and an image of being disembodied. Events perceived that are later verified are explained as ESP operating incidental to the hallucination, dream, altered state of consciousness, or image.

Parapsychologists have undertaken laboratory investigations into the existence of an externalized conscious and perceiving **Double.** In Charles Tart's experiment, a target five-digit number written on a piece of paper was placed on a shelf more than five feet above a bed in which a subject slept. The target could be seen only by someone looking down on the shelf. After four nights, the subject reported an out-of-body experience during which she floated above the number and could read it. She gave the correct number, 25132. The odds against guessing the number by chance were 99,999 to 1.

In an experiment by Robert L. Morris, Keith Harary who claimed the ability to induce an out-of-body experience was to to visit a location one-half mile from his room where there was a kitten. During the out-of-body experience claimed by the subject, the kitten became very quiet and did not meow at all in contrast to non-out-of-body control periods when it was very active and meowed thirty-seven times.

Karlis Osis carried out a physical detection study with Alex Tanous who was to induce an out-of-body experience and go into a room to look at target pictures. In order to see them he had to look through a viewing window in such a way that his point of view would be located in a shielded chamber in which sensor plates and strain gauges were installed capable of detecting any movement in the area in front of the viewing window. When the subject was supposed to be having an out-of-body experience and was correctly viewing the target pictures, the sensor plates became active suggesting a physical effect at the location where the out-of-body experience ostensibly was taking place.

BIBLIOGRAPHY: Besant, A. *Man and His Bodies,* 1900; Blackmore, S. J. *Beyond the*

*Body: An Investigation of Out-of-the Body Experiences,* 1981; Capel, M. 1978. "Las Experiencias Extracorporales: Revisión de la Casuista y Algunas Aportaciones Explicativas." *Psi Comunicación* 7–8:49; Crookall, R. *The Study and Practice of Astral Projection,* 1966; Delanne, G. *L'Âme Est Immortelle.* trans. into English as *Evidence for a Future Life,* 1904; Delanne, G. "La Psychologie Experimental." In P. Janet, ed., *IVe Congrès International de Psychologie,* 1901; Fox, O. *Astral Projection: A Record of Out-of-the Body Experiences,* 1962; Green, C. E. 1967. "Ecsomatic Experiences and Related Phenomena." JSPR 44:111; Hart, H. 1956. "Six Theories about Apparitions." PSPR 50: 153; Irwin, H. J. *Flight of Mind: A Psychological Study of the Out-of-Body Experience,* 1985; Monroe, R. A. *Journeys Out of the Body,* 1971; Moody, R. A., Jr. *Life after Life,* 1975; Morris, R. L. 1974. "PRF Research on Out-of-Body Experiences, 1973." *Theta* 41:1; Muldoon, S. and Carrington, H. *The Projection of the Astral Body,* 1973; Osis, K. and McCormick, D. 1980. "Kinetic Effects at the Ostensible Location of an Out-of-Body Projection during Perceptual Testing." JASPR 74:319; Palmer, J. 1978. "The Out-of-Body Experience: A Psychological Theory." *Parapsychology Review* 9:19; Tart, C. T. "A Psychophysiological Study of Out-of-the-Body Experiences in a Selected Subject." JASPR 62:3; Whiteman, J. H. M. 1956. "The Process of Separation and Return in Experiences Fully 'Out of the Body'." PSPR 50:240.

**Owen, Alan Robert George, 1919–.** British educator and parapsychologist. He was a Fellow of Trinity College, Cambridge, where he was a lecturer in genetics and mathematics when his interest in psychical research was kindled by his colleague, C.D. Broad. Dr. Owen became president of the Cambridge Society for Psychical Research and a member of the council of the Society for Psychical Research.

In 1963, he received an award from the Parapsychology Foundation for the best treatise on psychical research, his masterly study, later published as a book (Owen, 1965), dealing with various kinds of poltergeist phenomena. As a result of his survey, he concluded that there is no evidence that the poltergeist is a mysterious spirit from another dimension. He inclined toward the view that poltergeist disturbances may be produced by forces released from living poltergeist agents as a result of pent-up emotions.

In 1979, he moved to Canada where he taught mathematics and statistics at the University of Toronto and, with his wife, Iris Owen, founded the New Horizons Research Foundation and the Toronto Society for Psychical Research. Both organizations, however, discontinued their operations when Dr. Owen retired in 1988.

Selected Writing: *Can We Explain the Poltergeist?,* 1965.

**Owen, Iris.** Contemporary Canadian nurse. She co-authored a book (Owen and Sparrow, 1976) about her important experiment in which she applied the methods of Kenneth Batcheldor and which resulted in an imaginary ghost producing real physical phenomena.

A group in Toronto, none of them mediums, created a fictitious communicator they called "Philip." Meeting in weekly séances around a heavy table, they hoped to produce paranormal occurrences. Before long, there were levitations of the table and messages communicated by "Philip" by means of raps in answer to questions. The experiment, in which no true spirit was present, showed that the will, belief, and psychokinesis of living people can produce genuine paranormal phenomena and may explain table-tilting and rappings which Spiritualists attribute to spirits. See also **Owen Alan R. G.**

Selected Writing: and Sparrow, M. *Conjuring up Philip: An Adventure in Psychokinesis,* 1976.

**Owen, Robert Dale, 1801–1877.** Scottish-born editor, politician, and reformer. Inheriting utopian socialism from his famous father, Robert Owen, he came from Scotland to the United States in 1825 to help establish a socialist community in Indiana. Owen was elected to the Indiana legislature, edited a radical newspaper in New York, and opposed slavery.

Owen was a Spiritualist and took a general interest in the paranormal. He reported cases people told him in which strange and inexplicable phenomena had occurred ranging from precognition and poltergeists to apparitions (Owen, 1923). Psychical researcher F. W. H. Myers said that Owen "cannot be classed as a first rate *observer;* having been once at least grossly deceived by fraudulent mediums. Nor is his standard of what constitutes *evidence* very high . . . But, on the other hand, his own honesty and his strong wish to be accurate are undoubted. He wrote out the accounts given to him with care . . ." (Myers, 1889: 32n).

Selected Writing: *Footfalls on the Boundary of Another World,* 1923.

BIBLIOGRAPHY: Myers, F. W. H. 1889. "On Recognized Apparitions Occurring More Than a Year After Death." PSPR 6:13.

**Ozanne, Charles, 1865–1961.** American educator. A teacher of history at Harvard University and Radcliffe College, he became interested in psychical research in the 1920s. Of all the areas in that field, he felt, however, that the "Greatest of all the problems with which psychical research has to deal is the question of whether human personality can survive bodily death, and whether, if such survival is a fact, there is a possibility of communication between those who exist in that other realm and men still here on earth" (Ozanne, 1942:88–89).

ALthough Ozanne conducted experiments with the medium Mrs. Chenoweth, he served psychical research best as a philanthropist. In 1928 and 1929, his money permitted Walter F. Prince, then research officer of the Boston Society for Psychic Research, to conduct a large-scale inquiry into psychic experiences. In 1936, he gave financial aid to the BSPR again so that it could publish a study of Joseph G. Pratt's. In 1937 and 1938, he supported research done by Joseph B. Rhine and the Parapsychology Laboratory at Duke University and gave money toward the publication of its *Journal of Parapsychology.* On the advice of Gardner Murphy whom he greatly admired and as a gesture of American good will and cooperation (the British were after all our wartime allies), in 1943 he sent the sum of $500 to the Society for Psychical Research.

Ozanne was so interested in the work being done at the Parapsychology Laboratory that he moved from Cleveland, Ohio, to Durham, North Carolina. But when he perceived that his deep concern with the question of survival was not being addressed by Rhine or the Parapsychology Laboratory who seemed bent on what Ozanne thought were trivial areas of investigation (Berger, 1988), Ozanne provided money for the establishment in 1960 of the **Psychical Research Foundation.** This organization was to be devoted exclusively to the investigation of the survival question. Ozanne, who died in the year it began operations, bequeathed his estate to the PRF in the hope of ensuring that it would deal with this "greatest of all problems."

Selected Writing: 1942. "A Layman Looks at Psychical Research." JASPR 36:76.;

BIBLIOGRAPHY: Berger, A. S. *Lives and Letters in American Parapsychology,* 1988.

# P

**p (Probability).** The fraction of times that in a great number of **Chance** repetitions the observed result will be equaled or exceeded (JP).

**P (Probability).** The number which the fraction of successes approaches in the limit with a sufficiently large sucession of **Chance Trials;** that is, in chance matchings with five targets, P = 1/5, or one success in five trials (JP).

**Pact, Life After Death.** See **Life After Death Pact.**

**Padre Pio.** See **Pio, Padre.**

**Pagenstecher, Gustav, 1855–1942.** German-born Mexican medical doctor. With a degree from the University of Leipzig, Dr. Pagenstecher was a materialist whose discovery, when he was sixty-five years old, of the paranormal powers of a patient, Sra. **María Reyes de Zierold,** forced him to admit that there was something in the universe transcending matter. **Walter Franklin Prince** conducted one extremely striking psychometric experiment in Mexico with Sra. de Zierold in which she obtained information she could not have known. Both Pagenstecher and Prince published the results of work with her in the *Proceedings* and *Journal of the American Society for Psychical Research.*

Because of the loss of most of his money after World War I—it had been invested in Germany—Pagenstecher was forced to give up his work with psychometry and return to private practice. In November 1921 Sra. de Zierold in deep trance made some predictions that Pagenstecher sealed in three separate envelopes and sent to Prince to be kept unopened. In 1935 he wrote to Prince to open the envelopes since some of the predictions were apparently being fulfilled. Unfortunately, Prince had died in August 1934 and the experiment seems never to have been concluded.

Pagenstecher, an eloquent speaker, despite his unorthodox views was elected president of the Mexican Medical Society.

Selected Writings: 1922. "Past Events Seership: A Study in Psychometry." PASPR 16:1.

BIBLIOGRAPHY: Allison, L. W. 1943. "In Memory of Dr. Gustav Pagenstecher." JASPR 37:138; Prince, W. F. 1921. "Psychometrical Experiments with Señora Maria Reyes de Z." PASPR 15:189.

**Paine, Albert Bigelow, 1861–1937.** American author and biographer. He was authorized by Mark Twain (Samuel L. Clemens's pseudonym) to write his biography. Paine's three volume work, *Mark Twain, A Biography: The Personal and Literary Life of Samuel Langhorne Clemens* (1912), and other writings about Clemens, although considered uncritical by some writers, remain the principal sources of information about him.

Paine also was the author of *Joan of Arc—Maid of France.*

Paine tells about an incident of interest in psychical research that involved Clemens and himself: "[O]ne afternoon about five o'clock [I] fell over a coal-scuttle and scarified myself a good deal between the ankle and the knee . . . Next morning I received a note, prompted by Mr. Clemens, in which he said; 'Tell Paine I am sorry he fell and skinned his shin at five o'clock yesterday afternoon.' I was naturally astonished, and immediately wrote: 'I did fall and skin my shin at five o'clock yesterday, but how did you find it out?' I . . . learned at the same hour on the same afternoon Clemens himself had fallen up the front steps and, as he said, peeled off from his 'starboard shin a ribbon of skin three inches long.' The disaster was still uppermost in his mind at the time of writing, and the suggestion of my own mishap had flashed out for no particular reason."

It is possible that the two accidents were a coincidence and that no relationship exists between them. Yet the case looks like one of telepathy in which Clemens gained the paranormal knowledge of Paine's fall over the coal scuttle. If telepathy be accepted, Paine's experience makes him another **Noted Witness** for this phenomenon.

BIBLIOGRAPHY: Prince, W. F. *Noted Witnesses for Psychic Occurrences,* 1963, p. 219.

**Palingenesis.** See **Reincarnation.**

**Palladino, Eusapia, 1854–1918.** Famous Italian physical medium. She was an illiterate Neapolitan peasant. Her mother died giving birth to her; her father was murdered. She seems to have developed psychic gifts at puberty upon joining a Spiritualist group, her control when she was in deep trance being **"John King."** She was said to be "of such a decidedly erotic nature that . . . she thought of little else. . . . [The] unashamed exhibition of her erotic needs . . . [was] such that men were both impressed and attracted whereas women were repelled. Indeed it was suggested that . . . men . . . were rendered incapable of both criticism and judgment" (Dingwall, 1962:194).

Eusapia was discovered by **Enrico Damiani,** a Neopolitan Spiritualist. On his death, she disappeared to be rediscovered by **Ercole Chiaia** who brought her gifts as a medium to the attention of scholars and scientists outside Neapolitan circles. Over a period of twenty years, she was frequently studied by leading scientists and psychical researchers who differed over whether her phenomena—table levitations, grasps, touches, lights, materialization (usually of hands), blowing curtains, raps, movement of objects, playing of musical instruments, scents, and, occasionally, direct writing—were genuine. The skeptical Italian psychiatrist and founder of criminology Cesare Lombroso became convinced that they were. So did Prof. Enrico Morselli, a noted neurologist, who declared that the manifestations during her séances were genuine. However, neither Lombroso nor Morselli believed that the medium's phenomena required spiritistic explanations.

Prof. Charles Richet of France over a long period of investigation also concluded that, although Eusapia cheated from time to time, much of her phenomena were genuine. F. W. H. Myers was at first convinced, then changed his mind, but later came once more to believe that she produced at least some genuine phenomena. But Richard Hodgson, Henry and Eleanor Sidgwick and Alice Johnson as a result of what Fraser Nicol (1972) calls the "disastrous" (because, he says, ineptly handled) sittings in Cambridge, England, in 1895, all believed that she cheated and that "once a cheat, always a cheat." They thought that malobservation and a wish to believe deceived those who were convinced by Eusapia Palladino. As a result of their opposition the Society for Psychical Research refused to investigate her from 1898 until 1908.

In that year a careful study ("a classic of psychical research" [Nicol, 1972]) by Everard Feilding, Hereward Carrington and W. W. Baggally indicated that much of her phenomena were indeed genuine and produced by a force not known to orthodox science. There were eleven sittings during which occurred 470 instances of physical phenomena, including levitations of the séance table, movement of curtains, bulgings of Palladino's dress, psychokinesis (movement of objects), raps and sounds on musical instruments without contact, materialization of hands, unusual lights, and air currents. All the experimenters concurred that many of the phenomena were genuine. The séance room was set up in such a way that no accomplice could have entered it, and nothing could have been hidden without the experimenters' knowledge. They found that the better the experimental conditions, that is, when the light was good and the medium's hands and feet were under the tightest control, the best phenomena were produced.

In 1909, Carrington brought Eusapia Palladino to the United States. In December 1909 she was caught cheating by Prof. Hugo Münsterberg of Harvard and in April 1910 she was exposed again at Columbia University, this time by conjurers (Kurtz, 1985). In December 1910 in Naples Everard Feilding conducted another series of tests and this time concluded that all the phenomena produced were fraudulent (Feilding and Marriott, 1911). Carrington (who was not present at this last series of tests) remained convinced to the end of Eusapia's paranormal powers. And so we are left with the question of how much, if any, of her phenomena were genuinely produced.

BIBLIOGRAPHY: Dingwall, E. J. *Very Peculiar People,* 1962, pp. 18–214; Feilding, E., Baggally, W. W., and Carrington, H. 1909. "Reports on a Series of Sittings with Eusapia Palladino." PSPR 23:209; Feilding, E. and Marriott, W. 1911. "Report on a Series of Sittings with Eusapia Palladino at Naples." PSPR 25:57; Gauld, A. *The Founders of Psychical Research,* 1968; Kurtz, P. "Spiritualists, Mediums and Psychics." In his *A Skeptic's Handbook of Parapsychology,* 1985; Lombroso, C. *After Death—What?* 1909; Morselli, E. *Psicología e "Spiritismo,"* 1908; Nicol, F. 1972. "The Founders of the S.P.R." PSPR 55:341, 360–362; Sidgwick, H. 1894. "Disinterested Deception." JSPR 6:274.

**Palmer, John (Albert), 1944–.** American parapsychologist. Presently senior research Associate at the Institute for Parapsychology in Durham, North Carolina, Dr. Palmer first became interested in parapsychology when, in his senior year in high school, he read René Sudre's *Treatise on Parapsychology.* During his undergraduate years at Duke University, his interest was further developed by working as a research fellow at J. B. Rhine's Parapsychology Laboratory there.

Dr. Palmer's principal interests in the field are the psychological correlates of psi, altered states of consciousness (especially out-of-body experiences) and parapsychology as it relates to the philosophy of science, particularly with respect to its critics.

Dr. Palmer has co-authored a book (1986), contributed chapters to others, and has written numerous articles for scientific and parapsychological journals. He has received many grants including one from the Parapsychology Foundation for the study of extrasensory perception and OBEs, another from the McDonnell Foundation for the development of a parapsychology laboratory, and a third from the European Research Office of the United States Army for a critical review of parapsychology.

After receiving his Ph.D. in 1969 from the University of Texas at Austin, Dr. Palmer was an associate professor at McGill University, a research associate at the University of Virginia School of Medicine, an assistant research psychologist at the University of California at Davis, an associate professor and assistant dean of the Graduate School of Consciousness Studies at John F. Kennedy University, and a research associate at the University of Utrecht. He was president of the Parapsychological Association in 1979. He has been an editorial consultant for the *Journal of the American Society for Psychical Research* and chairman of the Publications Committee of the *Journal of Parapsychology.* He is also a member of the American Psychological Association and in April 1988 was elected president of the American Society for Psychical Research.

Selected Writings: 1983. "Sensory Contamination of Free-Response ESP Targets: The Greasy Fingers Hypothesis." JASPR 77:101; 1983. "In Defense of Parapsychology." *Zetetic Scholar* 11:39, 91; "ESP Research Findings." In S. Krippner, ed., *Advances in Parapsychology,* Vol. 2, 1979; "Attitudes and Personality Traits." In B. Wolman, ed., *Handbook of Parapsychology,* 1977; and Edge, H. L., Morris, R.L. and Rush, J. H. *Foundations of Parapsychology,* 1986.

**Palmistry.** Also known as Chiromancy, it is an art practiced since ancient times in India, Tibet, China, and Europe. Gypsy fortune tellers use it to predict the future and to read character by interpreting the patterns of lines, creases, loops, whorls, and arches on the palm and fingertips. Doctors have demonstrated that there are correlations between these patterns and patients' diseases. But while palm diagnosis may have some support, there is little empirical basis for claims that palms supply information about character or permit the palmist to divine future events. Walter F. Prince once called palmistry "another set of irrational assumptions rooted in the hoary past" and he assigned the subject to the "ash-pile" (Prince, 1930).

From the psychical researcher's viewpoint, this disposition of palmistry may be justified if a palmist's correct statements are the result of cues received from the behavior of the person whose palm is being read or of responses made by that individual. But if the palmist happens to be a psychic and the information received is the result of the palmist's psi, then palmistry becomes relevant and more interesting to psychical research. No experiments have been reported, however, to determine and confirm that psi operates in the ancient art.

BIBLIOGRAPHY: Prince, W.F. 1930. "Presidential Address." PSPR 39:247.

**Palm Sunday Case.** See **Balfour, Arthur J.**

**Paragnost.** Dutch term for a psychic.

**Paragnosy.** Dutch term for ESP.

**Paramnesia.** A falsification or distortion of memory or recognition. An alternative interpretation suggested by some researchers for cases of the reincarnation-type in which those purportedly reincarnated seem to be familiar with people, places, or names they normally could not have encountered. See also **Déjà vu.**

**Paranormal.** A term applied to phenomena that presently understood laws of cause and effect cannot explain. Synonymous with parapsychical, **psychic,** or paraspychological phenomena. Such phenomena are not supernatural. They are as much a part of nature as any other phenomena.

A paranormal event was defined by the British philosopher C. D. Broad as one that conflicts with any of the **"Basic Limiting Principles"** that we take for granted and on which we base both our scientific theories and our practical activities. For example, we take it for granted that we cannot know what experience another is having unless the second person tells us about it or somehow reveals it to one of our senses. Since **Extrasensory Perception** conflicts with this principle, it is a paranormal phenomenon.

**Paranormal Photography.** See **Spirit Photography; Thoughtography.**

**Parapsychical.** See **Paranormal.**

**Parapsychological Association.** Created in the United States in 1957 on the initiative of **J. B. Rhine,** the Parapsychological Association is an organization consisting of about 300 scholars and scientists from about thirty countries representing a wide spectrum of disciplines. It has as its principal objects the advancement of the field of parapsychology, dissemination of information about parapsychology, and the integration with other branches of science of the findings of parapsychology. In 1969, the Parapsychological Association became an affiliate member of the American Association for the Advancement of Science. The current address of the P.A. is P.O. Box 12236, Research Triangle Park, North Carolina 27709.

**Parapsychological Journal of South Africa.** Published twice a year by the South African Society for Psychical Research. It publishes articles intended primarily to reflect South African research and activity in parapsychology but it publishes as well papers from foreign contributors.

**Parapsychologischen Arbeitsgruppe Basel** (Parapsychology Work Group of Basel). Swiss organization founded in Basel in 1967 at the suggestion of **Hans Bender.** Under the direction of Matthias Guldenstein, a teacher, it conducts experiments, offers lectures, and cooperates with Schweizer Parapsychologische Gesellschaft (Swiss Parapsychology Society) in holding annual "Basel Psi Days," large international congresses on a variety of parapsychological subjects. Address: c/o Psi Zentrum Basel, Guterstrasse 144, CH-4053, Basel, Switzerland.

**Parapsychology.** The German word *parapsychologie* was coined by **Max Dessoir** of Germany. The prefix *para* meaning "beside" was meant to mark off an area of the field of psychology. **J. B. Rhine** with the approval of

**William McDougall** adopted the word in 1935. Increasingly, albeitly incorrectly, the term is used in place of psychical research. Strictly speaking, parapsychology is a division of science that uses experimental and quantitative techniques in the laboratory to investigate paranormal or psychic experiences or events involving living organisms. More specifically, it is concerned with cognitive or kinetic behavior that seems independent of the organs of sense and movement. This behavior includes extrasensory perception and psychokinesis. The stage was set for parapsychology as we know it in the twentieth century when Joseph B. Rhine, with his new concepts, test procedures, and statistical methods, "brought the experimental side of psychical research" (Berger, 1988) to the world. Because of the work done by Rhine and his successors parapsychology emerged out of the older field of psychical research as its scientific arm seeking experimental control of psi phenomena.

In order to maintain scientific respectability, orthodox parapsychology avoids at present any connections with topics considered "occult," such as unidentified flying objects, I Ching, tarot cards, palmistry, black magic, astrology, the Bermuda Triangle, Atlantis, and the Abominable Snowman.

Parapsychology asks us to accept behavior that simply does not fit into the time-space-energy-motion picture of the world that physical science has painted for us. Today therefore we find that parapsychology is "an outpost under siege" (Berger, 1988) assaulted by skeptics who maintain that it is a pseudoscience and by orthodox scientists and academic psychologists who are hostile or indifferent to it. Critics both inside and outside of parapsychology say that its experimental procedures are flawed and that its claims of the paranormal are without empirical foundation. For example, in 1987 the National Research Council of the National Academy of Sciences concluded in its report that "The Committee finds no scientific justification from research over the last 130 years for the existence of parapsychological phenomena" (Druckman and Swets, 1988). On the other hand, parapsychology remains a viable enterprise for many because "of all the sciences, it is the only discipline attempting to part the curtain of mystery drawn over human nature" (Berger, 1988). In addition, negative attitudes and reports to the contrary notwithstanding, it has collected data from the laboratory that seem to indicate the occurrence of phenomena outside the mechanisms of our organs of motion and sense.

BIBLIOGRAPHY: Berger, A. S. *Lives and Letters in American Parapsychology: A Biographical History, 1850–1987,* 1988; Druckman, D. and Swets J.A., eds., *Enhancing Human Performance. Issues, Theories, and Techniques,* 1988; Rhine, J. B. *Extrasensory Perception,* 1934; Wolman, B., ed., *Handbook of Parapsychology,* 1977.

**Parapsychology Abstracts International.** A semiannual of abstracts from both English and non-English journals and from articles on parapsychology in parapsychological reports, theses, and books and in non-parapsychological publications as well. It was founded by **Rhea A. White** and is published by **Parapsychology Sources of Information Center.**

**Parapsychology Foundation.** Established in 1951 by Eileen J. Garrett and Frances P. Bolton to further knowledge in parapsychology, the foundation encourages and provides financial assistance for research and laboratory experiments in the field. It has supported quantitative and qualitative studies by individual and groups of scientists, since 1953 has sponsored conferences both in the United States and abroad, and has published proceedings of its conferences, research studies in the form of parapsychological monographs and periodical such as *Parapsychology Review,* the *International Journal of Parapsychology,* and the magazine *Tomorrow* (the latter two now defunct). The foundation is not a membership organization and does no research of its own. It does, however, maintain an excellent library whose books are focussed on parapsychology. Staffed by a professional librarian, it is a fine resource for people seriously engaged in the study of parapsychology. The offices of the foundation are at 228 E. 71st St., New York, New York 10021.

**Parapsychology Laboratory.** With the approval of William McDougall, head of the Department of Psychology at Duke University, in 1935 **Joseph B. Rhine** organized and became the director of a separate Parapsychology Division of the Psychology Department called the Parapsychology Laboratory. In 1950, the Parapsychology Laboratory became autonomous and continued so until Rhine's retirement from Duke University in 1962 when it was transferred to the **Institute of Parapsychology.** From the mid-1930s on, the Parapsychology Laboratory was the scene in the United States of pioneering and extensive experiments in extrasensory perception and psychokinesis and the force that molded parapsychology into a branch of science.

**Parapsychology Review.** The former bimonthly official journal of the Parapsychology Foundation which ceased publication in 1990. It offered articles from scholars and scientists in all fields who have something to say about parapsychology. It also published news of conferences and current events, book reviews, and other matters of parapsychological interest anywhere in the world.

**Parapsychology Sources of Information Center.** Established by Rhea A. White, its object is to collect, catalogue and index all English language books, journals, and periodicals dealing with parapsychology, Jungian psychology, humanistic and transpersonal psychology, and mysticism. The information center runs computerized searches of authors and subjects and compiles bibliographies for researchers. The center also maintains collections of all the books and journals abstracted for *Parapsychology Abstracts International,* the council files of the Parapsychological Association, and the editorial records of *Theta* and *Research in Parapsychology.*

The office address is: 2 Plane Tree Lane, Dix Hills, N.Y. 11746.

**Parsons, Denys, 1914–.** Member of the British Skeptics, the British branch of the Committee for the Scientific Investigation of Claims of the Paranormal. Mr. Parsons has been a member of the Society for Psychical Research since 1942, was a member of its council for twenty years and joint honorary secretary of the SPR from 1948 to 1958. His principal interests in psychical research and parapsychology have been the investigation of telepathy, psychokinesis, retrocognition, radiesthesia, and dowsing. He writes that much of the fascination in parapsychological research lies in following every trail and that "research in parapsychology is akin to research in criminology and forensic medicine" (1985). His object has been to examine the cases and phenomena alleged to be paranormal and to present evidence that they have normal explanations. Insofar as his own investigations have been concerned, he seems always to have met this objective. He concludes that the layman does not know how to make a systematic investigation and, if such an investigation might disprove a claimed paranormal experience, does not want to make one.

Mr. Parsons was, until his retirement in 1979, head of press and public Relations at the British Library and, since then, has been doing research on behalf of authors.

Selected Writings: "Detective Work in Parapsychology." In P. Kurtz, ed., *A Skeptic's Handbook of Parapsychology,* 1985, pp. 599–609; 1982. "Dowsing—A Claim Refuted." JSPR 51:384; 1962. "A Non-Existent Building Located." JSPR 41:292; 1956. "Cloudbusting—A Claim Investigated." JSPR 38:352; 1948. "On the Need for Caution in Assessing Mediumistic Material." PSPR 48:344.

**Past Life Regression.** A subject under hypnosis is led back to the early years of childhood and then to the times prior to birth in order to obtain from the subject details of a prior life. *Prima facie* success of such regressions have brought fame and fortune to many hypnotists who have written best-selling books such as Morey Bernstein's *The Search for Bridey Murphy.* Unless valid criticisms of these regressions are met, however, it is difficult to take them seriously. Among these criticisms is the readiness of hypnotists and others to accept the assertions made by a subject without any effort to verify the details presented. If research has been done and an item or two verified, no negative data are given—such as that the records do not show the birth or death of the personality taken on by the subject or the existence of the family of the personality. A strong criticism always is that past life accounts under hypnosis are merely fantasies stimulated by the suggestions of the hypnotist. If facts are given that diligent research has verified, it is often possible that these details could have been learned by the subject in a normal manner at some time in the past, had been forgotten, and that the memories of them simply were revived and dramatized as a result of hypnosis and suggestion. See also **Bridey Murphy; Cryptomnesia.**

**Peak in Darien.** The title of a book written at the turn of the century by Francis P. Cobbe. The term is now applied to a form of deathbed vision in which a dying individual "sees" a dead person of whose previous death the one dying had no normal way of knowing.

A case of this kind was reported by F. W. H. Myers in his *Human Personality and its Survival of Bodily Death.* A woman had a guest named Julia X stay with her for a week. The guest had a beautiful singing voice and, in fact, was training to become a professional singer but never had a singing career. She and her hostess never saw each other again. Six or seven years later, the hostess, who had been seriously ill for a long time, was now dying. She was in her bed perfectly composed and discussing some business when suddenly she changed the subject and asked her companion, "Do you hear those voices singing?. . . I am sure they are the angels welcoming me to Heaven. . . . it is strange, there is one voice amongst them I am sure I know, and cannot remember whose voice it is." Then the woman stopped and pointed to the corner of the room. "[I]t is Julia X; she is coming on; she is leaning over you; . . . she is going. . . . She is gone." The companion thought that it was only a fantasy of the dying woman. But two days later, the *Times* recorded the death of Julia from puerperal fever. On the day of her death, she had started to sing in the morning and sang to the final moment.

The title "Peak in Darien" was adopted by F. R. Cobbe from Keat's sonnet *On First Looking into Chapman's Homer.* In the sonnet, "a peak in Darien" was the summit from which Cortez and his men first saw the great Pacific. The phrase was used in the book and is now used to indicate how dying people seem to see another reality for the first time.

**Pearce, Hubert.** Mid-twentieth-century American clergyman. He was convinced from his childhood in Arkansas of the existence of psychic powers because of his mother's psychic experiences and production of physical phenomena. Frightened by these powers, which he was afraid he shared, Pearce became "in [J. B.] Rhine's view, the greatest living proof of ESP" (Brian, 1982:119). Pearce first met Rhine in 1932 when the latter was trying to recruit students at Duke University to work either as subjects or experimenters in tests of extrasensory perception. Although Pearce was at first reluctant, Rhine persuaded him that he had nothing to fear and that, as a divinity student, he would have the opportunity of confirming some of the miracles reported in the Bible. From nul results in his early work with J. G. Pratt, Pearce began to score well, his culminating achievement being his twenty-five consecutive correct calls in an informal experiment with Rhine. The odds against a chance result such as this were, according to Rhine, 298,023,223,876,953,125 to 1!

Pearce is best known in parapsychology for the **Pearce-Pratt Experiments** which, although later severely criticized by Clarence E. M. Hansel (1966), are still considered among the most important experiments in clairvoyance ever conducted. William McDougall and Walter Franklin Prince on learning of Pearce's overall results in 10,300 trials of calling ESP cards (an average of 9.1 correct calls out of a possible 25 instead of 5 out of 25 expected by chance) found the results "almost too good to be true, even 'alarming'" (Brian, 1982:101). And "the chance odds [in the Pearce-Pratt experiment]s were 1 in $1^{11}$" (Pratt, 1977:60).

Pearce's abilities left him as rapidly as they had developed. A short time after the conclusion of the Pearce-Pratt experiments, Pearce had some bad news from home. From then on he was never able to score above chance in tests with ESP cards.

BIBLIOGRAPHY: Berger, A. S. *Lives and Letters in American Parapsychology,* 1988; Brian, D. *The Enchanted Voyager,* 1982; Hansel, C. E. M. *ESP: A Scientific Evaluation,* 1966; Pratt, J. G. *Parapsychology, An Insider's View of ESP,* 1977.

**Pearce-Pratt Experiments.** See **Pearce, Hubert; Pratt, Joseph G.**

**Pearl Tie-Pin Case.** Famous case in the annals of psychical research. Its evidence, said Sir Wiliam Barrett, "points unmistakably to a telepathic message from" a dead soldier (Barrett, 1918:185). In this case, a message was received by Geraldine Cummins ("Miss D. C.") and Hester Travers Smith who were playing with a ouija board. Geraldine Cummins's cousin had been an officer killed in France during World War I. It was nothing extraordinary when the cousin's name was spelled out for them on the board. But the next day a message came requesting the officer's mother to give his pearl tie pin to a girl he was going to marry. The name and address of the girl, both unknown to the women, were given. A letter sent to her was returned as incorrectly addressed and the ladies dismissed the entire matter as a piece of fiction. Six months later, however, when the military authorities returned his possessions to the family of the dead officer, they found out that he had been engaged to the girl whose name had come through the ouija board. Among his things were his pearl tie pin and his will in which the girl was named. Whether or not Barrett was right in thinking that the evidence necessarily pointed to a message from the dead officer, the case is a remarkable one requring some paranormal explanation.

BIBLIOGRAPHY: Barrett, W.F. *On the Threshold of the Unseen,* 1918.

**Pelham, George.** See **Piper, Leonora E.**

**Pendulum.** A device used by dowsers or others claiming psychic abilities. It consists of a ball, ring, or other object suspended by a thread which, when held, swings in one direction or another to indicate a location or an answer to a question.

**Penelhum, Terence, 1929–.** British philosopher. Professor of philosophy at the University of Calgary where he has also held the post of dean of arts and science, Penelhum focusses his attention on the hypothesis of discarnate survival after death and denies its logical possibility (Penelhum, 1970).

As a philosopher, Penelhum is not concerned with the religious teachings or empirical data bearing on the question but, rather, on the conceptual problems involved, especially the fundamental issue of personal identity and the criteria for identifying a disembodied postmortem person as being identical with a pre-mortem person. Penelhum rejects memory as a criterion and argues that only bodily continuity will do because that is something everyone can observe and recognize. In Penelhum's view, therefore, disembodied survival is an impossibility and no evidence, whether from mediums or otherwise, can be admitted for it. His position is shared by many who believe that identity cannot be shown in terms of personal memory.

To show that this position is incorrect evidence of personal memories from people postmortem would have to be unique in order to serve to identify them. An effort of this kind is **Arthur S. Berger**'s research and **Dictionary Test** in which the identification of select communicators depends on their memories of secret keys unknown to anyone living that would decipher messages they left behind (Berger, 1987). Philosopher Anthony G. N. Flew whose position with respect to disembodied survival is similar to Penelhum's has acknowledged that the memory criterion used in Berger's effort is a significant step forward in survival research (Flew, 1987). See also **Identity, Personal.**

Selected Writing: *Survival and Disembodied Existence,* 1970.

BIBLIOGRAPHY: Berger, A. S. *Aristocracy of the Dead,* 1987; Flew, A. Foreword. In A. S. Berger, *Aristocracy of the Dead,* 1987.

**Percipient.** A term correlative to "agent"; the individual to whom an impression is transmitted by an agent or who attempts to grasp what is in the agent's mind. Also one who experiences ESP or is a subject whose ESP ability or power of psychokinesis is tested. See also **Extrasensory Perception.**

**Perera Molina, Ramos, 1939–.** Spanish parapsychologist. The first professor of parapsychology ever appointed in a Spanish university (Universidad Autónoma de Madrid) and a founder of the Sociedad Española de Parapsicología, Perera created experimental techniques for inducing relaxation, mediumistic trances and other altered states of consciousness. He coined the term **"Psi-Omega"** to describe these techniques. He has also conducted field investigations into the practices of healers with an emphasis on the sociological aspects of their work. He continues as president of the Sociedad Española de Parapsicología.

**Perispirit.** See **Astral Body.**

**Perovsky-Petrovo-Solovovo, Count (Michael Solovioy), 1868–1954.** Russian nobleman. He joined the Society for Psychical Research in 1890 and collected Russian cases for the Census of Hallucinations. His main interest, however, was in physical phenomena.

In 1893 he wrote a letter to the *Journal* of the SPR in which he described how, with the second and third toes of his left foot, he produced spurious "spirit raps" identical to the raps the **Fox Sisters** were said to produce and which they claimed were made by spirit entities. He investigated the Russian physical medium S. F. Sambor who seemed to pass matter through matter (until Perovsky-Petrovo-Solovovo discovered that the simple expedient of passing a ribbon through the sleeves of the medium and those of his neighbors or of tying the medium's hands stopped the phenomena).

Although the count and his wife cooperated with Everard Feilding and W. Marriott in a short series of sittings with Eusapia Palladino in Naples in which some genuine phenomena seemed to have been produced, his experience with a cultivated, well-educated friend with an excellent reputation (he was the count's colleague at the Chancery of the Imperial Ministry of Foreign Affairs and a distinguished writer) was disillusioning for Perovsky-Petrovo-Solovovo. In 1910 he learned that for many years and without any apparent motive the friend was permitting mediums (including Sambor) to produce fraudulent phenomena by not controlling them properly. "Here, in this morbid tendency to deceive anonymously and systematically merely for the sake of deceiving, how much havoc may have been wrought in psychical research?" asked the count.

He wrote several articles for the *Proceedings* of the SPR in which he suggested that the conditions of the séance might cause such a state of mind in the sitter that either hallucinations might occur or fraud could be committed unobserved. He maintained that if the physical phenomena of Spiritualism exist, other mediums as talented as D. D. Home was reputed to have been would of necessity appear.

He owed his survival of the Russian Revolution to his being in Europe at the time, but his estates and excellent library (except for one book on psychical research which he had with him) were, of course, lost. See also **Mattiesen, Emil.**

Selected Writings: 1937. "My Experiments with S. F. Sambor." JSPR 30:87; 1911. "Les Phénomènes Physiques de Spiritisme." PSPR 25:413; 1909. "The Hallucination Theory as Applied to Certain Cases of Physical Phenomena." PSPR 21:436; 1893. "On the Production of Spurious 'Spirit Raps.'" JSPR 6:120.

**Perrott Studentship in Psychical Research.** Established in 1940 at Trinity College, Cambridge, England, to provide money to the person selected for research into mental phenomena or physical phenomena. Anyone at least twenty-one years of age may apply for the studentship and, to be considered, must submit the course of research, the names of three referees, and the candidate's qualifications. Students who have been selected in the past have included Celia E. Green, Samuel G. Soal and W. Whately Carington. The studentship has a tenure of one year during which the student may not pursue any other work that would interfere with the research. The studentship was made possible by a bequest to Trinity College by Frank D. Perrott in memory of Frederic W. H. Myers. It is now known as the Perrott-Warrick Studentship. Applications can be sent to Professor D. J. West, 32 Fen Road, Milton, Cambridge CB4 4AD, England.

**Perry, Michael Charles, 1933–.** British Anglican clergyman, presently archdeacon of Durham, England. Interested in psychical research and in parapsychology from childhood, he became a member of the Society for Psychical Research in 1951 and is now on its council. His main interests in psychical research and parapsychology are the relation of their data to the beliefs and practices of mainstream Christianity. To that end he has contributed articles and reviews to numerous parapsychological periodicals, including the *Journal of the Society for Psychical Research,* the *Journal of Religion and Psychical Research,* the *Parapsychology Review,* and *Theta.*

The Venerable Michael Perry has also written many books, some relevant to psychical research and parapsychology (1959, 1975, 1984). In the first of these works he maintained that the survival hypothesis is reasonable and that the resurrection of Christ cannot have been a resurrection of the flesh. In the second he tried "to show the link between the empirical evidence of psychical research and the claims of Christian theology." In the last, a collection of the author's essays, lectures, and sermons, the Ven. Michael Perry explores the implications of psychic phenomena for Christian thinking and tries to build bridges between psychical research and religion.

In a 1986 article in *The Christian Parapsy-*

*chologist* of which he has been editor since 1978, Perry writes: "Our knowledge of the paranormal makes it quite possible and sensible to aver that Moses and Elijah were in some real sense present and conversing with Jesus on the mountain of transfiguration . . . the disciples . . . were in an altered state of consciousness . . . which was probably psi-conducive . . .". He has also edited a book (1987) on psychic disturbances and occult involvement.

Recipient of an M.A. degree from Cambridge University in 1958, Perry in 1970, after holding various positions in the Church of England, assumed his present post of archdeacon of Durham and canon residentiary of Durham Cathedral. Since 1986 he has been chairman of the **Churches's Fellowship for Psychical and Spiritual Studies.**

Selected Writings: ed., *Deliverance,* 1987; 1986. "Parapsychology and the Transfiguration of Jesus." *The Christian Parapsychologist* 6:223; *Psychic Studies: A Christian's View,* 1984; *The Resurrection of Man,* 1975; *The Easter Enigma,* 1959.

**Persona Hypothesis.** To be distinguished from its normal meaning (i.e., a character in a novel or stage play), this term was invented by **Hornell Hart.** It describes his theory that a communicator in a mediumistic séance may be a personality structure or "persona" produced in part by the communicator and in part by sitters and mediums who unconsciously have used their histrionic powers to create the "persona." The personality structure may be the means by which the communicator is able to manifest consciousness and activity. The hypothesis can also explain apparitions of the living whose personalities may be constructed with the help of percipients.

**Personal Identity.** See **Identity, Personal.**

**Perty, Maximillan, 1804–1884.** Swiss professor at the University of Berne. In an effort to delve into the secret of human life and destiny, he was one of the earliest pioneers in the investigation of paranormal phenomena in his country. The author of many scholarly works, he was particularly drawn to the study of spontaneous cases over the centuries.

BIBLIOGRAPHY: Locher, T. "History of Psychical Research in Switzerland." *Proceedings of an International Conference. Parapsychology Today: A Geographic View,* 1971, p. 131.

**Phantasm.** Generally a visual hallucination or apparition, the word can refer to a broader range of sensory impressions, whether of hearing, taste, smell, or touch.

**Phantasms of the Living.** The title of a work, published in 1886, by Edmund Gurney (the principal author), F. W. H. Myers and Frank Podmore. It dealt with a class of apparition known as "crisis apparitions" in which one person believes that he or she hears the voice of or sees another person who is elsewhere and involved in some crisis, including death. The 1,300 page *Phantasms of the Living* included some experiments and set forth about 700 spontaneous cases "where there is reason to suppose that the mind of one human being has affected the mind of another without speech uttered, or word written or sign made"—in other words by telepathy.

The authors of the book believed that crisis apparitions were created by a telepathic message from the one undergoing the crisis that caused the recipient of the message to have an hallucination. The work is considered a classic and one of the high points in the early work of the Society for Psychical Research. Although many of the cases it reported have been shrugged off by skeptics, recent work has shown that many of their counterexplanations are incorrect.

**Phinuit.** See **Piper, Leonora E.**

**Phone Calls, Paranormal.** Messages received *via* the telephone (which may or may not be in working order) from someone the recipient knows to be dead or later learns was dead at the time the call was received. Although many of the calls are very brief, a few are lengthy and seem at the time quite normal. The problem from the pint of view of psychical research is that most of the cases reported are unsubstantiated stories. A few, however, give information unknown to anyone alive—for example, actress Ida Lupino's call from her dead father who told her where to find a deed. Some (including Ida Lupino's) are witnessed by one or more people: In one case the dead caller kept leaving messages for someone he was trying to reach.

D. Scott Rogo and Raymond Bayless who

co-authored a book (1979) on the subject argue that paranormal phone calls indicate that "we not only survive death, but can make contact with the living afterwards . . . [and] this contact can be made over the telephone!" (p.2.) Other explanations, excluding fraud, have been offered to explain these fascinating spontaneous cases: psychokinesis on the part of the living, telepathy at the moment of death, or hallucination.

BIBLIOGRAPHY: Rogo, D. S. and Bayless, R. *Phone Calls from the Dead,* 1979\1980.

**Photography, Paranormal.** See **Paranormal Photography.**

**Physical Medium.** See **Medium, Physical.**

**Physical Phenomena.** All at once the body of a man grows by several inches; an illuminated arm takes form and floats through the darkened room of a séance; in 1848, a child named Kate Fox claps her hands a number of times and an invisible entity, "Mr. Splitfoot," responds with an equal number of raps. These are some examples of physical phenomena, also called "telekinetic phenomena," generally associated with Spiritualism.

These phenomena occurring other than through the mind or muscles of a mental medium are supposed to demonstrate a force or unseen agency operating in the physical world. They are distinguished from mental phenomena and table-tilting and include: 1. **raps,** thumps, bangs or other percussive sounds that seem to suggest an unseen intelligence as in the case of the Fox Sisters; 2. **ectoplasm;** 3. **elongation;** 4. movements and **levitations** of human beings and physical objects without contact; 5. **materializations;** 6. the appearance of mysterious lights; 7. playing of apparently unheld musical instruments; 8. **direct voice;** 9. **slate-writing;** 10. **spirit photography;** 11. **apports;** 12. **fire tests** including handling or walking on red hot coals.

In spite of frequent discoveries of fraud and questionable experimental results, these phenomena occupied the attention of the early investigators of the Society for Psychical Research. The genuineness of these phenomena remains an open issue, especially in the light of evidence showing what poor witnesses people are (Hodgson and Davey, 1887; Besterman, 1932). Yet Stephen E. Braude writes (1986) that one "may not dismiss . . . accounts [of these phenomena] on the grounds that human testimony is unreliable, biased, and so forth. Moreover, when the conditions of observation are not conducive to malobservation . . . , appeals to faulty perception or memory are also of little utility. Likewise, last-ditch appeals to collective hallucination or hypnosis explain far too little. Finally, . . . assuming (plausibly) the accounts to be truthful, conjuring or fraud seem equally out of the question" (p. 85) because "allegations of detection of fraud, or of malobservation, or of misinterpretation of what was observed, or of hypnotically induced hallucinations, have to be scrutinized *as closely and as critically* as must the testimony *for* the reality of the phenomena" (Ducasse, 1958:22).

Other kinds of physical phenomena usually associated with saints and mystics are believed to prove that marvels and miracles have been brought about by the action of the Most High. Besides the already mentioned levitation and elongation, these include **incorruptibility, stigmata, luminous phenomena,** the "odour of sanctity," posthumous bleeding and the multiplication of food. See also **Ectoplasy; Poltergeists; Telekinesis.**

BIBLIOGRAPHY: Besterman, T. 1932. "The Psychology of Testimony in Relation to Paraphysical Phenomena: Report of an Experiment." PSPR 40:363; Braude, S. E. *The Limits of Influence,* 1986; Ducasse, C. J. 1958. "Physical Phenomena in Psychical Research." JASPR 52:3; Hodgson, R. and Davey, S. J. "The Possibilities of Mal-Observation and Lapse of Memory from the Practical Point of View." PSPR 4:381.

**Physics, Quantum.** See **Quantum Theories.**

**Pickering, Edward Charles, 1846–1919.** American astronomer and physicist. Inventor of the meridian photometer that measures the magnitude of stars, Pickering was also director of the Harvard College Observatory. When William James, also at Harvard College, promoted the organization of the American Society for Psychical Research in 1885, Pickering was made one of its vice presidents. He became a member of the ASPR's committee on telepathy, made careful mathematical analyses of experiments conducted to test the phenomenon and concentrated on demonstrating the possibility of telepathy-caused errors committed in many scientific researches (Pickering, 1885).

Selected Writing: 1885. "Possibility of Errors in Scientific Researches, Due to Thought-Transference." PASPR 1:35.

**Pickett, George Edward, 1825–1875.** Major-general under the stars and bars of the Confederacy during the American Civil War. "Pickett's Charge" on July 3, 1863, in the Gettysburg campaign in which three-quarters of his division were lost is regarded as the most spectacular and bloody defeat of the South in the war.

Over a year earlier, on the night before the first battle of Cold Harbor, known as the battle of Gaines's Mill, fought on June 27, 1862, Pickett had a dream he described in a letter to his wife: "All last night the spirit of my dear mother semed to hover over me . . . I wonder if, up there, she is watching over me, trying to send me some message—some warning. I wish I knew." Perhaps Pickett's mother was trying to warn him, for on the morning of the next day Pickett was shot and put out of action for several months. He is a **Noted Witness** for a spirit communication and a paranormal dream. See also **Dream, Paranormal.**

BIBLIOGRAPHY: Prince, W. F. *Noted Witnesses for Psychic Occurrences,* 1963, p. 99.

**Pictographic Process.** A term invented by **James H. Hyslop** to describe the kind of interaction he believed existed between a medium and a communicator. The latter did not communicate in words but in symbolic ideas that the medium translated into words. In Hyslop's language: "supernormal sensory experiences are all of the same type and reducible to a single law, expressed by the *pictograph process.* This process means, that the communicator manages to elicit in the living subject a sensory phantasm of his thoughts, representing, but not necessarily directly corresponding to, the reality" (Hyslop, 1919:111).

BIBLIOGRAPHY: Hyslop, J. H. *Contact with the Other World,* 1919.

**Picture Drawing Experiment.** Among the first experiments ever conducted to test for telepathy, the picture drawing experiment involves an agent who concentrates on an object or drawing while a percipient tries to draw the agent's mental image. As early as 1883, Malcolm Guthrie in England pioneered this kind of experiment with two female subjects who were able to make successful drawings of faces, chairs, animals, and fish.

A striking series of picture drawing experiments were reported in 1930 by American novelist Upton Sinclair. With the agent forty miles away drawing objects that occurred to him—a tree, flower, hat, helmet, bird's nest—and inserting the drawings in opaque envelopes, Sinclair's wife, Mary, acting as percipient, relaxed and fixed her mind on each target drawing. When she made her call, she also made a drawing of the object. Out of 290 drawings, 70 were failures, 155 were partly successful and 65 were totally successful. Equally impressive experiments were conducted by René Warcollier in France.

Two difficulties arise in connection with such experiments, however. It is possible that the ideas in the agents' minds are held in common with percipients so that the targets and responses are similar because of this commonality of ideas and not because of telepathy. It is also possible that, in determining whether the drawings resemble one another, we interpret them too favorably in order to find a correspondence between a target drawing and that made by the percipient. To meet these criticisms today a randomizing procedure is generally used to make a target selection and there is an objective evaluation by independent judges, ignorant of the sequence of the targets, who match targets to the responses. Their matchings are then analyzed statistically.

**Picture Test.** An apparent effort by a communicator to supply evidence of survival after death by drawing the attention of a sitter to a picture that will be linked to the communicator's life or to the sitting. See also **Book Test; Newspaper Test.**

**Piddington (Smith), John George, 1869–1952.** British psychical researcher. In 1899 he changed his surname from Smith to Piddington (his mother's name) to avoid confusion with all the other Smiths in the Society for Psychical Research which he had joined in 1890.

Along with Eleanor Sidgwick, Oliver Lodge, Alice Johnson and Gerald Balfour, he played an important part in psychical research through his interpreting the 3,000 or more scripts from the so-called "S.P.R. group of automatists" (Margaret Verrall, Helen Verrall, Leonora Piper, "Mrs. Willett" [Winifred Coombe-Tenant], "Mrs. Holland" [Alice Fleming], "Mrs. King" [Dame Edith Lyttelton] and Mrs. Stuart Wilson). These scripts over a period of thirty years made up the famous **Cross-Correspondences.** During much of this time Piddington and Mrs. Sidgwick (Gerald Balfour's sister) lived with Balfour at his home, Fisher's Hill, where they spent their time poring over these supposed communications from their dead friends and relatives.

Piddington also, because F. W. H. Myers' notes on the medium Rosalie Thompson had been destroyed and the chapter dealing with her mediumship had been deleted from *Human Personality and Its Survival of Bodily Death* (Myers, 1903), wrote the most important paper on Mrs. Thompson's phenomena. He concluded that they were paranormal. He wrote an outspoken obituary of Richard Hodgson whom Piddington described as being "full of fun" but "lacking in a sense of humour" and of being rather like an Old Testament figure.

In his Presidential Address to the SPR in 1924, Piddington made a distinction between the "High-and-Dry School" of psychical research to which he belonged, "those of cautious and conservative views who uphold the strictest methods of investigation" (p. 145) and the "Not-High-and-Dry School" who wished to "relax . . . the stringent precautions and the very high standards of evidence . . . and generally adopt a less suspicious and mroe genial attitude towards mediums, automatists . . . and so forth" (p. 146). It was this difference of views that in the 1920s caused tremendous dissension in the SPR and ultimately led to many resignations from the society, among them Sir Arthur Conan Doyle.

A successful businessman, Piddington was instrumental in the creation of the Research Endowment Fund which he hoped would eventually provide sufficient funds for the employment of a full-time research officer. In 1905 he helped with the financial and other negotiations between the Society for Psychical Research and the newly independent American Society for Psychical Research. He held a variety of positions in the SPR and was its president for the years 1924–1925.

W. H. Salter (1952) writes of Piddington's "human sympathy[,] . . . sense of humour . . . and his obvious trustworthiness (p.715), yet Alan Gauld tells us that, as "the abhorred destroyer of documents" (at least in Eric J. Dingwall's mind), he was the latter's *bête noire*.

Selected Writings: 1924. "Presidential Address." PSPR 34:131; 1916. "Cross-Correspondences of the Gallic Type." PSPR 29:1; 1908. "A Series of Concordant Automatisms." PSPR 22:19; 1907. "Richard Hodgson: In Memoriam. II." PSPR 19:362; 1904. "On the Types of Phenomena Displayed in Mrs. Thompson's Trance." PSPR 18:104; and Sidgwick, E. M. and Verrall, M. de G. 1910. "Further Experiments with Mrs. Piper in 1908." PSPR 24:31.

BIBLIOGRAPHY: Gauld, A. 1987. "Recollections of E. J. Dingwall." JSPR 54:230,233; Gauld, A. *The Founders of Psychical Research,* 1968; Salter, W. H. 1952. "J. G. Piddington and his Work on the 'Cross-Correspondence' Scripts." JSPR 36:708.

**Pike, James Albert, 1913–1969.** American clergyman. A lawyer who in 1944 turned to religion and the Episcopal church, Pike became a deacon, curate, and was ordained to the priesthood two years later. He became the head of the Department of Religion at Columbia University, dean of St. John the Divine in New York City, the world's largest Protestant church, and in 1958 was chosen Episcopal bishop of the diocese of California. Pike was the author of controversial books (Pike 1967, 1964) that candidly expressed his unorthodox views about many items of Christian beliefs, including the belief in virgin birth.

In 1966, his son, James, committed suicide. Soon strange phenomena began to occur: burned hair, postcards arranged at a 140 degree angle on the floor between twin beds, two paperback books lying in the same v-shaped angle between the beds, Jim's alarm clock whose hands were stopped at a similar angle—at 8:19, the hour that James had died. Pike thought that in some mysterious way his son was causing these occurrences (Pike, 1968). He saw mediums, including Ena Twigg, and, although he was very much aware of alternative explanations, came to believe that James was communicating with him. He also had sittings with the medium Arthur Ford. During a séance with Ford over Canadian television, Pike was convinced he had received evidential communications.

Pike's frank admissions of his mediumistic sittings and his belief in communication with the dead only added to the furor over the churchman who dared to question church teachings. His critics took his sittings as proof that the man really was unbalanced. An effort was made to try him for heresy but was abandoned in favor of censuring him. Shortly before his death in the desert near the Judean Hills in the Holy Land, Pike decided to leave the church.

Selected Writings: *The Other Side,* 1968; *If This Be Heresy,* 1967; *A Time for Christian Candor,* 1964.

**Pilot Case.** The case of an apparition called the "best-evidenced death coincidence" case of all (Sidgwick, 1922:152). A youthful British pilot named Lt. David E. M'Connel was killed when his airplane crashed in England on December 7, 1918, at 3:25 P.M. On the same day, a friend, Lt. James J. Larkin, who knew M'Connel well, was sitting in front of a stove in his room at the airfield some sixty miles from where his friend had crashed. Larkin was smoking and writing letters when the door to his room opened. He saw M'Connel in the doorway with his flying clothes and naval cap on. M'Connel smiled and said, "Hello boy!" Larkin replied, "Hello! Back already?" "Yes", said M'Connel. "Got there all right, had a good trip." Then M'Connel said, "Well, cheero!" and went out closing the door noisily. Larkin was sure that the event took place between 3:15 and 3:30 P.M. At 3:45 P.M. he told another officer that he had seen M'Connel in the room a few minutes before. Later, Larkin found out that M'Connel had been killed. A second officer confirmed that Larkin had told him exactly the account contained in a written report Larkin made afterward.

The case has been critically assessed (Berger, 1988) and remains one of the most cited and famous instances of a clearly externalized apparition seen at the time of the sudden and unexpected death of a person far from the percipient.

BIBLIOGRAPHY: Berger, A. S. *Evidence of Life After Death: A Casebook for the Tough-Minded,* 1988; Sidgwick, E. 1922. "Phantasms of the Living." PSPR 33:152.

**Pilot Experiment.** A small scale experiment preliminary in nature and conducted to pave the way for later and more conclusive experiments.

**Pio, Padre, 1887–1968.** Father Pio da Pietrelicina, Italian Capuchin priest. To his monastery in San Giovanni Rotondo in Foggia, Italy, millions of people—in 1967 alone over a million and a half—flocked in order to become Padre Pio's "spiritual children."

Padre Pio was an authentic stigmatic who received his wounds on September 20, 1918. In his words: "I was in the choir after the celebration of the Holy mass, when I was overcome with drowsiness as of a sweet sleep. . . . I discovered myself in front of a mysterious, exalted person *(personaggio)*. . . . [who] was spilling blood from his hands and feet and heart. . . . The vision of the person faded away, and I noticed that my hands and feet and chest had been pierced and were bleeding profusely" (Schug, 1976). He took the *personaggio* to be Jesus Christ himself.

The Rector of a Jesuit college visited the monk and wrote that Padre Pio "appears to have the stigmata. . . . I saw the five wounds. On Good Friday Dr. Schembri tells me that he and eleven other medical men saw these wounds wide open and bleeding. The Father Provincial told me that whenever he receives Holy Communion, blood flows copiously from his breast. . . . The bleeding began on the 1st of February last, and has continued on all Communion days since, except on Easter Sunday. The young man is in great pain, he is obliged to walk on his heels on account of the wound in the feet. . . . The marks of the scourges . . . were seen on his back. . . . It is undoubtedly a very extraordinary case . . . ."

Orthodox medicine could not help him. In a letter dated October 17, 1918, he said: "I have endured terrible and sorrowful hours. I die every moment, physically and morally. . . . Everything inside of me is raining blood, and sometimes even my bodily eyes are forced to submit to look on the bloody torrent of this stream. Please! Stop this torture for me, this condemnation, this humiliation, this confusion! My soul can no longer endure it . . ." (Schug, 1976). Yet he bled and continued to suffer for fifty years.

He also suffered from many strange ailments and fevers that made his bodily temperature rise to 125 degrees, so high that no thermometer could measure it. A temperature of 110 degrees is enough to kill any normal person, but the friar had tremendous recuperative powers that seem to have been matched by his psychic gifts. Many witnesses still living attest to the phenomena he produced: clairvoyance, precognition, levitation. Some sort of angelic telepathy is suggested by reports that he instructed his "spiritual children" to send him their "guardian angels" when they were at a distance in order to convey to him their needs and requests. Padre Pio had his own "guardian angel" who dictated and read letters in French and Greek, languages he did not speak and had not studied. This suggests the phenomenon of xenoglossy and perhaps a communicator familiar with such languages. How reliable the witnesses were who made these claims cannot be determined.

Padre Pio also apparently had an astonishing ability to bring about bilocation. There are many stories that the priest, while he was at San Giovanni Rotondo, gave the words of absolution to dying people in other locations. But the most striking story is about Padre Pio's friend, Msgr. Damiani, the vicar general of the diocese of Salto in Uruguay. The priest had vowed that he would be at Damiani's deathbed to assist him at the moment of his death. In 1941, Damiani was staying at the residence of the bishop of Uruguay, Cardinal Antonio Barbieri. One night, the cardinal was roused out of his sleep by a knock at the door. He could see a hooded Capuchin priest but not the priest's face. The cardinal dressed, entered the room where Damiani was staying and found him dying of a heart attack. On a table next to Damiani's bed, and at a time that Padre Pio was physically in the monastery in Foggia, was a piece of paper on which Damiani had written in Italian the words, "Padre Pio came." Damiani succumbed a short time later.

The claims made for Padre Pio make him a **Noted Witness** for the paranormal. More than that, they suggest that paranormal abilities may increase in direct proportion to spiritual development.

In 1959, Padre Pio predicted his own death at the age of eighty-two. He died on September 23, 1968. He was eighty-two. Nor did his wonders cease even at death. When his body was washed and clothed in the habit of a Capuchin, every one of the stigmata faded and vanished and from him arose an "odor of sanctity," the fragrant smell of orange blossoms.

BIBLIOGRAPHY: Grosso, M. 1982. "Padre Pio and the Paranormal." *Christian Parapsychologist* 4 (7):218, Schug, J. A. *Padre Pio*, 1976, pp. 31, 42, 68, 201–202, 240; Thurston, H. *The Physical Phenomena of Mysticism*, 1952, pp. 97, 212.

**Piper, Leonora E., 1857–1950.** Most renowned American medium. One of the two (the other being Gladys Osborne Leonard) most famous trance mediums of her time. An ordinary housewife of limited education, she was discovered by the American psychologist William James (she became his famous "white crow") who was impressed by sittings he and his family had with her. She was studied over a period of thirty years by the American and British Societies for Psychical Research, and many papers and reports were written about her trance phenomena, including Eleanor Sidgwick's monumental (657 page) report. She was also written about in the popular press, one example being an article about her from the woman's point of view published in July 1900 in *Harper's Bazaar.*

As one of the "peasants" (Nicol, 1972) she, unlike the "ladies and gentlemen" who were assumed incapable of cheating, was investigated thoroughly. It was concluded that she never resorted to fraud of any kind and that she possessed paranormal powers, the source of those powers being the only question. (All her sitters, however, notably Andrew Lang, were not equally impressed. In some of her poorer readings she [or her controls] definitely "fished" for information and she was often just plain wrong.)

Richard Hodgson, an extreme sceptic who had investigated and branded Mme Blavatsky fraudulent and had caught Eusapia Palladino cheating, studied Mrs. Piper for eighteen years. Despite their personal friction (Mrs. Piper found Hodgson cold and arbitrary and did not like working with him), Hodgson became gradually convinced, first, of the paranormality of Mrs. Piper's communications and, ultimately, that her controls were entities who had survived death. As a result of this belief, when the control "Rector," among others, prophesied a long life for Hodgson and when on June 29, 1905, a deceased friend of Hodgson's communicated through Mrs. Piper and told him that he would marry and have two children, Hodgson put off writing his long-promised third report on his investigations of Mrs. Piper. But, just six months later, on December 20, 1905, he was dead; the report was never finished and most of Hodgson's work was lost.

Mrs. Piper had many controls. The first important one was Phinuit who, from 1885 to 1892, was her principal control. He claimed to be the spirit of a Dr. Jean Phinuit Scliville, to have been born in Marseilles, to have studied medicine in Paris at a Merciana College and also at Metz, Germany, to have been married to one Marie Latimer and to have had no children. No trace of such a person could ever be found. In addition, Phinuit spoke little French and knew less about medicine. During his control, communication was entirely by voice.

Phinuit was gradually replaced by G. P. ("George Pelham," actually George Pellew) who, from 1892 to 1897, was Mrs. Piper's leading control. George Pellew had known Richard Hodgson who was studying Mrs. Piper at the time. G. P. seemed, despite some glaring errors, mainly to have known the things he should have known about the living G. P. He was also able to pick out of 150 sitters the 30 that he had known in life. During his control automatic writing began to replace voice communication.

In 1895, a communicator who said he was the English Spiritualist medium W. Stainton Moses who had died three years earlier began appearing during Mrs. Piper's trances. His controls, consisting of forty-nine spirit entities, were known as the "Imperator Band." Among them were Imperator (the prophet Malachi), Rector (St. Hippolytus), Doctor (Athenodorus) and Prudens (Poltinus). In 1896, the alleged Stainton Moses introduced these four members of his Imperator Band who gradually took over as Mrs. Piper's principal controls. They were never able, however, to identify themselves correctly in communications through Mrs. Piper. Nevertheless, many people, including Richard Hodgson who was said to have accepted their reality as surviving entities and to have modelled his life after their teachings, were impressed by them.

At the height of her powers Mrs. Piper was sometimes under double control with Phinuit communicating by voice on one subject while G. P. or another control wrote on another! She was also one of the mediums involved in the famous **"Cross-Correspondences."**

BIBLIOGRAPHY: Bull, K. T. 1900. "Mrs. Piper—A Study." *Harper's Bazaar* 33:741; Hodgson, R. 1892. "A Record of Observations of Certain Phenomena of Trance." PSPR 8:1; Hodgson, R. 1898. "A Further Record of Observations of Certain Phenomena of Trance." PSPR 13:284; James, W. 1897. "What Psychical Research Has Accomplished." In *The Will to Believe and Other Essays,* 1897; Piper, A. L. *The Life and Work of Mrs. Piper,* 1929; Sidgwick, E. M. 1915. "A Contribution to the Study of the Psychology of Mrs. Piper's Trance Phenomena." PSPR 28:1.

**Placement Test.** A technique for testing psychokinesis introduced by William E. Cox in which objects are released mechanically over a surface equally divided by a wire or line while a subject attempts to use psychokinesis to make the objects fall to one side or the other of the division.

**Planchette.** A small, heart-shaped wooden or metal device that rests on three casters and, while the fingers of an operator or operators are in light contact with it, moves on a **Ouija Board** to spell out letters or indicate numbers.

**Plant ESP.** See **Plantpsi.**

**Plantpsi.** Cleve Backster has raised the possibility that plants may have faculties akin to extrasensory perception. He reported significant activity on the part of plants when exposed to emotional situations. Several independent attempts to repeat Backster's experiments, however, have failed to replicate his results and suggest that claims of plantpsi are not justified.

**Plato, 427–347 B.C.** Greek philosopher. Disciple of Socrates, his works in the form of dialogues have made him, along with Aristotle, the most important and influential philosopher who ever lived. Besides his theory of eternal Forms or Ideas, of universals and of a utopian commonwealth, the views of the separation of body and mind can be traced back to this philosopher. His dualism, his theory of the immortal and immaterial soul and his scheme of rewards and punishments strongly influenced the early fathers of the Christian church, including Saint Augustine, Christian theology, and medieval thought. Spiritualism also was deeply influenced by Plato. The basic divorce of soul from body, his theory of spirit guides and of earthbound spirits haunting places where they lived or were buried—all were ideas incorporated into the movement.

As one of the first great thinkers to espouse reincarnation, he has given the doctrine the strength of his authority. As shown in the *Phaedo,* his belief in preexistence was based on reasoned arguments: Knowledge is only recollection and a soul must have existed before birth and obtained knowledge in a prior existence. A soul is born with eternal forms or ideas, such as justice and equality, that did not come to the soul at birth. The soul must therefore have acquired them in some previous life. After death, Plato maintained that the soul would survive because opposites are produced by opposites. Life and death are opposites. As life produces death, so will death produce life.

Through Socrates in the *Phaedo,* Plato pictured the after death existence. Souls follow a guide who leads them from the world of the living to a place where the dead gather to be judged for their virtuous or evil deeds. According to Plato, souls of true philosophers will live forever with the gods in heaven but impure souls will be earthbound spirits doomed to haunt their graves or places of death. Another guide will return souls to earth after many revolutions of ages. The kinds of rebirth will depend on how much truth a soul perceives. According to the *Phaedrus*: "the soul which has seen most of truth shall come to birth as a philosopher or artist, or musician or lover; that which has seen truth in the second degree shall be a righteous king or warrior or lord; the soul which is of the third class shall be politician or economist or trader; the fourth shall be a lover of gymnastic toils or a physician . . .". A soul in the last or ninth class will be a tyrant. Human souls, Plato thought, might be reincarnated as animals and from animals into human beings again. In *The Republic,* in the myth of Er, Plato reiterated that souls will be reborn but, according to what they have learned from previous lives, will be able to determine the conditions of their next lives.

**Playfair, Guy Lyon, 1935–.** British author. His books on the paranormal have focussed mainly on reincarnation and psychokinesis (Playfair, 1976) and on poltergeist phenomena both in Brazil (Playfair, 1975) and in a house in North London (Playfair, 1980). He considers the story of the poltergeist outbreak in the house his major contribution to psychical research because it is the first full-length and sustained study of a poltergeist case.

Selected Writings: *This House is Haunted,* 1980; *The Indefinite Boundary,* 1976; *The Flying Cow,* 1975.

**Plethysmograph.** An instrument that measures vasomotor activity. Attempts have been made to use it for testing for psi to see if any correlation exists between ESP response and vasomotor activity. No significant relationship has yet been established.

**PMIR.** See **Psi-Mediated Instrumental Response.**

**PMS.** Abbreviation for Postmortem Survival.

**Podmore, Frank, 1856–1910.** British psychical researcher and sceptic. William James called him "the prosecuting attorney of the S.P.R." As a young man Podmore was convinced of the reality of Spiritualism and its phenomena, but the more he investigated psychic phenomena, the more his scepticism grew. He came to believe that, with the exception of telepathy, all psychic phenomena, poltergeists, and all other physical phenomena could be explained by mistake, misinterpretation, credulity, or fraud. He felt that the cross-correspondences could be explained by telepathy from a living mind.

Although he was an honors student in classics and natural science at Oxford, he became a civil servant and worked in the General Post Office in London. He was not a charter member of the Society for Psychical Research but joined soon after its founding and worked closely with F. W. H. Myers and Edmund Gurney in the 1880s. He did much of the investigative work for *Phantasms of the Living,* which shows him as co-author with Gurney (who actually did most of the compilation and writing) and with Myers who wrote the Foreword. After Gurney's death in 1888 he became joint honorary secretary of the SPR, a post he held until 1896.

He did not believe, as Myers did, in communication by telepathy between embodied and disembodied minds (i.e., communications through mediums), but felt that telepathy between the living was a sufficient explanation for all paranormal phenomena. He had a keen analytical mind and pointed out that evidence, and not the social position of the people concerned, was important, that the SPR in its investigations ought not to use a "double standard"—differentiating the "peasants" who were not to be trusted from "ladies and gentlemen" who were assumed incapable of fraud (Nicol, 1972). Podmore believed that telepathy had been proved and was convinced of Mrs. Leonora Piper's paranormal powers. He also felt that Richard Hodgson was mistaken in considering Mrs. Rosalie Thompson a fraud. Although he seemed not to care about personal immortality, he wrote Henry Sidgwick that "I have at bottom some kind of inarticulate assurance . . . that our lives, our own conscious force, have some permanent value—and persist in some form after death."

Podmore was unhappily married and Trevor Hall (1964) raises the possibility of homosexuality (never confirmed). Ernest Rhys suggested that his problems could be traced to "his sadistic tendencies" (never elaborated).

On August 10, 1910, Podmore went to Lower Wyche, Malvern. On August 14 at 10:30 P.M. he left the cottage where he was staying and did not return. His body was found in a pond in Malvern several days later. Although Trevor Hall suggests suicide and there was the question of possible foul play, the coronor's inquest, without an autopsy, returned a verdict of "found drowned."

Selected Writings: *The Newer Spiritualism,* 1910; 1909. "The Report on Eusapia Palladino." JSPR 14:172; *Modern Spiritualism: A History and a Criticism,* 1902; 1898. "Discussion of the Trance-Phenomena of Mrs. Piper." PSPR 14:80; 1896–1897. "Poltergeists." PSPR 12:45; *Apparitions and Thought-Transference: an Examination of the Evidence for Telepathy,* 1894; and Gurney, E. and Myers, F. W. H. *Phantasms of the Living,* 1886.

BIBLIOGRAPHY: Berger, A. S. *Aristocracy of the Dead,* 1987; Dingwall, E. J. "Introduction." In F. Podmore, *Mediums of the Nineteenth Century,* 1963; Gauld, A. *The Founders of Psychical Research,* 1968; Hall, T. *The Strange Case of Edmund Gurney,* 1964; Nicol, F. 1972. "The Founders of the S.P.R." PSPR 55:341.

**Poincaré, Henri, 1854–1912.** Eminent French mathematician. A first cousin to Raymond Poincaré, president of France, his mathematical abilities were matched by no one. Although absentminded and nearsighted, his extraordinary ability to do complicated mental calculations, the diversity of his research in the pure and applied fields, and his prodigious memory of everything he ever read, made him the foremost mathematician of his day. Poincaré began his prolific output of writings about 1879. He produced more than thirty books and 500 papers on mathematical physics, celestial mechanics, and mathematics. The novel mathematical techniques he used in astronomy were described in three volumes of *Les Méthodes Nouvelles de la Mécanique Céleste* (1892, 1893, 1894). In 1887, he was elected to the Academy of Sciences in Paris.

Poincaré is a **Noted Witness** for automatism and the spontaneity of the creative process. In "Mathematical Creation," included in his *Foundations of Science,* he said: "It is time to penetrate deeper and see what goes on in the very soul of a mathematician. . . . I shall limit myself to telling how I wrote my first memoir on Fuchsian functions. . . . For fifteen days I strove to prove that there could not be any functions like those I have since called Fuchsian functions. . . . [E]very day I seated myself at my work table, stayed an hour or two, tried a great number of combinations and reached no results. One evening, contrary to my custom, I drank black coffee and could not sleep. Ideas rose in crowds; I felt them collide until pairs interlocked, so to speak, making a stable combination. By the next morning I had established the existence of a class of Fuchsian functions. . . . I had only to write out the results, which took but a few hours. . . . Just at this time I left Caen . . . to go on a geologic excursion. . . . Having reached Coutances, we entered an omnibus. . . . At the moment when I put my foot on the step the idea came to me, without anything in my former thoughts seeming to have paved the way for it, that the transformations I had used to define the Fuchsian functions were identical with those of non-Euclidian geometry. . . . On my return to Caen . . . I verified the result . . . ."

BIBLIOGRAPHY: Ghiselin, B. *The Creative Process,* 1952, pp. 36–37.

**Poltergeist.** When St. Dunstan, the tenth century archbishop of Canterbury, was a boy, he was the focal point of falling and flying stones. Similar poltergeist cases involving noises or the movement of objects have been reported and recorded over the centuries. William E. Cox analyzed forty-six such cases reported during the period 1850 to 1958 mainly from the United States and the United Kingdom while George Zorab has written about twenty more from Europe in the same period.

Two modern cases illustrate the poltergeist phenomenon. A few minutes before midnight, William G. Roll was following a twelve-year-old boy into the kitchen of his home in the Cumberland Mountains of Kentucky when, all at once, a kitchen table rose into the air, rotated and then settled easily on the backs of the chairs that had been around it. In the second case, called to investigate a Miami warehouse where souvenir items were stored, Roll and J. G. Pratt recorded 224 events that could not be explained normally (e.g., trays, glasses, and jars breaking, ashtrays and boxes falling, beer mugs, bottles, glasses, and boxes moving).

*Poltergeist* is a German term meaning "noisy spirit." And, in keeping with this term, some poltergeist phenomena consist of raps, thuds, and bangs on walls, doors, and furniture. Other reports or observations of poltergeist phenomena tell of glasses and dishes have jumped from their shelves; pictures have fallen from walls; objects have been thrown, transported or arranged in patterns; electrical equipment has been disrupted; and there have been inundations of water, outbreaks of destructive fire, and rocks have been made to rain down on or against houses.

The poltergeist has even assaulted people. In a poltergeist house in 1890, a policeman was struck with his own club and a priest who had come to exorcise the house was beaten with his Bible. From 1925 to 1927, a Romanian girl named Eleonore Zugun was victimized by a poltergeist as she was pricked, scratched, on the face, neck and arms, bitten on her arms and hands, and had her hair pulled out. In 1961, while investigating a poltergeist disturbance in New Jersey, Roll was hit on the head with a bottle.

The poltergeist phenomenon has always been in the "twilight area of delusion, fraudulent manipulation and genuineness. . . . Disbelievers reject the scandalous reports *in toto,* while believers gladly accept even spurious events as facts" (Bender, 1969). But when cases meet a high standard of evidence and when reports have been made by competent witnesses—and several cases meet this standard—they must be taken seriously. Laboratory investigations under controlled conditions of such occurrences have not been possible since generally they start unexpectedly and take place spontaneously in private homes or offices. The center of the occurrences is usually a living person, an adolescent, although there have been some cases where no such "focal person" or poltergeist agent exists.

"Noisy spirit," however, is probably not the best designation because it suggests some mysterious non-physical entity. The occurrences may be described better as examples of psychokinesis, a neutral term that does not suggest the source of the disturbances. To express the fact that poltergeist activity is spontaneous, unexpected, and recurring parapsychologists Roll and Pratt, with others following, describe poltergeist phenomena as "recurrent spontaneous psychokinesis" or RSPK. See also **Nickelheim Poltergeist; Rosenheim Poltergeist.**

BIBLIOGRAPHY: Bender, H. 1969. "New Developments in Poltergeist Research." *Proceedings of the Parapsychological Association,* 6:81; Cox, W. E. 1961. "Introductory Comparative Analysis of Some Poltergeist Cases." JASPR 55:47; Gauld, A. and Cornell, A. D. *Poltergeists,* 1979; Pratt, J. G. and Roll, W. G. 1971. "The Miami Disturbances." JASPR 65:409; Pratt, J. G. and Roll, W. G. 1958. "The Seaford Disturbances." JP 22:79; Roll, W. G. *The Poltergeist,* 1976; Price, H. *Poltergeist Over England,* 1945; Zorab, G. 1964. "A Further Comparative Analysis of Some Poltergeist Phenomena: Cases from Continental Europe." JASPR 58:105.

**Poltergeist Agent.** The person around whom poltergeist occurrences may be centered. While gender does not seem to be a determining factor, most poltergeist agents seem to be adolescents. William G. Roll and other parapsychologists believe that such occurrences are directly related to these focal persons's medical problems or their emotional, sexual, or psychological stresses. These problems or stresses when released in frustration or anger in certain provocative situations erupt in the form of unconscious psychokinesis, which, in turn, creates the poltergeist outbreaks.

There is not complete agreement on this interpretation, however, particularly in cases where objects are arranged in patterns or, while being transported through the air, suddenly change speed or angle of direction and take on a new trajectory. In such instances, it is difficult to conceive of the patterning or flight of the objects being produced by the unconscious psychokinesis of a living agent. It is tempting to think of a discarnate agency doing the arranging or manipulating the direction of flight. See also **Rosenheim Poltergeist.**

BIBLIOGRAPHY: Roll, W. G. *The Poltergeist,* 1972; Stevenson. I. 1972. "Are Poltergeists Living or Are They Dead?" JASPR 66:232.

**Pope, Dorothy Hampson, 1905–.** American editor. After receiving her B.A. degree *cum laude* from Brown University where she was a member of Phi Beta Kappa, she arrived in 1938 at J. B Rhine's Parapsychology Laboratory at Duke University. "At the time," she wrote, "I was at the end of a ten-year marriage. I needed to support my twin daughters, and I needed to find a career for myself. . . . As I look back at it now, the unexpected end of my marriage was the lucky break which forced me out of a quiet uneventful existence and into the livelier world in which I have lived ever since" (letter to authors, March 1986).

Mrs. Pope joined the staff of the Parapsychology Laboratory at a salary of ninety dollars a month mainly to work on the *Journal of Parapsychology,* a vocation that has lasted for fifty years. Whether as managing editor (1942–1963), co-editor (1964–1982), or consulting editor since her nominal retirement in 1982, Mrs.Pope's job has not changed in nature. She has maintained strict standards that have made the *JP* the prestigious publication that it is. From 1946 to 1965 she also researched and wrote all the material for the *Parapsychology Bulletin,* a companion publication to the *JP.* It published accounts of research not suitable for formal presentation in the *JP* and of foreign research as well as news of professional interest and portraits of leading parapsychologists.

Mrs. Pope considers that her special area of work is "to get the results of the research into print in whatever way I can." In 1942 Mrs. Pope co-authored two articles in the *JP* with J. Gaither Pratt. She was a member of the group whose discussions with Rhine led to the formation of the Parapsychological Association and was a member of the committee that drew up the original constitution of that body. In 1964 she became editor of the newly formed Parapsychology Press.

Mrs. Pope was not only an associate but a friend of J. B. Rhine (who, as she also wrote, "had inexhaustible drive; . . . expected a lot of others; . . . and [was] skimpy in the matter of praise and rewards") and his wife Louisa E. Rhine. Mrs. Pope was an invaluable help to them both professionally and personally. She has known all the greats, near-greats and not-so-greats of parapsychology since they have all, at one time or another, passed through Durham, North Carolina, the site of the original Parapsychology Laboratory and of its successor, the present Institute for Parapsychology. She is listed in *Who's Who of American Women.*

Selected Writings: *Parapsychology Bulletin,* 72 nos., 1946–1965; "The Search for ESP in Animals." *Tomorrow,* Summer 1953; with J. G. Pratt. "Five Years of the Journal of Parapsychology." JP March 1942; with J. G. Pratt. "The ESP Controversy." JP Sept. 1942.

BIBLIOGRAPHY: Berger, A. S. *Lives and Letters in American Parapsychology,* 1988; Rhine, L. E. *Something Hidden,* 1983.

**Position Effects.** Where a subject is aware of the location on the record sheet of trials in a psi experiment, it has been found that this awareness affects the rate of scoring success, most commonly causing the scoring rate to decline in the column of the record sheet where the run is recorded.

**Possession.** Also called "obsession." Commonly understood as the apparent invasion of and influence exerted on an individual's organism by an alien entity from another world, whether or not human. In most cases, however, it is likely that there is no discarnate spirit, human or otherwise, but, rather, a split-off of the individual's normal personality coming to the surface as an independent personality.

There are rare cases recorded, however, where the other-worldly interpretation may seem more plausible than any other. Such was the American case of the "Watseka Wonder" reported by E. W. Stevens (1887) and cited by William James (1901) as "perhaps as extreme a case of 'possession' of the modern sort as one can find." In this case Mary Roff, a young girl, died when Lurancy Vennum of Watseka, Illinois, was about one year old. When she was about fourteen, Lurancy claimed to be Mary Roff, said she was homesick and asked to see her parents and brothers. In the Roff's home she recognized and called by name people Mary had known and remembered events that had occurred during Mary's lifetime before Lurancy's birth. She remained Mary Roff for over three months during which she could not recognize the members or friends of the Vennum family. Curt J. Ducasse asked: "Just how, otherwise than as a case of paranormal 'possession' by a particular definitely identified mind having survived discarnate, is the case of for example the 'Watseka Wonder' to be explained?" But many other people have not found the evidence in the case conclusive. Critics such as Roger I. Anderson have suggested that Lurancy Vennum could have had ample opportunity to find out much about Mary Roff's life both in the small town where few secrets could be kept and also after having insinuated herself into the Roff's home.

There is also another kind of possession: demonic possession for which the cure was supposed to be exorcism. Its symptoms were the ability to speak an unknown tongue, the recoiling from "holy objects," and the responding to the Latin words of the exorcism rite.

BIBLIOGRAPHY: Anderson, R. I. 1980. "The Watseka Wonder: A Critical Evaluation." *Theta* 8:6; Ducasse, C. J. 1962. "What Would Constitute Conclusive Evidence of Survival after Death?" JASPR 41:401; James, W. *The Principles of Psychology.* Vol.I, 1901; McHarg, J. 1975. "Exorcism Past and Present." JSPR 48:232; Stevens, E. W. *The Watseka Wonder,* 1887.

**Poynton, John Charles, 1931–.** South African professor of biology at the University of Natal. He collects data on the incidence and demographic aspects of the out-of-body experience. In some surveys people report having had only one such experience. But Poynton found that 44 percent of the population he sampled seemed liable to have many out-of-body experiences. If individuals had one, they were likely to have multiple experiences. Poynton's contribution to knowledge about this phenomenon forces us to speculate that, because the effect of a single experience is so marvelously exciting, [i.e., that separation from the body means really living for the first time as Sylvan Muldoon (Muldoon and Carrington, 1973) and others claim, a person might try very hard to repeat it].

Poynton's interests in psychical research and parapsychology also include evaluating paranormal phenomena in black African cultures, conducting courses in parapsychology at the University of Natal, helping to run the South African Society for Psychical Research, and exploring the relation of parapsychology to ontology and to the philosophy of science.

Selected Writings: 1985. "Nonevident Psi and Phenomenology." *Parapsychology Review* 14:9; "Results of an Out-of-the-Body Survey." In J. C. Poyton, ed., *Parapsychology in South Africa,* 1975, p. 109.

BIBLIOGRAPHY: Muldoon, S. and Carrington, H. *The Projection of the Astral Body,* 1973.

**Prasad, Jamuna, 1915–.** Indian scholar. His research activities in the areas of reincarnation, extrasensory perception and yoga have made him one of the foremost leaders in psychical research in his country. His keen interest in the field brought him into contact with prominent Western parapsychologists and psychical researchers, such as Joseph Banks Rhine and Gardner Murphy.

In 1963, Dr. Prasad received the approval of the government of India to conduct an investigation of ESP in schoolchildren. Beginning in 1964, he collaborated with a leading Western researcher to conduct cross-cultural studies of spontaneous cases. He also acted as chief interpreter for studies by Western investigators of cases suggestive of reincarnation and himself carried out firsthand investigations and interviews of witnesses in the cases. In 1971, Dr. Prasad worked with Karlis Osis and helped him collect data in India for Osis's study of deathbed visions.

Dr. Prasad also has been a frequent participant in international conferences on parapsychology and has appeared on Italian television to discuss reincarnation research. He served as director of the Bureau of Psychology in Uttar Pradesh, was the director of the Allahabad Institute for Kundalini Research and the India Institute for Parapsychology. He is now research advisor for the Foundation for Reincarnation and Spiritual Research and is on the Advisory Board of the International Institute for the Study of Death.

**Pratt, Joseph Gaither, 1910–1979.** American parapsychologist. In his youth, Pratt's ambition was to become a Methodist minister. But, at Duke University, when one of his teachers, Joseph Banks Rhine, offered him fifty cents an hour to become research assistant in experiments on extrasensory perception, Pratt's new career in parapsychology began. He also worked with Gardner Murphy at Columbia University. After receiving his Ph.D., Pratt became a research associate in the Parapsychology Laboratory and, in 1964, joined the Department of Psychiatry at the University of Virginia.

Pratt was an experimenter in two classic experiments that are invariably cited as scientifically conclusive evidence of the occurrence of ESP. The Pearce-Pratt experiment was a card-guessing test of clairvoyance in which experimenter and subject were in separate buildings 100 yards apart. The results of the experiment far exceeded chance expectation. C. E. M. Hansel, however, who believes that ESP is impossible, noted in 1960 that the subject, Hubert Pearce, was under no observation and could have returned to the building where Pratt was and could have seen the target cards through the crack at the top of the door (a feat that Hansel demonstrated was possible—if improbable).

The Pratt-Woodruff series, also an experiment of the clairvoyance-type, used the screened touch matching technique and other precautionary controls as well. Joseph L. Woodruff was seated on one side of a table separated by an opaque screen from the subject who sat opposite him. Pratt, as an observer-experimenter, was seated behind the subject (and so was on the opposite side of the opaque screen from Woodruff). Woodruff shuffled a face down pack of ESP cards and never looked at their faces. He then recorded the subject's guesses of which key cards matched the top target card held by Woodruff. Pratt meanwhile kept his own record and altered the arrangement of the key cards hung on pegs on the subject's side of the screen. Using this procedure, Pratt had no contact with the target cards and Woodruff had no kowledge of the arrangement of the key cards. Both experimenters maintained independent data sheets. These interesting features of the experiment have made it one of the most elaborately designed of all time. It was supposedly so rigorously controlled that only the hypothesis of ESP was left as a reasonable explanation for the very significant results, yet Hansel thought the experimenter could have found out the value of the end key card.

Pratt also conducted important card-guessing experiments with Pavel Stepanek in Prague and later at the Division of Parapsychology, University of Virginia. He discovered in Stepanek a form of ESP known as the **Focussing Effect.**

Pratt also developed a method of evaluating mediumistic material objectively. Basically, his method consists of recording the statements made by a medium for each sitter and then submitting all the records to all sitters who do not know which records are theirs. The sitters then judge the records according to how they fit the sitters' particular cases. The resulting data are then analyzed statistically.

Pratt was interested, too, in the question of whether animals have ESP. In particular, the problem of pigeon-homing fascinated him. Because he thought that ESP might be the key to the problem, he contrived what he was sure would be the crucial test. A pigeon loft would be located on a ship at sea where there would be no landmarks. After pigeons had learned to fly to and from the loft, the ship would be moved to another location on the open sea while the pigeons would be released at some other distant point on the ocean. If the pigeons were to find the loft at its new location, their ESP would be demonstrated and the test would be passed with flying pigeons. To Pratt's great regret, however, lack of funds prevented his dream test from being carried out.

Pratt also investigated poltergeists and, in Leningrad, watched firsthand the psychokinetic effects produced by Nina Kulagina.

He was esteemed by his colleagues as a gentle man and a cautious investigator.

Selected Writings: *Parapsychology: An Insider's View of ESP,* 1977; *ESP Research Today,* 1973; *Towards a Method of Evaluating Mediumistic Material,* 1936; and Keil, H. H. J. 1973. "First Hand Observations of Nina S. Kulagina Suggestive of PK on Static Objects." JASPR 67:381; and C. Ransom. 1972. "Extrasensory Perception or Extraordinary Sensory Perception? A Recent Series of Experiments of Pavel Stepanek." JASPR 66:63; and Roll, W. G. 1971. "The Miami Disturbances." JASPR 65:409; and Rhine, J. B. 1954. "A Review of the Pearce-Pratt Distance Experiments of ESP Tests." JP 18:165; and Woodruff, J. L. 1939. "Size of Stimulus Symbols in Extrasensory Perception." JP 3:121.

BIBLIOGRAPHY: Berger, A. S. *Lives and Letters in American Parapsychology,* 1988; Hansel, C. E. M. *ESP: A Scientific Evaluation,* 1966; Keil, H. H. J. *Gaither Pratt: A Life for Parapsychology,* 1987; Thouless, R. 1961. "Review of the *Journal of Parapsychology, XXV, 2, June 1961, Durham, N.C.*" JSPR 41:212.

**Pratt-Woodruff Experiment.** See **Pratt, J.G.; Woodruff, Joseph L.**

**Prayer.** A serious communication, whether spoken or silent, addressed to a mysterious power; an integral part of religion in which people praise or give thanks to God or, feeling in great need of some favor or forgiveness for a wrong done, humbly appeal to the divinity. The state of mind of a person deep in prayer may be compared to that of a medium in trance, or of a mystic or to that achieved in meditation. In all a sort of altered state of consciousness or what Robert H. Thouless (1977) preferred to call "a changed state of consciousness" may be involved in varying degrees.

Prayer seems directly relevant to psychical research and parapsychology in that it assumes the existence of paranormal powers. "The process of communication takes place between the mind of the person who prays and the mind of God to whom the prayer is addressed, and by whom it is heard and answered. This corresponds to telepathy . . ." (Berger, 1989).

BIBLIOGRAPHY: Berger, A. S. "Religion and Parapsychology: Eight Points of Contact." In A. S. Berger and H. O. Thompson, eds., *Religion and Parapsychology,* 1989; Thouless, R. H. "Implications for Religious Studies." In S. Krippner, ed., *Advances in Parapsychological Research. Volume 1,* 1977, p.175.

**Precognition.** Without the possibility of inference from present evidence, the prediction or knowledge of random future events. The phenomenon is similar to **Clairvoyance** except that clairvoyance is extrasensory perception of objects or events in the present while precognition is ESP of the future. The phenomenon is not distinguishable from **Premonition** and differs from **Prophesy** only in that, in the latter, there is the additional element of information being given before an event in order to warn or comfort.

Of all the queer phenomena studied by psychical research and parapsychology, the queerest may be precognition. Forms of precognition of course occur everyday: The movements of the stars and planets are predicted by astronomers, weather forecasters tell us whether it will rain, snow, or be sunny, financial experts predict stock market trends and commodity futures. But all these predictions depend on inferences made from experience and educated guesses that what has happened in the past will happen again in the future. Psychical research and parapsychology are interested only in those types of precognitions that do not depend on inference or reasoning.

But do such paranormal precognitions exist? In her studies of over 2,500 saints, **Rhea A. White** found that precognitions formed the largest group of paranormal phenomena associated with very holy people. Saint Etheldrena, for example, forecast the pestilence that killed her and many others. Sinners, too, however, have foretold tragedies, disasters, deaths, and wars. Many **Noted Witnesses,** such as Charles Dickens, Joan of Arc, and Charles F. Oursler, have had precognitive experiences. The literature of psychical research supplies more examples, such as the sinking of the "unsinkable" Titanic and the Aberfan Disaster.

Many precognitions have been about war. For example, a letter postmarked October 2, 1973, was sent by an English housewife in Coventry, England, to the late Prime Minister Golda Meir of Israel. It described the housewife's vision of an Arab attack against Israel and specifically mentioned the "Heights of Golan." On October 6, Egypt and Syria did launch a surprise attack against Israel and the Syrians defeated the Israeli forces at the

Golan Heights. The letter was not received by the prime minister until after the war had started. She always wondered what she and Israel might have done if the letter had been received on October 2 instead of being postmarked on that date.

Two main factors led up to experiments in parapsychology to test precognition. Of the thousands of letters relating personal psychic experiences written to the Parapsychology Laboratory at Duke University Louisa E. Rhine found that precognitive experiences comprised about 40 percent. Also, when experiments revealed that extrasensory perception could extend over great distances and seemed unlimited by space, the logical suggestion was that ESP might not depend on time, either, and could be projected into the future. In 1938, Joseph B. Rhine used a modified card-guessing technique to test the hypothesis: He asked the subject to determine the order of the cards as it would be after the cards were shuffled. Soon this method was succeeded by mechanical shuffling techniques and later by vastly more sophisticated methods developed by Helmut Schmidt and others. Research continues today but enough significant results have been achieved to suggest that precognition really occurs.

Yet, while this is a parapsychological finding, it is disturbing for many in significant ways. For the phenomenon raises the most profound religious, philosophical and scientific questions. One is the question of causation. A knowledge of events that have not yet occurred and which could not have been inferred seems to imply backward causation. A future event has caused a person in the present to be aware of it. Other questions concern free will, fate and predetermination. How can the will be free in a world where our futures and fates are predetermined? The Stoics, who believed that all operations in the universe were totally determined, accepted precognition as possible and reasonable. As one way out of the problem, Louisa E. Rhine has argued that a precognized event need not necessarily be predetermined; "intervention" or an attempt by a percipient to prevent or avoid it may be successful (i.e., by not taking a train where its collision with another has been foreseen). Others (Angelos Tanagras [1938]; William G. Roll [1961]; Jule Eisenbud [1982] and Stephen E. Braude [1986], for example) to avoid precognition's involving retrocausation have hypothesized that the person has not foreseen what is going to happen but is actually making it happen by PK or telepathy. John Beloff (1987) prefers to think of precognition "as memory in reverse" (p. 75). See also **Anthony, Susan B.; Cayce, Edgar; Cargo Cult; Croiset, Gerard; Dixon, Jeane; Lincoln, Abraham; Kennedy, John F.; Nostradamus; Prophets, Religious.**

BIBLIOGRAPHY: Beloff, J. 1987. "The Limits of Influence: Psychokinesis and the Philosophy of Science by Stephen E. Braude." JSPR 54:72; Braude. S. E. *The Limits of Influence,* 1986; Eisenbud, J. *Paranormal Foreknowledge,* 1982; Livnen, G. 1986. "An Ostensible Precognition of the Arab Surprise Attack on the Day of Atonement." JSPR 53:383; Rhine, J. B. 1938. "Experiments Bearing on the Precognition Hypothesis." JP 2:38; Rhine, L. E. 1955. "Precognition and Intervention." JP 19:1; Rhine, L. E. 1954. "Frequency of Types of Experience in Spontaneous Precognition." JP 18:93; Roll, W. G. 1961. "The Problem of Precognition." JSPR 41:115; Tanagras, A. *La Destin, et la Chance,* 1938.

**Prediction.** See **Precognition.**

**Preexistence.** The question of human survival beyond death is bound up with the further question of whether we may not already have survived death. "If we have not existed in some form before this life, why should we exist in any form after it?" (Berger, 1983). Yet in the West even among believers in survival after death, the general assumption is that one's soul or spirit is created at birth. Although the early theologians of the ancient Church, including Origen and Justin Martyr, taught the preexistence of souls, the Church condemned the doctrine in its Fifth Ecumenical Council in 553 A.D.

Nevertheless, the doctrine has always had its adherents, ancient and modern: Pythagoras, Plato, Jewish mystics and the Kabbalah; writers, such as the Scottish author Chevalier Ramsay, and poets, such as Rudyard Kipling. Raynor C. Johnson believed that the tragic aspects of life—children who are born deaf, blind, defective or into conditions of squalor or of cruelty by their parents, for example—may be products of causes operating in their prior existences (Johnson, 1953:376–377). In short, preexistence is the basis of the belief in **Reincarnation** and its twin doctrine **Karma** and as such is a religious, philosophical, or poetic doctrine. But the attempt to find more conclusive evidence pointing toward the survival of the human personality after death bears directly on the doctrine of preexistence. As the philosopher John M. E. M'Taggart said: "[I]t seems to me that, if we succeed in proving immortality, it will be by means of considerations which would also prove pre-existence" (M'Taggart, 1970:74).

BIBLIOGRAPHY: Berger, A. S. "Concepts of Survival After Death: Toward Clarification, Evaluation and Choice." In *The Synergy of Religion and Psychical Research: Past, Present and Future, 1983. Proceedings of the Academy of Religion and Psychical Research,* 1984, 5:45; Johnson, R. C. *The Imprisoned Splendour,* 1957; M'Taggart, J. M. E. *Human Immortality and Pre-existence,* 1970.

**Preferential Matching.** A method of scoring responses to free material. A judge ranks the stimulus objects (usually pictures in sets of four) with respect to their similarity to, or association with, each response; and/or the judge ranks the responses with respect to their similarity to, or association with, each stimulus object (JP).

**Premonition.** A form of precognition. K. M. T. Hearne reports a premonition that came true: "In a dream I saw my uncle in a taxicab. The next thing I knew my uncle had been crushed to death inside the taxi. Two weeks later I did something very unusual for me—I went into the front room and switched on the TV to watch 'Calendar.' Within a minute it showed a railway line and gave out the grim news that my uncle had been killed on the line. I went to pieces and dashed into my neighbours' home." Hearne did research on premonitions and found that, in answer to his appeal in 1982 to readers of a national newspaper to send him stories of their premonitions, the overwhelming number came from females and that most of the premonitions were about death or injury to people close to the respondents. See also **Prophesy.**

BIBLIOGRAPHY: Hearne, K. M. T. 1984. "A Survey of Reported Premonitions and of Those Who Have Them." JSPR 52:261.

**Price, George Robert, 1922–1975.** American chemist and vigorous opponent of parapsychology. Price believed that if extrasensory perception were a reality, it would be of "enormous importance, both philosophically and practically" but, since it flew into the face of all current scientific theory, it was impossible. He maintained that, regardless of how improbable trickery might be in parapsychological experiments, it was still more probable than the phenomenon of ESP (Price, 1955). He reached this conclusion after reading the philosopher David Hume on "Miracles."

Miracles (and ESP was a miracle to Price) are not consistent with nature's laws which are based on a great body of evidence. So if we have to choose between the alternative of supposing the evidence of ESP to be false or that of nature's laws to be false, the first alternative is more probable than the second. With Tom Paine's words in mind—"Is it more probable that nature should go out of her course, or that a man should tell a lie?"—Price examined the experiments of Joseph B. Rhine and Samuel G. Soal that seemed to demonstrate the existence of ESP. He concluded that the results must be due to fraud committed by the experimenters or their subjects. At the very least, the experiments were marred by incompetence or statistical or clerical errors.

Price's charges were hailed by parapsychology's critics and his attacks on the field in general were published on the first page of *Science,* the most powerful scientific journal in the United States (Price, 1955). Naturally enough, Rhine and Soal and other parapsychologists counterattacked with charges that Price was wrong in arguing that ESP was not compatible with modern science. Rhine even seemed to enjoy Price's attacks. He thought it was better to be attacked than ignored (Berger, 1988:223). Sixteen years subsequent to the appearance of his article assailing Rhine, Soal, and parapsychology, Price had a complete change of heart, apologized for being "highly unfair" to Rhine and Soal and retracted his charges (Price, 1972). (Yet, as it turned out, he was right about Soal.)

Three years after his retraction, Price, still comparatively young, died. But his retractions and death did not end allegations of deception in parapsychology repeated even more vigorously by other sceptics, such as Charles E. M. Hansel.

Selected Writings: 1972. "Apology to Rhine

and Soal." *Science* 175:359; 1955. "Science and the Supernatural." *Science* 122:359.

**Price, Harry, 1881–1948.** Best-known British psychical researcher of his day. His "intense and sustained interest in occult phenomena" (Price, 1926b) began with an investigation in his youth of a haunt in Shropshire. He became a leading and controversial figure who brought the mystery and thrill of the paranormal to the attention of the man-in-the-street. His prolific pen contributed pieces to newspapers and magazines, including *Light.* These articles and his books on mediums (Price, 1925, 1930, 1975), poltergeists (Price, 1936, 1945), apparitions (Price, 1936) and haunts (Price, 1940, 1946) were avidly and widely read because he had a popular and engaging style of writing.

Price believed in the reality of clairvoyance, telepathy, precognition, and psychokinesis; yet he thought most mediums were frauds and made war against those he suspected (Price, 1922, 1931; Price and Dingwall, 1922). In the early 1920s Price's exposé of fraudulent "spirit" or psychic photographers, in particular William Hope, resulted in a lengthy, heated, and time-consuming controversy with Sir Arthur Conan Doyle (Price, 1922). Price examined many areas of psychical research from slate-writing to the conduct of sittings with famous mediums, including Mina S. Crandon ("Margery"), Helen Duncan, Stella C. and Eleonore Zugun. He was involved in experiments with Rudi Schneider whose phenomena he at first declared genuine. But later he produced a photograph, a double exposure, that he claimed showed Schneider cheating. Careful examination of the plate, however, revealed that it was not Schneider, but Price, who, for unknown reasons, had cheated.

On October 7, 1930, Price arranged a sitting with Eileen Garrett, a medium he was sure was completely honest, with the object of trying to reach Sir Arthur Conan Doyle who had died three months earlier. At this sitting a drop-in communicator identified himself as Captain Irwin who had died along with all the passengers and crew in the crash of the airship R-101 in France the day before. The remarkable information relating to the causes of the crash "Irwin" gave then and later made Eileen Garrett famous.

Another sensational case was that of Borley Rectory, according to Price the most haunted house in England. His famous investigation of Borley Rectory was attacked as fabrication on the one hand (Dingwall, Goldney, and Hall, 1956) and defended on the other (Hastings, 1969).

Price accumulated a library on psychical research amounting to some 20,000 volumes that he modestly called "the largest in the world on the subject" (Price, 1926a). Because he was convinced that the conduct of scientific experiments required apparatus, recording, and photographic equipment and a laboratory in which to use these instruments, Price founded the **National Laboratory of Psychical Research.** In 1925, he was appointed foreign research officer of the American Society for Psychical Research and served in that post for several years writing newsy communiqués from England that were published in the society's *Journal.*

Price was an amazing man of many talents. Educated as a mechanical engineer, he became a manufacturer of paper, a numismatist and magician and, as a photographer, helped improve the Royal Air Force's technique for taking aerial photographs during World War I. In 1922, he went with Eric J. Dingwall to Munich to observe mediumistic phenomena being investigated by Albert von Schrenck-Notzing. Persuaded of the genuineness of what he had seen, he came back to England determined to make himself the best-known writer and investigator in the field of the paranormal. In spite of accusations of poor investigating and downright trickery (Hope, 1933; Dingwall, Goldney, Hall, 1956), he succeeded.

Selected Writings: *Fifty Years of Psychical Research: A Critical Survey,* 1975; *The End of Borley Rectory,* 1946; *Poltergeist Over England,* 1945; *The Most Haunted House in England,* 1940; *Confessions of a Ghost Hunter,* 1936; "Regurgitation and the Duncan Mediumship." *Bulletin of the National Laboratory of Psychical Research,* 1931; *Rudi Schneider—A Scientific Examination of his Mediumship,* 1930; 1926a. "Some Early Works on False Mediumship." JASPR 20:120; 1926b. "A Strange Experience with a Shropshire Poltergeist." JASPR 20:77; *Stella C.,* 1925; 1922. "A Case of Fraud with the Crewe Circle." JSPR 20:271; and Dingwall, E. J. *Revelations of a Spirit Medium,* 1922.

BIBLIOGRAPHY: Dingwall, E. J., Goldney K. M., and Hall, T. H. 1956. "The Haunting of Borley Rectory: A Critical Survey of the Evidence." PSPR 55:1; Hastings, R. J. 1959. "An Examination of the 'Borley Report.'" PSPR 55:66; Hope, C. 1933. "Report of a Series of Sittings with Rudi Schneider." PSPR 41:255; "Obituary: Mr. Harry Price." 1948. JSPR 34:238; "Obituary: Mr. Harry Price." 1948. JASPR 42:152.

**Price, Henry Habberley, 1899–1984.** Eminent British philosopher. Wykeham professor of logic at Oxford University and author of many philosophical works, his contributions to psychical research have been likened to those of Henry Sidgwick and C. D. Broad. Like them, he came to psychical research, at least in part, through philosophy.

Prof. Price addressed the philosophical implications and questions psychical research raises, particularly telepathy (not "Why does Telepathy occur sometimes?" but rather "Why doesn't it occur all the time?"), clairvoyance (a phenomenon he found even more puzzling than telepathy) and apparitions (which he felt might be something like photographs or a moving picture) (Price, 1976\1940, 1939). He felt, however, that these phenomena had been proved and that this proof lessened "the antecedent impossibility of survival." He took the position that philosophers should design a conceptual framework for paranormal phenomena because he thought psychical research's hypotheses, rather than being too bold, were too timid.

Prof. Price had also come to psychical research by way of religion; for Price psychical research "seems sometimes almost to *be* a branch of religious apologetic . . ." (Cherry, 1985:198). He dealt with mediumship and the survival question and made "the most suggestive theoretical contribution of the last twenty years to the meta-parapsychology of post-mortem survival" (Cherry, 1985:18) in his formation of a concept of what disembodied human life might be like after death. He also urged that the West had a great deal to learn from the ideas and practices of the East.

Prof. Price was president of the Society for Psychical Research for the years 1939–1941 and again in 1960–1961.

Selected Writings: "Some Philosophical Questions About Telepathy and Clairvoyance." In J. M. O. Wheatley and H. L. Edge, eds., *Philosophical Dimensions of Parapsychology,* 1976. Originally published in 1940 in *Philosophy;* 1953. "Survival and the Idea of 'Another World.'" PSPR 50:1; 1939. "Presidential Address." PSPR 45:307.

BIBLIOGRAPHY: Cherry, C. "Obituary Professor Henry Habberly Price 1899–1984." JSPR 53:197.

**Prince, Walter Franklin, 1863–1934,** American clergyman and psychical researcher. "[H]onest, gentlemanly, scholarly, sincere and fussbudgety" (Berger, 1988:78), Prince initially came to psychical research through his interest in puzzles of all kinds. Later, while rector of All Saints Church in Pittsburgh, Prince encountered an unhappy young girl (in his writings he called her "Doris Fischer") with mercurial moods. She led him to his greatest writing and changed his life. One moment a bright, caring girl, another mischievous and vicious, the next sickly, he watched her daily and kept a detailed and exhaustive record of her alternating personalities. His observations of "Doris" culminated in the most prolonged, unusual, and detailed study of multiple personality ever recorded. After one of the personalities claimed to be a spirit, Prince began to correspond with James Hervey Hyslop and eventually became his assistant.

An earlier event had also helped push Prince into psychical research. In California where not a soul knew him, he and a young woman he had just met, out of curiosity, placed their hands on a planchette. As they did so, it began to move and correctly spelled out "Your father, W. M. Prince."

After Hyslop's death, Prince became director of research of the American Society for Psychical Research and editor of its publications. He was a first class investigator who called himself "a scrutinizing, analyzing and rationalizing monster." Accuracy was his religion and minute analysis his obsession. He was also a master of magic and quick to see how mediums sometimes used magician's methods to produce astonishing results. Before his resignation from the ASPR in 1925, Prince conducted significant experiments in Mexico in psychometry, attended the first International Congress on Psychical Research in Copenhagen, and investigated Mina S. Crandon ("Margery") who, he charged, produced her phenomena fraudulently. After his resignation from the ASPR, Prince became research officer of the Boston Society for Psychic Research and editor of its publications which gained the reputation of being among the most critical in psychical research. He was twice elected president of the Society for Psychical Research (1930 and 1931).

From Prince's pen came several books including *The Case of Patience Worth,* the study of the remarkable case of a housewife in St. Louis, Missouri, Pearl Lenore Curran, and the "spirit" who, through Mrs. Curran, created some of the most interesting and controversial literature of all time. Prince also wrote *Noted Witnesses for Psychic Occurrences,* a compilation of psychic experiences reported by more than 170 scientists, lawyers, doctors, high ranking military personnel, statesmen, diplomats, poets, and others.

Prince himself had a gruesome dream in 1917 that makes him a **Noted Witness,** too, whose testimony adds greatly to the evidence for precognition: "On the night following November 27, [1917] I dreamed that I had in my hands a small paper with an order printed in red ink, for the execution of the bearer, a woman. . . . The woman appeared to have voluntarily brought the order, and she expressed herself as willing to die, if I would only hold her *hand*. . . . [S]he was slender of the willowy type, had blonde hair, small girlish features, and was rather pretty. She sat down to die without any appearance of reluctance, seeming fully calm and resigned . . . I should have thought her about 35. Then the light went out and it was dark. I could not tell how she was put to death, but soon I felt her hand grip mine (my *hand*), and I knew that the deed was being done. Then I felt one *hand* (of mine) on the hair of the head, which was loose and severed from the body, and felt the moisture of blood. Then the fingers of my other *hand* were caught in her teeth, and the mouth opened and shut several times as the teeth refastened on my *hand,* and I was filled with the horror at the thought of a severed but living head. Here the dream faded out."

Through the newspapers on November 29 and other sources, Prince discovered that, on the night of November 28, a woman lay down on the tracks of the Long Island Railroad at Hollis, Long Island. Her name was Sarah A. Hand. She was slender, about thirty-one years old and had golden-brown hair. She placed her head on the tracks so that the wheels of the 11:15 P.M. train that had stopped at the station would cut off her head. After she was decapitated, a letter found in her purse and addressed "To whom it may concern" stated her belief in a life after death and that her severed head would live independently of her body. There are striking correspondences between Prince's dream and the actual event: Both dealt with a woman, in one thirty-five years old, in the other about thirty-one; in both she was slender and pretty; she had blonde hair in the dream and actually had golden-brown hair; in both the dream and the event she came voluntarily to die; death in both was bloody and by beheading; in the dream the woman was executed in darkness and she did die about 11:15 P.M.; throughout the dream there were constant references to "hand" and the suicide's name was Sarah A. Hand; in the dream the opening and closing mouth and Prince's idea that the head was living corresponded to the dead woman's theory that her head would not die after decapitation. See also **Pagenstecher, Gustav; Zierold, Maria Reyes de.**

Selected Writings: *The Case of Patience Worth,* 1964‹927; *Noted Witnesses for Psychic Occurrences,* 1963\1928; 1923. "Four Peculiarly Characterized Dreams." JASPR 17:82; 1921. "Psychometric Experiments with Señora Maria Reyes de Z." PASPR 15:189; 1915, 1916. "The Doris Case of Multiple Personality." PASPR 9:1, 10:701.

BIBLIOGRAPHY: Berger, A. S. *Lives and Letters in American Parapsychology: A Biographical History, 1885–1987,* 1988; *Walter Franklin Prince: A Tribute to His Memory,* 1935.

**Probability.** See **p; P.**

**Proceedings of the American Society for Psychical Research.** A publication of the American Society for Psychical Research, published irregularly. It consists of detailed or technical reports and major discussions of a scientific nature. To date, 31 volumes have been issued.

**Proceedings of the Society for Psychical Research.** Published by the Society for Psychical Research from time to time, when warranted by reports or discussions of major significance. The *Proceedings* contain many of the classics in the literature of psychical research and parapsychology. *Phantasms of the Living* is one example.

**Project Alpha.** The code name for a hoax devised by magician **James Randi.** In 1979 he had two young conjurors volunteer their services to the McDonnell Laboratory for Psychical Research at Washington University in St. Louis for a study into **Metal-Bending** by paranormal means. Randi theorized that: 1. no amount of financial support ($630,000 had been put up by the McDonnell Foundation for the establishment of the laboratory, but, according to Director Peter Phillips, only $6,000 was spent on the experiments in question) would improve the quality of work done by parapsychologists because of their pro-psychic bias; and 2. that parapsychologists would not pay attention to suggestions by magicians for improving controls and would be fooled by magic tricks. According to Randi, before experiments began with the two young men, he sent Dr. Phillips a list of warnings on things to avoid when testing subjects.

Nevertheless, no attempt was made to check into the young men's backgrounds and the original controls for the experiments were lax, the subjects being allowed very often to set up their own procedures. But the reasoning of the experimenters was that an atmosphere of trust had first to be established. Under these conditions, "both Alpha subjects produced 'spirit' photos on Polaroid film; bent spoons, keys and coat-hangers; turned tiny propellers inside bell-jars; moved objects around on a table; traced cryptic messages in ground coffee sealed in an upturned fish tank; caused ghostly inscriptions to appear on paper sealed in glass jars. . . . The mice were running the experiment" (Randi, 1985:341). Eventually, about 1982, Dr. Phillips heard rumors that the young men were tricksters sent by Randi. After controls were tightened, no phenomena occurred.

The damage, however, had already been done. Instead of pointing out to Dr. Phillips the mistakes he had made and the tricks that had been played, Randi released the whole affair to the media. One can but speculate that his motive was not to improve parapsychological experiments. Shortly thereafter the McDonnell Laboratory closed.

BIBLIOGRAPHY: Phillips, P. R. 1983. "A Brief Report on Recent Experiences with Fraudulent Subjects." (Privately circulated); Randi, J. "The Project Alpha Experiment." In K. Frazier, ed., *Science Confronts the Paranormal,* 1986; Randi, J. "The Role of Conjurers in Psi Research." In P. Kurtz, ed., *A Skeptic's Handbook of Parapsychology,* 1985.

**Projection.** A term used to describe the supposed withdrawal from the physical body of one's center of consciousness during an out-of-body experience. Also applied to the intentional production of one's own apparition or that of a third person's in order to make it visible to other people. See also **Apparition, Experimental.**

**Prophesy.** Knowledge of impending events that can neither be known through normal channels nor inferred from what is known. Prophesy is expressed in the form of a declaration, prediction, or teaching to warn, exhort, or advise. Plato considered it the noblest of the arts and Socrates called it a divine madness.

People have always asked: "What lies ahead for me?" "Will I marry?" "Will my father die?" "Will there be peace?" "Who will be elected president?" "Will my stocks go up or down?" "What horse will win the race?" Accompanying this universal concern to know what the future holds is the equally universal belief that the gods or selected people with god-given powers—from **Nostradamus** to **Jeane Dixon**—can forecast and reveal the future.

There have been other sources of revelation, too. The writings left by the historians of the past, including Herodotus and Ammianus Marcellinus, speak of omens and oracles, such as the **Delphic Oracle,** which were consulted constantly to obtain from the gods foreknowledge of the future. Prophetic dreams, according to Plutarch, were the "oldest oracle" in which divine messages opened the curtains of the future. Today, as psychical research and parapsychology have discovered, dreams remain the primary means of **Precognition.**

Fundamentally, the phenomenon of prophesy is not different from precognition, a field into which researchers in parapsychology entered in 1938 and where they have continued experimentation. The only respect in which prophesy and precognition differ is that the former involves warning, consolation, or some moral or religious theme. But the same word of caution about precognition needs to be given about prophesies. Pure accident may account for some declarations. Other prophesies may be self-fulfilling, that is, the event prophesied may be brought about deliberately by someone who knows the prophesy. Finally, the relation of time between an event and a prophesy is important. A prophesy must be reported or recorded by a trustworthy witness prior to and not after the event to which it relates.

**Prophesy, Religious.** While prophesy is almost indistinguishable from precognition, prophesy in religion contains an added element. The main meaning of the word "prophet," according to the Greek, is not "fore-teller" but "for-teller," that is, one who speaks *for* a divine being. Religious prophets were less concerned with predicting future events than with carrying out the will of God and functioning as the means of divine revelations. Nevertheless, the fundament in prophesy is the same as in precognition: the ability to make true forecasts of the future on the basis of paranormal knowledge.

The Old Testament contains several instances of this talent. The Hebrew prophet Samuel had precognitive abilities. Amos, who lived in the eighth century B.C., was a Minor Prophet of the Old Testament absolutely bent on forecasting doom for Israel: "Rejoice not, O Israel, for thou hast gone a whoring from God. . . . My God will cast them away, because they did not hearken unto him; and they shall be wanderers among the nations" (Hosea 9:1,7,17). Within a few years, his prophesy was fulfilled: The Assyrians overran Israel and dispersed over 27,000 Israelites throughout the Assyrian Empire. Thus the Jews became wanderers. Jesus Christ knew he would suffer in the future (Matt. 16:21; 17:22–23; 20:18–19). He forecast the destruction of Jerusalem in 70 A.D. (Luke 19:43–46; 21:20–24). Jesus knew who would betray him (John 13:18–21) and predicted the persecution of his disciples (John 16:2–4).

Religious claims of prophesy have been attacked as romantic tales based only on the unconfirmed testimony of the Bible. The importance of parapsychology to religion is that, by showing precognition to exist, it has provided an empirical basis for the prophetic experiences claimed and has made them more credible.

**Prophet, Mark, ?–1973, and Elizabeth Clare.** American channelers, called the "Twin Flames" by their followers. Both channeled "ascended masters," spiritually advanced discarnate beings who once were incarnate on earth and who bring the message of the individual Christ Self. Among the "masters" are Koot Hoomi Lal Singh, Djwal Kul, and the Master El Morya who were H. P. Blavatsky's enlightened masters (in her time allegedly alive and well and living in Tibet). Elizabeth now also channels the deceased Mark. The Prophets established their own community in southern California (Camelot) and their own publishing house (Summit University Press which has published dozens of volumes of the channeled material), but, because of cataclysms signalling the beginning of a new age which are about to take place, the community has moved to Oregon.

BIBLIOGRAPHY: Klimo, J. *Channeling,* 1987.

**Prosopopesis.** A term originated by the French psychical researcher **René Sudre** to indicate the assumption of an individual's organism by a different personality as in possession.

BIBLIOGRAPHY: Sudre, R. 1926. "The Role of Prosopopesis in Psychical Research." JASPR 20:129.

**Proxy Sitting.** A sitting in which, in order to avoid telepathy between the sitter and the medium, the sitter is a stranger to the ostensible communicator and is ignorant of the facts communicated. Some of the most impressive cases of proxy sittings were reported by the Rev. C. Drayton Thomas in sittings with the British medium Gladys Osborne Leonard. In one English case, the young girl communicator said that she had been on a journey, had made a detour, had made one or two changes in her original plan, that two awkward obstacles indirectly led to her death and that she had been with foreigners. All these items were later corroborated by the girl's mother. She said that her two daughters had planned to spend Saturday night with friends but instead (the first change in plan) stayed Sunday night. On the way back, the daughters had planned to drive to a luncheon date on Monday with friends but then decided (the second change in plan) to pick up their sister at a railway station and took a route different from the original one intended. After picking up the sister, they missed a turn and took an old road (probably the detour). While on the old road, children (the "awkward obstacles") suddenly ran on to the road from a cottage. The car swerved to avoid them and overturned. After the accident, the girl lingered on before she died attended by her mother, an Austrian friend, and two Austrian maids (the foreigners).

**Psi.** In the collection of stories sent to the Parapsychology Laboratory and L. E. Rhine by people who wanted to know what their puzzling experiences meant are many that seem to be stories of "psi." In one, a girl in Washington, D. C. dislocated her coccyx when she slipped on a marble staircase and fell. Although she did not telephone her parents in New York, her worried mother, who had had a dream the previous night that her daughter had fallen from a ladder and injured her back, called to ask the extent of her injuries. In another case, an unathletic young boy, in order to do better in sports, decided to try to control baseballs by getting a mental picture of them coming into contact with the bat and basketballs by imagining them going through the hoop. Once he began to hit home runs and sink baskets, he was invited to play with the other boys who had previously shunned him.

"Psi," then, is a term broad enough to encompass all the events and abilities of human beings and animals termed paranormal but should be used as a descriptive word only for events or abilities that may be paranormal. It does not mean or imply their paranormality in fact. In its cognitive aspect, "psi" includes clairvoyance, telepathy and precognition. It is an ability to learn things without using the sensory channels of information. In its kinetic aspect, it includes psychokinesis, the ability to affect physical objects with the mind alone.

The term psi, taken from the first letter of the Greek word *psyche* meaning "soul" or "mind," was proposed by **Robert H. Thouless.** Today "psi" has been widely adopted and seems to meet the objections to the terms "extrasensory perception" and "psychokinesis." They imply that what is happening is, on the one hand, some sort of perception or, on the other, that a mind is influencing an object—which may or may not be true. See also **Psi Gamma; Psi Kappa.**

BIBLIOGRAPHY: Rhine, L. E. *Psi: What is It?* 1975.

**Psi Component.** On the Cartesian assumption that each human being is made up of two components, one the ordinary body, the other a non-physical constituent capable of continuing beyond death, **C. D. Broad** coined this term to designate the latter.

**Psi Comunicacíón.** Published irregularly by the Sociedad Española de Parapsicología, this periodical, unlike others in Spain, is devoted exclusively to parapsychological subjects and does not mix discussions of occult subjects (e.g., satanism), with articles on parapsychology. It publishes editorials, scientific papers, book reviews, résumés of conferences, and general notices. In addition, abstracts in English of the principal papers are provided. The present editor is **Ramos Perera Molina.**

**Psi Dexterity.** Term originated by E. A. G. Knowles to describe the use of physical effort by a subject (shaking colored balls) combined with the use of psi ability to produce positive results in the experiment. In the absence of psi, there would have been no dexterity, just effort.

**Psi Differential Effect.** See **Differential Effect.**

**Psi Field Theory.** See **Field Theory.**

**Psi Gamma.** A theory-free term coined by **Robert H. Thouless** and B. P. Wiesner for the cognitive aspect of psi, such as clairvoyance, telepathy and precognition.

**Psi-Hitting.** Exercise of psi ability in such a way that subjects score positively in response to a target. See also **Extrasensory Perception.**

**Psi Kappa.** A neutral term coined by **Robert H. Thouless** and B. P. Wiesner for the kinetic aspect of psi in which a material object or system is influenced without the use of physical energy.

**Psilab//.** A computer hardware/software system prepared and used at the Psychophysical Research Laboratories. Its aim is to provide a tool for investigators of micro-PK, although geographically separated, to be able to collaborate, to develop common designs, and to standardize hardware protocols for testing hypotheses.

BIBLIOGRAPHY: Berger, R. E. and Honorton, C. "Psi Lab //: A Standardized Psi-Testing System." In R. A. White and J. Solfvin, eds. *Research in Parapsychology 1984,* 1985, p.68.

**Psi Mediated Instrumental Response.** Phrase invented by **Rex Stanford** to describe the unconscious and unintentional uses of psi by indivduals in order to serve their needs in daily life (e.g., a man forgets to transfer to another subway train and by "chance" meets the very friends he was travelling to visit and would not have met had he changed trains).

**Psi-Missing.** When a target at which subjects are directing their ESP is avoided to a significant degree. See also **Extrasensory Perception; Miss.**

**Psi News.** Now discontinued, it was from 1978 to 1986 the official bulletin of the Parapsychological Association. It was a quarterly publication containing articles and news relating to parapsychology for both the general public and parapsychologists.

**Psi-Omega.** A generic term introduced by **Ramos Perera Molina** and used principally in Spain to describe the procedures and techniques that facilitate entering into an altered state of consciousness (e.g., meditation or hypnosis).

**Psi Research.** A quarterly journal founded in 1982 by **Larissa Vilenskaya** and published by the Washington Research Center and Parapsychology Group in San Francisco, California. The journal presents theoretical and experimental papers in the field of parapsychology with an emphasis on research done in the Soviet Union, Eastern Europe, and China.

**Psi Science Institute of Japan.** Founded in 1976 in Tokyo, this organization consists of about 1,000 members. It investigates all paranormal phenomena as well as unidentified flying objects and publishes a monthly newsletter. Its office is located at Shibuya Business Hotel 6F, 12-5 Shibuyai-chome, Shibuya-ku, 150 Tokyo, Japan.

**Psi Trailing.** See **Anpsi.**

**Psyche.** A Greek word meaning "soul" or "mind" from whose first letter the word psi was taken.

**Psychiatry.** See **Doctrinal Compliance; Minus Function.**

**Psychic.** An elastic term. As a noun, it is used to refer to certain individuals who, in other cultures, would be called shamans, witches, or sorcerers. In the West, however, people who claim to be gifted with, or are observed to have, any types of psi abilities or experiences are called "psychics." The term is synonymous with "sensitive." Mediums are also psychics, but they generally are more narrowly limited to the production of physical phenomena or to acting as channels between the dead and the living.

Among leading (non-mediumistic) psychics are Uri Geller, Matthew Manning, Nina Kulagina, Pavel Stepanek, Gerard Croiset, Malcolm Bessent. Many psychics carry on lucrative businesses. They are consulted for different reasons: to solve problems, to heal, to peer into the future (Beverly Jaegers of St. Louis received the largest fee ever paid a psychic for predicting that the price of coffee would go up), to understand the past or to get into contact with higher levels of reality or powerful supernatural entities (not necessarily spirits of the dead) to which or to whom psychics are supposed to have access.

The tools and methods psychics use in order to carry on their occupations or use their abilities differ from psychic to psychic. Some use tea leaves, crystal balls, Tarot cards, or automatic speaking, writing or spelling while others may go into trance. No common factor such as sex, background, or intellectual attainment has been found to explain psychic ability.

As an adjective, "psychic" is used interchangeably with **Paranormal.** Any kind of paranormal event or experience is also a "psychic" phenomenon. Commonly, references are seen to the "psychic aura," to "psychic surgery" or to "psychic healing," "psychic archeaology" or "psychic photography."

The concept of "psychic" also has served as a vehicle for philosophical theories that might give the facts of psychical research and parapsychology some coherence. Gardner Murphy, for instance, proposed the idea of a "psychic sphere" between our time-space and a transcendent reality. In the "psychic sphere," psychic or paranormal phenomena, such as apparitions, ESP or psychokinesis, are supposed to occur and belong. It is through the "psychic sphere" that sometimes we can touch the transcendental reality.

**Psychical Research.** The objective investigation of the paranormal, a goal shared in common with **Parapsychology.** The term "psychical research" continues to be used widely in Great Britain. In the United States and many parts of Europe, it is commonly used interchangeably with the more dominant word "parapsychology." Strictly speaking, however, psychical research is different from parapsychology though their goal is the same; the former could be called "field psi," the latter "laboratory psi."

Using the methods of detectives, lawyers, judges, and historians to find evidence and interview and cross-examine witnesses, psychical research is the qualitative inquiry into, and the collection and evaluation of, spontaneous cases and phenomena relating to the question of survival after death such as cases of reincarnation, mediums, apparitions and haunts. These latter phenomena were the first to attract the attention of early investigators.

If we go back to the historical roots of psychical research, we find "that they spread wide and without limit and can be traced back to antiquity" (Berger, 1988). Paranormal experiences and events have existed in every place and time. Biblical literature is filled with them. Plato's *Phaedo* shows a concern with life after death and reincarnation. Possession and trance have occurred among primitive people in all ages. There are, however, some specific factors that contributed to the rise of psychical research. In the nineteenth century, mesmerism made people aware of phenomena later called telepathy and clairvoyance and Spiritualism stimulated awareness of mental phenomena and physical phenomena. Then there was the assault by science on the Christian teaching of a soul independent of the body that lived on after death. Many people wanted to know if facts could confirm this teaching.

Ever since the publication of J. B. Rhine's *Extra-sensory Perception* in 1934, the trend has been away from the survival question, mediums, apparitions, haunts, and psychical research in general and toward parapsychology and quantitative and experimental inquiry in the laboratory into the psi abilities of the living.

**Psychical Research Foundation.** Created in 1960 by **Charles E. Ozanne,** the Psychical Research Foundation was organized originally in Durham, North Carolina, as a scientific and educational center to carry out research into whether the human personality survives death. William G. Roll was and is its director. The scope of the studies of the Psychical Research Foundation includes meditation, haunts, poltergeists, out-of-body experiences, near-death experiences and mediums. The Psychical Research Foundation is now located at the William James Laboratory for Psychical Research, West Georgia College, Carrollton, Georgia 30118.

**Psychic Diagnosis.** See **Healing, Unorthodox.**

**Psychic Healing.** See **Healing, Unorthodox.**

**Psychic Photography.** See **Spirit Photography; Thoughtography.**

**Psychic Surgery.** See **Healing, Unorthodox.**

**Psychoenergetics.** Soviet term for **Parapsychology.**

**Psychogalvanometer.** A device to measure changes in skin resistance as a result of changes in the secretion of the sweat glands, it is one of several devices used in psi experiments. By its use some (but no significant) correlation has been found between galvanic skin response and positive ESP scores in card-guessing experiments.

**Psychograph.** A photographic message in the handwriting of a dead person allegedly received after the death of that person. Fred Barlow published psychographic exhibits that showed handwriting, unquestionably in the handwriting of dead people, on photographs obtained by sitters at séances. But, for fraudulent mediums or photographers, it is very easy to find specimens of a person's handwriting, to cut them out, to join them to make some message and then to photograph them. While a psychograph generally takes the form of words, it need not be limited to writing. It can also appear in the form of images. Thus Barbara M. Ivanova reported the case of a Soviet citizen who never studied art but created paintings in various styles "as if many painters were dwelling inside him" (Ivanova, 1986: 92).

BIBLIOGRAPHY: Ivanova, B. "Psychography and Parapictography as Ways of Receiving Intuitive Information." In Mir, M. and Vilenskaya, L., eds., *The Golden Chalice*, 1986.

**Psychokinesis (PK).** The response of objects such as dice or the environment to a person's wishes is commonly labelled "mind over matter." In psychical research and parapsychology, this effect is known as psychokinesis—the direct influence of the mind on an external physical system or object without the intermediation of any known physical energy. This term is used in preference to "telekinesis" in order to avoid the implication that an effect on an object or in the environment is produced by a deceased entity. Nevertheless, the term has been criticized, notably by **Robert H. Thouless,** because it commits us to the theory that force from an immaterial mind is being exerted on a material object. He thought that a neutral term such as **psi kappa** that did not commit us to any theory would be better.

The mental ability to affect the behavior of objects was used by ancient exorcists to show that they had succeeded in getting a victim rid of a diabolical entity. Eleazar, the Jewish exorcist, would place a bowl of water near the person possessed and instruct the entity to turn it over when it departed the victim's body. Nor was psychokinesis unknown to the Catholic church. Herbert Thurston reports several cases from the lives of religious figures over the centuries in which startled priests have seen the Sacred Host fly from an altar or from an officiating priest into the mouth of a communicant.

In the spontaneous physical effects observed in poltergeist disturbances, in some physical phenomena, such as floating musical instruments or levitating tables, and in reports of watches stopping and of objects falling or breaking at the time of someone's death lay a problem that cried out for parapsychological investigation. J. B. Rhine and Carroll B. Nash in the United States and George W. Fisk in England began experiments to test the ability of subjects to will the fall of the dice. Their experiments produced results greater than chance.

The early dice experiments were followed by placement tests developed by research associate W. E. Cox of Rhine's Parapsychological Laboratory and Haakon G. Forwald. These tests examined the ability of a subject to control the place where target objects would fall. Next living organisms were used as targets and, more recently, random number generators and radioactivity based random event generators have been used by **Helmut Schmidt** in the United States. A new tool for experiments in psychokinesis called the **tychoscope** has been invented in France.

Positive results in these well-conducted experiments suggest that psychokinesis and the ability of the mind to produce physical effects may be a real, if somewhat startling, phenomenon. A similar conclusion has been reached in the Soviet Union as a result of tests of **Nina Kulagina** conducted in 1978 at the USSR Academy of Sciences Institute of Radioengineering and Electronics. The purpose of the experiments was to test her ability to move objects without physical contact.

**Jule Eisenbud** (1982) has concluded that "PK is goal oriented, seems to operate directly, that is without the need of special computational machinery or information processing, and is virtually limitless in respect to 'target' materials and the situation in which it can manifest itself. . . . [T]here is no reason in principle to bar effects of any magnitude" (pp. 130, 132).

BIBLIOGRAPHY: Cox, W. E. 1951. "The Effect of PK on the Placement of Falling Objects." JP 15:40; Eisenbud, J. *Paranormal Foreknowledge*, 1982; Fowald, H. 1952. "A Further Study of the PK Placement Effect." JP 16:59; Nash, C. B. 1944. "PK Tests of a Large Population." JP 8:304; Rhine, L. E. and Rhine, J. B. 1943. "The Psychokinetic Effect: 1. the First Experiment." JP 7:20; Schmidt, H. 1970. "A Quantum Mechanical Random Number Generator for Psi Tests." JP 34:219; Thurston, H. *The Physical Phenomena of Mysticism*, 1952, pp.141–160; Vilenskaya, L. "On PK and Related Subject's Research in the U.S.S.R." In W. and M. J. Uphoff, *Mind Over Matter*, 1980, p.205.

**Psychometric Object.** See **Psychometry.**

**Psychometrist.** Distingushed from a psychometrician who administers psychological tests, a psychometrist uses the technique of psychometry or is a subject in psychometric experiments.

**Psychometry.** In psychological testing, tnis term means the method of mental measurement. In psychical research it means using extrasensory perception of a physical object to gain information about events or people once associated with it. Also called "object association," "object reading," or "token object reading," it may be another example of a motor **Automatism.**

Psychometric experiments have been carried out by Eugene Osty in France and Oskar Fischer of Prague. Among the most notable of these tests was an experiment conducted in Mexico by Gustav Pagenstecher and Walter Franklin Prince with the amateur Mexican medium **María Reyes de Zierold.** She was given a sealed envelope that contained a paper written under emotional circumstances. Another sealed envelope contained a description of the writer of the paper.

When the first envelope was put in the medium's hands, she began to describe a ship at night; many frightened screaming people on board; they spoke English; they were putting on life preservers; they heard an explosion. Then Señora de Zierold described a man in detail: He had a beard and moustache, black eyes and hair, and a scar over his right eyebrow; he held a small notebook from which he tore a leaf; on this he wrote as machine guns and an explosion like a bomb were heard; he placed the note in a bottle, corked it and threw it overboard; all the people were drowned. After she had finished, the first envelope was opened. It contained a slip of paper torn from a notebook. On it, in Spanish, were written: "The ship is sinking. Farewell my Louisa . . . your Ramon Havana . . . Farewell." This note had been discovered in a bottle picked up on the coast off the Azores.

An investigation disclosed that a Spanish political refugee using the name Ramon P. had left New York on a boat bound for Europe during World War 1 when many ships were being sunk by German U-boats. Ramon P.'s wife was named Louisa. When the second letter was unsealed, it was found that the medium's description of the man was correct also: He had black hair, black eyes, a full black beard, and a prominent scar over the right eye.

**Psychon Hypothesis.** Whately Carington's hypothesis that the mind consists of sensa and images, real non-physical entities which obey mental or psychical laws just as physical entities obey physical laws. He thought of them as constituents of mind in the same way that electrons and protons are the constituents of matter. The mind is therefore a psychon system in which all the psychons are linked, and, in Carington's theory, it is the psychon system that survives death.

**Psychophotography.** See **Thoughtography.**

**Psychophysical Research Laboratories.** Founded in 1979 in the Forrestal Research Center in Princeton, New Jersey, by James S. McDonnell. The Psychophysical Research Laboratory under its director, Charles Honorton, took over the work of the Division of Parapsychology and Psychophysics in the Department of Psychiatry at Maimonides Medical Center. The Psychophysical Research Laboratories research program has been directed toward observing extrasensory perception and psychokinesis under controlled laboratory conditions. One area of its research activities included the use of Ganzfeld procedures to produce relaxation and an altered state of consciousness; another area included the use of random number generators and computer games to study psychokinesis; a third area was the development of **Psi Lab//,** a computer hardware/software system. The Psychophysical Research Laboratories have closed because of lack of funds.

**Psychophysiological Responses.** See **Plethysmograph; Psychogalvanometer; Rapid Eye Movement.**

**Psychotronics.** Term used in Czechoslovakia and in France *(psychotronique)* for parapsychology.

**Puharich, Henry K. (Andrija), 1918–.** American physician, medical researcher, and psychical researcher. He has invented an artificial heart device and medical electronic systems.

Dr. Puharich was drawn to psychical research in 1947 when, during his residency in neurophysiological research, the subject of telepathy came up in a conversation. He said, "I didn't believe it; but I thought about it. If telepathy exists, then all the work I was doing in figuring out the circuitry of nerves was superfluous. So I took off two years to find out one thing—if telepathy was real . . .". He conducted experiments with medium Eileen Garrett, who convinced him that it was.

Dr. Puharich then went on to study the influence of mind-altering drugs on psi phenomena (Puharich, 1962). An interest in unorthodox healing led him to observe the Brazilian healer, Jose Arigo. Arigo used a dirty pocket knife to remove a tumor from Puharich's right elbow (Puharich, 1962) and made exact diagnoses in other cases. "Even though I couldn't prove it," said Puharich, "I was convinced that everything Arigo did was based on the action of some outside intelligence."

Puharich also investigated Uri Geller, the Israeli psychic (Puharich, 1974). Puharich developed a close friendship with Geller and considers him a miracle man with a mission to tell the world about extraterrestrials who want to help humankind. Dr. Puharich, an imaginative and ingenious researcher, seems to share Geller's mission as well as his belief in extraterrestrial forces and unidentified flying objects. Along with Geller, Dr. Puharich thinks that he also has been chosen by extraterrestrial entities to persuade the world of the reality of their existence and benevolence of purpose. In a cosmos about which we know practically nothing, it would be rash to dismiss even this possibility.

Selected Writings: "Psychic Research and the Healing Process." In E. D. Mitchell, ed., *Psychic Exploration,* 1974, p.333; *Uri: A Journal of the Mystery of Uri Geller,* 1974; *Beyond Telepathy,* 1962.

BIBLIOGRAPHY: 1973. "Interview: Andrija Puharich, M.D." *Psychic* 5(1): 6.

**Pure Telepathy.** See **Telepathy, Pure.**

**Pursel, Jach.** Contemporary American trance channeler. In 1975, Pursel, a State Farm Insurance Company representative, first "met" Lazaris during meditation. Deliberate attempts to reach Lazaris thereafter failed until Peny, Pursel's then wife, began asking simple questions, at which time Pursel would go into trance and Lazaris would take over. In 1976 Pursel (or Lazaris) began to give individual consultations. In 1976, also, Pursel gave up his business association with State Farm and became a full-time channeler. He is upset by the number of dubious channelers "coming out of the woodwork . . . [s]ome entities are not . . . credible or valuable" (Martin, 1987). In order to counter these alleged channelers, Pursel has become more visible by appearing, for example, on the "Merv Griffin Show" at the end of 1986. He is also making a great deal of money. See also **Channeling.**

BIBLIOGRAPHY: Martin, K. 1987. "The Voice of Lazaris." *New Realities* 7(6):26.

**Pygmalion Hypothesis.** In Greek legend, Pygmalion sculpted an ivory statue of Aphrodite which was animated when he prayed to the goddess to give it life. Jule Eisenbud has offered his "Pygmalion" theory as an explanation other than **Super ESP** to explain supposed survival evidence. He uses the Pygmalion hypothesis to explain the impression sometimes gained in sittings with mediums of a lifelike personality of a deceased person. His re-creation hypothesis holds that this personality is not any element of the deceased individual who has survived death. Instead, it is a re-creation by living people who have unconsciously and psychically organized some aspects of the dead person. The personality thus called into existence then assumes some degree of autonomy but continues to exist only while the living sustain that existence.

**Pyramid Power.** The ancient Egyptians built their royal tombs in the shape of pyramids. Mystics and seers have thought that the outline and measurements of pyramids contain secrets and predictions of world history, such as World War II and other events.

In Czechoslovakia, claims were made that dead animals placed inside a small scale model of the Great Pyramid, the tomb of Cheops, were mummified and that razor blades put inside it were sharpened (Ostrander and Schroeder, 1970). There wasn't a great demand in Czechoslovakia for mummified animals, but because Czech razor blades were of poor quality and razor blades could not be imported, the model pyramid was actually patented and marketed in Czechoslovakia as the "Cheops Pyramid Razor-Blade Sharpener." Soon in other countries pyramid energy generators were being sold to perform various functions from sharpening razor blades to improving the taste of wines.

People began to think that they, too, might

improve inside a pyramid, and many built their own pyramids by following exact specifications or purchased pyramid tents with opaque vinyl covers and wooden legs. They were supposed to give energy to people who sat inside them, perhaps by acting as a lens that focusses energy or as a resonator that collects it (Watson, 1973:99). (Advocates of **Crystals** claim similarly that the stones collect and channel powerful energy that can be used by people in their lives.)

In neither case is the form of energy identified so that the question raised for parapsychology by the pyramids (and crystals) is whether it is related to or may be a new form of psychokinesis. Normally, this phenomenon is understood as a mental ability possessed by human beings to affect matter. But the suggestion of the effects of the pyramidal shape, if they are real, is that psychokinesis may not be a personal force. Rather, it may be a cosmic force underlying all life that the pyramid has collected and channels. A theory of a cosmic force is not new. **Wilhelm Reich,** for example, posited a cosmic life force with his "orgone" theory. To date, however, all experiments to test for the presence of a cosmic energy in the pyramidal shape have produced only negative data. "Pyramid power" has eluded all laboratory attempts in Canada and France to verify its existence (Owen, 1975; Vincens, 1976).

BIBLIOGRAPHY: Ostrander, S.and Schroeder, L. *Psychic Discoveries behind the Iron Curtain,* 1970; Owen, A. R. G. *Psychic Mysteries of the North,* 1975; Vincens, R. *La Pyramide est Morte,* 1976; Watson, L. *Supernature,* 1973.

**Qigong.** See **Healing, Unorthodox.**

**Qualitative Method.** One of the ways psychical research studies paranormal phenomena; the method of observation by which reports of spontaneous cases are collected, investigated, classified, and interpreted. Supporters of this method maintain that such cases provide a natural field not found in the laboratory for the study of the paranormal and that these cases supply evidence of ESP and psychokinesis. See also **Quantitative Method.**

**Quantitative Method.** One of the ways parapsychology studies paranormal phenomena; the statistical method used to evaluate the results of psi experiments with targets. Supporters of this method claim that, among other advantages, it can address the questions of probability and chance and can persuade the scientific community of the validity of evidence for extrasensory perception and psychokinesis. Largely because of the work done by **J. B. Rhine,** the growth of the statistical method has been steady.

**Quantum Physics.** See **Quantum Theories.**

**Quantum Theories.** Governing the behavior of matter and radiation, quantum theories have been advanced that have implications for parapsychology, specifically extrasensory perception and psychokinesis. Evan Harris Walker, for example, considers the human mind to be an ongoing mechanical process. He believes that "all parts of the universe are connected on the sub-quantum level" (Gardner, 1985:589) and sees no reason for the mind (or "will") not being able to influence matter—regardless of distance.

Experiments have been and are being conducted to address some interesting aspects of these theories: 1. retroactive PK—a PK attempt in the future may be able to influence an event in the present; and 2. Feedback and observation—quantum effects may be merely potential. If future subjects receive feedback, their observations may exert a PK influence on these effects.

"In Walker's view, psi action is not a force that goes from brain to brain or brain to object, or object to brain. . . . A psi event occurs when one or more persons unite their quantum mechanical power to collapse a wave packet in such a way as to select a mutually desired future state . . ." (Gardner, 185:590). These attempts to tie quantum mechanics to psi, however, have been criticized as "only a collection of pious hopes" and "a caricature of a theory" (Gardner, 1985:594).

BIBLIOGRAPHY: Gardner, M. "Parapsychology and Quantum Mechanics." In P. Kurtz, ed., *A Skeptic's Handbook of Parapsychology,* 1985; Lauden, D. F. 1980. "Possible Psychokinetic Interactions in Quantum Theory." JASPR 50:399; Schmidt. H. 1981. "PK Tests with Pre-Recorded and Pre-Inspected Seed Numbers." JP 45:87; Walker, E. H. 1979. "The Quantum

Theory of Psi Phenomena." *Psychoenergetic Systems* 3:259; Walker, E. H. "Foundations of Paraphysical and Parapsychological Phenomena." In L. Oteri, ed., *Quantum Mechanics and Parapsychology,* 1975.

**Quarter Distribution (QD).** The distribution of hits appearing on a page of the ESP record sheet that has been divided horizontally and vertically into four equal quarters. On a tabulation of the hits, researchers have found that the fewest hits are in the lower right quarter and the largest number in the upper left quarter.

**Quimby, Phineas Parkhurst.** See **Mary Baker Eddy.**

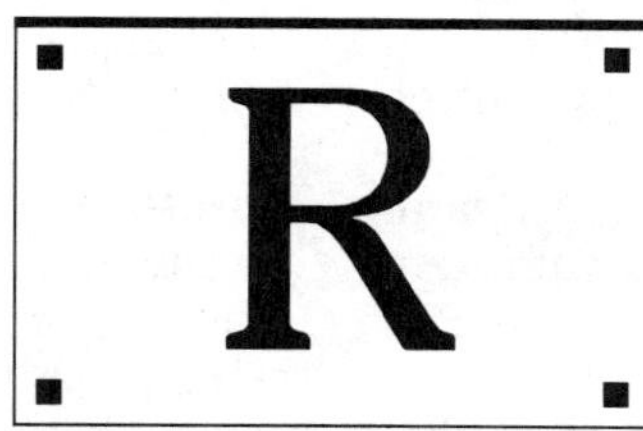

**Radclyffe Hall, Marguerite, 1880–1943.** British author. She is still famous for her *The Well of Loneliness* (1928), a novel about lesbianism that was promptly banned as obscene and so became a best-seller. Miss Radclyffe Hall was herself a lesbian (who called herself John in private).

After the death in 1916 of her first lover and in the hope of making contact with her, Miss Radclyffe Hall turned to psychical research and more particularly to the mediumship of Gladys Osborne Leonard. Miss Radclyffe Hall and her second lover, Una, Lady Troubridge, sat long and often with Mrs. Leonard, indeed as late as 1938, and reported their findings of evidential communications in two excellent reports published in the *Proceedings of the Society for Psychical Research* (1919, 1921). They also sat with George Valiantine and were favorably impressed.

Miss Radclyffe Hall was named to the council of the Society for Psychical Research in 1921 but resigned in 1925 because she felt she was being persecuted as a lesbian. She died of cancer in 1943 and was entombed with her first lover.

Selected Writings: and (Una) Lady Troubridge. 1919. "On a Series of Sittings with Mrs. Osborne Leonard." PSPR 30:339; and Una, Lady Troubridge. In Mrs. W. H. Salter, "A Further Report on Sittings with Mrs. Leonard." 1921. PSPR 32:44.

BIBLIOGRAPHY: Baker, M. *Our Three Selves—The Life of Radclyffe Hall.* New York: Morrow, 1985; Haynes, R. 1986. "Our Three Selves: A Life of Radclyffe Hall." JSPR 53:241; Rogo, D. S. 1986. "Our Three Selves—The Life of Radclyffe Hall." JASPR 81:309.

**Radiesthesia.** See **Dowsing.**

**Radin, Dean I., 1952–.** American psychologist and parapsychologist. A former concertmaster and first violinist with the University of Massachusetts Symphony Orchestra and director of the Human Information Processing Group at Princeton University, Dr. Radin, now associated with Contel Technology center in Virginia, became involved with parapsychology because of sceptics' frequent criticism that psi experiments are not repeatable. Dr. Radin concentrated on those experiments conducted with random number generators in attempts to replicate the psi phenomenon. When he reviewed and compared published data by meta-analysis, he found that a significant number had replicated psi and constituted strong evidence of psi (Radin, May, and Thomson, 1986). Dr. Radin believes, however, that regardless of the strength of the evidence, scientists will not accept its value unless persuasive and comprehensive theories are developed for the phenomenon. This task will require a broad study and understanding of many areas—the humanities, art, religion, philosophy, and other disciplines outside parapsychology. Dr. Radin's research was cited in 1984 on "Nova," a Public Broadcasting System television science program.

fore that, editor of *Research in Parapsychology* and visiting professor of parapsychology at John F. Kennedy University.

Selected Writing: and May, E. C., and Thomson, M. J. "Psi Experiments with Random Number Generators: Meta-Analysis Part I." In D. H. Weiner and D. I. Radin, eds., *Research in Parapsychology 1985,* 1986, p. 14.

**Radionics.** An instrumental method for detecting patterns of energy in the astral body, thereby diagnosing disease in the physical body. See also **De La Warr, George.**

**Ramtha (or Ram).** The spirit control of J. Z. Knight. Ramtha who, according to Marcello Truzzi "acts like a third-rate impression of Yul Brynner in a road tour of *The King and I,*" was first born 35,000 years ago in Atlantis or Lemuria but was also in a previous life the father of J. Z. Knight through whom he is channeled. His predictions for the next twenty years or so are bleak—hurricanes, earthquakes, and volcanic eruptions. To escape them he advises his followers to move to the Pacific Northwest. He also gives advice on practical matters—for example, he told Shirley MacLaine which vitamins to take.

Ramtha is one with God, not the Judeo-Christian God (he calls the Bible an "insidious book"), but the God of the process philosophers, such as Alfred North Whitehead and Charles Hartshorne. God "is the Absolute of Hegel, the Tao of Taoism, the Brahma of Hinduism. . . . God is 'the isness of All That Is'" (Gardner, 1987). God does not judge; he is entirely neutral. There is no evil; nothing is wrong; we have chosen our lives, no matter how wretched they are. We are gods through whom God experiences emotions and sensations. We can heal ourselves and can live forever in our present bodies. Normally, people die and are reincarnated but, if enlightened, they will ascend to union with God.

Although many people are willing to pay $400 to hear Ramtha, have spent millions on "his" lectures and tapes, and, by November 1986, according to the *New York Times,* about 1,500 of them had moved to the Yelm, Washington, area where Mrs. Knight lives, some "speculate that [the original Ramtha has] been replaced by a less benign entity" (Klimo, 1987).

BIBLIOGRAPHY: Klimo, J. *Channeling,* 1987; Gardner, M. *New York Review of Books,* April 9, 1987; *People,* January 26, 1987, pp. 30–31.

**Randi, James (Randall James Hamilton Zwinge), 1928–.** Canadian-born American magician, author, and lecturer, known professionally as "the Amazing Randi." He inveighs against faith healers, channelers, spoon benders, and psychics.

By using distraction and sleight of hand, he claims to have duplicated Uri Geller's metal-bending and other feats and maintains that, by setting up safeguards against cheating, he made Geller's appearance on the "Tonight Show" a complete failure. He created **Project Alpha** in which he sent two young magicians posing as psychically gifted subjects to the McDonnell Laboratory for Psychical Research at Washington University in St. Louis. Their cheating fooled the experimenters and the laboratory has since shut down.

Yet Randi does not deny the possibility of paranormal phenomena; he simply says that he has never seen any. He has a standing offer of a $10,000 prize "to any person or persons who will demonstrate any psychic, supernatural, or paranormal ability of any kind under satisfactory observing conditions [followed by twelve conditions]." He has, however, been accused of reneging both on a promise to pay Russell Targ and Harold Puthoff $1,000 in connection with incorrect statements he made about their Geller research and on his acceptance of a challenge to reproduce Ted Serios's Thoughtography (Braude, 1986).

He claims that he speaks "for rationality in what he sees as an increasingly irrational world" (Jaroff, 1988). Randi has suggested that parapsychologists need the expert help of conjurers (he has offered his own) "in tests on ESP, precognition, psychokinesis, and other unlikely—but not impossible—abilities" (Randi, 1985:339) because he believes that parapsychologists are unequipped to detect deception.

He has performed bogus "psychic surgery" on the *Tonight Show* in the course of which he seemed to be pulling bloody tissue and even organs from the abdomen of a volunteer. One of the founders of **CSICOP** (Committee for the Scientific Investigation of Claims of the Paranormal), he has also looked into the so-called powers of the Chinese masters of Qigong but could find no basis for their claims of paranormal healing. The Chinese children who supposedly read by putting the paper under their armpits or into their ears and who are supposed to mend broken matches inside tamper-proof sealed boxes are "cute, lovable, little guys," he says, but they cheat.

Randi's activities have been very profitable. In 1986 he received a $272,000 "genius" award from the MacArthur Foundation. He has been using the money mainly to discredit unscrupulous faith healers. He has driven TV evangelist and healer Peter Popoff into bankruptcy and caused Pat Robertson some embarrassment. In what seems to be a spoof of J. Z. Knight's Ramtha, he set up his protégé José Álvarez in Australia as the channeler of a 35,000 year old man who said things like "All answers are yes, and all questions can be answered thus" (Jaroff, 1988:71).

Randi started as a routine magician, then graduated to escape acts in which he duplicated some of Houdini's famous feats, such as escaping from a coffin submerged in water and releasing himself from a straitjacket while hanging upside down 110 feet over Broadway. He is a popular lecturer, has appeared frequently on the "Tonight Show" and has done three world tours as a performer and lecturer. He has written many articles and five books, one of them co-authored.

Selected Writings: *The Faith Healers,* 1987; "The Project Alpha Experiment." In K. Frazier, ed., *Science Confronts the Paranormal,* 1986; "The Role of Conjurers in Psi Research." In P. Kurtz, ed., *A Skeptic's Handbook of Parapsychology,* 1985; *The Truth about Uri Geller,* 1982; *Flim-Flam!,* 1980.

BIBLIOGRAPHY: Braude, S. E. *The Limits of Influence,* 1986, pp. 283, 284; Jaroff, L. "Fighting against Flimflam." *Time* June 13, 1988, pp. 70–71; "Psychic Tots of China." *Discover* July 1988, pp. 28–29.

**Random Behavior.** A concept originated by French experimenters **Rémy Chauvin** (under the pseydonym Pierre Duval) and Jean Mayer (under the pseudonym E. Montredon). In ESP tests with animals the experimenters perceived movements, differing from their normal behavior, made by the animals for no apparent reason. In an experiment with mice the movement of the mice to one side of a cage in order to avoid a mild electrical shock was significantly more frequent than had been expected by chance. These results were attributed to precognition or clairvoyance on the part of the mice.

**Random Event Generator. (REG).** An electronic noise-based device used increasingly as a research tool in parapsychology. With it, targets can be generated automatically and at different rates. It also provides immediate feedback to subjects in tests of both extrasensory perception and psychokinesis.

**Randomizer.** The person responsible for following a randomizing procedure.

**Randomizing Procedure.** A method followed to assure a haphazard selection of targets. Procedures have included use of random numbers tables and telephone directories whose numbers represent the symbols on ESP cards or the use of dice whose digits are translated into symbols.

**Random Number Generator (RNG).** An electronic noise-based device that generates random numbers from 0 to 255. Incorporated in computers, it is a new research tool in studies of psychokinesis, a considerable number of which have shown results of statistical significance.

**Random Numbers.** In a psi experiment, a random sequence of numbers is produced when no cause is in operation to place a particular digit in one position in the row instead of another or to have two particular digits stand in a special relation to one another.

**Random Order.** See **Chance.**

**Rao, Koneru Ramakrishna, 1932–.** Indian psychologist and parapsychologist. The attempt to reconcile the conception of the human being presented by Western psychology with the conflicting conception offered by the ancient philosophy of India (of a many-storied being within whom dwells a divine self) led Dr. Rao into parapsychology. His interest soon extended to the study of the nature of consciousness and the carrying out of extensive experimental studies of ESP.

Dr. Rao has worked in the United States with J. B. Rhine and L. E. Rhine at the Parapsychology Laboratory and, later, Institute for Parapsychology of which he became the director in 1977. In 1984, he left the institute to assume the post of vice chancellor of Andhra University in India where he had earlier been a professor of psychology and where, in 1967, he had established the Department of Psychology and Parapsychology. At the time of its establishment, it was the only university department of parapsychology in the world. Under his guidance, the department has been largely responsible for the existence in India of parapsychology as a field of inquiry and academic discipline. In 1985, Dr. Rao set up at Andhra University and became the director of the Institute for Yoga and Consciousness.

In 1987, Dr. Rao returned to the United States to resume his post as director of the Institute for Parapsychology. He was twice president of the Parapsychological Association and has been the editor of the *Journal of Parapsychology* and the *Journal of Indian Psychology*.

Selected Writings: *The Basic Experiments in Parapsychology*, 1984; *J B. Rhine: On the Frontiers of Science*, 1982; *Experimental Parapsychology*, 1966.

**Rao, P. V. Krishna, 1947–.** Indian psychologist. Professor of psychology at Andhra University and head of its Department of Psychology, his special interests are laboratory research into extrasensory perception and investigations into the relationship between psi and yogic meditation.

Selected Writings: with Rao, K. R. 1982. "Two Studies of ESP and Subliminal Perception." JP 46:185; with K. Harigopal. 1979. "The Three Gunas and ESP: An Exploratory Investigation." *Journal of Indian Psychology* 2:63.

**Rapid Eye Movement (REM).** A physiological measure that indicates when a sleeping subject is dreaming. It is used in the investigation of telepathy in dreams. Experimenters monitor the REM by means of electroencephalographic electrodes attached to the faces and skulls of subjects. During this possibly psi-conducive stage agents attempt to "send" target pictures to the dreamers. Following some minutes (10–20) of the REM, the subjects are awakened for a report and tape recording of their dreams. See also **Maimonides Medical Center, Dream Laboratory.**

**Raps.** Closely associated with the physical phenomena of Spiritualism and with poltergeist disturbances are mysterious knocking noises. These noises give the distinct impression of being made by an unseen intelligence.

A typical case of raps was investigated by William Barrett in a lonely cottage in Derrygonnelly, Ireland, occupied by a farmer and his family. They reported noises, scratchings and rappings each night after they went to bed. Rats were suspected but were exonerated when objects began to move and stones fall without any discernible reason. On Barrett's visit to the place, he heard coming from the ceiling, walls, various parts of the room, the chairs and bedstead faint raps, gradually becoming louder, accompanied by scratching or tearing sounds. In his presence, the source of the noises being asked to rap a certain number of times, it did so correctly. When one or more fingers were held up, the appropriate number of raps was given. The experiment was repeated four times with the same result.

Popular belief is that the phenomenon is produced by spirits of the dead as the word "geist" in "poltergeist" implies. Barrett believed that some intelligence was behind the raps and by means of telepathy was able to get into rapport with his mind and the minds of other people. Today parapsychologists tend to believe that raps and other poltergeist phenomena are usually produced by psychokinesis and express tensions or hostilities that have built up in a person who is the center of the disturbances and who is not able to release the tensions or hostilities in any normal way.

BIBLIOGRAPHY: Barrett, W. F. 1911. "Poltergeists, Old and New." PSPR 25:377.

**Raudive, Konstantin, 1909–1974.** Latvian philosopher and psychologist. He took the world by storm with his experiments with electronic voice phenomena and his book which made the extraordinary claim of having recorded more than 70,000 voices from the spirit world. In Raudive's better recordings, voices can be heard saying, "The dead live, Konstantin," "We are," "Please believe."

After reading Friedrich Jürgenson's book on the voice phenomena in 1967, Raudive sought out the author and did experiments with him for some years. Then Raudive began to conduct independent experiments ostensibly to determine if he could separate the phenomena from whatever influence Jürgenson might be exerting, although there are indications that, from Jürgenson's point of view, Raudive had decided to go into business for himself, as the saying goes. Some months later, Raudive heard what he thought was a whispered voice. Using microphone and radio methods and turning his radio to the "white noise" between radio stations, he began to collect more and more recorded voices and, by 1968, had added thousands to his archives.

Raudive's book, published in 1971, introduced the voice phenomena to the English-speaking world. It contained examples of the voices along with technical data and recording methods, some of which were designed by **Alex Schneider** who collaborated with him. Raudive believed that any individual exercising patience would be able to obtain results similar to his, a belief that may well have been borne out because in the last three decades numbers of enthusiastic amateurs as well as scientists have discovered the voice phenomena on their recordings, too. Most believe that the voices originate from another world.

Raudive was extremely stubborn in his methods and views and was convinced that his interpretations of the sounds on his tapes (not always easy to hear) were the only correct ones; he was oblivious to counterhypotheses. Nevertheless, whatever Raudive's faults may have been, "few can fail to admire the dedicated, patient and painstaking way Dr. Raudive pursued his studies" (Ellis, 1978:147).

Selected Writing: *Breakthrough,* 1971.

BIBLIOGRAPHY: Ellis, D. J. *The Mediumship of the Tape Recorder,* 1978.

**Raudive Voices.** See **Electronic Voice Phenomena; Raudive, Konstantin.**

**Rayleigh, Lord.** See **Stutt, John William.**

**Raymond.** Title of a book written by Sir Oliver Lodge (1916) in which he described his sittings with mediums in efforts to communicate with his son Raymond who was killed at the front on September 15, 1915 during World War I. Lodge, already convinced before his son's death of survival after death, was all the more persuaded by various incidents described in the book that his son was communicating from the beyond.

BIBLIOGRAPHY: Lodge, O. *Raymond,* 1916.

**Reader.** In psychical research a reader is a psychic, fortune-teller, or practitioner of I Ching, palmistry, taro cards, tea leaf, and other divinatory techniques who is consulted by people anxious about their personal problems, hopes, or fears or who want to know about their pasts or futures. Often these consultations take the place of the couch in sessions with a psychoanalyst. See also **Fortune-Telling.**

**Reading.** In psychical research a reading is the material a medium presents during a sitting or the information a reader provides.

**Reading, Cold.** Information a medium gives a sitter or a reader gives a client that is cast in terms so general that most sitters or clients will think it applies to them.

**Rebirth.** See **Reincarnation.**

**Recitative Xenoglossy.** See **Xenoglossy.**

**Rector.** See **Piper, Leonora E.; Moses, W. Stainton.**

**Recurrent Spontaneous Psychokinesis (RSPK).** See **Poltergeist.**

**Red Scratch Case.** Celebrated case that seemed to have involved an apparition conveying information not known to the percipient.

A salesman staying in a hotel room in St. Louis, Missouri, saw the apparition of his dead sister seated at a table. As he started forward in delight and called her name, she disappeared. The incident affected him so strongly that he took the next train home. When he told his parents that he had seen a bright red scratch on the right side of his sister's face, his mother nearly fainted. With tears streaming down her face, she told him that no one but herself had known that she had accidentally scratched her daughter's face as she lay in the coffin. The mother had used powder to obliterate all traces of the scratch. The salesman's mother was absolutely convinced that her son had seen his sister. She died in the belief that she would rejoin her daughter in the next world.

If the salesman did not receive information about the scratch by extrasensory perception from the mind of his mother, the case offers one of the most striking pieces of evidence of postmortem survival.

BIBLIOGRAPHY: Myers, F. W. H. 1889. "On Recognized Apparitions Occurring More Than One Year After Death." PSPR 6:13.

**Reese, Bert (also spelled "Ries"), 1851–1926.** Polish-born psychic. He was famous for his remarkable performances of billet-reading. He seemed able to tell people what was written on folded slips of paper even before they were given to him and convinced them that he possessed extraordinary paranormal powers. Among those who remained persuaded by Reese was Thomas A. Edison. Harry Houdini, however, who claimed to have found out Reese's trick, called him the "greatest billet-switcher" of all times and Walter F. Prince, who had a sitting with Reese, also detected Reese substituting one billet for another so that he was always one ahead and had already read in advance the billet that he answered before reading it aloud.

BIBLIOGRAPHY: Prince, W. F. 1932. "A Sitting with Bert Reese." JSPR 27:249.

**Reich, Wilhelm, 1897–1957.** Austrian-American psychoanalyst and discoverer of "orgone energy." A highly controversial figure some scientists consider to have gone completely insane, he was a Freudian psychoanalyst who was on the staff of the Vienna Psychoanalytic Institute. His first book, *The Function of the Orgasm* (1927), related the biological function of orgasm—the release of pent-up emotions and energies—to the sexual frustration of the working classes. His *Mass Psychology of Fascism* (1933), which blamed the sex-repressive German family system for the rise of Hitler, was published from Scandinavia. His *Character Analysis* (1933) is still used by analysts. In it Reich maintained that bioenergy that normally travels through the body in a specific circuit gets trapped wherever muscles are tight. This condition, if chronic, reduces the body's bioenergy and leads to sickness. From this grew Reich's theory of orgone (from "organism" and "orgasm") energy.

In 1933, Reich fled the Nazis and in 1934 differences with Freud and his followers led to his break with psychoanalysis. At this time he was living in Oslo, Norway, where he carried on experiments that led him to believe that he had discovered the origin of life ("bions"), which he believed developed from inorganic matter and were able to affect organic matter (kill certain cancer cells, cause eye inflammations, etc.) As the result of a press campaign against his work in Norway at this time (1939) he came to the United States. Here he continued his work with "bions" and developed boxes that "drew in" the "orgone energy," a non-electromagnetic force, the life force, which permeates all nature. Orgone is blue. That is why the sky, oceans, and lakes are blue, etc. Reich carried on experiments with an orgone motor, and by the early 1940s began to make orgone accumulators (orgone storage boxes) to use in experiments with unorthodox healing.

In 1948 Dr. Bernard Grad, the distinguished Canadian biochemist who has devoted much of his time to investigations of healing, began to sit regularly in an orgone accumulator. He writes that he "repeatedly experienced bioenergetic streamings on [his] back . . . and repeatedly felt being charged up after a half hour of its use." In 1949 Grad began a four-year study of the effect of orgone accumulators on lymphatic leukemia in mice. He "found that this treatment significantly lowered the incidence of this disease" (Grad, 1987).

Reich also experimented with the use of his orgone accumulators in weather control and this research continues.

From about 1947 on the federal Food and Drug Administration began to investigate the orgone accumulators. In 1954 Reich was brought to trial on charges of fraud. The proceedings dragged on for two years, Reich finally being sentenced to two years in prison for contempt of court. All his books and records dealing with orgone were ordered burned. (Some of these same books had already been burned by the Nazis.) Nine months later Reich died of a heart attack in prison.

His followers today believe that the "orgone discovery has emerged as the universal energic principle underlying all otherwise impenetrable paranormal phenomena . . ." (Constable, 1977).

BIBLIOGRAPHY: Constable, T. J. "Orgone Energy Engineering through the Cloudbuster." In J. White and S. Krippner, eds., *Future Science*, 1977, pp. 404–419; Gardner, M. *Fads and Fallacies in the Name of Science*, 1957,

250–262; Grad, B. R. "Experiences and Opinions of an Unconventional Scientist." In R. Pilkington, ed., *Men and Women of Parapsychology,* 1987, pp. 146–160; King, F. "Wilhelm Reich (1897–1957)." In Cavendish, R. *Encyclopedia of the Unexplained,* 1974, pp. 207–209; Mann, W. E. "Wilhelm Reich and Orgone Energy." In J. White and S. Krippner, eds., op. cit., pp. 103–112.

**Reichenbach's Experiments.** In the nineteenth century, Baron Karl von Reichenbach conducted experiments and made observations with subjects whom he called sensitives. They reported to him that from crystals, the human body, and some other materials there seemed to emanate a glow that produced curious sensory effects, sometimes cool, sometimes warm, sometimes pleasurable, sometimes painful, sometimes accompanied by abnormal mental states. Reichenbach believed that the phenomenon was physical and speculated that it was a cosmic force he called "Od" or "Odic force." Reichenbach also noted that many people reported peculiar sensations when a magnet was moved near their bodies. He observed that, in a dark room, flames coming from the poles of a magnet were visible.

Reichenbach's experiments and observations were considered sufficiently important by the early psychical researchers for them to make their own investigations. The Society for Psychical Research conducted many experiments but got only meager results to support the claim of luminous emanations that sound very much like the aura. Similarly, experiments of the American Society for Psychical Research conducted by Joseph Jastrow and G. F. H. Nuttall (Jastrow and Nuthall, 1886) and W. H. Pickering (Pickering, 1886) to test both the magnetic sense and the claim of flames were negative.

BIBLIOGRAPHY: Jastrow, J. and Nuttall, G. H. E. 1886. "On the Existence of a Magnetic Sense." PASPR 1:116; Pickering, W. H. 1886. "A Research on the Reality of Reichenbach's Flames." PASPR 1:127.

**Reincarnation.** The belief that each human being consists of a physical body and a spiritual or psychic component; that, after the death of the physical body, the spiritual or psychic component may persist for a time in an incorporeal state; and that, following this interval, it will be reborn in the physical body of a human being (in Hindu and Buddhist belief according to its **Karma**). Reincarnation has been variously called "metempsychosis," "transmigration," "rebirth," and "palingenesis" and interpretations of it vary. Among the Hindus, for example, rebirth may occur in the physical bodies of animals and, where Hinduism teaches that it is the soul that is reborn, the Buddhist doctrine of *anatta* teaches that it is a changing complex of states that persists. Rebirth is continuous until *moksha* is achieved in Hinduism or Nirvana in Buddhism.

Apart from these differences in the concept of reincarnation, the belief has possible applications to certain aspects of our lives,such as fears and dislikes. For example, a fear of water may be the consequence of having drowned in another existence, a dislike of one's parents may be the result of lingering memories of and feelings of a bond with other parents in a previous lifetime.

Reincarnation is highly relevant to psychical research because it is directly related to the question of survival after death, it being plain that reincarnation cannot take place unless some component of the human being survives death.

The belief in reincarnation frequently is tied in with a belief in karma, the moral link between lives that assures eventual justice to everyone by the operation of a retributive law. Another early support for the belief were child prodigies, such as Wolfgang Amadeus Mozart. The demonstration by young children of remarkable talents in some field could not be explained by heredity or previous training. But the reincarnation doctrine solved the problem by stating that child prodigies were reincarnations of individuals who, in former lives, had achieved virtuosity in these fields and carried their accomplishments into present lives. To these supports for reincarnation others were added including **Déjà Vu** experiences and **Past Life Regression.**

References prior to the last third of the twentieth century to spontaneous recalls of memories of past lives are rare but such recalls now form part of the current evidential base of the reincarnation belief. When an adult makes spontaneous statements about a previous life, it would not be unreasonable to think that he or she has acquired information normally about the life of the deceased person who is the subject of the claims. The case takes on a different complexion, however, when children of tender years make statements that they have lived before in places far from their homes and furnish details later investigation confirms. For this reason, evidence bearing on reincarnation mainly from the claims of young children of memories of prior lives has been collected.

Among cases from Lebanon is that of Imad Elawar who, as a two-year old child, one day recognized a strange man who had come from the village of Khriby, thirty kilometers from the child's home. The man had been a neighbor of the deceased Ibrahim Bouhamzy. This event was the culmination of a series of allegations Imad had been making about a previous life as a member of the Bouhamzy family in the distant village. Subsequent investigation of the case showed that of forty-seven items of information Imad gave about his former life, such as that he had had a woman named Jamile, forty-four were right.

In every case, however, the question is whether the reincarnation hypothesis is the best explanation for the facts or whether possession, fraud, cryptomnesia or extrasensory perception by which a child may have acquired information about a deceased person is a more likely explanation. In response to the last objection, however, apart from seeming to remember previous lives, the children investigated display no special psychic gifts. Nevertheless, the search goes on for cases in which children exhibit behavior traits or patterns pertinent to the prior life claimed and that could not so easily be attributed to ESP.

BIBLIOGRAPHY: Stevenson, I. *Cases of the Reincarnation Type Vols. I–IV,* 1975, 1977, 1980, 1983; Stevenson, I. 1974. *Twenty Cases Suggestive of Reincarnation,* 1974.

**Relaxation.** A state of deep mental and physical peace in which the mind is blank and passive and the body is rid of all tensions. This state seems to be directly related to psi performance. Investigators have found that such a state produces significantly higher success in experiments in extrasensory perception and psychokinesis in contrast to a non-relaxed state.

**Religion.** Sir Alister Hardy, a champion of religion and pioneer in the study of religious experiences, saw the great implications that psychical research had for religion. He wrote that "psychical research is one of the most important branches of investigation the human mind has ever undertaken" (Hardy, 1965). Its importance to religion arises out of their many interrelationships (Berger, 1989).

In religious texts there are recorded all kinds of paranormal phenomena. Many forms of religious activity assume the existence of paranormal abilities. Prayer seems to correspond to telepathy. Revelation corresponds to clairvoyance and **prophesy** corresponds to precognition. The phenomenon of psychokinesis corresponds to **miracles,** which suppose a spiritual power over the environment without physical mediation. Religion and psychical research also converge in what religion calls "immortality" or "eternal life." The quest of psychical research is for evidence that the human personality survives death for any period of time, the first condition for any of religion's teachings of a life eternal.

Finally, much research in parapsychology has been aimed at demonstrating that knowledge can be obtained without the use of the senses, by means of a psychic ability that may not be physical and which cannot be integrated into a physicalistic, materialistic picture of the world. It is this materialist concept that is fatal to everything that religion teaches and that parapsychological evidence seems to oppose.

BIBLIOGRAPHY: Berger, A. S. "Religion and Parapsychology: Eight Points of Contact." In A. S. Berger and H. O. Thompson, eds., *Religion and Parapsychology,* 1989; Hardy, A. *The Living Stream,* 1965.

**Religious Experience Research Unit.** See **Hardy, Sir Alister.**

**REM.** See **Rapid Eye Movement.**

**Remote Viewing.** A protocol to test for extrasensory perception originated by Russell Targ and Harold Puthoff. In remote viewing—a more neutral term than clairvoyance, telepathy or out-of-body experience—target locations are chosen at random. One experimenter goes to the targets while the subject remains with a co-experimenter and attempts to describe the targets verbally or by drawing. These descriptions are then evaluated by judges who visit the target locations and independently rank and document the responses. In various papers and in their book *Mind Reach* (1977), Puthoff and Targ reported remarkable success with this protocol. Not only did gifted sensitives describe the targets accurately, but everyone who attempted remote viewing with these experimenters was able to describe a target with some success. *Mind Reach* stimulated replications at parapsychological research centers around the world, most of which also reported success using the Targ-Puthoff protocol.

Sadly, critics (Kennedy 1979a, 1979b; Hyman 1986; Marks 1986) have shown that the judging procedure was tainted with cues. In one instance, judges 12,000 miles away in New Zealand, simply on the basis of the cues in the transcripts, were able to rank the targets correctly. Recently, however, Robert Jahn, dean of engineering and applied science at Princeton University, using a new method of scoring that can be analyzed by computer, has come up with confirmation of the remote viewing work (Beloff, 1988).

BIBLIOGRAPHY: Beloff, J. *The Importance of Psychical Research,* 1988; Hyman, R. "Outracing the Evidence: The Muddled 'Mind Race'." In K. Frazier, ed., *Science Confronts the Paranormal,* 1986, pp. 91–109; Kennedy, J. 1979a. "Methodological Problems in Free-Response ESP Experiments." JASPR 73:115; Kennedy, J. 1979b. "More on Methodological Issues in Free-Response Psi Experiments." JASPR 73:395; Marks, D. "Remote Viewing Revisited." In K. Frazier, op,cit., pp. 110–121; Targ, R. and Puthoff. H. *Mind Reach,* 1977.

**Repeatable Experiment.** An experiment that researchers anywhere, by following a prescribed procedure, can carry out by themselves in their laboratories with repeated success; in parapsychology a psi experiment that will produce a manifestation of psi on demand at any time. Sceptics charge that the evidence offered for psi has been through unrepeatable experiments. It is one principal reason mainstream scientists deny parapsychology admission into the halls of science. For science requires that, in order to be sure that results reached by one experimenter are real, the same results be repeatable and confirmed independently by other experimenters following the procedures prescribed.

Parapsychologist Joseph G. Pratt took the position that the repeatable experiment in parapsychology cannot be achieved and that the search for it should be abandoned because, he said, "Psi is a spontaneous occurrence in nature, and we can no more predict precisely when it is going to occur in our carefully planned and rigorously controlled experiments than we can in everyday life psychic experiences. . . . Predictable repeatability is unattainable because of the nature of the phenomena" (Pratt, 1978). After all, no one doubts the findings of astronomers and geologists even though they can never give repeatable laboratory demonstrations. Psi phenomena belong to the same realm of nature as stars and rocks and parapsychologists cannot be held responsible if nature will not do their bidding and perform on demand.

The assumption, however, that no repeatable experiments exist in parapsychology goes somewhat beyond the truth. One example are the home experiments with clocks carried out by W. van Vuurde that were repeated by Arthur E. H. Bleksley and confirmed by him. The use of the **Ganzfeld Procedure** has permitted a significant replication rate to be achieved. **Sheep-Goat Experiments** and **Remote Viewing** protocols also have been replicated. And while a trip to India, Sri Lanka, or Turkey is not a laboratory experiment, it is almost certain that one will find in these cultures several cases suggestive of reincarnation similar to cases found and reported earlier.

In spite of Pratt's urging, parapsychologists do recognize the importance of achieving a repeatable experiment. In the words of one: "Parapsychology will stand or fall on its ability" to find it (Honorton, 1981).

BIBLIOGRAPHY: Honorton, C. 1981. "Beyond the Reach of Sense: Some Comments on C. E. M. Hansel's *ESP and Parapsychology: A Critical Re-Evaluation.*" JASPR 75:155; Pratt, J. G. 1978 "Prologue to a Debate: Some Assumptions Relevant to Research in Parapsychology." JASPR 72:127.

**Resch, Andreas, 1934–.** Austrian Roman Catholic theologian and psychologist. He is the influential general secretary of **Imago Mundi** and editor of a publication of the same name. Professor of psychology, Father Resch has been called "Father of Paranormality" because he teaches a course in parapsychology at the Accademia Alphonsiana, an affiliate of the Pontifical Lateran University in Rome. The course, which is for Catholic priests and seminar directors studying clinical psychology and moral theology, has been very successful and seems to have the approval of the university and the Vatican.

While such a development should be applauded as an enlightened attitude by the Church toward parapsychology, some parapsychologists, for example Piero Cassoli, are "puzzled" by the course. After reviewing the subjects that are treated and the manner of treatment given them, Cassoli wrote: "I don't like to present this news as a conquest or as an Italian contribution to the achievements of parapsychology here and in the world" (Cassoli, 1971).

Father Resch believes that the Catholic church should be open to a dialogue with atheists and agnostics but that it should not conduct any dialogue with people who believe in Spiritualism or reincarnation. He also seems to think that all truly paranormal occurrences took place two thousand years ago. Any that occur now are the work of a diabolical agency. The question for any theologian, he believes, is whether a phenomenon has a natural or a supernatural cause. If the latter, the explanation for it lies in the Christian religion and in the judgment of the Church.

Selected Writings: 1969. *Parapsicología e Religióne Metapsíchica* 24:146.

BIBLIOGRAPHY: Cassoli, P. "Parapsychology in Italy Today." *Proceedings of an International Conference Parapsychology Today: A Geographic View,* 1971, p.187.

**Research in Parapsychology.** An annual publication of the Parapsychological Association that contains research briefs and papers, invited addresses, and abstracts presented at annual conferences held by the P.A. Editors in 1989 were Linda A. Henkel and Rick E. Berger.

**Research Institute for Psi and Psychics.** Dutch parapsychological organization established in 1980 to carry out theoretical and experimental investigations of psi phenomena and their relationship to biology, psychology, and, especially, to physics and observational theories. Along with the **Synchronicity Research Unit,** it produces most of the research done in the The Netherlands today. The address of the organization is Alexanderkade 1, 1018 CH Amsterdam, The Netherlands.

**Response Bias.** The inclination of subjects to call some target symbols more often and to call others less often than would be expected by chance. Some experimental results suggest that bias against a particular response increases the probability that this response, when made, will be an accurate, psi-mediated response.

**Responsive Xenoglossy.** See **Xenoglossy.**

**Retrocognition.** Non-inferential knowledge of past events.

**Revue Métapsychique.** Quarterly journal of the Institut Métapsychique International whose publication began in 1919. It publishes the research done by the institute as well as subjects of interest to parapsychology and psychical research ranging from laboratory experiments and spontaneous cases relating to extrasensory perception and psychokinesis to mysticism in Central Africa.

**Rhine, Joseph Banks, 1895–1980.** American pioneer in parapsychology. Sometimes called the "Father of Parapsychology" because his work was paradigmatic and for almost fifty years produced for parapsychology terms, concepts, and standardized research procedures the field continues to employ. Rhine made ESP (extrasensory perception) a household word. He was a person of enormous determination. For example, barred from the marines in World War I by a physical impairment, Rhine challenged the marine physician to a hike—and a marine uniform was his.

After the war, Rhine became a researcher in plant physiology and, from 1924 to 1926, was an instructor in that field at West Virginia University. After earning the degree of doctor of philosophy from the University of Chicago in 1925, he turned to psychical research in an effort to clear up the troubling questions of whether the human spirit survives death and whether the human being possesses any element not merely physical. In 1927, he and his wife **Louisa E. Rhine** abandoned their careers and went to work in the Department of Psychology under William McDougall at Duke University.

Rhine's investigations of the survival question and of medium Eileen Garrett raised the further question of the true source of information given by a medium that the medium could not have known normally. The possibility of telepathy between the mind of the medium and the sitter or the minds of other living people could not be discounted nor could the possibility that the medium received information by clairvoyance. Although these possibilities had been long considered, Rhine's experimental techniques with test cards designed by Karl Zener were new. So was the development of methods to eliminate sensory cues and to apply mathematical procedures to evaluate results.

Rhine's work with students using his ESP cards at Duke University obtained positive ESP data from a higher proportion of subjects than anyone else anywhere has ever obtained. Once, in order to provoke a subject to improve his score, Rhine bet $100 that the subject could not call a particular card correctly. Rhine repeated this bet twenty-five times, the subject got twenty-five straight hits and Rhine lost $2,500 (which he never paid since that sum was approximately his salary for an entire year).

In consequence of the ESP experiments at Duke, standard laboratory procedures for the testing of ESP evolved that came to be adopted throughout the world. Rhine's ESP experiments culminated in 1934 in his book *Extra-Sensory Perception.* This report of approximately 90,000 experiments with new research methodology to try to provide mathematical evidence of ESP, followed in 1937 by Rhine's *New Frontiers of the Mind,* brought fame to Rhine and Duke University. Rhine at that time chose a word Max Dessoir had originated over forty years earlier—"parapsychology"—to describe the research conducted at Duke. He then established there an autonomous **Parapsychology Laboratory** and the *Journal of Parapsychology,* which he co-edited with McDougall. Rhine also focussed on testing psychokinesis by throwing and influencing dice as targets. After nine years of experiments, he published results that he believed established PK.

Soon after *Extra-Sensory Perception* was published, Rhine was faced with criticism, principally from academic psychologists, who challenged the concept and evidence of ESP. Nevertheless, in 1940, with the cooperation of assistants, including Joseph G. Pratt, Rhine published *Extrasensory Perception after Sixty Years* which appraised the evidence for, and criticism of, ESP and effectively undermined critical assaults for a time. Rhine could not have known that, years later, opposition to the basic claims of parapsychology, and indeed to the field itself, would be renewed.

In 1957, at Rhine's initiative, the Parapsychological Association was founded. When in 1965 Rhine retired from Duke as professor of psychology, he set up the **Foundation for Research on the Nature of Man** and the **Institute for Parapsychology.** In the year of his death, he was elected president of the Society for Psychical Research.

Rhine did not discover ESP or psychokinesis. These phenomena have been reported for thousands of years. He did, however, originate certain terms now used regularly in parapsychology. He is also important because he placed ESP and PK in the controlled environment of the laboratory and because he made parapsychology into an experimental science.

Selected Writings: *New World of Mind,* 1953; *The Reach of the Mind,* 1947; *New Frontiers of the Mind,* 1937; *Extra-Sensory Perception,* 1934; with J. G. Pratt. *Frontier Science of the Mind,* 1957; with L. E. Rhine. 1943. "The Psychokinetic Effect: 1. The First Experiment." JP 7: 20; with J. G. Pratt, C. E. Stuart, B. M. Smith, and J. A. Greenwood. *Extrasensory Perception after Sixty Years,* 1940.

BIBLIOGRAPHY: Berger, A. S. *Lives and Letters in American Parapsychology,* 1988; Brian, D. *The Enchanted Voyager: The Life of J. B. Rhine,* 1982; Rao, K. R. *J. B. Rhine: On the Frontiers of Science,* 1982; Rhine, L. E. *Something Hidden,* 1983.

**Rhine, Louisa Ellen (Weckesser), 1891-1983.** American parapsychologist. Born into a strict Mennonite family, Louisa Weckesser learned young "that it's OK to be different if you know you are right, a lesson that certainly prepared her for her future role in life" (Feather, 1983:294). She is best remembered as the wife of **Joseph B. Rhine.** Yet it has been pointed out that although "[i]n both their personal and professional lives, they were a completely integrated team . . . Mrs. Louie . . . [b]efore she ever met Dr. JB was a person in her own right" (Feather, 1983:300—301) for she was four years his senior and was already teaching school when they met.

Although Louisa Rhine did a great deal of experimental work—in the first psychokinesis experiment (Rhine and Rhine, 1943) and in other laboratory tests—her main contribution to parapsychology is usually acknowledged to be her work with spontaneous cases of what seems to be psi, work which began in 1948 at the Parapsychology Laboratory at Duke University. Her spontaneous cases were sent in to her by thousands of people (15,000 over the years) who wanted either to share or to try to understand what had happened to them. She classified cases that seemed to indicate the influence of mind on matter as psychokinesis and those that seemed to involve extrasensory perception into sub-classes of telepathy, clairvoyance or precognition. Basing her work on G.N.M. Tyrrell's concept of **Mediating Vehicles** (1946) she developed "a two-stage model of psi. Like Tyrrell, she believed that Stage I (the receipt of information and the judgment that information is important) was close to conscious inspection and that Stage II (the process of mediating the information to consciousness) took forms common in psychological experience. . . . LER's [Louisa E. Rhine's] investigation of these mediating vehicles is perhaps the best known aspect of her work" (Weiner and Haight, 1983:306).

Dr. Rhine found that intuitions and hallucinations occurred only in the waking state. She found that information received in realistic dreams (or daydreams) was often precognitive, sometimes telepathic or clairvoyant. Unrealistic dreams could also contain elements of psi. She eventually concluded that dreams, hallucinations, intuitions, and even psychokinesis mediate ESP. In dealing with telepathy, Louisa Rhine came to believe that it was the percipient and not the so-called agent who initiated telepathic impressions. She also concluded that apparitions of the living or the dead were essentially the same, "merely creations and dramatizations by the mind of the living percipient. . ." (Berger, 1988). Louisa Rhine felt, too, that precognition was not essentially different from telepathy and clairvoyance, except for the deeper impressions caused by precognitive experiences and for their appearing most frequently in dreams that often involved forecasting death.

Since Louisa Rhine made no attempt to corroborate the cases sent to her—because she was collecting cases to provide clues for possible research, because common traits appearing in many cases would tend to be corroborative, and because, in any event, eventual experimental validation would be the ultimate corroboration—her methods have been attacked. It has been estimated that anywhere between 60 percent and 85 percent of her cases would be found to have normal explanations. Still, her work is provocative and intriguing.

Louisa Rhine's doctorate, received in 1923, was in botany—as was her husband's. When they found, however, that they were really not very interested in botany, they turned to psychical research in the hope that it would answer some of their questions about the human being. This interest eventually led them to Duke University under William McDougall where, beginning with mediumistic studies, they eventually turned to experimental and statistical work.

Louisa Rhine wrote many articles that were published in the *Journal of Parapsychology* and several books (1961, 1971, 1975, 1981) to explain parapsychology and psi to the general public. Her last book (1983), completed just weeks before she died, is the story of J.B. Rhine, Louisa E. Rhine, and their years together.

Selected Writings: *Something Hidden*, 1983; *The Invisible Picture*, 1981; *Psi: What Is It?* 1975; *ESP in Life and Lab*, 1967; *Hidden Channels of the Mind*, 1961; 1956, 1957. "Hallucinatory Psi Experiences: I, II, III." JP 20:233, 21:13, 186; 1954. "Frequency of Types of Experience in Spontaneous Precognition." JP 18:93; 1953. "Subjective Forms of Spontaneous Psi Experiences." JP 17:77; and J.B. Rhine. 1943. "The Psychokinetic Effect: I. The First Experiment." JP 7:20.

BIBLIOGRAPHY: Berger, A.S. *Lives and Letters in American Parapsychology*, 1988; Feather, S.R. 1983. "Something Different: A Biographical Sketch of Louisa E. Rhine." JP 47:293; Tyrrell, G.N.M. 1946. "The Modus Operandi of Paranormal Cognition." PSPR 48:65; Weiner D.H. and Haight, J. 1983. "Charting Hidden Channels." JP 47: 303.

**Richard Hodgson Memorial Fund.** See **Hodgson Memorial Fund.**

**Richardson, Mark Wyman, 1867–1947.** American physician. Following the deaths of his two young sons, this medical doctor who conducted laboratory investigations of typhoid fever at Massachusetts General Hospital began to read books on psychical research and to visit mediums.

A friend and colleague of Le Roi Crandon's, Richardson worked with Mina Crandon ("Margery") and, having an imaginative mind, created several ingenious devices to test her mediumship in experiments conducted by, among others, the American Society for Psychical Research. For example, in order to test for the independence of a direct voice heard in the Margery sittings, Richardson devised a "voice-cut-out-machine." It consisted of a U-tube, one end of which was connected by a flexible pipe to the mouth of the medium who, by blowing into the tube, was to keep a float in each arm of the tube "floating" during the production of the independent voice of "Walter," her control. If the floats "floated" while "Walter" was speaking, the voice had to be independent of the medium. Although Richardson's friendship with the Crandons could have biassed his judgment, he was truly convinced that "Margery's" phenomena, including "Walter's" voice, were genuine.

**Richet, Charles Robert, 1850–1935.** Renowned French physiologist and psychical researcher. Winner of the Nobel Prize in 1913 for his work on allergic reactions, he was a modern Renaissance man, being also a bacteriologist, pathologist, psychologist, medical statistician, pioneer in aviation, poet (he won the prize of the Académie Française for poetry in 1914), novelist, and playwright.

Early interested in psychical research (métapsychique—a term he coined with Jules-Blois), he was never sympathetic to Spiritualism but remained a positivist and materialist all his life. As early as 1873 his experiences with changes of personality in patients under hypnosis convinced him that communicators during a séance were not what they claimed to be but were rather some creation of the medium. As late as 1924, in his debate, published in the *Proceedings of the Society for Psychical Research,* with his friend Sir Oliver Lodge, he stated, as he had done for many years, that mental mediumship ("subjective metapsychics") indicated only "the perception of reality by extrasensorial channels" and that physical mediumship ("objective metapsychics") "gives no support whatever to the theory of survival."

René Warcollier felt that Richet's "first assays of psychical research . . . constitute . . . the special achievements of [his] genius, that is to say, his discovery of the objectification of characteristics [in hypnosis]; his prescience as to the importance of the percipient [rather than an agent] in telepathy; his invention of the device of the hidden alphabet in table-turning [some of the most interesting of the early experiments, reported in PSPR 2:239; 5:183], and his use of the calculus of probabilities to evaluate the significance of coincidences."

Richet held a series of sittings with Eusapia Palladino and was convinced that some of her physical phenomena were genuine. He studied materialization and ectoplasm (a word he invented) with Eva C. (Marthe Béraud) and, once again, was convinced of the phenomena. With Gustave Geley he conducted experiments at the Institut Métapsychique International with Franek Kluski in which paraffin casts, mainly of "spirit hands," were obtained, the wax having been carefully prepared by the experimenters so that no substitution was possible. The materializations therefore were apparently "neither fraudulent nor delusive." Richet concluded that materializations are "absurd . . . [but] true" (1923). He was certain that as a scientist he knew how to look for fraud and that he could not have been duped. The point has been made often, however, that scientists are frequently the most easily deceived because they do not know how to deal with illusionists (Brandon, 1983).

In 1905, Richet was president of the Society for Psychical Research. In 1923 he wrote his *Traité de Métapsychique* (Thirty Years of Psychical Research) "to introduce Psychical Research as a serious scientific study into the Universities, and to get it recognized as the beginnings of a real science" (Lodge, 1923). In 1926, upon his forced retirement because of age, his jubilee was celebrated by an international assembly of scientists and scholars. After his retirement he devoted his time to the writing of books on philosophy and parapsychology. He died suddenly and in the full possession of his powers at the age of eighty-five.

Selected Writings: 1924. "The Difficulty of Survival from the Scientific Point of View." PSPR 34:107; *Thirty Years of Psychical Research,* 1923; 1884, 1888. "The Hidden Alphabet." PSPR 2:239; 5:138.

BIBLIOGRAPHY: Brandon, R. *The Spir-*

*itualists,* 1983; Gauld, A. *The Founders of Psychical Research,* 1968; Jules-Bois, A.H. 1936. "Charles Richet: Father of Metapsychics." JASPR 30:1; Warcollier, R. (tr. by Renée Haynes) 1959. "Our Pioneers VII: Charles Richet." JSPR 40:157.

**Richmond, Kenneth 1882–1945.** Scottish educator and psychologist. He became interested in psychical research after reviewing Sir Oliver Lodge's book dealing with communications from his deceased son. Richmond conducted sittings with mediums, such as Gladys Osborne Leonard, and made a careful study of the material she produced during her trances (Richmond, 1936). His study was interrupted by his being called on during World War II to edit the *Journal of the Society for Psychical Research* and to act as secretary to the SPR in London. In recognition of his services, the SPR opened a fund to provide books for a special shelf in its library bearing an inscription in his memory.

Selected Writings: 1936. "Preliminary Studies of the Recorded Leonard Material." PSPR 44:17.

**Richmond, Zoë, 1888–1986.** British psychical researcher. Wife of Kenneth Richmond, she was his partner in investigations of mediums. She had many sittings with Gladys Osborne Leonard to whom she had gone after her brother had been killed in 1915 during World War I. Her most important contribution to psychical research, however, is a collection of well-authenticated experiences selected from the publications of the Society for Psychical Research. She believed that these experiences whether through mediums or spontaneous cases—as, for example, apparitions in dreams—could be attributed to the intention of a communicator who wanted to attract the attention of a percipient to something important (Richmond, 1938).

Selected Writing: *Evidence of Purpose,* 1938.

**Riess, Bernard F.** Mid-20-century American psychologist. A professor of psychology at Hunter College in New York, Riess was from the ranks of academic psychologists and, like them, was a sceptic concerning parapsychology and its phenomena. But unlike his colleagues, he was impressed by Joseph B. Rhine's work.

In 1936 and 1937 Riess began his own experiments in extrasensory perception in which an unnamed female psychic was the subject and ESP cards were used in targets. The subject was a quarter mile away from the target cards so that, when she made her calls, there could not have been any sensory cues. The results were fantastic, the highest scores ever achieved: 1,349 hits in 1,850 trials (Riess, 1937). After the subject became ill, however, her scores were no longer significant.

Riess's interest in the field did not cease, however. He became co-editor with Gardner Murphy of the *Journal of Parapsychology* from 1938 to 1941 in the hope of opening a channel of communication with psychologists. He was also elected to the Board of Trustees of the American Society for Psychical Research.

Selected Writings: 1937. "A Case of High Scores in Card-Guessing at a Distance." JP 1:260.

**Ring, Kenneth, 1935–.** American transpersonal psychologist. Professor of psychology at the University of Connecticut, he conducted the first scientific and systematic examination of the **Near-Death Experience** (Ring, 1980), which, until then, had been reported only in an anecdotal way by Elisabeth Kübler-Ross and Raymond A. Moody, Jr. Ring had no interest in parapsychology, but, as he wrote, "the NDE proved to be my avenue to the gateway of parapsychology" (letter to authors). He began his study because he was a psychologist concerned with altered states of consciousness but soon it became "evident to me that the NDE was a phenomenon with obvious paranormal aspects; second, it was equally clear that the early psychical researchers were the real pioneers in the field of study of which the NDE had become only the latest object of inquiry. . .".

Ring set out to examine the "core near-death experience" whose components include hearing oneself pronounced dead, feeling great peace, hearing a noise, and eight other elements characteristic of the NDE. Ring's aim was to answer several questions that Moody's work had not answered. Using a weighted index, Ring found, for example, that prior religiousness is not related to the occurrence or quality of an NDE and that the onset of an NDE is independent of the modes that bring it on, such as illness, accident, or suicide attempts. Ring's examination also, as he said, showed the phenomenon, with its out-of-body experience, deathbed visions and some precognition (which Ring calls "flashforwards") to be saturated with paranormal elements. Without parapsychology and its explanatory concepts and findings regarding this type of phenomenon, the NDE cannot be comprehended. In fact, Ring uses parapsychology to formulate a "parapsychological-holographic" explanation of the NDE (Ring, 1980: chap. 12).

In another study of the NDE, Ring focussed on what he perceives to be patterns among the experiencers of changed values and attitudes toward life. He sees in these patterns a powerful force: "The NDE is essentially a spiritual experience that serves as a catalyst for spiritual awakening and development. Moreover, the spiritual development that unfolds following an NDE tends to take a particular form. Finally, as a by-product of this spiritual development, NDErs tend to manifest a variety of psychic abilities afterward that are an inherent part of their transformation" (Ring, 1984:51).

Founder and first president of the **International Association for Near-Death Studies,** Ring continues to contribute to our expanding knowledge of the NDE.

Selected Writings: *Heading Toward Omega—In Search of the Meaning of the Near-Death Experience,* 1984; *Life At Death: A Scientific Investigation of the Near-Death Experience,* 1980.

**Ringger, Peter, 1923–.** Swiss psychologist and parapsychologist who sacrificed his health and financial resources to the furtherance of parapsychology in Swizerland. In 1951, he established and began publication of *Neue Wissenchaft,* a parapsychological journal. Under his editorship, the publication carried significant research reports. An appeal made by it for the establishment of a parapsychological organization resulted in the formation of the **Schweizer Parapsychologische Gesellschaft** (Swiss Parapsychological Society) with Ringger its president. He remained in that post until poor health compelled him to resign.

BIBLIOGRAPHY: Locher, T. "History of Psychical Research in Switzerland." *Proceedings of an International Conference Parapsychology Today: A Geographic View,* 1971, p.131.

**Roberts, Estelle, 1889–1970.** British medium. Her production of both mental phenomena and physical phenomena in performances in séances and on platforms in London over a period of forty years established her reputation. Her widely publicized book (Roberts, 1959) gives the story of her life and phenomenal powers and describes her as the most remarkable medium of all time. But, unlike other mediums such as Leonora E. Piper, Eileen Garrett, D.D. Home and Eusapia Palladino who willingly submitted to investigation under controlled conditions, she never did. Her reputation was largely based on séances held in complete darkness or platform demonstrations observed by untrained spectators and reported by the press. One can speculate on why she declined to sit with trained scientists who might test the genuineness of her claimed powers. Mrs. Roberts's own response to this question, however, and to an offer made by the Society for Psychical Research to investigate her and to award a prize for the demonstration of paranormal powers, was: "I am not interested in your offer of a prize for a demonstration of what I believe to be a religious belief" (JSPR 34:153).

Selected Writing: *Forty Years a Medium,* 1959.

BIBLIOGRAPHY: "Result of the Prize Offer to Physical Mediums." JSPR 34:153.

**Roberts, Jane, 1929–1984.** American trance channeller through whom modern **Channeling** began. In 1963 the aspiring novelist and poet had her first experience with channeling when she suddenly began to receive ideas about the physical universe. She and her husband, Robert Butts, then began to experiment with the ouija board. They eventually received messages from one "Frank Withers" who said he had spent most of his life in Elmira but in an earlier life had been a Turkish soldier who had known Jane and Robert in the Danish city of Triev. At their fourth ouija board session "Frank Withers" identified himself as **Seth,** the best-known of modern channeled entities. While Jane Roberts was in trance, Seth dictated (with Robert Butts taking notes) five fascinating best-selling books. Jane Roberts constantly pondered the question of who or what Seth was. In *The Seth Material* (1970:293), she wrote that "I am sure that Seth is my channel to revelational knowledge. . . . As to who or what Seth is, his term 'energy essence personality' seems as close to the answer as anyone can get. I don't believe he is a part of my subconscious. . . . It may be that Seth is the psychological personification of [a] supraconscious extension of my normal self." And again, "I am part of Seth, and . . . Seth must be a part of Jane . . . Seth represents that larger portion of the psyche from which our own kind of consciousness emerges" (Roberts, 1981).

On very rare occasions during trance, Roberts would break into "Sumari" during which "strange fluent musical notes . . . achiev[ing] an astonishing depth and richness, and cover[ing] a vocal range from soprano to bass" (Wambach, 1977:30) came through the normally tone-deaf Jane. Its meaning was interpreted by each listener for him or herself.

Jane Roberts also channeled "Seth Two," a group entity that contains Seth; the painter Paul Cézanne; and **William James,** the latter received automatically on the typewriter. This material, Roberts explained, was coming from a construct formed by her tuning in to James's reality and that it represented "whatever James's reality 'really is' now" (Roberts, 1978).

Selected Writings: *The Seth Material,* 1970; *Seth Speaks,* 1972; *The Unknown Reality, Vol.* 1, 1977\1988; *The After-Life of an American Philosopher: The World View of William James,* 1978; *The Unknown Reality, Vol. 2,* 1979\1989; *The Individual and the Nature of Mass Events, 1981.*

BIBLIOGRAPHY: Klimo, J. *Channeling,* 1987; Wambach, H. 1977. "A Session with Seth." *New Realities* 1(1):34.

**Roberts, Kenneth, 1885–1957.** American historical novelist. His novels—*Arundel* (1930) and *Rabble in Arms* (1933)—fictionalized and enlivened the American past. *Northwest Passage* published in 1937 was made into a spectacularly successful motion picture.

Known for his painstaking research into recondite aspects of American history, Roberts also earned another reputation that makes him a **Noted Witness** for Dowsing. He was convinced of its reality and wanted to interest the world in it. Roberts invited scientists to his farm in Kennebunkport, Maine, to see dowsers at work, and he published articles about dowsing in periodicals such as *Country Gentleman.* In 1951 Roberts wrote the best-selling *Henry Gross and His Divining Rod* whose subject was a game warden and dowser *par excellence.* In the book, Roberts said: "Not all the derision of all the geologists in the world can in any way alter the unfailing accuracy of the dowsing rod in Henry Gross's hands. . . . The man who sneers at the dowsing rod today would have scoffed, fifty years ago, at radio, television, and jet planes that travel at supersonic speed."

**Robertson, Morgan, 1861–1915.** American writer. As a youth, he ran away to sea. He sailed around the world and eventually wrote 200-odd stories and novels dealing with the lives and ships of seafarers. In his novel *Futility* published in 1898, Robertson described the construction of a large, supposedly unsinkable, steamship called *Titan.* On a voyage in the month of April, the fictional ship collided with an iceberg and "she rose out of the sea, higher and higher—until the propellers in the stern were exposed—then . . . she heeled, overbalanced, and crashed down to her side, to starboard." There were not enough lifeboats and the casualties were staggering.

This graphic picture could have been that of the **Titanic** going down. In other respects, too, the nonexistent *Titan* tallied with the real *Titanic* that sank in similar circumstances fourteen years later in April 1912. The 3,000 passengers and crew on the *Titan* who were lost compared to 2,207 aboard the *Titantic.* The *Titan* had twenty-four lifeboats, the *Titanic,* twenty. *Titan* struck an iceberg when she was making twenty-five knots; the *Titanic's* speed was twenty-three knots. Each ship had three propellers and the length of each ship was about the same (800 feet for the *Titan,* 882.5 feet for the *Titanic*). The hull of each had been designed with watertight compartments. When these six correspondences are combined with others—the close similarity of names (*Titan* and *Titanic*), the assumed unsinkability of both ships, the collision of both with an iceberg in the same month of April, the scarcity of lifeboats and the great loss of life—the case appears to be a remarkable example of precognition and Robertson is a **Noted Witness** for the phenomenon.

But it has been suggested that Robertson's case may have its Achilles's heel. For in true precognition inferences from available information or educated guesses must be ruled out. Robertson had been a sailor. In addition to his general knowledge of the sea and ships, perhaps he had studied the latters' engineering and construction aspects. He could have inferred from his experience and study the kind of marine disaster he wrote about. The question remains whether Robertson's novel was a projection fourteen years into the future of the author's extraordinary extrasensory perception, a highly successful use of his powers of inference or one of the most remarkable coincidences in history. It is noteworthy, however, that another of Robertson's stories, written in 1912, dealt with a sneak attack by the Japanese on the United States Navy. And another, published after the *Titantic* sank, concerns avoiding future disasters by the use of something like sonar.

Almost all of Robertson's stories deal with the future. They contain accounts of mesmerism, hypnosis, retrocognition, possession, reincarnation, telepathy, and dual personality. His great interest in psychic phenomena was well known and he himself was supposed to be a first-rate psychic. He believed that when he wrote he was possessed by some discarnate entity who sometimes abandoned him for months at a time during which he could not write a word.

Robertson claimed to have invented the periscope (but was unable to obtain a patent). He drank heavily and died in poverty and squalor. Yet he was regarded with affection and esteem by the writers and artists who knew him and who published *Morgan Robertson, The Man* (1915) after his death.

Selected Writings: Robertson, M. *Futility,* 1898.

BIBLIOGRAPHY: Eisenbud, J. *Paranormal Foreknowledge,* 1982, Chapter 6; Stevenson, I. 1960. "A Review and Analysis of Paranormal Experiences Connected with the Sinking of the *Titanic.*" JASPR 54:153.

**Robinson, Diana.** Contemporary British-born American psychologist, parapsychologist, and author. After studying in, and becoming a citizen of, the United States, she was drawn to parapsychology. Her efforts in the field have consisted in part of encouraging networking among members of the parapsychological community. But her main contribution has been her careful survey of psychokinesis that resulted in [illegible] book recognized as one of the b[illegible] tions in recent years to PK th[illegible] search. Ranging as it does from [illegible]ntal PK, poltergeists, miracles, ele[illegible] voice phenomena to thoughtography, [illegible] one of the most comprehensive [illegible]nson, 1981).

Selected Writings: *To Stretc[illegible] lank: A Survey of Psychokinesis,* 1981.

**Rochas, Albert De, 1837–[illegible].** French commandant of engineers and director of the École Polytechnique of Paris. He eventually devoted himself exclusively to psychical research and the study of hypnosis.

Colonel Rochas had sittings with the medium Eusapia Palladino and caught her in one of her customary tricks. When each of her hands was held by a sitter, she would manage to free one hand and substitute the other hand for it so cleverly that each sitter, now in control of only a part of the same hand, thought he or she was in control of one complete hand.

Primarily, however, Rochas conducted hypnotic experiments with subjects in which, after they awakened from their hypnotic trances, they obeyed commands given to them while hypnotized. He found to his dismay that some subjects, such as one Benoit, were extremely suggestible. For example, Rochas told the hypnotized Benoit: "Three and two make four." Rochas thought he had dispelled the idea from Benoit's mind at the end of the experiment. But the following day, after Benoit went back to work at the préfecture where he was a clerk, he continued to add three and two to make four. When his figures were sent back to him, he still could not see that he had made any error. When he was on the verge of being discharged, he returned to Rochas to find out what had been done to him to make him so stupid. Fortunately, Rochas was able this time to correct the situation he had created and save the man's job.

Rochas published several works and carried forward in France controlled experiments in hypnosis to a far greater degree than any work being done in England at the time.

Selected Writing: *Les Forces Non Definies,* 1887.

**Rockwell, Theodore, 1922–.** American chemical engineer and nuclear technologist.

After reading Sir James Jeans in college, he "was astounded at the idea that arcane scientific theories and experiments—quite apart from technology—could have a real impact on the everyday unscientific world around us" (Rockwell and Rockwell, 1988:359). This idea led him to his interest in parapsychology, particularly as it relates to the philosophy of science.

Mr. Rockwell has attacked those who, in the name of rationalism, have irrationally attacked parapsychology, in particular the Committee for the Scientific Investigation of Claims of the Paranormal and its sponsor, the journal *The Humanist.* He has pointed out that these attacks lump together satanists, astrologers, and psychical researchers and have attacked parapsychology in general on the basis, for example, of a particular researcher being a scientologist and another's father having owned a bookstore that sold "nut" books (Rockwell, Rockwell, and Rockwell 1978a). He has written that the "issue is not *acceptance* of the findings of parapsychology, but willingness to distinguish them from folk beliefs and to evaluate them objectively, applying the successfully tested tools of the scientific method. . . . [S]erious researchers [need] to obtain funding and publication, so that the scientific process can ultimately determine the nature and explanation of those phenomena now so unfortunately labeled 'paranormal' " (Rockwell, Rockwell, and Rockwell, 1978b:362,364).

Mr. Rockwell received his B.S. and M.S. degrees in chemical engineering from Princeton University and an honorary Sc.D. from TriState University for contributions toward the harnessing of nuclear power. From 1943 to 1949 he was with the Manhattan Project, from 1949 to 1953 he was in the Naval Reactor Headquarters (the last ten of these as technical director), and from 1953 to 1955 was director of the Nuclear Technology Divisions. He is presently a principal officer and director of a firm that provides engineering services in the energy field.

In addition to his many affiliations and memberships in his professional field, he is a member of the Parapsychological Association and was for many years its representative to the American Association for the Advancement of Science. He is also a member of the Society for Scientific Exploration, of the American Society for Psychical Research, of the American Society of Dowsers, and of the International Kirlian Research Association. His numerous papers in the field include four published in Japanese.

Selected Writings: and W.T. Rockwell. 1988. "Margins of Reality: The Role of Consciousness in the Physical World." JASPR 82:350; and R. Rockwell and W.T. Rockwell. 1978a. "Irrational Rationalists: A Critique of *The Humanist's* Crusade against Parapsychology." JASPR 72:23; and R. Rockwell and W.T. Rockwell. 1978b. "Part II. Context vs. Meaning: A Reply to Dr. Kurtz." JASPR 72:357.

**Rogo, D. Scott, 1950–1990.** American author and parapsychologist. This author of numerous books on parapsychology for the general reader, of a textbook on the subject, and of articles written for both parapsychological journals and popular magazines was drawn into the field as a teenager after reading a book on Spiritualism. Although he came to believe that parapsychology could best answer questions about life and the world, he took his undergraduate degree in musicology because he did not think it would be possible to earn a living in parapsychology.

He studied the out-of-body experience by making and analyzing case collections, by working in the summer of 1972 at the Psychical Research Foundation on their project with Keith (Blue) Harary and by exploring theoretical models for the experience. He also worked with the (former) Maimonides Medical Center and the Southern California Society for Psychical Research. He investigated poltergeists and hauntings. He concluded that not all poltergeist cases have a focal agent as is commonly supposed and that some hauntings are actually poltergeist cases. He was interested too in psi and its relation to altered states of consciousness, including sensory deprivation, and in what he called "bizarre forms of psychic phenomena," such as religious miracles, phone calls or other electronic messages from the dead and the effects of ostensible UFO encounters.

Mr. Rogo also taught college courses in parapsychology and presented papers at international conferences. He was a member of the Parapsychological Association and of the American Society for Psychical Research and the International Association for Near-Death Studies. See also **Phone Calls, Paranormal.**

Selected Writings: *The Evidence for Life after Death,* 1985; *Minds and Motion,* 1978; *The Haunted Universe,* 1977; 1976. "Aspects of Out-of-Body Experiences." JSPR 48:329; *An Experience of Phantoms,* 1974; *The Welcoming Silence,* 1973; with R. Bayless. *Phone Calls from the Dead,* 1979.

**Rol, Gustavo Adolfo, 1906–1987.** Italian man of letters and painter, he was also a medium. In full light, he has produced physical phenomena so impressive that Piero Cassoli, a veteran and cautious investigator, was constrained to write: "I can only say that what we saw that evening was something akin to miraculous" (Cassoli, 1971). The phenomena include levitations, materializations, apport of books, flowers, letters and coins, and direct writing or painting from a communicator.

While Rol was in the company of Remo Lugli, an Italian journalist, and others, "Rol told Remo Lugli to imagine a scene in the past, . . . and Lugli started describing a garret in Paris, with a writer living in it. This man, said Lugli, 'is writing an important book. . . .' 'With what is he writing?' asked Rol. 'With a quill pen, a beautiful, long, colored feather.' 'There it is!' cried Rol—and at the same moment a long, colored feather fell on the table. Five other people were present and all confirmed this description." (Giovetti, 1984).

"Demonstrations" or "exhibitions" rather than "experiments" are the more correct descriptive words for the manifestations in Rol's mediumship, for he would not submit to controlled tests. What Cassoli saw and Paola Giovetti described were phenomena apparently appearing under uncontrolled conditions. Since fraud and mediumship often go hand in hand, one must be cautious in accepting as conclusive mediumistic evidence produced without adequate controls.

BIBLIOGRAPHY: Cassoli, P. "Parapsychology in Italy." *Proceedings of an International Conference Parapsychology Today: A Geographic View,* 1971, p.187; Giovetti, P. 1984. "An Extraordinary Medium: Gustavo Adolfo Rol." *Theta* 12 (2):29.

**Rolf of Mannheim.** An Airedale terrier whose red coat, black nose, and playful disposition made him seem like all other dogs except for his most striking feature, "his almost human expression" (MacKenzie, 1919:219). He gained a world-wide reputation as one of the great "thinking" animals of all time.

In December 1911, in Mannheim, Germany, his mistress, Frau Moekel, being angry with her daughter for not being able to add 122 plus 2, turned to the dog and asked him, "What is 2 plus 2?" Rolf answered by tapping her arm four times. After that day, the dog was studied by scientists, priests, and scholars. As he sat by his mistress, he tapped out with his left paw in her hand or later on a piece of cardboard she held a code taught him by Frau Moekel. Frau Moekel was a fascinating woman, highly intelligent, who painted like a master and stopped runaway horses with a gesture. She taught Rolf how to rap a certain number of times for an object, say, six for a loaf of bread. Then she taught him to rap a certain number of times for a letter of the alphabet, say, ten for the letter "d." Nothing seemed to faze Rolf. He could solve mathematical problems, express religious ideas about the soul, become philosophical, or even joke.

That Rolf was able to learn and use the code of taps taught him by his mistress is evidence of his great intelligence. But a careful series of experiments with the dog showed that the dog's ability to answer questions was not due to a special intellect but, rather, his relation to his mistress. Rolf could not answer unless his mistress knew the answers to questions (MacKenzie, 1919).

It is here that the case has a bearing on psychical research and parapsychology. It is possible that the dog's success was due to his ability to use extrasensory perception to obtain information from his mistress. But in view of the fact that the dog's tapping was generally done in a mechanical way it is also possible that Rolf's performances were due to automatism, that is, the mistress's intelligence could have produced answers through the dog who was not conscious of what he was doing in the same way that mediums purportedly in contact with a discarnate personality write or speak automatically or operators of a ouija board unconsciously produce information from other living minds or from allegedly discarnate beings. See also **Anpsi; Chris the Wonder Dog; Clever Hans; Missy**

BIBLIOGRAPHY: MacKenzie, W. 1919. "Rolf of Mannheim—A Great Psychological Problem." PASPR 13:205.

**Roll, William George, 1926–.** American psychical researcher and parapsychologist. Born of American parents in Germany and educated through secondary school in Denmark, Roll's interest in psychical research and parapsychology, and in particular in poltergeists, was aroused by a neighbor, an author who was one of the foremost exponents of the subject in Denmark.

After receiving his B.A. in 1949 from the University of California at Berkeley, Roll went in 1951, thanks to a grant from St. Catherine's College, Oxford University, England, to that university to study parapsychology under philosopher and parapsychological theoretician Henry H. Price. This grant was succeeded by further grants from the Society for Psychical Research and the Parapsychology Foundation.

In 1958, while he was at J.B. Rhine's Parapsychology Laboratory at Duke University on a fellowship, he encountered his first parapsychological phenomena during a field investigation of a poltergeist case. Continuing research into poltergeist phenomena (or what has come to be known as RSPK—recurrent spontaneous psychokinesis) made Roll a leader in this branch of parapsychological investigation and led to his book (1972) on the subject that has been published around the world.

In 1960 Charles E. Ozanne, a high school and college teacher with a strong interest in the question of survival after death, provided funds for the reestablishment of the Psychical Research Foundation to investigate that question. Roll was named project director, a position he retains despite his being, since 1986, a part-time professor of psychology at West Georgia College in Carrollton, Georgia.

Beginning with studies of mediumship, Roll has gone on to investigate out-of-body experiences, psychometry, haunting phenomena, meditation, and consciousness. His contributions to the theoretical aspects of parapsychology include the psi field theory that states that traces are left in physical objects by mental or physical occurrences and "the psi system theory according to which psychic interactions occur on a level of the organismic system that encompasses individuals and their environment" (Berger, 1988).

Roll, who received his M. Litt. from Oxford in 1961, has written more than 100 papers, mainly for parapsychological journals, and has edited eleven volumes of *Research in Parapsychology.* He is editor of *Theta,* the *Journal* of the Psychical Research Foundation, and has been co-editor of the *Journal of Parapsychology.* He is a member of the American Association for the Advancement of Science and was on the founding council of the Parapsychological Association, of which he has been president.

Selected Writings: *The Poltergeist,* 1972; "Poltergeists." In B. Wolman, ed., *Handbook of Parapsychology,* 1977; "ESP and Memory." In J.M.O. Wheatley and H.L. Edge, *Philosophical Dimensions of Parapsychology,* 1976.

BIBLIOGRAPHY: Berger, A.S. *Lives and Letters in American Parapsychology,* 1988.

**Rolling Thunder (John Pope).** Contemporary Cherokee-born Shoshone medicine man. Eyewitnesses have reported all sorts of paranormal phenomena occurring in his presence: the production of lightning, rainmaking, and the cessation of rain, the production of a tornado funnel cloud that dissipated on command, apports, telepathy, clairvoyance, and even exorcism. He believes in reincarnation—death is just a transition—and in the law of karma. Both in conjunction with medical doctors in California, and at the Association for Research and Enlightenment in Virginia Beach, Virginia, he has effected healing of patients who were not helped by conventional medicine. He says that people are one with nature and cannot understand themselves until they understand nature.

His message to the non-Indian community is one of brotherhood and spiritual sharing. He says that "Indians are the keepers of the land. . . . We do not own the land, and certainly nobody else owns it. . . . [W]e are supposed to live as brothers and share. . . . [W]e do not believe in competition. We flow with nature and we are guided by the Spirit. . ." (Boyd, 1974:259,260). To Rolling Thunder, the resolution of karma—individual, racial, national, and global—is the way to enlightenment. On this way psychic powers and psychic phenomena will occur, but they are incidental and secondary.

BIBLIOGRAPHY: Boyd, D. *Rolling Thunder,* 1974.

**Romains, Jules** (*Nom de plume* of Louis-Henri-Jean Farigoule), 1885–1972. French poet and novelist. Founder of a French literary movement, Romaine was elected to the Académie Française because of his twenty-seven volume masterpiece *Les Hommes de Bonne Volonté* (1932—1946) and such internationally acclaimed works as *Dr. Knock* (1925).

Although known principally for his literary activities, Romain is also a **Noted Witness** for dermo-optic perception. He carried on experiments with blind or blindfolded subjects in which, without normal vision, they identified colors. The results convinced him of the existence of the phenomenon he called "extra-retinal vision" (Romaine, 1964). He believed that the ability to identify colors by means other than normal vision was possessed by all people and could be developed. But his findings were dismissed by the scientific world that attached no value to the work of a poet and novelist with no scientific training. Subsequent work in the field, however, has shown the dismissal of his work to have been mistaken.

Selected Writing: *La Vision Extra-Rétinienne et le Sens Paroptique,* 1964.

**R-101.** The R–101 was a great airship, a flying luxury hotel with a lounge, dining salons, and magnificent appointments. It left Cardington, England, on October 4, 1930 at 7 P.M. bound for India and crashed at Beauvais, France, on October 5 at 2:50 A.M. The forty-four passengers and crew on board were burned to death. Two days later, a séance, that had been arranged on October 2 by Harry Price to see if Sir Arthur Conan Doyle would communicate, was held in London with the trance medium Eileen Garrett.

The entranced medium's control mentioned the name "Irving" or "Irwin." The drop-in communicator, purporting to be the captain of the doomed airship, Flight Lieutenant H. Carmichael Irwin, spoke of the cause of the crash. He described the bulk of the dirigible, the capacity of the engine, the useful and gross lift, the elevator and tail pipe, the mix of the carbon and hydrogen, the load and cruising speed. The case is impressive because Irwin's name had not been mentioned before the séance, he was not the object of the experiment and neither Price nor the sitter were then occupied with the catastrophe. Neither they nor Mrs. Garrett were familiar with aeronautics or engineering, yet, to their surprise, Irwin made his appearance and all technical information was both relevant to the cause of the crash and correct. (Sceptics, however, have claimed that the troubles with the R–101 during construction could have come to Eileen Garrett's attention by normal means.)

The crash of the R–101 had also been the subject of two precognitive dreams (Lyttelton, 1937).

BIBLIOGRAPHY: Booth, J. *Psychic Paradoxes,* 1984; Lyttelton, E.L. *Some Cases of Prediction,* 1937; Price, H. 1931. "The R-101 Disaster. Case Record: Mediumship of Mrs. Garrett." *Psychic Research* 25:268.

**Roney-Dougal, Serena M., 1951–.** British psychologist. Dr. Roney-Dougal's main interests in parapsychology are the psychology of the psychic and building bridges across the various scientific and magical disciplines. Her thesis, on the basis of which she received her Ph.D. from Surrey University in 1987, was entitled "A Comparison of Psi and Subliminal Perception." Her work in this area was funded by the Society for Psychical Research.

In that same year in an article in the *Journal of the Society for Psychical Research* she wrote that "SP [subliminal perception] is as affected by psychological variables as other parapsychologists have found psi to be. . . . At both an objective and a subjective level, it was impossible to tell whether a particular session had been a psi or an SP one. . . . If one's motivations are other than those of enjoyment and curiosity, problems seem to occur" (pp. 174, 180).

Dr. Roney-Dougal has lectured widely and is currently teaching a course on parapsychology at Adult Evening Classes in Glastonbury, England, where she lives.

Selected Writings: 1987. "A Comparison of Subliminal and Psi Perception: Exploratory and Follow-up Studies." JASPR 81:141.

**Rope-Climbing Feat.** One of the most famous of all exploits attributed to the fakirs of India. Yet it is unique in that it seems never to have been seen by anyone who wants to see it. Firsthand accounts, sceptics say, do not seem to exist. Richard Hodgson, for example, who went to India to investigate Madame Helena Petrovna Blavatsky complained: "I sought in vain for an eye-witness, European or native, of the famous rope exploit." Still, there are a few eyewitness accounts. In one, the fakir is described as standing in front of a crowd as he coils a rope on the ground. He raises one end of it and, hand over hand, raises a portion of the rope. While the rest of the rope remains in a coil on the ground, the portion raised by the fakir seems to ascend into the air to a height of about twenty feet and remains erect in the air. The fakir then summons a small boy, speaks to him briefly, after which the boy starts to climb the rigid rope. He climbs hand over hand with legs twisted around the rope and when he reaches the top, he vanishes. Soon he becomes visible again as he climbs down. The rope then sinks to the ground.

If the exploit so reported is not a myth after all, some explanation of it must be found. Even if the rope is a trick one made out of rigid material that can be telescoped, how do we explain the disappearance of the boy? Can it be accounted for as some form of hallucination, a hypothesis familiar to psychical research? The hallucination might be induced by suggestion from the fakir who makes people think that the boy is invisible or visible again and to see or not see things the fakir wishes. Yet to suppose that a whole crowd of sane and honest people is hallucinating seems to strain credulity and the question of the rope-climbing feat remains as vexed and unsettled as ever.

BIBLIOGRAPHY: "An Account of the Indian Rope-Climbing Trick." 1904. JSPR 11:299; Hodgson, R. 1893. "Indian Magic and the Testimony of Conjurers." PSPR 9:354.

**Rope-Tying.** A test used by Harry Houdini, the Davenport Brothers and others, to baffle and astound audiences. Rope, ribbon, or tape was used to tie a medium's arms, legs, and body securely, perhaps to a chair on which the medium was seated inside a cabinet. In addition, sometimes the rope was tied around the medium's neck and fastened to the cabinet. After the lights were extinguished or the cabinet doors were closed, the medium's aim was to gain release from the bonds as quickly as possible. It might take ten or twenty minutes for a skilled maker of "sailor's knots" who was determined to conquer the medium with invincible knots to do his job, yet a clever medium would be free in only one minute and, stepping out of the cabinet carrying the now useless rope, would be greeted by cheers and applause from the gaping spectators. The medium's success depended on the use of several subtle ways of positioning body or hands so that the rope would be sufficiently slack to allow release subsequent to the tying process first of a hand, then of both hands, and finally of the entire body (Carrington, 1920).

BIBLIOGRAPHY: Carrington, H. *The Physical Phenomena of Spiritualism*, 1920.

**Rose, Ronald Kriss Hume, 1919–.** Australian psychologist, journalist, and writer. He was among the first to realize the enormous possibilities for parapsychology in Australia because of the beliefs and practices of the **Aborigines** and the claims that they use telepathy consciously. He was the first to enter an aboriginal settlement in Northern New Wales in order to conduct experiments in extrasensory perception and psychokinesis. The experiments were successful and the results significant. Rose also was aware that the atmosphere in Australia in the 1950s was not conducive to the nourishment of parapsychology there. Through lectures, writings and experiments, he endeavored to bridge the distance between Australia and faraway research centers and generally to promote parapsychological reearch in his country.

Selected Writings: 1950. "Psychical Research in Australia." JASPR 44:74; 1952. "Psi and Australian Aborigines." JASPR 46:17.

**Rose, Major W. Rampling, ?–1935.** British photographic expert. An investigator of so-called "spirit photography," he had spent more than thirty years in the industry and had founded and headed a large photographic business. With Fred Barlow, Rose, as the technical expert, investigated the spirit photographer William Hope. At first he thought that the "extras" that appeared on the plates were produced supernormally because he believed that he had kept the plates and slides under observation at all times. He later realized that there was always an interval of a second or two during which the photographer could, by sleight-of-hand, put the extras on the plate. He concluded: "I do not remember ever seeing a single abnormal photograph of all those which have passed through my hands that could not be explained by purely natural means."

At the time of his death he had been a member of the Society for Psychical Research for more than twenty years.

Selected Writing: and Barlow, F. 1933. "Report of an Investigation into Spirit Photography." PSPR 41:121.

**Rosen, Steven H., 1942–.** American philosopher, psychologist, and parapsychologist. Holder of a Ph.D. degree in experimental psychology from the City University of New York, Prof. Rosen's chief interest in parapsychology is its philosophical implications. He believes that in order to understand psi phenomena one must explore "alternatives to the philosophy of logico-empiricism and rationalism dominant in the West" because "psychic experiences are 'irrepresentable' within the framework of traditional Western thinking. . ." (Rosen, 1977:132). He has also pointed out that the physical world is "a living organism . . . which possesses mind" (p. 153).

Currently professor of psychology at the College of Staten Island of the City University of New York, Dr. Rosen is a voting member of the American Society for Psychical Research, is on the Board of Trustees of the Academy of Religion and Psychical Research, and is a member of the Parapsychological Association, the American Psychological Association, and the Association for the Study of Man/Environment Relations. He has, among others, served on the editorial boards of the *Journal of the American Society for Psychical Research* and the *Journal of Near Death Studies.* He has published scholarly papers in the field and has written a philosophical novel (1985) that dramatizes his point of view.

Selected Writings: "Psi and the Principle of Non-dual Duality." In B. Shapin, ed., *Parapsychology, Philosophy, and Religious Concepts,* 1987; *The Moebius Seed,* 1985; "Toward a Representation of the 'Irrepresentable.'" In J. White and S. Krippner, eds., *Future Science,* 1977.

**Rosenheim Poltergeist.** A case of seemingly inexplicable events until, as technicians, physicists, and parapsychologists worked together, it "reached the highest level of evidence" (Bender, 1969) of a poltergeist agent at work. In 1967, electrical malfunctions upset a usually calm and dignified law office in Rosenheim, a town in Bavaria. Hundreds of undialed telephone calls to the number 0119 were automatically registered by the telephone company and telephone bills soared. Neon lights kept going out. Light bulbs kept exploding, and automatic fuses blew continually. There were spillages of developing fluid from photocopying machines. The electric company technicians installed monitoring equipment to track down the cause of the problem but could not locate it. To make sure that electric current would not be interrupted technicians installed an emergency power apparatus. Still the disturbances went on.

Psychical researcher and parapsychologist **Hans Bender** was summoned to begin an investigation and noticed that when a nineteen year old secretary who had just been employed by the law office "walked through the passageway, the lamps began to swing behind her" (Bender, 1969). He suspected that she, as a poltergeist agent, caused all malfunctions, that they were triggered by her psychokinesis. Two physicists who supervised all voltage variations, loose contacts, external magnetic controls, and even kept an eye out for trickery concluded that there was no normal explanation for what was happening. They even disconnected the electrical circuit's monitoring device and supplied current from a battery without stopping the problem. "PK was objectively demonstrated" by this finding, said Bender.

The revelation that she might have been the real focus of the disturbances upset the secretary to the point of hysteria. Then different phenomena appeared: Paintings turned on walls, drawers slid open, and a huge storage unit weighing nearly 400 pounds moved from its place along a wall. It all ceased when the unfortunate secretary was dismissed. Later, when she and her fiancé visited a bowling alley, she may have been the cause of the electrical system that controlled the pins going crazy.

BIBLIOGRAPHY: Bender, H. 1969. "New Developments in Poltergeist Research." *Proceedings of the Parapsychological Association* 6:81.

**Rothschild, Friedrich, 1899–.** German-born psychiatrist dismissed from the institute of the University of Frankfurt, because he was a Jew. He immigrated to Palestine where he developed biosemiotics as a theory to cover psychophysical relationships and, specifically, metal-bending. Rothschild also wrote the introduction to a book on paranormal phenomena and their connection to the Jewish tradition (Rothschild, 1972).

Selected Writing: Introduction. In J. Bazak. *Judaism and Psychical Phenomena,* 1972.

**Royce, Josiah, 1855–1916.** American educator and philosopher. A professor of philosophy at Harvard College, he was an influential thinker and a leading force in the Idealistic school of thought in the United States. He interpreted the universe in terms of human ideas. Royce's philosophy also embraced loyalty, which he considered the *summum bonum,* the greatest good we can know.

Royce's interests also extended to psychical research. He served on the council of the American Society for Psychical Research. As chairman of its Committee on Apparitions and Haunts, he collected and criticized claimed accounts of apparitions of living or dead people. His interest in the ASPR and its work was "to search out God's truth in these obscurer realms. We need not fancy the truth to be in itself obscure, because its realms are still so. We need not add mysteries to things to make them more charming. The spiritual existence of this world, full of God's thoughts and ideals, is not more spiritual because we cannot read some of the thoughts, nor as yet glow with the realization of all the ideals. What we all want is more knowledge, and more enthusiasm. If this society offers to any of us a means whereby we can get either, for Heaven's sake let us not miss the opportunity!" (Royce, 1889: 427-428).

Selected Writings: "Report of the Committee on Phantasms and Presentiments." 1889. PASPR 1(4):350.

**RSPK.** See **Poltergeist**.

**RSPK Agent.** See **Poltergeist Agent.**

**Rubinstein, Anton Grigoryevich, 1829–1894.** Russian pianist and composer. Considered one of the outstanding artists of his day, he was admired by composers Frédéric Chopin and Franz Liszt, wrote six symphonies, many piano concerts and pieces, and several operas. He was the director of the St. Petersburg (now Leningrad) Conservatory and toured the United States. One evening he was having dinner in St. Petersburg with a pupil, Lillian Nichia. "The winds were howling around the house," she related. "and Rubinstein . . . inquired of me what they represented to my mind. I replied, 'The moaning of lost souls.' From this a theological discussion followed. 'There may be a future,' he said. 'There is a future,' I cried, 'a great and beautiful future, if I die first, I shall come to you and prove this.' He turned to me and with great solemnity. 'Good, Liloscha, that is a bargain; and I will come to you.'" Years later, Lillian Nichia was in Paris. "I woke one night," she said, "with a cry of agony and despair ringing in my ears. . . . Rubinstein's face was close to mine, a countenance distorted by every phase of fear, despair, agony, remorse, and anger. . . . I put fear from me and decided it was merely a dream. I had for the moment completely forgotten our compact." That afternoon she learned of the pianist's sudden death. Later, she found out that Rubinstein had died "with a cry of agony impossible of description."

The episode may suggest that Rubinstein tried to let his old pupil know by telepathy that he was dying and to fulfill his life after death pact. If so, he belongs in the box as a **Noted Witness** for these subjects.

BIBLIOGRAPHY: Prince, W.F. 1918. "Peculiar Experiences Connected with Noted Persons." JASPR 12:662.

**Run.** In ESP tests with ESP cards, successive calls of the twenty-five cards in the pack. In tests for psychokinesis with dice, twenty-four throws of one die.

**Run Score Variance.** See **Variance, Run-Score.**

**Rush, Joseph H., 1911–.** American physicist. He worked on the atomic bomb during World War II, was active in the scientists' political movement thereafter, and at the University of Colorado was a member of the Condon Committee that investigated UFOs.

His interest in parapsychology antedates all these activities, however, since it began in about 1936 when he discovered the shelf on psychical research in the Dallas Public Library, sat with an amateur psychic circle and learned about J.B. Rhine's statistical approach to experimental parapsychology. His interest has continued because he loves a mystery and because he has had apparently clairvoyant (for example, in a trance-like state he found his daughter's toy) and precognitive (dream) experiences that have convinced him of the reality of psi phenomena.

"From an investigation of survival through spontaneous and mediumistic experiences,"

Dr. Rush writes (1987), "parapsychology has become an esoteric field . . . literally a new field . . . of discrete concepts arranged by analogy with familiar sensori-motor functions: ESP and PK. . . . Null results do not invalidate positive results. . . ; they pose questions for further investigations" (pp. 68-69). Rush urges the use of teams of subjects, à la Kenneth Batcheldor, the creation of experimental conditions in which motivation and frustration are specific and a method for developing awareness of how psi functions. "The central impression that emerges from all the psi research is that these elusive phenomena are inextricably involved with mind" (p. 71)—which does not mean that psi is necessarily nonphysical but that we do not yet know everything about the physical (for example, the relationship between the observer and the observed) and that "psi phenomena should not be limited to living organisms" (p, 71).

For many years Dr. Rush worked at the National Center for Atmospheric Research in Boulder, Colorado, and has published widely in and out of parapsychology.

Selected Writings: "Parapsychology: Some Personal Observations." In R. Pilkington, ed., *Men and Women of Parapsychology,* 1987; "Problems and Methods in Psychokinesis Research." In S. Krippner, ed., *Advances in Parapsychological Research, Vols. 1 and 3,* 1977, 1982; "Physical Aspects of Psi Phenomena." In G.R. Schmeidler, ed., *Parapsychology: Its Relation to Physics, Biology, Psychology, and Psychiatry,* 1976; "Physical and Quasi-physical Theories of Psi." In J.H. Rush, H.L. Edge, J. Morris, and J. Palmer. *Foundations of Parapsychology: Exploring the Boundaries of Human Capability,* 1986.

BIBLIOGRAPHY: Batcheldor, K.J. 1984. "Contributions to the Theory of PK Induction from Sitter-Group Work." JASPR 78:105, Berger, A.S. *Lives and Letters in American Parapsychology,* 1988.

**Ruskin, John, 1819–1900.** English man of letters, artist, and art critic whose volumes of *Modern Painters* (1843-1860) and *The Stones of Venice* (1851-1853) revolutionized modern art and are some of the finest examples of Victorian prose. In his articles and letters, he rebelled against materialism and the social and economic conditions of Victorian England. He was a champion for the betterment of the human race but is best-known for his treatises on painting and painters. Not so well known is that he was a convert to Spiritualism, was a close friend of D.D. Home, and an honorary member of the Society for Psychical Research.

During a summer in Switzerland, Ruskin learned of a place in the valley of Chamonix that had the reputation of being haunted by the ghostly figure of a woman with a skull-like face who raked leaves and could be seen only by children. Ruskin took a child from another valley to the site of the alleged haunting. In those days of limited travel, no telephones, or mass media coverage, the boy was unlikely to have known of the legend. When Ruskin said to the child, "What a lonely place! There is nobody here but ourselves," the boy pointed and replied, "Yes, there is, there is a woman there raking leaves." According to the child, the woman looked up and he saw "only holes," but no eyes in her head.

Ruskin is a **Noted Witness** for the phenomena of haunt and apparition.

BIBLIOGRAPHY: Prince, W.F. *Noted Witnesses for Psychic Occurrences,* 1963, pp. 221-222.

**Ryerson, Kevin.** Contemporary American trance channeler. Catapulted to national attention (and fortune) by **Shirley MacLaine's** book *Out on a Limb* and by the television mini-series based on the book in which Ryerson played himself, he channels four entities: John, last incarnate at the time of Christ, who had been a member of the Essene Hebrew sect and is supposedly the most highly evolved of Ryerson's "entities"; Tom McPherson whose favorite incarnation was an Irish spy-pickpocket in Elizabethan times working for the English crown; Dr. Shangru, a Pakistani physician of several hundred years ago; and Obidaya whose favorite incarnation was as a Jamaican.

John's stilted and convoluted language is reminiscent of Edgar Cayce's trance language and, indeed, Ryerson was studying meditation with an Edgar Cayce group when, after six months, trance channeling began. Perhaps the most difficult thing to accept is that Ryerson was supposedly channeling his entities (as opposed to acting) for the mini-series *Out on a Limb*, so that they had to rehearse and to learn lines by "scanning" Ryerson's subsconscious and to stand by for innumerable "takes." Tom McPherson "hit the high points and the low points and even embellished his part a bit. . . . Tom . . . reminded us that he had done a great deal of Shakespearean street theater in his day. . . . After the rehearsal we [including Tom McPherson] sat and chatted" (MacLaine, 1987). The entities purportedly continued to perform on cue right through the actual filming.

BIBLIOGRAPHY: Klimo, J. *Channeling,* 1987, pp. 45-47; MacLaine, S. *It's All in the Playing,* 1987.

**Ryzl, Milan, 1928–.** Czechoslovakia-born physicist, biochemist, and parapsychologist. One of the great problems in research with extrasensory perception is that the faculty is not controllable consciously. Ryzl, however, maintained that he had developed a hypnotic procedure to train subjects to use their ESP abilities to such a degree that these powers were amenable to the will and control of experimenters and subjects (Ryzl, 1962). He spent a decade using his method of hypnosis in experiments with hundreds of subjects and succeeded in guiding and developing several star subjects, such as Pavel Stepanek, who were able to achieve significant scores in ESP tests.

Ryzl, who had been associated with the Institute of Biology of the Czechoslovakian Academy of Science, defected from Czechoslovakia in 1967. He came to the United States where he worked at the Parapsychology Laboratory and taught parapsychology in California. Ryzl has received the McDougall Award for Distinguished Work in Parapsychology.

Selected Writing: 1962. "Training the Psi Faculty by Hypnosis." JSPR 41:234.

# S

**Sabina, Maria Magdalena, 1889–1985.** Mexican *curandera* (shaman and healer) famed in Mexico and abroad for her use of the sacred or halucinogenic mushroom for unorthodox healing. In sacred rituals in Oaxaca, she ingested the mushroom *Psilocybe Mexicana* in order to diagnose and cure disease. Her fame brought many observers and investigators to Oaxaca who witnessed her rituals and even ate the mushrooms themselves. From its effects on them they predicted correctly that the drug extracted from the mushroom eventually would be put to use as a tool for the release of paranormal powers, for medical treatment and for the treatment of alcohol and narcotics addiction.

A film of María Sabina's life was made in the late 1970s by the sister of the then Mexican president, José López Portillo. Unfortunately, María Magdalena Sabina's fame had also spread to armies of hippies who poured into Oaxaca and brought great discredit upon the *curandera* in the eyes of her countrymen.

**Saints.** Individuals thought and officially recognized by the Catholic church to have special virtues and a close relationship to the transcendental realm. A saint is usually a mystic. To be canonized in the Catholic tradition a person must have lived with "heroic virtue" a joyous, loving, peaceful life with God and with others. In addition, two miracles must be shown to permit recognition as one particularly blessed as a Beatus and four miracles to be canonized a saint. The veneration of saints, such as martyrs, even their relics—personal articles, bones, or even corns—has been a practice long followed in Christianity. In the religions of the East, as well, holy men and prophets have received special attention and recognition and have been venerated as saints.

Because of their extraordinary psychic gifts, saints are of interest to psychical research and qualify as **Noted Witnesses** to the existence of paranormal phenomena. These gifts fall into several categories. Saint Philip of Neri, Saint Ignatius of Loyola, and Saint Francis of Sales all produced luminious phenomena: A brilliant aura surrounded them when they preached. Saint Ultan knew by telepathy or clairvoyance that robbers in the forest of Seneffe had killed Saint Follan. Saint Catherine of Siena, the patron saint of Italy, probably through telepathy, knew the thoughts of others. Saint Albertus Magnus, the thirteenth century scholar and theologian, in Cologne, Germany, knew, again either by telepathy or clairvoyance that Thomas Aquinas had died in the Italian town of Terracina. The patron saint of Sweden, Saint Bridget, demonstrated precognition by correctly predicting political matters and, similarly, Saint Aelfheah, the eleventh century archbishop of Canterbury, foretold the destinies of three men.

Rhea White (1981) found recorded in the biographies of saints in the *Acta Sanctorum* a seemingly endless line of other paranormal mental phenomena that included retrocognition, the out-of-body experience, xenoglossy and deathbed visions. Paranormal physical phenomena have not been ignored, either. Saint Alphonso of Liguori, experiencing the same state of levitation observed in the cases of almost ninety other saints, was seen off the ground by an amazed public when he preaching in Foggia in 1745. If psychokinesis is at the bottom of the multiplication of food by Saint John Bosco, the stigmata of Francis of Assissi and the travels of the Host through the air from the officiating Curé of Ars, then this aspect of the paranormal has been manifested, too.

White's study uncovered that 672 or 29 percent of a sample of 2,532 Christian saints demonstrated paranormal abilities. Although a mail survey of spontaneous cases made by John Palmer of 300 University of Virginia students and 700 adults in Charlottesville, Virginia, indicated that more than 50 percent of the people polled claimed at least one paranormal experience, a recent Gallup poll determined that only 10 percent of the general population reports such an experience. Twenty-nine percent is therefore a significant figure. But apart from statistics, White's observation was that, in some accounts, there were indications of far more conscious control of psychic abilities by saints than among the general population. And, in many cases, the evidence for the paranormal is even stronger than that from mediums and the séances of Spiritualism.

Do saintly psychics have paranormal powers because they are saints or would they have been psychically gifted even if they never had became extraordinary religious personages? Ms. White's finding was that the paranormal abilities of saints are linked to their spiritual growth. Such abilities may be linked also to the spiritual atmosphere in which saints live and work. There, where the spiritual world is isolated from the material one, contemplation may facilitate altered states of consciousness that, in turn, may facilitate psi. Most saints became psychic only after having entered the religious life. In addition, saints may be forced to employ psi both in their own personal religious lives and in order to connect with the spiritual realm. Studies of high level psychic experiences among religious personages may cast light on the entire psi process and furnish clues to be followed up and tested in the laboratory. Religion, as Ms. White said, maybe "the mother load [sic], the prime source of parapsychological phenomena" (White, 1981). See also **Bernadette, Saint; Bleeding, Posthumous; Catherine of Bologna, Saint; Catherine of Genoa, Saint; Food, Multiplication of; Gregory, Saint; Incorruptibility; Januarius, Saint; Joan of Arc, Saint; Joseph of Copertino, Saint; Mary, Saint; Teresa of Avila, Saint; Vincent De Paul, Saint.**

BIBLIOGRAPHY: Palmer, J. 1979. "A Community Mail Survey of Psychic Experiences." JASPR 73:221; White, R. 1981. "Saintly Psi: A Study of Spontaneous ESP in Saints." *Journal of Religion and Psychical Research* 4:157.

**Saint-Saëns, Charles Camille, 1835–1921.** French pianist, organist, and composer. He wrote melodic violin and cello concertos, operas, and symphonic poems. Among his works are the *Fifth Piano Concerto,* the opera *Samson et Dalila,* the suite *Le Carnaval des Animaux,* the symphonic poem *Le Rouet d'Omphales,* and that great symphonic spook, *Danse Macabre.* Franz Liszt admired him as the greatest organist of his day. Richard Wagner recognized his skill as a brilliant pianist.

Apart from his reputation in the musical field, he enters psychical research as a **Noted Witness** for the phenomena of telepathy and precognition. Saint Saëns wrote: "I, personally, have known cases of telepathy, of prescience of the future. . . .

"In the far-off days when I lived in the upper part of the Faubourg Saint-Honoré, I worked hard. When I was up to my ears in work, I suddenly thought of a lady of my acquaintance. Some moments afterward—the time it would take to pass through the courtyard and go up the stairs—some one rang: it was the lady of whom I had thought. The first four times I believed it was chance; but the twentieth time! This phenomenon lasted several years.

"In my youth, a painter, a friend of mine, showed me a picture he intended to submit for the annual exposition. He had not yet exhibited his work, and did not know whether the picture would be accepted. Looking at it, I saw it in the first room of the Palais de l'Industrie, in a certain place at the top of the stairs. On the day the Salon opened

I went there, and saw the picture placed just as I had foreseen."

Saint-Saëns, like Socrates, also had a personal daemon to whom he listened and who assisted him in his compositions. He is a **noted witness** as well for the creative process since, like other artists, he acknowledged a source of information and inspiration beyond his conscious control.

BIBLIOGRAPHY: Prince, W.F. *Noted Witnesses for Psychic Occurrences,* 1963, pp. 255-256.

**Salience.** The tendency of a subject to ESP tests to score significantly on the initial segment and final segment of a run.

**Salter, Helen (Woollgar) de Gaudrion Verrall (Mrs. W.H.), 1883–1959.** British psychical researcher. Daughter of the famous automatist and classical scholar Margaret Verrall, Helen Salter was herself both a classical scholar and an automatist. As a child she played at F.W.H. Myers's house, knew Richard Hodgson (as 'Hodge Podge') and played games with Eusapia Palladino who, she said, "cheated at every game she played." She was, as was her husband, W.H. Slater, very active in the Society for Psychical Research where she served variously as research officer, editor of both its *Journal* and *Proceedings* and as a member of the council.

Helen Salter (then Verrall) first experimented with automatic writing in 1903 and continued to produce script until about 1930. Her automatic writing formed part of many of the **Cross-correspondences;** some related to the Palm Sunday Case involving Arthur Balfour and some to the message in a sealed envelope F.W.H. Myers left in the hope of proving his survival of death. Helen Salter's first contribution to the *Proceedings* and the SPR in 1914 dealt with the cross-correspondences. From then on she contributed heavily to both the *Journal* and the *Proceedings* on a variety of subjects, including Eva C., telepathy, Mrs. C.S. Wilson, Mrs. Gladys Osborne Leonard, George Valiantine, and others. Her last publication in the *Journal* was an article on Eleanor Sidgwick. Her articles also appeared in the *Journal of the American Society for Psychical Research* and in the *Journal of Parapsychology.*

Helen Salter was, in addition, very active in public life. G.W. Lambert said that "to know her banished from one's mind any lurking suspicion that automatic writing was a practice disruptive of personality."

Selected Writings: 1958. "Our Pioneers. Mrs. Henry Sigdwick." JSPR 39:235; 1951. "Some Observations on the S.P.R. Group of Automatists." JSPR 45:47; 1932. "The History of George Valiantine." PSPR 40:389; 1930. "Some Incidents Occurring at Sittings with Mrs. Leonard Which May Throw Some Light on Their Modus Operandi." PSPR 39:306.

BIBLIOGRAPHY: Broad, C.D. 1959. "Obituary: Mrs. W.H. Salter," JSPR 40:129.

**Salter, William Henry, 1880–1969.** British barrister and historian. Salter (called "Willy" by his friends) was, according to C.D. Broad (1970), a "typical intelligent, cultured, Liberal Nonconformist; . . . [who] exhibited throughout [his life] the many virtues and the occasional angularities of that once powerful and now almost extinct Victorian species." Salter was probably introduced to psychical research by his wife **Helen De G. (Verrall) Salter** whom he married in 1915. From the end of World War I he donated most of his time to the service of the Society for Psychical Research of which he became a council member in 1919, its honorary treasurer (in 1920), and its honorary secretary (in 1924). In 1947–1948 he was president of the SPR and in later years a vice president. C.D. Broad said that Salter "enjoyed controversy, and could be trusted to give as good as he got."

He knew well almost all the important mediums—his wife was one—who produced the cross-correspondences which he believed to be both valid and important. He deposited with the library of Trinity College, Cambridge, unpublished material and scripts dealing with the cross-correspondences that are not to be opened until 1995 and material labelled "Reminiscences of The Society for Psychical Research" not to be opened until 1996. All this material is awaited eagerly.

Many reports and articles by Salter appear in the *Journal* and *Proceedings* of the SPR. A particularly interesting one deals with F.W.H. Myers's **Sealed Envelope Test** and suggests that, though the test literally failed, much paranormal information came through. He also published important books. In one he discussed apparitions (1938) and, in another (1961), survival phenomena, some of which he found impressive.

With Salter's death the last link with the founders of the SPR was severed.

Selected Writings: 1963. "The Rose of Sharon." PSPR 54:1; *Zoar, or the Evidence of Psychical Research Concerning Survival,* 1961; 1958-1960. "F.W.H. Myers' Posthumous Message." PSPR 52:1; *Ghosts and Apparitions,* 1938.

BIBLIOGRAPHY: Broad, C.D. 1970 "Obituary: Mr. W.H. Salter." JSPR 45:203; "W.H. Salter: Some Appreciations." 1970. JSPR 45:207.

**Saltmarsh, H.F., 1881–1943.** British psychical researcher. A businessman forced into early retirement because of poor health, he turned to the study of philosophical subjects that in turn led him into psychical research and his important contributions to the field.

In two of his writings on the problem of time and causation (1938, 1934) he surveyed the evidence for and advanced a theory for precognition which attracted him inexorably. It seemed to him "one of the most puzzling, the most mysterious of all the mysteries which are presented to the psychical researcher. That a human being, conditioned in space and time, should be able under certain rather rare and exceptional circumstances to acquire knowledge of future events raised problems of the utmost importance . . ." (1934:49).

A second philosophical problem—human survival and personal identity after death—produced three important writings. One dealt with the types of phenomena examined by psychical researchers in connection with the survival question and whether these phenomena are proof of survival (1932), a second dealt with experiments he conducted to see if the results of sittings could be attributed to chance (1929) and a third examined and explained the complicated scholarly cross-correspondences in terms laymen, who are not classical scholars, can understand (1938).

Saltmarsh, who joined the Society for Psychical Research in 1921 and was on its council, was also a key figure in the administration of its affairs until his death.

Selected Writings: *Foreknowledge,* 1938; *Evidence of Personal Survival from Cross-Correspondence,* 1938; 1934. "Report on Cases of Apparent Precognition." PSPR 37:49; 1932. "Is Proof of Survival Possible?" PSPR 40:105; 1929. "Report on the Investigation of Some Sittings with Mrs. Warren Elliott." PSPR 39:47.

**Sambor, Stephan Fomitch. ?–1902.** Russian physical medium. He held sittings in St. Petersburg, Russia, from about 1893 until his death in 1902. During this medium's séances, physical phenomena occurred: apports and one of his specialties, the production of a three-dimensional knot in a seamless leather ring. He was also known for another specialty, "chair threading" (i.e., during his séances a chair would be threaded on and would hang from one of his arms while both his hands were held).

Count Perovsky-Petrovo-Solovovo who over seven or eight years had 105 séances with him at first was sure that no trickery could have been practiced. He was quite impressed by the medium's phenomena until he found that one of the sitters in the circle failed to control Sambor's hands and so could have allowed some of the phenomena to be produced. This discovery forced the count to throw out some remarkable occurrences and one "chair threading" experiment. But in six other such experiments the guilty sitter had played no part. Perovsky-Petrovo-Solovovo had no explanation for the phenomena produced in these sittings. He explained "such curious episodes" as "some form of (mental) suggestion, possibly unconscious."

BIBLIOGRAPHY: Perovsky-Petrovo-Solovo, M. 1937. "My Experiments with S.F. Sambor." JSPR 30:87.

**Samuel, Hebrew Prophet, c. eleventh century, B.C.** Prophet, priest, judge, leader of Israel, and a man of not inconsiderable psychic abilities. He qualifies as a **Noted witness** for the paranormal. Like Joan of ARC, he, too, heard voices that he attributed to God but that might have been a monition, a guide, communicator, or his personal daemon. On one occasion as a child, Samuel heard a voice forecast the fall of the house of the priest Eli in whose service Samuel was (I Samuel, chap. 3). Around 1050 B.C., after the Philistines had badly defeated the Israelite forces and left the nation devastated, the elders pleaded with Samuel to name a king to rule over them (I Samuel 8:5). But he resisted in the belief that only God should be Israel's king and that the appointment of another would be blasphemous. But suddenly a voice came to him again and instructed him to anoint the young tribesman Saul, as king of Israel (1 Samuel 9:16).

Samuel could also find lost objects, perhaps by clairvoyance. For example, he told Saul correctly that his father's asses, lost for three days, had been found (1 Samuel 9:20). Samuel also demonstrated considerable precognitive gifts. He prophesied correctly that Saul would meet two men who would tell him that the lost asses had been found, that he would meet three men who would give him food to eat and that Saul would begin prophesying after he met other prophets (I Samuel, chap. 10). See also **Prophesy, Religious**.

**Sathya Sai Baba, 1926–.** Indian religious leader. He has followers in the millions around the world and is believed by many, especially in India, to be an avatar—a divine incarnation.

Born Sathyanarayana Ratnakaru Raju into a low caste in southern India, he was bitten by a scorpion in 1940 and was unconscious for many hours. When he came to, his entire personality had changed. He would sometimes fall into trance and expound on the ancient wisdom of India. Shortly thereafter, he left school and revealed himself as the reincarnation of Shirdi Sai Baba, a renowned holy man who died in 1918.

Although Sai Baba regards himself as a religious leader, he is widely revered for his production of "miracles," or paranormal phenomena: materialization of objects (gold rings and other beautiful pieces of jewelry, sacred ash, food, and fruits often out of season, statuettes, etc.), levitation, bilocation, telepathy, healing and paranormal light phenomena. He intentionally appears to his followers as well in their dreams, and they often, even at great distances, feel him near or smell characteristic odors.

Many scientists, among them C.T.K. Chari, Erlendur Haraldsson, Karlis Osis, and Michael Thalbourne, have tried to study Sai Baba, but he refuses to submit to testing under control. In his presence, however, they have seen what seem to be apports and materializations; objects have also seemed to change and dematerialize. Fraud in relation to Sai Baba's phenomena has never been demonstrated—although the possibility of regurgitation has been raised (Chari, 1973) and Hansen has stated that the types of observations made by Haraldsson and Osis in order to try to detect fraud to someone "knowledgeable in conjuring . . . would be unlikely to reveal fraud" (1987:186). "Sai Baba may be an avatar, or he may be a human being with unparalleled psychic ability, or he may be an unprecedently clever magician. But whatever he is, for the time being he is an enigma" (Thalbourne, 1982:64).

BIBLIOGRAPHY: Chari, C.T.K. 1973. "Regurgitation, Mediumship, and Yoga." JSPR 47:156; Hansen, G.P. "Examples of a Need for Conjuring Knowledge." In D.H. Weiner and R.D. Nelson, eds., *Research in Parapsychology, 1986,* 1987; Haraldsson, E. *Modern Miracles,* 1988; Thalbourne, M.A. 1982. "Correspondence." *The Journal of Religion and Psychical Research* 5(1):62.

**Scarpa, Vincenzo, ?–1898.** Italian leader of **Spiritualism.** Under the pseudonym of Niceforo Filalete, he was editor of the Spiritualist publication *Annàli dello Spiritísmo in Itàlia.* In 1840, Scarpa founded and actively directed the Società Torinése di Studi Spiritíci (Turin Society of Spiritualist Studies), possibly the first Spiritualist society in Italy.

**Sceptics. (Also skeptics).** From the philosophers of ancient Greece, who asserted that nothing could be known, to the eighteenth century philosopher David Hume, to the present, there have always been skeptics who doubt or are incredulous.

In the comparatively recent case of parapsychology, doubt and incredulity seem almost inevitable because some consider it "revolutionary," a challenge to prevailing notions of the world since "it is the only discipline that defies the materialist thesis that mental events are merely epiphenomena of brain processes" (Berger, 1988). So it is not surprising that the barrage from skeptics has been mounting until, by the 1980s, parapsychology has been described as "an outpost under siege" (Berger, 1988).

The term "skeptic" generally is applied to all critics of parapsychology. Yet, since skepticism basically is the absence of belief, the increasing number of critics who believe affirmatively that parapsychology is a pseudoscience are not skeptics.

As there are self-elected parapsychologists so there are self-elected skeptics who come in different kinds and categories. There is the soft-line group—the **Zetetic Scholar** is a possible if disputed example: It tends to be impartial, reasonable, responsible, contructive in criticism. Then there is the hard-line group, represented by the **Skeptical Inquirer**: It tends to be one-sided, dogmatic, cavilling, offering little constructive, and often misinformed in its efforts to discredit parapsychology.

Marcello Truzzi perceives three categories of skeptics: empirical, conceptual, and methodological (1982). Empirical skeptics think that any parapsychological data are obtained either by the fraud of subject or experiments or both or by experimenter incompetence or malobservation. Conceptual skeptics deny the idea of extrasensory perception and other paranormal phenomena on *a priori* grounds. They regard these phenomena as antecedent impossibilities that cannot fit into scientific theories and picture of the world. Philosophical skeptics in this group who are concerned with language think terms such as "extrasensory perception" are absurd or, with regard to the survival hypothesis, that it is not "coherent" because "no one has ever been able to explain how a separable and incorporeal soul might be identified" (Flew, 1988). Methodological skeptics repeatedly point out the painful fact that parapsychology has not solved the problem of the repeatable experiment and so fails to meet the fundamental requirement of repeatability that applies to all experiments in science. Skeptics also harp on the failure to establish any sort of theoretical framework for paranormal phenomena.

In addition, scientific journals and the media are always more willing to print criticisms and sensational exposure of incompetence, such as **Project Alpha,** than articles defending parapsychology. Yet from any objective point of view, parapsychologists should welcome criticisms wherever and whenever they appear. Criticism that is responsible and legitimate can be beneficial and can rid the field of bad data, poor methods, and incompetent personnel.

BIBLIOGRAPHY: Berger, A.S. *Lives and Letters in American Parapsychology: A Biographical History, 1850-1987,* 1988; Flew, A. Foreword to A.S. Berger. *Aristocracy of the Dead,* 1987, p.ix.; Truzzi, M. "J.B. Rhine and Pseudoscience: Some Zetetic Reflections on Parapsychology." In K.R. Rao, ed., *J.B. Rhine: On the Frontiers of Science,* 1982, p. 177.

**Schiller, Ferdinand Canning Scott, 1864–1937.** Anglo-American philosopher. Dr. Schiller was, like William James, a pragmatist. He joined the Society for Psychical Research in 1884, was its president in 1914, and maintained throughout his life an interest in psychical research.

Dr. Schiller wrote an enthusiastic review of F.W.H. Myers's *Human Personality and its Survival of Bodily Death.* He sat with the medium, Rudi Schneider and Mina S. Crandon ("Margery"). A wax fingerprint in his possession by showing fraud, helped to resolve the notorious controversy in the investigation of the latter.

He pointed out that the evidence of much psychic phenomena is historical, cannot be repeated any more than any other historical event can be, and is therefore not amenable to experimentation. He believed that there were no scientific, philosophical, or theological reasons for there not being a spirit world and that, if it exists, we need an SPR on the other side as well. He felt that we do not live in just one "real" world and that the scientific method should make it possible to "illumine the darkness that broods over the destiny of man."

Selected Writings: 1914. "Philosophy, Science, and Psychical Research. A Presidential Address." PSPR 27:191; 1905. "The Progress of Psychical Research." *Fortnightly Review* 77:60; 1900. "On Some Philosphical Assumptions in the Investigation of the Problem of a Future Life." PSPR 15:53.

**Schmeidler, Gertrude Raffel, 1912—.** Distinguished American psychologist and parapsychologist. Her interest in parapsychology dates from the winter of 1934-1935 when, as a graduate student at Harvard, she read J.B. Rhine's *Extra-Sensory Perception.* But her real involvement did not begin until 1942 when, teaching part time at Harvard (she had received her Ph.D. there in 1935), she audited a seminar on psychical research given by Gardner Murphy.

This involvement led to her beginning in 1942 her famous **"Sheep-Goat Experiments"** which suggest that those who believe in the possibility of ESP get better ESP scores than those who do not, with certain exceptions. Dr. Schmeidler has pointed out that a "shy, self-conscious sheep is likely to score low, as is a sheep who dislikes the experimenter or resents the particular method, or one with a bad headache; but on the other hand a goat who enjoys outlandish challenges might be expected to score high" (1987:80). This work was eventually described in a book (1958) co-authored with **Robert A. McConnell** who supplied the statistical analysis.

In later experiments in telepathy Dr. Schmeidler noticed that "a combination of two negative conditions resulted in positive ESP scores or else . . . a predicted difference between two groups reversed when test condition changed from pleasant to unpleasant" (1988a).

Precognition also fascinated her. The "clairvoyant precognition runs, where no one ever knew or would know the targets, showed scores significantly higher than chance," (1988a) which led her to conclude that "we need a theory of psi and time which includes mental access to at least some future events which will never be observed, by anyone" (1987:82).

Dr. Schmeidler also conducted experiments in psychokinesis with **Ingo Swann.** He turned out to be able at will to change the temperature of thermistors, and, remarkably, as Ingo made the target hotter, distant nontarget thermistors grew colder, and vice versa. Dr. Schmeidler notes that it looks as if the distribution of heat was being changed and, if so, perhaps we should not "ask about the source of the extra energy that PK uses to make objects move. . . [but instead] about how PK changes the energy patterns that it finds" (1988a).

Dr. Schmeidler devised a way to investigate haunts (1966) and a method, unfortunately untested, for investigating survival of personality after death (1977).

Dr. Schmeidler was research officer of the American Society for Psychical Research in 1945-1946. In 1947 she began teaching in the Psychology Department of the City College of New York (now the City College of the University of New York) where she became a full professor and is now professor emeritus. She continued to teach graduate courses in experimental psychology. She is a member of the American Psychological Association, the American Association for the Advancement of Science, the American society for Psychical Research whose president she was in 1981 to 1985, and of the Parapsychological Association whose president she was in 1958 and 1971. In 1988 she was given the latter's Career Achievement Award. Her personal papers consisting of over 24,000 items of correspondence, tests, and experiments are now at Duke University's Perkins Library where they are available for research.

Dr. Schmeidler has written literally hundreds of articles but was "shocked . . . to find that from the beginning to the end of [her] time at City College [had] published only eighteen articles not directed to parapsychology" (1988a). She has also written encyclopedia articles (1983, 1968) and several books, the most recent of which (1988b) "not only put[s] my ideas together but . . . also . . . argue[s] for them more convincingly than I have yet been able to do" (1988a). She concludes that psi is a psychological process but that we "need to know more about how psi relates to brain activity or to physical variables and physical theory . . . [P]arapsychologists have made a beginning at the work needed in a new science . . . but . . . there is much more work waiting to be done" (1988b:199).

Selected Writings: "Work in Progress." In A.S. Berger, *Lives and Letters in American Parapsychology,* 1988a; *Parapsychology and Psychology: Matches and Mismatches,* 1988b; "Questions and Attempts at Answers." In R. Pilkington, ed., *Men and Women of Parapsychology,* 1987; "Parapsychology." In B.B. Wolman, ed., *International Encyclopedia of Psychiatry, Psychology, Psychoanalysis, & Neurology,* 8, 1983, pp. 183-185; 1977. "Looking Ahead: A Method for Research on Survival." *Theta* 5:2; 1966. "Quantitative Investigation of a 'Haunted House.'" JASPR 60:137; "Clairvoyance." In the *Encyclopedia Americana,* 1968; with McConnell, R.A. *ESP and Personality Patterns,* 1958.

**Schmidt, Helmut Heinrich Wilhelm, 1928–.** German parapsychologist living in the United States. Recipient in 1954 of a Ph.D. in physics from the University of Cologne in Germany, his interest in parapsychology developed out of his study of theoretical physics and deals with the relationship of parapsychology to physics. He sees the borderline between physics and psi as an intellectual challenge.

Considered by arch-skeptic C.E.M. Hansel

(1985) "in terms of experimental sophistication . . . the successor to Rhine," Schmidt (1970) has conducted experiments in anpsi (with his cat and with cockroaches) that seem to show that animals can affect a random event generator. Robert L. Morris (1977), however, thinks the results can be attributed just as easily to human psi. Dr. Schmidt has developed automated ESP and PK (psychokinesis) test machines and has demonstrated that deviation from chance has occurred in repeated trials. He attributes this deviation to psychokinesis and has concluded that PK is goal oriented. He also found that subjects produce PK effects even though they do not know an experiment is being conducted.

Critics have questioned whether the deviations reported need to be the result of psi, and Hansel believes that any unexplained result that seems to be caused by psi must be fraudulent. Rex Stanford (1977), on the other hand, believes that Schmidt's development of and success with radioactivity-based random event generators in ESP and PK work "has provided evidence that an 'intrinsically unpredictable' quantum process can be both predicted and controlled through psi means" (p. 328).

Dr. Schmidt has further "integrated parapsychology with physics by conducting experiments to explore the apparent violation of causality by psi and [by developing] a theory based on quantum mechanics that a subsequent observer can have a retroactive PK effect on an event" (Berger, 1988).

Dr. Schmidt has held National Academy of Sciences research fellowships at the University of Michigan in Ann Arbor and at the University of California in Berkeley, has been a senior research scientist at Boeing Scientific Research Laboratories, and a research associate at the Institute for Parapsychology. He is presently researcher at the **Mind Science Foundation** in San Antonio, Texas. He is a member of the American Physical Society, the American Association for the Advancement of Science, and the Parapsychological Association on whose council he has served from time to time since 1973.

Selected Writings: 1976. "PK Effect on Pre-Recorded Targets." JASPR 70:267; 1975. "Toward a Mathematical Theory of Psi." JASPR 69:301; 1970. "PK Effects with Animals as Subjects." JP 34:255; 1969. "Quantum Processes Predicted?" *New Scientist* Oct. 16:114.

BIBLIOGRAPHY: Berger, A.S. *Lives and Letters in American Parapsychology,* 1988; Hansel, C.E.M. "The Search for a Demonstration of ESP." In P. Kurtz, ed., *A Skeptic's Handbook of Parapsychology,* 1985, 97-127; Morris, R.L. "Parapsychology, Biology, and ANPSI." In B.B. Wolman, ed., *Handbook of Parapsychology,* 1977, pp. 687-715; Stanford, R.G. "Experimental Psychokinesis." in B.B. Wolman, ed., *Handbook of Parapsychology,* 1977, pp. 324-381.

**Schneider, Alex, 1927–.** Swiss professor of physics, electronics engineer and psychical researcher. He became interested in psychical research in the 1950s and, in 1967, carried out experiments on electronic voice phenomena with Konstantin Raudive whom he helped in the development of a novel technique for recording. Prof. Schneider then began to do systematic research in the field and became vice president of **Imago Mundi** and president of the **Schweizer Parapsychologische Gesellschaft** (Swiss Parapsychological Society) in 1979. He is also president of "Psi Days," international conferences held every year in Basel on some aspect of parapsychology or psychical research and attended by large numbers of people from France, Germany, Italy, and the United Kingdom, as well as from Switzerland. Prof. Schneider has been a leading figure in the development of Swiss parapsychology and psychical research.

**Schneider, Rudi, 1908–1957.** Austrian physical medium. He demonstrated psychic ability from an early age. This medium's phenomena were produced while he was in trance and influenced by his control, "Olga." His phenomena included movement of objects, infra-red ray absorption, levitation, and materialization of hand-like or limb-like objects. He was investigated by the world's leading researchers, including Eugene Osty of France, Baron A. von Schrenck-Notzing of Germany, and Lord Charles Hope, Harry Price, Theodore Besterman, and C.C.L. Gregory of Great Britain. Price, who claimed that Schneider was guilty of cheating, has been held guilty of cheating to prove Schneider's guilt. Besterman wrote that in "a long series of sittings . . . held at the S.P.R. under my complete control . . . nothing whatever even remotely paranormal was observed," but he did not feel that Schneider ever tried to cheat. And seemingly paranormal phenomena that he did observe at other times he did not report because they were witnessed by no one else.

Dr. Gregory wrote that although "there is still no universally compelling evidence of levitation and materialization. . . in the case of Rudi Schneider,. . . . [the writer] is *himself* convinced of the genuineness of the Rudi phenomena. . . ." And most experimenters who had sittings with him concurred that Schneider was an honest medium who produced genuine physical phenomena.

BIBLIOGRAPHY: Gregory, A. *The Strange Case of Rudi Schneider,* 1985; Hope, Lord C. 1933. "Report of a Series of Sittings with Rudi Schneider." PSPR 41:255; "Rudi Schneider: Recollections and Comments." 1958. JSPR 39:206.

**Schneider, Willi (or Willy), 1903–1971.** Austrian physical medium. Older brother of Rudi Schneider, his mediumship developed when he was very young. He first came to the attention of Baron Albert von Schrenck-Notzing in 1919. He was then producing materializations. Shortly thereafter other phenomena, including psychokinesis, began. Schrenck-Notzing in 1921 brought the young man to Munich and arranged to investigate him in his own laboratory.

Among the many university professors, doctors, and other savants who attended Willi Schneider's twice weekly séances was Thomas Mann who, like all the others, was convinced of the paranormality of the phenomena produced. Although it was reported that Willi had been caught cheating in 1920 in his home town of Braunau, Eric J. Dingwall, then research officer of the Society for Psychical Research, was convinced that the control of the medium during the sittings in Munich and later at the SPR was so strict—Willi was undressed and then redressed in one-piece tights with luminous bracelets at the wrists, his arm was outlined with luminous pins and the objects to be moved were placed in a gauze cage—that only the complicity of a confederate, impossible under the conditions, could have caused the raps and movement of objects by normal means. Dingwall concluded that "the phenomena are in reality caused by supernormal agencies. . . . [T]his case stands almost alone in the history of mediumship. . . . Indeed, I cannot remember any medium who submits to such a control as does Willy Sch. . . . If the agency of the medium is excluded the only other hypotheses are hallucination, confederacy or collusion on the part of the investigators, sitter or others. . . . Collusion, confederacy and simple lying were all examined and shown to be untenable. . ." (Dingwall, 1922:369-370).

BIBLIOGRAPHY: Dingwall, E.J. 1926. "A Report of a Series of Sittings with Mr. Willy Schneider." PSPR 36:1; Dingwall, Eric J. 1922. "Physical Phenomena Recently Observed with the Medium Willy Sch. at Munich." JSPR 20:359; Perovsky-Petrovo-Solovovo, M. 1928. "Notes on Periodicals." JSPR 24:307.

**Schouten, Sybo Adrianus, 1940–.** Dutch parapsychologist who was the driving force behind the Parapsychological Laboratory at the University of Utrecht. "I became interested in parapsychology as a student . . . when reading philosophy," he wrote. "According to some philosophers, the existence of ESP would lead to an entirely different world-view. Therefore I wanted to know more about the subject" (Schouten, 1988).

His several contributions to parapsychology include important research on the two-volume *Phantasms of the Living,* a monumental work containing examples of one kind of apparition and often considered to have shown the existence of telepathy.

Schouten has been interested in seeing whether the usual explanations offered by skeptics are correct and if some assumptions are valid, such as that females are more likely to report spontaneous cases than are males. He made a systematic analysis of hundreds of cases described in the work and found, for example, that the majority of those reporting cases were female. Similarly, he was able to reject other normal counterhypotheses (Schouten, 1979).

He also observed that spontaneous cases from different countries and epochs are very similar in their patterns. He discovered that the patterns in the English cases in *Phantasms of the Living* reappeared in spontaneous cases occurring in Germany and in the large collection of such cases made by the Parapsychological Laboratory at Duke University and studied by Louisa E. Rhine. His finding signifies that cultural factors are not responsible for the patterns (Schouten, 1982).

There is always an important place for critics inside parapsychology because their expertise allows them to bring out problems beyond the competence of outside critics. Schouten is such a critic. For example, one of the respected experiments in extrasensory perception that is always cited in parapsychological literature as well-planned and outstanding because of its remarkable results was that conducted by Gerardus Heymans and others just after the First World War. Schouten and Edward F. Kelly reanalyzed the experiment, however, and found that the results could have been produced by normal means, i.e., motor automatism (Schouten and Kelly, 1978).

Selected Writings: September 12, 1988. Letter to authors; 1982. "Analysis of Spontaneous Cases: A Replication Based on the Rhine Collection." *European Journal of Parapsychology* 4:113; 1979. "Analysis of Spontaneous Cases as Reported in 'Phantasms of the Living.'" *European Journal of Parapsychology* 2:408; and Kelly, E.F. 1978. "On the Experiment of Brugmans, Heymans, and Weinberg." *European Journal of Parapsychology* 2:247.

**Schrenck-Notzing, Albert von, 1862–1929.** German psychical researcher. A medical doctor, forensic psychiatrist, and member of the German aristocracy, his early interest was in hypnosis. After meeting Henry Sidgwick and F.W.H. Myers of the English Society for Psychical Research at two international congresses held in Paris in 1889, he began to work in telepathy, the topic that was then being investigated by the SPR. Beginning in 1894, he turned his attention to physical phenomena.

Together with Charles Richet and Cesare Lombroso he sat in Rome with physical medium Eusapia Palladino. He also attended the Palladino sittings at Richet's estate on the Ile Ribaud (or Roubaud) and continued his investigations of her over a period of years for a total of fifty-five sittings. Although he caught her cheating on numerous occasions, he concluded that her cheating was never premeditated and that much of her phenomena were undoubtedly genuine.

His next subject for investigation was Eva C. (Marthe Béraud). He had attended her sittings in Algiers and now became a member of a circle in Paris to which she was giving materialization séances. His work with her "constituted [his] first irrefutable proof of the phenomena of materialization" (Sudre, 1929) and of ectoplasm. His "irrefutable proof" was not proof to others, however, who noted that the materialized figures were flat and looked exactly like cutouts of pictures of famous people that had appeared in a French tabloid. He reasoned that her flat "materializations" were "supernormal imitations of those engravings." Lambert (1954) who wrote that he "had had plenty of reason to doubt Schrenck's scientific integrity" noted, however, that "Schrenck had published . . . very suspicious pictures [of Eva C.'s materializations] and commented on them with surprising frankness. . .".

He worked also with physical mediums Willi and Rudi Schneider and many others including Einer Nielsen. "This time," writes Sudre, "the proof of the teleplastic [ectoplasmic] faculties of the human being was so well done that no further serious attempt at refutation was made." (Again this is Sudre's, and perhaps Schrenck-Notzing's, interpretation.)

In his later years Schrenck-Notzing became interested in spontaneous phenomena, particularly hauntings and poltergeists.

He did not feel that either physical or mental phenomena supported the spiritistic hypothesis. In the *Physical Phenomena of Mediumship* (1920) Schrenk-Notzing wrote, "It is not on a foundation of extra-corporeal beings that one will find the secret of the psychodynamical phenomena of these subjects, but rather through consideration of hitherto unknown transformations of the biophysical forces of the medium's organism."

Despite the doubts case upon his experimental methods, Schrenck-Notzing was the most influential German psychical researcher during the first three decades of this century.

Selected Writings: 1891. "Experimental Studies in Thought-Transference." PSPR 7:3; *Materialisationsphaenomene (The Phenomena of Materialization)*, 1914; *Physical Phenomena of Mediumship*, 1920; 1922. "Concerning the Possibility of Deception in Sittings with Eva C." PSPR 33:65.

BIBLIOGRAPHY: Lambert, R. "Dr. Geley's Report on the Medium Eva C." JSPR 37:682; "Obituary Notices: Freiherr Dr. von Schrenck-Notzing." JSPR 25:64; Sudre, R. "The Life and Works of Schrenck-Notzing." *Psychic Research* 23:250.

**Schumann, Robert Alexander, 1810–1856.** German pianist, conductor, music critic, and composer. He wrote chamber works, waltzes, lieder (songs), and piano pieces. Among his best-known piano pieces is *Fantasy in C Major.* He founded and became editor of the *Neue Zeitschrift für Musik.* His wife, Clara, was a fine concert pianist who interpreted his work. Two years before their marriage in 1840, he wrote to her: "I must tell you a presentiment I have had; it haunted me from the 24th to the 27th of March, during which I was absorbed in my new compositions.

"There was a certain passage which obsessed me, and some one seemed to be repeating to me from the depths of his heart: Ach Gott [Oh, my God]. While composing I visualized funeral things, coffins, sorrowing faces. . . When I had finished, I sought for a title. The early one which came to my mind was *Leichenphantasie* [Funeral Fantasy]. Is this not extraordinary? I was so overcome that the tears came to my eyes; I truly did not know why; it was impossible to discover the cause for this sadness. Then came Therese's letter, and all was clear. Her sister-in-law had notified her that her brother [the sister-in-law's] had just died."

Schumann's experience suggests possible telepathy from Therese or her sister-in-law or precognition of the brother's death and makes him a **Noted Witness** for these phenomena. (The composition he had entitled originally *Leichenphantasie* came later to be called *Nachtstücke* [Nocturne]).

BIBLIOGRAPHY: Prince, W.F. *Noted Witnesses for Psychic Occurrences,* 1963, pp. 256-257.

**Schurz, Carl, 1829–1906.** German-born American journalist and politician. After escaping from a German prison where he was jailed for having taken part in the revolution of 1848 in that country, he immigrated to Watertown, Wisconsin. He joined the antislavery movement, became a major general during the American Civil War, and Washington correspondent for the *New York Herald Tribune.* Subsequently, he became United States senator from Missouri and served as United States secretary of the interior from 1877 to 1881 in which office he reformed civil service and established a better policy toward the Indians.

In his reminiscences, he narrates that he happened to be at a friend's house in Philadelphia one evening when the group decided to hold a séance. He looked on casually as "spirits" were supposed to be in communication with a young automatist of about fifteen years of age. When he was requested to take part, he asked for the "spirit" of the great German poet, Johann Schiller, and, if it came, for a quotation from one of his works. The automatist wrote two lines in German which Schurz recognized as lines from the tragedy *Wallenstein.* The young girl denied ever having read the work.

Schurz then asked for the spirit of Abraham Lincoln. Soon the automatist wrote that the spirit had made its appearance and that it said that Schurz would be a United States senator from the state of Missouri. This seemed ridiculous to Schurz because his domicile was then in Wisconsin and he had never even thought of moving to Missouri. Yet two years later, circumstances brought him to St. Louis, and in 1869 he became a U.S. senator from Missouri. He is a Noted Witness whose testimony should be considered in connection with the concepts in psychical research of automatism, mediums, communicators, and survival.

BIBLIOGRAPHY: Prince, W.F. *Noted Witnesses for Psychic Occurrences,* 1963, p. 113-116.

**Schwartz, Stephen A., 1943–.** American director of the Mobius Society. Mr. Schwartz's work in psychic archeology (which he calls work in applied parapsychology) has been detailed in his books (1978, 1983). The first is a history and discussion of methodology of research "using intuitionally derived data in archeological explorations." The second is a general presentation of the use of psychics in archeology and of some of the successes achieved by this method. His interests generally have centered on consciousness, healing, and applied psi.

Mr. Schwartz is a visiting professor at John F. Kennedy University. He is a Fellow of the Royal Geographic Society, a member of the Explorers' Club of New York, and has been president of the Association for the Anthropological Study of Consciousness. He is also a member of the Advisory Board of *Phoenix, The Journal of the Association for Transpersonal Anthropology,* and is an associate member of the Parapsychological Association. Mr. Schwartz has written widely for the popular press and television and has also been the subject of television interviews and documentaries.

He has been a senior fellow of the Philosophical Research Society and special assistant for research and analysis to the chief of naval operations.

Selected Writings: *The Secret Vaults of Time,* 1978; *The Alexandria Project,* 1983.

**Schwarz, Berthold Eric, 1924–.** American psychiatrist. Dr. Schwarz believes that if we are to advance or even just survive we "must consider subjects like psi with an open mind rather than rejecting the data out of hand, or refusing to probe arbitrarily proclaimed sacrosanct areas, because of spurious authorities, discredited knowledge, unconscius taboos, or textbooks that tediously repeat errors and outworn doctrines of the past" (Schwarz, 1980:289).

Dr. Schwarz's openness to psychical research and psi began in 1945 when "I was on leave from the Navy in World War II. I was returning to my home when I became suddenly and progressively gripped with the horrible certainty that my younger brother Eric had been killed in action in General Patton's III Army in Germany. I couldn't shake off this thought . . . As I walked up to the door it was no surprise to learn that my premonition was all too true" (Schwarz, 1980:xii).

His interest awakened, he began to look more and more into the paranormal. He interviewed Henry Gross, the dowser Kenneth Roberts had written about, studied psychics and read the works of Jule Eisenbud and Jan Ehrenwald, other psychiatrists who had not rejected psi. Dr. Schwarz then made a study of paranormal dreams in their relation to psychotherapy (Schwarz, 1965) and kept a record of his children's telepathic episodes to show how they were linked to her relationship to her parents (Schwarz, 1971). He called to the attention of other psychiatrists situations in which psi had been in operation in psychiatric settings: in the patient-physician relationship, between parents and children, and the sensitivity to telepathy of elderly people whose sight and hearing are impaired. (Schwarz, 1980).

The belief that psi may link all of us is nowhere better illustrated than in the possibility that any psychosomatic disturbances may be brought on or aggravated by an unconscious telepathic stimulus from someone. Calling this effect a "telesomatic" reaction, Dr. Schwarz says that "telepathy offers an attractive hypothesis for the understanding of psychosomatic diseases" (Schwarz, 1980:114). He also believes that synchronicity is related to telepathy. From episodes in his life and practice, he holds that "understanding of synchronicity and telepathy can give wider dimensions to psychotherapy and show the unique interdependence of people and events" (Schwarz, 1980:177).

Since 1983 Dr. Schwarz has been working with a housewife who has reportedly produced apports, metal-bending, possible levitation of objects, stigmata, trance states in which independent entities communicate, direct writing in English and medieval French (although she is functionally illiterate), healings and materialization of copper foil (Schwarz, 1987).

A Fellow of the American Psychiatric Association, Dr. Schwarz is trying to persuade his colleagues in psychiatry to open their minds to the phenomena of psychical research and parapsychology. But the outlook is dim.

Selected Writings: 1987. "Apparent Materialization of Copper Foil. Case Report: Katie." *Pursuit* 20(4): 154; *Psychic-Nexus: Psychic Phenomena in Psychiatry and Everyday Life,* 1980; *Parent-Child Telepathy,* 1971; *Psychic-Dynamics,* 1965.

**Schweizerische Vereinigung für Parapsychologie (Swiss Association for Parapsychology).** Swiss parapsychological society founded in Biel in 1966 to disseminate information about parapsychology to the Swiss public through the establishment of high school courses in large towns and through lectures, information sheets *(Orientierungsblätter),* and its *Bulletin für Parapsychologie,* a biennial publication, sent to thousands of psychologists, clergymen, and psychiatrists. The association established the first exposition in Europe to deal with parpsychology and used an electronic test generator for its experiments. It also conducts research into electronic voice phenomena, haunts, levitation and unorthodox healing, investigates cases, and works with parapsychological groups in Switzerland and abroad. Since 1968, the organization has awarded prizes for research and experiments, some of which went to Swiss researchers—for example, Hans Naegli-Osjord. The majority, however, have gone to foreign parapsychologists, including Gertha Walther of Germany, Anita Gregory of the

United Kingdom, and Walter Uphoff of the United States. Address: Industriestrasse 5, 2555 Brugg, Switzerland.

**Schweizer Parapsychologische Gesellschaft (Swiss Parapsychological Society).** Swiss organization established in 1952 in Zurich. Its chief interests are the investigation of haunts and mediums and the organization in Zurich of lecture programs, workshops, seminars, and courses on various aspects of the paranormal. Since 1983, the society, with the cooperation of the **Parapsychologischen Arbeitsgruppe Basel** (Parapsychology Work Group of Basel) and the Schweizer Mustermesse (Swiss Industries Fair) has organized "Basel Psi Days," international conferences that each year focus on a special area of parapsychology or psychical research. The success and importance of these conferences is attested to by the fact that they draw large numbers of people from five countries, for example, almost 2,000 in 1988 alone. The society itself consists of 1,000 members and, with an extensive library, provides a valuable resource for archivists and researchers. Address: c/o Frau N. von Muralt, Weinhaldenstrasse 3, CH-8700, Kusnacht, Switzerland.

**Science Unlimited Research Foundation.** American organization established in 1972 to support original scientific research in parapsychology with an emphasis on random event generator studies. SURF is engaged also in testing the so-called compensatory hypothesis of psi. Basing its studies on a group of physically handicapped students from the area school systems, attempts are being made to see whether psi will be used by the students to compensate for their disabilities. Address: 311-D, Spencer Lane, San Antonio, Texas 78201.

**Scientific and Medical Network.** British organization established in 1973 with the aim of extending our ideas and assumptions beyond those accepted by orthodox science and to focus attention on parapsychological and other concepts and phenomena rejected by science as outside its concepts and physical laws. The organization is international and consists of about 500 physicians, economists, engineers, and other professionals. Address: The Old School House, Hampnett, Northleach, Glossop, England GL54 3NN.

**Score.** The number of hits made in any given unit of trials, usually a run (JP).

**Score, Average.** Total score divided by number of runs (JP).

**Score, Total.** Pooled scores of all runs (JP).

**Scott, Christopher, 1927–.** British psychologist and statistician. He was one of the first critics of the experiments conducted by Samuel G. Soal with Basil Shackleton. Scott's analysis of these experiments led him to charge that there was evidence that Soal had falsified data (Scott and Haskell, 1974). Many of Soal's defenders attacked Scott but his conclusion was later confirmed by the independent work of Betty Marwick. Scott insisted rightly in the opinion of many parapsychologists that since apparently respectable academics and scientists were willing to perpetrate fraud in their own experiments, parapsychologists must be extremely careful in the future about evaluating each other's work.

The Soal experiment seemed on its face to be tightly controlled with no fraud possible. The disturbing thing therefore is that none of us really knows when or under what circumstances fraud will be practiced. So, because a fraud-proof experiment is a delusion, Scott cautions "that sensible people should avoid total commitment to paranormal belief; some degree of scepticism should always be maintained—at least until we find a paranormal effect that can be demonstrated at will" (Scott, 1978:970).

Scott, who served on the council of the Society for Psychical Research, has done considerable other writing, including a discussion of the case of the "Jones Boys" and their possible use of supersonic whistles (Scott, 1960) and the suggestion of ideas for experiments to try to produce the elusive repeatable experiment (Scott, 1959). See also **Jones, Glyn** and **Ieuan**.

Selected Writings: 1978. "Correspondence." JSPR 49:968; 1960. "The Jones Boys and the Ultrasonic Whistle." JSPR 40:249; 1959. "In Search of a Repeatable Experiment." JSPR 40:174; and Haskell, P. 1974. "Fresh Light on the Shackleton Experiments." PSPR 56:43.

**Scott, Sir Walter, 1771–1832.** Scottish poet and novelist. He wrote narrative poems, his best known being *The Lady of the Lake*, and Scottish ballads. But he is famous as the leading romantic novelist of his time. Among his novels were *Ivanhoe*, *Kenilworth*, *The Bride of Lammermoor*, *Midlothian*, *Waverly*, and *Old Mortality*. He was imitated during his lifetime and after his death, but few imitators reached his heights of popularity and grandeur. Because peculiar things happened to him he is a **Noted Witness** for the *Paranormal*.

Some writers admit writing as if inspired by some external source. Scott, for example, read with surprise and could not recall having written *The Bride of Lammermoor* composed when he was ill.

The entry in his diary for February 17, 1828, suggests either déjà vu or an inclination toward a belief in reincarnation: "[Y]esterday at dinner time I was strangely haunted by what I would call the sense of pre-existence, with a confused idea that nothing that passed was said for the first time, that the same topics had been discussed and the same persons had stated the same opinions on them" (Shirley, n.d.).

Ten years earlier when his house at Abbotsford was being remodeled, he was roused one night by a "mysterious disturbance" that today we might classify as a poltergeist disturbance. In a letter dated April 30, 1818, he wrote: "The night before last we were awakened by a violent noise, like drawing heavy boards along the new part of the house. I fancied something had fallen and thought no more of it. This was about two in the morning. Last night, at the same witching hour, the very same noise occurred. Mrs. Scott, you know, is rather timbersome; so up I got, with Beardie's broadsword under my arm—'Bolt upright And ready to fight.' But nothing was out of order, neither can I discover what occasioned the disturbance."

It developed that, on the night and at the hour of the strange noise, George Bullock, who was in charge of redoing Scott's house, died suddenly. Scott was considerably "struck with the fantastical coincidence of our nocturnal disturbances at Abbotsford, with the melancholy event that followed."

BIBLIOGRAPHY: Prince, W.F. *Noted Witnesses for Psychic Occurrences*, 1963, pp. 172-173; Shirley, R. *The Problem of Rebirth*, n.d., p. 86.

**Screened Touch Matching.** An ESP card-guessing method in which a vertical opaque screen is placed between subject and experimenter seated opposite one another at a table. The screen prevents the subject from seeing the face-down pack of cards held by the experimenter on the other side of the screen. The subject, upon perceiving extrasensorially the top card in the pack, uses a pointer to point to a blank card beneath one of the five ESP cards suspended on the subject's side of the screen. The experimenter, who sees the pointer through an opening at the bottom of the screen, then places the top card opposite the blank card indicated and proceeds to the next card that then becomes the top card in the pack.

**Script.** The written record of material that comes through a medium. The text may be written by the medium, as it often was in the case, for example, of Mrs. Willett, when the medium is alone, awake, and in a normal state of consciousness. Other scripts may be written when a medium, awake and conscious or in a state of trance, is in the presence of a sitter or experimenter. Normally, when in trance, the medium neither writes out the record nor remembers the contents of a script that is taken down by the sitter or experimenter, or by a stenographer.

The scripts kept by James Hervey Hyslop during his sittings with Mrs. Leonora Piper show the techniques used in order to make a script accurate. Mistakes, bad grammar, or misspellings were all recorded exactly. Dots were used where a word or sentence was not completed. Sitters's or experimenters's statements, and their initials, were placed in parentheses to distinguish what they said from any statements made by or through the medium. See also **Automatic Writing, Speaking, or Spelling**.

**Scriven, Michael John, 1928–.** Anglo-Australian professor of philosophy now at the University of California at Berkeley. As a student at the University of Melbourne in Australia, he founded in 1948 the Melbourne University Society for Psychical Research, the first group in any Australian university and in the Southern Hemisphere for that matter to devote serious attention to parapsychology and psychical research. Subsequently, he became president of the Oxford University Society for Psychical Research.

As one of the few philosophers who consider that the paranormal has important theoretical and philosophical implications, he has contributed many papers to the *Journal of the American Society for Psychical Research* and the *Journal of the Society for Psychical Research.* Dr. Scriven believes that researchers in parapsychology and psychical research have been able to put together a factual basis for their science although a theory to incorporate and make sense of the facts still is lacking.

**Scrying.** See **Crystal-Gazing.**

**Sealed Envelope Test.** An experimental effort made by **F.W.H. Myers, Sir Oliver Lodge** and others to demonstrate that their personalities or consciousnesses had survived death. The usual method was to leave with a trusted person a sealed envelope containing a message or object that the person leaving the envelope hoped to describe correctly through a medium in a communication after death. The correct posthumous communication of the contents of the envelope would be evidence that the communication had come from the person who had deposited the envelope and that he or she had survived death.

This type of test proved not to provide clear-cut evidence, however, because, as happened both with Myers's and Lodge's tests, it can be difficult to judge whether a posthumous message and the contents of the envelope actually correspond. Cipher tests, and the combination lock test have therefore been developed to provide clear hit or miss tests. See also **Dictionary Test; Life After Death Pact**.

**Séance.** Usually thought of as a session with a medium who attempts to communicate with spirits of the dead, it can be held anywhere with any number of people present. A séance can also be a get-together of a group who meet regularly in an attempt to produce physical phenomena à la Kenneth Batcheldor. See also **Sitting.**

**Second Sight.** See **Clairvoyance.**

**Segment.** A unit of a run.

**Seki, Hideo, 1905–.** Japanese professor of information engineering at Tokai University. In quest of the dream of all parapsychologists to formulate some explanatory theory for psi, he has tried to conceive an original hypothesis of a psi information system to explain all psi phenomena. With an avid interest in all areas of parapsychology, he founded the **Psi Science Institute of Japan.**

Selected Writing: *Sai Kagaku no Zenbo* (Bird's Eye View of Psi Science), 1981.

**Sellers, Peter Richard Henry, 1925–1980.** British actor. In the 1960s and 1970s, he was acclaimed one of the great comic personalities of motion pictures. He was best known for his portrayal of the fumbling detective Inspector Clouseau in the *Pink Panther* films. His other films included *the Mouse That Roared, Heavens Above, What's New Pussycat,* and *Being There.*

In a conversation with Shirley MacLaine, he described what happened to him when his heart stopped beating and he was clinically dead: "Well, I felt myself leave my body. I just floated out of my physical form and I saw them cart my body away to the hospital. . . . I wasn't frightened or anything like that because *I* was fine; and it was my body that was in trouble. Then I saw Dr. Kennamer come. And he felt my pulse and saw that I was dead. He and some other people pushed down and up on my chest. . . . They did everything but jump up and down on me to get my heart beating again. Then . . . Rex . . . commanded somebody to carve me open right there on the spot. Rex took my heart out of my body and massaged the hell out of it. . . . Then I looked around myself and I saw an incredibly beautiful bright loving white light above me. I wanted to go to that white light more than anything. . . . I knew that there was love, real love, on the other side of the light which was attracting me so much. It was kind and loving and I remember thinking, 'That's God.' I tried to elevate myself toward it as Rex was working on my heart. . . . Then I saw a hand reach through the light. I tried to touch it, to grab onto it, to clasp it so it could sweep me up and pull me through it. Then I heard Rex say below me, 'It's beating again. I'm getting a heartbeat.' At the same moment a voice attached to the hand I wanted to touch so much said, 'It's not time. Go back and finish. It's not time.' The hand disappeared on the other side and I felt myself floating back into my body. I was bitterly disappointed. After that I don't remember anything until I regained consciousness back inside my body." (MacLaine, 1983.)

Sellers is another person who, while at the brink of death, went through the stages of the **Near-Death Experience**—the out-of-body-experience, the perception from outside his body of the scene in the hospital, the light he associated with love and a divinity, the return to his body—through which others have passed. He is a **Noted Witness** for this phenomenon.

BIBLIOGRAPHY: MacLaine, S. *Out on a Limb.* 1983, p. 171.

**Sender.** See **Agent.**

**Senkowski, Ernst, 1922-.** German physicist, electrical engineer, and leading authority on transcommunication. After World War II, he studied experimental physics at the University of Strasbourg, became a UNESCO expert in physics at the National Research Center in Cairo, Egypt, and later professor of physics at the University of Binghen/Rhine. His interest in the paranormal was "awakened around 1936 because of apparent contradictions against so-called physical laws but remained 'slumbering' till 1976. Practical work in EVP [electronic voice phenomena] started [at the] end of 1976 triggered by a TV-transmission in which pioneer Friedrich Jürgenson reported on voices of the dead" (letter to authors).

To his work on EVP, he has also added research into images allegedly produced by discarnate beings on video picture tubes. Senkowski said, "I have been a personal witness several times" to these transcommunications. "Even without sufficient understanding of paranormal phenomena from a physical point of view it is doubtless clear that the 'official' scientific system is incomplete. 'Extraordinary' interactions between mind and matter including transcommunication must be seriously considered, the contents of the latter demonstrating conscious personal survival of the so-called dead."

Selected Writings: 1979. "Voices on Tape." *Zeitschrift für Parapsychologie.* 29(3/4):201.

**Sensitive.** Synonym for **Psychic.**

**Sensory Automatism.** See **Automatism.**

**Sensory Deprivation.** See **Ganzfeld Procedure.**

**Series.** Several runs of experimental sessions that are grouped in accordance with the stated purpose and design of the experiment (JP).

**Serios, Ted, 1918–.** American subject. He was extensively investigated by Jule Eisenbud in original experiments with a Polaroid Land Camera. They were the first investigations of thoughtography since Tomokichi Fukurai.

Son of a Greek wrestler, Serios himself wrestled with the law and alcohol. But he was proud of himself. He once wrote, "Yes im a Drunk Bum Lo i.q. Steal but. . . . i say i do good Defend cats Dogs pigons Birds and small Kidds" (Eisenbud, 1967, p. 309). His world was divided into bums and bastards (people who did not like him) and great guys (those who did).

Apparently, Eisenbud was one of the great guys. He met Serios, then a bellhop in a Chicago hotel. They hit it off and from that time and for three years from 1964 to 1967 in Denver and Chicago Serios worked with Eisenbud. Before disinterested and trained observers and in ways that could not be explained by normal optical processes, Serios produced images of different kinds on the film of a camera, both film and camera having been furnished by Eisenbud. "When about to shoot, [Serios] seemed rapidly to go into a state of intense concentration, with eyes open, lips compressed, and a quite noticeable tension of his muscular system. His limbs would tend to shake somewhat. . . . His face would become suffused and blotchy, the veins standing out on his forehead, his eyes visibly bloodshot." (Eisenbud, 1967:25).

The phenomena produced by Serios have created a hot controversy. Although Eisenbud and some other parapsychologists believe absolutely that the phenomena are genuinely paranormal, sceptics charge fraud. Serios used in his demonstrations what he called a "gismo" a roll of paper or half-inch cut section of a plastic tube, which he held on or just over the lens of the camera while he looked at it. His stated reason was to limit the amount of light and surrounding objects. But critics maintain that he could have placed some optical device inside, perhaps microfilm, prepared beforehand, with a picture on it for the camera lens to shoot. James Randi claims that he duplicated Serios's feat by palming such an optical device.

On the other hand, the improbability of such cheating is indicated in the first place by the fact that dozens of pictures were produced by Serios when the camera was one to over sixty feet away from him. In addition, there were many distortions in the Serios pictures—for example, a blurred picture of an airplane hangar with the word "Cainadain" on the hangar instead of "Canadian." Such distortions could not have come from any actual picture somehow photographed and tend to establish paranormality rather than fraud.

Critics also claim that Serios confessed to fraud. But both Eisenbud and Serios deny the confession, Serios saying, "I'd be happy to get pictures by trickery if only someone would just show me how." (Eisenbud, 1975).

BIBLIOGRAPHY: Eisenbud, J. 1975. "On Ted Serios' Alleged 'Confession.'" JASPR 69:94; *The World of Ted Serios*, 1967; with Pratt, J.G. and Stevenson, I. 1981. "Distortions in the Photographs of Ted Serios." JASPR 75:143.

**Servadio, Emilio, 1904–.** Italian pioneer psychoanalyst and parapsychologist. Early interested in mesmerism and hypnosis, his doctoral thesis completed in 1926 dealt with the use of hypnosis in forensic medicine. His interest in psychical research, however, had already been stimulated by his reading of Charles Richet's *Traité de Métapsychique* published in 1922. When he read Sigmund Freud's *New Introductory Lectures on Psycho-analysis* published in 1933, he was stimulated to try to see if psychoanalysis could be used as a tool to study paranormal phenomena and found, as did Jan Ehrenwald and Jule Eisenbud, evidence of telepathy in the psychoanalytic setting.

During the war years (1938–1945), Servadio was in India where he immersed himself in Indian metaphysics and where he had "a cosmic experience which could not be expressed in words" (Servadio, 1987:92). In Rome, shortly after World War II, Servadio met Eileen Garrett. In 1953 he attended the first international conference on parapsychological Studies at Utrecht, Holland, organized by her and subsequently attended all the nineteen conferences sponsored by Mrs. Garrett's Parapsychology Foundation. She also funded his research in the United States, in Latin America, in Haiti and in Europe.

Servadio also experimented with LSD and psilocybin to see if their ingestion would stimulate extrasensory perception. The results were negative—except that once under the influence of LSD he had an ecstatic experience.

In addition to his membership in psychoanalytic societies, he co-founded in 1937 what later became known as the **Società Italiana Di Parapsicología** (Italian Society of Parapsychology) of which he was a member until 1981. In 1982 he became president of the Parapsychological Association of Italy. He is a member of the Parapsychological Association and is correspondent and adviser to the Parapsychology Foundation.

"I think," says Dr. Servadio (1987), "that paranormal phenomena give us some hints, as for thousands of years some of the great sages of the East have indicated, that this is a world of Maya, of appearance" (p. 96).

Selected Writings: 1971. "Eileen Garrett: A Personal Recollection." JSPR 46:61; 1958. "Telepathy and Psychoanalysis." JASPR 52:127; and R. Cavanna. *ESP Experiments with LSD 25 and Psilocybin: A Methodological Approach* (Parapsychological Monograph No. 5), 1964.

BIBLIOGRAPHY: Pilkington, R. "Emilio Servadio. Interview, Rome, August 24, 1985." In R. Pilkington, ed., *Men and Women of Parapsychology*, 1987.

**Session.** A sitting or experiment with a medium or an ESP test or experiment with psychokinesis. In the latter sense it signifies a unit of an experiment containing all the trials conducted on one occasion.

**Set.** A subdivision of the record page serving as a scoring unit for a consecutive group of trials, usually for the same target (JP). See also **Score**.

**Seth.** The entity that came through the trance channel **Jane Roberts** beginning in 1963 and continuing until her death in 1984. The Seth books have sold millions of copies. Jane Roberts's Seth (since her death other channelers claim to be channeling the same Seth) rarely but occasionally revealed paranormal knowledge about people who were present at the channeling sessions. He called himself an "energy essence personality." He said that we are not dependent on physical matter, that we are multi-dimensional and part of a larger, evolving "All That Is." We create our own reality and experience many incarnations, yet, since everything is taking place in an eternal and infinite present, we can affect our own past and future actual and probable selves (Klimo, 1987).

Jane Roberts wrote that Seth represents "the truth that we have allowed ourselves to forget [:] that our dreams come alive at midday; that our feelings and beliefs turn into the reality we experience; that . . . we are the events in which we participate . . . [;that w]e are of good intent. . . . Seth *is* a model of ourselves as we know we can be. . . . He is delivering to our conscious minds our deepest unconscious knowledge about ourselves, the world, the universe, and the source of Being Itself" (Roberts, 1981).

BIBLIOGRAPHY: Klimo, J. *Channeling,* 1987; Roberts, J. *Seth Speaks,* 1972; Roberts, J. *The Nature of Personal Reality,* 1974; Roberts, J. *The "Unknown" Reality, Vols. 1 and 2,* 1977, 1979; Roberts, J. *The Nature of the Psyche,* 1979; Roberts, J. *The Individual and the Nature of Mass Events,* 1981; Wambach, H. 1977. "A Session with Seth." *New Realities* 1(1):34.

**Sex (gender).** Strive though they may, "unisex" hair salons, clothing manufacturers, and other enterprises have not succeeded in eliminating some basic differences between men and women. Males are still superior in spatial orientation and females in acuity of perception and memory. Men continue to be more aggressive than women.

Parapsychology and psychical research raise another question about the sexes. Does gender have any connection with paranormal phenomena? Generally, there seems to be no relationship in spite of the popular belief that women are more intuitive. Nevertheless, what few clues there are suggest that one sex may perform better than the other in four areas: as mediums, in psi, in the out-of-body experience, and as communicators.

Mediumship is the second oldest of the female professions. While mediums may be both male or female, the great majority seem to be female. There have been outstanding male mediums—Emanuel Swedenborg and D.D. Home, for instance—but the greatest mediums during the "golden age" of mediumship and after, those who produced the most extraordinary and best-known results and were the foci of intensive and prolonged investigations were women: Leonora E. Piper, Gladys Osborne Leonard, Eusapia Palladino, Mina S. Crandon, "Mrs. Willett."

With respect to psi, Louisa E. Rhine points out (Rhine, 1961) that a far greater number of women than men report spontaneous cases. Females may, of course, just be less reluctant to discuss their psychic experiences than men. Yet several studies suggest a relation between psi and the female sex. A number of experiments show that girl students in school score much better in extrasensory perception tests than boys (Brier, 1969; Van Bussbach, 1961; Van de Castle, 1974; White and Angstadt, 1963). Another experiment in extrasensory perception indicates that the menstrual cycle may be linked to psi scores: women scored significantly better during the preovulatory phases of their cycles than during the postovulatory phases (Schmidt and Stanford, 1978). In experiments with psychokinesis, it was noted as well that female subjects scored significantly but that males did not (Dale, 1946).

On the other hand, out-of-body experiences may be linked to the male sex. It is noteworthy that more males than females claim an OBE (Blackmore, 1982). Robert Monroe, known for his OBEs, noticed first a direct relation between his sex drive and the start of his experience and that when he came back to his body he had a penile erection (Monroe, 1971).

Only one study has been made to determine whether there is any direct relation between sex and postmortem communication. It found that a significantly larger number of males made better communicators after death than females (Berger, 1987).

The body of data collected with regard to sex and the paranormal is small but is enough to suggest that the two are linked. With more openness to sex today, perhaps investigators will conduct more needed inquiries into this interesting and fundamental field.

BIBLIOGRAPHY: Berger, A.S. *Aristocracy of the Dead,* 1987; Blackmore, S.J. 1982. "Have You Ever Had an OBE: The Wording of the Question." JSPR 51:292; Brier, R.M. 1969. "A Mass School Test of Precognition." JP 3:125; Dale, L.A. 1946. "The Psychokinetic Effect: The First A.S.P.R. Experiment." JASPR 40:123; Monroe, R. *Journeys Out of the Body,* 1971; Rhine, L.E. *Hidden Channels of the Mind,* 1961; Schmitt, M. and Stanford, R.G. 1978.

"Free-Response ESP During Ganzfeld Stimulation: The Possible Influence of Menstrual Cycle Phase." JASPR 72:177; Van Bussbach, J.G. 1961. "An Investigation of ESP in First and Second Grades in American Schools." JP 25:161; Van de Castle, R.L. "An Investigation of Psi Abilities Among the Cuna Indians of Panama." In A. Angoff and D. Booth, eds., *Parapsychology and Anthropology*, 1974, pp. 80-97; White, R. and Angstadt, J. 1963. "Student Performance in a Two Classroom GESP Experiment with Two Student-Agents Acting Simultaneously." JASPR 57:32.

**Seybert, Henry, P. 1883–1983.** American philanthropist. This wealthy believer in Spiritualism left the University of Pennsylvania what was in the late nineteenth century a record amount of money to finance an investigation of the movement—$60,000. As a result of his gift, the **Seybert Commission** was appointed.

**Seybert Commission.** A commitee consisting of scientists and scholars appointed in the United States in 1894 by the University of Pennsylvania for the purpose of investigating "all systems of morals, religion, or philosophy which assume to represent the truth, and particularly of Modern Spiritualism." The appointment was made as a result of a generous gift by Henry Seybert to the University of Pennsylvania for the purpose of founding there a chair of philosophy, the gift being conditioned on the establishment by the University of a committee for the purpose mentioned. In the course of its existence, the commission examined many physical mediums, including Henry Slade and one of the Fox Sisters. The conclusion reached was that nothing was produced by these mediums that could not easily be explained by fraud.

**Shackleton, Basil, c.1900–1978.** South African star subject. He was best-known for his part in the most impressive experiments in extrasensory perception ever conducted on English soil. A creative portrait photographer by trade, Shackleton discovered when he was about twenty-three years of age that he had psychic talents as well. He used his abilities to amuse his friends in card-guessing games and to make money for himself by predicting the winners of horse races.

In early 1936 in London, Shackleton read in a Sunday newspaper about Samuel G. Soal and his experiments. In order to demonstrate his power of telepathy, Shackleton sought Soal out in his laboratory. In December 1940, Shackleton was discharged from the armed forces because of poor health (he had only one kidney and a duodenal problem). At that time Soal, with K.M. Goldney as collaborator, began experiments with Shackleton in which cards with pictures of animals were used. In these experiments from 1941 to 1943, cited innumerable times as part of the case for ESP because they were so striking, Shackleton's scores in over 4000 trials provided statistically overwhelming evidence in favor of ESP.

Shackleton, famous and satisfied, went back to South Africa in 1948. Thirty years later a bombshell hit as new evidence came to light of Soal's fraudulent manipulation of data in the experiments (Markwick, 1978). The whole series of tests with Shackleton was tainted and had to be removed as a support for ESP. And what of Shackleton's psychic powers? If indeed he had them, it is unfortunate that it happened to be Soal he read about in 1936 and on whom he depended for validation of his gifts. Some other investigator might have vindicated him and the years of effort he put into boring cards tests in order to supply evidence of ESP.

BIBLIOGRAPHY: Markwick, B. 1978. "The Soal-Goldney Experiments with Basil Shackleton: New Evidence of Data Manipulation." PSPR 56:250; Soal, S.G. and Goldney, K.M. 1943. "Experiments in Precognitive Telepathy." PSPR 47:21.

**Shakers.** Otherwise known as the United Socity of Believers in Christ's Second Coming. Called "Shakers" because of their worship in which they toss their heads from side to side with bodies twitching, jerking, and shaking. An extreme branch of the Quakers, their principal tenet is a life of celibacy. The sect does not accept marriage, considers celibacy the more perfect condition, and segregates the sexes in separate sections of houses. It preaches isolation from the world and an imminent Judgment Day with warning to all to change their lives to avoid being doomed to eternal Hell. The sect also believes that Christ's kingdom on earth started with the establishment of its church and considers that God has a dual nature, part male and part female.

The Shakers originated in England but, led by **Mother Ann** who founded their doctrine of celibacy, came to the colonies in America and became distinctively American. They arrived in New York City in 1774 and in 1776 went on to establish themselves in what is now Watervliet, New York. Expecting to find religious liberty, they instead encountered persecution: The American colonists believed that the Shakers were not on their side of the War for Independence. Nevertheless, the Shaker Society was organized in 1787 and increased in the years following with a growing reputation for industriousness and inventiveness. They produced the threshing machine, screw propeller, and clothespin, for example.

It is curious that the literature of psychical research has never noticed the paranormal phenomena produced by the Shakers between 1837 and 1847. The bodies of children and adults began to twitch uncontrollably, people claimed to be possessed by the spirits of the dead and went into trance to receive messages from communicators. These reported events are all the more interesting because they started eleven years before the famous manifestations at the home of the Fox Sisters that are generally thought to have given rise to Spiritualism and prior also to any publications by Andrew Jackson Davis. Spiritualist influence, therefore, cannot account for the psychic experiences of the Shakers that strongly support the teachings of Spiritualism.

The Shakers attracted more and more adherents and soon commanded 6,000 followers. As of the 1970s, however, the Shaker movement with its insistence on a life of celibacy had shrunk to only about twelve female members.

BIBLIOGRAPHY: Bird, J. M. 1929. "The Crisis in Psychical Research." *Psychic Research* 23:323; Evans, F. W. *Ann Lee, Shakers and Shakerism, a Compendium of the Origin, History, Rules and Regulations, Government and Doctrines of the United Society of Believers in Christ's Second Appearing,* 1859; Pierson, J. 1938. "Psychic Manifestations Among the Shakers—Part 1." JASPR 32:301.

**Shakespeare, William, 1564–1616.** English playwright and poet. He is considered by many as the greatest writer who has ever lived.

Shakespeare is of interest to psychical research because "[n]ever before and never since . . . has a writer revealed so deep and genuine an acceptance of psychic phenomena. . . . Shakespeare believed in prophecy, witchcraft, astrology, magic, and ghosts" (Yellen, 1962:17).

Shakespeare was a product of his times. As that product, says Yellen, he took for granted that everything that happened was rooted in the supernatural, that the stars predetermined events, that destiny could be controlled by magic, that ghosts were real (there are fourteen in Shakespeare's plays) and that in sleep one's mind made contact with the unseen world.

Gardner Murphy was fascinated by Shakespeare's "first efforts at scientific psychical research. . . showing the difference between a paranormal experience [the perception of ghosts] and an ordinary normal hallucination ["Is this a dagger which I see before me?]. . . . [T]he rough soldier, the gentleman, and the philosopher have three different interpretations of the ghost [in Hamlet]. . ." (1954:83) representing the three different points of view current in Shakespeare's day.

*Macbeth* can be looked upon as a story of a prophesy or, according to Jan (Hans) Ehrenwald, as "a classical instance of telepathy (1941:102), that is, the witches had, by telepathy, read Macbeth's suppressed desires. *Midsummer Night's Dream* and *The Tempest* deal with magic, in the latter "Prospero's farewell to magic [being regarded] as Shakespeare's farewell to the stage . . ." (Yellen, 1962:36).

Whether or not Shakespeare himself had had any psychic experiences we do not know, but his plays remain fascinating both to physical researchers and to lovers of fine literature.

BIBLIOGRAPHY: Ehrenwald, H. 1941. "Telepathy in Macbeth?" JSPR 32:99; Murphy, G. 1954. "International Collaboration in Psychical Research." JASPR 48:81; Yellen, S. 1962. "The Psychic World of William Shakespeare." *International Journal of Parapsychology* 4(3):17.

**Shaking Tent.** A séance conducted by the Chippewa Indians and the Woodland Algonkian Indians to summon spirits for answers to questions or predictions of the future. In the Indian séance, the spirits of deceased human beings usually are not invoked.

In the "shaking tent," a conjurer goes into a conjuring lodge that may shake when he is inside. While an audience remains outside waiting, he makes the attempt to communicate with animal spirits, such as the caribou, moose or Mikinak, the Great Turtle, who is the principal spirit. Mikinak is in a position similar to that of a control except that the Great Turtle is an animal spirit who acts as the intermediary with other animal spirits. Occasionally, however, a human spirit has been said to return in the "shaking tent." The Maidu in California sometimes hold séances to call on human spirits, but such attempts are rare among the Indians.

Phenomena similar to apports have taken place during a "shaking tent" séance. In one recorded case, a fifty-pound sack was transported a distance of 100 miles and in another case objects lost overboard during a canoe trip were returned. The skeptical among us may well think of trickery as an explanation for such phenomena or for the shaking of the lodge and the communictions claimed with spirits. But trickery in the mind of the Indian brings supernatural punishment and conjurers on their deathbeds swear that they have possessed the powers manifested. See also **American Indians.**

BIBLIOGRAPHY: Hallowell, A.I. "The Role of Conjuring in Saltean Society." *Publications of the Philadelphia Anthropological Society of Philadelphia,* 1942.

**Shaman.** Also called **Medicine Man** or witch doctor. One who enters into trance, converses with spirits, and possesses the power to cure the sick. Modern anthropologists and scientists in the West consider the belief in shamans without any foundation. For the psychical researcher, however, many of the beliefs, rites, and methods of shamanism are directly relevant to paranormal abilities and occurrences familiar to and studied by psychical researchers and obtain results similar to those obtained by mediums, psychics, and unorthodox healers. That shamans may have paranormal gifts seems suggested by research into the question. "A fairly large number of ethnographic documents has already put the authenticity of such phenomena [such as extrasensory perception] beyond doubt" (Eliade, 1966).

BIBLIOGRAPHY: Eliade, M. *Shamanism: Archaic Techniques of Ecstacy,* 1966.

**Shanker, Daya, 1929–.** Indian advocate of the High Court in Allahabad, India. He is as much concerned with death as he is with the law. Death, he believes, is a natural phenomenon that allows the soul to proceed to heaven, eventually to be born again to receive the unenjoyed portions of its rewards of past lives in accordance with the law of **Karma. Reincarnation** and karma are the twin pillars of his belief as they are for other Hindus but unlike them Shanker, as senior research fellow and general secretary of the **Foundation for Reincarnation and Spiritual Research,** works with Jamuna Prasad to put his beliefs to the test by making field investigations of reincarnation-type cases and collecting data to see if his beliefs can be verified. He is also a member of the International Institute for the Study of Death.

**Shapin, Betty, 1914–.** British editor of *Parapsychology Review* and of the *Proceedings* published by the Parapsychology Foundation of its annual international conferences. She joined the foundation in 1969 after having been a staff writer for the Research Institute of America, the National Foreman's Institute, and the National Tuberculosis Institute.

**Sheargold, Richard, 1911–1988.** British psychical researcher. A member of the Society for Psychical Research from 1955 until his death, Sheargold's interest in psychical research was mediumship and survival.

His earliest publication (1961) in the *Journal of the Society for Psychical Research* described an experiment in which he subjected sixteen mediums to card-guessing tests for telepathy. (They scored at chance.) He considered "The Haunting of Borley Rectory" by Eric J. Dingwall, Kathleen M. Goldney and Trevor H. Hall in which the authors attacked Harry Price the worst report ever published by the SPR. He believed, along with G.N.M. Tyrrell, that the underlying and ultimate truth about nature would probably seem to us fantastic and incredible and that we must not close our eyes to the reality of mystical experience in our examination of psi.

First chairman of the **Survival Joint Research Committee Trust** at the time of its creation in 1963, he believed in communication with the dead but thought of it "as an assemblage of memories of past earthly experiences drawn from material available in the minds of the sitters, and occasionally in the minds of other living persons, in addition to any relevant written or printed records. . . [and doubted] if such communication is a conscious act of the deceased in the sense that we understand consciousness. . ." (1963:35-36).

For the last twenty years of his life, perhaps because of experiences as a ham radio operator, he devoted much time to the electronic voice phenomena. He accepted their reality but felt, because of his own experiments, that they were produced psychokinetically by the experimenter. His last appearance in the JSPR was his kindly but negative review (1986) of *The Ghost of Twenty-Nine Megacycles* which describes George Meek's Spiricom.

Selected Writings: 1986. "The Ghost of Twenty-Nine Megacycle." JSPR 53:329; 1970. "The Psychology of Occultism." JSPR 45:318; 1963. "Survival and the Physical Basis of Memory." JSPR 42:35; 1961. "Experimental Card-Guessing Using Mediums as Percipients." JSPR 41:67.

**Sheep.** See **Sheep-Goat Experiments.**

**Sheep-Goat Experiments.** Experiments to investigate the attitudes and beliefs of subjects as they relate to ESP tests. The first and best-known was carried out by **Gertrude R. Schmeidler** in 1942. She divided her subjects into two classes: Those accepting the possibility of ESP were designated "sheep" and those who did not were called "goats." Under experimental safeguards, she found statistically significant differences between the two groups with the unmistakable trend toward higher scores for the sheep and toward scoring at or below mean chance expectation for the goats. The sheep-goat standard has been used widely and successfully to separate subjects who are high scoring from those who are not.

BIBLIOGRAPHY: Schmeidler, G.R. and McConnell, R.A. *ESP and Personality Patterns,* 1958.

**Sheldrake, Rupert, 1942–.** British biochemist and plant physiologist. Dr. Sheldrake has been a controversial figure in psychical research since the publication of a book (1981) subtitled "The Hypothesis of Formative Causation." This "formative causation" influences both the internal and external structure of things. Each thing is a "morphic unit" that has its own "morphogenetic field." Morphogenetic fields influence morphic units by "morphic resonance," which "depends on the systems's three dimensional structures and patterns of vibration" (Sheldrake, 1981:117) and can act across space and time.

The term morphogenetic field has been used by biologists in the past as a descriptive convenience, but Sheldrake thinks of them as actual structures and feels that his theory is empirically testable; for example, if a new task is learned by a species of animal or by a person, all other members of the same species should thereafter be able to perform that task. (An experiment with human subjects carried on simultaneously in Europe and the United States had positive results in Europe but negative results in the U.S.).

Although Sheldrake does not do so, the theory is clearly applicable to paranormal phenomena such as telepathy and clairvoyance and seems to explain Carl G. Jung's theory of synchronicity. It could be extended to explain "recurrent hauntings, the similar patterns manifested by poltergeist phenomena in various parts of the world, and experiences such as that of Miss Moberly and Miss Jourdain at Versailles" (Randall 1981:157).

John L. Randall calls Dr. Sheldrake's theory "a new philosophy of science . . . worthy of the most careful and impartial investigation" (1981:158). Stephen E. Braude on the other hand maintains that Sheldrake's theory is not viable and is not radical, either. He calls morphic resonance a "literally unintelligible mechanism" and says that it is Sheldrake's adoption of "the standard assumptions about what a scientific explanation of observable phenomena should look like (i.e., that phenomena should be analyzable in terms of unobservable subsidiary processes and mechanisms) . . . which . . . renders most . . . results [of behavioral scientists] worthless" (Braude, 1983:76). Nevertheless, Dr. Braude considers the work "serious and thought-provoking."

Dr. Sheldrake received his Ph.D. in biochemistry from Cambridge University. From 1967 to 1973 he was a Fellow of Clare College, Cambridge University, and director of studies in cell biology and biochemistry there. As a research fellow of the Royal Society he carried out research on the development of plants and the aging of cells. From 1974 to 1978 he was principal plant physiologist at the International Crops Research Institute for the Semi-Arid Tropics in Hyderabad, India, where he worked on the physiology of legume crops. He is now consultant plant physiologist to the same institute.

Dr. Sheldrake's latest book is entitled *The Presence of the Past.*

Selected Writings: *The Presence of the Past,* 1988; *A New Science of Life,* 1981.

BIBLIOGRAPHY: Braude, S.E. 1983. "Radical Provincialism in the Life Sciences: A Review of Rupert Sheldrake's *A New Science of Life.*" JASPR 77:63; Randall, J.L. 1981. "A New Science of Life: The Hypothesis of Formative Causation." JSPR 51:156.

**Shelley, Percy Bysshe, 1792–1822.** English lyric poet. His poems, marked by the quality of music and great imagination, are high points in English literature. His *Queen Mab* (1813) and *The Revolt of Islam* (1818) show his revolutionary spirit and his summons to revolt. His *Adonais* (1821), an elegy on John Keats, reveals his spirituality and concept of immortality. His other poems include *Prometheus Unbound* (1819), *The Cenci* (1819), *Ozymandias* (1817–1818) and *Ode to the West Wind* (1819). When his first wife committed suicide, Shelley married Mary Godwin, the daughter of William Godwin, who had already given birth to their child. A year later Mary Shelley wrote her famous *Frankenstein* and, in 1818, the couple left England permanently for Italy.

Shelley flowered on Italian soil; almost all his chief works were written there. In April 1822, the Shelleys took a house at San Terenzo on the Bay of Spezzia. One night loud cries were heard coming from the saloon. Shelley was found "staring horribly into the air" and evidently in a trance. They waked him and he related that a figure wrapped in a mantle came to his bedside and beckoned him. He must have risen in his sleep, for he followed the imaginary figure into the saloon when it lifted the hood of its mantle, ejaculated '*Siete sodis fatto?*' (Are you satisfied?) and vanished."

Shelley, a close friend of Lord Bryon's, had been shocked to learn that the latter's daughter, Allegra, had died in April. Then on May 6, Shelley was on his terrace looking down at the waters of the bay, when all at once he cried out and, in the words of his wife, "declared that he saw, as plainly as he saw me, a naked child [Allegra] rise from the sea and clasp its hands as in joy smiling at him."

We do not have Shelley's own analysis of these experiences. Mary Shelley called the beckoning figure "imaginary." Although it seemed real to him, the figure could have been produced by Shelley himself. Perhaps the figure was giving him an impression by means of precognition of something terrible that was going to happen to him. In May the reflecting waters of the bay could have produced the phenomenon of crystal gazing. Again, it is possible that the dead child rising from the bay was showing Shelley his fate. For on July 8, 1822, Shelley was drowned in the Bay of Spezzia when his little yacht was caught in a storm. So interpreted, these events bring Shelley to us as a **Noted Witness** for the paranormal.

BIBLIOGRAPHY: Prince, W.F. *Noted Witnesses for Psychic Occurrences,* 1963, p. 139.

**Sherman, Harold, 1898–1987.** American psychic. His reputation as a psychic, which continued over half a century, was established in 1937 with a sensational experiment in extrasensory perception he conducted with the famed Australian explorer of the Arctic, Sir Hubert Wilkins. While Wilkins was at the North Pole, Sherman, 3,000 miles away in his New York City apartment, noted his ESP impressions of Wilkins's expedition at the North Pole. The results were highly significant: Sherman's impressions were 70 percent accurate (Sherman, 1971). Once, for example, on one day out of a period of almost six months during which the experiment lasted, Sherman had the impression of a toothache. This was the very day Wilkins, with a severe tooth problem, had to fly to Edmonton for treatment.

Sherman founded the ESP Research Associates Foundation in Arkansas in 1963, where lectures and workshops were conducted in unorthodox healing and various psychic phenomena. In addition to his fame as a psychic, Sherman is known as a reporter, radio commentator, and the author of several popular books, including "how to" books to guide people in the development of their ESP abilities (1973;1964), a work on psychic surgery in the Phillipines (1967), and another on life after death (1972).

Selected Writings: *Harold Sherman ESP Manual,* 1973; *You Live After Death,* 1972; *Thoughts Through Space,* 1971; *"Wonder" Healers of the Phillipines,* 1967; *How to Make ESP Work for You,* 1964.

**Shin.** The twenty-first letter of the Hebrew alphabet. The symbol was adopted by Robert H. Thouless and B.P. Wiesner to describe their theory of an immaterial psychical component of the human being that operates in all our behavior and in all functions, both normal and paranormal. This component interacts with outside objects and outside brains and nervous systems and also with the brain and nervous system of the individuals in whom it is found. The Shin is a neutral term for what philosophy and religion call the "spirit" or "soul."

BIBLIOGRAPHY: Thouless, R.H. and Wiesner, B.P. 1947. "The Psi Process in Normal and 'Paranormal' Psychology." PSPR 48:177.

**Showers, Rosina Mary, (later Mrs. Nugent James), c.1857–?.** British private materializing medium. She was investigated by Sir Willam Crookes. Her principal spirit form was "Florence Maple" (supposedly the full form materialization of a spirit entity). On April 10, 1874, Crookes wrote that Florence Cook's "Katie" (the most famous full form materialization of all time) and Rosina Showers' "Florence" had been walking arm in arm, in strong light, in his laboratory. Rosina Showers was supposedly caught in fraud at Serjeant Cox's home and failed Cromwell Varley's electrical test. In 1875 Crookes reported that she confessed that "Florence" was a fraud and that she had had accomplices (after which her mother began a campaign of villification against Crookes).

The intriguing question remains how Crookes retained faith in Florence Cook and "Katie King" whom he had seen walking with the fraudulent "Florence" since the fraud of one seems to imply the fraud of the other.

BIBLIOGRAPHY: Hall, T.H. *The Spiritualists,* 1962; Medhurst, R.G. and Goldney, K.M. 1964. "William Crookes and the Physical Phenomena of Mediumship." PSPR 5:25.

**Shroud of Turin.** Also called Holy Shroud or, in Italian, *Santa Sindone.* Housed in a vault in the chapel of the Cathedral of St. John the Baptist in Turin, Italy, it is a famous Christian relic that has been known since it was first exhibited in 1357 in Lirey, France. On the cloth, 14 feet in length and 3½ feet wide, are impressed the blood-stained images of the front and back of a man. For centuries, the Shroud has been an outstanding religious image. Christians have believed that the Shroud is the cloth in which Jesus Christ was wrapped before he was entombed.

In 1978, thirty-five scientists from the United States, part of the Shroud of Turin Research Project, transported six tons of sophisticated equipment to Turin, used advanced technology to make an examination and computer and chemical analyses of the Shroud, took 30,000 photographs of it and, after working 120 hours over the Shroud, produced over twenty scientific papers setting forth their findings. At no time in the history of science has any religious relic received such rigorous, sustained, and painstaking attention.

The scientists concluded that the Shroud was a genuine artifact and, although Dr. Walter McGrone, who made microscopic examinations of surface material, maintained that the images had been painted on the cloth, the scientists rejected his argument. They maintained that there was no indication that the images were made by any human hands applying paint, stain, or coloring.

The images on the cloth are three-dimensional photographically negative pictures with dark and light reversed. They show a naked and bearded man, probably a Jew, of about thirty years of age who had been beaten savagely and then crucified. But, in spite of all their expertise and highly sophisticated equipment, the scientists were unable to answer clearly and definitively the great question of the true identity of the man in the burial shroud. But their findings seemed to suggest that the cloth was from the first century A.D. and generally to reinforce the centuries-old Christian belief that the corpse was Christ.

Ten years after the Shroud of Turin Research Project, three laboratories—at the University of Arizona, the Swiss Federal Institute of Technology of the University of Zurich, and at Oxford University—used the radiocarbon dating method to test three unmarked postage-stamp sized samples of cloth, including one, secretly coded, that had been taken from the Shroud. After this supposedly blind test, they reached a consensus that the Shroud could be dated to the thirteenth or fourteenth centuries. While the radiocarbon method cannot date with pinpoint accuracy, it is supposed to be accurate within plus or minus 100 years. The Shroud, therefore, according to the test, could not have been Christ's burial cloth. The inference is that the Shroud is a fake produced by some clever medieval trickery and to dismiss it.

Defenders of the shroud as Christ's burial cloth (Tyrer, Tribbe, Wilson, and Kendrick, 1989), however, have pointed out many improprieties in the testing of the Shroud: A new relatively untried method was used; the three laboratories were inexperienced (one, the Zurich lab, had been 1,000 years off in another test); the tests were not blind—each lab knew which piece of cloth came from the Shroud. In addition, the pieces of cloth were taken from one soiled, damaged and repaired corner of the Shroud so that the cloth might not even have been the original material. The Shroud had been subjected to intense heat (900 degrees Centigrade) in a fire in 1532 which could have altered the properties of the cloth. And how did pollen grains from Palestine get on the Shroud and, even more absorbing, how were the 3-D negative images of a man produced on the Shroud?

Joe Nickell, a magician and critic of the Shroud, has proposed that a technique of rubbing using a combination of myrrh and aloes—a technique known in the twelfth century—could have been used to produce the negative images. This technique cannot produce the fine details of the images such as Greek letters on coins or the eyelids of the face on the Shroud. It is also quite impossible to see how photographic images could have been made by a medieval artist before photography had been invented. Neither those who believe in the Shroud's authenticity nor those who believe it is a fake can explain the process or techniques that were used to make the images.

Since science cannot account for the markings on the Shroud either as man-made or as produced by any known natural event or process, psychical research and its interpretation of the mystery are extremely relevant to the enigma. If the Shroud is an authentic burial shroud of someone, even of a crucified medieval man—although by the fourth century A.D. crucifixtion had ceased to be used generally as a form of capital punishment—how could his corpse, whatever its identity, have produced on the cloth perfect photographic images of itself?

On the premise of the Shroud's having been someone's burial cloth, psychical researcher Frank C. Tribbe who examined the scientific data and findings offers an interpretation: that the images were produced by one great paranormal charge which, with microscopic accuracy and photographic negativity created the permanent images on the cloth as the body dematerialized. The possibility of dematerialization of the body in the Shroud would also interest psychical researchers. Materialization is a familiar enough phenomenon to psychical researchers but dematerialization or the disappearance of a physical object, while not unknown, is a phenomenon rarely encountered. Whatever body the Shroud wrapped, dematerialization and the resulting mysterious images on the cloth may have been the special products of his unique attributes and character.

BIBLIOGRAPHY: McGrone, W. "Shroud Image is the Work of an Artist." In K. Frazier, ed., *Science Confronts the Paranormal,* 1983, p. 344; Tribbe, F.C. 1986. "Twenty-one Enigmas of the Shroud of Turin." *Christian Parapsychologist* 6(5):162; Tribbe, F.C. *Portrait of Jesus? the Illustrated Story of the Shroud of Turin,* 1983; Tyrer, J. Tribbe, F. Wilson, I. and Kendrick R. 1989. "The Turin Shroud—Too Hasty an Epitaph?" *The Christian Parapsychologist* 8(1):2.

**Sidgwick, Eleanor Mildred (Balfour), 1845–1936.** Eminent British psychical researcher. The oldest of eight children, she was the sister of Arthur Balfour (a prime minister of England) and the wife of Henry Sidgwick, the first president of the Society for Psychical Research. She was a woman of great intellect and character.

Although she did not join the SPR until 1884, she had long been sitting with mediums who claimed to produce physical phenomena. She believed that such phenomena do occasionally occur but that the evidence for them was poor. In 1884 she considered the problem of postmortem apparitions (phantasms of the dead).

Because of her extraordinary ability to analyze and organize large masses of disorganized material, she was the chief author of the **Census of Hallucinations**—which enormous job she completed even after taking on the presidency of Newnham College, Cambridge, in 1892 (a position she retained until 1910). She was "an abler observer and more sensitive to small empirical details" than her husband and "with the use of her curiously small vocabulary" presented the results of her research "in such clear sentences that no one could fail to understand" (Nicol, 1972).

In 1888 Henry Sidgwick was appointed editor of the *Journal* and *Proceedings* of the SPR, which "meant," according to Alice Johnson (1936), "that Mrs. Sidgwick did practically all the work of editing. . . ." In 1915, she published her authoritative 657 page paper on Leonora Piper's mediumship.

She was methodical and unemotional in her approach to research, cautious and slow to make up her mind or to change it. For many years she, her brother Gerald Balfour, and J.G. Piddington maintained a household where, with Alice Johnson's help, they analyzed the communications, mainly those that made up the **Cross-Correspondences,** received over a thirty-year period supposedly from their deceased relatives and colleagues. Eleaor Sidgwick was president of the SPR in 1908–1909 and its president of honour in 1932.

Mrs. Sidgwick, a communicant in the Church of England and, according to Fraser Nico (1972), in the Church of Scotland all her life, thought that telepathy had been established and gradually came to believe in survival of death and in the reality of communication between the living and the dead.

Mrs. Sidgwick enjoyed pure mathematics very much and thought it "specially adapted to a disembodied existence." With her brother-in-law, Lord Rayleigh (who received the Nobel Prize in physics in 1904) she conducted some electrical experiments and is joint author with him of three papers published in the *Philosophical Transactions of the Royal Society.*

Selected Writings: 1915. "A Contribution to the Study of the Psychology of Mrs. Piper's Trance Phenomena." PSPR 28:1, 1885. "Notes on the Evidence, Collected by the Society, for Phantasms of the Dead." PSPR 3:69; and Johnson, A., Myers, F.W.H., Podmore, F., and Sidgwick, H. 1894. "Report on the Census of Hallucinations." PSPR 10:25; and Johnson, A. 1892. "Experiments in Thought-Transference." PSPR 8:536; and Sidgwick, H. and Smith, G.A. 1890. "Experiments in Thought-Transference." PSPR 6:128.

BIBLIOGRAPHY: Gauld, A. *The Founders of Psychical Research,* 1968; Johnson, A. 1936. "Mrs. Henry Sidgwick's Work in Psychical Research." PSPR 44:53; Nicol, F. 1972. "The Founders of the S.P.R." PSPR 55:341, 350; Salter, H. de G. 1958. "Our Pioneers, I: Mrs. Henry Sidgwick." JSPR 39:235.

**Sidgwick, Henry, 1838–1900.** British classical scholar and philosopher. A founding member and first president of the **Society for Psychical Research,** his intelligence, integrity, tact, patience and the extremely high standards of evidence he insisted on were his most important contributions to psychical research.

As an undergraduate he had already shown his interest in psychical research and for a number of years studied the phenomena of Spiritualism. In 1882 Frederic W.H. Myers and Edmund Gurney agreed to join what became the Society for Psychical Research only if their mentor Henry Sidgwick would also join and become its first president. He did so and brought with him into the SPR his wife, Eleanor Sidgwick, her brothers, Arthur and Gerald Balfour, and Lord Rayleigh.

Although he was not an innovative researcher, he did take part in some investigations. His interviews with Mme Blavatsky, Henry Steel Olcott and other Theosophists in London in 1884 led to Richard Hodgson's being sent to India to investigate the phenomena purportedly taking place there. In that same year Sidgwick's investigation of ghost stories resulted in his wife's paper entitled "Phantasms of the Dead." From 1889 to 1894 he collaborated with his wife and Alice Johnson on the extremely important **Census of Hallucinations**, which made it clear that there is a correlation between death and crisis apparitions. In 1889, also, his experiments with his wife in telepathy with hypnotized subjects gave results significantly above chance. (The possibility that these results were caused by the involuntary whispering of the hypnotist was investigated and discounted.)

In 1894 he and Eleanor Sidgwick were prevailed upon to join F.W.H. Myers and Oliver Lodge in their investigation of the controversial physical medium Eusapia Palladino at Charles Richet's château on the Île Ribaud (or

Roubaud) off the coast of France. Myers, Lodge, and Richet were extremely impressed by Eusapia's phenomena. Both Sidgwicks also felt at that time that the phenomena they saw produced were genuine. They were eventually persuaded by later sittings elsewhere that Eusapia Palladino was a fraud and thus anathema.

Sidgwick believed in Leonora Piper's telepathic powers but did not think any discarnate agency was needed to explain them. Although most parapsychologists and psychical researchers admire Sigdwick, some have criticized his refusal to continue investigating anyone ever caught cheating (Eusapia Palladino was the prime example) and his ready acceptance of Hodgson's damning report on Mme Blavatsky. After his death Sidgwick was purportedly a communicator in the **Cross-Correspondences** cases.

A brilliant classical scholar and philosopher, Sidgwick was made a fellow of Trinity College, Cambridge, in 1859, a position that required its holder to be a "*bona fide* [member] of the Church of England." Like so many of his generation, however, he had lost his faith as a result of Darwin's *The Origin of Species* and so resigned his fellowship in 1869. He then became a lecturer in moral science (no religious requirements). In 1883 he became Knightsbridge Professor of Moral Philosophy. In addition to philosophy, he also lectured (despite a stammer, he was an excellent lecturer) in history at Trinity College and on Shakespeare at Newnham College, Cambridge, a women's college he helped found. He was in addition deeply interested in religion, theology, morals, and ethics (his *Methods of Ethics* [1874] is considered one of the most important nineteenth century works), politics and political economy.

Selected Writings: 1896. "Involuntary Whispering Considered in Relation to Experiments in Thought-Transference." PSPR 12:298; and Johnson, A., Myers, F.W.H., Podmore, F., and Sidgwick, E.M. 1894. "Report on the Census of Hallucinations." PSPR 10:25; and Sigdwick, E.M. and Smith, G.A. 1890. "Experiments in Thought-Transference." PSPR 6:128.

BIBLIOGRAPHY: Broad, C.D. 1959. "Our Pioneers, VI: Henry Sidgwick." JSPR 40:103; Gauld, A. *The Founders of Psychical Research,* 1968; "Report of the Committee Appointed to Investigate Phenomena Connected with the Theosophical Society." 1885. PSPR 3:20.

**Significance.** A numerical result is significant when it equals or surpasses some criterion of degree of chance improbability. The criterion commonly used in parapsychology today is a probability value of .02 (odds of 50 to 1 against chance) or less, or a deviation in either direction such that the CR is 2.33 or greater. Odds of 20 to 1 (probability of .05) are regarded as strongly suggestive (JP).

**Silva Mind Control.** A world wide program that aims to develop, among other things, paranormal powers. Using sound, relaxation procedures, and light **Hypnosis,** the program purports to train participants to achieve their own special mental states, that is, more profound "levels of mind" or "levels of awareness," that will release and improve the ability to learn and to control some bodily functions and will increase psychic abilities, particularly the ability to make psychic diagnoses. Silva Mind Control students who graduate from the course are given the name, sex, and age of a stranger, asked to experience that person's deeper states of mind and then to make a "diagnostic reading" of the physical problems the stranger is having.

Because these readings have been reported to be highly successful, parapsychologists, always on the lookout for methods that will develop and strengthen the manifestation of extrasensory perception, have conducted controlled experiments with ten Silva Mind Control graduates. Fifty patients were selected from the files of a surgeon who had made full diagnoses of their disorders. Each subject was given an envelope containing the name, age, and sex of five patients. After the subjects had reached their particular levels of mind, they were asked to make diagnostic readings and to note on anatomical charts the locations of the patients's disorders. After the experiments were concluded, the main finding was that the Silva Mind Control graduates "showed no evidence of ESP in diagnostic readings" (Brier, Schmeidler, Savitz, 1975:270).

The parapsychologists concluded that the strikingly successful diagnostic readings were the results of cues given the graduates that influenced their correct diagnoses. In spite of this negative finding, however, people who have been trained in Silva Mind Control feel that their training has been "the main thing in allowing psi to emerge" (Roney-Dougal, 1984:381).

BIBLIOGRAPHY: Brier, B., Schmeidler, G.R., Savitz, B. 1975. "Three Experiments in Clairvoyant Diagnosis with Silva Mind Control Graduates." JASPR 69:263; Roney-Dougal, S. 1984. "'Occult' Conference Questionnaire." JSPR 52:379.

**Sinclair, Mary.** See **Sinclair Upton.**

**Sinclair, Nancy.** See **Johnson, Gertrude M.**

**Sinclair, Upton (Beall), 1878–1968.** American novelist and polemicist. Although his first published article appeared in a Theosophical magazine, he is best known for his "muckraking" novel *The Jungle,* his first success, published in 1906. Sinclair, a Socialist, had intended in the book to arouse sympathy for the workers in the meat-packing industry but instead aroused indignation at the quality of meat being passed off on the public. "I aimed at the public's heart," said Sinclair, "and by accident I hit it in the stomach."

Sinclair was always fascinated by ghosts and other strange happenings, read Edmund Gurney's *Phantasms of the Living* and was interested in Walter Franklin Prince's work. Martin Gardner (1957) considered him "a gullible victim of mediums and psychics" (p. 310).

His most important contribution to parapsychology and psychical research was his publication of *Mental Radio* (1930). In the book 290 tests of telepathy and clairvoyance with his second wife, writer Mary Craig Kimborough (died 1961), were described. In it Mary explained her technique for receiving clairvoyant impressions of drawings: "First . . . learn the trick of undivided concentration. . . .' Let go' of every tense muscle. . . . Then visualize . . . some pleasant . . . thing . . . Make the mind a complete blank. . . . Hold [the drawing] over your solar plexus. . . . Just wait expectantly and let something come. . ." William McDougall wrote the introduction to the English edition (Albert Einstein, a friend, wrote a kindly introduction to the German edition). The book received a good review in the *London Times.* But Martin Gardner called it "a highly unsatisfactory account of conditions surrounding the clairvoyance tests [because Sinclair was] exceedingly naive about the safeguards necessary to insure a controlled experiment" (pp. 310–311).

At one time, when Sinclair was writing in great detail about a fire, he heard the cry "Fire!" and looked out his window to see a cottage in flames. He was never sure whether the fire was merely a coincidence, a case of telepathy or clairvoyance, or even one of psychokinesis.

In 1934 Sinclair ran for governor of California (he lost) and in the 1940s won the Pulitzer Prize. He published thirteen plays and eighty-odd books translated into forty languages. He considered his being able to increase public interest in psychic phenomena one of his ten outstanding achievements.

Selected Writings: *Mental Radio,* 1930.

BIBLIOGRAPHY: "Book Notice." 1930. *Psychic Research* (JASPR) 34(9):426; Ebon, M. "Upton Sinclair's 'Mental Radio." In *They Knew the Unknown,* 1971, pp. 222-229; Gardner, M. *Fads and Fallacies in the Name of Science,* 1957; Price, H. "International Notes." *Psychic Research* (JASPR) 34(9):427-428; "Sinclair, Upton (Beall)." *New Encyclopaedia Britannica,* 1986.

**Singles Test.** A technique used in psychokinesis tests in which the aim of the subject is to try to influence a die to fall with a specified face up.

**Sitter.** An individual who has a séance or session with a physical or mental medium. See also **Absent Sitter.**

**Sitting.** A séance or session generally consisting of a medium and one or more sitters attempting to make contact with a communicator.

**Sixth Sense.** Used by the early French psychical researcher and particularly by **Charles Richet** as the title of a book, it is a popular term signifying some unknown physical sense with the power of clairvoyance and telepathy. But the term is contradictory. It implies the existence and function of a hidden human sense. But, by definition, through clairvoyance and telepathy knowledge is obtained without the use of any sensory organ. Moreover, no physiological locus in the human body for paranormal powers has ever been found so the supposition of some unknown organ with these powers is highly suspect.

**Skeptical Inquirer (originally The Zetetic).** Published quarterly in the United States, it is the official organ of the **Committee for the Scientific Investigation of Claims of the Paranormal.** It is a hard-line skeptical journal. Those sympathetic to parapsychology and psychical research label its articles on those subjects biased, unfair, emotional, misinformed, or uninformed. The publication with a circulation about ten times that of the pro-parapsychology publications combined (i.e., the *Journal of the American Society for Psychical Research* and the *Journal of Parapsychology*), presents criticisms of parapsychology and psychical research and denials of their claims. The *Skeptical Inquirer* with its large readership exerts considerable influence. Editor: Kendrick Frazier. See also **Sceptics.**

**Slade, Henry, ?–1905.** American medium. Greatest exponent of **Slate-Writing** in the history of Spiritualism. "Dr." Slade performed before the crowned heads of Europe and the uncrowned people of the United States and left them all gaping in astonishment at the inspiring spirit messages contained between the pair of slates he held. Professor Johann Zöllner, who investigated him, was convinced of the genuineness of his powers. So was Sir William Barrett who had many sittings with Slade. Barrett said that he "obtained what was alleged to be direct spirit writing on my own marked slate, in full daylight, and under conditions which certainly rendered any explanation of fraud or malobservation difficult to conceive. I believe Slade had genuine super-normal powers" (Barrett 1918:84).

But, with the exception of the Zöllner and Barrett investigations, Slade's reputation is stained with many reports or suspicions of outright fraud. The Seybert Commission, which had several sittings with him, detected him substituting slates surreptitiously and writing on slates beforehand while he scratched the undersides of slates to give off the sound of spirits writing. When Slade visited England in 1876, Eleanor Sidgwick conducted ten slate-writing séances with him. "The impression on my mind," she wrote, "is that the phenomena are produced by tricks" (Sidgwick, 1886:56). While in England, Slade also gave two sittings to a Professor Edwin Ray Lankester who, like the Seybert Commission, also discovered the medium writing a spirit message on a slate before the sitting. In October 1870, Lankester brought a notorious suit against Slade in which he charged Slade with fraudulently obtaining money from him. Slade was defended by Charles C. Massey and, although many famous witnesses appeared for the defense, including Alfred R. Wallace, Slade was convicted and sentenced to three months at hard labor.

It is curious that Slade should have been willing to give sittings to trained investigators, such as Zöllner, Barrett, the Seybert Commission, and Mrs.Sidgwick, and to risk a reputation that was already secure. Either he believed that he had real powers or he was so confident in his own skill at trickery that he felt he could easily deceive even experienced investigators. Since, like many other professional mediums, he seems to have resorted to trickery on occasion, this fact makes highly suspect all the phenomena he produced.

BIBLIOGRAPHY: Barrett, W.F. *On the Threshold of the Unseen*, 1918; Sidgwick, E. 1886. "Results of a Personal Investigation into the Physical Phenomena of Spiritualism. With Some Critical Remarks on the Evidence for the Genuineness of Such Phenomena." PSPR 4:45.

**Slate-Writing.** A phenomenon of independent writing on slate occurring in the presence of a physical medium during a séance or sitting and supposed to demonstrate that the spirits of deceased persons have sent messages in their own writing. In a typical séance or sitting of this kind, a sitter writes a note to a named spirit. The note is placed on the table and a slate pencil is placed between a pair of slates. When the medium believes that the moment has arrived for the spirit to whom the note is addressed to respond, the medium and the sitter take hold of the ends of the slates and sometimes hear the writing as it proceeds. When the slates are taken apart, the writing on the inside of one or both slates may be recognized by the sitter as that of the named deceased person.

While slate-writing has persuaded many sitters, especially when the characteristics of the writing seem without doubt to identify a dead relative, investigators have found the evidence generally unconvincing. The phenomenon has been attributed to fraud and trick mechanisms, and, indeed, Henry Slade and P.L.O.A. Keeler, both American slate-writing mediums with enormous reputations, were exposed as frauds time and time again. On the other hand, William Eglinton, the British counterpart of the Americans, was never caught fraudulently producing slate-writing. In his case, and in the cases of other slate-writing mediums not caught cheating, the phenomenon has been attributed either to clever conjuring or, from the work of Richard Hodgson and S.J. Davey, to lapse of memory or malobservation on the part of sitters and witnesses.

BIBLIOGRAPHY: Hyslop, J.H. 1921. "A Survey of American Slate-Writing Mediumship." PSPR 15:315; Hodgson, R. and Davey, S.J. 1887. "The Possibilities of Malobservation and Lapse of Memory." PSPR 4:381.

**Smith, H. Arthur, 1848–1922.** British lawyer, businessman, and administrator. Of deep religious convictions and strongly conservative, Smith had a life long interest in psychical research. He believed that the work of the Society for Psychical Research had made telepathy a household word. As a lawyer, however, he was particularly concerned with the evidence that investigations developed. He was accordingly not convinced of the source of messages allegedly from the dead (because of the problem of personal identity) although he felt that Alice Johnson's report on Mrs. Holland was a great step forward in that direction. He was president of the SPR in 1910 and made valuable contributions to its *Journal* and *Proceedings.*

He enjoyed cricket and played both the violin and the clarinet. His professional writings included *The Principles of Equity* and the *Married Women's Property Acts.*

Selected Writings: 1910. "Presidential Address." PSPR 24:330.

BIBLIOGRAPHY: Barrett, W. 1922. "Obituary Notices. I. H. Arthur Smith." JSPR 20:353; Johnson, A. 1908. "On the Automatic Writing of Mrs. Holland." PSPR 21:166.

**Smith, Helene (Catherine Elise Muller), 1861–1929.** Swiss medium. She became the celebrated focus of a prolonged and classic study by Theodore Flournoy who gained admittance to her circle in Geneva. In the course of her mediumship with him, as her own normal personality disappeared, she gave impressive dramatizations of lifelike personalities including that of a Hindu princess, claimed to be in communication with the spirits of famous deceased people, such as Marie Antoinette, and wrote in Sanskrit. Her most spectacular personality was the "Man from Mars" who described conditions on that planet and spoke in an incomprehensible language described as a Martian dialect.

The medium's powers might have been ranked as among the greatest in the history of psychical research were it not for Flournoy's findings that her strange languages had normal explanations and that her memories of past lives and spirit communications were mere fantasies from childhood, perhaps as an escape from an ordinary and unexciting life in Geneva.

BIBLIOGRAPHY: Flournoy, T. *From India to the Planet Mars,* 1901.

**Smith, Mary Justa.** Contemporary American Franciscan nun and educator at Rosary Hill College. She conducted important studies of the healer Oskar Estebany. She wanted to see if his method of laying-on-of-hands could affect the biological activity of the enzyme trypsin. She found that the activity in samples of trypsin solution he handled showed 15 percent more enzyme activity than the solution in test tubes he did not hold (Smith, 1968). This statistically significant difference suggests some paranormal effect produced by the healer.

Selected Writings: 1968. "Paranormal Effect on Enzyme Activity." *Proceedings of the Parapsychological Association* 5:15.

**Smith, Susy (Ethel), 1911–.** American writer. "My psychical research just kind of happened to me," Susy Smith wrote (1971:13). In 1955 she was a materialistic agnostic. Then, after reading Stewart Edward White's *The Unobstructed Universe* and *With Folded Wings,* she had a strong feeling of her dead mother's presence and decided to try to communicate with her. After using the ouija board, she began automatic writing and eventually automatic typewriting which, she became convinced, were produced by spirits communicating through her.

In an attempt to learn more about parapsychology she went to J.B. Rhine's Parapsychology Laboratory at Duke University but found that his statistical approach to ESP was not her cup of tea. She also learned there that both J.B. and Louisa Rhine were convinced that automatic writing was the product of the automatist's subconscious mind. Hornell Hart, however, who at that time was a professor of sociology at Duke University, did believe in survival and the possibility of spirit communication. He helped her understand physical and emotional problems she was having that some psychics had suggested were caused by malicious spirits.

Susy Smith has written widely on psychical research, most of it intended for the general reader. She gained recognition among researchers as well by her abridged and edited edition of F.W.H. Myers's *Human Personality and its Survival of Bodily Death* (1961-1903) for which Aldous Huxley wrote the Preface. Her *Mediumship of Mrs. Leonard* (1964) has been praised as a "well-documented account of the life and work of one of England's most gifted mediums . . ." (White 1977:914).

In 1971 Susy Smith founded the **Survival Research Foundation** whose purpose is the investigation of the possibility of the survival of human consciousness after bodily death.

**Selected Writings:** *Confessions of a Psychic,* 1971; *The Mediumship of Mrs. Leonard,* 1964.

BIBLIOGRAPHY: Myers, F.W.H. (Abridged and edited by S. Smith) *Human Personality and its Survival of Bodily Death,* 1961. (Originally published 1903, 2 vols.); White R.A. "Suggested Readings in Parapsychology." In B.B. Wolman, ed., *Handbook of Parapsychology,* 1977.

**Smythies, John Raymond, 1922–.** British psychiatrist and neurophysiologist now living in the United States. In 1951 Dr. (then Mr.) Smythies had already concluded that the "mind is able to abstract information from its present and future environment without the use of any of the recognized channels of sense" (Smythies, 1951:477) and was trying to give a theoretical basis for psi phenomena and their relationship to natural science.

The controversial theory that he began to work out then culminated in his essay (1967) based on non-Cartesian dualism. "Non-Cartesian dualism suggests that the world consists of the physical universe extended in physical space and a number of substantive minds extended each in a space of its own . . ., a *different* space from that of the physical world. . . . In this [multiple space theory] we postulate that the total human organism is extended in an *n*-dimensional space. . . . One section of this space contains his physical body and brain. The other contains his sense-data, images, etc. . . . The two may be linked by channels of information . . ." (Smythies, 1967:6-7). Dr. Smythies feels that this theory can not only explain ESP but possibly precognition as well. All we need to do is "suppose that the 'penumbra' of [the channel of information] (that we supposed might extend into the physical world outside the brain to account for telepathy and clairvoyance) extends [along the time axis of our multiple space] into the 'future' (Smythies, 1967:14).

Dr. Smythies received his B.A., M.B., B.Chir. (surgery), and M.D. in neuroanatomy, and M.Sc. in psychology from Cambridge University and a further M.Sc. in neuroanatomy, philosophy and anthropology from the University of British Columbia. A member of many learned societies, he is a Fellow of the Royal College of Psychiatrists, of the Royal College of Physicians, and of the American Psychiatric Association, and is a member of the American College of Neuropsychopharmacology.

Dr. Smythies is currently C.B. Ireland professor of psychiatric research, professor of biochemistry, at the University of Alabama at Birmingham and is senior vice-chairman of the external and international programs of the university's Department of Psychiatry and a member of its neuropsychiatry research program. He has been co-editor of the *International Review of Neurobiology* since 1958 and is on the editorial boards of *Psychopharmacologia, The British Journal of Psychiatry, Neuropsychobiology,* the *Journal of Neuroscience Research,* the *Journal of Receptor Research, Drug and Alcohol Abuse Research,* and *Psychological Medicine.* Since 1987 he has been president of the International Medical Administration Consultants.

Selected Writings: 1951. "The Extension of Mind: A New Theoretical Basis for Psi Phenomena." JSPR 36:477, "Is ESP Possible?" In J.R. Smythies, ed., *Science and ESP,* 1967.

**Soal, Samuel George, 1889–1975.** British mathematician and parapsychologist. His interest in psychical research began with his reading of Sir Oliver Lodge's book *Raymond,* which described communications through mediums from Lodge's son killed in World War I.

Soal himself began sitting with mediums and eventually sat for a prolonged period with Mrs. Blanche Cooper who produced the famous Gordon Davis communications. Davis, whom Soal believed to be dead but who turned out to be very much alive, supposedly communicated and gave a great deal of interesting information, some of which seemed to be precognitive. It has been said, however, that Mrs. Cooper spoke so softly and mumbled so indistinctly that no one except Soal was ever able to understand anything she was saying. And since Soal was given to altered states of consciousness and automatic writing, some of which was published in the *Proceedings of the Society for Psychical Research* under the pseudonym "Mr. V.," it was possible that he was the source of any veridical information supplied.

Soal was awarded a D.Sc. in 1945 by London University for his research work in parapsychology. During the years 1934-1939 he had tried unsuccessfully to replicate J.B. Rhine's card-guessing experiments. He was therefore extremely critical of Rhine's work until Whately Carington urged him to look for displacement in his results. And so Soal discovered his famous subject **Basil Shackleton** with whom he carried on from 1941 to 1943 his phenomenally successful experiments. Mrs. K.M. Goldney acted as co-experimenter. The controls in this series of experiments were supposed to be so rigorous and the precautions against every possible source of error so elaborate that parapsychologists agreed with Whately Carington who wrote (1945): "If I had to choose one single investigation on which to pin my whole faith in the reality of paranormal phenomena . . . I should unhesitatingly choose this series of experiments . . .".

As early as 1949, however, critics began to suggest that the only explanation for the remarkable results achieved by Shackleton had to be fraud—either collusion (G.R. Price) or substitution of cards (C.E.M. Hansel) or alteration of scores by Soal (Gretl Albert). Heated arguments continued over the years. In 1971 Dr. R.G. Medhurst made Mrs. Albert's accusations public and showed that there was some evidence in the scoring to support her. He also tried, in an attempt to exonerate Soal, to "reconstruct the target sequences using a computer in order to demonstrate that they were free from manipulation . . . but in every case the computer search failed" (Markwick, 1985:295).

The controversy continued to rage in the 1970s (the subject himself died in 1975), but it took Betty Markwick (1978; 1985) to show that manipulation of data had definitely taken place, perhaps after some initial genuine results. Renée Haynes, unconvinced, protested (1982) that "this lifelong investigator was tried by computer and found guilty of fraud."

Whether or not the fraud was intentional has been questioned. R.A. McConnell (1983:216) writes that Soal's was probably a case of multiple personality. But what is clear is that "manipulation has been etablished in some sections of the Soal-Shackleton data. . . . Of course manipulation established in any part of the data renders the whole evidentially worthless" (Markwick, 1985:305) and casts a shadow over Soal's entire career.

Selected Writings: 1925. "A Report on Some Communications Received through Mrs. Blanche Cooper." PSPR 35:471; and F. Bateman. *Modern Experiments in Telepathy,* 1954; and K.M. Goldney, 1943. "Experiments in Precognitive Telepathy." PSPR 47:21.

BIBLIOGRAPHY: Carington, W. *Telepathy,* 1945; Goldney, K. M. 1975. "Obituary Dr. S. G. Soal, M.A., D.Sc." JSPR 48:95; Haynes, R. *The Society for Psychical Research, 1882-1982,* 1982; McConnell, R.A. *An Introduction to Parapsychology in the Context of Science,* 1983; Markwick, B. 1978. "The Soal-Goldney Experiments with Basil Shackleton; New Evidence of Data Manipulation." PSPR 56:250; Markwick, B. "The Establishment of Data Manipulation in the Soal-Shackleton Experiments." In P. Kurz, ed., *A Skeptic's Handbook of Parapsychology,* 1985.

**Sociedad Española de Parapsicología (Spanish Parapsychological Society).** Created in 1973, this Spanish organization is the only one of several parapsychological groups to survive. It has become the most important center in Spain with a membership of about 2,500 and it monopolizes parapsychological activity there. It enjoys not only public recognition but that of universities which, under the auspices of the society, have given courses and degrees in parapsychology. Apart from its educational objective, the society does research in the field and laboratory. Its teams of researchers are the sources to which the media turn for information about the paranormal. Its publication is *Psi Comunicación.* Address: Belen 15 - 1 Derecha, 28004, Madrid, Spain.

**Sociedad Mexicana de Parapsicología (Mexican Parapsychological Society).** The only internationally respected parapsychological organization in Mexico. It performs services for the Catholic church in cases of alleged diabolical possession. Through the offices of the Catholic Archdiocese in Mexico City, people claiming to be so possessed are sent to the society for investigation, evaluation, and reports by parapsychologists, psychologists and psychiatrists.

The society was established in 1974 by Carlos Treviño B. and Marcela G. de Treviño at a time when there was on the rise in Mexico a variety of schemes to defraud the general public invented by self appointed "parapsychologists" and "psychics" reading coffee cups, performing *limpias* (a type of cleansing with herbs), or practicing witchcraft in many forms. The society also encountered resistance from the scientific community.

The goals of the organization are to fight trickery, public naïveté, and scientific hostility. To achieve these goals, the society carries out a broad program of education through lectures and courses in parapsychology, psychology, and the tricks of magicians and theatrical performers. In 1984, for example, at Centro Universitario México in Mexico City, it held its first symposium on parapsychology in which both Mexican and foreign parapsychologists participated. The address of the organization is Apartado 12-699, 03000 Mexico D. F., Mexico.

**Società Italiàna di Parapsicología (Italian Society of Parapsychology).** Italian organization founded in Milan in 1946 originally under the name "Associazióne di Metapsíchica" (Association of Metapsychics). Its activity is limited to providing an annual series of lectures on parapsychology and psychical research and the publication of a journal, *Rasségna Italiàna di Ricérca Psíchica* (Italian Journal of Psychic Research). The organization conducts no investigations or experimental research. Address: Via dei Montecatini 7, Rome, Italy.

**Society for Psychical Research (SPR).** Tales of haunts, ghosts, and of people who possess ways of knowing without using the five senses have been circulated since ancient times. But never were they studied objectively and scientifically to find out whether or not at the bottom of the tales were genuine phenomena.

In the mid-nineteenth century a "ghost society" was organized at Cambridge, England, to make some sporadic studies of this kind. But it was not until the Society for Psychical Research was organized in London in 1882 that critical and sustained investigation began. It was organized by eminent scholars and scientists among whom were Sir William F. Barrett, Henry Sidgwick, Frederic W. H. Myers and Edmund Gurney. Sidgwick became the SPR's first president, Barrett one of its vice presidents. Myers and Gurney served on the SPR's first council. The SPR commenced its work by classifying its subjects into several classes: telepathy, hypnotism, Reichenbach's phenomena, apparitions, haunts, and the physical phenomena of Spiritualism such as table-tilting and materializations.

The course of the SPR has not always been smooth. In the late 1920s, just as in its American cousin, the American Society for Psychical Research, a rift developed between the believers in physical phenomena (often Spiritualists) and the sceptics. Many of the former, including Sir Arthur Conan Doyle, left the SPR, but it survived.

Today, it continues its investigations into all types of paranormal phenomena, including telepathy, clairvoyance, precognition, retrocognition, psychometry, dowsing, apparitions, and survival. Its purpose, as stated in every issue of its *Journal,* is "to examine without prejudice or prepossession and in a scientific spirit those faculties of man, real or supposed, which appear to be inexplicable on any generally recognized hypothesis." In addition to the *Journal,* the SPR publishes *Proceedings.*

Of enormous value to researchers and archivists are the SPR's vast collections of papers left by great investigators: Sir William F. Barrett, Anita Gregory, Sir Oliver Lodge, Frederic W. H. Myers, William H. Salter, Samuel G. Soal, D. J. West. There are also the records of the great mediums Leonora E. Piper and Gladys Osborne Leonard. In addition, the SPR's library of parapsychological literature is one of the most complete in the world. The SPR is located at 1 Adam and Eve Mews, London W8 6UG.

**Society for Psychic Research.** Not to be confused with the Society for Psychical Research in England, this now defunct (since 1985) Spiritualist-oriented organization was founded in Australia in 1933 to carry out the primary object of **Spiritualism**—to prove that the human personality survives biological death. Its occasional reports of sporadic investigations produced nothing approaching proof but, in the course of about fifty years, it stimulated public interest in psychical research and succeeded in assembling an extensive library on psychical research and Spiritualism. In its latter years, the organization operated as a center for the development of personal growth and as a referral agency for mediums.

**Society for Scientific Exploration.** Founded in 1982 in the United States, it is an organization of scholars and scientists with doctoral degrees, several of whom are members of the National Academy of Sciences. It provides a forum for the open and critical discussion of anomalous phenomena, including parapsychology and psychical research, that are outside the mainstream of science. By discussing research on such phenomena, one of its aims is to advance the education of those in the mainstream of science. The organization publishes the *Journal of Scientific Exploration.* Address: c/o Peter A. Sturrock, Center for Space Science & Astrophysics, Stanford University, Stanford, CA 94305.

**Socrates, 469–399 B.C..** Athenian philosopher who taught philosophy without charge to the young and who was condemned to death as an impious subversive evildoer who corrupted the young. He was ugly, paunchy and snub-nosed but, as Plato pictured him for us, an extraordinary man of genius. He is also a **Noted Witness** for many aspects of the paranormal. He could have been a medium who received messages from a communicator or he could have had a guide or have been a psychic who received information by extrasensory perception. It all depends on how we interpret the source of the voice that, from early childhood, Socrates heard repeatedly.

He himself said in the *Phaedrus*: "I seemed to hear a voice." He could never be sure whether the voice was an actual one that came to him from an invisible source external to him—in which case his classification as a medium or psychic would be justified—or whether it was a monition, a voice that dwelt within him and came into his consciousness from a deep zone of his being. In the latter case, it would have been his personal daemon or guardian angel. In any case, it was a voice that he looked on as right and sure and that conveyed to him information generally to restrain him from some action he planned to take. If the voice did not speak to him, the action was approved.

In the *Phaedrus,* he said: "I am a prophet," and, if the report is correct, in the *Theages* he gave some evidence of precognition when he warned Timarchus not to leave the dinner table. The man rose a second time and again Socrates warned him. The third time, however, when Socrates' attention was diverted, Timarchus left and was slain by an assassin.

**Somerville, Edith Oenone, 1858–1949.** Irish writer. Her fourteen novels painted vivid and humorous pictures of life in Ireland in the nineteenth century. In collaboration with her cousin, Violet F. Martin (pseudonym "Martin Ross") she wrote *The Real Charlotte* (1894) and *Some Experiences of an Irish R. M.* (1899). After Martin died in 1915, Miss Somerville went on writing and all her books continued to show Martin Ross as co-author.

In her *Wheeltracks* (1923), Somerville explained: "In 1917, *Irish Memories* was published, and I told Constance (a cousin) what seemed incredible to some, and is to me the most natural thing in the world—that Martin's mind, blended with mine, no less now than in the past, has aided and made suggestions, taking, as ever, full share—and sometimes, I dare say, more than full share—in the task in hand. . .". Her conviction that Martin Ross's hand even after death still guided her pen makes Edith Somerville a **Noted Witness** for a communicator and for the creative process.

BIBLIOGRAPHY: Gibbes, E. G. 1939. "Influenced or Inspirational Writing." JASPR 33:270.

**Sorcerer.** One who uses magic for evil purposes; a practitioner of black magic.

**SORRAT (Society for Research on Rap-**

**port and Telekinesis).** A series of experiments in psychokinesis was begun in 1961 by John G. Neihardt—poet, expert in Indian history and culture, and professor at the University of Missouri—at Neihardt's nearby home, Skyrim Farm, and, eventually, at other locations as well. The purpose of the experiments was to try to manipulate matter by conscious mental effort (mind over matter).

The first of the series of experiments took place in 1961. Experimenters sat around a wooden table, their hands touching the surface of the table and their little fingers touching those of the people on either side. The first phenomenon, raps, took place on November 17, 1961, and thereafter vibrations and movements of the table began. In February 1966 Neihardt began receiving by way of the raps—one for yes, two for no—answers to questions and shortly after that levitations and "walking" of the table began. On one occasion Dr. Neihardt's chair was levitated with him in it and other objects were levitated. Apports were reported. At times some of the experimenters would go into trance and would receive messages from a variety of entities and a "composite entity" known as "Many Voices." Automatic writing sometimes took place.

In 1966 J. B. Rhine suggested to Neihardt the use of transparent boxes in which target objects could be locked. Movements of objects were observed. In 1969 W. E. Cox of Rhine's Foundation for Research on the Nature of Man became interested in the SORRAT experiments and, as a result, moved to Rolla, Missouri, in 1977. In 1979 the McDonnell Laboratory for Psychical Research funded Cox's experiments. Beginning in 1977 experiments revolved around a "mini-lab" of Cox's construction, a 5.5 gallon aquarium tank secured to a wooden platform, locked and sealed and further secured by heavy duty steel bands.

Various phenomena—movement of objects, writing of messages, interlocking of rings—have been filmed taking place in the "mini-lab," yet psychical researchers and parapsychologists in general (Cox who continues with the experiments is the exception) seem to feel that there is no evidence that anything paranormal has been taking place. Attempts at replication failed (Phillips and McBeath, 1983). Moreover, the film is activated only once movement has begun (so that it is never possible to see the beginning of the phenomenon) and the area filmed does not show the surroundings of the mini-lab (so that it is impossible to know if there is a natural explanation for the phenomenon). Indeed, a cruel parody of the SORRAT films was shown at the joint 1982 Parapsychological Association–Society for Psychical Research conference in Cambridge, England, whose serious object was to show that films of the SORRAT type can be faked.

In addition, letters have supposedly been "apported" and sent through the mail. One wonders why, if the phenomenon is genuine, the letters could not have been apported directly to the addressees. Too, a report that ESP cards had sorted themselves into suits was the subject of an unsuccessful experiment (Hansen and Broughton, 1983) and is reportedly only one of many failed tests.

Whether or not any or all of the phenomena reported are genuine, Neihardt's stated objective, "the controlled movement of selected target objects by conscious mental effort[,]" has not been realized.

BIBLIOGRAPHY: Cook, E. W. 1983. *"SORRAT: A History of the Neihardt Psychokinesis Experiments, 1961–1981."* JASPR 77:92; Cox, W. E. "Selected Static–PK Phenomena under Exceptional Conditions of Security." In R. A. White and Broughton, R. S., eds., *Research in Parapsychology, 1983,* 1984, pp. 107–110; Hansen, G. P. and Broughton, R. S. "An Investigation of Macro–PK: The SORRAT." In W. G. Roll, J. Beloff, and R. A. White, eds., *Research in Parapsychology, 1982,* 1983, pp. 115–116; Phillips, P. R. and McBeath, M. K. "An Attempted Replication of the Cox Films of PK." In W. G. Roll, J. Beloff, and R. A. White, eds., *Research in Parapsychology, 1982,* 1983, pp. 113–115; Richards, J. T. *SORRAT: A History of the Neihardt Psychokinesis Experiments, 1961–1981,* 1982.

**Soule, Minnie Meserve.** See **Mrs. Chenoweth.**

**South African Institute for Parapsychological Research.** Formed in 1968 by the South African Society for Psychical Research primarily to investigate all areas of parapsychology. It was also open to the public as a membership organization and thrived a few years until the dwindling support and finances caused the promising venture to fail.

**South African Society for Psychical Research.** Established in 1955 with headquarters at the University of Witwatersand, this organization was formed because great interest had been stimulated in Johannesburg by a small study group that had been set up to investigate paranormal phenomena. It followed the example of the Society for Psychical Research and aimed at the collection of information about, and the investigation of, all phenomena whether described as Spiritualistic or psychical.

Soon after the formation of the society, however, there was "dogmatic" opposition to it from "Marxists, atheists, and communists" (South African society, 1959) and the besieged society had to defend itself with a program of public education justifying itself and parapsychology in general. It managed to survive and thrive mainly because of the prestige of one of its founders, Arthur E. H. Bleksley, and became the center for parapsychology in South Africa. Functioning principally as an information channel, it formed the South African Institute for Parapsychological Research to perform investigative functions. The society in 1974 set up a branch at the University of Natal in Durban.

Unfortunately, because the participation of South African blacks has been extremely limited and the white population in South Africa is not large enough to justify a permanently functioning organization, the society holds meetings only irregularly and has no established premises. From 1957 to 1970, the society issued several publications containing essays on several aspects of parapsychology. It now publishes the *Parapsychological Journal of South Africa.* The address of the society is P. O. Box 23154, Joubert Park, Johannesburg, 2044, South Africa.

BIBLIOGRAPHY: 1959. "The South African Society for Psychical Research." JSPR 40:43.

**Space Brothers.** There have been many reports of people channeling "space brothers" or "extraterrestrials." This kind of channeling differs from "orthodox" channeling in that the entities channeled are not discarnate but are supposedly space beings from another dimension who are more spiritually and technologically evolved than we are. References to the "Confederation of Planets" or the "Intergalactic Confederation" sound like something out of *Star Trek* and the material transmitted is often highly technical and, for the present at least, unintelligible. It is interesting that information coming through different channels is remarkably similar. And it is startling that Andrija Puharich, Uri Geller and Ray Stanford, among others, have channeled "'Spectra,' . . . an 'extraterrestrial higher intelligence *from the future,*' possibly computerized"! (Klimo, 1987:56).

BIBLIOGRAPHY: Klimo, J. *Channeling,* 1987.

**Speaking in Tongues.** See **Gift of Tongues.**

**Spiegel der Parapsychologie.** Published quarterly by the Nederlandse Vereniging voor Parapsychologie, this Dutch periodical contains book reviews, notices, and experimental and theoretical papers on all aspects of parapsychology.

**Spiricom.** A word coined by **George Meek** who combined parts of the words "spirit" and "communication" to describe a device he has invented. It is supposed to be a breakthrough by means of which electronic communication with the dead without a séance or medium has been proved.

The "proof" consists of hours of two-way taped conversations in 1980 and 1981 between Dr. George Jeffrie Mueller, a physicist who died in 1967, and William J. O'Neil, the operator of the equipment. During these conversations, the dead scientist was said to have given specific instructions for dealing with electronic circuit problems with the device and for its improvement. The sceptical mind notes, however, that the conversations took place only when O'Neil was alone with the equipment. It is also curious that neither Mr. Meek nor other specialists were present when the dead Mueller was discussing electronics and supplying complicated technical instructions. On the other hand, the scientist is also said to have given details such as his social security number, where to find a copy of his death certificate, and facts concerning his academic life at Cornell University and the University of Wisconsin as well as about his jobs in government and industry. Mueller also furnished unlisted telephone numbers he requested be called. The details were verified and, after the numbers were called, there were "amazing results" (Meek, 1982a:14).

Accepting at face value the claim of evidential communications from Mueller, one must point out that, even if a spirit communication has been achieved, the aim and claim of dispensing with a medium to obtain the communication have not been. For O'Neil was not only an electronic technician. He also "had well developed clairvoyant and clairaudient capabilities. In other words, he had the ability to see and hear persons in other dimensions" (Meek, 1982a:12). So O'Neil seemed to be a medium whose powers were necessary to establish the communication with the deceased scientist. Spiricom, then, seems to consist of three basic components: a transceiver operating in the 30-130 Mhz range, a special combination of 13 audio frequencies from 21 to 701 cps, and the psychic abilities of the operator (Meek, 1982b).

Mr. Meek deliberately has not filed any patents on his device and is willing to provide a Spiricom technical manual to encourage others to replicate what he believes has been a breakthrough. A fairer offer could not be made.

BIBLIOGRAPHY: Meek, G. 1982a. "Spiricom: Electronic Communications with the 'Dearly Departed.'" *New Realities* 4(6):9; 1982b. "A Personal Statement from George W. Meek." *New Realities* 4(6):10.

**Spirit.** A word of various meanings. Generally signifying a vital principle that animates life or, in theology, the human soul, the divine influence of God in the human being, or the Holy Spirit that is one of the Trinity, in psychical research the concepts are different. For James H. Hyslop "spirit" is defined as "a stream of consciousness with its earthly memories intact" (Hyslop, 1918:115). Less specific popular thought conceives "spirit" merely as an incorporeal entity that once was incarnate and now survives in or is communicating from another reality (e.g., "spirit message," "spirit writings," "spirit possession," "spirit photography," "he is in spirit"). "Spirit" may also refer to an entity that never was incarnate, for example, some who purport to come through in channeling to make predictions or offer teachings.

BIBLIOGRAPHY: Hyslop, J. H. *Life After Death: Problems of the Future Life and its Nature,* 1918; Klimo, J. *Channeling,* 1987.

**Spirit Photography.** Photographs or "extras" of the faces or figures of people no longer alive on the same film or plate with the image of the living person who posed for the photograph. So-called "spirit photographers," such as William Mumler of Boston, Frederick A. Hudson and F. M. Parkes of London and Edouard Buguet of Paris, first flourished in the nineteenth century. Some consider spirit photographs experimental demonstrations of the objectivity of apparitions and of survival.

Fred Barlow and W. Rampling Rose, however, while not denying the possibility of genuine spirit photography, point out that in all their investigations they have never seen a spirit photograph that was not fraudulently produced. Defenders of the photographs argue that other competent observers of the whole photographic process have not detected trickery in some cases and that many spirit photographs have been taken by nonprofessional photographers experimenting for their own satisfaction with no pecuniary interest in their work.

**Spiritism.** A belief in the existence of spirits and in communicating with them through mediums. Although the term "Spiritism" is often used interchangeably with "Spiritualism," the two are not the same since the latter more correctly refers to a philosophical view that stresses mind or ideas as the only universal reality. Nevertheless, few of us distinguish between Spiritism and Spiritualism and today the latter term prevails.

Spiritism (or Spiritualism) must be distinguished, however, from the doctrine originating with **Allan Kardec** and which is widely embraced in Brazil where *Kardecismo* or his brand of Spiritism began in the late nineteenth century with the translation of Kardec's books into Portuguese. Kardecismo holds with the Spiritism (or Spiritualism) recognized outside of Brazil that the spirits of the dead live on and that the living can communicate with them through the process of mediumship. But unlike Spiritism or Spiritualism, *Kardecismo* maintains that spirits return to earth in a series of reincarnations.

**Spiritual Frontiers.** Quarterly journal published in the United States by **Spiritual Frontiers Fellowship.** It carries articles both by SFF members and others on spiritual growth, prayer, the relationship between religion and psychical research and parapsychology, and a variety of other topics ranging from reincarnation and survival to unorthodox healing, mystical experience, the shroud of Turin, and psychic phenomena in their various forms. It also contains research reports, book reviews, and correspondence. While many of the contributions lack critical analysis and must be taken with the proverbial grain of salt, others are interesting and important and evidence the constant effort of its longtime editor, Frank C. Tribbe, to maintain a high quality publication. Address: P. O. Box 7686, Philadelphia, PA 10101.

**Spiritual Frontiers Fellowship.** Organized in 1956 by clergymen and laymen active in many Christian denominations in the United States, the Spiritual Frontiers Fellowship aims at encouraging spiritual growth and at implementing, through lectures, meetings, and discussions, interest in paranormal phenomena that relate to survival, unorthodox healing, and prayer. Archivists and researchers will be pleased to learn that this organization has a large library on subjects relating to parapsychology and psychical research. The SFF publishes the journal *Spiritual Frontiers.* Its address is 10819 Winner Road, Independence, MO.

**Spiritual Healing.** See **Healing, Unorthodox.**

**Spiritualism.** A religion, system of philosophy or mode of thought based on a belief in God or an Infinite Intelligence, in the continuity of human existence and the personal identity of an individual beyond bodily death, and in a world of spirits who communicate with living people through mediums. Although it would be better to call this belief "spiritism" (not Kardecian spiritism) to distinguish it from a Spiritualist philosophy that is opposed to materialism, "Spiritualism" seems today to be the commonly accepted term.

Modern Spiritualism generally is considered native to the United States, its origin being the poltergeist phenomena that occurred in the house of the Fox Sisters in Hydesville, New York. But, in fact, the sources of Spiritualism antedate the raps at Hydesville. The philosophy of Spiritualism began with Andrew J. Davis who had a vision of Emanuel Swedenborg. Its belief in communication with the spirits of the dead began with the trance phenomena of Swedenborg who claimed to speak with the dead. The Fox Sisters, however, drew popular attention to Spiritualism after which it spread rapidly and claimed millions of adherents.

Many Spiritualists, notable among them William Barrett, gave impetus to the formation of the Society for Psychical Research, but today the majority of psychical researchers and parapsychologists consider that the Spiritualist movement has brought discredit on their fields by blurring the line between non-rigorous and rigorous experiment and between non-critical and critical conclusions.

**"Splitfoot, Mr."** Name the Fox Sisters gave to the invisible and mysterious source of **Raps** heard in their house in Hydesville, New York, on March 31, 1848. The mother of the children had just lain down to rest when rapping noises were heard in the bedroom where she, her husband, and the children slept. The children, who were in the other bed, tried to imitate the sounds by clapping their hands. Then, "My youngest child, Cathie, said: 'Mr Splitfoot, do as I do,' clapping her hands. The sound instantly followed her with the same number of raps. When she stopped, the sound ceased for a short time. Then Margaretta said, in sport, 'Now, do just as I do. Count, one, two, three, four,' striking one hand against the other at the same time; and the raps came as before." Then Mrs. Fox asked whether it was a human being that answered and there was no rap. When she asked if it was a spirit, there were two (Doyle, 1926). With Mr. Splitfoot, Spiritualism was born in the United States.

BIBLIOGRAPHY: Doyle, A. C. *The History of Spiritualism,* 1926, Vol. I, pp. 61–65.

**Spontaneous Cases.** A man dreams of an airplane crash prior to its happening. A woman is unaccountably aware of what her son is doing a thousand miles away. People sometimes have strange and unexpected experiences in everyday life that suggest they are psychic and have ways of knowing things they could not have known in any ordinary way.

Reports of such events and experiences received close attention from the early investigators of psychic phenomena and since have been received and collected by the thousands by the psychical research societies and parapsychological research centers. The largest collection of cases in the United States and perhaps in the world was accumulated at the Parapsychology Laboratory at Duke University and at its successor the Foundation for Research on the Nature of Man. Research workers, most notably Louisa E. Rhine, have studied the reports of spontaneous psi events and experiences in order to classify the kinds of phenomena they involve and to see what fresh insights and new lines of laboratory research they suggest.

**Spontaneous Psi Experiences.** See **Spontaneous Cases.**

**Spriggs, George, 1850–1912.** British physical medium. He specialized in materializations. Spriggs immigrated to Australia where he was investigated in a series of test séances arranged by William H. Terry, a Spiritualist and editor of a Spiritualist publication. In these tests, with the medium seated in a cabinet, materialized forms of different ages, appearances, and sex manifested and gave every apperance of being living beings: They touched sitters, drank water, and even ate biscuits. In several séances, the lower half of Sprigg's body was visible while a materialized form moved about so that he could not have been impersonating the "spirit." On other occasions, two or three forms were visible at the same time—and he could not have been impersonating them all at once. The forms permitted themselves to be weighed. Their weights sometimes varied by as much as 100 pounds so that again they could not all have been Spriggs.

The history of materializations is one in which physical mediums have often been caught in various kinds of fraud. So great care is needed before we can accept any evidence as conclusive. Some impressive evidence exists, for example in the cases of D. D. Home and Florence Cook. The provocative case of Spriggs may be considered in this light also.

BIBLIOGRAPHY: Donovan, W. D. C. *The Evidences of Spiritualism,* 1882.

**SRU-Bulletin.** See **Synchronicity Research Unit.**

**Stacking Effect.** In an ESP test, a similarity of preferences or habits among a group of subjects making calls for the same series of targets may cause a "stacking" effect (i.e., influence the result and exaggerate the scores).

**Stage Telepathy.** See **Mind-Reading Performance; Muscle-Reading.**

**Standard Deviation (SD).** Usually the theoretical mean square root of the deviations. It is obtained from the formula *NPQ* in which N is the number of single trials, *Q* the probability of failure (JP).

**Stanford, Ray, 1938–.** American psychic. The identical twin of psychologist and parapsychologist Dr. Rex G. Stanford with whom he often experienced spontaneous telepathy, Ray Stanford as a child recalled prior lives, including his most recent as a medical doctor named Clark. As a child he could also find lost objects, had precognitive dreams, and could see auras.

As a teenager he was fascinated with rockets and in 1955 received the Texas Academy of Science's highest award for a report entitled "Experiments with Multiple-Stage Principles of Rocketry." During this same period he saw many unidentified flying objects (UFOs), one of which was filmed.

In an example of psychic archaeology he located on a map an old Inca city that was discovered two years later. In 1960 during a group meditation he went into an ecstatic trance state in which he began channeling extraterrestrial entities that called themselves the "Brothers." One of them in 1961 materialized as a "glowing form over seven feet tall, complete with robe and metallic-like headpiece" (*Psychic,* 1974). Through the Brothers Stanford was able to make accurate medical diagnoses, prescribe treatment and give past-life readings. Some of the information that came through was precognitive.

In 1960 Stanford founded the Association for the Understanding of Man and was director of its Project Starlight International whose purpose was to construct technological systems for communication with extraterrestrial intelligences.

Mr. Stanford is no longer active in the psychic field.

BIBLIOGRAPHY: 1974. "Interview: Ray Stanford." *Psychic* 5(4):6,11.

**Stanford Research Institute.** American organization whose Electronics and Bioengineering Laboratory in Menlo Park,

California, investigates "those facets of human perception that appear to fall outside the range of well-understood perceptual or processing capabilities." To achieve this aim, SRI has conducted brain wave studies to see if paranormal functions are connected to brain functions. Experiments in telepathy, psychokinesis and remote viewing have also been carried out under controlled laboratory conditions to test the psychic abilities of many subjects, including Uri Geller and Ingo Swann. SRI is not affiliated with Stanford University.

BIBLIOGRAPHY: Targ, R. and Puthoff, H. E. *Mind-Reach: Scientists Look at Psychic Ability,* 1977.

**Stanford, Rex G., 1938–.** American psychologist and parapsychologist. Born into a psychically sensitive family (his brother Ray Stanford was for many years a practicing psychic; his mother and grandmother had had what seemed to be spontaneous ESP experiences as had he), he became interested in parapsychology during high school on hearing a paper presented by a fellow member of the Junior Section of the Texas Academy of Sciences on parapsychological research, including J. B. Rhine's. The "intellectual appeal of psi research, the evidence from experimentation (including my own), and opportunities to observe what might have been psi 'in the field' all combined to shape my interest and enthusiasm. . ." wrote Dr. Stanford in January 1986 (letter to authors).

During his undergraduate days, he visited Rhine's laboratory during several summers and, after graduation, had Summer Research Fellowships there in 1964, 1965, and 1966. After receiving his Ph.D. from the University of Texas in 1967 in Personality-Social Psychology, he held a Postdoctoral Fellowship at Rhine's Institute for Parapsychology. In 1968, Dr. Stanford conducted experimental studies of psi at the Division of Parapsychology, University of Virginia Medical School. From 1976 to 1980 he was director of the Center for Parapsychological Research in Austin, Texas. Since 1980 he has been a member of the Department of Psychology at St. John's University, and since 1983 as full tenured professor of psychology. He chose to teach at St. John's because the school was interested in having someone on the faculty with a background in parapsychology.

Dr. Stanford wrote further that "some of one's most valuable leads that need follow-up in systematic research are to be found in personal observations that may be related to psi events. The successful experimentalist will often have 'the field' as [a] teacher for the development of ideas to be tested in the laboratory." His research "which include[s] studies of the psychology of the Ganzfeld as an ESP-favorable setting . . . [is] among the most highly perceptive and respected in the field" (Berger, 1988).

Dr. Stanford wants to encourage aspiring parapsychologists to enter the field as a career and to that end has published the only general and systematic guidance in the area. He feels that the future of parapsychology depends upon parapsychologists' ability to contribute to disciplines other than their own (Stanford, 1987).

The author of numerous articles in parapsychological and other journals and of chapters in many books, he is an editorial consultant for the *Journal of the American Society for Psychical Research* and for the *Journal of Parapsychology.* He has been president of the Parapsychological Association (1973), is a member of the American Association for the Advancement of Science, of the American Psychological Association (Divisions 1, 8 and 36), and is a member of the Board of Trustees of the American Society for Psychical Research.

Selected Writings: "Ganzfeld and Hypnotic-Induction Procedures in ESP Research: Toward Understanding Their Success." In S. Krippner, ed., *Advances in Parapsychological Research 5,* 1987; "Recent Ganzfeld-ESP Research: A Survey and Critical Analysis." In S. Krippner, ed., *Advances in Parapsychological Research 4,* 1984; 1978. "Toward Reinterpreting Psi Events." JASPR 72:197; "Experimental Psychokinesis: A Review from Diverse Perspectives." and "Conceptual Frameworks of Contemporary Psi Research." In B. B. Wolman, ed., *Handbook of Parapsychology,* 1977, pp. 324–381, 823–858.

BIBLIOGRAPHY: Berger, A. S. *Lives and Letters in American Parapsychology,* 1988.

**Stanford, Thomas Welton, 1832–1918.** American businessman and benefactor. He made possible the second great stride toward recognition of psychical research by American universities after Harvard had done so in 1912 with the Hodgson Memorial Fund. He had a leaning toward Stanford University, founded in 1885 by his railroad tycoon brother, Leland, and gave it $400,000 (a huge sum in the World War I era) to create a fellowship to investigate whether communicators from the beyond and spirit messages really exist. Stanford University accepted the gift and set up the fellowship.

Thomas Stanford had become deeply interested and involved in Spiritualism after the unexpected death of his young wife in 1870. He became a zealous champion of the movement in Australia where he emigrated from the United States. It was there, in the country of the dingo and furry koala bear, that he made his fortune as the distributor of Singer sewing machines and where he encouraged and supported mediums and generally promoted the cause of Spiritualism. He helped to generate in Australia some interest in the paranormal and some spiritualistically oriented experimental séances.

Of all the mediums in Australia Charles Bailey was especially favored by Stanford's patronage. Stanford conducted séances with him for twelve years and left ten volumes of records so detailed as to make them, perhaps next to those left by James H. Hyslop, the most impressive ever prepared. These records he presented to Stanford University.

The sequel to Stanford's life was written by Stanford University and comprises one of the darker chapters in the history of American psychical research. A series of unsympathetic administrations has consistently failed to honor Stanford's wishes. John E. Coover was the first to receive a Stanford Fellowship and made a single study of telepathy in 1917. Charles E. Stuart was Thomas Walton Stanford Fellow in Psychical Research in 1942–1944. Yet officials have not supported investigations into the areas of psychical research for which the Stanford fund was created.

Selected Writing: *Psychic Phenomena: A Narrative of Facts,* 1903.

**Stanley, Sir Henry Morton, 1841–1904.** British-born explorer. It was he who spoke the famous words, "Dr. Livingstone, I presume," at the moment that he found and rescued the missionary David Livingstone in 1871 in what was then Zanzibar, East Africa.

Stanley's real name was John Rowlands. His life began in Wales, in the United Kingdom. Born out of wedlock, his mother had him baptized with his father's name. After boarding here and there, he signed up as a cabin boy on a ship that took him in 1859 to New Orleans where he was befriended and adopted by a business man named Henry Morton Stanley whose name he took. Stanley fought on the side of the Confederacy during the American Civil War. After the war ended, he enlisted in the United States Navy. He then became a journalist for several newspapers and was sent by the *New York Herald* to Ethiopia, Madrid and, finally, to search for Livingstone. The story of his discovery was published in 1872 in *How I Found Livingstone.* Queen Victoria rewarded him with a gold snuff box for his feat. After Livingstone's death in 1873, Stanley went back to Africa and, for his discovery of the Congo, was knighted in 1899.

During the Civil War Stanley was captured at the Battle of Shiloh and imprisoned at Camp Douglas not far from Chicago. It was there that he had either an out-of-body experience or a veridical telepathic or precognitive dream and is therefore entitled to be summoned to the box as a **Noted Witness.** According to Stanley: "[A]fter the morning duties had been performed, the cooks departed contented, and the quarters swept, I proceeded to my nest and reclined alongside of my friend Wilkes. . . . I made some remarks to him upon the card-playing group opposite, when, suddenly, I felt a gentle stroke on the back of my neck, and, in an instant, I was unconscious. The next moment I had a vivid view of the village of Tremeirchion, and the grassy slopes of the hills of Hirradog, and I seemed to be hovering over the rook woods of Byrnbella. I glided to the bed-chamber of my Aunt Mary. My aunt was in bed, and seemed sick unto death. I took a position by the side of the bed, and saw myself, with head bent down, listening to her parting words. . . . I put forth my hand and felt the clasp of the long, thin hands of the sore-sick woman. I heard a murmur of farewell, and immediately I woke. . . . On the next day, the 17th April, 1862, my Aunt Mary died at Fynnon Bueno [Wales]! . . . There are many things relating to my existence which are inexplicable to me, and probably it is best so; this death-bed scene, projected on my mind's screen, across four thousand five hundred miles of space, is one of these mysteries."

BIBLIOGRAPHY: Prince, W. F. *Noted Witnesses for Psychic Occurrences,* 1963, pp. 324–326.

**Stead, William Thomas, 1849–1912.** British journalist. Although he was deeply religious and looked on God as his "Senior Partner," Stead was also fervently committed to Spiritualism. In addition to his roles as manager of the *Pall Mall Gazette* and founder and editor of the monthly *Review of Reviews,* he was the publisher of *Borderland,* a Spiritualist journal. He himself was an automatist who conducted journalistic interviews (a technique he invented) with dead celebrities such as Catherine the Great and William E. Gladstone. One of Stead's chief communicators was Julia T. Ames, an American newspaperwoman, who inspired Stead to found in London in 1909 an institution for communicating with the dead. No charge was made to clients. Appropriately, it was called "Julia's Bureau."

Stead qualifies as a **Noted Witness** for precognition. In March 1903, he was at a séance when a medium predicted the assassination of the king and queen of Serbia. Although the Serbian minister in London was alerted and wrote to the king to take care, Alexander, king of Serbia, along with his queen, Draga, was murdered on June 11, 1903.

Stead had his own precognitive experiences, too. In 1880, he was editor of the *Northern Echo* in a town in the county of Durham, in northeast England. It was a position that he had no intention of surrendering. Suddenly, however, on January 1, 1880, he "knew for certain" that he would be giving up his post for a new position on the staff of a London paper. Unexpectedly, before the year was out, he had become assistant editor of the *Pall Mall Gazette* in London. Three years passed. There was no reasonable possibility of Stead's ever taking charge of the publication. Then, in October 1883, Stead wrote, "My wife and I were spending a brief holiday in the Isle of Wight. . . . One morning, about noon, we were walking in the drizzling rain. . . . Just as we were at about the ugliest part of our climb I felt distinctly, as it were, a voice within myself saying: 'You will have to look sharp and make ready, because by a certain date (which, as near as I can recollect, was 16th March of the next year), you will have sole charge of the *Pall Mall Gazette.*' . . . Mr. [John] Morley was then in full command and there was no expectation on his part of abandoning the post. . .". Nevertheless, Stead was so convinced of the truth of what the voice or personal daemon told him that he told Morley and the others on the staff what had happened. On February 24, 1884, Morley was elected to Parliament to replace a deceased member. Stead took over the *Pall Mall Gazette* just prior to the date he had recalled.

Stead was one of the passengers on the ***Titanic*** and was drowned. Yet he seemed to have had advance indications that he would go down with a vessel (although not specifically the *Titanic*). In the *Pall Mall Gazette* for 1886, there was a piece of fiction about the survivor of a shipwreck. His editorial note stated: "This is exactly what might take place if liners were sent to sea short of boats." (The great loss of life on the *Titanic* resulted from a shortage of lifeboats.) Six years after the *Pall Mall* article, Stead wrote a story published in 1892 in the *Review of Reviews* in which he talked of the threat of icebergs in the Atlantic and of an ocean liner that went down after colliding with one (just as the *Titanic* did). In that story, there was a fictitious vessel named the *Majestic.* In reality, there was a ship called *Majestic.* Her captain became the captain of the *Titanic* and drowned when she went down. Three years before the disaster, Stead gave a lecture to the Society for Psychical Research in which, to make a point, he presented himself to his audience as shipwrecked and crying out for help. Stead's references and imaginative and fictionalized pictures that so resembled the sinking of the *Titanic* might have been true forewarnings since the disaster could not have been anticipated or inferred.

BIBLIOGRAPHY: Brandon, R. *The Spiritualists,* 1983, pp. 190–205; "Note on the Alleged Prediction of the Servian Murders." 1903. JSPR 11:132; Prince, W. F. *Noted Witnesses for Psychic Occurrences,* 1963, pp. 224–226.

**Steiner, Rudolf, 1861–1925.** Austrian academic, philosopher, and founder of the Anthroposophical Society. Steiner was an avid admirer and student of the poet **Johann W. von Goethe** and spent seven years editing his writings. In 1894, Steiner published *The Philosophy of Freedom* and *The Philosophy of Spiritual Activity* and three years later settled in Berlin as the editor of a literary magazine and lecturer at a worker's college. He married but the marriage failed. For a while he found satisfaction in the arms of Theosophy because it seemed to him the closest expression of spiritual life. But soon his romance with it failed also as he began to formulate his own philosophy and teachings.

Steiner broke with the Theosophical Society and, in 1912, founded the Anthroposophical Society, and in the subsequent year designed and built the Goetheanum in Dornach, Switzerland, which was to be a school teaching and practicing through cultural and educational activities what he called a "spiritual science." Its aim is to show that "man can experience in his inner being in various ways how his spirit-eternal nature exists in relation to the spirit-eternal nature of the outer world, and that the great harmony between the human individuality and the universe is actually present in the human soul" (Steiner, 1971:62).

Among the ways of making spiritual science a certainty and of becoming conscious of and taking hold of the higher, spiritual world is something akin to a mystical experience—realizing that we have a spirit-eternal nature, becoming a spiritual being and making ourselves empty vessels into which the higher world flows. Another way of more direct interest to psychical research is "what may be called direct intercourse with beings of the spiritual world. . . Actual intercourse with an individual who has died is possible. . . Today men think: When a human being has passed through the gate of death, his activity ceases as far as the physical world is concerned. But indeed it is not so! There is a living and perpetual intercourse between the so-called [*sic*] Dead and the so-called Living. Those who have passed through the gate of death have not ceased to be present; it is only that our eyes have ceased to see them. They are there in very truth" (Steiner, 1973:12, 28).

Steiner's break with Theosophy did not signify that he had abandoned all its teachings in favor of his own. He retained, supported, and developed in his own way the ideas of reincarnation and karma. "It can truly be said that there are numbers of people today who believe in reincarnation and karma; but they act as if there were no such realities, as though life were actually confined to the one period between birth and death. . . . Only when we introduce into our lives right and concrete ideas of reincarnation and karma . . . shall we find how life can be fertilized by them. . . . A man who has assimilated these ideas knows: According to what I was in life, I shall have an effect upon everything that takes place in the future, upon the whole civilization of the future! . . . The feeling of responsibility will be intensified to a degree that was formerly impossible, and other mortal insights will necessarily follow" (Steiner, 1960).

Steiner died in Dornach in 1925. But today his Anthroposophy—meaning "man or human wisdom"—continues to spread out from there and from schools throughout the world.

Selected Writings: *The Dead Are With Us*, 1973; *Methods of Spiritual Research*, 1971; *Theosophy*, 1900.

**Stella C. (Cranshaw).** British physical medium discovered by Harry Price. She conducted a series of séances for him, beginning in 1923, at the National Laboratory of Psychical Research. They were marked by the burning of incense and were held in darkness except for a red light used for taking notes. Sounds from musical instruments, vivid flashes of light, movements of the cabinet, the ringing of a bell took place. Besides these physical phenomena, the rather commonplace stock-in-trade of most physical mediums, Stella C. was the first to cause the temperature of a séance room to drop. On one occasion Price measured a fall in temperature of eleven degrees while cool breezes fanned the sitters. Stella C. attracted the interest of famous investigators, among them Sir William Barrett and Charles Richet, and many thought her genuine.

Stella C. was not a professional medium; she had no special interest in things paranormal and had never sat in Spiritualist circles. She was simply a hospital nurse. After she had demonstrated her powers for Price and others for a number of years and when she felt her powers waning, she simply and wisely declined any more sittings and stepped off the mediumistic stage permanantly.

BIBLIOGRAPHY: Price, H. *Stella C.*, 1925.

**Stepanek, Pavel.** Czechoslovakian sensitive from Prague. He excelled in quantitative tests of extrasensory perception and was investigated by researchers from Holland, Sweden, India, Japan, and, in particular, by Milan Ryzl of Czechoslovakia and J. G. Pratt of the United States. The experiments with Stepanek extending over a period of ten years from 1961 to 1971 represent the most successful ESP trials ever conducted. A report of the test results with Stepanek appears in the *Guiness Book of World Records.*

A recent book by a hard-line skeptic (Gardner, 1989), however, claims that the tests were "[r]un by parapsychologists whose own careers were enhanced by this psychic celebrity [and were] characterized by a lack of controls, numerous opportunities for deception and highly erratic results. [They were] a classic example of self-interest conflicting with the interests of science, and ambition colliding with common sense" (flyer for book). The parapsychological community has not yet had an opportunity to answer these charges.

BIBLIOGRAPHY: Gardner, M. *How Not to Test a Psychic,* 1989; Pratt, J. G. 1973. "A Decade of Research with a Selected ESP Subject: An Overview and Reappraisal of the Work with Pavel Stepanek." PASPR 30:1.

**Stevenson, Robert Louis, 1850–1894.** High-ranking Scottish novelist and poet. His reputation began with descriptions in romantic prose of his journeys through France and Belgium. Although suffering from tuberculosis, Stevenson managed to write *The New Arabian Nights* in 1882 followed by *Treasure Island* in 1883, the story of piracy and adventure that established his fame. In spite of his illness, he continued to be creative. Even while searching for a cure in Switzerland, France, England, and the United States, he produced the unforgettable story of *The Strange Case of Dr. Jekyll and Mr. Hyde* (1886) and, in the same year, the adventure *Kidnapped,* both of which increased his reputation. Two years later, he was off for a journey to the Pacific. His final days were spent in Samoa.

In *Across the Plains* (1892) written in Samoa, Stevenson described his experiments with dreams. Just prior to sleep, by self-suggestion, he called on his never-failing "Brownies" to work for him in his dreams and to help him invent, write, and sell a story. The Brownies "have plainly learned to build the scheme of a considered story and to arrange emotion in a progressive order; one thing is beyond doubt—they can tell the dreamer a story, piece by piece, like a serial, and keep him all the time in ignorance of where they aim."

Stevenson's testimony as a **Noted Witness** for the creative process is a striking example of that uprising out of the unconscious of ideas, pictures and information that, without any conscious effort on the part of a creative person, produces writings and other creative achievements.

Selected Writing: *Across the Plains,* 1892.

**Stewart, Balfour, 1828–1887.** Highly reputed British physicist. A scrupulous and original experimentalist, Professor (of physics) Stewart was president of the Society for Psychical Research from 1885 until his sudden death in 1887 from a cerebral hemorrhage. He was involved in early experiments in thought-transference with the Creery Sisters and thought there was evidence for the occasional presence of telepathy. He believed that psychical research served the purpose of giving "insight into the principles which underlie . . . terrestrial occurrences."

In his capacity as a physicist, he wrote, among other works, *Treatise on Heat,* the standard work on the subject at the time of his death. The object of his book (written with Professor Tait) entitled *Unseen Universe,* of which there were twelve editions, was to establish that Christianity, far from being inconsistent with, was "the only intelligible solution of . . . the profounder problems of physical science."

In 1870 on his way to assume the chair of physics at Owens College, Manchester, he was crippled in a train accident. "He had . . . a simple-hearted and lovable nature, which endeared him to all his friends" (Barrett, 1888:198).

Selected Writings: 1885. "Presidential Address." PSPR 3:64; 1882. "Note on Thought-Reading." PSPR 1:35; and Tait, P. C. *The Unseen Universe or Physical Speculation on a Future State*, 1875.

BIBLIOGRAPHY: Barrett, W. 1888. "Professor Balfour Stewart." JSPR 3:197.

**Stewart, Gloria.** Mid-twentieth century British housewife. She gained a worldwide reputation as a high scoring subject in extrasensory perception tests conducted by Samuel G. Soal who had been on the lookout for psychics to use in ESP tests. In experiments with target cards conducted for four years beginning in 1936, Mrs. Stewart compiled an extraordinary record of hits. She seemed to have the most success when agents she liked and were her friends were looking at the cards. When she was not acquainted with the agents, her scores were not significant. Although she eventually got bored with the tests, her overall record over 37,100 trials was against enormous odds of more than 100,000 million to one that her guesses were attributable to chance (Soal and Bateman, 1954).

In spite of her success, however, the story of Soal's fraudulent manipulation of data in experiments with Basil Shackleton cannot be disregarded in judging whether the data obtained from Gloria Stewart's tests are genuine. If they were investigated as well, would they show fudging, too? The world will always wonder.

BIBLIOGRAPHY: Soal, S. G. and Bateman, F. *Modern Experiments in Telepathy,* 1954.

**Stigmata.** A plural form of the noun "stigma," it is a Christian term for markings on, or bleeding from, areas of the body corresponding to the wounds of the crucified **Jesus Christ,** that is, the palms (wounded by nails); the feet (similarly wounded); the side (wounded by a spear); the back and shoulders (the result of scourging and carrying a cross); the forehead (punctures from a crown of thorns).

From the sixth century B.C. to the fourth century A.D. when crucifixion was ended in Rome, it was the form of punishment used for pirates, captives, slaves, criminals, and trouble-makers. Sixteen centuries after it was abolished in Rome, crucifixion was renewed by the Nazis in the death camp at Dachau. Except for the punctures left by his crown of thorns, Christs's wounds, including scourging, were similar to those received by anyone who died on the cross. Yet it is an enigmatic historical fact that no manifestations have ever been reported on the bodies of non-Christians, have rarely appeared on the bodies of Protestants, but have been recorded almost always on the bodies of extremely religious Catholics.

Although stigmata are generally believed to date back to 1224 and **Francis of Assisi,** St. Paul might have been speaking about them when he said to the Galatians, "I bear on my body the marks of the Lord Jesus" (Galat. 6:17). Was Paul describing himself as the first stigmatic or was he referring to wounds he received from floggings, beatings, and stonings by those antagonistic to his teachings? In any case, since Francis, over 330 pious Roman Catholics have been stigmatics, among the most well known being the German nun Catherine Emmerich, the German Saint Lidwina of Schiedam, the German mystic **Therese Neumann,** and, most recently, the Italian priest **Padre Pio.**

While many Roman Catholics believe in the supernatural nature of the stigmata, the Catholic church has been cautious about accepting them as miraculous; it has canonized only sixty stigmatics. Even in the famous case of Father Pio's genuine stigmata, a Sacred Congregation of the Roman Curia declared on July 5, 1923, that, after formal investigation, the evidence had not established them as supernaturally caused and miraculous.

Although stigmata are associated with devout Catholics, it does not necessarily follow that they are strictly a religious phenomenon. The leading countertheory is auto-suggestion. The well-publicized stigmata of Francis caused many to yearn eagerly to be marked as Christ had been marked for the ecstacy of imitating or uniting with him. This obsession became what Herbert Thurston called the "crucifixion complex" and the marks differed depending on the suggestibility of each subject. The wounds of one woman matched in position and size those shown on the crucifix before which she prayed; another's wound might be on the right side, another's on the left. In Thurston's view, these differences point "to an auto-suggested effect rather than to the operation of an external cause" (Thurston, 1952).

If the stigmata appear on highly suggestible people, wounds should be induced by suggestions to a suggestible and sensitive person. The German physician Alfred Lechler asserted that he was able to induce artificially and by suggestion stigmata on the hands and feet of a twenty-nine year old patient, the markings of a "crown of thorns" on her forehead and the same bloody tears shed by Therese Neumann (Lechler, 1933).

But the explanation of "suggestion" is not alone enough to account for the stigmata. While stigmata have never been recognized as a paranormal phenomenon, psychical research offers an explanation to add to the psychological one. From the paranormal point of view, if the mind can cure as in Christian Science, or can kill as in voodoo death, it may be able to produce marks on the body. Studies of saints indicate that such people manifest and control paranormal abilities to an unusual degree. Devout people preoccupied with the Passion may be able through psychokinesis to produce physical effects on their bodies like Christ's.

BIBLIOGRAPHY: Lechler, A. *Das Rätsel von Konnersreuth im Lichte eines neuen Falles von Stigmatisation,* 1933; Thurston, H. *The Physical Phenomena of Mysticism,* 1952, pp. 122–123.

**Stimulus.** See **Target; Targets, Range of.**

**Stowe, Harriet Beecher, 1811–1896.** American novelist. Her *Uncle Tom's Cabin* in 1852 was a literary bombshell that incited anti-slavery feelings and helped lead to the American Civil War. She followed this book with additional anti-slavery literature: *A Key to Uncle Tom's Cabin* (1853) and *Dred: A Tale of the Great Dismal Swamp* (1856). Her popularity in the United States never diminished. She toured England, wrote about it in *Sunny Memories of Foreign Lands* (1854), and was popular until 1869 when, in an article entitled "The True Story of Lord Byron's Life," she accused him of committing incest with his sister.

Mrs. Stowe joins the ranks of those **Noted Witnesses** to the creative process who seem to have been inspired in their writings by some mysterious and unexplained source. In her case, this source at least in part produced *Uncle Tom's Cabin.* "Mrs. Stowe was seated in her pew in the college church at Brunswick during the communion service. . . . Suddenly, like the unrolling of a picture scroll, the scene of the death of Uncle Tom seemed to pass before her. At the same time, the words of Jesus were sounding in her ears, 'Inasmuch as ye have done it unto one of the least of these my brethren, ye have done it unto me.' It seemed as if the crucified, but now risen and glorified Christ, were speaking to her through the poor black man, cut and bleeding under the blows of the slave whip. She was affected so strongly that she could scarcely keep from weeping aloud.

"That Sunday afternoon she went to her room, locked the door, and wrote out, substantially as it appears in the published editions, the chapter called 'The Death of Uncle Tom'. . . . It seemed to her as though what she wrote was blown through her mind as with the rushing of a mighty wind."

BIBLIOGRAPHY: Stowe, C. E. and Stowe, L. B. *Harriet Beecher Stowe: the Story of Her Life,* 1911, pp. 144–145.

**Strutt, John William (third Baron Rayleigh), 1842–1919.** Brilliant British physicist and Nobel laureate (1904 for his isolation of the inert atmospheric gas argon). This Trinity College, Cambridge, graduate was, like many of his fellows of the period, interested in psychical research. He married Evelyn Balfour, sister of Eleanor Sidgwick and Arthur and Gerald Balfour. As a physical scientist, he was most interested in physical phenomena and, from sittings with Kate Fox (Jencken), one of the Fox Sisters, who spent time at his home, and Eusapia Palladino, was convinced that some physical phenomena could not easily be explained away. He was less convinced of the reality of telepathy. Lord Rayleigh became president of the Society for Psychical Research in 1919 and died that same year while still in office.

The world, of course, knows him as a physicist. His great book *The Theory of Sound* was written on a houseboat on the Nile where he was recuperating from an attack of rheumatic fever. His most significant early work resulted in a classic study of wave propagation. In 1879 to 1884 he served as second Cavendish Professor of Experimental Physics at Cambridge University. Rayleigh liked to work on several research projects at once, but "his work was consistently of high quality. . . . [H]e . . . opened up important new research frontiers . . . in acoustics and fluid dynamics." From 1908 until his death he was chancellor of Cambridge University.

Selected Writings: 1919. "Presidential Address." PSPR 30: 275.

BIBLIOGRAPHY: "Rayleigh (of Terling Place)," *The New Encyclopaedia Britannica,* 15th ed., 9:964; Lodge, Sir Oliver. 1920. "In Memory of Lord Rayleigh, O. M., F. R. S." PSPR 31: 1.

**Strutt, Robert John (fourth Baron Rayleigh), 1875–1947.** British physicist. Son of John William Strutt, third Baron Rayleigh, and, like his father, an experimental physicist, this Lord Rayleigh (who was a Balfour on his mother's side) was president of the Society for Psychical Research in 1937 and 1938.

His Presidential Address in which he discussed the history of and problems associated with physical mediumship illustrates his principal interest in psychical research. He pointed out that "failure to repeat can hardly constitute a disproof, when the identical conditions cannot be re-established" (1938a). Since we do not discard all communications through a mental medium because some are false, we should not dismiss a physical medium who has sometimes engaged in fraud. He discussed D. D. Home, Kathleen Goligher, Eusapia Palladino and Rudi Schneider and concluded that some physical phenomena must have been genuine. He initiated the method for using infrared rays in investigating physical mediums that were used to test Rudi Schneider and wrote a charming memoir (1938b) of his uncle Henry Sidgwick.

From 1908 to 1919 Lord Rayleigh was professor of physics at Imperial College, London, and did research on radioactivity in rocks. His "independent position and private laboratory . . . made it possible for him to explore some of the fascinating by-ways of science, closed to the industrial physicist, and fast closing to the academic physicist . . ." (1948:330).

Selected Writings: 1938a. "Presidential Address. The Problem of Physical Phenomena in connection with Psychical Research." PSPR 45:1; 1938b. "Some Recollections of Henry Sidgwick." PSPR 45:162.

BIBLIOGRAPHY: "Obituary. Lord Rayleigh, F. R. S." 1948. PSPR 48:330.

**Stuart, Charles E., 1907–1947.** American parapsychologist. He is best remembered for his statistical work in connection with experiments in extrasensory perception (with Greenwood, 1937). While a brilliant undergraduate major in mathematics at Duke University, he became interested in parapsychology. He met J. B. Rhine and began ESP experiments with friends, but his most striking experiments were in clairvoyance with himself as subject. In 1941 he received his Ph.D. in psychology from Duke for his thesis on an experimental study in ESP, the first of its kind ever awarded. In 1934 he had become a full-time research associate at the **Parapsychology Laboratory** and, except for the years 1942–1944 when he was Thomas Welton Stanford Fellow in Psychical Research at Stanford University, kept that job for the remainder of his life.

Dr. Stuart on Rhine's behalf answered many of the criticisms of the experimental work being done at the Parapsychology Laboratory. One of the most frequently raised was that the ESP cards used in card-guessing experiments could be read from the backs; Dr. Stuart pointed out that the commercially produced cards contained the warning: "Imperfections in the commercial production of the ESP cards preclude their unscreened use for experimental purposes." Dr. Stuart also indicated that errors in recording of scores in experiments were unlikely since the experiments were closely monitored and the results checked and rechecked. Another frequent criticism was the possibility of unconscious whispering of the symbol on the target card on the part of the agent, but Dr. Stuart explained that the order of the cards was usually unknown to the experimenter. The statistical criticisms were met by Dr. Stuart and by Joseph A. Greenwood.

In the mid-1940s Charles Stuart was attempting, as were Gertrude R. Schmeidler and Betty M. Humphrey, to distinguish between high-scoring and low-scoring subjects on the basis of attitude or personality (1946a; with Humphrey, Smith and McMahan, 1947). In addition, his drawing studies were the "only significant amount of free-response work ever to crack the *Journal of Parapsychology* . . . (e.g., Stuart, 1946[b], 1947)" (Palmer, 1982:46) because Rhine favored forced-choice rather than free-response methods of testing ESP. Dr. Stuart also coauthored two books (1937, 1940).

Selected Writings: 1946a. "An Interest Inventory Relation to ESP Scores." JP 10:154; 1946b. "GESP Experiments with the Free Response Method." JP 10:21; 1947. "A Second Classroom ESP Experiment with the Free Response Method." JP 11:14; 1947. with B. M. Humphrey, B. M. Smith, and E. McMahan. "Personality Measurements and ESP Tests with Cards and Drawings." JP 11:117; with J. B. Rhine, J. G. Pratt, B. M. Smith, and J. A. Greenwood. *Extrasensory Perception after Sixty Years,* 1940; with J. G. Pratt. *A Handbook for Testing Extrasensory Perception,* 1937b; 1937a. with J. A. Greenwood. "A Review of Criticisms of the Mathematical Evaluation of ESP Data." JP 1:295.

BIBLIOGRAPHY: Palmer, J. "Review of J. B. Rhine's ESP Research." In K. R. Rao, ed., *J. B. Rhine: On the Frontier of Science,* 1982; Pratt, J. G. 1947. "Obituary: Charles E. Stuart." JASPR 41:140; Rhine, L. E. *Something Hidden,* 1983.

**Studievereniging voor Psychical Research.** Founded in 1920, this Dutch Society for Psychical Research began the systematic investigation of telepathy and clairvoyance in The Netherlands and monopolized activity in parapsychology and psychical research in that country until World War II when it was compelled to discontinue its work. With the conclusion of the war, however, it returned to life and the domination of Dutch parapsychology. But in 1960 a rebellion took place against what was perceived as Wilhelm H. C. Tenhaeff's overly ambitious and arbitrary leadership of the organization. This revolt led to the departure of some key members, including George A. M. Zorab. Nevertheless the society continues today as a vehicle to promote education in both parapsychology and psychical research through lectures at the University of Utrecht and through the publication of its journal *TIJDSCHRIFT VOOR PARAPSYCHOLOGY.* Address: P. O. Box 786, 3500 AT Utrecht, The Netherlands.

**Subject.** The person being tested for psi ability.

**Subject Variance.** See **Variance, Subject.**

**Subliminal Self.** A term coined by **Frederic W. H. Myers.** He theorized that the normal consciousness has an ever-changing threshold *(limen)* and that there lies below it *(sub)* a Self with a capital "S." Some psychologists think that Myers's idea can be subsumed under that of the "unconscious." But his concept was much broader and suggests an abiding psychical entity that is the source of powers pertaining to genius, ecstacy, and a wide number of psychic phenomena and sometimes crosses over the threshold to make contact with the waking self. The waking self is only a small and always changing fragment of the larger Self.

**Sir Oliver Lodge** suggested a metaphor to describe Myers's complicated conception and distinguish it from the "unconscious": Every person is "the foliage of a tree which has its main trunk and its roots in another order of existence; but that on this dark inconspicuous and permanent basis, now one and now another system of leaves bud, grow, display themselves, wither and decay, while the great trunk and roots persist through many such temporary appearances, not independently of the sensible manifestations, nor unassisted by them, but supporting them, dominating them, reproducing them, assimilating their nourishment in the form of the elaborated sap called experience, and thereby growing continually into a more perfect and larger whole" (Lodge, 1903).

BIBLIOGRAPHY: Lodge, O. 1903. "Human Personality and its Survival of Bodily Death. By Frederic W. H. Myers." PSPR 18:22; Myers, F. W. H. *Human Personality and Its Survival of Bodily Death,* Vol. I, 1903.

**Sudre, René, 1880–?.** French psychical researcher and author. A frequent contributor to *Revue Métapsychique* and the *Journal of the American Society for Psychical Research.* Sudre wrote extensively on almost every topic relevant to psychical research—from the so-called "sixth sense" (1928a), clairvoyance (1928b), levitation (1928c), the subconscious mind (1930a), physics (1930b), and the soul (1931) to experiments with mediums (1928d). He also made a broad survey of the entire field in which other subjects, including telepathy, dowsing, hypnosis and psychokinesis were covered (1960).

Although sometimes Sudre seems insufficiently critical of some phenomena, one of his major contributions was his attempt to incorporate them into an all-embracing theory, the need for which has been recognized by many modern parapsychologists, including Gardner Murphy (Berger, 1988:173). Sudre, however, was an early advocate of a theory in opposition to experimentalists who cry for facts and more facts. As he wrote: "The establishing of [psychical research] as a legitimate science ranking with other sciences is retarded not so much because its phenomena may not be proved authentic as because the average man of science is unable to find a convincing explanation for them. That which might, for the whole range of facts, carry a coherent interpretation will have done more for [psychical research] than the work of a hundred qualified experimenters could accomplish, even if they were the greatest *savants* of their time" (1930b:117). Sudre's theory was that all paranormal phenomena can be subsumed under a great creative power that permeates all life and which he described as *"l'esprit."*

Sudre also participated in international conferences on parapsychology including the first one held at the University of Utrecht in 1953.

Selected Writings: *Treatise on Para-*

*psychology: Essay on the Scientific Interpretation of the Human Phenomenon Known as the Supernatural,* 1960; 1931. "Is the Soul Material?" *Psychic Research* 25:165; 1930a. "The Structure of the Sub-Conscious Mind." *Psychic Research* 24:77; 1930b. "Psychic Research and the New Physics." *Psychic Research* 24:117; 1928a. "Have We a Sixth Sense?" *Psychic Research* 22:158; 1928b. "Clairvoyance and the Theory of Probabilities." *Psychic Research* 22:63; 1928c. "The Phenomena of Levitation." *Psychic Research* 22:433; 1928d. "Recollections of Jean Gouzyk." *Psychic Research* 22:603.

BIBLIOGRAPHY: Berger, A. S. *Lives and Letters in American Parapsychology,* 1988.

**Sulzer, Georg, 1844–1929.** Swiss judge. Outside the courts of Zurich, he attended séances and worked with mediums to study their trance states and other phenomena. He believed in an invisible world peopled by spirits of the dead and, in his writings, focussed on the religious significance of psychical research.

BIBLIOGRAPHY: Locher, T. "History of Psychical Research in Switzerland." *Proceedings of an International Conference Parapsychology Today: A Geographic View,* 1971, p. 131.

**Summerland.** A radiant home in the spirit world that, according to **Spiritualism,** awaits us and from which spirits of the dead commune with the living. The word was coined in 1845 by **Andrew Jackson Davis,** the "Poughkeepsie Seer," whose writings had a profound impact on the development of Spiritualism in the United States.

**Super ESP.** A term coined by **Hornell Hart** to describe the extraordinary and unlimited powers of extrasensory perception that mediums or percipients purportedly possess. Through telepathy those with such powers can fish selectively and purposefully in the minds of living people anywhere, whether or not sitters, for special information about a deceased person, and, through clairvoyance, can fish with similar discrimination and control in all printed materials for needed information. Now, in order for any case to be evidence of survival after death, the information it furnishes either via a medium, apparition, or otherwise must be verified by some living person or by some written record. Applying the principle of Occam's razor, the Super ESP hypothesis is used to explain away every case that seems to suggest a message from a communicator on the ground that the staggering powers of Super ESP have been used to obtain the information either by tapping the memory of a living person or by tapping a document.

There is, however, virtually no evidence that the limitless and staggering powers assumed by the Super ESP hypothesis exist. Even if they do exist, there is no evidence that they can be used to produce the often lifelike character and spontaneous and animated conversations of some communicators. For this reason, other counterhypotheses to survival evidence, such as Akashic records, cosmic memory and the Pygmalion hypothesis, have been put forward.

**Supernatural.** Once used to describe psi faculties and phenomena, the word "supernatural," which suggests that such faculties are outside of nature, has been discarded in favor of "paranormal." There is no ground for the belief that psi faculties or phenomena are any less a normal part of nature than any other phenomena.

**Supernormal.** Invented by **F. W. H. Myers,** this word described a phenomenon or faculty related to a transcendental world or to faculties or phenomena transcending the level of ordinary experience. Replaced today by the word "paranormal."

**Super Telepathy.** See **Super ESP.**

**Surgery, Psychic.** See **Healing, Unorthodox.**

**Survival.** There are many kinds of and meanings for "survival": survivors of airplane crashes and plagues, soldiers who survive combat conditions, surviving widows and widowers, and people who just manage to survive from day to day. In psychical research, however, "survival" means personal survival of bodily death, the continuation beyond death for an indefinite period of the human mind, consciousness, or personality. See also **Survival Research.**

**Survival Joint Research Committee Trust.** British organization established in 1963 to bring about close cooperation between Spiritualists and psychical researchers in the scientific investigation of the question of survival. The trust uses a number of methods to test the survival hypothesis including analyses of the personalities of deceased people and studies of mediums. It also organizes public conferences. Address: 2 Greycoat Place, London SWIP ISD, England.

**Survival Research.** Investigations into the question of whether the human consciousness or personality survives physical death dominated much early psychical research. The members of the Society for Psychical Research were drawn to the subject and set out to collect systematically and completely all evidence that might throw light on it, such as psychic experiences that seemed to suggest contact with the dead. In the United States, William James had sittings with Mrs. Leonora Piper and, on behalf of the American Society for Psychical Research, Richard Hodgson devoted himself to studying her. James Hervey Hyslop conducted rigorous experiments with mediums.

After the 1930s, and the beginning of the era introduced by J. B. Rhine, parapsychologists mainly found the survival question less interesting than the laboratory investigation of extrasensory perception and psychokinesis.

The issue of whether personal survival after death is a reality remains controversial and complicated and has produced many different theories and types of investigations. The following major categories of phenomena have been subjects of research: apparitions of the dead; deathbed visions; drop-in communicators; electronic voice phenomena; mental and physical mediums; near-death experiences; out-of-body experiences; poltergeists; possession; cases suggestive of reincarnation; transcommunication; xenoglossy.

Although **Spiritualism** regards survival of death as already proven, there is no agreement among psychical researchers on this point. There are two lines of argument: On the one hand, since each of the categories of events or experiences can be explained by other than a survivalist explanation, the survival hypothesis has no leg to stand on; on the other hand, a belief in survival is warranted because it is not based on a lone category of evidence. It is based on a variety of categories all in line with the hypothesis, with some better explained by the hypothesis than others, but which all together point to survival. Still looking for new evidence, researchers (among them Arthur S. Berger who is training potentially powerful communicators for his dictionary test) continue to search for stronger cases in all categories including the reincarnation-type.

BIBLIOGRAPHY: Berger, A. S. *Aristocracy of the Dead,* 1987; Stevenson, I. *Cases of the Reincarnatoin Type Vols. I-IV,* 1975, 1977, 1980, 1983; Stevenson, I. 1977. "Research Into the Evidence of Man's Survival After Death." *Journal of Nervous and Mental Disease* vol. 165, No. 3:152.

**Survival Research Foundation.** Organized in the United States in 1971 by author Susy Smith and attorney-author Frank C. Tribbe as a private, non-profit scientific and educational research organization, the Survival Research Foundation studies, by objective methods, the question of human survival after death. Susy Smith was its first president and continued in that post until 1981 when Arthur S. Berger succeeded her.

The SRF has conducted investigations into the visions of the dying and those who have been at the brink of death, has initiated a long-term, large-scale research program based on dictionary, cipher, and combination lock tests, and has offered an award for innovative experiments and investigations. In 1985, the SRF created the International Institute for the Study of Death. The current address of the Survival Research Foundation is P. O. Box 8565, Pembroke Pines, Florida 33084.

BIBLIOGRAPHY: Berger, A. S. 1982. "Better Than a Gold Watch: the Work of the Survival Research Foundation." *Theta.* 10 (4): 82.

**Swann, Ingo, 1933–.** American artist and exceptionally successful subject in parapsychological experiments. He doesn't like to be called psychic because he doesn't "think that the word 'psychic' describes me. I've never gone into trance, nor do I give readings or consciously use telepathy" (*Psychic* 1973). But he has demonstrated remarkable other paranormal abilities that he has been willing to have tested in experiments in several areas.

One is psychokinesis. Since Swann believed that he could change the temperature of objects, Gertrude R. Schmeidler set up a test. "Ingo agreed to my rather tight conditions where order of trying for hotter or colder was counterbalanced and both length and number of trials were preset. He was pleased at each step of increasing rigor: Enclosing the sensor so that it was fully insulated and putting his target 15 feet away. Our series of sessions showed that he could indeed change the temperature recordings, toward either hotter or colder. And of course I was pleased, and rather awed, at working with someone who had such strong ability as he" (Schmeidler, 1988:276–277). Stella C. in the 1920s was also supposed to have been able to alter temperature, but until Dr. Schmeidler's experiments with Ingo Swann, the phenomenon had never been studied under rigorous conditions.

At the age of three Swann had his first out-of-body experience. Over the years he claimed to have trained himself to induce OBEs at will. In tests conducted at the American Society for Psychical Research, Swann's task was to observe in his out-of-body state targets located on a platform eight feet above the floor. When eight sets of targets and Swann's responses were randomized and studied by a blind independent judge, all eight sets were correctly matched. "The expectation of this happening by chance is about one in 40,000" (Mitchell, 1978:159). Perhaps Swann had succeeded in viewing the targets in an out-of-body state, but he might also have obtained knowledge of the targets through clairvoyance—in either case, however, an extraordinary performance.

Swann also excelled in remote viewing experiments at Stanford Research Institute. For example, using a double-blind protocol and the Palo Alto City Hall as a target, Swann, while closeted with an experimenter back at SRI, sketched a tall building with vertical columns, a fountain which he said he couldn't hear (it turned out that the fountain was not running) and four trees. An independent judge easily matched the target to the response. Swann's overall scores for a series of eight separate experiments were a significant 2,500 to one against chance. In addition, Swann's "contributions to paranormal research are not confined to his role as subject. He also is very articulate about his subjective experience, and slips easily into the role of co-researcher investigating the underlying laws of the phenomena" (Targ and Puthoff, 1977:37).

BIBLIOGRAPHY: "Interview: Ingo Swann." *Psychic* April 1973. 4 (4):6; Mitchell, J. "Out-of-the-Body Vision." In D. S. Rogo, ed., *Mind Beyond the Body: The Mystery of ESP Projection,* 1978; Schmeidler, G. R. "Work in Progress: Autobiographical Notes." In A. S. Berger. *Lives and Letters in American Parapsychology,* 1988; Schmeidler, G. R. 1973. "PK Experiments upon Continuously Recorded Temperature." JASPR 67:25; Targ,R. and Puthoff, H. E. *Mind-Reach: Scientists Look at Psychic Ability,* 1977.

**Swedenborg, Emanuel (Emanuel Swedborg), 1688–1772.** The most eminent Swedish savant of his time. He was also one of the strangest and greatest mystics of all time. The father of modern **Spiritualism,** he was the first leading man of science to gain insights into the spiritual realm. He also possessed paranormal gifts so unusual that they impressed no less a person than the philosopher Immanuel Kant.

Born in Stockholm, Sweden, Swedenborg became a scientific engineer, published Sweden's first scientific journal in 1715, and in 1716 was appointed by Charles XII as assessor of the Swedish Board of Mines. After his financée told him that she did not love him and broke off their engagement, the blow sent him reeling out of Sweden. When he returned, he was made a count by Queen Louisa Ulrica and his name was changed to Swedenborg. In 1734, he published the three volume treatise, *Philosophical and Metallurgical Works.* Six years later he published *The Economy of the Animal Kingdom* in which he dealt with the relation between soul and body.

In 1745, Swedenborg was visiting London. After dinner, he saw the apparition of a human being in his room. It said to him, "Don't eat so much," and disappeared. The following night, the apparition returned and identified itself as God. It told Swedenborg that his mission was to provide to the world an explanation of the Scriptures. For Swedenborg "heaven opened up to him" and the everyday practical world he had known was left behind in favor of the spiritual one. He withdrew more and more from society and lived simply. His experience also resulted in visions and trances and he became a **Noted Witness** for the creative process. As he wrote, "I am but the secretary. I write what is dictated to my spirit" (Dingwall, 1962).

He concentrated his energies on a reinterpretation of the Bible and on works on theology formed from things he had heard and seen in the spiritual world and from actual conversations with angels and with spirits of the dead. Within ten years after his death in 1772, the Swedenborgian church ("New Church" or "New Jerusalem Church") was established in the United States. It follows his teachings that the Bible should be interpreted spiritually, that any true marriage will continue in heaven, and that the spiritual realm and the earthly world are linked.

He influenced the "animal magnetism" movement started in the eighteenth century by Franz Anton Mesmer as mesmerized people went into trance and received spirit communications. Swedenborg was thus the first Spiritualist although the Spiritualism of today began in 1848 with the Fox Sisters. He influenced Andrew Jackson Davis who played a key role in the early development of Spiritualism. Davis claimed that Swedenborg's apparition came to him on March 7, 1844, and instructed him about the spiritual realm.

Swedenborg's trance communications differ markedly from those of ordinary mediums. In ordinary trances, the spirits are said to come to mediums from another world. In Swedenborg's trances, he claimed to go out to the spirits. Mediums normally remember nothing of their spirit encounters; Swedenborg, on the other hand, remembered his experiences in the other world and what the spirits, communicating not through the organs of speech but through telepathy, told him about the Bible.

The claims of converse with spirits has always raised the issue for psychical research of whether such a claim is the subjective product of the imagination or is an objective event supported by evidence. In Swedenborg's case, there is at least some evidential basis for the experiences he claimed. The first incident, in which he either went into the spirit world for information or used clairvoyance, was so impressive that it received the attention of Kant in his *Dreams of a Spirit Seer.* Kant related how "the widow of the Dutch Ambassador in Stockholm, some time after the death of her husband, was called upon by . . . a goldsmith . . . to pay for a silver service which her husband had purchased from him. The widow was convinced that her late husband had . . . paid his debt, yet she was unable to find this receipt." The widow then asked Swedenborg "if, as all people say, he possessed the extraordinary gift of conversing with the souls of the departed, he would perhaps have the kindness to ask her husband how it was about the silver service. . . . Three days afterward . . . Swedenborg . . . informed her that . . . [t]he debt had been paid . . . and the receipt was in a bureau in the room upstairs. . . . The bureau was opened; [a] compartment was found, of which no one had ever known before; and to the great astonishment of all, the papers were discovered there, in accordance with his description."

A second experience gives possible further evidence of Swedenborg's spirit communications. Three years after the death of her brother, the crown prince of Prussia, in 1758, Queen Louisa Ulrica heard rumors of Swedenborg's ability to converse with the dead. She charged him with a commission to communicate with her deceased brother. Swedenborg agreed. The following week Swedenborg again appeared in court. According to a member of the Swedish Senate, "Swedenborg not only greeted [the queen] from her brother, but also gave her [the brother's] apologies for not having answered her last letter; he also wished to do so now through Swedenborg; which he accordingly did. The queen was greatly overcome and said, 'No one, except God, knows this secret.' "

The third of Swedenborg's experiences makes him a noted witness for clairvoyance or, possibly, telepathy. Near the end of September 1759, Kant wrote, Swedenborg reached Gothenburg, Sweden, from England at 4 P.M. on a Saturday. About two hours later, he left the house where he was dining and came back looking pale and alarmed. Swedenborg told the guests that a dangerous fire had just broken out on Sodermalm in Stockholm (about 300 English miles from Gothenburg) where his house was located. The fire, he said, was spreading rapidly. He said that a friend's house had been burned to ashes already and that his own was in immediate peril. He came back about 8 P.M. to announce, "Thank God! The fire is extinguished, the third door from my house." The following morning, Sunday, Swedenborg was questioned by the governor of Gothenburg, to whom Swedenborg again described the fire in detail. On Monday, a messenger came from the Stockholm Board of Trade with letters confirming Swedenborg's description of the fire. On Tuesday, a royal courier arrived with details that again corresponded to Swedenborg's and stated that the fire had been extinguished at 8 P.M. Saturday. Swedenborg's gift, Kant said, was "Beyond all possibility of doubt."

BIBLIOGRAPHY: Dingwall, E. J. *Very Peculiar People, 1962;* Prince, W. F. *Noted Witnesses for Psychic Occurrences,* 1963, pp. 46–55.

**Swedenborgianism.** Views held by the "New Church" or "New Jerusalem Church" based on the teachings of **Emanuel Swedenborg** and dealing with salvation, the spiritual interpretation of the Scriptures, and the future state. The doctrines of Spiritualism coincide in many ways with those of Swedenborgianism whose founder, after all, influenced the rise and development of Spiritualism.

**Synchronicity.** Carl Gustav Jung's term for two contemporaneous events that, without any causal explanation, are related in a meaningful way. Since no causal explanation of psi phenomena seems at present forthcoming, the acausal connecting principle provided by the concept of synchronicity offers an explanation for some of these phenomena. Jung's case of the patient who, at the moment that a golden scarab appeared at the window, told him of dreaming of a golden scarab is an example of what Jung meant by synchronicity—a meaningful coincidence. In another similar case, a patient told of dreaming of a spectral fox just as a fox (Jung and the patient were walking in the woods) came out from the trees. "In the experience of a synchronistic event, instead of feeling ourselves isolated entities in a vast world we feel the connection to others and the universe at a deep and meaningful level" (Bolen, 1979:21).

BIBLIOGRAPHY: Bolen, J. 1979. "Synchronicity, Jung and the Self." *New Realities* 3(2):16; Jung, C. G. *Synchronicity: An Acausal Principle,* 1955.

**Synchronicity Research Unit.** This Dutch group consists of a core-team of researchers, including Brian Millar and Jeff C. Jacobs, its founder. They are supplemented from time to time by visiting researchers and all carry out theoretical and empirical research in parapsychology. Current programs include theoretical and experimental investigations of observational theories, psi-guided awakening from sleep, and case studies of synchronicity. The organization is responsible for much of the output of parapsychology in The Netherlands. It publishes the *SRU-Bulletin.* Address: P. O. Box 7625, 5601 JP Eindhoven, The Netherlands.

**Systems Theory.** A theoretical approach used by some parapsychologists to formulate a hypothesis for psi occurrences as taking place within a psychological, spatial, and temporal whole. Instead of the traditional view of an experiment, for example, that focussed on the experiment, experimenter, target, and subject using extrasensory perception or psychokinesis to hit the target as separate and objective entities interacting only during the experiment, the systems theoretical approach suggests that the experiment is a living system consisting of experimenter, experimental conditions, target, and subject, and the mutual interaction and influence of all.

# T

**Table-Tilting.** Synonym for "typtology," "table-tipping" and "table-turning." Movement, rotation or levitation of a table, which those seated around it sometimes interpret as messages.

The ancients were familiar with this phenomenon. Tertullian, a Christian theologian of the second century A.D., once rebuked some pagans: "Do not your magicians call ghosts and departed souls from shades below. . . . And how do they perform all this but by the assistance of angels and spirits, by which they are able to make stools and tables prophesy." Table-tipping was a practice of the Jews of the seventeenth century. Sabbatai Zebi, a Jewish mystic of that period who claimed to be the messiah, recognized it as the work of God: "for we sing at the table sacred psalms and songs, and it can be no Devil's work where God is remembered."

After the birth of Spiritualism, the phenomenon spread rapidly, almost as a craze, throughout the world. Today, in séances or sessions whose purpose is to receive communications from surviving personalities, members of the group seat themselves with their hands on or above a table, or, on occasion, with their hands behind the backs of their chairs. When the table tilts, dances, levitates, or moves in various directions, the belief is that the movements are produced by a surviving personality. Raps of a table leg or tilts when appropriate letters of the alphabet are called out are taken as messages from the beyond.

Michael Faraday showed that the phenomenon was created by the unconscious action of the fingers of the participants and not by spirits. But Faraday's experiment did not explain movements of the table when there was no possibility of contact with it. And the work of Kenneth Batcheldor and of a group of experimenters in Toronto in 1973 have demonstrated that table-tilting may be a psychokinetic effect since, after working together for a long time, both groups, by hoping and willing that they would do so, were able to make heavy tables rock and rap.

BIBLIOGRAPHY: Faraday, M. Letter to the Times, June 30, 1853; Owen I. M. with Sparrow, M. *Conjuring Up Philip,* 1976.

**Tanagras, Angelos, 1875–c.1970.** Greek high ranking naval officer with a lifelong interest in psychical research. Admiral Tanagras may have been the first to explain the phenomenon of precognition in a way that does not involve the disturbing implications of fate and predetermination. His explanation was that an event is caused by an individual's psychokinesis (Tanagras, 1938).

If, for example, someone foresees a train collision in a precognitive dream, it is the dreamer who brings about its actual occurrence by the use of PK, perhaps by interfering with the red warning lights on the track or by making the brakes of a locomotive defective. In Tanagras's view, precognitive and other phenomena and "bad luck" or "good luck" are all the results of "a hidden causality which springs from latent powers in man himself—powers which are imbedded in the remarkable human subconscious and which are liberated under certain conditions, causing man's impulses to act upon living or inorganic matter. Any force able to induce the latent powers of the subconscious to *gain ascendancy over the conscious mind* could achieve results exceeding all our materialistic expectations and giving the impression of being either *fate, fortune,* or a *miracle*" (Tanagras, 1967:7). To this force this reflective admiral in the Greek navy gave the name "psychoboly," a term borrowed from the Greek meaning "mind-throwing," that is, projecting the mind to influence people, objects, and events in a variety of situations.

Founder and president of the Greek Society for Psychical Research, Tanagras also carried out long-distance telepathy experiments between percipients in Athens and agents in Cambridge, England.

Selected Writings: *Psychophysical Elements in Parapsychological Traditions,* 1967; *Le Destin et la Chance,* 1938.

**Tanous, Alex.** Contemporary American psychologist and educator. He has been a star subject in out-of-body experience experiments conducted at the American Society for Psychical Research. Although as a child he was considered retarded, Dr. Tanous went on to receive several degrees, including an M.A. in philosophy and a doctor of divinity and to become a school psychologist.

He was discovered during Karlis Osis's fly-in experiment. Dr. Tanous was one of those who reportedly "flew in" from their homes (Dr. Tanous lived in Maine) to the ASPR's office in New York City to observe target objects arranged on a table there. He made a sketch of the objects he said he had seen from his position on the ceiling of the office. The sketch was certified correct by an ASPR assistant who went up a ladder next to the table to observe the targets as one would observe them from the ceiling.

With this success behind him, Dr. Tanous was called on to be the subject in another series of experiments at the ASPR. He was asked to go out of his body, project himself into a shielded chamber and look in a viewing window in the front of an optical image device that showed target images. Strain-gauge sensors had been placed in front of the viewing window to register any mechanical effects at the place where he was to project himself. There were 197 trials in which Dr. Tanous made 114 hits and 83 misses. More importantly, the strain-gauge level of activation for the period when he was supposedly looking at the targets and scoring hits was significantly higher than during the trials when he scored misses. Although the experimenters warned that "our interpretations must be very tentative," they believed that the results conformed to the out-of-body experience hypothesis and that something of Alex Tanous had left his body (Osis and McCormick, 1980).

Besides his participation in such experiments, Dr. Tanous has co-authored a book to tell parents how to deal with children who have psi abilities (Tanous and Donnelly, 1979).

Selected Writing: and Donnelly, K. F. *Is Your Child Psychic?,* 1979.

BIBLIOGRAPHY: Osis, K. and McCormick, D. 1980. "Kinetic Effects at the Ostensible Location of an Out-of-Body Projection During Perceptual Testing." JASPR 74:319.

**Targ, Russell, 1934–.** American physicist. A holder of patents on microwaves and lasers, his work in parapsychology (which he prefers to call by the Russian term psychoenergetics) seems to have begun in 1972. At that time he and Harold Puthoff co-founded a program at Stanford Research International for research and applications in remote viewing (a more scientifically acceptable term than clairvoyance, telepathy or out-of-body experience) for U.S. government clients. This controversial work eventually led to the publication of a book with Puthoff (1977) in which they set out the protocol for their experiments that they felt demonstrated the existence of paranormal ability. Replications of their experiments have apparently been carried out, but the judging procedures have often been criticized.

In 1982 Mr. Targ became a partner in Delphi Associates which applied remote viewing procedures for commercial clients and had success in predicting silver prices. Presently president of Bay Research Institute and senior staff scientist at Lockheed Research and Development, Mr. Targ is the author or coauthor of more than thirty articles in professional journals and of the first papers on psychoenergetic phenomena to appear in *The Proceedings of the IEEE* and in *Nature* and to be presented at a national meeting of the American Association for the Advancement of Science. He has also co-authored three books (1984, 1979, 1977).

Mr. Targ, who received his B.S. in physics from Queens College and did graduate work at Columbia University, has done experimental microwave work at Sperry Gyroscope Company, laser research at GTE Sylvania and was senior research physicist at SRI International until 1982. He is a senior member of the Institute of Electronics and Electrical Engineers, a member of the American Association for the Advancement of Science and of the Parapsychological Association, and is vice president of the International Association for Psychotronics Research. In 1977 he received the IEEE Franklin V. Taylor Memorial Award for his paper, "A Scientific Look at ESP." He has been the recipient of two National Aeronautics and Space Administration Awards and in 1983 addressed the Soviet Academy of Sciences on recent research in remote viewing.

Selected Writings: and K. Harary. 1985. "A New Approach to Forecasting Commodity Futures." *Psi Research* 5(3/4):79; and K. Harary. *The Mind Race: Understanding and Using Psychic Abilities,* 1984; and C. Tart and H. Puthoff, *Mind at Large: Institute of Electrical and Electronic Engineers Symposia on the Nature of Extrasensory Perception,* 1979; and H. E. Puthoff, *Mind Reach: Scientists Look at Psychical Research,* 1977.

BIBLIOGRAPHY: Berger, A. S. *Lives and Letters in American Parapsychology,* 1988.

**Target.** In ESP tests, the objective or mental events to which the subject is attempting to respond; in tests of psychokinesis, the objective process or object which the subject tries to influence (such as the face or location of a die) (JP). See also **Extrasensory perception.**

**Target Card.** The card which the percipient is attempting to identify or otherwise indicate a knowledge of (JP).

**Target Face.** The face of the falling die that the subject tries to make turn up by psychokinesis.

**Target Pack:** The pack of cards whose order the subject is attempting to identify.

**Target Preference.** See **Liking Effect.**

**Target, Quality of.** The range of targets is great. Are some targets better than others (i.e., do some targets provide subjects with stronger or sharper ESP impressions than others?) Some researchers suggest that natural targets are "good" because related to psi-hitting while unnatural targets (i.e., material objects such as mechanical, artificial, and concrete ones), are related to psi-missing and therefore "poor" ones. See also **Focussing Effect; Hit; Miss.**

**Targets, Range of.** Targets vary greatly in size, materials, color, and distance from the subject. The range of targets themselves is equally great. In ESP tests, targets have included: agents; animal pictures; art prints; baccarat cards; binary digits; colored lights; erotic pictures; ESP cards; geographical locations; IBM punch cards; music; pennies, photographs (black and white and in color); playing cards; prints (black and white and in color); roulette wheels; sounds; symbols; undeveloped film images; words. In tests of psychokinesis, targets have been: animals; Bakelite cubes; coins; dice; magnetometers; mechanical toys on wheels; microcellular organisms; plants; radioactive particles; random number generators; spheres (marbles or metal balls); water drops.

**Tarot Cards.** A deck of seventy-eight cards resembling playing cards, twenty-two of which contain pictures of lovers, death, emperors, jugglers, fools, the devil, and sundry other characters. Fifty-six cards have suits representing various matters such as money, journeys, love, and business. People seeking information about their personal problems or futures shuffle the deck and then cut it three times with the left hand. A reader places the cards in a pattern and interprets the meanings of the cards's symbols. The readings may take one of several forms. One may be a **Cold Reading,** that is, the reader may take advantage of hints provided by the conduct or statements of a client and use them to frame a reading. Or the way the cards are laid down or their interpretations may be the result of the reader's intuition or, if the reader is psychic, the result of psi used to obtain correct information about a client.

The one experimental effort by a parapsychologist to determine if psi is used in

Tarot card interpretations did not show any correlation between psi and the readings. Subjects "were unable to pick out their own Tarot card readings from among a group of others," and there was no reason to think anything paranormal was involved (Blackmore 1983:101).

BIBLIOGRAPHY: Blackmore, S. J. 1983. "Divination with Tarot Cards: An Empirical Study." JSPR 52:97.

**Tart, Charles T., 1937–.** American psychologist and parapsychologist. After two years of studies in electrical engineering at Massachusetts Institute of Technology, Charles Tart transferred to Duke University to study the human mind. While at Duke and then at the University of North Carolina from which he received his B.A., M.A., and Ph.D. degrees, he was a frequent visitor at J. B. Rhine's Parapsychology Laboratory.

Dr. Tart has written and done research on altered states of consciousness (including dreams, hypnosis and meditation), psychedelic drugs, mind/body relationships, and parapsychology (hauntings, poltergeists, psychometry, out-of-body experiences) and has invented ESP training machines to provide immediate feedback to subjects. He studied (1968) the famous "psychic" Peter Hurkos but found little psi ability.

Now a full professor of psychology at the University of California at Davis, Dr. Tart has served as a consultant at Stanford Research Institute (SRI) and worked with Harold Puthoff and Russell Targ in the widely discussed (and criticized) remote viewing projects.

Of his many books, he considers *Altered States of Consciousness* (1969) and *Transpersonal Psychologies* (1975) "classics," the latter having been translated into German and Spanish. He has written numerous chapters for books and articles for many scientific and parapsychological journals, including the *Journal of the American Society for Psychical Research,* the *Journal of the Society for Psychical Research,* and the *International Journal of Parapsychology.* He publishes a quarterly, *The Open Mind.*

In 1977 Dr. Tart was president of the Parapsychological Association and was a member of the American Association for the Advancement of Science. He is a member of the American Society for Psychical Research and of the International Association for Near-Death Studies, among others, and is a Fellow of the American Society for Clinical Hypnosis and the Society for Clinical and Experimental Hypnosis.

Selected Writings: *Transpersonal Psychologies,* 1975; *On Being Stoned,* 1971; *Altered States of Consciousness,* 1969 (rev. 1972); and Puthoff, H. and Targ, R. *Mind at Large: Institute of Electrical and Electronic Engineers Symposia on the Nature of Extrasensory Perception,* 1979; and Smith, J. 1968. "Two Token Object Studies with the 'Psychic,' Peter Hurkos." JASPR 62:143.

**Taylor, John, 1931–.** British physicist and mathematician. He is one of the few noted scientists who dared to tread into the field of parapsychology and to do an abrupt about-face after he got into it. "I started my investigations into ESP because I thought there could be something in it," he said (Taylor, 1980:vii). What attracted him even more than extrasensory perception and triggered his first book (Taylor, 1975) was metal-bending and the phenomena produced by Uri Geller. When he investigated Geller, the Israeli psychic performed one of his amazing feats with a spoon: Within a second, it softened, broke and became hard again. Dr. Taylor investigated other subjects and found the same "scrunches" or bending of paper clips which another physicist, John Hasted, had observed. Dr. Taylor was convinced of the authenticity of the metal-bending phenomenon and hypothesized that it was based on some kind of electromagnetic action (Taylor, 1975).

Subsequently, however, he did some more thinking and investigating and changed from believer to sceptic. "The evidence for paranormal spoon bending presented up to now," he wrote, "is suggestive but certainly not watertight" (Taylor, 1980:117). He now believes that the earlier test with Geller was faulty and that Geller's powers were not authentic: He was unable to perform in later tests in a controlled set up and with videotape and direct recordings of pressure applied to spoons. From his studies of other forms of paranormal phenomena, including clairvoyance, telepathy, precognition, and psychokinesis, Dr. Taylor concludes that there was nothing to them except "poor experimentation, shoddy theory and human gullibility" (Taylor, 1980:162). Perhaps most important for Dr. Taylor is his view that, except for unorthodox healing and spontaneous human combustion, "nearly all of the claimed paranormal phenomena are in complete contradiction to established science" (Taylor, 1980:162).

Dr. Taylor, a professor of mathematics at Kings College in London, presents the curious case of an academician and scientist who, in his first book, showed a belief in psychic phenomena and in his second, disbelief. The first probably angered academic and scientific colleagues: the second certainly placated them.

Selected Writings: *Science and the Supernatural: An Investigation of Paranormal Phenomena including Psychic Healing, Clairvoyance, Telepathy and Precognition by a Distinguished Physicist and Mathematician,* 1980; *Superminds (An Enquiry Into the Parnormal),* 1975.

**Telekinesis.** A term used by **Frederic W. H. Myers** to describe those physical phenomena of Spiritualism involving the movement of physical objects without the intermediation of any known physical energy. The Spiritualistic interpretation of telekinetic phenomena—that they are evidence of survival after death and of the existence of spirits—is usually not accepted in parapsychology or psychical research. The term "telekinesis" is therefore usually not used because of its Spiritualistic connotations. See also **Psychokinesis.**

**Telepathy.** Also called "mind-reading," "thought reading," "thought transference" and "mental telegraphy." This term, derived from the Greek and meaning "distant feeling," was introduced by **Frederic W. H. Myers** at the turn of the century to mean "the communication of impressions of any kind from one mind to another, independently of the recognized channels of sense."

Mind-to-mind communication has been reported since the time of Croesus. There are many instances in the Bible—Jesus Christ knew without being told that the woman of Samaria had had five husbands (John 4:18); the prophet Elisha always knew in advance what the king of Syria was planning in his war against the Israelites (2 Kings 6:8–12). From the eighteenth century comes the remarkable report of Emanuel Swedenborg's accurate vision of a great fire in Stockholm, some 300 miles from the city he was visiting. Subsequently, the practioners of mesmerism reported that mental impressions seemed to be received readily by people in a mesmeric state of trance.

No critical investigation of telepathy was made until the 1870s when experiments in telepathy were carried out by Sir William Barrett of England and Charles Richet of France. When the Society for Psychical Research was organized in 1882, telepathy was the first question the group investigated with, for example, picture drawing experiments. The SPR also collected spontaneous cases on a large scale in *Phantasms of the Living.* In one case, typical of thousands that have been collected since, at 7:00 A.M. one morning a woman woke up with a start with the sensation that she had been struck on her mouth and that she was bleeding under her upper lip—it was a dream and she was not bleeding. But her husband, who had been out sailing, at about seven o'clock that morning was hit by the tiller of the sailboat during a squall and his upper lip bled profusely.

Telepathy continues to be the subject of ongoing experimental investigations.

**Telepathy, Pure.** Term that distinguishes telepathy from clairvoyance. Although telepathy was one of the first objects of inquiry and experimentation by the early researchers, they did not realize that the tests they were conducting might not have been telepathic experiments at all. In all such experiments, the agent knew the target, whether a card, picture, number, or object so that, if the percipient correctly identified the impression of the target in the agent's mind, the result was taken as evidence of telepathy. Clairvoyance of the target itself by the percipient was not considered possible.

As this possibility became more appreciated, J. B. Rhine and his staff at the Parapsychology Laboratory tried to conceive of some experiment that would eliminate any objective target and even any written record of a target that could be "read" clairvoyantly. Rhine and Elizabeth McMahan, one of his research assistants, developed an experiment in which the symbols on ESP cards were converted into a personal code of numbers that was not written or spoken. When Elizabeth McMahan acted as agent during the experiment, she translated the number in her mind to the ESP symbol it represented. The subject's task was to guess the symbol, not the number, and record the guess. After many runs and a careful double-checking of hits and misses, extra chance results were found that seemed to suggest "pure telepathy."

Even so, the situation remains unclear: If the agent's thoughts of the symbols were physical brain processes at work, the subject might have been "reading" these processes by clairvoyance. If this is the case, the difficulty of finding an experiment for "pure telepathy" is greatly compounded.

**Teleplasm.** See **Ectoplasm.**

**Teleportation.** The paranormal transport of material objects or living bodies across a distance and through other objects and enclosed areas. Harry Price gave an account of a poltergeist case in India in which a young boy who had not come through the doorway was reported seen inside a house moving as if carried over the floor. The apparent transport of matter through matter remains one of the most perplexing and disturbing of all paranormal phenomena. See also **Apport; Nickelheim Poltergeist.**

BIBLIOGRAPHY: Price, H. and Kohn, H. 1930. "An Indian Poltergeist." *Psychic Research* 24:122.

**Telergy.** Word coined by **F. W. H. Myers** to denote some hypothetical power or energy that, in telepathy, permits an agent to initiate and effect a transmission of thought to the mind of a percipient. Whether this is the true psychical process or whether the precipient initiates the process and apprehends the mind of the agent is not certain today.

**Telesthesia.** Coined by F. W. H. Myers. See **Clairvoyance.**

**Tenhaeff, Wilhelm Heinrich Carl, 1894–1981.** Controversial Dutch parapsychologist. Until recently esteemed highly as a scrupulous researcher, he founded and edited the *Tijdschrift voor Parapsychologie,* the journal of the Dutch Society for Psychical Research. In March 1953 he was appointed to the chair of parapsychology at the University of Utrecht and made special professor of parapsychology—"professor extra ordinarius"—a position he held for twenty years. He was also director of the Parapsychological Institute at the University of Utrecht. Tenhaeff was the dominant force and acknowledged leader of the **Studievereniging voor Psychical Research** until 1960 when his dictatorial attitude and tactics created a schism within the organization so that many important figures in Dutch parapsychology resigned from it.

Tenhaeff wrote many books and papers that were published in his own and foreign journals. It was not until people began looking closely into his claims for his pet psychic Gerard Croiset that it became clear that Tenhaeff was doctoring the data. Dutch cases were changed and exaggerated for publication in foreign periodicals and investigations of Croiset were misrepresented in Dutch periodicals. Tenhaeff's excellent relations with the media made it possible for him to persuade people that he was "a prophet of a new, nonmaterialistic science. . . . He never failed to remind his audiences of the religious implications of his work or to allude darkly to possible bolshevik influences in skeptical circles" (Hoebens, 1986: 140). Yet, sadly, he is now looked on as a disgrace to the field. His fallen stature is clear from the fact that no major parapsychological journal reported his death. Tenhaeff died sad and embittered.

BIBLIOGRAPHY: Hoebens, P. H. "Croiset Mozart of 'Psychic Sleuths' " and "Croiset and Professor Tenhaeff: Discrepancies in Claims of Clairvoyance." In K. Frazier, ed., *Science Confronts the Paranormal,* 1986.

**Tennyson, Alfred, Lord, 1809–1892.** English poet. He succeeded William Wordsworth as poet laureate in 1850. His poetry represents the Victorian Age in England and appeals to both the deepest emotions and the highest intellect. He is buried in Westminster Abbey. Among his best-known poems are *The Lotus-Eaters* (1832), *The Lady of Shalott* (1832), *Ulysses* (1842), *In Memoriam* (1850), *The Charge of the Light Brigade,* (1855), *Idylls of the King* (1859), and *Crossing the Bar* (1889). He was an honorary associate of the Society for Psychical Research and there are verses in his *Early Sonnets No. 1* that show his belief in reincarnation:

So that we say, 'All this hath been before
All this hath been, I know not when or
  where:' . . .
Although I knew not in what time or
  place,
Methought that I had often met with you,
And either lived in either's heart and
  speech.

A letter written in 1874 shows him to be a **Noted Witness** also for a form of continuation beyond death, an altered state of consciousness or trance which he could induce: "[A] kind of waking trance (this for want of a better term) I have frequently had, quite up from boyhood, when I have been all alone. This has often come upon me through repeating my own name to myself silently till, all at once, as it were, out of the intensity of the consciousness of the individuality, the individuality itself seemed to dissolve and fade away into boundless being; and this is not a composed state, but the clearest of the clearest, the surest of the surest, utterly beyond words, where death was an almost laughable impossibility, the loss of personality (if so it were), seeming no extinction, but the only true life. I am ashamed of my feeble description. Have I not said the state was utterly beyond words."

BIBLIOGRAPHY: Prince, W. F. *Noted Witnesses for Psychic Occurrences,* 1963, p. 144.

**Teresa of Avila, Saint (Teresa Cepeda y Ahumada), 1515–1582.** Spanish mystic. Her writings are ranked among the greatest devotional books of the Roman Catholic church. In 1970, she became the first woman honored as doctor of the Church.

Born in Avila, Spain, one of eleven children, she left home with her brother to suffer martyrdom at the hands of the Moors because, said her brother, Teresa "wanted to see God." As it turned out, her wish was postponed. In 1531, she entered a convent in Avila and five years later the Carmelite convent there. In 1562, in order to reform Carmelite life, she founded the order of Discalced or Barefoot Carmelites to emphasize a life of contemplation and prayer for the nuns. Although frail and suffering constantly from bad health, Teresa traveled constantly and in all weather for the rest of her days to the scattered branches of the order. She herself meditated and prayed and yet was extraordinarily active and creative. Her works include *Interior Castle* (1588), *The Book of Foundations* (1610), and *Life of the Mother Teresa of Jesus* (1611).

She comes as an impressive **Noted Witness** for several kinds of paranormal phenomena. In support of levitation, for example, a phenomenon she called "the rapture" and which she experienced often while praying in her chapel, she recorded: "[Y]ou feel and see yourself carried away you know not whither . . . my soul was carried away, and almost always my head with it—I had no power over it—and now and then the whole body as well, so that it was lifted up from the ground. . . . It seemed to me, when I tried to make some resistance, as if a great force beneath my feet lifted me up. . . " Teresa's levitations were witnessed by her nuns, although one at a time and not collectively. Sister Anne of the Incarnation at Segovia gave her clear eye witness account: ". . . between one and two o'clock in the daytime . . . our holy Mother entered and knelt down. . . . As I was looking on, she was raised about half a yard from the ground without her feet touching it. . . . Then suddenly she sank down and rested on her feet . . .".

Teresa was plainly embarrassed by her levitations, desired no attention and sought no reputation. Teresa's body could also move from place to place above the ground. In her *Interior Castle,* she seems at first to be describing an out-of-body experience: "Sometimes the soul becomes conscious of such rapid motion that the spirit seems to be transported with a speed which, especially at first, fills it with fear . . .". This description is similar to **Yram's** who refers to his out-of-body experiences as "being lifted up by a whirlwind . . . sucked up violently by a sort of huge vortex" (Yram, 1976). In Teresa's continuing description: "Turning now to this sudden transport of the spirit, it may be said to be of such a kind that the soul really seems to have left the body . . .". But in the passage immediately following she expresses doubt about whether or not her soul was or was not in her body. Since this was exactly what St. Paul said (II Cor. 12:2–3), it is possible that Teresa was only following authority so that her experience would be more acceptable and understandable to the Church.

Teresa's death did not end the phenomena associated with her. Six years after she was buried, her body remained entire and in a state of incorruptibility observed in the cases of many religious figures. In addition, there issued from her corpse a marvellous sweet fragrance in the best religious tradition of the "odor of sanctity."

BIBLIOGRAPHY: Thurston, H. *The Physical Phenomena of Mysticism,* 1952, pp. 9–10, 11, 12; Yram. *Practical Astral Projection,* 1976, p. 60.

**Terry, William Henry, 1836–1913.** English Spiritualist. He immigrated to Australia where he played an important role in the history of Australian psychical research. As the result of a spirit message, he founded in Melbourne in 1870 a periodical called the *Harbinger of Light.* It became the voice of Spiritualism in Australia and, with its accounts of séances, sittings, and the investigations and phenomena of mediums, "became the primary record of Australian psychical research for many decades" (Irwin, 1988). Mr. Terry edited the organ for thirty-five years to advance the Spiritualist movement but, under his editorship, it was not merely a propaganda tool. He used it to stimulate others to conduct experimental research with mediums and when mediums were found to be fraudulent, William Henry Terry was courageous and objective enough to expose them.

BIBLIOGRAPHY: Irwin, H. J. 1988. "Parapsychology in Australia." JASPR 82:319.

**Thackeray, William Makepiece, 1811–1863.** English novelist, moralist, satirist, and journalist. After publishing the *National Standard,* a literary periodical, and writing for *Punch* and *Fraser's Magazine,* he became famous for his satirical novels (*Vanity Fair* [1847–1848] and later *Pendennis* [1848–1850], are examples) on the manners of English life in the Victorian age. In *Henry Esmond* (1852)—it and *Vanity Fair* were his best works—Thackeray produced an historical romance reminiscent of the genius of Sir Walter Scott.

Thackeray attended séances given by D. D. Home in London and New York and said that under circumstances where trickery was impossible he had seen a large heavy dining room table, loaded with dishes and glasses, rise two feet off the ground. Yet Thackeray was an extreme skeptic. Home called Thackeray the most skeptical man he had ever met.

Thackeray is also a **Noted Witness** for the creative process and for obtaining his inspiration from some source beyond his conscious control. "I have been surprised at the observations made by some of my characters. It seems as if an occult power was moving my pen." Once, when alluding to Becky Sharp, his famous woman character in *Vanity Fair,* Thackeray said: "I never thought she would say that."

BIBLIOGRAPHY: Gibbes, E. B. 1939. "Influenced or Inspirational Writing." JASPR 33:270; Inglis B. *Natural and Supernatural,* 1977, pp. 231–232.

**Thalbourne, Michael, 1955–.** Australian Ph.D. He is a parapsychologist who, in addition to having taught psychology, computers, and statistics at various universities in and out of Australia, has made important contributions to parapsychology and psychical research. These range from devising better methods of evaluating the data from experiments in extrasensory perception to weighing the factors that influence belief in psi and in the afterlife to a complete revision of the terminology used by parapsychologists, the last being a major achievement. A research associate at the McDonnell Laboratory for Psychical Research when Project Alpha forced it to close, Thalbourne returned to Australia and the Department of Psychology at the University of Adelaide.

Selected Writings: 1982. *A Glossary of Terms Used in Parapsychology.*

**Theodule, Adele Maginot, 1812–1886.** Remarkable French medium. Given, by a person neither she nor the experimenter had ever met, the name of a deceased person, completely unknown both to her and to the experimenter, she could describe that deceased individual perfectly. She also often reproduced the person's voice and movements. On one occasion she even became sunburned as the deceased had been, although she had not been exposed to the sun, and the condition lasted for twenty-four hours. See also **Cahagnet, Louis Alphonse.**

**Theosophy.** The concepts and doctrines of the Theosophical Society founded in 1875 by Madame **H. P. Blavatsky.** The tenets of the society are based mainly on world religions, particularly Hindu philosophy and the Upanishads. Its objects are to create a nucleus of universal brotherhood, to investigate unexplained laws of nature and powers of the human being, and to seek for divine knowledge.

The dramatic relation between Theosophy and psychical research, although short-lived and although it took place long ago, still continues to reverberate. In 1884, Madame Blavatsky, Colonel Henry Olcott, and others gave a committee of the Society for Psychical Research evidence of paranormal phenomena associated with the Theosophical Society that was supposedly taking place in India. The committee sent Richard Hodgson to India to investigate Madame Blavatsky and the phenomena. Hodgson's report in 1885 demolished her as far as the SPR was concerned, branded the phenomena fraudulent, and damned Theosophy in the eyes of psychical research for a hundred years. Now, however, this verdict is being contested, and not only by Theosophists. Vernon Harrison and others, including Robert H. Thouless, contend that Hodgson did not prove fraud and was neither legal nor scientific in his handling of the matter. On the other hand, Arthur S. Berger has defended Hodgson.

The Theosophical movement has "played a significant role in the independence movements and cultural renaissances of such countries as India, Sri Lanka, and Ireland. . . . Theosophy goes on, never surging dramatically in membership, never dying out" (Ellwood, 1983:111, 112).

BIBLIOGRAPHY: Berger, A. S. *Lives and Letters in American Parapsychology,* 1988; Ellwood, Jr., R. S. "The American Theosophical Synthesis." In H. Kerr and C. L. Crow, eds., *The Occult in America,* 1983; Harrison, V. 1986. "J'Accuse: An Examination of the Hodgson Report of 1885." JSPR 53:286.

**Theta.** Eighth letter of the Greek alphabet and first letter of *thanatos,* the Greek word meaning death. At the suggestion of **William G. Roll,** the word is used in several senses. As a noun, it denotes survival research. As an adjective, it denotes survival phenomena (i.e., "theta phenomena" or "theta evidence"). The terms "theta aspects" or "theta agent" are also used to refer to some aspects of the human being that may have survived death and may possibly manifest in cases of apparitions, mediums, communicators, haunts, or the unexplained movement of objects, as in apports or in some poltergeist disturbances.

**Theta Agent.** See **Apparition; Communicator; Theta.**

**Theta Aspects.** See **Theta.**

**Theta Journal.** Beginning in 1963, *Theta* has been published quarterly by the **Psychical Research Foundation.** It contains articles, personal experiences, book reviews and correspondence relating to survival, survival research, and survival phenomena. In 1986, its publication was undertaken by the Psychology Department of West Georgia College.

**Theurgy.** Hellenistic and pagan religion which, through magical rites and techniques, sought to communicate with the gods in order to influence their actions and to gain foreknowledge of the future. The doctrines of the theurgists were set forth in their sacred bible, the *Chaldean Oracles,* written in the second century A.D. by Julianus the Theurgist.

Theurgists used mediums to communicate with the gods in order to reveal the future. Porphyry, the Greek scholar and philosopher, noticed that the gods were slow to communicate in the beginning but, as the mediums practiced and gained more skill, the gods communicated more and more readily. Mediumistic methods varied. Some mediums, while fully conscious, seemed able to begin and end messages at will, a talent possessed by some modern mediums, such as "Mrs. Willett." Other mediums were placed in trance in which state they spoke automatically and in voices different from their normal voices. The mediums might remain perfectly still when divine communications were being received or they might move about. Violent movement meant that a medium had become possessed by a spirit.

In addition to precognition and possession, other paranormal phenomena were recognized as god-given signs. Described by Iamblichus, the third century Syrian philosopher, they included levitation of the mediums, the appearance of strange lights in the presence of the mediums, and, as the most significant of the divine signs, the materialization of the forms of spirits that would enter the bodies of the mediums. All these phenomena have their analogues in **Spiritualism** except that Theurgy associated them with the gods and not with deceased human beings. In this important respect, the beliefs of the Theurgists and Spiritualists are different.

**Thomas, Charles Drayton, ?–1953.** British clergyman and psychical researcher. A firm believer in Spiritualism, he sought in psychical research confirmation of his belief in survival after death. His principal contributions to the field were his sittings over a period of some twenty years with the noted medium Gladys Osborne Leonard.

Drayton Thomas believed that Feda, Mrs. Leonard's control, was an independent entity, the spirit of a young Indian girl as she claimed to be. His earliest sittings produced the book and newspaper tests (JSPR 20:89; 22:18; 23:118) that seemed to originate from a surviving mind on "the other side." He also conducted many proxy sittings with Mrs. Leonard, the most notable and most suggestive of survival after death being the **Bobbie Newlove Case** in which information unknown to anyone living was communicated.

The Rev. Mr. Drayton Thomas was a member of the council of the Society for Psychical Research for many years until his death.

Selected Writings: 1921. "Newspaper Tests." JSSPR 20: 89; 1933. "A Consideration of a Series of Proxy Sittings." PSPR 41:139; 1939. "A Proxy Case Extending over Eleven Sittings with Mrs. Osborne Leonard." PSPR 43:439.

BIBLIOGRAPHY: Allison, L. W. "Obituary: The Reverend C. Drayton Thomas." JASPR 48:37; Berger, A. S. *Evidence of Life after Death,* 1988, Chap. 2; Salter, H. de G. "Obituary: The Rev. C. Drayton Thomas." JSPR 37:677.

**Thomas, John Frederick, 1874–1940.** American public school administrator. History knows him as the recipient of the first Ph.D. awarded by an American university (Duke University) for a thesis on a topic related to psychical research: It dealt with mediumistic records. But Thomas also is the man who brought Joseph B. Rhine to Duke where he would do his historic work.

Thomas had been a graduate student at Duke under William McDougall. After Thomas's wife died in 1926, Thomas collected records of the sittings he had had with mediums in efforts to reach her. He wanted the records analyzed critically and interested J. B. and Louisa E. Rhine in the job of doing so. In 1927, he paid their way to Duke University to work as assistants to McDougall and evaluate the records (Berger, 1988). Thomas himself analyzed mediumistic material (Thomas, 1937, 1929). He threw new light on the phenomena and *modus operandi* of mediumship and proxy sittings. These sittings and the experiments conducted after his wife's death persuaded Thomas of the reality of survival after death.

Selected Writings: *Beyond Normal Cognition,* 1937; *Case Histories Bearing on Survival,* 1929.

BIBLIOGRAPHY: Berger, A. S. *Lives and Letters in American Parapsychology,* 1988.

**Thompson, Frederic Louis, 1868–?.** American goldsmith. He was the subject in a celebrated case investigated by James H. Hyslop. Robert Swain Gifford, an artist, died in January 1905. That summer, Thompson, who had no training or experience in painting, was overcome with a great desire to paint. In January 1906, he went to an art gallery in New York City, and while looking at Gifford's pictures, heard a voice say: "You see what I have done. Go on with the work" (Hyslop, 1909). Thereupon Thompson began to paint and sketch. His paintings and sketches were confirmed by competent experts to have Gifford's characteristics and to be recreations of the artist's style.

Hyslop used his method of **Cross-References** to try to determine if anything paranormal were going on. His sittings with mediums produced "phenomena which are undoubtedly supernormal and reflective of Mr. Gifford's personal identity" (Hyslop, 1909:462). The case suggests possession of Thompson by the dead Gifford.

BIBLIOGRAPHY: Hyslop, J. H. 1909. "A Case of Veridical Hallucinations." PASPR 3:1.

**Thompson, Rosalie (Mrs. Edmond), 1868–?.** British trance medium. Her mediumship began with physical phenomena—raps, lights, apports, levitation of chairs and tables. F. W. H. Myers who, from 1898 to 1900 had over 150 sittings with her, steered her into mental mediumship. She could see pictures and spirits, could write automatically both in trance and awake, and, most commonly, communicated by voice. Her chief control was her deceased daughter Nelly.

The most successful sittings with Mrs. Thompson seem to have been Myers's own, and, because of evidential material that he believed came from his dead love Annie Marshall, they convinced him of the reality of survival after death. Unfortunately, perhaps because he relied on Mrs. Thompson's prophesy that he would die on February 6, 1902 (he died on January 17, 1901), he did not live long enough to write his report of his sittings with her and, after his death, his wife destroyed his notes.

Myers had also written a lengthy chapter about Mrs. Thompson for inclusion in his posthumous *Human Personality and its Survival of Bodily Death,* but Alice Johnson, who with Richard Hodgson completed the manuscript after Myers's death, deleted this section from the book.

During one of her sittings Mrs. Thompson spoke Dutch, a language she did not know. Mrs. A. W. Verrall and Frank Podmore were also impressed by Mrs. Thompson, but Richard Hodgson was not. J. G. Piddington believed in the paranormality of Mrs. Thompson's communications but could not decide about their source. Mrs. Thompson was one of the mediums involved in the **Cross-Correspondences.**

BIBLIOGRAPHY: Gauld, A. *The Founders of Psychical Research,* 1968; Lodge, O. 1902. "Introduction to the Reports of Sittings with Mrs. Thompson." PSPR 17:61; Myers, F. W. H. 1902. "On the Trance Phenomena of Mrs. Thompson." PSPR 17:67; Piddington, J. G. 1904. "On the Types of Phenomena Displayed in Mrs. Thompson's Trance." PSPR 18:104; Van Eeden, F. "Account of Sittings with Mrs. Thompson." PSPR 17:75.

**Thompson-Gifford Case.** See **Thompson, Frederic L.**

**Thoughtography.** Word originated by **Tomokichi Fukuarai** who pioneered the first thoughtographic experiments. It denotes the apparent ability of a subject, deliberately and without using any photographic process, camera lens, or shutter, to imprint pictures on film plates or the film of a camera. In order to produce the effect, a subject seems to visualize an image, then to concentrate on a motion picture or Polaroid camera whose lens is capped, to assemble all his energy and, sometimes with a cry, to place the mental image on film.

Generally, the process of taking a picture with a camera involves the opening of a shutter that permits the lens to project an image on a negative from which a print is made. In thoughtography, a picture seems to be created with no lens or shutter. Thoughtographic or paranormal images are provocative since, if the mind, through psychokinesis, has the power to influence physical systems beyond the body (i.e., produce images on film), it makes us wonder what other and even greater powers it may have. Thoughtographic ability has been claimed in Japan by Masuaki Kiota and, in the United States, by Ted Serios.

**Thought-Reading.** See **Telepathy.**

**Thought Transference.** See **Telepathy.**

**Thouless, Robert Henry, 1894–1984.** Eminent British psychologist and parapsychologist. The man who invented "psi" and other important concepts in parapsychology, was a lecturer in psychology at Manchester and Glasgow universities and, later, at Cambridge. Dr. Thouless became interested in parapsychology because he loved puzzles and believed that psychic phenomena were puzzles to be solved, but he was drawn into the field in 1934 by the experimental work of J. B. Rhine.

Dr. Thouless soon realized that the very words used to describe parapsychological and psychic phenomena were loaded. For example, "extrasensory perception" or ESP, used to describe telepathy or clairvoyance, suggests that these phenomena involve some kind of perception such as seeing, smelling, or hearing. Perhaps a subject hazarding a guess on a target *was* "perceiving," perhaps not. Likewise, when we use the term "psychokinesis," we seem to be theorizing that a mind is exerting a direct influence on a physical object, which may or may not be the case. Thouless believed that it would be simpler and better to discard these terms and use instead something non-committal that offered no theory about what was really taking place. He coined the word **"psi"** to cover both ESP and psychokinesis. He and his colleague B. P. Wiesner also proposed the terms **"psi Gamma"** (for what are usually considered mental phenomena) and **"psi Kappa"** (for what are usually considered physical phenomena). Drs. Thouless and Wiesner also developed the theory of the **Shin** in an effort to accommodate both paranormal and normal events. Shin favors dualism with its concept of an immaterial component operating in the human being.

Dr. Thouless was president of the Society for Psychical Research from 1942 to 1944 wrote two books dealing with para psychology and about ninety articles for the

*Proceedings* and *Journal* of the SPR and the *Journal of Parapsychology.* He contributed to every major area of parapsychology and psychical research: Salience and decline effects; majority vote technique; unorthodox healing; precognition; feedback; and survival research. To the last, he contributed an ingenious **Cipher Test** to subject the difficult question of survival after death to experimental study. He also believed that parapsychology had religious implications and wrote: "Parapsychological research seems to reveal a world in which it is more reasonable to suppose that God and the supernatural play a part" (Thouless, 1977:176).

For fifty years, Dr. Thouless was a dominating figure in the fields of parapsychology and psychical research.

Selected Writings: "Implications for Religious Studies." In S. Krippner, ed., *Advances in Parapsychological Research, Vol. 1: Psychokinesis,* 1977, pp. 175–190; *From Anecdote to Experiment in Psychical Research,* 1972; *Experimental Psychical Research,* 1963; 1948. "A Test for Survival." PSPR 48:253; 1942. "The Present Position of Experimental Research into Telepathy and Related Problems." PSPR 42:1; and Wiesner, B. P. 1947. "The Psi Process in Normal and 'Paranormal' Psychology." PSPR 18:177.

BIBLIOGRAPHY: Berger, A. S. 1985. "Robert H. Thouless and His Work." JASPR 79:317; Berger, A. S. "A Tribute to Robert H. Thouless." In S. Krippner, ed., *Advances in Parapsychological Research, Vol. 4,* 1984.

**Thurston, Herbert, 1856–1939.** British Jesuit priest. He was the leading expert on psychical research among Roman Catholics in the United Kingdom. He made a survey of paranormal phenomena, including elongation, levitation, stigmata and psychokinesis, reported or observed among holy people or those canonized as saints (Thurston, 1955). His work, which reveals a sharp eye for evidential strengths and weaknesses and remarkable scholarship, is one of the best treatments of the subject ever made.

As a Jesuit, Father Thurston could not attend séances, but he read reports of them and other psychic phenomena and was an active member of the Society for Psychical Research. "Not many, perhaps, of his fellow members shared Fathers Thurston's standpoint," wrote his obituarist, "but there is none, however wide the difference in opinion, who will not deplore the loss of so courteous and learned a colleague" (Obituary, 1939).

Selected Writing: *The Physical Phenomena of Mysticism,* 1955.

BIBLIOGRAPHY: "Father Thurston's Work in Psychical Research." 1939. JSPR 31:118.

**Tibetan Book of the Dead.** See **Book of the Dead, Tibetan.**

**Tibón, Gutierre, 1905–.** Italian-born inventor of the small typewriter known as the "Hermes Baby." After taking up residence in Mexico in the mid-1940s, he achieved a reputation for his anthropological studies of Mexico's pre-Hispanic culture and for his investigations in psychical research. As a sceptical investigator, he transferred his inventive genius from devising a machine for printing letters to devising methods for exposing as a fraud the acclaimed physical medium Luis Martínez. To Tibón's utter amazement, in spite of all his ingenuity and many observations of the medium and experiments with him, he could find no evidence of trickery. Tibón came to regard Martínez's materializations as thought-forms of the medium objectified as ectoplasm.

**Tijdschrift voor Parapsychologie.** This Dutch journal published quarterly by the Studievereniging voor Psychical Research publishes general articles on parapsychology. It was founded in 1928 by P. A Dietz and W. H. C. Tenhaeff.

**Tillyard, Robin John, 1881–1937.** Anglo-Australian zoologist. Although British by birth, Australia beckoned to him after his graduation from Cambridge University in 1903. In Australia he first became a school teacher, subsequently a university lecturer in zoology and, finally, chief of the Division of Economic Entomology for the Australian government.

But while insects were his vocation, psychical research and mediums were his avocation. He visited England to work with Harry Price in the investigations of the mediums Stella C. and Eleonore Zugun and achieved his ambition of sitting with the spectacular Mina S. Crandon (Margery). The results of his several séances with her were published in the important British scientific journal *Nature* and in a publication of the American Society for Psychical Research. Of one séance, held in Boston in 1928, he wrote to Sir Oliver Lodge, "It was by far the most wonderful seance I have ever attended, and as far as I am concerned now I should not worry if I never had another sitting in my life . . . [because it had] the most marvelous result in the whole history of psychical research. . . . This séance is, for me, the culminating point of all my psychical research; I can now say, if I so desire, *'Nunc Dimittis,'* and go on with my own legitimate entomological work."

An auto accident ended his life in 1937. It is noteworthy that, eight and a half years earlier, one of the cases of precognition collected by A. W. Osborn predicted Tillyard's death in a car mishap. It is not clear whether he had notice of this prediction.

Selected Writings: 1931. "Dr. R. J. Tillyard's Notes of his Seance with 'Margery.'" *Psychic Research* 25:139; 1928. "Evidence of Survival of a Human Personality." *Nature* 122:243; 1926. "Science and Psychical Research." *Nature* 118:587.

BIBLIOGRAPHY: Evans, J. W. *The Life and Work of Robin John Tillyard 1881–1937,* 1963.

**Timm, Ulrich, 1938–.** German statistician. He is an outstanding authority on and developer of statistical tests used as a measure for evaluating the results of psi experiments. He developed a "psi-coefficient" that is employed widely to evaluate and compare experimental methods and results. He was a co-founder of the Wissenschaftliche Gesellschaft zur Förderung der Parapsychologie (Scientific Society for the Advancement of Parapsychology).

Selected Writing: 1973. "The Measurement of Psi." JASPR 67:282.

**Tischner, Rudolf, 1879–1961.** German historian and a doyen of German psychical research. He had long experience in and extensive knowledge of the field. Because he was frail as a youth, he spent his time in the study of philosophy and finally elected to enter the medical profession. But he turned to the paranormal when his interest was stimulated by an old friend who was investigating mediums. He tended to accept paranormal phenomena although he thought that survival after death, while a possibility, was impossible to prove.

Tischner conducted his own experiments in telepathy and wrote a book about them (Tischner, 1920). He also published monographs on Daniel D. Home and William Crookes and an account of Franz A. Mesmer and mesmerism. He acquired a broad knowledge of psychical research and published a history of it from the nineteenth century onward (Tischner, 1924). He was gratified when the Society for Psychical Research recognized his work by making him a corresponding member. But all his writings came to an end when Adolf Hitler's regime made it impossible to publish material dealing with the paranormal. And, during World War II, an air-raid destroyed his precious and extensive library.

Selected Writings: *Franz Anton Mesmer: Leben, Werk und Wirkungen,* 1928; *Geschichte der okkultistischen (metapsychischen) Forschung von der Mitte des 19. Jahrhunderts bis zur Gegenwart,* 1924; *Über Telepathie und Hellsehen. Experimentell-theoretische Untersuchungen,* 1920.

**Titanic.** White Star passenger liner which, on April 15, 1912, on its maiden voyage, struck an iceberg ninety-five miles south of Newfoundland and sank. A shortage of lifeboats resulted in over 1,500 passengers and crew perishing in the greatest peacetime maritime catastrophe of all time.

*Titanic*'s hull had been designed with sixteen watertight compartments and she had been regarded as unsinkable. Four compartments could be flooded without danger to the ship. Apart from her role in an appalling loss of life and her importance to the adoption of rules for safety at sea by international martime authorities, the *Titanic* is a special subject of study for psychical research because the ship was the seeming target of precognition on the part of many people.

One such case was that of J. Connon Middleton, a British businessman, who, on March 23, 1912, booked passage on the *Titanic.* Subsequently, he had two dreams in which he saw the ship floating keel upwards in the sea with passengers and crew swimming around her. Middleton cancelled his passage and told his friends and family of his dreams.

A second case is that of a woman in New York who was awakened by a frightening dream on the night of April 14–15. In the dream, her mother was in a rocking lifeboat crowded with many people. The woman did not know that her mother had been aboard the *Titanic*, and so, the next day, she was horrified to see her mother's name on the ship's passenger list. At the time of the dream, the mother was indeed in a lifeboat with other passengers.

The last example is that of Mr. and Mrs. Jack Marshall who were watching the ship as it sailed out of England bound for the United States. Mrs. Marshall suddenly cried out in alarm that the ship would sink and that hundreds of people would drown in the icy sea. Nothing said to her about the unsinkability of the *Titanic* would silence or calm the agitated woman.

These experiences came from percipients on both sides of the Atlantic who did not know one another, and they all seemed trained directly on one single target. In other words, these cases present one event experienced by several independent percipients and the collectivity of their experiences suggests that they may have been produced by some objective cause. Also, the fact that everyone considered the *Titanic* unsinkable is significant from the standpoint of psychical research and parapsychology because it raises a doubt about any explanation of chance or coincidence, renders highly improbable the use of inference from present knowledge in the forecasts of the tragedy, and seems to imply strongly that the experiences were truly precognitive. The peacetime disaster of the *Titanic* is therefore very much unlike that of the British liner *Lusitania* whose sinking by the Germans off Ireland in 1915 might have been easily forecast, during wartime and in waters where U-boats were active and had sunk many ships, by the many people who anticipated her sinking. See also **Robertson, Morgan; Stead, William Thomas.**

BIBLIOGRAPHY: Stevenson, I. 1960. "A Review and Analysis of Paranormal Experiences Connected with the Sinking of the Titanic." JASPR 54:153.

**Token Object Reading.** See **Psychometry.**

**Tomczyk, Stanislawa.** Early twentieth century Polish physical medium. She was discovered and studied extensively by Dr. Julien Ochorowicz. Baron von Schrenck-Notzing also investigated her as did Everard Feilding (whom she married in 1919). Ochorowicz, Feilding, and the medium herself all concurred that there was no spirit agency involved in the production of her phenomena but instead some force (psychokinesis). Feilding felt that the authentication of this psychokinetic force could explain all the phenomena of Spiritualism.

Stanislawa Tomczyk's phenomena, produced while she was in trance, were of two types: 1. spontaneous poltergeist-type phenomena; and 2. experimental psychokinetic phenomena that occurred while she was in a semi-trance. They involved the movement and levitation of small objects, such as matchboxes, tumblers, pencils, etc. (à la Nina Kulagina), the production of lights, effects on photographic plates and on a galvanometer, precipitation of chemicals held in solution, and vision through an opaque glass. The levitations sometimes were supposedly effected by a "fluid" thread—which skeptics say indicates fraud. Ochorowicz, Schrenck-Notzing, Charles Richet, and Theodore Flournoy all were convinced that her phenomena were genuine even though Flournoy was supposed to have caught her cheating.

After her marriage Stanislawa Tomczyk gave up her mediumship and reacted violently against it. Should private material on her mediumship in the possession of the Society for Psychical Research ever be made public we may then have enough information to decide whether or not her phenomena were indeed genuine.

BIBLIOGRAPHY: Feilding, E. 1915. "Note on the English Sittings with Miss Tomczyk." JSPR 17:28; Nicol, J. F. "Historical Background." In B. Wolman, ed., *Handbook of Parapsychology*, 1977, p. 320.

**Tongues, Gift of.** See **Gift of Tongues.**

**Torres, Penny, 1960–.** American trance channeler. She was called by *People* magazine in January 1987 "the hottest newcomer to channeling in Southern California." She channels "Mafu," an "entity from the seventh Dimension" who in his last incarnation was a leper in first century Pompeii. "Mafu" is to have the use of her body for seven years (beginning in February 1986) in exchange for taking care of the Torres's needs—Penny Torres charges $30 for day-long seminars and $125 for overnight retreats. "Speaking through Torres in a voice that sounds like Eartha Kitt doing Monty Python, Mafu tells his listeners, 'I am an enlightened entity and I come to you from the Brotherhood of Light.' " His purpose is to "bring the message of love to the human plane."

BIBLIOGRAPHY: "Voices from Beyond: The Channelers." *People* Jan. 26, 1987:30, 33.

**Total Score.** See **Score, Total.**

**Touch Matching.** A method of conducting an ESP test with cards in which a subject touches a key card to indicate a call of a target card. The experimenter then places the target card next to (or below if the screened touch matching technique is used) the key card indicated.

**Trance.** A state during which sensitivity to external stimuli has been reduced; an altered state of consciousness resembling a condition of deep hypnosis. It may be self-induced, induced by a hypnotist, or, in some cultures, by dancing, drumming, the inhalation of smoke from resinous plants or ingestion of yage or ayahuasca. During séances or sittings, mental mediums may remain in a conscious, waking state or pass into a state of trance.

It is difficult to lay down any hard and fast rule governing the trance process. Generally, however, a trance medium in a sitting or reclining position enters this state after a period of quiet with closed eyes. The state seems to begin after some deep breathing and restlessness with occasional whispers or moans. Once in a state of trance, the medium may give messages purporting to be from a deceased person. If a trance-personality is in control, the medium may speak in a trance voice, perhaps a contralto, or a masculine voice in the case of a female medium, talk like a child or use uncharacteristic vocabulary. The trance state may embrace different states of dissociation. With some trance mediums, such as Mrs. Willett, for example, normal consciousness seems to have disappeared only partially, for the medium needs to be able to transmit any supposed messages to sitters by automatic writing, speaking or spelling. With other types of trance mediums, a trance may occur in which another personality, either the trance-personality, a communicator or other entity independent of the medium seems to take over and possess the sensory and motor functions of the medium. Studies made by Gerald Balfour, W. H. Salter, Eleanor Sidgwick and C. D. Broad of the trance mediumships of the great mediums—Mrs. Leonora Piper, Mrs. Gladys Osborne Leonard and Mrs. Willett—throw light on the types and processes of trance mediumship. See also **Trance-Control.**

BIBLIOGRAPHY: Balfour, G. W. 1935. "A Study of the Psychological Aspects of Mrs. Willett's Mediumship and of the Statements of the Communicators." PSPR 43:41; Broad, C. D. *Lectures on Psychical Research,* 1962; Salter, W. H. 1921. "A Further Report on Sittings with Mrs. Leonard." PSPR 32:1; Sidgwick, E. 1915. "A Contribution to the Study of the Psychology of Mrs. Piper's Trance Phenomena." PSPR 28:1.

**Trance, Autonomous.** See **Trance.**

**Trance-Control.** A trance-personality that appears repeatedly in the trance states of a medium, or a dominating communicator who has taken the place of any trance-personality, either of which seem to replace or control a medium's motor and sensory mechanisms. See also **Control.**

**Trance Mediumship.** See **Trance.**

**Trance-Personality.** See **Control; Trance; Trance Control.**

**Transcendental Meditation (TM).** Brought to the West in 1959 by the Hindu monk Maharishi Mahesh Yogi, it is a program that teaches a technique of meditation based on a mantra (a sound that produces a spell or has special power). By repeatedly saying the mantra aloud or thinking of it, the mind is supposed to be stilled and the individual helped to enter a more profound level of consciousness.

The program spread rapidly. Thousands practiced it in the 1960s after celebrities including the Beatles, the famous British rock-group, took up the technique. People liked the monk's message: "Man is born to enjoy, to create, and to radiate happiness." TM also became popular because it was supposed to produce a deep state of rest, greater health, clarity of mind, freedom from tension, creative intelligence, and even a decrease in crime (Denniston and Williams, 1975).

The claim was made as well that advanced TM could produce *siddhis* involving paranormal abilities such as levitation or the finding of hidden objects with the power of clairvoyance. To see if there were empirical support for this latter claim, parapsychologists conducted experiments in clairvoyance with "siddhas," people who had been practicing meditation and the *siddhis* for years, and with ordinary TM meditators who had been practicing TM for some months. In card-guessing tests using the down through method and in tests with concealed pictures, none of the results with either group of subjects was significant, but, of the two groups, the "siddhas" obtained the lower scores (Harding and Thalbourne, 1981). According to independent judges who rated the targets and the images, thoughts and feelings of the subjects in other extrasensory perception experiments using target pictures, however, twenty TM graduates scored positively (Palmer, Khamashta, and Israelson, 1979). Perhaps further investigation is needed to clarify the meaning of these mixed results that find both negative and positive evidence of psi among transcendental meditators.

BIBLIOGRAPHY: Denniston, D. and McWilliams, P. *The TM Book,* 1975; Harding, S. E. and Thalbourne, M. A. "Transcendental Meditation, Clairvoyant Ability and Psychological Adjustment." In W. G. Roll and J. Beloff, eds. *Research in Parapsychology 1980,* 1981, p. 71; Palmer, J., Khamashta, K. and Israelson, K. 1979. "An ESP Ganzfeld Experiment with Transcendental Meditators." JASPR 73:334.

**Transcommunication.** Purported communications by means of audio, video, and computer systems with deceased people and other realities. An example of a transcommunication was reported to have occurred during an experiment in 1988. Physicist Ernst Senkowski addressed questions to a deceased scientist, and erudite and technical responses in German were received on a computer printout (Newsletter, 1988). Images of the dead also are said to be projected on video picture tubes even when television sets have no antennae.

BIBLIOGRAPHY: Unlimited Horizons Newsletter of Metascience Foundation, Spring 1988, 6 (1):4–6.

**Transmigration.** See **Reincarnation.**

**Traveling Clairvoyance.** See **Out-of Body Experience.**

**Treviño, Carlos B., 1935–.** Mexican doctor of medicine and psychoanalyst. He was drawn to parapsychology in 1967 and, seven years later with the help and advice of Joseph B. Rhine, co-founded the first parapsychological association in Mexico, the Sociedad Mexicana de Parapsicología. As its general director, he trains and organizes research teams, includes in each a medical doctor, a psychologist, or psychoanalyst and assigns paranormal phenomena to each team according to the interests or specialties of its members. Dr. Treviño appears frequently on Mexican television and writes books and articles concerning his own interests in possession and the relationship between psi and psychiatry.

Selected Writings: 1983. "'Possession, Psychiatry and Psi." *Psi Research 2 (2); Introducción a la Parapsicología,* 1976.

**Treviño, Marcela Gomezharper de, 1936–,** Mexican psychical researcher. She co-founded Mexico's largest parapsychological organization, the Sociedad Mexicana de Parapsicología, of which she has been the longtime bilingual secretary. One of her research interests has been Kirlian photography and its use as a tool for the diagnosis and assessment of physical and emotional conditions that the photographs may show. In order to find out about the relation between Kirlian technique and pregnancy, she had Kirlian photographs taken of the right index fingers of healthy non-pregnant and pregnant women. In the case of the women who were not pregnant, the photographs showed a dark egg-shaped mass with a thin glow around the periphery of the mass. The photographs of the pregnant women showed "pregnancy zones," the same egg-shaped structure but with emissions of energy that seemed to project from the center to the periphery to form a bright, broad ring around it with bright fingers extending outward all around the periphery. But Marcela Treviño points out that the "pregnancy zone" may not appear at all if a pregnant woman is under emotional or physical stress and she warns that the usefulness of Kirlian photography as a diagnostic tool remains in doubt.

BIBLIOGRAPHY: with Flores, A. C. 1985. "Kirlian Photography and Pregnancy." *Psi Research* 4 (3, 4): 232.

**Trial.** In ESP tests, a single attempt to identify

a target object; in PK tests, a single unit of effect, to be measured in the evaluation of results (JP).

**Tribbe, Frank C., 1914–.** American attorney and psychical researcher. He is the first and only researcher in the field to have subjected the **Shroud of Turin,** and the scientific findings and data in relation to it, to close examination.

Although carbon-dating in 1988 claimed to have established that the Shroud is no more than 728 years old and could not have been the burial cloth of Jesus Christ, scientists and church authorities continue to speculate about the mysterious images on the Shroud that are possibly the oldest "photographs" ever made although they were imprinted on the Shroud long before the invention of photography. Mr. Tribbe has cast doubts upon the results of the carbon-dating by pointing out problems with the way the tests were carried out (Tyrer, Tribbe, Wilson, and Kendrick, 1989). He also believes that logical minds are compelled to consider the spiritual or paranormal in order to explain the mystery of how the images got on the Shroud.

Mr. Tribbe's interest in the paranormal began in the 1930s and continued during the forty years he served as a U.S. government attorney. He co-designed a **Cipher Test,** was one of the organizers of the Survival Research Foundation and is a trustee on its board. He is also on the boards of the Academy of Religion and Psychical Research and Spiritual Frontiers Fellowship. He is editor of *Spiritual Frontiers* and also writes extensively in the field of the paranormal.

Selected Writings: (Editor) *The Ashby Guidebook for the Study of the Paranormal,* 1987; *Portrait of Jesus? The Illustrated Story of the Shroud of Turin,* 1983; and Tyrer, J., Wilson, I., and Kendrick, R. 1989. "The Turin Shroud—Too Hasty an Epitaph?" *The Christian Parapsychologist* 8(1):2.

**Trumpet Sitting.** See Direct Voice.

**Truzzi, Marcello, 1935–.** American sociologist and sceptic. Born in Copenhagen, Denmark, into an Italian circus family, he is known in parapsychology for his "soft-line" scepticism. He attended Florida State University from which he received his B.A., the University of Florida from which he received his M.A., and he took his Ph.D. at Cornell. Professor of sociology at Eastern Michigan University, he was a founding member and on the council of the Committee for the Scientific Investigation of Claims of the Paranormal (CSICOP) and first editor of its journal *The Zetetic* (now *The Skeptical Inquirer*). He resigned from CSICOP for what he considered its lack of impartiality. He is now the director of the Center for Scientific Anomalies Research (CSAR) and editor of its journal **Zetetic Scholar** which promotes interaction between critics and proponents of paranormal phenomena.

Dr. Truzzi (1982) distinguishes among empirical critics (who "take issue with the basic facts being alleged"), conceptual critics (who "call into question definitional congruence between ideas like psi, precognition, and clairvoyance"), and methodological critics (who "take issue with the operational and procedural aspects of research"). He is critical of J. B. Rhine's policy of publishing negative research results only if they contribute something constructive or novel. He feels that parapsychologists need to involve critics, especially conjurers (he is a member of the Psychic Entertainers Association), in the design of research and should try to integrate parapsychology more closely with psychology, statistics, sociology, and physiology. But most of all he asks for "openness to evidence and commitment to inquiry."

Dr. Truzzi's interest in criminology has led to the development of CSAR's Psychic Sleuths Project. He is the author of numerous articles for sociological, anthropological, and folklore journals.

Selected Writings: "J. B. Rhine and Pseudoscience: Some Zetetic Reflections on Parapsychology." In K. R. Rao, ed., *J. B. Rhine: On the Frontiers of Science,* 1982; 1980. "A Skeptical Look at Paul Kurtz's Analysis of the Scientific Status of Parapsychology." JP 44:35; 1978. "On the Extraordinary: an Attempt at Clarification." *Zetetic Scholar* 1:11; 1977. "Editorial: Parameters of the Paranormal." *The Zetetic* 1(2):4; *The Occult in America,* 1973; and Hoebens, P. H. "Reflections on Psychic Sleuths." In P. Kurtz, ed., *A Skeptic's Handbook of Parapsychology,* 1985.

**Tut-Ankh-Amen.** See **Curses.**

**Twain, Mark, nom de plume of Samuel Langhorne Clemens, 1835–1910.** American author and lecturer. He wrote humorous stories for "the mighty mass of the uncultivated people" who lived beneath "the thin top crust of humanity." His immensely popular books included *The Celebrated Jumping Frog of Calaveras County* (1865), *The Innocents Abroad* (1869), *Roughing It* (1872), *The Adventures of Tom Sawyer* (1876), *Huckleberry Finn* (1884). *A Tramp Abroad* (1880) and *A Connecticut Yankee in King Arthur's Court* (1889). Mark Twain was two people: one, the poet, dreamer and man of letters; the other, funny man, showman, and lovable platform and after-dinner speaker.

Mark Twain had an interest in the paranormal, especially in telepathy (he called it "mental telegraphy") and wrote about it long before the Society for Psychical Research (of which, as Samuel Clemens, he was a member) was organized. He narrated, for instance, several experiences in which he was able to induce people to write to him merely by writing, but not mailing, letters to them. He also told of being in Washington, D.C. He knew a friend was somewhere in the city but had no idea of his friend's exact whereabouts. He began to walk, went into a cigar store, stayed there a few minutes and decided to meet his friend by leaving the shop, going to the left and taking ten strides. He did so and he and his friend met face to face.

Albert Bigelow Paine, Twain's biographer, provided another impressive case of "mental telegraphy". Twain had been anxious to refer to an article he had written in 1885 for the *Christian Union*. But no copy of it could be found. Later, Twain was walking down Fifth Avenue in New York City when he thought again of the article and his wish to see it. At 42nd Street, as he waited to let automobiles go by, a stranger crossed the street, headed for him and thrust the clipping from the *Christian Union* into Twain's hand.

Among the most dramatic of Twain's personal experiences was his extraordinary precognitive dream of the death of his brother, Henry Clemens. Henry was about twenty years old when Twain, then staying at his sister's house, dreamed that his brother was lying in a metal coffin. The coffin rested on two chairs. A bouquet of flowers, with one crimson bloom in the center, was on the chest of the corpse. A few days later, Twain's brother lost his life, along with 150 others, when the steamboat *Pennsylvania* exploded on the Mississippi River near Memphis. Twain went to Memphis and found Henry in a metal casket positioned as in the dream, and, as Twain watched, a woman placed on the casket the bouquet he had seen in the dream.

Because so many creative people have psychic talents and experiences, we cannot discount the possibility that Mark Twain's also may have been produced or at least related to his tremendous creative gifts. In any case, he stands as a **Noted Witness** for several kinds of paranormal phenomena.

If some reports be believed, after Twain's death, he manifested as a communicator. Emily Grant Hutchings and Lola V. Hays of St. Louis claimed that Twain's spirit had dictated to them the books *Jap Herron* and *Brent Roberts*. Although the books were actually published and sold under his authorship, a close examination of the writings shows a very remote connection between the books and Mark Twain.

BIBLIOGRAPHY: Berger, A. S. *Aristocracy of the Dead*, 1987; Paine, A. B. "Mark Twain: A Biographical Summary." In the *Family Mark Twain*, Vol. 1, 1972.

**Twigg, Ena, 1914–late 1980s.** British medium. Born of psychic parents, she was one of the most famous mediums in the world. From her childhood, she had seen "misty" people with whom she formed lasting friendships. "I have always *known* things," she said, "I could go into a room and tell exactly what happened in that room, and what conversation had gone on there" (Vaughan, 1972).

Twigg's clients have included people as famous as she, including James A. Pike who consulted her after his son died. During the sitting, Pike was moved by a purported communication from someone with a German accent whom he believed to be the deceased theologian Paul Tillich (Pike, 1968). Pike was only one of many deeply impressed by this medium who describes other striking cases in her book (1973) and was judged by the Spiritualist National Union as the "1967 Spiritualist of the Year."

In her book, the medium shows more awareness than many of her clients of a counterhypothesis to the apparent spirit communications that impressed them. She wrote: "Sceptics and nonbelievers often attribute the medium's ability to produce information unknown to her to telepathy or clairvoyance. There remains, however, a large body of material, unknown to the sitter, which defies this explanation." While this statement is true, it must be borne in mind that the possibility of a medium's extrasensory perception having acquired information from a living person is not limited to a sitter. Super ESP goes far beyond a sitter, and other counterhypotheses such as cosmic memory and Akashic records require no sitter.

Selected Writing: with Brod, R. H. *Ena Twigg Medium,* 1973.

BIBLIOGRAPHY: Pike, J. A. *The Other Side,* 1968; Vaughan, A. 1972. "Interview: Ena Twigg." *Psychic* 4(2):7.

**Two-Tailed Test.** A measure of experimental results in which the movement of deviation below or above mean chance expectation has not been determined prior to the experiment. See also **One-Tailed Test.**

**Tychoscope.** A new apparatus (a "psychic toy") invented by Pierre Janin of Epernon, France, for experiments in psychokinesis. The name of the device comes from the Greek *tych* meaning chance and *scope* meaning to see or look. First described at an international conference of the Parapsychology Foundation held in Copenhagen in 1976, it is a vertical cylindrical battery-powered vehicle on wheels, about the size of a drinking glass. It moves at random while a tracing pen attached to it records a path. These tracings represent chance movements. In PK experiments, the subjects try to link with the machine and to enforce their will on it. When Remy Chauvin of Ivoy-le-Pré, France, used the device, mice, apparently bothered by the noise made by the machine, seemed to be able to influence the device to move away from them.

**Tyrrell, George Nugent Merle, 1879–1952.** British physicist, mathematician, and psychical researcher. Tyrrell was by profession a telegraphic engineer who, after World War I, devoted most of his time to psychical research. As early as 1921 he conducted statistically significant ESP experiments with his adopted daughter, Gertrude Johnson (Nancy Sinclair). In later experiments, conducted mainly in 1935 and 1936 with Gertrude Johnson and G. W. Fisk, he used an electrical apparatus of his own invention into which eventually a random element was introduced. In these experiments Gertrude Johnson still achieved results significantly above chance.

When the apparatus (and Tyrrell's home) was destroyed by a bomb during World War II—as a result of which the Tyrrell family lived for several years with Rosalind Heywood—instead of rebuilding the apparatus Tyrrell turned to the theoretical aspects of psychical research. He made a thorough scientific study of apparitions and constructed a model of the "perfect" apparition: It would be three-dimensional; it would obscure the background and would be heard breathing; its clothing would rustle, its shoes would shuffle, but it would leave no footprints; it would seem to be aware of us and might put its hand on our shoulder (when we might feel a sensation of cold); it might speak, but a long conversation would be impossible; it would be reflected in a mirror and might cast a shadow; it would be wearing appropriate clothing; it might seem to pick up an object or open and close a door; if we tried to touch it our hand would go through it; it could not be photographed and it would eventually disappear. Gardner Murphy (1953) said of Tyrrell's *Apparitions:* "It . . . is an amazingly close-thought, brilliant, integrated, all-around consideration of the problem of apparitions." He called it "exciting, serious reading on psychical research."

Tyrrell also wrote on the philosophical aspects of psychical research. "Tyrrell conceived of Psychical Research as 'the exploration of human personality', and he was deeply impressed by the *queerness* of the conclusions to which the exploration seems to commit u s. . ." (Price, 1953). An important theoretical work was his "The 'Modus Operandi' of Paranormal Cognition" (1946) in which he discussed **mediating vehicles** for ESP and in which he wrote: "Statistical experiments which appear . . . to point to the existence of . . . telepathy and . . clairvoyance, are misleading. . . . The attempt . . . to carry out statistical research in isolation from every other sort of research is in the highest degree unscientific, misleading and dangerous. . . . Statistical experiments . . . as a method of inquiry into the nature of paranormal cognition . . . [are of] very limited [value]" (pp. 118–119).

Tyrrell's works, for example, his published lecture, *Apparitions,* and his books *Science and Psychical Phenomena* and *The Personality of Man* were widely read and made psychical research accessible to the general reader. He was working on *The Nature of Human Personality* at the time of his death. It was prepared for publication by his wife and Nancy (Gertrude) Johnson with the advice of H. H. Price who wrote the Foreword.

Tyrrell was president of the Society for Psychical Research for the years 1945 and 1946.

Selected Writings: *Science and Psychical Phenomena,* 1961; *The Nature of Human Personality,* 1954; *Apparitions,* 1953; *The Personality of Man,* 1947; 1946. "The 'Modus Operandi' of Paranormal Cognition." PSPR 48:6.

BIBLIOGRAPHY: Broad, C. D. *Lectures on Psychical Research.* 1952; Murphy, G. 1953. "The Importance of Spontaneous Cases." JASPR 47:97–100; Salter, W. H., Fisk, G. W., and Price, H. H. 1953. "G. N. M. Tyrrell and his Contributions to Psychical Research." JSPR 37:63.

# U

**Ullman, Montague, 1916–.** American psychiatrist and parapsychologist. Best known in parapsychology for his work in telepathy and dreams at the Maimonides Medical Center Dream Laboratory, Dr. Ullman became interested in psychical research at the age of sixteen during his sophomore year in college when he sat with a group of friends. During these séances a variety of seemingly paranormal phenomena took place: levitations, psychokinesis, thoughtography and direct writing from a supposedly deceased communicator. Although Dr. Ullman believes that the phenomena were paranormal, he does not think they were caused by the spirit of a deceased communicator but rather that they were created out of the sitters' unmet needs.

Soon after opening his office for the practice of psychoanalysis, during which Dr. Ullman encountered instances of what seemed to be psi, he began to collaborate with Gardner Murphy in explorations of ESP under conditions of light trance and hypnosis. These sessions were Dr. Ullman's introduction to experimental parapsychology. In the late 1940s, encouraged by Gardner Murphy, Laura Dale and Dr. Ullman set up a Medical Section of the American Society for Psychical Research. It lasted until 1953 and included, among others, Jan Ehrenwald and Jule Eisenbud. In that year the REM (rapid-eye-movement) stage of sleep associated with dreaming was discovered. A few years later it occurred to Dr. Ullman to use this technique in a controlled dream telepathy experiment. Eileen Garrett and her Parapsychology Foundation provided the place, the equipment, and the funds for the study with Dr. Ullman, Karlis Osis, and Douglas Dean the experimenters.

The striking results obtained over a two-year period led in 1961 to the setting up, as the result of a grant arranged by Gardner Murphy, of the Dream Laboratory at Maimonides Hospital for the study of paranormal dreams. In 1962 Stanley Krippner joined the staff and developed the research methodology for the experiments. Nine of the twelve formal studies carried out "supported the hypothesis that altered states of consciousness, such as dreaming and hypnosis, can be associated with telepathic and precognitive effects" (Ullman, 1988).

More recently, as a result of lecturing and teaching in Sweden, Dr. Ullman has developed a way of making dream work accessible to everybody by means of dream-sharing sessions during which psi is sometimes evident and which can permit psi abilities to develop. In 1970 Ullman visited the Soviet Union, Czechoslavakia, and Bulgaria and learned something of their way of conducting psi research. During this trip he met Nina Kulagina who produced psychokinetic effects for him.

Dr. Ullman believes that psi "seems to be an emergency mechanism for the individual adrift in a technological society and an available and useful form of adaptation in societies that have escaped that evolutionar

route. . . . [P]si can evolve in natural systems when there is an interest in psi and a persistence in its pursuit. Essential . . . would be the humility and sensitivity to follow where psi effects lead us instead of . . . thinking we can trap psi by one of our ingenious experimental designs" (Ullman, 1987:28).

Selected Writings: "Autobiographical Notes." In A. S. Berger. *Lives and Letters in American Parapsychology,* 1988; "The World of Psychic Phenomena as I Came To Know It." In R. Pilkington, ed., *Men and Women of Parapsychology,* 1987; with Zimmerman, N. *Working with Dreams,* 1985; with Krippner, S. and Vaughan, A. *Dream Telepathy,* 1973; with Krippner, S. *Dream Studies and Telepathy,* 1970.

**Umbanda Cult.** An Afro-Brazilian possession trance cult, sometimes mistakenly called Macumba. It was established around 1904 and now has thousands of *centros* throughout Brazil. Each *centro* is directed by a person who has been trained and is experienced as a trance medium and who is knowledgeble about cult doctrine. While the spiritist doctrine of **Allan Kardec** appeals to the upper and educated class and the pure African Candomblé cult is oriented toward the lower and less educated class, the Umbanda appeals to both classes and to the middle class, too, combining as it does both Spiritist and African elements. One line of the cult follows the teachings of Kardec while another branch follows the beliefs and rituals of Africa.

In the *centros* advancing the Spiritist doctrines, quietly controlled ceremonies are marked by soothing music, sermons, and prayers for humankind and the ideas of Kardec. Standing in rows opposite one another, mediums go into trance at a signal, such as the sound of a small bell or the snapping of fingers. Sitters are positioned in the center of the row so that there are two entranced mediums to each sitter. In the African branch of the cult, sermons, prayers, and teachings give way to the sound of drums, chants, and the movements of the dance. Gone is the orderliness and calmness of the Spiritist ceremony. Here is spontaneity, color, drama, excitement as entranced mediums stand before an altar where they are found by sitters from the audience.

In spite of the contrast between them, both lines have a feature in common: the *consulta* or consultation. Trance mediums possessed by a *guia* or spirit guide make passes with their hands over or near sitters to force the perispirit into correspondence with the soul as the spirits talk to the sitters. In these consultations, sitters may seek from the spirits counselling or solutions for daily problems, the location of lost objects or the healing of physical ills.

The psychical researcher would explain the obtaining of information about events or situations independent of the sensory process on the basis of a psychic person's extrasensory perception. The belief of the Umbanda, however, is that each individual has a guide who obtains and conveys this information to the individual and makes that person aware of things, or makes the person do things, that could not have been known or done normally. The basic claim of the *Umbandanistas* is that the entities or spirits possessing mediums or generally watching over an individual have ESP and PK abilities that can be used for obtaining paranormal knowledge or for unorthodox healing purposes. Through training, the possession trance can be developed to bring forth more readily and strongly the psi abilities of the entity.

Before anyone scoffs at the Umbanda theory, it is well to remember that we still know little or nothing about how the psi or healing processes work. If one is willing to accept the existence of spirits as a tentative working hypothesis, the Umbanda theory is as good as any other in our present state of ignorance.

BIBLIOGRAPHY: Giesler, P. V. 1985. "Parapsychological Anthropology: II. A Multi-Method Study of Psi and Psi-Related Processes in the Umbanda Ritual Trance Consultation." JASPR 79:113.

**Unidentified Flying Objects (UFOs).** Known also as flying saucers. Mysterious objects of a variety of sizes and shapes, although generally disk-shaped, which, in the air, seem to violate all the laws of motion and physics. Over the last four decades there have been thousands of sightings. Ufologists around the world have collected sightings at night, in the daytime and on radar. The strange vehicles are said to be reconnoitering the earth, landing, and, after some inspection, zooming upward at shocking speeds. Burn marks and imprints on the ground, humanoids, and abductions of people have been described. There are also cases in which a UFO has been seen collectively by two or more people (Randles, 1983). In other cases, photographs of the vehicles have been taken and published in UFO periodicals.

On the other hand, a panel of scientists appointed by the Central Intelligence Agency to examine such reports concluded that 90 percent of the sightings were of natural astronomical or meteorological phenomena—bright planets, stars, meteors, weather balloons, airplanes, helicopters, globe lightning, Saint Elmo's fire, even a flock of birds. A commission organized in 1966 and a panel organized in 1968 by the U.S. Air Force at the University of Colorado and headed by the physicist E. U. Condon reached similar conclusions and recommended no further investigations. Earlier, the U.S. Air Force had started a top-secret study of reported sightings called Project Bluebook. In 1969, with over 12,000 reports in the file, the project was discontinued because of the position taken by the Condon commission.

The subject continues to be controversial. Ufologists and a large segment of the public defend the hypothesis that flying saucers come from planets more technologically advanced than earth. Uri Geller's claim of having been endowed with paranormal gifts from an intelligence from outer space fits into this idea. The opposing group hold that the whole ideas is sensational and unacceptable nonsense. Only a few, such as the late Josef A. Hynek, try to steer a middle course and remain open-minded.

Parapsychologists, psychical researchers, and other scientists are skeptical of UFOs and the extraterrestrial hypothesis for several reasons. Reports come from untrained observers and are anecdotal. Even reports from trained observers are doubtful because many provocative and distracting events may have been occurring at the same time. Although there have been thousands of sightings, not a single physical artifact has withstood "rigorous scrutiny" (Klass, 1981); there is no crashed spacecraft or defecting humanoid, not even a Venutian love potion which might have been brought back by men who claim they were abducted and seduced by exotic female extraterrestrials. Data are not reliable. Photographic evidence can be doctored. The most telling reason for continued scientific resistance may be that Hynek's Center for UFO Studies, after fifteen years of investigation, still has not come up with positive evidence.

In addition, parapsychology's resistance is a case of one fringe area of research rejecting another fringe area in order not to be associated with a craze, cult, or new religion. But parapsychology overlooks the possibility that UFOs may be directly related to its subject matter. All the phenomena in parapsychology and psychical research from extrasensory perception to psychokinesis are basically products of our minds. If UFOs exist, they may have origins in and also be dependent on human minds. Carl G. Jung, using his concept of synchronicity, hypothesized a psychophysical reality and wrote that "even if the UFOs are physically real, the corresponding psychic projections [of unhappy, desperate people seeking help from a cosmic intelligence] are not actually caused, but only occasioned, by them" (1969:115). Or, UFOs may not be objects in flight but phenomena produced by psychokinesis: They may be a species of materialization, or they may be thought-forms projected and physically objectified by observers.

If we allow for the possibility that there may be some genuine photographs of UFOs, they could not then be subjective or collective hallucinations. UFOs may be a new variety of paranormal entity. The cases in which a UFO has been seen by several independent witnesses at the same time should be interesting and even evidential for parapsychologists and psychical researchers because such cases compare favorably to cases in which two or more people see the same apparition, have the same dream, or perceive the same figures in a crystal ball (Hart and Hart, 1933).

In spite of the dismissal of 90 percent of sightings, a nucleus of cases nevertheless remains for which there is no satisfactory explanation and which offer the kind of mystery parapsychology and psychical research ought to explore.

BIBLIOGRAPHY: Hart, H. and Hart, E. B. 1933. "Visions and Apparitions Collectively and Reciprocally Perceived." PSPR 41:205; Jung, C. G. *Flying Saucers,* 1969; Klass, P. J. "UFOs." In C. Abell and B. Singer, eds., *Science and the Paranormal: Probing the Existence of the Supernatural,* 1981, p. 318; Randles, J. *UFO Reality: A Critical Look at the Physical Evidence,* 1983.

**University of Edinburgh.** See **Koestler Chair of Parapsychology.**

**University of Utrecht.** In 1953, this university became the first one anywhere to establish a chair for the teaching of parapsychology. In the same year, the university served as host to the First International Congress of Parapsychological Studies sponsored by the Parapsychology Foundation. A Parapsychological Institute was set up at the university under the direction of Wilhelm H. C. Tenhaeff to conduct tests in extrasensory perception, unorthodox healing, experiments in card-guessing, psychodiagnostic investigations of psychics, and the application of psi abilities to crime.

In 1973, a Parapsychology Laboratory was created within the university with Martin Johnson succeeding Tenhaeff as the holder of the chair of parapsychology. The laboratory provided an important training ground for young visiting researchers and, with workers such as Richard S. Broughton and Sybo Schouten, the laboratory soon achieved a reputation for high quality qualitative and quantitative research. It also published the *European Journal of Parapsychology.* Lack of funds, however, compelled the laboratory to shut its doors in 1988.

**Uphoff, Walter, H., 1913–.** American educator and psychical researcher. In the 1930s, when a senior at college, he was accused of being close-minded because he dismissed psychic phenomena without investigation. "That challenge made me embark on a lifelong exploration of psi phenomena, starting from a very skeptical position and gradually becoming less skeptical and more interested as I encountered evidence which could not easily be dismissed" (letter to authors). One of these non-dismissable pieces of evidence took place in 1965 "when my deceased secretary used the telephone to convey some unfinished business."

Since his retirement in 1976 from the faculty of the University of Colorado where he taught labor education and developments in psychical research, Prof. Uphoff has lectured, has written articles for foreign and domestic journals, and has co-authored with his wife, Mary Jo, books (1980, 1977) on the paranormal. He has also conducted extensive investigations of poltergeists, of mediums, among them Ena Twigg, Leslie Flint, Arthur Ford, Douglas Johnson, and of psychics, including Masuaki Kiyota and Uri Geller. Prof. Uphoff is also deeply involved in electronic voice phenomena and transcommunication.

President of the New Frontiers Center, he is known internationally and has received an award for his work from the Schweizerische Vereinigung für Parapsychologie (Swiss Association for Parapsychology).

Selected Writings: and Uphoff, M. J. *Mind Over Matter. Implications of Masuaki Kiyota's PK Feats with Metal and Film,* 1980; and Uphoff, M. J. *New Psychic Frontiers,* 1977.

**Up Through (UT).** Clairvoyance technique in which ESP cards are called up through the pack before any are removed or checked.

**Uvani.** See **Garrett, Eileen J.**

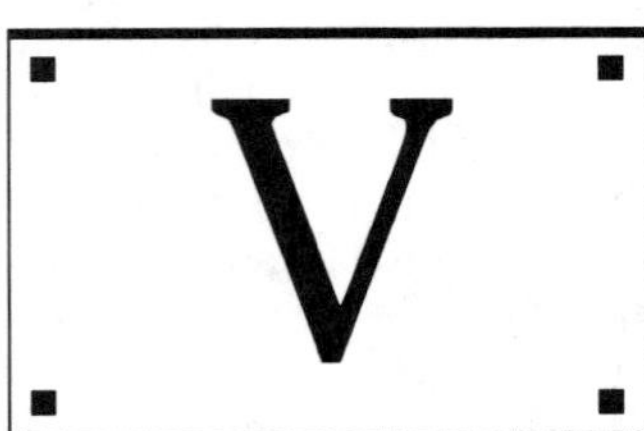

**Valiantine, George, 1874–?.** American physical medium. His supporters described him as "a remarkable example of 'direct voice' or trumpet mediumship" (Salter, 1932:389). During his sittings, sitters heard voices of the spirits of the dead through trumpets floating about the séance room. Two of his sitters were careful and experienced investigators from the Society for Psychical Research who observed every movement Valiantine made during a sitting in England in 1925. They heard the voices but could detect nothing suspicious. They apparently were persuaded that the voices provided evidential communications (Wooley, 1926).

Yet Valiantine undoubtedly cheated on many other occasions. For example, when the magazine *Scientific American* had appointed a committee two years earlier to investigate physical mediums, Valiantine was among them. The committee's report raised the clear inference that he had attempted trickery as he had before and after in Europe and elsewhere. His is an old problem in psychical research. If mediums have been fraudulent once, twice or several times, does this mean that they have no psychic ability and can produce no paranormal phenomena? Psychical researchers have universally followed the rule that they will have nothing to do with mediums once exposed.

If Valiantine held an authentic direct voice or trumpet sitting in 1925, if he then exhibited real paranormal powers and was the means of obtaining genuine spirit messages, then this policy of psychical researchers is wrong and misguided (Berger, 1988).

BIBLIOGRAPHY: Berger, A. S. *Evidence of Life After Death: A Casebook for the Tough-Minded,* 1988; Salter, Mrs. W. H. 1932. "The History of George Valiantine." PSPR 40:389; Wooley, V. J. 1926. "An Account of a Series of Sittings with Mr. George Valiantine." PSPR 36:52.

**Van Busschbach, John George, 1896–1974.** Dutch inspector of schools. As an educator, he wanted to know whether psi could be made to appear in the classroom. He carried out ESP tests with school children in Amsterdam and Utrecht and made the interesting discovery that only primary school children in the fifth and sixth grades produced significant scores. Pupils in secondary school scored only at chance (Van Busschbach, 1955). Thus, unless other conditions, such as teacher-pupil relations, in the classroom atmosphere influenced the outcome, age may be a factor in the manifestation of psi. Another of Van Busschbach's experiments showed that girls scored more significantly in ESP tests in both Dutch and American schools (Van Busschbach, 1959, 1961), thus suggesting that sex may have a relation to psi and that females may perform better than males.

Selected Writings: 1961. "An Investigation of ESP in the First and Second Grades in American Schools." JP 25:161; 1959. "An Investigation of ESP in the First and Second

Grades of Dutch Schools." JP 23:237; 1955. "A Further Report on an Investigation of ESP in School Children." JP 19:69.

**Van de Castle, Robert Leon, 1927–.** American psychologist and parapsychologist. Trained at the Parapsychology Laboratory, he became interested in discovering whether people in a non-scientific and non-technological society would score significantly in ESP tests. From 1968 to 1974, he conducted extensive ESP tests with 461 Cuna Indian junior high school students (Van de Castle 1974). The target pictures were of things with which they were intimately acquainted (i.e., a jaguar or canoe), as distinguished from the cold and unfamilar symbols used on ESP cards. But the special colored pictures did not seem to make any difference. The overall results for both the girls and boys, when combined, turned out to be only at chance. He discovered, however, that the scores of the girls were much better than those of the boys, a finding that suggests that in both non-technological and technological societies sex may be a correlate of psi.

Dr. Van de Castle also wondered about other correlates of psi performance. He studied hypnosis and concluded that it facilitated psi (Van de Castle, 1969). Along with other parapsychologists who tried to find personality correlates of psi, he developed a device (a questionnaire) to measure attitudes toward ESP and to replicate the work of Gertrude R. Schmeidler in relation to sheep-goat experiments. Subjects were to complete a series of incomplete questions. Responses were evaluated and subjects classified as "sheep" or "goat" (Van de Castle, 1957).

In addition to being an experimenter, Dr. Van de Castle participated as a percipient in well-known dream studies at the Maimonides Medical Center Dream Laboratory and made significant scores. He became professor of clinical psychology in the Department of Psychiatry at the University of Virginia Medical School and director of its Sleep and Dream Laboratory. He is now a psychologist at the Blue Ridge Hospital in Charlottesville, Virginia.

Selected Writings: 1974. "An Investigation of Psi Abilities Among the Cuna Indians of Panama." In A. Angoff and D. Barth, eds., *Parapsychology and Anthropology*, 1974, pp. 80–97; 1969. "The Facilitation of ESP Through Hypnosis." *American Journal of Clinical Hypnosis* 12(17):37; 1957. "Differential Patterns of ESP Scoring as a Function of Differential Attitudes Toward ESP." JASPR 51:43.

**Vandy, Edgar, c. 1895–1933.** British inventor and engineer. At the time of his death, he was working on an electrical drawing machine. Edgar Vandy was drowned in a swimming pool under rather mysterious circumstances. There were bruises on the body that seemed to indicate that he had suffered some kind of blow or accident prior to drowning.

In this famous case Vandy's brothers George and Harold, in the hope of learning more about the circumstances of his death, turned to mediums. C. Drayton Thomas held a proxy sitting with Gladys Osborne Leonard on the Vandys's behalf. They themselves had five sittings, one each with the medium Frances Campbell, one each with a Mrs. Mason, and George Vandy had a sitting with Miss Naomi Bacon. The sittings were held from August 1933 through November 1933 (later sittings added nothing), but their records did not come into the hands of the Society for Psychical Research until 1953. Kathleen Gay (1957) published a report on the sittings in the *Journal of the Society for Psychical Research* and C. D. Broad (1962) analyzed them in detail.

Athough the sittings shed no new light on the circumstances surrounding Edgar Vandy's death, yet "[i]t is quite incredible that the amount and kind of concordance actually found between the statements made by the various mediums at the various sittings should be *purely a matter of chance-coincidence*. . . . [after all] (i) What proportion of the male population of England are drowned *per annum* in open-air swimming-pools after mysteriously falling and getting a crack on the head? (ii) What proportion of the male population are skilled technicians, devoting themselves to inventions in general, and to designing and perfecting machines for the mechanical reproduction of drawing and lettering in particular? (iii) What proportion of the male population of England fall into *both* these categories"? (Broad, 1962:380–381)

The source of this apparently paranormal information remains the question—whether it came *via* telepathy from the minds of living people or from Edgar Vandy's surviving personality.

BIBLIOGRAPHY: Broad, C. D. *Lectures on Psychical Research,* 1962, pp. 350–383; Gay, K. 1957. "The Case of Edgar Vandy." JSPR 39:1.

**Variance, High.** Fluctuation of scores beyond mean chance expectation (JP).

**Variance, Low.** Fluctuation of scores below mean chance expectation (JP).

**Variance, Mean (Theoretical).** The expected variance of the theoretical mean score (JP). See also **Variance, High; Variance, Low; Variance, Run-Score; Variance, Subject; Variance, Theoretical.**

**Variance, Run-Score.** The fluctuation of the scores of individual runs around the theoretical mean (JP).

**Variance, Subject.** The fluctuation of a subject's total score from the theoretical mean of his series (JP).

**Variance, Theoretical.** A measure of the dispersal of a group of scores about their theoretical mean (JP). See also **Mean Chance Expectation.**

**Variance-Differential Effect.** Significant different between variances of run scores (or other units) in two experimental series designed to affect results differently. See also **Variance, High; Variance, Low; Variance, Mean; Variance, Run-Score; Variance, Subject.**

**Varley, Cromwell, 1828–1883.** British electrical engineer. Interested in Spiritualism, Varley, a Fellow of the Royal Society, was an expert in electric telegraphy. His inventions dealing with submarine cables made the construction of the transatlantic cable possible.

He is best known in psychical research for the construction of an electrical apparatus that was used in experiments with Florence Cook (and also with Rosina [Rosalie] Showers and Annie Eva Fay). He sat with Kate Fox (one of the Fox Sisters who produced a chorus of raps for him), investigated D. D. Home (he reported that "Deception was impossible") and contributed cases to *Phantasms of the Living.* He was involved in an experiment to test the existence of a "magnetic sense," reported in Reichenbach's experiments. None was perceived.

In the experiments using his electrical apparatus, it was supposed that any attempt at fraud on the part of the mediums would necessitate the breaking of the electrical circuits. The circuits not being broken, the inference was that the phenomena produced at the time were genuine. C. D. Broad, however, believed that in all instances the phenomena were fraudulent, someone very knowledgeable about electricity (Sir William Crookes, the experimenter, was such a person and there were few others in 1874) having acted as an accomplice.

Like Edmund Gurney, Varley used chloroform to relieve pain. Unlike Gurney, he did not die when the sponge from which he inhaled the chloroform failed to fall away from his nose and mouth when he lost consciousness. Fortunately, Varley's wife was in the house (Gurney had been alone in his hotel room in Brighton) and was able to remove the sponge in time.

BIBLIOGRAPHY: Broad, C. D. 1964. "Cromwell Varley's Electrical Tests with Florence Cook." PSPR 54:158; Nicol, F. 1972. "The Founders of the S.P.R." PSPR 55:341, 349.

**Vasiliev, Leonid Leonidovitch, 1891–1966.** Soviet professor of physiology at the University of Leningrad and founder of Soviet psychical research. He was an ardent advocate of hypnosis and extrasensory perception. In the 1930s, he conducted research that still stands as among the best pioneering work done in these areas and entitles him to be considered along with Joseph B. Rhine (whose work in the United States was done at about the same time) as one of the great figures of the period.

Vasiliev's experiments over long distances—between Leningrad and Sebastopol, 1000 miles apart—showed that it was possible through telepathy to place subjects in a hypnotic trance (Vasiliev, 1976). About half a century before, Pierre Janet had also conducted similar experiments. Although Vasiliev's work was fundamentally a replication of Janet's, it had a great impact in the Soviet Union and permitted psychical research to get a toehold there.

Ironically, it was also Vasiliev who caused it to slip again into obscurity. He went on to develop a "materialistic theory of telepathy" because he thought that the phenomenon could be accounted for by brain radiations. The theory may have been a prudent one because it made telepathy acceptable in the

Soviet Union and allowed his work to be financed. But soon "it became apparent that such a theory was not indicated by the results, quite the reverse; financial support and permission to publish were promptly withdrawn and the subject was abandoned in Russia for at least three decades" (Gregory, 1981:134). But when Vasiliev's writings finally were published in the 1960s, his reputation was restored and interest in psychical research and parapsychology regenerated.

Selected Writing: *Experiments in Distant Influence,* 1976.

BIBLIOGRAPHY: Gregory, A. 1981. "Psychical Research as a Social Activity." JSPR 51:789.

**Vaughan, Alan, 1936–.** American psychic. His interest in psychical research began in about 1967 when he played with a ouija board and for about twenty-four hours was apparently possessed by some entity. Shortly after that he began having psychic experiences.

Vaughan met medium Eileen Garrett who gave him a grant to study mediumship and prophecy in Europe. During that time he began to develop his own mediumistic abilities in London with the help of medium Douglas Johnson. He also began to make predictions and claims to have the greatest number of fulfilled prophesies of all those registered with the Central Premonitions Registry.

In 1983 while teaching at a psychic seminar in Sedona, Arzona, he began channeling a Chinese entity named Li Sung who claims to have been an herbalist and healer in China about 1200 years ago. Vaughan has channeled Li Sung for thousands of people who say they have been helped by "him." Li Sung has also helped Vaughan by showing him how to channel his own higher self and reach higher levels of creativity.

Vaughan has done dream work with Montague Ullman and Stanley Krippner and is currently working in psychic archaeology with the Mobius Society on a hunt for sunken treasure. He is also working on a computerized intuition trainer and a psychic video series.

Alan Vaughan was editor of *Psychic* magazine from 1972 to 1977 and of *Reincarnation Report* for the years 1982–1983. He has written over 200 articles on psychic phenomena for the popular press and is now working on a book on how to channel. He is the author of two books on precognition (1982\1988; 1973\1985), a book on synchronicity (1979\1980); a book on psychics (1972) and a chapter on the same subject (1974) and was a co-author of the book *Dream Telepathy* (1973\1988).

Selected Writings: *The Edge of Tomorrow,* 1982\1988; *Incredible Coincidence,* 1979\1980; *Patterns of Prophecy,* 1973\1985; "Famous Western Sensitives." In E. Mitchell with J. White, ed., *Psychic Exploration,* 1974; *Psychics,* 1972; and M. Ullman and S. Krippner, *Dream Telepathy,* 1973т1988.

**Veridical.** In psychical research when a percipient comes by information, perhaps in a dream, whose details correspond with the details of an actual event that, at the time of the experience, the percipient could not have known by any normal means, the experience is called veridical.

D. J. West reported a dream that turned out to be a veridical experience. In 1956, a husband and wife went on a journey from England to Italy. One night in Italy, the wife said, "I was restless and before dawn awoke with a terrific nightmare. I had dreamed . . . that my small daughter [in England] was crying for me, in terrible pain and trouble, and I had the clearest possible picture of her being put into an ambulance at our gate. There were many details of the picture which were unusual and yet extremely clear." A few days later, she received a telegram that her daughter had been taken violently ill with a suspected mastoid on the night of the nightmare and that she was rushed by ambulance to a hospital around dawn.

Other examples of veridical dreams are David Belasco's dream of his dying mother, Abraham Lincoln's dream foretelling his assassination, Sir H. Rider Haggard's telepathic dream of his dog's plight and the deathbed scene in the mind of Sir H. M. Stanley. All, except Lincoln's which was prophetic, illustrate that veridical experiences often take place at approximately the time when another person (or animal) is confronted by a critical situation—an accident, a grave illness, death—and that they correspond with the details of the situation.

Other illustrations of veridical experiences include out-of-body experiences or near-death experiences during which percipients seem to have obtained true and specific details of people or events at points distant from the physical body.

BIBLIOGRAPHY: West, D. J. 1963. "A Veridical

Dream by a Mother of Her Sick Child." JSPR 42:62.

**Verification.** See **Corroboration.**

**Verrall, Margaret de Gaudrion Merrifield (Mrs. A. W.), 1859–1916.** British medium. Margaret Verrall joined the Society for Psychical Research in 1889 after having had telepathic experiences with her young daughter Helen (the future Mrs. W. H. Salter). After F. W. H. Myers died in 1901 Mrs. Verrall tried and succeeded in writing automatically and continued to do so until right before her death. She became one of the most important of the automatists who received communications in the **Cross-Correspondences** cases.

Mrs. Verrall's account of her own work "throws light on the psychology of automatic writing and, to some extent, on the psychology of telepathy." She was a valuable investigator who combined sympathy with a highly critical faculty. She also wrote many reports on the works of others, and all the papers that appeared in the *Proceedings of the Society for Psychical Research* from 1894 onward passed through her hands as a member of the Committee of Reference. She gradually came to believe in the reality of survival after death.

She was among the first women students at Newnham College, Cambridge. In 1880 she was appointed lecturer in classics (to her chagrin instead of her friend Jane Harrison) and continued teaching on and off until shortly before her death despite her marriage in 1882 to classical scholar A. W. Verrall with whom her classical scholarship was a strong bond. She translated and collaborated on the text for *The Mythology and Monuments of Ancient Athens* 1890, published with Jane Harrison. After her husband's death in 1912, she edited his lectures on Dryden.

A descendant on her mother's side of an old French family, Margaret Verrall was bilingual and always maintained a French as well as an English outlook. Her friends called her "M. de G." (her husband called her "May") and were both admiring of and amused by her Frenchness. She was open-minded to rational arguments and "really believed in Freedom of Thought." Jane Harrison called her "the most civilised creature I have ever known. . . . In her character there were plenty of . . . little obvious, loveable and intensely logical absurdities, which allowed her friends to laugh at her, and so made her doubly dear." She wished to die and told her friend, "Sometimes I can scarcely bear to wait."

Selected Writings: 1906. "On a Series of Automatic Writings." PSPR 20:1; 1902. "Notes on the Trance Phenomena of Mrs. Thompson." PSPR 17:164; and Sidgwick, E. M. and Piddington, J. G. 1910. "Further Experiments with Mrs. Piper in 1908." PSPR 24:31.

BIBLIOGRAPHY: Harrison, J. 1917. "In Memoriam—Mrs. A. W. Verrall." PSPR 29:376; Sidgwick, E. M. 1916. "Obituary Notice: Mrs. A. W. Verrall." PSPR 29:170.

**Versailles, Apparitions At.** Versailles in northern France twelve miles from Paris is the scene of a grand palace, magnificent gardens, and the Grand Trianon and Petit Trianon, the former the retreat of Louis XIV, the latter the residence of Marie Antionette. C. A. E. Moberly and E. F. Jourdain, who at different times had been principals of St. Hugh's College in Oxford, were among the throngs of visitors to Versailles. On a hot summer's day (August 10, 1901), they experienced something there so uncanny that they eventually wrote a book about it and, in 1911, under assumed names, published *An Adventure.*

Basically, they narrated that, after walking a while, passing the Grand Trianon on their left, following the Chemin Creux and bearing around to their right, they entered the gardens of the Petit Trianon. All at once, they felt an eerie atmosphere. They saw two men working in the garden wearing three-cornered hats and gray-green coats. They came upon a rustic bridge and a kiosk. A woman and a girl, then an evil-looking man in a slouched hat and cloak sat by the kiosk and spoke to them in a strange accent. They followed a path that took them to a garden in front of the Petit Trianon where they saw a woman sketching and a lady seated on the grass dressed in a pale green fichu. Finally, they saw a young man come out of the Petit Trianon, the door banging behind him. They were not aware at the time of any kind of paranormal experience.

Subsequently, after a Frenchwoman told them of a local belief that the place was actually the haunt of Marie Antoinette and her Court, the two women decided, in November

1901, to make separate accounts of their experiences. In 1904, they visited Versailles and the Petit Trianon once more and found there no air of eerieness, no queerly dressed people, no path, bridge, or kiosk. The Petit Trianon was shut up tight so that no door could have been opened and banged shut. Everything was changed, nothing resembled what they had seen three years before. Then began eight years of research into French history and the Revolution. By the end of that time, the women came to believe that on that day in 1901 they had somehow stepped back in time and had seen the apparitions of people who had lived in the eighteenth century. They were persuaded that the lady in the shawl sitting by the Petit Trianon was not some tourist but Marie Antionette herself sitting in front of that building as she once did. And so they published their experiences in *An Adventure.*

The book caused and still causes both sensation and controversy. Many of its readers believed that these highly respected women were absolutely trustworthy and responsible and that they had indeed experienced the phenomenon of retrocognition. Other readers rejected the entire narrative as evidence of anything paranormal. Psychical Research takes its place in the hostile camp. From its vantage point, although there is no doubt that the woman were truthful and had the experiences they reported, the weakness of the case is that it does not come up to a minimum standard of evidence. Perhaps that is why, when the ladies sent their narratives in 1902 to the Society for Psychical Research, the accounts were rejected as not worth investigation. And the reviewer of *An Adventure* for the society said, "we cannot honestly say that [the authors] appear to us to have added anything of interest on the positive side of Psychical Research" (Review, 1911).

An important canon of evidence is that accounts of experiences must be written out while the memories of percipients are fresh in order to prevent the fading of memory and the introduction of things found out after the experience. In this case, the accounts were prepared three months later. In the meantime, the authors had learned that a body of belief existed that the place they had visited was haunted; this information could have influenced their memories and tainted their accounts. Their accounts, although made separately, were not truly independent because the two women discussed their experiences prior to writing them down. The additional weakness of the case is that there can be normal explanations for their experience. Perhaps what the women saw and later interpreted as people from another time were living people. Even in 1901, Versailles drew visitors from everywhere in all sorts of dress and speaking in all kinds of accents. All the individuals the women saw could have been real and became ghosts only because of tricks of memory and the knowledge of the haunting tradition.

This case bears some resemblance to the Dieppe Raid case: In both cases two women from England had possibly paranormal experiences while on visits to France. The cases are distinguished, however, because in this one the women failed to record their experiences immediately and could have mistaken living people for phantoms.

BIBLIOGRAPHY: Moberly, C. A. E. ("Miss Morison") and Jourdain, E. F. ("Miss Lamont"). *An Adventure,* 1911; "Reviews: *An Adventure.*" PSPR 25:353; Salter, W. H. 1950. "'An Adventure': A Note on the Evidence." JSPR 35:178.

**Victoria (Alexandrina Victoria), 1819–1901.** Queen of the United Kingdom and Ireland, empress of India, her reign began in 1837 and was the longest in the history of England. It encompassed a momentous era of prosperity, social legislation, and reform, the Industrial Revolution and territorial expansion. Victoria was idolized by her subjects, symbolized the power and glory of the empire, and endeared monarchy to the hearts of the common people.

Victoria was the adoring wife of Albert, prince of a small German state, whom she married in 1840 and to whom she bore nine children. When he died prematurely in 1861, it was a catastrophe for her. Hearing reports that Robert Lees had received communications from her dead husband, Victoria summoned the medium. In six séances with him, Victoria also reported receiving communications from her dead consort. But it was not Lees who persuaded her of spirit communication.

Two years before Spiritualism came into being in the United States in 1848, Victoria was already trafficking with mediums, attending séances, and generally showing herself to be a **Noted Witness** for mediumship and spirit communications. An object in the form of a gold watch provides concrete evidence.

A medium who impressed Victoria with marvelous phenomena received from the queen a gold watch on which was engraved: "Presented by HER MAJESTY to Miss Georgiana Eagle for her Meritorious & Extraordinary Clairvoyance Produced at Osborn House, Isle of Wight, July 17, 1846."

Beneath Victoria's queenly dignity and beyond the royal pomp and pageantry of her two Jubilees, she was little different from the humble female subjects she ruled—an adoring wife devastated by the death of her husband and who was perhaps too ready to believe.

**Vilenskaya, Larissa, 1948–.** Soviet-born parapsychologist. She believes that firewalking is one of the most interesting of human potentials. She has walked on red-hot coals in the United States and Europe and taught hundreds of people to do the same. She also is a healer and teacher who specializes in the development of psi abilities.

Before coming to the United States in 1981 and founding **Psi Research** a year later, she was deeply involved in research for almost ten years in Russia. She worked at the Bioinformation Laboratory of the Popov Scientific Technological Society for Radio Engineering, Electronics, and Communication at the Research Institute of General and Pedagogical Psychology of the U.S.S.R. Academy of Sciences. She was the secretary to Edward Naumov and worked with prominent Soviet parapsychologist Barbara Ivanova, Soviet researcher Victor Adamenko, and Soviet psychics Nina Kulagina and Rosa Kuleshova.

**Vincent de Paul, Saint, 1581–1660.** French founder of the Confraternities of Charity and the Sisters of Charity of St. Vincent de Paul whose women members help feed and nurse the sick and impoverished. One of the great saints of the Catholic church who manifested the phenomenon of incorruptibility, he was canonized in 1737. When his tomb was opened in 1712, fifty-two years after his burial, an eyewitness said that "everything was as when he had been laid there. The eyes and nose alone showed some decay. I counted eighteen teeth. The body was not disturbed, but those who approached it saw at once that it was entire and that the soutane was not in the least changed by time. No offensive odour was perceived, and the doctors testified that the body could not thus have been preserved for so long a period by any natural means" (Thurston, 1952).

BIBLIOGRAPHY: Thurston, H. *Physical Phenomena of Mysticism,* 1952, p. 237.

**Virginia, University of, Division of Parapsychology.** Through a bequest of Chester F. Carlson, who invented xerography, the Division of Parapsychology was founded in 1967 as an administrative unit of the Department of Behavioral Medicine and Psychiatry of the School of Medicine, University of Virginia. Investigations into cases suggestive of reincarnation formed part of its research activities as did the experiments conducted by J. G. Pratt with Pavel Stepanek. The Division of Parapsychology has now been absorbed by the Department of Personality Studies at the University of Virginia. Address: Box 152, Medical Center, University of Virginia, Charlottesville, Virginia 22908.

**Voice Phenomena.** See **Electronic Voice Phenomena.**

**Voodooism.** The belief in and practice of **Black Magic** and trance communications with deities and spirits of the dead through ceremonial dances and songs and the use of snakes, spells, and animal sacrifice. Originating in Africa, voodooism now is present in Cuba, Jamaica, Brazil, Haiti, and in the southern states of the United States.

The word "voodoo" comes from "vodun" which, in the language of the Fon people of Aboney, Benin, in West Africa, means god or spirit. In Cuba, it is called "Santería," in Jamaica "Obeah," in Brazil "Orisha," in Haiti "Vodun." In Haiti, for example, it is a public cult as well as an ancestor cult with private ceremonies. Although worshippers believe in Christian saints and one God, they acknowledge many other *loas* or deities. Among these are wild and cruel gods in a group called the Petro nation and gentle and good gods as well, such as Ogoun who is warlike, Loco the oracle, Legba the priest, Erzulie goddess of love, Simbi the magician and the ever-wise serpent, Damballah. The gods guide and protect, while priests *(hougans)* or priestesses *(mambos)* conduct ceremonies.

The voodoo ceremony consists of designs drawn in flour or ashes on the ground. While drums beat and songs are sung to the Christian saints and voodoo gods, worshippers dance. Soon one may waver, stumble, stagger, with a strange facial expression. The dancer may fall and then rise and act in a manner entirely familiar to all. At this point the heart of the voodoo religion has been reached. A *loa* has manifested itself by "mounting the head" as a rider mounts a horse. The affected individual loses consciousness and seems invaded by the god. Each god can be recognized by a familiar personality that has taken over that of the individual. Now the invaded person has reached the stage of voodoo called *hounsi canzo.* The next stage will be "the taking of the asson," a rattle used by the priests and priestesses. The final stage is "la prise des yeux" (taking hold of the eyes) when, after invasion by a god, the worshipper does not lose consciousness but now claims to be able to cure disease, induce an out-of-body experience and to possess the powers of telepathy and clairvoyance.

Observers may see voodooism as sinister mumbo-jumbo and find it difficult to achieve more than a shallow understanding of the religion, but the entire area is ripe for study by psychical research because the essence of it is **possession** by an other-world entity and because of the claimed gifts of extrasensory perception, unorthodox healing, and the ability to travel beyond the body.

The phenomenon of voodoo-death which follows a voodoo curse or ritual, such as casting a spell, sticking pins into dolls, or mutilating an effigy, has been studied by psychologists and psychiatrists. They theorize that the suggestion made to the intended victim by the curse or ritual leads to autosuggestion and a state of emotional overactivity that results in death. Victims literally worry themselves to death. The phenomenon is interesting from both personal and philosophical perspectives because it may signify that, if we believe that all is hopeless for us and that we have no control over our lives, we ourselves may be victims of death even when no voodoo is involved.

From the perspective of psychical research, the phenomenon is especially interesting because it underscores the same power of the mind to affect and control the body that is manifested in the stigmata and in the unorthodox healing at Lourdes and in Christian Science. The phenomenon of voodoo-death, however, is the other side of the coin and shows that the mind has the power not only to mark or cure the body but to kill it as well. Like **Bone-Pointing,** to kill by voodoo is the perfect murder since death is by natural causes.

BIBLIOGRAPHY: Deren, M. *Divine Horsemen: The Living Gods of Haiti,* 1953.

**Vuurde, Willem, van, 1909–.** Dutch parapsychological subject. Jeff D. Jacobs places him "in the gallery of the most outstanding subjects in the recorded history of parapsychology" (1985). Van Vuurde took part in Mr. Jacobs' and Arthur G. H. Bleksley's investigations of extrasensory perception during sleep. They seemed to demonstrate that ESP can be a guide to awakening over an extended period of time.

When van Vuurde saw war clouds gathering over Europe in 1936, he left The Netherlands to live in South Africa. But circumstances did not allow him to avoid the war he foresaw. He was made a prisoner-of-war by the Japanese and because of malnutrition lost much of his eyesight.

Back in South Africa he began to think about testing his belief that he could wake himself up at any unknown and randomly chosen time. He devised this simple test any one can try: "Two clocks (alarm clocks for cheapness) are fixed side by side in a box, the first one not wound, the second one going. The second clock can be stopped by pulling a string. The target time is set on the first clock by covering its face and turning the hands an unknown amount. The box is then closed and put under the bed. Pull the string on waking up [to stop the clock], and write the result down in the morning" (van Vuurde, 1956). In the morning, van Vuurde would record the time he had awakened and see if it corresponded with the target time. He ran this test 200 times between 1951 and 1954 and registered a hit if there was a difference between the wake up time and the target time of no more than two minutes plus or minus. From these tests, van Vuurde concluded that "I observe the clock while I am a sleep" (van Vuurde, 1956) and he believed that he made this observation by means of ESP.

When Jeff C. Jacobs made an objective evaluation of these home experiments, he found likewise "a highly significant psi effect" (Jacobs, 1985). It is possible, of course, that, because of his poor eyesight, van Vuurde could have misread either the wake up time or the target time and so made an error in the hits he recorded or that his home experiments were otherwise faulty or even doctored. An indication that they genuinely pointed to ESP directing awakening from sleep is a series of controlled experiments Bleksley conducted with van Vuurde between 1959 and 1967. They had such fantastic results that Bleksley was recognized by the Parapsychology Laboratory at Duke University for a distinguished research contribution of showing ESP during sleep.

W. van Vuurde is one of the exceedingly rare subjects who have demonstrated ESP ability and have produced an amazing number of hits over a lengthy stretch of time beginning with his own home experiments over a three-year period and for eight years of the series with Bleksley. Experiments continue with Jeff Jacobs. Van Vuurde had called his investigations "Project EASAN" (Ex Africa Semper Aliquid Novi: From Africa there is always something new). He indeed brought from South Africa a whole new kind of phenomenon that seems to show that ESP does not sleep when we do and that it tells us when to wake up.

Selected Writing: van Vuurde, W. 1956. "ESP During Sleep?" JSPR 38:282.

BIBLIOGRAPHY: Bleksley, A. E. H. 1963. "An Experiment of Long-Distance ESP During Sleep." JP 27:1; Jacobs, J. C. 1985. "PSI-Guided Awakening From Sleep 1: The Original Experiments of W. Van Vuurde." JSPR 53:159.

**W. T. Stead Borderland Library.** British Spiritualist organization established in 1914 by Estelle W. Stead, wife of **William T. Stead,** as a successor to "Julia's Bureau" set up by Stead to communicate with deceased people at no charge to clients. Mrs. Stead continued the work of the bureau until 1936 when the library ceased operations.

**Wallace, Alfred Russel, 1823–1913.** British naturalist. He is best known for having evolved the theory of the origin of species simultaneously with, but independently of, Charles Darwin. It was Wallace who popularized the phrase "the survival of the fittest." During a trip to the islands of modern Indonesia, he discovered the so-called "Wallace Line," to the west of which the flora and fauna are Oriental and to the east Australian. This discovery led to his theory of natural selection.

Wallace was a scientific materialist who was at first extremely sceptical of the claims of Spiritualism. In 1865, however, he began attending Spiritualist séances. Mrs. Mary Marshall, a London medium at whose sittings he observed levitation and apparently paranormal movement of objects and where his brother's name and place of death were spelled out, converted him. He "moved from Voltairean agnosticism to Spiritualism without embracing Christianity on the way . . ." (Inglis 1977:306).

Wallace sponsored the mediumship of Mrs. Agnes Guppy (at that time Miss Nichols) and testified to her levitation (which, he seems to have reasoned, must have been paranormal since she was enormously fat), to the production of musical sounds, and to apports of fresh flowers and fruits. He believed that as a result of spirit photography he had seen his dead mother's likeness. One photograph, he said, was unlike any that had ever been taken of her; the other on magnification showed a distinguishing facial characteristic. Because of his experiences he became a firm believer in contact with the dead, which he believed had been proved.

Like Sir Arthur Conan Doyle after him, he defended many mediums—for example, P. L. O. A. Keeler and Monck—who had been discredited and caught cheating. Indeed, in 1888, he carried on a running argument with Eleanor Sidgwick in the *Journal of the Society for Psychical Research* over the reality of certain materializations. For his entire life he witnessed and investigated psychic phenomena and in 1875 wrote *On Miracles and Modern Spiritualism.*

Wallace's scientific colleagues were so outraged and upset by his psychic claims that he was forced to lead two separate lives. In one, he was the esteemed biologist working and publishing in science. In the other he was a psychical researcher "in an entirely different world of individuals who were outcasts or non-entities with respect to the scientific establishment" (Hyman, 1982:160). So, while he was carrying on psychic investigations, he was lecturing and writing important scientific works, among them, *The Malay Archipelago* (1869), two essays in *Contributions to the*

*Theory of Natural Selection* (1871), his major book, *Geographical Distribution of Animals* (1876), and many more.

Perhaps because of his belief in Spiritualism, Wallace was certain that man's higher mental capacities are due, not to natural selection, but to some non-biological agency. Sadly, this same belief has harmed his reputation and fame so that, unlike Charles Darwin, he is scarcely remembered.

Selected Writings: 1888. "Correspondence." JSPR 16:312; *On Miracles and Modern Spiritualism,* 1875.

BIBLIOGRAPHY: Ebon, M. *They Knew the Unknown,* 1971, pp. 112–117; Hyman, R. "Pathological Science: Towards a Proper Diagnosis and Remedy." In R. A. McConnell, ed., *Encounters with Parapsychology,* 1982; Inglis, B. *Natural and Supernatural,* 1977; "Wallace, Alfred Russel." In *The New Encyclopedia Britannica,* Vol. 12, 1986, pp. 466–467.

**"Walter."** See **Mina S. Crandon.**

**Walther, Gerda, 1898–1977.** German psychical researcher. She was an outstanding figure in German psychical research for almost half a century. Daughter of two doctors of medicine, she seemed destined for a medical career also. But, as a young girl, she discovered that, at times, she seemed able to communicate by telepathy both with the dead and with the living. On one occasion, she saw a black aura surrounding the body of a man just before he died. In 1927, she officially entered the field when she became scientific assistant to Albert von Schrenck-Notzing. She went on to study telepathy, to write reviews of European parapsychological literature for the *Journal of the American Society for Psychical Research* and to investigate the medium Rudi Schneider whose gifts she was persuaded were genuine. Gerda Walther was also the author of two important books. During World War II, the German naval command, anticipating the present efforts of the military-scientific complexes of the great powers to use psychics for intelligence-gathering purposes, asked her to take charge of a program to train psychics to detect Allied submarines. But she refused and went back to her post in the Censor's Office in Munich where she put herself at risk on several occasions by trying, against Nazi decrees, to aid people from other countries—who had been sent to forced-labor camps—to get in touch with their families.

Selected Writings: *Zum anderen Ufer,* 1960; *Phaenomenologie der Mystik,* 1923.

**Warcollier, René, 1881–1962.** French pioneer in psychical research. His investigations convinced him of the unity of the human race. "We are the electrons in the atom of Humanity," he once said.

By profession a chemical engineer, he turned his attention to psychical research when the fervor of physical phenomena spread through Paris. He had some séances with Eusapia Palladino and Eva C. and thought some genuine phenomena might have occurred. But he preferred to concentrate his energies on mental phenomena and on telepathy, in particular, because, he wrote, "Research in telepathy may revolutionize our concept of mind as much as the discovery of radium revolutionized that of matter." He also believed that in telepathy lay the explanation for messages purporting to come from deceased communicators.

Warcollier conducted brilliant qualitative experiments that were published in *Revue Métapsychique,* in his book, *La Télépathie* (1926), and later in his *Experimental Telepathy* (1938). His technique was to encourage percipients to make their minds blank and to enter into a kind of reverie while, at the same time, agents concentrated on drawings. The percipients would then draw their impressions. The successes of his experiments matched those of Upton Sinclair with his wife, Mary.

In 1923 Warcollier and Gardner Murphy decided to work together in a series of transatlantic experiments with people in Paris and New York alternating as agents and percipients. In one experiment on the evening of March 14, 1925, Warcollier in Paris acted as the agent and, in a passive state at 9:30 visualized a glass funnel and tried to send it to the American group in New York. At the same hour, one percipient in New York drew a glass funnel. But another percipient in New York drew a large compote with handles, which she described as "like the horns of a stag," an image an agent three and a half hours earlier had been trying to transmit but Warcollier, as agent, at 9:30 tried to eliminate. This experiment shows Warcollier as both a researcher and a **Noted Witness** for telepathy.

His testimony should also be considered in relation to the phenomenon of death bed visions. In *La Télépathie,* he wrote: "My uncle . . . left Paris in 1893 for a trip to America, with my aunt and other members of the family. . . . [H]e died at Caracas on June 24, 1894. Just before his death . . . he had a prolonged dilerium, during which he called out the names of certain friends left in France, and whom he seemed to see." When the family returned to Paris, they found that the people Warcollier's uncle had seemed to have seen and had named had died before he had although the uncle had not known it.

From his work, Warcollier drew certain conclusions. Some psychical researchers, such as Walter F. Prince, believe that it is the agent in telepathy concentrating on a drawing or object who projects the thought, that is, that telepathy is "mental telegraphy." But Warcollier disagreed. "A large number of experiments have convinced us that the agent is not always very important, but that his action is not entirely negligible." Warcollier also believed with Frederic W. H. Myers that, at a deep level, we are all interdependent and at one with one another.

Warcollier was the editor of *Revue Métapsychique,* president of the Institut Métapsychique International, and a member of the Boston Society for Psychic Research.

Selected Writing: *Experimental Telepathy,* 1939.

**"Watseka Wonder."** See **Possession.**

**Weatherhead, Leslie D., 1893–1976.** British clergyman and author. Famous minister of the City Temple in London, he regarded psychical research as important in helping Christians answer questions about their faith. He believed that "in the country vaguely called 'Psychical Research,' lie discoveries which man desperately needs in his quest of reality. His poverty cries out for the riches which are at present hidden in the mental and spiritual parts of the universe . . ." (Weatherhead, 1959:14–15). Weatherhead found psychic phenomena in the Gospels and pointed out that the founder of Methodism, John Wesley, was taken with psychical research. He also examined the resurrection of Christ in the light of the phenomena of psychical research, such as apparitions and apports.

Selected Writing: *The Manner of the Resurrection in the Light of Modern Science and Psychical Research,* 1959.

**Weiner, Debra H., 1952–.** American parapsychologist. Interested in parapsychology from childhood, Ms. Weiner's first psi experiments were part of courses on design and statistics she took in 1974 as an undergraduate at Sonoma State University. At that time she also taught an undergraduate course on parapsychology. She attended the summer study program at the Institute of Parapsychology in 1976 where she returned in 1977, after receiving her B.A. degree, to join the institute's staff as a research fellow. Her mentor at the institute was critical parapsychologist James E. Kennedy who impressed her with his scholarship, creativity and thoroughness.

Among other articles for the *Journal of Parapsychology* she wrote (1983) a review of Louisa E. Rhine's collection of spontaneous cases. She is especially interested in laboratory experiments, particularly in micro-PK, and in empirical tests of observational theories (1986a). She has also examined parapsychologists' concepts and assumptions (1986b).

Ms. Weiner has presented numerous papers at parapsychological conferences and was senior editor of *Research in Parapsychology 1985* and *Research in Parapsychology 1986.* She was secretary of the Parapsychological Association (1983–1985) and its president in 1986.

Selected Writings: "Thoughts on the Role of Meaning in Psi Research." In D. H. Weiner and R. L. Nelson, eds., *Research in Parapsychology 1986,* 1987; "When Omniscience is Wrong: Psi Errors as a Clue to the Boundary of Psychic Functioning." In B. Shapin and L. Coly, eds., *Current Trends in Psi Research,* 1986b; and N. L. Zingrone. 1986a. "The Checker Effect Revisited." JP 50; and J. Geller. 1984. "Motivation as the Universal Container: Conceptual Problems in Parapsychology." JP 48:27; and J. Haight. 1983. "Charting Hidden Channels: A Review and Analysis of Louisa E. Rhine's Case Collection Project." JP 47:303.

BIBLIOGRAPHY: Berger, A. S. *Lives and Letters in American Parapsychology,* 1988.

**Wesley, John and Samuel.** See **Epworth Rectory.**

**West, Donald J., 1924–.** British forensic

psychiatrist and criminologist. His interest in psychical research dates from adolescence when he became fascinated by writings on that subject and on Spiritualism. As a result he joined the Society for Psychical Research when he was only seventeen. A few years later, from 1946 to 1949, he was the paid research officer of the Society.

Donald West and G. W. Fisk conducted the famous ESP experiments with clock cards that seem to show the importance of the role of the experimenter in obtaining positive results. (Fisk got the positive results, West the negative). He has in addition written many articles for the *Journal* and *Proceedings of the Society for Psychical Research* on both his experiments and on spontaneous cases: for example, on hallucinations, proxy sittings, haunts, a supposed case of xenoglossy (it wasn't), on mediums (he was impressed by Rudi Schneider's ability to produce PK phenomena), anpsi, and folklore. In 1958 he and G. W. Fisk were jointly awarded the McDougall Award for Distinguished Work in parapsychology.

Dr. West has also published a book on the miracles at Lourdes (1957) in which he concludes that the miraculous nature of the cases has not been established. Another book (1954\1962) is concerned mainly with the then contemporary experimental work in parapsychology and rejects Spiritualism and belief in survival. "In spite of his interest in the promotion of research," however, "he is known to have somewhat critical and ambivalent views on the evidential status of psi phenomena" (Letter to authors).

He is an elector and secretary for the Perrott Studentship in Psychical Research funds for the promotion of psychical research and is chairman of the SPR Research Grants Committee. He has twice been president of the SPR.

Dr. West holds the degrees of M.D. and Litt.D. and is a Fellow of the Royal College of Psychiatrists. He was director of the Cambridge University Institute of Criminology until 1984 and is now professor emeritus of clinical criminology research.

Selected Writings: *Eleven Lourdes Miracles,* 1957; *Psychical Research Today,* 1954; and G. W. Fisk. 1956. "ESP and Mood: Report of a 'Mass' Experiment." JSPR 38:320; and G. W. Fisk. 1953. "A Dual ESP Experiment with Clock Cards." JSPR 37:185.

BIBLIOGRAPHY: Haynes, R. *The Society for Psychical Research 1882–1982,* 1982; 1957. "Eleven Lourdes Miracles. by D. J. West." JSPR 39:90; Salter, W. H. 1954. "Psychical Research Today. By D. J. West." JSPR 37:348.

**Wheatley, James Melville Owen, 1924–.** Canadian philosopher and educator. While not a parapsychologist or psychical researcher, "My interest in psychical research," he writes, "is long-standing and has three sources: First, I was introduced to it by members of my family who had a strong interest in the field . . .; second, I was repeatedly led by my studies in philosophy of mind to consider questions that are of interest to psychical researchers; third my interest in psychical research was confirmed and sharpened by what I learned from [Curt J. Ducasse]—both through his writings and through conversations I had with him . . ." (Letter to authors).

In consequence of his interest, Wheatley has contributed several articles and book reviews to the *Journal of the American Society for Psychical Research* and a chapter on the implications of psychical research and parapsychology for philosophy (Wheatley, 1977). He has also co-edited for college and university courses on parapsychology a text that contains twenty-seven writings by philosophers, such as Ducasse, C. D. Broad, H. H. Price, and others dealing with psi and its relation to philosophy, cognition, precognition, survival, and science (Wheatley and Edge, 1976).

Selected Writings: "Implications for Philosophy." In S. Krippner, ed., *Advances in Parapsychological Research. Vol. I,* 1977; and Edge, H. L. *Philosophical Dimensions of Parapsychology,* 1976.

**White, John W., 1939–.** American author, editor, and educator in consciousness research. "I became interested in parapsychology in 1960 or 1961," he wrote, ". . . during my senior year at Dartmouth College. While browsing in the library stacks, I happened upon a copy of J. B. Rhine's *New World of the Mind.* It sparked a deep interest in me. As a young boy and teenager, I'd had a fascination with science fiction and fantasy stories, primarily those which dealt with the theme of psychic abilities, paranormal phenomena and supernatural powers . . . and when I discovered the world of parapsychology through a 'chance' meeting with

Rhine through his book, my interest in the human mind's supernormal capabilities was placed on a scientific basis" (letter to authors). His interest next extended into several areas: biofeedback, meditation, unidentified flying objects, and, finally, he said, "Parapsychology was the jumping-off point from which I dove into the realm of noetics and consciousness studies."

Mr. White helped Edgar D. Mitchell found the **Institute for Noetic Sciences** and became its director of education. He edited an anthology of all the topics of concern to psychical research and parapsychology (White, 1974) and co-edited another that deals with a variety of paranormal events that, although outside orthodox scientific models, are still within the realm of physics or psychology (White and Krippner, 1977).

One of Mr. White's most important contributions both to thanatology and psychical research is his guide to death and dying (White, 1980) that, as he says, "begins from a parapsychological base—the evidence for postmortem survival" which he is convinced can affect the quality of our lives. He also believes that it provides a rational basis for religious faith. Mr. White goes on to argue, however, in line with Eastern philosophy, that our aim is not personal survival but enlightenment to our real nature as a soul or *atman* that was never born and never dies. Now a freelance writer, Mr. White's articles and reviews have appeared in popular magazines and major newspapers.

Selected Writings: *A Practical Guide to Death and Dying,* 1980; ed., *Psychic Exploration,* 1974: and S. Krippner, eds., *Future Science: Life Energies and the Physics of Paranormal Phenomena,* 1977.

**White Magic.** The art or ritual of calling on and manipulating mysterious nonhuman powers for beneficial purposes.

**White, Rhea Amelia, 1931–.** American librarian, parapsychologist, and bibliographer. In the early 1950s she was keenly interested in mysticism. She came to believe, however, that science rather than religion was better equipped to understand man's evolving consciousness. Accordingly, instead of attending divinity school as she had planned, she joined the staff of J. B. Rhine's Parapsychology Laboratory at Duke University where she learned about testing for extrasensory perception and psychokinesis. She was particularly interested in the reactions of subjects who sometimes felt that they had been taken over by something outside themselves.

Another of Ms. White's interests has been in the creative process, particularly as seen in the lives of saints, and how this process may lead to a new psychophysical organism with "body being realized as a form of mind and mind as a form of body" (Gerald Heard quoted in White, unpublished ms.). These interests led to her writing *The Psychic Side of Sports* with Michael Murphy.

One of her most important contributions to parapsychology has been her annotated bibliographies on parapsychological subjects beginning in 1973 with *Parapsychology: Sources of Information* and continuing in each volume of *Advances in Parapsychological Research.* With Frederick C. Dommeyer she wrote a comprehensive study on psi research in universities in the United States and abroad. She has also written over seventy experimental and theoretical papers and has authored or co-authored several books. In 1981 she founded **The Parapsychology Sources of Information Center** and, in 1983, published *Parapsychology Abstracts International.* Her Psi Line Database System is the first computerized database of the parapsychological literature.

On the Founding Council of the Parapsychological Association, Ms. White was its president in 1984. She was editor of the *Journal of the American Society for Psychical Research* from 1959 to 1962, a task she resumed in 1984. She is a member of the American Association of University Women and was on the Board of Trustees of the Academy of Religion and Psychical Research.

Selected Writings: "A Select Bibliography of Books on Parapsychology, 1974–1976, 1976–1979, 1979–1982." In S. Krippner, ed., *Advances in Parapsychological Research: 1, 3* and *4,* 1977, 1982, 1984; 1981. "Saintly Psi: A Study of Spontaneous ESP in Saints." *Journal of Religion and Psychical Research* 4(3/4):157; and Dommeyer, F. C. 1963. "Psychical Research in Colleges and Universities, I, II, and III." JASPR 57:3, 57:55, 57:136; and Murphy, M. *The Psychic Side of Sports,* 1978.

**Whiteman, Joseph Hilary Michael, 1906–.** South African mathematician. He is not one of those doubters who wants proof of the reality of the out-of-body experience. For Dr.

Whiteman, the "proof of the pudding is in the eating." He has had numerous such experiences that he calls "full separation" in which his physical body seemed asleep or entranced while his mind was liberated from it and in another body and space.

Dr. Whiteman has described, for example, one such experience that was started by seeing a kind of round opening in the physical field of view: "I was in a state of relaxed watchfulness lying in bed, when the visual field opened out so that a scene was presented in bright light, inside a circular boundary. In the centre was a large rock of some substance like granite on a sandy beach. . . . The thought occurred to me that I might get through the opening on to the beach, and almost at once I left the body and approached the rock. No sooner had I arrived near the rock, however, than I became conscious of difficulty in breathing, which distracted me and brought me back in a few moments to the physical body" (Whiteman, 1956). His remarkable conclusion from his experiences is that he "and those who have experienced separation almost invariably state or imply that their conscious life has thereby become *purer* . . . and more truly their own, even sometimes to the extent of really finding themselves alive at last after a physical life that in comparison seems like a dream or prison" (Whiteman, 1956).

When Dr. Whiteman is back in his physical prison and normal space, he is emeritus associate professor of applied mathematics at the University of Capetown and the writer of many important papers on observational theories and the relationship between physics and parapsychology. Interested to see if any theory of paranormal phenomena can be found in physics, he himself has formulated a mathematic theory for this purpose. Dr. Whiteman sees in modern physics the possible legitimizing of parapsychology because he thinks that physics has now "reached the stage where the clear outlines of a new world-view and methodology are visible, and these provide an 'integral understanding' of the world and its psychological and mystical background. With the wider acceptance of such world-view and methodology, new fields of research may be expected to open out, and parapsychology may be considered to have become an established science" (Whiteman, 1977).

Selected Writings: "Parapsychology and Physics." In B. Wolman, ed., *Handbook of Parapsychology,* 1977, p. 730; 1956. "The Process of Separation and Return in Experiences Fully 'Out of the Body'." PSPR 50: 240, 252–253, 274.

**"Willett Mrs." (Mrs. Winifred [Pearce-Serocold] Coombe-Tenant), 1874–1956.** British automatist. She was a woman of great practical ability and interest in public affairs. As the first British woman delegate to the Assembly of the League of Nations she shows, says C. D. Broad, that "persons with mediumistic gifts are [not] invariably mere belfries hung with bats."

Mrs. Willett began automatic writing after the death of her daughter in 1908. In 1909 she largely stopped writing automatically because of an alleged communication from the deceased F. W. H. Myers to try to get direct impressions and to dictate them, first, to Sir Oliver Lodge, and, later, to Gerald Balfour. In 1910 she first sent into deep trance in which condition she both produced script and dictated her impressions. At times Mrs. Willett felt as if she were "almost becoming" the communicator. Broad writes that the "ostensible communications . . . are plainly the product of a highly intelligent and cultured mind or minds, with a keen interest in psychology, psychical research, and philosophy, and with a capacity for drawing subtle and significant distinctions," a description that did not fit Mrs. Willett.

She was one of the mediums through whom the **Cross-Correspondences** supposedly from Myers, Edmund Gurney, et al. were communicated. She was also the principal medium in the Palm Sunday case Involving Arthur Balfour. "In these communications, matters not known to any person present were unmistakably referred to (Gauld, 1977)." She is the purported communicator of the scripts published by Geraldine Cummins in *Swan on a Black Sea* to which C. D. Broad wrote the foreword.

BIBLIOGRAPHY: Balfour, G. W. 1935. "A Study of the Psychological Aspects of Mrs. Willett's Mediumship." PSPR 43:43; Balfour, J. 1960. "The 'Palm Sunday' Case: New Light on an Old Love Story." PSPR 52:79; Broad, C. D. *Lectures on Psychical Research,* 1962, pp. 287–314; Cummins, G. *Swan on a Black Sea: A Study in Automatic Writing,* 1965. Gauld, A. "Discarnate Survival." In B. B. Wolman, ed., *Handbook of Parapsychology,* 1977, p. 583; Lodge, O. 1911. "Evidence of Classical Scholarship and of Cross-Correspondences in

Some New Automatic Writings." PSPR 25:113.

**William McDougall Award.** See **McDougall Award for Distinguished Work in Parapsychology.**

**Williams, Charles, c.1850–?.** British materializing medium. From 1871 through at least 1873 he was in partnership with Frank Herne. During 1873 through February 1874, William Crookes sat weekly in his home with Williams. At these sittings, physical phenomena were produced including the materialization of **"John King"** under what Crookes reported as good conditions. D. D. Home who considered all mediums—except himself—fraudulent thought Williams was honest and in fact at one time they held joint sittings. Florence Cook also sat jointly with Williams and Herne and was described by Trevor Hall as their "protégée."

In September 1878 in Amsterdam Williams was caught using an accomplice, one A. Rita, who was impersonating John King. Nevertheless, Williams continued his sittings into the twentieth century and John King continued to materialize. R. G. Medhurst and K. M. Goldney quote part of an unpublished letter dated November 29, 1928, written to Sir Oliver Lodge by one "Arthur J. G. Fletcher of St. Paul's Vicarage, Thornton Heath, Surrey" in which the latter described a Spiritualist séance with Williams in about 1902. He described the materialization beginning as "a filmy irridescent cloud coming from the medium in a kind of spiral column; this, quite quickly, assumed the full length figure of a man. . . . [H]e came straight through the table. . . . I could see right through his hands. . . . I was conscious that he was a very real presence . . .".

BIBLIOGRAPHY: Hall, T. *The Spiritualists,* 1962; Medhurst, R. G. and Goldney, K. M. 1964. "William Crookes and the Physical Phenomena of Mediumship." PSPR 54:25; Podmore, F. *Studies in Psychical Research,* 1897.

**Wilson, Mrs. Charles Stuart, 1870–1956.** Anglo-American medium. Exposed in her youth to psychical research (her mother, a Mrs. Doane, was one of the earliest members of the Society for Psychical Research), Mrs. Wilson became an important figure in the **"Cross-Correspondences"** cases. She was married to British Brigadier General Charles Stuart Wilson, CB, and became an associate member of the SPR in 1901. She volunteered in 1915 to take part in telepathy experiments with Helen de G. Salter.

J. G. Piddington considered her an important member of the so-called SPR group of automatists who were producing the cross-correspondences, especially because she did not know any of the people involved in the cross-correspondences except Mrs. Salter. The latter described her as having a "lively sense of humour" and of maintaining "an impersonal and detached attitude toward her own phenomena. It was characteristic of her," Mrs. Salter added, "that she gave to her subconscious-self the name of 'Randolph,' after a small boy in Henry James's story 'Daisy Miller,' whose family couldn't live up to him."

BIBLIOGRAPHY: Salter, Mrs. H. de G. 1957. "Mrs. Stuart Wilson." JSPR 39:110; Salter, Mrs. H. de G. 1938. "A Sermon in St. Paul's." PSPR 45:25; Salter, Mrs. H. de G. 1917. "Some Experiments with a New Medium." PSPR 29:306.

**Windigo.** Sometimes called "Weetgo," "Wendigo," "Wintigo." A dreaded skeleton-like giant spirit with a craving for human flesh that the Chippewa Indians of the United States and the Ojibwa, Cree, and Algonkian-speaking Indians of northeastern Canada believe lives in the forests. While many spirits inhabit the forests of the Indians, the windigo is distinguished from the others by its heart of ice and its compulsive desire to devour Indians. Psychologists and anthropologists theorize that the windigo concept is a disorder resulting from the quest for food in the wintry reaches of the land occupied by Indians constantly struggling to survive. But for them, the monster is a living reality of their belief systems and daily life.

The primary paranormal factors in the windigo concept that make it a subject of interest to psychical research are the ideas of **possession** and the existence of spirit entities. For the Indians believe that the spirit of the monster can possess an individual who then becomes one or that someone can be transformed into a windigo by being selected by windigo spirit helpers. Possessed or transformed, the human windigo is overcome by a lust for human flesh and turns on his family. If such individuals are not cured, they are executed or even plead for their own execution.

In a typical case a twenty-two year-old man began to speak of eating his mother. His parents tried to reason with him unsuccessfully. The man insisted that he must have human flesh to eat. The whole camp was now aroused and a council was called. Its judgment was that the man had been possessed and turned into a cannibal by the evil spirit. He was sentenced to death. When he was advised of the sentence, he said, "I am willing to die", and his own father strangled him. The strength of the Indian belief in possession is indicated by the fact that his body (like the bodies of all those believed to have been transformed into windigos) was cremated to destroy the windigo spirit in it and to prevent it from coming back.

BIBLIOGRAPHY: Teicher, M. I. 1962. "'Windigo' Psychosis among Algonkian-Speaking Indians." *International Journal of Parapsychology* 4 (1):5.

**Wingfield, C. E. (Kate), ?–1927.** British automatist and trance medium. She was **Frederic W. H. Myers**'s "Miss A." This medium's séances always began with raps and often with table-tilting. In the early days of her mediumship, writing rapidly with a pencil, she produced scripts in different types of handwriting purporting to be that of guides who provided philosophical and religious teachings. Each "guide" had a distinct and characteristic handwriting that never varied regardless of the length of time that elapsed between communications. Besides automatic writing, Miss Wingfield by crystal gazing (i.e., by looking into a crystal or at a ring), would see a continuous series of pictures many of which were veridical. In one case, for instance, at 7:30 she saw in a crystal one Lady Radnor sitting in a red chair in a room Miss Wingfield had never seen. Then another woman in a black dress and white cap came into the room and put her hand on Lady Radnor's shoulder. Subsequently, all details were confirmed.

By 1900 Miss Wingfield had become a trance medium and was involved in the **Cross-Correspondences.** Sir Lawrence J. Jones sat with her some sixty-odd times from May 1900 to 1901 and felt that the thirty different guides and 108 communicators who came through at these sittings could be attributed to the medium's "powers of dramatic characterization" (1928:19). Miss Wingfield (Jones called her "K.") had no control but rather a "Master of Ceremonies" who served to introduce the communicators and to protect the medium. Her doctor guide Semirus seemed to Sir Lawrence to be an independent personality who knew things happening at a distance or even in the future. He was able to "find" his patients (à la Edgar Cayce) and to prescribe treatments. Medical doctors often consulted him.

C. D. Broad sat with Miss Wingfield and studied the records of her sittings. Although he concluded that they indicated that some constituent of the human mind seemed to have survived death (what he called a temporary mind-kin), Jones felt that full-blown survival fitted the facts better.

Miss Wingfield was an amateur medium always unwilling to seek publicity. She never received fees for her work and produced her phenomena only for her private circle of friends.

BIBLIOGRAPHY: Jones, L. J. 1928. "Presidential Address." PSPR 38:17; Myers, F. W. H. 1893. "I. The Subliminal Consciousness." PSPR 9:73–92; Myers, F. W. H. 1892. "III. The Subliminal Consciousness." PSPR 8:436, 485–516.

**Wissenschaftliche Gesellschaft zur Förderung der Parapsychologie. (Scientific Society for the Advancement of Parapsychology).** German membership organization founded in 1981 by Eberhard Bauer, Walter von Lucadou and others for the purpose of advancing high quality scientific research in parapsychology within the walls of universities and other institutions of higher learning. Although many attempts to form parapsychological organizations have been made in the postwar years in Germany, all have failed with the exception of this organization. A great majority of its members presently hold high academic positions in universities. Its objective is unique in Germany and in the rest of the world. The address of the organization is c/o Dipl. Psych Eberhard Bauer, Abteilung für Psychologie und Grenzgebiete der Psychologie, Albert Ludwigs-Universität, Freiburg i. Br., Belfortstr 16, 7800 Freiburg i. Br., West Germany.

**Witch.** From the old English *wicce* o "witch," a weird female who is supposed to possess inherent supernatural or paranormal powers. While generally a witch is thought c as using her powers for evil ("black witch raft"), some witches claim or are believed to se their powers for beneficial purposes 'white witchcraft"), such as curing those 'ho are ill. See also **Witchcraft.**

**'itchcraft.** From the Old English *wicca* neaning "wizard") and *wicce* (meaning vitch") plus *craeft* ("craft"), it is the use by 'itches (female) or wizards (male) of super-atural or paranormal powers inherent in em for good—the "white" kind of witch-raft—or for evil—the "black" kind of witch-raft. Witchcraft is not the same as magic. here was a belief in witchcraft in ancient reece, it is mentioned in the Old Testament Sam:28), and it persisted unhindered roughout Europe until the fifteenth century. rom that time to the eighteenth century, ome 300,000 people were put to death on harges of practicing witchcraft. Female itches or sorceresses and male warlocks, izards, and sorcerers supposedly in league ith the devil were condemned by the hurch, executed by the Inquisition in Eu-ope, and hunted in England under the uarts. During the colonial period in the nited States, there were persecutions in ew England, especially in Salem Village now Danvers, Massachussetts), where fifty-ve supposed witches were tortured and venty executed by hanging or being pressed death. No one was burned at the stake in alem as is popularly supposed. Witch-hunts ok place solely in New England where the uritans had settled and nowhere else in the olonies so that witch-hunting seems to have een a preoccupation of the Puritan mind nly.

Edmund Gurney, who examined 260 books nd records of the witchcraft trials, made a hastly discovery. He found "that there is a tal absence of respectable evidence, and almost total absence of any first-hand evi-ence at all . . ." (Gurney, Myers, Podmore, 386). In New Salem, for instance, witches ight be tried by tying their hands and feet nd throwing them into water to see if they ould sink or swim. Accusations made by ccusers who imagined themselves "be-itched" or who were motivated by malice or ite often were enough to convict.

Yet from our vantage point today, we can e there were some kernels of truth and fact nd many clear analogies to psychical re-earch. For example, the commonest case of itchcraft often involved some argument between an old woman of unpleasant appearance and the owner of a house. The old woman might have cursed the house after her request for a crust of bread had been refused or some complaint of hers denied. When strange noises, raps, or footsteps began to disturb the house, the old hag was held responsible for causing the phenomenon by witchery, tried, and executed. Today we would account for the disturbances as poltergeist manifestations and attribute them to a poltergeist agent in the house and not to a malevolent old woman. Indeed, the descriptions of a majority of witchcraft trials of the sixteenth and seventeenth centuries read like modern accounts of poltergeist investigations. Early cases of witchcraft also frequently involved adolescents just as do current poltergeist cases. In the famous seventeenth century case of the Demon Drummer of Tedworth, two little girls were the center of raps and noises and overturning furniture in their house, but William Drury, the drummer, was accused and imprisoned for having caused the disturbances.

Judges and accusers also were faced with other phenomena that have parallels in psychical research. The judges and accusers committed no error in thinking that the phenomena were real. Their error consisted in attributing to Satan the power of witches to know or do things they had no normal business knowing or doing. A woman was deemed a witch because she was able to describe an absent stranger just by handling an object, such as a tooth or coin, that belonged to the person. In Europe, another was burned because she could speak with spirits of the dead.

In the late fifteenth century, a pair of Dominican friars, Johann Sprenger and Heinrich Kraemer, determined to exterminate the black art in Germany, published a manual to guide judges and witchfinders. It was called *Maleus Maleficarum* or "The Witches' Hammer," spelled out methods for proving someone to be a witch and described witches and their manifestations. These included speaking in a strange tongue, describing events that had not yet taken place, causing the fog-shrouded appearance of dead people, and the ability to cure illness and sores. During the reign of James I, Agnes Simpson, charged as a witch, knew what the king had told his bride in intimate conversation. The king exclaimed "that all the

Devils in Hell could not have discovered same" (Williams, 1941).

These and similar observations about witches make it clear that many were psychics and mediums. Their accusers and judges were confronted by phenomena that included psychometry, mediumship, xenoglossy, precognition, materialization, healing and telepathy. The fear of such powers led the Church, the Inquisition, and the state to oppose them. In England, Statute 4 of the "Witchcraft Act" of 1735 expressly forbade anyone "to pretend from his or her skill or knowledge in any occult or crafty science, to discover where or in what manner any goods or chattels supposed to have been stolen or lost may be found" (i.e., clairvoyance). This statute was not repealed until 1951.

Psi has now been liberated from superstition because of the development of a rational and critical attitude which perceives that psi is not supernatural. The ability is not the work of the devil but is healthy and normal.

BIBLIOGRAPHY: Gurney, E., Myer. F. W. H., Podmore, F. *Phantasms of the Living,* 1886, Vol. 1, p. 172; Williams, C. *Witchcraft,* 1941.

**Witch Doctor.** See **Medicine Man; Shaman.**

**Woodruff, Joseph Leroy, 1913–.** American psychologist and parapsychologist. He received his training at the Parapsychology Laboratory at Duke University and became both a successful subject in tests of psychokinesis and a premier experimenter in many areas of parapsychology. His most famous experiment in clairvoyance was conducted with Joseph G. Pratt (Pratt and Woodruff, 1939).

Joseph B. Rhine thought, and parapsychologists continue to think, that the Pratt-Woodruff experiment was one of the best and most rigorously controlled ever carried out and that it gave significant evidence of extrasensory perception. Charles E. Hansel who speculated that the experimenters might have committed fraud (Hansel, 1980) attempted to lessen its evidential value. But his criticisms were vigorously answered (Pratt, 1976). Anyway, as has been observed: "The improbability of Dr Woodruff, a psychologist of impeccable respectability, having cheated for the very dubious advantage (for a psychologist) of having positive parapsychological results to his credit is, of cour[illegible] immense" (Thouless, 1961:213–214).

Woodruff also made a study of drugs [illegible] failed, as have other investigators, to find t[illegible] drugs brought out psi abilities (Woodru[illegible] 1943). He also tried to find out if psi i[illegible] correlate to any physiological activity in [illegible] body, but a study of ESP and the psyc[illegible] galvanic response showed no significant c[illegible] relation (Woodruff and Dale, 1952).

An instructor at City College of New Yo[illegible] he joined Gardner Murphy in the Departm[illegible] of Psychology to do work on ESP research[illegible]

Selected Writings: 1943. "ESP Tests Un[illegible] Various Physiological Conditions." JP 7:2[illegible] and Dale L. A. 1952. "ESP Function and [illegible] Psychogalvanic Response." JASPR 46:62; a[illegible] Pratt, J. G. 1939. "Size of Stimulus Symbols [illegible] Extrasensory Perception." JP 3:121.

BIBLIOGRAPHY: Berger, A. S. *Lives and L[illegible] ters in American Parapsychology,* 19[illegible] Hansel, C. E. M. *ESP and Parapsychology[illegible] Critical Reevaluation,* 1980; Pratt, J. G. 19[illegible] "New Evidence Supporting the ESP Interp[illegible] tation of the Pratt-Woodruff Experiment." [illegible] 40:217; Thouless, R. H. 1961. "The Journal [illegible] Parapsychology, XXV, 2 June 1961, Durha[illegible] N.C." JSPR 41:212.

**Worcester, Elwood, 1862–1940.** Americ[illegible] clergyman. James H. Hyslop having plan[illegible] the seed of psychical research in Worcest[illegible] mind, he joined the American Society [illegible] Psychical Research. When, after Hyslo[illegible] death, he believed that the ASPR was dev[illegible] ing from Hyslop's scientific standards, W[illegible] cester left the ASPR in 1925 and in that y[illegible] established in Boston the **Boston Soci[illegible] for Psychic Research.**

After receiving his D.D. degree from [illegible] University of Pennsylvania in 1898, Worces[illegible] held the chair of history of philosophy a[illegible] psychology at Lehigh University. He beca[illegible] rector of St. Stephen's in Philadelphia a[illegible] later rector of Emmanuel Church, one [illegible] Boston's most prestigious Episcopalian c[illegible] gregations. He established there a health p[illegible] gram, known as the Emmanuel moveme[illegible] which combined religion and medicine.

**Worrall, Ambrose Alexander, 1899–19[illegible]** British-born healer. With his wife, **Olga Worrall,** he attracted thousands to his h[illegible] ing services and was known throughout [illegible] world. Worrall discovered his gift soon a[illegible] World War I. His sister's twisted and pa[illegible] ed neck had been pronounced incurable the doctors. But when Worrall touched it, sister was cured.

The aftermath of the war brought mass employment to England so Worrall immiated to the United States in 1923. He rked in the aircraft industry and used his aling gifts for friends. With Olga, he set up New Life Clinic where they held their aling services. Worrall considered himself thing more than a channel for the divine wer of healing and, as a devout Christian, ed prayer in his healing in the belief that d was its true source.

While many others will agree with his relious interpretation of healing as God-given, other interpretation from the perspective of ychical research could be that prayer is the eans by which the blockage between mind d body and self-healing is eliminated or means by which psychokinesis is put into y.

Throughout his healing career, Worrall intained that people should not ignore hodox medicine and ought to take from it atever it could give them; it was another annel by which God used the divine power heal. Throughout his career Worrall used gift to help people without expecting paynt.

Selected Writing: with Worrall, O. N. *The t of Healing,* 1965.

**rrall, Olga Nathalie, 1906–1985.** Amern healer. Daughter of a Russian theolon, she was working as a secretary in eveland, Ohio, when, in 1928, she met and rried the healer Ambrose A. Worrall. But g before that she was aware of her own wer of healing. When, as a young girl, she ched her siblings, their pains or headnes would disappear. Her magic touch ed her mother of a kidney problem. With husband, she was impelled to use her ent and her laying-on-of-hands technique hout charge and for the benefit of others. n their New Life Clinic, she and her husnd shared the devout belief that they were annels for God's power to heal and there, ening their ministry with a prayer from the lect of the Protestant Episcopal Service of ly Communion, they conducted their heal- ministry to help thousands. For the hunds who could not be present but wanted aling, they prayed each night at 9 P.M. After husband's death, Olga Worrall continued the ministry and prayers without interruption.

Healing others was her life and absorbed all her energies to the exclusion of other areas in psychical research. "I am not at all interested in proving survival after bodily death," she wrote. "This is not my ministry, although in my field of Spiritual Healing I do receive, on rare occasions, proof of survival. This project of proof of survival is as old as the hills and if people cannot accept survival, my 'two cents worth' would not move them" (letter to authors). She was much more interested in proving her healing abilities and submitted to investigation under laboratory conditions.

In one experiment, bacteria had been exposed to an antibiotic. Those bacteria in a sealed test tube around which Mrs. Worrall cupped her hands showed a significantly greater growth then bacteria in control sealed test tubes that were taken out of the room and did not receive her treatment (Rauscher and Rubik, 1980). Olga Worrall was listed in *Who's Who in American Women* and went on with her healing ministry until her death.

Selected Writing: with Worrall, A. A. *The Gift of Healing,* 1965.

BIBLIOGRAPHY: Rauscher, E. and Rubik, B. A. "Effects on Motility Behavior and Growth Rate of Salmonella Typhimurium in the Presence of a Psychic Subject." In W. G. Roll, ed., *Research in Parapsychology 1979,* 1980, p. 140.

**"Worth, Patience."** See **Curran, Pearl Lenore.**

**Wriedt, Etta, 1859–1942.** American physical medium. She specialized in direct voice and in trumpet sittings. Voices claiming to be of dead people spoke through floating trumpets. The voices produced in her presence were particularly impressive because sometimes they conversed in several foreign languages and at other times there were reports of two voices speaking at the same time. (Holms, 1925). Etta Wriedt also seemed to have equally impressive powers as a mental medium aided by her control **"John King".**

On one occasion, a widow who could not locate her deceased husband's will came to her. The medium apparently received a message from the husband that the will could be found in a chest in a home in France. A search revealed that this information was correct (Fodor, 1964:14). Etta Wriedt held sittings with several famous people, including William MacKenzie King, the Canadian prime minister, and gave séances in William T. Stead's "Julia's Bureau" in London. If reports of the unusual phenomena she produced are correct, she was a remarkable medium.

BIBLIOGRAPHY: Fodor N. *Between Two Worlds*, 1964; Holms, A. C. *The Facts of Psychic Science and Philosophy*, 1925.

# X

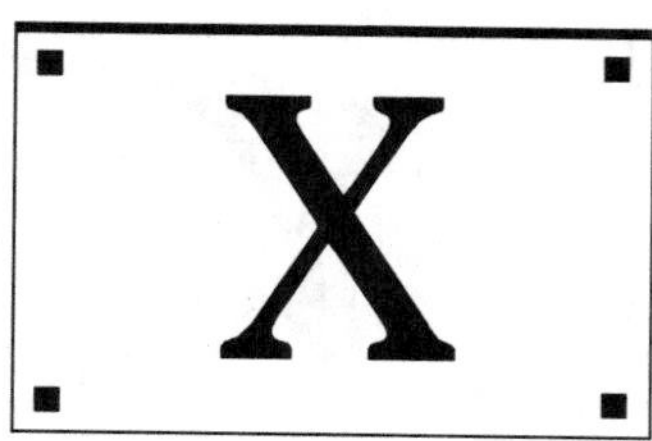

**Xenoglossy.** The speaking or writing of words or phrases in an unknown language by someone who could have had no normal means of learning the language. The term was first applied to this rare type of case by **Charles Richet** after he studied "Mme X" in Paris. She, while in a semi-trance, wrote long phrases in Greek.

The phenomenon generally is divided into two kinds: "recitative" in which a person seems to engage in merely a mechanical repetition of memorized language and "responsive" where people demonstrate an ability to carry on an active conversation in a foreign language they could not have learned normally. Explanations advanced for such cases include fraud, cryptomnesia, extrasensory perception, or the action of a discarnate personality who knew the language being spoken or written.

Although rare, some cases on record make plausible the theory of a surviving personality. Among the most outstanding of these is one that Frederic H. Wood wrote about in several books. A competent observer, Wood had sittings with an automatist whom he called "Rosemary." In the course of these sittings, a control appeared who said she was "Lady Nona," once a Babylonian princess who had lived in Egypt more than 3,000 years ago. Although the automatist's script was written in English, sometimes she spoke words and sentences impressed upon her by "Nona" in the language spoken in Egypt at the time of the Pharoah Amenhotep III. The words and phrases were translated by Howard Hulme, an Egyptologist. On one occasion, in order to test "Nona's" comprehension of the ancient language, Hulme gave Wood a question to ask in the old Egyptian tongue. In the question was a word that could be used in two separate senses. (In English, for example, the word "back" can mean the rear part of something or someone, or it can mean to support or uphold someone or something.) The Egyptian word meant either "hail" or "protect." Hulme used it in the sense of "Hail to thee Princess Nona." But the control responded with the second meaning: "Protected ones are we!" The case suggests a personality with a knowledge of the Egyptian language that the automatist did not possess.

BIBLIOGRAPHY: Kautz, W. H. 1982. "The Rosemary Case of Alleged Egyptian Xenoglossy." *Theta.* 10:26; Richet, C. 1905. "Xénoglossie: L'Écriture Automatique en Langues Étrangères." PSPR 29:162; Wood, F. H. *This Egyptian Miracle,* 1940; Wood, F. H. *After Thirty Centuries,* 1935.

# Y

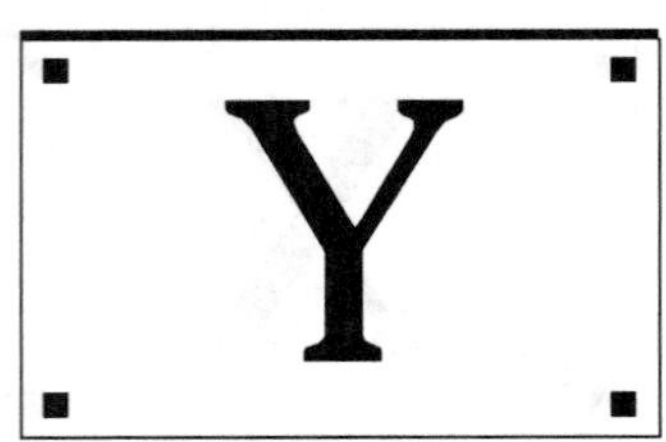

**Yeats, William Butler, 1865–1939.** Irish lyric poet and dramatist. Recipient of the Nobel Prize in Literature in 1923, he stimulated interest in Celtic culture and mystic ideas. He was the leading force in the Irish literary revival. Originally a painter, he became absorbed by the prophetic books and symbolic poetry of William Blake and soon replaced the brush with the pen. He published much verse and many plays. Yeats was also concerned with social and political problems and, in 1922, was elected to the Senate of the Irish Free State.

Yeats is a **Noted Witness** for the paranormal. By means of psychometry he got impressions from leaves and flowers and even from a cardboard symbol. He believed in spirits and Spiritualism. His wife was a medium through whom came some fifty notebooks of automatic writing. She spoke automatically as well. He was particularly impressed by what appeared to be xenoglossy when a medium, who did not know Italian, Greek, or Latin, spoke in these languages. In 1932, he had an equally impressive sitting with Mina S. Crandon, the famous "Margery," in whose presence wooden rings interlocked. Yeats sent the rings to England to be examined by Sir Oliver Lodge but the rings separated in transit. When he had a sitting with Geraldine Cummins, who was as thoroughly Celtic as he, he was astonished when her ouija board, either through telepathy or some communicator at work, produced the plot of a play he was then composing.

Yeats was attracted by Theosophy a Helena Petrova Blavatsky whom he admir although Richard Hodgson's condemnati of her troubled him. He wrote: "She sat the all evening, talking to whoever came—v and shapeless of body, and perpetually rc ing cigarettes—humorous and unfanatic, a displaying always, it seemed a mind th seemed to pass all others in her hones Unlike those about her, I had read with ca the Psychical Research Society's charge fraudulent miracle-working. . . . I could r accept this explanation, but finding tho charges, so weightily supported, incompa ble with what I saw and heard, awaited w impatience the explanation that never cam (Donoghue, 1972).

He was drawn to magic as well and interpenetrated much of his work. In 1892, wrote to a friend who had criticized his p occupation with it: "It is surely absurd hold me 'weak' or otherwise because I cho to persist in a study which I decided delib ately to make, next to my poetry, the m important pursuit of my life. . . . If I had r made magic my constant study I would r have written a single word of my Blake boc nor would *The Countess Cathleen* have ev come to exist . . . I sometimes forget that t word 'magic' which sounds so familiar to r ears has a very outlandish sound to oth ears" (Wade, 1954:210-211). He also believ in fairies.

Yeats is a witness to the **Creative Pr cess,** for he tapped into an external sour or into the "great memory" for his inform

n. When he read Oswald Spengler's *The* *cline of the West,* he was struck that engler's ideas had been his as well. Although he attributed this coincidence to the eat memory" which both had tapped, an ernative explanation might be telepathy.

Selected Writing: Yeats, W. B. *Per Amica* *entia Lunae,* 1918.

BIBLIOGRAPHY: Donoghue, D. *Memoirs,* 72, pp. 24–25; Ebon, M. *They Knew the* *known,* 1973; Wade. A., ed., *The Letters of* *B. Yeats,* 1954.

**ga.** Spiritual techniques, born in India, for aining a state of inner illumination and eration. The aim of yoga has been defined "the elevation of the narrow, fear-ridden d desire-tormented human consciousness a state of indescribable beauty, glory, and ss" (Krishna, 1972:19). In India, every sysn of yoga generally can be classified either Raja Yoga or Hatha Yoga.

There are few references to this ancient stem in the Vedas or the Upanishads, the in sources of religious and philosophic ought. The principal source for Raja Yoga the almost 2,000 year-old *Yoga Sutras* of tanjali and for Hatha Yoga the *Hatha Yoga* *adipka, Siva Samhita* and other works sed on Tantric philosophy and worship. In Raja Yoga system, there are eight "limbs" stages through which one must pass in der to still the mind and arrive at deepest **laxation** and **meditation.** When the final mbs" are reached the siddhis or paranorl powers and phenomena, such as levitan, are supposed to appear.

Although yoga seems to be a logical area study for psychical research, there has not en much investigation to test these claims psychic abilities and occurrences. The lack of hard data, therefore, leaves the claims without empirical basis. Nevertheless, considering the aim of yoga and what it might do for our mental states, there is little to be lost in trying it.

Yoga, of course, does not own the exclusive rights to the attainment of a higher level of consciousness. Even in India other methods, such as love and devotion to a divine power, are suggested in the Bhagavad-Gita.

BIBLIOGRAPHY: Krishna, G. *The Secret of Yoga,* 1972.

**Young, Meredith Lady** called "Agartha." Contemporary American channeler. While meditating, she began to feel (not hear or see) words from multidimensional beings from a plane more spiritually evolved than ours. Their purpose is to help humanity's development by showing the way to enlightenment, how to create one's own reality, how earth can survive, what healing is, what death is, and how we are all God.

Selected Writing: *A Journey to the Stars,* 1984.

BIBLIOGRAPHY: Klimo, J. Channeling, 1987, p. 59.

**Yram (Dr. Marcel Louis Forhan), 1884–1917.** French pioneer writer on astral projection. He reportedly travelled "astrally" from China where he lived for many years—and where he died—to visit friends. He was also an investigator of psychic phenomena and hypnotism and, from 1911, was a member of the Theosophical Society.

Selected Writings: Yram. *Practical Astral Projection* (Le Médecine de l'Âme), 1976.

BIBLIOGRAPHY: Pleasants, H. *Biographical Dictionary of Parapsychology,* 1964.

# Z

**Zeitschrift für Kritischen Okkultismus (Journal for Critical Occultism).** German quarterly journal. Under the editorship of Richard Baerwald it was a hard-line skeptical organ that published outstanding critical investigations of paranormal phenomena and attempted to provide a platform for a dialogue between skeptics and psychical researchers. The journal was published only from 1926 to 1928.

**Zen.** From the Sanskrit *dhyana* meaning "meditation." It is a technique taught by the Buddhist school in Japan of meditating with open eyes as distinguished from meditation with closed eyes as in **Yoga.** The aim of the Zen meditation technique is to achieve enlightenment.

Since meditation, relaxation and an altered state of consciousness seem to facilitate psi, Zen seems a logical subject for investigation by psychical research and parapsychology. Yet surprisingly little research has been done in this area. One positive experiment in psychokinesis has been reported, however. In this experiment, the subject used the Zen technique to meditate for twenty mintues prior to each session in which he tried to push the buttons on a random sequence generator in such a way that they would correspond with lamps that were going to light in a random sequence. "The scoring rate was 33 percent, where chance would predict 25 percent" (Schmidt H. and Pantas, L., 1971:51).

BIBLIOGRAPHY: Schmidt, H. and Pantas, L. 1971. "Psi Tests with Psychologically Equiv alent Conditions and Internally Different Ma chines." In W. G. Roll, R. L. Morris, J. D Morris, eds., *Proceedings of the Parapsy chological Association* 8:49.

**Zener, Karl E., 1903–1963.** American psy chologist. He designed the ESP cards. Al though Joseph B. Rhine often is credited with having conceived these cards, in reality the were designed by Zener who, in the 1930s was Rhine's colleague in the Department o Psychology at Duke University.

Rhine began by conducting many trials to test for telepathy with various target cards such as playing cards and cards with num bers or letters stamped on them. He then asked Zener, who had been trained in the psychology of perception, whether he could design symbols that could be distinguished and imaged more easily than the ones he had been using. Zener came up with geometric designs that were used on cards called "Zener Cards," later and more commonl called "ESP cards." These unusual card proved to be a noteworthy advance in the investigation of extrasensory perception.

Soon, however, Zener had another design He turned against Rhine and his ESP experi ments because he believed that Rhine and his work represented a danger to the Depart ment of Psychology and its program at Duke Zener worked with Helge Lundholm, anothe colleague in the department, to get rid o Rhine and his experimental schemes.

BIBLIOGRAPHY: Berger, A. S. *Lives and Letters in American Parapsychology,* 1988.

**Zener Cards.** See **ESP Cards; Karl E. Zener.**

**Zetetic Scholar.** Published irregularly in the United States by the Center for Scientific Anomalies Research to provide book reviews, bibliographies, and information about anomalies, including parapsychology. In the battle between sceptics and parapsychologists, it seems to be caught in no-man's land. Hard-line sceptics think the journal too soft on paranormal phenomena that they feel it tends to validate. Supporters of parapsychology think it is too hard on them in criticisms disguised as objective and constructive. Whichever side is right, the publication offers parapsychologists the needed opportunity to establish communication with sceptics. Editor: Marcello Truzzi.

**Zierold, María Reyes de, ?–1942.** Mexican upperclass housewife. She was an amateur psychometric medium. A large woman (she weighed 200 pounds) and the mother of a numerous family, she was a reluctant medium whose psychic gifts had been discovered by Dr. Gustav Pagenstecher during his use of hypnosis for therapeutic purposes.

Daughter of the governor of the state of Michoacán in Mexico during Porfirio Díaz's presidency, Sra. de Zierold was a woman of means, moderate education, and superior intellect. She was repelled by Spiritualism on account of an experience with fraud. She consented to Dr. Pagenstecher's experiments in psychometry only out of gratitude to him for saving her life.

In 1919, before a medical commission, Sra. de Zierold demonstrated her impressive ability to obtain from physical objects knowledge of facts beyond the reach of her normal powers. In 1921, her striking powers were again demonstrated in important psychometric experiments carried out in Mexico by Walter F. Prince. Remarkable results were obtained from a sealed letter. Sra. de Zierold was able to see the place and circumstances of the writer's death, and to describe him accurately. A "sea bean" seed, thought to be the seed of a tropical plant, was correctly identified as the seed of an inland tree. She also seemed to demonstrate precognition, but, because of Prince's death, these experiments were never concluded.

BIBLIOGRAPHY: Prince, W. F. 1921. "Psychometric Experiments with Senora Maria Reyes de Z." PASPR 15:189; Pagenstecher, G. 1922. "Past Events Seership: A Study in Psychometry." PASPR 16:1.

**Zöllner, Johann K. F., 1834–1882.** German professor of astronomy at Leipzig University. His work in the nineteenth century contributed to measuring the brightness of the moon compared to the sun and to estimating the brightness of stars that could be seen with the naked eye. In 1877–1878, in quest of discovering an empirical foundation for his theory of "space of four"–a hypothetical fourth dimension of space–he investigated the medium Henry Slade. In this space of four, Zöllner believed that the phenomena he observed during his séances with Slade could take place.

The phenomena consisted of knots tied in endless cords whose ends were sealed together and the materialization and dematerialization of objects. Another phenomenon observed and recorded by Zöllner was slate-writing in which spirits were supposed to have written directly on slates whose faces were locked together. Zollner described one experiment with the slates: "I took a book-slate, bought by myself; that is, two slates connected at one side by cross-hinges, like a book, for folding up. . . . We might have sat at the table in the brightly-lighted room for about five minutes, our hands linked with those of Slade in the usual manner *above* the table, when I suddenly felt on two occasions, the one shortly after the other, the slate pressed down on my lap, without my having perceived anything in the least visible. Three raps on the table announced that all was completed, and when I opened the slate there was within it, on the one side, the impression of a *right* foot, on the other side that of a left foot" (Zöllner, 1882:39).

Zöllner and his university colleagues who held sittings with Slade were convinced that the phenomena were authentic. But critics charged that one of his colleagues had a cataract, the other was over eighty years of age, and that Zöllner himself was mentally disturbed. This charge is what prompted one historian to write: "Of all the eminent men whose reputation has been undone by his decision to take psychical research seriously,

Zöllner is perhaps the most unfortunate" (Inglis, 1985:321).

Zöllner was, of course, fully competent and in mid-life. Nevertheless, although no explanation has ever been forthcoming for the phenomena he observed, the weight of his observations as evidence is diminished by the fact that Slade was detected in fraud on several other occasions and by the added fact that Zöllner was anxious to obtain experimental verification for his hypothesis of "space of four." Perhaps he was too ready to accept Slade's phenomena.

Selected Writing: *Transcendental Physics,* 1882.

BIBLIOGRAPHY: Inglis, B. *The Paranormal,* 1985.

**Zorab, George Avetoom Marterus, 1898–.** leading Dutch psychical researcher. The Netherlands' foremost (and oldest) worker in the field of psychical research, he was sent for an education at age eleven to The Netherlands from Java (now Indonesia) where he was born. Unexpectedly for him and his parents, Spiritualism, which had spread from the United States and engulfed Europe and The Netherlands, became part of his education. When he was twelve years old, he witnessed table-tilting for the first time, an experience that made him very happy "for I had solved one of my greatest problems"—the fear of death. For Spiritualism taught him that there is no death and that there could be communication with the spirits of those who have died. As he grew older, he read books in several languages on psychical research and became so interested in it that he took a copy of F. W. H. Myers's *Human Personality and its Survival of Bodily Death* along on his honeymoon. He became the editor of Spiritualist-oriented periodicals and a member of the Dutch Society for Psychical Research (Studievereniging voor Psychical Research). In 1936, he joined the Society for Psychical Research.

Just before the forces of Nazi Germany overwhelmed The Netherlands in the spring of 1940, Zorab's first book was published. It noted that the phenomena of Spiritualism did not require a spirit hypothesis and concluded that the evidence for survival beyond death was weak. He therefore changed his mind about the whole survival hypothesis which, as he still believes, "has not a leg to stand on." On the other hand, he is convinced that the materializations produced by the phys-ical mediums Florence Cook and Kate Coo were genuine and in no way distinguishabl from living people. He has written widely o that subject, including a book in Italian dedi-cated to the two mediums.

For over fifty years, Zorab has been a extraordinary figure in both European an international psychical research. Many hon-ors have come his way. When the Parapsy-chology Foundation and Eileen Garret planned the First International Conference o Parapsychological Studies in 1953, Zorab was charged with the task of organizing it When an International Committee for th Study of Spontaneous Paranormal Phe-nomena was established later at the Hague Zorab was appointed its chairman to coordi-nate studies of spontaneous cases in Europe He received the Perrott Studentship in Psychi-cal Research in 1961.

In 1986, he was paid a warm tribute by hi colleagues all over the world in a "Liber Ami-corum" that details his scholarly and scien-tific contributions to psychical research an gives a bibliography of over 350 books an articles he has written in many languages o one or another aspect of psychical researcl Editor of *Spiegel de Parapsychologie,* he con-tinues in his 90s to be active in the field.

Selected Writings: *Katie King: Donna Fantasma,* 1980; *De Jacht op het Spiritistic Bewijs,* 1940.

BIBLIOGRAPHY: F. W. J. J. Snel, ed., *In Honou of G. A. M. Zorab,* 1986.

**Zugun, Eleonore, 1913–.** Romanian phys-ical medium. In addition to raps in her pres-ence, she produced apports of toys ornaments, and chess pieces and poltergeis phenomena such as causing objects to mov or fly across a room. But her reputation rest-ed on stigmatic marks or abrasions, includ-ing scratches and teeth marks, that appeare suddenly on several parts of her body. He village priest, parents, and she herself be-lieved that their source was *Dracu* (th "Devil" in Romanian).

As a paranormal phenomenon, the stig-matic markings are suspect because the were on parts of the girl's body that she coul have scratched or bitten herself. In fact, th teeth-marks corresponded to those made b her own teeth. Yet no one ever observed he making any suspicious movement, and, ex-cept for possibly trying to impress or fo people, the question was never answered why she should wish to inflict painful bites and scratches on herself. And she was supposed to have been under constant observation by the countess with whom she lived in Vienna and who reported that on one occasion and "under the most rigorous conditions" she was bitten twenty-five times (Wassilko-Serecki, Z., 1926). Assuming the truthfulness of the countess, the lesions could have been of psychosomatic origin and cannot be dismissed as impossible.

BIBLIOGRAPHY: Price, H. 1926. "Poltergeist Phenomena of Eleonore Zugun." JASPR 20:449; Wassilko-Serecki, Z. 1926. "Observations on Eleonore Zugun—II." JASPR 20:593.

# ▪ APPENDIX A ▪

# Parapsychology and Psychical Research Around the World*

This appendix offers a brief overview of the history and current status of psychical research and parapsychology in countries where important developments in the field have taken or are taking place. For readers interested in pursuing their investigations further, the entries contain up-to-date listings for each country, including the principal research centers, membership organizations, members of the Parapsychological Association, major parapsychological publications, educational opportunities in parapsychology, and university departments of parapsychology.

## ARGENTINA

In South America the greatest interest and activity in psychical research and parapsychology has occurred in Argentina. It began in the latter part of the nineteenth century with the arrival of Spanish immigrants who, along with their other possessions, brought Spiritualism with them. Séances were held in Buenos Aires with prominent people such as the editor of the powerful newspaper *La Prensa.* In the 1900s famous mediums were being investigated in a more or less critical spirit and apparently some authentic phenomena were observed. In 1930 Argentinian universities became interested in psychical research, and in 1931 a department of paranormal psychology was created in the University of Buenos Aires by Professor Enrique Mouchet.

Other centers were started. By 1940, Joseph B. Rhine's card-guessing experiments had made their impact and his methods adopted. When Orlando Canavesio created a medical organization that focused on extrasensory perception, he stimulated interest in parapsychology. The Argentinian government in 1948 established the Institute for Applied Psychopathology and appointed Canavesio its head. The aim of the institute was to study the practices of Spiritualists and see if they were injurious to the public welfare. This unusual step mobilized the Spiritualists who, in 1949, established an Argentinian Society of Parapsychology that included many members of Spiritualist groups. Three years later, the Argentine Institute of Parapsychology was created to which many Spiritualists belonged, including José S. Fernandez and J. Ricardo Musso both of whom later became presidents of the group.

During the next two decades the progress of parapsychology in Argentina seemed to be advancing as academic interest in the subject increased, as courses in parapsychology were given at the national universities of Buenos Aires and of La Plata and as Musso received a provisional appointment to give courses at the Littoral National University. Private universities also gave courses such as the one taught by Enrique Novillo Paulí at the Catholic University of Córdoba.

Unfortunately, academic interest was short-lived. By 1970, for different reasons, all courses in parapsychology were canceled except for one at the University of Salvador where a Parapsychology Institute was created. Parapsychological organizations also carried on with public lectures and courses while individuals, such as Naum Kreiman, conducted experiments. The present parapsychological scene is as follows:

### RESEARCH CENTERS

Instituto de Parapsicología, Universidad del Salvador, Hipolito Yrigoyen 2025—Sarandi 65, 1081 Buenos Aires, Argentina.

Instituto Argentino de Parapsicología, Calle Ramon Lista 868, 1706 Domingo F. Sarmiento (Haedo) Prov. Buenos Aires, Argentina.

### MEMBERSHIP ORGANIZATION

Instituto Argentino de Parapsicología

### PARAPSYCHOLOGICAL ASSOCIATION MEMBERS

Lic. Enrique Novillo Paulí, Instituto de Para-

*Data supplied in part by the authorities from foreign countries named in the Preface and also drawn from Donna L. McCormick, ed., *Courses and other Study Opportunities in Parapsychology,* New York: American Society for Psychical Research, 1987.

psicología, Universidad del Salvador, Hipolito Yrigoyen 2025—Sarandi 65, 1081 Buenos Aires, Argentina.

MAJOR PARAPSYCHOLOGICAL PUBLICATIONS

*Cuadernos de Parapsicología.* (Instituto de Parapsicología)

EDUCATIONAL OPPORTUNITIES

Professor of Parapsychology Enrique Novillo Paulí gives a course at the Universidad del Salvador. The Instituto Argentino de Parapsicología also gives courses and lectures in parapsychology.

UNIVERSITY DEPARTMENTS IN PARAPSYCHOLOGY

Instituto de Parapsicología, Universidad del Salvador.

## AUSTRALIA

Paranormal phenomena are as indigenous to Australia as its aborigines in whose society and religion they play an important role. Yet although Australian scientists have always had a splendid opportunity for the objective observation and testing of the psychic powers claimed by the clever men of the aboriginal tribes, they lagged seriously for many years in the pursuit of this investigation as well as in the conduct generally of psychical research or research in parapsychology.

One of the reasons was Australia's history. After its colonization in 1788 by England both as a settlement for convicts and as a British base for trade with the East, the emphasis until the mid 1850s was on exploration, politics, and economic growth, especially in wool-growing and the discovery of copper and gold. Among the other reasons for the slow progress of Australian psychical research was the tendency of the public and press to confuse it with Spiritualism which made its appearance in Australia in the 1860s. In addition, Australia was remote from psychical research organizations in other parts of the world.

Psychical research flamed briefly in 1864 with William Archer's historic table-tilting experiment and died out just as quickly when his experiment ruled out any paranormal factor. A great opportunity for Australian psychical research was presented in the person of Richard Hodgson of Melbourne who had an interest in Spiritualism. But it was lost when he sailed for England in 1878. By the 1880s, William H. Terry had helped to promote the investigations of mediums and some psychical research groups appeared. But what research was done was carried out by small groups working at great distances from one another and mainly ignorant of one another's work. Anyway, the investigation of mediumship was discouraged and impeded once more by fraud, this time by the medium Charles Bailey.

In the 1900s, American Thomas W. Stanford's patronage helped push research of Australian mediums forward. A. W. Dobbie of Adelaide also played a positive role with his investigations of one of Stanford's mediums and his reports to Eleanor Sidgwick of some cases of clairvoyance. The only other Australian who generated serious research was Robin J. Tillyard but, with his death in 1937, what small forward movement there was came to a standstill. Not even the card-guessing experiments conducted at Duke University and which had created a furor elsewhere could get Australian parapsychology going.

After the Second World War, few Australian universities (mainly disinterested in or hostile to parapsychology), were disposed to carry out research although some experiments were conducted at Queensland University with negative results. No courses on parapsychology were given at university or college levels and, with one exception, there was not enough student interest to start research groups. The exception was Melbourne University where, in 1948, a Melbourne Society for Psychical Research was organized but it soon expired. In 1960, the only degree ever granted for research in parapsychology was the B.A. degree awarded by the University of Tasmania to Jurgen Keil.

In recent years two universities have offered courses in parapsychology and parapsychological organizations began to form. But Australian parapsychology continues to be sharply limited by the geography of the country and by an academic community unfriendly to it. It survives mainly through the work of individuals who have appeared on the scene. Ronald K. H. Rose pioneered in studies of the aborigines. Others, including Raynor C. Johnson, Michael John Scriven, Jurgen Keil, Harvey Jon Irvin and Michael A. Thalbourne, have made increasing contributions to parapsychology. The present parapsychological scene is as follows:

RESEARCH CENTERS

None

MEMBERSHIP ORGANIZATIONS

Australasian Institute of Psychic Research, P.O. Box 445, Lane Cove, NSW 2066.

Australasian Skeptics, P.O. Box 575, Manly, NSW 2095.

Australasian Society for Psychical Research, Professor J. Frodsham, School of Human Communication, Murdoch University, Murdoch WA 6153.

#### Parapsychological Association Members

M. K. Boyes, Inst. Ethnoscience Studies, Box 186, GPO, Blackwood, S. Australia 5051.

Dr. Harvey Jon Irwin, Dep't of Psychology, Univ. of New England, Armidale, NSW 2351.

Dr. H. H. J. Keil, Dep't of Psychology, Univ. of Tasmania, Box 252C, GPO Hobart, Tasmania 7001.

S. Knorles, P.O. Box 443, Armidale 2350.

Dr. M. Thalbourne, Department of Psychology, University of Adelaide, South Australia 5001.

#### Major Parapsychological Publications

*Psi.* Newsletter published by the Australasian Society for Psychical Research.

*Bulletin.* Australian Institute of Psychic Research.

#### Educational Opportunities in Parapsychology

Dep't of Psychology, University of New England, Armidale NSW 2531: First, second, and third year courses; also independent study/research can be arranged.

University of Tasmania, Hobart, Tasmania: undergraduate and graduate courses.

#### University Departments in Parapsychology

None.

## BRAZIL

Largest republic in South America, it leads the world in coffee crops. It also has the largest nominally Roman Catholic population in the world. Its fame in these respects is rivaled only by its leadership in the world of the paranormal. Voodooism is openly practiced. Healing methods are used in many countries, but Brazil is the world's foremost claimant to unorthodox healers and psychic surgeons. The ratio of conventional physicians to the general population is only about one per 1,200 people.

Surprisingly, even the 20 percent of Brazil's population of 145 million who are church-going Catholics who attend Mass and receive the sacraments are also *espiritistas* who beat drums, burn candles, and make offerings to pagan gods. Their Sundays may be spent in the Catholic church but, as followers of Spiritism, their Saturday nights are spent in Kardecian or cult churches along with the rest of the population. There are three principal cults: those that teach the doctrines of Allan Kardec; those, such as the Candomblé, that combine Afro-Christian religious beliefs; and the Umbanda cult with its two branches that offer Kardecian and Candomblé approaches. In the main, all agree on the existence of a spiritual body in addition to the physical body, on the existence of discarnate spirits, and in the use of spirit guides for healing the sick.

Here is a country where there is a preponderance of unorthodox healers, and conversations with the spirits of the dead and the belief in reincarnation are widespread. Yet there has been very little mainstream psychical research or parapsychology. One reason may be an historical difference between Brazil and other parts of the world. In the United Kingdom and United States, for example, psychical researchers broke with Spiritualists whose standards of evidence they considered low and whose methods of investigation seemed shoddy. It was the psychical researchers who did the investigating. In Brazil, on the other hand, there was no such schism. The Spiritists were the only researchers. But they were more concerned with evangelizing and unorthodox healing than with scientific work that remained sporadic except when Spiritism was attacked by the political establishment or by the Catholic church. At such times Spiritists made extra efforts to give their movement scientific respectability.

In the 1920s and '30s Carlos Mirabelli was proclaimed by the Cesare Lombroso Academy of Psychical Studies (set up specifically to study him) the greatest of all mental and physical mediums. Today some responsible Brazilian researchers seem to have emerged, including Waldo Vieira who is studying the out-of-body experience, and Hernani Guimares Andrade who studies cases of reincarnation and poltergeists. But while non-Brazilian psychical researchers and parapsychologists continue to travel to Europe, China and Mexico to conduct their studies, few venture into Brazil even though it leads other countries in the paranormal.

The present parapsychological scene is as follows:

#### Research Centers

Insituto Brasiliero de Informaçao e Pesquiza Parapsicologia (Brazilian Institute for Parapsychological Information and Research).

#### Membership Organizations

None

#### Parapsychological Association Members

None

#### Major Parapsychological Publications.

None.

EDUCATIONAL OPPORTUNITIES IN PARAPSYCHOLOGY.

None.

UNIVERSITY DEPARTMENTS IN PARAPSYCHOLOGY

None

## FRANCE

Psychical research got its start in France in the eighteenth century when the physician Franz Anton Mesmer brought mesmerism to Paris. Besides being cured during their "mesmeric" trances, people seemed to have paranormal perception and cognition. But a hostile report made by a commission of scientists and doctors established by King Louis XVI to look into Mesmer's method of treatment destroyed interest in it and its allied phenomena and broke up Mesmer's practice.

It was not until the mid-nineteenth century that psychical research received a new push as the work of Jean-Martin Charcot focussed the attention of the scientific world on hypnosis and on the unusual phenomena that accompanied it. In 1893, the first doctoral degree for a thesis on psychical research was granted by the University of Montpellier. Many great individual contributions have been made to the field by French psychical researchers: Charles Richet who investigated Eusapia Palladino and Eva C. and helped invent the term "métapsychique"; Gustave Geley who had sittings with Franek Kluski; René Warcollier, the foremost experimenter in telepathy; and the work of René Sudre and Robert Amadou.

In 1919, collective research and the use of the experimental method by people of the highest scientific standing began with the founding just after World War I of the Institut Métapsychique International. This represented the greatest advance in French psychical research. The institut carried out many tests, such as Eugene Osty's investigations of Pascal Forthuny, and, in 1933, joined with the British Society for Psychical Research in the study of the medium Rudi Schneider. Following World War II, however, there seemed to be a considerable slowing down of psychical research activity in France so that it was difficult for parapsychology to take hold. One reason may have been a dearth of suitable material and of subjects of the level of Schneider. Another important obstacle probably was the failure of French parapsychology to be accorded recognition as a branch of science in France and its inability to penetrate the walls of any university. Parapsychology was not and still is not included in any university curriculum.

This situation forced many parapsychologists with academic affiliations to go "underground" and to do their work and publish their results under pseudonyms to avoid injury to their academic reputations and careers. An example is Rémy Chauvin who conducted ESP tests.

The work done in dermo-optic perception and the experiments by Yvonne Duplessis, director of the Study Committee on Dermo-Optical Sensitivity, are most interesting, but they are not strictly parapsychological. It was because of dissatisfaction with the state of research in France that the Organisation pour la Recherche en Psyochtronique was established in 1987. The present parapsychological scene is as follows:

RESEARCH CENTERS

Institut Métapsychique International, 1 Place de Wagram, 75017, Paris, France.

Laboratoire Universitaire de Parapsychologie et d'Hygiène Mental de Toulouse, Yves Lignon, Parapsychologie, U.E.R. de Mathématiques, Université Toulouse-le-Mirail 31058, Toulouse, CEDEX, France.

MEMBERSHIP ORGANIZATIONS

Institut Métapsychique International.

Organisation pour la Recherche en Psychotronique, Yves Lignon—OEIL, Laboratoire de Parapsychologie, UER Mathématiques, Université Toulouse-le-Mirail 31058, Toulouse, CEDEX, France.

PARAPSYCHOLOGICAL ASSOCIATION MEMBERS

Dr. R. Amadou, 15 Rue Frédéric Sauton, Paris 75005.

Prof. R. Chauvin, Le Château, 18380 Ivoy-le Pre.

Dr. Y. Duplessis, 67 Ave. Raymond-Poincaré, Paris 75116.

Dr. C. Moreau, Ctr. Psychothérapique de Gireugn, St. Maur sur Indre 36250.

Dr. M. P. Varvoglis, 51 Bis Ave., Vaillant Couturier, Morsang S/Orge 91390.

E. Yerger, 28 Rue du Champ de Mars, Paris 75007.

MAJOR PARAPSYCHOLOGICAL PUBLICATIONS

*La Revue Française de Parapsychologie.* (Organisation pour la Recherche en Psychotronique, Yves Lignon—OEIL, Laboratoire de Parapsychologie, UER Mathématiques, Université Toulouse-le-Mirail, 31058 Toulouse, CEDEX, France.)

*Bulletin.* Organisation pour la Recherche Psychotronique.

Educational Opportunities in Parapsychology

None

University Departments in Parapsychology

None

## GERMANY

Germany is in a unique position. It has a rich past in psychical research and an uncertain future in that field as well as in parapsychology. As early as the 1830s, there were investigations by Justinus Kerner of cases of apparent possession by deceased individuals. In the middle of the nineteenth century German medical men, just as in France, began to study the usefulness of hypnosis as a tool and observed that sometimes in hypnotic trance patients manifested paranormal abilities.

In the 1870s, Professor Johann K. F. Zöllner had sittings with the notorious medium Henry Slade, and Alexander N. Aksakoff established a journal called *Psychische Studien* devoted to psychical research. In the 1880s Max Dessoir founded another similar publication, a society to study the paranormal, and carried out investigations of his own. To him we owe the very word "parapsychology." Starting in this century, Gustav Fechner came up with an unusual theory of immortality and, after World War I, there was considerable interest in Germany in physical phenomena. But the real progress in German psychical research in the years following the First World War was due primarily to prominent figures who were its theoreticians, critics, historians and investigators: Traugott K. Osterreich, Hans Driesch, Richard Baerwald, Rudolf Tischner, Gerda Walther, Albert von Schrenck-Notzing, Fritz Grunewald and Carl von Klinckowstroem.

Such progress as there was stopped dead in the Nazi regime: Publications were suppressed and important figures forced into retirement from academic positions or sent to concentration camps. The only exception was Hans Bender who, in 1936, received his Ph.D. for work in psychical research and parapsychology. After World War II with restrictions removed, Bender and his institute at Freiburg became the center of parapsychological activity, Karlis Osis was granted a doctorate for his work on extrasensory perception by the University of Munich, and a conference on paranormal physical phenomena was held at the University of Göttingen. Currently Germany is the focus of research in transcommunication and electronic voice phenomena in which Ernst Senkowski is a leading figure.

A new crop of parapsychologists is contributing to German parapsychology—Gerd H. Hövelmann, Eberhard Bauer, Walter von Lucadou, Klaus Kornwachs, Ulrich Timm and Hans D. Betz. But, in the face of harsh opposition, the emphasis is on individual not collective research as all efforts but one to form parapsychological organizations have been in vain. Parapsychology faces a future made dark by ignorance and extreme scepticism. The present parapsychological situation is as follows:

Research Centers

Institut für Grenzgebiete der Psychologie und Psychohygiene (Institute for Border Areas of Psychology and Mental Hygiene), Eichalde 12, 7800 Freiburg i. Br., West Germany.

Membership Organizations

Wissenschaftliche Gesellschaft zur Förderung der Parapsychologie (Scientific Society for the Advancement of Parapsychology), % Dipl.-Psych. Eberhard Bauer, Lehrstuhl für Psychologie und Grenzgebiete der Psychologie, Belfortstr. 16, 7800 Freiburg i. Br., West Germany.

Parapsychological Association Members

E. Bauer, Roemerstrasse 17, D—7814, Breisach 3, West Germany.

H. Bender, Institut für Grenzgebiete der Psychologie und Psychohygiene, Eichalde 12, 7800 Freiburg i. Br., West Germany.

G. H. Hövelmann, Im Sohlgraben 18, 3550 Marburg/Lahn 7, West Germany.

W. von Lucadou, Hildstr. 64, D 7800, Freiburg, West Germany.

U. Timm, Awaldstr. 98, D 7800, Freiburg, West Germany.

Major Parapsychological Publications

*Zeitschrift für Parapsychologie und Grenzgebiete der Psychologie.* Institut für Grenzgebiete der Psychologie und Psychohygiene.

Educational Opportunities in Parapsychology

Lehrstuhl für Psychologie und Grenzgebiete der Psychologie, Universität Freiburg, Belfortstr. 16, Freiburg i. Br. West Germany: course on the history and methods of parapsychology; course on the psychology of the occult wave; diplomas awarded to psychologists for completing a parapsychological topic.

University Department in Parapsychology

The Universität Freiburg has such a department.

## HAITI

Most impoverished republic in the West Indies. The language is a French-based creole and the national religious cult among the poor working class population who are descendants of African slaves is voodooism.

From the viewpoint of psychical research and parapsychology, the rituals and beliefs of voodoo present a mother lode, a rich region of paranormal phenomena ranging from possession and extrasensory perception to the power of the mind over the body. It is curious that, while teams of investigators interested in the paranormal will travel thousands of miles to test a psychic or see an isolated poltergeist disturbance, for instance, they studiously neglect an area 600 miles southeast of Florida that is a prime and ongoing source of material and subjects. The present parapsychological scene is as follows:

### Research Centers

None

### Membership Organizations

None

### Parapsychological Association Members

None

### Major Parapsychological Publications.

None.

### Educational Opportunities in Parapsychology.

None.

### University Departments in Parapsychology.

None.

## INDIA

"East is East and West is West," especially when we compare the way India and the West look at the paranormal. Whereas in Western culture, paranormal phenomena are, by definition, in conflict with principles we take for granted and with common sense, the culture of India considers them natural and normal and takes them for granted.

Jamuna Prasad has said: "Parapsychology in India has a long past but a brief history" (Letter to the authors). The belief in the paranormal is ancient and strong. It is very difficult to try to catalogue all the phenomena, beliefs, and practices in India that are of interest to psychical research and parapsychology. They cover a broad range: the celebrated rope-climbing feat; the belief in reincarnation; widespread fire-tests involving walking over hot coals; crystal-gazing as people look at the shiny-black surface of gum; the belief held in Northern India in possession by godlings or spirits; conjuring; hypnosis; levitation; meditation; yoga and yogis who claim powers to produce astounding paranormal phenomena of whom the supposed avatar, Sathya Sai Baba, is a modern example.

Beliefs in the paranormal are so much a part of people's lives that no one in India felt the need to conduct scientific investigations into this area. It was left to the West to initiate such investigations. Very soon after its organization, the Society for Psychical Research in England dispatched Richard Hodgson to India to investigate the marvels claimed by Helena Petrovna Blavatsky and the Theosophical Society.

Western psychical researchers and parapsychologists have influenced post-independence India. In 1951, theses on parapsychology were accepted on the postgraduate level in the Department of Psychology and Philosophy at Benares Hindu University. Several Indian scholars became interested. C. T. K. Chari began investigations into the paranormal and was president of a session of parapsychology in 1959 at a conference held at the University of Madras.

In 1957, K. Ramakrishna Rao published a book on the theories and evidence for extrasensory perception and, in the same year, Bhikhan L. Atreya of Benares Hindu University introduced parapsychology as a subject for study in Indian universities. In northern India some research was done at the University of Lucknow under Professor Kali Prashad, and later a Department of Parapsychology was established at Rajasthan University in Jaipur. In Allahabad, the Uttar Pradesh Bureau of Psychology was the first institution in Northern India to start a research project in parapsychology. In 1962 and 1963, the ESP experiments of Jamuna Prasad, the director of the bureau, attracted the attention of Joseph B. Rhine. Dr. Prasad had since remained active in psychical research, particularly in reincarnation studies, and in parapsychology. Several other universities, including the Universities of Bhagalpur, Madras and Mypore, as well as Madras Christian College, began to carry out experiments in ESP and psychokinesis.

By 1967, Andhra University had established a university department of parapsychology and the University Grants Commission created a parapsychological research center there. Several other scholars became active in psychical research and parapsychology, including Daya Shanker, Parmeshwar Dyal, Vasant V. Akolkar, Balbir Singh, and K. S. Rawat and a Foundation for Reincarnation and Spiritual Research was set up.

While parapsychological interest and activity began in India comparatively late, it led all other countries in Asia in the field for a long time. Now its leadership is being tested by Japan. The present parapsychological situation is as follows.

### Research Centers

Foundation for Reincarnation and Spiritual Research, 109 Rani Mandi, Allahabad 211003, U.P. India.

Institute for Yoga and Consciousness, Andhra University, Visakhapatnam 530003, A.P. India.

The Psychical Research Society, c-86, D.D.A. Flats, Saket, New Delhi 110017, India.

### Membership Organizations

Foundation for Reincarnation and Spiritual Research.

The Psychical Research Society.

Para Psychology Research Foundation, Mahavir Ganj, Beawar, 305901, Rajasthan, India.

### Parapsychological Association Members

Dr. N. K. Chadha, Dep't of Psychology, Univ. of Delhi, Delhi 110007.

Dr. S. Krishna, Dep't of Psychology and Parapsychology, Andhra University, Visakhapatnam, Andhra 530003.

Dr. L. P. Mehrotra, 346 Baghambari Housing Scheme, Allahpur-Allahabad, U.P. 211006.

Dr. S. Pasricha, Dep't of Clinical Psychology, Nimhans, Bangalore 560029.

Dr. V. Gowri Rammohan, Dep't of Psychology and Parapsychology, Andhra University, Visakhapatnam, Andhra 530003.

Dr. P. V. Krishna Rao, Dep't of Psychology and Parapsychology, Andhra, Univ., Visakhapatnam, Andhra 530003.

Dr. K. Ramakrishna Rao, Institute for Parapsychology, P.O. Box 6847, Durham, NC 27708.

Dr. V. Sudhakar, Dep't of Psychology and Parapsychology, Andhra Univ., Visakhapatnam, Andhra 530003.

### Major Parapsychological Publications

*Journal of Indian Psychology.* Andhra University, Visakhapatnam 530 003, A.P. India

*Kundalini.* Kundalini Research and Publication Trust, B-98, Sarvodaya Enclave, New Delhi 110017, India.

*Life Beyond.* H. L. Hingorani, Harnik House, 9 Sadhu Vaswani Road, Pune 411001, India.

*Occult India.* Occult India Publications, C–66/3, Phase II, Okhla, New Delhi 110020, India.

*Review of Darshan.* Ramnath Kaul Institute Library, Department of Philosophy, University of Allahabad, Allahabad 211001, India.

*Darshana International.* Dr. J. P. Atreya, Deewan, Bazar, Moradabad, India.

### Educational Opportunities in Parapsychology

Andhra University, Department of Psychology and Parapsychology, Visakhapatnam, Andhra 530003: instruction and research leading to M. Phil. and Ph.D. degrees; also possible to enroll in the university and do work at the Institute for Parapsychology in connection with the Ph.D. dissertation.

### University Departments in Parapsychology

Dep't of Psychology and Parapsychology, Andhra Univ., Visakhapatnam, Andhra 530003

## ITALY

Ruler of the ancient western world in Roman times and seat of the Renaissance from the fourteenth to the sixteenth centuries, Italy in the eighteenth century began its interest in psychical research with a study of the paranormal by Prospero Lambertini (Pope Benedict XIV). By the mid- and late nineteenth century, Vincenzo Scarpa and Enrico Damiani had organized Spiritualist societies and Ercole Chiaia, Cesare Lombroso, Enrico Morselli, and other Italian scholars and scientists were investigating an unlettered woman from the province of Bari who professed remarkable gifts as a medium: Eusapia Palladino. Among those who examined her was Ernesto Bozzano, another outstanding figure who left his imprint on Italian psychical research.

Around the turn of the century, the country that boasted of Galileo, Leonardo, Marconi, and other scientifically-minded people began to examine paranormal phenomena scientifically. In 1895, Giovanni Ermacora established a parapsychological journal with this aim and, sharing this same aim, in 1901 in Rome the Societa di Studi Psichica (Society of Psychic Studies) was founded. In 1937, Emilio Servadio, Ferdinando Cazzamalli, and others found the Societa Italiana di Metapsichica (Italian Society of Metaphysics), which four years later received the Italian government's recognition.

Following World War II, there was an explosion of interest in parapsychology: Individuals such as Gastone Di Boni, Piero Cassoli, Ugo Dettore and Giorgio Di Simone became active in the field; many parapsychological publications began to come off the presses; and an increasing number of parapsychological organizations were established, each operating on a different level of psychical research and parapsychology and each following different methods. Of these perhaps the most active is the Centro Studi Parapsicologici (Center for Parapsychological Studies). The present parapsychological situation is as follows:

### RESEARCH CENTERS

Associazione Italiana Scientifica di Metapsichica (Italian Scientific Association of Metapsychics), S. Vittore 9, Milan, Italy.

Centro di Ricerca Psichica del Convivio (Psychic Research Center of the Convivium), Via dei Serpenti, 100, 00184 Rome, Italy.

Centro Italiano di Parapsicologia (Italian Center of Parapsychology), Via Belvedere, 87/80127, Naples, Italy.

Centro Studi Parapsicologici, (Center of Parapsychological Studies), Via Valeriani, 39, 40134 Bologna, Italy.

Instituto "Gnosis" per la Ricerca sulla Ipotesi della Sopravvivenza (Institute "Gnosis" for Research on the Survival Hypothesis), Via Belvedere, 87/80127, Naples, Italy.

### MEMBERSHIP ORGANIZATIONS

Archivio di Documentazione della Ricerca Psichica, via Orfeo 15, Bologna, Italy.

Centro Italiano di Parapsicologia.

Centro Studi Parapsicologici.

Instituto "Gnosis" per la Ricerca sulla Ipotesi della Sopravvivenza.

### PARAPSYCHOLOGICAL ASSOCIATION MEMBERS.

Dr. P. Cassoli, Via Valeriani, 39, 40134 Bologna, Italy.

Prof. E. Servadio, Via Dr. Villa Emiliani 4 Int. 7, I 00197, Rome, Italy.

### MAJOR PARAPSYCHOLOGICAL PUBLICATIONS

*Bolletini.* Centro Studi Parapsicologici.

*Quaderni di Parapsicologia.* Centro Studi Parapsicologici.

*Informazioni di Parapsicologia.* Centro Italiano di Parapsicologia.

*Luce e Ombra.* Archivio di Documentazione Storica della Ricerca Psichica.

*Metapsichica.* Associazione Italiana Scientifica di Metapsichica.

*Rassegna Italiana di Ricerca Psichica.* Societa Italiana di Parapsicologia.

### EDUCATIONAL OPPORTUNITIES IN PARAPSYCHOLOGY

Except for a course given by Andreas Resch at Lateran University for students of moral theology, for the private teaching of parapsychology at the Academia Tibernia, and for courses in Bologna at the Centro Studi Parapsicologici, there are no educational opportunities in parapsychology provided by any academic institution.

### UNIVERSITY DEPARTMENTS IN PARAPSYCHOLOGY

None.

## JAPAN

Once the major religion of Japan, Shintoism, although considerably altered by the importation of Confucianism and Buddhism, still speaks to the Japanese of a world inhabited by phantoms of the living and dead and of gods entering into possession of people in order to convey information. Shrines to the spirits of the dead in every house reveal the conviction that spirits of dead relatives are still among the living and influence and control human events and actions.

In this land of ghosts and gods, psychical researchers began their studies of spontaneous cases in the nineteenth century. The first to investigate paranormal phenomena objectively was Atsutane Hirata who died in 1843. In 1886, Enryo Inoue organized Fushigi Kenkyukai (Society for Anomalous Phenomena) and also examined paranormal phenomena critically. In the 1900s, translations of the writings of Western psychical researchers stimulated interest. Tomokichi Fukurai started and continued experimental investigations in clairvoyance and thoughtography until controversy and tragedy ended them and temporarily halted the progress of psychical research in Japan.

Prior to World War II, Toranosuke Oguma introduced critical methods of research and, after the war, Soji Otani adopted Joseph B. Rhine's methods and established the Japanese Society for Parapsychology. Hiroshi Motoyama carried out tests of psychics and founded an institute to study Yoga and the paranormal. Since then a number of parapsychological organizations have been founded, including one by the disciples of Fukurai, which include some of the leading scientists in Japan. Among them is the psychologist Tosio Kasahara who focusses on psychokinesis and the study of gifted subjects, including Masuaki Kiyota, who appeared in the wake of a visit by Uri Geller to Japan. With increasing numbers of Japanese scientists now visiting Western parapsychological research centers, Japan now vies with India as the Asian country most active in parapsychology. The present parapsychological scene is as follows:

### Research Centers

Fukurai Shinrigaku Kenkyu-Jo (Fukurai Institute of Psychology), 10–3 Niizaka-machi, Sendai-shi, Miyagi-ken 980 Japan.

Japanese Society for Parapsychology, 26–14 Chuo 4–chome, Nakano-ku, Tokyo 164, Japan.

Kokusai Shukyo Cho-Shinri Gakkai (International Institute for Religion and Parapsychology), 11–7 Inokashira 4–chome, Mitaka-shi, Tokyo 180, Japan.

Nikon Nensha Kyokai (Japanese Association for Thoughtography), 21–12 Shumo-renjaku 4–chome, Mitaka-shi, 181 Tokyo, Japan.

Psi Science Institute of Japan, Shibuya Business Hotel 6F, 12–5 Shibuya 1–chome, Shibuya-ku, Tokyo 150, Japan.

### Membership Organizations

Fukurai Shinrigaku Kenkyu-Jo.

Japanese Society for Parapsychology.

Kokusai Shukyo Cho-Shinri Gakkai.

Psi Science Institute of Japan.

### Parapsychological Association Members

Dr. S. Harada, Azuma 3–18–18 Sakura Mura, Niihara Gun, Ibaraki Ken, T305, Japan.

T. Kasahara, Department of Psychology, Matui Hospital, 7–10 Ikegami 2–chome, Ota-ku, Tokyo 146, Japan.

Dr. A. Onda, 5–8–14 Minamisawa, Higashikurume-shi, Tokyo, Japan.

Prof. S. Otani, 26—14 Chuo 4 Nakano, Tokyo 164, Japan.

### Major Parapsychological Publications

*Bulletin.* The Fukurai Institute of Psychology.

*Journal of the Psi Science Institute* (of Japan).

*Newsletter.* The Japanese Society for Parapsychology

*Proceedings of the Japanese Society for Parapsychology. Shukyo to Cho-Shinri* (Religion and Parapsychology). Kokusai Shukyo Cho-Shinri Gakkai.

### Educational Opportunities in Parapsychology

None.

### University Departments in Parapsychology

None.

## MEXICO

The land South of the Border is also the land of the Lady of Guadalupe, the mysterious image many believe to be a miracle. Mexico is also the land where mushrooms are eaten to bring about visions and paranormal effects. In Oaxaca, the sacred mushroom is ingested to help divination and psychic powers. Peyotl, a small cactus that contains mescaline, also grows in Mexico. The Indians cut the plants into rings or buttons and eat them. Mexico is probably one of the areas of the world most thoroughly studied by psychical researchers and parapsychologists from the United States and elsewhere to determine the effects of hallucinogenic drugs.

Mexico appeals to psychical research and to parapsychology as well because *curanderos* and *curanderas* (male and female shamans and unorthodox healers), such as Maria Sabina or Barbara Guerrero, Mexico's most famous healer, abound.

Mexican psychical research, however, did not begin because of mushroom-eating or healing. Nor did it begin with large organizations for collective research, such as the American Society for Psychical Research in the United States or the Society for Psychical Research in the United Kingdom. The first twenty years of its existence depended on the isolated efforts of individuals. Gustav Pagenstecher, a German doctor living in Mexico, started Mexican psychical research in 1919 with his experiments in psychometry with María Reyes de Zierold. In 1937, another physician, Enrique Aragón, became the first investigator of poltergeists and haunts. It was not until 1939 that the Circulo de Investigaciones Metapsíquicas de México was established. During this period the medium Luis Martínez flourished and Gutierre Tibón did important work.

In 1974, an International Congress on Parapsychology was sponsored by the Association of Professors and Investigators of the Iberoamericana University in Mexico City and, in the same year, the important Sociedad Mexicana de Parapsicología (Mexican Parapsychological Society) was founded by Carlos Treviño B. and Marcela G. Treviño. Since then, many individuals have been active in the field, and, in 1988, parapsychology became an obligatory subject for future Catholic priests. The present parapsychological situation is as follows:

### Research Centers

Sociedad Mexicana de Parapsicología, Apartado 12–699, 03000 México, D.F., México.

### Membership Organizations

Sociedad Mexicana de Parapsicología.

Fundacíon International Subdud, Plutarco Elias Calles No. 702, Col. Club de Golf, Cuernavaca, Morelos 62030, México.

PARAPSYCHOLOGICAL ASSOCIATION MEMBERS

C. E. Cardena-Buelna, Nuevo León #138–10, 06100 México, D.F., México.

Dr. X. Tercero, Presa Reventada 110, San Jeronimo, Del. Contreras, 10200 México, D.F., México.

Dr. C. Treviño B., Apartado 12–699, 03000 México, D.F., México.

MAJOR PARAPSYCHOLOGICAL PUBLICATIONS.
None.

EDUCATIONAL OPPORTUNITIES IN PARAPSYCHOLOGY

Except for the teaching of parapsychology at the Instituto de Formación Sacerdotal de la Arquidiócesis de México (Institute for Priestly Education of the Archdiocese of Mexico) where Catholic priests receive their training, there are no educational opportunities provided at any academic institution. However, the Sociedad Mexicana de Parapsicología offers courses in parapsychology.

UNIVERSITY DEPARTMENTS IN PARAPSYCHOLOGY.
None.

## THE NETHERLANDS

For centuries, the people of The Netherlands have been familiar with paranormal phenomena. As early as the seventeenth century, the historian of the Dutch East India Company recorded that the Dutch governor-general in Batavia knew by extrasensory perception that a ship on which a friend was a passenger had met with disaster. In the nineteenth century, the impact of mesmerism was felt in The Netherlands as it was in the rest of Europe. People in mesmeric trance aroused interest with powers we now call telepathy and clairvoyance.

With the spread of Spiritualism at the turn of the twentieth century, interest in the paranormal mounted. Because of their interest in research, Professor Gerardus Heymans and H. I. F. Brugmans became key figures in the development of Dutch parapsychology. Later, with Dr. I. Zeehandelaar, Heymans founded the Studievereniging voor Psychical Research (Dutch Society for Psychical Research). In 1928, Paul A. Dietz and W. H. C. Tennhaeff founded the journal *Tijdschrift voor Parapsychologie.* In 1950, J. G. Busschbach conducted tests of telepathy in schoolchildren and, by means of the quantitative methods used by the Parapsychology Laboratory in the United States, reported positive results. In 1953, the First International Conference of Parapsychological Studies was held in Utrecht, and in the same year, at the University of Utrecht a chair of parapsychology under Tenhaeff's direction was established to extend and intensify research.

A controversy in the Dutch Society for Psychical Research (Studievereniging voor Psychical Research) resulted in the formation in 1960 of a second parapsychological organization, the Nederlandse Vereniging voor Parapsychologie (Dutch Society for Parapsychology). Other smaller groups also were formed to carry out research, including a student group known as Studie Centrum voor Experimentelle Para Psychologie (Study Center for Experimental Parapsychology). The group failed to survive but others came into being in one of which Jeff Jacobs and Brian Millar were active workers.

In 1973, a Parapsychology Laboratory was set up at the University of Utrecht where Martin Johnson and Sybo A. Schouten were important figures. Other prominent Dutch psychical researchers and parapsychologists are Jan Kappers and George Zorab whose active work in the conduct of research and the formulation of theories is recognized internationally. The present parapsychological scene is as follows:

RESEARCH CENTERS

Nederlandse Vereniging voor Parapsychologie, Laan van Meerdevoort 554, 2563 BL 's Gravenhage.

Research Institute for Psi and Physics, Alexanderkade 1, 1018, CH 1018 Amsterdam.

Studievereniging voor Psychical Research, P.O. Box 786, 3500 AT Utrecht.

Synchronicity Research Unit, P.O. Box 7625, 5601 JP Eindhoven.

MEMBERSHIP ORGANIZATIONS

Nederlandse Vereniging voor Parapsychologie.
Studievereniging voor Psychical Research.

PARAPSYCHOLOGICAL ASSOCIATION MEMBERS

Dr. D. J. Bierman, Dep't of Psychology, Univ. of Amsterdam, Alexanderkade 1, Amsterdam 1018 CH.

Dr. J. N. Houtkooper, Hendrick V. Avercampweg 23,1191 EW Ouderkerk Amstel.

J. C. Jacobs, Posbus 7625, 5601 JP Eindhoven.

Dr. M. Johnson, Hostagillesvagen 4, S–222 51 Lund, Sweden.

Dr. J. Kappers, Oosterpark 84, Amsterdam, 1092 Ave.

Dr. S. A. Schouten, University of Utrecht, Sorbonnelaan 16, 3584 CA Utrecht.

G. A. M. Zorab, Het Huis Te Palensteyn, Schoutenhoek, 240, Zoetermer.

MAJOR PARAPSYCHOLOGICAL PUBLICATIONS

*Spiegel der Parapsychologie.* (Nederlandse Vereniging voor Parapsychologie, Laan van Meedervoort 554, 2563 BL 's Gravenhage.

*SRU Bulletin.* Synchronicity Unit, P.O. Box 7625, 5601 JP Eindhoven.

*Tijdschrift voor Parapsychologie.* Studievereniging voor Psychical Research, P.O. Box 786, 3500 AT Utrecht.

EDUCATIONAL OPPORTUNITIES IN PARAPSYCHOLOGY

Department of Psychology, University of Amsterdam, Alexanderkade 1, Amsterdam 1018 CH: six-credit undergraduate course.

University of Utrecht, Sorbonnelaan 16, 3584 CA Utrecht: weekly lectures for psychology students; also supervision of doctoral degree.

UNIVERSITY DEPARTMENTS IN PARAPSYCHOLOGY.

The Parapsychology Laboratory at the Univ. of Utrecht has been discontinued for lack of funds.

## PANAMA

In Central America there is a virtual absence of any active interest in psychical research or parapsychology except in Panama. That country seems to be a paranormal melting pot into which a rich heritage of the beliefs and practices of many groups have been poured. There are the native groups, including the Cuna Indians, the Chocoes, and Guaymies, and a variety of cultures that appeared in Panama during the construction of the Panama Canal. Among these were the Africans who brought with them *Santería* or Voodooism and those who ascribe to the Brazilian Spiritism of Allan Kardec. In addition, the farmers of Panama have their *curanderos* ("healers") who are also purported to have psychic powers that go beyond unorthodox healing and extend to foretelling the future and exorcising haunts.

Nevertheless, it was not until 1982 that the Hispano-American Society for Philosophical and Metaphysical Research (Sociedad Hispano-Americano para la Investigación Filosófica y Metafísica) was founded by Roberto Manieri for the purpose of studying the phenomena from various perspectives. Under the auspices of this organization, several institutes were formed such as the Institute for Philosophical Research (Instituto para la Investigación Filosófica), which conducts philosophical studies, and the Institute for Parapsychological Studies (Instituto de Estudios Parapsicológicos), which does research in all areas of psychical research and parapsychology. The present parapsychological scene is as follows:

RESEARCH CENTERS

Instituto de Estudios Parapsicológicos, Apartado 8000, Panama 7, Panama.

MEMBERSHIP ORGANIZATIONS

Instituto de Estudios Parapsicológicos.

Sociedad Hispano-Americana para la Investigación Filosófica y Metafísica, Apartado 8000, Panama 7, Panama.

PARAPSYCHOLOGICAL ASSOCIATION MEMBERS

R. Mainieri, Instituto de Estudios Parapsicológicos, SINFIM, Apartado 8000, Panama 7, Panama.

MAJOR PARAPSYCHOLOGICAL PUBLICATIONS.

*Boletín Informativo.* Sociedad Hispano-Americano para la Investigación Filosófica y Metafísica.

EDUCATIONAL OPPORTUNITIES IN PARAPSYCHOLOGY.

There are no formal courses offered at any educational institution although it is reported that the Department of Psychology, National University of Panama, may be opening its doors to the possibility of such courses. The Instituto de Estudios Parapsicológicos presented courses from 1982–1985. These have been suspended for the time being, however, but reportedly are expected to resume in 1990.

UNIVERSITY DEPARTMENTS IN PARAPSYCHOLOGY

None.

## SOUTH AFRICA

With the reported occurrence of a large number of paranormal phenomena in South Africa, particularly among African black diviners, excellent opportunities for psychical research and studies in parapsychology have existed there. A South African Society for Psychical Research was established in 1910 in Capetown but a lack of interest kept it from developing from infancy. Some four decades later, however, interest increased.

The Psychology Department of the University of Rhodes conducted experiments in extrasensory perception in 1952 and offered an introductory course in parapsychology that required the completion of experimental work. The venture must have been successful because seven years later this university awarded a Ph.D. degree for research in parapsychology. In 1954, a group in Johannesburg established to investigate paranormal phenomena received such strong support that the South African Society for Psychical Research was formed there in 1955. Twenty years later, John C. Poynton established a branch of this society at the University of Natal. Among other leaders of South African parapsychology are Arthur E. H. Bleksley and Joseph H. M. Whiteman.

Although parapsychology has continued to survive through their efforts and those of others, it has not progressed to any great extent because the white population is too small to support any permanent research organization and because black Africans have not been supportive.

Scientific studies of black diviners, for example, have not been successful. The present parapsychological situation is as follows:

RESEARCH CENTERS

None.

MEMBERSHIP ORGANIZATIONS

South African Society for Psychical Research, P.O. Box 23154, Joubert Park, Johannesburg 2044.

PARAPSYCHOLOGICAL ASSOCIATION MEMBERS

Prof. J. C. Poynton, Biology Dep't, University of Natal, King George V Ave., Durban 4001.

MAJOR PARAPSYCHOLOGICAL PUBLICATIONS

Publications of the South African Society for Psychical Research 1959–1970.

*Parapsycholoigical Journal of South Africa.* South African Society for Psychical Research.

EDUCATONAL OPPORTUNITIES IN PARAPSYCHOLOGY

University of Natal, King George V Ave., Durban 4001: undergraduate course.

UNIVERSITY DEPARTMENTS IN PARAPSYCHOLOGY

None.

## SOVIET UNION

The Soviet Union is another country into which the interest in psychical research and parapsychology has spread. In the West, "parapsychology" is defined as the laboratory investigation of cognitive or kinetic behavior that is not dependent on the senses or muscles. In the Soviet Union, it is defined in a Soviet philosophoical dictionary as a "field of research studying forms of sensitivity which are not explained by the activity of known sense organs, as well as forms of influence of living beings upon surrounding phenomena, occurring without the intermediary of muscular forces."

While Soviet officialdom may not acknowledge that such research goes on there, the translation of Soviet and East European studies, correspondence and trips by Western scientists, scholars, and parapsychologists, such as Joseph G. Pratt, suggest that much research has indeed been conducted in the Soviet Union, although under the control of Soviet authorities. Research attempts, however, have encountered an ideological hurdle thrown up by Marxists. Since for the early British and American researchers the question of life after death was a principal concern and the emphasis was upon mediums, Marxists see psychical research and its supporters as guilty of "mysticism," "superstition," and "idealistic" propaganda that contradicts the materialism of Lenin and Marx and that only confuses the real economic and political issues that should concern people.

The interest the Soviets have shown, therefore, in many areas of the paranormal has been accompanied by theories appropriate to Soviet thought. Psi, which includes extrasensory perception and psychokinesis, is explained on the basis of mechanistic electromagnetic hypotheses. The Soviets account for unorthodox healing with the concept of a "biofield" introduced in 1946 by the biologist A. G. Gurvich. All living organisms are said to possess a bioenergetic field that reflects the condition of healthy or diseased organs and that can be detected as well as influenced by extrasensers and folk healers.

The Soviets have shown great interest in many areas: Long-distance telepathy experiments were conducted by Professor L. L. Vasiliev who had a materialistic theory for the phenomenon. Victor G. Adamenko investigated acupuncture, Kirlian photography and psychokinesis. Work was done in dermo-optic perception at the Moscow Academy of Science with Rosa Kuleshova. Experiments in psychokinesis were carried out with several subjects, including Nina S. Kulagina, who was studied over a period of ten years at the University of Leningrad and at the U.S.S.R. Academy of Sciences Institute of Radioengineering and Electronics. Healers such as Dzhuna Davitashvily and Barbara M. Ivanova (who is also a psychic) were the subjects of research in unorthodox healing. But, although there seems to be official support given to healers, there is also considerable official scepticism toward the phenomenon as debate continues in the Academy of Sciences of the U.S.S.R. about the validity of investigating it and whether any biofield exists that can be influenced.

From time to time, Westerners have heard that the Soviets are convinced that psychic abilities for intelligence gathering, for altering minds, for inducing death or sickness or for weapons application have military and intelligence potential and that they are well ahead of the West in the race to develop psi abilities. It is possible that the frightening reports of Soviet military and intelligence advances are clever pieces of misinformation calculated to mislead the West into science fiction investigations. So reports need to be viewed with caution.

The history of parapsychology in the Soviet Union is a story of ups, downs, and perhaps some ups again. It began in the 1920s at the University of Leningrad with experiments for testing telepathy in dogs. Vasiliev in that era promoted interest in parapsychology. In the next decades, little research was done and what laboratories there were were destroyed during World War II.

In 1960, however, a laboratory was established at the University of Leningrad to do work on telepathy or, as the Soviets would prefer to put it, electromagnetic emanations from the brain. For the next several years research blossomed in many places, including the Department of Psychology at the University of Moscow and the Ukrainian Academy of Sciences at Kiev. Western parapsychologists such as J. G. Pratt were welcomed, especially by Edward K. Naumov, a prime mover in the promotion of parapsychology in Moscow who carried on a friendly correspondence with foreign parapsychologists. Naumov was Pratt's host, in 1970 arranged a lecture for Montague Ullman, and acted as "P.R." man generally. In 1971, Stanley Krippner gave a lecture on parapsychology in the Soviet Union. But beginning around this period, increasing ideological opposition and a determined move to remove parapsychology from regular researchers impeded and changed parapsychology in the Soviet Union.

It is speculated that the KGB, which reportedly became extremely interested in the field, took it over. One of the initial victims of the takeover was Naumov who was sentenced to two years at hard labor in Siberia. In other developments, Barbara Ivanova was dismissed from her employment, and Adamenko was fired from his position and later left the Soviet Union. Larissa Vilenskaya, another parapsychologist, also left the country.

According to the *New York Times* of June 12, 1977, Robert Toth, correspondent for the *Los Angeles Times*, was arrested by the KGB for receiving a document on parapsychology from a laboratory of the Institute on Medical-Biological Problems. In 1982, Soviet speakers were invited to the Centenary-Jubilee Conference of the Society for Psychical Research and the Parapsychological Association in Cambridge, England, but were unable to attend. As of 1978, several research organizations continued to exist but, at the same time, much parapsychological research in the Soviet Union was shifted to a center in Acadamgoroduk, Siberia, where the research done and the data obtained are not accessible to Western observers.

In the 1980s, when the new Soviet policy of openness (glasnost) was established, some changes in the parapsychological scene in the Soviet Union began to appear. Apparently some recognition is being given to parapsychology as a respectable discipline. In March, 1987, for example, the widely read *Moscow News,* in the first article about poltergeists published in the Soviet Union, advocated more scientific studies of the subject, and in December 1987, Nina Kulagina sued a Soviet magazine for defaming her as a fraud. Russian scientists appeared as witnesses on her behalf and she won her suit. In 1988, an international conference on psychotronics was held at West Georgia College in the United States. Among the investigators from Europe, including Czechoslovakia, France, Italy, Norway, Poland, Romania, and West Germany, were five scientists from the Soviet Union.

It is impossible to know the exact status of parapsychology in the Soviet Union but it seems to be this:

### Research Centers

Acadamgoroduk, Siberia.

Bauman Higher Technology School (Moscow).

Division of Cybernetics, Leningrad Polytechnical Institute.

Division of Cybernetics, Moscow Engineering Physical Institute.

Division of Cybernetics of the Research Institute of Biophysics, U.S.S.R. Academy of Sciences, Pushchino.

Institute of Control Problems, U.S.S.R. Academy of Sciences.

Institute of Radio-Engineering and Electronics, U.S.S.R. Academy of Sciences.

Kazakh State University in Alma-Ata.

Leningrad State University.

Moscow Energetics Institute.

Research Institute of General and Pedagogical Psychology.

Academy of Sciences, Moscow.

Research Institute of Neurology and Psychiatry, Kharkov.

Tbilisi State University, Georgia.

Ukrainian Institute of Cybernetics, Kiev.

### Membership Organizations

None.

### Parapsychological Association Members

V. G. Adamenko, 13–15 A. Metaxa Str., Athens 10681, Greece.

E. K. Naumov, Mayakovsky Street 4, Apt. 16, 141400 Khimiki (Moscow Region), U.S.S.R.

MAJOR PARAPSYCHOLOGICAL PUBLICATIONS.
None.

EDUCATIONAL OPPORTUNITIES IN PARAPSYCHOLOGY.
None.

UNIVERSITY DEPARTMENTS IN PARAPSYCHOLOGY.
None.

## SPAIN

Although many countries have been for a long time concerned with and active in psychical research and parapsychology, Spain's interest in these subjects was negligible until comparatively recently. Sporadic attempts were made to organize parapsychological groups, such as the Asociación Espãnola de Investigactiones Parapsicológicas, but they all failed. The history of Spanish psychical research and parapsychology really began in 1971 when the Universidad Autónoma de Madrid opened its doors to the subject by allowing Ramos Molina Perera to offer courses. Then in 1973 scholars, newspaper reporters, and psychologists banded together to form the Sociedad Espãnola de Parapsicología, the country's leading organization in the field. The present parapsychological scene is as follows:

RESEARCH CENTERS

Sociedad Espãnola de Parapsicología. C/. Belen, 15–1 Dcha., 28004 Madrid.

MEMBERSHIP ORGANIZATIONS

Sociedad Espãnola de Parapsicología.

PARAPSYCHOLOGICAL ASSOCIATION MEMBERS

Miguel A. LaPuerta, Av. Ciudad Barcelona-138, Madrid ESC3BAJO 28007.

MAJOR PARAPSYCHOLOGICAL PUBLICATIONS

*Psi Comunicacíon.* Sociedad Espãnola de Parapsicología, C./ Belen, 15–1 Dcha., 28004 Madrid.

EDUCATIONAL OPPORTUNITIES IN PARAPSYCHOLOGY

None. Courses at the Universidad Autónoma have been discontinued.

UNIVERSITY DEPARTMENTS IN PARAPSYCHOLOGY
None.

## SWITZERLAND

A tourist and banking center, Switzerland is also known for its activity in and contributions to psychical research and parapsychology. High school adult education courses in parapsychology in many large towns and districts have paved the way for public interest and acceptance of the subject. Two parapsychological organizations offer lectures and meetings and strive to inform the Swiss population about psychical research and parapsychology. In addition, every year Basel is the scene of international congresses, each on a different phase of the field, to which foreign researchers as well as throngs of people from inside and outside Switzerland come. A considerable number of Swiss individual researchers have made contributions, including Maximilian Perty, Théodore Flournoy, Gebhard Frei, Peter Ringger, Carl G. Jung, Carl A. Meier, Hans Naegli-Osjord, Georg Sulzer, Fanny Hoppe Moser, Theo Locher, and Alex Schneider. The present parapsychological situation is as follows:

RESEARCH CENTERS

Schweizer Parapsychologische Gesellschaft, c/o Frau N. von Muralt, Weihaldenstrasse 3, CH–8700 Kusnacht, Switzerland.

Schweizerische Vereinigung für Parapsychologie, Industriestrasse 5, 2555 Brug, Switzerland.

MEMBERSHIP ORGANIZATIONS

Schweizer Parapsychologische Gesellschaft

Schweizerische Vereinigung für Parapsychologie

Parapsychologischen Arbeitsgruppe Basel, c/o Psi Zentrum, Guterstrasse 144, CH–4053 Basel, Switzerland.

PARAPSYCHOLOGICAL ASSOCIATION MEMBERS

Dr. C. E. Meier, 8032 Zurich, Steinwiestr. 37, Switzerland.

MAJOR PARAPSYCHOLOGICAL PUBLICATIONS

*Bulletin für Parapsychologie.* Schweizerische Vereinigung für Parapsychologie.

EDUCATIONAL OPPORTUNITIES IN PARAPSYCHOLOGY

Except for high school adult education courses, there are no educational opportunities provided in any academic institution.

UNIVERSITY DEPARTMENTS IN PARAPSYCHOLOGY
None.

## UNITED KINGDOM

The first foundations of psychical research and parapsychology were laid in the UK in the 1850s when a few individuals formed a Ghost Society. By

1882, the Society for Psychical Research was formed around the nucleus of scholars and scientists, among them Sir William Barrett, Henry Sidgwick, Frederic W. H. Myers and Edmund Gurney. Also contributing to the early work of the society were Eleanor Sidgwick, William Crookes and Frank Podmore. The subjects they set out to investigate were telepathy, hypnosis (or mesmerism), apparitions, haunts, and physical phenomena.

In connection with this last class of phenomena, some of the notable events of the late nineteenth century included Crookes's investigations of mediums Florence Cook and D. D. Home and the appointment by the SPR of Richard Hodgson to investigate the physical phenomena claimed by Helena Petrovna Blavatsky and her Theosophical Society. This latter investigation still arouses controversy. Other mediums were also studied—Leonora E. Piper, Eusapia Palladino, and Rosalie Thompson.

One of the great contributions of the SPR during its early period was the publication *Phantasms of the Living* which focussed the attention of workers on telepathy, both in the form of experiments and spontaneous cases. Other landmark publications were the *Census of Hallucinations* and Myers's *Human Personality and its Survival of Bodily Death* which set forth his theory of the subliminal self. The deaths of Sidgwick (1900) and Myers (1901) almost wrecked the SPR, but Sir Oliver Lodge took over its leadership. In this period automatists, such as Margaret de G. Verrall, were studied and the phenomenon known as the cross-correspondences, said to be the most formidable of all evidence of survival, discovered.

In the war years (1914–1918) when relatives and friends sought contact with those who had fallen, one of the main activities of the SPR and psychical researchers was the investigation of other outstanding mediums, including "Mrs. Willett" and Gladys Osborne Leonard with whom C. Drayton Thomas conducted proxy sittings. During this period other figures emerged, among them Whately Carington, Eric J. Dingwall, and the controversial investigator Harry Price. There was also a renewed interest in physical phenomena as manifested by physical mediums, including Eva C. and Rudi Schneider. Soon there was a shift from studies of mediumship to quantitative lines of inquiry that continue to the present day into psychokinesis and extrasensory perception. New chapters in theory and experiment, both good and bad, were written by Robert H. Thouless, Samuel G. Soal, G. N. M. Tyrrell, W. H. Salter, Donald West, John Beloff, and others, and star subjects were found, among them Basil Shackleton. C. D. Broad and H. H. Price contributed philosophical studies. As new workers, including Susan J. Blackmore, keep coming on the scene, the story of British psychical research and parapsychology continues to unfold. The present scene is as follows:

### Research Centers

Alistair Hardy Research Centre (formerly Religious Experience Research Unit), Manchester College, Oxford OX1 3TD.

Brain and Perception Laboratory, Medical School, University of Bristol, Bristol BS8 1TD.

International Institute for the Study of Death, UK Branch, David Lorimer, Director, The Old School House, Hampnett, Northleach GL54 3NN.

Parapsychical Laboratory, Downton, Wilshire.

Society for Psychical Research, 1 Adam & Eve Mews, London W8 6UG.

### Membership Organizations

Alister Hardy Research Centre.

Internationl Institute for the Study of Death.

Society for Psychical Research.

### Parapsychological Association Members

Dr. K. N. Banham, Hockley Rise, Stoke Poges, Bucks SC2 4QE.

Dr. J. Beloff, Dep't of Psychology, Univ. of Edinburgh, 7 George Square, Edinburgh EH8 9JZ, Scotland, U.K.

Dr. D. J. Benor, 4a/3 Belsize Park Gardens, London NW3 4LB.

Dr. S. J. Blackmore, Pear Tree Cottage, Greyfield Rd., High Littelton, Avon BS18 5YB.

Dr. T. J. Brodbeck, Wild Carr Barn, Gressingham, Lancaster.

Dr. B. J. Carr, 39 Windsor Road, Wanstead, London E11 3Q4.

M. Cassirer, 38 Christchurch Ave., London NW6 7BE.

Dr. A. J. Ellison, 10 Foxgrove Ave., Beckenham, Kent BR3 2BA.

Dr A. Gauld, Department of Psychology, University of Nottingham, Nottingham NG7 2RD.

K. M. Goldney, 154 Rivermead Court, Hurlingham, London SW6.

P. M. Huby, 14 Marine Terrace, Wallasey, Merseyside I45 7RE.

Dr. B. Inglis, Garden Flat, 23 Lambolle Road, London NW3 4HS.

K. M. Wilson Korner, 3 Brantwood Ave., Isleworth, Middlesex TW7 7EX.

A. J. Mayne, 29 Fairford Crescent, Downhead Park, Milton Keynes MK1 59AF.

Dr. J. F. McHarg, 33 Hazel Ave., Dundee, Scotland DD2 1QD.

Dr. J. Milton, Department of Psychology, University of Edinburgh, 7 George Square, Edinburgh EH8 9JZ, Scotland, UK.

J. Morris, 2 Strathalmond Green, Edinburgh EH4 8AQ, Scotland, U.K.

Dr. R. L. Morris, Department of Psychology, University of Edinburgh, 7 George Square, Edinburgh EH8 9JZ, Scotland, UK.

Dr. A. B. Phillip, 7 Bracknell Gardens, London NW3 7EE.

A. W. Robertson, 359 Mearns Road, Newton Mearns, Glasgow G77, Scotland, U.K.

Dr. S. M. Roney-Dougal, 14 Selwood Road, Glastonbury, Somerset.

Dr. A. R. Sheldrake, 20 Willow Road, London NW3 1TJ.

Dr. D. Stevenson, 22 Blacket Place, Edinburgh EH9 1RL, Scotland, U.K.

Dr. D. J. West, 32 Pen Road, Milton, Cambridge CB4 4AD.

MAJOR PARAPSYCHOLOGICAL PUBLICATIONS.

*Christian Parapsychologist.* Churches' Fellowship for Psychical and Spiritual Studies, St. Mary Abchurch, Abchurch Lane, London EC4 7BA.

*Journal of the Society for Psychical Research.* Society for Psychical Research, 1 Adam & Eve Mews, London W8 6UG.

*Proceedings of the Society for Psychical Research.* Society for Psychical Research.

EDUCATIONAL OPPORTUNITIES IN PARAPSYCHOLOGY.

Department of Psychology, Edinburgh University, 7 George Square, Edinburgh EH8 9JZ, Scotland: Supervision of graduate research leading to a PH.D. in psychology with emphasis on parapsychology.

University of Loughborough, Loughborough, Leicestershire LE11 3TU: 5 week extension course on the paranormal.

UNIVERSITY DEPARTMENTS IN PARAPSYCHOLOGY.

Koestler Chair of Parapsychology, University of Edinburgh.

## UNITED STATES

Spiritualism began in the USA in the middle of the nineteenth century and attracted a huge number of adherents. But collective scientific research into the paranormal did not start until several decades later after a tour by Sir William Barrett who stimulated scholars, one of whom was William James, to form a society with purposes similar to those of the Society for Psychical Research in England. The American Society for Psychical Research was organized in 1885.

During this period occurred the discovery of Leonora E. Piper who over the next thirty years was the trance medium most investigated by the English and American societies. The organization inquired into telepathy, hypnosis, mediums, apparitions, and haunts. Richard Hodgson was brought from England to become secretary of the ASPR and to manage it. The organization could not survive, however, and it became a branch of the Society for Psychical Research.

After Hodgson's death in 1905, the ASPR was reorganized by James H. Hyslop who set high scientific standards and managed it exclusively for twenty years. During this period, the principal activity of the ASPR was the investigation of mediumship and the question of survival. With Hyslop's passing (1920), William McDougall and Walter F. Prince became the mainstays of the ASPR but were soon alienated by a lowering of Hyslop's scientific standards and by the controversy in the 1920s over the medium Mina S. Crandon ("Margery"). McDougall and Prince therefore joined Elwood Worcester who had formed the Boston Society for Psychic Research. The major emphasis of the ASPR during this time was on mediumship and psychical research.

Beginning in the 1930s, however, the direction of inquiry into the paranormal changed. Joseph Banks Rhine began experiments in extrasensory perception at Duke University, soon made "ESP" a household word, and converted psychical research into a science with an experimental methodology for which he adopted the name "parapsychology." Experiments in psychokinesis also were conducted at Duke and Louisa E. Rhine studied thousands of case reports of spontaneous cases.

In the 1940s, Gertrude R. Schmeidler conducted her historic sheep-goat experiments and the ASPR was reorganized under the leadership of Gardner Murphy who restored it to Hyslop's standards. In the 1950s, the Parapsychology Foundation was organized and the Parapsychological Association was formed. The 1960s and '70s saw Montague Ullman and Stanley Krippner conduct dream studies, Rhine's establishment (after he left Duke University) of the Foundation for Research on the Nature of Man, and the organization of other research laboratories and groups. There was a decided emphasis on quantitative and statistical methods of investigation into extrasensory perception and psychokinesis, on remote viewing, and the Ganzfeld procedure, on new models and theories of psi, and on finding the elusive repeatable experiment.

In the 1980s, American parapsychology staggered under a barrage of attacks from academic psychologists and groups such as the Committee for the Scientific Investigation of Claims of the Paranormal and from criticisms by both internal and external sceptics concerning its experimental procedures. The present parapsychological scene is as follows:

### Research Centers

American Society for Psychical Research, 5 West 73rd St., New York, N.Y. 10023.

Center for Scientific Anomalies Research, Dr. Marcello Truzzi, P.O. Box 1052, Ann Arbor, Michigan 48103.

Division of Parapsychology (now Division of Personality Studies), University of Virginia, Box 152, Health Sciences Center, Charlottesville, VA 22908.

Foundation for Research on the Nature of Man, Box 6847, College Station, Durham, NC 27708.

Institute for Parapsychology, Box 6847, College Station, Durham, NC 27708.

Metascience Foundation, P.O. Box 737, Franklin, NC 28734.

Mind Science Foundation, 8301 Broadway, Suite 100, San Antonio, Texas 78209.

Mobius Society, 7801 Wilshire Blvd., Los Angeles, CA 90010.

Psychical Research Foundation, West Georgia College, Carrollton, GA 30118.

Science Unlimited Research Foundation, 311–D Spencer Lane, San Antonio, Texas 78201.

SRI, 333 Ravenswood Ave., Menlo Park, CA 94025.

Survival Research Foundation, P.O. Box 8565, Pembroke Pines, FL 33084.

### Membership Organizations

Academy of Religion and Psychical Research, P.O. Box 614, Bloomfield, CT 06002.

American Society for Psychical Research, 5 West 73rd St., New York, N.Y. 10023.

International Institute for the Study of Death, P.O. Box 8565, Pembroke Pines, FL 33084.

Parapsychological Association, P.O. Box 12236, Research Triangle Park, NC 27709.

Society for Scientific Exploration, Peter A. Sturrock, Center for Space Science & Astrophysics, Stanford University, Stanford, CA 94305.

Spiritual Frontiers Fellowship, 10819 Winner Road, Independence, MO 64052.

Survival Research Foundation, P.O. Box 8565, Pembroke Pines, FL 33084.

### Parapsychological Association Members

Dr. C. B. Akers, 1493 Clairmont Rd., Decatur, GA 30033.

C. S. Alvarado, Inst. for Parapsychology, Box 6847, Durham, NC 27708.

L. M. Auerbach, 2330 Pleasant Hill Rd., #6, Pleasant Hill, CA 94523.

J. A. Ballard, PhD., 1610 Hillside Dr., Beavercreek, OH 45432.

S. Baumann, 121 Dolphin, Galveston, TX 77550.

R. Bayless, 11348 Cashmere St., Los Angeles, CA 90049.

A. S. Berger, P.O. Box 8565, Pembroke Pines, FL 33084.

Dr. R. E. Berger, 7027 Settlers Ridge, San Antonio, TX 78238.

Dr. J. L. Bosworth, 191 Gothic Court, Gahanna, OH 43230.

N. L. Bowles, Box 69454, Los Angeles, CA 90069.

Dr. W. Braud, 8301 Broadway, #100, San Antonio, TX 78209.

Dr. L. W. Braud, Route 5, Box 633, Conroe, TX 77304.

Dr. S. E. Braude, 7350 Mossy Brink Court, Columbia, MD 21045.

Dr. B. Brier, Department of Philosophy, C. W. Post College, Greenvale, N.Y. 11548.

Dr. R. W. Brooks, Department of Philosophy, Oakland University, Rochester, MI 48063.

Dr. R. S. Broughton, Foundation for Research on the Nature of Man, P.O. Box 6847, Durham, NC 27708.

M. L. Carlson, 3933 Lincoln Ave., Oakland, CA 94602.

Dr. J. Carpenter, 727 Eastowne Dr., Suite 300B, Chapel Hill, NC 27514.

Dr. R. J. Chevako, RR #1, Kiley Road, New Woodstock, N.Y. 13122.

Dr. I. L. Child, 2 Cooper Road, North Haven, CT 06473.

Dr. T. K. Clark, 121 Crandon Circle, Beaver, PA 15009.

E. Coly, 228 E. 71st St., New York, N.Y. 10021.

F. D. Conlon, Box 148, Steamboat Springs, CO 80477.

E. Cook, 528 Locust Ave., Charlottesville, VA 22901.

W. E. Cox, 20 Southbrook Drive, Rolla, MO 65401.

Dr. J. C. Crumbaugh, Tally Arms #32, Church & 16th., Gulfport, MS 39501.

Dr. L. E. Curry, P.O. Box 542, Metter, GA 30439.

F. David, W. Pa. Eastern Star Home #217, 226 Bellevue Rd., Pittsburgh, PA 15229.

J. W. Davis, 717 Chalice St., Durham, NC 27705.

Dr. D. Dean, P.O. Box 377, Princeton, NJ 08542.

R. J. DeMattei, 4801 Wilshire Blvd., Suite 320, Los Angeles, CA 90010.

P. B. Derr, 10 Deleon #D5, El Paso, TX 79912.

M. L. Dickstein, 4 Sawyer Road, Bolton, MA 01740.

Dr. F. B. Dilley, Dep't of Philosophy, University of Delaware, Newark, DE 19711.

A. A. Drewes, 4 Capital Drive, Washingtonville, N.Y. 10992.

Dr. S. A. Drucker, 818 N. Buchanan Blvd., Durham NC 27701.

Dr. H. Edge, Campus Box 2659, Rollins College, Winter Park, FL 32789.

Dr. J. Eisenbud, 4634 E. 6th Ave., Denver, CO 80220.

G. F. Ellwood, 2011 Rose Villa St., Pasadena, CA 91107.

S. R. Erwin, P.O. Box 643, Coshocton, OH 43812.

Prof. L. A. Foster, Jr., 66 James Square, Williamsburg, VA 23185.

R. Franklin, Box 611, Jefferson, NC 28640.

Dr. L. L. Gatlin, 706 Tolman Dr., Stanford, CA 94305.

K. Gaynor, 3536 Centinela #12, Los Angeles, CA 90066.

Dr. R. W. George, 302 N. 10th St., Tarkio, MO 64491.

R. Gerber, 69-66 230 St., Bayside Hills, N.Y. 11364.

P. V. Geisler, Department of Anthropology, Brown 228, Brandeis University, Waltham, MA 02254.

D. E. Graff, 168 Windcliff Road, Prince Frederick, MD 20678.

Dr. T. N. E. Greville, Box 152, Health Science Center, University of Virginia, Charlottesville, VA 22908.

Dr. B. C. Greyson, 1179 Farmington Ave., West Hartford, CT 06107.

Dr. D. H. Gross, Rd. 6 Scaife Road, Sewickley, PA 15143.

Dr. M. Grosso, 5400 Fieldston Road, Riverdale, N.Y. 10471.

Dr. J. A. Hall, 8215 Westchester Dr., Ste. 244, Dallas, TX 75225.

G. Hansen, Princeton Arms North 1, Apt. 59, Cranbury, NJ 08512.

Dr. K. Harary, I.F.A.P., 1550 California St., San Francisco, CA 94109.

Dr. A. Hastings, 2451 Benjamin Dr., Mountain View, CA 94043.

Dr. J. Healy, 74-03 Commonwealth Blvd., Bellerose, N.Y. 11426.

Dr. S. F. Hendrickson, 165 Madison Pl., Ridgewood, NJ 07450.

Dr. G. Heseltine, Science Unlimited Research Fdn, 311–D Spenser Lane, San Antonio, TX 78201.

M. D. Hill, 50 Portsmouth Road, Amesbury, MA 01913.

C. Honorton, 301 College Road East, Princeton, NJ 08540.

J. A. Hornaday, 22446 Estallens, Mission Viejo, CA 92692.

G. S. Hubbard, NASA Ames Research Center, Mail Stop 244–14, Moffett Field, CA 94035.

F. J. Hynds, Box 69454, Los Angeles, CA 90069.

Dr. A. Imich, 305 West End Ave., New York, N.Y. 10023.

C. P. Irwin, 454 Fernwood Dr., Moraga, CA 94556.

Dr. J. D. Isaacs, 11 La Plaza, Orinda, CA 94563.

Prof. W.H. Jack, RFD Box 619, Marlborough, NH 03455.

Dr. R. Jeffries, 3946 Ocean Hills Court, Virginia Beach, VA 23451.

Dr. E. Jenkins, 820 Mt. Vernon Ave., Charlotte, NC 28203.

Dr. C. B. Jones, 6435 Shady Lane, Falls Church, VA 22042.

Dr. B. K. Kanthamani, Box 6847, College Station, Durham, NC 27708.

P. Keane, 43-22 63rd St., Woodside, N.Y. 11377.

Dr. E. F. Kelly, Rt. 1, Box 76C, Durham, NC 27705.

Dr. A. Khilji, FRNM, Box 6847, College Station, Durham, NC 27708.

E. Kinkead, 522–A Heritage Village, Southbury, CT 06488.

L. F. Knipe, 117 W. 57th St., New York, N.Y. 10019.

Dr. S. Krippner, Saybrook Institute, 1550 Sutter St., San Francisco, CA 94109.

E. Leyhe, 4317 Mainfield Ave., Baltimore, MD 21214.

Dr. J. K. Long, Plymouth State College, Plymouth, NH 03264.

R. W. Lowrie, 101 Lowrie Lane, Dade City, FL 33525.

Dr. M. C. Maher, 400 W. 43rd St., Apt. 39–S, New York, N.Y. 10036.

J. Matlock, 2021 Englewood Ave., Durham, NC 27705.

Dr. E. C. May, SRI International, 333 Ravenswood, Menlo Park, CA 94025.

Dr. E. E. McAdams, 450 N. Rossmore Ave., Los Angeles, CA 90004.

M. K. McBeath, Department of Psychology, Bldg 420, Stanford University, Stanford, CA 94305.

Dr. D. McCarthy, 1365 E. 52nd St., Brooklyn, N.Y. 11234.

Dr. J. McClenon, 1001 Jones Ave., Elizabeth City, NC 27909

Dr. R. A. McConnell, 430 Kennedy Ave., Pittsburgh, PA 15214.

T. McConnell, 430 Kennedy Ave., Pittsburgh, PA 15214.

D. L. McCormick, ASPR, 5 West 73rd St. New York, N.Y. 10023.

Rev. D. A. McKnight, P.O. Box 76, Greenville, VA 24440.

Dr. E. A. McMahan, Department of Biology 046A, University of North Carolina, Chapel Hill, NC 27514.

Dr. J. Mishlove, 48 Saint Francis Lane, San Rafael, CA 94901.

R. J. Munson, 1724 Laurel Ave #3, Knoxville, TN 37916.

Dr. M. J. Nanko, 3709 Ocean Crest, Santa Ana, CA 92704.

Dr. C. S. Nash, 16493 Horado Court, San Diego, CA 92128.

Dr. C. B. Nash, 16493 Horado Court, San Diego, CA 92128.

Dr. R. D. Nelson, Princeton Eng. Anomalies Research, Princeton University, Princeton, NJ 08544.

Dr. V. M. Neppe, Department of Psychiatry RP10, University of Washington, Seattle, WA 98195.

M. L. Nester, 262 Central Park West, #10D, New York, N.Y. 10024.

Dr. R. C. Neville, 2380 Country Club Dr., Flagstaff, AZ 86001.

Dr. K. Osis. 10 Douglas Road, Glen Ridge, NJ 07028.

Dr. J. A. Palmer, P.O. Box 6847, College Station, Durham, NC 27708.

J. R. Perlstrom, 701 Boulder Springs Dr. #B6, Richmond, VA 23225.

Dr. D. T. Phillips, 5107 Calle Asilo, Santa Barbara, CA 93111.

Dr. P. R. Phillips, Department of Physics, Washington University, St. Louis, MO 63130.

Dr. R. Pilkington, 30 Donna Court, Apt. 5, Staten Island, NY, 10314.

D. H. Pope, 3405 Windsor Way, Durham, NC 27707.

K. F. Powell, 85 Cross Ridge Road, Chappaqua, N.Y. 10514.

Dr. H. E. Puthoff, Inst. of Advanced Studies, 1301 Capitol of Texas Hwy S., Austin, TX 78746.

R. P. Quider, 607 Tailwind Dr., Sacramento, CA 95838.

Dr. D. Radin, 10221 Martinhoe Dr., Vienna VA 22180.

Dr. H. H. Rao, Box 6847, Durham, NC 27708.

Dr. K. R. Rao, Box 6847, Durham, NC 27708.

R. A. Reinsel, 305 W. 13th St., Apt. 2J, New York, N.Y. 10014.

O. B. Rivers, 3003 Farm Road, Alexandria, VA 22302.

D. Robinson, Department of Psychology, University of Rochester, Rochester, N.Y. 14627.

Dr. T. Rockwell, 3403 Woolsey Dr., Chevy Chase, MD 20815.

Dr. D. P. Rogers, FRNM, P.O. Box 6847, Durham, NC 27708.

D. S. Rogo, 18132 Schoenborn St., Northridge, CA 91324.

W. G. Roll, Department of Psychology, West Georgia College, Carrolltown, GA 30118.

J. G. Ruiz, 1901 Ocaso Camino, Fremont, CA 94539.

Dr. J. H. Rush, 1765 Sunset Blvd., Boulder, CO 80302.

Dr. E. I. Schechter, 2805 Regis Dr., Boulder, CO 80303.

M. Schlitz, 8301 Broadway, Suite 100, San Antonio, TX 78209.

Dr. G. R. Schmeidler, 17 Kent Ave., Hastings-on-Hudson, NY 10706.

Dr. H. Schmidt, 131 Shannon Lee, San Antonio, Texas 78216.

S. A. Schwartz, 4801 Wilshire Blvd., Suite 320, Los Angeles, CA 90010.

Dr. B. E. Schwarz, 642 Azalea lane, Vero Beach, FL 32963.

E. Shields, 5455 Eight St. #10, Carpinteria, CA 93013.

Dr. E. Shrager, 140 Eighth Ave., Brooklyn, N.Y. 11215.

C. Siegel, 336 Blue Ridge Dr., Martinez, CA 94553.

M. F. Smith, 226 Almondtree Lane, Oakley, CA 94561.

J. Solfrin, 56 Joaquin Miller Ct., Oakland, CA 94611.

N. Sondow, 789 West End Ave., Apt. 5D, New York, N.Y. 10025.

Dr. R. L. Sprinkle, Box 3708, University Station, Laramie, WY 82071.

Dr. R. G. Stanford, St. John's University, Marillac Hall, SB15, Jamaica, N.Y. 11439.

Dr. D. M. Stokes, 219 Sugartown Rd. P 303, Wayne, PA 19087.

W. C. Stone, W. Clement Stone Enterprises, P.O. Box 649, Lake Forest, IL 60045.

R. A. Strong, 7514 Belleplain Drive, Huber Heights, OH 45424.

Prof. P. A. Sturrock, Ctr. for Space Science & Astrophysics, Stanford University, ER L306, Stanford, CA 94305.

R. Taetzch, 12 Colburn Road, East Brunswick, NJ 08816.

R. Targ, 80 Hayfield Rd., Portola Valley, CA 94025.

Dr. C. T. Tart, 1675 Visalia, Berkeley, CA 94707.

W. H. Tedder, 3288 S. Dudley Ct., Lakewood, CO 80227.

F. C. Tribbe, Route 1, Box 134, Penn Laird, VA 22846.

S. V. Tringali, 81 Bellingham St., Chelsea, MA 02150.

Dr. M. Truzzi, Dep't of Sociology, Eastern Michigan University, Ypsilanti, MI 48197.

Dr. M. Ullman, 55 Orlando Ave., Ardsley, N.Y. 10502.

Dr. J. Utts, Div. of Statistics, University of California, Davis, CA 95616.

Dr. M. R. M. Van Blaaderen, Department of Social Sciences, Eastern Montana College, Billings, MT 59101.

Dr. R. L. Van de Castle, 6 East, Blue Ridge Hospital, Charlottesville, VA 22901.

A. Vaughan, 3223 Madera Ave., Los Angeles, CA 90039.

L. Vilenskaya, Psi Research, 484-B Washington St., #317, Monterey, CA 93940.

Dr. M. W. Wagner, Department of Psychology, State University of New York—Oswego, Oswego, N.Y. 13126.

Dr. E. H. Walker, 834 Paradise Road, Aberdeen, MD 21001.

D. H. Weiner, 13 Hamilton Rd., Chapel Hill, NC 27514.

R. A. Wells, P.O. Box 8033, U T Station, Knoxville, TN 37916

R. A. White, 2 Plane Tree Lane, Dix Hills, N.Y. 11746.

M. Witunski, McDonnell Foundation, P.O. Box 516, St. Louis, MO 63166.

Dr. W. O. Wolfson, 3000 Seminole, Detroit, MI 48214.

H. M. Zimmerman, 903 Chahootkin Dr., Alexandria, VA 22308.

N. Zingrone, 4635-E Hope Valley Rd., Durham, NC 27707.

C. E. Zsambok, 5464 Sherfield D., Dayton, OH 45426.

### Major Parapsychological Publications

*Journal of the American Society for Psychical Research.* **American Society for Psychical Research, 5 West 73rd St, New York, NY 10023.**

*Journal of Parapsychology.* **Foundation for Research on the Nature of Man, Box 6847, College Station, Durham, NC 27708.**

*Journal of Religion and Psychical Research.* **Academy of Religion and Psychical Research, Box 614, Bloomfield, CT 06002.**

*Journal of Scientific Exploration.* **Society for Scientific Exploration, Peter Sturrock, Center for Space Science & Astrophysics, Stanford University, Stanford, CA 94305.**

*Parapsychological Monographs of the Parapsychology Foundation.* **Parapsychology Foundation, 228 E. 71st St., New York, N.Y. 10021.**

*Parapsychology Review.* **Parapsychology Foundation.**

*Proceedings of the American Society for Psychical Research.* **American Society for Psychical Research.**

*Proceedings of the International Conferences of the Parapsychology Foundation.* **Parapsychology Foundation.**

*Research in Parapsychology.* **Parapsychological Association, 12236 Research Triangle Park, NC 27709.**

*Spiritual Frontiers.* **Spiritual Frontiers Fellowship, P.O. Box 7686, Philadelphia, PA 19101.**

*Theta.* **Psychical Research Foundation, West Georgia College, Carrollton, GA 30118.**

*Zetetic Scholar.* **Center for Scientific Anomalies Research, P.O. Box 1052, Ann Arbor, MI 48103.**

### Educational Opportunities in Parapsychology

Antioch University, Dep't of Psychology, 300 Rose Ave., Venice, CA 90291

Graduate courses in transpersonal psychology and parapsychology; also master's degree program in psychology with concentration on parapsychology or transpersonal psychology.

Athens State College, Dep't of Psychology, Athens, AL 35611

Five-credit undergraduate course in experimental parapsychology; seminars in parapsychology; supervision of research for credit.

American Society for Psychical Research, 5 West 73rd St., New York, N.Y. 10023

Lectures, seminars, classes in parapsychology.

Bridgewater State College, Dep't of Psychology, 5401 Wilkens Ave., Baltimore, MD 21228

Three-credit undergraduate course; and supervision of independent study/research.

East Texas State University, East Texas Station, Commerce, TX 75428

Non-credit continuing education courses.

Eastern Michigan University, Dep't of Sociology, 712 Pray-Harrold Bldg., Ypsilanti, MI 48197

Three-credit undergraduate course; also supervision of independent study/research.

Fairlawn Community School, P.O. Box 8, Fair Lawn, NJ 07410

Non-credit course.

Fordham University, Dep't of Theology, Bronx, NY 10458

Four-credit course on religious implications of parapsychology.

Forest Institute of Professional Psychology, Dep't of Psychology, 1717 Rand Road, Des Plaines, IL 60016

Credit graduate course.

Foundation for Research on the Nature of Man, Box 6847, College Station, Durham, NC 27708

Summer School study program; also residential training for credit toward degrees in institutions in which students are enrolled.

Idaho University, Dep't of Psychology, Moscow, ID 83843

Three-credit undergraduate course; also supervision of independent study/research.

Institute for Transpersonal Psychology, 250 Oak Grove, Menlo Park, CA 94025

Courses available (Write for more information.)

JFK University, 12 Altarinda Road, Orinda, CA 94563

Interdisciplinary studies of consciousness leading to master's degree with emphasis on parapsychology.

Kingsborough Community College, Dep't of Behavioral Sciences, 2001 Oriental Blvd., Brooklyn, NY 11235

Three-credit undergraduate course.

Lyndon State College, Dep't of Philosophy and Religion, Lyndonville, VT 05851

Three-credit undergraduate course.

Maryland, University of, Dep't of Philosophy, 5401 Wilkens Ave., Baltimore, MD 21228

Three-credit undergraduate and graduate courses.

Miami, University of, Dep't of Psychology, Coral Gables, FL 33129

Three-credit undergraduate course; also supervision of independent study/research.

Maine, University of Southern, 60 High St., Portland, Maine 04101

Non-credit introductory course.

Missouri, University of, Dep't of Psychology, 5319 Holmes St., Kansas City, MO 64110

Three-credit undergraduate introductory course.

Nassau Community College, Garden City, NY 11530

Non-credit course.

New School for Social Research, Social Science Division, 66 W. 12 St., New York, NY 10011

Three-credit undergraduate course.

North Carolina, University of, Dep't of Psychology, Chapel Hill, NC 27514

Supervision of independent undergraduate study/research.

Our Lady of the Lake University, Providence Building, Rm. 2A, 411 SW 24th St., San Antonio, TX 78285

Non-credit course

Rollins College, Dep't of Philosophy, Winter Park, FL 32783

Three-credit undergraduate course; also supervision of independent study/research.

Saybrook Institute, 1550 Sutter St., San Francisco, CA 94109

Correspondence course leading to Ph.D. with emphasis on parapsychology.

Slippery Rock University, Dep't of Philosophy, Slippery Rock, PA 16057

Three-credit undergraduate course.

Southwestern College, Dep't of Mathematics & Sciences, 900 Otay Lakes Road, Chula Vista, CA 92010

Three-credit undergraduate course; supervision of independent study/research.

St. John's University, Dep't of Psychology, Grand Central & Utopia Parkways, Jamaica, NY 11439

Three-credit undergraduate course; also supervision of independent study/research.

Staten Island, College of, Department of Psychology, 715 Ocean Terrace, Staten Island, NY 10301

Four-credit course.

St. Bonaventure University, Dep't of Theology, St. Bonaventure, NY 14778

Three-credit undergraduate course.

State University of New York-Geneseo, Dep't of Psychology, Geneseo, NY 14454

Three-credit undergraduate course; also supervision of independent study/research.

State University of New York-Oswego, Dep't of Psychology, Oswego, NY 13126

Three-credit undergraduate course; also four-credit undergraduate course with laboratory research.

Virginia, University of, Dep't Behavioral Medicine & Psychiatry, Box 152, Health Science Center, Charlottesville, VA 22908

Courses are not available; however, there are fellowships for university faculty members with advanced degrees for the study of spontaneous cases.

Virginia Commonwealth University, Dep't of Psychology, Richmond, VA 23284

Three-credit undergraduate course.

Western Connecticut State University, Dep't of Psychology, White St., Danbury, CT 08801

Three-credit undergraduate course.

West Florida, University of, Dep't of Psychology, Pensacola, FL 32514

Undergraduate and graduate BA and MA courses in psychology with emphasis on parapsychology.

West Georgia College, Dep't of Psychology, Carrollton, GA 30118

Credit undergraduate and graduate courses; also supervision of independent study/research.

Wichita State University, Dep't of Religion, Box 76, Wichita, KS 67208

Three-credit undergraduate course; supervision of independent study/research.

Winward Community College, 45–720 Keaahala Road, Kaneohe, HI 96744

Non-credit general course.

Wisconsin, University of, Dep't of Psychology, Stevens Point, WI 54481

Three-credit undergraduate course.

Wyoming, University of, Dep't of Psychology, Box 3708, University Station, Laramie, Wyoming, 82071

Three-credit undergraduate course; supervision of independent study/research.

## University Departments in Parapsychology

A Department of Parapsychology founded as an administrative unit of the Department of Behavioral Medicine & Psychiatry of the School of Medicine at the University of Virginia has now been absorbed into a Division of Personality Studies at that institution.

## ▪ APPENDIX B ▪

# Country Index

Countries are listed alphabetically. The headings under each country refer to the entries in the text in which the country is mentioned.

## CHINA



## CUBA



## CZECHOSLOVAKIA



## DENMARK



## EGYPT



## FINLAND



## FRANCE

(See also "History and Current Situation", p. 481.)

Institut Métapsychique International
Janet, P.
Joan of Arc
Kardec, A.
Laboratoire Universitaire de Parapsychologie et d'Hygiène Mental de Toulouse
Loudun, Demons of
Lourdes, Miracles of
Mary, Saint
Mesmerism
Metagnone
Metapsychics
Organisation pour la Recherche en Psychotronique
Osty, E.
Ouija Board
Palladino, E.
Picture Drawing Experiment
Piper, L. E.
Poincaré, H.
Prospopesis
Psychokinesis
Psychometry
Psychotronics
Pyramid Power
Random Behavior
*Revue Métapsychique*
Richet, C.
Rochas, A. de
Romains, J.
R-101
Rubinstein, A. G.
Saint-Saens, C. C.
Schneider, R.
Shroud of Turin
Sidgwick, H.
Spirit Photography
Stevenson, R. L.
Sudre, R.
Telepathy
Theodule, A. M.
Thoughtography
Tychoscope
Verrall, M. de G.
Versailles, Apparitions at
Vincent de Paul, Saint
Warcollier, R.
Xenoglossy
Yram

## GERMANY

(See also "History and Current Situation", p. 482.)

Aksakoff, A.
Baerwald, R.
Bender, H.
Betz, H.
Boehme, J.
Carington, W. W.
Chari, C. T. K.
Clever Hans
Coleridge, S.
Crime Detection
Dessoir, M.
Driesch, H.
Ebon, M.
Extrasensory Perception
Eysenck, H.
Geller, U.
Goethe, J. W. von
Gregory, A.
Grunewald, F.
Helmholz, H. von
Hanussen, E.
Hitler, A.
Hövelmann, G. H.
Institut für Grenzgebiete der Psychologie und Psychohygiene
Jaffé, A.
Kant, I.
Keil, H. H. J.
Klinckowstroem, C. von
Kornwachs, K.
Leibniz, G. W.
Lucadou, W. von
Luther, M.
Mann, T.
Mattiesen, E.
Münsterberg, H.
Neumann, T.
Nickleheim Poltergeist
Nietzche, F. W.
Osterreich, T. K.
Ouija Board
Pagenstecher, G.
Parapsychology
Piper, L. E.
Poltergeist
Price, H.
Rolf of Mannheim
Rosenheim Poltergeist
Rothschild, F.
Saints
Schmidt, H. W.
Schneider, R.
Schneider, W.
Schrenck-Notzing, A. von
Schumann, R. A.
Schurz, C.
Schweizerische Vereinigung für Parapsychologie
Senkowski, E.

## GREECE



## HAITI

(See also "History and Current Situation", p. 483.)


## HUNGARY



## ICELAND



## INDIA

INDIA

(See also "History and Current Situation", p. 483.)


## INDONESIA



## IRELAND

## ISRAEL



## ITALY

(See also "History and Current Situation", p. 484.)



## JAMAICA



## JAPAN

(See also "History and Current Situation", p. 485.)



## LATVIA

## LEBANON



## MARTINIQUE



## MELANESIA



## MEXICO

(See also "History and Current Situation", p. 486.)



## THE NETHERLANDS

(See also "History and Current Situation", p. 487.)



## NEW GUINEA



## NEW ZEALAND



## NORTH AFRICA



## NORWAY



## PANAMA

(See also "History and Current Situation", p. 488.)



## PHILLIPINES



## POLAND



## PORTUGAL

## PUERTO RICO

Alvarado, C. S.

## ROMANIA

Eliade, M.
Poltergeist
Zugun, E.

## SAMOA

Stevenson, R. L.

## SCOTLAND

(See also United Kingdom.)

Brougham, H. P.
Duncan, H. V.
Jonson, B.
Knox, J.
Koestler Chair of Parapsychology
Lang, A.
Owen, R. D.
Millar, B.
Muirs, J.
Richmond, K.
Scott, Sir W.
Stevenson, R. L.

## SOUTH AFRICA

(See also "History and Current Situation", p. 488.)

Bleksley, A. E. H.
Home, D. D.
Jacobs, J. C.
!Kung
Lang, A.
Mitchell, T. W.
Murray, G. G.
Parapsychological Journal of South Africa
Poynton, J. C.
Shackleton, B.
Sidgwick, E. M.
South African Institute for Parapsychological Research
South African Society for Psychical Research
Stewart, B.
Whiteman, J. H. M.

## SOVIET UNION

(See also "History and Current Situation", p. 489.)

Acupuncture
Adamenko, V. G.
Aksakoff, A.
Anpsi
Blavatsky, H. P.
Coffins, Disturbed
Dermo-Optic Perception
Duplessis, Y.
Extrasenser
Gregory, A.
Home, D. D.
Hypnosis
Ivanova, B.
Keil, H. H.
Kirlian Photography
Kulagina, N. S.
Kuleshova, R. A.
Levitation
Messing, W.
Mushroom Cult
Ouspensky, P. D.
Perovsky-Petrovo-Solovovo, M.
Pratt, J. G.
Psychoenergetics
Psychokinesis
Raudive, K.
Rubinstein, A. G.
Sambor, S. F.
Vasiliev, L. L.
Vilenskaya, L.
Worrall, O. N.

## SPAIN

(See also "History and Current Situation", p. 491.)

Gavilán Fontanet, F.
Jordan Peña, J. L.
Perera Molina, R.
*Psi Comunicación*
Psi-Omega
Sociedad Española de Parapsicología
Teresa of Avila, Saint

## SWEDEN

Brougham, H. P.
Forwald, H. G.
Jacobson, N. O.
Johnson, M.
Jonsson, O.
Jürgenson, F.
Linnaeus, Carolus
Psychokinesis
Stepanek, P.
Swedenborg, E.
Telepathy

## SWITZERLAND

Calvin, J.

## SYRIA



## TIBET



## UNITED KINGDOM

(See also "History and Current Situation", p. 491.)

Doyle, Sir A. C.
Duncan, H. V.
Dunne, J.
Duplessis, Y.
Edwards, H.
Eglinton, W.
Eliot, G.
Ellison, A. J.
Epworth Rectory
Extrasensory Perception.
Eysenck, H. J.
Faraday, M.
Fay, A. E.
Feilding, E. F.
Fisher, Sir R. A.
Fisk, G. W.
Fleming, A. M.
Flew, A. G. N.
Flint, L.
Fodor, N.
Ford, A.
Forthuny, P.
Fortune-Telling
Galloway, D. D. G.
Galsworthy, J.
Gauld, A.
Gay, K.
Ghost
Ghost Society
Gladstone, W. E.
Glanvil, J.
Goldney, K. M.
Goodrich-Freer, A.
Grattan-Guinness, I.
Green, C.
Gregory, A.
Gregory, C. C. L.
Grunewald, F.
Guppy, A.
Gurney, E.
Haggard, Sir H. R.
Hall, T.
Hansel, C. E. M.
Hardy, Sir A.
Haunt
Haynes, R.
Herne, F.
Hettinger, J.
Hodgson, R.
Holmes, N., Mr. and Mrs.
Holmes, O. W.
Home, D. D.
Hope, C.
Hope, W.
Housman, A. E.
Huby, P. M.
Hudson, F.
Hugo, V. M.
Huxley, A.
International Association for Near-Death Experiences
International Institute for the Study of Death.
Iredell, I.
Jacks, L. P.
Jack the Ripper
Jephson, I.
Johnson, A.
Johnson, D.
Johnson, G. M.
Johnson, S.
Jones, L. J.
Jonson, B.
*Journal of Paraphysics*
*Journal of the Society for Psychical Research*
KIB Foundation
Kilner, W. J.
Kipling, R.
Koestler, A.
Koestler Chair of Parapsychology
Lambert, G. W.
Lang, A.
Lawrence, T. E.
Leadbeater, C. W.
Leaf, W.
Leek, S.
Lees, R.
Leonard, G. O.
Levitation
Lodge, O.
London Dialectical Society
London Spiritualist Alliance
Lorimer, D.
Lowell, A.
Lyttelton, D. E.
MacKenzie, A.
Manning, M.
Markwick, B.
Massey, C. C.
Mayne, A.
McDougall, W.
McHarg, J.
McKenzie, J. H.
Mead, G. R. S.
Medhurst, R. G.
Mellon, A.
Metal-Bending
Mitchell, T. W.
Moses, W. S.
Moss, G.
Mother Ann
Mundle, C. K. M.
Munnings, F. T.

## UNITED STATES

(See also "History and Current Situation", p. 493.)

Adamenko, V. G.
Allison, L. W.
Alvarado, C. S.
American Association—Electronic Voice Phenomena
American Indians
American Institute for Scientific Research
American Society for Psychical Research
*Amityville Horror, The*
Anderson, M.
Anderson, R. I.
Angoff, A.
Anthony, S. B.
Apparition
Ashby, R. H.
Association for Research and Enlightenment
Bach, R.
Backster, C.
Balfour, A. J.
Bangs, L.
Bangs, M.
Batcheldor, K.
Bayless, R.
Bergen, E.
Belasco, D.
Berger, A. S.
Berger, R.
Bessent, M.
Bird, J. M.
Bishop, W. I.
Blavatsky, H. P.
Bleeding Pictures and Statues
Bond, F. B.
Bowditch, H. P.
Braud, W. G.
Braude, S.
Brier, R.
Bristol, J. I. D.
Broughton, R.
Browning, E. B.
Bull, T.
Burbank, L.
Calvin, J.
Carey, K.
Carlson, C. F.
Carpenter, W. B.
Carrel, A.
Carrington, H.
Cassadaga
Center for Scientific Anomalies Research
Chaffin Will Case
Chari, C. T. K.
Chenoweth, Mrs.
Child, I. L.
Christian Science
Christopher, M.
Clark, W. H.
Coly, E.
Coly, L.
Committee for the Scientific Investigation of the Claims of the Paranormal
Conley Case
Coover, J. E.
"Course on Miracles, The"
Cox, W. E.
Crandon, L. R. G.
Crowley, A.
Crying Pictures and Statues
Curran, P. L.
Dale, L. A.
Davenport Brothers
Deathbed Visions
Dermo-Optic Perception
Dixon, J.
Ducasse, C. J.
Duke University
Duplessis, Y.
Ebon, M.
Eddy, M. B.
Edge, H.
Edison, T. A.
Edmonds, J.
Ehrenwald, J.
Eisenbud, J.
Esalen Institute
Estabrooks, G.
Extrasensory perception
Fay, A. E.
Feola, J. M.
Flew, A. G. N.
Fodor, N.
Ford, A.
Fort, C. H.
Fortune-telling
Foundation for Research on the Nature of Man
Fox, G.
Fox Sisters
Funk, I.
Gardner Murphy Research Institute
Geller, U.
Greeley, H.
Greenwood, J. A.
Greville, T. N. E.
Grof, S.
Grosso, M.
Grunewald, F.
Hall, G. S.
Hall, P. F.
Hand Trembling
Hansen, G. P.
Harary, K.
Hare, R.

Ozanne, C.
Paine, A. B.
Palmer, J.
Parapsychological Association
Parapsychology Foundation
Parapsychology Laboratory
Pickering, E. H.
Pickett, G. E.
Picture Drawing Experiment
Piddington, J. G.
Pike, J. A.
Piper, L. E.
Poltergeist
Pope, D.
Possession
Pratt, J. G.
Precognition
Price, G. R.
Prince, W. F.
Psi
*Psi Research*
Psychical Research
Psychical Research Foundation
Psychokinesis
Psychophysical Research Laboratories
Puharich, H. K.
Pursel, J.
Quincy, J.
Radin, D.
"Ramtha"
Randi, J.
Rao, K. R.
Red Scratch Case
Reich, W.
Rhine, J. B.
Rhine, L. E.
Richardson, M. W.
Riess, B. F.
Ring, K.
Roberts, J.
Roberts, K.
Robertson, M.
Robinson, D.
Rockwell, T.
Rogo, D. S.
Roll, W. G.
Rolling Thunder
Royce, J.
Rubinstein, A. G.
Rush, J. H.
Ryzl, M.
Saints
Schiller, F. C.
Schmeidler, G. R.
Schurz, C.
Schwartz, S. A.
Schwarz, B. E.
Schweizerische Vereinigung für Parapsychologie
Science Unlimited Research Foundation
Scriven, M.
"Seth"
Seybert, H.
Seybert Commission
Shakers
Shaking Tent
Sherman, H.
Shroud of Turin
Sinclair, M.
Sinclair, U.
*Skeptical Inquirer*
Slade, H.
Slate-Writing
Smith, M. J.
Smith, S.
Society for Scientific Exploration
SORRAT
Spiricom
Spirit Photography
*Spiritual Frontiers*
Spiritual Frontiers Fellowship
Spiritualism
"Splitfoot, Mr."
Spontaneous Cases
Stanford, Ray
Stanford Research Institute
Stanford, Rex
Stanford, T. W.
Stanley, Sir H. M.
Stead, W. T.
Stepanek, P.
Stevenson, R. L.
Stowe, H. B.
Stuart, C. E.
Summerland
Survival Research Foundation
Swedenborg, E.
Tanous, A.
Targ, R.
Tart, C.
Thomas, J. F.
Thompson, F. L.
Thoughtography
Tillyard, R. J.
*Titanic*
Tribbe, F. C.
Truzzi, M.
Twain, M.
Ullman, M.
Uphoff, W.
Valiantine, G.
Van de Castle, R. L.
Vasiliev, L. L.

## URUGUAY



## YUGOSLAVIA



## WEST INDIES

# ▪ Appendix C ▪

# Bibliography


Adams, F. C. 1957. "The Possible Bearings of the Psychology of C. G. Jung on Psychical Research." JASPR 50:25.

Akers, C. "Methodological Criticisms of Parapsychology," In S. Krippner, ed. *Advances in Parapsychology, Vol. 4.* Jefferson, NC: McFarland, 1984, pp. 112–164.

Akasakoff, A. N. *Animisme et Spiritisme.* Paris: Libraire des Sciences Psychiques, 1985.

———. *Animism and Spiritism: an Attempt at a Critical Investigation of Mediumistic Phenomena, with Special Reference to the Hypothesis of Hallucination and of the Unconscious: An Answer to Dr. E. von Hartmann's Work, 'Der Spiritismus'.* Leipsig: Oswald Mutze, 1890. 2 Vols.

Allison, L. W. 1957. "In Memory of Waldemar B. Kaempffert." JASPR 51:84.

———. 1954. "Obituary: The Reverend C. Drayton Thomas." JASPR 48:37.

———. 1934. "Proxy Sittings with Mrs. Leonard." PSPR 42:104.

———. *Leonard and Soule Experiments in Psychical Research.* Boston: Boston Society for Psychic Research, 1929.

"Obituary and Tributes to Mrs. E. W. Allison." 1959. JASPR 53:81.

"Obituaries. Mrs. Lydia Allison." 1959. JSPR 40:98.

Alvarado, C. S. 1987. "The Life and Work of an Italian Psychical Researcher: A Review of *Ernesto Bozzano: La Vita e l'Opera* by Gioanni Iannuzzo." JASPR 81:37.

———. 1987. "Observations of Luminous Phenomena around the Human Body: A Review." JSPR 54:38.

———. 1986. "ESP During Spontaneous Out-of-Body Experiences: A Research and Methodological Note." JASPR 53:393.

———. 1986. "Ernesto Bozzano, Une Nota Bibliografica in Tre Reviste Straniere." *Luce e Ombra* 86:9.

———. 1982. "Historical Perspective in Parapsychology: Some Practical Considerations." JSPR 51:265.

———. 1980. "Joseph Banks Rhine (1895–1980). Pionero en la parapsicología experimental." *Psi Comunicación* 6:9.

Amadou, R. *Les grand médiums.* Paris: Editions Denoel, 1957.

———. *La Parapsychologie.* Paris: Editions Denoel, 1954.

"An Account of the Indian Rope-Climbing Trick." 1904. JSPR, 11:299.

Anderson, M. 1966. "The Use of Fantasy in Testing for Extrasensory Perception." JASPR 60:150.

———. 1957. "Clairvoyance and Teacher-Pupil Attitudes in Fifth and Sixth Grades." JP 21:1.

Anderson, M., and E. Gregory. 1959. "A Two-Year Program of Tests for Clairvoyance and Precognition with a Class of Public School Pupils." JP 23:149.

Anderson, M., and R. A. McConnell. 1961. "Fantasy Testing for ESP in Fourth- and Fifth-Grade Class." *Journal of Psychology* 52:491.

Anderson, M., and R. White. 1957. "A Further Investigation of Teacher-Pupil Attitudes and Clairvoyance Test Results." JP 21:81.

———. 1956. "Teacher-Pupil Attitudes and Clairvoyance Test Results." JP 20:141.

Anderson, R. I. 1986. "Reincarnation: Can Christianity Accommodate It?" *Journal of Religion and Psychical Research* 9:189.

———. 1985. "The Life and Works of James H. Hyslop." JASPR 79:167.

———. 1984. "Psychometry or Survival, Parts I & II." *Parapsychology Review* 15(3,4):6,10.

———. 1984. "Cahagnet's Contributions to Psychical Research." *Theta* 12:74.

———. 1983. "The Mediumship of Geraldine Cummins." *Theta* 11:50.

———. 1981. "Contemporary Survival Research: A Critical Review." *Parapsychology Review* 12(5):8.

———. 1980. "The Watseka Wonder: A Critical Evaluation." *Theta* 8:6.

Anderson, R. I., with W. L. Anderson. 1982. "Veridical and Psychopathic Hallucinations: A Comparison of Types." *Parapsychology Review* 13(3):17.

Angoff, A. *Eileen Garrett and the World Beyond the Senses.* New York: Morrow, 1974.

Angstadt, J., and R. White. 1963. "Student Performance in a Two Classroom GESP Experiment with Two Students-Agents Acting Simultaneously." JASPR 57:32.

Annual Report. 1949. JSPR 35:2.

Aragon, E. O. *Historia del Alma.* Mexico City: Imprenta Aldina, 1943, Vol. II.

Archer, W. 1864. "Observations on Table-Moving." *Proceedings of the Royal Society of Tasmania* 4:86.

Artley, J. L., J. E. Lenz, and E. F. Kelly. 1980. "A Computer-Based Laboratory Facility for the Psychophysiological Study of Psi." JASPR 74:149.

Artley, J. L., and W. T. Joines. 1969. "Study of a Haunted House." *Theta* 27:2.

Ashby, R. H. 1982. "Personhood." *Spiritual Frontiers* 14 (1): 7.

———. *The Guidebook for the Study of Psychical Research.* New York: Samuel Weiser, 1972.

Averill, R. L., and J. B. Rhine. 1945. "The Effect of Alcohol upon Performance in PK Tests." JP 9:32.

Averill, P. L., J. B. Rhine, and B. M. Humphrey. 1945. "An Exploratory Experiment on the Effects of Caffeine Upon Performance in PK Tests." JP 9:80.

Azuma, N., and I. Stevenson. 1987. "Difficulties Confronting Investigations of 'Psychic Surgery' in the Phillipines." *Parapsychology Review* 18(2):6.

Backster, C. 1968. "Evidence of a Primary Perception in Plant Life." *International Journal of Parapsychology* 10:329.

Backus, J. M. "Parapsychology and Literature." In B. Wolman, ed. *Handbook of Parapsychology.* New York: Van Nostrand Reinhold, 1977.

Baerwald, R. "Die intellektuellen Phänomene." In M. Dessoir, ed. *Der Okkultismus in Orkunden.* Berlin: Ullstein Verlag, 1925.

Baggally, W. W. 1914. "Report on Experiments with 'Amy Joyce.'" JSPR 16:168.

———. 1910. "The Naples Report on Eusapia Palladino." JSPR 14:213.

———. 1910. "Some Sittings with Carancini." JSPR 14:193.

Baggally, W. W., E. Feilding, and H. Carrington. 1909. "Report on a Series of Sittings with Eusapia Palladino." PSPR 23:309.

Bagnall, O. *The Origin and Properties of the Human Aura.* New Hyde Park, New York: University Books, 1970.

Balfour, G. 1935. "A Study of the Psychological Aspects of Mrs. Willett's Mediumship, and of the Statements of the Communicators Concerning Process." PSPR 43:43.

———. 1917. "The Ear of Dionysius: Further Evidence Affording Evidence of Personal Survival." PSPR 29:197.

———. 1905–1907. "Presidential Address." PSPR 19:373.

Balfour, J. 1960. "The 'Palm Sunday' Case." PSPR 52:79.

Ballou, R. O. and G. Murphy. *William James on Psychical Research.* London: Chatto and Windus, 1960.

Bander, P. *Voices from the Tapes.* New York: Drake Publishers, 1973.

Barbanell, M. *Across the Gulf.* London: Psychic Press, 1940.

Barendregt, J. T., with M. Ryzl, J. Kappers, and P. R. Barkema. 1965. "An Experiment in Prague." JP 29:176.

Barham, A. 1988. "Dr. W. J. Crawford, His Work and His Legacy in Psychokinesis." JSPR 55:113.

———. 1988. "The Crawford Legacy, Part II." JSPR 55:196.

———. *Strange to Relate.* London: Colin Smythe, 1980/1984.

———. *Life Unlimited.* London: Volturna Press, 1982.

Barkema, P. R., Van Asperen de Boer, and J. Kappers. 1966. "Is It Possible to Induce ESP with Psilocybine? An Exploratory Investigation." *International Journal of Neuropsychiatry* 2 (5): 447.

Barkema, P. R., with J. T. Barendregt, M. Ryzl, and J. Kappers. 1965. "An Experiment in Prague." JP 29:176.

Barker, D. R. 1978. "Reviews. Psychic Archeology: Time Machine to the Past. By Jeffrey Goodman." JASPR 72:186.

Barker, J. C. *Scared to Death: An Examination of Fear, its Causes and Effects.* London: Frederick Muller, 1968.

———. 1967. Premonitions of the Aberfan Disaster."JSPR 44:169.

———. 1967. "Disaster Early Warning System." JSPR 44:107.

Barlow, F., and W. Rampling-Rose. 1933. "Report of an Investigation into Spirit-Photography." PSPR 41:121.

Barnouw, V. 1946. "Paranormal Phenomena and Culture." JASPR 40:2–21.

Barrett, L. *Psi Trek.* New York: McGraw Hill, 1981.

Barrett, W. *Death-Bed Visions.* London: Methuen, 1926.

———. 1924. "Some Reminiscences of Fifty Years of Psychical Research." PSPR 34:275.

———. 1922. "Obituary Notices. I. H. Arthur Smith." JSPR 20:353.

———. 1920. "In Memory of Sir William Crookes, O.M., F.R.S." PSPR 31:12.

———. 1919. "Report on Dr. Crawford's Medium." PSPR 30:334.

———. *On the Threshold of the Unseen.* New York: E. P. Dutton Co., 1918.

———. 1918. "Evidence of Super-Normal Communications through Motor Automatism." PSPR 30:230.

———. 1911. "Poltergeists, Old and New." PSPR 25:377.

———. 1905. "Obituary. C. C. Massey." JSPR 12:95.

———. 1904. "Address by the President." PSPR 18:323.

———. 1900. "On the So-Called Divining Rod: A Psycho-Physical Research on a Peculiar Faculty Alleged to Exist in Certain Persons Locally Known as Dowsers." PSPR 15:130.

———. 1897. "On the So-Called Divining Rod, or Virgula Divina: A Scientific and Historical Research as to the Existence and Practical Value of a Peculiar Human Faculty Unrecognized by Science, Locally Known as Dowsing." PSPR 13:2.

———. 1888. "Professor Balfour Stewart." JSPR 3:197.

———. 1887. "On Some Physical Phenomena, Commonly Called Spiritualistic, Witnessed by the Author." PSPR 4:25.

Barrett, W., E. Gurney, and F. W. H. Myers. 1882. "First Report on Thought Reading." PSPR 1:13.

Barrington, M. R. 1976. "A Poltergeist Revived: The Flying Thermometer Case Again." JSPR 48:293.

———. 1973. "A Free Response Sheep/Goat Experiment Using an Irrelevant Task." JSPR 47:222.

———. 1971. "Obituary. Dr. R. G. Medhurst 1920–1971." JSPR 46:124.

———. 1966. "Swan on a Black Sea: How Much Could Miss Cummins Have Known?" JSPR 43:289.

———. 1965. "The Case of the Flying Thermometer." JSPR 43:11.

Batcheldor, K. J. 1984. "Contributions to the Theory of PK Induction from Sitter-Group Work." JASPR 78:105.

———. 1982. "Obituary C. H. W. Brookes-Smith." JSPR 51:403.

———. 1966. "Report in a Case of Table Levitation and Associated Phenomena." JSPR 43:339.

Bauer, E. 1984. "Criticism and Controversies in Parapsychology." *European Journal of Parapsychology* 5:141.

Bayfield, M. A. 1913. "Andrew Lang and Psychical Research." PSPR 27:419.

Bayless, R. 1959. "Correspondences." JASPR 53:35.

Bayless, R., and E. E. McAdams. *The Case of Life after Death: Parapsychologists Look at the Evidence.* Chicago, Ill: Nelson Hall, 1981.

Bayless, R., and D. S. Rogo. *Phone Calls from the Dead.* Englewood Cliffs, NJ: Prentice-Hall, 1979.

Beard, P. *Living On.* New York: Continuum, 1981.

———. *Survival of Death.* London: Hodder and Slaughton, 1966.

Bechterev, W. 1949. "'Direct Influence' of a Person Upon the Behavior of Animals." JP 13:166.

Beloff, J. *The Importance of Psychical Research.* London: Society for Psychical Research, 1988.

———. 1988. "Advances in Parapsychological Research, Vol. 5." JSPR 55:157.

———. "Parapsychology and the Expectation of Progress." In D. H. Weiner and D. I. Radin, eds. *Research in Parapsychology, 1985.* Metuchen, NJ: Scarecrow Press, 1986.

———. "George Zorab and 'Katie King.'" In F. W. J. J. Snel, ed., *In Honour of G. A. M. Zorab.* Amsterdam: Nederlander Vereniging voor Parasychologie, 1986.

———. "What Is Your Counter-Explanation? A Plea to Skeptics to Think Again." In P. Kurtz, ed. *A Skeptic's Handbook of Parapsychology.* Buffalo, NY: Prometheus Books, 1985.

———. "Historical Overview." In B. Wolman, ed. *Handbook of Parapsychology.* New York: Van Nostrand Rheinhold Company, 1977.

———. *Psychological Sciences.* New York: Barnes & Noble, 1974.

———. *The Existence of Mind.* New York: Citadel, 1964.

———, ed. *New Directions in Parapsychology.* Metuchen, NJ: Scarecrow Press, 1975.

———. 1969. "Review of Periodical Literature 1968." JSPR 45:60, 72.

———. 1966. "Review. *Towards a New Philosophical Basis for Parapsychological Phenomena.*" JSPR 32:317.

———. 1963. "Explaining the Paranormal." JSPR 42:101.

Beloff, J., with J. Smythies, eds. *The Case for Dualism.* Charlottesville, VA: University of Virginia Press, 1988.

Bender, H. "A Positive Critic of Superstition." In R. Pilkington, ed. *Men and Women of Parapsychology: Personal Reflections.* Jefferson, NC: McFarland, 1987.

———. "Poltergeists." In I. Grattan-Guiness, ed. *Psychical Research: A Guide to Its History, Principles and Practices.* Wellingborough, Northamptonshire: Aquarian Press, 1982.

———. *Unser sechster Sinn.* Stuttgart: Wilhelm Goldmann Verlag, 1982 (originally published 1972).

———. "Modern Poltergeist Research: A Plea for an Unprejudiced Approach." In J. Beloff, ed. *New Directions in Parapsychology.* London: Elek Science, 1974.

———. 1969. "New Developments in Poltergeist Research." *Proceedings of the Parapsychological Association* 6:81.

Bender, H., R. Hampel, H. Kury, and S. Wendlandt. 1975. "The 'Geller-effect'—An Investigation on Interviews and Questionnaires Part 1." *Zeitschrift für Parapsychologie und Grenzgebiete der Psychologie* 17:219.

Bender, H., R. Vandrey, and S. Wendlandt. "The 'Geller Effect' in Western Germany and Switzerland: A Preliminary Report on a Social and Experimental Study." In J. D. Morris, W. G. Roll, and R. L. Morris, eds. *Research in Parapsychology 1975.* Metuchen, NJ: Scarecrow Press, 1976.

Bennett, E. W. 1936. "In Memory of Everard Feilding." PSPR 44:5.

Berendt, Heinz C. "A New Israeli Metal-Bender (with Film)." In W. G. Roll, J. Beloff, and R. W. White, eds. *Research in Parapsychology 1982.* Metuchen, NJ: The Scarecrow Press, 1983, p. 43.

Berger, A. S. "Three Views of Death and Their Implications for Life." In P. Badham, ed. *The Value of Human Life.* New York: Paragon House, (in press).

———. "Religion and Parapsychology: Eight Points of Contact." In A. S. Berger and H. O. Thompson, eds. *Religion and Parapsychology.* New York: UTS, 1989.

———. *Evidence of Life after Death: A Casebook for the Tough-Minded.* Springfield, Ill.: Charles C. Thomas, 1988.

———. 1988. "Two Unrecognized Problems in Survival Research." In D. H. Weiner and R. L. Morris, eds. *Research in Parapsychology 1987.* Metuchen, NJ: The Scarecrow Press, 1988, p. 140.

———. *Lives and Letters in American Parapsychology: A Biographical History, 1850–1987.* Jefferson, N.C.: McFarland & Co., 1988.

———. *Aristocracy of The Dead.* Jefferson, NC: McFarland & Co., 1987.

———. "Bridging the Gap: A Critical Survey of the Latest Types of Prima Facie Survival Evidence." In P. and L. Badham, eds. *Death and Immortality in the Religions of the World.* New York: Paragon House, 1987.

———. 1985. "The Early History of the ASPR." JASPR 79:39.

———. 1985. "Robert H. Thouless and His Work." JASPR 79:327.

———. "A Tribute to Robert H. Thouless." In S. Krippner, ed. *Advances in Parapsychological Research 4.* Jefferson, NC: McFarland and Co., 1984.

———. 1984. "Experiments with False Keys." JASPR 78:41.

———.. "Concepts of Survival After Death: Toward Clarification, Evaluation and Choice." In *The Synergy of Religion and Psychical Research: Past, Present and Future, 1983. Proceedings of the Academy of Religion and Psychical Research,* 1984 5:45.

———. 1982. "Better Than a Gold Watch: the Work of the Survival Research Foundation." *Theta* 10(4):82.

Berger, R. "Psi Effects without Real-Time Feedback." In D. H. Weiner and R. L. Morris, eds. *Research in Parapsychology 1987.* Metuchen, NJ: The Scarecrow Press, 1988, p. 14.

Berger, R., and C. Honorton. "Psi Lab//:A Standardized Psi-Testing System." In R. A. White and J. Solfvin, eds. *Research in Parapsychology 1984.* Metuchen, NJ: The Scarecrow Press, 1985, p. 68.

Bergier, J., and L. Pauwels. *The Morning of the Magicians.* New York: Avon Books, 1968. (First published in France in 1960 by Editions Gallimard as *Le Matin des Magiciens*).

Bergson, H. 1913. "Presidential Address." PSPR 26:462.

Bernstein, M. *The Search for Bridey Murphy.* Garden City, NJ: Doubleday, 1956.

Besant, A. *Man and His Bodies.* London: Theosophical Press, 1900.

Besant, A., and C. W. Leadbeater. *Occult Chemistry.* Adyar, Madras: Theosophical Publishing House, 1919.

"Annie Besant." *Encylopaedia Britannica,* 1958, pp. 470–471.

Besterman, T. *Collected Papers on the Paranormal.* New York: Garrett Publications, 1968.

———. 1935. "The Mediumship of Carlos Mirabelli." JSPR 29:141.

———. 1933. "An Experiment in 'Clairvoyance' with M. Stefan Ossowiecki." PSPR 41:345.

———. 1932. "The Psychology of Testimony in Relation to Paraphysical Phenomena: Report of an Experiment." PSPR 40:363.

———. 1930. "Review of *Modern Psychic Mysteries, Millesimo Castle, Italy.*" JSPR 26:10.

Besterman, T., and G. Heard. 1933. "Note on an Attempt to Locate in Space the Alleged Direct Voice Observed in Sittings with Mrs Leonard." JSPR 28:84.

Besterman, T., with I. Jephson, and S. G. Soal. 1931. "Report of a Series of Experiments in Clairvoyance Conducted at a Distance under Approximately Fraud-proof Conditions." PSPR 39:375.

Betz, H. D. 1975. "Experimentelle Untersuchung ungewohnlicher Metall-Biegeeffekte." *Zeitschrift für Parapsychologie und Grenzgebiete der Psychologie* 17:241.

Bierman, D. 1981. "An Open Letter to Julian Isaacs." JSPR 51:183.

Bird, C. 1982. "Fruitful Searches." *New Realities* 4(5):45.

Bird, J. M. 1929. "The Crisis in Psychical Research." *Psychic Research* 23:323.

———, ed. 1928. "The Margery Mediumship." PASPR 20–21, Vol. 1.

———. 1926. "Observations on the Moss Case." JASPR 20:41.

———. *Margery the Medium.* New York: Maynard Co., 1925.

Birge, W. R., and J. B. Rhine. 1942. "Unusual Types of Persons Tested for ESP. I. A Professional Medium." JP 6:85.

Blackmore, S. J. "A Theory of Lucid Dreams and OBEs." In J. Gackenbach and S. LaBarge, eds. *Lucid Dreaming.* New York: Plenum Press, 1988.

———. 1987. "A Report of a Visit to Carl Sargent's Laboratory." JSPR 54:186.

———. *The Adventures of a Parapsychologist.* Buffalo, NY: Prometheus Books, 1986.

———. "The Adventures of a Psi-Inhibitory Experimenter." In P. Kurtz, *A Skeptic's Handbook of Parapsychology.* Buffalo, NY: Prometheus Books, 1985.

———. 1984. "ESP in Young Children." JSPR 52:311.

———. 1983. "Divination with Tarot Cards: An Empirical Study." JSPR 52:97.

———. 1982. "Have You Ever Had an OBE: The Wording of the Question." JSPR 51:292.

———. *Beyond the Body: An Investigation of Out-of-the-Body Experiences.* London: Heinemann, 1981.

———. *Parapsychology and Out-of-the-Body Experiences.* London: Society for Psychical Research, and Hove: Transpersonal Books, 1978.

Blatty, W. P. *The Exorcist.* New York: Harper & Row, 1971.

Blavatsky, H. P. *The Voice of the Silence.* London: Theosophical Publishing Society, 1892. Originally published 1889.

———. *Secret Doctrine.* London: Theosophical Publishing Society, 1888.

———. *Isis Unveiled.* London: Theosophical Publishing Society, 1877.

Bleksley, A. E. H. "Creativity in the Mathematical Field." In A. Angoff and B. Shapin, eds. *Psi Factors in Creativity.* New York: Parapsychology Foundation, 1970, p. 85.

———. 1963. "An Experiment of Long-Distance ESP During Sleep." JP 27:1.

Boirac, E. *Psychologie Inconnu: Introduction et Contribution à l'Etude Experimentale des Sciences Psychiques.* Paris: 1908.

Bolen, J. 1978. "Kreskin: Mind Star in a Universe of Realities." *New Realities* 1(6):8.

———. 1974. "Interview: Richard Bach." *Psychic* V (6) No. 6: 6–10, 25–27.

———. 1973. "Interview: Shafica Karagulla, M.D." *Psychic* 4(6):6.

Bond, F. B. 1935. "Editorial Notes: 'Walter' Thumbprints: Dr. Cummins's Report." JASPR 29:130.

———. *The Gospel of Philip the Deacon.* New York: Macoy, 1932.

———. *The Gate of Remembrance: The Story of the Psychological Experiment Which Resulted in the Discovery of the Edgar Chapel at Glastonbury.* Oxford: B.A.B.H. Blackwell, 1918, 1921.

"Book Notice." 1930. *Psychic Research* (JASPR) 34(9):426.

Booth, J. *Psychic Paradoxes.* Los Alamitos, CA: Ridgeway Press, 1984.

Borzymowski, A. 1965. "Experiments with Ossowiecki." *International Journal of Parapsychology.* 7(3):259.

Bose, J. C. *Growth and Tropic Movements of Plants.* New York: Longmans, Green Co., 1929.

Boswell, J. (ed. A. Birrell) *Life of Samuel Johnson, LL.D.* Philadelphia, PA: 1901.

Bowden, H. T., and Soal S. G. *The Mind Readers.* London: Faber and Faber, 1959.

Boyd, D. *Rolling Thunder.* New York: Dell Publishing Co., 1974.

Bozzano, E. *Popoli Primitivi e Manifestazioni Supernormali.* Milan: Armenia Editore, 1974.

———. (tr. I. Emerson) *Polyglot Mediumship.* London: Rider, 1932.

———. *Phénomènes Psychiques au Moment de la Mort.* Paris: Editions de la B.P.S., 1923.

———. *Les Phénomènes de Hantise.* Paris: Alcan, 1920.

Brandon, R. *The Spiritualists.* New York: Alfred A. Knopf, 1983.

Braud, W. G. 1987. "Dealing with Displacement." JASPR 81:209.

———. "The Two Faces of Psi: Psi Revealed and Psi Obscured." In B. Shapin and L. Coly, eds. *The Repeatability Problem in Parapsychology.* New York: Parapsychology Foundation, 1985, pp. 150–182.

———. 1983. "Psychokinetic Influence on Electrodermal Activity." JP 47:95.

———. "Lability and Inertia in Psychic Functioning." In B. Shapin and L. Coly, eds. *Concepts and Theories of Parapsychology.* New York: Parapsychology Foundation, 1981, pp. 1–36.

———. "Psi Conducive Conditions: Explorations and Interpretations." In B. Shapin and L. Coly, eds. *Psi and States of Awareness.* New York: Parapsychology Foundation, 1978, pp. 1–41.

Braud, W. G., and R. Wood. 1977. "The Influence of Immediate Feedback on Free-Response GESP Performance during Ganzfeld Stimulation." JASPR 71:409.

Braude, S. E. *The Limits of Influence: Psychokinesis and the Philosophy of Science.* London: Routledge & Kegan Paul, 1986.

———. 1985. "The Enigma of Daniel Home." JSPR 53:40.

———. 1983. "Radical Provincialism in the Life Sciences: A Review of Rupert Sheldrake's *A New Science of Life.*" JASPR 77:63.

———. 1982. "Precognitive Attrition and Theoretical Parsimony." JASPR 76:143.

———. 1981. "The Holographic Analysis of Near-Death Experiences: The Perpetuation of Some Deep Mistakes." *Essence: Issues in the Study of Aging, Dying and Death* 5:53.

———. *ESP and Psychokinesis: A Philosophical Examination.* Philadelphia, PA: Temple University Press, 1979.

———. 1979. "The Observational Theories in Parapsychology: A Critique." JASPR 73:349.

———. 1979. "Objections to an Information-Theoretic Approach to Synchronicity." JASPR 73:179.

Brian, D. 1982. *The Enchanted Voyager: The Life of J. B. Rhine.* Englewood Cliffs, NJ: Prentice Hall Inc., 1982.

Brier, R. M. 1969. "A Mass School Test of Precognition." JP 3:125.

Brier, R. M., and W. V. Tyminski. "Psi Application." In J. B. Rhine, ed. *Progress in Parapsychology.* Durham, NC: The Parapsychology Press, 1971, p. 36.

Brier, R. M., and J. B. Rhine. *Parapsychology Today.* New York: Citadel Press, 1968.

Briggs, K. C. 1976. "The Great Beast: The Legend of Aleister Crowley." *Psychic* 7(5):39.

Broad, C. D. 1970. "Obituary: Mr. W. H. Salter." JSPR 45:203.

———. 1964. "Cromwell Varley's Electrical Tests with Florence Cook." PSPR 54:158.

———. *Lectures on Psychical Research.* New York: The Humanities Press, 1962.

———. 1959. "Obituary: Mrs. W. H. Salter." JSPR 40:129.

———. 1959. "Our Pioneers, VI: Henry Sidgwick." JSPR 40:103.

———. *Personal Identity and Survival.* (The Thirteenth Frederic W. H. Myers Memorial Lecture) London: The Society for Psychical Research, 1958.

———. 1955. "The Phenomenology of Mrs. Leonard's Mediumship." JASPR 49:47.

———. *Religion, Philosophy and Psychical Research.* London: Routledge and Kegan Paul, 1953.

———. 1950. "Immanuel Kant and Psychical Research." PSPR 49:79.

———. *The Mind and its Place in Nature.* London: Routledge and Kegan Paul, 1925.

"In Memoriam: Professor C. D. Broad 1887–1971." 1971. JSPR 46:103.

Brod, R. H., and E. Twigg. *Ena Twigg Medium.* London: W. A. Allen, 1973.

Brookes-Smith, C. 1973. "Data-Tape Recorded Experimental PK Phenomena." JSPR 47:69.

Broughton, R. S. "Brain Hemisphere Specialization and ESP: What Have We Learned?" In R. A. White and R. S. Broughton, eds. *Research in Parapsychology 1983.* Metuchen, NJ: Scarecrow Press, 1984.

———. "The Use of Computers in Psychical Research." In I. Grattan-Guinness, ed. *Psychical Research: A Guide to Its History, Principles and Practices.* Wellingborough, UK: Aquarian Press, 1982, Chapter 19.

———. 1975. "Psi and the Two Halves of the Brain." JSPR 47:133.

Broughton, R. S. and J. R. Perlstrom. "A Competitive Computer Game in PK Research: Some Preliminary Findings." In R. White and J. Solfvin, eds. *Research in Parapsychology 1984,* Metuchen, NJ: The Scarecrow Press, 1985, pp. 74–81.

Broughton, R. S., and G. P. Hansen. "An Investigation of Macro-PK: The SORRAT." In W. G. Roll, J. Beloff and R. A. White, eds., *Research in Para-*

*psychology, 1982.* Metuchen, NJ: The Scarecrow Press, 1983, pp. 115–116.

Broughton, R. S., B. Millar, and M. Johnson. 1981. "An Investigation into the Use of Aversion Therapy Techniques for the Operant Control of PK Production in Humans." *European Journal of Parapsychology* 3:317.

Brown, R. *In Her Own Write: A Note on Rosemary Brown. The Rosemary Brown Piano Album.* London: Paxton, 1974.

Brugmans, H. J. F. W. 1923. "De 'Passieve Toestand' van een Telepaath door het Psychogalvanisch Phenomeen Gecontroleerd." *Overdruck vit Mededeelingen Der Studievereeniging voor Psychical Research* 7.

Brugmans, H. J. F. W., G. Heymans, and A. Weinberg. "Une communication sur des expériences télépathiques au laboratoire de psychologie à Groningue." *Compte Rendu Officiel du Premier Congrès International des Recherches Psychiques.* Copenhagen, 1922, p. 396.

———. "Some Experiments in Telepathy Performed in the Psychological Institute of the University of Groningen." *Compte Rendu du Premier Congrès International des Recherches Psychiques,* 1921.

Bucke, R. M. *Cosmic Consciousness.* New York: E. P. Dutton Co., 1923.

Budge, E. A. *The Egyptian Book of the Dead.* New York: Bell Publishing Co., 1950.

Bull, K. T. 1900. "Mrs. Piper—A Study." *Harper's Bazaar* 33:741.

Bull, T. 1938. "Mental Obsession and the Latent Faculty." JASPR 32:260.

———. 1927. "Resistance to Metaphysical Science." JASPR 17:645.

Burdick, D. S., and E. F. Kelly. "Statistical Methods in Parapsychology Research." In B. Wolman, ed. *Handbook of Parapsychology.* New York: Van Nostrand Reinhold, 1977.

Burt, C. "The Implications of Parapsychology for General Psychology." In R. Van Over, ed. *Psychology and Extrasensory Perception.* New York: New American Library, 1972, p. 344.

———. *Psychology and Psychical Research.* London: Society for Psychical Research, 1968.

———. "Psychology and Parapsychology." In J. R. Smythies, ed. *Science and ESP.* London: Routledge & Kegan Paul, 1967, p. 61.

———. 1963. "Jung's Account of his Paranormal Experiences." JSPR 42:163.

Burton, L., W. Joines, and B. Stephens. 1975. "Kirlian Photography and its Relevance to Parapsychology." In *Research in Parapsychology 1974.* Metuchen, NJ: The Scarecrow Press, 1975, p. 77.

Cadbury, H. J. *George Fox's 'Book of Miracles'.* Cambridge: Cambridge University Press, 1948.

Cadoret, R. J. 1964. "An Exploratory Experiment: Continuous EEG Recording During Clairvoyant Card-Guessing." JP 28:226.

———. 1955. "The Reliable Application of ESP." JP 19:203.

Cahagnet, L. A. *Arcanes de la Vie Future Dévoilés.* Paris: Bailliere, 1860.

———, tr. F. F. Pearson. *The Sanctuary of Spiritualism.* London: George Peirce, 1851 (originally published in France 1850).

———. *The Celestial Telegraph.* London: George Peirce, 1850 (originally published in France 1848–1849).

Caldwell, T. "Epilogue by Taylor Caldwell." In J. Stearn, *The Search for a Soul: Taylor Caldwell's Psychic Lives.* Garden City, NY: Doubleday & Co., 1973.

Campbell, J. L. 1969. "Correspondence. Strange Things and Ada Goodrich-Freer." JSPR 45:183.

Campbell, J. L., and T. H. Hall. *Strange Things.* London: Routledge & Kegan Paul, 1968.

Cantwell, R. 1977. "Win, Place and Glow." *Sports Illustrated* 47:32.

Capel, M. 1978. "Las Experiencias Extracorporales: Revisión de la Casuista y Algunas Aportaciones Explicativas." *Psi Comunicación* 7-8:49.

Carington, W. W. *Telepathy: An Outline of its Fact, Theory and Implications.* New York: Gordon Press, 1972 (originally published 1945 Methuen & Co.).

———. *Matter, Mind and Meaning.* London: Methuen & Co., 1949.

———. 1944. "Experiments on the Paranormal Cognition of Drawings: III. Steps in the Development of a Repeatable Technique." PASPR 24:3.

———. 1944. "Experiments on the Paranormal Cognition of Drawings. IV." PSPR 47:155.

———. 1934. "The Quantitative Study of Trance Personalities, Part I." PSPR 42:173.

———. 1935. "The Quantitative Study of Trance Personalities, Part II." PSPR 43:319.

———. 1937. "The Quantitative Study of Trance Personalities. Part III." PSPR 44: 189.

———. (W. Whately Smith). 1919. "'The Reality of Psychic Phenomena.'" PSPR 30:306.

"Obituary: Mr. W. Whately Carington, M.Sc." 1947. PSPR 48:197.

Carlson, D. 1969. "The Beginnings of Chester Carlson's Interest in Parapsychology." PASPR 28:5.

Carpenter, W. Boyd. 1912. "Presidential Address." PSPR 26:2.

Carr, J. D. *The Life of Sir Arthur Conan Doyle.* New York: Harper & Bros., 1949.

Carrington, H. n.d. "An Instrumental Test of the Independence of a 'Spirit Control'." *Bulletin I,* American Psychical Institute.

———. *The Case for Psychic Survival.* New York: Citadel Press, 1957.

———. 1925. "Experiences in Psychic Photography." JASPR 19:258, 263.

———. *The Problems of Psychical Research.* New York: Dodd, Mead Co., 1921.

———. *Physical Phenomena of Spiritualism.* New York: Herbert B. Turner, 1907, republished 1920.

———. 1907. "An Examination of Mons. Aksakoff's 'Case of Partial Dematerialization of a Medium's Body'." PASPR 1:131.

Carrington, H., and F. Nandor. *The Story of the Poltergeist down the Centuries.* London: Rider & Co., 1953.

Carrington, H., with S. J. Muldoon. *The Phe-*

*nomena of Astral Projection.* London: Rider & Co., 1951.

———. *The Projection of the Astral Body.* London: Rider & Co., 1929. Republished New York: Samuel Weiser, 1973.

Carrington, H., with E. Feilding, and W. W. Baggally. 1909. "Report on a Series of Sittings with Eusapia Palladino." PSPR 23:309.

Carrithers, W. A., Jr. 1962. "Madame Blavatsky: 'One of the World's Great Jokers'." JASPR 56:131.

"Case of the Will of James L. Chaffin." 1927. PSPR 36:517.

"Case: Forecasts of Horse Races." 1947. JSPR 34:63.

"The Cases of Mr. Moss and Mr. Munnings." 1926. JSPR 23:71.

"Cases Received by the Literary Committee." 1885. JSPR 1:487.

Cassirer, M. 1985. "Helen Duncan: A Reassessment." JSPR 53:138.

———. 1983. "The Fluid Hands of Eusapia Palladino." JSPR 52:105.

Cassoli, P. "Parapsychology in Italy." *Proceedings of an International Conference Parapsychology Today: A Geographic View.* New York: Parapsychology Foundation, 1971, p. 187.

Casteñeda, C. *The Teachings of Don Juan.* New York: Simon & Schuster, 1968.

Cavanna, R., and E. Servadio. *ESP Experiments with LSD 25 and Psilocybin: A Methodological Approach* (Parapsychological Monograph No. 5). New York: Parapsychology Foundation, 1964.

Cavendish, R., ed. *Encyclopedia of the Unexplained.* New York: McGraw Hill, 1974.

Cerminara, G. 1973. "Missie the Psychic Dog of Denver." *Psychic* 5(1):37.

Chari, C. T. K. "Some Generalized Theories and Models of Psi: A Critical Evaluation." In B. Wolman, ed. *Handbook of Parapsychology.* New York: Van Nostrand Reinhold Co., 1977, p. 803.

———. 1973. "Regurgitation, Mediumship and Yoga." JSPR 47:156.

Chauvin, R. 1988. "'Built upon Water' Psychokinesis and Water Cooling: An Exploratory Study." JSPR 55:10.

———. 1986. "A PK Experiment with Mice." JSPR 53:348.

Chauvin, R. (Duval, P.), and E. Montredon (J. Mayer). 1968a. "ESP Experiments with Mice." JP 32:153.

———. 1968b. "Further Psi Experiments with Mice." JP 32:260.

(Mrs. Chenoweth). PASPR Vols. 3, 4, 5, 6, 7, 9, 14 (1909–1920).

Cherry, C. "Obituary Henry Habberly Price 1899–1984."JSPR 53:197.

Child, I. L. "Criticism in Parapsychology." In S. Krippner, ed. *Advances in Parapsychological Research 5.* Jefferson, NC: McFarland, 1987.

———. 1985. "The Question of ESP in Dreams." *American Psychologist* 40 (11):1219.

———. "Implications of Parapsychology for Psychology." In S. Krippner, ed. *Advances in Parapsychological Research 4.* Jefferson, NC: McFarland, 1984.

———. *Humanistic Psychology and the Research Tradition.* New York: Wiley, 1973.

Christopher, M. *Mediums, Mystics and the Occult.* New York: Thomas Y. Crowell, 1975.

Clark, W. H. "Parapsychology and Religion." In B. Wolman, ed. *Handbook of Parapsychology.* New York: Van Nostrand Reinhold, 1977, p. 769.

———. *Chemical Ecstacy: Psychedelic Drugs and Religion.* New York: Sheed and Ward, 1969.

Coe, M. R. J. 1958. "Fire-Walking and Related Behavior." JASPR 52:85. (Originally published in *The Psychological Record* in 1957).

Cohen, D. *The Encyclopedia of Ghosts.* New York: Dodd Mead, 1984.

Coleman, M. H. 1987. "Correspondence." JSPR 54:158.

———. "William Crookes to Charles Blackburn." JSPR 47:306.

———. 1956. "Borley Rectory: Some Criticisms." JSPR 38:249.

"A Fictitious Communicator." 1924. JSPR 21:306.

Constable, T. J. "Orgone Energy Engineering through the Cloudbuster." In J. White, and S. Krippner. *Future Science.* Garden City, NY: Doubleday, 1977, pp. 404–419.

Cook, E. W. 1983. *"SORRAT: A History of the Neihardt Psychokinesis Experiments, 1961–1981."* JASPR 77:92.

Coover, J. E. *Experiments in Psychical Research.* Palo Alto, CA.: Stanford University Press, 1917.

Cornell, A. D. 1959. "An Experiment in Apparitional Observation and Findings." JSPR 40:120.

Cornell, A. D. and A. G. Gauld. *Poltergeists.* London: Rouledge & Kegan Paul, 1979.

———. 1961. "The Geophysical Theory of Poltergeists." JSPR 41:148.

———. 1960. "A Fenland Poltergeist." JSPR 40:343.

*A Course in Miracles.* Tiburon, CA: Foundation for Inner Peace, 1975.

Cox, W. E. 1985. "An Invited Rebuttal to George Hansen's 'Critique' of Mr. Cox's Mini-Lab Experiments." *Archaeus* 3:25.

———. "Selected Static-PK Phenomena under Exceptional Conditions of Security." In R. A. White and R. S. Broughton, eds. *Research in Parapsychology, 1983.* Metuchen, NJ: The Scarecrow Press, 1984, pp. 107–110.

———. 1979. "A Comparison of Two Machines Using Water Bubbles as PK Target." JP 43:44.

———. 1963. "Reviews. Psychic: The Story of Peter Hurkos." JSPR 57:44.

———. 1961. "Introductory Comparative Analysis of Some Poltergeist Cases". JASPR 55:47.

———. 1957. "The Influence of 'Applied Psi' upon the Sex of Offspring." JSPR 39:65.

———. 1951. "The Effect of PK on the Placement of Falling Objects." JP 15:40.

Cranston, S. L., and J. Head, eds. *Reincarnation.* New York: Causeway Books, 1967.

Crawford, W. J. *The Psychic Structures of the Goligher Circle.* London: John Watkins, 1921.

———. *The Reality of Psychic Phenomena.* London: John Watkins, 1916.

Crookall, R. *The Study and Practice of Astral Projection.* New Hyde Park, New York: University Books, 1966.

———. *More Astral Projections.* London: Aquarian Press, 1964.

———. *The Supreme Adventure.* London: James Clarke Co., 1961.

Crookes, W. 1896. "Address by the President." PSPR 12:338.

———. 1889. "Notes of Seances with D. D. Home." PSPR 6:98.

———. *Researches in Spiritualism.* London: J. Burns, 1875.

———. *Researches in the Phenomena of Spiritualism.* London, 1874.

Cross, J. W. *George Eliot's Life as Related in Her Letters and Journals.* New York: Harper Bros., 1885.

Cummins, G. *Swan on a Black Sea: A Study in Automatic Writing.* London: Routledge and Kegan Paul, 1965.

Dale, L. A. 1946. "The Psychokinetic Effect: The First A.S.P.R. Experiment." JASPR 40:123.

———. 1941. "Henri Bergson, Realist." JASPR 35: 57.

Dale, L. A., and R. A. White. *Parapsychology: Sources of Information.* Metuchen, NJ: Scarecrow Press, 1973.

Dale, L. A., and G. Murphy. *Challenge of Psychical Research.* New York: Harper and Row, 1966.

Dale, L. A., and J. L. Woodruff. 1952. "ESP Function and the Psychogalvanic Response." JASPR 46:62.

Dale, L. A., and E. Taves. 1943. "The Midas Touch in Reverse." JASPR 37:57.

Davey, S. J. 1887. "The Possibilities of Malobservation &c. from a Practical Point of View." JSPR 3:8.

Davey, S. J., and R. Hodgson. 1887. "The Possibilities of Malobservation and Lapse of Memory from a Practical Point of View." PSPR 4:381.

Davis, A. J. *The Great Harmonia: Being a Philosophical Revelation of the Natural, Spiritual, and Celestial Universe,* 5 vols. New York and Boston: Various publishers, 1850–1855.

———. *The Principles of Nature, Her Divine Revelations, and a Voice to Mankind.* New York: S. S. Lyon and W. Fishbough, 1847.

Day, L., in collaboration with G. De La Warr. *New Worlds Beyond the Atom.* London: Vincent Stewart Publishers, 1956.

Dean, E. D. *The Mystery of Healing: Still a Mystery after 60,000 Years.* N.Y.: Search, 1987.

———. "Precognition and Retrocognition." In E. D. Mitchell (J. White, ed.) *Psychic Exploration.* New York: Putnam's, 1974, pp. 173–178.

———. "The Kirlian Aura." In S. Krippner and D. Rubin, eds. *The Energies of Consciousness.* New York: Doubleday, 1974, Chapter 5.

———. 1966. "Plethysmographic Recordings as ESP Responses." *International Journal of Neurospsychiatry* 2:439.

Dean, E. D., with J. Mihalasky, L. Schroeder and S. Ostrander. *Executive ESP.* Englewood Cliffs, NJ: Prentice Hall, 1974.

Delanne, G. *Documents pour Servir à l'Etude de la Reincarnation.* Paris: Editions de la B.P.S., 1924.

———. *L'Ame Est Immortelle.* (trans. into English as *Evidence for a Future Life,* New York: G. P. Putnam's Sons, 1904).

———. "La Psychologie Experimental." In P. Janet, ed. *IVe Congrès International de Psychologie.* Paris: Felix Alcan, 1901.

De La Warr, G., in colloboration with L. Day. *New Worlds Beyond the Atom.* London: Vincent Stewart Publishers, 1956.

Demarest, D., and C. Taylor, eds. *The Dark Virgin.* New York: Coley Taylor Inc. (n.d.)

Denniston, D., and P. McWilliams. *The TM Book.* New York: Warner Books, 1975.

Deren, M. *Divine Horsemen: The Living Gods of Haiti.* London: Thames & Hudson, 1953.

Dessoir, M. 1889. "Die Parapsychologie. Eine Entgegnung auf den Artikel 'Der Prophet'." *Sphinx* 7:341.

———. 1886. "Experiments in Muscle-Reading and Thought-Transference." PSPR 4:111.

Dettore, U., ed. *L'Uomo e l'Ignoto.* Milan: Armenia, 1979. 5 vols.

———. *L'Altro Regno.* Milan: Bompiani, 1973.

Dingwall, E. J. "The Need for Responsibility in Parapsychology." In P. Kurtz, ed. *A Skeptic's Handbook of Parapsychology.* Buffalo, NY: Prometheus Books, 1985.

———. 1970. "Responsibility in Parapsychology." *Parapsychology Review* 1:13.

Dingwall: ———. 1970. "D.D. Home and the Mystery of Iniquity." JSPR 45:31.

———. "Introduction." In F. Podmore, *Mediums of the Nineteenth Century.* New Hyde Park, NY: University Books, 1963.

———. "Introduction." In E. Feilding, *Sittings with Eusapia Palladino and Other Studies.* New Hyde Park, NY: University Books, 1963.

———. *Some Human Oddities,* New Hyde Park, NY: University Books, 1962.

———. *Very Peculiar People.* New Hyde Park, NY: University Books, 1962.

———. 1936. "Correspondence. The Mediumship of Mirabelli." JSPR 29:169.

———. *Ghosts and Spirits of the Ancient World.* London: Kegan Paul, 1930.

———. 1930. "An Amazing Case: The Mediumship of Carlos Mirabelli." *Psychic Research* 24(7):296.

———. 1926. "A Report of a Series of Sittings with Mr. Willy Schneider." PSPR 36:1.

———. 1926. "A Report on a Series of Sittings with the Medium Margery." PSPR 36:79.

———. 1924. "An Experiment with Polish Medium Stefan Ossowiecki." JSPR 21:259.

———. 1924. "Telekinetic and Teleplastic Mediumship." PSPR 34:324.

———. 1922. "Einer Nielsen." JSPR 20:327.

———. 1922. "The Hypothesis of Fraud." PSPR 32:309.

———. 1922. "Physical Phenomena Recently Observed with the Medium Willy Sch. at Munich." JSPR 20:359.

———. 1921. "The Psychic Structures at the Goligher Circle." PSPR 32:147.

Dingwall, E. J., K. M. Goldney, and T. H. Hall. 1956. "The Haunting of Borley Rectory: A Critical Survey of the Evidence." PSPR 55:1.

Di Simone, G. *Rapporto dalla Dimensione X.* Rome: Edizioni Mediterranee 1973–1986.

———. *Dialoghi con la Dimensione X. (Beyond Death).* Rome: Edizioni Mediterranee, 1981.

Dodds, E. R. 1972. "Gilbert Murray's Last Experiments." PSPR 55:371.

———. 1971. "Supernormal Phenomena in Classical Antiquity." PSPR 55:189.

———. 1962. "Experimental Research at the Universities and in the Society." PSPR 53:247.

———. 1957. "Obituary. Gilbert Murray, O.M." JSPR 39:150.

———. 1934. "Why I Do Not Believe in Survival." PSPR 42:147.

Dommeyer, F. C., and R. A. White. 1963. "Psychical Research in Colleges and Universities, I, II and III." JASPR 57:3, 57:55, 57:136.

Donnelly, K. F., and A. Tanous. *Is Your Child Psychic?* New York: Macmillan Publishing Co., 1979.

Donoghue, D., ed. *Memoirs.* London: n.p., 1972.

Donovan, W. D. C. *The Evidences of Spiritualism.* Melbourne, Australia: Terry, 1882.

Douglas, A. *Extra-Sensory Powers.* New York: Overlook Press, 1977.

Doyle, A. C. *The Edge of the Unknown.* New York: Berkley, 1968 (originally published 1930).

———. *The Complete Sherlock Holmes.* Garden City, NY: Garden City Publishing Co., 1938.

———. "The Psychic Question as I See It." In Murchison, C., ed. *The Case for and against Psychical Belief.* Worcester, Mass.: Clark University, 1927.

———. *The History of Spiritualism.* London: Cassele & Co., 1926. 2 Vols.

———. *The Case for Spirit Photography.* New York: George H. Doran Co., 1923.

———. *The Coming of the Fairies.* New York: George H. Doran Co., 1921 (Reprinted New York: Weiser, 1975).

Driesch, H. "Die wissenschaftliche Parapsychologie der Gegenwart." In H. de Geymuller, ed. *Swedenborg und die übersinnliche Welt.* Stuttgart: Deutsche Verlagsanstalt, 1936.

———. 1930. "The Mediumship of Mirabelli." *Psychic Research* 24(11): 486.

———. "Psychical Research and Philosophy." In C. Murchison, ed. *The Case for and Against Psychical Belief.* Worcester, Mass: Clark University, 1927.

———. "Presidential Address: Psychical Research and Established Science." 1926. PSPR 36:171.

Druckman, D., and J. A. Swets, eds. *Enhancing Human Performance. Issues, Theories, and Techniques.* Washington, D.C.: National Academy of Sciences, 1988.

Ducasse, C. J. 1962. "What Would Constitute Conclusive Evidence of Survival After Death?" JASPR 41:401.

———. *A Critical Examination of the Belief in a Life After Death.* Springfield, Ill: Charles C. Thomas, 1961.

———. 1958. "Physical Phenomena in Psychical Research." JASPR 52:3.

———. 1954. "Some Questions Concerning Psychical Phenomena." JASPR 48:3.

———. *Nature, Mind and Death.* La Salle, Ill: Open Court Pub. Co., 1951.

Duke, D. M., and L. B. Williams. "Qualities of Free Response Targets and Their Relationship to Psi Performance." In W. G. Roll, ed. *Research in Parapsychology 1979.* Metuchen, NJ: The Scarecrow Press, 1980.

Dunne, B. J., R. G. Jahn, and R. D. Nelson. 1985. *Princeton Engineering Anomalies Research.* Technical Note PEAR 85003.

Dunne, B. J., and R. G. Jahn. "Analytical Judging Procedure for Remote Perception Experiments." In W. G. Roll and J. Beloff, eds. (J. McAllister, ass't ed.) *Research in Parapsychology, 1980.* Metuchen, NJ: Scarecrow Press, 1981.

Dunne, J. W. *An Experiment with Time* New York: MacMillan, 1927.

Dunraven, Earl of. 1924. "Experiments in Spiritualism with D. D. Home." PSPR 35:1.

Duplessis, Y. 1985. "Dermo-Optical Sensitivity and Perception." *International Journal of Biosocial Research* 7(2):76.

———. *La Vision Parapsychologique des Couleurs.* Paris: Epi, 1974.

Duval, P. (Chauvin, R.), and E. Montredon (J. Mayer). "ESP Experiments with Mice." In J. B. Rhine, ed. *Progress in Parapsychology.* Durham, NC: The Parapsychology Press, 1971, p. 17.

Eastman, M. 1964. "Apparitions and Precognition." JSPR 42:303.

Ebon, M. *Psychic Warfare: Threat or Illusion.* New York: McGraw Hill, 1983.

———. 1982. "In Memoriam—Ashby Remembered." *Spiritual Frontiers* 14 (1):3.

———. *The Evidence for Life After Death.* New York: New American Library, 1977.

———. *The Satan Trap.* Garden City, New York: Doubleday & Co., 1976.

———. *The Devil's Bride: Exorcism, Past and Present.* New York: Harper & Row, 1974.

———. 1974. "Exorcism beyond the Chaos." *Psychic* 5(6):50.

———. *They Knew the Unknown.* New York: New American Library, 1971.

———. *Prophecy in Our Time.* New York: The New American Library, 1968.

Edge, H. L. 1985. "The Dualist Tradition in Parapsychology." *European Journal of Parapsychology* 53.

———. 1985. "Parapsychology and Atomism." JSPR 53:78.

———. 1978. "A Philosophical Justification for the Conformance Behavior Model." JASPR 72:215.

———. "The Place of Paradigms in Parapsychology." In B. Shapin and L. Coly, eds. *The Philosophy of Parapsychology.* New York: Parapsychology Foundation, 1977.

Edge, H. L., R. L. Morris, J. Palmer, and J. Rush. *Foundations of Parapsychology: Exploring the Boundaries of Human Capability.* London: Routledge & Kegan Paul, 1986.

Edge, H. L., and J. M. O. Wheatley, eds. *Philosophical Dimensions of Parapsychology.* Springfield, IL: Charles Thomas, 1976.

Edwards, H. *The Healing Intelligence.* New York: Taplinger, 1971.

———. *Evidence for Spirit Healing.* London: Psychic Press, 1952.

Ehrenwald, J. "An Autobiographic Fragment." In R. Pilkington, ed. *Men and Women of Parapsychology.* Jefferson, NC: McFarland, 1987.

———. *Anatomy of Genius.* New York: Human Sciences Press, 1984.

———. *The ESP Experience: A Psychiatric Validation.* New York: Basic Books, 1978.

———. 1975. "The Devil's Bride." JASPR 69:292.

———. 1968. "Human Personality and the Nature of Psi Phenomena." JASPR 62:366.

———. 1957. "The Telepathy Hypothesis and Doctrinal Compliance in Psychotherapy." *American Journal of Psychotherapy.* 11:359.

———. *New Dimensions of Deep Analysis.* New York: Grune and Stratton, 1954 (2nd ed. New York: Arno Press, 1975).

———. *Telepathy and Medical Psychology.* New York: W.W. Norton, 1948.

Eilbert, L., and G. Schmeidler. 1959. "A Study of Certain Psychological Factors in Relation to ESP Performance." JP 14:53.

Eisenberg, D., with L. T. Wright. *Encounters with Qi.* New York: W.W. Norton, 1985.

Eisenbud, J. "My Life with the Paranormal." In R. Pilkington, ed. *Men and Women of Parapsychology: Personal Reflections.* Jefferson, NC: McFarland, 1987.

———. *Paranormal Foreknowledge: Problems and Perplexities.* New York: Human Sciences Press, 1982.

———. 1982. "Some Investigations of Claims of PK Effects on Metal: The Denver Experiments." JASPR 76:218.

———. 1975. "On Ted Serios' Alleged 'Confession.'" JASPR 69:94.

———. 1973. "A Transatlantic Experiment in Precognition with Gerard Croiset." JASPR 67:1.

———. 1972. "Discussion of Professor Flew's Paper. 1. the Dilemma of the Survival Data." JASPR 66:145.

———. *The World of Ted Serios.* New York: Morrow, 1967.

———. 1946. "Telepathy and Problems of Psychoanalysis." *Psychoanalytic Quarterly* 15:32 (Reprinted in G. Devereux, ed. *Psychoanalysis and the Occult.* New York: International Universities Press, 1953.)

Eisenbud, J., with J. G. Pratt, and I. Stevenson. 1981. "Distortions in the Photographs of Ted Serios." JASPR 75:143.

"Eleven Lourdes Miracles. by D. J. West." 1957. JSPR 39:90.

Eliade, M. *Shamanism: Archaic Techniques of Ecstacy.* Princeton, NJ: Princeton University Press, 1966.

Ellis, D. J. *The Mediumship of the Tape Recorder.* Pulborough, West Sussex, England: D. J. Ellis, 1978.

Ellison, A. J. *The Reality of the Paranormal.* New York: Dodd, Mead, 1988.

———. 1982. "Psychical Research: After 100 Years What Do We Really Know?" PSPR 56:384.

———. "Kirlian Photography." In I. Grattan-Guinness, ed. *Psychical Research—A Guide to Its History, Principles and Practices.* London: Aquarian Press, 1982.

———. 1978. "Mind, Belief and Psychical Research." PSPR 56:236.

———. 1962. "Some Recent Experiments in Psychic Perceptivity." JSPR 41:355.

Ellison, J., and A. Ford. *The Life beyond Death.* New York: Berkley Publishing Corp., 1971.

Ellwood, R. S., Jr. "The American Theosophical Synthesis." In H. Kerr and C. L. Crow, eds. *The Occult in America.* Urbana and Chicago, IL: University of Illinois Press, 1983.

Esser, A. H., J. Forster, and L. LeShan. 1969. "A Transatlantic 'Chair Test'." JSPR 45:167.

Estabrooks, G. H. 1927. "A Contribution to Experimental Telepathy." *Bulletin of the Boston Society of Psychic Research* 5:1. Reprinted in 1961 in JP 25:190.

Evans, C. C., and E. Osborn. 1952. "An Experiment in the Electroencephalography of Mediumistic Trance." JSPR 36:578.

Evans, F. W. *Ann Lee, Shakers and Shakerism, a Compendium of the Origin, History, Rules and Regulations, Government and Doctrines of the United Society of Believers in Christ's Second Appearing.* New York: D. Appleton & Co., 1859.

Evans, J. W. *The Life and Work of Robin John Tillyard 1881–1937.* St. Lucia: University of Queensland Press, 1963.

Evans-Wentz, W. Y. *The Tibetan Book of the Dead.* New York: Oxford University Press, 1960.

"Extract from J. E. de Mirville's 'Des Esprits et de Leurs Manifestations Fluidiques'." 1899. PSPR 14:373.

Eysenck, H. J. 1967. "Personality and Extrasensory Perception." JSPR 44:55.

Eysenck, H. J. and C. Sargent, *Know Your Own PSI-IQ.* New York: World Almanac Publications, 1983.

———. *Explaining the Unexplained.* London: Weidenfield and Nicholson, 1982.

Faraday, M. Letter to the *Times,* June 30, 1853.

Farmer, J. S. *'Twixt Two Worlds: A Narrative of the Life and Work of William Eglinton.* London: n.p., 1886.

"Father Thurston's Work in Psychical Research." 1939. JSPR 31:118.

Feather, S. R. 1983. "Something Different: A Biographical Sketch of Louisa E. Rhine." JP 47:293.

Feilding, E. *Sittings with Eusapia Palladino & Other Studies.* New York: University Books, 1963.

———. 1915. "Note on the English Sittings with Miss Tomczyk." JSPR 17:28.

Feilding, E., W. W. Baggally, and H. Carrington. 1909. "Report on a Series of Sittings with Eusapia Palladino." PSPR 23:309.

Feilding, E., and W. Marriott. 1911. "Report on a Series of Sittings with Eusapia Palladino at Naples." PSPR 25:57.

Feola, J., and K. R. Rao. "Alpha Rhythm and ESP in a Free Response Situation." In W. G. Roll *et al.*, eds. *Research in Parapsychology 1972.* Metuchen, N.J.: Scarecrow Press, 1973.

Fischer, O. 1926. "Zür Nomenklatur und Systematik des Okkultismus." *Zeitschrift für Parapsychologie* 1:304.

Fisher, R. A. 1929. "The Statistical Method in Psychical Research." PSPR 39:189.

Fisk, G. W. 1953. "A Dual ESP Experiment with Clock Cards." JSPR 37:185.

Fisk, G. W., and D. J. West. 1956. "ESP and Mood: Report of a 'Mass' Experiment." JSPR 38:320.

Fisk, G. W., W. H. Salter, and H. H. Price. 1953. "G. N. M. Tyrrell and his Contributions to Psychical Research." JSPR 37:63.

FitzSimons, R. *Death and the Magician: The Mystery of Houdini.* New York: Atheneum, 1980.

Flammarion, C. 1935. "The Unknown of Yesterday is the Truth of Tomorrow." JASPR 29:339.

———. *Death and Its Mystery: Before Death.* New York: Century Co., 1921.

Flew, A. Foreword to A. S. Berger. *Aristocracy of the Dead.* Jefferson, NC: McFarland & Co., 1987.

———. *The Logic of Mortality.* Oxford: Blackwell, 1987.

———. 1972. "Is There a Case for Disembodied Survival?" JASPR 66:129.

———. *A New Approach to Psychical Research.* London: C. A. Watts, 1953.

Flores, A. C., and M. G. de Treviño. 1985. "Kirlian Photography and Pregnancy." *Psi Research* 4 (3,4): 232.

Flournoy, T. *Esprits et Médiums.* Geneva: Libraire Kundig, 1911.

———. *From India to the Planet Mars.* New York: Harper, 1901.

Fodor, N. *Between Two Worlds.* New York: Paperback Library, 1964.

———. *The Haunted Mind: A Psychoanalyst Looks at the Supernormal.* New York: Garrett Publications, 1959.

———. *On the Trail of the Poltergeist.* New York: Citadel Press, 1958.

———. *New Approaches to Dream Interpretation.* New York: Citadel Press, 1951.

———. 1938. "Letter from England—The Ghost of Lawrence of Arabia." JASPR 32:311.

———. 1938. "A Letter from England—The Man Who Heard the Banshee." JASPR 32:286.

———. *The Mysterious People.* London: Rider, 1935.

———. *Encyclopedia of Psychic Science.* London: Arthurs Press, 1934.

Fodor, N., and H. Carrington. *The Story of the Poltergeist down the Centuries.* London: Rider, 1953.

Ford A. *Nothing So Strange.* New York: Harper & Bros., 1958.

Ford A., with J. Ellison. *The Life beyond Death.* New York: Berkley Publishing Corp., 1971.

Forster, J. *The Life of Charles Dickens.* London: n.p., 1874. 3 Vols.

Fort, C. *Lo!* New York: Dover, n.d. Originally published 1931.

———. *New Lands.* New York: Ace Books, n.d. Originally published New York: Boni & Liverwright, 1923.

———. *The Book of the Damned.* New York: Dover, n.d. Originally published 1919.

Forwald, H. *Mind, Matter and Gravitation: A Theoretical and Experimental Study. Parapsychological Monographs No. 11.* New York: Parapsychology Foundation, 1970.

———. 1955. "A Study of Psychokinesis and Physical Conditions." JP 19:133.

———. 1952. "A Continuation of the Experiments in Placement PK." JP 16:273.

———. 1952. "A Further Study of the PK Placement Effect." JP 16:59.

Forwald, H., and R. A. McConnell. 1967. "Psychokinetic Placement: I. A Re-examination of the Forwald-Durham Experiment." JP 31:51.

———. 1968. "Psychokinetic Placement: III. Cube-Releasing Devices." JP 32:9.

Forwald, H., and J. G. Pratt. 1958. "Confirmation of the PK Placement Effect." JP 22:1.

Fox, O. *Astral Projection: A Record of Out-of-the Body Experiences.* New Hyde Park, NY: University Books, 1962.

"Frances P. Bolton Dies." 1977. *Parapsychology Review* 8 (2): 1.

Frazer, J. G. *The Golden Bough.* New York: Macmillan Co., 1951.

Freud, S. 1912. "A Note on the Unconscious in Psycho-Analysis." PSPR 26:312.

———. "Dreams and Telepathy." In G. Devereux, ed. *Psychoanalysis and the Occult.* New York: International Universities Press, 1953. Originally published 1922.

———. "The Occult Significance of Dreams." In *Psychoanalysis and the Occult,* New York: International Universities Press, 1953. Originally published 1925.

———. "New Introductory Lectures on Psycho-Analysis." In *Psychoanalysis and the Occult,* New York: International Universities Press, 1953. Originally published 1933.

Friedrich, O. 1987. "New Age Harmonies." *Time* 130 (23):62.

Fujiwara, S. *Senrigan Jikkenroku* (Record on Experiments of Clairvoyance). Tokyo: Dainippon Tosho, 1911.

Fukurai, T. *Toshi to Nensha.* Tokyo: Hobunkan, 1913, republished as *Clairvoyance and Telepathy.* London: Rider, 1930.

Fuller, J. G. *The Airmen Who Would Not Die.* New York: G. P. Putnam's Sons, 1979.

Gardner, F. L. *Fairies.* London: Theosophical Publishing House, 1945.

Gardner, M. *How Not to Test a Psychic: A Study of the Unusual Experiments with Renowned Clairvoyant Pavel Stepanek.* Buffalo, NY: Prometheus Books, 1989.

———. "Parapsychology and Quantum Mechanics." In P. Kurtz, ed. *A Skeptic's Handbook of Parapsychology.* Buffalo, NY: Prometheus Books, 1985.

———. *Fads and Fallacies in the Name of Science.* New York: Dover, 1957.

Garland, J., and R. Montgomery. *Ruth Montgomery: Herald of the New Age.* Westminster, MD: Random House, 1986.

Garrett, E. J. *My Life as a Search for the Meaning of Mediumship.* New York: Oquaga Press, 1938.

———. *Awareness.* New York: Creative Press, 1943.

———. *Many Voices: The Autobiography of a Medium.* New York: Putnam, 1968.

Gasteiger, E. L., K. A. Horowitz, and D. C. Lewis. 1975. "Plant 'Primary Perception': Electrophysiological Unresponsiveness to Brine Shrimp Killing." *Science* 189:47.

Gauld A. 1987. "Recollections of E. J. Dingwall." JSPR 54:230.

———. 1983. "Andrew Lang as Psychical Researcher." JSPR 52:161.

———. *Mediumship and Survival.* London: Heinemann, 1982.

———. "Discarnate Survival." In B. Wolman, ed. *Handbook of Parapsychology.* New York: Van Nostrand Reinhold Company, 1977.

———. *The Founders of Psychical Research.* New York: Schocken Books, 1968.

Gauld, A., and A. D. Cornell. *Poltergeists.* London: Routledge & Kegan Paul, 1979.

———. 1961. "The Geophysical Theory of Poltergeists." JSPR 41:148.

———. 1960. "A Fenland Poltergeist." JSPR 40:34.

Gauquelin, M. *Cosmic Influence on Human Behavior.* N.p.: Garnstone Press, 1974.

Gavilan, F. F. 1978. "Los Factores Motivacionales del Investigador en Parapsicología." *Psi Comunicación* 7–8:9.

Gay, K. 1957. "The Case of Edgar Vandy." JSPR 39:1.

Gay, K., and G. W. Lambert. 1952. "The Dieppe Raid Case." JSPR 36:607.

Geley, G. *L'Ectoplasmie et la Clairvoyance.* Paris: Alcan, 1924.

———. *From the Conscious to the Unconscious.* New York: Harper and Bros., n.d. (originally published 1919.)

———. 1923. "Experiments in Materialization." JASPR 17:233; 17:423; 17:555; 17:630; 17:677.

Geller, J., and D. H. Weiner. 1984. "Motivation as the Universal Container: Conceptual Problems in Parapsychology." JP 48:27.

Gengerelli, J., and T. S. Moss. 1967. "Telepathy and Emotional Stimuli: A Controlled Experiment." *Journal of Abnormal Psychology* 72:341.

Ghiselin, B. *The Creative Process.* New York: The New American Library, 1952.

Gibbes, E. B. 1939. "Influenced or Inspirational Writing." JASPR 33: 271.

Giesler, P. V. 1988. "Kenneth J. Batcheldor: Friend, Colleague and Teacher." *ASPR Newsletter* 14(4):32.

———. 1986. "GESP Testing of Shamanic Cultists: Three Studies and Evaluation of Dramatic Upsets during Testing." JP 50:123.

———. 1984. "Parapsychological Anthropology: I. Multi-Method Approaches to the Study of Psi in the Field Setting." JASPR 78:289.

———. 1984 and 1985. "Batcheldorian Psychodynamics in the Ubanda Ritual Trance Consultation: Part I and II." *Parapsychology Review* 15(6):5 and 16(1):11.

———. 1985. "Parapsychological Anthropology: II. A Multi-Method Study of Psi and Psi-Related Processes in the Umbanda Ritual Trance Consultation." JASPR 79:114.

Glanvil, J. *Saducismus Triumphatus.* London: Tuckyr, 1700.

Goodrich-Freer, A. 1889. "Recent Experiments in Crystal Vision." PSPR 5:486.

Grad, B. "Experiences and Opinions of an Unconventional Scientist." In R. Pilkington, ed. *Men and Women of Parapsychology: Personal Reflections.* Jefferson, NC: McFarland, 1987.

———. 1981. "Paranormal Healing and Life Energy." *ASPR Newsletter* 7:21.

———. "The Biological Effects of the 'Laying-on of Hands' in Animals and Plants: Implications for Biology." In G. Schmeidler, ed. *Parapsychology: Its Relation to Physics, Biology, Psychology and Psychiatry.* Metuchen, NJ: Scarecrow Press, 1976.

———. 1965. "Some Biological Effects of the 'Laying on of Hands'." JASPR 59:95.

Grad, B., with R. J. Cadoret and G. I. Paul. 1961. "An Unorthodox Method of Treatment of Wound Healing in Mice." *International Journal of Parapsychology* 3:5.

Grant, K. "Aleister Crowley (1875–1947)." In R. Cavendish, ed. *Encyclopedia of the Unexplained.* New York: McGraw Hill, 1974.

Grattan-Guinness, I. ed., *Psychical Research—A Guide to Its History, Principles and Practices.* London: Aquarian Press, 1982.

Green, C. *Lucid Dreams.* Oxford: Institute of Psychophysical Research, 1968.

———. *Out-of-Body Experiences. Proceedings of the Institute of Psychophysical Research.* 1968.

———. 1967. "Ecsomatic Experiences and Related Phenomena." JSPR 44:111.

———. 1960. "Analysis of Spontaneous Cases." PSPR 53:97.

Green, H. J. M. "Correspondence." JSPR 45:428.

Greenwood, J. A. 1940. "A Reply to Dr. Feller's Critique." JP 4.

———. 1939. "Some Mathematical Problems for

Future Consideration Suggested by ESP Research." JP 3.

———. 1937. "Mathematical Techniques Used in ESP Research." JP 1.

Greenwood, J. A., with J. G. Pratt, J. B. Rhine, B. M. Smith, and C. E. Stuart. *Extra-sensory Perception after Sixty Years.* New York: Henry Holt, 1940. (Republished Boston: Bruce Humphries, 1966 with a new foreword by J. B. Rhine).

"Joseph A. Greenwood 1906–1988." *FRNM Bulletin* 37:2, Spring 1988.

Gregory, A. *The Strange Case of Rudi Schneider.* Metuchen, NJ: Scarecrow Press. 1985.

———, ed. 1982. "London Experiments with Matthew Manning." PSPR 56:283.

———. 1981. "Psychical Research as a Social Activity." JSPR 51:789.

———. 1979. "Cyril Burt—Psychologist. By L. S. Hearnshaw." JSPR 50:249.

Gregory, C. C. L., and A. Kohsen. 1958. "A Cosmological Approach to a Theory of Mental Images." PSPR 52:33.

———. *Physical and Psychical Research.* London: Omega Press, 1954.

Gregory, E., and M. Anderson. 1959. "A Two-year Program of Tests for Clairvoyance and Precognition with a Class of Public School Pupils." JP 23:149.

Grensted, L. W. "Is God Evident? An Essay towards a Natural Theology. By Gerald Heard." JSPR 35:346.

Gresham, W. L. *Houdini: The Man Who Walked Through Walls.* New York: Holt, Rinehart and Winston, 1959.

Greville, T. N. E. "Some Views of Survival." In W. G. Roll, J. Beloff, R. A. White, eds. *Research in Parapsychology 1982.* Metuchen, NJ: The Scarecrow Press, 1983, p. 120.

———. 1949. "On the Number of Sets Required for Testing the Significance of Verbal Material." JP 13:137.

———. 1944. "On Multiple Matching with One Variable Deck." *Annals of Mathematical Statistics* 15:432.

———. 1941. "The Frequency Distribution of a General Matching Problem." *Annals of Mathematical Statistics* 12:350.

Gribbin, J., and S. H. Plagemann. *The Jupiter Effect.* New York: Walker, 1974.

Grof, S., and J. Halifax. *The Human Encounter with Death.* New York: E. P. Dutton, 1978.

Grosso, M. "St. Paul's *Metanoia:* An Essay in Psycho-History." In A. S. Berger and H. Thompson, eds. *Religion and Parapsychology,* New York: UTS, 1989.

———. "A Post-Modern Mythology of Death." In A. S. Berger, J. Berger, A. H. Kutscher, et al., eds. *Perspectives on Death and Dying.* Philadelphia, PA: The Charles Press, 1989.

———. *The Final Choice: Playing the Survival Game.* Walpole, New Hampshire: Stillpoint Press, 1985.

———. 1982. "Padre Pio and the Paranormal." *Christian Parapsychologist* 4(7):218.

———. 1979. "The Survival of Personality in a Mind-Dependent World." JASPR 73:367.

Grünewald, F. *Physikalisch-mediumistische Untersuchungen.* Pfullingen: Johannes Baum Verlag, 1920.

Guarino, R. 1975. "The Police and Psychics." *Psychic* 6(2):9.

von Gulat-Wellenberg with H. Rosenbusch and C. von Klinckowstroem. "1: Der physikalische Mediumismus." In M. Dessoir, ed. *Der Okkultismus in Urkunden.* Berlin: Ullstein Verlag, 1925.

"Note on the Gunther-Geffers Case." 1928. JSPR 24:306.

Gurney, E. 1889. "On Apparitions Occurring Soon after Death." PSPR 5:403.

———. 1889. "Remarks on Mr. Peirce's Rejoinder." PASPR 1:285.

———. 1888. "Note Relating to Some of the Published Experiments in Thought-Transference." PSPR 5:269.

———. 1888. "Hypnotism and Telepathy." PSPR 5:215.

———. 1884. "The Problems of Hypnotism." PSPR 2:265.

Gurney, E., F. W. H. Myers, and F. Podmore. *Phantasms of the Living.* London: Trubner, 1886.

Gurney, E., F. W. H. Myers, and W. F. Barrett. 1882. "First Report on Thought Reading." PSPR 1:13.

Guthrie, M. 1883. "Experiments in Thought-Transference." PSPR 2:24.

Haight, J., and D. H. Weiner. 1983. "Charting Hidden Channels: A Review and Analysis of Louisa E. Rhine's Case Collection Project." JP 47:303.

Halifax, J., and S. Grof. *The Human Encounter with Death.* New York: E. P. Dutton, 1978.

Hall, G. S. Preface. In A. E. Tanner, *Studies in Spiritism.* New York: D. Appleton Co., 1910.

Hall, P. F., ed. 1914. "Experiments with Mrs. Caton." JASPR 8:1.

Hall, T. H. *The Enigma of Daniel Home.* Buffalo, NY: Prometheus Books, 1984.

———. *The Strange Case of Edmund Gurney.* London: Duckworth, 1964.

———. *The Spiritualists.* New York: Helix Press, 1963 (reissued as *The Medium and the Scientist.* Buffalo, NY: Prometheus Books, 1984).

Hall, T. H., and J. L. Campbell. *Strange Things.* London: Routledge & Kegan Paul, 1968.

Hall, T. H., and E. J. Dingwall. *Four Modern Ghosts.* London: Duckworth, 1958.

Hall, T. H., E. J. Dingwall, and K. M. Goldney. 1956. "The Haunting of Borley Rectory: A Critical Survey of Evidence." PSPR 51:1.

Hallowell, A. I. "The Role of Conjuring in Saltean Society." *Publications of the Philadelphia Anthropological Society.* Philadelphia: University of Pennsylvania Press, 1942.

Hampel, R., H. Bender, H. Kury, and S. Wendlandt. 1975. "The 'Geller-effect'—An Investigation on Interviews and Questionnaires. Part 1." *Zeitschrift für Parapsychologie und Grenzgebiete der Psychologie* 17:219.

Hankey, M. 1970. "Mrs. Eileen Garrett." JSPR 45:406.

———. 1969. "Mrs. Gladys Osborne Leonard: Some Reminiscences." JSPR 45:105.

———. *James Hewat McKenzie. A Personal Memoir.* Wellingborough: Aquarian Press, 1983.

Hansel, C. E. M. *ESP: A Scientific Evaluation.* New York: Charles Scribner's Sons, 1966.

———. *ESP and Parapsychology: A Critical Reevaluation.* Buffalo, NY: Prometheus Books, 1980.

———. "The Search for a Demonstration of ESP." In P. Kurtz, ed. *A Skeptic's Handbook of Parapsychology.* Buffalo, NY: Prometheus Books, 1985, pp. 97–127.

Hansen, G. P. "Examples of a Need for Conjuring Knowledge." In D. H. Weiner and R. D. Nelson, eds. *Research in Parapsychology, 1986.* Metuchen, NJ: Scarecrow Press, 1987.

———. 1982. "Dowsing: A Review of Experimental Research." JSPR 51:343.

Hansen, G. P., and R. S. Broughton. "An Investigation of Macro-PK: The SORRAT." In W. G. Roll, J. Beloff and R. A. White, eds. *Research in Parapsychology, 1982.* Metuchen, NJ: The Scarecrow Press, 1983, pp. 115–116.

Haraldsson, E. *Modern Miracles.* New York: Fawcett Columbine, 1988.

———. 1985. "Representative National Surveys of Psychic Phenomena: Iceland, Great Britain, Sweden, USA and Gallup Multinational Survey." JSPR 53:145.

———. 1981. "Some Determinants of Belief in Psychical Phenomena." JASPR 75:297.

———. 1980. "Confirmation of the Percipient-Order Effect in a Plethysmographic Study of ESP." JP 44:105.

———. 1980. "Apparitions of the Dead: A Representative Survey in Iceland." In W. G. Roll and J. Beloff, eds. *Research in Parapsychology 1980.* Metuchen, N.J.: Scarecrow Press, 1981, pp. 3–5.

Haraldsson, P., and L. R. Gissurarson. 1989. "The Icelandic Medium Indridi Indridason." PSPR 57:1.

Haraldsson, E., and K. Osis. *At the Hour of Death.* New York: Avon Books, 1977 (Rev. ed. New York: Hastings House, 1986).

Haraldsson, E. and I. Stevenson. 1975. "A Communicator of the 'Drop In' Type in Iceland: The Case of Gudni Magnusson." JASPR 69:245.

———. 1975. "A Communicator of the 'Drop In' Type in Iceland: The Case of Runolfur Runolfsson." JASPR 69:33.

Harary, K. (Stuart Blue). "Psi as Nature." In W. G. Roll, R. L. Morris, and R. A. White, eds. *Research in Parapsychology, 1981.* Metuchen, NJ: Scarecrow Press, 1982, pp. 75–78.

———. "The Marshmallow Ghost: A Group Counseling Approach to a Case of Reported Apparitions." In W. G. Roll, R. L. Morris, and R. A. White, eds. *Research in Parapsychology, 1981.* Metuchen, NJ: Scarecrow Press, 1982, pp. 187–189.

———. "A Personal Perspective on Out-of-Body Experiences." In D. Scott Rogo, ed. *Mind Beyond the Body: The Mystery of ESP Projection.* New York: Penguin Books, 1978.

Harary, K. (Stuart Blue), and P. Weintraub. *The Free Flight Program.* New York: St. Martin's Press, 1989a.

———. *The Creative Sleep Program.* New York: St. Martin's Press, 1989b.

Harary, K., and R. Targ. 1985. "A New Approach to Forecasting Commodity Futures." *Psi Research* 5(3/4):79.

———. *The Mind Race: Understanding and Using Psychic Abilities.* New York: Villard Books, 1984.

Harding, S. E., and M. A. Thalbourne. "Transcendental Meditation, Clairvoyant Ability, and Psychological Adjustment". In W. G. Roll and J. Beloff, eds. *Research in Parapsychology 1980.* Metuchen, NJ: Scarecrow Press, 1981, p. 71.

Hardy, A. C. *The Divine Flame.* London: Collins, 1966.

———. *The Living Stream.* London: Collins, 1965.

———. 1953. "Biology and Psychical Research." PSPR 50:96.

———. 1950. "Telepathy and Evolutionary Theory." JSPR 35:225.

Hardy, A. R. Harvie and A. Koestler. *The Challenge of Chance. Experiment and Speculations.* London: Hutchinson, 1973.

Hardy J., and Searls, D. 1978. "Impressions of Elisabeth." *Theta* 6(2/3):1.

Hare, R. *Experimental Investigation of the Spirit Manifestations.* New York: Partridge & Brittan, 1855.

Harigopal, K., and P. V. K. Rao. 1979. "The Three Gunas and ESP: An Exploratory Investigation." *Journal of Indian Psychology* 2:63.

Harper, S., and C. Honorton. 1974. "Psi-Mediated Imagery and Ideation in an Experimental Procedure for Regulating Perceptual Input." JASPR 68:156.

Harrison, J. 1917. "In Memoriam—Mrs. A. W. Verrall." PSPR 29:376.

Harrison, V. 1986. "J'Accuse: An Examination of the Hodgson Report of 1885." JSPR 53:286.

Hart, H. N. *Toward a New Philosophical Basis for Parapsychological Phenomena.* Parapsychology Monographs No. 6. New York: Parapsychology Foundation, 1965.

———. *The Enigma of Survival.* Springfield, IL: Charles C. Thomas, 1959.

———. 1956. "Six Theories About Apparitions." PSPR 50:153.

———. 1955. "Traveling ESP." In *Proceedings of the First International Conference of Parapsychological Studies.* New York: Parapsychology Foundation, pp. 91–93.

———. 1953. "The Psychic Fifth Dimension." JASPR 47:3 and 47:47.

Hart, H. N., and E. B. Hart. 1933. "Visions and Apparitions Collectively and Reciprocally Perceived." PSPR 41:205.

Harvie, R., A. Hardy and A. Koestler, *The Challenge of Chance. Experiments and Speculations.* London: Hutchinson, 1973.

Hasted, J. B. *The Metal Benders.* London: Routledge & Kegan Paul, 1981.

———. 1976. "An Experimental Study of the Validity of Metal-Bending." JSPR 48:365.

Hastings, A. 1987. "Therapeutic Support for Initial Psychic Experiences." *ASPR Newsletter* 13(2):11.

———. "The Study of Channeling." In D. H. Weiner and R. D. Nelson, eds. *Research in Parapsychology 1986.* Metuchen, N.J.: Scarecrow Press, 1987, pp. 152–153.

———. 1983. "A Counseling Approach to Parapsychological Experience." *Journal of Transpersonal Psychology* 15:145.

Hastings, R. J. 1969. "An Examination of the 'Borley Report'." PSPR 55:66.

Haynes, R. "Aspects of Psychical Research." In R. Pilkington, ed. *Men and Women of Parapsychology: Personal Reflections.* Jefferson, NC: McFarland, 1987.

———. 1985/1986. "A Life-Long Look at Psi." *Theta* 13/14:14.

———. *The Society for Psychical Research 1882–1982: A History.* London: MacDonald & Co., 1982.

———. 1982. "Are Unusual Phenomena Signs of the Paranormal?" *The Christian Parapsychologist* 4(6):179.

———. 1980. "Rosalind Heywood 1895–1980." JSPR 50:521.

———. *The Seeing Eye, the Seeing I: Perception, Sensory and Extra-sensory.* New York: St. Martin's Press, 1976.

———. *Philosopher King: The Humanist Pope Benedict XIV.* London: Weidenfeld & Nicolson, 1970.

———. *The Hidden Springs: An Enquiry into Extra-Sensory Perception.* London: Hollis and Carter, 1961. (Rev. ed. pub. Boston: Little, Brown, 1972.)

Head, J., and S. L. Cranston, eds. *Reincarnation.* New York: Causeway Books, 1967.

Healy, J. 1987. "Correspondence." JSPR 53:286.

Heard, G. 1953. "A Philosophical Scrutiny of Religion. By C. J. Ducasse." JASPR 47:119.

———. *Is Another World Watching? The Riddle of the Flying Saucers.* New York: Bantam Books, 1953. Originally published Harper & Brothers, 1951.

Heard, G., and T. Besterman. 1933. "Note on an Attempt to Locate in Space the Alleged Direct Voice Observed in Sittings with Mrs Leonard." JSPR 28:84.

Hearne, K. M. T. 1984. "A Survey of Reported Premonitions and of Those Who Have Them." JSPR 52:261.

Hearnshaw, L. S. *Cyril Burt—Psychologist.* London: Hodder and Stoughton, 1979.

Heiden, K. *Der Fuehrer.* Boston: Houghton Mifflin Co., 1944.

Henry, T. S. *"Spookland!": A Record of Research and Experiment in the Much Talked of Realm of Mystery, with a Review and Criticism of the So-called Spiritualistic Phenomena of Spirit and Materialisation, and Hints and Illustrations as to the Possibility of Artificially Producing the Same.* Sydney: Maclardy, 1894.

Herbert, B., H. H. Keil, M. Ullman, J. G. Pratt. 1976. "Directly Observable Voluntary PK Effects: A Survey and Tentative Interpretation of Available Findings from Nina Kulagina and Other Known Related Cases of Recent Date." PSPR 56:197.

Hettinger, J. *Exploring the Ultra-Perceptive Faculty.* London: Rider, 1941.

———. *The Ultra Perceptive Faculty.* London: Rider, 1940.

Heymans, G., H. J. F. W. Brugmans, and A. Weinberg. "Une communication sur des expériences télépathiques au laboratoire de psychologie à Groningue." *Compte Rendu Officiel du Premier Congrès International des Recherches Psychiques* Copenhagen, 1922, p. 396.

Heywood, R. "Autobiography." In R. A. McConnell, ed. *Encounters with Parapsychology.* Pittsburgh: R. A. McConnell, 1982, pp. 58–80.

———. 1979. "Professor E. R. Dodds, D.Litt., F.B.A." JSPR 50:171.

———. 1978. "Mrs. Muriel Hankey." JSPR 49:824.

———. 1973. "G. W. Fisk and ESP." JSPR 47:24.

———. 1969. "Mrs. Gladys Osborne Leonard: A Biographical Tribute." JSPR 45:95.

———. 1969. "Obituary. The Hon. Mrs Cyril Gay." JSPR 45:92.

———. 1962. "Lord Charles Hope." JSPR 41:395.

———. *The Sixth Sense: An Enquiry into Extrasensory Perception.* London: Chatto & Windus, 1959, reissued London: Pan Books, 1971. (American edition entitled *Beyond the Reach of Sense*.)

———. *The Infinite Hive.* London: Chatto & Windus, 1964, reissued London: Pan Books, 1972. (American edition entitled *ESP: A Personal Memoir.* New York: Dutton, 1964.)

Hodgson, R. 1898. "A Further Record of Observations of Certain Phenomena of Trance." PSPR 13:284.

———. 1895. "The Value of the Evidence for Supernormal Phenomena in the Case of Eusapia Paladino." JSPR 7:36.

———. 1893. "The Defence of the Theosophists." PSPR 9:129.

———. 1893. "Indian Magic and the Testimony of Conjurers." PSPR 9:354.

———. 1892. "Mr. Davey's Imitations by Conjuring of Phenomena Sometimes Attributed to Spirit Agency." PSPR 8:252.

———. 1892. "A Record of Observations of Certain Phenomena of Trance." PSPR 8:1.

———. 1885. "An Account of Personal Investigations in India, and Discussion of the Authorship of the 'Koot Hoomi' Letters." PSPR 3:207.

Hodgson, R., and S. J. Davey. 1887. "The Possibilities of Malobservation and Lapse of Memory from a Practical Point of View." PSPR 4:381.

Hoebens, P. H. "Sense and Nonsense in Parapsychology." In K. Frazier, ed. *Science Confronts the Paranormal.* Buffalo, NY: Prometheus Books, 1986, pp. 29–39.

———. "Investigation of the Mozart of 'Psychic Sleuths'." and "Gerard Croiset and Professor Tenhaeff." In K. Frazier, ed. *Science Confronts the Paranormal.* Buffalo, NY: Prometheus Books, 1986, pp. 122–132; 133–141.

Hoebens, P. H., with M. Truzzi. "Reflections on Psychic Sleuths." In P. Kurtz, ed. *A Skeptic's Handbook of Parapsychology.* Buffalo, N.Y.: Prometheus Books, 1985.

Hoebens, P. H., with G. Hövelmann, and M. Truzzi. "Skeptical Literature on Parapsychology An Annotated Bibliography." In P. Kurtz, ed. *A Skeptic's Handbook of Parapsychology.* Buffalo, N.Y.: Prometheus Books, 1985, p. 449.

Hoffman, E(dward). *The Way of Splendor: Jewish Mysticism and Modern Psychology.* Boulder, Colorado: Shambala, 1981.

Hoffman, E. *Huna: A Beginner's Guide.* Rockport, MA: Fara Research, 1976 (Revised 1981).

Holms, A. C. *The Facts of Psychic Science and Philosophy.* London: Kegan Paul, French, Trubner, 1925.

Holt, H. *On the Cosmic Relations.* London: Williams & Margate, 1915.

Holzer, H. *Window to the Past, Exploring History through Extra Sensory Perception.* London: Leslie Frewin, 1970.

Honorton, C. 1985. "Meta-Analysis of Psi Ganzfeld Research: A Response to Hyman." JASPR 49:59.

———. 1981. "Beyond the Reach of Sense: Some Comments on C. E. M. Hansel's *ESP and Parapsychology: A Critical Re-Evaluation.*" JASPR 75:155.

———. "Science Confronts the Paranormal." In J. D. Morris, W. G. Roll, and R. L. Morris, eds. *Research in Parapsychology 1975.* Metuchen, NJ: Scarecrow Press, 1976.

———. 1971. "Automated Forced-Choice Precognition Tests with a 'Sensitive'." JASPR 65:476.

———. 1969. "Relationship Between EEG Alpha Activity and ESP Card-Guessing Performance." JASPR 63:365.

Honorton, C., and R. Berger. "A Standardized Psi-Testing System." In R. A. White and J. Solfvin, eds. *Research in Parapsychology 1984.* Metuchen, NJ: Scarecrow Press, 1985, p. 68.

Honorton, C., and S. Harper. 1974. "Psi-Mediated Imagery and Ideation in an Experimental Procedure for Regulating Perceptual Input." JASPR 68:156.

Honorton, C., S. Krippner, and M. Ullman. 1973. "A Long-Distance ESP Dream Study with the 'Grateful Dead'." *Journal of the American Society of Psychosomatic Dentistry and Medicine* 20:9.

———. 1971. "A Precognitive Dream Study with a Single Subject." JASPR 65:192.

Honorton, C., and L. Rubin. 1971. "Separating the Yins from the Yangs: An Experiment with the I Ching." *Proceedings of the Parapsychological Association* 8:6.

Hope, Lord C. 1958. "Rudi Schneider: Recollections and Comments." JSPR 39: 214.

———. 1933. "Report of a Series of Sittings with Rudi Schneider." PSPR 41:255.

Horowitz, K. A., D. C. Lewis, E. L. Gasteiger. 1975. "Plant 'Primary Perception': Electrophysiological Unresponsiveness to Brine Shrimp Killing." *Science* 189:478.

Houdini, H. "A Magician among the Spirits." In C. Murchison, ed. *The Case for and against Psychical Belief.* Spencer, MA: The Heffernan Press, 1927.

Houston, J., and R. L. Masters. *The Varieties of Psychedelic Experience.* London: Turnstone Books, 1973.

Hövelmann, G. H. "Neglected Figures in the History of Parapsychology. I. Some General Reflections." In F. W. J. J. Snel, ed. *Liber Amicorum in Honour of G. A. M. Zorab.* The Hague: Nederlandse Vereniging voor Parapsychologie, 1986, pp. 94–126.

———. 1984. "Are Psi Experiments Repeatable?" *European Journal of Paraspychology* 5:285.

———. 1983. "Cooperation Versus Competition: In Defense of Rational Argument in Parapsychology." *European Journal of Paraspychology* 4:483.

———. 1983. "Some Recommendations for the Future Practice of Parapsychology." In W. G. Roll, J. Beloff, R. A. White, eds. *Research in Parapsychology 1982.* Metuchen, N.J.: The Scarecrow Press, 1983, p. 137.

Hövelmann, G. H., with M. Truzzi, and P. H. Hoebens. "Skeptical Literature on Parapsychology An Annotated Bibliography." In P. Kurtz, ed. *A Skeptic's Handbook of Parapsychology.* Buffalo, N.Y.: Prometheus Books, 1985.

Huby, P. M. "Some Aspects of the Problem of Survival." In S. C. Thakur, ed. *Philosophy and Psychical Research.* London: Allen & Unwin, 1976.

———. 1970. "New Evidence About 'Rose Morton.'" JSPR 45:391.

Huby, P. M., and C. W. M. Wilson. 1961. "The Effects of Centrally Acting Drugs on ESP Ability in Normal Subjects." JSPR 41:60.

Hudson, T. J. *Scientific Demonstration of a Future Life.* Chicago, IL: A. C. McClurg, 1895.

———. *The Law of Psychic Phenomena.* London: G. P. Putnam's Sons, 1893.

Humphrey, B. M., C. E. Stuart, B. M. Smith, and E. McMahan. 1947. "Personality Measurements and ESP Tests with Cards and Drawings." JP 11:118.

Humphrey, B. M., J. B. Rhine, and R. L. Averill. 1945. "An Exploratory Experiment on the Effects of Caffeine upon Performance in PK Tests." JP 9:80.

Hurkos, P. *Psychic: The Story of Peter Hurkos.* London: Arthur Barker, 1962.

Huxley, A. *Heaven and Hell.* New York: Harper & Row, 1956.

———. *The Doors of Perception.* New York: Harper & Bros., 1954.

———. *The Devils of Loudun.* New York: Harper & Bros., 1952.

———. *Themes and Variations.* New York: Harper & Bros., 1950.

Hyman, R. 1986. "Parapsychological Research: A Tutorial Review and Critical Appraisal." *Proceedings of the IEEE* 74:823.

———. "Outracing the Evidence: The Muddled 'Mind Race'." In K. Frazier, ed. *Science Confronts the Paranormal.* Buffalo, NY: Prometheus Books, 1986, pp. 91–109.

———. 1985. "The Ganzfeld Psi Experiment: A Critical Appraisal." JP 49:3.

———. "Pathological Science: Towards a Proper Diagnosis and Remedy." In R. A. McConnell, ed. *Encounters with Parapsychology.* Pittsburgh, PA: R. A. McConnell, 1982, pp. 156–164.

Hynek, J. A. *The UFO Experience.* Chicago, Illinois: H. Regenery Co., 1972.

Hyslop, J. H. 1921. "A Survey of American Slate-Writing Mediumship." PSPR 15:315.

———. *Contact with the Other World.* New York: The Century Co., 1919.

———. *Life After Death: Problems of the Future Life and its Nature.* New York: E. P. Dutton Co., 1918.

———. 1912. "A Record and Discussion of Mediumistic Experiments." PASPR 6:1.

———. 1910. "A Record and Discussion of Mediumistic Experiments." PASPR 4:85–86.

———. 1909. "A Case of Veridical Hallucinations." PASPR 3:1.

———. 1909. "Editorial." JASPR 3:191.

———. 1909. "Professor Newcomb and Occultism." JASPR 5:255.

———. 1909. "Observations on the Mediumistic Records in the Thompson Case." PASPR 3:593.

———. *Psychical Research and the Resurrection.* Boston: Small, Maynard and Co., 1908.

———. 1908. "Professor Muensterberg and Dr. Hodgson." JASPR 2:23.

———. 1901. "A Further Record of Observations of Certain Phenomena of Trance." PSPR 16:1.

Imai, S., Y. Ro, N. Kohri, T. Kasahara, S. Otani. "A Study on PK Ability of a Gifted Subject in Japan." In W. G. Roll and J. Beloff, eds. *Research in Parapsychology, 1980.* Metuchen, NJ: The Scarecrow Press, 1981, p. 39.

Inglis, B. 1988. "Sir William Barrett (1844–1925)." JSPR 55:16.

———. *The Hidden Power.* London: Jonathan Cape, 1986.

———. *The Paranormal: An Encyclopedia of Psychic Phenomena.* London: Granada Publishing Co., 1985.

———. *Science and Parascience: A History of the Paranormal, 1914–1939.* London: Hodder and Stoughton, 1984.

———. "Retrocognitive Dissonance." In W. G. Roll, J. Beloff and R. White, eds. *Research in Parapsychology 1982.* Metuchen, NJ: The Scarecrow Press, 1983, p. 69.

———. "Power Corrupts: Skepticism Corrodes." In W. G. Roll and J. Beloff, eds. *Research in Parapsychology, 1980.* Metuchen: NJ: Scarecrow Press, 1981, p. 143.

———. *Natural Medicine.* London: Collins, 1979.

———. *Natural and Supernatural: A History of the Paranormal from the Earliest Times.* London: Hodder and Stoughton, 1977.

Inoue, E. *Shinkai* (Real Mystery). Tokyo: Shiseido, 1919.

"Interview: Uri Geller." *Psychic* June 1973. 4(5):6.

"Interview: Sybil Leek." *Psychic* November 1969 1:6.

"Interview: Thelma S. Moss." *Psychic* August 1970 2:4.

"Interview: Andrija Puharich, M.D." *Psychic* October 1973. 5(1):6.

"Interview: Ingo Swann." *Psychic* April 1973. 4(4):6.

Irwin, H. J. 1988. "Parapsychology in Australia." JASPR 82:319.

———. 1987. "Charles Bailey: A Biographical Study of the Australian Apport Medium." JSPR 54:97.

———. *Flight of Mind: A Psychological Study of the Out-of-Body Experience.* Metuchen, NJ: Scarecrow Press, 1985.

———. 1985. "Parapsychological Phenomena and the Absorption Domain." JASPR 79:1.

Isaacs, E. "The Fox Sisters and American Spiritualism." In H. Kerr and C. L. Crow, eds. *The Occult in America: New Historical Perspectives.* Urbana and Chicago: University of Illinois Press, 1983.

Israelson, K., K. Khamashta, and J. Palmer. 1979. "An ESP Ganzfeld Experiment with Transcendental Meditators." JASPR 73:334.

Ivanov, A. 1964. "Soviet Experiments in 'Eyeless Vision'." *International Journal of Parapsychology* 6:5.

Ivanova, B. "A Letter from Barbara Ivanova." In M. Mir and L. Vilenskaya, eds. *The Golden Chalice.* San Francisco, CA: H. S. Dakin Co., 1986, p. 43.

Jacks, L. P. 1917. "Presidential Address: The Theory of Survival in the Light of its Context." PSPR 29:287.

———. 1915. "Dramatic Dreams, an Unexplored Field for Psychical Research." JSPR 17:178.

Jacobs, J. C. 1985. "PSI-Guided Awakening from Sleep 1: The Original Experiments of W. Van Vuurde." JSPR 53: 159.

Jacobson, N. O. *Life without Death? On Parapsychology, Mysticism, and the Question of Survival.* Trans. by Sheila La Farge. New York: Delacorte Press/ Seymour Lawrence, 1971.

Jaffé, A. "C. G. Jung and Parapsychology." In J. R. Smythies, ed. *Science and ESP.* London: Routledge & Kegan Paul, 1967.

———. *Apparitions and Precognition.* New York: University Books, 1963.

———, ed., Jung, C. G. *Memories, Dreams, Reflections.* London: Collins, Routledge & Kegan Paul, 1963.

Jahn, R. G. "On the Representation of Psychic Research to the Community of Established Science." In R. A. White and R. S. Broughton, eds. *Research in Parapsychology 1983.* Metuchen, NJ: Scarecrow Press, 1984, pp. 127–138.

Jahn, R. G., and B. J. Dunne, and R. D. Nelson. 1985. *Princeton Engineering Anomalies Research.* Technical Note PEAR 85003.

Jahn, R. G., and B. J. Dunne, and E. G. Jahn. "Analytical Judging Procedure for Remote Perception Experiments." In W. G. Roll and J. Beloff, eds. (J. McAllister, ass't ed.) *Research in Parapsychology, 1980.* Metuchen, NJ: Scarecrow Press, 1981.

James, W. *The Varieties of Religious Experience.* New York: New American Library, 1958. (First published London: Longmans, Green & Co., 1902.)

———. "What Psychical Research Has Accomplished." In *The Will to Believe and Other Essays.* New York: Dover Publications, 1956. (First published 1897).

———. 1909. "Report of Mrs. Piper's Hodgson-Control." PSPR 23:2.

———. 1903. "Reviews: Human Personality and its Survival of Bodily Death." PSPR 18:22.

———. *The Principles of Psychology.* London: Macmillan Co. 2 Vols., Vol. I, 1901.

James, W., O. Lodge, W. Leaf, and F. W. H. Myers. 1890. "A Record of Observations of Certain Phenomena of Trance." PSPR 6:436.

Janet, P. 1886. "Deuxième Note sur la Sommeil Provoqué à Distance et la Suggestion Mentale Pendant l'Etat Somnambulique." *Revue Philosophique de la France et de l'Etranger.* August 21:212.

Janin, P. "Psychism and Chance." In B. Shapin and L. Coly, eds. *The Philosophy of Parapsychology: Proceedings of an International Conference Held in Copenhagen, Denmark August 25–27, 1976.* New York: Parapsychology Foundation, 1977.

Jastrow, J. "The Animus of Psychical Research." In C. Murchison, ed. *The Case for and against Psychical Belief.* Worcester, Mass: Clark University, 1927, p. 281.

———. 1923. "A Reply to Mr. Prince." JASPR 17:15.

Jastrow, J., and G. E. H. Nuttall. 1886. "On the Existence of a Magnetic Sense." PASPR 1:116.

Jay, R. *Learned Pigs and Fireproof Women.* New York: Villard Books, 1986.

Jenkins, E. *The Shadow and the Light: A Defence of Daniel Dunglas Home, the Medium.* London: Hamish Hamilton, 1982.

Jephson, I. 1954. "Psychoanalysis and the Occult." JSPR 37:235.

———. 1933. "A Behaviourist Experiment in Clairvoyance." PSPR 41:99.

———. 1928. "Evidence for Clairvoyance in Card-Guessing: A Report on Some Recent Experiments." PSPR 38:223.

Jephson, I., S. G. Soal, and T. Besterman. 1931. "Report of a Series of Experiments in Clairvoyance Conducted at a Distance under Approximately Fraud-proof Conditions." PSPR 39:375.

Johannet, R. 1938. "Dr. Eugene Osty." JASPR 32:363.

Johnson, A. 1936. "Mrs. Henry Sidgwick's Work in Psychical Research." PSPR 44:53.

———. 1914. "A Reconstruction of Some 'Concordant Automatisms.'" PSPR 27:1.

———. 1908–1909. "On the Automatic Writing of Mrs. Holland." PSPR 21:297.

———. 1910. "Second Report on Mrs. Holland's Script." PSPR 24:201.

———. 1911. "Third Report on Mrs. Holland's Script." PSPR 25:218.

Johnson, A., E. M. Sidgwick, H. Sidgwick, F. W. H. Myers, A. T. Myers, and F. Podmore. 1894. "Report on the Census of Hallucinations." PSPR 10:25.

Johnson, M. *Parapsychologie, Onderzoek in de Grensgebieden van ervaring en Wetenschap.* Baarn, Holland: DeKern, 1982.

———. "ESP and Subliminality." In W. G. Roll, R. L. Morris, and J. D. Morris, eds. *Research in Parapsychology 1973.* Metuchen, NJ: Scarecrow Press, 1974, pp. 22–24.

———. 1971. "An Attempt to Manipulate the Scoring Direction of Subjects by Means of Control of Motivation of the Subjects." *Research Letter,* Parapsychological Division of the Psychological Laboratory of the University of Utrecht (Mar.):1.

———. 1968. "Relationship between Dream Recall and Scoring Direction." JP 32:56.

Johnson, M., and B. K. Kanthamani. 1967. "The Defense Mechanism Test as a Predictor of ESP Scoring Direction." JP 31:99.

Johnson, M., B. Millar, and R. S. Broughton. 1981. *European Journal of Parapsychology.* 3:317.

Johnson, M. and B. Nordbeck. 1972. "Variation in the Scoring of a 'Psychic' Subject." JP 36:311.

Johnson, R. C. *The Imprisoned Splendour.* Wheaton, Ill.: The Theosophical Publishing House, 1953.

Joines, H., L. Burton, and B. Stephens. 1975. "Kirlian Photography and its Relevance to Parapsychology." In *Research in Parapsychology 1974.* Metuchen, NJ: The Scarecrow Press, p. 77.

Joines, W. T., and J. L. Artley. 1969. "Study of a Haunted House." *Theta* 27:2.

Jones, L. J. 1928. "Presidential Address." PSPR 38:17.

Josephson, M. "Edison." In *The New Encyclopedia Britannica,* 15th ed. Chicago: Encyclopedia Britannica, 1986.

Jourdain, E. F. ("Miss Lamont"), and C. A. E. Moberly ("Miss Morison"). *An Adventure.* London: Macmillan, 1911.

Jules-Bois, A. H. 1936. "Charles Richet: Father of Metapsychics." JASPR 30:1.

Jung, C. G. *Synchronicity.* London: Routledge, 1972.

———. *Kryptomnesie.* In *Psychiatrische Studien.* Gesammalte Werke Vol. 1. Freiburg: Walter-Verlag, 1966. Originally published 1905.

———. *Memories, Dreams, Reflections.* New York: Pantheon Books, 1963.

———. *Archetypes and the Collective Unconscious.* Princeton: Princeton University Press, 1959.

———. "Synchronicity: an Acausal Connecting Principle." In C. G. Jung and W. Pauli. *The Interpretation of Nature and the Psyche.* Princeton: Princeton University Press, 1955.

———. 1920. "The Psychological Foundations of Belief in Spirits." PSPR 31:75.

Jürgenson, F. *Sprechfunk mit Verstorbenen.* Freiburg i. Br.: Herman Bauer, 1967.

Kaempffert, W. 1956. "Dr. James H. Hyslop and Psychical Research." JASPR 50:134.

Kahn, S. D. 1980. *"Ave Atque Vale:* Gardner Murphy." JASPR 74:37.

———. "Myers' Problem Revisited." In G. R. Schmeidler, ed. *Parapsychology: Its Relation to Physics, Biology, Psychology, and Psychiatry.* Metuchen, NJ: Scarecrow Press, 1976.

———. 1962. "The Enigma of Psi: A Challenge for Scientific Method." JASPR 56:114.

———. 1952. "Studies in Extrasensory Perception." PASPR 25:1.

Kanthahamani, B. K., and M. Johnson. 1967. "The Defense Mechanism Test as a Predictor of ESP Scoring Direction." JP 31:99.

Kappers, J., with van Asperen de Boer and P. R. Barkema. 1966. "Is It Possible to Induce ESP with

Psilocybine? An Exploratory Investigation." *International Journal of Neuropsychiatry* 2(5):447.

Kappers, J., with M. Ryzl, J. T. Barendregt, and P. R. Barkema. 1965. "An Experiment in Prague." JP 29:176.

Karagulla, S. *Breakthrough to Creativity.* Santa Monica, CA: DeVorss & Co., 1967.

Kardec, A. *Le Livre des Médiums.* Paris: Didier, 1861.

Kasahara, T. *Sai no Senjo (The Battlefield of Psi).* Tokyo: Heibonsha, 1987.

Kasahara, T., N. Kohri, Y. Ro, S. Imai, S. Otani. "A Study on PK Ability of a Gifted Subject in Japan." In W. G. Roll and J. Beloff, eds. *Research in Parapsychology, 1980.* Metuchen, NJ: Scarecrow Press, 1981, p. 39.

Katz, R. 1973. "Education for Transcendence: Lessons from the !Kung Zhu/Twasi." *Journal of Transpersonal Psychology* 5:136.

Kautz, W. H. 1982. "The Rosemary Case of Alleged Egyptian Xenoglossy." *Theta* 10:26.

Keil, J. 1987. *Gaither Pratt: A Life for Parapsychology.* Jefferson, NC: McFarland & Co., 1987.

———. 1971. "A Wider Conceptual Framework for the Stepanek Focusing Effect." JASPR 65:75.

Keil, J., B. Herbert, M. Ullman, J. G. Pratt. 1976. "Directly Observable Voluntary PK Effects: A Survey and Tentative Interpretation of Available Findings from Nina Kulagina and Other Known Related Cases of Recent Date." PSPR 56:197.

Keil, J., and J. G. Pratt. 1973. "First Hand Observations of Nina S. Kulagina Suggestive of PK on Static Objects." JASPR 67:381.

———. 1969. "Further ESP Tests with Stepanek in Charlottesville Dealing with the Focusing Effect." JASPR 63:253.

Kellog, C. E. 1937. "The Problems of Matching and Sampling in the Study of Extra-Sensory Perception." *Journal of Abnormal and Social Psychology* 32:462.

Kelly, E. F. 1983. "A Psychobiological Framework for PSI Research." *Proceedings: Symposium on Applications of Anomalous Phenomena, November 30–December 1, 1983,* pp. 365–405.

———. 1982. "On Grouping of Hits in Some Exceptional Psi Performers." JASPR 76:101.

———. "Converging Lines of Evidence on Mind/Brain Relations." In B. Shapin and L. Coly, eds. *Brain/Mind and Parapsychology.* New York: Parapsychology Foundation, 1979.

Kelly, E. F., and S. A. Schouten. 1978. "On the Experiment of Brugmans, Heymans, and Weinberg." *European Journal of Parapsychology* 2:247.

Kelly, E. F., and D. S. Burdick. "Statistical Methods in Parapsychology Research." In B. Wolman, ed. *Handbook of Parapsychology.* New York: Van Nostrand Reinhold, 1977.

Kelly, E. F., J. E. Lenz, and J. L. Artley. 1980. "A Computer-Based Laboratory Facility for the Psychophysiological Study of Psi." JASPR 74:149.

Kelly, E. F., and R. G. Locke. "Altered States of Consciousness and Psi: An Historical Survey and Research Prospectus." *Parapsychology Foundation Monograph.* New York: Parapsychology Foundation, 1981.

———. 1981. "A Note on Scrying." JASPR 75:220.

Kelly, H. A. 1970. (quoted in M. Ebon. 1974. "Exorcism beyond the Chaos." *Psychic* 5(6):50).

Kenawell, W. W. *The Quest at Glastonbury: A Biographical Study of Frederick Bligh Bond.* New York: Garrett Publications, 1965.

Kendrick, R., I. Wilson, F. Tribbe, and J. Tyrer. 1989. "The Turin Shroud—Too Hasty an Epitaph?" *Christian Parapsychologist* 8(1):2.

Kennedy, J. E. 1979. "Methodological Problems in Free-Response ESP Experiments." JASPR 73:115.

———. 1979. "More on Methodological Issues in Free-Response Psi Experiments." JASPR 73:395.

Kennedy, J. L. 1938. "A Methodological Review of Extra-Sensory Perception." *Psychological Bulletin* 36:59.

———. 1938. "The Visual Clues from the Backs of ESP Cards." *Journal of Psychology* 6:149.

Khamashta, K., J. Palmer, and K. Israelson. 1979. "An ESP Ganzfeld Experiment with Transcendental Meditators." JASPR 73:334.

Kilner, W. J. *The Human Aura.* New Hyde Park, New York: University Books, 1965.

King, F. "Wilhelm Reich (1897–1957)." In R. Cavendish, ed. *Encyclopedia of the Unexplained.* New York: McGraw Hill, 1974, pp. 207–209.

Klass, P. J. "UFOs." In C. Abell and B. Singer, eds. *Science and the Paranormal: Probing the Existence of the Supernatural.* New York: Charles Scribner's Sons, 1981, p. 318.

Klemme, H. L., and G. Murphy. 1966. "Unfinished Business." JASPR 60:306.

Klimo, J. *Channeling: Investigations on Receiving Information from Paranormal Sources.* Los Angeles: Jeremy P. Tarcher, Inc., 1987.

von Klinckowstroem, C. 1958. "Ist Die Wünschelrute ein Aberglaube?" *Erfahrungsheilkunde* 3:211.

von Klinckowstroem, C. with H. Rosenbusch, and W. von Gulat-Wellenberg. "1: Der physikalische Mediumismus." In M. Dessoir, ed. *Der Okkultismus in Urkunden.* Berlin: Ullstein Verlag, 1925.

Kline, M. V. *A Scientific Report on 'The Search for Bridey Murphy'.*" New York: Julian Press, 1956.

Kmetz, J. 1977. "A Study of Primary Perception in Plant and Animal Life." JASPR 71:157.

Knowles, E.A.G. "Psi Dexterity in a Mixing Experiment." In J. B. Rhine and R. Brier, eds. *Parapsychology Today.* New York: The Citadel Press, 1968.

Koestler, A. "J. B. Rhine's Impact." In K. R. Rao, ed. *J. B. Rhine: On the Frontiers of Science.* Jefferson, NC: McFarland & Co., 1982, p. 144.

———. *The Roots of Coincidence.* London: Hutchinson, 1972.

Koestler, A., A. Hardy and R. Harvie. *The Challenge of Chance. Experiments and Speculations.* London: Hutchinson, 1973.

Kohn, H., and H. Price. 1930. "An Indian Poltergeist." *Psychic Research* 24:122.

Kohr, R. L. 1980. "A Survey of Psi Experiences

among Members of a Special Population." JASPR 74:395.

Kohri, N., T. Kasahara, Y. Ro, S. Imai, S. Otani. "A Study on PK Ability of a Gifted Subject in Japan." In W. G. Roll and J. Beloff, eds. *Research in Parapsychology, 1980.* Metuchen, NJ: Scarecrow Press, 1981, p. 39.

Kohsen, A., and C.C.L. Gregory. 1958. "A Cosmological Approach to a Theory of Mental Images." PSPR 52:33.

———. *Physical and Psychical Research.* London: Omega Press, 1954.

Kornwachs, K., and W. von Lucadou. 1983. "On the Limitations of Psi—A System-Theoretical Approach." In W. G. Roll, J. Beloff, R. A. White, eds. *Research in Parapsychology 1982.* Metuchen, N. J.: The Scarecrow Press, 1983, p. 85.

———. 1980. "Development of the Systemtheoretic Approach to Psychokinesis." *European Journal of Parapsychology* 3 (3):297.

Kreskin. *The Amazing World of Kreskin.* New York: Random House, 1973.

Krieger, D. 1976. "Healing by the 'Laying-On' of Hands as a Facilitator of Bioenergetic Change: The Response of In-Vivo Human Hemoglobin." *Psychoenergetic Systems* 1:121.

———. 1976. "A Second Experiment in 'Laying-on-of-Hands'." *Psychoenergetic Systems* 7.

Krippner, S. *Song of the Siren: A Parapsychological Odyssey.* New York: Harper & Row, 1975.

———. 1968. "Experimentally-Induced Telepathic Effects in Hypnosis and Non-hypnosis Groups." JASPR 62:387.

Krippner, S., and M. Ullman, with A Vaughan. *Dream Telepathy.* New York: Macmillan, 1973.

Krippner, S., C. Honorton, and M. Ullman. 1973. "A Long-Distance ESP Dream Study with the 'Grateful Dead'." *Journal of the American Society of Psychosomatic Dentistry and Medicine* 20:9.

Krippner, S., M. Ullman, and C. Honorton. 1971. "A Precognitive Dream Study with a Single Subject." JASPR 65:192.

Krippner, S., and M. Ullman. "Dream Studies and Telepathy." *Parapsychological Monographs No. 12.* New York: Parapsychology Foundation, 1970.

Krippner, S., and A. Villoldo. *The Realms of Healing.* Millbrae, CA: Celestial Arts, 1976.

Krishna, G. *The Secret of Yoga.* New York: Harper & Row, 1972.

Kübler-Ross, E. "Epilogue." In D. Gill's *Quest: The Life of Elisabeth Kübler-Ross.* New York: Harper & Row, 1980.

———. *To Live until We Say Goodbye.* Englewood Cliffs, NJ: Prentice Hall, 1978.

———. "Foreword." In S. Grof, and J. Halifax. *The Human Encounter with Death.* New York: E. P. Dutton, 1978.

———. "Foreword." In R. Moody. *Life after Life.* New York: Bantam Books, 1976. Originally published Covington, GA: Mockingbird Books, 1975.

———. *On Death and Dying.* New York: Macmillan, 1969.

Kuhn, T. *The Structure of Scientific Revolutions.* Chicago: University of Chicago Press, 1962.

Kurtz, P., ed. *A Skeptic's Handbook of Parapsychology.* Buffalo, N.Y.: Prometheus Books, 1985.

———. "Spiritualists, Mediums and Psychics." In his *A Skeptic's Handbook of Parapsychology.* Buffalo, NY: Prometheus Books, 1985.

———. 1978. "Is Parapsychology a Science?" *The Skeptical Inquirer* 3:14.

———. 1978. "The Humanists' Crusade against Parapsychology: A Discussion. Part One. On the Art of Quoting Out of Context: A Response to the Rockwells' Critique." JASPR 72:349.

Kury, H., R. Hampel, H. Bender, and S. Wendlandt. 1975. "The 'Geller-effect'—An Investigation on Interviews and Questionnaires. Part 1." *Zeitschrift für Parapsychologie und Grenzgebiete der Psychologie* 17:219.

Lambert, G. W. 1976. "D. D. Home and the Physical World." JSPR 48:298.

———. 1968. "Stranger Things: Some Reflections on Reading 'Strange Things' by John L. Campbell and Trevor H. Hall." JSPR 45:43.

———. 1966. "The Quest at Glastonbury." JSPR 43:301.

———.1968. "Johannes, the Monk: A Study in the Script of J.A. in 'The Gate of Remembrance'." JSPR 44:271.

———. 1962. "Richard's Garden Revisited." JSPR 41:279.

———. 1958. "The Cheltenham Ghost: A Reinterpretation." JSPR 39:267.

———. 1956. "The Use of Evidence in Psychical Research." PSPR 50:275.

———. 1955. "Poltergeists: A Physical Theory." JSPR 9:37.

Lambert, G. W., and K. Gay. 1952. "The Dieppe Raid Case." JSPR 36:607.

Lambert, R. 1954. "Dr. Geley's Report on the Medium Eva C." JSPR 37:682.

Lang, A. "Edmund Gurney." In *Encyclopaedia Britannica,* 11th ed. Cambridge, 1911.

———. 1911. "Presidential Address." JSPR 25:364.

———. 1903–1904. "The Poltergeist at Cideville." PSPR 18:454.

———. 1903–1904. " 'The Nineteenth Century' and Mr. Frederic Myers." PSPR 18:62.

———. 1903. "The Poltergeist, Historically Considered." PSPR 17: 305–326.

———. 1900. "Discussion of the Trance Phenomena of Mrs. Piper." PSPR 15:39.

———. *Cock Lane and Common-Sense.* London: Longmans, Green and Co., 1894/1896.

———. 1895. "The Voices of Jeanne d'Arc." PSPR 11:198.

Lauden, D. F. 1980. "Possible Psychokinetic Interactions in Quantum Theory." JASPR 50:399.

Leadbeater, C. W. and A. B. Besant. *Occult Chemistry.* Adyar, Madras: Theosophical Publishing House, 1919.

Leaf, W. 1903. "Review of *Human Personality and Its Survival of Bodily Death.*" PSPR 18:53.

———. 1890. "A Record of Observations of Certain Phenomena of Trance. Part II." PSPR 6:558.

"Obituary: Dr. Walter Leaf." 1927. JSPR 24:52.

Lechler, A. *Das Rätsel von Konnersreuth im Lichte eines neuen Fälles von Stigmatisation.* Elberfeld: *Licht und Leben,* Verlag, 1933.

LeClair, R. C. *The Letters of William James and Théodore Flournoy.* Madison, WI: University of Wisconsin Press, 1966.

Lenz, J. E., E. F. Kelly, and J. L. Artley. 1980. "A Computer-Based Laboratory Facility for the Psychophysiological Study of Psi." JASPR 74:149.

LeShan, L. *From Newton to ESP.* Wellingborough, VK: Turnstone, 1984.

———. *The Mechanic and the Gardener: Understanding the Wholistic Revolution in Medicine.* New York: Holt, Rinehart, 1982.

———. *You Can Fight for Your Life: Emotional Factors in the Development of Cancer.* New York: Evans, 1976.

———. *The Medium, the Mystic and the Physicist.* New York: Viking Press, 1974.

———. 1968. "The Vanished Man: A Psychometry Experiment with Mrs. Eileen J. Garrett." JASPR 62:46.

———. 1967. "A 'Spontaneous' Psychometry Experiment with Mrs. Eileen Garrett." JSPR 44:14.

LeShan, L., and A. H. Esser. 1969. "A Transatlantic 'Chair Test'." JSPR 45:167.

Lewis, D. C., E. L. Gasteiger, K. A. Horowitz. 1975. "Plant 'Primary Perception': Electrophysiological Unresponsiveness to Brine Shrimp Killing." *Science* 189:47.

Lewis, L. S. May 11, 1936. Correspondence. *Morning Post.* London.

Litvag, I. *Singer in the Shadows: The Strange Story of Patience Worth.* New York: MacMillan, 1972.

Liverziani, F. *La reincarnazione e i suoi fenomeni—"chi" o "cosa" si reincarna.* Rome: Edizioni Mediterranee, 1985. (English edition: *Reincarnation and its Phenomena—"Who" or "What" Become Reincarnated.* London and New York: Regency Press, 1988.)

———. *La esperienze di confine e la vita dopo la morte.* Rome: Edizioni Mediterranee, 1986.

Livnen, G. 1986. "An Ostensible Precognition of the Arab Surprise Attack on the Day of Atonement." JSPR 53:383.

Locher, T. *Parapsychologie in der Schweiz.* Biel: Schweizerischen Vereinigung für Parapsychologie, 1986.

———. "History of Psychical Research in Switzerland." *Proceedings of an International Conference Parapsychology Today: A Geographic View.* New York: Parapsychology Foundation, 1971, p. 131.

Locke, R. G., and E. F. Kelly. 1981. "A Note on Scrying." JASPR 75:220.

———. "Altered States of Consciousness and Psi: An Historical Survey and Research Prospectus." *Parapsychology Foundation Monograph.* New York: Parapsychology Foundation, 1981.

Lodge, O. 1924. "In Memoriam—Gustave Geley. 1868–1924." PSPR 34:201.

———. 1922. "On the Making of Test Plates by Previous Exposure." JSPR 20:370.

———. 1920. "In Memory of Lord Rayleigh, O.M., F.R.S." PSPR 31:1.

———. *Raymond, or Life and Death.* London: Methuen, 1916.

———. 1916. "Recent Evidence about Prevision and Survival." PSPR 29:111.

———. 1911. "Evidence of Classical Scholarship and of Cross-Correspondences in Some New Automatic Writings." PSPR 25:113.

———. 1903. "Human Personality and its Survival of Bodily Death. By Frederick W. H. Myers." PSPR 18:22.

———. 1902. "Introduction to the Reports of Sittings with Mrs. Thompson." PSPR 17:61.

———. 1890. "A Record of Observations of Certain Phenomena of Trance—Part I." PSPR 6:443.

Lodge, O., W. Leaf, F. W. H. Myers, and W. James. 1890. "A Record of Observations of Certain Phenomena of Trance." PSPR 6:436.

Lodge, O., and C. Richet. 1924. "For and against Survival." PSPR 34:107.

Lombroso, C. *After Death—What?* Boston: Small, Maynard, 1909.

———. 1906. "The 'Haunted Houses' Which I Have Studied." *Annals of Psychical Research* 3:361.

London, J. *The Star Rover.* New York: Macmillan, 1963. Originally published 1915.

Long, M. F. *The Secret Science behind Miracles.* Santa Monica, CA: DeVorss, 1948.

Lorimer, D. *Survival? Body, Mind and Death in the Light of Psychic Experience.* London: Routledge & Kegan Paul, 1984.

Loth, D. *A Long Way Forward: The Biography of Congresswoman Frances P. Bolton.* New York: Longmans, Green, 1957.

von Lucadou, W., and K. Kornwachs. 1983. "On the Limitatins of Psi—A System-Theoretical Approach." In W. G. Roll, J. Beloff, R. A. White, eds. *Research in Parapsychology 1982.* Metuchen, NJ: The Scarecrow Press, 1983, p. 85.

———. 1980. "Development of the Systemtheoretic Approach to Psychokinesis." *European Journal of Parapsychology* 3(3):297.

Ludwig, L., M. Reiser, S. Saxe, and C. Wagner. 1979. "An Evaluation of the Use of Psychics in the Investigation of Major Crimes." *Journal of Police Science and Administration* 7:18.

Lungin, T. (tr. C. Rosenberger and J. Glad; English version ed. by D. S. Rogo). *Wolf Messing: The True Story of Russia's Most Famous Psychic.* New York: Paragon House, in press.

Lyttelton, E. *Some Cases of Prediction: A Study.* London: Bell, 1938.

———. *Our Superconscious Mind.* London: n.p., 1931.

MacCarthy, C. W. *Rigid Tests of the Occult: Being a Record of Some Remarkable Experiences Through the Mediumship of Mr. C. Bailey with a Critical Examination of the Origin of the Phenomena.* Melbourne, Australia: Stephens, 1904.

MacKenzie, A. *Hauntings and Apparitions.* London: Heinemann, 1982.

———. 1980. "Talks with Rosalind Heywood." JSPR 50:523.

———. *Apparitions and Ghosts.* New York: Popular Library, 1971.

———. *Frontiers of the Unknown.* London: Anchor Books, 1968.

———. *The Unexplained: Some Strange Cases of Psychical Research.* London: Anchor Books, 1966.

MacKenzie, W. 1919. "Rolf of Mannheim—A Great Psychological Problem." PASPR 13:205.

MacLaine, S. *Out on a Limb.* New York: Bantam, 1983.

———. *Dancing in the Light.* New York: Bantam, 1985.

———. *It's All in the Playing.* New York: Bantam, 1987.

MacRobert, A. F. 1954. "Proxy Sittings: A Report of the Study Group Series with Arthur Ford." JASPR 58:71.

McAdams, E. 1984. "Reported Near-Death Observations in a Hospice in California." *1983 Annual Conference Proceedings of the Academy of Religion and Psychical Research: "The Synergy of Religion and Psychical Research: Past, Present and Future"* 57.

McAdams, E., and R. Bayless. *The Case of Life after Death: Parapsychologists Look at the Evidence.* Chicago, IL: Nelson Hall, 1981.

McBeath, M. K. and P. R. Phillips. "An Attempted Replication of the Cox Films of PK." In W. G. Roll, J. Beloff, and R. A. White, eds. *Research in Parapsychology, 1982.* Metuchen, NJ: The Scarecrow Press, 1983, pp. 113–115.

McClenon, J. *Deviant Science: The Case of Parapsychology.* Philadelphia, PA: University of Pennsylvania Press, 1984.

McConnell, R. A. *Parapsychology in Retrospect: My Search for the Unicorn.* Pittsburgh, PA: R. A. McConnell, 1987.

———. *An Introduction to Parapsychology in the Context of Science.* Pittsburgh, PA: R. A. McConnell, 1983.

———. *Parapsychology and Self-Deception in Science.* Pittsburgh, PA: R. A. McConnell, 1982.

———. *Encounters with Parapsychology.* Pittsburgh, PA: R. A. McConnell, 1982.

———. *ESP Curriculum Guide.* New York: Simon & Schuster, 1970.

McConnell, R. A., and M. Anderson. 1961. "Fantasy Testing for ESP in Fourth- and Fifth-Grade Class." *Journal of Psychology* 52:491.

McConnell, R. A., and H. Forwald. 1967. "Psychokinetic Placement: I. A Re-examination of the Forwald-Durham Experiment." JP 31:51.

———. 1968. "Psychokinetic Placement: III. Cube-Releasing Devices." JP 32:9.

McConnell, P. A., and G. R. Schmeidler. *ESP and Personality Patterns.* New Haven, CT: Yale University Press, 1958.

McCormick, D. L., ed. *Courses and Other Study Opportunities in Parapsychology.* New York: American Society for Psychical Research, 1987.

McDougall, W. "Psychical Research as a University Study." In C. Murchison, ed. *The Case for and against Psychical Belief.* Worcester, Mass.: Clark University, 1927.

———. *Body and Mind: A History and Defense of Animism.* London: Methuen, 1911.

McGrone, W. "Shroud Image Is the Work of an Artist." In K. Frazier, ed. *Science Confronts the Paranormal.* Buffalo, NY: Prometheus Books, 1983, p. 344.

McHarg, J. 1986. "A Course in Miracles." *The Christian Parapsychologist* 6:109.

———. "Psychose und Synchronizität." In *Grenzgebiete der Wissenschaft, I.* Innsbruck: Resch Verlag, 1985, pp. 23–31.

———. "Cryptomnesia and Paranormal Personation: Two Contrasting Examples." In W. G. Roll, J. Beloff, and R. A. White, eds. *Research in Parapsychology 1982.* Metuchen, NJ: Scarecrow Press, 1983, p. 207.

———. "Psychical Research and Psychiatry." In I. Grattan-Guiness, ed. *Psychical Research, A Guide to Its History, Principles and Practises.* Wellingborough: Aquarian Press, 1982, pp. 316–324.

——. 1978. "A Vision of the Aftermath of the Battle of Nechtanesmere, AD 685." JSPR 49:938.

———. "A Poltergeist Case from Glasgow." In J. D. Morris, W. G. Roll, and R. L. Morris, eds. *Research in Parapsychology, 1976.* Metuchen, NJ: Scarecrow Press, 1977, pp. 13–15.

———. 1975. "Exorcism Past and Present." JSPR 48:232.

———. "Poltergeist and Apparitional Haunting Phenomena Affecting the Family and Associates of an Adolescent Girl with Well-controlled Epilepsy." In J. D. Morris, W. G. Roll, and R. L. Morris, eds. *Research in Parapsychology, 1972.* Metuchen, NJ: Scarecrow Press, 1973, pp. 17–19.

McMahan, E. "Joseph Banks Rhine: Teacher and Friend." In K. R. Rao, ed. *J. B. Rhine: On the Frontiers of Science.* Jefferson, NC: McFarland, 1982, p. 13.

———. 1946. "An Experiment in Pure Telepathy." JP 10:224.

McMahan, E., C. E. Stuart, B. M. Humphrey, and B. M. Smith. 1947. "Personality Measurements and ESP Tests with Cards and Drawings." JP 11:118.

M'Taggart, J. M. E. *Human Immortality and Pre-existence.* New York: Kraus reprint 1970 (Originally published London: Edward Arnold, 1916).

McVaugh, M. R., and S. H. Mauskopf. *The Elusive Science.* Baltimore, MD: Johns Hopkins University Press, 1980.

McWilliams, P., and D. Denniston. *The TM Book.* New York: Warner Books, 1975.

"Maeterlinck, Maurice." In *The New Encyclopedia Britannica,* Vol. 7, 1986.

Mann, T. "Thomas Mann and the Occult: An Unpublished Letter." *Encounter,* April, 1976, pp. 21–24.

Mann, W. E. "Wilhelm Reich and Orgone Energy."

In J. White and S. Krippner, eds. *Future Science.* Garden City, NY: Doubleday, 1977.

Manning, M. *The Strangers.* London: W.H. Allen, 1978.

———. *The Minds of Millions.* London: W.H. Allen, 1977.

———. *The Link.* New York: Holt, Rhinehart & Wilson, 1975.

Manning, W. E. 1968. "Collected Papers on the Paranormal." JSPR 44:407.

Marks, D. "Remote Viewing Revisited." In K. Frazier, ed. *Science Confronts the Paranormal.* Buffalo, NY: Prometheus Books, 1986, pp. 110–121.

Markwick, B. "The Establishment of Data Manipulation in the Soal-Shackleton Experiments." In P. Kurtz, ed. *A Skeptic's Handbook of Parapsychology.* Buffalo, NY: Prometheus Books, 1985.

———. 1978. "The Soal-Goldney Experiments with Basil Shackleton: New Evidence of Data Manipulation." PSPR 56:250.

Markwick, B., and J. Beloff. "Dream States and ESP." In D. H. Weiner and R. D. Nelson, eds. *Research in Parapsychology 1987.* Metuchen, NJ: The Scarecrow Press, 1988.

———. "Dream States and ESP." In W. G. Roll, J. Beloff, and R. A. White, eds. *Research in Parapsychology 1982.* Metuchen, NJ: The Scarecrow Press, 1983.

Marriott, W. A. 1911. "A Mediumistic Trickster." *Mainly About People,* June 24:777.

Marriott, W. A., and E. Feilding. 1911. "Report on a Series of Sittings with Eusapia Palladino at Naples." PSPR 25:57.

Martin, K. 1987. "The Voice of Lazaris." *New Realities* 7(6):26.

Masters, R. E. L. and J. Houston. *Mind Games.* New York: Viking, 1972.

———. *The Varieties of Psychedelic Experience.* New York: Holt, Rhinehart & Winston, 1966.

Massey, C. C. 1886. "The Possibilities of Mal-Observation in Relation to Evidence for the Phenomena of Spiritualism." PSPR 4:75.

Mattiesen, E. *Das persönliche Überleben des Todes. Eine Darstellung der Erfahrungsbeweise.* Berlin: Walter de Gruyter, 1936–1939.

———. 1929. "A Reply to Count Perovsky-Petrovo-Solovovo." JSPR 25:27.

Mauskopf, S. H., and M. R. McVaugh. *The Elusive Science.* Baltimore, MD: Johns Hopkins University Press, 1980.

May, E. C., D. I. Radin, and M. J. Thomson. "Psi Experiments with Random Number Generators: Meta-Analysis Part I." In D. H. Weiner and D. I. Radin, eds. *Research in Parapsychology 1985.* Metuchen, NJ: Scarecrow Press, 1986, p. 14.

Mayne, A. 1963. "The Promotion of Research." JSPR 42:202.

Mead, M. "Preface." In J. Belo, *Trance in Bali.* New York: Columbia University Press, 1960.

———. *Coming of Age in Samoa.* New York: William M. Morrow, 1961. Originally published 1928.

"Margaret Mead." *The New Encyclopaedia Britannica,* Vol. 7. Chicago: Encyclopedia Britannica, Inc., 1986.

Meade, M. *Madame Blavatsky: The Woman Behind the Myth.* New York: Putnam's, 1980.

Medhurst, R. G. 1971. "The Origin of the 'Prepared Random Numbers' Used in the Shackleton Experiments." JSPR 46:39.

———. 1967. "New Light on Old Ghosts." JSPR 44:94.

Medhurst, R. G., and K. M. Goldney. 1964. "William Crookes and the Physical Phenomena of Mediumship." PSPR 54:25.

"Mediumship of Mr. C. Bailey." 1905. JSPR 12: 77, 109.

Meek, G. 1982. "Spiricom: Electronic Communications with the 'Dearly Departed'." *New Realities* 4(6):9.

———. 1982 "A Personal Statement from George W. Meek. *New Realities* 4(6): 10.

———. 1982. "The Significance of the Spiricom Breakthrough." *New Realities* 4(6):14.

———. *After We Die What Then?* Franklin, N.C.: Metascience Foundation, 1980.

Meier, C. A. "Obituaries. C. G. Jung." JSPR 41:216.

Michell, J., and R. J. M. Rickard. 1977. *Phenomena: A Book of Wonders.* New York: Pantheon Books.

Millar, B. "The Observational Theories: A Primer." *European Journal of Parapsychology* 2(3):304.

———. "Correspondence." 1974. JSPR 47:461.

Millar, B., R. S. Broughton, and M. Johnson. 1981. "An Investigation into the Use of Aversion Therapy Techniques for the Operant Control of PK Production in Humans." *European Journal of Parapsychology* 3:317.

Mir, M., and L. Vilenskaya, eds. *The Golden Chalice.* San Francisco, CA: H. S. Dakin Co., 1986.

Mitchell, E. D. "Introduction: From Outer Space to Inner Space. . . ." In E. D. Mitchell, *Psychic Exploration: A Challenge for Science.* New York: G. P. Putnam's Sons, 1974.

———. *Psychic Exploration: A Challenge for Science.* New York: G. P. Putnam's Sons, 1974.

Mitchell, J. "Out-of-the-Body Vision." In D. S. Rogo, ed. *Mind Beyond the Body: The Mystery of ESP Projection.* New York: Penguin Books, 1978.

Mitchell, P., and I. Owen. 1979. "The Alleged Haunting of Borley Rectory." JSPR 50: 149, 161.

Mitchell, T. W. 1939. "Obituary Professor Sigmund Freud." PSPR 45:344.

———. 1939. "Sigmund Freud. *Moses and Monotheism.*" PSPR 45:347.

———. 1931. "Beneath the Threshold." Myers Memorial Lecture.

———. 1922. "Presidential Address." PSPR 33:1.

———. 1920. "The Doris Fischer Case of Multiple Personality." PSPR 31:30.

———. 1912. "Some Types of Multiple Personality." PSPR 26:257.

———. 1912. "A Study in Hysteria and Multiple Personality, with Report of a Case." PSPR 26:286.

Moberly, C. A. E. ("Miss Morison"), and E. F. Jourdain ("Miss Lamont"). *An Adventure.* London: Macmillan, 1911.

Monroe, R. A. *Far Journeys.* Garden City, NY: Doubleday, 1985.

———. *Journeys out of the Body.* Garden City, NY: Doubleday, 1971 (reissued 1977).

Montgomery, R. In Editors of *Body, Mind and Spirit. The New Age Catalogue.* New York: Doubleday, 1988.

———. *Threshold to Tomorrow.* Westminster, MD: Random House, 1982.

———. *Strangers Among Us.* Westminster, MD: Random House, 1979.

———. *A World Beyond.* Westminster, MD: Random House, 1971.

———. *Here and Hereafter.* Westminster, MD: Random House, 1968.

———. *A Search for the Truth.* Westminster, MD: Random House, 1967.

———. *A Gift of Prophecy: The Phenomenal Jeane Dixon.* New York: William Morrow & Co., 1965.

Montgomery, R., with J. Garland. *Ruth Montgomery: Herald of the New Age.* Westminster, MD: Random House, 1986.

Montredon, E. (Jean Meyer), and P. Duval (Rémy Chauvin). "ESP Experiments with Mice." In J. B. Rhine, ed. *Progress in Parapsychology.* Durham, NC: The Parapsychology Press, 1971, p. 17.

Moody, R. A., Jr. *The Light Beyond.* New York: Bantam Books, 1988.

———. *Life after Life.* Covington, GA: Mockingbird Books, 1975.

———. *Reflections on Life after Life.* New York: Bantam Books, 1977.

Moore, R. L. "The Occult Connection? Mormonism, Christian Science and Spiritualism." In H. Kerr and C. L. Crow, eds. *The Occult in America: New Historical Perspectives.* Urbana and Chicago IL: University of Illinois Press, 1983.

———. *In Search of White Crows.* New York: Oxford University Press, 1977.

Moran, R., and J. Peter. "The Amityville Horror Hoax." 1978. *Fate* 31(5):43.

Morris, R. L. 1982. "Assessing Experimental Support for True Precognition." JP 46:321.

———. "A Survey of Methods and Issues in ESP Research." In S. Krippner, ed. *Advances in Parapsychological Research 2: Extrasensory Perception.* New York: Plenum Press, 1978.

———. 1970. "Psi and Animal Behavior: A Survey." JASPR 64:242.

———. "Parapsychology, Biology and ANPSI." In B. Wolman, ed. *Handbook of Parapsychology.* New York: Van Nostrand Reinhold Co., 1977.

———. 1974. "PRF Research on Out-of-Body Experiences, 1973." *Theta.* 41:1.

Morris, R. L., with H. Edge, J. Palmer, and J. Rush. *Foundations of Parapsychology: Exploring the Boundaries of Human Capability.* London: Routledge & Kegan Paul, 1986.

Morrison, J. S. 1948. "Greetings from Australia." *Harbinger of Light* 79(3):8.

Morselli, E. *Psicologia e 'Spiritismo': Impressioni e note critiche sui fenomeni medianici di Eusapia Paladino.* Turin: Fratelli Boca, 1908, 2 vols.

Morton, R. C. 1892. "The Record of a Haunted House." PSPR 8:311.

Moser, F. H. *Okkultismus, Täuschungen und Tatsachen.* Munich: E. Reinhart, 1935.

———. *Spuk—Irrglaube oder Wahrglaube?* Baden bei Zurich: Gyr Verlag, 1950.

Moses, W. S. ("M. A. Oxon."). *Spirit Teachings.* London: n.p., 1949\1883.

Moss, T. S. 1969. "ESP Effects in 'Artists' Contrasted with Non-Artists." JP 33:57.

Moss, T. S., and G. R. Schmeidler. 1968. "Quantitative Investigation of a 'Haunted House' with Sensitives and a Control Group." JASPR 62:399.

Moss, T. S., and J. Gengerelli. 1967. "Telepathy and Emotional Stimuli: A Controlled Experiment." *Journal of Abnormal Psychology* 72:341.

Motoyama, H. *Psi to Ki no Kankei* (The Correlation between Psi Energy and Ki). Tokyo: Shukyo Shinri Shuppan, 1987.

———. 1977. "Physiological Measurements and New Instrumentation." In G. W. Meek, ed. *Healers and the Healing Process.* Wheaton, IL: Theosophical Publishing House, 1977.

"Mr. Browning on D. D. Home." 1903. JSPR 11:11.

Muldoon, S. J. *The Case for Astral Projection.* Chicago, IL: Ariel Press, 1935.

Muldoon, S. J., with H. Carrington. *The Phenomena of Astral Projection.* London: Rider & Co., 1951.

———. *The Projection of the Astral Body.* London: Rider & Co., 1929. Republished New York: Samuel Weiser, 1973.

Muller, K. E. *Reincarnation Based on Facts.* London: Psychic Press, 1970.

Mundle, C. K. M. "On the 'Psychic' Powers of Non-Human Animals." In S. C. Thakur, ed. *Philosophy and Psychical Research.* London: Allen & Unwin, 1976.

———. 1973. "Strange Facts in Search of a Theory." PSPR 56:1.

———. 1965. "The Explanation of ESP." *International Journal of Parapsychology* 7(3):221.

———. 1950. "The Experimental Evidence for PK and Precognition." PSPR 49:61.

Münsterberg, H. 1899. "Psychology and Mysticism." *Atlantic Monthly.*

Murphy, G. 1970. "Are There Any Solid Facts in Psychical Research?" JASPR 64:3.

———. 1966. "Research in Creativeness: What Can It Tell Us about Extrasensory Perception?" JASPR 60:8.

———. 1957. "Triumphs and Defeats in the Study of Mediumship." JASPR 52:125.

———. 1957. "Notes for a Parapsychological Autobiography." JP 21:173.

———. 1953. "The Importance of Spontaneous Cases." JASPR 47:89.

———. *Personality: A Biosocial Approach to Origins and Structure.* New York: Harper and Row, 1947.

———. 1945. "An Outline of Survival Evidence." JASPR 39:2.

———. 1945. "Difficulties Confronting the Survival Hypothesis." JASPR 39:67.

———. 1945. "Field Theory and Survival." JASPR 39:181.

———. 1943. "Psychical Phenomena and Human Needs." JASPR 37:163.

———. 1941. "W. Whately Carington: In Memoriam." JASPR 41:123.

———. *Historical Introduction to Modern Psychology.* New York: Harcourt, Brace and World, 1929.

Murphy, G., and H. L. Klemme. 1966. "Unfinished Business." JASPR 60:306.

Murphy, G., and R. O. Ballou, eds. *William James on Psychical Research.* London: Chatto and Windus, 1961.

Murphy, G., with L. A. Dale. *The Challenge of Psychical Research.* New York: Harper and Row, 1961.

Murphy, M. *Golf in the Kingdom.* New York: Viking, 1972.

Murphy, M. and R. A. White. *The Psychic Side of Sports.* Reading, MA: Addison-Wesley, 1978.

Murray, G. 1952. "Presidential Address." PSPR 49:155.

———. 1916. "Presidential Address." PSPR 29:46.

Myers, A. T., W. Crookes, V. Horsley, W. C. Bull. 1885. "Report on an Alleged Physical Phenomenon." PSPR 3:460.

Myers, A. T., and F. W. H. Myers. 1893. "Mind-Cure, Faith-Cure, and the Miracles of Lourdes." PSPR 9:160.

Myers, F. W. H. *Human Personality and its Survival of Bodily Death.* London: Longmans, Green, 1903.

———. 1902. "On the Trance Phenomena of Mrs. Thompson." PSPR 17:67.

———. 1898. "The Right Hon. W. E. Gladstone." JSPR 8:260.

———. 1893. "The Experiences of W. Stainton Moses.—I." PSPR 9:245.

———. 1893. "I. The Subliminal Consciousness." PSPR 9:3, 12–15, 73–92.

———. 1892. "III. The Subliminal Consciousness." PSPR 8:436, 485–516.

———. 1892. "On the Indications of Continued Terrene Knowledge." PSPR 8:200.

———. 1892. "Prefatory Note. Record of a Haunted House." PSPR 8:311.

———. 1892. "Supplement." PSPR 8:597.

———. 1891–1892. "On Alleged Movement of Objects, without Contact, Occurring Not in the Presence of a Paid Medium." PSPR 7:383.

———. 1889. "On Recognized Apparitions Occurring More Than a Year ater Death." PSPR 6:13.

———. 1889. "Postscript on Mr. Gurney's Reply to Professor Peirce." PASPR 1:300.

———. 1885. "Automatic Writing." PSPR 3:1.

Myers, F. W. H., and H. Sidgwick, E. M. Sidgwick, A. Johnson, A. T. Myers, and F. Podmore. 1894. "Report on the Census of Hallucinations." PSPR 10:25.

Myers, F. W. H., and A. T. Myers. 1893. "Mind-Cure, Faith-Cure and the Miracles at Lourdes." PSPR 9:160–209.

Myers, F. W. H., and O. Lodge, W. Leaf, and W. James. 1890. "A Record of Observations of Certain Phenomena of Trance." PSPR 6:436.

Myers, F. W. H., and E. Gurney, and F. Podmore. *Phantasms of the Living.* London: Trubner, 1886.

Myers, F. W. H., E. Gurney, and W. F. Barrett. 1882. "First Report on Thought Reading." PSPR 1:13.

Naegeli-Osjord, H. *Possession and Exorcism.* Gerrards Cross, UK: New Frontiers Center and Colin Smythe, 1988.

Nanko, M. 1985. "A Report on the Case of Natuzza Evolo." *Journal of the Southern California Society for Psychical Research* 3:5.

Nash, C. B. *Parapsychology: The Science of Psiology.* Springfield, IL: Charles C. Thomas, 1986.

———. 1986. "Comparison of Subliminal and Extrasensory Perception." JSPR 52:435.

———. 1984. "Test of Psychokinetic Control of Bacterial Mutation." JASPR 78:145.

———. 1983. "An Extrasensory Observational Theory." JSPR 52:113.

———. *Science of Psi: ESP and PK.* Springfield, IL: Charles C. Thomas, 1978.

———. 1978. "Correspondence. Aura, Kirlian Photography and Acupuncture." JSPR 49:764.

———. 1969. "Cutaneous Perception of Color." JASPR 63:83.

———. 1944. "PK Tests of a Large Population." JP 8:304.

Nash, C. B., and C. S. Nash. 1962. "Negative Correlations Between the Scores of Subjects in Two Contemporaneous ESP Experiments." JASPR 56:80.

Nelson, R. D., B. J. Dunne, and R. G. Jahn. 1985. *Princeton Engineering Anomalies Research.* Technical Note PEAR 85003.

Newbold, W. R. 1920. "An Estimate." JASPR 14:493.

———. 1898. "A Further Record of Observations of Certain Phenomena of Trance. Part II." PSPR 14:6.

———. 1897. "Demon Possession and Allied Themes. By John L. Nevius, D.D." PSPR 13:602.

———. 1896. "Subconscious Reasoning." PSPR 12:11.

"New Case of Disturbed Coffins in the Barbados." 1947. JSPR 34:11.

Newcomb, S. 1886. "Address of the President." PASPR 1:84.

*New Realities* eds. 1979. "Matthew Manning beyond Spoon Bending." *New Realities* 2(6):28.

Nicol, B. H. 1960. "The Jones Boys: A Case for Telepathy Not Proven." JASPR 54:118.

———. (then Humphrey) 1949. "ESP Subjects Rated by Two Measures of Personality." JP 4:274.

———. *Handbook of Tests in Parapsychology.* Durham, NC: Parapsychology Laboratory, 1948.

———. 1947. "Simultaneous High and Low Aim in PK Tests." JP 11:160.

Nicol, B. H., and J. F. Nicol. 1955. "The Feeling of Success in ESP." JASPR 49:3.

———. 1953. "The Exploration of ESP and Human Personality." JASPR 47:133.

Nicol, J. F. "Historical Background." In B. Wolman,

ed. *Handbook of Parapsychology.* New York: Van Nostrand Reinhold, 1977, pp. 317–318.

———. 1972. "The Founders of the S.P.R." PSPR 55:341.

———. 1966. "The Silences of Mr. Trevor Hall." *International Journal of Parapsychology* 8(1):5.

———. 1967. "Obituary: Professor Hornell Hart." JSPR 44:165.

———. 1948. "The Fox Sisters and the Development of Spiritualism." JSPR 34:271.

Nicol, J. F., and B. Humphrey. 1955. "The Feeling of Success in ESP." JASPR 49:3.

———. 1953. "The Exploration of ESP and Human Personality." JASPR 47:133.

Nielsen, E. *Solid Proofs of Survival.* London: Spiritualist Press, 1950.

Nordbeck, B., and M. Johnson. 1972. "Variation in the Scoring of a 'Psychic' Subject." JP 36:311.

"Note on the Alleged Prediction of the Servian Murders." 1903. JSPR 11:132.

"Note on the 'Gunther-Geffers Case.'" 1928. JSPR 24:306.

"Notes on Periodicals." 1930. JSPR 26:87.

Nouvomeysky, A. S. 1963. "The Nature of the Dermo-Optical Sense." *The Problems of Psychology* 5. Eng. Trans. *International Journal of Parapsychology.* 6:5.

Novillo Paulí, E. *Los Fenómenos Parapsicológicos—Psi en el Laboratorio.* Buenos Aires: Editorial Kapelusz, 1984.

Nuttall, G. E. H., and J. E. Jastrow. 1886. "On the Existence of a Magnetic Sense." PSPR 1:116.

Ochi, Y. 1982. "Some Observations on Metal Bending of Pure Aluminum Plate by Psychokinesis." *Journal of the Psi Institute of Japan* 17:7.

Ochi, Y., A. Tokaoka, and A. Sasaki. 1978. "Some Observations with Scanning Electronic Microscope (SEM) of Fracture Surface of Metals Fractured by Psychokinesis." *Journal of the Psi Institute of Japan* 2:15.

Oguma, T. *Shinrei-Gensho no Mondai* (Problems of Psychical Research). Tokyo: Shinrigaku Kenkyyukai, 1918.

Onda, A. 1964. "A Study of the Relationship Between Creativity and ESP." *Bulletin* of Tokyo University 18:1.

Osborn, A. W. *The Meaning of Personal Existence.* London: Sidgwick and Jackson, 1966.

———. *The Future is Now: The Significance of Reincarnation.* New York: University Books, 1962.

Osis, K. "The Paranormal: My Window to Something More." In R. Pilkington, ed. *Men and Women of Parapsychology.* Jefferson, NC: McFarland, 1987.

———. 1987. "A Tribute to Margaret L. Anderson, 1920–1985" [sic]. JASPR 81:257.

———. 1985. "The American Society for Psychical Research 1941–1985: A Personal View." JASPR 79:501.

———. "Out-of-Body Research at the American Society for Psychical Research." In D. Scott Rogo, ed. *Mind Beyond the Body: The Mystery of ESP Projection.* New York: Penguin Books, 1978, p. 162.

———. 1970. "ESP over Long Distances: In Search of Transmitted Energy." Paper presented at the 137th Meeting of the American Association for the Advancement of Science.

———. 1966. "Linkage Experiments with Mediums." JASPR 60:91.

———. *Deathbed Observations by Physicians and Nurses.* (Parapsychological Monographs No. 3). New York: Parapsychology Foundation, 1961.

Osis, K., and D. McCormick. 1980. "Kinetic Effects at the Ostensible Location of an Out-of-Body Experience during Perceptual Testing." JASPR 74:319.

Osis, K., and E. Haraldsson. *At the Hour of Death.* New York: Avon Books, 1977. (Rev. ed. New York: Hastings House, 1986).

Osterriech, T. K. "Kathleen Goligher" and "Stanislawa Tomczyk." In A. Schrenck-Notzing, ed. *Die physikalischen Phänomene der grossen Medie. Eine Abwehr.* Stuttgart, Berlin & Leipzig: Union Deutsche Verlagsgellschaft, 1926, pp. 105, 171.

———. *Die Besessenheit.* Langensalza: Wendt & Klauwell, 1921. (English edition *Possession: Demoniacal and Other, among Primitive Races, in Antiquity, the Middle Ages, and Modern Times.* E.T. D. Ibberson. New Hyde Park, NY: University Books, 1966).

Ostrander, S., and L. Schroeder. *Handbook of Psychic Discoveries.* New York: Berkeley Medallion Books, 1974.

———. 1971. "Psychic Enigmas & Energies in the U.S.S.R." *Psychic* 2(6):8.

———. *Psychic Discoveries behind the Iron Curtain.* New York: Bantam Books, 1970.

Osty, E. *Une Faculté de Connaissance Supra-Normal. Pascal Forthuny.* Paris: Felix Alcan, 1926.

———. (trans. by S. de Barth). *Supernormal Faculties in Man.* London: Methuen & Co., 1923.

Osty, M. 1959. "Eugene Osty: Pioneer Researcher." *Tomorrow* 7(1):96.

Otani, S. "Effect of Short-Term Stimulus upon ESP Functions." In J. Beloff and W. G. Roll, eds. *Research in Parapsychology 1980.* Metuchen, N.J.: The Scarecrow Press, 1981, p. 89.

Otani, S., S. Imai, Y. Ro, N. Kohri, T. Kasahara. "A Study on PK Ability of a Gifted Subject in Japan." In J. Beloff and W. G. Roll, eds. *Research in Parapsychology, 1980.* Metuchen, NJ: The Scarecrow Press, 1981, p. 39.

Oteri, L., and R. van Over, eds. *William McDougall: Explorer of the Mind.* New York: Garrett Publications, 1967.

Ouspensky, P. D. *Strange Life of Ivan Osokin.* New York: University Books, 1966.

———. *In Search of the Miraculous.* London: Routledge and Kegan Paul, 1950.

van Over, R., and L. Oteri, eds. *William McDougall: Explorer of the Mind.* New York: Garrett Publications, 1967.

Owen, A.R.G. *Psychic Mysteries of the North.* New York: Harper & Row, 1975.

———. *Can We Explain the Poltergeist?.* New York: Garrett Publications, 1965.

Owen, I., and P. Mitchell. 1979. "The Alleged Haunting of Borley Rectory." JSPR 50: 149, 161.

Owen, I., with M. Sparrow. *Conjuring Up Philip.* New York: Harper and Row, 1976.

Owen, R. D. *Footfalls on the Boundary of Another World.* Philadelphia, PA: Lippincott, 1923.

Ozanne, C. "A Layman Looks at Psychical Research." JASPR 36:76.

Pagenstecher, G. 1922. "Past Events Seership: A Study in Psychometry." PASPR 16:1.

Paine, A. B. "Mark Twain: A Biographical Summary." In the *Family Mark Twain,* Vol. 1. New York: Harper and Row, 1972. (Originally published 1894).

Palmer, J. 1983. "Sensory Contamination of Free-Response ESP Targets: The Greasy Fingers Hypothesis." JASPR 77:101.

———. 1983. "In Defense of Parapsychology." *Zetetic Scholar* 11:39, 91.

———. "Review of J. B. Rhine's ESP Research." In K. R. Rao, ed. *J. B. Rhine: On the Frontier of Science.* Jefferson, NC: MacFarland, 1982.

———. "ESP Research Findings." In S. Krippner, ed. *Advances in Parapsychology,* Vol. 2. New York: Plenum, 1979.

———. 1979. "A Community Mail Survey of Psychic Experiences." JASPR 73:221.

———. 1978. "The Out-of-Body Experience: A Psychological Theory." *Parapsychology Review* 9:19.

———. "Attitudes and Personality Traits." In B. Wolman, ed. *Handbook of Parapsychology.* New York: Van Nostrand Reinhold, 1977.

Palmer, J., H. Edge, R. L. Morris, and J. Rush. *Foundations of Parapsychology: Exploring the Boundaries of Human Capability.* London: Routledge & Kegan Paul, 1986.

Palmer, J., K. Khamashta, and K. Israelson. 1979. "An ESP Ganzfeld Experiment with Transcendental Meditators." JASPR 73:334.

Parsons, D. "Detective Work in Parapsychology." In P. Kurtz, ed. *A Skeptic's Handbook of Parapsychology.* Buffalo, NY: Prometheus Books, 1985, pp. 599–609.

———. 1982. "Dowsing—A Claim Refuted." JSPR 51:384.

———. 1962. "A Non-Existent Building Located." JSPR 41:292.

———. 1961. "The Black Boxes of Mr De La Warr." JSPR 41:12.

———. 1956. "Cloudbusting—A Claim Investigated." JSPR 38:352.

———. 1948. "On the Need for Caution in Assessing Mediumistic Material." PSPR 48:344.

Passeron, A. 1983. "Trances and Dances." *Revue Métapsychique* 17:9.

Pauwels, L., and J. Bergier. *The Morning of the Magicians.* New York: Avon Books, 1968. (First published in France in 1960 by Editions Gallimard as *Le Matin des Magiciens*).

Penelhum, T. *Survival and Disembodied Existence.* New York: Humanities Press 1970.

Perlstrom, J. R., and R. S. Broughton. "A Competitive Computer Game in PK Research: Some Preliminary Findings." In R. White and J. Solfvin, eds. *Research in Parapsychology 1984.* Metuchen, NJ: Scarecrow Press, 1985.

Perovsky-Petrovo-Solovovo, M. 1937. "My Experiments with S. F. Sambor." JSPR 30:87.

———. 1928. "On Some 'Critical' Methods." JSPR 24:361.

———. 1928. "Notes on Periodicals." JSPR 24:307.

———. 1911. "Les Phénomènes Physiques de Spiritisme." PSPR 25:413.

———. 1909. "The Hallucination Theory as Applied to Certain Cases of Physical Phenomena." PSPR 21:436.

———. 1903. "Obituary—Mr. A. N. Aksakoff." JSPR 11:45.

———. 1893. "On the Production of Spurious 'Spirit Raps'." JSPR 6:120.

Perry, M., ed. *Deliverance.* London: SPCK, 1987.

———. 1986. "Parapsychology and the Transfiguration of Jesus." *The Christian Parapsychologist* 6:223.

———. *Psychic Studies: A Christian's View.* Wellingborough: Aquarian Press, 1984.

———. *The Resurrection of Man.* London: Mowbray's Library of Theology, 1975.

———. *The Easter Enigma: An Essay on the Resurrection with Special Reference to the Data of Psychical Research.* London: Faber & Faber, 1959.

Peter, J., and R. Moran. 1978. "The Amityville Horror Hoax." *Fate* 31(5):43.

Pfungst, O. *Clever Hans.* New York: Holt, Rinehart and Winston, 1965. (Originally published and translated from the German in 1911 by Henry Holt Co.)

Phillips, P. R. 1983. "A Brief Report on Recent Experiences with Fraudulent Subjects." (Privately circulated.)

Phillips, P. R., and M. K. McBeath. "An Attempted Replication of the Cox Films of PK." In W. G. Roll, J. Beloff, and R. A. White, eds., *Research in Parapsychology, 1982.* Metuchen, NJ: The Scarecrow Press, 1983, pp. 113–115.

Pickering, E. C. 1885. "Possibility of Errors in Scientific Researches, Due to Thought-Transference." PASPR 1:35.

Pickering, W. H. 1886. "A Research on the Reality of Reichenbach's Flames." PASPR 1:127.

Piddington, J. G. 1924. Presidential Address." PSPR 34:131.

———. 1923. "Forecasts in Scripts Concerning the War." PSPR 33:438.

———. 1916. "Cross-Correspondences of the Gallic Type." PSPR Research 29:1.

———. 1908. "A Series of Concordant Automatisms." PSPR 22:19.

———. 1907. "Richard Hodgson: In Memoriam. II." PSPR 19:362.

———. 1904. "On the Types of Phenomena Displayed in Mrs. Thompson's Trance." PSPR 18:104.

———. 1903. "Le Temple Enseveli, by Maurice Maeterlinck." PSPR 17:411.

Piddington, J. G., E. M. Sidgwick, and M. de G. Verrall. 1910. "Further Experiments with Mrs. Piper in 1908." PSPR 24:31.

Pierson, J. 1938. "Psychic Manifestations Among the Shakers—Part 1." JASPR 32:301.

Pike, J. A. *The Other Side.* Garden City, New York: Doubleday & Co., 1968.

———. *If This Be Heresy.* New York: Harper & Row, 1967.

———. *A Time for Christian Candor.* New York: Harper & Row, 1964.

Pilkington, R. "Emilio Servadio. Interview, Rome, August 24, 1985." In R. Pilkington, ed. *Men and Women of Parapsychology: Personal Reflections.* Jefferson, NC: McFarland, 1987.

———. "Eileen Coly: Interview, January 20, 1986." In R. Pilkington, ed. *Men and Women of Parapsychology: Personal Reflections.* Jefferson, NC: McFarland, 1987.

Piper, A. L. *The Life and Work of Mrs. Piper.* London: Kegan Paul, 1929.

Plagemann, S. H., and J. Gribbin. *The Jupiter Effect.* New York: Walker, 1974.

Playfair, G. L. *This House is Haunted.* London: Souvenir Press, 1980.

———. *The Indefinite Boundary.* London: Souvenir Press, 1976.

———. *The Flying Cow.* London: Souvenir Press, 1975.

Pleasants, H., ed. *Biographical Dictionary of Parapsychology.* New York: Helix Press, 1964.

Podmore, F. *Mediums of the Nineteenth Century.* New Hyde Park, NY: University Books, 1963.

———. *The Newer Spiritualism.* London: Fisher Unwin, 1910.

———. 1909. "The Report on Eusapia Palladino." JSPR 14:172.

———. *Modern Spiritualism: A History and Criticism.* London: Methuen, 1902.

———. 1899. "Correspondence." JSPR 38:49.

———. 1898. "Discussion of the Trance-Phenomena of Mrs. Piper." PSPR 14:80.

———. *Studies in Psychical Research.* London: Kegan Paul, Trench, Trubner & Co., 1897.

———. 1896–1897. "Poltergeists." PSPR 12:45.

———. *Apparitions and Thought-Transference: an Examination of the Evidence for Telepathy.* New York: Putnam's, 1894.

Podmore, F., H. Sidgwick, E. M. Sidgwick, A. Johnson, F. W. H. Myers, and A. T. Myers. 1894. "Report on the Census of Hallucinations." PSPR 10:25.

Podmore, F., E. Gurney, and F. W. H. Myers. *Phantasms of the Living.* London: Trubner, 1886. 2 vols.

Pollack, J. H. *Croiset the Clairvoyant.* Garden City, NY: Doubleday, 1964.

Pond, M. B. *The Unwilling Martyrs.* London: Spiritualist Press, 1947.

Pope, D. H. *Parapsychology Bulletin,* 72 nos., 1946–1965.

———. "The Search for ESP in Animals." *Tomorrow,* Summer 1953.

Pope, D. H., with J. G. Pratt. 1942. "Five Years of the Journal of Parapsychology." JP 6.

———. 1942. "The ESP Controversy." JP 6:174.

Poynton, J. C. 1985. "Nonevident Psi and Phenomenology." *Parapsychology Review* 14:9.

———. "Results of an Out-of-the-Body Survey." In J. C. Poynton, ed. *Parapsychology in South Africa.* Johannesburg: South African Society for Psychical Research, 1975, p. 109.

Pratt, J. G. 1978. "Prologue to a Debate: Some Assumptions Relevant to Research in Parapsychology." JASPR 72:127.

———. *Parapsychology: An Insider's View of ESP.* Metuchen, NJ: The Scarecrow Press, 1977.

———. *ESP Research Today: A Study of Developments in Parapsychology Since 1960.* Metuchen, NJ: The Scarecrow Press, 1973.

———. *On the Evaluation of Verbal Material in Parapsychology.* Parapsychological Monograph No. 10. New York: Parapsychology Foundation, 1969.

———. 1947. "Obituary: Charles E. Stuart." JASPR 41:140.

Pratt, J. G., B. Herbert, H. H. Keil, and M. Ullman. 1976. "Directly Observable Voluntary PK Effects: A Survey and Tentative Interpretation of Available Findings from Nina Kulagina and Other Known Related Cases of Recent Date." PSPR: 56:197.

Pratt, J. G., with J. Eisenbud, and I. Stevenson. 1981. "Distortions in the Photographs of Ted Serios." JASPR 75:143.

Pratt, J. G., and H. H. J. Keil. 1973. "First Hand Observations of Nina S. Kulagina Suggestive of PK on Static Objects." JASPR 67:381.

Pratt, J. G., with C. Ransom. 1972. "Extrasensory Perception or Extraordinary Perception? A Present Series of Experiments with Pavel Stepanek." JASPR 66:63.

Pratt, J. G. and W. G. Roll. 1971. "The Miami Disturbances." JASPR 65:409.

"President Lincoln's Manifesto for the Abolition of Slavery: The Narrative of Colonel Kase." 1930. *Psychic Research* 24:115.

Price, G. R. 1972. "Apology to Rhine and Soal." *Science* 175:359.

———. 1955. "Science and the Supernatural." *Science* 122:359.

Price, H. *Fifty Years of Psychical Research: A Critical Survey.* New York: Arno Press, 1975.

———. *The End of Borley Rectory.* London: Harrap, 1946.

———. *Poltergeist over England.* London: Country Life, 1945.

———. *The Most Haunted House in England.* London: Longmans, Green, 1940.

———. *Confessions of a Ghost Hunter.* New York: G. P. Putnam's, 1936.

———. 1936. "A Report on Two Experimental Fire Walks." *Bulletin II, University of London Council for Psychical Investigation.*

———. 1931. "Regurgitation and the Duncan Mediumship." *Bulletin of the National Laboratory of Psychical Research.*

———. *Rudi Schneider—A Scientific Examination of His Mediumship,* London: Methuen & Co., 1930.

———. 1931. "The R-101 Disaster (Case Record): Mediumship of Mrs. Garrett." JASPR 25:268.

———. 1930. "International Notes." *Psychic Research* 34(9):427–428.

———. 1926. "Some Early Works on False Mediumship." JASPR 20:120.

———. 1926. "A Strange Experience with a Shropshire Poltergeist." JASPR 20:77.

———. 1926. "Poltergeist Phenomena of Eleonore Zugun." JASPR 20:449.

———. *Stella C.* London: Hurst and Blackett, 1925.

———. 1926. "Science in the Séance Room." JASPR 20:202.

———. 1922. "A Case of Fraud with the Crewe Circle." JSPR 20:271.

Price, H., and H. Kohn. 1930. "An Indian Poltergeist." *Psychic Research* 24:122.

Price, H., and E. J. Dingwall. *Revelations of a Spirit Medium.* London: Kegan Paul, 1922.

"Obituary: Mr. Harry Price." 1948. JSPR 34:238.

"Obituary: Mr. Harry Price." 1948. JASPR 42:152.

Price, H. H. "Some Philosophical Questions about Telepathy and Clairvoyance." in J. M. O. Wheatley and H. L. Edge, eds. *Philosophical Dimensions of Parapsychology.* Springfield, IL: Charles C. Thomas, 1976. (Originally published in 1940 in *Philosophy.*)

———. 1954. "Professor C. D. Broad's *Religion, Philosophy and Psychical Research.*" JASPR 48:56.

———. 1953. "Survival and the Idea of 'Another World'." PSPR 50:1.

———. 1941. "Henri Bergson." PSPR 46:271.

———. 1939. "Presidential Address. Haunting and the 'Psychic Ether' Hypothesis; With Some Preliminary Reflections on the Past and Present Condition and Possible Future of Psychical Research." PSPR 45:307.

Price, H. H., W. H. Salter, and G. W. Fisk. 1953. "G. N. M. Tyrrell and His Contributions to Psychical Research." JSPR 37:63.

Prince, M. *The Dissociation of Personality.* New York: Longman, Green and Co., 1906.

Prince, W. F. *The Case of Patience Worth.* New Hyde Park, NY: University Books, 1964. (Originally published 1927 by Boston Society for Psychic Research.)

———. *Noted Witnesses for Psychic Occurrences.* New York: University Books, 1963. (Originally published 1928 by Boston Society for Psychic Research.)

———. 1932. "A Sitting with Bert Reese." JSPR 27:249.

———. 1930. "Presidential Address." PSPR 39:247.

———. 1923. "Four Peculiarly Characterized Dreams." JASPR 17:82.

———. 1921. "Psychometric Experiments with Señora Maria Reyes de Z." PASPR 15:189.

———. 1920. "Peculiar Experiences Connected with Noted Persons." JASPR 14:362.

———. 1918. "Peculiar Experiences Connected with Noted Persons." JASPR 12:678.

———. 1915, 1916. "The Doris Case of Multiple Personality." PASPR 9:1, 10:701.

*Walter Franklin Prince: A Tribute to His Memory.* Boston: Boston Society for Psychic Research, 1935.

Progoff, I. *The Image of an Oracle: A Report on Research into the Mediumship of Eileen J. Garrett.* New York: Garrett Publications, 1964.

Protti, G. 1934. "Accertamente e Considerazione Esguite a Pirano sulla Cosidetta 'Donna Luminosa.'" *Riforma Medica* 50:841.

*Psychic* eds. 1975. "Interview Matthew Manning." *6(5):58.*

"Psychic Tots of China." *Discover* July 1988, pp. 28–29.

Puharich, H. K. 1974. "Psychic Research and the Healing Process." In E. Mitchell, and J. White, eds. *Psychic Explorations.* New York: G. P. Putnam Son's, 1974, p. 333.

———. (Andrija). *Uri: A Journal of the Mystery of Uri Geller.* New York: Anchor/Doubleday, 1974.

———. *Beyond Telepathy.* Garden City, NY: Doubleday & Co., 1962.

Puthoff, H. E., and R. Targ. *Mind-Reach: Scientists Look at Psychic Ability.* New York: Delacorte Press/Eleanor Friede, 1977.

Puthoff, H. E., R. Targ, and C. T. Tart. *Mind at Large: Institute of Electrical and Electronic Engineers Symposia on the Nature of Extrasensory Perception.* New York: 1979.

Quing Nan, Z. 1985. "Qigong—Ancient Way to Good Health." *China Reconstructs.* Vol. 34, No. 7. July 1985, p. 56.

Radin, D. I., E. C. May, and M. J. Thomson. "Psi Experiments with Random Number Generators: Meta-Analysis Part I." In D. H. Weiner and D. I. Radin, eds. *Research in Parapsychology 1985.* Metuchen, NJ: The Scarecrow Press, 1986, p. 14.

Raeder, K. "Klaus Maria Brandauer." 1988. *European Travel & Life* 4(4):57.

Randall, J. L. 1981. "A New Science of Life: The Hypothesis of Formative Causation." JSPR 51:156.

Randi, J. *The Faith Healers.* Buffalo, NY: Prometheus Books, 1987.

———. "Project Alpha Experiment." In K. Frazier, ed. *Science Confronts the Paranormal.* Buffalo, NY: Prometheus Books, 1986.

———. "The Role of Conjurers in Psi Research." In P. Kurtz, ed. *A Skeptic's Handbook of Parapsychology.* Buffalo, NY: Prometheus Books, 1985.

———. *The Truth about Uri Geller.* Buffalo, NY: Prometheus Books, 1982. (Originally pub. as *The Magic of Uri Geller.* New York: Ballantine Books, 1975.)

———. *Flim-Flam!* New York: Lippincott & Crowell, 1980.

Randles, J. *UFO Reality: A Critical Look at the Physical Evidence.* London: Robert Hale, 1983.

Ransom, C., with J. G. Pratt, 1972. "Extrasensory Perception or Extraordinary Perception? A Present Series of Experiments with Pavel Stepanek." JASPR 66:63.

Rao, K. R. *The Basic Experiments in Parapsychology.* Jefferson, NC: McFarland & Co., 1984.

———. *J. B. Rhine: On the Frontiers of Science.* Jefferson, NC: McFarland & Co., 1982.

———. *Experimental Parapsychology.* Springfield, IL: Charles C. Thomas, 1966.

Rao, K. R., and P. V. K. Rao. 1982. "Two Studies of ESP and Subliminal Perception." JP 46:185.

Rao, P. V. K., and K. R. Rao. 1982. "Two Studies of ESP and Subliminal Perception." JP 46:185.

Rao, P. V. K., and K. Harigopal. 1979. "The Three Gunas and ESP: An Exploratory Investigation." *Journal of Indian Psychology* 2:63.

Rao, P. V. K., and J. Feola. "Alpha Rhythm and ESP in a Free Response Situation." In W. G. Roll *et al.,* eds. *Research in Parapsychology 1972.* Metuchen, NJ: Scarecrow Press, 1973.

Raudive, K. *Breakthrough.* New York: Taplinger Pub. Co., 1971.

Rauscher, E., and B. A. Rubik. "Effects on Motility Behavior and Growth Rate of Salmonella Typhimurium in the Presence of a Psychic Subject." In W. G. Roll, ed. *Research in Parapsychology 1979.* Metuchen, NJ: Scarecrow Press, 1980, p. 140.

Rauscher, W. F., with A. Spraggett. *Arthur Ford: The Man Who Talked with the Dead.* New York: New American Library, 1973.

Rayleigh, Lord (John William Strutt). 1919. "Presidential Address." PSPR 30:275.

"Rayleigh (of Terling Place)." 1986. *The New Encyclopaedia Britannica,* 15th ed., 9:964.

Rayleigh, Lord (Robert John Strutt). 1938. "Presidential Address. The Problem of Physical Phenomena in connection with Psychical Research." PSPR 45:1.

———. 1938. "Some Recollections of Henry Sidgwick." PSPR 45:162.

"Obituary. Lord Rayleigh, F.R.S." 1948. PSPR 48:330.

Reiser, M., L. Ludwig, S. Saxe, and C. Wagner. 1979. "An Evaluation of the Use of Psychics in the Investigation of Major Crimes." *Journal of Police Science and Administration* 7:18.

Rejdak, Z. 1971. "Phenomena: Nina Kulagina's Mind over Matter." *Psychic* 2(6):24.

———. 1969. "The Kulagina Cine Films: Introductory Notes." *Journal of Paraphysics* 3:64.

"Report on the Census of Hallucinations." 1894. PSPR 10:25.

"Report of the Committee Appointed to Investigate Phenomena Connected with the Theosophical Society." 1885. PSPR 3:201.

"Report on the Oliver Lodge Posthumous Test." 1955. JSPR 38:121.

"The Result of the Prize Offer to Physical Mediums." JSPR 34:153.

"The Rev. Arthur Ford." 1928. JSPR 24:357.

"Reviews: *An Adventure*." PSPR 25:353.

Rhine, J. B. "History of Experimental Studies." In B. Wolman, ed. *Handbook of Parapsychology.* New York: Van Nostrand, Reinhold Co., 1977, p. 25.

———. 1974. "A New Case of Experimenter Unreliability." JP 38:215.

———. 1971. "Eileen J. Garrett as I Knew Her." JSPR 46:59.

———. *New World of the Mind.* New York: William Sloane Associates, 1953.

———. *The Reach of the Mind.* New York: William Sloane Associates, 1947.

———. 1938. "Experiments Bearing on the Precognition Hypothesis." JP 2:38.

———. *New Frontiers of the Mind.* New York: Farrar and Rinehart, 1937.

———. *Extra-Sensory Perception.* Boston: Boston Society for Psychic Research, 1934. Also published Boston: Bruce Humphries.

———. 1934. "Telepathy and Clairvoyance in the Normal and Trance States of a 'Medium.'" *Character and Personality* 3:91.

Rhine, J. B., and R. Brier *Parapsychology Today.* New York: Citadel Press, 1968.

Rhine, J. B., and J. G. Pratt. 1954. "A Review of the Pearce-Pratt Distance Series of ESP Tests." JP 18:165.

Rhine, J. B., and R. L. Averill. 1945. "The Effect of Alcohol upon Performance in PK Tests." JP 9:32.

Rhine, J. B., B. M. Humphrey, and R. L. Averill. 1945. "An Exploratory Experiment on the Effects of Caffeine upon Performance in PK Tests." JP 9:80.

Rhine, J. B., and L. E. Rhine. 1943. "The Psychokinetic Effect: 1. The First Experiment." JP 7:20.

Rhine, J. B., J. G. Pratt, C. E. Stuart, B. M. Smith, and J. A. Greenwood. *Extrasensory Perception After Sixty Years.* New York: Henry Holt, 1940. (Republished Boston: Bruce Humphries, 1966, with a new foreword by J. B. Rhine.)

Rhine, J. B., and L. E. Rhine. 1929. "An Investigation of a 'Mind-Reading Horse.'" *Journal of Abnormal and Social Psychology* 23:449.

———. 1929. "Second Report on Lady, the 'Mind-Reading' Horse." *Journal of Abnormal and Social Psychology* 24:287.

———. 1927. "One Evening's Observation on the Margery Mediumship." *Journal of Abnormal and Social Psychology* 21:401.

Rhine, L. E. *Something Hidden.* Jefferson, NC: McFarland, 1983.

———. *Psi: What Is It?* New York: Harper & Row, 1975.

———. *ESP in Life and Lab: Tracing Hidden Channels.* New York: Macmillan, 1967.

———. *Hidden Channels of the Mind.* New York: William Sloane, 1961.

———. 1956. "Hallucinatory Psi Experiences: I. An Introductory Survey." JP 20:233.

———. 1957. "Hallucinatory Psi Experiences: II. The Initiative of the Percipient in Hallucinations of the Living, the Dying, and the Dead." JP 21:13.

———. 1957. "Hallucinatory Psi Experiences: III. The Intention of the Agent and the Dramatizing Tendency of the Percipient." JP 21:186.

———. 1955. "Precognition and Intervention." JP 19:1.

———. 1954. "Frequency of Types of Experience in Spontaneous Precognition." JP 18:93.

———. 1953. "Subjective Forms of Spontaneous Psi Experiences." JP 17:77.

Rhine, L. E., and J. B. Rhine. 1943. "The Psychokinetic Effect: I. the First Experiment." JP 7:20.

———. 1929. "An Investigation of a 'Mind-Reading Horse'." *Journal of Abnormal and Social Psychology* 23:449.

———. 1929. "Second Report on Lady, the 'Mind-Reading' Horse." *Journal of Abnormal and Social Psychology* 24:287.

———. 1927. "One Evening's Observation on the Margery Mediumship." *Journal of Abnormal and Social Psychology* 21:401.

Rhys, E. *Everyman Remembers.* New York: ———, 1931.

Richards, J. T. *SORRAT: A History of the Neihardt Psychokinesis Experiments, 1961–1981.* Metuchen, NJ: The Scarecrow Press, 1982.

Richet, C. 1925. "Des Conditions de la Certitude." PSPR 35:422, 433–438.

———. *Thirty Years of Psychical Research.* New York: Macmillan, 1923 (republished New York: Arno Press, 1975).

———. 1905. "De Quelques Phénomènes dits de Materialisation." *Annales des Sciences Psychiques.*

———. 1905. "Xenoglossie: L'Ecriture Automatique en Langues Etrangères." PSPR 29:162.

———. 1889. "Further Experiments in Hypnotic Lucidity or Clairvoyance." PSPR 6:66.

———. 1884. "La Suggestion Mentale et Le Calcul des Probabilités." *Revue Philosophique* 18:608.

Richmond, K. 1936. "Preliminary Studies of the Recorded Leonard Material." PSPR 44:17.

Richmond, Z. *Evidence of Purpose.* London: G. Bell & Sons, Ltd. 1938.

Rickard, R.J.M., and J. Michell. *Phenomena: A Book of Wonders.* New York: Pantheon Books, 1977.

Riess, B. F. 1937. "A Case of High Scores in Card-Guessing at a Distance." JP 1:260.

Ring, K. *Heading Toward Omega—In Search of the Meaning of the Near-Death Experience.* New York: William Morrow, 1984.

———. *Life At Death: A Scientific Investigation of the Near-Death Experience.* New York: Coward, McCann & Geoghegan, 1980.

Ro., Y., N. Kohri, T. Kasahara, S. Imai, and S. Otani. 1981. "A Study on PK Ability of a Gifted Subject in Japan." In J. Beloff and W. G. Roll, eds. *Research in Parapsychology, 1980.* Metuchen, NJ: Scarecrow Press, 1981, p. 39.

Roberts, E. *Forty Years a Medium.* London: Herbert Jenkins, 1959.

Roberts, J. *The Seth Material.* Englewood Cliffs, NJ: Prentice-Hall, 1970.

———. *Seth Speaks.* Englewood Cliffs, NJ: Prentice-Hall, 1972.

———. *The Nature of Personal Reality.* Englewood Cliffs, NJ: Prentice-Hall, 1974.

———. *The Unknown Reality, Vol. 1.* Englewood Cliffs, NJ: Prentice-Hall, 1977 (Reissued by Bantam Books, 1988).

———. *The After-Life of an American Philosopher: The World View of William James.* Englewood Cliffs, NJ: Prentice-Hall, 1978.

———. *The Unknown Reality, Vol. 2.* Englewood Cliffs, NJ: Prentice-Hall, 1979 (Reissued by Bantam Books, 1989).

———. *The Nature of the Psyche.* Englewood Cliffs, NJ: Prentice-Hall, 1979.

———. *The Individual and the Nature of Mass Events.* Englewood Cliffs, NJ: Prentice-Hall, 1981.

Robertson, M. *Futility.* New York: M.F. Mansfield, 1898 (Reprinted in J.W. Hannah. *The Futility God.* Mansfield, OH: The Didactic Publishing Associates, 1975).

Robinson, D. *To Stretch a Plank: A Survey of Psychokinesis.* Chicago: Nelson Hall, 1981.

Rochas, A. *Les Forces non Définies.* Paris: Masson, 1887.

Rockwell, T. and W. T. Rockwell. 1988. "Margins of Reality: The Role of Consciousness in the Physical World." JASPR 82:359.

Rockwell, T., R. Rockwell, and W. T. Rockwell. 1978. "Irrational Rationalists: A Critique of *The Humanist*'s Crusade against Parapsychology." JASPR 72:23.

———. 1978. "Part II. Context vs. Meaning: A Reply to Dr. Kurtz." JASPR 72:357.

Rogo, D. S. 1989. "Book Review. Lives and Letters in American Parapsychology—A Biographical History, 1859–1987 by Arthur S. Berger." *Parapsychology Review* 20(3):12.

———. 1985. "Book Review. The *Paranormal* by Brian Inglis." JSPR 53:180

———. *The Evidence for Life after Death.* Wellingborough, UK: Aquarian Press, 1985.

———. *Miracles: A Parascientific Inquiry into Wondrous Phenomena.* New York: Dial Press, 1982.

———. *Minds and Motion.* New York: Taplinger, 1978.

———. *The Haunted Universe.* New York: New American Library, 1977.

———. 1976. "Aspects of Out-of-Body Experiences." JSPR 48:329.

———. *An Experience of Phantoms.* New York: Taplinger, 1974.

———. *The Welcoming Silence.* New Hyde Park, NY: University Books, 1973.

———. 1973. "Fakers and Fakirs." *Psychic* 5(2):50.

Rogo, D. S., with R. Bayless, *Phone Calls from the Dead.* Englewood Cliffs, NJ: Prentice-Hall, 1979.

Roll, W. G. *The Poltergeist.* Metuchen, NJ: The Scarecrow Press, 1976. (Originally published New York: New American Library, 1972.)

———. "Poltergeists." In B. Wolman, ed. *Handbook of Parapsychology.* New York: Van Nostrand Reinhold, 1977.

———. "ESP and Memory." In J. M. O. Wheatley and H. L. Edge, eds. *Philosophical Dimensions of Parapsychology.* Springfield, IL: Charles C. Thomas, 1976.

———. 1964. "The Psi Field." *Proceedings of the Parapsychological Association* 1:32.

———. 1961. "The Problem of Precognition." JSPR 41:115.

Roll, W. G. and J. G. Pratt. 1971. "The Miami Disturbances." JASPR 65:409.

———. 1958. "The Seaford Disturbances." JP 22:79.

Romains, J. *La Vision Extra-Rétinienne et le Sens Paroptique.* Paris: Gallimard. (Eng. Trans. *Eyeless Vision.* New York: Putnam, 1964).

Roney-Dougal, S. M. 1987. "A Comparison of Subliminal and Psi Perception: Exploratory and Follow-up Studies." JASPR 81:141.

———. 1984. "'Occult' Conference Questionnaire." JSPR 52:379.

Rose, L. 1955. "Some Aspects of Paranormal Healing." JSPR 38:105.

Rose, R. 1952. "Psi and Australian Aborigines." JASPR 46:17–28.

———. 1950. "Psychical Research in Australia." JASPR 44:74.

Rosenbusch, H., with C. von Klinckowstroem, and W. von Gulat-Wellenberg. "1: Der physikalische Medi-umismus." In M. Dessoir, ed. *Der Okkultismus in Urkunden.* Berlin: Ullstein Verlag, 1925.

Rothschild, F. Introduction. In J. Bazak. *Judaism and Psychical Phenomena.* New York: Garrett Publications, 1972.

Royce, J. 1889. "Report of the Committee on Phantasms and Presentiments." PASPR 1(4):350.

Rubik, B. A., and E. Rauscher. "Effects on Motility Behavior and Growth Rate of Salmonella Typhimurium in the Presence of a Psychic Subject." In W. G. Roll, ed. *Research in Parapsychology 1979.* Metuchen, NJ: The Scarecrow Press, 1980, p. 140.

Rubin, L., and C. Honorton. 1971. "Separating the Yins from the Yangs: An Experiment with the I Ching." *Proceedings of the Parapsychological Association* 8:6.

Rush, J. H. "Parapsychology: Some Personal Observations." In R. Pilkington, ed. *Men and Women of Parapsychology.* Jefferson, NC: McFarland, 1987.

———. "Physical and Quasi-physical Theories of Psi." In J. H. Rush, H. L. Edge, J. Morris and J. Palmer, eds. *Foundations of Parapsychology: Exploring the Boundaries of Human Capability.* London: Routledge and Kegan Paul, 1986.

———. "Problems and Methods in Psychokinesis Research." In S. Krippner, ed. *Advances in Parapsychological Research, Vols. 1 and 3.* New York: Plenum Press, 1977, 1982.

———. "Physical Aspects of Psi Phenomena." In G. R. Schmeidler, ed. *Parapsychology: Its Relation to Physics, Biology, Psychology, and Psychiatry.* Metuchen, NJ: Scarecrow Press, 1976.

———. 1971. "Mind, Matter, and Gravitation: A Theoretical and Experimental Study." JASPR 65:223.

Ryzl, M. 1962. "Training the Psi Faculty by Hypnosis." JSPR 41:234.

Ryzl, M., J. Kappers, J. T. Barendregt, and P. R. Barkema. 1965. "An Experiment in Prague." JP 29:176.

Ryzl, M., and J. Ryzlova. 1962. "A Case of High-Scoring ESP Performance in the Hypnotic State." JP 26:153.

Ryzlova, J., and M. Ryzl. 1962. "A Case of High-Scoring ESP Performance in the Hypnotic State." JP 26:153.

Sage, M. 1909. "The Alleged Miraculous Hailstones of Remiremont." PSPR 21:405.

Salter, H. de G. 1958. "Our Pioneers, I: Mrs. Henry Sidgwick." JSPR 39:235.

———. 1957. "Obituary. Gilbert Murray, O.M." JSPR 39:154.

———. 1957. "Mrs. Stuart Wilson." JSPR 39:110.

———. 1953. "Obituary: The Rev. C. Drayton Thomas." JSPR 37:677.

———. 1951. "Some Observations on the S.P.R. Group of Automatists." JSPR 45:47.

———. 1938. "A Sermon in St. Paul's." PSPR 45:25.

———. 1932. "The History of George Valiantine." PSPR 40:389.

———. 1930. "Some Incidents Occurring at Sittings with Mrs. Leonard Which May Throw Light on Their *Modus Operandi.*" PSPR 39:306.

———. 1927. "Notes on Periodicals." JSPR 24:125, 127.

———. 1917. "Some Experiments with a New Medium." PSPR 29:306.

———. 1915. "An Enquiry Concerning 'The Angels of Mons.'" JSPR 17:106.

Salter, W. H. 1963. "The Rose of Sharon." PSPR 54:1.

———. *Zoar, or the Evidence of Psychical Research Concerning Survival.* London: Sidgwick and Jackson, 1961.

———. 1958–1960. "F. W. H. Myers' Posthumous Message." PSPR 52:1.

———. 1955. "Obituary: Sir Lawrence J. Jones." JSPR 38:48.

———. 1954. "Psychical Research Today. By D. J. West." JSPR 37:348.

———. 1952. "J. G. Piddington and His Work on the 'Cross-Correspondence' Scripts." JSPR 36:708.

———. 1950. "'An Adventure': A Note on the Evidence." JSPR 35:178.

———. 1944. "Obituary. II. T. W. Mitchell, M.D." PSPR 47:258.

———. *Ghosts and Apparitions.* London: G. Bell & Sons, 1938.

———. 1921. "A Further Report on Sittings with Mrs. Leonard." PSPR 32:1.

Salter, W. H., G. W. Fisk, and H. H. Price. 1953. "G. N. M. Tyrrell and His Contributions to Psychical Research." JSPR 37:63.

"W. H. Salter: Some Appreciations." 1970. JSPR 45:207.

Saltmarsh, H. F. *Foreknowledge.* London: Bell, 1938.

———. *Evidence of Personal Survival from Cross-Correspondences.* London: Bell, 1938.

———. 1934. "Report on Cases of Apparent Precognition." PSPR 37:49.

———. 1932. "Is Proof of Survival Possible?" PSPR 40:105.

———. 1929. "Report on the Investigation of Some Sittings with Mrs. Warren Elliott." PSPR 39:47.

Sandburg, C. *The War Years, 1864–1865. Vol. III.* New York: Dell Publishing Co., 1959, pp. 823–826. (Originally published by Harcourt, Brace Co., New York, 1939)

Sargent, C., and H. J. Eysenck. *Know Your Own Psi-IQ.* New York: World Almanac Publications, 1983.

———. *Explaining the Unexplained.* London: Widenfield and Nicholson, 1982.

Sasaki, S., Y. Ochi, and A. Tokaoka. 1978. "Some Observations with Scanning Electronic Microscope (SEM) of Fracture Surface of Metals Fractured by Psychokinesis." *Journal of the Psi Institute of Japan* 2:15.

Savitz, B., B. Brier, and G. R. Schmeidler. 1975. "Three Experiments in Clairvoyant Diagnosis with Silva Mind Control Graduates." JASPR 69:263.

Saxe, S., L. Ludwig, M. Reiser, and C. Wagner. 1979. "An Evaluation of the Use of Psychics in the Investigation of Major Crimes." *Journal of Police Science and Administration* 7:18.

Schaffer W. 1988. "Miss Seminole Blends Cultures Old and New." *The Miami Herald* (Neighbors, 8/14/88), p. 14.

Schiller, F. C. S. 1921. "Vom Jenseits der Seele." PSPR 32:146.

———. 1899. "Psychology and Psychical Research. A Reply to Professor Munsterberg." PASPR 14:348.

Schmeidler, G. R. "Work in Progress." In A. S. Berger, *Lives and Letters in American Parapsychology.* Jefferson, NC: McFarland & Co., 1988.

———. "Questions and Attempts at Answers." In R. Pilkington, ed. *Men and Women of Parapsychology.* Jefferson, NC: McFarland & Co., 1987.

———. "Parapsychology." In B. Wolman, ed. *International Encyclopedia of Psychiatry, Psychology, Psychoanalysis, & Neurology,* 8, 1983, pp. 183–185.

———. "Clairvoyance." In the *Encyclopedia Americana.* New York: Americana Corp., 1968.

———. 1977. "Looking Ahead: A Method for Research on Survival." *Theta* 5(1):2.

———. 1973. "PK Experiments upon Continuously Recorded Temperature." JASPR 67:25.

———. 1970. "High ESP Scores after a Swami's Brief Instruction in Meditation and Breathing." JASPR 64:100.

———. 1966. "Quantitative Investigation of a 'Haunted House'." JASPR 60:137.

Schmeidler, G. R., B. Savitz, and B. Brier. 1975. "Three Experiments in Clairvoyant Diagnosis with Silva Mind Control Graduates." JASPR 69:263.

Schmeidler, G. R., and T. S. Moss. 1968. "Quantitative Investigation of a 'Haunted House' with Sensitives and a Control Group." JASPR 62:399.

Schmeidler, G. R., and R. A. McConnell. *ESP and Personality Patterns.* New Haven and London: Yale University Press, 1958.

Schmeidler, G. R., and L. Eilbert. 1950. "A Study of Certain Psychological Factors in Relation to ESP Performance." JP 14:53.

Schmidt, H. 1981. "PK Tests with Pre-Recorded and Pre-Inspected Seed Numbers." JP 45:87.

———. 1976. "PK Effect on Pre-Recorded Targets." JASPR 70:267.

———. 1975. "Toward a Mathematical Theory of Psi." JASPR 69:301.

———. 1970. "PK Effects with Animals as Subjects." JP 34:255.

———. 1970. "A Quantum Mechanical Random Number Generator for Psi Tests." JP 34:219.

———. 1969. "Quantum Processes Predicted?" *New Scientist* Oct. 16:114.

Schmidt, H., and L. Pantas, 1971. "Psi Tests with Psychologically Equivalent Conditions and Internally Different Machines." In W. G. Roll, R. L. Morris, J. D. Morris, eds., *Proceedings of the Parapsychological Association* 8:49.

Schmitt, M., and R. G. Stanford. 1978. "Free-Response ESP During Ganzfeld Stimulation: The Possible Influence of Menstrual Cycle Phase." JASPR 72:177.

"Rudi Schneider: Recollections and Comments." 1958. JSPR 39:206.

Schouten, S A. 1982. "Analysis of Spontaneous Cases: A Replication Based on the Rhine Collection." *European Journal of Parapsychology* 4:113.

———. 1979. "Analysis of Spontaneous Cases as Reported in 'Phantasms of the Living'." *European Journal of Parapsychology* 2:408.

Schouten, S. A., and E. F. Kelly. 1978. "On the Experiment of Brugmans, Heymans, and Weinberg." *European Journal of Parapsychology* 2:247.

von Schrenck-Notzing, A. *Materialisationsphänomene.* Munich: Ernst Reinhardt, 1914.

Schroeder, L., and S. Ostrander. *Handbook of Psychic Discoveries.* New York: Berkley Medallion Books, 1974.

———. 1971. "Psychic Enigmas & Energies in the U.S.S.R." *Psychic* 2(6):8.

———. *Psychic Discoveries Behind the Iron Curtain.* New York: Bantam Books, 1970.

Schug, J. A. *Padre Pio.* Huntington, IN: Our Sunday Visitor, 1976.

Schwartz, E. K. 1952. "The Phenomena of Astral Projection." JASPR 46:161.

Schwartz, S. A. *The Alexandria Project.* New York: Delacorte Press/Eleanor Friede, 1983.

———. *The Secret Vaults of Time.* New York: Grosset & Dunlap, 1978.

Schwarz, B. E. 1987. "Apparent Materialization of Copper Foil. Case Report: Katie." *Pursuit* 20(4):154.

———. *Psychic Nexus: Psychic Phenomena in Psychiatry and Everyday Life.* New York: Van Nostrand Reinhold, 1980.

———. *Parent-Child Telepathy.* New York: Garrett Publications, 1971.

———. *Psychic-Dynamics.* New York: Pageant Press, 1965.

Scott, C. 1978. "Correspondence." JSPR 49:968.

———. 1960. "The Jones Boys and the Ultrasonic Whistle." JSPR 40:249.

———. 1959. "In Search of a Repeatable Experiment." JSPR 40:174.

———. 1949. "Experimental Object-Reading: A

Critical Review of the Work of Dr J. Hettinger." PSPR 49:16.

Scott, C., and P. Haskell. 1974. "Fresh Light on the Shackleton Experiments." PSPR 56:43.

Searls, D., and J. M. Hardy. 1978. "Impressions of Elisabeth." *Theta* 6(2/3):1.

Seki, H. Sai Kagaku no Zenbo (Bird's Eye View of Psi Science). Tokyo: Kosakusha, 1981.

Senkowski, E. 1979. "Voices on Tape." *Zeitschrift für Parapsychologie.* 29(3/4):201.

Servadio, E. 1971. "Eileen Garrett: A Personal Recollection." JSPR 46:61.

———. 1967. "Psychoanalysis and Parapsychology." In J. R. Smythies, ed. *Science and ESP.* London: Routledge and Kegan Paul, pp. 255–261.

———. 1958. "Telepathy and Psychoanalysis." JASPR 52:127.

Servadio, E., and R. Cavanna. *ESP Experiments with LSD 25 and Psilocybin: A Methodological Approach* (Parapsychological Monograph No. 5). New York: Parapsychology Foundation, 1964.

Sheargold, R. 1986. "The Ghost of Twenty-Nine Megacycles." JSPR 53:329.

———. 1980. "A Drop-in Communicator." JSPR 50:420.

———. 1970. "The Psychology of Occultism." JSPR 45:318.

———. 1963. "Survival and the Physical Basis of Memory." JSPR 42:35.

———. 1961. "Experimental Card-Guessing Using Mediums as Percipients." JSPR 41:67.

Sheldrake, R. *The Presence of the Past.* New York: Times Books, 1988.

———. *A New Science of Life: The Hypothesis of Formative Causation.* London: Blond & Briggs; Los Angeles, CA: Tarcher, 1981.

Sherman, H. *Harold Sherman ESP Manual.* Little Rock, Arkansas: Human Development Associates, 1973.

———. *You Live After Death.* Greenwich, CT: Fawcett Books, 1972.

———. *Thoughts through Space.* London: Frederick Muller, 1971.

———. *"Wonder" Healers of the Phillipines.* London: Psychic Press, 1967.

———. *How to Make ESP Work for You.* Los Angeles, CA: DeVorss, 1964.

Shields, J. 1988. "Obituary Kenneth J. Batcheldor." JSPR 55:110.

Shirley, R. *The Problem of Rebirth.* London: Rider Co., n.d.

Sidgwick, E. M. 1925. "In Memory of Sir William Fletcher Barrett, F.R.S." PSPR 35:413.

———. 1924. "Report on Further Experiments in Thought-Transference Carried Out by Professor Gilbert Murray, LL.D., Litt.D." PSPR 34:212.

———. 1922. "Phantasms of the Living." PSPR 33:23.

———. 1921. "An Examination of Book Tests Obtained in Sittings with Mrs. Leonard." PSPR 31:241.

———. 1916. "Obituary Notice: Mrs. A. W. Verrall." PSPR 29:170.

———. 1915. "A Contribution to the Study of the Psychology of Mrs. Piper's Trance Phenomena." PSPR 28:1.

———. 1900. "Discussion of the Trance Phenomena of Mrs. Piper." PSPR 15:16.

———. 1891. "On Spirit Photographs; A Reply to Mr. A. R. Wallace." PSPR 7:268.

———. 1886. "Results of a Personal Investigation into the Physical Phenomena of Spiritualism. With Some Critical Remarks on the Evidence for the Genuineness of Such Phenomena." PSPR 4:45.

———. 1885. "Notes on the Evidence Collected by the Society for Phantasms of the Dead." PSPR 3:69.

Sigdwick, E. M., J. G. Piddington, and M. de G. Verrall. 1910. "Further Experiments with Mrs. Piper in 1908." PSPR 24:31.

Sidgwick, H. 1896. "Involuntary Whispering Considered in Relation to Experiments in Thought-Transference." PSPR 12:298.

———. 1894. "Disinterested Deception." JSPR 6:274.

Sidgwick, H., A. Johnson, F. W. H. Myers, F. Podmore, and E. M. Sidgwick. 1894. "Report on the Census of Hallucinations." PSPR 10:25.

Sigwick, H., E. M. Sidgwick, and G. A. Smith. 1890. "Experiments in Thought-Transference." PSPR 6:128.

Sinclair, U. *Mental Radio.* Pasadena, CA: Upton Sinclair, 1930 (Republished Springfield, IL: Charles C. Thomas, 1962).

"Sinclair, Upton (Beall)." *New Encyclopedia Britannica,* 1986.

Sitwell, S. *Poltergeists.* London: Faber, 1940.

Slawinski, J. 1987. "Electromagnetic Radiation and the Afterlife." *Journal of Near-Death Studies* 6:79.

Smith, B. M., C. E. Stuart, B. M. Humphrey, and E. McMahan. 1947. "Personality Measurements and ESP Tests with Cards and Drawings." JP 11:118.

Smith, B. M., J. B. Rhine, J. G. Pratt, and C. E. Stuart. *Extrasensory Perception after Sixty Years.* New York: Henry Holt, 1940. (Republished Boston: Bruce Humphries, 1966, with a new foreword by J. B. Rhine.)

Smith, H. A. 1910. "Presidential Address." PSPR 24:330.

Smith, J., and C. T. Tart, 1968. "Two Token Object Studies with the 'Psychic,' Peter Hurkos." JASPR 62:143.

Smith, M. J. 1968. "Paranormal Effects on Enzyme Activity." *Proceedings of the Parapsychological Association* 5:15.

Smith, S. *Confessions of a Psychic.* New York: Macmillan, 1971.

———. *The Mediumship of Mrs. Leonard.* New Hyde Park, NY: University Books, 1964.

Smith, W. W. (Carington) 1919. "The Reality of Psychic Phenomena." PSPR 30:306.

Smythies, J. R. "Is ESP Possible?" In J. R. Smythies, ed. *Science and ESP.* London: Routledge and Kegan Paul; New York: Humanities Press, 1967.

———. 1951. "The Extension of Mind: A New Theoretical Basis for Psi Phenomena." JSPR 36:477.

Smythies, J. R., and J. Beloff, eds. *The Case for*

*Dualism.* Charlottesville, VA: University of Virginia Press, 1988.

Snel, F. W. J. J., ed. *In Honour of G. A. M. Zorab.* Amsterdam: Nederlander Vereniging voor Parapsychologie, 1986.

Soal, S. G. 1953. "My Thirty Years of Psychical Research." PSPR 50:67.

———. 1932. "Experiments in Supernormal Perception at a Distance." PSPR 40:165.

———. 1925. "A Report on Some Communications Received through Mrs. Blanche Cooper." PSPR 35:471.

Soal, S. G., and F. Bateman. *Modern Experiments in Telepathy.* New Haven, CT: Yale University Press, 1954.

Soal, S. G., and H. T. Bowden. *The Mind Readers.* London: Faber and Faber, 1959.

Soal, S. G. and K. M. Goldney. 1943. "Experiments in Precognitive Telepathy." PSPR 47:21.

Soal S. G., I. Jephson and T. Besterman. 1931. "Report of a Series of Experiments in Clairvoyance Conducted at a Distance under Approximately Fraud-proof Conditions." PSPR 39:375.

"The South African Society for Psychical Research." 1959. JSPR 40:43.

Sparrow, M., and I. M. Owen. *Conjuring up Philip.* New York: Harper and Row, 1976.

Spraggett, A., with W. F. Rauscher. *Arthur Ford: The Man Who Talked with the Dead.* New York: New American Library, 1973.

"Interview: Ray Stanford." *Psychic.* 1974. 5(4):6, 11.

Stanford, R. G. "Ganzfeld and Hypnotic-Induction Procedures in ESP Research: Toward Understanding Their Success." In S. Krippner, ed. *Advances in Parapsychological Research 5.* Jefferson, NC: McFarland & Co., 1987.

———. "Recent Ganzfeld-ESP Research: A Survey and Critical Analysis." In S. Krippner, ed. *Advances in Parapsychological Research 4.* Jefferson, NC: McFarland & Co., 1984.

———. 1978. "Toward Reinterpreting Psi Events." JASPR 72:197.

———. "Experimental Psychokinesis: A Review from Diverse Perspectives." In B. Wolman, ed. *Handbook of Parapsychology.* New York: Van Nostrand Reinhold, 1977, pp. 324–381.

———. "Conceptual Frameworks of Contemporary Psi Research." In B. Wolman, ed. *Handbook of Parapsychology.* New York: Van Nostrand Reinhold, 1977, pp. 823–858.

———. 1974. "An Experimentally Testable Model for Spontaneous Psi Events. I. Extrasensory Events." JASPR 68:34.

Stanford, R. G., and M. Schmitt. 1978. "Free-Response ESP during Ganzfeld Stimulation: The Possible Influence of Menstrual Cycle Phase." JASPR 72:177.

Stanford, T. W. *Psychic Phenomena: A Narrative of Facts.* Melbourne, Australia: Bruce and Davies, 1903.

Steiger, B. *The Psychic Feats of Olof Jonsson.* Englewood Cliffs, NJ: Prentice-Hall, 1971.

Steiner, R. *The Dead Are with Us.* London: Rudolf Steiner Press, 1973.

———. *Methods of Spiritual Research.* Blauvelt, NY: Rudolf Steiner Publications, 1971.

———. *Theosophy.* London: Kegan Paul, 1900.

Stevens. E. W. *The Watseka Wonder.* Chicago, Ill: Religio-Philosophical Pub. House, 1887.

Stevenson, I. *Cases of the Reincarnation Type Vols. I–IV.* Charlottesville: University Press of Virginia, 1975, 1977, 1980, 1983.

———. 1983. "Mediumship and Survival." JSPR 52:203.

———. 1977. "Research into the Evidence of Man's Survival after Death." *Journal of Nervous and Mental Disease* 165(3):152.

———. "Reincarnation: Field Studies and Theoretical Issues." In B. Wolman, ed. *Handbook of Parapsychology.* New York: Van Nostrand Reinhold Co., 1977, p. 631.

———. *Twenty Cases Suggestive of Reincarnation.* (2nd Rev. Ed.) Charlottesville: University Press of Virginia, 1974.

———. 1972. "Are Poltergeists Living or Are They Dead?" JASPR 66:233.

———. 1971. "Eileen Garrett—An Appreciation." JASPR 65:336.

———. 1970. "A Communicator Unknown to Medium and Sitter." JASPR 64:53.

———. 1968. "The Combination Lock Test for Survival." JASPR 62:246.

———. 1967. "An Antagonist's View of Parapsychology." JASPR 61:254.

———. 1960. "A Review and Analysis of Paranormal Experiences Connected with the Sinking of the Titanic." JASPR 54:153.

Stevenson, I., and N. Azuma. 1987. "Difficulties Confronting Investigations of 'Psychic' Surgery in the Phillipines." *Parapsychology Review* 18(2):6.

Stevenson, I., with J. Eisenbud, and J. G. Pratt. 1981. "Distortions in the Photographs of Ted Serios." JASPR 75:143.

Stevenson, I., and E. Haraldsson. 1975. "A Communicator of the 'Drop In' Type in Iceland: The Case of Gudni Magnusson." JASPR 69:245.

———. 1975. "A Communicator of the 'Drop In' Type in Iceland: The Case of Runolfur Runolfsson." JASPR 69:33.

Stewart, B. 1885. "Presidential Address." PSPR 3:64.

———. 1882. "Note on Thought-Reading." PSPR 1:35.

Stewart, B., and P. C. Tait. *The Unseen Universe or Physical Speculation on a Future State.* London: ———, 1875.

Stowe, C. E., and L. B. Stowe. *Harriet Beecher Stowe: The Story of Her Life.* Boston: Houghton Mifflin, 1911.

Stratton, F. J. M. 1958. "Four Modern Ghosts." JSPR 39:288.

———. 1955. "Obituary: Dr. L. P. Jacks." JSPR 38:100.

Strutt, J. W. See Lord Rayleigh.

Strutt, R. J. See Lord Rayleigh.

Stuart, C. E. 1946. "An Interest Inventory Relation to ESP Scores." JP 10:154.

———. 1946. "GESP Experiments with the Free Response Method." JP 10:21

———. 1947. "A Second Classroom ESP Experiment with the Free Response Method." JP 11:14.

Stuart, C. E., B. M. Humphrey, B. M. Smith, and E. McMahan. 1947. "Personality Measurements and ESP Tests with Cards and Drawings." JP 11:117.

Stuart, C. E., J. B. Rhine, J. G. Pratt, B. M. Smith, and J. A. Greenwood. *Extrasensory Perception after Sixty Years.* New York: Henry Holt, 1940. (Republished Boston: Bruce Humphries, 1966, with a new foreword by J. B. Rhine.)

Stuart, C. E., and J. G. Pratt. *A Handbook for Testing Extrasensory Perception.* New York: Farrar and Rhinehart. 1937.

Stuart, C. E., and J. A. Greenwood. 1937. "A Review of Criticisms of the Mathematical Evaluation of ESP Data." JP 1:295.

Sudre, R. *Treatise on Parapsychology.* New York: Citadel Press; London: George Allen & Unwin, 1960.

———. 1931. "Is the Soul Material?" *Psychic Research* 25:165.

———. 1930. "The Structure of the Sub-Conscious Mind." *Psychic Research* 24:77.

———. 1930. "Psychic Research and the New Physics." *Psychic Research* 24:117.

———. 1929. "The Case of Victor Hugo and the Collective Psychism." *Psychic Research* 23:337.

———. 1928. "Have We a Sixth Sense?" *Psychic Research* 22:158.

———. 1928. "Clairvoyance and the Theory of Probabilities." *Psychic Research* 22:63.

———. 1928. "The Phenomena of Levitation." *Psychic Research* 22:433.

———. 1928. "Recollections of Jean Gouzyk." *Psychic Research* 22:603.

———. 1926. "The Ideas of Hans Driesch." JASPR 20:193.

———. 1925. "The Philosophy of Geley." JASPR 19:30.

———. 1926. "The Role of Prosopopesis in Psychical Research." JASPR 20:119.

Supplemental Number. 1935. JASPR 29 (5, sup.):153.

Swain, B. 1982. "Metascience News." *New Realities* 4(6):8.

Swets, J. A., and D. Druckman, eds. *Enhancing Human Performance. Issues, Theories, and Techniques.* Washington, D.C.: National Academy of Sciences, 1988.

Symonds, J. *The Lady with the Magic Eyes.* New York: Thomas Yoseloff, 1960.

Tanagras, A. *Psychophysical Elements in Parapsychological Traditions.* New York: Parapsychology Institute, 1967.

———. *Le Destin et la Chance.* Athens: n.p., 1938.

Tanous, A., and K. F. Donnelly. *Is Your Child Psychic?* New York: Macmillan Publishing Co., 1979.

Targ, R., and K. Harary. 1985. "A New Approach to Forecasting Commodity Futures." *Psi Research* 5(3/4):7.

———. *The Mind Race: Understanding and Using Psychic Abilities.* New York: Villard Books, 1984.

Targ, R., and H. E. Puthoff. *Mind-Reach: Scientists Look at Psychic Ability.* New York: Delacorte Press/Eleanor Friede, 1977.

Targ, R., H. E. Puthoff, and C. T. Tart. *Mind at Large: Institute of Electrical and Electronic Engineers Symposia on the Nature of Extrasensory Perception.* New York: Praeger, 1979.

Tart, C. "Psychological Resistance in Research on Channeling: A Discussion of the Channeling Panel." In D. H. Weiner and R. D. Nelson, eds. *Research in Parapsychology 1986.* Metuchen, NJ: Scarecrow Press, 1987.

———. 1985. "Psychics' Fears of Psychic Powers." In D. H. Weiner and D. I. Radin, eds. *Research in Parapsychology 1985.* Metuchen, NJ: The Scarecrow Press, 1986, p. 151.

———. *Transpersonal Psychologies.* New York: Harper & Row, 1975.

———. *On Being Stoned: A Psychological Study of Marijuana Intoxication.* Palo Alto, CA: Science & Behavior Books, 1971.

———. *Altered States of Consciousness.* New York: John Wiley & Sons, 1969 (rev. 1972).

———. 1968. "A Psychophysiological Study of Out-of-Body Experiences in a Selected Subject." JASPR 62:3.

Tart, C., H. Puthoff, and R. Targ. *Mind at Large: Institute of Electrical and Electronic Engineers Symposia on the Nature of Extrasensory Perception.* New York: Praeger, 1979.

Tart, C., and J. Smith. 1968. "Two Token Object Studies with the 'Psychic,' Peter Hurkos." JASPR 62:143.

Taves, E., and L. A. Dale. 1943. "The Midas Touch in Reverse." JASPR 37:57.

Taylor, J. *Science and the Supernatural: An Investigation of Paranormal Phenomena including Psychic Healing, Clairvoyance, Telepathy and Precognition.* New York: E.P. Dutton, 1980.

———. *Superminds (An Enquiry into the Paranormal).* London: Macmillan, 1975.

Teicher, M. I. 1962. "'Windigo' Psychosis among Algonkian-Speaking Indians." *International Journal of Parapsychology* 4(1):5.

Tenhaeff, W. H. C. 1960. "The Employment of Paragnosts for Police Purposes." Proceedings of the Parapsychological Institute of the State University 1:15.

———. *Beschouwingen Over het Gebruik van Paragnosten Voor Politiele en Andere Praktische Doeleinden (Observations on the Use of Paragnosts for Police and Other Practical Purposes).* Utrecht: Byleveld, 1957.

Tenhaeff, W. H. C., and G. D. H. van Woudenberg. 1964. "Practical Achievements of Sensitives." *Zeitschrift für Parapsychologie und Grenzgebiete der Psychologie.* 7:159.

Thalbourne, M. 1982. *A Glossary of Terms Used in Parapsychology.* London: William Heinemann, 1982.

———. 1982. "Correspondence." *The Journal of Religion and Psychical Research* 5(1):62.

Thalbourne, M., and S. E. Harding. "Transcendental Meditation, Clairvoyant Ability and Psychological Adjustment." In W. G. Roll and J. Beloff, eds. *Research in Parapsychology 1980.* Metuchen, NJ. Scarecrow Press, 1981, p. 71.

1981, p. 71.

Thibaudet, A., and O. A. Bird. "Bergson, Henri(-Louis)." In the *New Encyclopaedia Britannica,* Vol. 2, 1986, pp. 129–131.

Thomas, C. D. 1939. "A Proxy Experiment of Significant Success." PSPR 45:257.

———. 1939. "A Proxy Case Extending over Eleven Sittings with Mrs. Osborne Leonard." PSPR 43:439.

———. 1933. "A Consideration of a Series of Proxy Sittings." PSPR 41:139.

———. 1928. "The Modus Operandi of Trance Communication According to Descriptions Received through Mrs. Osborne Leonard." PSPR 38:49.

———. 1921. "Newspaper Tests." JSPR 20:89.

Thomas, J. F. *Beyond Normal Cognition.* Boston: Boston Society for Psychic Research, 1937.

———. *Case Studies Bearing upon Survival.* Boston: Boston Society for Psychic Research, 1929.

Thomson, M. J., E. C. May, and D. I. Radin. "Psi Experiments with Random Number Generators: Meta-Analysis Part I." In D. H. Weiner and D. I. Radin, eds. *Research in Parapsychology 1985.* Metuchen, NJ: The Scarecrow Press, 1986, p. 14.

Thouless, R. H. "Implications for Religious Studies." In S. Krippner, ed. *Advances in Parapsychological Research. Volume I.* New York: Plenum Press, 1977, p. 175.

———. *From Anecdote to Experiment in Psychical Research.* London: Routledge & Kegan Paul, 1972.

———. 1968. "Review of *Obituary—The 'Hodgson Report' on Madame Blavatsky.*" JSPR 44:341.

———. 1966. "Swan on a Black Sea: A Study in Automatic Writing." JSPR 43:267.

———. 1963. "Correspondence." JSPR 42:203.

———. *Experimental Psychical Research.* Baltimore, MD: Penguin Books, 1963.

———. 1961. "Journal of Parapsychology, xxv, 2 June 1961, Durham, N.C." JSPR 41:212.

———. 1959. "The Mind Readers. By S. G. Soal and H. T. Bowden." JSPR 40:84.

———. 1955. "The Oliver Lodge Posthumous Test of Survival: Some Comments." JSPR 38:172.

———. 1949. "Report of a Visit to the United States." JSPR 35:14.

———. 1948. "A Test of Survival." PSPR 48:25.

———. 1942. "The Present Position of Experimental Research into Telepathy and Related Phenomena." PSPR 42:1.

———. 1937. "A Review of Mr. Whately Carington's Work on Trance Personalities." PSPR 44:223.

———. 1935. "Dr Rhine's Recent Experiments in Telepathy and Clairvoyance and a Reconsideration of J. E. Coover's Conclusions on Telepathy." PSPR 43:24.

Thouless, R. H., and B. P. Wiesner. 1947. "The Psi Process in Normal and 'Paranormal' Psychology." PSPR 48:177.

Thurston, H. *The Physical Phenomena of Mysticism.* London: Burns Oates, 1955.

Tietze, T. R. 1976. "Ursa Major: An Impressionistic Appreciation of Walter Franklin Prince." JASPR 70:1, 14–15.

———. 1974. "The Great Physical Mediums, Part II." *Psychic* 5(3):30–33.

———. *Margery.* New York: Harper and Row, 1973.

Tiller, W. A. "Devices for Monitoring Nonphysical Energies." In E. G. Mitchell, *Psychic Exploration.* New York: G. P. Putnam, 1974, p. 488.

Tillett, G. *The Elder Brother: A Biography of Charles Webster Leadbeater.* London: Routledge & Kegan Paul, 1982.

Tillyard, R. J. 1931. "Dr. R. J. Tillyard's Notes of His Seance with 'Margery'." *Psychic Research* 25:139.

———. 1928. "Evidence of Survival of a Human Personality." *Nature* 122:243.

———. 1926. "Science and Psychical Research." *Nature* 118:587.

Timm, U. 1973. "The Measurement of Psi." JASPR 67:282.

Tischner, R. *Franz Anton Mesmer: Leben, Werk und Wirkungen.* Munchen: Verlag der Muncher Drucke, 1928.

———. *Geschichte der okkultistischen (metapsychischen) Forschung von der Mitte des 19. Jahrhunderts bis zur Gegenwart.* Pfullinge: Johannes Baum Verlag, 1924.

———. *Über Telepathie und Hellsehen. Experimentell-theoretische Untersuchungen.* Munchen: J. F. Bergmann, 1920.

Tokaoka, A., S. Sasaki, and Y. Ochi. 1978. "Some Observations with Scanning Electronic Microscope (SEM) of Fracture Surface of Metals Fractured by Psychokinesis." *Journal of the Psi Institute of Japan* 2:15.

Treviño, C. B. 1983. "'Possession', Psychiatry and Psi." *Psi Research* 2(2).

———. *Introducción a la Parapsicología.* Mexico City: Socieded Mexicana de Parapsicología, 1976.

Treviño, M. G. de, and A. C. Flores. 1985. "Kirlian Photography and Pregnancy." *Psi Research* 4(3, 4): 232.

Tribbe, F. C., ed. *The Ashby Guidebook for the Study of the Paranormal.* York Beach, Maine: Samuel Weiser, 1987.

———. 1986. "Twenty-one Enigmas of the Shroud of Turin." *Christian Parapsychologist* 6 (5):162.

———. *Portrait of Jesus? The Illustrated Story of the Shroud of Turin.* New York: Stein and Day, 1983.

———. 1982. "Research Report: Robert Ashby and the Super ESP Hypothesis." *Spiritual Frontiers* 14 (1):33.

———. 1980. "The Tribbe/Mulders Code." *Journal of the Academy of Religion and Psychical Research* 3:44.

Tribbe, F., J. Tyrer, I. Wilson, and R. Kendrick. 1989.

"The Turin Shroud—Too Hasty an Epitaph?" *Christian Parapsychologist* 8(1):2.

Trubo, R. 1975. "Psychics and the Police." *Psychic* 6(2):8.

Truzzi, M. "J. B. Rhine and Pseudoscience: Some Zetetic Reflections on Parapsychology." In K. R. Rao, ed. *J. B. Rhine: On the Frontiers of Science.* Jefferson, NC: McFarland & Co., 1982.

———. 1980. "A Skeptical Look at Paul Kurtz's Analysis of the Scientific Status of Parapsychology." JP 44:35.

———. 1978. "On the Extraordinary: an Attempt at Clarification." *Zetetic Scholar* 1:11.

———. 1977. "Editorial: Parameters of the Paranormal." *The Zetetic* 1(2):4.

———. *The Occult in America.* New York: Charles Scribner's Sons, 1973.

Truzzi, M. and P. H. Hoebens. "Reflections on Psychic Sleuths." In P. Kurtz, ed. *A Skeptic's Handbook of Parapsychology.* Buffalo, NY: Prometheus Books, 1985.

Truzzi, M., with G. Hövelmann, and P. H. Hoebens. "Skeptical Literature on Parapsychology: An Annotated Bibliography." In P. Kurtz, ed. *A Skeptic's Handbook of Parapsychology.* Buffalo, NY: Prometheus Books, 1985.

Tubby, G. O. 1941. "Mrs. Chenoweth (In Memoriam)." JASPR 35:31.

Twigg, E., with R. H. Brod. *Ena Twigg Medium.* London: W. A. Allen, 1973.

Tyrer, J., F. Tribbe, I. Wilson, and R. Kendrick. 1989. "The Turin Shroud—Too Hasty an Epitaph?" *Christian Parapsychologist* 8(1):2.

Tyrrell, G. N. M. *Science and Psychical Phenomena & Apparitions.* New Hyde Park, N.Y.: University Books, 1961. Originally published 1953 by the Society for Psychical Research.

———. *The Nature of Human Personality.* London: Allen & Unwin, 1954.

———. 1948. "The O.J.L. Posthumous Packet." JSPR 34:269.

———. *The Personality of Man.* Harmondsworth, UK: Penguin Books, 1947.

———. 1947. "The 'Modus Operandi' of Paranormal Cognition." PSPR 48:65.

———. 1936. "Further Research in Extra-Sensory Perception." PSPR 44:99.

———. ("Mr. T.") 1922. "The Case of Miss Nancy Sinclair." JSPR 20:294.

Ullman, M. "Autobiographical Notes." In A. S. Berger. *Lives and Letters in American Parapsychology.* Jefferson, NC: McFarland, 1988.

———. "The World of Psychic Phenomena as I Came to Know It." In R. Pilkington, ed. *Men and Women of Parapsychology.* Jefferson, NC: McFarland, 1987.

Ullman, M., and N. Zimmerman. *Working with Dreams.* Los Angeles, CA: J.P. Tarcher, 1985. Originally pub. 1979.

Ullman, M., J. G. Pratt, B. Herbert, and H. H. Keil. 1976. "Directly Observable Voluntary PK Effects: A Survey and Tentative Interpretation of Available Findings from Nina Kulagina and Other Known Related Cases of Recent Date." PSPR: 56:197.

Ullman, M., and S. Krippner, with A. Vaughan. *Dream Telepathy.* New York: Macmillan, 1973.

Ullman, M., S. Krippner and C. Honorton. 1973. "A Long-Distance ESP Dream Study with the 'Grateful Dead'." *Journal of the American Society of Psychosomatic Dentistry and Medicine* 20:9.

Ullman, M., S. Krippner, and C. Honorton. 1971. "A Precognitive Dream Study with a Single Subject." JASPR 65:192.

Ullman, M., and S. Krippner. "Dream Studies and Telepathy." *Parapsychological Monographs No. 12.* New York: Parapsychology Foundation, 1970.

Unlimited Horizons Newsletter of Metascience Foundation, Spring 1988, 6 (1):4–6.

Uphoff, M. J., and W. Uphoff. *Mind Over Matter. Implications of Masuaki Kiyota's PK Feats with Metal and Film.* Oregon, WI: New Frontiers Center; Gerrard's Cross, UK: Colin Smythe, Ltd., 1980.

———. *New Psychic Frontiers.* Gerrard's Cross, UK: Colin Smythe, Ltd., 1977.

Uphoff, W., and M. J. Uphoff. *Mind Over Matter. Implications of Masuaki Kiyota's PK Feats with Metal and Film.* Oregon, WI: New Frontiers Center; Gerrard's Cross, UK: Colin Smyth, Ltd., 1980.

———. *New Psychic Frontiers,* Gerrard's Cross, UK: Colin Smythe, Ltd., 1977.

Vahle, N. 1987. "The Spiritual Legacy of Edgar Cayce." *New Realities.* 8(2):34.

Van Asperen de Boer, J. Kappers, and P. R. Barkema. 1966. "Is It Possible to Induce ESP with Psilocybine? An Exploratory Investigation." *International Journal of Neuropsychiatry* 2 (5): 447.

Van Bussbach, J. G. 1961. "An Investigation of ESP in First and Second Grades in American Schools." JP 25:161.

———. 1959. "An Investigation of ESP in the First and Second Grades of Dutch Schools." JP 23:227.

———. 1955. "A Further Report on an Investigation of ESP in School Children." JP 19:69.

Van de Castle, R. "An Investigation of Psi Abilities among the Cuna Indians of Panama." In A. Angoff and D. Barth, eds. *Parapsychology and Anthropology.* New York: Parapsychology Foundation, 1974, pp. 80–97.

———. 1969. "The Facilitation of ESP through Hypnosis." *American Journal of Clinical Hypnosis* 12(17):37.

———. 1957. "Differential Patterns of ESP Scoring as a Function of Differential Attitudes Toward ESP." JASPR 51:43.

Van Eeden, F. "Account of Sittings with Mrs. Thompson." PSPR 17:75.

Van Vuurde, W. 1956. "ESP During Sleep?" JSPR 38:282.

Vasiliev, L. L. *Experiments in Mental Suggestion.* Church Crookham, Hampshire, UK: Study of Mental Images Publications, 1963. Orig. published in the Soviet Union in 1963.

———. *Experiments in Distant Influence.* London: Wildwood House, 1976.

Vaughan, A. 1987. "Channeling." *New Realities* 7(3):43.

———. *The Edge of Tomorrow.* New York: Coward, McCann, 1982 (rev. ed. New York: Dodd, Mead, 1988).

———. *Incredible Coincidence.* New York: Lippincott, 1979; NAL, 1980.

———. *Patterns of Prophecy.* New York: Hawthorn, 1973; Sun, 1985.

———. "Famous Western Sensitives." In E. Mitchell (with J. White, ed.) *Psychic Exploration.* New York: Putnam, 1974.

———. 1973. "Interview; Rosalind Heywood." *Psychic* 5(2):6.

———. 1972. "Interview: Ena Twigg." *Psychic* 4(2):7.

———. *Psychics.* New York: Harper & Row, 1972.

Vaughan, A., M. Ullman, and S. Krippner. *Dream Telepathy.* New York: Macmillan, 1973.

Verrall, Helen de G. (Salter) 1914. "The History of Marthe Béraud." PSPR 27:333.

Verrall, M. de G. 1916. "Report on a Series of Experiments in 'Guessing.'" PSPR 29:64.

———. 1906. "On a Series of Automatic Writings." PSPR 20:1.

———. 1902. "Notes on the Trance Phenomena of Mrs. Thompson." PSPR 17:164.

Verrall, M. de G., J. G. Piddington, and E. M. Sidgwick. 1910. "Further Experiments with Mrs. Piper in 1908." PSPR 24:31.

Vilenskaya, L. 1984. "Investigation and Application of Telepathy, Clairvoyance and Psychokinesis in the USSR and in the West." Paper presented at the Second International Congress on Interdisciplinary Discussions of Border Area Problems of Science, Basel, Switzerland, November 1984.

———. "On PK and Related Subjects' Research in the U.S.S.R." In W. Uphoff and M. J. Uphoff, *Mind Over Matter.* Oregon, WI: New Frontiers Center, 1980, p. 205.

Vilenskaya, L., and M. Mir. eds., *The Golden Chalice.* San Francisco, CA: H.S. Dakin Co., 1986.

Villoldo, A. and S. Krippner. *The Realms of Healing.* Millbrae, CA: Celestial Arts, 1976.

Vincens, R. *La Pyramide est Morte.* Marseilles: Prospectus du Cercle Parapsychologique, 1976.

Wade, A. *The Letters of W. B. Yeats.* London: Rupert Hart-Davis, 1954.

Wagner, C., L. Ludwig, M. Reiser, and S. Saxe. 1979. "An Evaluation of the Use of Psychics in the Investigation of Major Crimes." *Journal of Police Science and Administration* 7:18.

Walker, E. H. 1979. "The Quantum Theory of Psi Phenomena." *Psychoenergetic Systems* 3:259.

———. "Foundations of Paraphysical and Parapsychological Phenomena." In L. Oteri, ed. *Quantum Mechanics and Parapsychology.* New York: Parapsychology Foundation, 1975.

Walker, N. 1930. "The Tony Burman Case." PSPR 39:1.

Wallace, A. R. 1899. "Mr. Podmore on Clairvoyance and Poltergeists." JSPR 9:22.

———. 1888. "Correspondence." JSPR 16:312.

———. *On Miracles and Modern Spiritualism: Three Essays.* London: James Burns, 1875.

"Wallace, Alfred Russel." In *The New Encyclopedia Britannica,* Vol. 12, 1986, pp. 466–467.

Wallis, W. K. "Spiritualism in Australia." *Harbinger of Light* 77(5):36.

Walsh, W. T. *Our Lady of Fatima.* London: Macmillan, 1949.

Walther, G. *Zum anderen Ufer.* Remagen: Otto Reichel, 1960.

———. *Phaenomenologie der Mystik.* Freiburg: Walter-Verlag Olten, 1923.

Wambach, H. 1977. "A Session with Seth." *New Realities* 1(1):34.

Warcollier, R. *Experimental Telepathy.* London: George Allen & Unwin, 1939.

Wassilko-Serecki, Z. 1926. "Observations on Eleonore Zugun—II." JASPR 20:593.

Watkins, A. M., and G. K. Watkins. 1971. "Resuscitation of Anesthetized Mice." JP 35:251.

Watkins, G. K., and A. M. Watkins, 1971. "Resuscitation of Anesthetized Mice." JP 35:251.

Watson, L. *Supernature.* Garden City, NY: Doubleday, 1973, p. 75.

Weatherhead, L. D. *The Manner of the Resurrection in the Light of Modern Science and Psychical Research.* New York: Abingdon Press, 1959.

Webb, J. *The Occult Underground.* La Salle, IL: Open Court Publishing Co., 1974.

———. "Carl Gustav Jung." In R. Cavendish, ed. *Encyclopedia of the Unexplained.* New York: McGraw-Hill, 1974a.

———. "Synchronicity." In R. Cavendish, ed. *Encyclopedia of the Unexplained.* New York: McGraw-Hill, 1974b.

Weinberg, A., H. J. F. W. Brugmans, and G. Heymans. "Une communication sur des expériences télépathiques au laboratoire de psychologie à Groningue." *Compte Rendu Officiel du Premier Congrès International des Recherches Psychiques* Copenhagen, 1922, p. 396.

Weiner, D. H. "Thoughts on the Role of Meaning in Psi Research." In D. H. Weiner and R. L. Nelson, eds. *Research in Parapsychology 1986.* Metuchen, NJ: Scarecrow Press, 1987.

———. "When Omniscience is Wrong: Psi Errors as a Clue to the Boundary of Psychic Functioning." In B. Shapin and L. Coly, eds. *Current Trends in Psi Research.* New York: Parapsychology Foundation, 1986.

Weiner, D. H., and N. L. Zingrone. 1986. "The Checker Effect Revisited." JP 50.

Weiner, D. H., and J. Geller. 1984. "Motivation as the Universal Container: Conceptual Problems in Parapsychology." JP 48:27.

Weiner, D. H., and J. Haight. 1983. "Charting Hidden Channels: A Review and Analysis of Louisa E. Rhine's Case Collection Project." JP 47:303.

Weintraub, P. and K. (Stuart Blue) Harary. *The Free Flight Program.* New York: St. Martin's Press, 1989a.

———. *The Creative Sleep Program.* New York: St. Martin's Press, 1989b.

Wendlandt, S., H. Kury, R. Hampel, and H. Bender. 1975. "The 'Geller-effect'—An Investigation on Interviews and Questionnaires. Part 1." *Zeitschrift für Parapsychologie und Grenzgebiete der Psychologie* 17:219.

West, D. J. 1973. "Obituary: G. W. Fisk." JSPR 47:21.

———. 1958. "Sigmund Freud: Life and Work. Vol. III. The Last Phase." JSPR 39:242.

———. *Eleven Lourdes Miracles.* London: Gerald Duckworth, 1957.

———. 1956. "Centenary of Sigmund Freud." JSPR 38:265.

———. *Psychical Research Today.* London: Duckworth, 1954 (Reissued Penguin, 1962).

———. 1950. "The Parapsychology Laboratory at Duke University, and the American Society for Psychical Research: Some Impressions." JSPR 35:165, 169.

———. 1949. "The Identity of 'Jack the Ripper'." JSPR 35:76.

———. 1946. "Trial of Helen Duncan." PSPR 48:32.

West, D. J., and G. W. Fisk. 1956. "ESP and Mood: Report of a 'Mass' Experiment." JSPR 38:320.

———. 1953. "A Dual ESP Experiment with Clock Cards." JSPR 37:185.

Wheatley, J. M. O. "Implications for Philosophy." In S. Krippner, ed. *Advances in Parapsychological Research. Vol. I.* New York: Plenum Press, 1977.

——— and H. L. Edge, eds. *Philosophical Dimensions of Parapsychology.* Springfield, IL: Charles C. Thomas, 1976.

White, J. *A Practical Guide to Death and Dying.* Wheaton, IL: Quest Books, 1980.

———, ed. *Psychic Exploration.* New York: G. P. Putnam's Sons, 1974.

White, J., and S. Krippner, eds. *Future Science: Life Energies and the Physics of Paranormal Phenomena.* Garden City, NY: Doubleday & Co., 1977.

White, R. 1981. "Saintly Psi: A Study of Spontaneous ESP in Saints." *Journal of Religion and Psychical Research* 4:157.

———. "Suggested Readings in Parapsychology." In B. Wolman, ed. *Handbook of Parapsychology.* New York: Van Nostrand Reinhold, 1977.

———. "A Select Bibliography of Books on Parapsychology, 1974–1976." In S. Krippner, ed. *Advances in Parapsychological Research: 1.* New York: Plenum Press, 1977.

———. "A Select Bibliography of Books on Parapsychology, 1976–1979." In S. Krippner, ed. *Advances in Parapsychological Research: 3.* New York: Plenum Press, 1982.

———. "A Select Bibliography of Books on Parapsychology, 1979–1982." In S. Krippner, ed. *Advances in Parapsychological Research: 4.* Jefferson, NC: McFarland, 1984.

———. 1976. "The Limits of Experimenter Influence on Psi Test Results: Can Any Be Set?" JASPR 78:333.

———. 1966. "A Gift of Prophecy: The Phenomenal Jeane Dixon." JASPR 60:297.

White, R. and J. Angstadt. 1963. "Student Performance in a Two Classroom GESP Experiment with Two Student-Agents Acting Simultaneously." JASPR 57:32.

White, R., and M. Anderson. 1956. "Teacher-Pupil Attitudes and Clairvoyance Test Results." JP 20:141.

White, R., and M. Anderson. 1957. "A Further Investigation of Teacher-Pupil Attitudes and Clairvoyance Test Results." JP 21:81.

White, R., and L. A. Dale. *Parapsychology: Sources of Information.* Metuchen, NJ: Scarecrow Press, 1973.

White, R., and F. C. Dommeyer. 1963. "Psychical Research in Colleges and Universities, I, II and III." JASPR 57:3, 57:55, 57:136.

White, R., and M. Murphy. *The Psychic Side of Sports.* Reading, MA: Addison-Wesley, 1978.

Whiteman, J. H. M. "Parapsychology and Physics." In B. Wolman, ed. *Handbook of Parapsychology.* New York: Van Nostrand Reinhold Co., 1977, p. 730.

———. 1956. "The Process of Separation and Return in Experiences Fully 'Out of the Body.'" PSPR 50:240, 252–253, 274.

Wiesner, B. P., and R. H. Thouless. 1947. "The Psi Process in Normal and 'Paranormal' Psychology." PSPR 48:177.

Williams, C. *Witchcraft.* London: Faber, 1941.

Williams, G. M. *Madame Blavatsky: Priestess of the Occult.* New York: Alfred A. Knopf, Inc., 1946.

Williams, L. B., and D. M. Duke. "Qualities of Free Response Targets and Their Relationship to Psi Performance." In W. G. Roll, ed. *Research in Parapsychology 1979.* Metuchen, NJ: The Scarecrow Press, 1980, p. 74.

Wolman, B., ed. *Handbook of Parapsychology.* New York: Van Nostrand Reinhold Company, 1977.

Wilson, C. W. M. and P. H. Huby. 1961. "The Effects of Centrally Acting Drugs on ESP Ability in Normal Subjects." JSPR 41:60.

Wilson, I., F. Tribbe, J. Tyrer, and R. Kendrick. 1989. "The Turin Shroud—Too Hasty an Epitaph?" *Christian Parapsychologist* 8(1):2.

Wood, F. H. *This Egyptian Miracle.* Philadelphia, PA: McKay Co., 1940 (2nd Rev. Ed. London: John M. Watkins, 1955).

———. *After Thirty Centuries.* London: Rider, 1935.

Wood, R., and W. G. Braud. 1977. "The Influence of Immediate Feedback on Free-response GESP Performance during Ganzfeld Stimulation." JASPR 71:409.

Woodruff, J. L. 1943. "ESP Tests under Various Physiological Conditions." JP 7:264.

Woodruff, J. L., and L. A. Dale. 1952. "ESP Function and the Psychogalvanic Response." JASPR 46:62.

Woodruff, J. L., and J. G. Pratt. 1939. "Size of Stimulus Symbols in Extrasensory Perception." JP 3:121.

Woolley, V. J. 1931. "The Visit of M. Pascal Forthuny to the Society in 1929." PSPR 39:347.

———. 1926. "An Account of a Series of Sittings with Mr. George Valiantine." PSPR 36:52.

Worrall, A. A., with O. N. Worrall. *The Gift of Healing.* New York: Harper & Row, 1965.

Worrall, O. N., with A. A. Worrall. *The Gift of Healing.* New York: Harper & Row, 1965.

Woudenberg, G. D. H. van, and W. H. C. Tenhaeff. 1964. "Practical Achievements of Sensitives."

*Zeitschrift für Parapsychologie und Grenzgebiete der Psychologie* 7:159.

Wright, L. T., and D. Eisenberg. *Encounters with Qi.* New York: W. W. Norton, 1985.

Wright, M. 1944. "Obituary. II. T. W. Mitchell, M.D." PSPR 47:259.

Yarbro, C. Q. *Messages from Michael.* New York: Playboy Paperbacks, 1979.

———. *More Messages from Michael.* New York: Berkley Books, 1986.

Yeats, W. B. *Per Amica Silentia Lunae.* London: Macmillan Co., 1918.

Yellen, S. 1965. "Sir Arthur Conan Doyle: Sherlock Holmes in Spiritland." *International Journal of Parapsychology* 7(1):33.

———. 1962. "The Psychic World of William Shakespeare." *International Journal of Parapsychology* 4(3):17.

Young, M. L. *Agartha: A Journey to the Stars.* Walpole, NH: Stillpoint Publishing, 1984.

Yram. *Practical Astral Projection.* New York: Samuel Weiser, 1976, p. 60.

Zimmerman, N., and M. Ullman. *Working with Dreams.* Los Angeles, CA: J. P. Tarcher, 1975. Orig. pub. 1979.

Zingrone, N. L., and D. H. Weiner. 1986. "The Checker Effect Revisited." JP 50.

Zöllner, J. K. F. *Transcendental Physics.* London: W. H. Harrison, 1882.

Zorab, G. A. M. *Katie King: Donna o Fantasma.* Milan: Armenia Editore, 1980.

———. 1970. "Test Sittings with D. D. Home at Amsterdam." JP 34:47.

———. 1965. "Croiset the Clairvoyant." JSPR 43:209.

———. 1964. "A Further Comparative Analysis of Some Poltergeist Phenomena: Cases from Continental Europe." JASPR 58:105.

———. 1962. "Reviews. Psychic: The Story of Peter Hurkos." JSPR 41:429.

———. *De Jacht op het Spiritistich Bewijs.* The Hague: Boucher, 1940.

Zuromski, P. 1987. "A Conversation with Shirley MacLaine." *Body, Mind and Spirit* 6(5):19.